THE NAVAL WAR OF 1812

A Documentary History

Perry's Victory on Lake Erie.

THE NAVAL WAR OF 1812

A Documentary History

Volume II
1813

WILLIAM S. DUDLEY
Editor

CHRISTINE F. HUGHES
TAMARA MOSER MELIA
Associate Editors

CHARLES E. BRODINE, Jr.   CAROLYN M. STALLINGS
Assistant Editors

With a Foreword by
DEAN C. ALLARD
Director of Naval History

NAVAL HISTORICAL CENTER
DEPARTMENT OF THE NAVY
WASHINGTON, D.C.
1992

SECRETARY OF THE NAVY'S ADVISORY
COMMITTEE ON NAVAL HISTORY

Library of Congress Cataloging-in-Publication Data
(Revised for vol. 2)

The Naval War of 1812.

Includes bibliographical references and indexes.
1. United States—History—War of 1812—Naval
Operations—Sources. I. Dudley, William S.
II. Crawford, Michael J. III. Naval Historical
Center (U.S.)
E360.N35 1985   973.5'25   85–600565
ISBN 0–945274–06–8

For sale by the Superintendent of Documents, U.S. Government Printing Office
Washington, D.C. 20402

Foreword

In the first volume of *The Naval War of 1812: A Documentary History,* published in 1985, the reader was provided a summary view of American naval history from 1775 to 1805, a selection of documents representing the events that led to war, followed by a theater-by-theater grouping of some 300 naval documents describing the course of major and minor events that occurred during the first six months of the war.

For the small United States Navy, numbering sixteen ships in readiness at the start of the conflict, these early months were encouraging. American frigate commanders outfought several worthy British opponents on the high seas. These American naval victories had the important intangible effect of raising the morale of the American people and government after a series of military reverses on the Canadian frontier. The Royal Navy was much more powerful as a whole, and even the force initially on station in North America was measurably larger in resources than the American squadrons. Despite this, the Royal Navy was initially unable to blockade the U.S. Navy. For the later months of 1812 and the early part of 1813, this situation held. Gradually, however, the British naval and military reinforcements sent to Halifax and Quebec would change the fortunes of war in North America.

In the present volume, over 500 documents vividly relate the second campaign of the War of 1812 as it affected the U.S. Navy. The war at sea in 1813 brought unexpected disappointment as well as elation to those accustomed to the great celebrations of the previous year. Thus the sloop of war *Hornet's* victory over H.M.S. *Peacock* in February 1813 brought James Lawrence into the fold of heroes; yet only three months later Lawrence died following the *Shannon-Chesapeake* action. The frigate *Constellation,* Captain Charles Stewart, was unable to break out through the British blockade of the Chesapeake Bay, and the ship remained at Norfolk for the duration of the war. Commodore Stephen Decatur's squadron composed of the frigates *United States, Macedonian,* and the sloop *Hornet* likewise failed to break through the blockade of Long Island Sound.

On the eastern Great Lakes, the naval picture was different. Commodore Isaac Chauncey pressed with great energy to establish naval shipbuilding programs on Lakes Ontario and Erie during the winter and spring of 1813. This policy paid dividends, for it enabled the squadrons under Chauncey's command on Lake Ontario and under Master Commandant Oliver Hazard Perry on Lake Erie to seize the initiative and allowed American military commanders to bring their troops into the field. Chauncey's combined attacks on York and Fort George and Perry's victory on Lake Erie put the enemy into retreat in Canada. The military prospects for the United States improved greatly due to these applications of landlocked sea power.

As these events grasped the public imagination, American sailors were busy in other theaters as well. Captain David Porter's frigate *Essex,* sailing independently, rounded Cape Horn and entered the Pacific. Porter devastated British whaling fleets off the western coast of South America. Before the year was out, British warships were cruising Pacific waters to hunt him down.

On the Gulf Coast, an area given little thought by Madisonian strategists, naval and military commanders struggled to prepare for whatever the war might bring. The Creek War smoldered and flared up in Alabama; American military forces under Major General James Wilkinson captured Mobile from the Spanish; and Captain John Shaw, commanding the New Orleans Station, repeatedly warned Washington of the vulnerability of the Mississippi delta. Just as frequently, the navy secretary scolded Shaw for spending too much money on defensive measures. Shaw's nightmares came to life only one year later, as the British targeted New Orleans for a major amphibious assault.

On Chesapeake Bay, another segment of the American population learned only too well what war could bring. British amphibious attacks laid waste the coastal areas of the Chesapeake in Virginia and Maryland. Regular American army forces were virtually nonexistent, naval forces were too slender to oppose their ably led enemy, and the Virginia and Maryland militias had limited effectiveness. Under Admiral Sir John Borlase Warren and Rear Admiral George Cockburn, the British had their way in the Chesapeake during the spring and summer of 1813. The events of 1813, if read correctly, foretold of more and worse to come in the next campaign season.

The second year of the war brought a great challenge to the United States. The nation that declared war in 1812 began to taste its bitter fruit in 1813. The United States Navy learned more about its strengths and weaknesses in this more difficult phase. The strengthening enemy blockade, the lack of American ships of the line, the drain of warfare on at least two fronts, and inadequate preparations for war by the Jefferson and Madison administrations limited the U.S. Navy's capabilities in the face of superior force. It is difficult to build a navy during a war. But it may be built beforehand, thus delaying or even deterring armed conflict. Perhaps the most important lesson drawn from the second year of the war was the need for preparedness—in order for the United States to conduct a war at sea successfully, its navy must have adequate manpower, training, equipment, and ships.

As in our first volume, we particularly hope that this work will attract a wide and varied audience. The general reader, the earnest student, the professional scholar, and the serving officer can all use this book with interest and profit. We hope, as well, that the documents presented in this series will stimulate a better understanding of the historical lessons of sea power for the United States.

I wish to express gratitude to Dr. William S. Dudley, senior historian and previously head of the Early History Branch, for the dedicated leadership and professional skill that he has devoted to the War of 1812 series since 1978. The present volume's preface identifies many additional historians, editors, librarians, archivists, and officials who supported and shaped this work. Among them I especially thank Rear Admiral John D. H. Kane, Jr., the former director of naval history, who initiated the project thirteen years ago; and Christine F. Hughes, Carolyn M. Stallings, and Charles E. Brodine, Jr., the able editorial staff of this volume. It is obvious that *The Naval War of 1812* results from the combined talents and interests of many people. It also reflects the longstanding faith of the United States Navy in the value of historical understanding for the well-being of the American naval service and for the nation as a whole.

DEAN C. ALLARD
Director of Naval History

Preface

This is the second volume of three in a documentary series on the history of the United States Navy in the War of 1812. It contains documents that reflect the substance of maritime warfare between the United States and Great Britain from 1812 to 1815. We have drawn heavily on naval records held by the National Archives and Records Administration. To these we have added others reflecting a variety of viewpoints: the plans and reports of British naval and army officers who engaged our forces, newspaper columns of the day, statements of civilian officials who were charged with direction of the war, and the papers of private citizens who chose to go to war for personal profit though at great risk. To guide the reader in the use of these documents and as a unifying medium, brief essays and headnotes are provided.

The historical materials are arranged chronologically by topics within theaters of operations. Each theater is preceded by an introductory essay that provides a context for the documents that follow. We have expanded the number of theaters treated in the first volume. To the Atlantic, Northern Lakes, and Gulf Coast theaters, we have added ones for the Chesapeake Bay and the Pacific, reflecting the drift and expansion of war as determined by the main participants. The documents contained in this volume will cover the period from January through December 1813. This arrangement is logical because it best illustrates the tempo of warfare during a time when the change of seasons and sudden changes of weather persuaded combatants to slow or halt operations to avoid the increased risks of catastrophe that frequent storms, freezing temperatures, and excessively muddy roads would bring. The final volume of this series will deal with the events of 1814–15.

This documentary history is more than a recounting of battles from eyewitness reports. Many documentary works have dealt with the War of 1812, but none is currently in print and very few have focused solely on naval affairs as this series does. The objective of this work is to display the underpinnings of the U.S. Navy during the war. In this way, we hope to explain its successes and failures at a formative period in its institutional history. While battles are the stuff of war and cannot be ignored, this volume also attempts to explain through documents the concerns of policy makers as well as commanding officers, of ordinary sailors and marines, and of common citizens who had opinions about the course of the war. It is hoped that the documents in this volume will provide glimpses of the U.S. Navy long forgotten or perhaps unknown to a majority of its readers. Specialists will be familiar with much of the material, but its variety should stimulate research in new directions.

This documentary project has been underway since 1978 and has involved the efforts of many dedicated individuals working within and outside of the Naval Historical Center. A former director of naval history, Rear Admiral John D. H. Kane, Jr., made the decision for the Historical Research Branch to commence the project in keeping with the wishes of President Franklin Delano Roosevelt, who had urged an earlier director, Captain Dudley W. Knox, to print the naval manuscripts of the War of 1812. The first volume of these documents was in distribution when Dr. Ronald Spector became director of naval history. His support of the project was constant and appreciative. Dr. Dean C. Allard, the present director, has enthusiastically urged completion of these and other documentary projects. Dr. William J. Morgan, senior historian emeritus of the Naval Historical Center, has lent his wisdom and experience from years as editor of *Naval Documents of the American Revolution* in offering welcome advice to a younger project.

Since the publication of Volume I, several staff members who gave invaluable assistance toward the editing of Volume II have transferred to other branches of the Naval Historical Center or have gone on to other walks of life. Nonetheless, they helped assemble our documentary base extending into 1815, established the professional editorial practices that the Early History staff follows today, and set our standards through publication of the first volume of this series. These include Dr. Tamara Moser Melia, the first associate editor of Volume II, and assistant editors Lieutenant Donna Geiger Nelson, Dr. Michael A. Palmer, Lieutenant Marycarol Hennessy, and Joye Leonhart Durant. Of the present Early History Branch staff, I am most indebted to our superb War of 1812 editorial team, led by associate editor Christine F. Hughes, and aided by assistant editors Carolyn M. Stallings and Charles E. Brodine, Jr. These are the individuals whom I guided in the selection, transcription, annotation, and writing of headnotes for the documents printed in this volume. They also shared the arduous task of copy editing before final submission to the printer, correcting galleys and page proofs, selecting illustrations, and indexing the volume. Dr. Michael J. Crawford, head of the Early History Branch, and staff historian E. Gordon Bowen-Hassell contributed their expert knowledge of early American naval history and offered their assistance whenever it was needed. Charlotte Marie Knowles, the branch secretary, quietly and patiently took care of many details essential to the smooth running of the office during this demanding period. As usual in publishing a book such as this, many Naval Historical Center employees were called upon for assistance. To Stanley Kalkus, librarian of the navy, John Vajda, director of the Navy Department Library, and others on the library staff, we are indebted for efficient service and willing cooperation with the many requests made for obscure works, difficult citations, and liaison with the Library of Congress. Charles Haberlein, Agnes Hoover, and Edwin C. Finney, Jr., of the Curator Branch's Photographic Section provided advice and information concerning the many possibilities for illustrating the volume. The staff members of Bernard Cavalcante's Operational Archives Branch assisted by making available the biographical data in their Early Naval Records Collection ("ZB" Files).

Many archival institutions and libraries provided us with information and copies of documents and illustrations from their repositories. Most notably included in this category are the Military Reference Branch of the National Archives whose naval specialists, Richard Von Doenhoff and Barry Zerby, were most helpful in the search for obscure documents and in expediting their availability for proofreading. The Library of Congress, the National Archives of Canada, the Public Archives of Nova Scotia, the National Library of Scotland, the Public Record Office in London, and the National Maritime Museum of Greenwich, England, are repositories of large collections of naval documents that we frequently consulted. Of special assistance to us was Mary Z. Pain of London, whose unparalleled knowledge of holdings and painstaking research provided documentation available nowhere else. As with all documents obtained from the Public Record Office, unpublished Crown Copyright materials are reproduced in this volume with the permission of Her Majesty's Stationery Office. Other helpful institutions included: the Buffalo and Erie County Historical Society, the Chicago Historical Society, the Historical Society of Pennsylvania, the William L. Clements Library at the University of Michigan at Ann Arbor, Michigan, the Essex Institute and Peabody Museum of Salem, Massachusetts, the Franklin Delano Roosevelt Library, the Maryland Historical Society, the New-York Historical Society, the New York Public Library, the Rhode Island Historical Society, the Massachusetts Historical Society, the Pennsylvania Academy of Fine Arts, and libraries at the University of North Carolina at Chapel Hill and the University of South Carolina. The United States Naval Academy Museum provided us with assistance and access to their collections, as did the Special Collections Division of the Nimitz Library at the Naval Academy. Other individuals who deserve mention here are William Clipson of Annapolis, Maryland, who provided us an excellent set of specially drawn maps for illustrations; Emily Cain of the *Hamilton-Scourge* Project in Hamilton, Ontario, for advice based on her research on the U.S. Navy schooners *Hamilton* and *Scourge*; and Dr. William M. P. Dunne of Hampton Bays, Long Island, New York, researcher and bibliophile extraordinary, for access to his collection of naval documents and books and for generously sharing his wide knowledge of naval history.

A most important group that has provided us with encouragement over the years are the members of the Secretary of the Navy's Advisory Committee on Naval History who gave us sympathetic support and advice. I am also grateful to Dr. Harold D. Langley of the Smithsonian Institution and Professor Christopher McKee of Grinnell College; they have provided us with friendly advice and constructive criticism in reading our documents in manuscript form. We value their sage advice on matters dealing with the American sailing navy. As editor, I accept full responsibility for any mistakes or errors of fact or misinterpretations found in essays, headnotes, or annotations. As in any selection of documents, others may differ with us about what was included or omitted. I believe that those we have selected fairly represent the concerns of the Navy Department in the second year of the War of 1812.

W. S. DUDLEY
Naval Historical Center
Washington Navy Yard
Washington, D.C.

Contents

Descriptive List of Illustrations

Maps

Editorial Method

This documentary series is a selective edition of naval records. The reader familiar with Volume I will notice a change in Volume II's layout. Desiring to provide more documents, the editors have redesigned the page style and used a lighter weight paper—all in the interests of gaining more print per page and more pages in the book. We have also saved space by grouping more documents into themes, thereby writing fewer, but more comprehensive headnotes. The result has been a substantial increase in documents printed.

The editors direct the reader to Volume I for a full explanation of the editorial method. The following are the major changes that have been implemented.

Source Note

The National Archives and Records Administration (NARA) has microfilmed many of the record groups used in this series. The typical researcher is not permitted to use the original manuscripts except in special cases. NARA allowed us to check our transcriptions against the originals, thus ensuring us the most accurate transcription possible. We have provided in the source note the microfilm designation for the documents as an aid to the researcher. For example, M125 is the microfilm group for captains' letters sent to the secretary of the navy.

We have expanded our symbols for designating copied material to include one for a letter book copy (LB Copy).

Transcription

We have continued the policy established in Volume I to adhere as closely as possible to the original in spelling, capitalization, punctuation, and abbreviation. In order to preserve the author's original writing style, we retained the dashes used in place of periods, commas, and semicolons. We do not abbreviate the complimentary close as was done in Volume I, but in the interest of saving space, have run it at the end of the last paragraph rather than as a separate paragraph.

Missing and Indecipherable Words

A bracketed question mark indicates illegible or mutilated material.

Unlike Volume I, we no longer add in square brackets the first names of persons mentioned in a document. We consider this to be an unnecessary editorial intrusion. The interested reader is directed to the index for full names.

Abbreviations Used to Describe Manuscripts

AD   Autograph Document
ADS   Autograph Document Signed
AL   Autograph Letter
ALS   Autograph Letter Signed
D   Document
DS   Document Signed
LB   Letter Book
LS   Letter Signed

Repository Symbols and Other Abbreviations

A&R   Appointments and Resignations
Adm.   Admiralty
AF   Area File
BC   Letters from Officers of Rank Below that of Commanders Received
            by the Secretary of the Navy
CaOOA   National Archives of Canada, Ottawa, Ontario
CGO   Circulars and General Orders, Navy Department
CL   Captains' Letters to the Secretary of the Navy
CLS   Confidential Letters Sent by the Secretary of the Navy
CM   Records of General Courts-Martial and Courts of Inquiry of the
            Navy Department
CMC   Office of the Commandant, U.S. Marine Corps
CNA   Letters Sent by the Secretary of the Navy to Commandants of Navy
            Yards and Navy Agents
CSmH   Henry E. Huntington Library, San Marino, Calif.
CtY-M   Yale Medical Library, Yale University, New Haven, Conn.
DLC   Library of Congress, Washington, D.C.
DNA   National Archives and Records Administration, Washington, D.C.
DNR   Naval Historical Center, Washington, D.C.
InU   Indiana University, Bloomington, Ind.
MC   Masters Commandant Letters Received by the Secretary of the Navy
MdAN   U.S. Naval Academy Museum, Annapolis, Md.
MdHi   Maryland Historical Society Library, Manscripts Division,
            Baltimore, Md.
MHi   Massachusetts Historical Society, Boston, Mass.
MiU-C   William L. Clements Library, University of Michigan,
            Ann Arbor, Mich.
MLR   Miscellaneous Letters Received by the Secretary of the Navy
MLS   Miscellaneous Letters Sent by the Secretary of the Navy

NBuHi	Buffalo and Erie County Historical Society, Buffalo, N.Y.
Nc-Ar	North Carolina State Archives, Raleigh, N.C.
NcD	William R. Perkins Library, Special Collections Department, Duke University, Durham, N.C.
NCooHi	New York State Historical Association, Cooperstown, N.Y.
NcU	University of North Carolina, Chapel Hill, N.C.
NHi	New-York Historical Society, New York, N.Y.
NHpR	Franklin D. Roosevelt Library, Hyde Park, N.Y.
NN	New York Public Library, New York, N.Y.
PHi	Historical Society of Pennsylvania, Philadelphia, Pa.
RG	Record Group
RHi	Rhode Island Historical Society, Manuscript Collection, Providence, R.I.
R.N.	Royal Navy
RNHi	Newport Historical Society, Newport, R.I.
RPB	Brown University Library, Providence, R.I.
ScU	South Caroliniana Library, University of South Carolina, Columbia, S.C.
SNL	Secretary of the Navy Letters to Officers, Ships of War
UkLPR	Public Record Office, London
U.S.A.	United States Army
U.S.M.C.	United States Marine Corps

Short Titles

Adams, *History of the United States.*   Henry Adams. *History of the United States of America during the Second Administration of James Madison.* 2 vols. New York: Charles Scribner's Sons, 1891.

Analectic Magazine.   *The Analectic Magazine, Comprising Original Reviews, Biography, Analytical Abstracts of New Publications.* . . . 16 vols. Philadelphia: M. Thomas, 1813–20.

Apgar, "U.S. Brig *Argus.*"   Wilbur E. Apgar. "The Last Cruise of the U.S. Brig *Argus.*" *U.S. Naval Institute Proceedings.* Vol. 65 (May 1939), pp. 653–60.

ASP: Military Affairs.   *American State Papers. Documents, Legislative and Executive, of the Congress of the United States.* . . . Class V. *Military Affairs.* Vol. 1. Washington, D.C.: Gales and Seaton, 1832.

Barbary Powers.   U.S. Office of Naval Records and Library. *Naval Documents Related to the United States Wars with the Barbary Powers.* 6 vols. Washington, D.C.: Government Printing Office, 1939–44.

Belovarac, "Brief Overview."   Allan Belovarac. "A Brief Overview of the Battle of Lake Erie and the Perry-Elliott Controversy." *Journal of Erie Studies.* Vol. 17 (Fall 1988), pp. 3–6.

Brannan, *Official Letters.*   John Brannan. *Official Letters of the Military and Naval Officers of the United States during the War with Great Britain in the Years 1812, 13, 14, & 15.* . . . Washington, D.C.: Way & Gideon, 1823.

Bridgwater, "John Jacob Astor."   Dorothy Wildes Bridgwater. "John Jacob Astor relative to His Settlement on Columbia River." *Yale University Library Gazette.* Vol. 24 (Oct. 1949), pp. 47–69.

Cain, *Ghost Ships.*   Emily Cain. *Ghost Ships:* Hamilton *and* Scourge: *Historical Treasures from the War of 1812.* New York: Beaufort Books, 1983.

Calderhead, "Naval Innovation."   William L. Calderhead. "Naval Innovation in Crisis: War in the Chesapeake, 1813." *American Neptune.* Vol. 36 (July 1976), pp. 206–21.

Chapelle, *American Sailing Navy.*   Howard I. Chapelle. *The History of the American Sailing Navy.* New York: W. W. Norton, 1949.

Chapelle, *Fulton's "Steam Battery."*   Howard I. Chapelle. *Fulton's "Steam Battery": Blockship and Catamaran.* Washington, D.C.: Smithsonian Institution, 1964.

Claiborne, *Letter Books.*   William C. C. Claiborne. *Official Letter Books of W. C. C. Claiborne, 1801–1816.* 6 vols. Edited by Dunbar Rowland. Jackson, Miss.: State Department of Archives and History, 1917.

Clanin, "Correspondence of Harrison and Perry."   Douglas E. Clanin. "The Correspondence of William Henry Harrison and Oliver Hazard Perry, July 5, 1813–July 31, 1815." *Northwest Ohio Quarterly.* Vol. 60 (Autumn 1988), pp. 153–80.

Coggeshall, *American Privateers and Letters-of-Marque.*   George Coggeshall. *History of the American Privateers, and Letters-of-Marque, during Our War with England in the Years 1812, '13, and '14.* . . . 3d ed. New York: George P. Putnam, 1861.

Cooper, *Ned Myers.* James Fenimore Cooper. *Ned Myers; or, A Life before the Mast.* 1843. Reprint. Edited by William S. Dudley. Classics of Naval Literature Series. Annapolis: Naval Institute Press, 1989.

Crawford, *Journal.* William H. Crawford. *Journal of William H. Crawford.* Edited by Daniel C. Knowlton. Smith College Studies in History. Vol. 11 (Oct. 1925), pp. 5–64.

Crowninshield, "*America* of Salem." Bowdoin B. Crowninshield. "An Account of the Private Armed 'Ship' *America* of Salem." *Historical Collections of the Essex Institute.* Vol. 37 (Jan. 1901), pp. 1–76.

Cushman, "Columbia Alumni." Paul Cushman. "Columbia Alumni Serving as Naval Surgeons in the War of 1812." *Bulletin of the American Academy of Medicine.* Vol. 47 (1971), pp. 50–66.

Dietz, "Cartel Vessels." Anthony G. Dietz. "The Use of Cartel Vessels during the War of 1812." *American Neptune.* Vol. 28 (July 1968), pp. 165–94.

Dietz, "Prisoner of War." Anthony G. Dietz. "The Prisoner of War in the United States during the War of 1812." Ph.D. diss., American University, 1964.

Drake, "Loss of Mastery." Frederick C. Drake. "A Loss of Mastery: The British Squadron on Lake Erie, May–September 1813." *Journal of Erie Studies.* Vol. 17 (Fall 1988), pp. 47–75.

Drake, "Yeo and Prevost." Frederick C. Drake. "Commodore Sir James Lucas Yeo and Governor General George Prevost: A Study in Command Relations, 1813–14." In *New Interpretations in Naval History: Selected Papers from the Eighth Naval History Symposium,* edited by William B. Cogar. Annapolis: Naval Institute Press, 1989, pp. 156–71.

Dudley, "Chauncey and Joint Operations." William S. Dudley. "Commodore Isaac Chauncey and U.S. Joint Operations on Lake Ontario, 1813–14." In *New Interpretations in Naval History: Selected Papers from the Eighth Naval History Symposium,* edited by William B. Cogar. Annapolis: Naval Institute Press, 1989, pp. 139–55.

Dudley, *Naval War of 1812.* William S. Dudley, ed. *The Naval War of 1812: A Documentary History.* Vol. 1. Washington, D.C.: Naval Historical Center, 1985.

Dunne, "Inglorious First of June." W. M. P. Dunne. "'The Inglorious First of June': Commodore Stephen Decatur on Long Island Sound, 1813." *Long Island Historical Journal.* Vol. 2 (Spring 1990), pp. 201–20.

Dye, "Maritime Prisoners." Ira Dye. "American Maritime Prisoners of War, 1812–15." In *Ships, Seafaring and Society: Essays in American Maritime History,* edited by Timothy J. Runyan. Detroit: Wayne State University Press, 1987, pp. 293–320.

Ellison, "David Wingfield." David Ellison. "David Wingfield and Sacketts Harbour." *Dalhousie Review.* Vol. 52 (1972), pp. 407–13.

Essex Institute, *American Vessels.* Essex Institute. *American Vessels Captured by the British during the Revolution and War of 1812: The Records of the Vice-Admiralty Court at Halifax, Nova Scotia.* Salem, Mass.: Essex Institute, 1911.

Estes and Dye, "Death on the *Argus.*" J. Worth Estes and Ira Dye. "Death on the *Argus:* American Medical Malpractice *versus* British Chauvinism in the War of 1812." *Journal of the History of Medicine and Allied Sciences.* Vol. 44 (April 1989), pp. 179–85.

Everest, *War of 1812.* Allan J. Everest. *The War of 1812 in the Champlain Valley.* Syracuse, N.Y.: Syracuse University Press, 1981.

Friedman and Skaggs, "Jesse Duncan Elliott." Lawrence J. Friedman and David C. Skaggs. "Jesse Duncan Elliott and the Battle of Lake Erie: The Issue of Mental Stability." *Journal of the Early Republic*. Vol. 10 (Winter 1990), pp. 493–516.

Garitee, *Republic's Private Navy*. Jerome R. Garitee. *The Republic's Private Navy: The American Privateering Business as Practiced by Baltimore during the War of 1812*. Middletown, Conn.: Wesleyan University Press, 1977.

Goldowsky, *Yankee Surgeon*. Seebert J. Goldowsky. *Yankee Surgeon: The Life and Times of Usher Parsons (1788–1868)*. Boston: The Frances A. Countway Library of Medicine and the Rhode Island Publications Society, 1988.

Gough, *Royal Navy*. Barry Gough. *The Royal Navy and the Northwest Coast of North America, 1810–1914: A Study of British Maritime Ascendancy*. Vancouver: University of British Columbia Press, 1971.

Guernsey, *New York City*. Rocellus S. Guernsey. *New York City and Vicinity during the War of 1812–'15. . . .* 2 vols. New York: Charles L. Woodward, 1889.

Hallahan, *Craney Island*. John M. Hallahan. *The Battle of Craney Island: A Matter of Credit*. Portsmouth, Va.: Saint Michael's Press, 1986.

Heine, *Ninety-six Years*. William C. Heine. *Ninety-six Years in the Royal Navy*. Hantsport, Nova Scotia: Lancelot Press, 1987.

Hickey, "American Trade Restrictions." Donald R. Hickey. "American Trade Restrictions during the War of 1812." *Journal of American History*. Vol. 68 (Dec. 1981), pp. 517–38.

Hickey, *War of 1812*. Donald R. Hickey. *The War of 1812: A Forgotten Conflict*. Urbana: University of Illinois Press, 1989.

Hitsman, "Alarum on Lake Ontario." J. Mackay Hitsman. "Alarum on Lake Ontario, Winter 1812–13." *Military Affairs*. Vol. 23 (1959), pp. 129–38.

Hitsman, "Spying." J. Mackay Hitsman. "Spying at Sackets Harbor, 1813." *Inland Seas*. Vol. 15 (1959), pp. 120–22.

Hitsman and Sorby, "Independent Foreigners." J. Mackay Hitsman and Alice Sorby. "Independent Foreigners or Canadian Chasseurs." *Military Affairs*. Vol. 25 (Spring 1961), pp. 11–17.

Hobbs, "Congreve War Rockets." Richard R. Hobbs. "Congreve War Rockets, 1800–1825." *U.S. Naval Institute Proceedings*. Vol. 94 (March 1968), pp. 80–88.

Hogg, *Artillery*. Oliver F. G. Hogg. *Artillery: Its Origin, Heyday and Decline*. Hamden, Conn.: Archon Books, 1970.

Horsman, *War of 1812*. Reginald Horsman. *The War of 1812*. New York: Alfred A. Knopf, 1969.

Humphries, "Capture of York." Charles W. Humphries. "The Capture of York." *Ontario History*. Vol. 51 (1959), pp. 1–21.

Hussey, *Voyage of the* Racoon. John A. Hussey, ed. *The Voyage of the* Racoon: *A 'Secret' Journal of a Visit to Oregon, California and Hawaii, 1813–1814*. San Francisco: Book Club of California, 1958.

Hutcheon, *Robert Fulton*. Wallace Hutcheon, Jr. *Robert Fulton: Pioneer of Undersea Warfare*. Annapolis: Naval Institute Press, 1981.

Inderwick, *Journal*. James Inderwick. *Cruise of the U.S. Brig* Argus *in 1813: Journal of Surgeon James Inderwick*. Edited by Victor H. Paltsits. New York: New York Public Library, 1917.

Jacobs. *U.S. Army*. James R. Jacobs. *The Beginning of the U.S. Army, 1783–1812*. Princeton, N.J.: Princeton University Press, 1947.

James, *Naval History.*   William James. *The Naval History of Great Britain.* . . . 6 vols. London: Richard Bentley & Son, 1886.

Johnston, *Three Years in Chili.*   Samuel Burr Johnston. *Letters Written during a Residence of Three Years in Chili, Containing an Account of the Most Remarkable Events in the Revolutionary Struggles of that Province.* . . . Erie, Pa.: R. I. Custis, 1816.

Langley, *Social Reform.*   Harold D. Langley. *Social Reform in the United States Navy, 1798–1862.* Urbana: University of Illinois Press, 1967.

Lavery, *Nelson's Navy.*   Brian Lavery. *Nelson's Navy: The Ships, Men and Organisation, 1793–1815.* Annapolis: Naval Institute Press, 1989.

Leech, *Thirty Years from Home.*   Samuel Leech. *Thirty Years from Home; or, A Voice from the Main Deck.* . . . Boston: Tappan & Dennet, 1843.

Lemmon, *Frustrated Patriots.*   Sarah M. Lemmon. *Frustrated Patriots: North Carolina and the War of 1812.* Chapel Hill: University of North Carolina Press, 1973.

Long, *Nothing Too Daring.*   David F. Long. *Nothing Too Daring: A Biography of Commodore David Porter, 1780–1843.* Annapolis: Naval Institute Press, 1970.

Long, *Sailor-Diplomat.*   David F. Long. *Sailor-Diplomat: A Biography of Commodore James Biddle, 1783–1848.* Boston: Northeastern University Press, 1983.

Lossing, *Pictorial Field-Book.*   Benson J. Lossing. *The Pictorial Field-Book of the War of 1812.* . . . New York: Harper & Brothers, 1869.

Ludlum, *Early American Hurricanes.*   David M. Ludlum. *Early American Hurricanes, 1492–1870.* Boston: Lancaster Press, 1963.

McKee, C. *U.S. Naval Officer Corps.*   Christopher McKee. *A Gentlemanly and Honorable Profession: The Creation of the U.S. Naval Officer Corps, 1794–1815.* Annapolis: Naval Institute Press, 1991.

McKee, L. "Portsmouth."   Linda A. M. McKee. "Captain Isaac Hull and the Portsmouth Navy Yard, 1813–1815." Ph.D. diss., St. Louis University, 1968.

Maclay, *American Privateers.*   Edgar S. Maclay. *A History of American Privateers.* 1899. Reprint. New York: D. Appleton, 1924.

Maclay, *United States Navy.*   Edgar S. Maclay. *A History of the United States Navy from 1775 to 1894.* 2 vols. New York: D. Appleton, 1897.

Mahan, *Sea Power.*   Alfred T. Mahan. *Sea Power in its Relation to the War of 1812.* 2 vols. 1905. Reprint. New York: Haskell House, 1969.

Maloney, *Captain from Connecticut.*   Linda M. Maloney. *The Captain from Connecticut: The Life and Naval Times of Isaac Hull.* Boston: Northeastern University Press, 1986.

Marshall, *Royal Navy Biography.*   John Marshall. *Royal Naval Biography.* . . . 4 vols. in 8. London: Longman, Hurst, Rees, Orme, and Brown, 1823–35.

Melville, *White Jacket.*   Herman Melville. *White Jacket; or, The World in a Man-of-War.* 1850. Reprint. Edited by William L. Heflin. Classics of Naval Literature Series. Annapolis: Naval Institute Press, 1988.

Mouzon, "*General Armstrong.*"   Harold A. Mouzon. "The Unlucky *General Armstrong.*" *American Neptune.* Vol. 15 (Jan. 1955), pp. 59–80.

Mouzon, *Privateers of Charleston.*   Harold A. Mouzon. *Privateers of Charleston.* Charleston, S.C.: Historical Commission of Charleston, 1954.

Napier, *Journal.*   Henry E. Napier. *New England Blockaded in 1814: The Journal of Henry Edward Napier, Lieutenant in H.M.S.* Nymphe. Edited by Walter M. Whitehill. Salem, Mass.: Peabody Museum, 1939.

Naval Chronicle.   *The Naval Chronicle,* . . . *Containing a General and Biographical History of the Royal Navy of the United Kingdom.* . . . 40 vols. London: Joyce Gold, 1799–1818.

Naval Documents. U.S. Naval History Division. *Naval Documents of the American Revolution.* 9 vols. to date. Edited by William B. Clark and William J. Morgan. Washington, D.C.: Government Printing Office, 1964–.

Nelson, "Ghost Ships." Daniel A. Nelson. "Ghost Ships of the War of 1812." *National Geographic.* Vol. 163 (Mar. 1983), pp. 289–313.

Norway, *Post-Office Packet Service.* Arthur S. Norway. *History of the Post-Office Packet Service, between the Years of 1793–1815.* London: Macmillan, 1895.

Pack, *Man Who Burned the White House.* James Pack. *The Man Who Burned the White House: Admiral Sir George Cockburn, 1772–1853.* Annapolis: Naval Institute Press, 1987.

Padfield, *Broke and* Shannon. Peter Padfield. *Broke and the* Shannon. London: Hodder and Stoughton, 1968.

Patrick, *Florida Fiasco.* Rembert W. Patrick. *Florida Fiasco: Rampant Rebels on the Georgia-Florida Border, 1810–1815.* Athens: University of Georgia Press, 1954.

Paullin, *John Rodgers.* Charles O. Paullin. *Commodore John Rodgers: Captain, Commodore, and Senior Officer of the American Navy, 1773–1838.* 1910. Reprint. Annapolis: Naval Institute Press, 1967.

Picking, Enterprise *and* Boxer. Sherwood Picking. *Sea Fight off Monhegan:* Enterprise *and* Boxer. Portland, Me.: Machigonne Press, 1941.

Pleadwell, "Edward Cutbush." Frank L. Pleadwell. "Edward Cutbush, M.D." *Annals of Medical History.* Vol. 5 (Dec. 1923), pp. 337–86.

Pleadwell, "James Inderwick." Frank L. Pleadwell. "James Inderwick: Surgeon, United States Navy, 1813–1815." *United States Naval Medical Bulletin.* Vol. 1 (1922), pp. 2–15.

Porter, *Journal of a Cruise.* David Porter. *Journal of a Cruise Made to the Pacific Ocean, by Captain David Porter, in the United States Frigate* Essex, *in the Years 1812, 1813, and 1814.* . . . 2 vols. Philadelphia: Bradford and Inskeep, 1815.

Pratt, *Expansionists of 1812.* Julius W. Pratt. *Expansionists of 1812.* New York: Macmillan, 1925.

Pullen, Shannon *and* Chesapeake. Hugh F. Pullen. *The* Shannon *and the* Chesapeake. Toronto: McClelland and Stewart, 1970.

Ralfe, *Naval Biography.* James Ralfe. *The Naval Biography of Great Britain: Consisting of Historical Memoirs of Those Officers of the British Navy Who Distinguished Themselves during the Reign of George III.* 4 vols. London: Whitmore & Fenn, 1828.

Rippy, *Joel R. Poinsett.* J. Fred Rippy. *Joel R. Poinsett, Versatile American.* Durham, N.C.: Duke University Press, 1935.

Ritchie and Ritchie, "Laker's Log." Margaret K. and Carson I. A. Ritchie. "A Laker's Log." *American Neptune.* Vol. 17 (July 1957), pp. 203–11.

Robinson, "Prisoners." Ralph Robinson. "Retaliation for the Treatment of Prisoners in the War of 1812." *American Historical Review.* Vol. 49 (1943), pp. 65–70.

Roland, *Underwater Warfare.* Alex Roland. *Underwater Warfare in the Age of Sail.* Bloomington: Indiana University Press, 1978.

Roosevelt, *Naval War of 1812.* Theodore Roosevelt. *The Naval War of 1812.* 1882. Reprint. Edited by Edward K. Eckert. Classics of Naval Literature Series. Annapolis: Naval Institute Press, 1987.

Rosenberg, *Building Perry's Fleet.* Max Rosenberg. *The Building of Perry's Fleet on Lake Erie, 1812–13.* Harrisburg: Pennsylvania Historical and Museum Commission, 1987.

Roske and Donley, "Perry-Elliott Controversy." Ralph J. Roske and Richard W. Donley. "The Perry-Elliott Controversy: A Bitter Footnote to the Battle of Lake Erie." *Northwest Ohio Quarterly*. Vol. 34 (1962), pp. 111–23.

Skaggs, "And They Are Ours." David C. Skaggs. "And They Are Ours." *Timeline*. Vol. 6 (Apr.–May 1989), pp. 20–27.

Skaggs, "Joint Operations." David C. Skaggs. "Joint Operations during the Detroit–Lake Erie Campaign, 1813." In *New Interpretations in Naval History: Selected Papers from the Eighth Naval History Symposium*, edited by William B. Cogar. Annapolis: Naval Institute Press, 1989, pp. 121–38.

Skeen, *John Armstrong*. C. Edward Skeen. *John Armstrong, Jr., 1758–1843: A Biography*. Syracuse, N.Y.: Syracuse University Press, 1981.

Statutes at Large. *The Public Statutes at Large of the United States of America, from the Organization of the Government in 1789, to March 3, 1845. . . .* 8 vols. Edited by Richard Peters. Boston: Little, Brown, 1846–67.

Stevens, *Affair of Honor*. William O. Stevens. *An Affair of Honor: The Biography of Commodore James Barron, U.S.N.* Chesapeake, Va.: Norfolk County Historical Society, 1969.

Symonds, *Navalists and Antinavalists*. Craig L. Symonds. *Navalists and Antinavalists: The Naval Policy Debate in the United States, 1785–1827*. Newark: University of Delaware Press, 1980.

Tyler, "Fulton's Steam Frigate." David B. Tyler. "Fulton's Steam Frigate." *American Neptune*. Vol. 6 (Oct. 1946), pp. 253–74.

Valle, "Navy's Battle Doctrine." James E. Valle. "The Navy's Battle Doctrine in the War of 1812." *American Neptune*. Vol. 44 (Summer 1984), pp. 171–78.

Valle, *Rocks & Shoals*. James E. Valle. *Rocks & Shoals: Order and Discipline in the Old Navy, 1800–1861*. Annapolis: Naval Institute Press, 1980.

Watson, *Commodore James Barron*. Paul B. Watson. *The Tragic Career of Commodore James Barron*. New York: Coward-McCann, 1942.

Wilkinson, *Memoirs*. James Wilkinson, *Memoirs of My Own Times*. 3 vols. Philadelphia: Abraham Small, 1816.

Chapter One

The Atlantic Theater:
January–December 1813

Many Americans whose congressmen had declared war against Great Britain in June 1812 probably regretted the decision by the end of December. The military campaigns had gone badly. The militia system was ineffective, and the regular army barely existed. The states with the largest prepared militias, those of New England, had populations that were critical of the war and their governors refused to send troops outside their state boundaries. Recruiting for the regular army had failed to produce a sufficient number of soldiers and the supply system was in chaos. President Madison's strategy was to launch a three-pronged, coordinated assault with the objective of seizing and holding a portion of Upper Canada until Great Britain had come to terms, agreeing to halt impressment of seamen and seizure of American merchant ships under the authority of the Orders in Council. New legislation had authorized a 35,000 man regular army, but less than 7,000 were on hand in June. The president was authorized to enlist 50,000 volunteers and to call up 100,000 state militia; the latter were paper armies only. The call for enlistments went out too late, and state militias were not prone to fight outside of their states. Troops that did exist were scattered at garrisons throughout the country.

Of the three small armies that were hastily assembled in 1812, all were poorly equipped, ill trained, and led by timid, aging officers. Major General Henry Dearborn, who commanded the eastern armies, took personal command of an army bivouacked near Albany. Brigadier General William Hull, who commanded the northwestern army, attacked the British surrounding Detroit but was forced to surrender. Dearborn's army, intending to attack Montreal, briefly crossed the border near Lake Champlain and then retreated to Plattsburg after the first signs of resistance.

Dearborn's subordinates, Major General Stephen Van Rensselaer, New York militia, and Brigadier General Alexander Smyth, U.S. Army, commanded successively at Buffalo on the Niagara. In October 1812, Van Rensselaer attacked Queenston Heights from Niagara but was driven back. Smyth made a similar attempt in November, with the same result. In January 1813, a contingent of British troops and Indians badly mauled General James Winchester's Kentucky militia south of Detroit at Frenchtown on the River Raisin. Consequently, General William H. Harrison's Northwest Army was stalled near Fort Meigs in northern Ohio.

To this disheartening situation, one must add the depletion of the national treasury. Revenues had fallen off sharply as a result of the British blockade. Fewer ships in foreign trade meant reduced customs receipts on imports. Treasury Secre-

tary Albert Gallatin employed desperate measures to float loans in order to finance the war. Under these circumstances, it should not be surprising that President Madison would want to take advantage of the offer of the Russian czar in
early 1813 to mediate the "dispute" between the United States and Great Britain.

The arrival of this offer in February prompted Madison and Gallatin into action. Madison entered into discussions with the Russian minister Andrei Ia.
Dashkov, feeling there was little to lose. Gallatin proceeded to use the offer to woo
investors who might lend money to the United States government. The way the war
was going, the Russian mediation offer presented at least a possibility of peace,
and therefore, a decreased investment risk. To attract investors, Gallatin offered an
increase in the interest rate from 6% to 7.5%. As a result, he was successful in obtaining sufficient financing for another year of war.

Were it not for the brilliant performance of the U.S. Navy in the first months of
the war, Americans would have had every reason to seek a negotiated peace. The
navy raised the nation's morale in a series of ship-to-ship engagements on the high
seas and perhaps gave the president and Congress the fortitude to continue the
struggle they had begun the previous spring. The Essex-Alert, Constitution-
Guerriere, Wasp-Frolic, United States-Macedonian, and Constitution-
Java battles were fought between August and December 1812. By the end of the
year, this succession of victorious naval engagements raised the reputation of the
navy to its highest level in years. Only five years before, the American frigate
Chesapeake had been humiliated by H.M.S. Leopard off the Virginia Capes.
The Royal Navy soon recognized that American ships and seamen were a force to
be respected. On Lake Ontario, Commodore Chauncey established American dominance by late November, demonstrating the efficacy of a lake navy. Despite its
small size, the United States Navy was professional and full of fight. The question
was: How to use this force in the face of likely British reinforcements in the Atlantic and on the Northern lakes?

The navy's strategy, as stated by Secretary Paul Hamilton in September 1812,
was to divide the frigates and smaller vessels into three squadrons. Thus, Commodore William Bainbridge, commanding Constitution, 44 guns, was to sail in
company with Captain David Porter's Essex, 32, and Master Commandant James
Lawrence's sloop of war Hornet, 18. These plans were frustrated when Essex, re-
quiring extensive refitting after a successful cruise, returned to the Delaware. As
Constitution and Hornet were ready for sea, Bainbridge departed, ordering
Porter to rendezvous at either the Cape Verde Islands or the island of Fernando de
Noronha off the northern Brazilian coast; failing this, he was to use his discretion
in determining how best to employ his ship. A second squadron was comprised of
Commodore Stephen Decatur's frigate United States, 44, Captain Samuel
Evans's Chesapeake, 38, and Master Commandant Arthur Sinclair's brig
Argus, 18. As it happened, Chesapeake was not ready, departed later, and
cruised independently. The third squadron was to be Commodore John Rodgers's
President, 44, Captain John Smith's frigate Congress, 36, and Master Com-
mandant Jacob Jones's sloop of war Wasp, 18. Detained because of repairs, Wasp

sailed later, intercepted a convoy of merchant ships, and captured H.M. sloop of war Frolic, *only to be herself captured hours later by H.M.S.* Poictiers, 74.

While the squadrons were at sea, Secretary Hamilton took the opportunity of suggesting to Congress the building of a class of 74-gun ships of the line and additional frigates. On 23 December, after more than a month of debate, Congress authorized the construction of four 74-gun ships and six 44-gun frigates. The bill, signed into law on 2 January 1813, was the first major naval construction bill in more than a decade. Unfortunately, the events and shortages of the war retarded construction and reduced the projected number of ships. The 74-gun ships Independence, Washington, *and* Franklin, *and the frigates* Java *and* Guerriere *would not be completed until after the war. When nearly finished, the frigate* Columbia *was burned at the Washington Navy Yard in 1814.*

The slow progress of the war and the elections of November 1812 wrought changes among those responsible for naval and military administration. Madison's reelection gave him the confidence he needed to replace Hamilton with William Jones as secretary of the navy and William Eustis with John Armstrong as secretary of war. The navy had done well up to that point, but Madison asked Hamilton to resign because he had become personally unable to manage the rapidly growing pressures of office. It was common knowledge that Hamilton had a drinking problem and that this was affecting his work.

Madison chose William Jones to be secretary of the navy because he thought that, as a former sea captain, merchant, and banker, Jones would be skilled at managing naval officers, ships, and naval finance. He had also served a term in Congress and was a loyal Republican. Jones inherited from Hamilton a skeleton staff of civilians, led by chief clerk Charles Goldsborough, with no professional naval officers to serve as military advisers or to whom he could delegate technical tasks. Jones occasionally consulted nearby officers, such as Captain Thomas Tingey, the commandant of the Washington Navy Yard, and Captain Charles Morris, *whose ship* Adams *was being repaired at the Washington Navy Yard.* Jones was a personal friend of Commodore Bainbridge's, from whom the new secretary may have acquired knowledge of the navy's inner workings. When Jones arrived in office, he set about his task with a will, establishing himself as the final authority. He was determined not to be a figurehead with a small staff of long-tenured clerks running the office.

One of his first acts was to replace chief clerk Goldsborough with Benjamin Homans, a man recommended by Elbridge Gerry, the newly elected vice president from Massachusetts. Soon after, he requested from Captain Morris a list of reforms that could be made in the Navy Department. Jones proved to be a competent administrator in an overburdened department, though not a naval strategist. These professional matters he usually left to his senior commodores and captains. John Armstrong, at the head of the War Department, took the opposite course and involved himself in battlefield command, with disastrous results in late 1813.

The navy had stations at major seaports from Portland, Maine, to New Orleans, Louisiana. The commandants of these stations had to contend with the scarcity of men, armament, vessels, and provisions, never knowing when or where the mobile

British would present themselves. Local citizens along the seaboard usually had no one else to rely on for protection. Officers who found themselves in this position were anxious to escape to a command at sea, but the opportunities rarely came. Thus, the Atlantic theater presents a varied maritime geography and the navy's forces ranged from large frigates to gunboat flotillas. The navy's offensive cruising strategy gradually withered as the British strengthened their blockade of key ports.

Initially, British land and sea forces were deployed in Europe and in the Caribbean, where the requirements of war against Napoleonic France and her colonies demanded their presence. The British struggle against revolutionary France and her dominions had been underway since 1793. By the end of 1805, British naval victories had swept the allied French and Spanish navies from the seas, but the blockade of the French ports in the English Channel and the North, Baltic, and Mediterranean Seas remained in effect to prevent naval resurgence and to obstruct the enemy's seaborne trade. The new war in America was an added threat, if not an absolute danger to the British Empire. Any ships sent to the western Atlantic to deal with American naval squadrons and privateers would weaken Britain's military posture in the Mediterranean, Bay of Biscay, and the English Channel. The shortage of regular troops in Canada and the lack of ships of the line on the North American Station can largely be explained by these considerations. Yet the European picture had begun to change by late 1812.

Napoleon's armies invaded Russia in June, reached Moscow by September, and were forced into retreat by October. In Spain, the Duke of Wellington's armies were gradually pushing French armies from Iberian soil. He scored a major victory at Salamanca, suffered a setback at Burgos, but recovered at the Battle of Vitoria on 21 June 1813, the turning point of the Peninsular War. The course of events had begun to run against the French emperor. Within a year he abdicated and departed for exile on Elba. The Lords Commissioners of the Admiralty reversed their initial reluctance to release additional ships for operations against the United States as fewer ships were needed on European stations. The early successes of the U.S. Navy and the slow progress of Admiral Warren in stemming the American tide of heavy frigates and privateers in the first year of war precipitated a more aggressive British stance by mid-1813. Although the impact of British reinforcements was not felt for several months, Navy Secretary William Jones soon faced his severest challenge because the improvement in British military affairs in the European war released troops and ships for use in North America.

Squadron Cruise Reports

The year 1813 opened with the return of three U.S. warships that had left on cruises in October 1812. Commodore John Rodgers and Captain John Smith, in President *and* Congress, *arrived at Boston on 31 December after making a circuit of the western Atlantic. They sighted but five British vessels and captured only two. Master Commandant*

Arthur Sinclair in Argus, *after parting company with Commodore Stephen Decatur, cruised near Barbados, Brazil, and Bermuda. Because he took just five merchant prizes, Sinclair considered his cruise unsuccessful. All three ships needed extensive repairs.* President *and* Congress *did not depart again until the end of April. Refitting and a special mission delayed* Argus's *sailing until June.*

COMMODORE JOHN RODGERS TO SECRETARY OF THE NAVY PAUL HAMILTON [1]

U.S. Frigate *President*
Boston   Jany. 2nd 1813

Sir

I wrote you on the 31st ult informing you of my arrival with this Ship and the *Congress*—

It will appear somewhat extreordinary when I inform you that in our late cruise we have sailed by our log nearly 11'000 Miles, that we chased every thing we saw, yet that we should have seen so few Enemies Vessels and more particularly when we have from time to time been in the track of his whole commerce to every part of the Globe.

In the hope of being afforded an opportunity of adding additional reputation to our little Navy, we did not return until I may say our Provisions were nearly indeed entirely expended.

Of the last month we cruised about three weeks between Halifax and Bermuda, and the remainder of the time between the latter place and the Chesapeak, without seeing a single Enemy's Vessel: Having experienced much bad weather, both Ships will require considerable outfit, particularly in Spars, Sails, and rigging; and the *President's* Copper appearing defective in several places, will make it necessary to heave her out to repair the same, and which I shall make arrangements for, so as to commence the opperation by the time I can receive your approbation.

I am anxious to get to Sea again, and no time shall be lost in refitting both Ships.— The *President* having sprung her Main mast, will require a new one.— I am in hopes on examination that the *Congress* will not be found to require any essential repairs further than in her Sails and rigging.

I forgot to mention to you in my last communication that on the 16th ult in Latd. 35° 51'. Longd. 66° 34' we fell in with and sent back for adjudication, the Ship *Bedford,* of Portsmouth (N.H.) sailing under a British licence, bound from Baltimore to Lisbon, with a cargo of Flour.

Herewith you will receive a chart shewing our track during the last cruise   I have the honor to be With the greatest respect Sir Your obet. Servt.

Jn⁰ Rodgers

LS, DNA, RG45, CL, 1813, Vol. 1, No. 4 (M125, Roll No. 26). Chart not located.

1. Paul Hamilton resigned on 31 December 1812. William Jones accepted the appointment to be the new secretary of the navy on 14 January 1813.

Map 1. *Atlantic and Gulf Theaters*

MASTER COMMANDANT ARTHUR SINCLAIR TO
SECRETARY OF THE NAVY HAMILTON

U States Brig *Argus*　Newyork—Jany. the 2d 1812 [*1813*]—

I have the Honor, Sir, to inform you of my arrival here after a long, unpleasant and, considering the track I have taken, unsuccessful cruize. I was ordered by Comdr. Decatur to cruize far to windward of Barbadoes, unless circumstances should render a deviation from those orders advisable, in which event I was to use my own judgement— In running for this ground I kept well to the Eastward in hopes of falling in with some of the Brazile ships, and on the 27th of October I captured one from that quarter— From her Commander I learned that news of the war had not reached them until two days before his departure, and that there were a number of valuable ships homeward bound from thence— I, by mutual consent, shortened our allowance and kept my wind for the Longd. of Cape St. Rogue, the Eastern point of the Brazile, where most of them pass

Strong S E winds prevailing, by the time I reached it, I found the state of my provisions would not admit of my remaining long in any one place, being <u>particularly</u> ordered to return <u>to the U States</u> to replenish— My crew also began to grow sickly from the excessive heat and short allowance of Water

I then shaped my course under easy sail along down the Line, in hopes of intercepting vessels bound to and from the north part of the Brazile; and particularly down about Surinam I felt sure of meeting some of Value— After passing this ground as low down as would just admit of my weathering Barbadoes, and not falling in with a single sail, I hauled across to the northward, and spent all the time which the state of my provision would admit— I then shaped my course for Bermudas, and past just to the Eastward of it, hoping to fall in with some of their Small cruizers, who could not be employed on our Coast at this boistrous Season and would probibly be here abouts in search of our homeward bound Eastindia ships— Here I had one continued and heavy gale of Wind, which distrest us very much; the *Argus* begining to shew her age in every joint, keeping one pump employed and leaking in every seam and nail head in her upper works— During this gale I fell in with two large ships laying too— Taking them for Enemies Ships of War, who had either not seen me from the thickness of the weather, or were prevented by the gale from chasing me, I wore Ship and stood to windward of them, and after convincing myself they were Ships of War, I hauled again to the Northward under cover of the night— The next morning, the gale having moderated, I chased a small vessel of war, which from her Rig I took to be one of their cruizers, and gained so much on her, that I kept her in sight until a 11 Oclock that night when she got off in a Squall— A few hours more light would have made him ours

Finding continual gales from the Westward I began to feal considerable apprehentions as regarded our provision, I therefore took the necessary precautions in time and went upon little more than would support Nature— The *Argus* being too deep to acquit herself properly in sailing, with 75 days water and provision, which is as much as she can stow, the Commodore ordered me to take in 60 days, and my having been sent out two days before we sailed in company with the other ships in order to reconnitre the enemy; it had brought my cruize up to 70 days upon 60 of provision, where I fell in with a Squadron of the Enemies ships consisting of six Sail of Line of Battle ships and Frigates, and was closely chased for three days, and run several hundred miles out of my Course with the only favourable wind I had had since leaving the Trades— This remarkable chase and wonderful escape, commenced on the 15 of December in Longd. 61.30—Lattd 35.40; for the particulars of which I beg leave to refer you to the enclosed abstract from my journal; which I feal confident will satisfy you that no expedient or exertion in my power to make, was left untried, and serious as our loss has been, it was indispensably necessary for the preservation of the Ship and did save her from the Enemy—[1] Since that period I have been continually beating about and laying too, between Bermuda and the Continent, and have experienced some as long and heavy gales as are generally met with; which added to the chase and its effects has made a complete wreck of the *Argus* both in Hull and Rigging

So very badly has she leaked in her upper works that there has not been one single dry spot between decks for the last 15 days— The water has been six inches on her Magazine floor, having come first from above into my Cabbin and the ward room, oweing to her Beams and decks being rotten and opening while she was labouring in those heavy gales; our sail room has also been full of water, and what was more serious than all, what little bread we had left after having lived since the chase upon four ounces each man for 24 Hours, was totally spoiled, and we have barely made out to keep soul and body together upon a less quanty of Peas and Rice— What has made it infinitely worse for us, has been the vessel affording us no shelter from the wet and cold when below deck— Thirty or forty of those poor improvident fellows have resorted to drinking Salt water, which has completely knocked them up, and some of them have been rendered delirious

They have had not a drop of Spirits in all this hard weather which appears to be one of their greatest wants— We must have perished for want of water before this time had we not been lucky in frequent and heavy rains about the Line where we saved near two thousand gallons.

However there is no doubt but a short time will restore them all, as nourishment is all they want— I feal sensibly mortified, Sir, in having returned from such a lengthy cruize without an opportunity having offered by which I might have added some few Laurels to the number so recently and so gallantly acquired by some of my brother Officers; as I confidently think, from the merits of the Officers and Crew I have the honor to Command that opportunity is all that is wanting to insure them an equal share— I feal much pleasure in saying that in all our difficulties and hardships there has been nothing like a murmer onboard; ~~but~~ such has been their zeal for the service that they have always met the reduction of allowances with cheerfulness, while it appeard to hold out a prospect of meeting an opportunity of sharing in the glory of their brother Tars— I annex you the particulars of five prizes maned by the *Argus* this Cruize, and it is with heart fealt regret that I am compeld to state that only two of them are Ships of the Enemy.

As the *Argus* must undergo a thorough repair before she can take a cruize of any length; I will make a correct statement of her state by the next mail— I have the honor to sign myself with respect, Sir, Your Obt. Servt.

A Sinclair

ALS, DNA, RG45, MC, 1813, No. 1 (M147, Roll No. 5). This letter was sent with two enclosures, "A list of Vessels Captured by the United Sts Brig *Argus*, under my command, in the months of October, November, and December 1812—," and excerpts from the log of the *Argus*, 15–18 December 1812.

1. John Borlase Warren in *San Domingo* chased *Argus*; see Warren to Croker, 25 Jan. 1813, pp. 15–16.

Naval Medicine Ashore and at Sea

Philadelphia naval surgeon Edward Cutbush expressed his frustrations in attempting to provide medical care for a group of undisciplined seamen. Cutbush, a proponent of establishing rules for the government of naval hospitals, reiterated his plea for regulatory measures.[1] Dr. Amos A. Evans, Constitution*'s surgeon, showed great solicitude for the sick and wounded who were returning home after "Old Ironsides'" engagement with* Java.[2]

1. Pleadwell, *"Edward Cutbush,"* pp. 369–73; and Dudley, Naval War of 1812, Vol. 1, pp. 140–43.
2. See Dudley, Naval War of 1812, Vol. 1, pp. 639–49, for the 29 December 1812 action.

SURGEON EDWARD CUTBUSH TO CHARLES W. GOLDSBOROUGH [1]

Sir,

In pursuance of an order, I received from the Department, dated Novr. 19 1812,[2] I removed the men who had been landed from the *Essex* to Philada., two of them, being in a situation to do duty, were sent to New York with a draft from this place; two have deserted, John Francis, Peter Johnson, they are useless men—of the remainder one refuses to submit to the necessary treatment of his case, *Fistula in Perineo*,[3] which does not prevent him from committing great excesses.[4] Commodore Murray thinks that they should be discharged—it is also my opinion; as they are so extremely unruly, there is no prospect of any good to be derived either to themselves or the public service. Two are the most hardened villians, I have had under my care since I have been in service; the black hole of the Yard, Clog and chain—have no terrors—in fact, from a circumstance which has occurred, I am very apprehensive, that their conduct during the night, and from a disposition to resist the sentinels at the Gates of the Yard, that blood will be shed. The sentinels must do their duty in the night.

As Capt. Porter by letter stated his intention of "discharging them from service had time and circumstances permitted", I beg leave to solicit permission to discharge such of them as are in the habit of going over the fence and returning intoxicated. Commodore Murray declines issuing an order respecting them as they were brought to Philada. by direction of the Department. It appears to me that it would be incurring a needless expense, by keeping a guard of Marines over these men, five in number, especially as they will be useless, and having diseases that were not contracted, except one case, in the line of their duty. Should permission be obtained to discharge the most ungovernable, the Purser, I presume, has the power to discharge the pay that may have become due, since they have been in the Hospital.

On remonstrating with one of these men, an Englishman, on the impropriety of his conduct, and stating that the Government would not support men, who were thus injuring themselves, he had the impudence to say that he knew of no Government in the U.S.—

The above circumstances render it necessary that regulations, sanctioned by the Navy Department, should be adopted for the Government of men in sick quarters; the conduct, of which I complain, is subversive of all discipline, but I have no remedy. I will thank you to communicate the contents of this letter to the Secretary and obtain an order thereon, addressed to me or Commodore Murray.[5] I have the honor to remain your sert.

E Cutbush
Jany. 4, 1812 [1813]

ALS, DNA, RG45, BC, 1813, Vol. 1, No.5 (M148, Roll No. 11).

1. Charles W. Goldsborough of Maryland had been connected with the Navy Department since 1798, becoming its chief clerk in 1801.

2. Hamilton had ordered Cutbush to care for the men David Porter left behind at the hospital at New Castle, Delaware, when he sailed on his cruise in the fall of 1812. The secretary could not order their discharge until the state of their accounts could be ascertained; see Hamilton to Cutbush, 19 Nov. 1812, DNA, RG45, SNL, Vol. 10, p. 205 (M149, Roll No. 10).

3. Passage leading to the urinogenital duct.

4. For more background on these men, see Dudley, *Naval War of 1812*, Vol. 1, pp. 591–92.

5. William Jones directed Alexander Murray to discharge them if "the good of the service requires it." See Jones to Murray, 27 Jan. 1813, DNA, RG45, SNL, Vol. 10, p. 235 (M149, Roll No. 10).

Extract of Medical Prescription Book of Surgeon Amos A. Evans[1] Kept on Board the U.S. Frigate *Constitution*

Sunday Jany 10th

Particular attention must be paid to the sick & wounded: & see that they get their medicines drink &cas ordered.

Johnson must attend to the cooking & procuring water for the sick—

Williams must wash all the bandages &c in Boiling water, & have them ready rolld up. He must also scrape lint & pay a general attention to the sick. He must make the poultices.

Bowen must give all the medicines.

Stephen Vee must make all drinks & give them. He must also see that any man has Lemonade when he wants it. They must all keep their regular watch at night except Bowen who is subject to all calls for medicine &c at night. Johnson must keep his watch.

AD, CtY–M, Medical Prescription Book of Dr. Amos A. Evans kept on board the U.S. Frigate *Constitution*. This is an extract from 1813.

1. Amos A. Evans held surgeon's rank dating from 20 April 1810.

British Reassess Naval War in America

The new year ushered in a period of reexamination for the British. Admiral Sir John Borlase Warren, after just three months as head of the North American Station, quickly concluded that more ships were required if he was to conduct successful naval operations against the United States. The Admiralty informed Warren that it was economically impossible to establish a force everywhere to prevent attacks. In early 1813, however, it relented to the admiral's request for reinforcements, agreeing to supply him with more ships and a force of Royal Marines—but with the full expectation that the war would soon be over and they could be returned to their own stations.

ADMIRAL SIR JOHN B. WARREN, R.N., TO
FIRST SECRETARY OF THE ADMIRALTY JOHN W. CROKER

No. 67

San Domingo at Sea
5th January 1812 [*1813*]

Sir

I have enclosed for their Lordships information the statement of the loss of His Majesty's late Gun Brig *Plumper* Lieutenant Bray; [1] and in consequence of the Enemies Privateers becoming daily more numerous, and the assembling a Force of Three thousand Men at East Port on the Frontiers of New Brunswick and menacing that Province with attacks; I am induced again to earnestly solicit their Lordships to send eight of the large Gun Brigs for this particular service, as well as other ships to answer the very many and serious applications made upon me for aid, and protection for the Coats [*coasts*] of British America and the west Indies; and the reduced state of the Squadron under my Command   I have the honor to be Sir Your most obedient humble Servant

John Borlase Warren

LS, UkLPR, Adm. 1/503, pp. 139–40.

1. Lieutenant William Mackenzie Godfrey, R.N., commander of the sloop *Emulous*, reported that *Plumper* had wrecked on 5 December 1812 off Point Lepreau, New Brunswick, with her commanding officer, Lieutenant James Bray, and about sixteen of the crew surviving; see Godfrey to Senior Naval Officer, Halifax, 7 December 1812, UkLPR, Adm. 1/503, pp. 141–43. *Plumper* had captured several American privateers in 1812.

ADMIRAL SIR HENRY E. STANHOPE, R.N.,[1] TO FIRST LORD OF THE ADMIRALTY
VISCOUNT ROBERT SAUNDERS DUNDAS MELVILLE

Private

Stanwell House   Staines   Jan 5. 1813

My Lord

The recent Events incident to the American War lead me to hope for your Lordship's Indulgence for committing my thoughts to Paper, which, but for a Moments unexpected Indisposition I intended Myself the Honor of soliciting Permission to have named personally this Day

Admiral Sir John Borlase Warren, R.N.

I think the Americans will be so elated by their unexpected Success that a more than usual Spirit of Enterprize will stimulate, even the Federalists, to the Equipment of Men of War of large Dimensions under the Character and name of Frigates; and altho it be true that at this Instant They have only Three of great Force, the Ease with which They can run up any Number from the Plenty of Materials within Themselves, will I suspect rapidly encrease their Force together with a Host of minor Frigates and other armed vessels— adverting to the just Adage of "*Venienti occurrite Morbo*",[2] I would submit for your Lordship to direct a Survey upon the Sixty four, and small Class of Seventy four Gun Ships in Ordinary, to ascertain their State of Condition for speedy Service, and such as should be so considered might be cut down, selecting Such whose Lines would encourage the Hope of their sailing well, when by the Removal of an immense Weight from aloft, they would be lifted much out of the Water while their Stability would be rather increased as the Weight below would continue the same, and their Force should be left as Efficacious as Circumstances would admit, which would place them far above the Americans— Your Lordship will perceive I suggest this merely upon the Spur of the Moment until the Ships ordered to be built could be brought forward; And with Respect to their Annoyance upon the Coast I would humbly submit that any Attack upon the principal Sea Port Towns would be unavailable and disastrous without such a Land Force as the Circumstances of the Country could not perhaps readily admit—but I would effectually blockade them by such a well connected Chain of commanding Force as They should not be able to oppose, composed of small Squadrons under the Command of active intelligent officers; And as these different Squadrons might be exposed accidentally to Attack from Galleys, Gun boats, and similar Craft it would be proper for the Ships to be supplied with Boats of a certain Description for such Emergencies. But as the Coast of America in its vast Extent, has innumerable small Harbours and Inlets as well for Trade, as for the building and equipping of armed Vessels I would suggest smaller cruizing Squadrons to be a continual Watch and Annoyance, and that a certain additional Force of Marines well appointed be attached so as to destroy with certain effect whatever might grow up in these Harbours—totally regardless of Capture, so that no Impediment should be to the speediest Reembarkation before any opposing Force of Consequence could be collected. I conceive moreover, by the Way of keeping them in perpetual Alarm, the Demonstration of serious Attack might be made at any particular Port, and when their Force was drawn to it the Squadrons so collected might separate instantly for real Execution upon any Spot where it might have been previously determined. I would submit to your Lordship that even now such Ships as could be spared might be appointed to this Service, and I am fully persuaded the Success would equal the best Expectation—

These are simply Outlines of any future better digested Plan, which I have the Honor to submit to your Lordship's Indulgence, and Pardon for this Intrusion if Such it should appear, arising from much Experience in the Command of small Vessels on that Coast as a Lieutenant and Captain, exclusive of Opportunity from traversing many hundred Miles in various Situations and Disguise upon two Attempts to escape when a Prisoner in the American Contest.[3] I am well aware, from whence I speak with great Deference to their distinguished Merit and Abilities that no Men can have greater preeminent Merit than my Brethren at the and Nautical Friends at the Admiralty, while Local knowledge can only be attainable by personal Experience, which has thus brought me to adventure so much in Submission to your Lordship but still I beg to be understood in due Deference to these distinguished officers who form a Part of that Board, to which, particularly during the Presidency of the late Lord Melville, I stood so highly indebted and attached.

Committing myself to your Lordship's Indulgence, I have the Honor to be My Lord Your Lordship's most humble, and obedient Servant,

H. E. Stanhope

ALS, CSmH, Melville Papers.

1. Sir Henry Edwin Stanhope, a naval veteran of the Revolutionary War, was promoted to admiral on 12 August 1812.
2. An ounce of prevention is worth a pound of cure.
3. *Naval Documents*, Vol. 2, pp. 1268–69 and Vol. 4, pp. 1304 and 1422.

FIRST SECRETARY OF THE ADMIRALTY JOHN W. CROKER TO ADMIRAL SIR JOHN B. WARREN, R.N.

Copy   No. 2

Admiralty Office
9th Jany. 1813.

Sir

My Lords Commissioners of the Admiralty had hoped that the great force placed at your disposal as stated in my letter of the 18th November would have enabled you to obtain the most decided advantages over the Enemy, and to blockade their Ships of War in their Ports, or to intercept and capture them at Sea if they should escape the vigilance of your blockading Squadrons.—

In this expectation their Lordships have been hitherto disappointed, and tho' they hope that the measures you have taken for the employment of your forces may have already been attended with success, yet as it is of the highest importance to the Character and interests of the Country that the Naval Force of the Enemy, should be quickly and completely disposed of, my Lords have thought themselves justified at this moment in withdrawing Ships from other important Services for the purpose of placing under your orders a force with which you cannot fail to bring the Naval War to a termination, either by the capture of the American National Vessels, or by strictly blockading them in their own Waters.—

For this purpose H.M. Ships named in the Margin are ordered to proceed to join you, in addition to the 6 Sail of the Line already under your Orders.—

As the force under your Command will thus consist of upwards of ten Sail of the Line, my Lords have thought fit to appoint a Captain of the Fleet to serve with your Flag, and as they are not aware of any individual among the Senior Captains of the Navy to whom the appointment must be limitted, who would be more acceptable to you, they have appointed Captain Henry Hotham to that Situation, and have directed him to hoist a broad Pendant & putting to Sea with H.M. Ships *La Hogue* and *Valiant* proceed to join your Flag, putting himself under your Command as soon as he shall enter the limits of your Station.—

The *Sceptre* & *Plantagenet* the former intended for the Flag of Rear Adml. Cockburn, will follow as soon as possible.—

Such addition will also be made to your force in frigates and Sloops as will place 30 of the former and 50 of the latter at your disposal.—

It has not been without interfereing for the moment with other very important Services that my Lords have been able to send you this reinforcement and they most anxiously hope that the vigorous and successful use you will make of it, will enable you shortly to return some of the Line of Battle Ships to England, which, if the heavy American frigates should be taken or destroyed, you will immediately do, retaining with you the four Line of Battle Ships which you may consider as best fitted for the service of your Station, sending the rest in this case under the orders of Commodore Hotham, whose Functions as Captain of the Fleet will then cease, to Spithead, authorizing him to hoist a Broad Pendant when he shall be thus detached.

My Lords command me to acquaint you that they have been surprized to learn that the *Spartan,* which you had ordered to accompany the *Africa,* was seen on the 28th Novr. in Latitude 39°.41.—North Longitude 25 West; and they desire you will call for and transmit to me for their information a Report of the *Spartan*'s Proceedings from her parting with the *Africa* 'till she returned to your station and rejoined your Flag or some of the Ships under your Command as my Lords are strongly impressed with the opinion, intimated to you in my Letter of the 18th November, that it is highly desireable that Ships should not, by being detached singly, be exposed to the risk of meeting a superior force of the Enemy; and they cannot suppose that with a knowledge that Commodore Rogers and Bainbridge with their respective Squadrons were likely to be at sea, you could have authorized the Captain of the *Spartan* to expose himself to the danger of meeting them, unnecessarily and out of your Station.

Their Lordships command me to acquaint you that as soon as the other important Services on which they were employed permitted, two Battalions of the Royal Marines were recalled to England in order to be completed, refreshed, disciplined, and equipped with a view to their being sent as soon as possible to Bermuda to be employed by you in such manner as may in your judgment most tend to the advantage of H.M. Service and the annoyance of the Enemy.

The Battalions will each consist of about 640 Rank and File with a due proportion of Officers and Non Commissioned Officers, and an Artillery Company with Guns and all the usual equipments for field Service.

They will be conveyed to you in Troop Ships which will be directed to follow your orders. I am &c.

J W Croker

Copy, National Library of Scotland, Alexander F. I. Cochrane Papers, MS 2340, fols. 37–42. Another copy is in UkLPR, Adm. 2/1375, pp. 365–73. Names of ships written in the margin were *La Hogue, Valiant, Sceptre,* and *Plantagenet,* all 74-gun ships of the line.

ADMIRAL SIR JOHN B. WARREN, R.N., TO
FIRST SECRETARY OF THE ADMIRALTY JOHN W. CROKER

<u>private</u>   *San Domingo*
                                                             Off N. York
                                                          Janry. 25th 1813

My Dear Sir

I have sent for their Lordships Information Two Dispatches in Cypher from the French Consul in Carolina to the Minister for Foreign Affairs at Paris. The Cypher may be Discovered at the Office in Downing Street by my old friend Broughton, or some of the Gentlemen in that Department:

I was very near falling in with Rogers a short Time ago, having Taken & burnt a privateer that spoke him in the morning of the Day she fell in with us:

The *Argus* Sloop of War was chaced by this Ship, & only escaped by Throwing her Boats & spars overboard & starting her water: you are aware that the *Dragon* 74 *Statira* 38 & *Collibri* Brig are with me: we have Taken & burnt since our being out 16 sail of Ships & Vessels.— I may probably produce some Deficit ere long in the Revenue of the United States: If all my other Divisions are equally active & successful: I am anxious to Take or Destroy some of the Enemys Frigates as they are called, but in reality they are small Two Decked Ships: I trust their Lordships will not be Displeased with my having enclosed a Newspaper containing an Official Report of the Committee upon their Naval Affairs; & particularly the size Descripsion and Force of the American Frigates:— As it occurred the Information might not yet have arrived in England: I wish you would send me some Razees of the Descripsion I have stated:[1] & the *Indefatigable*, as well as 8 Gun Brigs for New Brunswick the Gulph of St Lawrence; and another Ship or Two of the Line would render our Force here more useful & respectable. will you have the kindness to present my best wishes & respects to Lord Melville & believe me to be with much esteem My Dear Sir Most sincerely your obed servt

John Borlase Warren

P S. I hope you have received my Letter communicating my having Taken Captain Thompson from the *Collibri* to act in this ship instead of Gill; who I have placed in the *Loupcervier*, the American *Wasp*, as a post ship & Lieut. G. Pechell my Flag Lieut. to act in *Collibri*: There will be a Regular Vacancy in the *Renown* in all probability as the Capt was given over as Sir F. Laforey wrote the word: I could not go on with Gill, he is not equal to the Situation of my Captain: & I cannot say more than has been the case: with so many Demands upon me: & *Cleopatra* has never joined me. Thompson is a Deserving Officer & was my Lieut in the *Renown*, When in the Fleet off Ushant, & as Third in Command in the Mediterranean. Do what you can therefore upon this occasion for me.

I shall be obliged to you in sending the enclosed Letter to Lady Warren.

I return in a few Days to Bermuda

ALS, owned by Ira Dye, Virginia Beach, Virginia. No enclosures were found.

1. "Any of our Old Ships of the line cut down, taking Off their Fore Castle, Poop and Quarter Deck and Manned with 380 men, would answer as Cruizers upon this Coast, to meet the Ships building in America, better than any other description of Vessels"; see Warren to Croker, 25 Jan. 1813, UkLPR, Adm. 1/503, pp. 241–42.

FIRST SECRETARY OF THE ADMIRALTY JOHN W. CROKER TO
ADMIRAL SIR JOHN B. WARREN, R.N.

Secret   10th Feby 1813

Sir

I have received your letters as per margin[1] and have it in command from my Lords Coms of the Admiralty to make to you the following observations on the several points of your communications—

In reply to the demands for increase of force which you have made, you will observe by my letter of the 9th of last month that their Lordships have, not without inconvenience to other Services, placed under your command a force much greater in proportion than the National Navy of the Enemy opposed to you would seem to warrant—

Their Lordships have not received from you any account of the number, strength, or preparations of the American Navy; nor have they any reason for believing that it much exceeds what it was at the date of my letter of the 16th November; vizt about fourteen sail of Vessels of all descriptions; to oppose which you have at this moment under your orders, Eleven Sail of the Line, one Ship of 50 Guns, thirty four frigates, Two *en flutes*,[2] thirty eight sloops, and twelve smaller Vessels; in all a total of 97 Pendants—[3]

From the circumstance of your having been at the date of your last letters so long without hearing from England, which their Lordships cannot account for, you cannot have been aware of the several reinforcements ordered to join you, and most of which must before this time have put themselves under your orders.

And from your having again omitted to send an account of the disposition of the fleet under your command, my Lords are ignorant of what ships you may actually have with you, particularly as they observe that one of your frigates the *Spartan* has lately been refitting at Gibraltar.

It is true that several of the Ships included in the foregoing statement may not have actually joined your flag; but such as have not, are employed in the Convoy Services of your Station; and the necessity of sending such heavy Convoys arises from the facility and safety with which the American Navy has hitherto found it possible to put to Sea.

It is stated in your letter to me of the 5. Novr. last, that you expected that Commodore Bainbridge would about that day sail from Boston with the ships under his command, and intended to form a junction with the *Constellation* off the Chesapeake; you neither on that occasion acquainted me for their Lordships information of what steps you had taken to intercept them or to frustrate their object; nor do you again in your letters lately received, though dated a month later, state whether or not Commodore Bainbridge had sailed, and whether or not he formed the intended junction off the Chesapeake.

The uncertainty in which you left their Lordships in regard to the movements of the Enemy and the disposition of your own force has obliged them to employ six or seven sail of the line and as many frigates & sloops, not included in the beforementioned number, in guarding against the possible attempts of the Enemy.

Captain William Prowse, with two sail of the line, two frigates, and a sloop, has been sent to St Helena in the apprehension of the American Squadrons having proceeded to that quarter.

Rear Admiral Lord Amelius Beauclerk, with two sail of the line, two frigates, and two sloops, is station'd in the neighbourhood of Madeira and the Western Islands, lest Commodore Bainbridge should have come into that quarter to take the place of Commodore Rodgers, who was retiring from it about the time you state Commodore Bainbridge was expected to sail.

Commodore Owen, who, with one ship of the Line, one frigate, and two sloops, had preceded Lord Amelius Beauclerk, is not yet returned from the cruize on which the appearance of the Enemy near the Western Islands had obliged their Lordships to send this force.

The *Colossus* and *Elephant* with the *Rhin* & *Armide* are but just returned from similar services; so that it is obvious that large as the force under orders was, and is, it is not all that has been opposed to the Americans, and that these Services became necessary only because the chief weight of the Enemy's force has been employed at a distance from your station.

Under these circumstances their Lordships are not only not prepared to enter into your opinion that the force on your station was not adequate to the duties to be executed, but they feel that, consistently with what other branches and objects of the public Service require, it may not be possible to maintain on the Coast of America for any length of time a force so disproportionate to the Enemy as that which, with a view of enabling you to strike some decisive blow, they have now placed under your orders.

In reply to your statement that the Crews of Privateers and letters of Marque, which now amount to six hundred, have in several instances landed at the points of Nova Scotia and the Leeward Islands, and cut out Vessels from the Harbours;[4] I am commanded to observe that my Lords never doubted that the Privateers of the Enemy would become extremely numerous, as most, if not all, of their commercial Marine would probably be diverted to privateering; but they were convinced of the impracticability of the remedy for this evil which you seem to propose, namely, the meeting them with an equal number of ships. The only measures which with any attention to economy, and any reasonable prospect of success can be opposed to the Enemy's privateering system, are those of blockading their Ports, and of not permitting our Trade to proceed without protection; and for the execution of these purposes the force under your command will, no doubt, by judicious arrangement be found adequate.

My Lords wish that you had stated the particulars of the landings made on many parts of the Leeward Islands and Nova Scotia, that they might have conveyed the information to H.M. Secretary of State for the Colonial Department, whose duty it is to attend to the Shore Defences of the Colonies; as it is not to be expected that in such extensive and detached Provinces a naval force can be stationed at every point of the Coast to prevent the occasional landings of plunderers and privateers; and upon this part of the subject and with reference to Sir Geo. Beckwith's letter inclosed in yours, I have to refer you to the copy (sent herewith) of my letter to Mr. Goulburn, some time since.

You have also stated in very strong terms that our Trade is threatened with absolute ruin. On this subject my Lords desire me to report their opinion, and to signify to you their positive direction that no Merchant Vessels should be permitted to sail without Convoy, & that frequent and regular protection should be afforded between the different Ports of your command; and you will see by the Extract of the Convoy Act, herewith sent, that when regular Convoys are appointed, and no persons are authorized to grant Licences to sail without Convoy, no Vessel can <u>run</u> without being subject to the penalties of that Act; which you are to give due notice at all the Ports that it is their Lordships intention to enforce. An attention to this circumstance will, it is hoped, prevent all serious injury to the Trade, and the execution of the arrangement communicated to you in my Letter of the 14h January will afford it all the facility which the Merchants themselves appear to desire.

My Lords cannot but hope that the reports which you state of <u>swarms</u> of American Privateers being at Sea, must be, in a great degree exaggerated; as they cannot suppose that you have left the principal Ports of the American Coast so unguarded as to permit such multitudes of Privateers to escape in and out unmolested; and their Lordships are quite sure that by preventing our Merchant Ships from running and by carefully blockading the principal Ports the trade of privateering will be made so hazardous and expensive that its objects will be in most instances frustrated; and that of course the general system will be very considerably checked.

On the subject of the Razees proposed in your letter of the 29th December, I have to acquaint you that their Lordships have already turned their attention to this point; and had ordered four 74 Gun Ships to be cut down & fitted in the manner you recommend, with a view to their being employed on the American Station in lieu of Line of Battle Ships.

Their Lordships had also resolved to send, as soon as the Season would permit, a force of small Vessels to be employed in the Bay of Fundy & on the Coast of Nova Scotia. Their Lordships had considered that six Brigs commanded by Commanders would be sufficient for their Service; but if two more can be spared they shall be sent agreeably to your request. Three of these Brigs will be attached to the Newfoundland Convoy from the Channel on the 25th Instant, and three others to the Nova Scotia Convoy from Cork on the 1st of March.

The *Sceptre* is now at Spithead, and only waiting for a fair wind to proceed to your Station. Her Captain[5] will deliver to you a copy of the orders he has received from their Lordships, together with this letter.

The *Forester* Sloop is attached to the *Sceptre* for the purpose of protecting the Trade down to Jamaica, where she is ordered to follow Admiral Stirling's orders, and to replace the *Brazen* which yesterday arrived at Spithead from that Station.

A Sloop will also, if she can be provided in time to sail with the *Sceptre*, accompany her to Barbadoes, and on her arrival there be directed to follow the orders of Sir Francis Laforey.[6] I am &c.

J W C.

Admiral Sir J. B. Warren Bt K. B.
Bermuda. By the *Sceptre*.

Copy, UkLPR, Adm. 2/1376, pp. 73–87.

1. From No. 53, 21 Dec. 1812, to No. 67, 5 Jan. 1813, inclusive.
2. A large warship used as a transport, with lower deck guns removed to make more room, was said to be "*en flute.*"
3. The list totals 98 vessels.
4. See Warren to Croker, 29 Dec. 1812, in Dudley, *Naval War of 1812*, Vol. 1, pp. 649–51.
5. Charles Baynton Hodgson Ross, R.N.
6. Rear Admiral Sir Francis Laforey, R.N., commanded the Leeward Islands Station.

Navy Department Administrative Problems

Mounting criticism of his stewardship of the Navy Department, as well as personal misgivings concerning his own administrative talents, prompted Secretary Hamilton to resign 31 December 1812. Two weeks later, William Jones, a successful Philadelphia merchant and former sea captain, accepted President Madison's offer to fill the vacant post. Jones immediately faced practical questions of supply, such as those confronting Nathaniel W. Rothwell, the newly appointed purser on the St. Marys Station, and congressional ag-

itation for a reorganization of the department. Jones would spend much of 1813 en-
meshed in the minute details of directing the nation's war effort at sea.

PURSER NATHANIEL W. ROTHWELL TO SECRETARY OF THE NAVY HAMILTON

St Marys   January 8th 1813

Sir

I arrived here and took charge of Mr. Harris[1] business on the 1st. Inst. and was astonished to find the difficulty so great in procuring Funds Provisions, Slops &c in fact evry article for the maintanance of the Flotilla— There is now a considerable amount due officers & Seamen & in February half the men on this Station will be discharg'd.

There is not one Hundred Barells of Salt Provisions in Savannah & none of moment in Store— Flour can not be purchas'd, & I am therefore directed by Comdr Campbell to request one years Salt Provisions & a few Barrells Flour— All the Provisions will be exhausted by the time a supply could arrive— Say Three Hundred Barrells Pork & Two Hundred Barrells Beef.[2] It is of the utmost importance to keep up a supply, a deficiency would cause detention & a purchase at extravagant prices— The Whiskey received from Savannah comes higher & is not of so good a quality as the whiskey to the northward—

I will now Sir solicit you to point out the plan I am to adopt in procuring Funds. I cannot negotiate a Bill in this place for $1000— I can pursue Mr Harriss plan, and use the Bank in Savannah, consequently must pay a discount which I shall be compeld to do until I hear from you, receive a remittance, or directions how to proceed— I have a demand on me from the Commanding Officer of Marines, which I shall comply with as soon as in funds, Altho not authoris'd by letter I feel a confidence the act will not be sensur'd, particularly as Mr. Harris has been authoris'd to supply the marine officers with what money they want— You will have the goodness Sir to forward me the proper authority for my Government if you wish me to connect that business with my Pursership. I have the Honor to be Sir Your Obdt Hble St

N W Rothwell

ALS, DNA, RG45, BC, 1813, Vol. l, No. 8 (M148, Roll No. 11).

1. Gwinn Harris was the former purser at St. Marys.
2. Jones subsequently contracted for 200 barrels of beef and 200 barrels of pork to be delivered to Savannah; see Jones to Hugh Campbell, 26 Jan. 1813, DNA, RG45, SNL, Vol. 10, p. 236 (M149, Roll No. 10).

LIEUTENANT CHARLES MORRIS TO CONGRESSMAN LANGDON CHEVES [1]

Washington Navy Yard   Jany. 9. 1813

Sir,

I had the honour to receive your letter of Decr. 28th 1812 requesting any information I might possess, which might expose the present causes of mismanagement in the naval establishment, and suggestions as to the best means of reform.

My opinion is also particularly requested as to the existence of great abuses, waste, and extravagance in the present mode of building, repairing, equiping and supplying the Naval force of the U. States.

The causes of such abuse, waste and extravagance if they exist, and what the remedy?

You are also pleased to submit to my consideration some particular suggestions, which had been made to the committee, and as those suggestions comprehend nearly all the objects of your enquiry, I proceed to remark upon them in their regular order.

1st. "The present mode of supplying the navy through navy agents, is one great source of abuse & extravagance."

This mode of supplying the navy, is in my opinion liable to strong objections.— The compensation of the agents being derived from commissions on the purchases made by them for the government, is an inducement for them to purchase at high prices. I do not mean to say, that such is their practice, but that the present regulations makes it for their interest to pursue such a system.

The limits of $2000 a year can operate but on few, as the commissions of few amount to that sum.

Whether extravagant prices have or have not been given for different articles by Navy agents, is in the power of the committee to ascertain from other sources.

Remedy. It is recommended that agents should receive fixed salaries, instead of commissions. That in all purchases they should advertise for seald proposals, and be bound to accept those most favourable to the government; and that they shall regularly make oath at the settlement of their quarterly accounts, that they have complied with the above regulations.

2d. The manner in which contracts are made and carried on, is believed to be another great source of abuse and expence."

This is believed to be correct, under an impression that, in many instances no advertisements are made for sealed proposals. That the contracts are made in too loose a manner. That ample security is not required for their faithful performance, or that it is not properly exacted. And that an indiscreet advance of money is sometimes made to the contractors without due security for the government.

Remedy. Advertisements for sealed proposals. The contracts to be made as explicit and as precise as possible. To require good security for their complete performance and to make no advances, but on such security as should ~~make~~ render the government safe.

3d. The want of regular system and allowance for vessels of each class, in stores and furniture and outfits, is another source of extravagance and waste.

This is unquestionably correct. Most of our commanders have or at least exercise the privilege of following their own ideas of propriety on these subjects, but a greater inconvenience is felt in the <u>armament</u>, <u>equipment</u>, and internal arrangements of the vessels. On these points also commanders are frequently left at liberty to exercise their discretion, and as few are precisely of the same opinion, it sometimes happens, that, vessels of the same dimensions are differently armed, equiped and arranged, so that spare stores prepared for one will not answer for another.

Remedy. To class the different vessels, to regulate the armament, complete equipments and allowances of the various stores for each class.

4. "The delay of ships wanting repairs, spars and other articles, form another article of expence, while the public at the same time looses the service of the vessels."

Very considerably inconvenience has resulted in some instances from such delays. These delays have generally been owing apparently to an incorrect view of the importance of magazines in different ports supplied with such articles as are most commonly wanted for the services requiring considerable time for their construction or collection, and such magazines or <u>depots</u> is the only adequate remedy for this inconvenience.

5. The employment of more artificers, workmen, and labourers in the Navy Yards, than can be employed to advantage, is another source of great expence.

On this subject I can only say, that, comparing the expence of labour in some of the yards, with the service performed, induces me to believe that it is at least injudiciously directed. Horses and oxen I should presume might be substituted for men, to great advantage, for the removal of heavy articles. And I am disposed to believe that, many articles might be attained by contracts, of equal quality and at much less expence, than by having them made by artificers employed in the yard on daily pay.

6. "The discretion which officers exercise in altering their vessels when in commission, is another source of extravagance and waste."

The alteration of vessels when in commission has heretofore been attended with very considerable expence. In some instances the improvements made, have compensated for their cost: but in most cases, the alterations have been attended with no good consequences, and in some, have been very injurious.

Remedy. A regulation forbidding any commander to alter in any degree the vessel under his command, unless by particular permission or order from the Secrety. of the Navy; or when on foreign service, from the commanding officer of the squadron: and that no such order or permission shall be given, but upon the recommendation of a majority of three or more commanders, previously ordered to examine & report the advantages which would probably result from such alteration.

7. The want of accountability in the warrant officers before they are discharged from the ship they have served on board of, is an other source of loss to the public.

This I believe is not strictly correct. If a loss has been sustained by the public, through the warrant officers, it must have been from the neglect of their commanders, who are required by existing regulations to audit their accounts weekly, and keep check books of their receipts and expenditures; which if performed, would prevent loss to the public.

An additional and very considerable expence is believed to have been incurred by a neglect to carefully preserve the various stores and equipment landed from vessels laid in ordinary. Great inconvenience has been felt, and the expence of repairs been very much increased from the want of dry docks in some of our ports to which vessels requiring repairs or examinations below light water mark, might have been taken, instead of pursuing the only other mode of repairing them, which is heaving them down. In calculating these inconveniences and expences: the removal of all their armaments, stores ballace [*ballast*] &c. The expence of additional preparations for heaving down; & the increased detention of the vessel, must be taken into consideration, together with the injury the vessel unavoidably sustains under the strain of the operation; and the risque of those she may probably sustain from accident.

The advantages which it is conceived would result from such an establishment are such as in my opinion require the earliest attention to the subject, particularly since it is contemplated to build ships of the line.

The practice of repairing vessels at yards situated on long rivers of tedious and difficult navigation, is believed to have caused very considerable expences, beyond what would have been incurred if the repairs had been made at yards more conveniently situated.

In estimating the amount of these expences, attention must be paid to the time necessarily lost in the navigation; to the difference of freight for those articles usually procured from the coast, or by water. The difficulty and expence of procuring seamen to man vessels at such places—and when the vessels require lightening to pass shoals between the sea and those yards; the trouble and expence of transporting her stores and equipments in other vessels.

It is also believed, that, for several years past, a very considerable portion of the naval expences has been caused by the gun boats. A discription of force, which though it may be serviceable in some particular situations, does not appear sufficiently important to warrant its continuance at the great expence it has hitherto occasioned.

If however it is deemed expedient to continue the use of gun boats; I beg leave to suggest the propriety of detaching them from the regular naval Establishment— From their size and construction they are only proper for harbour defence, and even then, they can only act with effect in two situations; one is, under the protection, or in conjunction with land batteries. The other, when they can occupy a situation on, or behind some shoal, fairly within range of point-blank shot, and where they can not be approached by the enemy's vessels within the range of grape—for if the vessels are beyond point-blank range the fire from the boats would do very little injury; and if within grape distance, the boats must either retire, surrender or have all their men swept from their unsheltered decks. A very small portion of naval knowledge is necessary for their management in the harbours: while on the skill and ability of those charged with the service of their artillery depends almost the whole of their utility. Their force will not authorise the employment of experienced naval officers to command them, and they offer no opportunity for the inexperienced to improve in naval knowledge. I would propose, that, the gun boats in the different harbours, should be placed under the direction of the military commanders at those places who, from their knowledge of the batteries under their command, are best qualified to assign them their proper stations. Let an officer acquainted with naval affairs have a general superintendance of their movements as ordered by the military commander. To each boat assign two petty officers, four seamen and four ordinary seamen, to take care of and manouvre her; and when they may be wanted for action, let a requisite number of artillery be detached to each boat, for the proper management of the gun. The person performing the naval part of the duty in the boats might be made subject to the army or naval laws, as should be deemed most expedient. The officers superintend the naval duties in the establishment, should be considered as distinct from the regular naval service, and as having no right or claim for promotion in it, but might be eligible to an adoption in it as a reward for particular acts of bravery or good conduct. By adopting some arrangement of this kind, the military commanders will always have the control of that floating force, but adapted for their particular purposes; without having occasion to consult with any other officer.

The regular naval ~~establishment~~ service will be relieved from an establishment which, without even having formed one good officer, has ruined a great number of promising young men: and the country it is believed, will receive equal advantages from the gun boat establishment at a very reduced expence.

To your general question "as to the present causes of mismanagement in the naval establishment;" I can only offer an opinion, which I give with much diffidence, as it has been formed from the limited observations, I have been able to make, while attending to the details of service in a subordinate capacity.

One of the great causes of the present mismanagement is in my opinion owing to the want of an efficient and uniform system for the government of all the different branches of service. A system which, should fully and clearly establish the duties of every officer, and the mode in which those duties should be performed; a system which should control the expenditures of the public monies in all the minute details, as well as in more general expenditures: which should prescribe the armaments and equipments & the proper allowances of every description, for vessels of each class, and which should enable the department at all times to ascertain with precision the actual state & condition of the whole establishment; and provide in season for its probable wants.

Another and perhaps, greater cause of the present mismanagement is, the want of a board of professional men, to advise the head of the department on questions merely professional, and to superintend the details of service; and particularly to see that, all established regulations shall be carried into complete and full effect. To this board might be assigned also, the duty of making all contracts, of examining the accounts of all officers charged with stores (pursers excepted) to examine midshipmen & certify to their qualifications for promotion.

The proper persons to constitute such a board at present, are conceived to be three naval men, having under their direction a surgeon general and contractor general. With the greatest respect I have the honour to be Yours &c &c &c

Honble. Langdon Cheves
Chairman of the Committee of Naval Enquiry

Copy, PHi, U. C. Smith Collection, Papers of William Jones. Morris forwarded a copy of his response to Cheves's inquiry to Jones shortly after his appointment as secretary of the navy.

1. Langdon Cheves was chairman of the House of Representatives' naval affairs committee during the first session of the Twelfth Congress. Burwell Bassett chaired it during the second session.

Secretary of the Navy William Jones to Congressman Burwell Bassett

Honorable Burwell Bassett   Navy Depart.
Chairman of the Naval Committee   2d Feby 1813
House of Repr.

Permit me to revive the Suggestions I had the honor to make to you in conversation relative to the better organization of the Navy Department, and though it would be premature in me to offer any general system of improvement yet in my view there are some prominent defects in the establishment

Secretary of the Navy William Jones

which are susceptible of a simple remedy similar to that which necessity urged the adoption of in relation to the War Department.

The vital error appears to me to consist in loading the Chief of the Department with the Cognizance of details and with the execution of duties which divert his attention from the sound direction of the great & efficient objects of the establishment, or the inevitable alternative is to submit the execution of those duties to subordinate Agents whose responsibility does not afford a sufficient guarantee to the public for the judicious & faithful discharge of the trust of this nature is the duty of forming Contracts, making purchases and the effective controul and accountibility of Navy Agents now spread over the interior as well as the Atlantic Coast, and which I conceive would employ to great public advantage a distinct department directed by a responsible and able head. If in the present state of our Navy this view of the subject is in any degree correct the increase as now provided for by Law must render it indispensable.

I would therefore respectfully suggest the idea of a Naval Purveyors Department with deputies as many as may be necessary to be nominated by the President to the Senate. The Purveyor to reside in some of our Central Sea port towns, where the state of the market & the information necessary to form Contracts to advantage can be best known and effected with the best Security: the Secretary of the Navy retaining the controul and general direction of all important contracts to be formed by the purveyor.

Permit me also to ask of you to consider the propriety of encreasing the appropriation for Clerks in the Navy Department so as to admit of the addition of two able Clerks to the number now employed. I would also suggest the propriety of providing for the appointment of an additional number of Captains in anticipation of those authorized by the Act for building the 74s— There is not now a single vacancy and unless a Captain is taken from one of the Navy Yards, there is no Commander for the *Macedonian* although a distinguished Master Commandant has been designated for that promotion and command;[1] indeed we have none to provide for Casualties or the fate of Battle.

I would also draw your attention to a species of force of vast importance for short Coasting Convoys as well as for the annoyance of the enemy. I mean Corvettes such as the *Hornet* or rather larger (such as the enemy employs) of this valuable class of vessels we are almost destitute.

I think Six vessels of this class would be desirable. They can be built by Contract on favorable terms and in service in four months. Orders have been given to construct and equip two Corvettes at Erie and one at Sacketts Harbour with a view to the complete command of the whole of the Lakes. I think Sir the public could be amply remunerated for the additional Six Corvettes, by a reduction of the number of gunboats now in Service and of the officers and Crews of those that may be retained in Situations admitting of such diminution. I have the honor to be very respectfully &c.

W Jones.

LB Copy, DNA, RG45, Letters to Congress, Vol. 2, pp. 147–48.

1. On 1 February 1813, Master Commandant Jacob Jones was ordered to New York to supervise the repair and equipping of *Macedonian*. He was promoted to captain on 3 March 1813.

Privateer Activity

American privateers menaced the high seas throughout the war, wreaking havoc on British merchantmen and forcing the Admiralty to send out more naval vessels for the protection of British trade. Highflyer *and* Comet *from Baltimore and* America *from Salem all had successful careers as privateers. Although* Highflyer *was captured early in 1813, she had netted her owners an estimated $187,000. The British capture of* Highflyer *was a great coup.* Comet *earned her Baltimore investors about $220,000 before being sold in 1814 to a group of New Yorkers.[1]* America *brought in six prizes valued at $158,000 after her first cruise from September 1812 to January 1813.[2] The following grouping documents* Highflyer*'s capture, alleged mutinous activity on board* America, *and a day in the privateering career of* Comet.

1. *Garitee,* Republic's Private Navy, *p. 272.*
2. *Maclay,* American Privateers, *p. 333; for an account of* America*'s career, see Crowninshield, "*America *of Salem."*

CAPTAIN JOHN P. BERESFORD, R.N.,[1] TO ADMIRAL SIR JOHN B. WARREN, R.N.

His Majesty's Ship *Poictiers*
at Sea, 9th Jany. 1813—

Sir,

I beg leave to acquaint you that His Majesty's Ship under my Command in Company with the *Acasta* Captured this day the American Schooner Privateer *High Flyer*, mounting five Guns and having on board a Compliment of 72 men; She was on her return from the West Indies where she had made several Captures, is a particularly fine Vessel, Coppered and Copper fastened, and sails remarkably fast.[2] I have the honor to be Sir, Your most Obedient humble Servant

Signed　J P Beresford　Captain

Copy, UkLPR, Adm. 1/503, p. 281.

1. John Poo Beresford had been sent to the North American Station at the beginning of the war.
2. The British used *Highflyer* in their Chesapeake operations, retaining her name. U.S.S. *President* recaptured *Highflyer* in September 1813.

DEPOSITION OF JOSEPH ROPES

To the Honorable the Secretary of the Navy
of the United States of America,

Joseph Ropes Esquire Commander of the Private Armed Ship *"America"* of Salem[1] in the County of Essex and Commonwealth of Massachusetts, in pursuance of an Act of the said United States entituled "An Act concerning Letters of Marque, Prizes and Prize goods" passed the 26th day of June AD 1812, and the fifteenth section of said Act,[2] respectfully represents that he the said Joseph Ropes as Commander of the said Ship *America*, and by virtue of a Commission or Letter of Marque under the seal of the said U. States, and the hand of the President of the same bearing date the second day of September AD 1812, sailed from said <u>Salem</u> on the seventh day of September in the year aforesaid on a Cruise, that <u>Charles Still</u>, entered on board the said Ship for the said Cruise as a quarter master, that on the twentieth day of October AD 1812, while on the said Cruise on the high seas and from 12, to 15, leagues to the Westward of St. <u>Michaels</u> he the said Ropes fell in with the Ship *Eliza* of <u>Philadelphia</u>, bound to <u>Cadiz</u>, after closely examining the papers of the said the *Eliza*, he the said Ropes suffered her to proceed on her voyage; shortly after, on the same day, the said Still came to him the said Ropes Commander as aforesaid, then being aft, on the poop deck, and in a very insolent manner demanded in the name of the crew, from the sd. Ropes the reason why he the sd. Ropes had not manned out the said *Eliza*—to which the sd. Ropes replied that he the sd. Still might inform the ships's company that he did not think proper to send her in— the said Still then said to him the said Ropes that they (the crew) did not come for pleasure and were not to be put off so— he the said Ropes then ordered the said Still forward and commanded him to say no more— the said Still then in a very mutinous manner and with much indecent language said to the said Ropes that this was the third good and lawful prize to his the sd. Still's knowledge which he the sd. Ropes had let go and that if he the sd. Ropes chose he might order him the sd. Still in irons— the sd. Ropes then ordered the first Lieutenant of the said Ship to call the Master at Arms and put the said Still in irons— the said Still on hearing this immediately went forward and thirty or forty of the Crew set up a loud shout and immediately the ship was in much confusion— the sd. Ropes told the sd. first Lieutenant to take but little notice of it but to see that the said Still was put in irons— the sd. first Lieutenant then went forward with the Master at Arms (after calling the sd. Still to come aft a number of times without effect) but shortly returned and informed him the sd. Ropes, that many of the Crew appeared determined to resist the putting the sd. Still in irons— Upon this the marines were paraded aft and the officers of the sd. Ship called on deck with their pistols— while this was doing, the said Still with some little assistance, began to cast loose the bow gun, saying, at the same time, that the Captain and officers were arming themselves but if they (the Crew) would join him the sd. Still, he the sd. Still would blow them the sd. Officers all to damnation— the said Still was then stopped by the Boatswain from proceeding further— the Crew were then called aft and after a few words were said to them upon the folly of their conduct, he the said Ropes ordered the Master at Arms to put the said Still in irons which was done accordingly one man only making any opposition to it who desisted upon being spoken to— the said Still was confined in irons on board the sd. Ship until her arrival in Salem aforesaid which was on the seventh of January Instant, he the sd. Ropes not having met with any public ship of war of the said United States at sea. The said Ropes would further represent that the sd. Still is now in the custody and safe keeping of John Rodgers Esquire Commodore, and Commander of the public Ship of War of the sd. United States and also a squadron of public ships now lying in the harbour of Boston in the sd. Commonwealth he the said Ropes having, upon the above representation, requested the said Commodore, to take into his custody the said Still to abide the order of the Secretary of the Navy, of the sd. United States, upon the representation which he the sd. Ropes, should make to the sd. Secretary touching the sd. Still, and agreeably to the Act aforesaid. Whereupon the sd. Ropes, and in consideration of the premises, requests the Honorable the Secretary of the Navy of the said United States to call a Court Martial for the trial of the said Still for mutiny and for exciting and endeavoring still further to excite among the Crew aforesaid a mutiny on board the said Ship "*America*" against the authority of him the said Ropes Commander as aforesaid, and the officers acting under his Command and authority, agreeably to the Act aforesaid and the fifteenth section thereof. And the sd. Ropes would further represent that the witnesses to substantiate the above facts on the trial of the sd. Still are John Kehew, first Lieutenant, John Harris, Prize Master & Capt. of the Bow gun, Thomas Poor, Boatswain, & Jesse Brown Seaman and Benjamin West, Seaman of and on board the Said ship *America* during her said Cruise, some of whom are bound again to sea, and he the sd. Ropes would therefore respectfully represent that it might be for the security and advancement of justice if the Court Martial for the trial of the sd. Still should be called without much delay and as speedily as possible. All which is respectfully submitted

Salem   January 15th AD 1812 [*1813*]   By Jos. Ropes
Commonwealth of Massachusetts
Essex

Personally appeared this sixteenth day of January AD 1813, the said Joseph Ropes and made oath that the facts contained in the foregoing representation are true
Before me   John Pitman Jun.   Justice of the Peace.

Copy, DNA, RG45, MLR, 1813, Vol. 1, No. 26 (M124, Roll No. 53). Joseph Ropes probably copied the deposition.

1. George Crowninshield & Sons of Salem owned *America*, a 350-ton vessel built in 1804; she usually carried 20 guns. This was *America*'s first cruise as a privateer; Joseph Ropes, a very capable and well-known sea captain, commanded her; see Maclay, *American Privateers*, p. 328.
2. Section fifteen was reprinted in Dudley, *Naval War of 1812*, Vol. 1, p. 169.

COURT-MARTIAL OF CHARLES STILL[1]

[Extract]
Marine Barracks, Navy Yard Charlestown   Tuesday the 9th of March 1813

The Court met pursuant to adjournment, and having deliberately considered the evidence for the prosecution, and that of the prisoner, and the statement made by the prisoner in his defence, are of opinion that he is not guilty of Mutiny nor of exciting or attempting still further to excite a mutiny on board said private armed Ship *America*; but that he is guilty of such parts of the charge as fall within the meaning of the last clause of the Thirteenth Article of the rules and regulations for the government of the Navy of the United States in as much as he is guilty of having uttered Seditious and Mutinous words, and that he treated with contempt his superior officers, while in the execution of their duty, as charged in the complaint of Joseph Ropes commander of said Ship *America*, and do therefore adjudge that the said Charles Still receive one hundred lashes on his naked back, alongside or on board such Ship, or Ships, and at such time, and place as Commr. John Rodgers shall direct.

signed
Isaac Hull   President
L. Warrington
Tho Gamble
John H. Elton
B. V. Hoffman

Thomas Welsh Junr
Judge Advocate

Copy, DNA, RG125, CM, Vol. 4, No. 131 (M273, Roll No. 4).

1. On 9 February, Jones ordered Commodore Rodgers to convene a court-martial of Charles Still; see Jones to Rodgers, 9 Feb. 1813, DNA, RG45, SNL, Vol. 10, p. 249 (M149, Roll No. 10).

LOGBOOK ENTRY OF PRIVATE ARMED SCHOONER *COMET* OF BALTIMORE, CAPTAIN THOMAS BOYLE,[1] COMMANDER

Remarks on Saturday 30th January 1813

The first of these 24 hours light winds & pleasant weather in chase of the be-fore mentioned Ship   @ 1/4 past 12 maridian hoisted American Coulars & began fireing at her in hopes to cut away Something to impede her way as She Sailed fast which we Soon did & approached her verry fast when She began fire-ing the action then became general we endeavouring to close with her a fast as possible   @ thirty minutes past maridian we opened our whole battery of big Guns & musketry upon her   at forty minutes past maridean they hauled down the English Coulars in Submission to the *Comet* we having one man killed & three wounded one with the loss of his leg by a Round Shot came in through the quick work between the fore riging & Bridle Port   on boarding found her to be the Ship *Adelphia* of abberdeen from Liverpool with Salt & Dry Goods for St. Salvador   put Wm. Barlet prize master on board with eleven men & ordered for america   at 7 PM Parted with the prize She mounting Eight Eighteen pound Caronades   middle & latter parte Pleasant. Lattd. Obsd. 13" 30 South

D, MdHi, Ships' Logbooks and Papers, MS. 748.

1. Thomas Boyle settled in Baltimore when he was nineteen. In July 1812, he took *Comet*, a 187-ton schooner built by Thomas Kemp in 1810, on a three month cruise. This log entry is for Boyle's second cruise in *Comet*, December 1812 to March 1813. Just before capturing *Adelphi*, a 361-ton ship out of Liverpool, Boyle had driven off a Portuguese warship escorting three well-armed English vessels. *Comet* took the latter as prizes; see Garitee, *Republic's Private Navy*, pp. 149–51.

Commodore Hull–Anaconda Affair

By early 1813, Liverpool Packet, *a very successful British privateer operating off New England, had menaced the American coastal trade for months. Boston merchants enlisted the navy's support to end this scourge by privately purchasing a schooner and lending it to Commodore John Rodgers to man and use as a coastal convoy. While entering Provincetown harbor on 16 January 1813, this schooner,* Commodore Hull, *Acting Lieutenant Henry S. Newcomb, commanding, encountered the American privateer brig* Anaconda. *Some fishing vessels informed Newcomb that she was a New York privateer. The lack of a viable signalling system between public and private warships, however, resulted in the privateer ship's firing on* Commodore Hull, *she being mistaken for the greatly feared* Liverpool Packet.[1]*

A court-martial acquitted Anaconda's *Lieutenant George W. Burbank of the charges of insulting the flag and of deliberately wounding Newcomb and two crewmen from* Commodore Hull. *The court concluded that there was reasonable doubt about the schooner's nationality.*

1. *The 18-gun brig* Anaconda, *owned by New Yorkers Peter H. Schenck and Francis H. Nicoll, was commanded by Captain Nathaniel Shaler. On the day of the incident with* Commodore Hull, *Shaler was conducting business on shore and had left the vessel in the charge of his first lieutenant, George W. Burbank.*

COMMODORE JOHN RODGERS TO SECRETARY OF THE NAVY HAMILTON

U.S. Frigate *President*
Boston   Jany. 13th 1813

Sir

It being represented to me, by a Committee of Merchants, of this place, that the coasting Trade between here and Martha's Vineyard had of late sustained great injury by the depridations of a certain British privateer Schooner called the *Liverpool Packet*; they at the same time having offered to equip, and furnish a suitable vessel for the purpose of affording Temporary protection to said trade, provided I would employ her to that effect: I have in consequence acceded to their proposal, and shall employ in the completion of the before mentioned object the Schooner *Capt. Hull* [1] which they yesterday purchased, until your pleasure shall be known—

The *Capt. Hull* is about 100 Tons, and was built for a Privateer. She is armed with Four carriage Guns (Six Pounders) 50 Muskets, 50 Pistols, and 50 Sabres, and officered and manned from this Ship, in the character of a Tender, by one Lieutenant, Four Midshipmen, the Coasting Pilot, and Forty five men— She will sail tomorrow for Martha's Vineyard, to convoy to this place a number of Coasting Vessels, now waiting there, and afraid to put to Sea, it being represented that the *Liverpool Packet* is laying wait for them in the vicinity of Cape Cod

I should not have taken upon myself to have employed this Vessel, as before stated, without having the approbation of the Secretary of the Navy, would not the delay which must unavoidably ensue, before I could receive his instructions, entirely defeat the object in view.

In the present situation of the *President*, refitting as she is, the before mentioned Fifty officers and men could not be more advantageously employed, and

I hope the same may meet your approbation   I have the honor to be with the greatest respect Sir Your Obdt. Servt.

Jn⁰ Rodgers

LS, DNA, RG45, CL, 1813, Vol. 1, No. 20 (M125, Roll No. 26).

1. Rodgers meant *Commodore Hull.*

COMMODORE JOHN RODGERS TO SECRETARY OF THE NAVY JONES

U.S. Frigate *President.*
Boston   Jany 19th 1813

Sir

I regret being under the necessity of requesting that you will authorise me to order a Court Martial to try George W. Burbank, First Lieutenant of Private armed Brig *Anaconda,* on the charge set forth in the enclosed paper—

The *Commr. Hull* is the Schooner which I informed you on the 14th Inst.[1] that I should employ for the protection of the Coasting trade to this place, until your pleasure should be made known to me . . . The *Commr. Hull* I had given the command of to Lieut. Newcomb, of this Ship, and on his passage from this to Holmes Hole, to afford Convoy to Coasting vessels, fell in with the Privateer Brig *Anaconda* of New York.

The enclosed will shew the cause of my request for authority to order a Court Martial— I have taken the advice of Mr. Blake, the district attorney, in the business, and he agrees with myself that the First Lieutenant of the Privateer (and who was commanding officer of the *Anaconda* at the time the accident happened) is subject to a trial by Naval Martial Law. . . . Perhaps it might have been as proper for me to detain the Privateer until I could be informed of your determination, but my repugnance to injure the owners of the vessel for the rash act of her officer, will induce me to permit her to proceed on her cruise . . .

The *Commr. Hull* left Cape Cod this morning with a small convoy to proceed as far as Holmes' Hole, and to afford such vessels as she may find there convoy to this place.

Lieut. Newcomb I have reason to hope is not badly wounded. I have the honor to be With the greatest respect Sir Your Obdt. Servt

Jn⁰ Rodgers

LS, DNA, RG45, CL, 1813, Vol. 1, No. 24 (M125, Roll No. 26). Ellipses are the writer's.

1. Rodgers meant 13th.

[Enclosure]

To George W. Burbank, 1st Lieutenant of the Private Armed Brig *Anaconda,* now at anchor in the Harbour of Boston

By authority vested in me by certain Laws passed on the 26th day of June 1812, concerning Letters of Marque and reprisal: I do hereby arrest you, that you may be held to appear before a Court Martial, to answer to the charge of having unjustifiably fired into a Vessel in the service of the United States, called the *Commodore Hull,* and thereby wounding the Commanding Officer and Two Seamen belonging to said Vessel.

Specification

Namely, that you George W. Burbank did on, or about the 16th of the present month, while laying in Cape Cod harbour, and while acting in your capacity of First Lieutenant, and Commanding Officer of the private armed Brig *Anaconda,* whereof Nathaniel Shaler is commander (but who was not at the time on board) direct, cause, or permit certain cannon of said Brig, which were loaded with Powder and Balls, to be fired at the Schooner *Commodore Hull,* commanded by Henry S. Newcomb, a Lieutenant in the Navy of the United States, and thereby wound, by said Shots so fired, the said Henry S. Newcomb and Two Seamen, belonging to the said Schooner *Commodore Hull,* and that you did thus proceed to insult the Flag of the United States, and to wound and maim her said ~~commander~~ officer and Seamen without any justifiable cause whatever

Captn. Greenleaf, commanding the Marines of the U.S. Frigate *President,* is to serve this arrest, and you are to be confined to the limits of said Frigates decks, until the decision of the Honble. the Secretary of the Navy shall be made known to me, relative to the further proceedings necessary in your case

Jn⁰ Rodgers
Comd'g the U.S N forces
at Boston

U.S. Frigate *President*
Harbour of Boston, Jany. 19th 1813

Copy, DNA, RG45, CL, 1813, Vol. 1, No. 24, enclosure (M125, Roll No. 26). This copy was signed by Rodgers.

Testimony of George W. Burbank at his Court-Martial

[Extract]
6 March 1813   10 A.M.   Marine Barracks   Charlestown Navy Yard

I sent Lt. Miller on board the Schooner to ascertain what she was, our people in the mean time was conversing on the subject, and from the appearance of her sails, which appeared to made of English Duck, the fur caps of the men[1] & the refusal of the officer to tell us what she was, it was generally believed it was the *Liverpool packet* and a determination was impressed amongst us to ascertain beyond doubt, what she was, on Lt. Millers return he informd me he could get no satisfacttion that the commanding officer refused to tell the name of the schooner or any thing about her except that her colours & his uniform ought to satisfy him that she was a United States vessel and he a United States officer. The schooner then began to get underway. . . . Believeing it to be my duty to prevent the escape of the Schooner till I knew what she was, I ordered the shot to be drawn from the Bow Gun, the Cannister was drawn but they were not able to get out the round shot, and I then ordered the gun to be so elevated that the shot would not strike the Town & I gave orders to fire the Bow Gun a head of the Schooner with the intention of preventing her from getting underway—. the three guns were then fired which occasioned the accident. That I did not direct cause or permit a gun to be fired into the Schooner I believe is fully proved from the evidence and that I did not insult the flag of the United States is also true, because at the time I ordered the gun to fired ahead of the schooner I thought her an enemy and at no time had I supposed her to be a vessel of the United States.

That Lt. Newcomb meant to conceal the name & character of the schooner from me while I had given him Satisfaction respecting the Brig is evident . . . . [2]

Signed   G. W. Burbank

Copy, DNA, RG125, CM, Vol. 4, No. 131 (M273, Roll No. 4). This is an extract of a lengthy court-martial proceeding that lasted from 27 February to 11 March 1813. Burbank read this defense statement and then presented a copy of it to the court.

1. Previous testimony at the court-martial indicated that this type of fur cap was popular in Halifax, raising doubts about *Commodore Hull*'s nationality.
2. On 11 March Commodore Rodgers concurred in the acquittal of Burbank and ordered his release.

Secretary Jones's Reflections on His New Position

Less than two weeks after receiving his appointment from the president, Jones arrived in Washington energetic and confident to undertake the new challenge. Unlike Hamilton, Jones had a maritime background, having sailed in a Pennsylvania privateer during the Revolution. He had developed ties with Congress while serving a term as Philadelphia's Republican representative in the Seventh Congress (1801–3). As a vocal war hawk he had promoted the American declaration of war. Jones realized that he would make enemies but was optimistic that he could effect change as secretary of the navy. In the following letter to his wife, Jones noted his intention not to shrink from necessary reforms.

SECRETARY OF THE NAVY JONES TO ELEANOR JONES

Washington   23d Jany 1813

My dear Wife

I arrived safe here after an agreeable journey at 3 Oclock this afternoon and for the moment have put up at Davis' Hotel until I can look about for agreeable permanent quarters. Genl Armstrong had written on to a friend and has taken the rooms offered to me by Mrs. Wilson— I have this evining heard of a place that I think will suit me better. I called for a moment on the President who indeed expressed great pleasure— I am to see him in the morning on business, and take a family dinner with him. This eving. I called on Mr Gallatin and had some interesting conversation relative to public measures connected with my department. I have not seen my friend Macon yet. Those of my friends whom I have casually met with greet me with pleasure and express great confidence, but commisserate me in the Herculean task I have to encounter.

Be it so, but I am sure it will give you pleasure to learn that though the report of its difficulties increase as I advance my hope and confidence is strengthened and the terrors appear to diminish with the serious contemplation I have given to the subject. Having accepted the trust with reluctance, but with the purest motives and most ardent zeal for the sacred cause of our Country why should I despair? My pursuits and studies has been intimately connected with the objects of the department and I have not been an inattentive observer of political causes and effects. The truth is that the difficulties I have to encounter are artificial, but they are not the less difficult on that account. They arise from the corruption of self interested men who have taken root in the establishment and like the voracious poplar nothing can thrive in their shade. But (as we did in our yard) we can cut it down replace the fair pavement, and let in the cheering beams of the sun of truth and honesty. I shall take care however not to cut rashly and indiscriminately. If I cut off the noxious plants, I will cherish the useful trees.

But of what avail you will say is honest intention, and faithful services if assailed by the breath of calumny and faction. I answer, if I am incompetent & grossly negligent it will not be calumny— If I am faithful and reasonably competent the consciousness of virtue and fidelity I hope will sustain me. To expect to pass without lashing would be idle. I have only to request you not to mind it when it does occur. My love to all friends. Your ever affectionate Husband.

Wm Jones

ALS, PHi, U. C. Smith Collection, Papers of William Jones.

Charleston Station and Force Report

Captain John H. Dent, commanding officer at Charleston, South Carolina, began 1813 with a force composed of barges and four schooners: Alligator, Carolina, Ferret, *and* Nonsuch.[1] *In response to enemy harassment of the coast, he deployed those vessels that were adequately manned, but lack of men and officers hampered his operations. Having received approval from the former secretary to make necessary repairs and improvements to the rented navy yard, Dent spent the winter collecting supplies. Writing to Jones on 16 February about the anticipated work, Dent obviously had not received the secretary's letter of 9 February in which the latter had ordered Dent to suspend all permanent improvements at the navy yard.[2] Dent, along with Surgeon George Logan, would press Jones throughout the first half of 1813 to establish better and less expensive medical care for the station.[3]*

1. Alligator *was the former gunboat No. 166. For background on* Carolina *and* Ferret, *see Dudley,* Naval War of 1812, *Vol. 1, pp. 583–86.* Nonsuch, *formerly the successful Baltimore privateer of the same name, owned by George Stiles, was purchased in 1812 at Charleston for $15,000; see Garitee,* Republic's Private Navy, *pp. 87, 271, 279.*

2. *See Dent to Hamilton, 5 Dec. 1812, in Dudley,* Naval War of 1812, *Vol. 1, p. 589 and Jones to Dent, 9 Feb. 1813, SNL, Vol. 10, p. 249 (M149, Roll No. 10).*

3. *See pp. 121–22.*

Captain John H. Dent to Secretary of the Navy Jones

Charleston   30th January 1813.

Sir

Official information having been received here that ten or twelve coasters with full cargoes of rice had been chased into Bull's Bay by an Enemy's Brig of War, on Saturday, and were exposed to be cut out by her boats, I immediately manned from the Guardship two Barges, and dispatched them for their protection, they have not yet returned. I also transfered the crew of the Schooner *Carolina* to the *Nonsuch,* and directed her commander, Sailing Master Mork,[1] to proceed to Sea, and remain off Bulls Bay, and protect as far as practicable the vessels therein, or draw the attention of the enemy from that point. The weather has been extremely thick and boisterous since, the enemy could not have remained near the coast, the vessels are still safe, and I expect them all in to day.

I have dispatched a barge to convoy an Army transport, loaded with ordinance, inland to Savannah. It will be impossible to man, the Schooner or Barges, what few men are here, are either taken by the privateers, or engaged for France, at 45 dollars pr month. The Schooner *Alligator* sails this morning for her station in Port Royal Sound, to protect the inland trade. I Have the Honor to be With great respect Your most Obt. Svt.

J H Dent

ALS, DNA, RG45, CL, 1813, Vol. 1, No. 40 (M125, Roll No. 26).

1. Sailing Master James Mork was Dent's second in command.

Captain John H. Dent to Secretary of the Navy Jones

The Honorable William Jones   Charleston   16th Feby. 1813
Sir

The Season has been so cold, that little more has been done to the wharf at the Navy Yard than collect the materials, the weather begins to break, and I shall tomorrow commence with the workmen, and continue until compleated. The Artificers Houses are in a State of forwardness and will be compleated in three weeks. I have applied at different times, to the Marine officer on this Station for a guard to be placed at the Yard for the protection of the public Stores therein, and he has not been able to supply one, without breaking up the guard at the barracks, I beg leave to suggest the moving of the present Marine Barracks to the Navy Yard, where suitable and good accommodations can be had untill proper barracks are built; they are now paying a high rent for a House in the environs of the City, and if removed to the yard, would save considerable expence to the department, and be rendering important Service at the same time. I suggested this arrangment, at the establishment of the Yard. Also our Hospital is in the city the Surgeon having orders to rent quarters for the Sick, and disabled Seamen attatched to this Station; the expence attending this establishment has been greater than was necessary, and if removed to the yard, where there is a house calculated to receive for the present the Sick & wounded. The late fire destroyed his House, with Several sets of instruments, and considerable medicine belonging to the Station.

There has not been a commissioned Officer attatched to this Station for the last year. The Schooner *Carolina* is ready for Sea, half manned, and requires an Active Lieutenant for a Commander, She is a very fine vessel, and I think will Sail fast: eight Midshipmen, and two Surgeon's mates are much wanted on this Station. I have been obliged to appoint my clerk Mr Matthew Reardon to act as purser of the *Carolina*. Since in commission, he has performed that Service much to my satisfaction, and is in every respect qualified, to do that duty, I shall feel particularly gratified if his appointment is confirmed, knowing that he will be an acquisition to the Service. Muster Rolls of the different vessels and boats under my command will be immediately forwarded for your information. I Have the Honor to be With great respect your obt Svt.

J H Dent

ALS, DNA, RG45, CL, 1813, Vol. 1, No. 76 (M125, Roll No. 26).

Lack of Adequate Medical Care and Regulations

Dissatisfaction with the medical treatment provided for the gunboat crews at Beaufort, North Carolina, induced the sailing master who was in charge there to recommend contracting for the services of a local private practitioner. Having to rely on the naval surgeon at Ocracoke was inconvenient and medical care suffered.

The complaints at Beaufort were representative of problems throughout the naval community. On 26 February 1811, Congress recognized the need for more uniform medical care for seamen and passed a law providing funding for separate naval hospitals through various revenue sources.[1] Secretary of the Navy Hamilton solicited the recommendations of several naval surgeons in drafting rules and regulations for the government of those hospitals. Dr. Edward Cutbush headed this naval commission, and Hamilton presented its findings to the Twelfth Congress. The measure languished throughout the war. In the second document that follows, Cutbush apprises the new secretary, William Jones, of the need for reforms in the naval medical establishment.

1. Statutes at Large, *Vol. 2, Stat. 3, Chap. 26, pp. 650–51.*

SAILING MASTER JOHN C. MANSON[1] TO SECRETARY OF THE NAVY JONES

William Jones Esqr.   Beaufert N. Ca.   Febry. 1st 1813
Sir

We have been here nearly six months, in which time the Crews of U. States Gun Boats *No. 147 & 148* have been very sickly oweing to the severity of the winter several of them have had the Desintery & Plurisy, but by taking great care of them have not lost but one man who died after a short illness of the latter disease. Sir I have now 3 on board sick and one on shore & Mr. Haddaway has on board his Boat *No. 147* about the same complaining.

I am sorry to say during the time above mentioned we have not been visited by Doctor Morrison but once, from Ocricock.

Sir I have taken the liberty which I hope you will excuse to send inclosed a copy of a Contract made between the U. States, and a Doctor James Manney who lives at this place, who wishes if you approve of the same to furnish Medicine & attend both Boats regularly for $30. pr. Month.

Sir as the people still continue sick & thought it would be much the cheapest way and I hope will meet with your approbation, as it is not convenient for Doctor Morrison to attend to this station & the Ocricock Station.

Sir you will please to have the goodness to drop me a line to inform me whether I shall employ Doctor Manney or not.[2] I have the Honor to be Sir Respectfully Yr. Mo. Obt. Servt.

John C. Manson, S. M.

P.S. Sir there is no Hospital at this place & we have to give $2 a week for the sick on shore. Respect. Yr. Mo. Obt. Svt.

John C. Manson

ALS, DNA, RG45, BC, 1813, Vol. 1, No. 42 (M148, Roll No. 11).

1. John C. Manson was a sailing master from 15 July 1812 until his discharge, 10 June 1815.
2. No response by Jones to either Manson or Dr. James Manney was found.

SURGEON EDWARD CUTBUSH TO SECRETARY OF THE NAVY JONES

Sir,

A System of rules and regulations for the government of Naval Hospitals, drawn up by myself, and concurred in by Drs. Davis, Marshall and Ewell, were presented to Congress at the last session by Mr. Hamilton; they were examined by a Committee appointed for the purpose, and reported to the house with some amendments, July 11. 1812, but were not finally acted upon. Although there is no law authorizing the establishment of Naval Hospitals,[1] yet as temporary buildings have been appropriated at different places, for the reception of the sick and wounded belonging to the Navy, I conceive that some rules and regulations for their government are necessary. The want of a system of rules, authorized by an act of Congress, was sensibly felt by me, during the last summer, in the small hospital at New Castle under my direction; I therefore beg leave to solicit your attention to the subject, for, without regulations, it is impossible to restrain the convalescents from acts injurious to themselves, to the service and to the inhabitants, who reside in the vicinity of those establishments. I likewise beg leave to state, that a certain number of Hospital Surgeons are appointed for the army, but none are authorized for the Navy!! With due deference, I conceive that the responsibility attached to those who act in that capacity in the Navy, not only entitles them to the rank, but to the same pay and emoluments, received by an Army Hospital Surgeon, Whilst engaged in attendance on the Hospital at New Castle, I was only authorized to charge the extra expenses incurred in my visits, between the Navy Yard at Philada. and that place. Permit me, Sir, (as the subject of the rank of Officers has been brought before Congress) to solicit your attention to that of the surgeons of the Navy, when you take into consideration the relative rank of Officers. Although, it is apparently of little consequence, yet, I can assure you, that the description of a Naval Surgeon, by the pen of the celebrated Dr. Smollett in his Roderick Random,[2] has prevented many men of professional abilities from entering our service, under an idea, that the surgeons and mates, were considered in the same menial situation, and I must add that the pay is not a sufficient inducement. There is scarcely a village in the U S where a practitioner of medicine and surgery, does not receive a greater compensation than a Naval Surgeon. There is not a sufficient degree of respectability attached to the Surgeons of our Navy. In the British service, at present, the pay increases with the number of years that a surgeon serves, and the rate of the ship to which he is advanced; it is considered a promotion to be advanced from a sloop of war to a Frigate, and so on to a first rate; he likewise ranks with Sea Lieutenants and Captains of the Army, subject, however, to the orders of the Lieuts in the line of his duty as a surgeon. In the French Service, I believe the rank has been made still more respectable. I hope, Sir, for the honor of our Navy and the profession of Medicine that, (although the army surgeon receives more pay) you will permit no invidious distinction in point of rank.

As to Naval Hospital Surgeons, I humbly conceive that they ought to rank with Hospital Surgeons of the army, and with the same grade of officers with whom they are ranked. I have the honor to remain your humble Servant.

E Cutbush
Philada.   Feby. 13 1813

ALS, DNA RG45, BC, 1813, Vol. 1, No. 60 (M148, Roll No. 11).

1. The 26 February 1813 act authorized a board of naval commissioners to procure sites and construct buildings for naval hospitals. Nothing was done until the 1820s, however.
2. *Roderick Random*, 2 vols. (London, 1748) is a novel about the adventures of a picaresque hero who enters the service of a physician, by popular British novelist Tobias George Smollett (1721–71). Smollett received an M.D. from Marischal College, Aberdeen, in 1750.

Jacob Lewis and the New York Flotilla

Jacob Lewis, captain of the privateer Bunker Hill *early in the war, was appointed master commandant in the U.S. Navy in November 1812. He was given the command of all the gunboats and fire ships stationed at New York. Lewis accepted this new challenge and set out immediately to assess the status of his flotilla. He found it undermanned and "in a pitiable State owing to the prejudice which has existed against it." Lewis knew that he had local support because the committee for harbor defense, fearful of a swarm of British ships in the spring, exhorted the state legislature for money for defense. Unsure of Jones's support, Lewis enlisted the aid of Secretary of State James Monroe in convincing the Navy Department that gunboats used in coastal defense freed frigates for sea duty. He feared the flotilla would become emasculated through drafts of its crews for other duties. His fears were realized when Jones asked him to recruit for the Lake Champlain service; more importantly, the secretary did not spare New York from the gunboat reduction order. Lewis was ordered on 26 February to reduce to 15 gun vessels. As on other stations, public reaction was adverse.[1]*

1. *Paul Hamilton to Lewis, 27 Nov. 1812, DNA, RG45, SNL, Vol. 10, p. 211 (M149, Roll No. 10); Lewis to Jones, 10 Feb. 1813, DNA, RG45, MLR, 1813, Vol. 1, No. 115 (M124, Roll No. 53); Jones to Lewis, 9 Feb. 1813, and 26 Feb. 1813, DNA, RG45, SNL, Vol. 10, pp. 249 and 281–83 (M149, Roll No. 10).*

MASTER COMMANDANT JACOB LEWIS TO SECRETARY OF THE NAVY JONES

Sir

I have to inform you that the Flotilla under my Command requires about three hundred and fifty men to compleat the number required for that servise, the Rendezvous in this City is clos'd for the want of monies to pay the recruits, I am very apprehensive that the Flotilla which I have the honor to Command will fall very short of that state of preparation which may be expected, by the month of Apl. I have the honor to assure you of my high Confd. & Regs.

J Lewis
Comg U.S. Flotilla

N Yk.   Feby. 6th <u>1813</u>

ALS, DNA, RG45, MLR, 1813, Vol. 1, No. 96 (M124, Roll No. 53).

MASTER COMMANDANT JACOB LEWIS TO SECRETARY OF STATE JAMES MONROE

Honble. James Monroe   Private

Sir

I am very desirous of possessing the confidence of the present Secretary of the Navy as I did of the late Mr Secy. Hamilton. I am now very much occupied in raising and organising the Crews of the Flotilla under my Command, it is my intention to make them land as well as Sea Soldiers,—and I trust when my Crews Shall be compleated I shall be able to throw on shores at Sandy hook one thousand effective men (in Case of emergency) and at the same time place the flotilla in a place of perfect safety where the Enemy could not possibly get at them—

I will exercise and train the Crews on the hook to landing, Embarking, Marching, forming and displaying Colloms— They <u>shall be amphibious Soldiers</u>, But in order to render this force thus formidable and effective, it will be necessary I should have the good opinion of the Secretary of the Navy, and that he should offer me prompt and ample support,   Gun Boats hitherto have been held in the utmost contempt, owing to a false prejudice the inhabitants of this vast City now begin to believe, that the City cannot be defended without the Auxillary force of this floating defence, and great deal I now expected from it, in the event of an attack, the new arrangement made in the Flotilla has already brought it into [respect as?] any number of the first Masters of Ships out of this Port are Constantly tendering their Servises to me, I <u>could chuse out of one hundred</u>,

The prejudice of the Navy against G. Boats has arisen from an Idea that the appropriations made for Gun Boats, in Case of their non-Existance, would have gone to the Increase of the Navy, (in fact) they have viewed it as a substitute for a Navy &c   The fact is very different, Gun Boats take the place of Frigates in the defence of harbours therefore frigates instead of being employ'd for that purpose go on the bosom of the Ocean and Cruize for Glory & pelf— The Flotilla including the fire vessels would have been in compleat readiness for Servise Ere this moment, had it not been for a system of drafting from them, or enticing them to Volunteer for the Ships or Lakes, hundreds have been taken out of the boats in this way, and altho the men that I have recruited has been under special Contract, that they shall not go on any other Service other than the defence of the harbour of New York, yet I know an attempt is now on foot to take men from the flotilla, allow me to assure you Sir that such a procedure, will not only astonish disgust and damp the ardour of the officers, but produce a Cabal among the Inhabitants of this City, and for myself I assure you I shall feel very much mortified,   I am perfectly aware of the importance of Gun Bs so much so, that I would, suggest a plan to take from the two frigates which are and will remain Blockaded in the Chesapeake their Crews & send them to the Lakes they will make all Canada tremble,—

The mode of doing it, would be to order the ships put in ordinary, afterwards call on the Crews to volunteer, the men will all go, and where ever our Ships are Blockaded be it here, or Elsewhere, I would send all their Crews on to the Lakes—

I have taken the liberty of thus freely addressing you, from the best of motives, as well to Solicite your good offices near the Secretary of the Navy. Come. Chauncey has done <u>wonders</u>, he had Carte Blance, from the late Secretary; the Present has <u>renewed</u> it—

it was most certainly the intention of Mr Hamilton to place the whole Flotilla for the defence of the harbour of New York under my distinct Command, and I have reason to believe that it was the Presidents also,

I am perfectly satisfied to Command what has been always despised by the Navy, and thus I make it useful, I ask nothing more than the smiles of my Country—and the approbation of my Government,   I have the honor to be with the hight. Cnsi. & Respt. your very Obt. & Huml. Sert.

J Lewis
Come. U.S. Flotilla

New Yk, Feby. 27th 1813

ALS, DNA, RG45, MLR, 1813, Vol. 2, No. 11 (M124, Roll No. 54).

Lieutenant Drayton Reports the Loss of *Vixen*

Because of the illness and death of Vixen's *commander, Master Commandant George W. Reed, the Navy Department did not receive an official report on the capture of* Vixen *by* Southampton *in November 1812. Lieutenant Glen Drayton,* Vixen's *second in command, recounts here the unequal contest between the two ships, the subsequent loss of both vessels, and the lack of sufficient funds to support the American prisoners while in captivity. Drayton and most of his officers left Jamaica in April, arriving at Cape May on 2 May. The remaining officers and crew gave up waiting for a cartel ship and took passage on the American merchant ship* William Penn, *arriving at Little Egg Harbor, New Jersey, about a month after Drayton.*

LIEUTENANT GLEN DRAYTON[1] TO SECRETARY OF THE NAVY HAMILTON

Spanish Town (Jamaica)
February 8th 1813

Sir,

I am extremely sorry that by the Death of Capt. G. W. Reed, (late of the U.S. Brig *Vixen*) it devolves on me as Senior Officer of said Vessel, to inform you her Capture and Subsequent loss by Shipwreck, the particulars of which are as follows.

Being on our return from a Cruise of Thirty days without meeting any of the Enemey's Vessels, having ranged along the West India Islands from as far Eastward as

Turk's Island, on the 22d Novr. being in the Lat of 30° 30' N and Long. 79° W at 7 A.M. discovered a Sail to the Northd. the wind being light from the Eastd.; which we soon discovered to be a large Ship, apparently a Frigate standing for us,   We immediately made sail and hauled our wind to the Southd., finding her gaining on us fast, Capt. Reed ordered the water started, and the wind becoming light we got out our Sweeps, by the means of which at first hoped to escape. about 1. P.M. the wind freshened and became more steady, when she again overhauled us,   Our private Signal being made, which was not answer'd Capt. Reed directed the Anchors to be cut from the Bow, the Bow Guns, Kedge Anchors, Shot, and all lumber to be hove overboard in order to lighten the Vessel, slacken'd up the Stays, & started the Wedges of the Masts, all of which proved ineffectual,   we then bore up, in hopes of eluding her untill Night, but from her superior sailing she soon got within Gunshot when she commenced firing, her shot then passing over us, and there appearing no possible chance of escape, Capt. Reed called us together, where conceiving that any resistance against so superior a force would be a Wanton and useless Sacrafice of a brave Crew, we were compelled after firing two Guns to surrender.— She proved to be His Majesty's Frigate *Southampton* of 38 Guns, Sir James Lucas Yeo, (commander). Capt. Reed went on board the Frigate & tendered his Sword, which was immediately returned him, the Officers and Men being taken on board the Ship, both Vessels filled away, steering to the Southd. & Eastd. from the 22d. to the 25th. the wind blowing fresh and Sea running high could have no Communication with the Brig, consequently could not get our Trunks &c from on board. On the night of the 26th. about 1/2 past 12, being at Meridian in Lat. 24° 54' N. Lon. 74° 30' W. the Ship Struck on a reef of Rocks, immediately afterwards, the Brig struck on our Starboard Bow about a quarter of a Mile from us. At 3 A.M. The Officer and Crew of the Brig deserted her, she having bilged. At daylight on the 27th we saw the land astern which proved to be Little Windward, or Conception Island, where we were fortunate enough to land the Crews of both Vessels in safety. Our Officers and Crew however were unable to save anything from the wreck of the Brig, she having settled so quickly. Boats were then dispatched to New Providence and the neighbouring Islands to procure relief, on the 6th Decr. H.M. Brig *Rhodian* with two Transports arrived to our assistance on board of which the two Crews were embarked and Sailed on the 9th for this Island where we arrived on the 14th and were put on parole, the Men being put on board the Prison Ship at Port Royal.

I am extremely sorry, Sir, that much to be lamented Death of Capt. Reed who died of a Fever in this place on the 5th of January, prevents his recommending his Crew (which I know to have been his intention), their orderly & decorous behaviour during the time of the Ships striking, and afterwards, on the Island, was such as to induce Sir James, to assemble them, before his own Crew, and thank them publickly for their Service, and I trust Sir, that tho' they have been unfortunate, they have not been inactive, and should it please their Country to call them out again, they will support the dignity of her Naval Character which has so recently and generally been established—

On our arrival at this place Capt. Reed drew a certain Sum of Money in order to supply the Officers & Crew with cloathing &c. Since his death I have also been compelled to draw, as the scarcity & high price of provisions will not permit us to live on the allowance made by the British Government— I feel it a duty incumbent on me Sir, to inform you that there are upwards of Four Hundred American Prisoners now at this place, who I beleive would willingly enter the Service should a Cartel arrive.—

Mr. Satterwhite ~~late~~ purser of the late Brig, I have entrusted this to, who also has the several Indents, and Vouchers respecting the Monies drawn, he has obtained permission to return home from the Admiral, being considered a noncombatant, the Surgeon & Clerk have also applied, and I have no doubt, will allow permission—

Trusting Sir, that upon our arrival in America, and the usual enquiries being made into our conduct, it may meet your approbation. I have the honor to be, Sir, Yr. most, Obt. Servt.

Glen Drayton,
Lieut. U.S. Navy

ALS, DNA, RG45, BC, 1813, Vol. 1, No. 46 (M148, Roll No. 11). The original document has been corrected grammatically in pencil in another hand. These corrections have been omitted. When Lieutenant Drayton was paroled, he returned George Reed's papers to his brother Joseph Reed. Among them was a copy of his official letter on the surrender which the Navy Department had not received. Joseph Reed sent an undated, unaddressed, and unsigned copy of this letter to Jones; see DNA, RG45, MLR, 1813, Vol. 3, No. 95 (M124, Roll No. 55). For the British account, see Dudley, *Naval War of 1812*, Vol. 1, pp. 594–95.

1. Glen Drayton had served as acting lieutenant in *Vixen* since reporting for duty in May 1811. In January 1813, while he was still a prisoner, the Senate confirmed his appointment as lieutenant.

Naval Construction in 1813

A desire to continue the blue water victories of 1812 spurred passage of the naval expansion act of 2 January 1813, authorizing the building of four 74-gun ships and six 44-gun frigates. Three American ships of the line were eventually begun under this act: Franklin *at Philadelphia,* Washington *at Portsmouth, and* Independence *at Charlestown. Construction of three frigates was undertaken in 1813:* Columbia *at the Washington Navy Yard,* Guerriere *at Philadelphia, and* Java *at Baltimore.*

Fully expecting that the British would enforce a strict blockade of the coastline in 1813, Jones believed that smaller vessels could be built faster, would be better commerce raiders, and might succeed in diverting the blockaders from their stations. Congress approved an act authorizing construction of six additional sloops of war on 3 March 1813.[1] Argus *was begun at the Washington Navy Yard;* Erie, Ontario, Wasp, Peacock, *and* Frolic *were built under private contract, the first two at Baltimore, and the last three at Newburyport, New York, and Boston, respectively.[2]*

In letters to William Doughty, newly appointed naval constructor at the Washington Navy Yard,[3] and the navy agents at Boston and Philadelphia, Secretary Jones stressed the importance of inventorying and purchasing materials for ship construction as expeditiously as possible.

1. For the January and March acts, see Statutes at Large, Vol. 2, Stat. 2, Chap. 6, p. 789; and Vol. 2, Stat. 2, Chap. 54, p. 821.
2. For a full description of the design and construction of American vessels during the war, see Chapelle, American Sailing Navy, chapter 5.
3. William Doughty operated a small shipyard at Georgetown, District of Columbia. He was the principal designer for several of the new frigates and sloops.

SECRETARY OF THE NAVY JONES TO WILLIAM DOUGHTY

Mr. William Doughty   Navy Depart.
Constructor, Navy Yard   feby: 8th 1813
Washington

On application to Captain Tingey Commandant of the Navy Yard, he will put into your possession the Mould loft, together with a convenient office, and all the Draughts, plans, Books, Instruments and every other thing appertaining to the Constructor's department, and will afford to you every facility and assistance you may require in the discharge of the duty assigned to you for which you will receive instructions from this Department. As I wish to form an approximate estimate of the timber, plank, thickstuff &c now in the yard (exclusive of what may be necessary to complete the work on hand and the Live Oak for the 74) in order to ascertain what may be necessary to procure without delay for laying down and building a Frigate, you will by exhibiting this letter to Capt. Tingey receive such information as may facilitate your estimate of what may be in the yard, as well as of what may be expected under existing Contracts within a reasonable time for the object in contemplation

The draughts of the 74 and of the Frigate *Congress* I presume are among the number in the Navy Yard—these I wish to inspect. You will also ascertain whether there are any half breadth models of the Frigates or other vessels.

W Jones.

LB Copy, DNA, RG45, CNA, Vol. 1, pp. 354–55 (M441, Roll No. 1).

SECRETARY OF THE NAVY JONES TO NAVY AGENT AMOS BINNEY

Amos Binney Esq   Navy Depart.
Boston.   9. feb. 1813

You will, without delay, procure on the best terms in your power all the necessary plank, thickstuff and other materials of wood for a 74. gun ship, which it intended to build at Boston. Consult Capt. Hull as to the best means of procuring these materials of the choicest quality. If the plank &c can not be had, <u>let the trees be cut down immediately</u>.

A bill of Scantling will be sent on, as soon, as the Constructor has it prepared. Mean time as delay must be avoided, you can obtain from some experienced builder a general description, and proceed to act upon it.

Among other considerations, which induce me to urge your proceeding <u>without delay</u>, in the execution of these instructions, the fact that this is the proper season for cutting the timber, and that it is rapidly passing away is very important. Should we not avail ourselves of this Season, we may be compelled to suspend our operations till next winter, and thus lose that time, during which it is hoped, by proper & prompt arrangements, the object may be accomplished. I am respy.

W Jones

LB Copy, DNA, RG45, MLS, Vol. 11, pp. 186–87 (M209, Roll No. 4).

SECRETARY OF THE NAVY JONES TO SENATOR SAMUEL SMITH[1]

The Honorable S. Smith   Navy Depart.
Chairman of the Naval Committee   Feb: 22d 1813.
Senate.

It has so happened, that I did not see the Bill which you enclosed in your Note of the 20th until after it had passed the House of Representatives. Some of its provisions may have been suggested by a letter I addressed to the Honorable Chairman of the Naval Committee of the H. R.[2]

We have now in Service but one Sloop of war of the class (but smaller) of those contemplated by the Bill now pending before the Senate.[3]

Of the utility of such vessels the practice of the enemy is pretty strong evidence and as applied to our Circumstances, they will be found still more so. Their force is inferior only to a frigate—their cost and expenditure only about one third in actual Service; and in pursuit of the Commerce and light cruisers of the enemy three Sloops of the class proposed may reasonably be expected to produce a much greater effect than a single Frigate.

Moreover they may be very useful in our own waters and for the protection of our Coasting trade against the depredations of the enemy's light Cruizers.

Aided by these vessels our Frigates would be enabled to take a wider range in pursuit of higher game. I propose to rate them 18 guns, to mount 18–32 pd. Carronades and 4 long 12 pdrs.

The cost of such a Sloop of war including two months wages in advance, and four months provisions I estimate at 75,000 Dollars. The 2d Section of the Bill I presume was suggested by a similar one in the "Act concerning the Naval Establishment" passed the 30th March 1812 and from some doubts, whether the authority to put a vessel in Commission the creating an additional Captain &c though the construction and practice has I believe been in the affirmative hitherto. In respect to the 44s some doubts have been suggested, whether the authority given by the "Act to encrease the Navy of the U States" viz as soon as suitable materials can be procured therefor to cause to be built &c would warrant the building by Contract with private Builders.

These are merely my own ideas on the subject without presuming to explain those which prevailed at the passing of the Bill, and are submitted with great deference and respect. I have the honor &c

W Jones.

LB Copy, DNA, RG45, Letters to Congress, Vol. 2, pp. 162–63.

1. Samuel Smith, Republican senator from Maryland, was chairman of the Senate naval affairs committee during the second session of the Twelfth Congress.

2. Smith asked Jones to clarify some points in the House bill relating to the construction of sloops; see Smith to Jones, 20 Feb. 1813, DNA, RG45, MLR, 1813, Vol. 1, No. 152 (M124, Roll No. 53). Jones is probably referring to his 4 February 1813 letter to Burwell Bassett; see DNA, RG45, Letters to Congress, Vol. 2, pp. 149–50.

3. *Hornet.*

SECRETARY OF THE NAVY JONES TO NAVY AGENT GEORGE HARRISON

George Harrison Esqr.   Navy Depart.
Philadelphia.   5th March 1813

I have received your letter of the 1st inst. with the Note from Mr. Dallas on the subject of the Navy Yard, and when I receive the report of Messrs. Humphreys Penrose [1] & Davis, I shall determine what course to pursue.

The obstacles which induced Mr. Penrose to decline a participation in the building of the 74 having been removed. He will unite with Mr. Humphreys for that purpose and I have desired them to confer together and fix upon an equitable compensation for their Services. It is a heavy undertaking & I am sure the public Service will be benefitted by their joint talents, and public confidence & Satisfaction conciliated.

Messrs. J. & F. Grice [2] having proposed to superintend & direct the building of one of the 44 gun Frigates upon the terms (copy) enclosed and having stated to me that they had a considerable quantity of timber at their refusal and some live oak timber of their own fit for the purpose, You are hereby authorized to enter into an engagement with them on the terms proposed to superintend & direct the building of and completing to a cleat a 44 Gun frigate of such materials, dimensions & form, and in such a manner as shall be directed by this Department and also under your direction to purchase & collect the timber necessary for the purpose.

I also agree to purchase all the Live Oak they may have suitable for the purpose at such valuation as competent and disinterested persons, chosen with your approbation, may determine. If Live Oak for the Main transom, upperpiece of Stern apron Hawse pieces &c are not to be had in Philadelphia, there is a prime Cargo of Mahogany in Baltimore lately purchased by my order out of which these principal pieces or a part of them may be selected & sent round by way of French town—no time should be lost in procuring the Timber materials. I am &c

                                                             W. Jones.

LB Copy, DNA, RG45, MLS, Vol. 11, pp. 215–16 (M209, Roll No. 4).

1. Samuel Humphreys, son of former naval constructor Joshua Humphreys, and Charles Penrose designed and built ships in Philadelphia.
2. Joseph and Francis Grice, brothers, were Philadelphia shipbuilders.

Lieutenant Crane Seeks Promotion

William M. Crane's naval career was in a state of flux during the winter of 1812–13. In November he was ordered by Hamilton to command the Charlestown Navy Yard. Then in February 1813 Jones transferred him to the New York Navy Yard to replace Charles Ludlow. This was to be a temporary assignment, for Isaac Chauncey was expected to return to the post. No doubt dissatisfied with these shore positions after a long naval service, Crane, while visiting his family in New Jersey, decided to solicit senatorial assistance in obtaining a promotion. Crane was appointed master commandant in March 1813.

LIEUTENANT WILLIAM M. CRANE TO SENATOR THOMAS WORTHINGTON [1]

Elizabethtown. N Jersey   10 Feby. 1813

Sir

I have just received a letter from my brother Joseph H. Crane of Dayton in the State of Ohio. He informs me that you had been good enough to assure him that whenever the expected promotions are made in the Navy you will give your aid in obtaining such promotion as I may be entitled to—for this promise Sir I beg you to receive my thanks—

It may not be improper for me to state that I have been in the Service near fourteen years— Was at Tripoli with Commodore Preble and actively engaged in all the attacks made on that place—in which service I had the Command of a gun boat— In 1805 I received from Commodore Rodgers the command of a Cutter Sloop of 8 guns in which I cruised a year and then returned in her from Mediterranean to the U States.— I have served as first Lieut. to Capt. Hull and Commodore Decatur & Have commanded the Sloops of War *Argus* and *Nautilus*— I may further say that from the time of my entering the Service until now I have been constantly employed in Service, and at least one half the time on foreign stations— I am personally known by all the Captains and Commanders in the Navy and should in all cases wish to refer to them for every information which may be thought necessary with regard to my character & professional acquirements— I trust Sir that it is considered by the government, that I have on all occasions endeavoured to serve my country with zeal and firmness and hope soon to have an opportunity of shewing that I am not unworthy of the Station in which the President & Senate may choose to place me— With much respect I am Sir Yr. Hl. Servt.

W. M. Crane

ALS, DNA, RG45, MLR, 1813, Vol. 1, No. 175 (M124, Roll No. 53). Crane's letter was enclosed with Worthington's 24 February 1813 letter of recommendation to Jones; see DNA, RG45, MLR, 1813, Vol. 1, No. 174 (M124, Roll No. 53). Worthington noted that Crane lacked "influential relations to press his claims."

1. Thomas Worthington served Ohio in the Senate, 1803 to 1807 and 1810 to 1814.

Orders to Cruise Singly

Fearful that the British blockade would prevent American vessels from getting to sea, Jones wrote to several of his officers requesting details of their proposed cruises and inquiring when they expected to sail. Captain Charles Stewart, whose Constellation *was already blockaded in the Chesapeake, proposed a coastal cruise to South Carolina and then Newfoundland, across the Atlantic to Portugal, and then westward to the West Indies and home. Commodore John Rodgers had several alternatives for* President: *cruising from Newfoundland to Nova Scotia, Ireland to France, Norway to Denmark, or into the mid-Atlantic. Commodore Stephen Decatur's projected cruise plan included intercepting the British blockading squadron off Charleston, South Carolina, and then sailing between Newfoundland and the Azores to menace British merchant vessels coming from the East and West Indies and Brazil.*

After receiving responses from his commanders, Jones expressed his own views that they should consider cruising near the West Indies. The anticipated British buildup of naval force along the Atlantic coast of the United States would deplete the enemy's strength in the Caribbean, leaving the area unprotected and ripe for commerce raiding.[1]

1. See Jones to Stephen Decatur and Jacob Jones, 17 Mar. 1813, SNL, Vol. 10, pp. 306–309 (M149, Roll No. 10).

CIRCULAR FROM SECRETARY OF THE NAVY JONES TO COMMANDERS OF SHIPS NOW IN PORT REFITTING

Circular

Comre. Rodgers Boston }	Navy Department
" Bainbridge " }	22. Februy. 1813
" Decatur N. York } To Commanders of Ships	
Capt. Stewart Norfolk } now in port refitting [1]	
" Morris Present }	

There is good reason to expect, a very considerable augmentation of the Naval force of the enemy on our coast the ensuing Spring; & it will be perceived that his policy will be to blockade our Ships of War in our own harbors; intercepting our private cruisers, prizes and trade, and Harrass the seaboard.

Our great inferiority in naval strength, does not permit us to meet them on this ground without hazarding the precious Germ of our national glory.— we have however the means of creating a powerful diversion, & of turning the Scale of annoyance against the enemy. It is therefore intended, to dispatch all our public ships, now in Port, as soon as possible, in such positions as may be best adapted to destroy the Commerce of the enemy, from the Cape of Goodhope, to Cape Clear, and continue out as long as the means of subsistence can be procured abroad, in any quarter.

If any thing can draw, the attention of the enemy, from the annoyance of our coast, for the protection of his own, rich & exposed Commercial fleets, it will be a course of this nature, & if this effect can be produced, the two fold object of increasing the pressure upon the enemy and relieving ourselves, will be attained.

Cruizing singly, will also afford to our gallant Commanders, a fair oppertunity of displaying distinctly their Judgement, skill & enterprize, and of reaping the laurel of Fame, and its solid appendages, which so extended a field of Capture, without impairing the means of continuing the persuit, cannot fail to produce,—with this view, I wish to be apprized, (a short time in anticipation) of the period when each Ship, now refitting, will be ready for Sea, in order that instructions may be forewarded from this Department.

Your own ideas of a Cruize, with this general view, will be acceptable to me.

W. Jones.

LB Copy, DNA, CGO, Vol. 1, pp. 99–100 (M977, Roll No. 1).

1. John Rodgers in *President* left Boston in late April for a cruise; see pp. 250–55 for a discussion of his return. William Bainbridge decided to wait for *Independence*, 74, to be built; see Bainbridge to Jones, 1 Mar. 1813, PHi, U. C. Smith Collection, Papers of William Jones. Stephen Decatur in *United*

States left New York in May, but was forced to put in at New London in early June, where he remained blockaded by the enemy for the remainder of the year. Charles Stewart took command of *Constellation* in late 1812. The British blockade prevented his escape early the next year, forcing him to seek refuge in Norfolk. Jones reassigned Stewart to *Constitution* in early May, but Stewart did not leave Boston on a cruise until December 1813. *Constellation* never got to sea during the war. No response from Charles Morris was found. Because he was in Washington, he might have spoken to Jones directly. His ship, *Adams,* did not slip through the blockade until 1814.

CAPTAIN CHARLES STEWART TO SECRETARY OF THE NAVY JONES

United States frigate *Constellation*
Norfolk Harbour   March 2. 1813

Sir/

I have received your letter of 22d ult. and observe the desire you have of giving our ships of war, singly, the most extensive range for the annoyance of the Enemy's Commerce, which fully accords with my ideas of the subject since the commencement of the war. Our Naval means are truly limited, but no doubt much may be effected, small as they are, by the exertions and enterprise of the Officers when judiciously scattered over an extensive field of operations; and each ship, separately, will be more on their guard and better enabled to take care of themselves should they be endangered by too great a superiority of force. The difficulty of remaining out a sufficient length of time, owing to the small quantity of provisions and stores they can carry, will be a great objection to their proceeding into distant seas, and the difficulty of returning to the ports of the United States will increase daily, as the enemy are now making arrangements to block up our waters. How far we can rely on supplies from other places I do not know, but most of the ports we dare go into among the allies of England are incompetent to furnish them. The greatest advantages would be derived by the frigates having a small fast sailing schooner with them as a tender; they would facilitate the procuring supplies, and prevent often times the necessity of putting the frigate to great hazard: my ideas, therefore, would be to attach to each of the frigates, a vessel of that description, calculated to carry six or eight light guns, which in the first instance could be put in the hold, the schooner then stowed full of provisions and stores, with a sufficient number of men to navigate her, and to proceed from the United States and keep company with the frigate. But in case of separation to proceed to a fixed rendezvous, which each Commander could fix on; and when they were relieved sufficiently from their cargo, they could mount their guns, and be officered and manned from the frigate, and cruise with her, and on all occasions would do away the necessity of the frigates going into port for supplies. There are other advantages to be derived from them; in case of capturing valuable property they would afford the means of securing it on some desolate island untill the cruise was over. I will here beg leave to illustrate this observation, by observing, how useful such a vessel would have been to Commodore Bainbridge, as all the valuables on board the frigate *Java* could thereby have been saved to the gallant *Constitution*.

My plan for the *Constellations* cruise, could I have got to sea, was to have proceeded off the coast of South Carolina, and endeavoured to have picked up some of the Enemy's small cruisers, from thence off the Western Islands, from thence off Cape St. Vincent and Cadiz, from then off Madeira and the Cape de

Verds, from thence off to windward of the Caribbean Islands, then down through the West Indies to the Gulf passage and home; my stay on each station being prolonged or shortened according to success, information, the state of my supplies, and other circumstances; but should a small vessell be given the ship as a tender, my cruise could be much lengthened and varied to greater advantage.

The *Constellation* will be in readiness to sail as soon as we can get one suit of her sails enlarged; (most of her sails being one third too small, and all our spare canvass has been used to alter what is done), which will I hope be accomplished in the course of this week. I have the honor to be Very Respectfully Sir Your obedient Servant

Ch^S. Stewart

ALS, DNA, RG45, CL, 1813, Vol. 2, No. 6 (M125, Roll No. 27).

COMMODORE JOHN RODGERS TO SECRETARY OF THE NAVY JONES

U.S. Frigate *President*
Boston   March 8th 1813

Sir

As you suggested (in your circular of the 22nd ult) that my ideas of a cruise would be acceptable, permit me to say, that there are in my opinion Five different stations where our Ships might be employed with much advantage in capturing and destroying the Enemie's commerce—Namely—On the Eastern edge of the Banks of Newfoundland, in the direction of their Trade between England and Nova Scotia, and Newfoundland—Between the Manilla reef and the Southwesternmost part of the Banks of Newfoundland—Between Cape Clear and Ushant—Between the Naze of Norway and Jutland, and on the Equator, between the Longtd. of 24° and 31° West.

By stationing a Ship or Ships, at each of these places, all the Enemie's East India and South American trade would twice on its passage, both outward and homeward, have to pass in the direction of our cruisers— All her West India commerce once going out and thrice returning— All her Newfoundland and Nova Scotia trade twice going out and twice returning home: and all her trade to the Baltic once going out and once returning.

The Ships stationed near the Bank of Newfoundland, and Between it and Manilla reef, being near our own Coast, might easily receive their supplies from the U. States. Those stationed near the English Channel receive the like from France— Those stationed near the Cattegat from Sweeden and Denmark: and those stationed on the Equator from various ports in Brazil, provided the policy of England does not induce her to oblige the Portuguese to shut their Ports against our Ships of War, when they have for their object the procuration of Supplies.

It is a matter of indifference to me which of these stations shall fall to my lot— Indeed I should have no objection to remaining on our Coast, if I am to cruise alone, as I flatter myself that I shall have the *President* in such order, so far as relates to her sailing qualities, as to have nothing serious to apprehend from any force that she is not equal to encounter— perhaps by being Stationed on our own Coast, and having an understanding with the Commanders of the Frigates *Constellation* and *Adams*, I might be enabled to draw the Enemies Blockading

Squadron so far off from the Chesapeak, as to enable them to get to Sea; and without which they may perhaps be kept in port during all the next Summer.

The weather, since I wrote you last, has been so intollerably cold, and the Country so covered with Ice and Snow, that we have been able to do but very little towards the Ships completion for sea— The mercury in the Thermometer stands to day Six degrees above Zero—a degree of cold scarcely ever known here at this Season   I have the honor to be with great respect Sir your Obdt. Servt.

Jn° Rodgers

LS, DNA, RG45, CL, 1813, Vol. 2, No. 150 (M125, Roll No. 27). This letter is bound with those for April 1813. It was originally dated "Feby" but changed to March.

COMMODORE STEPHEN DECATUR TO SECRETARY OF THE NAVY JONES

New York   March 10. 1813

Sir

Your instructions to select the Lieutenants for my ship from the commissioned officers have been received. I am unacquainted with any of the Lieutenants holding commissions, at present unemployed and shall be much obliged if you will furnish me with the names of those from whom it is intended I shall select— Having obtained Captain Smiths consent that Mr. Warrington should join me I shall have him for my first Lieutenant with Mr. Nicholson & Mr Gallagher—

The new mainmast for my ship will be finished to day and the principal cause of my detention so long in port being thus removed I have the honour to comply with your request by submitting to your consideration my thoughts on our next cruise—It appears by the newspapers that Lord Townsend in the *Eolus* [*Æolus*] with some smaller vessels is employed off Charleston in the blockade of that port— The *Argus* being in great forwardness will be ready about the same time with the *United States*—and with this force (if that of the enemy be no greater than I suppose it, a frigate and two sloops) I am confident by taking a circuit to the Eastward of Bermuda, the cruisers to the northward may be avoided and a successful blow struck at his Lordship. This subordinate enterprize (to be undertaken only on certain information of the blockading force) being complete I would proceed in pursuit of the main object of my cruise to the Eastern edge of the Grand Bank in about the Latitude of 42 and cruise in the direction of Ushant to about 20 West Longitude— Here I would continue cruising until compelled to go in for refitment or refreshment— I shall be in the track of all the British Commerce returning from beyond the Cape of Good Hope from the Brazils & the West Indies and shall probably find their Merchantmen separated from their convoys as they commonly are dispersed before they have so far completed their voyage home—

From the information I have of the preparation of the enemy there is no doubt that our whole coast will be lined with his men of war during the summer months— This presents but little difficulty to our going out but will render our return during the mild season extremely hazardous— I would prefer to remain out as long as possible & by all means untill the approach of the autumnal equinox when the attention of the Enemy will be occupied in providing for his own safety. To enable me to do this I shall take between three & four months provisions which is as large a supply as my ship can carry and would recommend, that the Government should employ some confidential agent to take up a neutral vessel, lade her with provisions and proceed in her to one of the Cape de Verd Islands—there they may be retained ostensibly for sale but at prices to prevent purchases— St. Iago would be preferred because water can be obtained there with the greatest facility and altho' considerably distant from the proposed cruising ground I should both in going & returning be in the way of the Enemys outward bound Indiamen and by sweeping along the coast of Portugal would be constantly in the way of annoying their Mediterranean trade and occasionally intercepting their supplies for the Peninsula— I am perfectly satisfied of the advantages which will result from our vessels cruising singly as you propose— After the attempt on Lord Townsend (should that be deemed expedient) I think the *Argus* had better separate from me & continue by herself but take up the same ground as that contemplated by me for a cruise— All which is with the utmost deference submitted by Sir your most obedient & very humble servant

Stephen Decatur

ALS, DNA, RG45, CL, 1814, Vol. 2, No. 31 (M125, Roll 35); bound at 10 March 1814.

Gunboat Reduction Order

In late February Jones made arrangements for reducing and apportioning gunboats among the stations. This was an economy measure, for he considered them to be "scattered about in every creek and corner as recepticles of idleness and objects of waste and extravagance without utility."[1] The gunboats in actual service were poorly manned and recruiting efforts had stalled. Jones proposed the following distribution of gunboats: fifteen at New York, five in the Delaware, fourteen for the Chesapeake, six at Georgia, and ten at New Orleans.[2] All others were to be laid up in ordinary—ready for emergency service. According to Jones, the government could not be expected to defend every point of the long coast. The stations must make do with a small naval force. Jones realized that a mix of ship sizes was essential to meet the anticipated British blockade. He strongly supported the Congressional bill authorizing construction of sloops of war. Jones recognized that reducing the number of gunboats in service would save on maintenance expenditures. These savings could help pay for the sloops' construction.[3] Individual station commanders and coastal residents, however, disapproved of the reductions.

1. *Jones to his brother, Lloyd Jones, 27 Feb. 1813, PHi, U. C. Smith Collection, Papers of William Jones.*
2. *For gunboat reductions at New Orleans, see pp. 638–39; 661–63.*
3. *Symonds,* Navalists and Antinavalists, *p. 186.*

SECRETARY OF THE NAVY JONES TO COMMODORE HUGH G. CAMPBELL

Hugh G Campbell Esqr   Nav. Deptmt.
Commg. Naval Officer   St. Marys Ga.   26 Feb. 1813

It has been determined that no more than Six gunboats shall be retained in commission on the station under your command; & that all the residue, together with all the barges, shall be laid up in ordinary, but kept in a state of readiness, to receive crews on an emergency—which in such event will consist principally of volunteers, of & near the places where they shall be laid up. The whole number of gunboats at other places, are to be proportionately reduced.[1]

Each of the six gunboats to be retained in commission under your command must have a crew to consist of a commander at 40$ 2 midshipmen a 19. or 2 masters mates, at 20$ 1 acting gunner. 1 steward. 1 cook each a 18$. 8 able seamen, at 12$. 16 ordinary seamen & boys. at 6 to 10$ total 30. All the other gunboats & barges must be laid up together, at such places as may in your opinion be the most suitable—& to take care of them.—one master & one cook for the whole, & one seaman for each. For all the gunboats including those in commission, as well as those in ordinary, there will further be allowed, one surgeon, one surgeons mate & 1 purser. No other officer or man of any description will be allowed, either the boats in commission, or those in ordinary.

For the gunboats in commission, or rather for those to be retained in commission, you will select Six of the most approved masters, & if you have them at present on board of gunboats, 12 of the most promising midshipmen— The names of the other masters, & of the remaining midshipmen, should there be any, with your opinion of each, you will be pleased to transmit to me. The masters, & if they should be undeserving, the midshipmen, I shall dismiss

The *Troup* may remain at Savannah for the protection of that harbor, her crew must consist of, a Lieut: commanding a 40$, a master, 4 midshipmen, 1 boatswain, 1 gunner a 18$ 2 masters mates a 20$, 4 qt. gunners, 2 qr. masters, 1 coxswain, 1 armourer, 1 master at arms, 1 steward, 1 cook, each a 18$ 1 caps. clerk a 25$ 30 able seamen at 12$ & 40 ordinary Seamen & boys at 6 to 10$ & 1 Surgeons mate may be attached to her— The purser provided above, must keep the accounts of the *Troup*, as well as the accounts of the gunboats, & barges in ordinary.

All the officers, other than those herein authorised to be retained, or required to be reported to me—& all the Petty officers, able seamen, ordinary seamen & boys (unless they should be required for the *Enterprize*,[2] are to be discharged & paid off, & you will accordingly, have them discharged & paid off— If the *Enterprize*, or any other cruizing vessel should require any of these officers or seamen, you will of course turn them over to such vessel, in preference to discharging them.

For yourself, you may retain a clerk at 25$ per month—& should you judge them necessary for the public good, a small boats crew, not to exceed 1 coxswain & 4 oarsmen; & you may also retain an ordinary seaman, as your porter.

You will be pleased to report to me the names of all the officers retained in Service, & transmit to me a general roll of every person on the station—whether on board the *Enterprize*, the gunboats in commission—The *Troup*—or attached to the boats & barges in ordinary—after you shall have executed the above instructions; & you will execute them without delay. You will also report particularly the state &

condition of the gunboats, retained in commission; & the numbers of Boats & Barges retained in ordinary, with their condition, should you want any officers under this arrangement. You will report to me the number &c.

W. Jones

LB Copy, DNA, RG45, SNL, Vol. 10, pp. 280–81 (M149, Roll No. 10).

1. See Jones to Jacob Lewis, Alexander Murray, and Thomas N. Gautier, 26 Feb. 1813; Jones to John H. Dent, 28 Feb. 1813; and Jones to John Shaw, 1 Mar. 1813; all in DNA, RG45, SNL, Vol. 10, pp. 281–87 (M149, Roll No. 10); and Jones to Isaac Hull, 26 Feb. 1813, DNA, RG45, CNA, Vol. 1, pp. 364–65 (M441, Roll No. 1) for similar orders.
2. *Enterprise*, Johnston Blakeley commander, departed the New Orleans Station in company with *Viper* on 2 January. She parted company with *Viper* on the seventh and arrived at St. Marys eleven days later; see Blakeley to Hamilton, 23 Jan. 1813, DNA, RG45, MLR, 1813, Vol. 1, No. 49 (M124, Roll No. 53).

Navy Department Personnel Changes

Upon taking office, William Jones found the office of the secretary of the navy severely disorganized and partially blamed its chief clerk, Charles W. Goldsborough. As early as 5 February, Secretary of State James Monroe sought information about Benjamin Homans as a possible replacement. Jones had probably asked Monroe's advice about prospective candidates, and the latter wrote to Vice-President-elect Elbridge Gerry about Homans. Gerry reported that Homans was a good Republican, a former commercial ship captain, and an honest, diligent administrator. Gerry, a Massachusetts native, extolled Homans's bureaucratic acuity in organizing the office of secretary of that commonwealth. Jones firmly but compassionately obtained Goldsborough's resignation and appointed Homans to the post of chief clerk.[1]

1. The chief clerk of the Navy Department ensured the safety and accuracy of that office's records; drafted reports, annual budgets, and responses to correspondence; and oversaw the daily operation of that office. Goldsborough was chief clerk from April 1802 until March 1813. Homans succeeded him and retained that position until December 1823.

NOTES MADE BY SECRETARY OF THE NAVY JONES REGARDING A VISIT BY CHIEF CLERK CHARLES W. GOLDSBOROUGH

Notes

Mr. Goldsborough called at 5 Oclock and expressed himself much satisfied with the liberal manner in which I had made known to him my determination—felt great anxiety lest it should bear the appearance of an abrupt dismissal which might countenance the idea that I had discovered in him a want of integrity or breach of duty, and afford to his enemies a triumph, to the prejudice of his Character and future pursuits; declared that he had faithfully discharged the trust reposed in him and instead of having accumulated property by his situation in the Department was absolutely poor and should have to dispose of his house & furniture and seek a support elsewhere and as the prospect during war was dull solicited the appointment of Storekeeper at Portsmouth N H—requested a postponement of his resignation if convenient until the end of the quarter which would give to the affair a favorable aspect and in the interem he would announce to his friends his intention to resign.

On my part really wishing to render the manner of his retiring as little irksome to him as possible and my determination to dispense with his services being founded upon the excessively disordered and confused state in which I have found every Branch of the Department of which he has been the principal Director for twelve years, and at the same time witnessing his capacity and facility of business am compelled to attribute it to some other cause than the want of the requesite qualifications, I am justified in selecting another and this he readily admits.

I have agreed that he shall continue and pursue his own course for ten days in the meantime stating publicly his resignation and which I am also to mention.

He also expressed a wish that I would purchase some of his furniture which would strengthen the appearance of an amicable seperation, and declared that so far from feeling any irritation on the occassin he was thankful for the candid course I had observed towards him and declared that if he had entered the Department under circumstances similar to myself he would have acted in the same manner. He said that he had long contemplated the subject of reform and prepared and degested a system secured from the information he had received from Commodore Preble and others as well as from his own observation which he hoped I might find worthy of perusal and approbation.

His manner was such as to excite regret for the necessity of his resignation rather than any opposite sentiment

AD, PIIi, U. C. Smith Collection, Papers of William Jones. Jones decided to replace Goldsborough as head clerk in the Navy Department on 27 February. Goldsborough called on Jones the morning of the 28th, but because Jones was not available, left a note saying he would return at 5 p.m.; see Jones to Goldsborough, 27 Feb. 1813 and Goldsborough to Jones, 28 Feb. 1813, PHi, U. C. Smith Collection, Papers of William Jones. Jones indicated in this undated memorandum that Goldsborough called at 5 o'clock— most likely on the 28th as he had said he would. Jones probably wrote these notes after their meeting, the evening of 28 February.

Benjamin Homans to Secretary of the Navy Jones

In examining into the State of the Navy Department, I find much of the important business so blended with the Accountants Office,[1] that it becomes necessary to have free personal Communications with him, and through him to obtain information, as well as free access to the Documents, and mode of transacting business in the various payments and money concerns; this will require time, and requires also a Corresponding disposition on his part, to afford me a knowledge of the routine and distinct operations of his office—independently of the usual jealousy of office, the political antipathies of party, and the personal pride of those who feel the superiority of knowledge from long experience, are among the obstacles to the speedy attainment of these objects.

To obtain a knowledge of the state of the Contracts, and of the actual supplies of Naval Stores, provisions &c, I must depend in great measure on the aid of Mr. Turner, and I frequently find that important Documents when wanted, are in the Accountant's Office; it would therefore facilitate the business of the Department to have a general statement from the Accountant; with a schedule of such papers and Documents generally, as he keeps constantly in his custody.— To know the exact state of expenditures on the specific appropriations, some rule must be adopted in passing accounts, so as not to over-charge a particular head of appropriation, is this the sole business of the Accountant?—or what concern have I in directing the filling of Warrants?—as I conceive it will be proper to balance the appropriations every day, in order to keep in view the state of the funds, to meet further drafts.—

The Store Keepers returns are irregular, and many deficient & some of them greatly overcharged with details of small articles not worth enumerating;—if a regular form of Returns were adopted, it would aid them, and simplify the entry, under Classification of the most important Supplies.

There are no Returns (that I have seen) of Gun powder in the Navy Magazines.— nor do I know of any rule for supplying each Ship. The Captains in the Navy, have not made regular returns of their Muster Rolls on Sailing, and of their Prisoners on arriving in Port, if such have been made to the Accountant, ought they not to be first sent through the Department, & then passed over to the Accountant. It is a question, in what manner and to whom the report is made, of the fulfilment of each Contract agreably to its tenor— Many of the Store Returns, mention damaged and perishable provisions—ought they not be sold,—or enquired into?— If another Room could be procured for the Clerks to write & record in, they would be more free from interruption and save much time—the former habits & Customs of the offices are detrimental to the discharge of business, and any innovation attempted on my part now, would be illy received, and add to the jealousy, and ill-will that appear to prevail against me— The Cases in the room I occupy, are badly constructed, and <u>almost useless</u> for filing away letters & papers, they could be sold for near as much as would pay for convenient pine Cases, where all the Documents & Papers and letters of one or two years could be kept for immediate uses, until filed away with old papers in order, for future references— There is an upper Room filld with Books old Letters & papers of various kinds (some important) in great disorder & dirty.— all the intervals of time, after Office hours & public business, I purpose to devote, to put every thing in good order, and to take cognizance of the documents & Affairs of Office— that it has not already been done, is owing to my state of health, anxiety of mind to get myself settled, and to find the means of temporarily providing for my family, and to pay off my expenses here for Six Months past, destitute as I have been of a Dollar, and a prey to many mortifications, disappointments and consequent low Spirits and almost habitual despondency—with a little encouragement, I shall recruit, and my whole time will be faithfully devoted to the office, and to reduce by degrees everything to a systematic operation—

I <u>cannot</u>, and I <u>ought not</u> after the experience I have had, doubt of my ability to give satisfaction in the performance of any and all the duties that may devolve upon me,— I want <u>only</u> that confidence that most men have <u>enough</u> of, and my disposition would lead to render the duties easy and agreable to all connected with me—but as a perfect Stranger, labouring under some disadvantages, and finding an Office in such a State, that time alone can enable me to become acquainted with its routine of duties, and to remedy defects.—

My great object and desire are to be essentially useful, to support all in my power the honour & reputation of the Government, and to prove myself a faithful & attentive servant.—

Benjamin Homans

ALS, PHi, U. C. Smith Collection, Papers of William Jones. This unaddressed, undated letter was probably written in late March after Goldsborough had vacated his post.

1. Thomas Turner served as accountant of the navy from 9 January 1800 until his death on 15 March 1816.

Charleston Station Report—March 1813

By March 1813, Captain John H. Dent reported increased British activity off South Carolina. He was discouraged by obvious American collaboration with the enemy. Dent employed Nonsuch *as a coaster against privateers and complied with Jones's order to reduce the number of gunboats and barges. Jones mistakenly thought that there were still gunboats on that station, but earlier orders had sent them southward to assist the Georgia station. Dent commanded barges and four schooners, but, as with other station commanders, he was unable to man them with full complements. This was one reason why Jones advocated gunboat reductions, because maintaining undermanned vessels was a waste of money. Coming just as the British were increasing their blockade, the cutbacks in local naval forces angered citizens in vulnerable ports.*

CAPTAIN JOHN H. DENT TO SECRETARY OF THE NAVY JONES

The Honble William Jones   Charleston   1st March, 1813

Sir

I have the honor to inform you that the *Nonsuch* arrived here on Saturday with the ordinance & Stores from fort Johnson (N.C.) She fell in with an Enemy's Gun Brig, off Cape Roman,[1] exchanged a few Shot in reconnoitering, and escaped easy by Superior Sailing. The Frigate *Eolus* [*Æolus*] and Brig *Sophie* with the two Small Privateers are Still off our bar, by information received from the fishing Smacks, they have made no Captures of Consequence. five Schooners & Several Ships Sailed on Saturday for france, unobserved by the blockading Squadron; it appears that Lord Townsend is perfectly acquainted, with the State of this harbor, and also the destination of every vessel in it, with the politics of their owners &c. he sent in yesterday some prisoners taken in a small vessel from the Southward, I regret that I am not authorized to prevent the fishing smacks from going out while the Enemy remains off the bar, no doubt but all the information goes through that channel, altho rigidly searched at the Guard vessel.

The *Nonsuch* will sail the first wind with orders to cruize between Savannah and Cape Fear, and endeavor if possible to destroy the privateers, or oblige them to keep with the Frigate, she will cruize on the outer edge of the Gulf Stream, in order to recapture their prizes bound to Bermuda & Providence. Sailing Master Mork commanding the *Nonsuch* is an active, intelligent, officer well acquainted with that class of vessel, and I think if possible Should be promoted[2] I Have the Honor to be With great respect Your most obt. Sevt.

J H Dent

ALS, DNA, RG45, CL, 1813, Vol. 2, No. 3 (M125, Roll No. 27).

1. Cape Romain is 37 miles northeast of Charleston.
2. James Mork, a sailing master since July 1812, was commissioned a lieutenant on 27 April 1816.

CAPTAIN JOHN H. DENT TO SECRETARY OF THE NAVY JONES

Charleston   15th March 1813

Sir

I had the honor to receive your letter of the 28th ult. directing me to lay up in ordinary all the Gun boats of every discription and barges under my command, and discharge from the service the Petty officers, Seamen &c not wanted to complete the crews of the Schooners, *Carolina* and *Nonsuch*.[1] The Guard vessel coming under, that class, I have ordered her to the Navy Yard, with the Barges, and shall immediately have them placed in ordinary and have directed Mr. Gautier Senior Officer at Wilmington to do the Same, with the two boats under his orders, and after discharging the petty Officers, send the seamen, Ordinary Seamen & boys, here under the care of the Midshipmen, by the first safe conveyance to complete the crews of the Schooners. I presume the Schooners *Ferret* & *Alligator*, the one stationed in Port Royal, the other in St Helena Sound to protect, the Inland Navigation, which is very much exposed at those points, as not coming within this order, and shall wait your further orders relative to them.[2] the Gun Boats at Newbern & Beaufort (N.C.) I do not consider under my command having received no instructions to that effect altho' the officers have occasionally made me reports of their proceedings having no purser or no channel through which they could receive their pay, and having received many complaints on that head, I directed Mr. Halsey Purser, on the Wilmington Station, to advance them one quarters pay, should it be due, and to act as purser for them, until further orders.

The Guard vessel in this port was commanded by Sailing Master Joseph Taylor with an Acting Master and two mates, no midshipmen. Mr. Taylor also attended the recruiting service, his is a new appointment, and little acquainted with the etiquette & routine of the Service, other wise a Smart active officer: The barges have but two regular Masters, Drew & Lord, the others are acting. Mr. Drew is an old Master in the service, and formerly commanded a Gun Boat on the Wilmington Station, but was arrested, and tried by a Court Martial, for violence committed on the inhabitants & City of Wilmington, in part found guilty, and suspended from his rank &c for two months, he is a man of no education, with violent & ungovernable passions; Mr. Lord has held several warrants as Master in the Service, when inconvenient to him to perform any Service he resigns, and after some time obtains a new appointment, he is a man of good connections, and education & if possessed of Stability would make a good officer. Mr. Gautier was formerly Lieutenant in the Service and resigned on the reduction of the Navy, was appointed Sailing Master in 1806 or 7,[3] and since has been in charge of the Wilmington Station, he is an active good officer, and is on board Gun boat *No. 167.* Sailing Master Levy commanding Gun Boat *No. 7,* is neither a seaman or officer, there are two midshipmen, Mr. Robert Rogerson & Mr. Archibald Campbell attatched to these boats.

To keep the barges on duty, I have been compelled for the want of officers, to appoint a few Masters of vessels to command them, with the rank & emoluments of Masters—all such I have ordered discharged. I Have the Honor to be with great respect your obt Svt.

J H Dent

ALS, DNA, RG45, CL, 1813, Vol. 2, No. 43 (M125, Roll No. 27).

1. Jones to Dent, 28 Feb. 1813, DNA, RG45, SNL, Vol. 10, pp. 285–86 (M149, Roll No. 10). There were barges, not gunboats, on the Charleston Station.

2. Jones evidently had intended that Dent retain *Ferret* and *Alligator*, for they were used throughout the spring of 1813 to protect South Carolina's coastal and inland waterways.

3. Thomas N. Gautier was warranted a sailing master on 4 August 1807.

British Gunnery Exercises

The defeats suffered by the Royal Navy at the hands of the much smaller American navy shocked the Admiralty into a reexamination of naval policy. Attributing some of the American victories to superior gunnery, the Lords Commissioners directed Admiral Sir John B. Warren to emphasize gunnery exercise. The court-martial of the captain and crew of Peacock *attributed one of the causes of her capture by* Hornet *in February 1813 to a "want of skill in directing the Fire, owing to an omission of the Practice of exercising the crew in the use of the Guns for the last three Years. . . ."* [1]

1. *For the sentence handed down at the 7 June 1813 court-martial, see University of Hull, Brynmor Jones Library, Hull, England, Hotham Collection, DDHO/7/98. See pp. 68–75 for after-action reports of this engagement.*

ADMIRAL SIR JOHN B. WARREN, R.N., STANDING ORDERS ON THE NORTH AMERICAN STATION

Genl. Order

The Lords Commissioners of the Admiralty having in their examination of the Logs of His Majestys Ships & Vessels deserned that in too many instances the Captains & Commanders of His Majestys Ships & Vessels appear to have omitted to exercise their respective Crews at the Great Guns and in the use of the small Arms as frequently as the importance of this part of their Duty requires, and directed me to call the attention of the Captains & Commanders of His M Ships & Vessels under my Orders to the 9th 10th and 11th Articles of the 4th Chapter of the General Printed Instructions; you are hereby strictly enjoined to cause the same to be duly carried into execution.

Their Lordships trust that all the Officers of His Majestys Naval Service must be convinced that upon the good discipline and the proper training of their Ships Companies to the expert management of the Guns, the preservation of the high character of the British Navy most essentially depends, and that other works on which it is not unusual to employ the Men are of very trifling importance, when Compared with a due preparation (by instruction and practice) for the effectual Services on the day of Battle. On these and all other suitable occasions the respective Officers should earnestly endeavour to impress on the minds of the Men that the issue of the Battle will greatly depend on the cool, steady and regular manner in which the Guns shall be loaded, pointed & fired, and that nothing but the most perfect discipline and practice in these particulars can insure proper effect from their fire upon the Enemy and prevent accidents to themselves.[1]

You will be careful that the times of exercising the Great Guns and small Arms be always entered in the Ships Log conformable to the General printed Instructions.

Bermuda   6 March 1813
Signed)   J B Warren

LB Copy, University of Hull, Brynmor Jones Library, Hull, England, Hotham Collection, DDHO/7/45.

1. In a 23 March 1813 circular to the admirals, Croker reiterated this admonition by ordering that scouring the iron stanchions and ring bolts "be gradually discontinued and abolished, and that the time thrown away on this unnecessary practice be applied to the really useful and important points of discipline and exercise at Arms." See UkLPR, Adm. 2/1376, pp. 164–65.

Gunboats in Ordinary—North Carolina Station

Sailing Master Thomas N. Gautier, commander of the Wilmington, North Carolina, naval station, considered himself under the authority of Captain John H. Dent of Charleston. When Jones ordered Gautier to lay up all the gunboats in North Carolina and discharge many of their crews, the sailing master responded that he would await Dent's orders concerning the dismissals because Dent might need seamen at Charleston. Jones answered that this was unnecessary because Gautier must obey Navy Department orders only. Gautier's official response to the gunboat reduction order was efficient and courteous. Privately, Gautier complained to Dent that once he had laid up all vessels, "I then shall sit down in sullen retirement and view the Boats in the mud and to reflect on the situation of my state not a single armed vessell allotted for her defence."[1]

1. *Gautier to Dent, 29 Mar. 1813, NcU, Wilson Library, Southern Historical Collection, Gautier Papers, #273.*

SAILING MASTER THOMAS N. GAUTIER TO SECRETARY OF THE NAVY JONES

Smithville N.C.   March 10th 1813

Sir

Have this day the honour of receiving yr orders of 26th Ulto. Have written Capt. Dent respecting the men & shall await his orders conserning their discharge. Have also written the Comdg. Officers of all the Gun Boats stationd in the waters of No. C. & to Surgeons Mt. E. D. Morrison ordering them to this place, on their arrival shall proceed according to yr orders. I would beg leave Sir to represent the necessity of my retaining a Clerk for the purpose making returns issuing provisions &c, shall take the liberty to await yr further orders respecting his discharge. The Boats are commanded viz

Sailg. Mastr J. M. Levy on this Station[1]

Ditto	George Evans }	Ocracock
Ditto	J Wolfenden }	Station
Ditto	Manson }	Beaufort
Midsn.	E Hadaway }	Station

On this Station an Surgeon J. Cowdery, a Gentleman of great inteligence in his profession, was taken in the *Philadelphia* at Tripoli and has seen much active service; he is in an infirm state of health; has a family of 5 children at Norfolk, to which place he is desireous of being ordered.

James Moore has been rated Gunner 14 years. Midshipmen Archibald S. Campbell & Robert Rogerson (By last returns there were no midshipmen on either the other Stations except E Hadaway) Mr. Campbell is an intelligent young man of firm & steady habits, obedient to orders, & promises to make a valuable officer. R. Rogerson is a boy, has behaved Correctly & given me much Satisfaction, he posseses the qualifications requisite for a good officer.

Was there a Navy Yard at Wilmington no doubt or hesitation could arise with me in laying the Boats in ordinary, but as it is private property, beg leave to submit the following.

Shall the Boats have sheds over them & their Hull preserved with varnish &c.

I have also a fine Guard Boat, clinker built ader bottom, 40 ft long 8 wide; shall she be hauled up & put under a shed; are the Guns to be landed. The Stores &c shall deliver to the Agent.

Is it not most elegible to rent a wharf which can be had low at this juncture. Have the honour to remain Sir very Respectfully Yr. Ob. Svt.

T. N Gautier

ALS, DNA, RG45, BC, 1813, Vol. 1, No. 111 (M148, Roll No. 11).

1. Wilmington Station.

SECRETARY OF THE NAVY JONES TO SAILING MASTER THOMAS N. GAUTIER

T. N Gautier   Nav: Deptmt.
Commdg. Officer.   Wilmington NC.   19 March 1813

I have your letter of the 12th[1] respecting gunboats &c. on your station. You will observe the orders from this Department supercede the necessity of waiting orders from Capt. Dent. I cannot see the necessity of a clerk for a few gunboats in ordinary with one Master for the whole, & one man for each boat let the master see to the issuing provisions, or perhaps the Master & men may board at a rate, not exceeding the value of their rations, which if you find practicable, it will save the trouble of issuing rations. You will order Doct. Cowdery to Norfolk, & order James Moore, gunner, Midshipmen Campbell & Rogerson to report themselves to the commanding officer at Charleston.

If the gunboats cannot be moored in a tier along the shore, you will inform me of the lowest rate, for which they can be laid up at a wharf

You will have the gunboats & guard boats covered to preserve them from injury by the weather & the guns & Stores will remain on board, under care of the officer & men, where they can be preserved as well as on Shore.

W. Jones

LB Copy, DNA, RG45, SNL, Vol. 10, pp. 310–11 (M149, Roll No. 10).

1. Gautier's letter is dated the 10th.

SAILING MASTER THOMAS N. GAUTIER TO SECRETARY OF THE NAVY JONES

Wilmington   April 2d 1813

Sir

I have the honor of reporting to you the Boats in Ordinary: viz *No. 167–No. 7–No. 146–147–148–150*

Doctor Jonathan Cowdery is orderd to Norfolk. Mr. Morrisson discharged, James Moore Gunner, Midsn Campbel and Rogerson under Orders for Charleston and will sail in a Day or two—

Great difficulty arises in regard to the Officers and men, attached to the Boats from Ocracock and Beaufort, and untill there accounts come on from Norfolk they will be an expense to Government—

I have retained for the Boats in ordinary Six Seaman, one for each Boat, one Cook for the Whole, one Acting Gunner, one Sailing Master, Makeing Nine in the Whole,—

As no Purser will be on the Station will you Sir be pleased to Order Mr. J. Potts, Navy Agent to pay my requestions Quarterly for payment of Officers, men and contingencies—

A Mr. Machesnay [*McChesney*], Midn. attached to *No. 147* (under command of Midn. Haddaway) is I understand Adicted to liquor, his appearance Slovenly, and in his manners nothing prepossessing—

I have an Offer of the very uppermost wharf in Town detached from all Others, it has a shed and a Building formerly occupied as a Blacksmith and Turners shop, and a Dwelling House, for the Occupancy of the whole Three hundred & fifty Dolls. per annum paid Quarterly, but without the Buildings it will be Two hundred & fifty, it is by far the best station for the Boats, and if the whole is taken the House will serve to Mess in and for a hospital and the Sheds to put our Boats under, The property could be purchased for $3.500 at three years Credit by Instalments, the details I did not enter into—[1] I have the honor to be Sir Yr. Obt. Servt.

T. N. Gautier

ALS, DNA, RG45, BC, 1813, Vol. 1, No. 162 (M148, Roll No. 11). A letter book copy of this letter dated 3 April is held by NcU, Southern Historical Collection, Gautier Papers, #273.

1. Jones authorized Joshua Potts, navy agent for Wilmington, to pay the rent for the wharf and sheds that Gautier had recommended if Potts thought they were reasonable; see Jones to Gautier, 22 May 1813, DNA, RG45, SNL, Vol. 10, p. 406 (M149, Roll No. 10).

Mutiny on Board *General Armstrong* [1]

A naval court-martial required at least five commissioned officers to adjudicate a case. This created major problems at small stations where there often were not enough officers to try a case expeditiously. Naval courts-martial had jurisdiction over offenses committed on board private armed vessels. When the privateer ship General Armstrong *put into Wilmington, North Carolina, on 17 April, her captain, John Sinclair, accused the officers and most of the crew of confining him, taking possession of the vessel, and engaging in acts of piracy. Sailing Master Thomas N. Gautier took the accused into custody and held them on board the gunboats then laid up in ordinary, although as a warrant officer he lacked this authority. Because there were no officers at or near Wilmington, Jones was faced with the dilemma of either permitting the prisoners to suffer indefinite incarceration or of requiring five officers to abandon their posts. Before Jones had the chance to get legal advice, a misunderstanding occurred between the keeper of the privateer and one of the sailing masters in charge of a gunboat where some of the mutineers were confined. Jones ordered the prisoners released, basing his decision on the lack of naval jurisdiction over piratical offenses.*

1. This General Armstrong, *captained and partly owned by John Sinclair, should not be confused with the very successful New York schooner of the same name, commanded at this time by Guy R. Champlin. For an excellent secondary account of this affair, see Mouzon,* "General Armstrong."

MEMORIAL OF THE CREW OF THE PRIVATEER GENERAL ARMSTRONG TO JOHN SINCLAIR

Copy of the Memorial handed Captain Sinclair, on board the American privateer armed ship General Armstrong, *latitude 22, 03, N. longitude, 25 W. at Meridian, Thursday, 18th March, 1813*

Captain John Sinclair,

Sir—

Eleven days have now elapsed since we left the Isle of Brava, all of which time we have been endeavoring to get to the Eastward; but our prospects are *now* no better than they were in our opinion of effecting such a thing when we started— For the ground we *gained* the evening before our coming to anchor in Brava, convinced us fully of the impracticability of our ever being able to work to windward among those islands, without getting a slant or two of wind, and should your object have been to touch at one of the Canaries, you would doubtless have stood well to northward first, so as to have got out of the Trade Winds, your intention surely cannot be to touch at one of the Cape de Verds, when you were apprised of a British Squadron being among those Islands which caused you to quit Brava in the manner you did, without purchasing any supplies for the remainder of the cruise; well knowing the situation of our stores, not now having above *100 lbs. Bread, two and a half tierces of rice, two barrels of Cow-Peas, and one barrel of Flour,* water we had abundance of, say upon a moderate calculation 6000 gallons, and yet allowed only 2 quarts per man a day, and one quart per week to boil rice or pease with. Great discontent (and God knows not without sufficient cause) which has for some time past prevailed on board, among officers and men. *STARVATION now staring us in the Face, for we are fully convinced your intention is to go on the coast of Africa. Langor and weakness* already having possession of half of the crew, and that among the best of us, induces us to apprise you that we are aware of the situation we are likely to be placed in, even allowing that fortune should throw another prize within our grasp and she be of half the force of the one we lost; we hesitate not to say, that she will also slip through our fingers. If your intention has not been of a nature that may prove fatal to us, it has excited much alarm. Why did you not purchase (for you said you could) sufficient supplies at Brava? and not attempt to *gull* us with the *story* of a

"British Squadron being off those Isles." But, Sir, we are fully convinced that *all is not clear on your part.* The privations we have put up with from the commencement of the cruise, will convince mankind, when they come to be fully stated, (and that they will one day or other) that we have done more than any commander of a private cruising ship could or would have expected from his crew, and still *you* would wish to make us more than slaves. Allowing Sir, you were at Africa, *You could purchase no more there than what you could at Brava; & the time that it will take us to get on the coast will terminate our cruise,* & (from threats you have thrown out) there is no doubt many there are among us that you may have in your power, on whom you will execute them, *if we have or may take any step,* that *you* may think improper. Be it so. In our *native country,* we are ready *at any and all times* to have an investigation of our proceedings; *but not trust to your clemency* in a strange land, among a set of Turks, or Africans. But, Sir, a presumption as strong as Holy Writ and the *first law in nature* bids us *shape our course home,* and that presumption is, sir, *that there are a hundred chances to one, but we will fall in with one or more English cruisers on the coast;* and then, sir, would it take much philosophy to tell what would become of us? A prison ship, for life; for there would be no exchange under two years, and it is not likely one of us would weather that time out; or if by superior sailing, we should run away, we must starve to death. *The crisis demands that we go to the Westward and the prospect far better, both for owners and crew.* In fact in taking the one (going home) we have great hopes of doing better. In the other; *The Horrors of a Prison Ship on a coast that is known to be fatal to Strangers at the coming season, or starvation on board our own ship;* by standing to the Westward, should we fall in with any supplies, *Let us stay out until the cruise expires;* if not, let us proceed to the United States. Trusting you will consider seriously the dreadful situation you are about placing us in, and without the most singular interposition of Divine Providence *will prove a total loss to yourself and owners;* We say, *we trust you will shape our course towards the United States,* or if you think we can get to France before our provisions be out, go thither; in so doing, *we are willing and at all times ready to obey your commands.*

[Here follow the names of sixty-three persons who signed the above]

Unidentified newspaper clipping of an article attributed to the *Wilmington Gazette* (N.C.) enclosed in DNA, RG45, MLR, 1813, Vol. 3, No. 142 (M124, Roll No. 55).

SAILING MASTER THOMAS N. GAUTIER TO SECRETARY OF THE NAVY JONES

19th April 1813
Wilmington NC

Sir

I have the honor of informing you of the arrival of the private armed Ship *Genl. Armstrong* John Sinclair Esqre. commander at this Port the 17th Inst.

I submit to you the copies of letters addressed to me & of my proceedings & wait your orders   I have divided the mutineers in Number Sixty one on board *N. 148* J. C. Manson S M *N. 147* E. H. Haddaway Mids. *N. 150* George Evans S. M. & *N. 146* John Wolfenden S. M.

I have ordered the Boats out in the Stream for the better safety of the Prisoners to merit your approbation is my highest ambition & am Sir most respectfully your Obedt. Sevt.

T N Gautier

ALS, DNA, RG45, BC, 1813, Vol. 1, No. 201 (M148, Roll No. 11). For Gautier's instruction to his subordinate sailing masters regulating the prisoners' confinement and his arrest order, see DNA, RG45, BC, 1813, Vol. 1, between Nos. 194 and 195 (M148, Roll No. 11).

[Enclosure]
Copy of a letter received from Captn. St. Clair of the private armed Ship *General Armstrong* dated Wilmington NC   17. April 1813

Sir

You will perceive by my declaration made & sworn to before two Justices of the Peace at the Court house of this Town & now furnished you that the private Ship of War *General Armstrong* of which I am the only legal Commander and largely concernd in as owner and which Ship is now lying at Anchor in the Stream in this Port Was on the 18th. March last forcibly, feloniously & Piratically taken possession of by the officers, Seamen &c in said declaration named who at same time confined me & others of my officers & crew and who have since kept me confined in the most vigorous, wanton cruel & unprovoked manner from said 18th, day of March untill this day when I was relieved by the Civil Authorities   they in the mean time directing & Converting my said Ship, on such courses, and to such purposes as they saw fit Capturing, detaining boarding overhauling & plundering such vessels as they may meet without any legal authority to such acts I have therefore to request you as Commandant of the Naval force of the United States on this Station to cause said Offenders to be arrested & confined in such manner and in such place as you may judge expedient untill they be brought before a Court Martial then to answer for the crimes & felonies & piracies, they have respectively done & committed I am very respectfully Yr. most obedt. hble Servt.

John St Clair

Thomas N Gautier Esqr. Commandant of the
United States Naval force   Port of Wilmington NC

Copy, DNA, RG45, BC, 1813, Vol. 1, between Nos. 194 and 195 (but an enclosure to No. 201 above) (M148, Roll No. 11). The copyist misspelled Sinclair's name.

SAILING MASTER THOMAS N. GAUTIER TO SECRETARY OF THE NAVY JONES

Wilmington N.C.   April 28th 1813

Sir

It is with great regret that in performing my Duty I report to you an unfortunate event that has raised the public mind to a high pitch and wounded my feelings as Commanding Officer— On the Evening of the 26 Inst a few minutes after 8 O. Clock glass was set the guard Boat was on the Tour to watch the Privateer *General Armstrong* and all the Mutineers or Pirates on Board the Gun Boats, and to bring too and examine all Boats passing to and fro from said ship or Passing the

Boats.— The said guard Boat Commanded by S. M. Evans,[1] soon after started from along side *No. 150* espied a Boat putting of from the *Genl. Armstrong* (of which Ship a Capt. J. S. Oliver was keeper) and consequently excited some suspition (as their were still a few Mutineers on Board of her)   he ordered his men to row towards her and when sufficient near hailed who goes there and received for answer that it was Capt. Olliver whom they all Knew very well and that he was going across the River Mr. Evans informed him he could Know no one at Night that he only wanted him to step on Board *No. 147* and if all was Clear, should be treated like a Gentleman and allowed to pass over— Capt. O replyed he would not come along side and that he was in a Damnable hurry at any rate— Mr. Evans answered he was in no hurry, but that he must come along side and be examined or if he did not he would make his painter fast and tow him up— Olliver replyed that any man that attempted to touch the painter of my Boat I will Knock him Down and I will not go on Board— Mr. Evans said if he did not he would have to fire on him— Oliver answered fire and be damned You are nothing but a set of cut throats and villians and I'll see you all Damned first before I go—with which Mr. Evans Snaped a Pistole at him to deter him but it Mised fired and he laid it down— Then Mr. Cunningham Masters Mate a Board of *No. 147* asked Mr. Evans what was the matter. Mr. Evans informed him their was a man that resisted his authority and the execution of his Orders. Mr. Cunningham immediately in his Boat and they tied Olivers Boat to the stern of the Guard Boat. while they were fastening the painter, O. took one of his oars and aimed at two men which struck one in his side— Mr. Cunningham then gave O several strokes with the flat part of his Cutlass— Oliver jumpt forward in his Boat to the stern of the guard Boat and seized a Pistole in the stern sheets of said guard Boat and snaped her twice the third time it went of and Mr. Cunningham and a coloured man fell over board which Mr. Evans seeing (as he had got on Board *No. 147*) ordered fire (meaning the alarm gun. Mr. Macchesney Midn. did fire which accidently wounded him (Oliver) so mortally that he expired in less than 15 Minutes— Mr. Macchesney was arested by me soon after and Delivered him & Mr. Evans over to the Demand of Civil Authority, on Tuesday Morning the Court of Justices after due examination and herd the pleading of his Counsil for bail declared their offence not bailable and consequently committed them to a filthy hole of a Dungeon. Mr. Evans Sailing Master & Mr. Macchesney Midn. of the U. States Navy from which I hope they will be releived by Genl. W. W. Jones & John London Esqr. their Council applying immediately for bail and Authorized in Asserting that they can obtain security to any amount, unfortunately the form is that not only the Prisoners but all the securities must appear in Raleigh before the Judge to sign their which I fear is impossible from the Distances— Myself & Mr. Evans feel as much Distresed as others that so melancholly a Circumstance has happened— but if he executed his orders it has been from no bad Motive (as he is a good officer) but he imagined that a Boat comeing from the Pirates ship should be particular examined and the trgical issue is owing to the rashness and hardehood of the deceased—who was herd to say by some Gentn. in town (upon reading a notice I had posted up under the Public Court House of my having issued orders to bring too and examine all Boats and hopeing no one would refuse to conform as any accident would be regretted by the execution of them particularly situated as we were with the Prisioners and Ship *Genl. Armstrong* in Charge) that he would be Damned if ever he would come too for any of them (Meaning the Officers) and that he would make the experiment but Mr. Evans knew not at the time that Oliver had ever expressed himself in that Manner & positively knew not Oliver personly Subjoining are two Orders refering to this Case both the 19th Inst. for your investigation and fear the Officers will have to be confined untill next superior Court in October without bail can be procured at Raleigh,—

29th Cunningham the m. mate was yesterday taken up as accessary & committed I am with respect your Obedt. Servt

T N Gautier

ALS, DNA, RG45, BC, 1813, Vol. 1, No. 217 (M148, Roll No. 11).

1. George Evans, a native of Philadelphia serving under a sailing master's warrant dated 11 June 1812, was a brother of Captain Samuel Evans, U.S.N.

[Enclosure]

(Coppy)

Mr. Manson   (Circular)   19th April 1813

I need not point out to you how necessary it is that every care should be taken that none of the Prisioners escape for which purpose I request a guard to be rowed round the boats & Ship *Genl. Armstrong* every Night During the hours of Eight at Night and Day light alternately— You will Direct the guard Boat to Night

Mr. Haddaway   2nd.
Mr. Evans   3rd.
Mr. Wolfendon   4th.

You will suffer no intercourse between the Prisioners from one Boat to the other   no shore Boat to but by your permission to Come along Side, You will Keep it in view   I expect the Assistance of all the Officers in the execution of the Duties devolved on us, I shall give the officer of the Night the Guard word at 4 O Clock each evening,—

T N G.

Copy, DNA, RG45, BC, 1813, Vol. 1, No. 217, enclosure (M148, Roll No. 11).

[Enclosure]
Copy
Mr. Manson   (Private)   19th. April 1813

Sir
You will in case of sudden alarm, mutiny, rescue or dissobedience fire one of your small guns or large muskets upon which signall the Boats manned & armed will proceed to the Gun Vessell giving the Alarm

a Copy of this you will give to each officer (as Private) of course no gun, musket or pistol will be fired from any of the Gun Vessells but on alarm or attack &c.

T N G.

Copy, DNA, RG45, BC, 1813, Vol. 1, No. 217, enclosure (M148, Roll No. 11).

SECRETARY OF THE NAVY JONES TO JOHN SINCLAIR

John Sinclair, Esqr.   Navy Department,
Commdr. of Privateer   June 7. 1813.
General Armstrong, Wilmington N C

Sir,

Your letter, of the 29th ultimo,[1] and the papers which accompanied it are before me. Without touching the merits of the case, it may be remarked, that the arrest of the persons alluded to was irregular, as Mr. Gautier is only a Warrant Officer, whose command and authority did not embrace the case; and moreover, under the previous orders from this Department, which he was bound to execute, the naval force there being laid up in ordinary, he had no force to take or to keep the offenders in custody.

The Act of Congress which gives jurisdiction over such offences committed on board privateers, as are cognizable by a Court martial, "did not mean to interfere with, or supersede the constitutional jurisdiction of the courts of the United States, and the most serious crime which the offenders appear to have committed after the mutiny, was that of <u>Piracy</u>, which is exclusively within the jurisdiction of the U.S. Courts. Besides, the Act of Congress does not contemplate impossibilities, or mean to subject the public interest to peril and injury. A Court Martial of commissioned officers could not have been assembled for the trial of the offenders without leaving their Stations in the time of War, to the great danger and injury of the service and of the Public.

There are, it is conceived, abundant reasons for the course which has been pursued. Without the most distant application of the suggestion to your case, a contrary doctrine would subject the officers of the Navy and the Public interest to the caprice, passion, or resentment of any individual who may command a private armed Ship, and demand the arrest and trial of an indefinite number of persons in the remote corner of the Union. I am, respectfully Your Obedt. Servant

W. Jones.

LB Copy, DNA, RG45, SNL, Vol. 10, pp. 456–57 (M149, Roll No. 10). Another copy of this letter is in DNA, RG45, MLS, Vol. 11, pp. 298–99 (M208, Roll No. 4).

1. Sinclair was angry that Gautier had released the alleged mutineers on Jones's order and that the civil authorities in Wilmington refused to take cognizance. See Sinclair to Jones, 29 May 1813, DNA, RG45, MLR, 1813, Vol. 3, No. 142 (M124, Roll No. 55).

Hornet vs. *Peacock*

Constitution *and* Hornet *left the United States together in October 1812. Commodore William Bainbridge, after setting fire to the severely damaged* Java, *returned* Constitution *to America on 6 January, leaving James Lawrence behind to blockade Bahia as long as he could.* Hornet *was then to cruise along the northeastern coast of South America.*[1] *There she met H.M. brig sloop* Peacock *at the mouth of the Demerara River. Several*

*Medal Commissioned by Congress Commemorating the Victory of
U.S. Sloop of War* Hornet *over H.M. Brig Sloop* Peacock

naval historians have attributed Peacock*'s loss to the British ship's ineffective gunnery. The well-trained and disciplined crew of* Hornet *defeated the so-called polished "yacht."* [2]

1. For Bainbridge's revised cruising order, see Bainbridge to Lawrence, 5 Jan. 1813, DNA, RG45, CL, 1813, Vol. 1, No. 7 1/2 (M125, Roll No. 26).
2. Roosevelt, Naval War of 1812, p. 169; and Mahan, Sea Power, Vol. 2, pp. 7–8.

CAPTAIN JAMES LAWRENCE [1] TO SECRETARY OF THE NAVY JONES

U.S. Ship *Hornet*
Holmes' Hole, March 19, 1813

Sir,

I have the honour to inform you of the arrival at this port, of the U.S. Ship *Hornet,* under my command, from a cruize of 145 days, and to state to you that after Commodore Bainbridge left the Coast of Brazils (Jany. 6) I continued off the harbour of St. Salvadore, blockading the *Bonne Cityonne* until the 24th, when the *Montague* 74 hove in sight, and chased me into the harbour; but night coming on I wore and stood out to the southward.— Knowing that she had left Rio Janeiro for the express purpose of relieving the *Bonne Cityonne* and the Packet (which I had also blockaded for 14 days, and obliged her to send her mail to Rio in a Portuguese smack) I judged it most prudent to shift my cruizing ground, and hauled by the wind, to the eastward, with the view of cruizing off Pernambucco, and on the 4th Feby. captured the English brig *Resolution* of 10 guns from Rio Janeiro, bound to Maranham [*Maranhão*], with coffee, jerked beef, flour, fustic, and butter, and about $23,000 in specie. As she sailed dull, and I could ill spare hands to man her, I took out the money and set her on fire. I then run down the coast for Maranham, and cruized there a short time, from thence run off Surinam. After cruizing off that coast from the 15th until the 22d. of February, without meeting a vessel I stood for Demerara with an intention, should I not be fortunate on that station, to run through the West Indies on my way to the U. States; but on the 24th, in the morning, I discovered a brig to leeward, to which I gave chase—run into quarter less four, and not having a pilot, was obliged to haul off. The fort at the entrance of Demerara river, at this time bearing S.W. dist. about 2 1/2 leagues. Previous to giving up the chase I discovered a vessel at anchor, without the bar, with English colours flying, apparently a brig of war. In beating round Corobana bank, in order to get to her, at 1/2 past three P.M. I discovered another sail on my weather quarter, edging down for us— at 4.20 she hoisted English colours, at which time we discovered her to be a large man-of-war Brig, beat to quarters and cleared ship for action, and kept close by the wind, in order if possible, to get the weather guage.— At 5.10 finding I could weather the enemy, I hoisted American colours & tacked. At 5.25 in passing each other, exchanged broadsides within half pistol shot. Observing the enemy in the act of wearing, I bore up, received his starboard broadside, run him close on board on the starboard quarter, and kept up such a heavy and well-directed fire, that in less than fifteen minutes he surrendered (being literally cut to pieces) and hoisted an ensign union down from his fore rigging, as a signal of distress. Shortly after, her main-mast went by the board. Dispatched Lieut. Shubrick on board, who soon returned with her first Lieut. who reported her to be his Britannic majesty's late brig *Peacock,* commanded by Capt. Wm. Peake,[2] who fell in the latter part of the action,—that a number of her crew were killed and wounded and that she was sinking fast, she having then six feet water in her hold. Dispatched the boats immediately for the wounded, and brought both vessels to anchor. Such shot holes as could be got at were then pluged, guns thrown overboard, and every possible exertion used to keep her afloat until the prisoners could be removed, by pumping and bailing, but without effect as she unfortunately sunk in 5 1/2 fathoms water, carrying down thirteen of her crew; and three of my brave fellows, viz. Jno. Hart, Joseph Williams, and Hannibal Boyd. Lieut Conner, and Mid. Cooperer, and the remainder of my men employed in removing the prisoners, with difficulty saved themselves by jumping into a boat that was lying on the booms as she went down. Four men of the thirteen mentioned, were so fortunate as to gain the fore top, and were afterwards taken off by our boats. Previous to her going down, four of her men took to her stern boat, that had been much damaged during the action, whom I sincerely hope reached the shore; but from the heavy sea running at the time, the shattered state of the boat, and the difficulty of landing on the coast, I am fearful they were lost. I have not been able to ascertain from her officers the exact number of killed. Capt. Peake and four men were found dead on board. The Master, one Midshipman, Carpenter and Captain's Clerk, and twenty-nine men wounded, most of them very severely, three of which died of their wounds after being removed, and nine drowned. Our loss was trifling in comparison. John Place killed, Samuel Coulson and Joseph Dalrymple, slightly wounded; Geo. Coffin & Lewis Todd severely burnt by the explosion of a cartridge. Todd survived only a few days. Our rigging & sails were much cut. One shot through the foremast and the Bowsprit slightly injured. Our hull received little or no damage—

At the time I brought the *Peacock* to action, the *Espiegle* (the brig mentioned as being at an anchor) mounting 16 two and thirty pound caronades, and 2 long nines, lay about 6 miles in shore of me, and could plainly see the whole of the action. Apprehensive she would beat out to the assistance of her consort, such exertions were used by my officers and crew, in repairing damages &c. that by 9 o'clock our boats were stowed a new set of sails bent, and the ship completely ready for action. At 2 A.M. got under way, and stood by the wind to the northward and westward, under easy sail. On mustering next morning, found we had two hundred and seventy-seven souls on board (including the crew of the American brig *Hunter* of Portland, taken a few days before by the *Peacock)* and as we had been on two-thirds allowance of provisions for some time, and had but 3,400 gallons of water on board, I reduced the allowance to three pints a man, and determined to make the best of my way to the United States.

The *Peacock* was deservedly styled one of the finest vessels of her class in the British navy. I should judge her to be about the tonnage of the *Hornet.* Her beam was greater by five inches, but her extreme length not so great by four feet. She mounted 16 four and twenty pounds caronades two long nines, and twelve pound caronades on her top-gallant forecastle as a shifting gun, and one four or six pounder, and two swivels mounted aft. I find by her quarter-bill that her crew consisted of one hundred and thirty-four men, four of whom were absent in a prize.

The cool and determined conduct of my officers and crew during the action, and their almost unexampled exertions afterwards, entitle them to my warmest acknowledgments and I beg leave, most earnestly, to recommend them to the notice of government.

By the indisposition of Lieut Stuart, I was deprived of the services of an excellent officer. Had he been able to stand the deck, I am confident his exertions would not have been surpassed by any one on board. I should be doing injustice to the merits of Lieut. Shubrick, and acting-lieutenants Connor & Newton, were I not to recommend them particularly to your notice. Lieut. Shubrick was in the actions with the *Guerierre* and *Java*— Capt. Hull and Commodore Bainbridge can bear testimony as to his coolness and good conduct, on both occasions. With the greatest respect, I remain, sir, your obt. servt.

                                                                    Jas Lawrence

P.S. At the commencement of the action my sailing master and seven men were absent in a prize, and Lieut. Stuart and six men on the sick list— As there is every appearance of the winds coming from the E'd I shall stand for N. York in the morning.

ALS, DNA, RG45, CL, 1813, Vol. 2, No. 61 (M125, Roll No. 27).

    1. James Lawrence was promoted to captain on 4 March 1813.
    2. William Peake, R.N., had been a commander since 22 January 1806.

LIEUTENANT FREDERICK A. WRIGHT, R.N., TO LORDS COMMISSIONERS OF THE ADMIRALTY

                                                    New York   26th March 1813.

Sir

The much to be lamented death of Captain William Peake who fell gallantly fighting his Ship while engaged with the United States Ship of War *Hornet,* places me in the painful situation of announcing to you the Capture of His Majesty's Brig *Peacock* while on a Cruize of the Coast of Demerary. On the 24th February, Entrance of the Harbor bearing SW distance nine or ten Leagues At 3.30 PM observed a Ship on the Lee Bow standing to the westward made all Sail in chase. on nearing observing her to have the appearance of a Man of War made the Private Signal Strange Sail tack'd from us and shewed English Colours finding her unable to answer Signal clear'd Ship for Action   At 4.10 Strange Sail tack'd towards us and hoisted American Colours bore up with the intention of bringing him to close Action   At 4.45 Commenced the Engagement by exchanging broadsides within half Pistol Shot distance on contrary Tacks *Peacock* passing to Leeward immediately Wore and gave Starboard Broadside   Action was continued by both Vessels at close distance keeping nearly before the Wind. At 4.55 Vessel forging ahead Enemy took up a position on our Starboard Quarter where he poured in a destructive fire from his whole Broadside while we were unable to bring more than the two after Guns to bear on him and owing to this every Man stationed at the Four After Guns was either Killed or Wounded by this incessant discharge of Grape and Small Shot which was fired from the Musquetry and Swivels placed in his Tops and which from the closeness of the Ships at this time made every person on the Quarter Deck a Distinct Object. The Topsail and Gaff halyards being Shot away the Topsails fell on the Cap and Boom   Mainsail was rendered useless, at this period of the Action Captain Peake was wounded by a Musquet Shot and by a Splinter which knocked him down he continued however to retain the Command of the Ship for some Minutes longer when he gallantly fell nobly defending his Ship by a Cannon Shot which instantly deprived him of Life, and the Service of a Meritorious and brave Officer   The Command of the Ship now devolving on me the Action was continued with an ardour characteristic of British Seamen but the injury the Vessel had sustained from the Enemys Shot under the Quarter made it apparent we could not long sustain so Unequal a Contest   At 5.10 it was reported to me by the Carpenter that the Vessel had six feet water in her Hold and was fast sinking the four after Guns were rendered unserviceable the whole of the Standing and Running Rigging cut away the Main Mast badly wounded and without support yet as the fire was briskly kept up by the Waist Guns I was determined to support the honor of the British Flag as long as defense was practicable but the Main Mast going close by the board a few minutes afterwards and the Enemy again taking up his raking position and the Vessel an unmanageable and sinking Wreck, I was at length to save the lives of the remaining Crew however reluctant and painful it was compeld to wave my Hat in acknowledgement of having struck the Ensign having fallen with the Gaff into the Water   When we came to compare the disparity of Force between the two Vessels with the extraordinary Number of Men on board the Enemy which allowed them to keep a large number in their Tops who supported an incessant galling and destructive Fire. I hope it will appear that every thing was done to support the honor of His Majesty's Arms while defence was practicable.[1] The Enemy have nothing to boast of in this conquest except the possession of a few Prisoners as the Vessel went down in half an hour after their getting on board her although they used every means in endeavouring to keep her afloat by the Pumps bailing at the Hatchway heaving the Guns overboard Cutting away the Anchors & lightening her in every possible manner. I regret to add that eight of the unfortunate Survivors of the Action are supposed to have gone down in her it being impossible from the removal of the numerous Wounded who were first attended to and the short time the Vessel remained above Water to save them all as she sank in five fathoms Water many of the People who got into the Fore Top were afterwards picked up by a Boat which floated off the Booms   Three of the Enemy went down in the Brig   The Casualties I regret to say are extremely numerous three Men besides the Captain were killed five have since died of their Wounds & thirty three wounded most of them severely as will be seen by the enclosed return   It is impossible for any language of mine to do justice to the merits of the surviving Officers and Ships Company or to the spirit they shewd throughout the whole of this unfortunate affair which had they not been opposed to an overwhelming force would under more favourable circumstances and with any thing like equality of Guns or Men have ensured success they were every thing an Officer could wish for & I feel happiness in bearing testimony to their determinate resolution and bravery which was beyond all praise   The Comparative force of the Vessels I give underneath. I have the honor to be Sir Your Obedient Servant

(Signed)   Frederick A Wright   Senr. Lieut.

Peacock Sixteen 24 Pounder Carronades & two long 6 Pounders and one Hundred and twenty two Men

Hornet. Eighteen 32 Pounder Carronades & two long 9 Pounders and one Hundred and Seventy Men

Copy, UkLPR, Adm. 1/503, pp. 491–93.

1. The officers and crew of *Peacock* were honorably acquitted because of their bravery and zeal during the action and because the ship was sinking when they surrendered. The court criticized their gunnery. See *Peacock* court-martial, 7 June 1813, University of Hull, Brynmor Jones Library, Hull, England, Hotham Collection, DDHO/7/98.

[Enclosure]

List of Killed Wounded and Missing of His Majesty's Sloop *Peacock* in Action with the United States Ship *Hornet* on the 24 February 1813.

Killed

William Peake Esqr.	Commander
Richard Physk	Seamen
Peter Solly	Do
James Cotte	Private Marine

Wounded

Mr. Edward Lott	Master	Slightly
Mr. C. D Unwin	Purser	Do
Mr. George Marr	Carpenter	Do
Mr. William Stone	Mid	Severely
Mr. John Wordsworth	Do	Slightly
Mr. William Isaac	Clerk	Do
James Manson	Boatsn. Mate	Severely
Thomas Roberts	Sail Maker	Do
Edward Brady	Captain Mast	Do (since dead)
John Smith	Quarter Master	Do
William Lourey	Carps. Crew	Do
James Medcalf	Quarter Master	Do
John Evans	Captn. M Top	Slightly
Thomas Harding	Seaman	Do
Barny Higgins	Do	Severely (since dead)
James Massey	Do	Do
Richard Williams	Coxwain	Do
James Steele	Seaman	Slightly
William Watt	Do	Do
John Beer	Do	Do
William Evans	Do	Do
Edward Mckellap	Do	Severely
James Boyle	Do	Do
William Blackwell	Private Marine	Do
Daniel Regan	Do	Do
Peter Hunter	Do	Do (since dead)
Robert Mansell	Private Marine	Slightly
Henry Beard	Do	Do

William King	Boy	Severely
Thomas Trithowen	Do	Do
Samuel Johnson	Do	Do
George Adams	Do	Do (since dead)
George Harris	Do	Do (since dead)

Supposed to have sunk in the Brig

Joseph Medcalf	Quarter Master
James Ekin	Captain Fore Top
James Rolston	Do
James Kett	Seaman
Evan Williams	Do
James Redgrove	Do
Robert Robertson	Do
John Langmead	Private Marine

(Signed)   Frederick A. Wright   1st Lieut
(Signed)   John Whitaker   Surgeon

Copy, UkLPR, Adm. 1/503, pp. 495–96.

British Naval Strategy

The Admiralty's strategy in 1813 for winning the American war combined a strict block-ade to cripple the U.S. economy with a convoy system to protect British commerce. The Lords Commissioners of the Admiralty had dispatched four additional ships of the line to Warren and they now believed, considering the weak state of the American navy, that the admiral had ample resources to accomplish his mission. They rejected Warren's comparison of ship strength during the Revolution with the current war as fallacious because Warren had no French fleet with which to contend; they questioned his failure to blockade Boston more closely and refused to accept bad weather as an excuse; and they enjoined him to make do with available resources and then increased the area he must blockade to encompass the ports from Rhode Island to the Mississippi. The proposed division of ships that Warren sent the Admiralty in late March was outdated a month later, demonstrating how difficult it was to keep current with changing circumstances on both sides of the Atlantic.

FIRST SECRETARY OF THE ADMIRALTY JOHN W. CROKER TO ADMIRAL SIR JOHN B. WARREN, R.N.

[Extract]

20th March 1813

Sir

I have this day received your several despatches numbered in the margin, dated the 20th and 26th of last month; and as the subjects to which they relate are very much connected and blended together, I have received the commands of my Lords Commissrs of the Admiralty to communicate to you in one despatch their general observations and Instructions on the whole. . . .

With regard to the watching Boston, I am to state to you that my Lords are aware that this Port cannot be effectually blockaded from November to March, but they must also observe that Commodore Rogers with the *United States, Congress,* and *Argus,* and Commodore Bainbridge with the *Constitution and Hornet* appear to have sailed in the month of October, and in the month of December, tho' it was not possible perhaps to have maintained a permanent watch on that Port, yet having as you state in your letter of the 5th Novr last precise information that Commodore Bainbridge was to sail at a given time, my Lords regret that it was not deemed practicable to proceed off that Port (at a reasonable and safe distance from the land) and to have taken the chance at least of intercepting the Enemy if the weather should not have permitted you to blockade him.

With regard to your future operations and the disposal you propose to make of your force, I have to express to you their Lordships approbation of the general arrangement. They observe however that this arrangement was made before you were aware that four additional Sail of the Line were given to your command, two of which join'd in the interval between the writing & despatching your letters.

This accession of force will enable you to establish a better system of relief than you contemplated at the time you wrote.

On the details of your proposed distribution my Lords command me to state their opinion that in each separate Squadron which you may form, there should, if possible, be one Line of Battle Ship at least; but as your measures must necessarily depend on the state and disposal of the Enemy's Ships, and on many considerations which cannot be anticipated, they must leave to your own judgement and discretion the appropriation of your force and the measures which it may be right to adopt in counteraction of the Enemy's views.

My Lords are glad to think that you will consider the amount of force now under your orders as most ample— It exceeds very much what on a mere comparison with the means of the Enemy would appear necessary; and in addition to this great force not less than Ten sail of the Line, as many heavy Frigates, and double the number of sloops are employed for the protection of the Trade against the Americans, some of them occasionally within the limits of your Station, the rest in situations to which it appears most probable that the Enemy, escaping from your Station, should direct his operations.

The comparison which you make between the amount of force employ'd in the last American war & the present is by no means just; you will recollect that at the former period the fleets of France were actually in the West Indies and American Waters, and it was chiefly to oppose them that so great a force was then necessary.

If the french (as is perhaps not improbable) should push out a force to succour the Americans, my Lords would & will feel it their duty to increase your Squadron in an equal or even greater proportion; but the force now permanently under your orders of upwards of 100 Pendants and 16– or 1700 Men,[1] they have placed at your disposal to be employed against an Enemy whose principal Ports are capable of being blockaded, and whose force according to the statement inclosed in your letter No. 78 consists of 4 large & 3 smaller frigates, and 1 Sloop & 4 Brigs in Commission, manned by 3400 men, and of two or three small frigates in a state of forwardness.

With regard to the state of the Squadrons under your orders, as to their Complements of men, which you represent as being very short, my Lords observe from your state and condition of the 21st Feby. and from those of Jamaica & the Leeward Islands of the 31st Jany. that on a full Complement of 14673 your fleet was only 727 short, while on the other hand there appear to have been 1388 Supernumeraries in the Squadrons, leaving (if the accounts be correct) 661 men over & above the full Complements of the several ships. . . .

With respect to the observation which you take occasion to make on Admiral Stirling's proceedings, and the opinion which you intimate that the several Commands should be so far separated, as that while you retain'd a general authority over the whole, the divisional flag officers should have a greater share of responsibility than is at present, as you conceive, imposed upon them, I am on the first point to observe to you, their Lordships agree with you in disapproving Admiral Stirling's proceedings in the particulars referred to, and will not fail to acquaint him that they do so;[2] and on the subject of the conveyance of Specie they direct you to give orders that in future no Sum exceeding £100,000 be sent home in less than a heavy frigate; and if a Sum of £500,000 should be likely to be collected, you are to appropriate a Line of Battle Ship to it's conveyance— But on the 2nd point, my Lords command me to say that they do not exactly comprehend your proposition, or how the Junior Officers can be at once under your orders & separately & distinctly responsible—[3]

You observe that all that you would wish to consider as being within your power, are the general Stations of the force, the power of withdrawing or adding to the force on each Station, & the Convoys being regularly attended to— These, my Lords agree with you, are the principal points on which the interference of the Commander in Chief is likely to be called for; but how these most important subjects are to be separated from the general responsibility of an Admiral their Lordships do not see.

It was with the view of giving unity & effect to our operations against a single Enemy that the stations were united into a single command. If you should find that you are unequal to the management of so extensive a duty, it would be better, in their Lordships opinion, to have again three distinct and responsible Commanders in Chiefs, than to have three Officers with divided authority and mixed responsibility. . . .

The obvious course is that you should allot to the divisional Admirals such force as from your view of the state and disposition of that of the Enemy you may judge necessary or expedient; that you should give them express orders on such subjects as may admit of them, and discretional orders where they may be most proper; and for the execution of these and for the due employment of the force you entrust to them, they must be held responsible in the first degree to you, but thro' you to their Lordships and His Majesty in the same manner that all other divisional Admirals now are, and at all times, and in all situations, have been; and while my Lords recommend and expect the most conciliatory conduct on the one part, and cordial cooperation on the other, they command me to say that they will not fail to visit any contravension of your commands as strongly as of their own. . . .

Finally my Lords command me to recall to your attention my several letters of the dates named in the margin, and to recommend to you the most active and vigorous prosecution of the War during the Season when the whole of the

American Coast is accessible by your Squadron, and which will admit of your placing all the Enemy's Ports in a state of close and permanent Blockade. . . .

J W C.

P.S. I am further to signify their Lordships particular approbation of the measures you propose to take for the protection of the Trade & Convoys destined for the River St Lawrence—

Copy, UkLPR, Adm. 2/1376, pp. 341–67.

1. Croker no doubt meant 16,000 to 17,000 men.

2. The Admiralty recalled Vice Admiral Charles Stirling in the spring of 1813 to face charges of corruption in the letting of Royal Navy ships for convoy. Specie was always transported in the king's ships for safety; when this was done a charge of 2 1/2 percent was levied, of which the admiral and the captain of the ship received a share. Stirling was accused of levying upon petitioners for convoys a charge for freighting specie even when there was no specie. On 9 May 1814 a court-martial determined that the charges had been proved in part and sentenced Stirling to remain on the half pay list and to be excluded from promotion. See Ralfe, *Naval Biography*, Vol. 3, pp. 73–107.

3. Because of the distance of the West Indies from the "seat of war" and Warren's inability to have full and current information on the situation there, he had recommended that the Lords Commissioners of the Admiralty consider the "expediency of placing upon the Admirals Commanding in the West Indies both to Windward and Leeward, the entire responsibility and governance of their own Stations, empowering me only to Command the Force under them, in the event of necessity requiring a consolidation." Warren to Croker, 26 Feb. 1813, UkLPR, Adm. 1/503, pp. 223–26.

First Lord of the Admiralty Viscount Robert Saunders Dundas Melville to Admiral Sir John B. Warren, R.N.

<u>Private.</u>   Admiralty
                                                    26th. March 1813
Dear Sir,

I mentioned in my letter to you of the 23d. Inst. that we intended to dispatch a Sloop with our replies to your letters; but as the Troop Ships with the Marine Battalions are on the point of sailing & will probably make their passage nearly in as short a time, we shall detain the Sloop till she can be attached to a convoy. She may possibly go with the *Asia* which is intended to sail on that service for the West Indies on the 10th. April.

You will receive by the present opportunity an order for blockading all the principal Ports in the United States to the southward of Rhode Island & including the Mississippi, and we calculate that your force is amply sufficient to enable you to execute this service effectually.[1]

We do not intend this as a mere <u>paper</u> blockade, but as a complete stop to all trade & intercourse by Sea with those Ports, as far as the wind & weather, & the continual presence of a sufficient armed Force, will permit & ensure. If you find that this cannot be done without abandoning for a time the interruption which you appear to be giving to the internal navigation of the Chesapeake, the latter object must be given up, & you must be content with blockading its entrance & sending in occasionally your cruisers for the purpose of harrassing & annoyance. I do not advert to enterprizes which you may propose to undertake with the aid of the Troops, as these will of course be directed with an adequate force to special objects. I apprehend also that it is scarcely necessary for me to request your most particular attention to the leaving an adequate force on the Jamaica & Leeward Islands stations for the purpose of guarding the various points which are likely to be assailed by Privateers; the clamour has been great here, though apparently unfounded, on your withdrawing a large portion of the West India force to the northward. The providing of sufficient convoys between Quebec & Halifax & the West Indies will not escape your attention, nor the husbanding & refitting your Force by having a certain number only engaged in cruising, so that the whole may be kept as effective as possible, & your blockading vessels be occasionally relieved. You have under your command some of the most active & intelligent Officers in the Navy, & I rely on your rendering them available to the public Interest.— I have the honor to be, Dear Sir, your very faithful & obedient Servant

Melville.

ALS, InU, Lilly Library, War of 1812 Manuscripts.

1. A few days later the Admiralty ordered Warren to "institute a strict and rigorous Blockade of the Ports and Harbours of New York, Charleston, Port Royal, Savannah and of the River Mississippi." See Admiralty to Warren, 26 Mar. 1813, National Library of Scotland, Alexander F. I. Cochrane Papers, MS 2340, fols. 49–50.

COAST OF AMERICA, PROPOSED DIVISION OF SHIPS & THEIR STATIONS

No.	Ships' Names	Rate	Station & No.	Remarks
1	Marlborough	74	No. 1	To intercept the Enemies' Trade and Cruizers from Washington &
2	Victorious	74	Blockade of the	Baltimore & to prevent the produce of Virginia from going to market.
3	Maidstone	36	Chesapeake	To destroy their Revenue & Resources, there being the greatest
4	Junon	38		No. of Privateers from those Ports upon the whole Coast of America.
5	Laurestinus	26		
6	Fantome	18		
	a Tender	8		
1	Poictiers	74	No. 2	Ditto Ditto
2	Narcissus	32	Blockade of the	
3	Paz	10	Delaware	
1	Dragon	74	No. 3	Do. Do. This Port may be Blockaded by taking possession of Sandy
2			Off New York	Hook with Troops & anchoring some Ships within it, & by another
1	Belvidera	36	No. 4	Squadron off Montuck Point to anchor, Water & Refit in Gardiners Bay
2	Acasta	40	Off Nantucket Shoal,	E. end of Long Island where 18 Sail of the Line under Adml. Abuthnot
			Block Island,	in the old American War used to lay.
			Montuck Point	
1	Rattler	18	No. 5	To protect the Coast of New Brunswick from Invasion.
2	Emulous	14	In the Bay of Fundy	
3	Nova Scotia	12		
4	Bream	6		
5	Herring	6		

#	Ship	Guns	No.	Station	Remarks
1	*Shannon*	38	No. 6	For the protection of Nova Scotia	To cruize upon St. Georges Bank, off the Gulf of St. Lawrence & on the Banks of Newfoundland.
2	*Tenedos*	38			
3	*Nymphe*	38			
1	*Aeolus*	32	No. 7	Off Charleston, Beaufort, Ocracoke & Roanoke	To intercept the Trade, Privateers & destroy the Revenue, several additional Vessels must be added to distress this part of the Enemy's Coast.
2	*Sophie*	18			
1	*Viper*	14	No. 8	Savannah & St. Augustine	The most implacable & virulent people in the whole Union.
1	*San Domingo*	74	No. 9	To relieve the Ships in Chesapeake and Delaware	To unite to meet an Enemy, or to Cruize occasionally whenever an additional No. of Frigates or Sloops arrive so as to afford relief upon the several Stations here alluded to, two Frigates & two Sloops of War will be added to my Division to enable me to detach upon the space of the occasion to any given point wanting Force or in search of any of the Enemy's Ships. In the month of March it will be necessary to add a new Squadron to attend to Boston & Rhode Isld., as the weather will then be sufficiently mild to admit of Ships keeping that Station. The Three heavy Frigates under Captain Broke will be wanted off the great bank of Newfoundland and from thence to Cape Race, and in the opening of the Gulf of St. Lawrence to cover the Canadian Convoys and Re-inforcements of Troops and Stores for those Provinces and Nova Scotia.
2	*Ramillies*	74			
3	*Statira*	38			
4	*Orpheus*	32			
5	*Colibri*	18			
	a Tender	8			

J B Warren

DS, UkLPR, Adm. 1/4359, Warren enclosed this document with his letter numbered 104 of 28 March 1813 to Croker.

Bibles for Seamen

Through its chaplains the navy attempted to provide religious instruction for enlisted men. A chaplain's duties in the early nineteenth century were to read prayers at specific times, preach to the crew on Sundays, and instruct the midshipmen and volunteers in writing, arithmetic, navigation, and lunar observations.[1] Dr. Andrew Hunter was the chaplain at the Washington Navy Yard, where he had taught navigation to the midshipmen. He had accepted an appointment as chaplain and mathematician in the navy in March 1811.

1. *Andrew Hunter to Jones, 29 Apr. 1813, DNA, RG45, MLR, 1813, Vol. 2, No. 116 (M124, Roll No. 54).*

CHAPLAIN ANDREW HUNTER TO SECRETARY OF THE NAVY JONES

Navy-yard, Mar. 31st 1813.

Sir,

Since my connection with the Navy, and particularly since my arrival in this city, I have endeavoured to supply every public ship that went out of the harbour with a number of bibles for the use of the seamen. The marine barracks have also been furnished with a number of New-testaments and religious tracts. The effects produced by their spending their spare time in reading those books have been visible to a number of the officers. If some plan could be adopted for supplying the ships at regular periods with the scriptures and some small religious and moral tracts I have no doubt it would produce an amelioration of their morals and increase their civilization. For notwithstanding chivalry and the increase of moral & physical science have had great effects in civilizing a portion of mankind yet I think it might easily be demonstrated that the Old and New testaments have done infinitely more, and at a much smaller expense. My long acquaintance with soldiers warrants me in saying that the greater number of them as well as of sailors value highly what they call religion, however great and culpable their aberrations from it may be. Public opinion seems to look for the adoption of some general rule on this subject, and christianity would certainly give its approbation. Our seamen and marines would be more attached to their government and their country if they found themselves regarded as rational beings, independent of the services which we demand and expect from them in defence of our country and its precious rights. My limited situation has not enabled me to furnish so ample and regular a supply of books as circumstances seemed to require. The manner of procuring the books which have been distributed has been by my ardent application to individuals in the state from whence I came, and to different Bible-societies. How long these supplies will be afforded is uncertain, therefore I thought it my duty as a chaplain to lay these remarks and this information before the Head of our beloved Navy for his consideration. And in the event of our not being able to supply the ships in the above way to request some aid from the public. I have recently received advice that a hundred new-testaments had been shipped for me by the Bible-Society of Philadelphia. These are daily expected to arrive, and shall be distributed as opportunity may offer. When that society shall have stricken off an edition of the Bible with the stereotypes which they have lately imported, we shall I hope be able to procure another supply. I have been endeavouring to procure some assistance from the Bible-society at Boston, but am not able to say anything as to the success of the attempt. The want of a free water-transportation impedes our designs in this as well as in many other things. With great respect I am, Dr. Sir, your obedient servant

Andw. Hunter

ALS, DNA, RG45, BC, 1813, Vol. 1, No. 160 (M148, Roll No. 11).

James Biddle and the Delaware Flotilla

Jones authorized the retention of only five gunboats for the Delaware flotilla in his February reduction order.[1] He refused to give Alexander Murray, commander of the Philadelphia Station, any more gunboats until local pressure and fears of a British buildup in the area made Jones change his mind. At the end of March, Jones asked Master Commandant James Biddle[2] to take command of the Delaware flotilla, consisting of ten gunboats. Later he purchased two cutters, which were converted into the block sloops Buffalo *and* Camel. *By the end of April, Biddle had manned only four of his ten gunboats. After convoying two vessels with military stores down the Delaware River, Biddle reported the British strength in the bay and the enemy's efforts to reconnoiter using the stratagem of a flag of truce.*

Jones had intended the flotilla command to be a temporary assignment for Biddle; when Hornet *required a new commander, he offered that ship to Biddle on 30 April. Lieutenant Samuel Angus replaced Biddle in the Delaware command.[3]*

1. *Jones to Alexander Murray, 26 Feb. 1813, DNA, RG45, SNL, Vol. 10, p. 283 (M149, Roll No. 10).*

2. *Biddle was promoted to master commandant early in March 1813. He had been captured in the action between* Wasp *and* Poictiers *and was inactive for four months after being paroled in November 1812. See Dudley, Naval War of 1812, Vol. 1, pp. 536–41 and 579–83 for the* Wasp-Frolic *action and* Wasp's *subsequent capture by* Poictiers. *See Long, Sailor-Diplomat, pp. 39–59, for additional background on Biddle.*

3. *For the orders concerning the Delaware command, see Jones to Biddle, 30 Apr. 1813, DNA, RG45, SNL, Vol. 10, p. 387 (M149, Roll No. 10), and Jones to Angus, 1 May 1813, DNA, RG45, SNL, Vol. 10, p. 389 (M149, Roll No. 10).*

Secretary of the Navy Jones to Master Commandant James Biddle

(private)

Navy Department
March. 31. 1813

Sir

Do you not think that the command of ten of the best of the Gun Boats at Philada. with 35 men each officers included would afford you an opportunity of chastising the invaders of your native stream with credit to yourself and infinite satisfaction to your fellow citizens? If you have an inclination to try the experiment I will give you an official order.[1] A popular officer whose spirit and enterprize attracts public confidence may recruit men when ordinary means fail. A judicious position under cover of night or in a calm would enable you to inflict such wounds as would teach the enemy caution and perhaps terminate their annoyance of the Delaware. With 350 men you would have nothing to apprehend from boarding but on the contrary under favorable circumstances might become the assailant yourself.

As this service would be but temporary and as five of the Boats are I presume already manned could not the other five be manned with volunteers and commanded by some of our popular and spirited ship masters to whom I would grant temporary Warrants as Sailing Masters for that purpose. I am respectfully Your Obdt. Servt.

W. Jones

ALS, PHi, Letters of Commodore James Biddle, Vol. 1, No. 2620.

1. See Jones to Biddle, 6 Apr. 1813, PHi, Letters of Commodore James Biddle, Vol. 1, No. 2622.

MASTER COMMANDANT JAMES BIDDLE TO SECRETARY OF THE NAVY JONES

Philadelphia   April 4th 1813

Sir

I am honored with your letter of the 31. ulto. I am decidedly of the opinion that Gun boats are a species of force calculated to render important Service in still waters; and with a force of ten Boats in the Bay of Delaware, well equipt, judiciously applied, & under favorable circumstances, I should think there was a reasonable ground to expect that the Enemy's Ships could be either destroyed, or compelled to evict their anchorage and put to Sea. I have the honor therefore to state that I shall be happy to receive your orders to command the flotilla fitted out for the defence of the Delaware—

With regard to Volunteers, I should think that while an Enemy was in the Bay, a sufficient number of them might be procured, for a short period, to man at least the five Boats, especially if popular & respected masters of vessels of this port were employed in them. Many volunteers certainly could be had from this city; and as the conduct of the Enemy has been such as to excite exasperation in the minds of the people on both shores of the Delaware, I should think that many could be procured also from below. This opinion is confirmed to me by the Bay-Craft-Men with whom I have conversed. Permit me to add that no exertion shall be wanting on my part to procure the volunteers, & that all my endeavours shall be used towards effecting the objects for which the flotilla is Equipt— I have the honor to be With great Respect Sir Yr. hbl. Obt. St.

J. Biddle

ALS, DNA, RG45, MC, 1813, No. 45 (M147, Roll No. 5).

SECRETARY OF THE NAVY JONES TO MASTER COMMANDANT JAMES BIDDLE

Navy Department
April 25, 1813

Sir

The two cutters, the *Buffaloe* & the *Camel* now fitting out at Philadelphia for the Service of the U S Navy on the Delaware are to be attached to your command.[1] They are to be fitted with a solid enclosed bulwark 5 feet 10 Inches high covered with gratings shod with Iron so as to be proof against any number of boarders and are to be armed with two long 18s. and two 24 pd. carronades (if such of the latter as are used in the Navy are to be had) to shift over so as to fight one long 18 and the two carronade of a side and the two long 18s. through the thwartship bulwarks forward or aft as occasion may require.

The after part of the bulwark may be fitted up so as to afford you excellent accommodations.

With respect to the bulwark Mr. Penrose the builder has my particular directions and Come. Murray is directed to attend to their armament &c but as you are to command and fight them it will be well to attend to their equipment. I wish the original appearance of these vessels to be retained and when the guns are housed and ports in, the bulwark painted yellow will resemble a deck load of lumber (when painted of that colour) which those vessels are accustomed to carry and may answer an excellent purpose of deception night or day. I am satisfied that these vessels thus fitted are the best calculated for the defence of the Delaware of any that can be devised.

They are known to sail remarkably fast even with a heavy deck load of lumber—they work well, draw little warter, have a great Beam are very stiff, and able to bear a very heavy armament, and will also row remarkably well.

The great object is the complete defence against boarders, any number of which they can repel or destroy by a proper use of the Battery and musketry. The practice of the enemy in our waters is to send powerful boarding parties.

In the attack and capture of the *Dolphin* Privateer & others lately in the Rappahanock there were 21. Boats averaging 40. men each.[2] I am respectfully yours &c.

W. Jones

ALS, PHi, Letters of Commodore James Biddle, Vol. 1, No. 2624.

1. Jones ordered George Harrison, Philadelphia navy agent, to purchase two river vessels. They were converted into the block sloops, *Camel* and *Buffalo*, and served as commissioned vessels with the Delaware flotilla throughout the war; see Jones to Murray, 22 Apr. 1813, DNA, RG45, SNL, Vol. 10, pp. 362–63 (M149, Roll No. 10).
2. See pp. 339–40 for this account.

MASTER COMMANDANT JAMES BIDDLE TO SECRETARY OF THE NAVY JONES

Philadelphia   April 28th 1813

Sir

I have the honor to acquaint you that Genl. Bloomfield[1] some days since asked of Commodore Murray to furnish a Convoy for the protection down the Bay of two vessels containing Military Stores for Lewistown & Cape May, & that at the request of Come. Murray I proceeded down on this service with four Gun Boats, using all that are as yet equipt and manned. Owing to unfavorable weather I was absent twelve days, & returned to the city last Evening having seen one of the Vessels safely up Duck Creek & the other to Bridgetown on the Cohansey.

By information from the inhabitants below it appears that the Enemy have two small Schooners one Sloop, and three barges, which have occasionally been up as high as the upper end of Bombay hook. The barges are the Ship's launches with one small carronade; the Schooners & Sloop are of a slight armament tho' generally full of men. I was disappointed as well as mortified at finding that notwithstanding the depredations committed by these Vessels, yet the people, who from the interruption of the Navigation are at present without employment, are not sufficiently excited to enter on board the Gun Boats. While below with the Boats I recruited only two men. It is proper however to add that I was not in Maurice River, the place where it is said, we should most probably be enabled to collect men.

While off Cohansey I received information that there was at Bridgetown a vessel bearing a flag of truce from Come. Beresford,[2] in consequence of which I anchored in the Creek & sent an officer up to make Enquiry into her circumstances. It appeared that she was the Sloop *Betsy* of Bridgetown, regular packet to and from Philadelphia which had been captured by the Enemy's boats and now sent to Bridgetown, ostensibly for the purpose of arranging an Exchange of Prisoners. She had onboard nine men including a Lieutenant of Marines & a Midshipman; had 6 muskets, 2 pistols, 3 Cutlasses & 101 Musket Cartridges, and sixty two water casks, 17 of which they had filled on their way up the Creek. I therefore addressed a Note to the Collector of Bridgetown, stating that this vessel could not be considered as having any claim to the protection guaranteed to a regular flag of truce, & that it was my duty to see that She was not permitted to return to the *Poictiers,* until the orders of the Government could be had with regard to her. By the return of the Officer who was the bearer of my letter, I received a Communication from General Bloomfield who had just arrived at Bridgetown, & stating that he had detained the flag of truce. I have the honor to be with much Respect Sir Your Hlb. Ob. St.

J Biddle

ALS, DNA, RG45, MC, 1813, No. 54 (M147, Roll No. 5).

1. Brigadier General Joseph Bloomfield, U.S.A., commanded the 4th Military District, encompassing west New Jersey, Pennsylvania, and Delaware, in 1813.

2. Captain Sir John Poo Beresford, R.N., in *Poictiers*, 74, commanded the Delaware blockading squadron.

Ships for Cartels and Special Missions

Cartel ships and flags of truce were used during the War of 1812 to transport prisoners and persons with special missions. The Department of State had jurisdiction over the exchange of prisoners and diplomatic negotiations. The belligerents agreed to provide two public vessels for repatriation of prisoners. Not wishing to deplete its already small naval force, the Americans purchased several vessels—Analostan in December 1812 and Perseverance and Neptune in the following spring. Chandler Price, a prominent Philadelphia businessman and friend of William Jones's, offered to sell the latter two ships to the navy. The British blockade restricted egress from the Atlantic seaboard for most merchant vessels and ship owners like financially-pressed Price had to reduce their inventories. Jones negotiated the sales at terms favorable to the government and supervised the manning and provisioning of the vessels, but the State Department financed them.[1]

1. For a discussion of cartel vessels, see Dietz, "Cartel Vessels," pp. 165–94.

SECRETARY OF THE NAVY JONES TO NAVY AGENT GEORGE HARRISON

George Harrison Esquire
Navy Agent, Philadelphia.

Navy Department,
April 3rd 1813.

Sir,

The Secretary of State having requested me to procure a Vessel suitable for a Cartel to proceed to Jamaica and bring home the Prisoners there; and, also, a good and convenient Ship to proceed as a flag to Europe; after due enquiry, I offered Mr. Chandler Price 8000 dollars for his Ship *Perseverance,* for the former, and 13000 dollars for his Ship *Neptune* for the latter object; he having asked 9000 dollars for the *Perseverance,* and 15000 dollars for the *Neptune.*— He has accepted my offer for the *Perseverance* and forwarded a bill of Sale, and means, I presume, to accept my offer for the *Neptune,* but has filled up the bill of Sale with 15000 dollars.— I now return it, and you will please to have a new bill of Sale executed, with the consideration money 13,500 dollars, and forward it to this Department. I enclose Mr. Price's letter which will explain his meaning. You will please to take charge of these ships immediately, and until further orders their respective commanders can continue in charge.— These vessels are represented to me to be extremely well found, requiring little, or nothing, to put them to sea, and every thing belonging to them is included in the Sale.—

The *Perseverance* you will put in order immediately, and in good Sailing trim, with Stone ballast, 130 Punchions of water and 20,000 Rations, of the United States Navy, except of whiskey, which will be half allowance.—

Over the water must be a Platform of boards, and in the hold, between Decks and Cabbin, accommodations for 400 persons, say two thirds below at one time.—

She will be commanded by a Sailing Master, of the United States Navy, (perhaps her present Master if he is clever)[1] two Mates, Boatswain, two Cooks, a Carpenter, Surgeon & Mate (and Medicines) and 10 Seamen.—

Having more Navy Beef, Pork and whiskey, at this Station than is required, I shall order these articles for both ships from this to New Castle, if time will admit. The Ship will be put in good condition, but nothing superfluous; and you will get her in readiness as fast as possible.—

The *Neptune* is to be put in very complete order with a particular view to the comfortable accomodation of three or four passengers of distinction, and their domestics.[2] Her accommodations are good, but if the rooms require enlarging, or any alteration can add to their comfort and Convenience, you will have it done.— Indeed, I will refer you, in confidence to Mr. Gallatin, and will thank you to converse with him, both as to the accommodations and Stores, which you will provide accordingly, and I know he could not be in better hands. I wish you could get him to look at the Ship: I know her to be an excellent vessel, of convenient size—an excellent Seaboat and Sailer. She will touch at New York if he wishes it. I shall be particular in selecting a commander, who will also be an officer of the United States Navy—a Lieutenant, if I can find a clever fellow unemployed.[3] Dispatch is very desirable in this object. You will keep the accounts of these vessels distinct from your account with this Department, and the Department of State will supply the funds as wanted.

As soon as the bill of Sale of the *Neptune* is corrected and received, I will remit the amount of Purchase money of both vessels to you. I am, very respectfully, your Ob: Servant.

W Jones.

LB Copy, DNA, RG45, CLS, 1813, pp. 3–5.

1. Jones appointed Sailing Master Joseph H. Dill, formerly a seaman in the merchant service, to command *Perseverance.*
2. *Neptune* sailed in May, carrying the two peace commissioners, Albert Gallatin and James A. Bayard, to Europe for mediation talks sponsored by the Russian czar.
3. Jones named his brother, Lloyd Jones, to captain *Neptune,* giving him the temporary rank of master commandant.

St. Marys Station—April 1813

When Secretary of the Navy Jones ordered a reduction of the number of gunboats, Commodore Hugh G. Campbell had twelve gun vessels on the St. Marys Station: four on the St. Johns River cooperating with the army; four about St. Marys; and four stationed at different inlets along the Georgia and South Carolina coasts. Campbell's inability to man some of his barges made them unserviceable.[1] Receiving no response from the department regarding a cruise for Lieutenant Johnston Blakeley in Enterprise, *Campbell ordered him to transport provisions to the army in Florida. The following letter from Blakeley to Jones epitomizes the restlessness of a naval officer anxious to cruise against the enemy.*

The other brig on the station, Troup, *purchased by Acting Lieutenant Charles F. Grandison, was discovered to be rotten and unfit for service. Grandison had been under suspension since the beginning of the year for misbehavior. A court of inquiry convened on 19 April sustained the charges of unofficerlike and ungentlemanly conduct. Jones dismissed him from the navy, however, not because of these charges but for the unauthorized purchase of the brig* Troup.[2]

1. Campbell to Jones, 6 Mar. 1813, DNA, RG45, CL, 1813, Vol. 2, No. 17 (M125, Roll No. 27).
2. Court of inquiry relating to Charles F. Grandison, DNA, RG125, CM, Vol. 4, No. 133 (M273, Roll No. 4); Jones to Grandison, 1 May 1813, DNA, RG45, SNL, Vol. 10, p. 388 (M149, Roll No. 10).

LIEUTENANT JOHNSTON BLAKELEY TO SECRETARY OF THE NAVY JONES

U S Brig *Enterprize*
Savannah River   8th April 1813

Sir

With no feigned reluctance and much real regret do I intrude upon your attention at this time. A period of almost ten months of war has elapsed, without this vessel being permitted to cruize a single day. While in the Mississippi the opportunity to do so was withheld, until an application, in consequence of that refusal, was made to the Navy Department and we were ordered to this station. On 18th January we arrived; since which, I have repeatedly applied for permission to make a cruize and altho I expected every day to receive orders to that effect, no such order could be obtained. I have been too long in the habits of subordination to question the propriety of those placed over me in command; but when it is considered that I have already lost rank and am likely to lose more and when the means of obtaining reputation is not only denied, but the certain consequence will be the diminution of any little I might possess; I trust will plead my apology for troubling you. Thirteen years have I been in service; almost the whole of which time has been actively employed, and now only ask, to enjoy in common with the rest of the Navy an opportunity to go against the Enemy. While every vessel of the United States every revenue cutter and every privateer are or have been engaged in cruizing this one alone remains chained to her moorings. To the magnanimity and justice of the Honourable the Secretary of the Navy I look, in the fullest confidence, that I may no further be a sufferer in rank and reputation: tho the former is only desirable as it may tend to increase the latter. I have the honour to be very respectfully yr mot Obt Servt.

J. Blakeley

ALS, DNA, RG45, MLR, 1813, Vol. 3, No. 6 (M124, Roll No. 55).

COMMODORE HUGH G. CAMPBELL TO SECRETARY OF THE NAVY JONES

Duplicate   St Mary's   14th April 1813

Sir,

I cannot rest in silence on the subject of the *Troup* lately purchased on Government account at Savannah— It is to be regreted that Mr. Grandison ever had any thing to do with her, he may be qualified to fit out the cabin of a Merchant ship, but to the outfits of a ship of war he appears a stranger.

The *Troup* has been some old French Privateer or sharp built vessel Risen on and literally speaking rotten from Keel to Gunwale, her upper works much better than her lower frame— I have examined her and had most of her Timbers boared, but have not found five that are sound— Mr. Grandison unship'd the Mizenmast and stowed the cambouse on deck, which while a British Packet was camped below   This change left no room for a boat on deck, which induced me to have the Mainmast, pumps and Topsail sheet Bitts moved farther aft to give room for that purpose— In making this alteration we find the want of new channels all of which the Carpenter has agreed to make good for sixty dollars— On striping the Mainmast, we find the Maintop entirely rotten and part of the Masthead defective, the latter we can make good, the former is to be made for thirty four dollars—

The timely arrival of Lieutenant Walpole relieved me much, as I had not an officer on board on whom I could depend— Mr. Edwards whom I found acting Lieut. on board the *Troup* appears so totally ignorant of his duty as to render it absolutely necessary to supersede him in the command by Mr. Walpole, with whom I have left positive instructions not to expend a dollar upon her but what is absolutely necessary, which by every calculation of mine will be Trifling, there being already near twelve thousand dollars expended on her exclusive of the purchase— On an overhaul of all the spare rigging Blocks &ca I find in addition to a full rigged ship as far as shrouds, stays, Backstays, Bowlines, &c, &c, from the lower dead eye to the Top Gallant Truck, flying & ring bound Ends, seven spare Topmast, Backstays, three hundred and twenty spare Blocks, Eight spare Marlin spikes and other articles— Mr. Grandison has a new suit of sails of much larger size than her present spars—it was his intention to new mast and spar her in his own way, all of which I have forbid, having found in the Hull of the *Troup* nothing more than a small armed Transport or Guard ship for a Harbor   I have the Honor to be With Great Respect Sir Your obedient Servant

Hugh G. Campbell

LS, DNA, RG45, CL, 1813, Vol. 2, No. 182 (M125, Roll No. 27).

SECRETARY OF THE NAVY JONES TO COMMODORE HUGH G. CAMPBELL

Hugh G. Campbell, Esqr.   Navy Department.
Commanding Naval Officer,   April 24. 1813.
Savannah, Gea.

Sir,

Enclosed is my answer to the letter of the Mayor of the City of Savannah, relative to the naval force limited for the protection of the district under your command which you will please to peruse and deliver sealed.—[1] Its contents are also intended for your information and government.

I wish to write you much at large on the subject of your command, but time, at this moment, does not admit. I however rely fully on your prudence and judgment for the correction of the extravagant expenditure which has marked all our Southern Stations.—

You will confine yourself to the force already limited, and enter into no new contract, purchase or expenditure, without special authority from this Department.—

Should the military forces of the United States be withdrawn from Florida, the naval force will return from that station to St. Mary's, but of this movement you will be apprized in due time.[2] You will, in all cases, cooperate with the Military Commander, but of the manner and extent of such co-operation you will be the judge.—

On that subject I enclose to you a joint regulation of the war & navy Departments for your government.[3] You will immediately order the United States Brig *Enterprise* to proceed, without delay, direct to Portsmouth, New Hampshire, or the first convenient port in that vicinity, and report to Captain Isaac Hull at Portsmouth, Commanding Naval Officer of that district, whose further orders Captain Blakeley will obey.—[4] I am, very, respectfully &ca.—

W. Jones.

LB Copy, DNA, RG45, SNL, Vol. 10, pp. 370–71 (M149, Roll No. 10).

1. See Jones to George Jones, 23 Apr. 1813, MLS, Vol. 11, pp. 252–53 (M209, Roll No. 4). Jones responded in the same vein in answering all such entreaties for more naval support—that resources were limited and stations must make do with less.
2. See pp. 153–54.
3. See Agreement Governing Joint Operations, 8 April 1813, pp. 434–35.
4. Not having received this letter from Jones, Campbell had ordered Blakeley on a short cruise in mid-May to intercept merchant vessels; see Campbell to Blakeley, 15 May 1813, DNA, RG45, CL, Vol. 3, No. 130 1/2 (M125, Roll No. 28).

Building the 74s

Shipbuilding burgeoned during April, while the government found itself competing for supplies with shipbuilders who were constructing large privateers. William Jones rewarded Commodore William Bainbridge with the command of the Charlestown Navy Yard after his victory over Java. He was to superintend construction of a 74-gun ship, Independence. *Bainbridge replaced Captain Isaac Hull, who took charge of the long-neglected yard at Portsmouth, New Hampshire, where he spent the second quarter of 1813 attempting to collect enough timber to build a 74. It was mistakenly thought that there were sufficient supplies at both the Portsmouth and Charlestown stations to build two ships of the line. The materials left over from the unfinished building program of the late 1790s, however, had suffered from appropriation over the ensuing years. Hull found his inventory very low of critical items, especially the live oak which could be obtained only from southern forests.*

Drafting the designs for the 74s and the frigates occupied several months that spring, as Secretary Jones and William Doughty at Washington, Charles Penrose, Joshua and Samuel Humphreys at Philadelphia, William Bainbridge at Boston, and Isaac Hull at Portsmouth all expressed their views on construction. Former naval constructor Joshua Humphreys swayed Jones, arguing that "By making our ships large, it is the only plan by which this country can in any wise be formidable with a small comparative number of Ships, it will in some degree give us the lead in naval affairs." [1]

1. Joshua Humphreys to Jones, 24 Apr. 1813, PHi, Joshua Humphreys Letter Book, pp. 117–18. For background on the building of the 74 at Portsmouth, see L. McKee, "Portsmouth."

SECRETARY OF THE NAVY JONES TO CAPTAIN ISAAC HULL

Isaac Hull Esq.   Navy Depart.
Commandant of the Navy Yard.   april 9th 1813.
Portsmouth N.H.

I have received your letter of the 3rd announcing your arrival at your Station. I wish you immediately to prepare the ways for laying down the 74, which is to be built under your inspection with as much dispatch as may be consistent with the careful collection of the best materials and the faithful execution of the workmanship. The copy of the original draught of the 74 I presume must be in possession of the Navy Agent and as the entire frame is cut to moulds and rough bevelled, it therefore cannot be deviated from. Their proportions and lines are good and fair, they will be noble ships, but too crooked, and their top side tumbles home too much, this however cannot now be helped except the sheer which I intend to straighten by raising it amidships and dropping at each end. The upper deck is to be flush without poop. A Mr. William Badger has been mentioned to me as the most experienced & respectable builder in Portsmouth. I wish you to ascertain his qualifications and that of others and let me know the terms or rate per annum, at which any one or two of them will engage to direct the work as master builders. You will require a Smith's shop and some other necessary improvements in the yard, and I should like to have an estimate of the cost of the improvements absolutely requisite.

On your taking charge of the Navy Yard and effects attached to it the functions of Mr. Langdon will be simply that of Navy Agent with no other perquisite or allowance than that allowed by Law viz. One per Cent on the amount of his expenditure. You will have to engage a complete master Ship Smith to execute the work in the yard.

The entire Superintendance and controul of the Navy Yard and everything attached to it is with you, and I rely with perfect confidence upon your judicious arrangement and economical management, to prove to the public that establishments of this nature are not necessarily scenes of extravagant waste and expenditure.

You will if you think proper remove all the public Stores to the navy yard and give up the Stores that have been hired. In a former letter I authorized you to continue such of the masters of the Gun Boats as appeared to you to merit their Stations and to report to me those of a contrary character if any in order that they may be discharged from the Service.

In your estimate of the improvements you may include the probable cost of the Stores you suggest the propriety of building.

Mr. Langdon made a return on the 27 Feby last of the timber on hand, which you will please examine and compare with the Stock actually on hand—also a return of articles belonging to the Navy Department at Portsmouth copies of which you can obtain. I am respectfully Your obt. Servt.

W. Jones.

LB Copy, DNA, RG45, CNA, Vol. 1, pp. 393–94 (M441, Roll No. 1).

Captain Isaac Hull to Secretary of the Navy Jones

U.S. Navy Yard   Portsmouth   23 April 1813

Sir

I find it impossible to ascertain precisely the particular pieces of live oak Timber there is in this Yard. Consequently we cannot tell what will be wanting, untill we begin to work, and get it all out of the sheds; there can be no doubt, but there will be many pieces wanting. Indeed from what I can now see, I should suppose that we have not more than two thirds of the frame of live oak— Will you be pleased to inform me how the deficiency is to be made up, when a particular piece is found wanting? I should suppose that the white oak of this Country would answer for floor timbers should any of them be wanting, which I have no doubt will be the case. I should be much pleased to know your wishes particularly on this subject as the distance from this to Washington is so great that the Service may suffer very much before I could write to the Department and get an answer relative to a particular piece of timber that might from time to time be found deficient. Indeed at such a distance it will be impossible for me to consult you on every thing that relates to the building of the Ship, without some inconvenience to the service. If therefore I should use my own ~~judgement~~ discretion in little matters, and should be so unfortunate as not to meet your approbation, I pray you to be assured that it will be only from an error in judgement, and not from the want of proper care and zeal for the service. Very respectfully, I have the honor to be Sir, Your obedient Servant

Isaac Hull

LS, DNA, RG45, CL, 1813, Vol. 3, No. 34 (M125, Roll No. 28).

SECRETARY OF THE NAVY JONES TO COMMODORE WILLIAM BAINBRIDGE

Commre. William Bainbridge   Navy Depart.
Commandant of the Navy Yard,   april 28th 1813.
Charlestown, Masstts.

You cannot be more desirous than I have been to increase the dimensions of the 74s. not so much on account of defective proportions as a desire to make them superior to their Class of the Enemy's Ships. The moulded beam of our 74s. is 48 f 6 which is exactly equal to 49 f 2 inches according to the British naval rule of measurement, as they include a 4 inch plank on each side. If there is a 74 Gun ship, old or new, in Europe of 49 ft 2 inches beam and 19 ft 6 inches depth from the Ceiling, to the top of the lower Gun deck Beam, I do not know it, and will thank you to point to the authority. I know that a Ship may be destroyed as effectually by an excess of Beam, as by any other disproportion.

The formation of floating bodies, their relative dimensions and complicated connection with the multifarious objects of force, velocity capacity, strength, stability, ease and safety, requires a life of study and practice tested by the experience of those nations who have attained the highest emminence in the art, illustrated by that of our own, in which every variety of form and fancy has been indulged even to excess. It is therefore at least problematical whether we are correct in finding fault with their relative proportions of the French Ships of War, for it is notorious, that the Science and system of that Nation has led the way to all the improvements in the art of Naval Construction, and that as other Nations have adopted those principles of Construction, so have they attained that degree of excellence, for which modern naval architecture is so justly admired. Mr. Hartt[1] exhibited a draught of a large line of battle ship of his own Construction, in which the principal object appeared to be the greatest possible Stability and capacity but in my judgment carried to such an extreme, both as to extravagant breadth of Beam, and excessive fullness, of the 2nd futtock, that no arrangement of the Ballast and Stores could possibly prevent the destruction of her rigging and masts, if not of the Ship. Yet Mr. Hartt is an ingenious and excellent Builder, and his error arises from his endeavouring to encrease those two essential qualities, without sufficiently considering the effect upon the other no less important properties. My only embarrassment with respect to extending the dimensions of the 74s. arose from information and a belief, that the timber was cut very close to the moulds and bevelling, and being sufficiently acquainted with the principles and practice of Construction, to know the difficulty of converting timber under such circumstances, I despaired of making any essential alteration and having the entire responsibility, I was not disposed to hazard any thing upon speculative opinion. I however have been relieved by information derived from Mr. Joshua Humphreys, the original Constructor of our Navy, under whose direction the timber was cut, who says "The Timber being cut large, it will be sufficient, unless great alterations are made in their Shape." In conformity with this opinion and my own judgment, I have written this day to Captain Hull at Portsmouth on the subject as follows, which I will quote for your government.[2]

"I therefore desire that the length of Keel for straight rabbet may be increased from 150 to 155 feet and the moulded breadth from 48.6 to 50 feet and the original depth continued the same as it now is. The increase of length is a simple operation, but the Builder will understand me; as to the increase of breath by supposing the midship frame to be cut through the middle line and spread <u>horizontally</u> (not by running the frames up upon the ribbands) to the desired breadth, and the other frames fore and aft, in the same manner by gradually diminishing by a waterline to a point at the rabbit and the Stem and post. The Sheer to be straightened as much as possible, by raising it amidships, and dropping if forward and aft, so as to approach the line of the gun decks, as near as may be, and avoid cutting the thick stuff with the Port cills forward and aft; also the tumbling home of the topside to be diminished as much as the timber will admit. The form of body with these alterations will be very good, indeed the moulded timber will admit of but little alteration in that respect, if we were disposed to improve it. This increase of dimensions will admit of 15 ports of a side on the lower deck and 16 on the 2nd Deck. I wish the Builder to attend to these general ideas relative to the alterations, and accommodate his new draught as nearly as may be to the original <u>Body</u> and Horizontal planes. If the lines of the fore body can be swelled a little as high as the 3rd or 4th Horizontal Section, the form and qualities of the Ship will be improved; the after body is in fair proportion. With the dimensions thus extended, the Poop will be retained; you will observe that the increased length and breadth are in the precise proportions of those relative dimensions in the original draught. I shall send you a copy of the original Bill of Scantling, in detail, as given by Mr. Humphreys, the gentleman, who was then naval Constructor.[3] I am very respectfully your obt. St.

W. Jones

LB Copy, DNA, RG45, CNA, Vol. 1, pp. 400–402 (M441, Roll No. 1).

1. Jones is probably referring to Edmund Hartt, who, with his son Edward, was building the 74 at Boston until a dispute with William Bainbridge in the summer of 1813 resulted in their resignation and dismissal respectively.
2. Jones to Isaac Hull, DNA, RG45, CNA, Vol. 1, pp. 364–65 (M441, Roll No. 1).
3. The end quotation mark is missing.

SECRETARY OF THE NAVY JONES TO CAPTAIN ISAAC HULL

Isaac Hull Esqr.   Navy Depart.
Commandant of the Navy Yard.   April 30th 1813
Portsmouth N.H.

In reply to your letter of 23rd Current, I can not but express my regret that so great deficiency in the timber at Portsmouth should be discovered at this late period, particularly as the transportation by water is almost entirely cut off by the enemy. A complete frame was deposited originally at Portsmouth, and I cannot suppose much of it to have been actually consumed; if the deficiency could be ascertained as the work progresses without causing delay, it might probably be supplied from the Navy Yard at Charlestown, as two frames were deposited there.

It is very desirable not to mix the common White Oak with the Live Oak, if it can be avoided, particularly in those parts most exposed to decay. Those that may be wanting in the floor being less exposed to decay than those above, may be readily supplied with White Oak; indeed if some of the Live Oak floor timbers can be converted into such pieces as may be deficient elsewhere, they can be replaced without inconvenience by the White Oak.

In cases not of essential importance in the progress of the Ship, you will exercise your own best judgment in supplying deficiencies as they occur. I am respectfully your obedt. Servt.

W. Jones.

LB Copy, DNA, RG45, CNA, Vol. 1, p. 405 (M441, Roll No. 1).

Charleston Station—Admonitions and Complaints

By April 1813, Jones had had almost three months to study the naval strategies and financial accounts of the various stations. In a highly critical letter to Captain John H. Dent, Jones questioned his decision to deploy Nonsuch *beyond the Carolina coastal waters when Charleston citizens were demanding more naval protection. Moreover, the secretary found Dent's navy yard improvements and the establishment of a naval agent at Beaufort to be fiscally irresponsible. Dent had been so discouraged with the reductions on his station that even before receiving this reprimand he had requested transfer to a seagoing command. He further expressed his unhappiness with Jones's orders when, in a letter ordering William Joyner, Beaufort navy agent, to disband that station, he said, "I must thank you for the interest and satisfaction you have given in that Station & am sorry to say our new Secretary, has so far curtailed, the force on this Station, that I shall have little or nothing to do."[1]*

Nonsuch, *the vessel Dent had permitted to cruise to Florida, returned with a privateer prize captured off Savannah. As ordered, Dent would now keep* Nonsuch *within South Carolina's territorial waters.*

1. *Dent to Jones, 5 Apr. 1813, CL, Vol. 2, No. 132 (M125, Roll No. 27); quotation from Dent to William Joyner, 23 Apr. 1813, ScU, John H. Dent Letter Book.*

SECRETARY OF THE NAVY JONES TO CAPTAIN JOHN H. DENT

John H. Dent, Esquire   Navy Dep'tm't
Commanding Naval Officer,   April 9. 1813.
Charleston, So. Ca.

Sir,

Your three letters of the 2nd have just appeared, and I find that the Schooner *Non-such* has been dispatched upon a cruize on the coast of Florida,[1] instead of being employed for the protection of the trade & harbour of South Carolina; and this at the very moment when the City of Charleston is complaining of the want of Naval protection by the reduction of a few Barges.— The latitude of discretion you have been in the habit of exercising is altogether inadmissible, and must not be repeated. You are within Six days post of this Department, and on every occasion of importance can readily consult with, and ask instruction from, me.— The expenditure on your station has been very extravagant and must be corrected; and for every expense not authorised by law, or the sanction of this Department, previously obtained, you will be held accountable.

The Schooners *Non-such, Carolina* and *Ferret,* and the Gun Boat at Beaufort,[2] are to be employed for the protection of the coast and harbours of South Carolina, and are not to go off soundings,[3] or leave that coast, without orders from this Department. The agency you have created at Beaufort must be instantly abolished, as well as the establishment of the Navy Yard at Charleston, and all persons employed therein discharged. In short your command and authority are limited to the four vessels above mentioned, and to those in ordinary; and no other expenses or charge will be allowed. You will not undertake to appoint or employ, any person, in any capacity whatever, not specially authorised by this department. The Public property and improvements at the Navy Yard I shall direct the Navy Agent, Mr. Robertson, to dispose of, either by sale, or compromise with the proprietor of the yard, and pay the rent up to the time. You will, therefore, carry into execution, forewith, the orders I have given you on this subject. I am, respectfully, yours &ca.

W. Jones

P.S. When it may be necessary to replenish the supplies, or refit the vessels employed near Beaufort, both, or one, may repair to Charleston for that purpose.

LB Copy, DNA, RG45, SNL, Vol. 10, pp. 342–43 (M149, Roll No. 10).

1. Dent instructed Sailing Master James Mork to take *Nonsuch* out as far south as Cape Canaveral to intercept five merchant vessels reportedly sailing without an escort from Havana; see Dent to Jones, 2 Apr. 1813, DNA, RG45, CL, 1813, Vol. 2, No. 119 (M125, Roll No. 27).
2. Jones meant the other schooner, *Alligator.*
3. Off soundings means in water too deep to be fathomed by a hand sounding line.

SAILING MASTER JAMES MORK TO CAPTAIN JOHN H. DENT

Savannah   11th April 1813.

Sir

Having according to your orders finished my cruize, and on my way back on Friday the 9th inst at 5 P.M. Savannah light House in sight from the mast head, I made four sail, a head two standing for me, when near enough saw one to be a Schooner, the other a Sloop finding them to be enemies. I engaged them when near enough the Schooner Keeping long ways to Windward, and after firing one broadside into the sloop, she struck her Colours. I am happy she proved to be the privateer Sloop *Caledonia* of Nassau mounting Eight guns and forty men, I arrived safe in with her last evening. The Schooner escaped when I took possession of the cutter. She was the *Mayflower* privateer of two guns & forty men, belonging to Nassau, the other two vessels were a Spanish Schooner & a Pilot boat. The *Caledonia* besides her eight guns mounted has eleven in her hold, of different sizes, as soon as I can give up the Prisoners, I shall return to Charleston. I Have the Honor to be with great respect your obt Svt.

James Mork

The *Caledonia* has
3 Killed
7 Wounded (2 dangerously)
3 Missing

The *Nonsuch* has
Alexr. Markinson, O. S. Wounded dangerously.
William Herringbroke Seaman
                                    Wounded Slightly
Joseph Sacket   do.

LB Copy, ScU, John H. Dent Letter Book. Another copy of this letter is found in DNA, RG45, CL, Vol. 2, No. 184, enclosure (M125, Roll No. 27).

CAPTAIN JOHN H. DENT TO SECRETARY OF THE NAVY JONES

The Honble. Wm. Jones   Charleston   May 8th. 1813

Sir

Our port continues Blockaded by a sloop of war & two Brigs, they have in company the Privateer *Dash* of one gun, they have made a number of captures, principally coasters, by the prisoners landed here to day, I learn the privateer was to an anchor yesterday in Bull's Bay, and made some captures inland, if the Blockading Squadron should leave the coast, I shall direct the *Nonsuch* to look into the different inlets, and endeavour to capture the privateer, I regret I have not the use of two Barges, to take advantage of vessels of that class that will occasionally infest those exposed rivers & particularly Bulls Bay when all the trade from the North pass immediately in view, the Boats belonging to the Schooners are too small to attempt any expedition—[1] I have the honor to be very respectfully yr. obd. Servt.

                                                    J H Dent

ALS, DNA, RG45, CL, 1813, Vol. 3, No. 105 (M125, Roll No. 28).

1. Jones replied that Dent must expect the enemy to visit all U.S. ports and therefore must make do with the vessels he had; see Jones to Dent, 14 May 1813, ScU, John H. Dent Letter Book or DNA, RG45, SNL, Vol. 10, p. 415 (M149, Roll No. 10).

Chesapeake's Cruise Report

United States *and* Argus, *under squadron commodore Stephen Decatur, left Boston in October 1812, but the third ship in the group,* Chesapeake, *under Captain Samuel Evans,*[1] *was still refitting and did not sail until 17 December. Evans headed for his designated cruising ground near the equator between 24° and 30° west longitude. By mid-January* Chesapeake *captured two British merchant ships that had left their convoy and proceeded alone to South America. Evans decided to remain in his cruising area instead of venturing out after the rest of this convoy, but after taking only one vessel during a three-week span in February, he decided to leave these barren waters for Surinam. Two weeks there proved fruitless as well. Turning northward to Barbados and running a Boston-bound course parallel to the east coast of America proved more successful.*

Returning to a Navy Department under new leadership, Evans soon learned that Secretary Jones expected him to refit as expeditiously and economically as possible for another independent cruise. Evans was no doubt tired after sailing for almost four months; a recurring problem with his left eye from an old wound spurred him to request shore duty.[2] The resignation from the navy of the commandant of the New York Navy Yard, Charles Ludlow, and Evans's decision to forego another cruise created employment problems and opportunities. The command of the New York Navy Yard finally devolved on Evans, and James Lawrence was assigned Chesapeake.

1. *Samuel Evans's service in the navy dated from 1798. His past assignments included commanding* Nautilus, Siren, Argus, John Adams, *and the gunboat flotilla at Baltimore, as well as being a naval inspector proving guns and shot. Before taking charge of* Chesapeake *in August 1812, Evans commanded the Gosport Navy Yard.*

2. *Evans to Jones, 30 Apr. 1813, DNA, RG45, CL, 1813, Vol. 3, No. 70 (M125, Roll No. 28).*

Captain Samuel Evans to Commodore Stephen Decatur

(Copy)   U.S. Frigate *Chesapeake*
                                                                        Boston   April 10th 1813

Sir,

I avail myself of the termination of the *Chesapeakes* Cruize which has ended by her arrival in this Port, to inform you of the principal transactions thereof. I believe it is known to you that we Sail'd from Boston on the 17th December last— On the 31st at 3 P M. We discover'd the first Sail, to which we gave chase, but night Coming on We lost Sight of her— On the first of January at half past 3 P M. being in Lat. 34° N. and Long 32° West we discover'd another Sail to which we gave Chase— At 5 Lieut Page boarded her and discover'd that She was the American Brig *Julia* of Boston from Lisbon bound to Boston— And that she was Sailing under a British License—which the Captain deliver'd to him— In consequence of this I determin'd to place her papers in the hands of a Midshipman and send him in her, to her port of destination, that she might be proceeded against if proper, but the night being now advanc'd, and the weather boisterous, I concluded to Lay by with her until morning. When at 1/2 past 8 A M—while about despatching her—Two Sails were discover'd in the Winds Eye of us—Standing directly for our weather bow— About 1/2 past 9, I discover'd by their Sails they were vessels of War, one of which appear'd to be a large Ship— Midn. Blodget and the Captain of the Brig were now despatch'd to her with direction to Steer his course by doing which he Would go large, and some Distance from them— And on the return of the Boat, I wore round and Stood under Double reef'd topsails and fore topmast Stay Sail, so as to bring them about three points on our Weather Quarter, with the double purpose of drawing them from the Brig— And by Compelling them to haul more up, to be enable'd to ascertain more Correctly the force of them— After standing some distance from the Brig I back'd the Mizen Topsail to let them approach us; but finding they bore directly up and that by remaining with it aback they would be quite Near us before we could discover their force, I fill'd it again and Stood one point higher than before. And they again haul'd up but not so that we could discover more than the round of their bows, and nearly in this position, they kept untill about 11 A M. when we lost sight of them in a heavy Squall— About this time our Fore top mast was discover'd to be Sprung and by Meridian the Sea and Wind had increase'd to that degree that it was necessary to bring the Ship to a reef'd foresail and main topsail with hous'd Top Gallant masts— At 2 P M having every thing snug and being desirous to ascertain their force so that if there was not a great disparity I might endeavour to obtain a position to bring them to Action on the Weather's moderating, I wore and Stood in the direction we had last seen them until 5 P M. When having discover'd nothing of them, I again Wore and proceeded towards our place of destination— On the 9th We made the Island of St Anthony one of the Cape De Verds— Here it may be proper to mention that our passage until the 10th of January when we were in Lat. 15°30' N. and Long. 25°11' W had been uncommonly boisterous— We had by that day lost Two topmasts And from the Day of our Sailing untill then the Gun Deck had not been dry— On the 12th at 6 A M we discover'd a Sail bearing N b E to which we gave chace, and at 10. brought her too and boarded her. She proved to be the British Ship *Volunteer* from Liverpool to Biaha [*Bahia*], one of a Convoy of 12 Sail bound to different part of South America, and the Pacific Ocean under charge of the *Cherub* Sloop from which she had parted five days previous to our falling in with her. She had on board a considerable invoice of Dry Goods and I put a Crew on board her and despatch'd her to America— The next day at 6 A M we discover'd another Sail bearing W b N. to which we gave Chase and at 11. boarded her. As she was known to be the Brig *Liverpool Hero* one of the convoy, I boarded her under English Colours, in hopes of being enabled to gain such information as would bring us in Sight of the fleet, I found that she had left them the day after the *Volunteer,* that she had but little that was valuable in her, and as her Main Mast would make us an excellent Main topmast, which we were much in want of, I determin'd to take out the Valuable part of her Cargo and Destroy her. While in the execution of this at 4 P M. another Sail was Discoverd. On seeing us she made Sail from us, and as the Wind was light and no possiblilty of coming up with her before dark— I judged it best to take what we could from the Brig While day lasted and to run part of the night to the Southd. and Westward in hopes to intercept her next day— This I did and lay by the latter part of the Night and most of next morning. When seeing nothing of her I bore up and Stood in a direction to intercept the fleet, if they had passed the inside of the Cape De Verds which from the course they were Steering when the Brig Separated from them, and the information I was enable'd to glean from the Capt. and Crew of her before I inform'd them who we were, I was Strongly impress'd with the Idea they had done but I regret to say that after pursuing this course until I arriv'd on our Cruizing ground we saw nothing of them— Perhaps Sir, the idea may suggest itself to you, that taking into Consideration the lattitude allotted in my instructions, it would have been proper for me to have pursued them further, and I will therefore give you my reasons for not doing so— As I have mention'd heretofore I boarded the Brig under English Colours. I believe the Captain had not the Smallest Suspicion of our being other than an English Frigate until I undeceived him— By different questions I learnt that there was not the smallest apprehension in the fleet of falling in with American Cruizers, between where they were and their places of Destination; and that it was very possible that they had nearly all separated, as the evening when he last saw the Commodore they were much scatter'd

some a considerable distance astern of the Brig and others as far ahead, And by
the papers I obtain'd I learnt they were bound to nearly as many ports as there
was Vessels   These Considerations operated forcibly to determine me to abide
on the ground alloted me, and I reason'd thus— It is evident that by this time
they must be Separated, and the only probable chance I can have of falling in
with any of them will be to proceed, directly, and Cruize off a Neutral harbour—by doing this I may possibly fall in with one or two that are bound to the
most northerly ports—but while I am occupied looking for those Vessels which
may be in Shore of me When I see them and escape— The chance is the others
will be safely arrived in port—besides at this period an alarming Malignant fever
had made its appearance in the Ship, Which threatn'd to be epidemical and, I
was apprehensive that by going into the Sultry lattitudes when we might Calculate
upon almost continual rain, there would be no possibility of checking it— Again;
this was only one fleet, and from one port; we were in the track they saild, both
homeward & outward— The Newspapers we had obtain'd announc'd that the
Governor General of India would sail in a few Weeks, in a Frigate for his Command— By remaining where we were, was it not possible we might be so fortunate as to intercept him? Finally taking into consideration all those circumstances
I determined to remain on our cruizing ground, be the event what it would; and I
have now to regret that I must inform you I could scarcely have made a more unhappy determination for after Cruizing there untill the 23d of February, We discover'd but one Sail which proved to be the British Brig *Earl Percy* from Bonavista
to Brazils with a Cargo of Salt; Her I manne'd and order'd in— It now remains
for me to relate to you the Transactions since we left our Cruizing ground—
From the 5th of Feby when we took the *Earl Percy* and were in the Long. of 24°.30'
W. and Lat. 2°32' N. untill the 23rd—the Weather had been such as to deprive us
of the benefit of Lunar Observations— Apprehensive that we had a Westerly Current, I had part of the time been plying to the Eastward. When on the 23d we
found ourselves by a Lunar in 30°.30' W. As we were now in my opinion to the
Westward of the General track, and it would take all the time We could allow ourselves to remain to the Southd.—to gain three or four degrees of Easting. I concluded we could do no better than abandon the ground we had been so unfortunate on— And on the 24th bore up for the Coast of Surrinam— Here we arriv'd
on the 2d March and remain'd until the 6th—without seeing any thing— When
we made Sail to the Northd, and pass'd about a Degree to the Eastd. of Barbados
and the other Caribbee Islands—untill to the Northward of them, When we
Steer'd to the Westd parrallel to the Different passages until Long 75°—when we
hauld to the Nord. & Eastd. along our coast; In this route we fell in with the following vessels which we Boarded—and we chased one Ship and one Sloop— The
former of which escap'd us in the night and the other in thick Weather. In Lat
25°.51' N. Long 66°.56' W. March 19th boarded a Spanish Schooner from Porto
Rico to Cadiz. In Lat 25°.58' N. Long 68°.15' W. March 21 boarded the Ship
Charleston & Liverpool Packet, from Cadiz to New York. In Lat 26°.20' N. Long 70°.6'
W March 23d—boarded the Cartel Schooner *Thetis*, from St. Bartholomews to
New York, out of which we obtain'd seven volunteers— On the 3d of April in Lat.
37°.51' N Long 71°.9' W boarded the Portuguese Brig *St Antonio De Invego* from
Lisbon to Wilmington (NC) on the 5th April. Lat. 40°.18' Long 68°.24' W
boarded the Ship *Virgin* from Lisbon to New York— On the 7th April Lat 41°.55'
N. Long. 68°.7' W retook the Schooner *Valerius*, in the Possession of an English
Prize master, who Stated that he cut her out of Tarpaulin Cove. On the 8th April

Lat. 42°.57' N Long 68° West boarded the Brig *Jane* of Portland for St. Bartholo-mews— I am happy to inform you that independent of the fever I have before al-luded to, the Ship has been unusually healthy for a New Crew. We have not now so many on the Sick list as we sail'd with— And owing to the judicious arrange-ments of the First Lieut Page, and the Surgeon, and the Zeal with which they were carried into execution by all the Officers, We were fortunate enough to check it in a Short time, with the loss of Seven men, who all died in from three to seven Days illness—

The Ship will require a new Main Mast, the one in being decay'd and in work-ing in yesterday a heavy flaw carried away the Main topmast by which we unfor-tunately lost three men, and Sprung the head of the Mizen Mast which I expect will have to be replac'd likewise— We have on board between forty & fifty Pris-oners. The Masters of the *Volunteer* & *Liverpool Hero* I permitted to proceed in the *Earl Percy* on parole— I am with respect Sir your Obed. Svt.

sign'd   Samuel Evans

Copy, DNA, RG45, CL, 1813, Vol. 2, No. 166, enclosure (M125, Roll No. 27). Evans for-warded to Jones this copy of the cruise report that he had sent to Decatur.

Secretary of the Navy Jones to Captain Samuel Evans

Samuel Evans, Esquire   Navy Dep'tm't.
Commdg. the U.S. Frigate, *Chesapeake,*   April 19. 1813
Boston

Sir,

I have received your letter, of the 10th instant, covering a copy of your report of the cruize of the United States Frigate *Chesapeake*, under your command, and con-gratulate you on your safe arrival in port, as your return being anticipated much solicitude had been excited for your safety, on account of the powerful force maintained by the Enemy on our coast, of which, possibly, you might not have been apprized. If, from fortuitous circumstances, your cruize has been less bril-liant than your zealous efforts merited, it has not been ineffectual, and I have the most perfect confidence that if fortune had thrown an enemy in your way worthy of a contest for glory, the commander, officers and crew of the *Chesapeake* would have rendered her name as conspicuous in the annals of fame as any of her more fortunate sisters. It is of great importance that not a moment should be lost in re-fitting the *Chesapeake* for a separate cruise, for which you will receive instructions from this Department in due time. I regret the necessity you mention for delaying your outfit for a new main mast, & perhaps, a mizen mast. The expense, though very great, (for indeed, those frequent repairs cut deep into the naval resources) is not the only evil—time is still more precious; for the effect of our limited force depends upon its constant activity and enterprize. I, therefore, trust that if it is possible to render your present masts fit for service, and avoid the ruinous delay consequent upon the procuring new masts, you will immediately repair them and prepare for sea: and I further trust that in your whole equipment the strictest economy, consistent with real utility, will be strictly observed. The last equipment of the *Chesapeake* was, in many respects, highly extravagant; particularly for the luxurious indulgence of the fancy of her commander and officers, much of which will never be allowed by this Department.

In illustration of this I refer you to the accounts signed by yourself for the splendid equipage of the cabbin and wardroom. I am very respectfully, your Ob. Servant.

W. Jones.

LB Copy, DNA, RG45, SNL, Vol. 10, pp. 356–57 (M149, Roll No. 10).

Pension Certificate

An officer, seaman, or marine who was disabled in the line of duty was entitled to receive a pension for life or during his disability. The amount of the pension depended on the nature and degree of the disability but was not to exceed one-half the person's monthly pay. Funding for these payments came from the money accrued from the sale of prizes. The government pledged to make up any deficiency in the fund and any surplus was earmarked for the further comfort of those who had served their country. A board, the Commissioners of the Navy Pension Fund, composed of the secretaries of the navy, war, and treasury, administered the fund and presented an annual report to Congress regarding its status.[1] This document is representative of pension certificates issued during the war.

1. *"An Act for the Better Government of the Navy of the United States," April 23, 1800; Statutes at Large, Vol. 2, Stat. 1, Chap. 33, Sec. 9 and 10, p. 53.*

PENSION CERTIFICATE FOR WILLIAM LONG

William Long of Wiscassett in the State of Massachusetts Late seaman on board the United States Frigate *Constitution* having been wounded in his left arm & Shoulder in the action with the British Frigate *Java* on the 29th day of December 1812 and having been disabled in the service of the United States while acting in the line of his duty, he is entitled to receive Six Dollars per month from the Commissioners of loan of the State of Massachusetts, payable half yearly on the first day of January and first day of July, in every year during his life or the continuance of such Disability to Commence the Eightenth day of march 1813.

The same will be paid to the said William Long in person or on his legal power of Attorney, but no payment will be made on a power of Attorney unless the said William Long appeared before the said Justice in the month next preceeding that in which the payment is to be made and that his disability still continued.

Given under my hand and Seal of the Navy Department the 13th day of April 1813

Registered   W. Jones
    Benja. Homman [*Homans*]
    Secretary to the board of Commissioners
    of the navy pension fund

Copy, DNA, RG45, AF4 (M625, Roll No. 4).

Secret Mission of *John Adams*

John Jacob Astor, the wealthy fur trade entrepreneur, had established a foothold in the Pacific Northwest in 1811 with his Pacific Fur Company. Citing both economic and strategic reasons, Astor persuaded the Madison administration to send an American vessel to his outpost, Fort Astoria on the Columbia River in the Oregon territory. He hoped an American presence would prevent the Northwest Company (a Montreal-based fur company) from setting up a trading post there. Secretary Jones decided to send Master Commandant William M. Crane in John Adams *on this special mission. Since secrecy was essential, Jones ordered Crane to Washington in early April to receive oral orders. Excited about finally getting a sea command, Crane spent the next two months repairing, refitting, and manning* John Adams, *which had been undergoing repairs since the war began.*[1]

1. For background on Fort Astoria and the navy, see Gough, Royal Navy, *pp. 8–28; and Bridgwater, "John Jacob Astor."*

SECRETARY OF THE NAVY JONES TO MASTER COMMANDANT WILLIAM M. CRANE

William M. Crane, Esquire,   Navy Dep'tm't.
U.S. Navy,   April 16th 1813.
Baltimore

Sir,

You will proceed immediately to New York and take the Command of the United States Ship *John Adams,* destined, by the President, for a special and confidential object, and in order to render her fit for service it will be necessary to cut down her top side, and re-convert her into an efficient Corvette, as she was previous to the last repair and outfit at Boston.

About 16 or 17 feet of the after part of the quarter deck and the top gallant forecastle will be retained, but without armament, or any thing above, other except the Crane Irons and ridge Rope. Her armament will be 20 heavy 12 pounders and four long 18's. The nature of the service requires very great attention to the equipment, Stores and provisions, with a view to the utmost possible extension of time, and of such nature and quality as will occupy the least space, be least liable to decay, and comprehend the most vegetable and antiscorbutic substances. Your hospital Stores must be laid in with great judgment, and your provisions should comprehend a large proportion of Rice, kilndried Indian Meal, Molasses, Sourcrout, essence of spruce, Cremtartar, Slops, vinegar, beans, flour packed in tight barrels, with the inside of the Staves and heads chared to a Coal, pickled Cucumbers, &c &c, and a great abundance of dried herbs, pressed into boxes, for culinary and medicinal purposes.

Of your salted provisions a large proportion should be pork, which, in some convenient part of the Ship, will not only go further, but is very convenient and economical when supplies of fish may be had. The flour of which your bread is made should not be bolted too close, and the bread should be <u>rebaked</u> before it is packed in the Rooms.

Your Military Stores must be of the best description, and put up with care. You will require a very good Armourer and a good Smith, with tools and conveniences for erecting a forge, with a supply of bar, bolt & hoop Iron.

Your Naval Stores should not only be of the best kind, but should be so apportioned as to provide for the consumption of those articles in remote situations, where commerce and the arts do not furnish the means of replenishing.

With these general views you will proceed to equip & prepare the Ship for Sea, and on your arrival at New York you will suggest to me the means which appear to you best calculated to furnish you with Officers and Crew fit for this special service, & of every thing which may expedite and facilitate the Progress of the equipment.[1] Your final instructions will be prepared in due time, with the deliberation due to the importance of the object which has been, in confidence, developed to You. I am, very respectfully, &ca.

W. Jones

LB Copy, DNA, RG45, CLS, 1813, pp. 11–13.

1. Crane's first report to Jones on the state of *John Adams* indicated his desire to improve the quality of her crew and to change her armament; see Crane to Jones, 21 Apr. 1813, DNA, RG45, MC, 1813, No. 48 (M147, Roll No. 5).

President Escapes Boston

Commodore John Rodgers spent the first quarter of 1813 refitting, manning, and provisioning President *for another cruise. There would be no squadron for him to command that year, because Jones had ordered single cruises only. The department emphasized commerce raiding over ship engagements. After spending a month in Halifax refitting, H.M.S.* Shannon, *38, commanded by Philip B. V. Broke, returned to blockading Massachusetts Bay in late March accompanied by Captain Sir Hyde Parker in H.M.S.* Tenedos, *38. Broke sent challenges to Rodgers via fishing vessels, but* President *and* Congress *slipped out of the harbor at the end of April, taking advantage of a change of wind during squally weather. For greater protection, the American captains decided to leave jointly and then depart on separate cruises.[1] Just before sailing, Rodgers sent Jones his latest cruising plans, which the secretary approved, except for sailing to the Far East, where Jones believed Rodgers would be overextending himself.[2]*

1. Padfield, Broke and *Shannon, pp. 130–37.*
2. *Jones to Rodgers, 29 Apr. 1813, DNA, RG45, CLS, 1813, p. 14.*

COMMODORE JOHN RODGERS TO SECRETARY OF THE NAVY JONES

U.S. Frigate *President*
April 22nd 1813

Sir

Owing to contrary winds I was prevented leaving Boston until this morning:— I am now preparing the Ship in the best possible manner for hard service, and shall sail upon a certainty on Sunday next if the wind will admit of my getting out.

On leaving here I intend steering for Halifax; off which after alarming and doing the Enemy all the injury in my power, I have it in contemplation to take a direction to fall in with his Store Ships &c coming from England; and after producing alarm and distraction in the neighbourhood of the Eastern part of the Grand Bank, shall shape my course for Corvo; a little to the Westward of which, and in Latitude from 37° to [?°][1] intend cruising three, or perhaps four weeks;—thence along to the Northward of the Azores off Cape St. Vincent;—thence along the Coast of Portugal and in a northerly direction to meet his Commerce going into the Channel at which point, after remaining ten or fifteen days, pass, according to circumstances, either North about round Ireland, or through St. George's Channel, and cruise some days in the vicinity of Raughlin Island and the Mull of Cantyre.[2] From this I propose steering to intercept his trade coming from and going to the Baltic, in a situation on Jutland reef; where it is probable I shall cruise until it will become necessary to replenish my water and Provisions; and which I presume I shall find no difficulty in doing in some of the Ports of Denmark.

Having made such a cruise as that which I have mentioned, and finding that hostilities are still continued, it is probable I may proceed into the China Seas, and from thence back to the United States.

You will perceive, Sir, that I have given myself a wide range, and if things turn out as I hope they will, I flatter myself that I shall be enabled on my return to give you a pleasing account of my cruise.

The *Congress* is, and will continue with me until I get clear of Boston Bay. I have the honor to be with great respect Sir Your Obdt. Servt.

Jn⁰ Rodgers

LS, DNA, RG45, CL, 1813, Vol. 3, No. 28 (M125, Roll No. 28).

1. Torn document.
2. Rathlin Island is located in the North Channel off the northeastern coast of Northern Ireland. The Mull of Cantyre or Kintyre is a cape on the southern extremity of Kintyre Peninsula off the southwestern coast of Scotland, projecting into the North Channel.

CAPTAIN THE HONORABLE THOMAS BLADEN CAPEL, R.N.,[1] TO ADMIRAL SIR JOHN B. WARREN, R.N.

H.M. Ship *La Hogue*
at Sea   11th May 1813

Sir

It is with great mortification I am to acquaint you, that since my letter of the 25th of April last, two of the Enemy's Frigates (the *President* and *Congress*) have escaped from Boston. I deeply lament the circumstance, but trust you will be satisfied that every exertion was made by the Ships under my orders to prevent the Enemy putting to Sea—indeed it is impossible for more zeal and perseverance to have been shewn by any Officer than by Captain Broke, who with the *Tenedos* has been invariably as close as possible off the Port of Boston as the circumstances of the weather would permit, but the long continued Fogs that prevail on this part of the Coast at this Season of the year give the Enemy great advantage. It appears that they put to Sea on the morning of the 30th April with the wind at S b E and from all I have been able to learn stood far to the Northward, having been seen (by a Vessel spoken by the *Emulous*) to the Northward of the Isle of Shoals they then crossed to the Southward. I have Stationed the *Shannon* and *Tenedos* between Cape Anne and Cape Cod in the Bay of Boston—the *Nymphe* between the Latd. 43° 40' Longde. 60° 01 and Latde. 42° 30' Longde. 69° 00' and occasionally communicate with the above named Frigates, while I myself with the *Curlew* Cruized in a line South from Cape Sable to St. George's Bank, and occasionally also to communicate with the Frigates, but I am sorry to say the Enemy succeeded in escaping without being discovered by any of us except the *Curlew* who had parted company.

On the 6th Inst. I spoke the English Privateer *Retaliation*, who the day previous had been boarded by the *Curlew* in Latde. 40° 16' Longde. 66° 30' Captain Head informed the Master of her that he had been Chased the day before by the Enemy's Frigates, and that the last he saw of them was Steering about S by E with the wind Easterly.

I joined the *Shannon, Tenedos* and *Nymphe* again on the 10th, of May off Cape Cod and I have the honor to transmit to you a Copy of the Log of my proceedings since the 25th of April, together with Captain Broke's for the same period, and shall forward to you by the earliest opportunity a sketch of the various positions taken by the different ships of this Squadron to intercept the Enemy— The *Shannon* and *Tenedos* has again proceeded to reconnoitre Boston.

The *Chesapeake*'s masts are all on end, but I do not apprehend she is near ready for Sea. I have the honor to be Sir your very Obt. Hble. Sert.

(Signed)   Thos. Bladen Capel   Captain

Copy, UkLPR, Adm. 1/504, pp. 171–73.

1. Thomas Bladen Capel spent all of the War of 1812 on the North American Station.

New Yorkers Provide Support for Gunboats

By April 1813, the British had begun to menace New York City in force. Jacob Lewis found himself in the unenviable position of having to placate both the economy-minded Secretary Jones and the frightened New York citizenry. Jones's gunboat reduction order was based on the premise that vessels that lacked a full complement were inefficient and should be eliminated. Distraught coastal residents, however, sought more gunboats for protection. When the British appeared off Sandy Hook in early April, Lewis called up the gunboats in ordinary. But he soon realized he lacked the sailors to man them.[1]

1. See Lewis to Jones, 11 Apr. 1813, MLR, 1813, Vol. 3, No. 10 (M124, Roll No. 55).

SECRETARY OF THE NAVY JONES TO MASTER COMMANDANT JACOB LEWIS

Jacob Lewis, Esqr.
Commanding U.S. Flotilla,
New York Harbour.

Navy Departm't,
April 23. 1813.

Sir,

A few days absence, at Baltimore, has delayed my reply to your letter of the 11th instant.

The discretion vested in you to call the Gunboats laid up in ordinary into service upon any sudden and real emergency, <u>manned with volunteers</u>, did not contemplate calling them into Service upon the mere appearance of the enemy off
the Hook; and why call them into service when you have no men to man
them?—for you are not authorized to ship a single man, nor is it intended you
shall. You appear extremely importunate to increase and extend your force and
command, but the force allotted to you must be with reference to the relative
force employed at other places, and to the general naval wants and resources, of
which you will permit this Department to be the exclusive judge. I, therefore, disapprove of your taking the Gunboats out of ordinary on the emergency you
mention, and if any expense has been incurred on that account I shall consider
it improper, and you will again replace them in ordinary, there to remain until
such an emergency as shall <u>clearly indicate</u> an immediate attack by the enemy on
the harbour of New York; when, if volunteers offer to man them, you will call
them into service, and not otherwise without orders from this Department. Till
then you will consider your command as confined to the fifteen Gunboats officered and manned as directed in my order of the 26th of February last.

As to a "Flag Ship, Hospital Ship and Store Ship", they are appendages with
which you must dispense: and, permit me to observe that whilst you keep the 15
Gun Boats in the most efficient condition, you will do it with the strictest economy and good management, otherwise the whole of them will be placed in ordinary. For, it is proper that you, and every officer in the Navy should know,
that, if the loose and extravagant expenditure which has hitherto prevailed shall
continue, the naval resources will not meet the exigencies of the service.—

If it is not convenient for the Flotilla to leave the Hook in order to replenish
the provision and water, the Navy Agent can employ a shallop, occasionally, to
convey the supplies to the Flotilla.—

I deem it proper to be thus explicit with you, and, at the same time, to express my confidence in your qualifications as a Commander, and my personal
regard and respect. I refer you to my letter of the 26th of February, the last
paragraph of which you appear not to have noticed.— The passage of the
sound being intercepted the Gunboats at Rhode Island will remain on that station.—[1] I am, respectfully &ca.

W Jones.

LB Copy, DNA, RG45, SNL, Vol. 10, pp. 367–69 (M149, Roll No. 10).

1. Jones had requested a list of the gunboats in commission and in ordinary, their condition, and
the names of their commanders and crew. In the earlier letter, Jones had ordered all the gunboats
at Newport, Rhode Island, to leave for New York; see Jones to Lewis, 26 Feb. 1813, DNA, RG45,
SNL, Vol. 10, pp. 281–83 (M149, Roll No. 10).

SECRETARY OF THE NAVY JONES TO NICHOLAS FISH [1]

Nicholas Fisk Esqr.   Navy Depart.
New York   May 15th 1813.

In the distribution of the Naval force of the U.S. with a view to active offensive
operations and the defence of our extensive waters and numerous harbours,
with the limited force and resources at the disposal of this Department, such a

disposition has been made, as to give to each according to its relative importance and local Security either natural or artificial, such proportion as appeared to comport with the obligations of the government for the general defence of all.

The increase of the force at any one point, must therefore necessarily reduce that of another or diminish the force and effect of our gallant Navy on the Ocean by employing the Seamen and resources of the Department in mere preparations for defence and arresting the progress of the efficient increase of the Naval force now in operation, the completion of which is so much to be desired.

In this view of the subject and aloof from any local influence or excitement has the force at New York been limited to fifteen Gun Boats in active Service, the residue to be kept in ordinary in a perfect state of preparation, and called into Service upon any real emergency under the command of Captain Lewis, provided Volunteers are offered to man them free of expense to the United States, and who shall be subject to the laws and regulations for the Government of the Navy of the United States while in Service. This order was given to Capt. Lewis on the 26th of Feby. last, and the supernumerary Gun Boats were laid up in ordinary accordingly; but on a late occasion and merely on the appearance of the Blockading Squadron off New York, Captain Lewis informed me that he had taken the Boats from ordinary into Service, but said not a word about men, to man them, and until the receipt of your letter I was ignorant of the proposition of the Corporation of the City, to furnish, pay, and provide for, the crews of 15 additional Boats, which I most readily assent to and authorize Captain Lewis to accept and put the additional Boats into Service whenever the Corporation shall deem it necessary. This Department will provide a Commander for each Boat and furnish the equipment and military Stores. This arrangement, I trust, under existing circumstances will be considered just and reasonable particularly when the very great proportion of the national resources employed for the defence of and expended in New York, and the utter impracticability of defending our extensive coast on all points against the Superior force of an enemy, who can at pleasure concentrate the whole of that force upon any one point, is duly appreciated. I am very respectfully Sir your obedt. Servt.

W. Jones.

LB Copy, DNA, RG45, MLS, Vol. 11, pp. 277–78 (M209, Roll No. 4). Jones's clerk misspelled Fish's name.

1. Nicholas Fish, a retired lawyer, was a Federalist alderman on the New York City Common Council and the chairman of its Committee of Defense during the War of 1812.

MASTER COMMANDANT JACOB LEWIS TO SECRETARY OF THE NAVY JONES

Honble. William Jones

Sir

After the severe and unmerited reprimand contained in your letter of 23d of last month, I had concluded that for some cause or other to me <u>unknown</u>, a Total silence on my part (in future) would be most desireable to you I therefore had determined not to trouble you or cause your displeasure either with or by suggestions or questions but confine my self to formal reports such as my duty made necessary, and the service required—

Yours of the 23d. Ulto. contains another censure equally unmerited, charging me with omission, immediately on receiving it, I left the Hook & waited on the Corporation, with a view of acting on the arrangements gone into between you & them instantly, but to my great disapointment was inform'd by that honorable body that you had misconceived their intentions (which were) to advance the pay for the officers and Crews of fifteen Gun boats, that it was expected the Goverment would furnish rations, that it ought not to be expected by the Govt. that men would volunteer & find themselves &c and observed to me that nothing could be done at <u>present</u> to comport with my instructions—

Consequently my visit hither has proved abortive immediately after closing this I shall again return to my position at Sandy Hook and there await my destiny—where the Enemy are constantly menacing—and <u>where</u> he I believe meditates an attack—and <u>where</u> most Military men believe he will be <u>successful</u>, to the great injury of the Country and the administration, unless <u>Major Means, are used instead of the existing Minor</u> I would undertake to give you a correct statement of the situation of that very Important post, If I did not fear that it would be call'd <u>super arrogance</u>—or construed into <u>Egotism</u>—thereby <u>again</u> incur your displeasure.

I will proceed to offer a few remarks In vindication of my Conduct, for which I have been so severely reprimanded, with a hope that the prejudice you appear to have imbibed against me, (from false representations I trust) will be somewhat allay'd if not Totally <u>disputed</u>, firstly—with respect to calling the Vessels again into actual servise which had been placed in ordinary—I have the honor to observe, that they were not moved, nor did any expence occur, in consequence   It was done in consequence of the Enemys menacing Sandy Hook when a number of men were at work erecting a Battery totally unprotected.

The universal cry of the City was, the Enemy are at the Hook—all the works will be destroy'd & all the Mechanicks & others will be made prisoners, This by every person with whom I consulted from the Commander in Chief down, was considered a <u>Case of Emergency</u> & I confess I was of the same opinion—that it was one in a <u>superlative degree</u>, I have cause however to regret that I so construed it; my humble apology is, that the term being in some measure indefinite admits of different interpretations, I have great pleasure in assuring you that no Ill come from it (on the contrary) it served to prove incontrovertably that volunteers can not be depended on, altho invited not one appeared, and it was on this occasion that the Corporation were induced to take into Consideration, the necessity of coming forward & furnishing the means to <u>produce Volunteers</u>—believing as I did the case an imergent one,—

<u>Secondly</u>—as to the letter you allude to dated 26 feby—I have to assure you no such letter has been recd. by me,[1]

<u>Thirdly</u>—with respect to Econimy, be assured Sir, that system enters into all my plans and regulations—but in this as well in other indefinite things, I may err in judging as to what constitutes, or may be consider'd Econimy—in my particular Case my Idea is—to render the Flotilla sufficiently Strong & efficient for the purpose it is intended without useless expense or Extravagance is true Economy—<u>thus far would I go & no farther</u> with deference I herewith hand you a scetch of my proceedings—since I had the honor to command the Flotilla, for either your approbation, or disapprobation on taking Command—inquired into the Cause

of one of greatest evils which appeared to exist which was desertion, I found it and applied the remedy— Since which no desertions have taken place, I have obliged every officer in the Flotilla to repair at <u>his own expense</u>, all damages done, by carelessness or neglect, even the loss of masts Cable & anchors this regulation has prevented the repeated accidents formally happen'd,—

And for extravagance or useless expense, I have invariably either furlough'd or discharged the officer—

I have returned the hammocks and built berths—because the former cost a great deal more, & soon ware out—the latter will last as long as the Boat and are never missing— I have changed several of the Circles to the Guns—because they were mounted upon a false principle therefore in a great measure useless—

I have alter'd one of the double Boats—because she could not be made to ware or Stay (in fact) as she was could not be made useful—and having two 32 lb. and having room for a furnace for heating shot, I deemed it proper to render her efficient if possible, <u>I have compleatly Succeeded</u>—she has a furnace, and now sails faster than any thing in the Flotilla— I have established at Spermecetee Cove at the Hook, with the expense of a few Refuse boards a forge, & with the smiths found on board the Flotilla do all its iron work— I have also a Carpenters Shed and do all that work without expense to the Govt. other than the cost of the materials—

and from imperious necessity I am now about erecting at the same place a temporary Hospital—for the Sick, which will Cost the U.S. five hundred board & 100 lb. nails I deem'd it absolutely inhumane to be cruizing about, with four or five sick person on Board a Gun Boat, groaning—& supplicating to be put on Shore some were, that they may receive comfort & necessary aid—

As to the privations which the Flotilla suffer from being obliged to keep their stations at the hook, I will omit comment—

I am willing to believe that its owing to the alternate manner in which the Command of the Navy Yard has devolved—<u>for Example</u>

From Chauncey to Ludlow—
From Ludlow to Hull—
From Hull back to Ludlow—
From Ludlow to Crane—
From Crane to Ludlow—
From Ludlow to Lawrence—

From Lawrence—to the Deputy Store Keeper &c—these unavoidable Changes must naturally produce more or less inconvenience to the Service I am willing to bear my proportion without a murmer—excuse this hasty & incoherent Scrawl and allow me to assure Sir, that my servises are devoted to my Country—that my attachment <u>is now as it ever has been</u>, indelible, for my Government and Mr. Madisons Administration. I live with the fond hope to deserve well of my Country—and that I shall retain <u>undiminished</u> the Consideration & friendship with which I long have been honor'd by the President of the U. States—as well as the Secretaries of State & War, and I assure you Sir it shall be study if <u>possible</u> to deserve your approbation instead of concur with respt. to the proposals from the Corporation they were forwarded to you as soon after being proposed to me as <u>possible</u>—it was my wish that the proposition should be made direct to you as the proper person to answer it and that it would save time to do so—which I <u>consider'd all important</u>— I have the honor to be with high consr. & respt. yr. faithful Humle. St.

J Lewis

New York   May 23d 1813

ALS, DNA, RG45, MLR, 1813, Vol. 3, No. 123 (M124, Roll No. 55). See also No. 124 for note from Nicholas Fish stating that the New York City Common Council had agreed to help pay expenses for defense.

1. In his 11 April letter to Jones, Lewis had mentioned receiving Jones's instructions authorizing him to bring gunboats into service in case of an emergency. Lewis may therefore have received the February gunboat reduction order, but conveniently forgotten it; see 11 Apr. 1813, MLR, 1813, Vol. 3, No. 10 (M124, Roll No. 55).

Fulton's Ordnance Experiments

The increase in British naval operations in 1813 prompted proposals to counter enemy attacks. Congress on 3 March 1813 mandated a monetary incentive by authorizing payment to any person who destroyed a British ship equal to one half the value of that ship.[1] In enlisting Jones's support for torpedo experiments, Robert Fulton asserted his view that "every Physical operation which is not contrary or at Varience with the laws of nature is practicable for man to perform; this admitted and torpedoes with practice must succeed, for there is no Physical impossibility to prevent it."[2] Fulton asked Jones in April to loan him a fire ship at New York so he could gain experience in using torpedoes at the ends of spars. By June Jacob Lewis reported Fulton's success in using columbiads under water.

1. Statutes at Large, Vol. 2, Stat. 2, Chap. 47, p. 816.
2. Fulton to Jones, DNA, RG45, MLR, 1813, Vol. 3, No. 18 (M124, Roll No. 55). For further documentation on Fulton, see pp. 210–12, 354–56.

Robert Fulton to Secretary of the Navy Jones

New York   April 27th 1813.

Sir

I am anxious to make some interesting experiment on the practice of Torpedoes and for that purpose require a Vessel and some hands which is too expensive for my private purse. You have here several fire Ships which are idle and the Gun boats have many men which do little. Commodore Lewis and I will go into the experiments if you will have the goodness to order that we may take one of the best of the fire Ships for that purpose and some of the Gun boat men.[1] it is not intended to blow her up or in any way injure her but to use her for experience on the mode of attacking with Torpedoes in the end of Spars as mentioned in one of my letters to you for which purpose She will be anchored with the Gun boats to have the men handy and near their permanent duty. this will be gaining useful experiences without any expence to Government. Your granting this request by return of post will promote a useful art and much oblige   your most obedient

Robert Fulton

Robert Fulton

ALS, DNA, RG45, MLR, 1813, Vol. 3, No. 58 (M124, Roll No. 55).

1. When Fulton did not get a prompt response from Jones, he wrote to him again on 8 May. Jones ordered Jacob Lewis to assist Fulton by providing one fire vessel and some men but insisted that the navy "incur no expense whatever on account of these experiments." See Fulton to Jones, 8 May 1813, DNA, RG45, MLR, 1813, Vol. 3, No. 82 (M124, Roll No. 55) and Jones to Lewis, 16 May 1813, DNA, RG45, SNL, Vol. 10, p. 420 (M149, Roll No. 10).

MASTER COMMANDANT JACOB LEWIS TO SECRETARY OF THE NAVY JONES

Sir

Your letter which you did me the honor to write to me of the 11th Ulto— reached me at Sandy Hook, Its <u>contents was as balm to a wound</u>—the *Argus* left Sandy Hook at 5 Ock Friday Eve—with a prosperous breese,

The Port remains unblockaded, I have for several days been attending to Experiments such as firing one hundred pound Columbiad—five feet under water, The first experiment was made by immersing a six pounder four feet below the Surfice, placing a target 10 feet distance through which the ball pass'd—

The question which then suggested itself was, whether—the Gun would not burst if the Muzzle of the Gun was immersed and the other part remain out of water, (accordingly) a hundred pounder was placed In a box with the Muzzle through its side the water prevented from entering. Into the box, the Gun charged with Ten pounds of powder, and a ball—the box sunk in five feet of water—a Target placed at 25 feet distance under water, and the Peace discharged, without Injury—the Ball entered a very Considerable distance into the Target, which was of three feet thickness.

It is therefore ascertained that Cannon can be Exploded under water with as much Certainty as above, it remains to be known how far ~~the ball~~ from the Ship the ball can be drove through the bottom of a Ship—

I am of opinion that a 42 p—will pass through the bottom of <u>any Vessel</u> at twenty feet distance, this Mr. Fulton will prove In a few days—if he should be successful I think submarine Batteries can be turned to a good Accot.— with the highest Consn. & Respect I am yr very Obt Servt.

J Lewis
Comg. U.S. Flotilla
New York   20th June 1813

ALS, DNA, RG45, MLR, 1813, Vol. 4, No. 67 (M124, Roll No. 56).

MASTER COMMANDANT JACOB LEWIS TO SECRETARY OF THE NAVY JONES

Sir

We have again made an experiment with a 100 lb. Columbiad under water, at a Target six feet distance—the Ball pass'd through three feet of solid oak— we had fired a twenty four pounder, with 10 lb. of powder, the same quantity which was given to the Columbiad and were astonished to find it did not pirce the Target farther than the Columbiad did—it proves that the momentum of weight is greater under water in proportion than in the air—

Previous to the last experiment it was believed that the 24 lb. having much less water & wood to displace & being impell'd by the same ignited force, would have pass'd infinitely farther through the Target than the Columbiad— by Experiments Columbiads are preferable to any other Calibre for submarine Batteries—with which together Torpedoes—and Torpedo locks fire Ships & <u>Boats enough</u> to keep the Enimies Boats in—there largest Ships can be driven out of our rivers— I have the honor to be with the highest Resp. Yr. obt. St.

J Lewis
Comg. U.S. Flotilla
N Yk.   June 28th 1813

ALS, DNA, RG45, MLR, 1813, Vol. 4, No. 106 (M124, Roll No. 56).

British Naval Activity off Block Island

By April 1813, the British were tightening their grip around Long Island Sound. Captain Sir Thomas Masterman Hardy[1] commanded a squadron off Block Island, harassing the coastal trade and privateers. H.M. frigate Orpheus, *one of the ships in his squadron, often sent her smaller boats after enemy vessels when her size prevented effective pursuit herself. In this way, the British were able to maintain a strong blockade.*

1. *Sir Thomas Masterman Hardy, R.N., Vice Admiral Horatio Nelson's flag-captain at Trafalgar, was appointed to* Ramillies *in August 1812.*

CAPTAIN HUGH PIGOT, R.N.,[1] TO CAPTAIN SIR THOMAS M. HARDY, R.N.

Copy   His Majestys Ship *Orpheus*
Off Block Island
April 29th 1813.

Sir

At daylight yesterday morning we chased a ship steering for Rhode Island and there being little wind I sent a Boat armed with Mr. Dance (Acting Lieutenant), to cut her off, this service he effectually performed in a most gallant and judicious Manner— observing her great superiority of force he waited untill it was time she tacked off shore and then made an attempt to board under a very heavy fire from four long six pounders and repeated volleys of Musketry and by thus engaging the attention of her Crew she ran upon the Rocks about three Miles up the West River[2] when he returned on board having a few Men only scratched with sluggs. We soon after Anchored within gunshot and observing her Crew land with their Musquets and joined by a strong party on shore, I sent Lieutenant Collins in the Launch with her Cannonade to keep them in check, while Mr Dance with two Boats boarded the ship and turned her Guns upon the Enemy who had kept up a brisk fire from behind the Rocks and Stone Walls.

Lieutt. Collins having advanced with most determined bravery within a few yards of the shore the Enemy instantly directed the whole of their fire at his Boat, but were soon dispersed.

The only person hurt on this occasion was that excellent and brave Officer Lieutt. Collins who received a shot in his Body and one through his right Arm of which I sincerely lament to add he survived but twenty four hours.

Mr. Dance now finding the ship bulged [*bilged*] and with a few Casks of Brandy only on board set her on fire. By the papers found on board I learn she was the *Wampoc* American letter of Marque from L'Orient with eight Guns mounted, and I judge from there being fresh beef on board she had touched at Nantucket or Marthas vineyard and landed the principal part of her Cargo.

Permit me Sir to request you will acquaint the Commander in Chief with the highly praiseworthy conduct of Acting Lieutenant Dance whom I truly wish may be confirmed in his appointment to this ship. I have the honor to remain Sir your most obedient & very Humble Servant

H. Pigot   Captain

To: Captain Sir Thos. Hardy   Bart.
    Senior Officer   Off Block Island

Copy, UkLPR, Adm. 1/503, pp. 629–31.

1. Hugh Pigot, a captain in the Royal Navy since 1804, followed in the naval footsteps of his captain father and admiral grandfather.
2. The west passage of Narragansett Bay.

Delaware Flotilla

Commodore Alexander Murray commanded the Delaware flotilla during an interim period in May 1813, after Master Commandant James Biddle departed for Hornet *and before Lieutenant Samuel Angus took charge later that month. Meanwhile, two citizens' groups, the Committee for the Defense of Wilmington, Delaware, and the Committee for the Defense of the Delaware, were bombarding Jones with requests for increases in naval assistance. Jones reproved Manuel Eyre, his personal friend and member of the latter committee, for wanting to divert department funding from offensive to defensive operations, but eventually the secretary accepted the citizens' proffer of help. Jones's initial response to Eyre documents the secretary's strategic planning for the limited forces available to him.*

Lieutenant Angus took command of the flotilla in May and, after reconnoitering the Delaware River, reported his great satisfaction with the handling of the block sloops. Obviously concerned with the American gunboats, Admiral Sir John B. Warren ordered Captain Hassard Stackpoole to use rowboats to attack the gunboats and to take care in boarding them.

MANUEL EYRE TO SECRETARY OF THE NAVY JONES

Philada.   May 9th. 1813

My Dear Sir

Ever since my return from Washington I have been endeavouring to rouse the feelings & patriotism of our citizens to aid the General Government in the defence of the Bay & River Delaware. After many unsuccessful attempts, I think this desirable object is accomplished. Enclosed you have the proceedings of a general meeting of our Citizens at the Coffee house on 6th inst. when Charles Biddle[1] was chairman and John Sergeant secretary. Altho patriotism actuated many yet the Majority are governed by fear or self interest. The City Councils will I believe appropriate thirty thousand Dollars towards this defence and from individual subscription we shall perhaps raise as much more, these funds will in part if not altogether be put at the disposition of the Managing Committee. It is most probable that this Committee will send a deputation to Washington to call on the General Government for further aid. I have conversed with persons who were some time on board the *Poictiers* and there is every reason to believe an attempt will be made in less than three or four weeks (their reinforcement may arrive) to destroy New Castle & perhaps Wilmington—[2] The quantity of powder and military stores in the United States arsenal and the State Magazine in the Vicinity of this city makes it very probable that some attempt may be made to destroy them both but my opinion is that more danger is to be apprehended from incendiaries lurking in & about our City than from any attempt of the open enemy. Most of the Englishmen have been suffered to return to this City or its vicinity and some of them the most worthless characters. At a crisis like the present the public safety and the safety of so much public property demands in my opinion an immeadiate order from the General Government for every English subject without distinction to remove immeadiately at least from fifty to sixty miles into the interior of the country.

The Committee of Management have it in contemplation and no doubt will build six or eight launches or Row Galleys to be partially manned at the expense of the city unless the General Government will man them— The proposed plan for the defence of the Bay & River by the Committee is to call upon the General Government to put all the Gun boats here say 19 in immeadiate commission these with the two Sloops to be manned at the expense of Government. The Government to be at no greater expense than the usual allowance to seamen &ca. in the United States service any additional bounty and other expences in obtaining the men will be paid by the Committee. The Committee propose to build six or eight launches or Row Galleys in aid of the Gun boats from 40 to 70 feet long which shall be placed under the officers of the General Government and be manned by the Government if it deems proper if not, the Committee will partially mann them & place them under the controul of the United States officers and when required can be manned by volunteers or from the Gun boats for any particular emergency. The Committee also propose to procure a ship or vessel as a store ship for the Gun boats to be always anchored in the rear of the flotilla and I think they would also furnish a very fast sailing schooner as a tender on the flotilla to be manned in the same manner as the gun boats. These are the General out lines of the plan to be proposed by the Committee and if you think well of them and will write me immediately it may be the means of preventing a Committee going down to Washington to call on the General Government, as I know the constant calls and importunities upon the heads of the departments I wish to save you all the trouble in my power— I think there is nothing in this plan but what the Government will and ought to grant.

On a consultation with Genl. Bloomfield it appears a verry desirable object with him either to sink a hulk or to have one ready to sink in the Channel back of Fort Miflin to prevent any attack in the rear— There are other objects which the Committee will direct and will be attended with considerable expence & will be paid by the Committee but shall not trouble you with them.

I shall feel gratified if by return of post you would inform me that you agree to put in commission immediately the whole 19 Gun boats & the two shallops and mann the Row Galleys & a fast sailing schooner at the expence of Government. The Committee to pay every expence of extra bounty &ca to procure the men but the Government to furnish all the cannon firearms munitions of war & rations—

If you put the boats all in commission and appoint sailing masters I mention the names of a number of Masters of vessels in addition to those you had when I last saw you, who I believe would accept of the command. Norris Hanley, Capt. Hughes, Isaac Silliman, Capt. Donaldson, Capt. Sheed, James McCullough (if exchanged) James Boviar, James Ramage Daniel McPherson, Capt. Myrrick, William Waters, & perhaps Patrick Hays & Thos. Ruby— The Characters of nearly all these you know perhaps as well as I do and will select such as you deem most proper.

Permit me to suggest an idea that forcibly presses on my mind that you would appoint one of the Captains in the Navy now remaining at home to take command (if only for a short time) of this flotilla in the Delaware, such as Capt. Lawrence or any other whose popularity would give such spirit to the enterprize as to accomplish some thing honorable to our country and be the means of strengthening the friends of the administration here. Altho C Biddle and others are friendly to Murray yet the Committee will do every thing in their power both with the funds at their disposal as well as their personal attention to promote so desireable an object. If you will express your opinion as to the best mode of constructing these Row Galley or any other part of this defence it will be highly acceptable. There is a report of the capture of the Brig *Lightning* in the Bay of Biscay about the first of April altho it is not certain yet the report bears every appearance of being true it was just about the time she must have been in the Bay. It is highly gratifying to me that you are placed in such a situation as not to incur any loss by the capture and all the accounts can now soon be closed—[3]

I hope Mrs. Jones with her two nieces arrived in safety at Washington are pleased with it and enjoy good health. Mrs. Eyre & my respects to Mrs. Jones and accept my sincere regard. ever truly yours

Manuel Eyre

ALS, PHi, U. C. Smith Collection, Papers of William Jones.

1. Eyre is referring to Master Commandant James Biddle's father.
2. On 29 May, boats from *Statira*, *Spartan*, and *Martin* under the orders of Commander Humphry Fleming Senhouse of H.M. Sloop *Martin* moved up and swept the Delaware and its creeks, returning on the 31st after taking and destroying some twenty American vessels; see Hassard Stackpoole to George Cockburn, 8 June 1813, UkLPR, Adm. 1/506, pp. 147–50.
3. Jones was a part owner of the brig *Lightning*.

SECRETARY OF THE NAVY JONES TO MANUEL EYRE

<u>Private</u>   Washington   12 May 1813

My dear Sir

I have received your favor of the 9th. and the friendship that exists between us will I trust tolerate a free and candid reply. Indeed the subject of your letter

is altogether of a public nature involving the plans and operations of the Department over which I preside and may be considered as addressed officially
though directed privately. I shall follow your example in the form of a private
letter but as I never write in private that of which I ought to deprecate the pub-
licity you are at liberty to make use of it as you think proper by way of information to the Committee of which you are a member. The laudable zeal displayed
in the proceedings of the meeting the copy of which you enclosed, does credit
to our City and proves that in the event of real danger the spirit and resources
of the people will be equal to the crisis, but upon a dispassionate view of the
force and probable designs of the enemy the alarm appears to transcend the
real cause of apprehension. My public duty having in a particular called my attention and observation to the movements of the enemy, the result of my reflec-
tions may not be unacceptable to you. When the hostile squadron first entered
the Chesapeake in force I expected a thousand men would have been landed
and by a forced march from Lynnhaven Bay have destroyed Norfolk before a
force could have been collected to repel them but after 48 hours delay with a
fair opportunity to land I was satisfied they did not mean to attempt it in that
way. The Naval force collected there at one time was very formidable and had
every appearance of a determination to force the passage of the narrows.

The destruction of the *Constellation,* the Navy Yard Gun Boats and shipping
and property at Norfolk was a very strong temptation. Captain Stewart however
by a single movement with seven Gun Boats & two small tenders compelled them
to slip and run from the station they had taken, and they never again seriously
menaced the place, but their object was in part accomplished, for they had
caused a very considerable concentration of the public force and a great expense in preparation for defence. They then moved off and proceeded to menace Baltimore in the same way exciting a great alarm and expense and then
moved down to Annapolis in the same attitude and producing the same effect.
They have finally abandoned that and gone down the Bay perhaps to Sea to
watch our squadron or it may be a part of them to the Delaware to play off the
same game there with the same effect. Their plan of operation appears to me
clearly to be that of a rigorous Blockade and harassing exciting and depredating
with the hope of diverting our attention from the ocean and the Lakes by employing our troops and our Seamen in the preparation for the defence of our
Sea port towns and innumerable Bays harbours rivers and creeks, and surely if
they could reduce us to act on the defensive only while they vary the scene of action by their superior force and keep up the excitement and alarm and constant
preparation from North to South their object would be gained, for it is idle to
suppose we can be prepared at all points to meet the concentrated force of the
enemy, and also act with vigor and effect upon the Ocean and the Lakes.

From what has passed I am warranted in concluding that they do not mean to
hazard the safety of their ships or the loss of masts, in intricate and narrow
channels in the face of even a very moderate force.

As to the burning of French town, Havre de Grace Hughs's furnace Geo,town
cross roads and Frederick there was nothing to oppose them but poor ONeill at
Havre, and in the Chesapeake they are in a spacious open Bay of safe and easy
navigation free from shoals and shallow flats and with scarcely any tide. It is remarkable that ever since the Blockade they have carefully avoided entering our
narrow rivers and have never attempted any thing by Land where they would
not have been beaten by two hundred men. But it appears they annoy our Bay

trade and thereby produce great loss and inconvenience to our Cities. This in the event of War with Britain must have been expected by every rational man for it is the natural result of our extensive and navigable waters and their great naval superiority.

Our only plan is to keep up a reasonable force at the several principal points according to the relative importance and exposure of each, without impairing our active operations against the enemy and with a constant view to the <u>attainable</u> means and resources of the Government and to the continuance of the War. If we act like an unskillful combatant urged by his fears or his passions to exhaust his strength in a furious onset we may expect to share his fate.

With this view of the subject who is to decide upon the nature extent and distribution of the public force of the United States?—those immediately interested in local safety and under the influence of that feeling—or the constituted authorities who have the whole subject before them and whose duty it is to watch over and apply the public force for the common defence of all?

I know you too well to doubt your answer. The present distribution of the Naval force of the U.S. for harbour defence contemplates ten Gun Boats and two Block Sloops with two long 18s ~~and~~ two 24 pound carronades and 50 men in each.

This force I did and still do think if well managed, competent not only to the complete defence and protection of the Delaware river and Bay but to the severe annoyance of the enemy. I therefore deem it necessary to inform you explicitly, that the <u>Naval force and expenditure</u> on the Delaware cannot under existing circumstances be increased beyond what I have thus stated— Indeed it would be an unjust diversion of the resources of the Navy Department from places less protected than the Delaware and whose inhabitants are not less urgent and certainly with not less reason.

You will recollect that the force above mentioned is not more than half manned—that one rendezvous is open and every effort employed to procure men for the special service of the Delaware, and that the competition for men which you contemplate may have the effect of closing our rendezvous and enhancing the difficulty and expense of procuring men for other branches of the public for it is in vain that we increase our Navy if our physical means of employing them shall be absorbed in preparations for mere local defence.

I do not approve of Barges or launches for harbour defence or for convoy; they require a vast number of men and are entirely exposed which we ought to avoid. I would not give one of the Block Sloops with 50 men for five times their number in launches. Whom are you to attack with launches? not the enemys ships, but his launches and tenders full of men, and this may prove an unprofitable work of slaughter. The Gun Boats and <u>Sloops particularly</u> form strong convoys and may by taking favorable positions may cut the enemys ships to pieces. I am fearful that in manning your Barges and launches you will unman our Gun Boats and Sloops and I must be permitted to think that the public good would not be promoted by that effect. These ideas you may make known to the committee and I hope they will be received in the spirit in which they are written. My predilections and attachments secure me from the suspicion of a want of disposition to defend my native city and stream. I am very sincerely and respectfully your friend[1]

W Jones

ALS, MiU–C, War of 1812 Papers.

1. Two weeks later Jones did accept the launches offered by the Committee for the Defense of the Delaware and attached them to the flotilla. He directed Murray to officer and man them from the flotilla when necessary for selected service. See Jones to Murray, 27 May 1813, DNA, RG45, SNL, Vol. 10, p. 443 (M149, Roll No. 10).

LIEUTENANT SAMUEL ANGUS TO SECRETARY OF THE NAVY JONES

Private   U.S. Flotilla on the Delaware
                                                        off Egg Island—Sloop
                                                    Buffalo   June 9th 1813

Sir

I rec'd your polite and friendly letter dated April 26 mark'd <u>private</u> which from the circuitous rout it had did not come to hand before   When I rec'd it from the New Castle post office the Seale was broke

I greatly apreciate your good advice and shall endeavor always to merit the character as an officer you say I possess— It is a source of much regret to me that my promotion has been hindred by an error of judgment and that an officer younger than myself in <u>commission</u> (Captn. Biddle) should have been promoted over my head although I must confess at the same time that he merits any thing the goverment can bestow— I hope sir as the dificulty between Comr. Chauncey and myself is now settled to your satisfaction it may not prove a future hindrance to my promotion—[1] the Command you have assign'd me on the Delaware as you justly observe is an important one and I am in hopes before long and when we get our flotilla properly man'd to be a considerable annoyance to the british— my reason for leaving New Castle was to afford the river navigation protection which I hope you will approve off our Night rendezvous since leaving New Castle has been Cohanzy Creek, I have stood down some distance below the Flotilla and can see the british squadron from the deck consiting off 2 frigate the *Spartan* & *Statira* ~~and~~ *Martin* sloop and 8 or 9 sail of shallop and two masted boats (which from Information recd. by the pilot of the Spanish ship *Minerva* which the british Squadron have turn'd back (having taken out their provision and water consiting 9 casks of water and 4 lbs. of provision) having informed him that they will suffer no vessel to go out ~~as the~~ the Delaware being blockaded, I shall for the future suffer no spanish or portugees vessel to go down without a positive order from you or Comr. Murray) which they are now mounting Guns on and observe when they return reinforcement they intend to pay New Castle a visit—

The block sloops are far superior to what could have possibly been expected carrying their Guns well and being remarkably stiff their is but one improvement that possibly could be made to them—the <u>Iron</u> bands or bars on the gratings make it dificult to ship and unship them if Sir you would grant me permission to take the Iron off the grating and raise the midship combings about 6 Inches above the others so that loop holes might be cut through them for musket or the long pike it would make them utterly impregniable—they sail far superior to the Gun boat and equal to almost any of the finest light (without load) shallops—as the barges are to be attatch'd to the flotilla (from what Comdr. Murray informs me) would it not sir be well to let the Gun boat carry forty and the block sloops 60 men (the Sailors are highly pleased with the block sloops having excellent and roomy accommodation)—and by that means we shall be able to man the barges from the flotilla and still have sufficient men on board for mannagin the Guns and five aditional Lieuts. or masters to officer them. I left Phila. on the 29 of May and have been cruizing up and down the bay ever since, I shall leave Chanzy [*Cohansey*] for New Castle to morrow or the next day as they provissions will then be on out

the flotilla consists of 7 Gun boat from 8 to 10 men short and the *Buffalo* and *Camble* [*Camel*] blocksloops fully mand— In hopes Sir you will grant my requests and suffer me to put two 18 lb carrondaides on the *Buffalo* as she will carry them perfectly well the Iron on her grateing weing nearly as much as two 18 lbs. carron aides would   I have the honor to subscribe my self very respecty. your much oblig'd and most obt. Sert.

Saml. Angus
Lt. Comg. U.S. D.F.

ALS, DNA, RG45, BC, 1813, Vol. 2, No. 122 (M148, Roll No. 11).

1. For information on the Chauncey-Angus feud, see Dudley, *Naval War of 1812*, Vol. 1, pp. 371–74, and, Vol. 2, pp. 438–39.

ADMIRAL SIR JOHN B. WARREN, R.N., TO
CAPTAIN HASSARD STACKPOOLE, R.N.

Copy   *San Domingo*, Hampton
Roads   Chesapeake   June 28th 1813

Sir,

I have to acknowledge the receipt of your Letter of the 19th Instant communicating the movements of the Enemy's Gun Boats in the Delaware, I recommend to you not to permit any of the vessels under your Orders to be drawn among the Shoals in situations where they cannot close with the Enemy, but rather if any attack is made upon the Gun Boats, that it should be with rowing Boats, and that in boarding the Enemy care should be taken that it is done by entering at the Bow or Stern as many of them have Nettings and a mode of tieing up their oars so as to prevent people entering by the Broadside of the Gun Boats

I very much approve of your having sent the *Spartan* to Halifax to refit and to rejoin you, but so soon any Frigate arrives here, I shall in the mean time send her to reinforce you   I have the honor to be, Sir, Your Obedient, humble Servant

Signed   John Borlase Warren

Copy, UkLPR, Adm. 1/506, pp. 159–60.

Naval Medicine

George Logan, surgeon on the South Carolina Station since 1810, tried to convince Jones in the spring of 1813 that a naval hospital was needed at Charleston. Before

Logan's appointment to the station, the proprietor of a private infirmary cared for the sick, charging 75 cents per day and extra for surgical operations. Logan contended that he had saved the navy money by taking them under his own care, and he indicated through his sick list report that the Charleston Station required a hospital. After consulting Dent, Jones decided to engage a guard vessel for the accommodation of the sick because it would be more economical.[1]

Dr. Edward Cutbush was dissatisfied with his post as surgeon on the Philadelphia Station, which included the gunboats at New Castle and in the Delaware River and Bay. He wrote to Jones soon after the new secretary arrived in Washington about a surgeon's position at the Washington Navy Yard. Jones appointed Cutbush to the Washington post and outlined for him the responsibilities and emoluments of the job.[2] The following letters contrast the naval hospital establishment at Washington with a recommendation for creating one at Charleston, South Carolina.

1. Logan to Jones, 10 May and 11 June 1813, DNA, RG45, BC, 1813, Vol. 2, Nos. 33 and 129 (M148, Roll No. 11); and Jones to Logan, 26 June 1813, SNL, Vol. 10, p. 483 (M149, Roll No. 10).
2. Cutbush to Jones, 21 Jan. 1813, DNA, RG45, BC, 1813, Vol. 1, No. 15 (M148, Roll No. 11).

SURGEON GEORGE LOGAN TO SECRETARY OF THE NAVY JONES

Charleston, S. C.

Sir!

I have the honor to enclose a report of clinical & other sick of the U.S. Seamen, occurring* under my care since the 19 Novr. last, with a desire to shew the expediency of a Hospital Establishment on this station. It may be proper to remark that the conditions of the several Invalids <u>herein mentioned</u> were such as to occasion much annoyance to the Crew, & rendered <u>their removal into sick quarters</u> absolutely necessary.

I have to regret that the destruction of my papers & Books (with other property) on the night of the 19th Novr. prevents my furnishing a report anterior to that date.[1] I am Sir very respectfully your obt. &c.

19th May 1813.   Geo Logan

ALS, DNA, RG45, BC, Vol. 2, No. 59 (M148, Roll No. 11).

1. A fire in Surgeon Logan's house in Charleston on 19 November 1812 destroyed medical supplies, books, and documents. See Dudley, *Naval War of 1812*, Vol. 1, p. 587.

[Enclosure]

Report of the U.S. Invalid Seamen admitted into Hospital quarters on the Charleston Station during Six months ending the 19th May 1813.— viz.

Names	Where from	Diseases & When recd.	When discharged
Elias Wigfal	Guardship	Rheumatism	19th Novr. 1812. Relieved
Andrew Miller	Schr. *Ferret*	Syphilis. 1st Decr. 1812	23d. Decr. 1812. cured
Andrew Noles	Guardship	Ulcer 7th Jany. 1813	23d Jany. 1813. cured
John Henley	Guardship	Burn. 9th Jany. 1813	23d. Jany. 1813. cured
Christir. Beekman	Guardship	Pulmy. Consumpn. 23d Decr. 1812	15th April 1813 dead
Willm. Miller	Guardship	Paralysis. 29th Jany. 1813.	14th Mar. 1813. dead
James S. Lyons	Gun Boat '153' (Alcorn Commg.)	Ulcers & diseased scapel[1] 15. Jany. 1813.	1st Apl. 1813. relieved
Gardner	Navy Yard	Diarrhea 17th. Feby. 1813	25th Feby. 1813 cured
Peter Rochester	Schr. *Carolina*	Catarrl. Fever[2] 2d Mar 1813	12th Mar 1813 cured
David Callum	Schr. *Carolina*	Pneumonia 3d Mar 1813	12th Mar 1813 cured
Samuel Waters	Schr. *Carolina*	Phthisis[3] 27th Mar 1813	15th April 1813 relievd.
Walter Hosman	Schr. *Carolina*	Diarrhea 24th Apl. 1813	10th May 1813 relievd.
John Wentstrom	Schr. *Carolina*	Catarrhl. Fever 10th May 1813	14 May 1813 cured

Cured & relieved 11. dead 2. total 13.

*(of Invalids admitted into Hospital quarters.)

Geo. Logan

ALS, DNA, RG45, BC, 1813, Vol. 2, No. 59, enclosure (M148, Roll No. 11).

1. Probably scapula, a shoulder blade.
2. Catarrhal fever is an inflammation of a mucous membrane.
3. Pulmonary tuberculosis.

SECRETARY OF THE NAVY JONES TO SURGEON EDWARD CUTBUSH

Doctor Edward Cutbush   Navy Depart.
Surgeon U.S. Navy.   23rd May 1813
Navy Yard Washington

You are hereby appointed to the charge and direction of the Marine and
Navy Hospital establishment in this City and of the medical and hospital Stores,
which may from time to time be required for the use of the hospitals, or for the
vessels of the United States equipped at this place, with the issue whereof you
will be charged and held accountable quarter yearly.

The Commandant of the Navy Yard and the Commandant of the Marine
Corps will each provide for you a Store room for the preservation of the medi-
cal & hospital Stores, of which you will keep the keys and have the exclusive
Charge and direction of the issues.

Until the Establishment of the Navy hospital is matured, you will adopt such
regulations for the management and direction of the hospitals and of the officers and persons under your authority, as shall appear to you best adapted, to
promote the public interest, and the objects of the institutions under your
charge. You will observe that none but persons entitled by Law to the benefit of
the Navy or Marine medical and hospital Stores, are to participate in the use
thereof. It his however to be understood, that if any Master or laboring Me-
chanic, or common laborer employed in the Navy yard, shall receive any sudden wound or injury, while so employed in the Yard, he shall be entitled to temporary relief. But if the person sustaining such injury be a Slave, his master shall
allow out of his wages a reasonable compensation for such medical and hospital
aid as he may receive, and if the injury of disability shall be likely to continue,
the master shall cause such Slave to be removed from the public hospital. The
Commandant of the Navy Yard and the Commandant of the Marine Corps or
the late Surgeon of those establishments will cause to be delivered to you all the
medical and hospital Stores and Surgical instruments now on hand, for which
you will give duplicate receipts, one of which you will forward to the accountant
of the Navy Department, in order that you may be charged with the same.

All requisitions made either by the Commandant of the Navy Yard or the
Commander of any vessel of the Navy of the United States, for medical Stores,
hospital Stores or Surgical instruments, are to be carefully examined by yourself, which if found correct and reasonable you will approve, but if otherwise,
you will reduce the requisition to what you may deem proper for the occasion.

You will make out such requisitions for medical and Hospital Stores and Surgical instruments from time to time, as may be necessary to meet in due time,
the demands of this Station, and present the same to this Department, in order
that measures may be taken to procure them of the best quality and at the most
reasonable rate, by ascertaining the cost at other places and comparing it with
the prices at this place. On the arrival of any vessel of the Navy of the United
States at this place, for the purpose of refitting, the Surgeon of any such vessel
will furnish you with an exact inventory of all the medical and Hospital Stores
and Surgical instruments, remaining on board of said vessel, to be certified by
the signing officers, which Stores and Surgical instruments you are to receive
and deposit in the Store room, and furnish a Copy of the said certified Inven-

tory to the accountant of this Department, in order that you may be charged with the same.

If the Surgical instruments so delivered shall require cleaning or repairing, you will cause the same to be put in order, fit for use, and the medical chests and implements to be cleansed, repaired, or replaced, as the case may require. All that can be performed by the mechanics in the Navy Yard, or Marine Barracks either in making or repairing or other work for the hospital Department, will be done on your application to the Commandant of the Navy Yard, or Commandant of the Marine Corps. You will carefully enquire into and take notes of the present practice in the Hospital Department at this Station, and correct whatever may appear to you, upon a careful investigation, contrary to Law, or incompatible with the public interest and real objects of the institutions.

You will be allowed, for your care, management and direction of all the objects thus committed to your Charge as follows.

By the act of the 27th of march 1804, vol. 7, chap. 53, page 148 the Surgeon attached to the Navy Yard and Vessels in Ordinary at Washington is entitled to the same pay rations and emoluments, as are allowed to a Surgeon in the army of the United States viz

45 dollars per month for twelve months is	$540.00
3 Rations per day at 20 Cents for ditto do.	219.00
10 dollars per month for forage ditto do.	120.00

The pay, rations & clothing of a Servant if not taken from the line amounting in 12 months to 237 $\frac{48\ 3/4}{100}$ dollars viz

Pay at 8 dollars per month	$96.00
Rations at 20 Cents per day	73.00
Clothing	68.48 3/4
	$237.48 3/4

He is also allowed quarters, fuel, candles, to be furnished by the quarter master of the army: but as that is not applicable to the present case, the following is considered an equitable allowance for those objects at this Station to wit;

For quarters per annum dollars	250.00
For fuel and Candles	150.00
	400.00

In addition to the Pay rations &c allowed under this act, you will be entitled to receive, as superintendent of medical stores

400.00

Making together, the Sum of   Dollars   1916.48 3/4

Your Pay and Emoluments are to commence here with the date of the letter, by which you were ordered to repair to this Station. I am very respectfully your obedt. Servt.

W. Jones

LB Copy, DNA, RG45, CNA, Vol. 1, pp. 423–26 (M441, Roll No. 1).

Chesapeake vs. *Shannon*

After returning triumphant from the Hornet-Peacock *engagement, Captain James Lawrence was appointed to the post of commandant at the New York Navy Yard, and then soon after ordered to command* Constitution. *He was reassigned, however, to* Chesapeake *in early May, when Captain Samuel Evans's health problem created a command vacancy in the frigate. Jones, ever anxious to see American vessels cruising rather than in port refitting, directed Lawrence to leave immediately for Boston to oversee her refitting. Lawrence was commander of* Chesapeake *fewer than two weeks before he met* Shannon, *whereas Captain Philip B. V. Broke had the advantage of commanding his ship for seven years. Broke, recognizing that* Shannon *would soon be recalled for extensive repairs, desperately wanted to engage an American frigate as the capstone to his long naval career; he wrote the following letter, cleverly describing the "advantages" of meeting in single combat, but Lawrence had already sailed by the time the letter arrived at Boston.*

Some historians have criticized Lawrence for sailing before first working his untrained crew and raw officers into a team. Ordered by Secretary Jones to depart as expeditiously as possible, Lawrence took the first opportunity to sail. Although there is merit to the charge that Chesapeake *was not ready, ultimately,* Shannon*'s expertise in broadside gunnery defeated the Americans.*[1]

1. *For more background on this engagement, see Padfield,* Broke and Shannon, *especially chapters six and seven; and James,* Naval History, *Vol. 6, pp. 50–68. For an American point of view, see Roosevelt,* Naval War of 1812, *pp. 176–90.*

CAPTAIN PHILIP B. V. BROKE, R.N., TO CAPTAIN JAMES LAWRENCE

His Britannic Majesty's Ship
Shannon off Boston   1813[1]

Sir,

As the *chesapeake* appears now ready for Sea, I request you will do me the favor to meet the *Shannon* with her, Ship to Ship, to try the fortune of our respective Flags; to an Officer of your character, it requires some apology for proceeding to further particulars, be assured Sir, that it is not from any doubt that I can entertain of your wishing to close with my proposal, but merely to provide an Answer to any objection which might be made, and very reasonably, upon the chance of <u>our</u> receiving an unfair support,—

After the diligent attention which we had paid to Commodore Rodgers, the pains I took to detach all force, but *Shannon* and *Tenedos*, to such a distance that they could not possibly join in any Action fought in sight of the Capes, and the various <u>Verbal</u> messages which had been sent into Boston to that effect, we were much disappointed to find that the Commodore had eluded us, by sailing on the first change, after the prevailing Easterly winds had obliged us to keep an offing from the Coast; <u>he</u>, perhaps, wished for some <u>stronger</u> assurance of a fair meeting; I am therefore induced to address <u>you</u> more particularly, and to assure you that what <u>I write</u> I pledge my <u>honor to perform</u> to the utmost of my power,—

The *Shannon* mounts twenty four Guns upon her broadside, and one light Boat Gun, <u>Eighteen pounders</u> on her Main deck, and Thirty two pound Carronades on her Quarter deck and Forecastle; and is manned with a Complement of <u>Three Hun-</u>

Master Commandant James Lawrence

Captain Philip Bowes Vere Broke, R.N.

dred Men and Boys, (a large proportion of the latter), besides Thirty Seamen, Boys, and Passengers which were taken out of re-captured Vessels lately. I am thus minute, because a report has prevailed in some of the Boston papers, that we had one Hundred and Fifty Men additional lent us from *La Hogûe*, which really never was the case;—*La Hogûe* is now gone to Halifax for Provisions, and I will send all other Ships beyond the power of interfering with us, and meet you wherever is most agreable to you, within the limits of the undermentioned Rendezvous, viz: from Six to Ten leagues east of Cape Cod light House;—"from Eight to Ten Leagues East of Cape Ann lights,—"on Cashe's ledge in Lat. 43°:00' No. or, at any bearing and distance you please to fix; off the South breaker of Nantucket, or the Shoal on St. George's bank.

If you will favor me with any plan of Signals, or Telegraph, I will warn you, (if sailing under this promise) should any of my Friends be too nigh, or any where in sight,—until I can detach them out of our way;—or I would sail <u>with you</u>, under a truce Flag, to any place you think safest from our Cruisers, hauling it down when fair to begin Hostilities;—

You must, Sir, be aware that my proposals are highly advantageous to you, as you cannot proceed to Sea singly in *chesapeake* without imminent risque of being crushed by the superior force of the numerous British squadrons which are now abroad, where all your efforts, in case of a rencontre, would, however gallant, be perfectly hopeless;

I entreat you, Sir, not to imagine that I am urged by mere personal vanity to the wish of meeting the *chesapeake*, or that I depend only upon your personal ambition for your acceding to this Invitation, we have both nobler motives,— you will feel it as a compliment if I say that the result of our meeting may be the most grateful Service I can render to my Country,— and I doubt not that you, equally confident of success, will feel convinced that it is only by continued triumphs in <u>even combats</u>, that your little Navy can now hope to console <u>your</u> Country for the loss of that Trade it can no longer protect.— favor me with a speedy reply,— we are short of Provisions and Water, and cannot stay long here; I have the honor to be Sir Your obedient humble Servant.

Captain of His Britannic
Majesty's Ship *Shannon*
P B V Broke

N.B.— For the <u>general</u> service of watching your Coast, it is requisite for me to keep another Ship in Company, to support us with her Guns and Boats, when employ'd near the Land, and particularly to Aid each other, if either Ship in chase should get on shore;— you must be aware that I cannot consistently with my duty, wave so great an advantage for this <u>general service</u>, by detaching my Consort, without an assurance on your part of meeting me directly, and that you will neither seek, or admit Aid from any other of <u>your</u> armed Vessels, if <u>I</u> detach <u>mine</u> expressly for the sake of meeting you;— should any special order restrain you from thus answering a formal challenge, you may yet oblige me by keeping my proposal a secret, and appointing any place you like to meet us (within Three Hundred Miles of Boston) in a given number of days after you sail. as, unless you agree to an Interview, I may be busied on other service,—and perhaps be at a distance from Boston, when you go to Sea.— choose your terms, <u>but let us meet</u>.

Captain.

To the Captain of the United States Frigate *Chesapeake.*

LS, DNA, RG45, CL, 1813, Vol. 4, No. 12a (M125, Roll No. 29). The postscript was not signed by Broke. Broke's letter to Lawrence was enclosed in William Bainbridge to Jones, 3 June 1813, DNA, RG45, CL, 1813, Vol. 4, No. 12 (M125, Roll No. 29).

1. Broke did not date his letter, but it is probable that he wrote this challenge to Lawrence on 31 May and that it was taken to the Boston post office on 1 or 2 June.

AN ACCOUNT OF THE *CHESAPEAKE-SHANNON* ACTION [1]

Copy　Thos. Bladen Capel　　　　　　　　　*Shannon*　Halifax
　　　　　　　　　　　　　　　　　　　　　　June 6th 1813

Sir,

I have the honor to inform you that being close in with Boston Light House in His Majestys Ship under my Command on the 1st inst.—I had the pleasure of seeing that the United States Frigate *Chesapeake* (whom we had long been Watching) was coming out of the Harbour to engage the *Shannon*— I took a position between Cape Ann and Cape Cod, and then hove to for him to join us—the Enemy came down in a very handsome manner, having three American Ensigns flying—when closing with us he sent down his royal Yards— I kept the *Shannons* up, expecting the breeze would die away— At half past five P M the Enemy hauled up within hail of us, on the Starb. side & the Battle began—both Ships steering full under the Topsails; after exchanging between two and three Broadsides, the Enemys Ship fell on board of us—her mizen channels locking in with our fore rigging— I went forward to ascertain her position, and observing that the Enemy were flinching from their Guns, I gave orders to prepare for boarding— Our gallant bands appointed to that Service immediately rushed in under their respective Officers, upon the Enemys Decks driving every thing before them with irresistable fury.— the Enemy made a desperate, but disorderly Resistance— The firing continued at all the Gangways and between the Tops, but in two minutes time the Enemy were driven, Sword in hand from every Post. The American flag was hauled down and the proud old British Union floated triumphant over it— in another minute they ceased firing from below and called for quarter— the whole of this Service was atchieved in fifteen minutes from the commencement of the Action.

I have to lament the loss of many of my gallant Shipmates, but they fell exulting in their Conquest.

My brave first Lieutenant Mr. Watt was slain in the moment of Victory, in the act of hoisting the British Colours—his Death is a severe loss to the Service— Mr. Aldham the Purser, who had spiritedly Volunteered the charge of a Party of small armed men, was killed at his Post on the Gangway— My faithful Old Clerk Mr. Dunn was Shot by his Side.— Mr. Aldham has left a Widow to lament his loss— I request the Commander in Chief will recommend her to the protection of the Lords Commissioners of the Admiralty.—

My Veteran Boatswain, Mr. Stephens has lost an Arm—he fought under Lord Rodney on the 12th April. I trust his Age and Services will be duly rewarded— I am happy to say that Mr. Samwell a Midshipman of much merit, is the only other Officer Wounded besides myself, and he not dangerously. Of my gallant Seamen & marines We had twenty three Slain, and fifty six Wounded— I subjoin the Names of the former— No expressions I can make use of can do justice to the merits of my Valiant Officers and Crew.— the calm courage they dis-

"H.M.S. Shannon commencing the BATTLE with the
AMERICAN FRIGATE Chesapeake on the 1st June 1813"

"H.M.S. Shannon leading her PRIZE the
AMERICAN FRIGATE Chesapeake into HALIFAX HARBOUR on the 6th June 1813"

played during the Cannonade, and the tremendous precision of their fire, could only be equalled by the ardour with which they rushed to the assault.— I recommend them all warmly to the protection of the Commander in Chief—

Having received a severe Sabre Wound at the first onset, whilst charging a party of the Enemy who had rallied on their forecastle, I was only capable of giving Command 'till assured our Conquest was Complete, and then, directing Second Lieutenant Wallis to take charge of the *Shannon,* and secure the Prisoners, I left the third Lieutenant Mr. Falkiner (who had headed the Main Deck boarders) in charge of the Prize— I beg to recommend these Officers most strongly to the Commander in Chiefs patronage, for the gallantry they displayed during the Action, and the Skill and judgment they evinced in the anxious duties which afterwards devolved upon them—

To Mr. Etough the acting Master—I am much indebted, for the steadiness in which he Conn'd the Ship into Action— The Lieutenants Johns and Law of the Marines bravely boarded at the head of their respective Divisions.

It is impossible to particularize every brilliant deed performed by my Officers and Men, but I must mention when the Ships Yard Arms were locked together, that Mr. Cosnahan who Commanded in our Main Top, finding himself screened from the Enemy by the foot of the Topsail, laid out at the Main Yard Arm to fire upon them, and Shot three men in that situation— Mr. Smith who Commanded in our foretop, & stormed the Enemys foretop from the fore Yard Arm, and destroyed all the Americans remaining in it— I particularly beg leave to recommend Messrs. Etough the acting Master, Smith & Leake midshipmen as having already passed their examination for Lieutenants and Messrs. Clavering, Raymond and Littlejohn as equally qualified, and being within a few weeks of their time— this latter Officer is a Son of Captain Littlejohn who was Slain in the *Berwick.*

The loss of the Enemy was about Seventy killed, and One hundred Wounded— amongst the former were the fourth Lieutenant, a Lieut. of marines, the Master and many other Officers— Captain Lawrence is since Dead of his Wounds.—[2]

The Enemy came into Action with a Compliment of four hundred and forty men— the *Shannon* having picked up some re Captured Seamen had three hundred and thirty.

The *Chesapeake* is a fine frigate, and mounts forty nine Guns—Eighteens on her main Deck—two and thirties on her quarter Deck & forecastle—both Ships came out of Action in the most beautiful order—their Rigging appearing as perfect as if they had only been Exchanging a Salute.— I have the honor to be Sir, Your most Obedient humble Servant

P. B V. Broke

List of Killed on board His Majesty's Ship Shannon

G. T. L. Watt	1t Lieut.
G. Aldham	Purser
John Dunn	Captain's Clerk
G. Gilbert	Able Seaman
Wm. Berilles	Do.
Neil Gilchrist	Do.
Thos. Selby	Do.
Jas. Long	Do.
John Young	Do.

	Jas. Wallace	Do.
	Joseph Brown	Do.
	Thos. Barr	Ordy.
	Mickl. Murphy	Do.
	Thos. Molloy	Do.
	Thos. Jones	Do.
	Jno. Oconnelly	Do.
	Thos. Barry	1t Class Boy
Marines	Saml. Millard	Corpl.
	Jas. Jayms	Private
	Dominique Saden	Do.
	Wm. Young	Do.
Superys.	Wm. Morrisay	
	Jno. Moriarty	
	Thos. German	

(Signed)   P. B. V. Broke Capt.
Alexr. Jack   Surgeon.

Copy, UkLPR, Adm. 1/503, pp. 645–53. Edgar S. Maclay, in his study of the U.S. Navy, found that this letter lacked Broke's sanction because the British captain's wounds prevented him from writing or even dictating. On 6 June, the day *Shannon* and *Chesapeake* entered Halifax, Broke lay motionless and spoke only in monosyllables. Maclay asserted that while he was in England, from 1885 to 1886, he received documents from Admiral Sir Provo Wallis, second lieutenant on *Shannon*, that proved that this letter was concocted by Captain the Honorable Philip Wodehouse, commissioner of the Halifax Dockyard, Captain the Honorable Thomas Bladen Capel and Captain Richard Byron in order to get an official account of the victory off to London as soon as possible. Wallis indicated to Maclay that this letter contained inaccuracies relating to the performance of several people and the condition of the rigging. See Maclay, *United States Navy*, Vol. 1, pp. xix–xxi. For a recent account of this controversial letter, see Heine, *Ninety-six Years*, pp. 54–60.

1. Captain the Honorable Thomas Bladen Capel, R.N., was the senior naval officer at Halifax.
2. Peter Padfield computed 146 casualties out of 395 officers and men on board *Chesapeake*: 50 killed outright; 19 wounded, since dead; and 75 wounded and recovered. "This casualty proportion was quite sufficient to ensure the defeat of any man-of-war of the day. No dereliction of duty or cowardice need be attributed to the Chesapeakes." See Padfield, *Broke and* Shannon, p. 233.

LIEUTENANT GEORGE BUDD [1] TO SECRETARY OF THE NAVY JONES

Halifax   June 15th 1813

Sir

The unfortunate death of Captain James Lawrence and Lieutenant Augustus C. Ludlow has rendered it my duty to inform you of the Capture of the late United States Frigate *Chesapeake*. On Tuesday June 1st at 8 A.M. we unmoored Ship and at Meridian got under way from President's Roads, with a light wind from the Southward and westward, and proceeded on a cruise. A Ship was then in sight, in the offing which had the appearance of a Ship of War, and which from information received from pilot boats and craft we believed to be the British Frigate *Shannon*. We made sail in chase and cleared Ship for action. At 1/2 past 4 P.M. she hove to, with her head to the Southward and eastward. At 5 P.M. took in the royals and top gallant Sails, and at 1/2 past 5 hauled the courses up. About 15 minutes before 6 P.M. the action commenced within pistol shot. The first broadside did great execution on both sides, damaged our rigging, killed among others Mr. White the sailing master, and wounded Captain Lawrence— In about 12 minutes after the commencement of the action, we fell on board of the enemy, and immediately after one of our arm chests on the quarter deck was blown up by a hand grenade thrown from the enemy's Ship.[2] In a few minutes one of the Captain's aids came on the gun deck to inform me that the boarders were called. I immediately called the boarders away and proceeded to the Spar deck, where I found that the eneny had succeeded in boarding us and had gained possession of our quarter deck. I immediately gave orders to haul on board the fore tack, for the purpose of shooting the Ship clear of the other, and then made an attempt to regain the quarter deck, but was wounded, and thrown down on the gun deck. I again made an effort to collect the boarders, but in the mean time the enemy had gained complete possession of the Ship. On my being carried down to the cockpit, I there found Captain Lawrence and Lieutenant Ludlow both mortally wounded; the former had been carried below previous to the Ship's being boarded; the latter was wounded in attempting to repel the boarders. Among those who fell early in the action was Mr. Edward J. Ballard the 4th Lieutenant and Lieutenant James Broome of Marines.

I herein enclose to you a return of the killed and wounded, by which you will perceive that every Officer, upon whom the charge of the Ship could devolve, was either killed or wounded previous to her capture.[3] The enemy report the loss of Mr. Watt their first Lieutenant, the Purser, the Captain's Clerk, and 23 seamen killed, and Captain Broke, a Midshipman, and 56 seamen wounded.

The *Shannon* had, in addition to her full complement an officer and 16 men belonging to the *Belle Poole*, and a part of the crew belonging to the *Tenedos*. I have the honor to be, with very great respect &c. Sir, Your Most Obt. Servt.

George Budd

ALS, DNA, RG45, BC, 1813, Vol. 2, No. 138 (M148, Roll No. 11).

1. George Budd's commission as lieutenant dated from 23 May 1812. As second lieutenant of *Chesapeake*, Budd became the senior surviving officer after the death of Lawrence and First Lieutenant Augustus C. Ludlow.

2. British historian William James disputes this, saying only that an arms chest "caught fire and blew up, but did no injury whatever." See James, *Naval History*, Vol. 6, p. 56.

3. No list was found with Budd's letter. For a printed version, see Pullen, Shannon *and* Chesapeake, pp. 143–46.

Blockade Frustrates *United States, Macedonian,* and *Hornet*

The British established a tight blockade around New York during April and May 1813. Captain Robert Dudley Oliver,[1] senior British naval officer, positioned Valiant, *74, and* Acasta, *44, near Sandy Hook to prevent any southerly escape. Captain Sir Thomas Masterman Hardy blockaded the eastern exit between Montauk Point and Block Island with* Ramillies, *74, and* Orpheus, *36. In their initial cruising plans, Commodore Stephen Decatur in* United States *and Lieutenant William H. Allen in* Argus *were to leave New York together and proceed to attack the British blockaders off Charleston, South Carolina, before separating. Just before Argus sailed, President Madison ordered her to return to port for a special diplomatic mission.*[2] *The refitted British frigate* Macedonian, *38, under Captain Jacob Jones, joined* Decatur *on 13 May; and* Hornet, *20, under Master Commandant James Biddle, followed on 22 May. The three American ships attempted to sortie through Lower New York Bay but were frustrated by weather conditions. Impatient with waiting and convinced that Hardy's squadron was less formidable than Oliver's, Decatur, the senior American officer, decided to venture his squadron through the narrow and treacherous Hell Gate into Long Island Sound. Captain Oliver, anticipating Decatur's plan, ordered Hardy to switch stations with him so that he could confront the Americans.*

1. Robert Dudley Oliver, a captain since 1796, commissioned Valiant in 1810, and commanded her on the American coast from 1813 to 1814.
2. See pp. 140–42.

COMMODORE STEPHEN DECATUR TO SECRETARY OF THE NAVY JONES

U.S.S. *United States.*   New London   June 1813[1]

Sir,

On tuesday the 18th Ult. we got under way at New York in company with the *Macedonian* & *Hornet* with a view of passing Hurl [*Hell*] Gate, but in our approach to it this ship took the ground slightly, which detained us untill it was too late for that tide but without doing the ship any damage— The wind continued Easterly and light untill the 24th when we all got under way & stood through Hurl Gate without the least difficulty— On the 26th we came down Sound and continued in the neighbourhood of Fishers Island, changing our situation occasionally, untill the lst Instant. We had various information of the force of the Enemy off Montaug but were only certain of his having a line of battle ship & a frigate there— On the first we stood through the race there being then no vessel of war in sight beside the Seventy-four & a frigate & they a long distance to the Southward & Westward of Montaug— As we approached Block Island we discovered two men of war under it and finding the ships which were in chase of us to Leeward hauling their wind to cut us off from New London and those in Block Island channel manoeuvring to prevent our reaching Newport we hauled our wind & beat back through the Race up to this harbour.[2] Two of the Enemy's ships, the names of which I had not been able to ascertain, a line of battle ship and a frigate are now off here and it is said three of his men of war one or two of them of the line are off Block Island.

On inquiry I found Fort Trumbull the only work here mounted or garrisoned was in the most unprepared state & that only one or two cannon were to be had in the neighbourhood for any temporary work which should be erected— I immediately directed my attention & all my exertions to strengthening the defences of the place— Groton Height has been hastily prepared for the reception of a few large guns & they will be mounted immediately— a small outwork in advance of it has also been mounted with two of the dismounted carronades of this ship and the militia of the vicinity are out in abundant numbers to garrison them— The Enemy has declared his intention to cut us out— and when it is considered how important the destruction of these ships is to him I think if he could detach a force sufficient to secure it there is no doubt it would be attempted— with the force off here I do not believe it will be & have no great apprehension of the result if it should—

If twenty pieces of heavy cannon, 18 or 24 pounders (the latter to be preferred) mounted on travelling carriages could be sent here from New York or elsewhere with authority to lay platforms & incur the expences incident to their being fitted for use, I think the place might be made impregnable; but the hostile force on our coast is so great, were the Enemy to exert all his means or a large portion of them in an attack here I do not feel certain that he could be resisted successfully with the present defences of the place— I am Sir with great respect your very humble Servant

Stephen Decatur

LS, DNA, RG45, CL, 1813, Vol. 4, No. 3 (M125, Roll No. 29).

1. Decatur did not date his letter, but Jacob Jones and James Biddle wrote their accounts to Secretary Jones on 2 June.

2. Jacob Jones and James Biddle reported seeing "a man of war" and "a large Sail . . . apparently a Ship of the Line", respectively. See Jacob Jones to William Jones, 2 June 1813, DNA, RG45, CL, 1813, Vol. 4, No. 9 (M125, Roll No. 29); and James Biddle to William Jones, 2 June 1813, DNA, RG45, MC, 1813, No. 67 (M147, Roll No. 5). W. M. P. Dunne carefully studied British records and found no evidence of any enemy vessels in the area except for *Valiant* and *Acasta*. He concluded that the three American commanders, their judgments tainted by false intelligence reports, mistook some vessels near Block Island for British warships. See Dunne, "Inglorious First of June," pp. 214–16.

COMMODORE STEPHEN DECATUR TO SECRETARY OF THE NAVY JONES

U.S. Frigate United States   New London.   June 6. 1813

Sir

Since I had the honour of writing you I have ascertained that the ships blockading the Sound, are the *Valiant* and *Ramillies,* Seventy fours, the *Acasta* & *Orpheus* Frigates, a sloop ship and some tenders,— They are now at anchor within our view a little to the Westward of the Race— The boats of the *Valiant* landed yesterday on Gardiners Island and took from thence some stock— the officers stated, that they had dispatched a tender for a reinforcement, and that when they should obtain it, they intended an attack—

Our present position (from the state of the batteries and the few guns that are mounted on Fort Griswold) is not such, as to inspire me with much confidence as to the result of an attack made by such a force as they can command;—for although I am satisfied, that we should destroy two or three of their leading ships, there is no doubt, but the remaining force of the Enemy would be sufficient to secure the capture of our vessels or their destruction— It has therefore been my determination, in case no favourable opportunity should offer to proceed to sea, to avail myself of the first good wind and dark night, to return to New-York by the way of the Sound— If the Ships of the Enemy in sight maintain their present position we shall be enabled to pass up Sound without risk— if however they should take anchorage off the mouth of this harbour (which there is nothing to prevent) it will be hardly possible that we can pass them— In this event, I shall proceed up the river about [six?] miles, to do which, I shall have to lighten some and bring my ship upon an even keel— At this point we shall be perfectly secure, as the channel is very narrow and intricate and not a sufficient depth of water to enable large ships to follow—

If some of the twenty four pounders in the Navy Yard at New York with carriages could be sent here, and a few of the Gun Boats stationed there, could be removed here, I feel satisfied our position would be rendered so formidable that no attack of the enemy need be apprehended.

Enclosed is the copy of a letter addressed to me by the Governour of Connecticut—& another from the Collector of Sag Harbor   With the highest respect I am Sir your very humble servant

Stephen Decatur

LS, DNA, RG45, CL, 1813, Vol. 4, No. 21 (M125, Roll No. 29). Enclosures are not printed.

CAPTAIN ROBERT DUDLEY OLIVER, R.N., TO ADMIRAL SIR JOHN B. WARREN, R.N.

Copy   *Valiant* at Sea   13th June 1813

Sir

On the 16 May the American Frigates *United States* and *Macedonian* & *Argus* Brig [1] after laying several days at Sandy Hook, and finding no chance for making their escape, that way returned up the North River— On the 20th I received information that they had entered the East River, and that the *United States* had been aground but without receiving any damage,— On the 22d the *Martin* called off the Hook in her way to Block Island & the *Valiant*, and *Acasta*, being reduced to 10 days water (as the only resource within my reach) I sent orders by the *Martin* to Sir Thomas Hardy to join me off Sandy Hook, until I could get water.— On the 25th having received information which I thought certain that the Enemy's Ships had been under weigh in the East River the day before and had probably passed Hell Gates, I pushed for Montuck Point and reached it the Morning of the 26th and learnt from Capn. Pigot of the *Orpheus* that the *Ramilies* was gone off Sandy Hook, I sent her to join her— I anchored the next day off Block Island and procured 20 tons of water, the weather then became so bad I was obliged to desist watering and it was so foggy that I could not reconnoitre the entrance of the Sound till the 30th when I saw the Enemy's Frigates and the *Hornet* Sloop at Anchor to the westward of Fishers Island, the wind was from the westward the floodtide done and As they had the Port of New London so near to them I had no hopes of approaching them in that situation so I returned off Montuk— On the morning of the first of June at 9 O Clock as we were rounding Montuk Point with the *Acasta* the above Ships were seen directly to Windward at about 7 or 8 Miles distance coming down with studding sails set steering S.E the wind at N[W?]   As soon as ever they made us out they hauled close upon a wind with every sail they could carry, and altho, we were flying light there not being 40 Tons of water in both Ships we neared them considerably by the time they entered the Race which they effected by 12 O Clock—we both passed it about 3 quarters past 12, by this time the Wind had Changed to W.S.W. and had brought the *Acasta* so near the *United States* that they had a shot each tho' scarcely within distance, the latter had then her studding sails set on both sides steering for New London which she entered soon after two O Clock, the *Macedonian* and *Hornet* kept a head and appeared to sail much better.— I extremely regret it was not in my power to prevent their reaching a Port; there was no person in either of our Ships that had ever been thro' the Race before, and it certainly is a Navigation from the great strength of the tide and other cir-cumstances that requires some local knowledge—

We repassed the Race and anchored off Gardiners Island, from whence we could see the Enemy's Ships in New London River & I sent the *Acasta* to Fort-pondbay where she got wood and water with great ease also a few Cattle.—

On the 2d. June I pressed a fishing smack and sent an express to Sir Thos. Hardy to join me with the *Ramilies* and *Orpheus* in the hope that something might be done with those Ships at New London, light winds prevented his ar-rival till the 7th. By this time the Enemy's Ships had moved up the River 5 or 6 Miles to Gales Ferry where I understand there is little more water than they draw— the Forts on each side had been considerably strengthened and Two or three Regiments had Arrived in the Town and it was the unanimous opinion of Captains Sir T Hardy Pigot and Kerr that the destructions of those Ships could not be effected with any prospects of saving our own without having a superior Force to take the place and even then it was very doubtful if the Line of Battle Ships could go up the River, upon no Chart do I see more than 4 fathoms marked and that only at the entrance. The *Macedonian* grounded the first day going in and the *Hornet* was obliged to lighten before she could get off where she touched— On the 8th we Anchored off the West End of Fishers Island within 4 or 5 miles of New London where I continued Sounding and annoying the Coasting trade of the Enemy as much possible till the 12th when leaving the *Ramilies* & *Orpheus* there having previously supplied them with all the Provisions we could possibly spare— I sailed with the *Acasta* and am now making the best of my way to Halifax to replenish, the wind precluding our going to Bermuda with our present supplies much as I feel disappointed in not having been able to do more against the Enemy yet I have great consolation in having prevented their getting to sea from both ends of Long Island and from knowing that they are now in a situation where perhaps they can be more easily watched than in most others.— I have the honor to be Sir Your most obedient humble servant

Signed   Rt. Dudley Oliver   Capn.

Copy, UkLPR, Adm. 1/504, pp. 223–26. Original is incomplete and badly damaged; see UkLPR, 1/504, pp. 179–81.

1. *Hornet* replaced *Argus.*

COMMODORE STEPHEN DECATUR TO SECRETARY OF THE NAVY JONES

U.S.F. *United States*   New London
June 18th 1813

Sir,

Since I last had the honor of writing you, two of the Enemys ships, (a seventy four & a Frigate) have left their anchorage off this place; it is reported that they have sailed for Hallifax.

The vessels remaining are a Seventy four & frigate, they are at anchor off the Mouth of this Harbor about four miles distant there is also a Frigate cruising be-tween Montague & Fishers Island.— The Gun Boats have not yet arrived from New York, the moment they do, & the weather will permit, I contemplate an attack with them on the enemy;[1] The position they have chosen is the best that could have been for our purpose.—

I have requested the Navy Agent to forward to this place two Forges that were at the Navy Yard New York. They have arrived at New Haven, & will be here in the course of today, I intend placing them on the Gun Boats.—

I am sorry to inform that notwithstanding the vigilance of our guard boats, there is constant communication kept up with the enemy.— One person has been detected in going alongside of the enemys ships, he is now confined by order of the Marshall, there is little doubt that he was employed by Mr. Stewart the Agent for Prisoners at this place. It appears by his own acknowledgement that he is an Alien Enemy. I do trust this man may be tryed as a spy; something should certainly be done to put a stop to this communication.

Mr. Stewart the gentleman above spoken of, appears to have great influence here, he has it in his power, & it is said uses it, to do much injury.— I am informed by many persons entitled to credit, that Mr. Stewart has been in the practice of loading (through his agents) Neutral vessels with stock cleared out for St. Bart's, but discharged their cargoes alongside the enemies ships— I have the honor to be most respectfully your obt. St.

Stephen Decatur

ALS, DNA, RG45, CL, 1813, Vol. 4, No. 85 (M125, Roll No. 29).

1. After learning that Decatur had retreated several miles up the Thames River, Jones told Jacob Lewis not to hazard the New York gunboat flotilla to aid Decatur unless it was absolutely necessary; see Jones to Lewis, DNA, RG45, SNL, Vol. 10, p. 464 (M149, Roll No. 10).

Admiralty Orders for Warren

The Admiralty's correspondence with Admiral Sir John B. Warren indicated a lack of confidence in his ability to oversee the vast North American Station under his charge. They urged him to deploy more force to protect the seasonal convoys to Quebec and New Brunswick and to enforce a closer blockade off Boston. Furthermore, the Lords Commissioners directed Warren to exchange the ships stationed in the West Indies and North America as the weather necessitated, thus employing his limited force to the best advantage.

FIRST SECRETARY OF THE ADMIRALTY JOHN W. CROKER TO ADMIRAL SIR JOHN B. WARREN, R.N.

3 June 1813.

Sir

I am commanded by my Lords Commrs. of the Admiralty to acknowledge the receipt of your Letter of the 20th. of April, transmitting a return of the Disposition of the Ships and Vessels under your orders, and to acquaint You that tho' it does not appear that you have appropriated any Ships or Vessels for the protection of the Lands to the Northward of Halifax, in the neighbourhood of the Gut of Canso, the Island of St. John, and other parts of the Gulf of St. Lawrence within the limits of your Command, their Lordships trust that a sufficient force will arrive there, agreeably to your intention communicated in your Letter of the 20th. Feby. by the time the first Ships and Convoys from England bound to the different Ports of that Part of New Brunswick and Quebec may be expected to approach the entrance of the Gulf of St. Lawrance where they must unavoidably separate to proceed to their several Ports consequently it is very desirable that the Privateers should be prevented from occupying that ground during the Season in which the Trade is carried on between that part of North America and England.

Their Lordships also hope that in making your Arrangements for annoying the Enemy, you have been able to afford a more considerable force off Boston, where the greatest number of his Ships of War appear at present to be.

I am further to acquaint you that tho' their Lordships are obliged to send a great many Ships and Vessels to the West Indies with Convoy, with directions to follow the orders of either of the Flag officers on the Leeward Island & Jamaica Stations, they trust to you for giving those Flag officers Instructions with respect to what number of them should be kept under their Orders respectively, more particularly during the Hurricane Months, where but little Trade is carrying on in those Seas, and some of the Force may probably with propriety be employed to more advantage, on the Coast of America until the fall of the Year, and the time the West India Trade from this Country may be expected to arrive, by which period, and when operations cannot be so well carried on in America, a sufficient force should be there for the protection of the Outward bound Trade to the Islands, and to the late Dutch Colonies. I am &c

J W C

LB Copy, UkLPR, Adm. 2/1377, pp. 65–67.

New Mission for *Argus*

Lieutenant William H. Allen had served with Decatur in United States *from 1809 until early 1813, when he was ordered to superintend the refitting of* Argus. *Allen received orders from Jones in early May to sail that brig in company with Decatur's* United States *on a cruise against the blockaders off Charleston, South Carolina, and then to separate on individual voyages. But President Madison required a ship to take the new minister to France, William H. Crawford, to his post. On 28 May 1813, Jones directed Allen to prepare* Argus *to accommodate the minister and drafted new orders for the vessel while in European waters. Jones, ever the proponent of an offensive naval policy, instructed Allen to make* Argus *a commerce raider, harassing the British coastal trade and the homeward-bound West Indian fleet. The secretary hoped to bring a taste of the war to the British Isles.*[1]

1. For documentation on Argus's cruise, see pp. 217–24.

SECRETARY OF THE NAVY JONES TO LIEUTENANT WILLIAM HENRY ALLEN

Lieut. W. H. Allen   Navy Department
Comg the U.S Brig *Argus*   June 5th 1813.
New York.

Sir,

When the Honourable Mr. Crawford, Minister Plenipotentiary from the U. States to France, is ready for departure, you will receive him and his suite on-board, and proceed, with the first favourable opportunity to Sea,[1] directing your course, without deviating for any other object, to the first Port you can make in France. In all probability, you will find Brest, or L'Orient, the easiest of access; but should you have an opportunity of landing the Minister, on any part of the coast of France, you may thereby avoid much risk, in attempting to enter a Port, before which you may find a hostile squadron. But in whatever way you may effect the first object of your destination, you will then proceed upon a cruize, against the commerce, and light cruizers of the enemy, which you will capture, and destroy in all cases, unless their value, and qualities shall render it morally certain, that they may reach a safe, and not distant Port. Indeed, in the present state of the enemy's force, there are very few cases that would justify the manning of a prize; because the chances of reaching a safe port are infinitely against the attempt, and the weakening the crew of the *Argus,* might expose you to an unequal contest with the enemy.

It is exceedingly desirable that the enemy should be made to feel the effect of our hostility, and of his barbarous system of warfare; and in no way can we so effectually accomplish that object, as by annoying, and destroying his commerce, fisheries, and coasting trade. The latter is of the utmost importance, and is much more exposed to the attack of such a vessel as the *Argus,* than is generally understood. This would carry the war home to their direct feelings and interests, and produce an astonishing sensation. For this purpose the cruizing ground, from the entrance of the British Channel, to Cape Clear, down the coast of Ireland, across to, and along the N.W. Coast of England, would employ a month or six weeks to great advantage. The coasting fleets, on this track, are immensely valuable; and you would also be in the way of their West India homeward fleet, and of those to and from Spain, Portugal, and the Mediterranean. When you are prepared to leave this ground, you may pass round the N.W. of Ireland towards fair Island passage, in the track of the Archangel fleets, returning home in August and September.

When it shall be absolutely necessary to return home, you will pursue such route as may best promote the objects of your cruize; and endeavour to make some Eastern port, perhaps Portsmouth may be as easy of access, and as convenient, in other respects, as any other. On your arrival in France, you will, with the aid of Mr. Crawford, be better able to form an opinion of the expediency of attempting to send prizes into France, or of touching there, to replenish your stores, in order to protract your cruize.

Your own disposition, and the amiable character of the Minister, insure to him the kindest attention on your part; and I am persuaded, that you will derive the most ample gratification from such an intercourse. Your talents, and honourable services, are deeply impressed upon this Department, and will not cease to excite its attention. Wishing you a prosperous, and honourable cruize, I am, very respectfully, Your Obedient Servant,

Wm Jones.

LB Copy, DNA, RG45, CLS, 1813, pp. 29–31.

1. Allen left New York on 18 June, taking the southerly route past Sandy Hook.

Charleston Station at Midyear

Jones reversed his gunboat reduction order in late May 1813 after he received many requests from the citizenry of Charleston and after Captain Dent explained the grave situation there. On 27 May Jones ordered four barges out of ordinary to protect merchant vessels against the small British cruisers. When he learned that Dent actually had six barges out of service, Jones reinstated all of them.[1] Dent now had more vessels under his command, but no sailors to fill the complements. Jones rebuffed Dent's efforts to open a rendezvous at Wilmington, North Carolina, and told him to try Savannah instead. Furthermore, Dent reiterated his request for his own ship because he saw others of lesser rank who were given command of frigates.[2] His dissatisfaction with his command was so severe that he asked to be returned to Washington, but to no avail.

1. *Jones to Dent, 27 May 1813, DNA, RG45, SNL, Vol. 10, p. 442 (M149, Roll No. 10).*
2. *Jones to Dent, 17 June 1813, DNA, RG45, SNL, Vol. 10, p. 468 (M149, Roll No. 10); Dent to Jones, 8 June 1813, DNA, RG45, CL, 1813, Vol. 4, No. 32 (M125, Roll No. 29).*

Captain John H. Dent to Secretary of the Navy Jones

Charleston   5th June, 1813

Sir

I have had the honor to receive your two letters of the 27th May. There are no Gun Boats here, I presume you must have meant Barges, and shall have four immediately put in Commission and manned. They are of large dimensions & carry a twelve pound carronade, with accommodations, for one months provisions for thirty men, they are better calculated to act in the inlets against the Small privateers, that infest them, than Gun Boats and move with greater facility, from one point to another; I shall use every exertion to have them immediately manned, and shall station two in the neighbourhood of Bulls Bay & the other two in Stono & North Edisto, and will no doubt give great Security, to the inland coasting trade of this State. There are three Masters here Drew, Jervey and Lord. I shall want a fourth, also two Midshipmen for the *Carolina*, her compliment shall be increased, to that of the *Nonsuch* immediately, There are but few Seamen here, and I am afraid it will be difficult to man the Barges as soon as I wish, most of them are in privateers, and letters of Marque to France. I Have the Honor to be With great respect yr obt Svt.

J H Dent

ALS, DNA, RG45, CL, 1813, Vol. 4, No. 17 (M125, Roll No. 29).

SECRETARY OF THE NAVY JONES TO CAPTAIN JOHN H. DENT

John H. Dent　　　　　　　　　　　　　　　　Navy Department
Charleston, S.C.　　　　　　　　　　　　　　　June 11, 1813,

Sir,

I have received yours of the 5th instant. When part of the Gun Boats formerly on the Charleston Station were ordered to the southward, the transfer was not noted on the records of the Department, and hence it was supposed that some still remained there. According to the information possessed by this Department, there are six Barges, under your command, which you will man and employ in the most effectual manner, for the protection of the Waters of So. Carolina.— These Barges, together with the *Nonsuch, Carolina, Ferret* and *Alligator,* I trust, will afford complete protection.[1]

Should there be any difficulty in procuring men, the crews of the Schooners while kept in port by a superior force, may be employed to man the Barges as occasion may require.— I am respectfully, Your Obdt. Servt.

W. Jones

LB Copy, DNA, RG45, SNL, Vol. 10, p. 462 (M149, Roll No. 10).

1. Two weeks later Dent ordered *Alligator* back to Charleston for necessary repairs; see Dent to Sailing Master R. Bassett, 24 June 1813, ScU, John H. Dent Letter Book.

CAPTAIN JOHN H. DENT TO SECRETARY OF THE NAVY JONES

Charleston.　27th June 1813.

Sir

I have the honor to forward for your information the Copy of a letter from Lieut. Kearney Comg. the U.S. Schooner *Carolina,* detailing his proceedings during his late cruize.[1] Should the port not be blockaded by a Superior force I shall send the *Nonsuch* out in a few days in quest of the privateers, A barge has this morning returned from Bulls Bay where She has been five days protecting, & keeping the enemy's boats from cutting off the inland trade, the officer reports that the privateer, had made several unsuccessfull attempts to enter that Bay, and had once grounded in the attempt, but the tide rising enabled her to get off, several Coasters had been chased into the Bay by the above vessel, and protected by the barge when they were convoyed clear of all danger, and arrived here yesterday & this morning. I shall man two barges from the *Carolina,* and direct one to proceed as far inland as Georgetown & Santees, the other to remain in Bulls Bay. Midshipman Cuthbert has reported himself, & has been ordered to join the *Nonsuch.* I Have the Honor to be With great Respect Your Most Ob Svt

J H Dent

LS, DNA, RG45, CL, 1813, Vol. 4, No. 123 (M125, Roll No. 29).

1. Lawrence Kearny (not Kearney) had been an acting lieutenant in *Enterprise* for several years and wished a transfer "to a vessel on the Northern Station." He was commissioned lieutenant 6 March 1813 and ordered to command *Carolina* at the end of April; see Kearny to Jones, 17 Mar. 1813, DNA, RG45, BC, 1813, Vol. 1, No. 123 (M148, Roll No. 11); and Dent to Kearny, 30 Apr. 1813, ScU, John H. Dent Letter Book.

[Enclosure]
(Copy)   U.S. Schooner *Carolina*
                                    Rebellion Roads   27th June 1813

Sir

   In compliance with your orders of the 17th inst,[1] I proceeded to Bulls Bay in
quest of the enemy's Privateer of 14 Guns which was said to be there, but not finding her I stood off towards Cape Roman and in a Short time discovered her ahead
& gave chase for three hours & was coming up with her very fast when a man of
War Brig of 18 Guns (supposed to be the *Sophie*) stood down for the chase and intercepted me I tacked at a leagues distance from her, when she and the Privateer
both made all Sail in chase of me, which continued for two hours & eight minutes,
when they finding they were losing ground, discontinued the chase. On the 21st
Standing off from Charleston bar, I discovered a man of War Brig, & ran down for
her, and found her to be the same vessel which had chased us on the day before,
She made all Sail in chase but could not Come up with me. On the 22nd I anchored in St Helena's sound and on the 23rd stood out again, after endeavoring to
get some fresh water, the water on board being very bad, I ran off Bulls and on the
24th at 4 P.M. I again had the fortune to discover the Privateer. I made all sail in
chase, but being late in the afternoon and the heavy Squalls that came on in the
evening afforded her an opportunity of effecting her escape which she did.

   My cruize having expired, I have returned under the impression you would
indulge me with a few more Days, when I may be more fortunate, but I may save
myself & you the trouble of that request, as I find (though with the deepest regret) I am displaced.[2] I Have the Honor to be With Much esteem Yr Obt Servt

                              (Signed)   Lawrence Kearney

Copy, DNA, RG45, CL, 1813, Vol. 4, No. 123, enclosure (M125, Roll No. 29).

   1. See Dent to Kearny, 17 June 1813, ScU, John H. Dent Letter Book, in which Dent enjoined
Kearny "not to go off soundings" in compliance with Jones's strictures. For Jones's orders, see Jones
to Dent, 9 Apr. 1813, p. 96. In other words, Kearny was not to stray from the coastal waters he was
supposed to protect.
   2. Jones reassigned Kearny to *Ferret* because he wanted a more senior lieutenant, John D. Henley,
to command *Carolina*; see Dent to Kearny, 29 June 1813, ScU, John H. Dent Letter Book; and Jones
to Dent, 4 June 1813, DNA, RG45, SNL, Vol. 10, p. 453 (M149, Roll No. 10).

Harbor Defense

   *Senator Samuel Smith of Maryland, as chairman of the select Senate committee on the
naval establishment, requested information from Jones regarding the number of gunboats
in service along the coast. He sought to win approval for purchasing a number of barges
to protect the entrances of harbors from enemy penetration. Jones suspected that Smith had
a self-interest in this issue because the city of Baltimore, having purchased several barges
at the height of the recent British incursions along the Chesapeake, now wished to sell these
vessels to the government. Jones considered barges less cost efficient than gunboats because
they required more men to fill their complements than did gunboats. As there was already
a critical shortage of available seamen to man the vessels on hand, purchasing more vessels with little prospect of manning them was a waste of valuable resources.*

SECRETARY OF THE NAVY JONES TO PRESIDENT JAMES MADISON

Navy Department
June 6. 1813

Sir

The enclosed report is prepared in consequence of a call from the Chairman of the Naval Committee of the Senate for a return of the number of Gun Boats in service and their stations, with a view as I understood him in conversation to propose an additional special defence for Baltimore of a number of Barges or Galleys which the City of Baltimore during the late excitement built and now wish to charge them upon the general Government. I deemed it proper on this occasion to exhibit a general view of our coast & harbour defence which I think you will believe with me is amply sufficient to absorb all the resources of the Department applicable to that branch of the Service. I have had a great deal of correspondence with corporations and committees from Maine to Georgia which I did not think necessary to trouble you with. It became my duty to resist their claims and I believe I have addressed arguments and reasoning which has satisfied the most of them. I consider it indispensable to resist the pretensions of local bodies who undertake to prescribe not only the extent but the natures and manner of employing the public force.

As you have repeated applications on this subject the enclosed paper may be a useful reference— I am very respectfully your obdt. Servt.

W Jones

ALS, DLC, James Madison Papers, Ser. I, Vol. 52, No. 50.

[Enclosure]

Exhibit shewing the number of Gun Boats and vessels substituted for Gun Boats, in Service for harbour and coast defense at the several naval stations and elsewhere in the U States

Stations	Number of Gun Boats	Number & description of force substituted for Gun Boats	Explanations & Remarks
New Orleans and Coast adjacent	7	2 despatch Boats 1 Block Ship building—	progress not ascertained
Georgia	6	2 Barges 1 Ship 18 Guns	
So Carolina	5[1]	2 Barges. . . . . 2 Schooners 16 Guns ea 1 Schooner 10 Guns	4 of the Gun Boats and the 2 Barges recently ordered into Service
Norfolk	20	. . . . 2 tenders 1 Bomb vessel	9 of which are fully manned the others partially manned & progressing as men may be procured

Stations	Number of Gun Boats	Number & description of force substituted for Gun Boats	Explanations & Remarks
Potowmac	3	1 Cutter................ 1 Schooner............. 2 Scows ea a 32 pdr	a heavy gun in each
Baltimore	1	3 first rate Schooners 1 smaller.... do.........	Well armed—Loaned to the US by the owners for the defence of the Bay and the River Patapsco—The US. stipulate to return them safe to the owners in the condition they were received. They are manned with about 350 men paid and provisioned by the US. & commanded by N. officers
Delaware Bay & River	10	2 Block Sloops	With solid covered Block Houses proof against boarding—armed one with 4 long 18s. the other 2 long 18s and 2 24 pd. carronades manned each with 50 men sail remarkably fast, row with facility and draw but 6 feet water.
		6 Barges................	Well armed—furnished by the City of Philada. partially manned and attached to the Delaware flotilla under the command of the Navy officer
New York	31	.... The *Alert* Sloop of War 5 fire vessels	15 of which are manned provisioned and paid by the City and under the command of the U S officer commanding the flotilla— the U S furnishing only the Boats military stores & commanders
Waters of Rhode Island Connecticut & the Sound	11	....	....

Stations	Number of Gun Boats	Number & description of force substituted for Gun Boats	Explanations & Remarks
Boston Harbour	4	....	To be manned generally with the crews of the U S vessels whilst under repairs in that port.
Portsmouth NH	2	....	For the protection of the Harbour and Navy Yard, the crews to be employed in the duty of the Navy Yard.
		U.S. Brig *Siren* U.S. Brig *Enterprize*	Ordered to this Station from the Southward but were out on a short cruize when the order arrived which will delay their arrival on that station for some time.
			As the US. Brigs *Nautilus Vixen* and *Viper* have been captured it is contemplated to purchase immediately 2 Brigs of 16 Guns ready equipped to be employed for the protection of the coast of Maine New Hampshire & Massachusetts, as depredations have greatly encreased there and Gun Boats are not applicable to that coast
Lake Champlain	2	4 armed schooners[2]	
Presque Isle or Erie	4	....	

total <u>106</u> Gun Boats in Service. The residue of the Gun Boats that are fit for service are kept in ordinary ready to be put in service on any sudden emergency—those that are decayed and unfit for service are laid up. Respectfully submitted[3]

W Jones
Navy Department
June 7. 1813

The Hon. Samuel Smith
Chairman of the Naval
Committee of the Senate of the U S.

Copy, DLC, James Madison Papers, Ser. I, Vol. 52, No. 53. This copy was written and
signed by Jones.

1. There were no gunboats at Charleston, only barges and schooners; see pp. 35–37 and 57–59.
2. Jones meant sloops. He did not know of the capture of two of the sloops on 3 June; see pp.
488–92, 513.
3. The vessels in North Carolina were still in ordinary when Jones forwarded this report of the gunboats in service to Madison. Jones ordered all six returned to active service on 11 June; see p. 143.

SENATOR SAMUEL SMITH TO SECRETARY OF THE NAVY JONES

                                              Senate Chamber   10th June 1813
Sir,
    The Committee of Senate to whom has been referred so much of the Presi-
dent's Message as relates to the Navy of the United States, have directed me to
request of you to inform them, whether you consider yourself authorised to
hire or purchase vessels as Hulks to be sunk in the Entrances of the harbours of
the United States, or to prepare Booms or other impediments to prevent the
entry of the ships of the enemy into such harbours.[1] The Committee appear to
be disposed to employ large Barges, capable of carrying 18 and 32 pounders,
and of such a construction as that they may row as fast as the Barges of the
enemy. The committee wish to know how many such Barges would be necessary
for the ports of the U.S.—And how much such Barges of 50 feet long, and 70
feet long would cost. I have the honor to be your obt. servt.

                                              S. Smith   Chairman

LS, DNA, RG45, MLR, 1813, Vol. 4, No. 37 (M124, Roll No. 56).

1. On 16 July Congress approved an act for the defense of ports and harbors that authorized the
president to hire or purchase hulks to be sunk at such entrances; see *Statutes at Large*, Vol. 3, Stat. 1,
Chap. 13, p. 18.

SECRETARY OF THE NAVY JONES TO SENATOR SAMUEL SMITH

Honble. Samuel Smith   Navy Department
Chairman of the Naval   June 17. 1813.
Committee—Senate.

    In reply to your letter of the 10th instant I have the honor to state that "the au-
thority to hire or purchase vessels as Hulks, to sink in the entrance of the Harbours of the United States, or to prepare Booms or other impediments to prevent the entry of the Ships of the enemy into such Harbours" is not considered
as vested in this Department. It is believed that such preparations have hitherto
been under the direction of the War Department (under whose authority chains
or Booms have in some places been long since prepared,)   The Islands piers &c

in the several rivers and harbours, which have been ceded to the United States by the individual States, and which are necessary for the purpose of extending Booms, having been under the exclusive direction of either the War or Treasury Department. Moreover I am not certain that any Department of the government of the United States, is vested with authority to obstruct the Channel of a River or harbour, by sinking hulks or by other impediments, without the previous sanction of the State having Jurisdiction over the same.

The Barges (or rather Galleys) contemplated by the Committee are certainly a very useful Class of Vessels as an auxiliary force, attached to vessels calculated to afford accommodations necessary for the health and comfort of the crews, without which it would be impracticable to procure them, or to retain them if procured.

The form necessary to produce the greatest celerity of movement by the impulse of the oar, must be long, narrow, and shallow; consequently such vessels being open and of small capacity, cannot afford to a numerous Crew, the accommodations necessary to lodge and protect them from the weather, or to prepare their provisions and carry the necessary Supplies. Hence it results that if these vessels are to be employed distinctly, a given number will require a Store Ship—Hospital ship and receiving ship, in which to prepare the provisions, and shelter the Crew from the inclemency of the weather, otherwise disease will be the inevitable consequence.

But if attached to the Vessels now employed in harbour defence, and manned from those vessels, as the nature of the Service may require, the utility of both Classes of Vessels would be retained; the difficulty of procuring additional Crews obviated; and the expenditure but moderately increased: as the same Crews would perform the alternate duty of both classes of Vessels and the accommodation and comfort of both would be improved.

The only advantage to be derived from Barges is in calm or very moderate weather, for when the wind blows strong, any fast Sailing Vessel can with ease escape from or overtake them. It is impracticable to combine in the same vessels the qualities of very fast rowing and Sailing.

The obstacles to manning Barges are want of accommodations, labor of the Oar, and the absence of pecuniary advantage; whilst they are tempted into the Ships of the Navy, and private armed vessels, by the Stimulus of prize money, the eclat of our Naval Victories, and the preference which Seamen naturally give to Vessels better adapted to their habits and Comfort; and I am satisfied that these causes will be found to operate so powerfully as to prevent any considerable extension of this species of force. We have the capacity to encrease the number of Vessels of every description to any extent, but experience proves that the means of manning them is not so unlimited and therefore policy requires that we should husband our resources. In Philadelphia they have been recruiting nearly three months and with the aid of the bounty given by the Citizens have manned only 7 Gun Boats. In Baltimore Captain Gordon was nearly three months manning one Gun Boat. In Norfolk the recruiting for the Gun Boats has entirely failed. In Charleston, where I have ordered Six Barges into Service, Captain Dent despairs of manning them, and the same difficulty elsewhere but too generally prevails.

It may be said that prejudices exist against Gun Boats which do not apply to Barges; this is yet to be determined. Gun Boats have much better accommodations and afford more comfort to their Crews than Barges, and I think I hazard nothing in predicting, that the difficulty of manning Barges will equal that of Gun Boats. Certain it is that this species of force can be carried but to a very limited extent under the Naval Establishment. The number of men required in proportion to the efficient force of a Barge is excessively great, and it will be recollected that a vast number of our seamen are still employed in licensed merchantmen abroad and in our public and private armed vessels.

This small and scattered species of force is the most expensive and least susceptible of the economical controul of this department of any that can be devised. The rank and character of the persons commanding on detached and remote Stations ensure no responsibility. Small agencies and offices must be multiplied, and in every view the nature of the Service is incompatible with the rank, duties and indispensable acquirements of the officers of the Navy, and of the existing regulations of the Naval Establishment.

If this system of Harbour defence is to be extended, the public interest will be promoted by rendering the system distinct from that of the Naval Establishment.

If Congress under existing circumstances shall determine to employ a certain number of Barges, I would recommend their being attached to and manned from the force already employed for Harbour defence, as occasion may require. In this way and this way only, does the enemy employ his launches and Barges.

Then with a view to the force alluded to as now provided for Harbour defence the following number and apportionment of Barges may resolve your inquiry viz

Mississippi & Waters of Mobile	8 Barges	
Georgia	4	
South Carolina	6	
North Carolina	5	
Lower part of Chesapeak	8	
Upper part of Do.	8	
Delaware Bay & River	6	
New York	6	
Waters of R Island &	4	
Long Island Sound		
total	55	

To the Coast and Harbours east of Rhode Island Gun Boats and Barges are inapplicable.

From a comparison of the actual cost of Barges lately built for the Committee of the Citizens of Philada. the largest Class mentioned in your letter say 70 feet long 14 feet wide and 4 feet deep measuring about 36 Tons would cost with Sails, rigging, Oars and every thing complete except armament about $2500
The Second Class viz 50 feet long 12 feet wide
     & 3 1/2 feet deep measuring about 19 tons
     complete except armament $1250
The 3rd Class viz 36 feet long 8 feet wide
     3 feet deep, measuring about 9 tons $ 625
The first Class is capable of carrying a long 24 pd. in one end and a 32 pd. Carronade in the other—would row 36 Oars double banked, and require a Crew of 54 men Officers included.

The 2nd Class a long light 18 pounder, would row 28 oars, double banked, and require a Crew of 42 men, officers included.

The 3rd Class a 12 pd. Carronade, would row 20 Oars double banked and require a Crew of 30 men officers included.

They should be constructed both ends alike to row with equal facility and velocity either way.

Those employed in the Southern waters would require to be copper fastened & coppered, to secure them from the worms, which would increase the cost of

the 1st Class	$750
of the 2nd Class	$500
of the 3rd Class	$300

I am very respectfully Sir, your obedt. Servt.

W. Jones.

LB Copy, DNA, RG45, Letters to Congress, Vol. 2, pp. 177–81.

Defense of North Carolina

The British blockade of the Chesapeake was so effective by May 1813 that some of the bay area trade moved south to North Carolina. Desiring to close this new outlet in late May, the British sent a schooner, the former Baltimore privateer Highflyer, *to reconnoiter off Ocracoke. The British departed after taking a sloop, but left the coastal towns greatly alarmed. Local residents wrote to North Carolina's Governor William Hawkins demanding the return of the two gunboats laid up in ordinary by Secretary Jones's February reductions. Jones soon found himself inundated with requests for coastal protection. The collector of the port of Ocracoke, Thomas S. Singleton, and Congressman William Rufus King[1] solicited gunboats from Jones after receiving many letters from coastal residents.[2]*

1. William Rufus King, a North Carolina lawyer, served that state in Congress from 1811 to 1816.
2. John Gray Blount to William Hawkins, 25 May 1813, Nc–Ar, Governors' Papers (William Hawkins), 1 Jan.–4 June 1813, pp. 189–90; Thomas S. Singleton to Jones, 21 May 1813, DNA, RG45, MLR, 1813, Vol. 3, No. 113 (M124, Roll No. 55). For more background on North Carolina during the war, consult Lemmon, Frustrated Patriots.

CONGRESSMAN WILLIAM RUFUS KING TO SECRETARY OF THE NAVY JONES

House of Representatives

Sir

Your engagements having prevented my seeing you at your office, I have taken the liberty of calling your attention to the exposed situation of the Sea coast of North Carolina— Leaving Ocracoke, Beaufort & Swansborough out of the question; I wish to direct your view to the Town of Wilmington situated on the bank of the Capefear river, now (in consequence of the dismantling of the Gun Boats) altogether destitute of any protection, except what is afforded by a sandy mound, called a <u>Fort</u>; which even were it repaired, and rendered competent to the defence of the Inlet it was ment to guard, would still (for the want of some naval force stationed in the river) leave the Town greatly exposed— The Capefear makes its entrance into the Ocean by two separate Channels, so distant from each other that the Fort intended to guard the one can have no bearing on the other— The Channel of this other called the new Inlet continues to

deepen, and even now will afford admittance to Vessels of sufficient force to effect the entire destruction of the Town— The country around is thinly populated; The Town is not adequate to its own defence even against the most inferior force. There are no Troops stationed either there or in the Vicinity; such an enterprize would be safe and easy— It may be said that our coasts will be a protection. That there is no sufficient object to induce an attack— To the first I will barely remark that we are much indebted to nature for the portion of security we now enjoy; none other having been afforded us— To the second I must be permitted to state, that there is in Wilmington two Banking establishments— In consequence of the Blockading of the Chesapeake it is the nearest and supposed to be the safest southern port; it is as might be expected crowded with shiping, and will thus attract the attention of the Enemy. There are several salt manufactorys in the vicinity of the Town; the destruction of which would not only be a serious loss to the proprietors, but would be greatly detrimental to the state— I trust sir nothing more need be said to convince you that objects are not wanting to stimulate the avarice of the Enemy— Without greatly exceeding the due limits of expenditure a military force could not be so stationed as to guard to points exposed— A small naval force is alone wanting and from the shallowness of our waters Gun Boats are peculiarly fitted to be useful— I hope you will take the subject under consideration; and oblige me with an answer—[1]
Your most Obt. Huml. Servt.

W. R. King

ALS, DNA, RG45, MLR, 1813, Vol. 4, No. 94 (M124, Roll No. 56). Jones received King's letter on 12 June, which suggests that the congressman probably wrote it on or before that date.

1. Jones ordered two vessels for Ocracoke and one for Beaufort; see Jones to William R. King, 14 June 1813, DNA, RG45, MLS, Vol. 11, p. 310 (M209, Roll No. 4).

SECRETARY OF THE NAVY JONES TO SAILING MASTER THOMAS N. GAUTIER

T. N. Gautier Esqr.   Navy Department
Comg. Naval Officer,   June 22nd 1813.
Wilmington N.C.
Present.

Sir,
    You will repair to Wilmington, North Carolina with the least possible delay, and prepare for immediate service six of the Gun boats under your command; and will recruit the following number of petty Officers, Seamen, and ordinary Seamen for each boat viz.

1 Acting Gunner at	$20 pr. mo. & 2 rations pr. day.	
2 Acting Master's Mates at	20 Do.	Do.
1 Carpenter's Mate at	19 Do.	Do.
1 Cook	18 Do.	Do.
1 Acting Steward at	18 Do.	Do.
8 Seamen at	12	and 1 Do.
16 Ordinary Seamen at	10 Do.	Do.

Of this force <u>three</u> are to be stationed at Wilmington, <u>one</u> at Beaufort, and <u>two</u> at Ocracoke. Your command will extend to the whole, and you will give such instructions to the several commanders, as the good of the service may require. You will act under the immediate orders of and communicate directly with, this Department, on all subjects relative to your command;[1] and I expect of you, the utmost vigilance and attention, as well to protect the waters and coast assigned to your command, as to guard against the abuses, and regulate the expenditures with the strictest economy, and accountability of all those under your command.

Doctor Morrison will resume his station, and you will employ an acting Surgeon's Mate, (who will be entitled to the pay and emoluments of a Surgeon's Mate in the Navy) for the Boats at Ocracoke &c.

Sailing Master Taylor will proceed with you, to command one of the Boats at Wilmington. Sailing Master Manson is ordered to rejoin you at Wilmington; and as you go through Norfolk, Captain Cassin, upon shewing him this letter, will order four <u>good</u> sailing masters, from the Boats that are not manned, to proceed, under your command, to your station.

Mr. Potts, the Agent, who will also act as Purser for the station, until further ordered, will provide you with the necessary means to carry these orders into effect, and you will exhibit to him, this letter as his authority for the same. You will also man, and employ the Barge, and occasionally visit, and inspect the several stations, with care and scrutiny and report briefly, from time to time, whatever may be interesting. I am, Sir, respectfully, your Obt. Servant,

Wm. Jones

You will be allowed a Clerk for the station, who will receive the pay and rations of a Midshipman. W. J.

LB Copy, DNA, RG45, SNL, Vol. 10, pp. 475–76. (M149, Roll No. 10).

1. Jones officially made North Carolina separate from the Charleston Station.

American Forces Leave East Florida

The Madison administration had sought congressional approval for the occupation of the Floridas from the commencement of the war. The Senate narrowly defeated such a measure in July 1812, and the act that passed on 12 February 1813 authorized occupation of West Florida only.

The administration did not immediately order the removal of troops from East Florida, but ultimately it had to acknowledge defeat. Major General Thomas Pinckney, military commander in East Florida, received on 18 March the order from the War Department to evacuate. The army embarked from the St. Johns River on 26 April and evacuated Fernandina on 6 May. Commodore Campbell's gunboats convoyed the troops to St. Marys.[1] In writing Campbell about the changes he was to implement as a result of the military departure from East Florida, Jones queried the commodore about consolidating the Georgia and South Carolina Stations.

1. For more background on East Florida, see Patrick, Florida Fiasco, *especially chapters 19 and 20.*

Secretary of the Navy Jones to Commodore Hugh G. Campbell

Hugh G. Campbell, Esqr.   Navy Department.
Commdg. Naval Officer   June 12. 1813.
St. Marys Ga.

Sir,

The naval and military forces of the United States having withdrawn from Florida, the naval force assigned for the protection of the Waters of Georgia, will consist of the ship *Troup*, six Gun Boats and the Barges on that station. The Barges are to be attached to the Gun Boats, or to the *Troup*, and manned from those Vessels as occasion may require, but they are not to have distinct Crews.

You will not confine the Gun Boats to St. Marys or to any particular Station, but so distribute the force under your command as to protect the coast and several Inlets in the most effectual manner.

The evacuation of Florida appears to supersede the necessity of a distinct Naval Station at St. Mary's, which has greatly increased the expenditures.—

You will please to communicate your ideas on the subject, and let me know whether, in your opinion, the entire business of the station cannot be transacted to more advantage, and with more complete control, at Savannah, so as to abolish the establishment at St. Marys, and when the several vessels may want supplies, employ either one of the public vessels, or a craft, for the purpose of conveying them. If the public interest will admit this arrangement, I contemplate extending your Command so as to embrace the naval force on the So. Carolina and Georgia Stations, as a Captain on each of those Stations is thought superfluous. In this event, you would reside at Charleston, and have a trusty Commandant of the Ship *Troup* to superintend the force on the Georgia Station, under your immediate controul.—[1]

The Hospital vessel may be continued, and stationed so as to afford the greatest advantage to the whole force.— I was pleased to learn that the *Enterprize* had sailed for her destination.— I am, respectfully, Your obdt. servt.

                                                            W. Jones.

LB Copy, DNA, RG45, SNL, Vol. 10, pp. 463–64 (M149, Roll No. 10).

1. When Jones did not receive a response from Campbell regarding this station consolidation, he wrote to him again on 25 June 1813; see DNA, RG45, SNL, Vol. 10, p. 480 (M149, Roll No. 10).

Commodore Hugh G. Campbell to Secretary of the Navy Jones

                                                    St. Marys   16th July 1813
Sir

I have the honor to acknowledge the receipt of your letter dated the 25th Ult, expressing a desire to break up the naval establishment at this place and observing that you want to hear from me before you determine

In reply I beg leave to observe that the alteration you propose may promote the Public good in a pecuniary way to a small amount, but how far that would compensate for the want of an establishment on the Frontier, where we have daily in view and very near neighbors, a Foreign nation, allied to the greatest enemy we have, and that the continuance of the war may induce the enemy to take advantage of the unprotected situation of these waters, into which they may pass with little concern and cut off all communication between this place and savannah by water, likewise, the encreased Trade that is likely to recommence at Fernandina, well calculated to promote smuggling, which without a good lookout will be practised with ease across this narrow water, and will likely Bring on frequent misunderstandings between us and the spaniards, that may require some person on the spot to govern our officers commanding Gun Vessels, the most of whom frequently stand in need of advice and correction.

In other respects the plan you propose is economical and compact from which might result a small deduction of Public expence, and should you determine to break up this establishment would not savannah on account of its central Situation be the most proper residence for a commanding officer, where he could communicate more readily with the two extremities of his command   I have honor to be With Great Respect Sir Your obedient servant

Hugh G Campbell

LS, DNA, RG45, CL, 1813, Vol. 5, No. 5 (M125, Roll No. 30).

Secret Mission of *John Adams*—Status Report

By June John Adams *was almost ready to sail on her secret mission to reinforce the American fur trading post on the Columbia River. John Jacob Astor was concerned that the Royal Navy would become involved. He was correct, for the Northwest Company's vessel,* Isaac Todd, *escorted by H.M. frigate* Phoebe, *had left Portsmouth, England, on 25 March 1813 for Fort Astoria. The Northwest Company had convinced the Admiralty that it was in Britain's national interest to stop this American encroachment. On 26 June, almost on the point of departure, the American mission was indefinitely postponed. Faced with a critical manpower shortage on Lake Ontario, Jones sent William M. Crane and the crew of* John Adams *to assist Commodore Isaac Chauncey. Despite continued remonstrances from Astor that national security and American interests were at stake, the short-term exigencies of winning the war prevailed. The nation's resources were stretched too thin to warrant such an expedition.*[1]

1. *For background on Fort Astoria, see Gough,* Royal Navy, *pp. 8–28; and Bridgwater, "John Jacob Astor." Jones directed Crane to communicate to Astor the "temporary change" in plans and "to suspend the collateral arrangements." See Jones to Crane, 26 June 1813, DNA, RG45, SNL, Vol. 10, pp. 481–82 (M149, Roll No. 10).*

JOHN JACOB ASTOR TO SECRETARY OF THE NAVY JONES

New York   17 June 1813

Sir

I had the Honnour to address a few Lines to you on the 6th not haveng reicd any Reply I feare the Same has escaped your noties— understanding that Capt. Crane is nearly ready for Sea it would be very Satisfactory to me to be informd as Soon as may be convenient whether it be your wish that I should prepare a ship for the voyage in contemplation and for the purpose of caring Such Suplys for the use of Captn. Crane as he may be in need of & which he can not carry in his owen ship— I have the pleasure to Inform you that I have a few Days Sence Recd Dispatches over Land—from the mouth of Columbia River there Dates are of the 26 & 29 June last from there I had the Happiness to Learn that the party which went over land had Safly Reached our fort there & that the ship *Beaver* which Saild from here on the 16 octr. 1811 with men & suplys had also arvid & was Laying in Columbia River when the Dipatches came away—all ware well the pepal felt Secure from the natives and our prospects are most flattering and no Doubt of success is entertaind unless Interupted by the British of which I have Some feares— Mr. Stewart the Bearer of these Dispatches has not yet arvid here but I exspect him in 10 or 12 Days & he will no Doubt give Some Intersting Information   I will thank you Sir to make this known to the president

I think it very Important that if a Ship is Send in aid of Capt. Crane that the Commander should be a man of experiens of confidence & Integritay & abilitys—one who is acquainted with the coast with the Rivers & the country generally such mean are Sccars [*scarce*] there is one only whom I know Mr. John Ebbetts & he will not go unless he can be made acquainted with the object of the voyage hitherto. I Did not feel myself at Liberty to make it Known to any one but if I am to Send a Ship I would thank you to permit me to comunicate with him— I have the Honnour to be Resptfuly Sir your obd Servt.

John Jacob Astor

ALS, DNA, RG45, MLR, 1813, Vol. 4, No. 58 (M124, Roll No. 56).

SECRETARY OF THE NAVY JONES TO JOHN JACOB ASTOR

John Jacob Astor Esqr.   Navy Dept.
New York   June 22nd 1813.

Sir,

My reply to your favours of the 6th and 17th had been delayed, as well by the pressure of Official business, as by the desire I entertained to have a full and final conversation with the President, on the subject of Captain Crane's destination, and the objects connected with it. His indisposition has, however, precluded the opportunity I had desired; but I still hope that the health of the President will be sufficiently restored, before my final instructions to Captain Crane shall be closed. The bulk of the extra articles, which Captain Crane has desired you to prepare, exceeds my expectation, and I have suggested to him, the expediency of substituting rice for a considerable portion of the Bread. Will you please to furnish me with a list of the extra articles, ordered by Captain Crane—of the manner, and the terms on which you proposed to ship them, and of the conditions, on which you proposed to take any surplus articles at the place of destination, which Captain Crane may not require for the use of the United States. You will please provide the articles Captain Crane may have required, and furnish me with the information I solicit, in order that I may lay the same before the President; as it is a contingent affair, requiring your confidential aide, instead of the usual agency of the regular Agent of the Department, in order to keep the destination and object of the voyage unknown. As to the character of, and conditions on which you may engage a vessel, for the purpose of conveying the extra stores, and such things on your own account, as you may think proper, I shall submit it entirely to your judgment and discretion, satisfied that you will, in this case, act for the United States as you would for yourself. I have some knowledge of Captain Ebbetts, having seen him in Canton, and consider him every way qualified for the command you contemplate for him, and have no objection to your communicating to him, in confidence, the object and destination. I am very much gratified with the information you have received from the settlement, and I sincerely hope, as well for the benefit of the enterprizing individuals concerned, as for the future prosperity of an interesting and important branch of the trade of our country, that the destined succours may arrive in time, to afford permanent security to the settlements. I am, very respectfully, Your Obedient Servant,

Wm. Jones.

LB Copy, DNA, RG45, CLS, 1813, pp. 34–35.

Cartel Agreement

After five weeks of sighting no enemy vessels, Commodore John Rodgers captured four ships during the second week of June. The British packet brig Duke of Montrose *surrendered to* President *on 10 June, northwest of the Azores. Rodgers arranged a cartel agreement with the captain of the packet. The Admiralty, however, refused to honor it, affirming that they had informed the American government that exchanges made on the high seas were invalid.[1] The following documents are the packet captain's account of the capture and the cartel agreement between the two commanders.*

1. *Norway,* Post-Office Packet Service, *pp. 240–42.*

AARON GROUB BLEWETT TO CHRISTOPHER SAVERLAND[1]

C. Saverland Esqr.   Falmh.   June 23. 1813

Sir,

I beg leave to acquaint you for the information of their Lordships the Post Masters General, that H M late Hired Packet *Duke of Montrose,* under my command, being in the prosecution of her voyage to Halifax with the Mails, on the 9th Inst. on Lat. 44.0. Long 29 1/2 at 7 h. 30 m. we discovered a strange sail on our weather bow, at 8 A M perceived her to be a Schooner, under all possible sail in chase of us, and coming up very fast, we mustered all hands to Quarters, and got all ready for Action, the Quarter & Waste Nettings filled with Sails & Hammocks, the Mails ready for sinking got the Stern Boat in & run out the Stern Chase Guns. half past Meridian the Schooner hoisted American Colours, and fired 3 Guns at us, we still keeping our course, waiting for the Enemy to close, in order to get our Guns to bear more effectually, but finding her to keep on our Quarter at long shot distance, we bore up and got the Stern Guns to bear, & fired them, then hauled across her Bows and discharged our Starboard Broadside at her & again wore to close her, at the same time firing our Larboard Broadside at her, & again wore to close her, at the same time firing our Larboard Broadside at her as they came to bear, the Schooner also tacked to the N.E. & the Action became General, with all Sail set, at 1 P M. the Schooner tacked to the Westward to keep at long shot, we still kept up our fire with our long Guns, at 1.45 the Schooner tacked to the Eastward & bore up to close us, when the Action was continued until 20 minutes past 2, She then being out of Gun shot, and making all Sail to the Eastward, we ceased firing & tacked to the Westward keeping our course, at 6 lost sight of the Enemy, this Schooner was pierced for 14 Guns & appeared to have a great number of Men. I am happy to say that in this Action no one was hurt on board the *Duke of Montrose*, nor did the Ship receive any material damage.

On the 10th Inst. in Lat. 43.4 Long. 31.40 at 11.45 we discovered a large Ship ahead, at noon we tacked Ship to avoid her, apparently in chase of us, at 2.30 made the private signal for the day to the Chase, which was not answered, at 2.45 the chase was fast coming up with us, and made a Signal at her fore which we did not understand, at 5 she hoisted a broad blue Pendant, at the main & commenced firing at us, at 6 P M. we hoisted an Ensign & Pendant, at 6.30 we discovd. an American Ensign flying on board the chasing ship, she being then within musket shot with all her Crew at Quarters, the Tompions out of her Guns and apparently intended to fire directly into us. I thought it proper to sink the Mails and haul down the Colours, as it was impossible for us to escape, shortly after the *Duke of Montrose* was taken possession of by an Officer from the United States Frigate *President* Commanded by Commodore Rogers. I was immediately removed on board the American Frigate, where I remained until 8 P M when it was ordered by Commodore Rogers, that the Officers, Passengers & Crew of the Packet, together with the Crews of the Brigs *Kitty* & *Maria* (two Prizes taken by the Commodore) should return to England in the *Duke of Montrose* as a Cartel, and consider themselves Prisoners of War until regularly exchanged. We parted from the American Frigate on the 12th inst. at 8 A M then in Lat. 43.12 Long 29.45 & arrived here this day.

It gives me much pleasure to say that in the Action on the 9th Inst. with the Schooner, the Crew of the *Duke of Montrose* behaved with the greatest spirit & entirely to my satisfaction & their conduct since their Capture has been such as I could wish.

I cannot close this Letter without bearing evidence to extreme liberality of Commodore Rogers who would not allow the Crew of the *Duke of Montrose* to be plundered of the least trifle. I am &c.

(Signed)   A G Blewett

LB Copy, General Post Office, London, GPO, Post 48/7, pp. 443–45.

1. Aaron Groub Blewett, captain of the British Post Office Service temporary packet *Duke of Montrose*, reported his capture to Christopher Saverland, agent for the postal service at Falmouth.

CARTEL AGREEMENT [1] FOR *DUKE OF MONTROSE*

United States Frigate *President*
at Sea.   June 10. 1813

1. We the undersigned being the Officers, Crew & Passengers of H B Majesty's Packet Brig the *Duke of Montrose* this day captured by the United States Frigate *President,* Commanded by John Rodgers Esqr. so obligated ourselves & pledge our sacred Honor in Consideration of said Packets being permitted to return to England, with us on Parole not to serve in Arms against the United States of America during the present War or not until we are regularly exchanged as Prisoners of War.

2. And we do also obligate ourselves to proceed direct for England on said Brig observing strictly her character as a Cartel & that, on our arrival in England she shall be placed in the Hands of the Agent for American Prisoners & subject to his Orders as a Cartel.

3. And we do further obligate ourselves that the said Brig shall be permitted to leave England with a similar number of American Prisoners and also allowed to proceed to the United States of America without molestation or hindrance under the direction of Mr. David West (Private Secretary to Commodore Rogers) who is placed on board the said Brig for the purpose of seeing the above obligation carried into effect.

Signed by Captn, Officers, Crew & Passengers

LB Copy, General Post Office, London, GPO, Post 48/7, pp. 446–47.

1. Christopher Saverland forwarded Aaron Groub Blewett's letter and the cartel agreement to Francis Freeling, secretary of the Post Office in London, and expressed his misgivings with Article 3. Receiving word that the Admiralty had disavowed the agreement, Saverland ordered Blewett to fit out *Duke of Montrose* immediately for another voyage; see Saverland to Freeling, 26 June and 2 July 1813, General Post Office, London, GPO, Post 48/7, pp. 446 and 455.

Enterprise at Portsmouth

Captain Isaac Hull's command encompassed the defense of Portsmouth harbor and the coastal area adjoining it to the east, as well as superintendence and construction of a 74-gun ship. Jones ordered the brigs Siren *and* Enterprise *to aid Hull in protecting his station.* Enterprise *arrived in mid-June, but* Siren *was still laid up at Charlestown undergoing repairs. Distressed by the strong British presence off the coast, Hull now worried that these ships might easily succumb to the larger British force and recommended that they be sent instead on cruises to the St. Lawrence and Halifax.*

CAPTAIN ISAAC HULL TO SECRETARY OF THE NAVY JONES

U.S. Navy Yard   Portsmo.
24th June 1813

Sir

I had the honour a few days since to inform you of the arrival of the *Enterprize* at this place. She is still here, but is ready for sea, and will sail the first wind provided that nothing appears off to prevent it. Two days after she arrived, a Frigate, the *Rattler* Sloop of War and two Brigs were close in with the harbour, and some one of them has been near ever since. That and the want of a good pilot has prevented her from sailing.

When these vessels[1] were first ordered to this Station I believed they would be very useful in protecting the Coasting trade, but since I find the Enemy's Cruizers so much stronger than we are that we can hardly promise securety to the trade if we undertake to convoy it. Indeed by sending these vessels into the ports to the Eastward that are not well guarded, they will be in danger of being taken out by superior force, and will probably be the cause of the destruction of other property, if not the towns where they are. With this view of the situation of the Coast, I submit to you whether they would not be more usefully employed taking a cruize near the Southern edge of the Grand Bank, or between that and the entrance of the Gulph of St. Lawrence; they would there be out of the way of cruizers on the coast and would probably fall in with captured Ships bound in or with ships bound to Europe, or to Halifax.

When I am made acquainted with your wishes on this subject I shall act accordingly.[2] I have the honour to be With great respect Sir, Your obedient Servt.

Isaac Hull

Since writing the above, the *Rattler* and a Brig have appeared off.

LS, DNA, RG45, CL, 1813, Vol. 4, No. 111 (M125, Roll No. 29).

1. *Enterprise* and *Siren*.
2. Jones responded that the fears of the local populace demanded their use as convoys until such time when he could reconsider moving them to another station; see Jones to Hull, 5 July 1813, DNA, RG45, CNA, Vol. 1, p. 454 (M441, Roll No. 1).

A Deadly Trap in Long Island Sound

In March Congress passed what became known as the "Torpedo Act." Under the provisions of this law, the government pledged to pay to any individual who burned, sank, or destroyed a British warship, a bounty amounting to half the value of the destroyed craft plus half "the value of her guns, cargo, tackle and apparel."[1] The government's offer of financial reward spawned a number of efforts by enterprising citizens to destroy enemy vessels.[2] Although none of these attempts ever resulted in the loss of a British warship, the Royal Navy did experience several close calls. The deadliest and most frightening of these occurred on 25 June off New London.

1. Statutes at Large, *Vol. 2, Stat. 2, Chap. 47, p. 816.*
2. *For brief treatments of this aspect of the naval war against Great Britain, see* Hutcheon, Robert Fulton, *pp. 120–26, and* Roland, Underwater Warfare, *pp. 120–25.*

MASTER COMMANDANT JACOB LEWIS TO SECRETARY OF THE NAVY JONES

Sir

I have Inform you that on finding some Persons, who were willing To try their Fortunes, in an attempt to distroy one of the Enimies Ship before New London, I assisted them in their project,   a vessel[1] was prepared for the purpose, partly loaded with peas & other Articles such as the Enimy were supposed to be in want of. some naval Stores &c. I had frequently witness'd the Enimies hawling Coasting Vessels alongside for the purpose of hoisting out such articles that they were in want of in preferance to discharging them with their Boats— (the plan was therefore) that if the Enimy should do with this Vessel as they were in the habit of doing with others—that of hawling her along Side of the Ship The Ship should be distroy'd

To effect the object, a Quantity of powder with a great Quantity of Combustables were placed beneath, the articles which the Enimy were to hoist out— the act of displacing these Articles was to Cause an Explosion, by a Cord fasten'd to the striker of a Common Gun lock—which ignited with a train of powder,—the first or Second Hogshead moved the Cord— my plan was to have obtained a Vessel having a mast calculated to make a Top mast for one of their largest Ship and to have conected the Cord to the heel of it—(this because) they could not have taken it out in any other way than geting the Vessel alongside,   (however) the expence prevented it, I could not afford the means,   (As it is) the result as follows—

This vessel proceeded off New London   the Barges as was expected, went in pursuit of her,   the persons on board after discharging several vollies of small arms on the Launches abandon'd, in their boat— the Enimy very Triumphantly took possession and stood Towards the Ship evidently with a view of taking her alongside of her

the tide running strong. & the wind failing they were prevented, after great exertion in towing with several of their Launches from getting alongside, and was obliged to bring the Vessel to Anchor & began discharging with their Launches— when the explosion took place, and it is believed distroy'ed every Soul as well the Launches— I am unable to give the probable numbers— you may expect that in a day or two— I am about driving or distroying the Frigate In the Delaware— Ships can be Kept out of our narrow waters and tides way—this is Certain.—[2] and I trust Ere long I shall devise the Means— I have the honor to Assure you of my high Consr. & respt.

J Lewis
Come. U.S. Flotilla
New Yk.   June 28th. 1813

ALS, DNA, RG45, MLR, 1813, Vol. 4, No. 107 (M124, Roll No. 56).

1. Schooner *Eagle* was fitted out by John Scudder, Jr. See Guernsey, *New York City*, Vol. 1, pp. 279–81.

2. Perhaps because of the near success of Lewis's scheme, Secretary Jones received a nearly identical plan from Mr. A. Anderson of Middletown, Connecticut. See Anderson to Jones, 13 July 1813, DNA, RG45, MLR, 1813, Vol. 4, No. 160 (M124, Roll No. 56).

Admiral Sir John B. Warren, R.N., to
First Secretary of the Admiralty John W. Croker

San Domingo, Potowmac River,
in the Chesapeake   July 22nd 1813—

Sir,

I request you will communicate the enclosed Letter from Sir Thos. Hardy to their Lordships, containing a most Melancholy event of the loss of a most Gallant officer and Ten Brave Seamen, by a Diabolical and Cowardly contrivance of the Enemy; Indeed the Dayly attempts practised by Commodore Decatur and the americans against that valuable officer Sir Thos. Hardy and the Ships under his orders now Blockading the Enemy's Frigates in the Port of New London; by means of Torpedoes Fire Vessels and other Infernal Machines, are beyond conception— I have the honor to be Sir, Your most Obedient humble Servant—

John Borlase Warren

LS, UkLPR, Adm. 1/504, p. 49.

[Enclosure]

Ramillies off New London
26th June 1813

Sir,

I beg to acquaint you, that yesterday morning at 10 oClock, Mr. McIntyre Master's mate was sent from this Ship in one of her Boats to cut off a Schooner that standing for New London, as there was but little wind he easily effected his purpose: but not until the Schooner had reached the Shore, and the Crew, who immediately deserted her, had let go her only anchor— She was taken possession of at 11. oClock by our Boat under a sharp musquetry from the Shore, but without doing any mischief— at 1. PM. I was hailed from the Schooner by Mr. McIntyre, and informed her name was the *Eagle* of New York, and was laden with Naval Stores and provisions—that he had cut her Cable—and as she had no other anchor on board, Lieutenant Geddes, with the Pinnace was (ordered to relieve the other Boat) and directed to take her alongside a Sloop we had Captured a few days before— at half past 2 o'Clock, whilst in the Act of furling her sails; and taking in moorings, the Schooner blew up with a most tremendous explosion, and I lament to say Lieutenant Geddes, and ten Valuable Seamen fell a sacrifice to this new mode of Warfare— Three Seamen who happened to be on the Foretopsail yard are very much burnt; but in a fair way of recovery— The Service will experience a great loss in Lieutenant Geddes, whose gallant and meritorious Conduct I have frequently witnessed—he having served with me at different periods for more than eight Years—and he has left a Widow to lament his loss—

Under the Circumstances, it is most providential that the Schooner was not taken alongside this Ship, as it appears to me quite evident that the Naval Stores and Provisions were placed in her as an Inducement for us to do so—

I enclose a list of the persons who unhappily lost their lives, and of those wounded. I have the honor to be Sir Your most obedient humble Servant

signed   T M Hardy
Captain

Copy, UkLPR, Adm. 1/504, pp. 51–53.

[Enclosure]

A List of One Officer & ten Seamen belonging to H:M: Ship *Ramillies* who were killed by an Explosion onboard a Enemy's Vessel Off New London, 25th June 1813.—

No. on SB	Names	Qualy.	Where Born	Remark.
23	John Geddes	Lieutt.	Aberdeen	Wife living in Portsmouth Hants.—
78	Willm. Bentley	LM	London	
131	Peter Dass	Ab	Orkney	Wife & Child living in Shields Northumberland.—
166	Chas. Welch	Ab	London	
167	Jas. Curtis	Ab	Penryn	
277	Philip Petree	Captain Af Guard	Wesel on the Rhine	
288	Jas. Spence	Ab	Orkney	
301	John Williams	Ab	London	
313	Allen McDougal	LM	Campbelltown (Argylle.	
328	Robt. Bean	Ab	London	
357	Wm. Darby	Ord	Dublin	

A List of 3 Seamen Wounded by the above Explosion.

No. on SB	Names	Qualy.	Where Born	Remark.
124	John Good	Ab	Exwell (Warwick)	Much Scorched in the Face, Arms, & Legs, but
143	Patk. Farrell	Ab	Cork	at present doing well
361	Alexr. Keith	Ord	London	

         "Signed—"   T. M. Hardy Captain

A Copy.—

Copy, UkLPR, Adm. 1/504, p. 55.

General Orders of Admiral Sir John B. Warren, R.N.

Genl. Order N 87   *San Domingo* in the Chesapeake
                                                              19 July 1813

   In consequence of the unfortunate accident which has lately taken place by
the blowing up of an American Prize some time after she was taken possession
of, by which His Majestys Service has been deprived of Lieut. Geddes a brave
and experienced Officer and ten valuable Seamen belonging to His Majesty's
Ship *Ramillies,* from which it appears the Enemy are disposed to make use of
every unfair and Cowardly mode of Warfare, such as Torpedoes. It is the Commander in Chiefs directions that no Prize or Boat shall be permitted to be
brought alongside of His Majestys Ships & Vessels (but that any American Vessel
or Boat with whom it may be necessary to communicate shall be Kept at a
proper distance or Anchored) before an examination shall take place.

                                                        Signed   H. Hotham
                                                        Captn. of the Fleet

LB Copy, University of Hull, Brynmor Jones Library, Hull, England, Hotham Collection,
DDHO/7/45.

New Signals for Naval Warships

   The British gained two prizes the day Chesapeake *struck her colors to* Shannon*: a
powerful new frigate, and a set of the American navy's signal books. Potentially, the latter
represented the greater of the two prizes, for with them, superior British vessels could lure
U.S. warships under their guns.*[1] *Recognizing the threat* Chesapeake*'s signal books
posed in enemy hands, Secretary Jones acted quickly to prepare a new signal system for distribution to all his commanding officers. To assist him in this task, the secretary called on
Commodore William Bainbridge.*

   1. Less than six weeks after the capture of Chesapeake, *the Admiralty was providing copies of the American
frigate's signals to vessels preparing to cruise in the Atlantic. See Admiralty to Captain Charles Paget, 10 July
1813, UkLPR, Adm. 2/1377, pp. 145–48.*

Secretary of the Navy Jones to Commodore William Bainbridge

Commodore Wm. Bainbridge   Navy Depart.
U.S. Navy   June 30. 1813.
Charlestown Masstts.

   Your letter of the 24 instant has been received.
   It is indeed, a subject of regret, that our Signals should have fallen into the
hands of the enemy; and it is certainly of the utmost importance that they
should be so constructed, as that the private Signals would be unintelligible to

him. They can readily be made so that a simple change of Signification such as can be easily retained in the memory, would render the written significations not only useless to him but of advantage to us, if they should fall into his hands, as the deception would be detected in the first display.

I wish you immediately to confer with Captains Hull and Decatur on the subject, and to prepare such new Signals and Significations as may effectually guard against the evil in future: And also to embrace every opportunity to inform the Commanders of our vessels abroad that the Enemy is in possession of our Signals. To send a vessel in search of them would be so precarious and uncertain as to afford no prospect of success; but, by fast sailing vessels going to France or the North of Europe, if any, it can be communicated through our public agents abroad.— It may, likewise, be conveyed by friendly persons going to Lisbon or Cadiz; and particularly to Brazil, where, I fear the *Essex* is blockaded. The *President* Frigate is probably by this time in the North Sea and the *Congress* perhaps between the Western Islands, and the Coast of Spain and Portugal and Madeira or the Cape de Verds.

The *Argus*, when she lands the Minister at Brest, or L'Orient, will cruize in the mouth of the Irish Channel.

What do you think of making it public in the Newspapers? Some of them might find their way to our Commanders. I am very respectfully your obedient Servt.

W. Jones.

LB Copy, DNA, RG45, CNA, Vol. 1, pp. 450–51 (M441, Roll No. 1).

COMMODORE WILLIAM BAINBRIDGE TO SECRETARY OF THE NAVY JONES

Navy Yard   Charlestown
16th July 1813

Sir

I have the honor of sending to you, by Lieut George Parker—a code of Private Signals which I have made, and the code of Numerical Signals which I have digested Captain Hull approves of them. As yet I have not heard from Comr. Decatur on the Subject to whom I immediately wrote in pursuance to your directions— But considering it important that the Signals should be as speedily arranged as possible, I have declined waiting any longer to hear from Comr. Decatur respecting them.

The Private Signals are so arranged as, in my opinion, to make a discovery of them impossible—except wantonly done— Each Commander of our vessels on receiving them, ought to be directed after reading them, to immediately destroy them and only to communicate them to his first Lt. on the probability of getting into Action, and then to do it, with the strictist injunction of Secrecy. In case of his illness he should then inform his first Lieutenant what the private Signals are. In the present order of the arrangement of the Numerical Signals 363 Numbers and their expressd significations, are fully and much better supplied by the introduction of the Compass Signal. This reduction of numbers, not only lessens the bulk of the Numerical Signals, but brings them within the power of three flags, instead of 4 as formerly required. By transposing the numbers of the late Signal flags (as I have done, and altering the repeaters, and answering flags, the Signals are so changed, as to make them compleatly unintelligable to the Enemy by their having the late ones—

I recommend the Day and night Signals, to be in one Book—and only one Signal Book to be allowed to each Vessel and that to be kept always in the Captains Possession.

I also send by Lieut. Parker (a most worthy officer, who was my first Lt. in the Action with the *Java*—and whom I have the honor of recommending particularly to your Notice) the flags taken from the British Frigate *Java* after her surrender to the U.S. Frigate *Constitution* under my command. I have the honor Sir, to be with the greatest respt. yr obt. St.

Wm Bainbidge

P.S. For some time past Lt. Parker has been by my orders, superintending the building of the Sloop of war [1] near this Yard—

NB. I enclose a Card of the old flags, and one as I have altered them. I did not put the new ones in the Signal Book. presuming that you would send it. to have new Books printed by it— And if you should. the leaf that has the drawing of the Night Signals ought to be taken out previously so that neither the flags or Shapes of Lights should be seen at the printing office— I also enclose a brief code of Fog Signals which I recommend to be written in the Signal Book Confidentially at the Department in preference of being printed—

LS, DNA, RG45, MLR, 1813, Vol. 4, No. 167 (M124, Roll No. 56).

1. *Wasp.*

SECRETARY OF THE NAVY JONES TO COMMODORE WILLIAM BAINBRIDGE

Commodore W. Bainbridge,   Navy Department
Charlestown Massachusetts.   Augt. 1st 1813.

Sir,

Master Commandant Parker [1] is charged with a packet to be delivered to you, containing the General and Private Signals now prescribed for the use of the Navy of the U.S. until countermanded. [2]

The System is, with some exceptions, that devised by, and received, a short time since, from yourself. Capt. Morris had prepared a set, upon nearly similar principles; but instead of one common number, as in yours, he had a varying number for each day of the week, which, as it would burthen the memory more than yours, the latter was preferred.

The old flags are retained, but with different values, and will save the expense and trouble of new ones.

You will observe some other minor alterations and substitutes in the New Code.

You will please furnish the Commanders, on your station, with copies; under the strictest injunction of caution and care, to confine the mental key to themselves, until the approach of danger, shall render it indispensible to communicate it to their first Lieutenants, only, with like confidence and precaution. My attention has been so engrossed, by important public measures, toward the close of the Session of Congress, that I have been drawn off from some objects, in your quarter, that will now, I trust, receive notice. Master Comdt. Parker will command the *Siren*, which vessel you will, when repaired, prepare for a cruise of as long duration, as her capacity for provisions, water and stores will admit, without prejudice to her sailing.

It is a little extraordinary, that, North of the Delaware, there is not a Boring Mill and Foundery fit for Naval purposes, which is a serious objection, in time of war, to extensive Naval building and equipment in the Eastern States; and if they had the Foundery and Machinery, the iron must still be brought from Jersey, and it is as easy to send the guns as the iron. We shall be under the necessity of sending the 24 pd. Carronades, for the *Siren*, from this place or Baltimore, through Delaware, Jersey, and the Sound, if clear, or to New Haven, and from thence by land. I shall send you the Drawings, proportions, & minute description of Carronade carriages, of various sizes, and of the Iron work, attached thereto, which, if you have it not already, will be useful to you.

It is probable I may send 10 or 12 of the carronades ready mounted, but of this you shall soon be informed.

The new sloops of war are to be armed with 20. 32 pd. carronades, and two long 18 pounders; for which you may prepare the carriages. The carronades will soon be ready and sent on. If you have the long 18 pounders it will save so much expense of transportation. I am, very respectfully, Your Obedient Servant,

W. Jones.

LB Copy, DNA, RG45, SNL, Vol. 11, pp. 32–33 (M149, Roll No. 11).

1. George Parker was promoted to master commandant on 24 July 1813.
2. A copy of this signal book may be found in DNA, RG45, Signal Books, 1813–June 1865.

British Naval Strength in North America

When the United States declared war on Great Britain, the Royal Navy had eighty-three vessels of all types in the western Atlantic and Caribbean.[1] While this was more than enough force to counter the threat of the infant republic's navy, it was adequate neither for blockading the American coast nor for combating privateers. Over the next twelve months, the Admiralty acted to increase this force with a steady infusion of ships and men, so that by the summer of 1813 British naval strength in North America stood at one hundred and twenty-nine vessels. The Royal Navy's growing strength spelled greater difficulties for the U.S. Navy and additional economic hardship for the nation.

1. For a listing of these vessels and the stations to which they were attached, see Dudley, Naval War of 1812, *Vol. 1, pp. 179–82.*

Ships in Sea Pay

[Extract]
Admiralty Office }
1st. July 1813.

The present disposition of His Majesty's
Ships and Vessels in Sea Pay

Leeward Islands
Rear Admiral Sir Francis Laforey Bart:

Rate	Ships	Guns	Men	Commanders	When Commissd.	When sailed from England
3	Cressy	74	590	C. Dashwood	26 Jany. 1811	31 Feb. 1813
"	Bedford	74	590	Jas. Walker	17 Sep. 1807	3 Apl. 1813
4	Grampus	50	343	F. A. Collier	8 Jany. 1810	2 Sep. 1812
5	Statira	38	315	H. Stackpoole	30 July 1807	3 Oct. 1808
"	Surprize	38	315	Sir T. J. Cochrane	19 Sep. 1812	19 Dec. 1812
"	Rhin	38	315	C Malcolm	17 June 1809	3 Apl. 1813
"	Orpheus	36	284	H. Pigot	22 Aug 1809	24 Nov 1809
"	Pique	36	284	Hon: A Maitland	9 Aug. 1811	22 Sep. 1813
"	Venus	32	270	K. MacKenzie	24 Sep 1808	24 Dec. 1812
"	Circe	32	215	E. Woolcombe	24 Nov 1804	15 Nov 1812
6	Lightning	20	121	B. C. Doyle	25 Mar 1807	2 Feb 1812
"	North Star	20	121	T. Coe	25 June 1810	6 June 1813
"	Coquette	20	121	J Simpson	8 May 1812	14 Dec 1812
Sloop	Surinam	18	121	J. E. Watt	19 Mar 1805	15 Dec 1808
"	Charybdis	18	121	J Clephane	18 Feb 1809	23 June 1809
"	Crane	18	121	J. Stuart	13 Sep 1809	29 Sep 1812
"	Espiegle	18	121	J. Taylor	7 Sep 1812	22 Jany. 1813
"	Peruvian	18	121	Geo. Kippen		
"	Epervier	18	121	Rd. Wales	Jany. 1813	23 Mar 1813

Type	Guns	Tons	Ship	Commander		
"	18	121	*Rifleman*	J. Pearce	12 Sep 1809	23 Mar 1813
"	18	121	*Indian*	Hy. Jane		6 Feb. 1813
"	18	121	*Persian*	C. Bertram	27 May 1809	3 Apl. 1813
"	18	121	*Heron*	W. McCulloch	16 Nov. 1812	28 Mar. 1813
"	18	121	*Eclipse*	H. Lynne	4 Sep 1809	6 Feb 1813
"	18	121	*Musquito*	J. Tomkinson	26 June 1811	24 Apl. 1813
"	18	121	*Arachne*	C. H. Watson	16 May 1808	9 May 1809
"	18	121	*Childers*	J. Bedford	20 July 1812	29 Sep 1812
"	18	121	*Arab*	R. Standley	17 Sep 1812	13 Dec 1812
"	16	100	*Vautour*	P. Lawless	20 Sep 1810	22 Jany. 1813
"	16	90	*Bustard*	C. B. Strong	12 Apl. 1808	3 Apl. 1813
"	14	85	*Spider*	F. G. Willock		
"	14	62	*Dominica*	G. W. Barrette	29 May 1811	23 Nov 1811
"	14	76	*Opossum*	Tho. Wolrige	24 Nov 1808	13 Oct. 1809
Gun Brig	14	55	*Momefortunée*	Lt. J. Steele	Commissd. abroad	
"	10	55	*Elizabeth*	" E. F. Dwyer	Do. Do.	
Schooner	4	20	*Ballahou*	" N. King	Do. Do.	
"	10	50	*Swaggerer*	" Guise	Do. Do.	
"	10	50	*Maria*	" Dickson	Do. Do.	
Cutter	10	60	*Liberty*	" Senhouse		

Jamaica
Rear Admiral Brown

Rate	Guns	Tons	Ship	Commander		
3	74	590	*Vengeur*	T. Dundas	1 Sep. 1810	22 Jany. 1813
"	74	590	*Asia*	G. Scott	29 Jany. 1812	22 Apl. 1813
5	44	340	*Argo*	C. Quinton	17 July 1802	22 Jany. 1813
6	22	175	*Garland*	R. P. Davies	23 Mar 1807	11 Nov 1807
"	22	175	*Cossack*	F. Stanfell	24 Sep 1803	7 June 1812
"	22	175	*Cyane*	T. Forrest	25 Mar 1807	
"	20	121	*Fawn*	T. Fellowes	25 Mar 1807	
"	20	121	*Herald*	C. Milward	12 Mar 1807	4 July 1812

Rate	Ships	No. of Guns	Men	Commanders	When Commissd.	When sailed from England
Sloop	Moselle	18	121	G. Mowbray	21 Nov 1807	16 Jany. 1808
"	Frolic	18	121	A. Mitchell	1 Apl. 1807	25 Feb. 1808
"	Sappho	18	121	H. OGrady	4 Feb. 1807	22 June 1808
"	Sapphire	18	121	Hy. Haynes	4 Feb. 1807	24 Sep. 1810
"	Forester	18	121	A. Kennedy	13 Apl. 1806	23 Mar. 1813
"	Doterel	18	121	W. W. Daniel	26 Oct. 1808	22 Apl. 1813
Gun Brig	Decouverte	10	50	Lt. Williams	Commissd. abroad	
"	Variable	10	50	Lt. Yates	Commissd. abroad	
Recg. Ship	Shark		70	J. Gore	23 June 1806	

North America
Admiral Sir John Borlase Warren

Rate	Ships	No. of Guns	Men	Commanders	When Commissd.	When sailed from England
3	St. Domingo	74	640	Admiral Sir J. B. Warren / S. J. Pechell	21 Mar 1809	14 Aug. 1812
"	Dragon	74	640	R. Barrie	1 Sep 1810	31 Oct. 1810
"	Ramillies	74	590	Sir T. M. Hardy	7 Oct 1812	16 Dec. 1821[1]
"	Poictiers	74	590	Sir J. P. Beresford	11 Jany. 1810	14 Aug 1812
"	Marlborough	74	590	R Adml. Cockburn / R. Honyman	30 July 1807	23 Sep 1812
"	Valiant	74	590	R. D. Oliver	23 Mar 1807	14 Jany. 1813
"	Hogue	74	590	Commre. Hotham / Hon. T. B. Capel	Dec. 1811	14 Jany. 1813
"	Victorious	74	590	J. Talbot	29 Dec. 1808	20 Nov 1812
"	Plantagenet	74	590	R. Lloyd	29 Dec. 1808	20 Nov 1812
"	Sceptre	74	590	C. B. H. Ross	6 Mar 1809	23 Mar 1813
"	Majestic	58	491	J. Hayes	26 Jany. 1813	2 June 1813

Rate	Ship	Guns		Captain		
5	*Acasta*	44	340	A. R. Kerr	10 Apl. 1811	14 June 1812
"	*Loire*	40	340	T. Brown	31 Oct 1807	22 Apl. 1813
"	*Nymphe*	38	315	F. P. Epworth	1 May 1812	9 July 1812
"	*Junon*	38	315	J. Sanders	30 Mar 1812	8 Aug. 1812
"	*Tenedos*	38	315	H. Parker	20 Apl. 1812	28 Aug. 1812
"	*Spartan*	38	315	E. P. Brenton	15 Aug. 1805	25 July 1811
"	*Shannon*	38	315	B. P. V. Broke	14 Jany. 1806	9 Aug. 1811
"	*Armide*	38	315	Sir E. T. Troubridge	21 Aug. 1809	25 Mar. 1813
"	*Lacedemonian*	83	315	S. Jackson	23 Dec. 1812	2 June 1813
"	*Maidstone*	36	284	G. Burdett		19 June 1812
"	*Belvidera*	36	284	R. Byron	14 Jany. 1810	27 Oct. 1810
"	*Barrosa*	36	284	W. H. Shirreff	28 Oct. 1812	31 Jany. 1813
"	*Narcissus*	32	254	J. R. Lumley	20 June 1812	29 Sep 1812
"	*Æolus*	32	254	Lord J. Townshend	3 Sep 1802	16 Aug 1807
"	*Cleopatra*	32	215	C. Gill		11 Dec 1811
"	*Minerva*	32	215	R. Hawkins	25 Nov 1804	9 Nov 1812
6	*Laurestinus*	24	175	T. Graham	3 May 1811	20 Sep 1812
"	*Wanderer*	20	121	F. Newcombe	23 Dec 1806	28 Aug 1812
Sloop	*Sophie*	18	121	N. Lockyer	26 Oct. 1809	28 Aug. 1812
"	*Curlew*	18	121	M. Head	3 July 1812	28 Aug 1812
"	*Rattler*	18	121	Hon. H. D. Byng	13 Dec 1803	1811
"	*Nimrod*	18	121	N. Mitchell	12 Aug 1812	22 Sep 1812
"	*Atalante*	18	121	Fred. Hickey	Commissd. Abroad	9 Nov 1812
"	*Fantome*	18	121	J. Lawrence	Do.	4 Dec 1812
"	*Columbia*	18	121	J. K. Kinsman	Do.	
"	*Morgiana*	18	121	D. Scott	Do.	
"	*Loup Cervier*	18	121	W. B. Mends	Do.	
"	*Sylph*	18	121	W. Evans	Do.	
"	*Recruit*	18	121	G. R. Pechell	19 Mar 1809	19 Nov 1811
"	*Raleigh*	18	121	G. W. Hooper	10 Mar 1807	18 Mar 1813
"	*Wasp*	18	121	T. Everard	28 Aug 1812	22 Apl. 1813
"	*Ringdove*	18	121	W. Dowers	17 Sep 1806	2 June 1813

Rate	Ships	No. of Guns	Men	Commanders	When Commissd.	When sailed from England
"	*Martin*	18	121	H. F. Senhouse	26 Mar 1807	
"	*Colibri*	16	100	J. Thomson	Commissd. abroad	
"	*Mohawk*	12	95	W. [H] Litchfield	Do.	
"	*Emulous*	16	95	Wm. Godfrey	Do.	
"	*Thistle*	12	60	J. K. White	15 Aug 1812	23 Mar 1813
"	*Manly*	14	60	E. Collier	31 Aug 1812	Do.
"	*Borer*	12	60	R. Coote	13 Sep 1812	Do.
"	*Bold*	12	60	J. Skekel	29 July 1812	17 Apl. 1813
"	*Boxer*	12	60	S. Blyth	22 Aug 1812	Do.
"	*Conflict*	14	60	H. L. Baker	7 Nov 1812	17 Apl. 1813
"	*Contest*	14	60	J. Rattray	Dec 1812	22 Apl. 1813
Schooner	*Paz*	10	50	Lt. Dumaresq	15 Oct. 1808	22 Apl. 1811
"	*Cuttle*	4	20	" Saunders	Commissd. abroad	
"	*Bream*	4	20	" Hare	Do.	
Rec Ship	*Centurion*		36	" Brand	20 Nov 1808	1809
"	*Ruby*		90	Comre. Evans	7 Oct 1810	25 July 1811
				Lt. Ward		
Prison Ship	*Ardent*		97	J Cochet		

Newfoundland

Vice Admiral Sir Richd. Goodwin Keats KB

Rate	Ships	No. of Guns	Men	Commanders	When Commissd.	When sailed from England
3	*Bellerophon*	74	590	V. Admiral Sir R. G. Keats } E. Hawker	25 June 1811	22 Apl. 1813
5	*Sybille*	40	340	C. Upton	19 July 1803	25 Mar 1813
"	*Crescent*	38	315	J. Quilliam	28 Dec 1810	4 Apl. 1813
"	*Hyperion*	36	284	W. P. Cumby	21 Jany. 1808	13 May 1812

	Ship			Captain			Station
"	*Dryad*	36	284	E. Galwey	9 Sep. 1802	23 Apl. 1813	North America
6	*Comet*	20	121	G. W. Blamey	9 Jany. 1808	4 Apl. 1813	Mediterranean
"	*Rosamond*	20	121	D. Campbell	25 Mar 1807	23 Mar 1811	Do.
Sloop	*Hazard*	18	121	Jno. Cookesley	27 June 1802	5 June 1813	Do.
"	*Pheasant*	18	121	J. Palmer	4 June 1798	17 Mar 1813	North America
"	*Electra*	14	95	W. Gregory	7 Feb 1812	17 Mar 1813	Mediterranean
"	*Muros*	14	86	T S Griffinhoofe	Dec. 1811	17 May 1813	Do.
Cutter	*Adonis*	10	42	Lt. Buchan	8 Mar 1806		Do.
Prison Ship	*Triton*		11	" Bishop		1809	North America

Troop Ships

	Ship			Captain		Station
3	*Diadem*	28	200	J. Phillimore	19 June 1810	North America
"	*Leyden*	28	200	J. Davie	15 June 1810	Mediterranean
"	*Bristol*	28	200	G. Wyndham	16 July 1810	Do.
4	*Leopard*	26	175	W. H. Dillon	5 Mar 1811	Do.
"	*Diomede*	26	175	C. M. Fabian		North America
5	*Regulus*	22	135	J. Tailour	9 June 1810	Mediterranean
"	*Melpomene*	22	135	G. Falcon	13 July 1810	Do.
"	*Brune*	22	135	W. L. [S] Badcock	30 July 1810	Do.
"	*Romulus*	22	135	G. W. H. Knight	12 Sep 1810	North America
"	*Freija*	22	135	W. I Scott	26 Jany. 1810	To Lisbon
"	*Woolwich*	22	135	T. B. Sulivan	11 Feb. 1813	To Quebec
"	*Mermaid*	18	115	D. Dunn	12 Jany. 1810	Mediterranean
"	*Fox*	18	115	D. Paterson	21 May 1812	North America
"	*Dover*	12	115	A. V. Drury	22 June 1812	Mediterranean
"	*Success*	16	115	T. Barclay	Aug. 1812	North America
6	*Mercury*	16	105	Sir H. Richardson	28 May 1810	Leeward Islands
"	*Vestal*	16	105	S. Deckar	30 July 1810	Do.
"	*Nemesis*	16	105	Hon. J. A. Maude	27 Feb. 1812	North America

Admiralty Office ⎫ Abstract of the Monthly List.
1 July 1813 ⎭

	Rate	No. of	
		Ships	Men
East Indies	3	2	1180
	5	11	3105
	Sloops	5	605
	Hos. & Rec. Ship	1	52
		19	4942
Cape of Good Hope	3	1	491
	5	3	852
	Sloops	2	242
		6	1585
South America	3	1	590
	5	5	1479
	6	3	431
	Sloops	3	363
	Cutters &c	2	95
		14	2958
Leeward Islands	3	2	1180
	4	1	343
	5	7	1998
	6	3	363
	Sloops	20	2228
	Gun Brigs	6	290
		39	6402
Jamaica	3	2	1180
	5	1	340
	6	5	767
	Sloops	6	726
	Gun Brigs	2	100
	Receiv. Ship	1	70
		17	3183
North America	3	11	6491
	5	16	4675
	6	2	296
	Sloops	25	2525

	Rate	No. of	
		Ships	Men
	Schooners	3	90
	Receivg. Ships	2	126
	Prison Ship	1	97
		60	14300
Newfoundland	3	1	590
	5	4	1223
	6	2	242
	Sloops	4	423
	Cutter	1	42
	Prison Ship	1	11
		13	2531
Mediterranean	1	4	3424
	2	4	2952
	3	21	12750
	5	19	5483
	6	6	834
	Sloops	28	3067
	Bombs	3	223
	Gun Brigs	4	160
	Receiv. Ship	1	121
	Hosp. Ship	1	121
		91	29135
Portugal	3	1	491
	5	2	589
	6	4	646
	Sloops	8	756
	Gun Brigs	5	252
	Receiv. Ship	1	380
		21	3114
Baltic	3	8	4664
	4	1	343
	5	2	579
	6	2	296
	Sloops	14	1285
	Bombs	3	212
	Gun Brigs	15	772
		45	8151

	Rate	No. of	
		Ships	Men
Channel Fleet	1	3	2511
	3	13	7820
	5	8	2427
	Sloops	6	610
	Gun Brigs	3	150
		33	13518
Ireland	5	2	599
	Sloops	10	1149
	Gun Brigs	3	150
		15	1898
Downes	Staty. Ship	1	280
	Sloops	10	868
	Gun Brigs	7	405
		18	1553
Guernsey & Jersey	6	1	140
	Sloops	2	221
	Gun Brigs	5	255
		8	616
Plymouth	Receivg. Ship	1	320
	Sloops	8	755
	Gun Brigs	4	200
		13	1275
Portsmouth	Receivg. Ship	2	464
		2	1180
	5	3	914
	Sloops	8	685
	Gun Brigs	3	142
		18	3385
Sheerness	Receivg. Ship	1	250
	Sloops	4	280
	Gun Brigs	2	100
		7	630

	Rate	No. of	
		Ships	Men
Yarmouth	Receivg. Ship	2	168
	Sloops	4	314
	Gun Brigs	3	125
		9	607
Off the Texel and Scheld	2	1	738
	3	11	6760
	5	2	499
	Sloops	9	715
	Gun Brigs	7	350
		30	9062
Leith	Flag Ship	1	200
	5	1	215
	6	1	135
	Sloops	7	715
	Gun Brigs	4	200
		14	1465
Convoys & Particular Services	3	4	2460
	5	10	2950
	6	3	417
	Sloops	10	1165
	Cutters	4	190
		31	7182
Unappropriated	2	1	738
	3	9	5310
	4	2	930
	5	14	4196
	6	4	484
	Sloops	12	1391
	Bomb	1	67
	Schooners	4	155
		47	13271
Troop Ships	3	3	600
	4	2	350
	5	10	1270
	6	3	315
		18	2535

| | Rate | No. of ||
		Ships	Men
Prison Ships	Yachts	6	117
Stationary Ships &ca	Prison Ships	12	1152
	Pris. Hos. Ships	1	58
	Hosp. Ships	4	230
	Conval. Ship	1	70
	Slop & Conv. Ship	3	267
	Sta. & Recg. Ship	8	580
	Tenders	3	117
		38	2591

General Abstract

| Rate | No. of ||
	Ships	Men
1st.	7	5935
2d.	6	4428
3d.	92	53737
4th.	6	1966
5th.	120	33393
6th.	39	5366
Sloops	205	21088
Bombs	7	502
Gun Brigs Cutters &c	87	4223
Yachts	6	117
Stationy. & Receivg. Ships	22	3011
Prison Ships	14	1260
Prison Hospital Ships	1	58
Hospital Ships	5	351
Convalescent Ship	1	70
Conv. & Slop Ships	3	267
Tenders	3	117
	624	135889

D, UkLPR, Adm. 8/100, Ships in Sea Pay, 1813. These charts have been condensed, eliminating columns that are virtually blank. In the manuscript, Lieutenant Ward appears in a column "Lieutenants," which is between "Commanders" and "When Commission'd."

1. 1812.

A Question of Authority:
The Philadelphia Navy Yard

Commodore Alexander Murray had been the commanding officer at Philadelphia since 1808. With the declaration of war against Great Britain in 1812, his responsibilities at that station multiplied severalfold. Despite these increased burdens, one area that remained outside Murray's authority was the construction of ships at the Philadelphia Navy Yard. That was the responsibility of the yard's naval constructors.

In the summer of 1813, the building of two new warships—a 74-gun ship of the line and a 44-gun frigate—was underway at the Philadelphia yard, and Murray found himself in the middle of a dispute between the naval constructors[1] and the commanding officer of marines[2] at the navy yard. The squabbling between these parties threatened progress on the new ships. Unsure of his authority to act, Commodore Murray appealed to Secretary Jones to clarify the extent of his jurisdiction over activities at the yard.

1. *Samuel Humphreys and Charles Penrose supervised the construction of the 74-gun ship of the line* Franklin, *and Joseph and Francis Grice supervised the construction of the 44-gun frigate* Guerriere.
2. *Captain Anthony Gale, U.S.M.C.*

COMMODORE ALEXANDER MURRAY TO SECRETARY OF THE NAVY JONES

Philada.   July 3rd. 1813

Sir.

The duties incumbent on me as Naval Commander on this station, requires my constant attendance at the Navy Yard, where extensive operations are now going on, I wish to have some precise rule to guide my conduct; at present I have no jurisdiction beyond the flotilla, references, & questions are often made to me on subjects out of my powers to answer,

This observation is now made to you, in consequence of frequent bickerings, & complaints, between the Naval Constructors, & the Marine Officer of the Yard, who thinks himself authorised to act at his discretion, & in no instance has he ever consulted me, nor do I feel myself at liberty to instruct him; I think some regulations ought now to be adopted to prevent confusion, & to relieve me from the awkward situation in wch. I now stand—

Capt. Gale in a former instance behaved very disrespectfully to me, when I fitted out the *Constellation,* for wch. he received a severe reproof from his Commanding Officer, since wch. there has been no cordiality between us, & he has not treated Mr. Penrose with that respect due his present station requires, he assumes a high tone, & I must beg leave to suggest to you the propriety of having one out let to the Navy Yard only, he & his Sergeant hath built a Tavern opposite the upper Gate by the Barracks, wch. I fear will become a nuisance & occupies a Centinal extraordinary merely for their convenience—[1]

The flotilla have been down the Bay & removed all the Buoys; there was but one Frigate on the Brown, & she moved out of their way, I hope the Enemy will pay respect to our little fleet in future, we have not had any interuption to our Bay Craft since we first shewed them our faces—

Commodore Alexander Murray

I beg leave to enclose you the letter from the managing Committee respecting the *Northern Liberty* Galley[2] for your consideration— I have the honr to be Your Mo. Obt.

A Murray

ALS, DNA, RG45, CL, 1813, Vol. 4, No. 141 (M125, Roll No. 29).

1. In the spring of 1816, a court of inquiry reviewed several charges against Gale, including operating a grog shop in the Philadelphia Navy Yard in partnership with his orderly sergeant, John D. Maher. Gale was acquitted of all charges. For the record of this court-martial see DNA, RG127, CM, Vol. 7, No. 237 (M273, Roll No. 7).
2. *Northern Liberties* was one of several subscription ships built by the city of Philadelphia for the defense of the Delaware and purchased by the Navy Department. For additional documentation see pp. 231–32.

SECRETARY OF THE NAVY JONES TO COMMODORE ALEXANDER MURRAY

Alexander Murray Esqr.   Navy Department
Commg. Naval Officer   July 8th 1813.
Philadelphia

As the various and important objects now in operation at the Navy Yard within your Station, require order, regularity and authority in the direction & controul of the persons employed therein, you are hereby vested with the command of that establishment for the government of which you will prescribe such rules and regulations, as may be reasonable and proper for conducting the public business therein, to the best advantage, and preserving harmony and Satisfaction among the individuals employed

You are perfectly aware, that the Mechanics who are employed in the Navy Yard, are a valuable and independent class of men, over whom it is neither proper nor practicable, to exercise a rigorous controul; and your own experience and disposition, will point out to you, the nature of the regulations which command their ready acquiescence and respect.

The Master Builders are charged with the construction of the 74, and with the general direction of all the Mechanics, in the execution of all the work for the 74. and also with the management and conversion of the timber, and other materials employed in the improvement of the Wharf and Slip, and in the construction of the Slip and buildings necessary for the same; for which purpose they will receive instructions from this Department. These Gentlemen are well known to you. Their personal Standing and abilities and the importance of the work in which they are engaged entitle them to confidence and respect, which I am sure they will receive from you, and through you, from all who are under your command.

The nature of their charge renders it necessary that they should have free access, at all times, to the yard, and the Centinels should be instructed, to permit the free ingress and egress at all times of the Master Builders, and those they may introduce.

The Store keeper[1] will render the monthly returns of the public property, within the Navy Yard as usual.

The authority of the officer of Marines, extends only to his subordinate officers and men and their particular garrison & duty.

He is to furnish at your requisition, such Sentinels as you may deem necessary for the protection of the Navy Yard, and of the public property therein;

and shall cause them to execute such orders, while on their posts, as you shall require of him in writing from time to time.

You will designate such avenues and permit such only to be kept open, as you may deem necessary for the public interest, and prohibit all improper intercourse, or communication, which may come to your knowledge. I am respectfully your obdt. Servt.

W. Jones

LB Copy, DNA, RG45, CNA, Vol. 1, p. 455 (M441, Roll No. 1).

1. Robert Kennedy.

COMMODORE ALEXANDER MURRAY TO SECRETARY OF THE NAVY JONES

Philada.   July 12th. 1813

Sir,

I have just recd. your letter of the 8th. Inst. & shall pay every attention in my power to the regulation, & duties assigned me over the Navy yard, & adopt such a system as shall be approved of by all concerned in the various operations going on there,— hope to prevent any future descensions & that we shall maintain that cordiality so essential

I have just returned from an excursion down the Delaware to visit the flotilla, wch. I found in excellent order, the Barges excepted, they are now ordered up to undergo some alterations, their Guns were too heavy, & badly arranged, we now are putting Carronades in them, & placing them more in the center of the boat, the one that was sunk has been recovered with the loss of her Gun, & she has undergone the necessary alterations, & joined the flotilla, the block sloops[1] are the favorite Vessels, they sail well, & much dryer than would have been expected, they had some good tryals in stiff breeses, when last down the Bay, the G. boats are also in fine condition, & all their Crews under good discipline, & order, but we have not as yet recruited our compliment of men, only eight of the boats are full Manned; Lt. Mitchell this day reported himself to me to take the station of Lt. Stewart yet in a very bad state of health, & I have permetted him to take his quarters somewhere in the Country to try what can be done for him, Lt. Mitchell is also in a bad state of health, but he goes down tomorrow; Sailg. Master Elberson is reported to me by Doctr. Kearney, as being in a bad state of health, & will be unfit for duty for a long time; we of course stand in need of another Sailg. Master, & Lt. Angus presses very hard to be allowed one to ease him of part of the charge now on him, he has conducted himself uniformly very well & very industriously—

After a scene of vexation, & trouble with the Sailors of the *Vixen*,[2] & their landlords, they have come down in body, turned out by the Rascal that has boarded them, when they found they coud not play upon me, & requested to be sent on to New York, about 50 in number, wch. I have this done in a G. boat to Burlington under the charge of Midn. Renshaw, their landlords are now to look for their money as they please, some of the Men whose time of service has expired I have reshipped & sent on with the others to wait the issue of their exchange & your further orders— I have the honor to be Your Mo. Obt.

A Murray

ALS, DNA, RG45, CL, 1813, Vol. 4, No. 191 (M125, Roll No. 29).

1. *Buffalo* and *Camel.*

2. U.S. brig *Vixen* was captured in November 1812 by H.M. frigate *Southampton.* See Dudley, *Naval War of 1812,* Vol. 1, pp. 594–95. Her crew arrived in a cartel off Cape May on 2 May 1813. After their arrival in Philadelphia, they became a source of great aggravation to Murray.

The Admiralty's Prohibition against Single-Ship Combats

As news of the American frigate victories of 1812 reached Great Britain, the Admiralty was subjected to a storm of public criticism. To a nation whose navy had mastered the fleets of Europe and numbered well over six hundred vessels of all types, it was incomprehensible that any warship, let alone an American one, could defeat one of the Royal Navy's own. While a number of reasons were advanced by the Admiralty and its defenders to explain the Royal Navy's losses, some commentators had no difficulty in singling out the true authors of these naval defeats. As one anonymous critic declared, "it is those men who are at the head of the government, and those who have the regulating of naval affairs, that the opprobrium will be cast upon."[1] Stung by the censure directed at them from all quarters, the Admiralty took the unprecedented step of forbidding frigate commanders from engaging their American counterparts in single-ship combat.

1. *Oceanus [pseud.],* Naval Chronicle, *Vol. 29 (Jan.–June 1813), p. 12.*

FIRST SECRETARY OF THE ADMIRALTY JOHN W. CROKER TO STATION COMMANDERS IN CHIEF

Secret & Confidential   10 July 1813

Sir

My Lords Comrs. of the Admiralty having received intelligence that Several of the American Ships of War are now at Sea, I have their Lordships Commands to acquaint you therewith, and that they do not conceive that any of His Majestys Frigates should attempt to engage, single handed, the larger Class of American Ships; which though they may be called Frigates, are of a size, Complemant and weight of Metal much beyond that Class, and more resembling Line of Battle Ships.

In the event of one of His Majestys Frigates under your orders falling in with one of these Ships, her Captain should endeavour, in the first instance, to secure the retreat of His Majestys Ship, but if he finds that he has advantage in sailing, he should endeavour to manouvre, and keep company with her, without coming to action, in the hope of falling in with some other of His Majestys Ships with whose assistance the Enemy might be attacked with a reasonable hope of success.

It is their Lordships further directive that you make this known as soon as possible to the Several Captains Commanding His Majestys Ships.

J W C

To the Several Commander in Chief
on the Home Station and to
Vice Admiral Martin   Lisbon   By Packet   Dup. by Packet   3d: Augt.—

Vice Admiral Sir E. Pellew Bt.   Medeterranean
            Sent under cover to R. A. Linzee by *Echo*   Dup. by the *Boyne*—
Admiral Sir J. B. Warren   Bermuda   By *Bramble*   Dup. by *Endymion*

Rear Adml. Sir F. Laforey   Barbadoes   By *Galatea*
Rear Adml. Brown   Jamaica   By *Goliath*
Vice Adml. Sir R. Keats   Newfoundland   By *Talbot*
Rear Adml. Dixon   South America—   By *Akbar*
Rear Adml. Tyler   Cape of Good Hope   By *Acorn*
Vice Admiral Sir S. Hood   East Indies—   By *Acorn*

LB Copy, UkLPR, Adm. 2/1377, pp. 154–56.

The British Attack on Ocracoke

Admiral Sir John B. Warren followed up his attacks on Craney Island and Hampton, Virginia, with a raid on the North Carolina coast. To this end, he dispatched seven vessels and five hundred troops under the command of Rear Admiral George Cockburn to Ocracoke with orders to destroy American shipping there. Cockburn's force arrived off Ocracoke bar on the night of 12 July. Early the next morning the British launched their assault.

REAR ADMIRAL GEORGE COCKBURN, R.N., TO
ADMIRAL SIR JOHN B. WARREN, R.N.

No. 20   *Sceptre* off Ocracoke Bar
                                                    the 12th. July 1813
Sir,
    I have the honor to inform you that His Majestys Ships under my Orders, with the Detachment of Troops under the Orders of Lieutenant Colonel Napier took up this Anchorage last Night after dark and the Lt. Colonel agreeing with me in an Idea of the advantages which we were likely to derive from carrying your further Orders into Execution at once, and thereby prevent the Enemy collecting any Force from the Neighbourhood, or exerting additional Means of Defence in consequence of our appearance, I directed Preparations to be instantly commenced for the Debarkation of the Troops, and for making the intended Attack, although the weather was not so favorable as I could have wished, and from its having been dark before we approached the Place, it had been out of our Power to ascertain the exact Positions occupied by the Enemy or the Means of Defence he actually possessed.
    Under these circumstances the following Arrangements were quickly made and forthwith proceeded on; an advanced division of the best pulling Boats with

armed Seamen, and some Marines of this Ship was directed to precede the others for the purpose of attacking the Enemy's Shipping, and of occupying and diverting the fire of any Armed Vessels which might be stationed at the Place for assisting in its defense, To Lieutenant Westphal 1st. of my Flag Ship (who had just recovered from the wound he received at Havre-de-Grace) I entrusted this Division, and the carrying into effect the objects of it, directing Captain Russell to sustain and support him with the Rocket Boats.

The Flat and heavier Boats with as many of the 102nd Regt. Artillery &c &c as they could carry, followed the advanced Division as quickly as possible, and were destined to attack and occupy such positions on the surrounding Lands as Circumstances and the Enemy's means of Defence might point out the Propriety of after Daylight, and Captain Paterson of the *Fox* was charged with the Care and management of this Division— The Third and last Division was composed of the *Conflict* the armed Tenders and small Vessels which were directed to take on board the Remainder of the Troops, and to follow the Boats into the Harbor as fast and as far as might be found practicable Captain Ross of this Ship was charged with the general superintendence of the whole Arrangement, and Captains Knight and Maude with much laudable Zeal also attended to render me their personal assistance wherever Circumstances might require it.

The whole moved from the Ships towards the Shore about 2 O'clock this morning, but owing to the great Distance from the Bar to the Harbour, and the heavy swell which was running, it was considerably after Daylight before the advanced Division turned a projecting Shoal Point, behind which the Vessels lay, and round which is the only possible way by which the Shore can be approached with Safety. the Enemy therefore had some little Time to prepare for Defence, which he did not fail to avail himself of, and immediately the Boats doubled this Point a heavy fire was opened on them from a Brig and Schooner which hoisted American Colours, and were soon discovered to be the only armed Vessels here.— Lt. Westphal therefore with his Division pulled directly and resolutely for these, under Cover of some Rockets which were thrown by Captain Russell with admirable precision.

The fire of the Brig now began to slacken, and on Mr. Westphal's approaching her Bow with the advanced Boats, the Enemy cut her cable and abandoned her, and the Schooner immediately struck her Colours, when they were both almost instantly boarded and taken Possession of. The rest of the Vessels in the Harbor proving to be Neutral Merchant Vessels the advanced Divisions was immediately dispatched in chace of some small Vessels which had brought down Goods to load the Vessels laying here, but which had made off up the River on our being first discovered, these however our Boats unfortunately failed in their Endeavours to overtake owing to frequently grounding on the Shoals, from want of Knowledge of the Navigation, and the American Vessels having been much favored by the Breeze.

The Troops in the mean time having divided into two Divisions effected a landing on and without further Opposition took Possession of the Portsmouth and Ocracock Island, where all immediately submitted to our Mercy, and therefore according to the principle hitherto pursued in such cases, the Lt. Colonel and myself have directed that no mischief shall be done to the unoffending Inhabitants and that whatever is taken from them shall be strictly paid and accounted for, They are now driving in Cattle &c. for the Refreshment of our Troops and Ships, and as we learn that there neither is at Washington nor Newbern any Vessel of any size nor other object worthy our attention, this Harbor being the only Anchorage for Vessels drawing more than Eight feet Water loading from or trading to any Place within these Extensive Inlets, the passages of Roanoke and Carrituck being now filled up and impassable, We propose in obedience to your Orders to rejoin you with the least possible Delay after having embarked the Cattle &c and got the Prizes out of the Harbour.

The Brig captured proves to be the *Anaconda*,[1] mounting 18 Nine Pound long Guns, just refitted and complete in every Respect, has made but one Cruize since she was built, is Copper bottomed, a most beautiful Vessel and perfectly fit for His Majesty's Service.—

The Schooner is the *Atlas*, a Letter of Marque of about 240 Tons mounting Ten Guns, a very fine Vessel has just been completely refitted, is coppered, and from her Character for Superior Sailing, would also probably prove a useful Vessel for His Majesty's Service.—

It now becomes my pleasing Duty to mention to you Sir the good behaviour on this Occasion, of the several Officers and Men you placed under my Command. Captain Ross of this ship, Captains Paterson, Knight, Maude and Baker, of the *Fox, Romulus, Nemesis* & *Conflict*, have been indefatigable in their Exertions and the assistance they have afforded me in effecting and carrying forward the Service, and to Lieutenant Westphal who so gallantly and resolutely pulled up with the few Boats to so formidable a Brig and Schooner under a heavy fire, my warmest Encomiums are due, and I trust you will permit me Sir in consequence thereof again to recommend this highly deserving officer to your favourable Notice, Lieutenants Hutchinson & Urmston Commanding the *Highflyer* and *Cockchafer*[2] likewise merit by their exertions that I should express to you how highly satisfied I am therewith.

It is also with the highest Gratification that I feel myself called upon prior to concluding this letter, to mention to you the truly cheerful, ready, and able cooperation I have invariably experienced from Lieutenant Colonel Napier of the 102nd Regt. and the Officers and Troops under his Orders, which must have ensured to us Success had the Enemy opposed us with his utmost means, and has tended to establish a Confidence and Understanding between our respective Services which cannot fail to have the happiest Effect on such future conjunct Operations as may be hereafter undertaken by these Forces I have the honor to be &c

                                        (Sd.)   G Cockburn   Rr. Admiral

LB Copy, DLC, Papers of George Cockburn, Container 9, Letters Sent 3 Feb. 1812–6 Feb. 1814, pp. 217–21.

  1. For additional documentation on *Anaconda*, see pp. 31–34.
  2. *Highflyer* and *Cockchafer* were schooner tenders mounting five guns each.

JOHN O. FARNUM TO NATHANIEL SHALER

Captn. Shaler   Newbern   1813

Sir,

With Sorrow & pain I inform you the *Anaconda* is in possession of ~~by~~ the English

On Sunday Evening at About 11 O Clock, I was informed by A boat from Ocracock that Several vessels had Ancored of the bar,,— I immediately got Every thing prepared for action, and in the mean time prepared to Sink the vessel, if we where drove of, and got the boats ready with all of our things in them,—

At 4 A.M. Saw A number of boats Coming Over the bar,, As they got within reach of Our Shot, we Commenced firing upon them, and Continued So untill, I Saw, and Counted 30 or, 32, boats, and two Schoners the boats had, 9 & 12 pounder, in their bow, and from, twenty five to thirty Five men in Each boat,

[I?] immediately fired two nine pounders through her bottom, and Cut her cables, and run up her jibbs to Cant her on Shore,

We immediately took to the boats, (the Hellish Expedition come up very quick and took possestion of the brig,) Some continued on after us, and we where Obliged to through over board, Our Cloathing &c. to Clear Ourselves, your Obedient & Humble Servent

John O. Farnum

NB. the bearer of this, is just a going, and I have not time to give to give you the particulars in full, we have just Arrived here, and fatiged complety but as we have we are destitute of money and with nary Cloaths, if you will be so good as to send me on Some money, [?] how we can get it will oblige [?].

ALS, PHi, Shaler Papers. Farnum probably wrote this letter on 13 July. The bracketed question marks represent between two and three indecipherable words.

Lieutenant Kennedy's Refusal to Cruise in *Nonsuch*

When Lieutenant Edmund P. Kennedy refused to cruise in Nonsuch *because there was no surgeon on board, Captain John H. Dent referred the matter to the Navy Department, asking whether he should arrest Kennedy for disobedience of orders or await the assignment of a surgeon to* Nonsuch. *Secretary Jones's response indicates that the department drew a distinction between the medical needs of naval vessels ordered on foreign cruises and those assigned for the protection of home waters.*

CAPTAIN JOHN H. DENT TO SECRETARY OF THE NAVY JONES

The Honorable William Jones   Charleston   19th July 1813

Sir

I have the honor to transmit for your information a letter from Lieut Comdt Kennedy, and my answer thereto, relative to a Surgeon for the U.S. Schooner *Nonsuch*. It is unnecessary for me to make any comment on this letter, as the department has long Since been informed of the want of that class of officers on this station, the consequences that would ensue in the event if, an engagement, (not taking into view the ordinary occurrences on board) would be serious and fatal to many. I should find no difficulty in obtaining the services of a mate, but your order of the 9th April directs me not to appoint or employ, any person in any capacity whatever, not specially authorized by the department.

In my letter of this morning I enclosed you my orders to Lieut Kennedy, to proceed to sea, for the purpose of transporting Lieut Sevier & his detachment to Beaufort NC, I have not as yet heard any thing from Lieut Sevier, but was desirous to have the vessel ready at Beaufort to prevent any detention that might arise from head winds, or the port being blockaded at the moment, her Services might be wanted. Should a Surgeon not arrive, I see no prospect of getting the *Nonsuch* to Sea, and I have been verbally informed by Lieut. Kennedy, that he would be arrested sooner than proceed without one, In this case Sir you will be enabled to judge fully of the merits of Lieut Kennedy's deportment, and decide whether he can be charged with disobedience of orders or insubordination. I Have the Honor to be With great respect Your most Obt. Svt.

J H Dent

LS, DNA, RG45, CL, 1813, Vol. 5, No. 19 (M125, Roll No. 30).

[Enclosure]

United States Schooner *Nonsuch*
Rebellion Roads—   19th. July 1813
Sir—

I have the honour to acknowledge the receipt of yours of the 17th inst Ordering me to repair immediately to Sea— I should have replyed to that order before Sir, but indisposition prevented it

You certainly must be aware Sir, of the dreadful Consequences that might result from my proceeding to Sea on a Cruise, without having a Medical Man on board, the object of cruising I presume is to meet the enemy, & indeed I see no possibility of avoiding a fight, as my track will be precisely on the Cruising ground of the Enemy, & to lead men into Battle without having a Surgeon on board to assist the maimed, I think would mark but little feeling; altho' I should only be obeying orders of my Superior Yet should any unfortunate accident arise from it I should reflect on it but with horror, and the deepest concern for the Sufferers—

There is not an officer or man in the Vessell Sir, but feels gloomy on the occasion. I do not, cannot think it the intention of the Honble. Secry. of the navy that any National Vesell should proceed to Sea on a Cruise, particularly on this Station where Men are so subject to Sickness without a Medical Man on board—

After a Service of Thirteen Years with Honr., I should be extremely sorry to be charged with disobedience of orders or insubordination; I do not mean it shall be so if you persist in my proceeding to Sea under present circumstances. I will go sir, but Permit me to say, that I think it equally cruel & illegal that the lives of so many Officers & Men should be so little Considered

If you will do me the favor Sir, to Assure me that Mr. Jones directs that the *Nonsuch* shall proceed to Sea with or without a Surgeon, rather than not go I will Employ one at my own expence— I've the Honr. with the highest respect to remn. Yr. most Obt. Sv't.

Edmd. P. Kennedy

Comdr. J H Dent
US Navy Charleston—

ALS, DNA, RG45, CL, 1813, Vol. 5, No. 19, enclosure (M125, Roll No. 30).

[Enclosure]
(Copy)   Charleston   19th July 1813

Sir

Your letter of to day, stating the want of a Surgeon, for the *Nonsuch*, with remarks thereon has been received. I Shall only observe, that the department is in
possession of every information on that subject, and must be fully capable of
judging of the Situation of your vessel, in the event of an engagement. I am Sir
very respectfully yrs

                                        (Signed)   J H Dent

Lieut Comdt Kennedy
Comg U. S. Schr. *Nonsuch*   Rebellion Roads

Copy, DNA, RG45, CL, 1813, Vol. 5, No. 19, enclosure (M125, Roll No. 30).

SECRETARY OF THE NAVY JONES TO CAPTAIN JOHN H. DENT

John H. Dent Esqr.   Navy Department
Comg. Naval Officer,   August 7th 1813.
Charleston S. C.

Sir,

Your letters of 19th July, enclosing one from Lt. Kennedy are received. The
Surgeons Mates would have been ordered to the *Nonsuch* and *Carolina*, but
none have been at immediate command; New appointments, however, have
taken place, a few days since, and they will be ordered on. In the meantime, I
may observe, that the style of Lt. Kennedy's Letter, while it displays very acute
feelings, appears not to mark the distinction between a vessel, bound on a foreign Cruize, and that of the *Nonsuch*, intended to keep close in with the land, so
as to have access to medical aid in a few hours. Upon the same principle, the
commander of a Barge, or Gun Boat, may remonstrate against proceeding to
Bull's Bay, or Georgetown, without a Surgeon. The gloomy aspect of the Crew,
described by Lieut. Kennedy, upon the prospect of running a few miles along
shore without a Surgeon, is not very characteristic of a Seaman, and may have
been merely the effect of sympathy with their Commander. This Gentleman,
lately commanded the *Scorpion* Cutter, in the Chesapeake, as much exposed to
battle and wounds, as he now is, and had no Surgeon's Mate.

However, sooner than press upon his feelings, I would rather relieve him
from a situation so irksome; in the meantime, & until a Surgeon's mate arrives,
her Officers and crew will be quite as usefully employed in the Barges where the
terror of wounds may not be so great, as on board a first rate. I am, respectfully,
Yours, &c.

                                              W. Jones

LB Copy, DNA, RG45, SNL, Vol. 11, pp. 40–41 (M149, Roll No. 11).

Barron's Plea for Command

After receiving a five-year suspension from the navy for his role in the Chesapeake-Leopard Affair,[1] *Captain James Barron turned to the merchant service to support himself and his family. When the United States declared war on Great Britain, Barron was serving as master on board an American-owned brig sailing between Lisbon, Gothenburg, and Copenhagen.[2] At the end of his term of suspension, Barron wrote a heartfelt letter to Secretary of the Navy Jones requesting to be restored to active command.*

1. *See Dudley,* Naval War of 1812, *Vol. 1, pp. 26–34.*
2. *Watson,* Commodore James Barron, *p. 81; see also Stevens,* Affair of Honor, *pp. 98–107.*

CAPTAIN JAMES BARRON TO SECRETARY OF THE NAVY JONES

Private   Copenhagen   22 July 1813

Dear Sir,

Inclosed you will find a letter addressed to you as Secretary of the Navy of the U.S. which I hope you will consider proper and containing all that is—necessary on the present occasion, but as it has not been my good fortune to have had a personal acquaintance with you;—the only knowledge of my Character you may have, may possibly be derived from sources not very friendly to me. Should this be the case I have only to rely on the strength of your mind and the justice & liberality of your disposition, to decide on a case perhaps envelloped in as much obscurity and heretofore treated with as much Injustice & Inhumanity as any that ever came under your inspection.— I never can, nor never will, acknowledge that the sentence under which I have laboured for these five years was just, or that it was not, the result of malice, and not the sound and disinterested opinion of just and impartial Judges.— It is not in human nature for a brave man to neglect his duty in the hour of need and such is the sentence of the court on this occasion their opinion relative to neglect was founded on a paper* written by myself, at ~~the~~ a time when I was in a state of distraction both of body & mind, and merely states an impression which the result of the British Commander's conduct made on my mind after the affair was ended, but which the paper alluded to, did not contain namely the words <u>to take by force</u> any british deserters found on board the *Chesapeake* thus was this cruel sentence past and inflicted without mercy on a man who had spent the prime of his life in the service of his country and the truly guilty set at liberty and protected from censure or punishment.

If an officer having preferred charges against his Commander fails to produce other proof and when brought to his own oath, prevaricates as to the facts, is he not guilty of falsehood and in some measure of mutiny? Is not perjury punishable?

Mr. Babit,[1] was proved so by four witnesses and the sentence of the court proves that the charges exhibited against me by the officers of the *Chesapeake* were without foundation and yet they escaped punishment and were protected from any discription of Governmental displeasure. Capt Gordon and his officers contrary to my opinion previously expressed, gave two entertainments on board the *Chesapeake* in hampton roads while she was laying, and only waiting for their exertions to proceed on her cruize.—indeed when I am addressing myself to a Gentleman whose knowledge and experience enables him to decide on facts, it is only necessary to request your reference to the log book of that ship, to prove that the unpunished are the guilty, for when you observe that she laid twenty two days in Hampton roads with her whole crew on board, and her orders ready, argument is unnecessary to prove the inattention of those dishonorable accusers, whose only shift·was to take some advantage, and remove the blame to some more important person. It would however be imposing too much on your time and patience now to call your attention to a review of those very unpleasant circumstances, and my only wish in life is to have an opportunity to prove to the world in general and my Country in particular that I have suffered without Just cause for there are circumstances known to those intimately acquainted with the particulars of that affair, that would in my humble opinion convince the world, that I was, to say the least of it, cruelly sacrificed. but if on the contrary, some of my friends enjoy the happiness of your acquaintance, it is possible I may have a greater share of your commisseration than I am aware of, let that be as it may I have great confidence in the correctness of your head and the goodness of your heart, and hope and trust that this communication will meet with that delicacy which my more than ordinary situation entitles me to, being fully impressed with this belief, I shall conclude, only adding my prayer, that the navy may be cherished and protected by the nation and guided by nautical wisdom. very Respectfully I have the Honor to be Your Obt. Sevt.

James Barron

*This paper was Lost, on the day the affair happened, and was Referd. to on Memory

ALS, DNA, RG45, CL, 1813, Vol. 5, No. 28 (M125, Roll No. 30).

1. Fitz Henry Babbit was serving as a midshipman on board *Chesapeake* during her rencontre with H.M.S. *Leopard*. He was promoted to lieutenant 5 June 1810.

[Enclosure]

Copenhagen   22 July 1813

Sir,

The term of my suspension having expired, the object of the present letter is to inform you that the first wish of my heart has always been to render service to my Country in an honourable way.— If therefore they are wished and will be employed to that end, your commands will be readily obeyed.[1] A letter directed to the care of J. M. Forbes[2] Esqr. will find me here or in St. Petersburg. very respectfully I have the honor to be, Your obedt. Servt.

James Barron

ALS, DNA, RG45, CL, 1813, Vol. 5, No. 27 (M125, Roll No. 30).

1. Jones apparently did not wish to avail himself of the controversial captain's services, for Barron's letter went unanswered. Barron remained in Copenhagen until 1818 when he returned to the United States. He would have to wait until 1824 before the Navy Department gave him another command—the Philadelphia Navy Yard.
2. John M. Forbes was consul general to Denmark.

British Sailors in American Service

Death by hanging was the punishment prescribed for any British subject captured while serving on an American man-of-war.[1] Despite that sanction, many British seamen were willing to take the risk of serving on board U.S. naval vessels or privateers. Some, when captured, sought clemency by asserting that they had been forced to serve on the American ships against their will. Needful of seamen, Royal Navy officers were willing to consider clemency in return for enlistment.

1. For documentation on the punishment meted out to British deserters, see pp. 273–74.

Admiral Sir John B. Warren, R.N., to First Secretary of the Admiralty John W. Croker

> San Domingo, Potowmac
> River in the Chesapeake,
> July 22nd 1813.—

Sir,

I enclose a Report from the Senior Officer at Halifax of several British Subjects found serving in the Enemy's Frigate *Chesapeake,* and I beg leave to request their Lordship's orders upon the Subject.—

The Voluntary confession and open statement of these men entitle them to some attention: especially those who appear to have been inveighled or forced into the Enemy's Service previous to the declaration of War; and I well remember in the former American War various instances of a similar kind occurred, when it was the practice to admit of any open or reasonable Excuse, and after an Engagement to be faithful in future to divide them into several Ships in the West Indies and otherwise, that they might not be lost to their Country; and perhaps such Examples of Clemency would have a good effect amongst those Seamen the Enemy have in their Service. I have the honor to be Sir, Your most Obedient humble Servant.

John Borlase Warren

LS, UkLPR, Adm. 1/504, pp. 73–74.

[Enclosure]
Copy.   H:M. Ship *Valiant* in
J B Warren   Halifax Harbour, 23d June 1813.

Sir,

The men named below late of the *Chesapeake* have given themselves up as British Subjects, they relate as follows; It is supposed there are many others of the same description amongst the Crew of the *Chesapeake.*

Thomas Jones—23 Years of Age, had been 9 months in the *Chesapeake,* & before that onboard the *John Adams* where he had been two Years, was born in London where his Father resides in Lambeth. Spital Fields, but he has not heard from his friends these ten Years. he reported himself to Captn. Evans when he Commanded the *Chesapeake* & told him that he was an Englishman, but he threatened to put him in Irons.

Henry Simpson 27 Years of Age had been 9 months onboard the *Chesapeake,* was made drunk at New York & taken onboard the *Chesapeake,* was born in England at Liverpool & was married at Dublin (in the Year 1811) where his Wife now resides in Sutton's Court Rogertsons Quay

John Pearce 21 Years of Age had been about 7 months in the *Chesapeake,* was born at Ipswich in England, which he left 10 Years since in the *Frances & Joseph* English Merchant Ship belonging to London which he left soon after his arrival in Philadelphia after being a considerable time in the Coasting Trade he Shipped onboard the *Chesapeake* last September The day they Sailed from Boston Capt: Lawrence told them they were going out to fight the *Shannon,* they asked to have their Prize Money for the last Cruize when he damned them for a set of Rascals, then they went down & hove the anchor up, but very unwillingly.— Thos. Arthur 24 Years of Age had been 8 months in *Chesapeake* which he Joined at Boston, was born at Ulverstone [?] miles from Lancaster— Came from Liverpool to Pensacola in the English Ship *James.* He declared himself a British Subject to Mr. Bell Mate of the English Ship *Volunteer* which the *Chesapeake* took last Cruize, and so did Jones & Simpson, & he promised to get them clear by speaking to the British Agent at Boston— he says that Thomas Carpenter Willm. Martin and several other Englishmen now in Prison belonged to the *Chesapeake.* I have the honor to be Sir, Your most Obedt. Servant

Signed   Robt. Dudley Oliver—   Captain

Copy, UkLPR, Adm. 1/504, pp. 75–77.

ADMIRAL SIR JOHN B. WARREN, R.N., TO
FIRST SECRETARY OF THE ADMIRALTY JOHN W. CROKER

San Domingo   Potowmac
River Chesapeake, 25th
July 1813.—

Sir,

Enclosed herewith I beg leave to transmit for the Information of their Lordship's a Copy of a Letter from Captain Oliver of His Majesty's Ship *Valiant,* enclosing the Copy of a Deposition respecting four British Subjects taken onboard the United States Frigate *Chesapeake.*— I have the honor to be Sir, Your most Obedient humble Servant.

John Borlase Warren

LS, UkLPR, Adm. 1/504, p. 269.

[Enclosure]
Copy   His Majesty's Ship *Valiant*
J B Warren   Halifax Harbour   30th. June 1813,

Sir,

I beg leave to enclose the Deposition of Mr. John Bell late Mate of the English Ship *Volunteer,* respecting four British subjects taken on Board the *Chesapeake* who are sent herewith by the *Armide,* for your disposal, They gave themselves up to Lieutenant Miller the agent for Prisoners,—

Another Man Named George Williams gave himself up to Lord James Town-send from the *Chesapeake*, I also send him he has been in America since he was 7 years of age, had been 9 months in the *Chesapeake* and some time before that on Board the *United States*, he is certain that there were 10 or 12 Englishmen Killed on board the *Chesapeake* and that a great many more are now in the Prison, I think many of those Men would give themselves up if it was thought right to offer them any hope of pardon and on the other hand to discover them may be ex-tremely difficult.— I have the honor to be Sir, Your most obedient Servant

(Signed)   Robt. Dudley Oliver   Captain

Copy, UkLPR, Adm. 1/504, pp. 271–72.

[Enclosure]

Deposition relative to the British
Subjects on board the *Chesapeake*.—

Halifaxss
Copy.—
J B Warren

The deposition of John Bell a native of England, of the Age of Thirty five Years, who being duly sworn., says that he is a Mariner, and that on the 12th day of January last past he was mate of the British Ship *Volunteer* on a Voyage from Liverpool in England to St. Salvador's in the Brazils, on which day the said Ship was Captured by the United States Frigate *Chesapeake* in which Ship the Depo-nent remained a Prisoner from that date until the 9th day of April following, when the said Ship arrived in Boston, that during the time he was onboard the said Ship, he became acquainted with ten British Sailors, to whom soon after Deponents arrival in Boston, he communicated the intelligence that the Right Honble. Sir J. B. Warren had issued a Proclamation offering a Pardon, to all British Sailors who should return to the British Dominions, and read the Procla-mation to them early in the Month of May following, that the said ten Sailors, All declared that they were desirous of leaving the Service of the United States and return to Halifax and requested the Deponent to apply to Mr. Prince the Marshall at Boston to obtain their release, That deponent in consequence of their request did apply to Mr. Prince, and stated to him that the said Ten Sailors whose Names deponent delivered to Mr. Prince were British Subjects, and were desirous of leaving the *Chesapeake*, and requested Permission to go to Halifax in a Cartel, which was then about to sail for this Port, or that they might be permit-ted to surrender themselves Prisoners of War, That Mr. Prince said he was too much engaged in Business at that time to attend to Deponents application and nothing could be done in behalf of the said sailors, by the deponent as he then came in a Cartel for Halifax, where he arrived about the 15th. day of May last,

That yesterday deponent went to the Prison upon Melville Island, were he saw Thomas Arthur, Henry Simpson, and Thos. Jones, three of the said British Sailors whom he knew to be the same, who were onboard the said Ship *Chesa-peake*, while deponent was a Prisoner onboard the same Ship, That he does not know that the said Persons went by their real Names, he thinks they did not as

when they made application to the deponent to solicit the Marshall for their release, they gave different Names as their true, and real Names.—

"Signed"   John Bell

A Copy   W. Miller   Agent

for Prisoners of War

Sworn before me
the 22d June 1813
("Signed") Henry H. Cogswell.—
Not. Pub.—

Copy, UkLPR, Adm. 1/504, pp. 273–75.

Building the 74 at Portsmouth

*Through the spring and early summer, progress on the 74-gun ship of the line building
at Portsmouth was painfully slow.[1] While a number of problems retarded work on the 74,
no obstacle proved more vexing or less readily soluble than the shortage of timber at the
Portsmouth yard, especially live oak timber. By July, this shortage had become so acute that
Captain Isaac Hull was forced to lay off most of his carpenters and to substitute white oak
for live oak in portions of the ship's construction. It was at this moment of crisis in the
74's construction that Hull proposed an important addition be made to the works at the
Portsmouth yard—a shiphouse.*

1. *For an extended treatment of the construction of the 74-gun ship of the line* Washington *at Portsmouth,
see Maloney,* Captain from Connecticut, *Chapter 9.*

Captain Isaac Hull to Secretary of the Navy Jones

U S Navy Yard   Portsmo.

24th July 1813

Sir,

I have had the honour to receive your letter of the 17th, instant, and have
taken measures for the purchase of the Timber. Mr. Blake[1] thinks from what he
saw, that the other two cargoes are nearly or quite as good as the one purchased, or at any rate may be made so by taking out the shorter pieces, which
the owners are willing to do. The Timber that is out of these ships is not quite
so large but we are assured that what remains in them is larger, and there is
none of it but what will make excellent plank Stock to saw 12 inches wide,
which is quite as wide as we could wish them— I have written Mr. Storer the
Agent at Portland and directed him to make an offer for the Timber not exceeding 10 1/2 Dols. I think they will take that when they find you are determined not to give more and as we have one cargo we can dispense with the
other for a short time untill we see what they will do. Should they not take the
10 1/2 and we give more, I shall not purchase it untill the owners take it all out,
that we may see it, and should it not be so good, they must let us take such only
as is equal in quality—

I regret extremely that we should be obliged to break off our Carpenters for want of timber, but it must be done. I shall discharge all but ten or fifteen to-day. We have some more timber coming from Boston but not near enough to make up the deficiency. What we shall do for the remainder I know not. There is a large quantity of Timber at Boston and many pieces of it belong here, but there is such a deficiency in the Frames that Commodore Bainbridge takes such as will not work into one place to make up another, Say Floors belonging midships to make up sharp Floors aft and forward, and for making Breast hooks Transoms &c &c which will work up many of them. We have been obliged to make all the sharp floors forward and aft of White Oak in consequence of not having a spare piece of <u>live oak</u> in the Yard. The White Oak is however of the best quality and has been in dock ten or twelve years; so that in the bottom of the Ship I have no fears about it, as it is perfectly seasoned. We have now thirteen Frames up, and have all the timber in the Yard laid out some frames wanting one piece and some two or three. Our Carlings, Stanchions &c are nearly all out, and of the best white Oak I ever saw, perfectly seasoned. Our plank is good and well seasoned, and more of them than we shall want. We have also seasoned Oak that will make nearly all the lower deck Beams. Will they not be much stronger and better for that deck than pine? I should like them much better, particularly as we have them so well seasoned—

I shall visit Commodore Bainbridge again in a day or two and after getting every piece he will spare me I shall send a Memorandum of the deficiency to New York, to meet your order for its being furnished from that place—

As the Winters here are very cold and large quantities of Snow falls, may I be permitted to suggest the idea of covering the Ship after she is framed. The cost to build a permanent cover, would probably be two thousand dollars, and I believe a great part of it would be saved in building this ship and others could be built under it, so that by having one much would be saved in labour besides the injury the Frame would receive by being exposed to the winter and the sun the next summer. I should be much pleased to know your wishes on that subject—

I am anxiously waiting your orders about building the Store houses, Magazine &c. and your wishes relative to spare spars for the Frigates mentioned in your letter some time since. With very great Respect I have the honour to be Sir Your Obedient Servant.

Isaac Hull

LS, DNA, RG45, CL, 1813, Vol. 5, No. 40 (M125, Roll No. 30).

1. Joshua Blake, a member of an influential Bay State family, had served under Hull as first lieutenant of *Argus* from May 1803 to March 1805. The two men remained friends after Blake resigned his commission in April 1809. On 26 June 1813, Hull appointed Blake acting master of the Portsmouth Navy Yard. See Hull to Jones, 26 June 1813, in DNA, RG45, CL, 1813, Vol. 4, No. 117 (M125, Roll No. 29); and Maloney, *Captain from Connecticut*, pp. 223–24.

SECRETARY OF THE NAVY JONES TO CAPTAIN ISAAC HULL

Captain Isaac Hull   Navy Depart.
U.S. Navy   Commandant   Augt. 10. 1813.
of Navy Yard.   Portsmouth N.H.

Other pressing duties have delayed my reply to several of your late letters. I shall now embrace them all in substance.

I am pleased to learn that you have obtained an additional Supply of timber (live oak) from Boston and I hope the residue may be procured at New York where I have desired Captain Evans to deliver it to your order. If however the interruption and danger of transportation continues I have concluded not to wait for a supply from New York, and in that case you will decline that supply and substitute White Oak which I am induced to admit in consequence of your assurance that it has been 10 or 11 years in dock, is perfectly sound and seasoned, and of the very best quality. I feel great responsibility in building those Ships and wish to construct them of such Materials and with such fidelity as to ensure their durability and remove the prejudice which has taken such deep root in consequence of the enormous repairs and loss of time which has so seriously impaired the resources and efficacy of the Establishment

I rely upon good timber, good work and thoroughly <u>dry Salting</u> to produce this effect.

The lower Deck Beams you may make of prime White Oak which I presume you will have to scarph in the middle and it will be well to slit a small tongue out of the ends to let the Salt penetrate.

The Knees should be kept an Inch & quarter below the upper edge of the Beams so that the air may circulate and the Salt rest upon the upper surface of the Knee.

The Oak ought to be very excellent or I should prefer the Pitch pine.

The Cargo at Bath will be entirely for your Station. Tell Mr. Wood I will not give a Cent more than for that at Bath.

I have bought another large Cargo at New York for $13. but it is near the Navy Yard and will only require to be removed as it may be wanted for use, therefore it is cheaper than the other. You will take measures to procure two sets of Masts and Spars for each of the classes of Ships viz. 74 . 44 . 36 & <u>large Sloops</u> and also to erect the Store houses you mention, but only of such dimensions as will answer present purposes, with a view to future extension; and a magazine of a moderate Size. In giving you this authority I feel that nothing but absolute necessity could justify me in outrunning the appropriations, and pray you to observe the strictest economy. If you can erect a good substantial permanent Cover over the Ship after she is framed, for the sum you mention $2000—it will be money well laid out and I authorize you to contract for or build one as the public interest may direct.

You will recollect that I want for the use of the Department a fair and correct Draught of the Ship as taken from the <u>Mould loft</u>.

I agree to allow Mr. Craven[1] for his Services while Clerk of the Yard at the rate of $700. per annum. Thus I believe I have embraced all the objects of your present enquiry and solicitude. I am very respectfully your obedt. Servt.

W. Jones.

LB Copy, DNA, RG45, CNA, Vol. 1, pp. 469–70 (M441, Roll No. 1).

1. Tunis Craven, the son-in-law of Commodore Thomas Tingey, was acting purser at Portsmouth Navy Yard from August 1812 until April 1813, when his appointment was revoked by Secretary Jones. Through Hull's intercession, Craven was able to obtain the dual appointments of storekeeper and clerk of the yard at Portsmouth. See Hull to Jones, 20 Apr. 1813, in DNA, RG45, CL, 1813, Vol. 3, No. 21 (M125, Roll No. 28); and Maloney, *Captain from Connecticut,* p. 225–26.

CAPTAIN ISAAC HULL TO SECRETARY OF THE NAVY JONES

U S. Navy Yard   Portsmouth   29th August 1813

Sir,

I have had the honour to receive your letter of the 10th instant in answer to my letters previous to that date.

Measures will be immediately taken to procure timber for the Masts, but as it can be got at less expence, in winter and delivered here early in the Spring, I shall contract only for one set for each class to be delivered here this fall; the other set in the Spring—

The season is now so far advanced that I fear the frost will be injurious to the storehouses should we build them this fall, I have therefore pretty much determined to collect the materials and have them on the spot, to commence early in the spring. They can then be built by the time we shall want them for our stores. Should I find however that the materials can be collected in time to run them up before the frost sets in, I shall do it on account of the price of labour, which will be less now than in the Spring.

Believing that the Magazine was absolutely necessary, as the powder for all the Gun Boats and the Yard was stowed in one of the Gun Boats, there being no other place to put it, I had commenced the building it previous to the receipt of your letter, and it is now about half done. The body of it is round, twenty five feet in the clear, with a wall three feet thick and the height ten and an half or eleven feet, with an arch thrown over it of brick— The main magazine to contain from seven to nine hundred Bbls. and the Arch to contain the filled Cartridges, Powder horns &c. that may be necessary to keep on the Island. This building will cost little more than the labour of laying the stone and brick as the stone is collected by the Gun Boat men on the Island. The cost will be sent you as soon as completed. Should I not build the Stores this fall I shall, with the Sailors in the Yard, run out the two launching piers about forty feet which must be done before the ship can be launched, and these by carrying into twenty four feet at low water, will make a wharf for the Ship to lie at when launched, and sufficiently large by covering over the launching slip with square timber, which can be easily removed when another ship is built.

The Agent is now looking for some one to undertake the building of the Cover over the Ship, agreeably to a plan I have given him, but I fear however it will cost a little more than the sum named to you; if it does, I must endeavour to save it in some other way, for I think it all important that it should be done in this yard what ever they may do in the others, as the climate is much more severe, and the Navy Yard being on an Island, the weather will be much colder than otherwise.[1]

I pray you to be assured that whatever is done under my direction shall be at the least possible expense, and nothing shall be done but what is for the good of the service. With great Respect I have the honour to be Sir, Your Obedt. Servant

Isaac Hull

LS, DNA, RG45, CL, 1813, Vol. 5, No. 173 (M125, Roll No. 30).

1. The shiphouse was completed by the first week of December and would continue in use for well over four decades; for a contemporary visual representation, see Maloney, *Captain from Connecticut*, p. 253.

Fiasco off Cape May

On the morning of 29 July, Master Commandant Samuel Angus[1] received word that a British sloop of war had taken a prize off Cape May. Angus immediately sortied with the Delaware flotilla to investigate. On arriving at the mouth of the bay, Angus found the enemy vessel, H.M. sloop Martin, *lying aground in shoal waters. As he anchored his vessels in a battle line opposite the exposed and unmaneuverable* Martin, *the American commander must have felt assured of an easy victory.*

1. *Angus was promoted to master commandant on 24 July 1813.*

MASTER COMMANDANT SAMUEL ANGUS TO COMMODORE ALEXANDER MURRAY

Public Service   U. States Flotilla, Cape May
                                                                              July 29th 1813.
Sir.

Laying off Dennis's Creek this morning I discovered that an Enemy's Sloop of War, had chased a small vessel, and taken her near the Overfalls.[1] I immediately got under weigh, and stood down the Bay. The Sloop of War stood so near the Overfalls, that she grounded slightly on the Outer ridge of Crows Shoals. I thought proper to endeavour to bring him to action, I succeeded and got within three quarters of a mile & anchored the Boats (Consisting of eight Gun Boats, and two Block Sloops.)—in a Line ahead.[2] A heavy Frigate[3] had by this time, anchored about a half mile further out. After a Cannonade of one hour, and forty five minutes, in which the Ships Kept up a constant, and heavy firing, heaving their Shot, from a half, to three quarters of a mile over us, they doing us but little damage, their shot seldom striking us

The Sloop of War, and Frigate finding our Shot to tell on their hulls, manned their Boats ten in number (two Launches, the rest large Barges, and Cutters) with from thirty to forty Men in each, and dispatched them after Gun Boat *No. 121*, Sailing Master, Shead which had unfortunately, fell a mile, and a half out of the Line; although it had been my positive and express orders to anchor at half cables length apart, and not farther. from the strong Ebb tide they succeeded in capturing her, after a gallant resistance, (for three times did *121* discharge her long gun, apparently full of Cannister, among the whole line of Boats when at a very short distance, which must have done great execution, and not till after She was boarded did the colours come down). before any assistance could be given her, however we got near enough to destroy three or four of their Boats, and must have Killed a vast number of Men, it being a calm they succeeded in getting her away, by sending all their Boats ahead and towing her; but have paid dearly for their temerity; they must at least have had one third of their Men Killed and Wounded— All of our ammunition is expended. Five of the Gun Boats have their Gun carriages disabled. The Enemy had a decided superiority over us, from the goodness of their powder, although they struck but two of the Vessels, they put one Shot through the foot of the *Buffaloe*'s jib, and one through the under part of the bow sprit. And cut Gun Boat *No 125*, Sailg. Master L. Moliere's rigging in several places, and an Eighteen pound shot, struck her long gun and indented it several inches; but happy am I to say that not a man was wounded in any of the Boats, except the one captured— And have not yet learn't their fate.—. The Sloop of War must have been entirely cut to pieces, if the powder in the Gun Boats had been but only commonly good— I feel much indebted to Lt. Mitchell, and Officers, Comg. Gun Boats for their spirited exertions, in carrying into execution, my orders and if I may judge from the Gallant resistance made by Sailg. Master Sheed, in engaging when Surrounded by the Boats of the Enemy that every Officer, and Man, of the Flotilla will do their duty in all situations. I have the honor to be respecty. your Most Obt. Servt.

Saml. Angus
Comg. US Delaware Flotilla

PS the action commenced 7 M. before 1 PM & ended 37 M after 2 PM

ALS, DNA, RG45, MC, 1813, No. 91 (M147, Roll No. 5).

1. The Overfalls is an area of shoal water just off Cape May.
2. Gunboats *No. 116*, Vincent Lowe; *No. 120*, John Kitts; *No. 121*, William W. Sheed; *No. 122*, John T. Wade; *No. 125*, Lucas Moliere; *No. 129*, [George Binder?]; *No. 132*, William Pluright; and *No. 135*, James Ramage. Block sloops *Camel*, Francis J. Mitchell, and *Buffalo*, Samuel Angus.
3. *Junon.*

COMMODORE ALEXANDER MURRAY TO SECRETARY OF THE NAVY JONES

Phila.   Augt. 2nd 1813

Sir

Since my letter to you yesterday enclosing Lt. Anguss letter to me relative to the Action, & loss of the G. boat, I have conversed with sailg. Master Wade on the subject. I expressed my surprize that none of the Flotilla went down to her assistance, as she could not get up to them, he tells me it was the wish of all the Officers, & they all got ready at a moments warning expecting a signal from Lt. Angus, but no signal was made during the action, he tells me that sailg. Master Shed behaved most nobly, & he fears most of his Crew must have fallen, & great execution on both sides—

This Moment the *Camel* has arrived with her decks much injured in the action, I shall put as many Carpenters to work on her as are necessary, & hope to get her & a boat to replace the one lost down tomorrow, Lt. Mitchel who Commands her, corroborates what Mr. Wade says, they both think the boat might have been saved, Lt. Angus writes in high applause of Lt. Mitchels behavior as a very gallant officer.

I have written down to Mr. Angus putting many questions to him relative to this affair, as I wish to give you a satisfactory detail of the business.

The Schr. that attends the Barge has gone down as a Flag of Truce under the charge of sailg. Master Ramage to enquire into the state of our Prisoners & wounded Men, on her return I shall give you further particulars, Doctr. Kearney has also gone down with her. I have the honor to be Your Mo. Obt.

A Murray

ALS, DNA, RG45, CL, 1813, Vol. 5, No. 64 (M125, Roll No. 30).

Sailing Master William W. Sheed to
Master Commandant Samuel Angus

On Board his Majesty's Sloop *Martin*
off Providence Rhode Island   August 6th 1813

Sir

It is with the deepest regret that I have to Announce to you the Capture of the U.S. Gun Boat *No. 121* under my Command, by the Boats of the *Junon* Frigate & *Martin* Sloop of War, Eight in Number, three of Which mounted 12 pound Carronades & Carrying in All 150 men,   at 10 Minutes before Meredian on the 27th of July I received orders from you to form aline a head & to fire on the Enemy, but finding myself drove Away from the Squadron by the Wind dying Away & a Strong Ebb tide, I remained Sweeping & firing the thirty two pounder at the same time. finding My Shot did not reach I placed all hands to the sweeps to endeavour to gain the Squadron,   At 20 Minutes past 12, I perceived the Enemy's Barges making for me they now being out of Gun Shot. I still endeavoured to sweep up to the Squadron,   at 20 Minutes before 1 I commenced firing at the Enemys Boats & Sweeping at the Same time, but finding I could gain nothing, I Anchored to Receive them as American Tars have been Accustomed to,   the Enemy now getting Within Grape, I commenced it. but unfortunately the Pintle of the Larger Gun gave Way the first round,   I again Charged & got her to bear again, which discharge did considerable damage, but tearing my Gun Carriage all to peices,   I again loaded with the hope of getting her to bear Again but found it utterly impossible,   the Enemy now being Close on board discharging Volleys of Shot from the Carronades & Muskets, I Call'd the Boarders & Small Arms Men Away to repel the Enemy   the Enemy now Surrounding us they Pour'd a heavy fire on us which We returned with as much promptness as our feeble Number would admit   Several of my men having now fell our Ensighn hallyards shot away, My Men [ ] [1] altho, I endeavour'd to Cheer them. but Seeing the Superiority of the Enemy's force In the Act of Boarding us in Every Quarter they began to fire briskly except five or Six of them. I found it necessary for the preservation of those few valuable lives to surrender to seven our ~~few~~ number the Enemy boarding loading our decks with Men, We were all driven below and it was with the utmost difficulty that the Officers could Satiate the revenge of the Seamen who seemed to thirst for Blood & Plunder   the Last of Which they took Care to rob us of Everything,   We had None Killed but Seven wounded five Slightly the Enemies loss by us was Seven Kill'd and twelve Wounded. 4 of Which has since died, they have Conquer'd Me but they have paid dearly for it And I trust Sir when you come to view the disadvantages that I labour'd under having not been but Seven days on Board of my Boat[2] & Scarcely time to Station my men And the Misfortune of entirely disabling My Gun the Superiority of Numbers to oppose me you will be convinced that the flagg I had the honour to wear has not lost any of that National Courage that has ever been Attach'd to it   I have the honour to be With the Greatest Respect Sir your most Obedient Svt.

William Shead

Copy, DNA, RG45, MLR, 1813, Vol. 5, No. 68 (M124, Roll No. 57). The copyist spelled Sheed's name incorrectly.

1. Blank space in document.
2. Sheed had accepted his warrant as sailing master scarcely two months before the action on the Delaware.

American Gunboat Flotilla Attacking H.M. Sloop of War Martin in Delaware Bay, 29 July 1813

Master Commandant Samuel Angus to Secretary of the Navy Jones

To the Honorable Wm. Jones   U S Flotilla Delaware bay
Secy. of the Navy   laying of the thumb caps [1]
                                              Western shore   Augt. 8 1813

Sir,

from the publications I have seen in the papers of my letter address'd to Commodore Murray relative to the action of the 29 July of Cape May induces me to believe that a correct Copy was not sent you, for the honor of myself and officers I have thought it advisable to send you a copy of three letters [2] addressed to Commodore Murray respecting the action of the 29 of July.— be assured Sir it was no trifling excuse about the badness of the powder for I had wrote to Comme. Murray frequently respecting it— the following is an extract from one letter— "the powder is very bad it will not heave a shot at the greatest degree of elevation more than one mile"— an extract of another to Commre. Murray— "our powder (let me again mention) is shamefully bad I have seen a hot loger head roll'd over the touch hole of a Gun and the powder flash by grains for half a minute before the Gun exploded"— to this I was answerd that he found the boats had condem'd powder on board— an extract of another letter to the Commodore— "I shall leave the boats that are not properly organized at New Castle as ruin and disgrace would attend them in their present unorganized and deficient state in case they should fall in with the enemy—

In fact Sir, it gives me pain to mention (although I am in duty bound to my own character) the Shamefull way Comre. Murray has sent the boats down— as many of them are now undergoing repairs at Phila.   let me respecty. request leave to come to washington as I have many things I should wish to relate to you that would not be proper through the medium of a letter— the british have all left the bay they have taken the mast out of *121* and sunk her— they acknowledge to have 5 Killd and 13 wounded on the 29 July and several shot through their sloop of war very respecty. I have the honor to be your most obt. Servt.

                                                          S. Angus

PS   I have enclos'd for your perusal a copy of the orders issued to the different Comre. of the flotilla on the day of action

ALS, DNA, RG45, MC, 1813, No. 98 (M147, Roll No. 5).

1. Thrumcap is a point of land on the eastern shore of Bombay Hook Island.
2. These enclosures, all copies of letters from Angus to Murray, were mistakenly bound following DNA, RG45, MC, 1813, No. 91 (M147, Roll No. 5). The first enclosure, marked "letter no. 1", is a duplicate of Angus's letter of 29 July printed above. The second enclosure, marked "letter no. 2." and also dated 29 July, complains of the poor quality of the flotilla's gunpowder. The third enclosure, marked "letter N. 3" and dated 3 August, is a response to several queries made by Murray respecting Angus's failure to assist Sheed, his failure to employ the flotilla's barges, and the quality of the flotilla's gunpowder.

Commodore Alexander Murray to Secretary of the Navy Jones

                                              Philada.   Augt. 25th. 1813
Sir,

I am much in want of some of the rules & regulations for the Government of the Navy, such as I had was distributed amongst the different Officers that have been on this station, who have taken them away with them, I wish also to have a correct list of the Officers of our Navy, if you will do me the favor to have ordered up to me,

I am sorry to observe to you in my defence, that <u>Mr. Angus</u> has been striving hard to vindicate himself in the failure of his attack on the *Martin* Sloop of War, by indirect hints that his Powder was not good, & that the Gun slides gave way, as to first complaint, except some old Powder sent to exercise his Guns, it was of Duponts manufactory, & of the first quality, when sent on board, but as I am informed by his Officers, not an atom of it has been turned, or air'd since he has had command, <u>wh</u>. in such damp confined Magazines will readily account for its loosing its strength, but I have had it proved since returned, & I do not find it much depreciated, the G. slides, & pintles were made according to directions recd. from the N. dept., & I believe were as substantial as any in the service, but what could stand thirty successive rounds, fired from those 32 lbs. in <u>wh</u>. was expended more than 3000 lbs. of Powder, not a shot of <u>wh</u>. took effect, from the great distance they fired, some of his Officers tell me, that they wished to have ceased in fir'ing, knowing it to be of no effect, & hailed him requesting that they might be permitted to go to the relief of the G boat that was taken, but refused 'till too late to succour her, he has been very pettish to me for making my remarks, & comments to him; <u>censure has gone abroad</u>, he never in his life may have such another opportunity of distinguishing himself, the *Martin* lay aground 24 hours, & we have lost a noble Officer by his oversight, who did his duty; I hope his next adventure will be more successful, & do away the unfavorable opinions impressed on the minds of many; for my own part I wish not to criminate him, but as his Senior Officer I deem it my duty to investigate; & make my observations on his general conduct[1]

The Flotilla is now in good order & gone down the Bay, I have directed Mr Angus to bring up the wounded Men from Cape May if in condition to move   I have the honor to be Your Mo. Obt.

A Murray

ALS, DNA, RG45, CL, 1813, Vol. 5, No. 152 (M125, Roll No. 30).

1. Initially Secretary Jones voiced support for Angus despite criticism of him by Murray and others, noting that Angus's "reputation as a well qualified and intrepid officer" stood "too high to admit of any supposition unfavorable to his character.—" But as the controversy surrounding the loss of Gunboat *No. 121* persisted, Jones must have concluded that a court of inquiry was necessary to put the matter to rest. On 4 September he ordered a court convened "to inquire into the conduct of the Commanding and other Officers of the U.S. Flotilla in the attack on the Enemy near Cape May." The court, presided over by Captain Charles Morris, met on board the block sloop *Buffalo* at New Castle from 10–15 September. While the court did not find Angus guilty of cowardice, it did find him guilty of errors in judgment. Quoted material from DNA, RG45, CNA, Vol. 1, pp. 467, 491 (M441, Roll No. 1). The record of Angus's court of inquiry may be found in DNA, RG125, CM, Vol. 4, No. 146 (M273, Roll No. 4).

Combatting Smugglers

One of the most frustrating problems the Madison administration had to contend with as it directed the nation's war effort was the growing trade in contraband goods between Americans and the enemy. This illegal traffic was a matter of concern not only because it enabled the British army and navy to fight more effectively, but because it made the U.S. government appear to have little control over its own citizenry. When Congress balked at an embargo to bring this commerce under control, President Madison resorted to his powers as chief executive for a solution. Thus, in late July, he directed Secretaries Jones and Armstrong to issue orders to all naval and military officers to interdict illegal trade with the enemy.[1]

1. *For a discussion of the Madison administration's efforts to bring commercial traffic with the enemy under control, see Hickey, "American Trade Restrictions."*

NAVY DEPARTMENT CIRCULAR

Circular.

Navy Department.
July 30th 1813.

Sir,

You will perceive, that the object of the enclosed General Order, is, to prevent <u>intelligence and succours</u> being carried to the enemy, hovering off our Harbours, or within the waters and jurisdiction of the United States; and that none, but Vessels or Craft, proceeding, or apparently intending to proceed, towards the enemy, so as to pass within the reach of his power, and from which he might "derive succours or intelligence", are intended to be stopped.

With a vigilant execution of the order, you will be careful to guard against injuring those, who may be pursuing their lawful occupations, without intending to violate the object of the General order. I am, respectfully, your Obedient Servant,

W. Jones.

	John Shaw
Wm. Bainbridge	John Cassin
Stephn. Decatur	Alexr. Murray
Saml. Evans	Saml. Angus
Charles Gordon	Jacob Lewis
Charles Morris	Isaac Hull
J. H. Dent	T. N. Gautier
H. G Campbell	I Chauncey
Thos. McDonnough	O. H. Perry

LB Copy, DNA, RG45, SNL, Vol. 11, p. 30 (M149, Roll No. 11).

NAVAL GENERAL ORDER.

The palpable and criminal intercourse, held with the enemy's forces, blockading and invading the waters and shores of the United States, is, in a Military view, an offence of so deep a dye, as to call for the vigilant interposition of all the Naval Officers of the United States.

This intercourse is not only carried on, by foreigners, under the specious garb of friendly flags, who convey provisions, water, and succours of all kinds, (ostensibly destined for friendly ports, in the face, too, of a declared and rigorous blockade,) direct to the fleets and stations of the enemy, with constant intelligence of our Naval and Military force and preparation, and the means of continuing and conducting the invasion, to the greatest possible annoyance of the Country; but the same traffic, intercourse and intelligence, is carried on, with great subtlety and treachery, by profligate citizens, who, in vessels ostensibly navigating our own waters, from port to port, under cover of night, or other circumstances favouring their turpitude, find means to convey succours, or intelligence to the enemy, and elude the penalty of the law. This lawless traffic and intercourse, is also carried on, to a great extent, in craft, whose capacity exempts them from the regulations of the revenue laws, and from the vigilance, which vessels of greater capacity attract.

I am, therefore, commanded by the President of the United States, to enjoin and direct, all Naval commanding Officers, to exercise the strictest vigilance, and to stop & detain, all vessels, or craft, whatsoever, proceeding, or apparently intending to proceed, towards the enemy's vessels, within the waters, or hovering about the harbours of the United States; or towards any station, occupied by the enemy, within the jurisdiction of the United States, from which vessels, or craft, the enemy might derive succours or intelligence.

Wm. Jones.

Navy Department
July 29th 1813.

LB Copy, DNA, RG45, SNL, Vol. 11, p. 29 (M149, Roll No. 11).

MASTER COMMANDANT JACOB LEWIS TO SECRETARY OF THE NAVY JONES

Sir

I had the honor of addressing you a few hasty lines yesterday giving an account of my Cruise down long Island Sound, since which my mind has dwelt much on the subject of the general order Contained in your note of the 30th—and find great difficulty. in executing it, to the extent of its object—owing to the running of the Enimy and the peculiar situation of this port it having two outlets— the Enimy have excluded in their Edict the Port of New Haven, (the Consequence is) that place has become the St. Bartholemews of America, in my excursion down Sound I visited that Port and found it the Rendesvouz of Sweads Spanyard & Portuguese (Alias Englishmen) all Vessels of this discription pass in and out by that passage, stop and get franchised at N. Haven, after which they meet with no difficulty, from the Blockade Squadron— from the Contiguous situation of the State of Conecticut and the disposition of Its Inhabitants, the Enimies wants are render'd as few as they would be if in the River Thames Gardners Island affords water, has on it one thousd. Head of Cattle, one do. of Sheep &c. an Ample supply of fresh provisions, are found there, the Enimies Barges appear to have the whole range of the lower part of the Sound, for twenty miles, they after having Satiated their ferocity in burning and otherwise destroying the Coasting Vessels have in Violation of their Own laws. now began to ransom, all the Vessels they take, and divide the moneys arising thereto (on the head of the Capstan,) if the Conecticut people were the only person who suffer'd by these Maurauders—it would not be a matter of regret, but I am sorry to see the good people of long Island who are the fast friends of the administration, suffering prodigiously allow me to solicit your permission, to fit out an expedition, on the following plan— to wit to emply two Coasting Sloops—which can be had at a very trifling expence,   I will load a tier of Bundles of [Saw'd] hay around the deck— Cover the out side of the bundles with old Canvis to make them appear like Bales of Cotton,   these will not only serve to decoy. but a bull work for the men   Cotton is Constantly going from this City to the different cotton factorys in R. Island State— therefore the deception will be perfect, the Value very inviting &c I will have a boat and the number of men generally attached to such a Vessel, leave the Vessel run for the Shore on approach of the Enimy— this is the usual practice, when it is found they may be overtaken by the Enimy— with these Vessels I can go through Hell Gate unnoticed by Keeping the men out of sight, therefore the Enimy's friends could not give them information   (a rouse de guerre) could not fail,   cut off the Enimies Barges once & the Coasting trade of the sound would be free,   Gun Boats can not perform this Kind of Service by reason their being too well Known, & Sluggish in movement   these Coasting Sloops Sail superiorly fast   superiority can be hired for about 10 dollars per day the expedition could be performed in a Week—and if successful would reduce the price of Wood in this City six Shillings on the Cord—and gratify the people on long Island exceedingly—who Volunteer their Servises to go as pilots— and in the event of its being Compleatly successful—good must come out of it,   it would alarm the Enimy—& Keep them in, and ~~above all gratify the good people of L. Island~~: Sr. Ths. hardy has been informed by his friends that the object of my Visit down Sound was to place Torpedoes—in plum gut—and I am informed that he boasts of having received the information   with the highest Consr. & respt. yr. very Obt Servt.

J Lewis
Come. U.S. Flotilla
N Yk.   9th Augt. 1813

Excuse the Style of this letter its written in great haste—

ALS, DNA, RG45, MLR, 1813, Vol. 5, No. 77 (M124, Roll No. 57).

Secretary Jones's Rationale on Promotion

The Navy Department considered seniority in rank an important factor in determining which officers merited promotion.[1] But as the following letters from Secretary Jones reveal, seniority was not the sole criterion, nor the most important one, guiding the department's decisions on promotion.

1. It is worth noting that only commissioned officers were ranked according to seniority, with rank being determined by the date of commission. This was not the case among warranted officers. As Secretary Jones informed one young midshipman, "If you have conceived the idea of Rank among Midshipmen, you are mistaken, no such principle has prevailed, nor ought to prevail. They are all Novitiates, and the rule is, to promote them according to their several merits, acquirements, and services." See Jones to Thomas T. Webb, 17 Nov. 1813, DNA, RG45, SNL, Vol. 11, p. 11 (M149, Roll No. 11). For a discussion of promotion in the early sailing navy, see C. McKee, U.S. Naval Officer Corps, pp. 271–325.

SECRETARY OF THE NAVY JONES TO SENATOR JOSEPH ANDERSON [1]

The Honorable   Navy Depart.
Jos. Anderson   July 30, 1813
Senate Chamber

In respect to the selections from the Roll of Officers for promotion submitted to the President I have endeavoured to obtain as correct information as the nature of the case will admit and with the utmost care & impartiality have named those who appeared from their Services and opportunities of acquiring professional knowledge to merit a preference.

The good of the Service has been my only guide. Almost all the gentleman are personally unknown to me, and the interest of the Service excepted, it is to me a matter of entire indifference which of them are promoted.

If Seniority of date was the absolute rule, the task would be very simple and less irksome to the Secretary but it never has been—it ought never to be, except when merit and knowledge are equal in the candidate. The promotion from Lieutenants to Masters Commandant is a most important step indeed—A distinct and important Command requiring the highest degree of professional knowledge and experience.

The gentlemen whom the Hon Mr. Brown [2] mentions deserve all the commendation he has given them but it is not my fault if they have been confined for some years almost exclusively to gun Boat Service and have seen little else since their last promotion. The question is Are they now qualified to command a Ship of War? or does not the interest of the Service require that they should previously serve as senior Lieutenants on board some of the frigates or as Lieutenants Commanding some of the smaller vessels, as Lieutenant Henley has done for some considerable time past.

There are three Lieutenants older than Mr. Dexter and five older than Mr. Alexis not nominated or noticed in the inquiry. They cannot all be promoted.

The oldest Lieutenant on the Roll (including those nominated for promotion) Mr. Carroll is on the New Orleans Station.

This Case has not been noticed.

Mr. Patterson has I believe seen only flotilla Service since his promotion and being senior to Messrs. Dexter & Alexis he has frequently been Commanding Officer of that Station for which he is perfectly qualified.

A Brother of Mr. Henley senior to himself and to Mr. Dexter & Alexis is not nominated. [3] I believe there are as many Masters Commandant nominated at this time as the Service will require between this and the next Session; and I would rather have seen them reduced than to have them increased at this time.

If Messrs. Dexter and Alexis desire it, I will with pleasure, endeavour to find commands for them more favorable to their views. I am very respectfully your obedt. Servt.

W Jones

LB Copy, DNA, RG45, Letters to Congress, Vol. 2, pp. 186–87.

1. Joseph Anderson represented Tennessee in the U.S. Senate from 1797 to 1815.
2. Senator James Brown from Louisiana. Brown paid Secretary Jones a visit to remonstrate against the department's failure to include Daniel T. Patterson, Daniel S. Dexter, and Louis Alexis among those nominated for master commandant. See Brown to Patterson, 31 July 1813, NHpR, Naval History Manuscript Collection. For additional documentation on Brown's efforts on behalf of Lieutenant Dexter, see pp. 672–73.
3. Lieutenant Robert Henley.

Secretary of the Navy Jones to Lieutenant James Renshaw [1]

Lt. James Renshaw,   Navy Department
Comg. U.S. Ship *Alert,*   Septr. 15th. 1813.
New York.

Sir,

The desire of promotion is not only natural but laudable, and therefore the desire, and the claim, is universal in Naval and Military life; and great allowance should always be made, for the zeal with which Candidates urge their claims.

I have received your letter of the 11th Inst., soliciting the command of the *Enterprize,* or her prize, the *Boxer.* To this I can give no definite answer at present; but am very much disposed to give you an opportunity, by an active command, to signalize yourself.

I have also received several letters from yourself and Brother,[2] complaining of injustice done to you in the late promotions; and urging your claims, with much zeal and perseverance, with the avowed object of extorting from the Department, a pledge of promotion, either immediate, or at the next session. Both the manner, and the purpose, are too exceptionable to command acquiescence, or pass without notice.

Whatever may be the views of the Department, it would be a dereliction of duty, and sound policy to anticipate its purposes by premature pledges.

Officers frequently, in urging their pretensions to preferment, tacitly violate the principles for which they contend, by losing sight of the rights and claims of others upon the same principle.

The extent of promotions is not governed by the pleasure of this Department, but by the necessities of the Public service;—this criterion limited the late promotions of Lieuts. to Master Comdts. to <u>fifteen</u>. Upon your own absolute principle of seniority, this number could not have reached you; and therefore, to do what you call justice, in promoting you, the rights and claims of five Lieutenants, Senior to yourself must be overlooked; Viz. Messrs M. B. Carroll, J. M. Gardner, Robt. Henley, Stephen Cassin, and D. S. Dexter.

But the absolute rule of seniority has at no time prevailed, as may be seen by early promotions of Junior Officers, over those of long standing, and with this you must be perfectly acquainted.

The only Officer, Junior to yourself, that has been promoted to the rank of M. Comdt. is Mr. Downes, nine days your Junior. Mr. Parker was specially promoted for the gallant action with the *Java.* If you imagine, that any partialities, or prejudices, influence the selections in this Department, you are greatly mistaken.

Mr. Downes is to me an entire stranger; but I understood from the most respectable sources, that he was an Officer of uncommon merit, second to no Lieut. in the Navy, had had great advantages of enterprizing service, having been actively employed long before the War, and ever since on one continued cruize, the termination of which is probably still very remote.

My personal knowledge, and local feelings were naturally on your side; but I hope I have not greatly erred, in supposing that Mr. Downes might, possibly, have superior claims to promotion. But at all events, (Mr. Downe's out of the question,) your claim to participate in the late promotions can rest only on your superior merit over five of your Seniors, and not from the date of Commission; which I pray may never become the absolute rule, for I should, from thence,

date the decline of our Infant Naval Hercules; unless as in some other countries, the Executive could promote an indefinite number, to get at an Officer of
distinguished merit and talents. But, Sir, in regard to the promotion of Lieutenants, the rule of Seniority is by no means absolute in any Naval Service. If it
is, how happens it that there are so many grey headed Lieutenants, and youth-
ful Captains, in the most celebrated Naval Service in the World. In our Military
service the rule is but partial. Officers rise regimentally; but only in their own
regiments. If new regiments are to be raised, new Officers are appointed.

The analogy however is not strict. Naval promotions, above the rank of Lieutenants, become immensely important. The honour of the Nation, is, as completely involved in the command of a Sloop of War, as in that of a Frigate.

The Commander is, <u>in chief</u>, and without controul; every thing depending
upon his skill, judgment and prowess. These observations are not applied personally to any one; they go to support a general principle, and to shew the absur-
dity of rendering the rule of seniority absolute. As to yourself, I have shewn, that
according to that rule, you could not have participated in the late promotions.

The rule of Seniority, under equal circumstances, always will, and ought to
prevail. I am, respectfully, Your Obedt. Servt.

W. Jones.

LB Copy, DNA, RG45, SNL, Vol. 11, pp. 87–90 (M149, Roll No. 11).

1. James Renshaw was commissioned a lieutenant on 25 February 1807. At the beginning of the
war he was attached to the flotilla at New York. On 21 May 1813 he was ordered to assume command of *Alert*, and on 15 September 1813 he was given command of *Enterprise*.

2. See Richard Renshaw's letter of 9 August 1813 to Secretary Jones in DNA, RG45, MLR, 1813,
Vol. 5, No. 89 (M124, Roll No. 57).

Fulton's Proposal for Steam-Powered Warships

*In the summer of 1813, Robert Fulton redirected his energies from experiments with tor-
pedoes and submarine guns [1] into a different project, the development of a steam-powered
warship. In a correspondence conducted with Commodore Stephen Decatur, the famed in-
ventor refined his ideas for this vessel. Had she been completed before peace was declared,
steam frigate* Fulton I *might have proven an effective weapon. Her construction presaged
a new age in naval warfare.[2]*

1. *See pp. 111–14.*
2. *The most detailed treatments of this craft are* Tyler, *"Fulton's Steam Frigate," and* Chapelle, *Fulton's*
"Steam Battery." *See also* Hutcheon, *Robert Fulton, Chapter 5.*

ROBERT FULTON TO COMMODORE STEPHEN DECATUR

Commodore Decatur   New[1]   August 5th 1813

Dear Sir

in answer to your letter of 29 July if there be no Serious difficulty other than
entangling the masts of our Vessel with the yards of the enemy that may be obviated,   ~~Before~~ while making out my drawings for the patent I ~~have~~ composed a

boat Ship with a Steam engine the engine within the wooden walls and two wheels in her body toward her Stern where neither engine or wheels can be [hurt?] If such a Vessel of 250 or 300 Tons were Schooner riged the masts could be lowered as in our steam boats and raised at pleasure, the practice then would be to use the masts and sails at sea as usual and when in sight of the enemy get up the steam when within one mile lower the masts and run in the Bowsprit they would then lie snug on the main deck within the Wooden walls, as though guarded by barbet batteries thus A masts when down

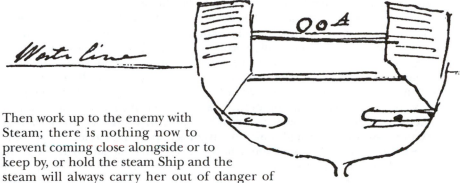

Then work up to the enemy with Steam; there is nothing now to prevent coming close alongside or to keep by, or hold the steam Ship and the steam will always carry her out of danger of being sunk by the sinking enemy Thus suppose you to command a 74 and one Such Steam Sub marine Shot Vessel and about to engage a 74 She must either run away or sink for while engaged with you on one side the Steam Ship could work up under her quarter on the opposite side and Sink her. In like manner It appears to me that 4 Steam Ships could destroy a 74 as She could not bring her guns to bear on the whole of them— In fact in fact the Steam Seems to give per-fection to this system, of as to the mechanism and operation of the steam en-gine I have no doubt It is one of my best combinations I mentioned it in my letter of 29 June to Mr. Jefferson he was highly pleased and as I told you of-fered all his support to have a fair experiment Hence as Steam I can lay the Vessel close within 12 or 6 feet and can carry her off out of danger after her fire is given—do any serious difficulties remain— if not let us immediately urge it upp upon the government.

What is the kind of torpedo experiment which is preparing at New London what the name of the parties, is not Mr Scudder and Riker concerned in it who were concerned in the *eagle?*[2] how do the mean to act Many persons in-sist that Halseys project was all a farce to create alarm in the enemy and that he never actually attempted to go to sea in his Boat did you see him and it? On philosophical principles I have strong doubts that he could not remain so long under water as you suppose or go to a sufficient depth to get under the bottom of a 74 without the water pressing his machine together and drowning him, at 22 feet under water there would be a pressure of 1400 pound on each Superfi-cial foot of his boat on deck ends and all round, a Boat only 2 feet diameter and 10 feet long would have a pressure on her of 45 tons—

AL, MdAN, Zabriski Collection, Robert Fulton Manuscripts.

1. Probably New York.
2. See pp. 160–64.

Commodore Stephen Decatur to Robert Fulton

Augt 9th. 1813

My Dear Sir,

Yours of the 5th Inst. I have received   (The principle difficulties to our project appears now to be removed; the only thing that at present strikes me which remains to be guarded against is the boarding of our vessel from boats,   on this score there will be much danger & unless completely secured from this will be useless,)   a 74 will be able to send 200 men in her boats.

I am of the opinion, that she will be completely defended from such risque in the following manner—her gunwail to be within 3 feet of the water, her decks to have considerable slope, & the whole Surface of the deck to be covered with Iron spikes, very sharp & about 3 inches apart   it would in fact be a hackel,   on such a deck men could not walk,   this deck we could keep covered with boards, until going alongside of the enemy,   In addition to this I would have along the gunwail, 8 or 10 feet apart extending entirely around her, magazines, say thirteen inch shells, charged with powder, & musket balls, with a gun barrel leading through the vessels side, through which the train is to pass, so that let a boat come alongside, where she might, she would have a shell bursting on board her,   In like manner I would have ~~one of~~ these shells laid on the deck, one for every 10 or 12 square feet— The hatchway to admit the mast to lay down should be narrow, the coamings 2 feet thick, with loop holes for musketry & to observe the enemy, & to observe when to discharge the shells, the hatchway between the coamings to be covered with stout gratings, to admit musketry to fire through

The Torpedo expedition fiting her I know nothing about,   a Major Frink, & Mr. Richard, are the proprieters,   your man Welden is here,   the moon (unless overcast) will prevent any immediate attempt. any aid in my power I will give him,   he appears to be prudent & percervering— I shall offer some more remarks on the submarine business shortly   yors truely

S Decatur

ALS, MdAN, Rosenbach Collection.

A New Strategy for Defending the Charleston Station

By August the number and size of enemy ships operating off Charleston had become so great that Captain John H. Dent could no longer send the schooners Nonsuch *and Car- olina on cruises with any degree of safety. These new circumstances forced Dent to reassess the deployment of men and vessels on his station.*

Captain John H. Dent to Secretary of the Navy Jones

The Honorable William Jones.   Charleston.   18th August. 1813.

Sir

I have the honor to report that the Enemy's Boats from the Squadron entered Dewees's Inlet on monday, and destroyed two or three small inland traders yesterday, they landed on long island, committed some depredations, and took off a few head of Cattle, and sheep.

I have brought the Schooners *Carolina* and *Nonsuch* from the roads, taken the officers and crew from the latter, put them on board barges *No. 7 & 9* and placed them under the direction of Lieut Haddaway,[1] with orders to proceed inland to Bulls Bay, and cruize in its vicinity, for the protection of the inhabitants on those islands, and the inland trade, they Sailed this evening, on this service, I shall place the remaining men, on board barge *No. 11*, make up her complement from the *Carolina*, and send her into Stono, to remain with the *Ferret*, as that vessel is too weakly manned to protect herself against a detachment of Boats, the other two barges I retain in the harbor to do guard duty, manned from the *Carolina*,   this Sir, is the best disposition I can make with the force under my command, which employs every man on the Station, and I trust it will meet your approbation.

I am sorry to say the Militia will not volunteer on board the barges, and the Garrisons in this harbour are already too weak to authorize the commanding officer, detaching any part thereof for our expedition in the inlets. The situation of this coast is such, that I am now satisfied the *Nonsuch* and *Carolina* cannot render any Service, as they will not be able to cruize while so superior a force remains on the coast, and it is not probable that it will be less during the war; the only means of protecting this Seabord is by barges, or heavy row gallies to be kept in divisions, traversing the river and inland passages, which will afford an opportunity of meeting the enemy on an equal footing. I Have the Honor to be with great respect your Most Obt Svt.

J H Dent

LS, DNA, RG45, CL, 1813, Vol. 5, No. 117 (M125, Roll No. 30).

1. Edward H. Haddaway was warranted a midshipman on 20 June 1806. On 26 June 1813 he was appointed acting lieutenant on board *Nonsuch*.

Capture of H.M. Sloop *Dominica*

Most decisive naval actions fought during the War of 1812 were determined by seamanship and gunnery. An exception to this was the engagement between the American privateer schooner Decatur [1] *and H.M. sloop* Dominica *in which hand-to-hand combat decided the result. On 5 August,* Decatur *overwhelmed* Dominica *in a boarding action that left nearly three-quarters of the British sloop's crew killed or wounded. Besides being one of the bloodiest and hardest-fought actions of the war, it was one of the few sea fights in which an American privateer bested and captured a Royal Navy vessel.[2]*

1. Decatur *was built at the Charleston shipyard of Pritchard and Shrewsbury. She was launched on 13 March 1813, and, at 240 tons, was the largest privateer to sail from the South Carolina port. She departed Charleston on her maiden voyage on 27 May and was captured in 1814 by H.M. frigate* Le Rhin. *See Mouzon,* Privateers of Charleston, *pp. 21–22, 25.*

2. *For details of the engagement between* Decatur *and* Dominica, *see Coggeshall,* American Privateers and Letters-of-Marque, *pp. 172–7; Maclay,* American Privateers, *pp. 311–17; and Mouzon,* Privateers of Charleston, *pp. 22–24.*

DISTRICT COURT JUDGE JOHN DRAYTON TO
SECRETARY OF STATE JAMES MONROE

So: Carolina.   Augt., 24th: 1813.

Sir.

I have the pleasure to inform you, that by the Capture of his Britannic Majesty's Sloop of War *Dominica*, command by the Late George Wilmot Barrette Esqr. the <u>British Naval Signals</u>, & various military Orders And other important informations have come into my hands, as prize of the Court of Admiralty of this State: and which I now have the honor & satisfaction of forwarding, for the information of the President of the United States—.

The above Vessel was taken after a severe engagement by, the <u>Privateer De-catur</u> of this Port, Commanded by <u>Captain Dominique Diron</u>.[1] It is with pleasure I announce him to the notice of Government: as it appears, that he & his whole Crew fought nobly: took the Sloop by boarding: and treated the prisoners with the utmost humanity—

The prize, is completely fitted up as a Sloop of War; 14 twelve pound Carronades 1 thirty two pounder Carronade midships, & one brass four pounder— Coppered up to the beams, and would be an useful addition to the navy of the United States— As the Capture was by boarding, little or no damage by cannon shot has occurred—

With congratulations on this occasion I have the honor to subscribe myself in haste Sir respectfully yr. mo. ob. st.

John Drayton
Judge of the District Court
of South Carolina.

NB. The *Decatur* had 6 twelve pound Carronades & one Long 18 pounder: & 103 men— The *Dominca* had 83 men.

ALS, DNA, RG45, MLR, 1813, Vol. 5, No. 132 (M124, Roll No. 57).

1. Earlier in his career, Captain Diron had commanded the French privateer *Superbe*. According to Maclay, he was considered "one of the most celebrated privateersmen . . . [of] his day." See Maclay, *American Privateers*, p. 311.

CHARLES R. SIMPSON[1] TO THOMAS BARCLAY[2]

Charleston,— South Carolina
24 August, 1813—

Sir,

My attention has been So Completely engaged in attending to the Wounded, obtaining Paroles for the officers and permission for the Surgeon, and Secretary to Land with other matters incidental to the unfortunate occurrence it is now my painfull Duty to Communicate, and not being myself a Resident in the City that I have not before had time to make Known to you the Capture of His Majestys Late Sloop (a Philadelphia Schooner formerly called the *Glee* I believe, Captured on an Illegal Voyage) *Dominica* commanded by George Wilmote Barrett Esquire on the 5 inst by the American Privateer *Decatur*, Capt Dominique Diron belong-

American Privateer Schooner Decatur Captures H.M. Sloop Dominica, 5 August 1813

ing to this Port and the arrival of both Vessels, with the British Ship *London Trader* of London from Surinam bound to London, on the morning of the 20 inst.— Mortifying as is the Result of this unfortunate Affair. I trust His Majestys Government will never for a moment doubt that the Crew of the *Dominica* which consisted of 85 Men, among whom was a Sergeant & Corporal and Thirteen Marines, did their Duty, when they are informed that when this Vessel was taken possession of there were not more than Three Men able to do Duty. and Every officer Killed or Mortally Wounded excepting Mr. Nicholls a Midshipman, slightly wounded and a Young Gentleman of the Name of Lindo a Volunteer and Supernumerary—. I have not yet seen Mr. Nicholls in consequence of his being on board of one of the United States Schooners appointed for the defence of this harbor. and laying at a Considerable Distance from the City so that I have been able to learn no particulars from him, but from those I have seen it seems very evident that the Loss of this vessel is to be attributed entirely to the Want of Knowledge of and Experience in the Management of a Schooner, on the part of Captain Barrette, who had been Second Lieutenant of the *Dragon* and made in the West Indies. and immediately appointed to the *Dominica*. and the Vessel herself being extremely difficult to Work.—. of these two very Serious disadvantages Capt. Diron. a Frenchman. and complete Privateersman. with a very large Crew consisting Chiefly of his own Countrymen who amounted in Number I believe to 93 chiefly if not all Blacks. & Mulattoes. and in Ferocity and cruelty <u>exceeded by none</u>. as will be Shewn on the Return of the remainder of the crew to His Majestys Dominions, more fully availed himself and after a most desperate Discharge of Musketry succeeded in Boarding when a Scene of Cruelty was exhibited which has perhaps been never equalled. the Boarders Killing in the most merciless manner all the Wounded on the Decks.— I have requested the Surgeon Mr. David Watson an officer whose ~~whom~~ anxious Care of and Generous attention to his Wounded Countrymen will I trust recommend him very Strongly to His Majestys Government, in Case of his Seeing Mr. Nicholls before I should to Solicit him to write to the Admiral a Letter communicating the Fate of this unfortunate Vessel. and to convey it to me that I may forward it to you to be transmitted by the earliest opportunity. of which request I hope you will not disapprove.— I have the pleasure to inform you that Since their arrival the Wounded have been taken every Care of. and are all excepting Two or three, very desperately Wounded. and of whose recovery there is some doubt. but great hopes, in a fair Way of Recovery. For the Surgeon and Clerk. I have obtained permission to land. and to return to His Majestys Dominions. by the earliest Conveyance, and I am very hopefull of Soon finding one for them for Bermuda in a Neutral. I have not yet Obtained ~~for~~ Paroles for Messrs. Nicholls and Lindo. but hope to do So to day. although I find much difficulty in So doing in Consequence of there being no Such provision in the Agreement. and so with Masters & Merchantmen. who think it very hard to be Confined in a Prison Ship which is at this moment the Case with Mr. Lindo. and Capt Sinclair of the *London Trader.*—. I should be much obliged to be made acquainted with the Custom of Nations on these occasions.—. I have been at Some loss how to act in Consequence of the Privateersmen having retained all the Bedding belonging to the *Dominica,* and the prisoners being entirely without it. and its Cost being now so very extravagant. but in order to be as economical as possible. I propose if I cannot obtain it Gratis, to endeavour to buy the Bedding from the Privateersmen.— As the number of Prisoners in the Prison Ship is now considerable. you would do me a great favor by reminding General Mason of the Repairs it requires. and also. and particularly of the Awning or Shed over the Deck which it so very much wants. and I would most earnestly Solicit the favor of you to expedite as much as possible their Return to His Majesty Dominions. I observe Two cartels are hourly expected at the Northward from Halifax and should be much pleased if you could order one of them here. or obtain permission for an American vessel to proceed. which I little doubt I could procure on Good Terms. I have the honor to be Sir Your most obedient humble Servant

Charles R Simpson

ALS, NHi, Barclay Collection.

1. Simpson was probably one of the numerous agents Barclay employed at U.S. seaports to process British prisoners.
2. Barclay was the principal agent for British prisoners in the United States.

Cruise of the U.S. Brig *Argus*

On 18 June, the U.S. brig Argus, *Lieutenant William H. Allen[1] commanding, departed New York on what was to be the single most destructive cruise undertaken by an American naval vessel during the war. On board* Argus *was the new U.S. minister to France, William H. Crawford, whom Allen was charged with conveying to Europe. Though beset by boisterous seas for much of the voyage,* Argus's *Atlantic transit was a quick one, taking only three and a half weeks. After landing Minister Crawford at L'Orient, France, Allen quickly reprovisioned his ship, putting to sea again on 20 July. From 23 July to 13 August, the American commander enjoyed spectacular success cruising between the mouth of the English Channel and the coast of Southern Ireland, even conducting a raid up the River Shannon. All told, nineteen prizes were taken and the British merchant marine was thrown into a state of panic. But the intrepid Allen was a victim of his own success. On the morning of 14 August,* Argus *fell in with H.M. sloop* Pelican, *one of several powerful enemy vessels sent in search of the American brig. After an action of forty-five minutes, in which Allen himself was mortally wounded,* Argus *struck to* Pelican.[2]

1. *Allen was at sea when the Senate confirmed his commission as master commandant on 24 July 1813.*
2. *The best secondary account of* Argus's *final cruise is Apgar, "U.S. Brig* Argus. *"*

JOURNAL OF MINISTER TO FRANCE WILLIAM H. CRAWFORD

[Extract]

Wednesday 30th.[1] The wind increases to a storm. The *Argus* marches "o'er the mountain wave." The rain descends in torrents and drives me from the deck. The guns on the lee side are constantly under water, and every heavy sea washes the deck with its mountain billows. It is impossible to stand on the deck without clinging to a rope. It is extremely difficult to keep dry even in the cabbin, unless I get into the berth, which I am the more inclined to do from the violent wretching which the motion of the vessel communicates to my stomach. I however do not cascade, as the wretching subsides on getting into the berth. In the evening I

Master Commandant William Henry Allen

visited the deck, and remained on it as long as I could keep dry by the aid of a great coat. The storm raged with increasing violence, the waves swelled into little mountains, continually varying their forms and relative positions. Presented a magnificent prospect. The dashing of the ship, its alternate elevations, and depressions excited apprehensions that she might be swallowed up in the immense chasms intervening the billows, or might upset by the violence of the winds. All the sails had been taken in except the main foresail, and still we made eleven knots an hour. Thro the night, wave after wave, and billow after billow, continued to land the deck of the *Argus*. Every minute the rushing of the waters over my head reminded me of the violence of the storm and kept me awake, tossed from side to side of by [*my*] birth [*berth*] by the rocking of the vessel. . . .

Tuesday, 6th.[2] Cold, cloudy, showery, and the gale rather stiff. At 4 P.M. saw sail[3] on the lee bow, wished Capt. Allen to speak her, to learn a little of what had been done in Europe, as we had no expectation of learning anything shortly of what has been done, and is now doing on the Western side of the Atlantic. A contest immediately commenced between the *Argus* and the strange sail which was ascertained to be a schooner to obtain the weather gage. The *Argus* succeeded and hoisted Portuguese colors, the other hoisted British. The *Argus* then hoisted British colors, the schooner did the same. A gun was then fired from the *Argus* ahead of the schooner, and another astern. American colors were then hoisted, and shot was fired directly at the schooner, and orders given to prepare for giving a broad-side. The British colors were hauled down. She was pierced for 16, and had 6 guns. She was an American built schooner, captured on her first voyage from New York, in the bay of Biscay, by a British cruiser, and sold in London, where she was coppered and sailed in April for Newfoundland. She sailed the first of June with a cargo of fish for Oporto, which port she left on the 1st inst. in ballast. Capt. Allen burnt her, and proceeded on his voyage. The master informed us that Lord Wellington had passed the Ebro without fighting a battle, and was within a few leagues of the main army which it was believed would risk a general battle. The wind increased in the evening, and the sea became rough which retarded the removal of the prisoners and their baggage on board the *Argus*.

Crawford, "Journal," pp. 18, 20.

1. 30 June 1813.
2. 6 July 1813.
3. The British privateer schooner *Salamanca*, formerly the American privateer *King of Rome*.

JOURNAL OF SURGEON JAMES INDERWICK[1]

[Extract]

August 12th Thursday—   at Sea—
off the Saltees Ireland

*Jas Hall—Better—
Jno Tamer   Pains Rather increased. Continue the P Doveril   make assiduous
        use of the liniment—
*Fred Hyatt—
*Mr. Jamison—
Jno Bladen—

*Joshua Jordan   Doing Better—
 Robert Jamison—
 Discharged Wm. Young.   sent as mate to Mr. Levy[2] in the Ship *Betsy*—
 [Total] 7

Captured a new Brig called the *Ann* from Cardigan to London with Slate and Welsh Woolens. Sunk her Brought too a Portuguese Brig bound to Cork— Sent the Prisoners from the 2 last prizes on board of her. Gave chace to two large Ships and a Brig to leeward— Allowed the Brig to Pass us and continued the chase after the large vessells. All showing English colors. One ship showing 18 ports the other 16. apparently preparing for action. Brought them too and sent Mr. Allen[3] on board the largest the Captain of which refused to come on board us; and before our boat had returned the both made sail keeping close to each other. Made sail and Engaged them both. The large one struck after receiving 2 broadsides— chased the other close in and she escaped among the Saltese rocks. The large one proved a Scotch Ship the *Defiance* mounting 14 long nines 21 men—from Greenock to Newfoundland.

August 13th. Friday—   idem

*Jas Hall—Better. is now employed in day duty.
 Jno Tamer
*Fred Hyatt
*Mr. Jamison   Continue the Infus Amar with wine
 Jno Bladen
*Josh Jordan Let him continue the friction with more Oint (and use the
    Dover's Powder as before directed
 Robert Jamison
 Jno Freeman Recd. a large wound with an adz across the instep near the ancle
    joint. 2 sutures were passed thro the edges and the lips brought together
    with the assistance of adhesive Plaster & roller bandage— The Hemmor-
    rhage was considerable but I did not find it necessary to take up any ves-
    sel. enjoined perfect quiet.—
 [Total] 8

At 2 oClk A.M.. Captured a large Brig the *Baltic* one of the W.I. fleet laden with Sugar bound to Dublin.— at 5. Sloop laden with deal boards— at 6. burnt the *Defiance* and the *Baltic*— threw overboard the cargo of the Sloop and sent her away with the Prisoners at 9 PM fired a gun and brought too a large Brig the *Belford*—which nearly ran aboard of us— She proved to be from Dublin bound to London laden with linen Wine &c worth 100,000 £— Took out of her a box of Plate and at 12oClk burnt her.—

August 14th   Saturday   St George's Channel

Early this morning came to action with a large english Brig She captured us after an action of 45 minutes she proved to be the *Pelican.*—[4]

August 15th   Sunday   at Sea

The following list comprehends the number of killed and wounded on board of our vessel as far as can be at present ascertained.

Mr. Wm. W Edwards—Midshipman.[5]   Killed by shot in the head.
Mr. Richd. Delphy—Midshipman—   Do.   Had both legs nearly shot off at the knees   he survived the action about 3 hours
Joshua Jones—Seaman—Killed—
Geo Gardiner—Seaman—His thigh taken off by a round shot close to his body. he lived about 1/2 an hour—
Jno Finlay—Seaman—His head was shot off at the close of the action.—
Wm. Moulton [*Knolton*]—Seaman   Killed—
Total 6.

The following were wounded. viz.

Wm. H Allen Esq—Commander—His left knee was shattered by a cannon shot. Amputation of that thigh was performed about 2 hours after the action— an Anodyne was previously administered—an Anodyne at night—
Lieut Watson—1st.[6] Part of the Scalp on the upper part of the head torn off by a grape shot,—the bone denuded. It was dressed lightly and he returned and took command of the deck.— now on board the *Pelican*.—
Mr. Colin McCloud—Boatswain—Received a severe lacerated wound on the upper part of the thigh. a slight one on the face and a contusion on the right shoulder. Dressed simply with lint and roller Bandage—
Mr. James White—Carpenter—Shot near the upper part of the left thigh—bone fractured. Hemmorrhage considerable— Dressed the wound with lint imbued with Ol olivar— Applied bandage and Splints— Anodyne at night has also an incised wound in the head—Dressing—Suture—Adhesive plaster & Double headed roller—
Joseph Jordon—Boatswains Mate Has a large wound thro the left thigh the bone fractured and splintered,—the back part of the right thigh carried off—and nearly the whole of the fleshy nates carried away— Dressed with lint imbued with Ol Olivar—gave a large anodyne—repeated it at night.— Case hopeless—
Jno. Young—Quarter Master—Received a severe shot wound in the left breast seeminly by a glancing shot. The integuments and part of the extensor muscles of the hand torn away— Dressed lightly with oil and lint with appropriate bandages—gave him an anodyne at night—
Francis Eggert—Seaman—Has a very severe contusion of the right leg with a small gunshot wound a little above the outer ancle   no ball discoverable— Dressed the wound with lint & bandage & directed the leg to be kept constantly wet with Aq. Veg. Mineral.— 3 hours after reception the leg was swelled and very painful gave him an anodyne— Proposed Amputation but he would not consent. This morning the leg excessively tense—swelled— vesicated—and of a dark color about the outer ancle.— Has considerable fever Directed the saline mixture with occasional anodyne To Continue the Lotion.—
John Nugent—Seaman—Gun Shot wound in the superior part of the right thigh about 2. inches from the groin.— Thigh bone fractured and much Splintered—ball Supposed to be in— Several pieces of bone were ex-

tracted but the ball was not found— Dressed lint Bandage with Splints— Anodyne— Rested considerably well last night but there has been a large oozing from the wound— Applied fresh lint. no fever—

Charles Baxter—Seaman—Has lacerated wound of the left Ancle— The lower part of the fibula Splintered—apparently affecting the joint. Has much hemmorrhage from this wound.— He has also a Gun Shot wound of the right thigh. The ball has passed obliquely downwards thro the back part of the thigh. I proposed the Amputation of his left leg but he would not give his consent. Dressed both wounds with lint & Roller Bandages— Made considerable compression on the left foot in order to restrain the bleeding— Has some fever this morning. H. Mist. Salin.— Tamarind water for drink—low diet

James Kellam O Seaman—Lacerated wound of the calf of the right leg—also a wound in the ham of the Extremity— Dressing Simple— To day the leg somewhat Swelled and painfull—slackened the bandage—

Wm. Hovington—Seaman—Complains much of pain & Soreness in the Small of the back and nates— It is suspected that he has received a severe contusion on the parts H. Anodyne at night— N.S. ad $\bar{3}$xvi Apply continually Aq. Veg. Min to the parts—

Jas. Hall—Seaman Has a Slight wound above the left eye—I suspect caused by a Splinter— Dressing Simple—

Total ascertained—12.

Owing to the disordered state of the vessel the wounded have wretched accommodation—if that term may be used— I endeavoured to make their condition as comfortable as possible— Divided, those of our people who remained on board, and were well, into watches—in different parts of the vessel— Mr. Hudson[7] Mr. Dennisson[8] & myself sitting up with the Captain— Directed Lemonade & Tamarind water to be kept made and served to the Wounded—

*Able to go to Quarters

AD, NN, Astor, Lenox and Tilden Foundations, Rare Books and Manuscripts Division, James Inderwick Journal, 1813. An edited version of Inderwick's journal was published by the New York Public Library in 1917. See Paltsits, *Journal of Surgeon James Inderwick.*

1. James Inderwick was appointed *Argus*'s acting surgeon by Stephen Decatur. He reported for duty on board *Argus* on 8 May 1813 and was at sea when the Senate confirmed his commission as surgeon on 24 July. For more on Inderwick's naval career, see Pleadwell, "James Inderwick," and Estes and Dye, "Death on the *Argus*."

2. Uriah P. Levy was warranted a sailing master on 21 October 1812. He served on *Argus* as a supernumerary. Levy and nine other men were placed on board *Betsy* with orders to take her as prize to France. She was recaptured by H.M. frigate *Leonidas* on 12 August 1813.

3. William Howard Allen, Jr., no relation to *Argus*'s commander, was promoted to lieutenant on 24 July 1813.

4. *Pelican*, sloop of war, 18 guns.

5. For additional documentation on Edwards, see p. 428.

6. William H. Watson was promoted to lieutenant on 7 March 1813.

7. John Hudson was appointed acting master on 5 December 1812 while serving on the New York flotilla. He is entered on *Argus*'s muster roll as sailing master. There is no record of the Navy Department confirming his appointment with a warrant.

8. Henry Dension served as purser on board *Argus*.

COMMANDER JOHN F. MAPLES, R.N., TO
VICE ADMIRAL SIR EDWARD THORNBOROUGH,[1] R.N.

[Extract]

H.M. Sloop *Pelican*, St. David's-head, East five Leagues,
August 14, 1813.

I have the honour to inform you, that in obedience to your orders to me of the 12th instant to cruise in St. George's channel, for the protection of the trade, and to obtain information of an American sloop of war, I had the good fortune to board a brig, the master of which informed me, that he had seen a vessel, apparently a man of war, steering to the N.E.; at 4 o'clock this morning, I saw a vessel on fire, and a brig standing from her, which I soon made out to be a cruiser, made all sail in chase, and at half past five came alongside of her (she having shortened sail, and made herself clear for an obstinate resistance), when, after giving her three cheers, our action commenced, which was kept up with great spirit on both sides forty-three minutes, when we lay her alongside, and were in the act of boarding, when she struck her colors. She proves to be the United States sloop of war *Argus*, of three hundred and sixty tons, eighteen twenty-four pounder carronades, and 2 long twelve-pounders; had on board when she sailed from America, two months since, a complement of one hundred forty-nine men, but in the action one hundred and twenty seven,[2] commanded by Lieutenant Commandant W. H. Allen, who, I regret to say, was wounded early in the action, and has since suffered the amputation of his left thigh.

No eulogium I could use would do sufficient justice to the merits of my gallant officers and crew, which consisted of one hundred and sixteen; the cool courage they displayed, and the precision of their fire, could only be equalled by their zeal to distinguish themselves; but I must beg leave to call your attention to the conduct of my first lieutenant Thomas Welsh, of Mr. William Ganville, acting master, Mr. William Ingram, the purser, who volunteered his services on deck, and Mr. Richard Scott, the boatswain.

Our loss, I am happy to say, is small, one master's-mate, Mr. William Young, slain in the moment of victory, while animating, by his courage and example, all around him, one able seamen, John Emery, besides five seamen wounded, who are doing well; that of the enemy I have not been able to ascertain, but it is considerable, her officers say, about forty killed and wounded.[3] I have the honor to be, &c.

J. F. MAPLES, Commander.

Naval Chronicle, Vol. 30 (July–Dec. 1813), pp. 216–17.

1. Edward Thornborough was commanding officer of the Irish Station.

2. *Argus* departed New York with a complement of 151 men. At the time of her engagement with *Pelican*, *Argus*'s crew, due to the manning of several prizes, had been reduced to 131, 127 of whom were fit for duty.

3. *Argus*'s known casualties totaled six killed and eighteen wounded, five mortally. The casualty reports of Surgeon James Inderwick and Lieutenant William H. Watson are published in *Niles's Weekly Register*, Vol. 7 (Sept. 1814–Mar. 1815), p. 39 and Vol. 8 (Mar.–Sept. 1815), pp. 43–44.

John Hawker to William Allen

PLYMOUTH, 19th AUGUST, 1813.

SIR—The station I have had the honor to hold for many years past, of American vice consul, calls forth my poignant feelings in the communication I have to make to you of the death of your son, captain Allen, late commander of the United States' brig of war *Argus*, which vessel was captured on saturday last, in the Irish channel, after a very sharp action of three quarters of an hour, by his Britannic majesty's ship *Pelican*.

Early in the action he lost his left leg, but refused to be carried below, till from loss of blood, he fainted. Messrs. Edwards and Delphy, midshipmen, and four seamen, were killed; and lieutenant Watson, the carpenter, boatswain, boatswain's mate, and seven men wounded. Captain Allen submitted to amputation, above the knee, while at sea. He was yesterday morning attended by very eminent surgical gentlemen, and removed from the *Argus* to the hospital, where every possible attention and assistance would have been afforded him had he survived; but which was not, from the first moment, expected, from the shattered state of his thigh! At eleven, last night, he breathed his last! He was sensible at intervals until within ten minutes of his dissolution, when he sunk exhausted, and expired without a struggle! His lucid intervals were very cheerful; and he was satisfied and fully sensible that no advice or assistance would be wanting. A detached room was prepared by the commissary and chief surgeon, and female attendants engaged, that every tenderness and respect might be experienced. The master, purser, surgeon, and one midshipman, accompanied captain Allen, who was also attended by his two servants.

I have communicated and arranged with the officers respecting the funeral, which will be in the most respectful, and at the same time economical manner. The port admiral has signified that it is the intention of his Britannic majesty's government that it be <u>publicly</u> attended by officers of rank, and with military honors. The time fixed for procession is on Saturday, at eleven, A.M. A lieutenant-colonel's guard of the royal marines is also appointed. A wainscoat coffin has been ordered; on the breast plate of which will be inscribed as below.* Mr. Delphy, one of the midshipmen, who lost <u>both</u> legs, and died at sea, was buried yesterday in Saint Andrew's church yard. I have requested that captain Allen may be buried as near him, on the right (in the same vault, if practicable) as possible. I remain, respectfully, sir, your most obedient, humble servant.

(Signed)   JOHN HAWKER
Cidevant American vice consul

To general Allen, &c. &c. &c. Providence, R. Island.

*Tablet, whereon will be recorded the name, rank, age and character of the deceased, and also of the midshipman, will be placed (if it can be contrived) as I have suggested; both having lost their lives in fighting for the honour of their country.

Niles's Weekly Register, Vol. 5, supplement (Sept. 1813–Mar.1814), p. 49.

The New Sloops of War: Launching *Peacock*

Peacock was one of six new sloops of war authorized by Congress in March 1813.[1] *She was built at New York by Adam and Noah Brown*[2] *with her keel being laid on 9 July. To command* Peacock, *Secretary Jones selected Master Commandant Lewis Warrington,*[3] *a capable and combat-tested naval veteran of thirteen years. Warrington arrived in New York to superintend the sloop's construction the last week in August. As the following documents illustrate,* Peacock's *new commander had to attend to innumerable details in preparing his ship for launch. The exploits of the powerful and swift-sailing* Peacock *in 1814 and 1815 would confirm Jones's faith in the new sloop as the ideal class of vessel for waging war against the enemy's commerce.*

1. See pp. 43, 45.

2. *The Browns also designed and built several well known privateers, among them* General Armstrong, Prince de Neufchatel, *and* Paul Jones. *According to maritime historian Howard Chapelle, the ships designed by Adam and Noah Brown "were usually noted for speed." See Chapelle,* American Sailing Navy, *p. 260.*

3. *Warrington was promoted to master commandant on 24 July 1813.*

MASTER COMMANDANT LEWIS WARRINGTON TO SECRETARY OF THE NAVY JONES

New-York   August 26th 1813

Sir

I have the honor to inform you that I have arrived at this place agreably to order, and find the Sloop progressing pretty rapidly; all her Beams, and the framing of the gun Deck being nearly completed—

As expedition in her equipment, is doubtless a primary consideration, I take the liberty of suggesting, the propriety of commencing, on the spars, carriages, rigging and sails all of which I apprehend might be nearly completed by the time she is launched— In the mean time, a rendezvous, might at this moment, be opened for her with success; as I find that there are now here a number of Seamen—

As the next important consideration, that presents itself, is the selection of Officers, and as much depends on a reciprocal knowledge of each other's qualifications, I had previous to leaving the *United States,* some conversation, with Com: Decatur, who has agreed, (provided it meet your approbation) to Lieut: Nicholson's joining the vessel as her first, when he himself shall have got the vacancies in his own ship supplied. There is also a Midshipman (Philip Voorhees) of Trenton New-Jersey, whose abilities are so well known to me, from a long course of service together, that it would afford me much satisfaction, to have him with me now With much respect I am Your Obdt: Servt:

L. Warrington

ALS, DNA, RG45, MC, 1813, No. 113 (M147, Roll No. 5).

MASTER COMMANDANT LEWIS WARRINGTON TO
SECRETARY OF THE NAVY JONES

New-York   September 6th 1813

Sir

I yesterday received the two letters, which you transmitted, containing the different statements, for the outfits of the *Peacock*: and have communicated with the Agent on the subject; who is now making his arrangements for the completion of them

With respect to the Kentucky Hemp, which you have mentioned to Dr. Bullus, I have heard such general complaint from the Officers here at this time, and during the last winter, whose experience rendered them judges that I have deemed it proper to state it to you; and also that the persons who have agreed to contract for the furnishing it, are remark'able for finesse and slight work whenever they think it will escape detection

There are now on hand here, nearly an hundred Tons of that Hemp, which on account of its inferiority, have not been manufactured, and which has occasioned my being so explicit, as you seem to leave it optional, and I should not wish to be at the expence of Russia, if the other would answer

With respect to the Boats, I observe that the 1st. Cutter or Launch, is to be clinker built, which I should suppose would render her much weaker, than a Carvel built boat; would be more difficult to repair when injured, as well as much more expensive, and for the purpose of boating an anchor, which may sometimes be necessary, she will not be as convenient as a Launch, which might be built of pine, to render her light as has been done in several instances   I also submit to your judgement, the propriety of having another small boat, as at sea, in the event of having our only one injured, the inconvenience of having to take out a large Cutter with the yards, would be great, as well as the delay sometimes occasioned thereby—

Mr. Voorhees as acting Lieut: and Mr. Parker[1] as master have joined the Sloop The former is entirely idle; and if we could open a rendezvous, we should not only get some fine fellows; but also give an active young man employment

As we shall soon want a Carpenter, and as I cannot expect a warranted one, (there being so few) I should like much to have your approbation to engage one who is strongly recommended and whose brother is Carpenter of the *United States* and is in high estimation there for his qualifications— In taking the liberty to offer my opinions about the Hemp and Boats; I beg that you will not suppose, it any thing but a wish to render every assistance in my power, in the line of my profession has been my motive   I am respectfully Your Obdt. Servt.

L. Warrington

ALS, DNA, RG45, MC, 1813, No. 120 (M147, Roll No. 5).

1. James Parker was warranted a sailing master on 17 August 1813. Upon learning that Secretary Jones had received a published report that he was "an imposter, and an infamous Character," Parker set out for the capital to clear his name. The sailing master deserted the service after failing to convince Jones of his honest reputation with several bogus letters of recommendation. Quoted text from Jones to Bainbridge, 17 Jan. 1814, DNA, RG45, SNL, Vol. 11, p. 194 (M149, Roll No. 11). See also Jones to Warrington, 27 Jan. 1814, DNA, RG45, SNL, Vol. 11, p. 202 (M149, Roll No. 11).

MASTER COMMANDANT LEWIS WARRINGTON TO
SECRETARY OF THE NAVY JONES

New-York   September 13th. 1813

Sir

In conformity to the wish contained your last letter, of knowing when the *Peacock* will be launched; I have the honor to inform you, that the Builders calculate on putting her into the water, on the 22d or 23d of the present month— This is on the supposition that she will be coppered afloat; and I am now going to the yard, to ascertain the quantity of sheathing copper, that may be on hand, for that purpose— Although there have been no directions issued, for joiner's work: yet as I suppose it is your wish, that every thing should be under way; I have ~~given~~ requested the Agent, to fix upon some man, in whom he can place confidence, and make an arrangement with him for the speedy completion of it— She will I suppose, be fitted by riggers, as there are not men in the yard to do it— I am much pleased, that my observations with respect to the Boats, meet your approbation: ~~and~~ but as it regards the Kentucky Hemp, my remarks applied to the parcel in possession of the manufacturer, whose name was mentioned— Mr. Clarke as Purser, has reported himself under orders of the 16th. Ult: and Mr. Thorn, under orders of the 4th of the present month, has also reported himself, as attached to the Sloop; which I apprehend must be a mistake and as I am at a loss to ascertain which it is your intention, I should retain, I have to request your commands on that head[1]   I have the honor to be respectfully

L. Warrington

Although I understand, that in your directions about the gun-carriages every thing appertaining to them is to be supplied by the maker of them, yet as a question has arisen amongst the persons disposed to contract, whether the screws and cast iron plates, which receive the navel bolt to secure the gun to the carriage, will or will not be sent with the guns, as thus has been frequently the case, I have also to request your intention on that head and more particularly as the Agent seems to be of that opinion

ALS, DNA, RG45, MC, 1813, No. 125 (M147, Roll No. 5).

1. Both James H. Clark and Herman Thorn were commissioned pursers on 24 July 1813. Thorn remained with *Peacock* and Clark was ordered on to *Frolic.*

MASTER COMMANDANT LEWIS WARRINGTON TO
SECRETARY OF THE NAVY JONES

New-York   Septr. 22d 1813

Sir

As it seems Commodore Decatur is anxious to retain Lt. Nicholson as first with him; and as Lt. Saunders of the *Constellation,* has requested me to apply for his joining the *Peacock;* I take the liberty of asking for him as 2d, under the impression that that ship, will scarcely be able to get to sea this season, and independent of Lt. S:, is better off for Officers than any other that I know of— Mr. Williams[1] who has been for some time an acting Mid: of the *United States,* who was in her at the time she captured the *Macedonian,* but who left her some time since, to settle some private business that required his personal attendance, is anxious to be ordered to the *Peacock* in the same capacity, if it does not interfere with any regulation which you may have adopted— I should be pleased to have him, as I have tested his capability and knowledge, and can speak well of him, from experience— In the arrangement of Officers for this Sloop, I should be gratified in being left without a Marine Officer, as without him the, Gun-room will contain a sufficient number of cabins to obviate the necessity of hanging a Cot in it; and the Detachment may be reduced from 25, the ordinary number, to 20 the number fully sufficient; by which we should acquire five additional Seamen; and to prevent the loss that might accrue to Government in the cloathing accounts, the clerk could very well take charge of them, and make the proper statements— I subjoin the following statement for the ship's Company, supposing it to be about 160, and should it meet your approbation and ideas, it will give me great pleasure

1	Captain
3	Lieuts:
1	Master
1	Surgeon
1	Purser
4	Midsn:
1	Clerk
3	Master's Mates
1	Boatswain
1	Gunner
1	Carpenter
1	Ship's Steward
4	Quarter Masters
6	Quarter Gunners
2	Boatswain's Mates
1	Cook
20	Marines
108	Seamen, Ordinary, and Boys, including other Petty Officers not
160	mentioned— I have omitted a Sail-Maker because I can get a very good man

who is willing to go as Mate and it will be reducing the number of Officers and ~~the~~ increasing the number of working hands   Very respectfully I am Your Obdt. Servt.

L. Warrington

ALS, DNA, RG45, MC, 1813, No. 131 (M147, Roll No. 5).

1. Benjamin S. Williams was warranted a midshipman by the Navy Department on 9 November 1813.

Master Commandant Lewis Warrington to Secretary of the Navy Jones

New-York   Septr: 30th 1813

Sir

I have the honor to inform you of the launch of the Peacock on Monday last; [1] which I should have earlier communicated, but for a severe indisposition for the two last days— We have opened a rendezvous and are going on with it well— We have entered seventy two men already—

The weather has been, and is now so stormy, that we have not yet been able, to transport the Sloop to the yard— I am respectfully Your Obdt. Svt.

L. Warrington

ALS, DNA, RG45, MC, 1813, No. 133 (M147, Roll No. 5).

1. 27 September 1813.

Hurricane Damage to the Southeastern Stations

Over a three-week period in August and September, the naval stations at Charleston and St. Marys were rocked by two successive hurricanes.[1] Damage caused by these gales would hamper naval operations along the southeastern coast well into the new year.

1. *For additional information on the first of these two storms, consult Ludlum,* Early American Hurricanes, *pp. 58–59.*

CAPTAIN JOHN H. DENT TO SECRETARY OF THE NAVY JONES

The Honorable William Jones   Charleston   28th Augt 1813

Sir,

It is with regret, I have to inform you, that the weather for some time past has indicated a gale—which came on yesterday about noon from the N.E. and by 9. P.M. increased to a hurricane, which blew with greater violence untill 12, than I have ever recollected, to have experienced; the City and wharves present this morning a melancholy aspect; it is impossible as yet to give any idea of the damage, but it has been greater than that Sustained in 1804, the *Nonsuch, Carolina,* and Hospital Ship, are the only vessels safe, the latter dismasted, some of the barges in seeking safety in the docks were carried in the streets, of with the general Wreck, and are much damaged, the tide rose so high that Ships are now on the wharves— the beautiful new Bridge over Ashley river is entirely destroyed, and washed away. the Prison Ship parted her cable and is now on shore at James Island, a wreck of a vessel on fort reef—not Known whether the people on board were saved.

I had the honor to inform you in my letter of yesterday that I should proceed to port Royal with the barges, the weather prevented it, at the moment of departure, which I consider a fortunate escape. I shall be able tomorrow to give you a correct report of the damage sustained by the Schooners & Barges under my command. I Have the Honor to be With great respect Yr. most obt Svt

J H Dent

LS, DNA, RG45, CL, 1813, Vol. 5, No. 165 (M125, Roll No. 29).

COMMODORE HUGH G. CAMPBELL TO SECRETARY OF THE NAVY JONES

St Mary's   18th Sept. 1813

Sir

We had yesterday morning and night proceeding one of the most severe Gales I have ever witnessed— It commenced about 6 PM at NNE and veered to NBW when it blew with the greatest force and continued until about 1 A,M, at which time the Tide, which had Risen to an uncommon hight ceased to flow, and for about one hour we were favored with a calm— About two oclock the Gale recommenced at sw and blew until daybreak with equal, indeed I think encreased violence— here the destruction commenced, every Vessel in harbor drove on shore or sunk at their moorings— Gun Vessel No. *164* Jno. R Grayson commander, that had just returned from convoying Troops to Beaufort, upset at an anchor and of 26 souls on board at the time she went down only six were saved— Mr Grayson and two men reached the marsh on the Florida side and with Great difficulty supported themselves through the night and until 11 oclock next day, when they were discovered and taken off— Mr Lecompt mids. on board, and two men were taken off from an old wreck about 2 1/4 miles down the River between this place and Point Peter, to which place they were taken No. *161* in ordinary Lies sunk a little above the harbor, I am in hopes she will be got up— *No 62* the Vessel which was reported as condemnable, which Lay off the Town, having on board the men attached to vessels in ordinary, sunk at her anchors, but fortunately no lives were lost— Nos. *160, 158, 63* and *165* are on shore above high water mark, they will be got off with little damage the two former are in ordinary— No. *3* Hospital Vessel parted her cables and drifted over abody of marsh about 3 miles, and is now on the Florida shore   have sent her assistance and hope she will be got off *No 168* John Hulburd commander Laying off the south End of cumberland, not being able to fetch into this river above Point Peter, run for the harbor of Fernandina and anchord. above the Town, from which situation he driven some miles over a marsh and is now on shore about 6 or 7 miles from this place with the loss of his mainmast— The damage attending the Gun Vessels on shore, I flatter myself will be trifling— a few new Boats and 3 or 4 Cables & anchors will be required, some canvas and carpenters work— The Gun Vessels and almost every Vessel on shore lay in the street— No. *63* has lost her rudder and channels, Nos. *160* and *165* the Iron work of their rudders— the *saucy Jack*, Privateer of Charleston Laying ready to sail is now laying high and dry on a marsh that must be at least 5 feet above the line of Low Tide   She draws 14 feet, seven feet being the common Rise

This town has suffered much Seven Inhabited houses blown down and several in frame, but no lives Lost,— much more fortunate than its neighboring town Fernandina, where I am told by a gentleman Just from that place, that 20 houses are blown, down every Vessel in port drove on shore, except a Swedish Brig, and a considerable amount of Mercantile property destroyed   I have the honor to be With Great Respect Sir your obedient servant

Hugh G Campbell

LS, DNA, RG45, CL, 1813, Vol. 6, No. 67 (M125, Roll No. 31).

Philadelphians Contribute Ships to the Navy

In May, the Common Council of Philadelphia voted monies to construct six barges for the defense of the Delaware River.[1] The council's action reflected the fears of many Philadelphians that the federal government was incapable of defending their city and its mercantile trade. It was the council's intention, once these craft were completed, to turn them over to the navy for use in conjunction with other public warships. Work on the barges was completed before the end of spring, but it was not until September that they were finally transferred to the navy where they proved a welcome addition to the Delaware flotilla.

1. *For documentation relating to the council's decision, see pp. 115–17.*

THOMAS LEIPER TO SECRETARY OF THE NAVY JONES

Philada.   September 2d. 1813

Dear Sir

This day the Committee of the Corporation Flotilla assigned to George Harrison Esqr. Navy Agent Three of their Barges viz *No. 1, 2 & 3* It would be an agreeable thing to the Committee could they get clear of the whole Flotilla belonging to the Corporation and clear I am it would be an advantage to the service if the property was invested in the Navy Department—

Your Navy Agent Mr. Doughty objected to the Barge *No. 4* not on account of Her size but as not being sufficiently built. This Barge was built under the direction of Mr. Emanual Eyres the method he took he concieved to be an improvement but Captain Hawkins informs with the expence of a very few dollars she might be fitted up like to the others— *No. 5 & 6* your Mr. Doughty objected to them because they were under the size the Law required but cannot you apply to some other purpose— The Barges without the schooner *Helen* cannot exist for the Barge men have no place to sleep or screen their stores but on board the schooner and as you must have a Vessel of the Kind you cannot procure one on better terms— I am informed on a peace establishment she would sell for almost double the money she cost viz 5000$ As for the Gun Boat[1] built and fitted out under the direction of Captain Gustavus Conyngham[2] who has seen and examined every Timber in her there is but one opinion of her here viz that she so far exceeds any of our Gun Boats here as a 74 that of a Frigate— Captain Conyngham informs she will Row Fifty two oars and that she equal to any Four Gun Boats on this station   We are extremely interested here to see this Gun Boat properly man'd by men who will fight her and if she is found so very supperior to those in being they will be discharg'd and others on the same Construction built for the First Cost of this Vessel $6500 is nothing in Comparison when we take into View Bounty Pay and Rations of men for seven Years for that is the period I affix to the War unless Great Britain should get in the Gutter sooner— My reason you will observe their minds are made up to establish certain Claims and Our's are made up <u>never</u> <u>never</u> to admit them from that circumstance no[thing] remains but to Fight it Out— Respectfully I am Your most Obedient St.

Thomas Leiper
Chairman

ALS, DNA, RG45, MLR, 1813, Vol. 6, No. 22 (M124, Roll No. 58).

1. A reference to the galley *Northern Liberties.*
2. Gustavus Conyngham had earned great fame during the American Revolution as commander of the Continental Navy cutter *Revenge.* During the War of 1812, he was a member of the Common Council of the City of Philadelphia.

SECRETARY OF THE NAVY JONES TO THOMAS LEIPER

Thomas Leiper Esqr.   Navy Depart.
Chairman of the Committee   Septr. 16. 1813.
of the Philadelphia Corporation Flotilla

I have delayed answering your favor of 2d. inst. until I could finally determine upon the propositions it contains in respect to the Barges and Schooner belonging to the Corporation of the City of Philadelphia and I have directed the Navy Agent to negotiate with you for the purchase of the large Gun Boat, and of Barges *No. 5* & *6*—also of the Schooner *Helen.*

The rule by which this Department must be governed in carrying into effect the Laws providing for Building or procuring of Barges, is the intrinsic value or what such vessels properly constructed and fitted for the required Service would cost the Department if built under its direction. Having recently built at this Navy Yard and by Contract elsewhere a number of large Barges or galleys of a very Superior kind and Construction, I am induced to believe from a comparison of the Cost of those with that of your Gun Boat and allowing for the difference of size—that your Boat cost more than a similar one could be built for by the government; and moreover I do not approve of the manner in which the Gun carriages and Slides are constructed, as the Guns cannot be pointed to the object in a horizontal direction by the Carriage, but by the movement of the entire Boat. Some alterations may therefore be necessary which will add to the cost. I mention these things for your consideration. I have felt it to be my duty to take the Barges built by the City in preference to building, because a very considerable expense had been incurred by its inhabitants with very patriotic motives. The Navy Agent will confer with you on the subject and I have no doubt that a compromise will readily be made upon just and equitable principles.

The Barge *No. 4* is reported to me to be too slightly built for the Service and would probably cost more in repairs from time to time than she is worth. I therefore decline the purchase of that Barge. I am very respectfully your obedt. Servt.

W. Jones.

LB Copy, DNA, RG45, MLS, Vol. 11, p. 433 (M209, Roll No. 11).

Enterprise vs. *Boxer*

Lieutenant William Burrows relieved Master Commandant Johnston Blakeley as commander of Enterprise *on 21 August.[1] A native of Pennsylvania, Burrows was son of the Marine Corps' first commandant, William W. Burrows, and had served in the navy for more than thirteen years. Although he was viewed "as something of an odd fish in the serv-*

ice," the twenty-seven-year-old lieutenant was a thoroughly accomplished seaman and a ca-
pable officer.[2] *As he put to sea on what was to be his first and last cruise in* Enterprise,
Burrows may have felt a particularly strong sense of mission, for only three months before
he had lain in a British prison at Barbados. On 5 September he would avenge his captivity
when Enterprise *fell in with H.M. brig* Boxer.

1. *Blakeley was ordered on to Charlestown to superintend the construction of one of the new sloops of war*
building there. See Jones to Blakeley, 6 Aug. 1813, DNA, RG45, A&R, Vol. 11, p. 26.

2. *Maloney,* Captain from Connecticut, *p. 232. For contemporary appraisals of Burrow's character and*
career, see Analectic Magazine, *Vol. 1 (Nov. 1813), pp. 396–403; and* Niles's Weekly Register, *Vol. 5, sup-*
plement (Sept. 1813–Mar. 1814), pp. 36–41.

CAPTAIN ISAAC HULL TO LIEUTENANT WILLIAM BURROWS

U.S. Navy Yard   Portsmouth   28th Aug. 1813

Sir,

You having reported to me that the U S. Brig *Enterprize* under you command
is ready for service, I have to direct, that you proceed to sea on a Cruise along
the coast to the Eastward as far as Kennebeck River calling off the different
ports between this place and Kennebeck and taking a good look in shore.

As the object of your cruise is to protect the coasing trade to the eastward
which has been so much interrupted by small cruisers of the enemy of late, you
will keep as close along the land as the safety of your vessel will admit, and by all
means keep so close as not to let the large Cruisers of the Enemy get in shore of
you to cut you off, and great care must be taken to keep so near a port that your
vessel will enter as to be sure of reaching it in a few hours chace as the enemy's
cruisers are so numerous that you hardly hope to be long out without being
chaced by a superior force, in which case it would be desirable to have a port
under your lee or near you, that you may run for.

As it is the practice of the Enemy to man out small coasting boats for the purpose
of deceiving and capturing the vessels running along the shore, and as these vessels
are often made use of by our own citizens for the purpose of conveying supplies to
the enemy and for carrying on an unlawful trade with them, you will examine all
suspicious vessels hovering about the coast and should you find any that cannot give
a proper account of themselves they must be sent in for examination—

Should you find it necessary, from bad weather, being chaced by an enemy, or
any other cause, to enter a harbour you will not remain there any longer than is
absolutely necessary for the safety of your vessel and the good of the service.

You will give convoy and every other aid in your power to vessels wanting it
and keep me advised of all your proceedings as opportunities offer—

Enclosed you have a set of signals for your vessel which you will receive and
be particularly careful that they do not fall into the hands of the Enemy or any
one that will make a bad use of them, and as soon as you shall have made yourself acquainted with the private signals sufficiently to retain them in your memory you will destroy the memorandum that accompanies them.

You will return this place in two weeks unless the service should require you
to remain on the Eastern coast longer, in which case you will advise me. Very respectfully I am, Your Obedt. Servant.

LB Copy, NHi, Isaac Hull Letter Books, 25 Feb. 1813–13 Mar. 1814, pp. 112–13.

LIEUTENANT DAVID MCCRERY, R.N., TO
COMMANDER ALEXANDER GORDON, R.N.

Copy   Portland, United States
Edw: Griffith R. Adml: 6th: of September 1813.

Sir,

I have to acquaint you for the information of the Commander in Chief, with the Capture of His Majestys late Brig *Boxer*, by the United States Brig *Enterprize*, Yesterday, between Seguin and Manheagan, distant East from Portland about ten leagues.

I lament it becomes my duty, from the death of Captain Blyth, who fell the first broadside, to state that on the 4th. Instant the *Boxer* being at anchor at the Island of Manheagan sent her boats towards Demoscota in chase, and having captured a Schooner, which was immediately recaptured by an American Privateer, she weighed so suddenly as to leave the Assistant Surgeon with two Midshipmen onshore, and having chased the Privateer until night the wind became so light as to prevent our return for those Officers. The next morning we observed a man of War brig in the Offing. At 9 AM, discovered her to be the *Enterprize*, gave chase which she observed, and made all possible sail from us distant about six miles, beating to the Westward with a light breeze. Shewed our Colours and fired a Gun. At 2°.40 PM. coming up with the Enemy fast, who fired her stern Gun at us, and shewed American Colours at each Mast head. At 3°.10' she shortened Sail, and bore up to close us, then distant about one mile. At 3°.35' we commenced action within half pistol Shot, and continued it within that distance until 4°.45' P.M. when we were a complete wreck; all the Braces and Rigging shot away, the Main top Mast and top gallt. Mast hanging over the side, Fore and MainMasts nearly gone, and totally unmanageable; with only our Quarter Deck Guns manned; Three feet water in the hold; No Surgeon to attend the Wounded; and the Enemy at that moment gaining a raking position I deemed it proper, with the advice of the Officers, to hail the Enemy telling them we would strike having our Ensigns nailed by that brave and good Officer Captn. Blyth who entered the action with the most noble and determined bravery, and fell cheering and giving confidence to his Crew.

I now have to speak in every good terms of the brave and cool conduct of Mr. John Read, Actg. 2nd: master (who has passed his examination for Lieutenant) and Mr. Francis Gould, the Purser; the former for his judicious conduct in laying us alongside the Enemy, and working the Guns after the ship was disabled the latter, who commanded the Quarter Deck Guns by his own, and by the wish of his late Captain, for keeping up to the last a steady and resolute fire. I likewise beg to mention Mr. John McA[ulay] Clerk, for his attention to the wounded.

I have now to hope that my Superiors will not conceive that the British flag has been disgraced by this action. The *Boxer* had sixty six persons onboard (including the beforementioned Officers and eleven boys) out of which four are Killed, and eighteen wounded.

The *Enterprize* carries fourteen 18 Pound Carronades, and two long nines, with a Complement of One hundred and two men; being two Guns and Thirty six men in her favour. She is much damaged in Hull and Rigging:—both lower masts nearly gone, her Captain and three men killed, and fourteen wounded.

I feel it my duty to mention that the Bulwarks of the *Enterprize* were proof against our Grape, when her Musquet Balls penetrated thro' ours. I enclose a List[1] of the Killed and wounded.—and have the honor to be, Sir, Your most obedient humble Servant,

signed, David McCrery.
Lieutt. late of the Boxer.

Captain Gordon,
His Majesty's Sloop *Ratler*

Copy, UkLPR, Adm. 1/504, pp. 301–3.

1. This enclosure lists four men killed and eighteen wounded.

LIEUTENANT EDWARD R. McCALL[1] TO CAPTAIN ISAAC HULL

United State's Brig Enterprise
Portland, 7. September, 1813

Sir,

In consequence of the unfortunate death of Lieutenant Commandant William Burrows, late Commander of this vessel, it devolves on me to acquaint you with the result of our Cruize after sailing from Portsmouth on the 1st. instant. We steered to the eastward, and on the morning of the 3d. off Wood Island, discovered a Schooner which we chased into this harbour where we anchored. On the morning of the 4th. weighed anchor and swept out and continued our course to the eastward. Having received information of several Privateers being of Monhagan we stood for that place, and on the following morning in the bay near Penequid Point discovered a brig getting under way which appeared to be a vessel of war, and to which we immediately gave chase. She fired several guns and stood for us, having four Ensigns hoisted. After reconnoitering and discovering her force and the nation to which she belonged we hauled upon a wind to stand out of the bay, and at 3 o'clock shortened sail tacked and ran down with an intention to bring her to close action. At twenty minutes after 3. pm. when within half pistol shot, the firing commenced from both, and after being warmly Kept up, and with some manoeuvring, the enemy hailed and said they had surrendered about 4 p.m., their colours being nailed to the Masts could not be hauled down. She proved to be his B. Majesty's late Brig *Boxer* of fourteen guns, Samuel Blythe Esquire Commander, who fell in the early part of the engagement having received a cannon shot through the body. And I am sorry to add that Lieutenant Burrows who had gallantly led us to action fell also about the same time by a musket ball which terminated his existance in eight hours.

The *Enterprise* suffered much in Spars and Rigging and the *Boxer* both in Spars Rigging and hull, having many shot between wind and water.

It would be doing injustice to the merit of Mr. Tillinghast second Lieutenant, were I not to mention the able assistance I received from him during the remainder of the engagement, by his strict attentions to his own division and other departments. And the Officers and Crew generally I am happy to

Engagement between U.S. Brig Enterprise and H.M. Brig Boxer off Pemaquid Point, Maine, 5 September 1813

add, from their cool and determined conduct, have my warmest approbation and applause.

As no Muster roll that can be fully relied on has come into my possession, I cannot exactly state the number killed aboard the *Boxer,* but from information received from the officers of that vessel, it appears there were between twenty and twenty five, and fourteen wounded. Enclosed is a list of the killed and wounded aboard the *Enterprise.* I have the honour to be with great respect Sir, Your Most Obedt. Servt.

Edward R. McCall
Senior Officer

ALS, DNA, RG45, CL, 1813, Vol. 6, No. 19, enclosure (M125, Roll No. 31).

1. McCall was commissioned a lieutenant on 11 March 1813.

[Enclosure]

List of the killed and wounded aboard the U.S. Brig *Enterprise* in the engagement with the British Brig *Boxer* the 5th. Sept. 1813.

Killed

Nathl. Garren	O. Seam.

Wounded

Wm. Burrows Esqr.	Commr. since dead
Kervin Waters	Midsh. mortally
Elisha Blossom	Carptrs. mate, Since dead
David Horton	Qr. Master
Russel Coats	Qr. Master
Thomas Owings	Qr. Master
Benja. Gannon,	Boat's. Mate
Scuiler Bradley	Seam.
James Snow	Seam
Snow Jones	Seam.
Peter Barnard	O Seam
Wm. Thomas 2d.	Seam
John Fitzmere	Marine

Edwd. R. McCall
Senior Officer

Wounded aboard the *Boxer*

John Fuller	Seam
John Pollock	Seam
Benja. Jackson	Seam
Robert Collier	Seam
George Lachman	Seam
John Hagan	Seam
Robert Header	O Seam

John Bell	O Seam
John Savage	Marine
Edward Watts	Marine
Henry Labet	Marine
Thomas Ritches	Marine
Henry Purdy	Carpenter's Mate
Robert Durian	Seaman

Edwd. R McCall
Senior Officer

ALS, DNA, RG45, CL, 1813, Vol. 6, No. 19, enclosure (M125, Roll No. 31).

DEPOSITION OF LIEUTENANT JOHN A. ALLEN, BRITISH ARMY

[Extract]

Monhegan Island—
7th: September 1813.

I certify on the Word and honor of an Officer, and a Gentleman, the following to be a correct statement of facts:—

"That navigating for a short period from St. John's in H:M S *Boxer* for the benefit of my health; when off the Island of Monhegan—on Saturday the 4th: Inst:, understanding the inhabitants of that Island to be Neutrals, and would not molest those who deported themselves in a peaceable and friendly manner;— I landed on the same day for the purpose of taking a short walk, accompanied by Messrs: Pile & Nixon, Midshipmen.

"That Mr: Anderson Surgeon of the Vessel came on shore at the same time, with the intention of visiting and prescribing for a Cripple son of Mr. Starling an inhabitant of the Island, whom he had been requested to see on a former occasion when belonging to H:B:M:S. *Rattler.*—

"That after remaining a few hours on the Island we waited for a Boat from the *Boxer* to take us on board; at which time, she suddenly & unexpectedly got under weigh, and stood off to the Westward with the intention (as it afterwards appeared), of returning in the evening to take us on board.

"That the vessel was nearly becalmed in the night a considerable distance from us, which prevented her speedy return; when the following morning a Brig was discovered in sight to which the *Boxer* gave chase: An Action took place the same day between the Vessels;—before its termination we obtained a Small Boat, and endeavoured to get on board, but after the Engagement the vessels having borne away, we found it impossible to come up with them, and therefore returned to Monhegan.

"On Monday the 6th: Inst: a number of Armed Men, whom we understood to be Fishermen from various places surrounded the house in which we were, meaning to convey us away Prisoners:—but being apprehensive of violence, and ill treatment from them, we voluntarily put ourselves under the protection of Two Gentlemen who happened to land on the Island requesting them to take us to whatever part of the United States they might judge proper—their names were Capt: Sampson & Mr: Thomas

J. A: Allen
lt: 64t: Regt.

Certified

W. Anderson	Surgeon	*Boxer*
J. N. Pile	Midshipman	Do.
J. Nixon	Do.	Do.

DS, MHi, Frederick Lewis Gray Papers.

CAPTAIN ISAAC HULL TO SURGEON SAMUEL AYER[1]

Portland   6th Sept. 1813

Sir,

There being a number of sick and wounded men now at this place landed from the United States Brig *Enterprize* and British Brig *Boxer*, and Doctor Washington[2] having requested of me some assistance to attend them, I have to direct that you give him as ~~he~~ much assistance as he may require and ~~see~~ that you visit the sick and wounded as often as the state they are in require, and see that no distinction is made between the Crew of the *Enterprize* and that of the *Boxer* as to the treatment they receive. You will every week make report to me the state the British prisoners are in and when any of them are so far recovered as to enable them to desert you will deliver them over to the Marshal[3] taking his receipt for the same.

In furnishing Hospital stores and Medicines for them you will you will see that they are purchased at the least possible expense, and that they are of a good quality, and that proper care is taken of them— With great Respect I am Sir Your Obedt. Servant

LB Copy, NHi, Isaac Hull Letter Books, 25 Feb. 1813–13 Mar. 1814, p. 121.

1. Ayer was commissioned a surgeon on 29 December 1812.
2. Bailey Washington was commissioned a surgeon on 24 July 1813.
3. Thomas G. Thornton.

ACTING CARPENTER JOSEPH ROBINSON[1] TO CAPTAIN ISAAC HULL

Report of the damages Sustained in the Carpenters Department, on board this Vessel, in the late Action with H.B.M.'s Brig *Boxer*, on the 5th. Augt. 1813—[2]

1. Fore Mast
1. Main Mast
1. Main Boom
6. Sweeps
1. Royal Yard
2. Studdingsail Booms
1. Main Topgallant Mast
1: Boat
The Taffarel cut away
The Bulwarks Slightly damaged

Joseph Robinson
Carpenter

ALS, DNA, RG45, CL, 1813, Vol. 6, No. 34, enclosure (M125, Roll No. 31). Robinson's report was probably written on 9 or 10 September.

1. Joseph Robinson was first entered on *Enterprise*'s muster roll on 28 August 1813. He was never warranted by the Navy Department.
2. Robinson meant 5 September.

ACTING BOATSWAIN JOHN BALL[1] TO CAPTAIN ISAAC HULL

Report of damages Sustained in the Boatswain's Department, on board this Vessel, in the late Action with H.M.B.'s Brig *Boxer*, on the 5th. August 1813—[2]
7. pair of Shrouds in the lower Rigging
3. pair " Ditto   " " Topmast rigging
the Main Stay stranded—
the jib Stay—do—
fore Topgallant Stay—
Main lifts—
Main boom Topping lifts
3. Topmast backstays—
1 Topgallant Backstay—
Chief Part of the running rigging—

Sails

1: Square Main Sail
1: Fore & aft do Ditto—Ditto
1. Main Topsail
1. fore Topsail
1. Fore Topgallant sail
1. main Staysail
1. Jib

John Ball
Boatswain

ALS, DNA, RG45, CL, 1813, Vol. 6, No. 34, enclosure (M125, Roll No. 31). Ball's report was probably written on 9 or 10 September.

1. John Ball was appointed acting boatswain on board *Enterprise* sometime between March and May 1813. His appointment was confirmed by the Navy Department with a warrant on 18 October 1814.
2. Ball meant 5 September.

ACTING GUNNER HORATIO EWART[1] TO CAPTAIN ISAAC HULL

Report of damages Sustained in the Gunners Department on board this Vessel in the late engagement with the B. Brig *Boxer*, on the 5th. Augt. 1813—[2]

1. 18 Pound Carronade
8. Ships Muskets
7. Pistols

1. 9 pound worm & ladle
5 Marine Muskets
3 Cutlasses
2. 18 Pound Breeching
4. fire Buckets

Horatio Ewart
Gunner

ALS, DNA, RG45, CL, 1813, Vol. 6, No. 34, enclosure (M125, Roll No. 31). Ewart probably wrote this report on 9 or 10 September.

1. Horatio Ewart was appointed acting gunner on board *Enterprise* on 11 August 1812. His appointment was never confirmed with a warrant from the Navy Department.
2. Ewart meant 5 September.

LIEUTENANT EDWARD R. MCCALL TO CAPTAIN ISAAC HULL

U. Brig Enterprize
Portland   September

Sir

I have to request that you will be pleased to Apply for a Court Martial for the purpose of Trying Mr William Harper[1] Sailing Master of this Vessel, and Mr Isaac Bowman Captains Clerk, on the following Charges   Vizt.,

Mr William Harper, Charged with Cowardice
Specification 1st

In as much as he left his Station in the early part of the engagement between the U.S. Brig *Enterprize* and the British Brig *Boxer,* and endeavored to screen himself from the Shott of the Enemy by getting behind the Foremast and under the heel of the Bowsprit while the enemy lay on our quarter,—by doing which he set an Example to the Crew of the *Enterprize* that might have led to her surrender and desgrace to the American Character.

Specification 2nd.

For having Advised me to haul down the Colours at a time when the fireing from the Enemy was much deminished and ours could be continued with unabated Effect,—

Specification of Charges against Mr Bowman Clerk[2]

For leaving his station during the engagement with his Majestys late Brig *Boxer* on the 5" inst. and going below into the Shott Locker. I am with great respect Sir Your Obedt. Servt.

Edward R McCall

ALS, DNA, RG45, CL, 1813, Vol. 6, No. 38, enclosure (M125, Roll No. 31). McCall probably wrote this letter on 11 September.

1. For more on Harper and his court-martial, see pp. 289–92.

2. Shortly after his arrest, Isaac Bowman wrote a letter to Captain Hull explanatory of his conduct on the day of the battle. Hull forwarded this letter to Secretary Jones, observing that Bowman appeared "to be a poor, innocent lad and as little acquainted with the world, as he is with a Ship." On 26 October, *Enterprise*'s new commander, Lieutenant James Renshaw, lifted Bowman's arrest. The young clerk continued on the brig's muster roll through mid-April 1814. See Hull to Jones, 18 Sept. 1813, DNA, RG45, CL, 1813, Vol. 6, No. 68 and enclosure (M125, Roll No. 31); and Renshaw to Hull, 26 Oct. 1813, DNA, RG45, BC, 1813, Vol. 4, No. 62 (M148, Roll No. 12).

The Problem of Desertion

As the war with Great Britain moved into its second year, the navy's desertion rate steadily increased. It was a problem that, despite the department's best efforts, defied ready solution. Not even the threat of one hundred lashes was enough to stem the flight of seamen and marines from the service. The rate of desertion was particularly high at naval stations where duty, owing to climate, geography, or remoteness, was especially onerous. Charleston was one such station.

Captain John H. Dent to Secretary of the Navy Jones

The Honble. Wm. Jones   Charleston   Septr. 11th. 1813

Sir

Desertion had become so prevalent on this station,[1] and often from the wanton neglect of the Officers, that I directed the Purser[2] (in such cases, when the men were in debt to the US.) to stop the amt. from the Officers pay, this has been done, and given considerable offence to Sailing Master Lord, who suffered a man to run from neglect, that had entered the service the day before, recd. two months advance & Bounty; This punishment has generally been adopted by the Comdrs. to induce officers to be more careful of the men under their charge, and to prevent loss to the U S. by the neglect. it appears the officers on this station have determined not to abide by this regulation, and I have appealed to you sir for the sanction of the Dept.— if it meets your approbation, if not that you will adopt some other mode of punishment, by which this frequent neglect of duty can be rectified— I have the honor to be with great respect Yr. Obdt. Servt.

J H Dent

LS, DNA, RG45, CL, 1813, Vol. 6, No. 37 (M125, Roll No. 31).

1. Dent had complained earlier of desertion at Charleston. See, for example, Dent to Jones, 3 July 1813, DNA, RG45, CL, 1813, Vol. 4, No. 145 (M125, Roll No. 29). The frustrating dimensions the desertion problem could assume are illustrated in Lieutenant John D. Henley's letter to Dent of 2 July 1813, in which Henley informs his superior that two deserters made off with the schooner *Carolina*'s cutter. See Henley to Dent, 2 July 1813, ScU, John H. Dent Letter Book.

2. John H. Carr.

SECRETARY OF THE NAVY JONES TO CAPTAIN JOHN H. DENT

John H. Dent Esqr.   Navy Department
Comg. Naval Officer,   October 8th 1813.
Charleston S.C.

Sir,

I have received your letters of the 11th and 12th Septr.. The careless conduct of Officers, as represented by you, is certainly very reprehensible; and they certainly, in cases of such palpable neglect, ought to be liable for the amount of bounty, &c. but as there is no regular authority to stop their pay, that remedy cannot be applied; but in future, if representation is made of such neglect, the Officer shall be made amenable to a Court Martial, or be dismissed from the service. I am, respectfully, Your Obedt. Servant,

W. Jones.

LB Copy, DNA, RG45, SNL, Vol. 11, p. 110 (M149, Roll No. 11).

CAPTAIN JOHN H. DENT TO OFFICERS COMMANDING
U.S. NAVY VESSELS ON THE CHARLESTON STATION

Charleston   16th October 1813

General Orders.

Serious inconveniences and great loss having arisin to the Service from desertion and in most cases from the inattention of the officers in charge of Boats &c. I am directed by the Honble. the Secretary of the Navy on representation being made of such neglect the officer Shall be amenable to Court Martial or dismissed from the service,

You will cause this order to be made public among the officers of your vessel and in cases of desertion a report made me as early as possible embracing the particulars.

J H Dent

LB Copy, ScU, John H. Dent Letter Book.

Legal Guidance for Naval Officers

Secretary Jones's general order of 29 July[1] thrust naval officers to the fore in the battle against smugglers. It was not long before legal questions arose as to how far naval officers could go in their pursuit of contraband trade.

1. See pp. 205–6.

ASHER ROBBINS [1] TO SECRETARY OF THE NAVY JONES

Honble Wm. Jones   Newport.   14 Sepr. 1813—
Sec'ry of the Navy   District Attorney's office

Sir

A coasting vessel has been cleared out from this port, for Wilmington in No. Carolina with a Cargo of potatoes, cheese, Onions and apples. There is strong reason to suspect that her object is to supply the Enemy. The Commander of the Flotilla. here. Mr. Nicholson has, referred to me for advice, whether under your orders of the 29 July last he would be warranted in stopping and detaining this vessel. After an attentive consideration of your orders, I have been obliged to give it as my opinion that he would not. This vessel by her <u>papers</u>, does <u>not appear</u> to be entending to proceed "towards the Enemy's vessels in the waters or hovering about the Harbors of the United States: or towards any station occupied by the Enemy within the Jurisdiction of the U.S." The track of her ostensible destination is wide, of the blockading. vessels of the Enemy; yet she may easily deviate to those vessels, & I have, no doubt will.— I respectfully therefore submit to your consideration whether it would not be proper to add to your orders. the further instruction, to stop and detain all vessels & craft, suspected to be destined for the, supply of the Enemy, whatever the ostensible destination might be. If this, or something like this, is not done, it will be easy to elude the effect of these orders, by giving to those vessels and craft. a colorable destination, to which the orders will not apply.

The Navy officers here appear. perfectly disposed to stop this profligate trade carrying on with the Enemy, but they are afraid of prosecutions if they pass the line of their instructions and in that case, no doubt. prosecutions would be commenced against them.—[2] I have deemed it my duty to make this communication & hope it may be acceptable.— I have the honor to be your respectful servt.

Asher Robbins

ALS, DNA, RG45, MLR, 1813, Vol. 6, No. 50 (M124, Roll No. 58).

1. Robbins was the U.S. district attorney at Newport, Rhode Island.
2. See Master Commandant Jacob Lewis's comments regarding the practice of ransoming vessels, in Lewis to Jones, 28 Nov. 1813, DNA, RG45, MLR, 1813, Vol. 7, No. 69 (M124, Roll No. 59). Lewis believed this practice was being used as a screen by American merchants to cover illegal intercourse with the enemy. When Lewis detained the schooner *Betsy* because he suspected her owner of trading with the enemy under the guise of arranging a ransom, the owner, Charles W. Gordon, threatened to prosecute the master commandant for damages. Soliciting the advice of the department, Lewis was instructed to release *Betsy* to her owner.

SECRETARY OF THE NAVY JONES TO ASHER ROBBINS

Asher Robbins Esqr.   Navy Department
Newport, R I.   October 2 1813.

Other very pressing matter has prevented an earlier reply to your favour of the 14th. ultimo.

In the present ineffectual state of our laws in relation to the nefarious inter-course which it is so desirable to check and to punish the aggressors, it becomes a matter of some difficulty to frame an Executive order, in consonance with Constitutional and legal authority, so as to embrace cases of the kind you have described. It was foreseen at the time, but, it was conceived, that the exercise of the military power, founded upon mere suspicion, might lead to error, or abuse, and involve the officer in difficulty and litigation

The President will, in a few days return to the Seat of government, when the case will be presented to his view, and if punishable, a remedy applied.[1] I have the honor to be, Sir very respectfully your obedt. Servt.

W Jones

LB Copy, DNA, RG45, MLS, Vol. 11, p. 454 (M209, Roll No. 11).

1. The absence of further correspondence between Robbins and Jones in the Navy Department records suggests that a remedy was never found.

Retaliation against British Prisoners of War

No sooner had Captain Sir Thomas M. Hardy survived one attempt to blow up his ship, Ramillies,[1] *than he learned that another such plot was in the offing. To foil this scheme, Hardy had one of the alleged saboteurs, Joshua Penny, taken from his home and placed in irons aboard* Ramillies. *President Madison's response to this brazen seizure and imprisonment of a private U.S. citizen was quick and unequivocal. He ordered the American commissary general of prisoners, John Mason, to place a British prisoner of war in "the same state, of degradation & suffering" as Joshua Penny.[2] It was incidents such as this one involving Penny that contributed to the escalating use of retaliatory measures against prisoners of war by both belligerents.[3]*

1. *In late June, John Scudder, Jr., attempted to sink* Ramillies *by rigging a prize ship to explode after she was brought alongside the British vessel. For documentation, see pp. 160–64.*
2. *Madison to Mason, 23 Sept. 1813, pp. 248–49.*
3. *For additional background on retaliation against American and British prisoners of war, consult Dietz, "Prisoner of War," pp. 248–68, and Robinson, "Prisoners."*

MAJOR BENJAMIN CASE TO
CAPTAIN SIR THOMAS M. HARDY, R.N.

SIR THOMAS HARDY, *Commander of H.B.M. squadron off Gardiner's Island:*

Sir:—The inhabitants of the town of East Hampton have requested of me a flag, which I now authorize, for the purpose of demanding Joshua Penny, a nat-ural-born citizen of the township of Southold on this island, and a resident of the town of East Hampton.

He is demanded as a non-combatant, being attached to no vessel as a mariner or corps of military whatever, but was taken by force by your men from his bed in his own house unarmed.

The bearer of this flag is Lieut. Hedges, an officer under my command, in government service. You will have the goodness to deliver Mr. Penny to Lieut.

Hedges, as he cannot consistently be retained as a prisoner of war by any article in the cartel agreed on, ratified and confirmed by the agents of each of our governments for the exchange of prisoners.

Given under my hand, at the garrison of Sag Harbor, the 23d day of August, 1813.

BENJ. CASE
Major commanding the troops in United States
service at Sag Harbor.

Guernsey, *New York City*, Vol. 1, pp. 284–85.

CAPTAIN SIR THOMAS M. HARDY, R.N., TO
MAJOR BENJAMIN CASE

HIS BRITANNIC MAJESTY'S SHIP *Ramillies*,
IN GARDINER'S BAY, *Aug.* 24, 1813.

Sir:—As it was late yesterday afternoon when I had the honor of receiving your letter of the 23d inst., requesting the release of Joshua Penny, I did not judge it proper to detain Lieut. Hedges for my reply.

I now beg leave to inform you I had received certain information that this man conducted a detachment of boats, sent from the United States squadron, under the command Com. Decatur, now lying in New London, from that port to Gardiner's Island on the 26th of July last, for the express purpose of surprising and capturing the captain of H.B.M.'s frigate *Orpheus* and myself, and having failed in that undertaking, but making prisoners of some officers and men belonging to the *Orpheus,* he went with the remaining boats to Three Mile Harbor. The next account I had of him was his being employed in a boat contrived for the purpose, under the command of Thomas Welling, prepared with a torpedo to destroy this ship, and that he was in her at Napeng Beach when this ship and the *Orpheus* were in Port Pond Bay, last week. He has also a certificate given him on the 18th of this month, by some of the respectable inhabitants of East Hampton, recommending him to Com. Decatur as a fit person to be employed on a particular service by him, and that he has for some time been entered on the books of one of the frigates at $40 per month;[1] add to which, this notorious character has been recognized by some of the officers and men of this ship as having been on board here two or three times with clams and fruit—of course as a spy to collect information of our movements.

Having been so well acquainted with the conduct of this man for the last six weeks, and the purpose for which he has been so actually employed in hostilities against his Britannic Majesty, I cannot avoid expressing my surprise that the inhabitants of East Hampton should have attempted to enforce on you a statement so contrary to fact. I therefore cannot think of permitting such an avowed enemy to be out of my power, when I know so much of him as I do. He will, therefore, be detained as a prisoner of war until the pleasure of the commander-in-chief is known.

Robert Gray, an inoffensive old man who was taken with Penny, I have landed, as it does not appear that he is one of his accomplices in the transactions alluded to.

I think proper to enclose a copy of my letter to Justice Terry,[2] to warn the inhabitants of the coast against permitting the torpedo to remain anywhere near them.

I have the honor to be, sir, your most obedient, humble servant,

THOMAS M. HARDY
Captain of H.M.'s Ship *Ramillies*

Guernsey, *New York City*, Vol. 1, pp. 285–87.

1. When queried by Secretary Jones as to whether Penny was entered on *United States'* muster roll, Commodore Decatur replied that he was not. He did state, however, that Penny had been paid to serve as a pilot for the expedition to Gardiner's Island. See Jones to Decatur, 30 Sept. 1813, DNA, RG45, SNL, Vol. 11, p. 104 (M149, Roll No. 11); and Decatur to Jones, 6 Oct. 1813, DNA, RG45, CL, 1813, Vol. 6, No. 130 (M125, Roll No. 31).

2. Enclosure not printed.

PRESIDENT JAMES MADISON TO SECRETARY OF THE NAVY JONES

Montpelier   Sept. 6. 1813.

Dear Sir

Among the letters which will go of course to Mr. Sheldon's file of candidates, is one from Dr. Sage, stating circumstances of another sort, which claim a prompt & rigid attention. It is probable that you will have recd. the information from some official source; or that it may have been forwarded to the Dept. of State. It is equally due to Mr. Penny, and to the most obvious policy. that the putting him in Irons for the cause alledged, should be instantly retaliated, and notice given to the British Commander, that the orders for that purpose will continue to be executed, untill Penny shall be relieved. Should no other evidence of the transaction. than the statement of Dr. Sage. have come to hand, that appears to be a sufficient basis for the order of retaliation, which will of course be rescinded, in the event of a disclaimer or correction of the treatment of Mr. Penny. The questions to be decided are 1. whether one or two British subjects prisoners shall be put into the situation of P. 2. who the individual or individuals shall be. On these points, be so good as to communicate with the Secry. of State if still with you. Should he have left Washington, your own decision will be sufficient. It would be premature to take up the question, how far. on a failure of the ordinary subjects of retaliation. resort may be had to British subjects not Prisoners. But it may possibly be fortunate that this resort exists, agst. the extraordinary proceedings of the Enemy agst. Citizens of the U. States. Accept my esteem & best wishes

James Madison

ALS, PHi, U. C. Smith Collection, Papers of William Jones.

PRESIDENT JAMES MADISON TO
COMMISSARY GENERAL OF PRISONERS JOHN MASON [1]

Montpelier   Sept. 23—1813.

Sir

I have this day reced. your letter of the 21t. instant, with the letters & papers from our Agent for prisoners of War at Halifax.[2] The encouragement which the Enemy seem to derive from our reluctance to retaliate their cruelty towards our military citizens in captivity, requires that an appeal should be made without delay, to their feelings for their own unfortunate people, as they have none for ours. You will proceed therefore to have a corresponding number and grade of British prisoners of war in our hands, placed under a rigor of treatment, corresponding with that authenticated to be used towards American prisoners of war, in their hands; reserving a disproportionate retaliation, for the necessity which may be produced by the inefficacy of a numerical one.

The peculiarity of the case of Mr. Penny which was the subject of my late letter to the Secey. of the Navy, marks it for a distinct notice and vindication. You will meet it by putting into the same state, of degradation & suffering, a British prisoner at least equivalent in estimation. It would seem that an extraordinary spite is indulged against the Commanders of our privateers; whose gallantry & success entitle them the more to the protection of their Country. The situation not only of the six mention'd by Mr. Mitchell but of others reported by Mr. Beasly, should be immediately retaliated on Commanders of British privateers, or on other persons as nearly equivalent in number & grade as may be. The sending to England from Halifax, of the crews of Privateers, or indeed of other prisoners of war, cannot be justified; their continuance within the reach of proper supplies and a quick exchange, being opposed by no plea of necessity or safety. It is proper therefore that the practice should be arrested, by a strict confinement of equal numbers. we cannot adopt a precise retaliation by sending British prisoners beyond sea, and it is certain, that a harsh confinement here will not exceed that which will be inflicted on American prisoners, during their passage & after their arrival.

It is necessary also that the pretext of a voluntary surrender of individuals, as British subjects, should at least be firmly remonstrated against. A confession of that sort, under the duress of their situation, and the means said to be used to extort it, cannot avail, especially where an opportunity of verifying it is refused to an American Agent claiming them as American Citizens. If the Cartell is not to be respected, the course pointed out by that, comes also into veiw.

The British conduct with respect to non-combatants, to seamen on board their Ships at the commencement of the war &c &c will be taken into consideration, after my return to Washington. It is probable that delays & disappointments in the case of such sea men are studiously sought out; these being the men, particularly the impressed seamen, who would bring into the service of their Country, a capacity & feelings most to be dreaded by its Enemies.

I have intimated to the Secey. of the Navy, that you will communicate with him on the steps you are to take. You will of course do the same with the Secey. of State should he be on the spot. Accept my esteem & best respects

James Madison

ALS, MiU–C, War of 1812 Papers.

1. John Mason was appointed to the dual post of Commissary General of Prisoners and Superintendent of Alien Enemies in the spring of 1813.
2. John Mitchell.

The Question of Prisoner Exchanges

Under the terms of the cartel agreement concluded between the United States and Great Britain on 12 May 1813, no military or naval officer placed on parole could take up arms again until he had been officially exchanged.[1] The scrupulousness with which the Navy Department observed this regulation is illustrated in the following interchange between Purser Joseph Wilson, Jr., and Secretary William Jones.

1. The principal prisoner exchanges arranged in 1813 were negotiated on 12 May and 9 November of that year; see Dietz, "Prisoner of War," p. 79.

PURSER JOSEPH WILSON, JR.,[1] TO SECRETARY OF THE NAVY JONES

U.S. Brig *Rattle Snake* Portsmouth September 23rd 1813

Sir

When I received the Commission of Purser, in the U.S. Navy, with which you Honoured me—together with an order to Report myself to Capt. Creighton as Purser of the U.S. Brig *Rattle Snake*—I was a Prisoner of War on Parole— I sailed on a cruise as prize master in the Private armed Ship *America*[2] belonging to Messrs. Crowningshield[3] of Salem in the month of March last—was ordered as prize master on board a vessel captured by the *America* on the First of May & recaptured by the *Sir John Sheerbrook* (an English private armed Brig) in Boston Bay about the 15th of May— one or two days after capture I was sent on shore near Boston on Parole— When I received my Commission I calld on James Prince Esquire Marshall of that District who informed me it was his opinion I could accept my Commission with propriety as he should write immediately to General Mason & he had no doubt but my certificate of exchange would be forward immediately— A Month has now elapsed & I have received nothing from General Mason— Mr. Prince continues to assure me that he expects it daily, but as I now think it possible I may not obtain my exchange before the *Rattle Snake* sails on a Cruise I consider it my duty to make known to you my situation & if I have errd in not making it known to you before, I hope Sir, you will have the goodness to pardon it, as an error of Judgement—

Will you Sir, be pleased, to inform me whether I can remain on board the *Rattle Snake* as Purser, without my exchange, with propriety & if I cannot, to order me to some station on shore, or to remain on shore until I am exchanged— as I should be very sorry to feel myself guilty of any thing which even my enemies could consider Dishonourable— I have the Honour to be With the Greatest Respect Your Most Obedient Humbl. Servt.

Joseph Wilson Junior

ALS, DNA, RG45, BC, 1813, Vol. 3, No. 180 (M148, Roll No. 12).

1. Joseph Wilson, Jr., was commissioned a purser on 24 July 1813.
2. For documentation on *America*, see pp. 27–30.
3. George Crowninshield, George Crowninshield, Jr., and Benjamin W. Crowninshield.

SECRETARY OF THE NAVY JONES TO PURSER JOSEPH WILSON, JR.

Joseph Wilson Junr. Esqr.   Navy Department
Purser U.S. Navy.   Septr. 28th 1813.
Portsmouth N.H.

Sir,

You certainly were very much in error not to inform me you were a Prisoner of War. You cannot act under your Commission, nor can you receive pay or emolument until you are exchanged.[1]

You were commissioned because your services were required, and as you are not in a situation to render those services, by being a Prisoner of War, not taken in the service of the Navy of the United States, you cannot receive pay or emolument as an Officer thereof.

Whatever you may have received will, therefore, be charged against you, and you will pay over to the Purser of the Station, whatever public monies or effects you may have received, as he will act as Purser for the *Rattle Snake* until another shall be ordered. I am, respectfully, yours, &c.

                                                            W. Jones.

LB Copy, DNA, RG45, SNL, Vol. 11, p. 100 (M149, Roll No. 11).

1. Wilson was finally exchanged on 9 November 1813. On 20 December he was ordered again by Jones to report to *Rattlesnake*.

Return of the U.S. Frigate *President*

On 26 September, Commodore John Rodgers arrived at Newport in President, *concluding an arduous, five-month-long cruise in the North Atlantic. Despite the capture of a dozen prizes, Rodgers expressed disappointment over the results of his voyage. He had hoped to achieve a victory similar to those obtained by Hull, Decatur, and Bainbridge in 1812; but the opportunity of meeting an enemy frigate in single-ship combat never presented itself. Secretary of the Navy Jones had no such reservations about the success of Rodgers's cruise. He praised the commodore for the damage he had wrought on the enemy's commerce, reminding him that his cruise had accomplished an objective far more important than winning additional laurels for the republic's navy—it had forced the Admiralty to occupy a disproportionate share of its resources in a fruitless hunt for* President. *It is worth noting that of the cruises made in 1813 by U.S. naval vessels, only* Essex *and* Argus *made more captures than* President. *Unlike* President, *however, neither* Essex *nor* Argus *returned home safely. Both were captured by the enemy.[1]*

1. This assessment of Rodgers's cruise in President *draws upon Paullin,* John Rodgers, *pp. 271–72, 275–77.*

COMMODORE JOHN RODGERS TO SECRETARY OF THE NAVY JONES

U.S. Frigate *President*
New Port   Septr. 27th. 1813

Sir

Your having been informed of my leaving Boston on the 23rd of April last, and of my departure from President Road, in company with the *Congress,* on the 30th of the same month, it now only remains for me to make you acquainted with my proceedings since the latter date—

In a few hours after getting to Sea, the wind, which had been light, from the Westward, shifted to the S.E. and obliged us to beat, consequently prevented our getting clear of the Bay until the 3rd of May, when in the afternoon, while in chase of a British Brig of War, near the Shoal of George's Bank, we passed to windward of Three Sail; Two of which from their appearance, and the information previously received, I judged to be the *La Hogue* 74, and *Nymphe* Frigate, and the Third a Merchant Brig

After getting clear of George's Bank the wind veered to the North Eastward and we continued a long East Southerly, in the direction of the Southern edge of the Gulf Stream until the 8th of May in Longitude 60°W. Latd. 39°30'N. when I parted company with the *Congress*.— After parting company I shaped a course, as near as the wind would permit, to intercept the Enemy's West India commerce passing to the southward of the Grand Bank; Not meeting with any thing in this direction, except American Vessels from Lisbon and Cadiz, I next pursued a route to the northward on a parrallel with the Eastern edge of the Grand Bank, so as to cross the tracks of his West India, Halifax, Quebec and St. John's trade: In this route, experiencing constant thick fog for a number of days, and not meeting any thing, after reaching the Latitude of 48 N. I steered to the S.E. towards the Azore's, off which, in different directions, I continued until the 6th of June, without meeting a Single Enemy's Vessel, or any others, except Two Americans:— At this time falling in with an American ship bound to Cadiz, and receiving information that She had, Four days before, passed an Enemy's convoy from the West Indies bound to England, I crowed. [*crowded*] Sail to the N.E. and altho' disappointed in falling in with the Convoy, I nevertheless made Four Captures between the 9th and 13th of June.

Being now in the latitude of 46°N. and Longtd. 28°W. I determined on going into the North Sea, and accordingly shaped a course that afforded a prospect of falling in with Vessels bound to Newfoundland from St. George's Channel, by the way of Cape Clear, as well as others that might pass North about to the Northward of Ireland: to my astonishment however in all this route I did not meet with a single vessel, until I made the Shetland Islands, and even off there nothing but Danish Vessels trading to England under British Licences:— At the time I reached the Shetland Islands a considerable portion of my Provisions and water being expended it became necessary to replenish these, previous to determining what course to pursue next; and I accordingly, for this purpose, put into North Bergen on the 27th of June, but, much to my surprize and disappointment, was not able to obtain any thing but water, there being an unusual scarcity of Bread in every part of Norway, and at the time not more in Bergen than a bare sufficiency for its inhabitants for Four or Five weeks; this being the case, after replenishing my water, I departed on the 2nd of July, and stretched over towards the Orkney Islands, and from thence toward the North Cape for the purpose of intercepting a Convoy of 25 or 30 Sail, which it was said would leave Archangel about the middle of July under the protection of Two Brigs or two Sloops of War; and was further informed by Two Vessels I captured on the 13th and 18th of the same month:— In this object however the Enemy had the good fortune to disappoint me by a Line of Battle Ship and a Frigate making their appearance off the North Cape on the 19th of July, just as I was in momentary expectation of meeting the Convoy: On first discovering the Enemy's Two Ships of War, not being able, owing to the haziness of the weather, to ascertain their character with precision, I stood toward them until making out what they were I hauled by the wind on the opposite tack to avoid them; but owing to faint, variable winds, Calms, and entire day light (the Sun in that Latitude, at that Season, appearing at midnight several degrees above the Horrison) they were enabled to continue the chase upwards of 80 hours; during which time, owing to the different changes of the wind in their favor, they were brought quite as near to as was desirable:— At the time of meeting with the Enemies Two Ships the Privateer Schooner *Scourge*, of New York, which I had fallen in with the day before, was in company; but their attention was so much engrossed by the *President* that they permitted the *Scourge* to escape without appearing to take any notice of her

Being thus disappointed in meeting with the Convoy, and a still further portion of my Provisions being expended, I determined to proceed to a more westerly station, and accordingly Steered to gain the direction of the Trade passing out of and into, the Irish Channel:— In this position between the 25th of July and the 2nd of August, I made Three Captures, when finding that the Enemy had a superior force in that vicinity I found it expedient to change my ground; and, after taking a circuit around Ireland, and getting into the Latitude of Cape Clear, Steered for the Banks of Newfoundland, near to which I made Two more Captures, and by the latter one found the *Belleropan* 74 and *Hyperion* Frigate were on the Eastern part of the Bank and only a few miles to the westward of me; I however did not fall in with them:— From the Eastern edge of the Grand Bank to which I had beat all the way from the N.W. Coast of Ireland (the wind having prevailed, without intermission from the lst of August to the middle of September, from West to South West) I steered for the United States, without seeing a single Vessel of any kind until the 22nd of the present Month, being near the South Shoal of Nantucket, I met with a Sweedish Brig, and an American Cartel (the Russian Ship *Hoffnung*) from London bound to New Bedford

By this time my Provisions, and particularly Bread, was so nearly consumed as to make it indispensably necessary that I should put into the first convenient Port, after gaining the requisite information of the disposition of the Enemy's cruisers as could enable me to steer clear of a Superior force; and this I was enabled to do in a manner which I shall communicate in another letter:— On the 23rd Inst. I captured His Britannic Majesty's Schooner *High Flyer* (Tender to Admiral Warren) with which Vessel I now have to inform you of my arrival at this Port

Annexed is a list of vessels captured and destroyed in which were made 271 Prisoners: I have now however only 55 Prisoners on board; having sent to England, on Parole, 78 in the *Duke of Montrose*.[1] 76 in the Greenland Ship *Eliza Swan*, and 60 in the Barque *Lion*, of Liverpool

During my cruise altho' I have not had it in my power to add any additional lustre to the character of our little Navy, I have nevertheless rendered essential Service to my country, I hope, by harassing the Enemies Commerce and employing, to his disadvantage, more than a dozen times the force of a single Frigate.

My Officers, and crew have experienced great privations since I left the United States, from being nearly Five Months at Sea, and living the last Three Months of that time upon a Scanty allowance of the roughest fare, and it is with peculiar pleasure I acquaint you that they are all in better health than might be expected; altho' you may well suppose that their scanty allowance has not been of any advantage to their Strength or appearance.

The *High Flyer* was commanded by Lieut. Hutchison, Second of the *St. Domingo*; She is a remarkably fine Vessel of her class, sails very fast, and would make an excellent light cruiser, provided the Government has occasion for a Vessel of her description

Just at the moment of closing my letter, a news-paper has been handed me containing Captn. Broke's challenge to my late Gallant friend Captn. Lawrence, in which he mentions with considerable <u>emphasis</u> the pains he had taken to meet the *President* and *Congress* with the *Shannon* and *Tenedos*.

It is unnecessary at present to take further notice of Captn. Broke's observations than to say, if that was his disposition his conduct was so glaringly opposite as to authorise a very contrary belief:— Relative to Captn. Broke I have only further to say that I hope he has not been so severely wounded as to make it a <u>Sufficient</u> <u>reason</u> to prevent his reassuming the command of the *Shannon* again. I have the honor to be With Great Respect Sir Your Obdt. Servt.

Jn⁰ Rodgers

LS, DNA, RG45, CL., 1813, Vol. 6, No. 100 (M125, Roll No. 31).

1. For documentation on the capture of *Duke of Montrose*, see pp. 157–59.

[Enclosure]
List of Vessels Captured and destroyed

9th of June Brig *Kitty*,[1] of Greenock, Robert Love Master, of 2 guns and 11 Men, from Newfoundland bound to Alicant (Spain) with a Cargo of Cod fish:— Ordered her for France

10th June Packet, Brig *Duke of Montrose*, A. G. Blewett Commander, of 12 Guns and 34 Men, from Falmouth bound to Halifax: Sent her to England, as a Cartel, with 78 Prisoners

11th June Letter of Marque Brig *Maria*, of Port Glasgow (Scotland) John Bald Master, of 14 Guns and 35 Men, from Newfoundland bound to Spain, with a Cargo of Cod fish: Ordered her for France

12th June Schooner *Falcon*, of Guernsey, John Manger Master, of 2 Guns and 10 Men, from Newfoundland bound to Spain, with a cargo of Cod fish:— ordered her for France

12th July Brig *Jean and Ann* of Salt Coats, Robert Caldwell Master, from Cork bound to Archangel in Ballast, took out her Crew and Sunk her

18th July Brig *Daphne* of Whitby, William Gales Master, of 2 Guns and 9 Men, from South Shields bound to Archangel, in Ballast: took out her Crew and Sunk her

July 24th Ship *Eliza Swan*, of Montrose, John Young Master, of 8 Guns and 48 Men, from a Greenland Whaling Voyage, bound to Montrose with Fish Blubber ransomed her for £5000 Sterling

July 29th Brig *Alert*, of Peter Head, George Shand Master, from Archangel bound to Aporto (via England) with a cargo of Pitch and Tar: took out her crew and Burnt her

August 2nd Barque *Lion*, of Liverpool, Thomas Hawkins Master, of 8 Guns and
    52 Men, from a Greenland Whaling Voyage bound to Liverpool, with Fish
    Blubber:— ransomed her for £3000 Sterling
August 30th Hermophraedite Brig *Shannon*, of St. Kitts, John Perhings Master,
    from St. Kitts bound to London, with a Cargo of Rum, Sugar and Mo-
    lasses:— Ordered her for the United States—
Sept. 9th Brig *Fly*, of Bermuda, James Bowey Master, of 6 Guns and 9 Men, from
    Jamaica bound to London, with a cargo of Coffee: ordered her to the
    United States
Sept. 23rd His Britanic Majestys Schooner *High Flyer*, Lieut. George Hutchison
    Commander, of 5 Guns, 5 Officers, and 34 Men.

D, DNA, RG45, CL, 1813, Vol. 6, No. 100, enclosure (M125, Roll No. 31).

1. *Kitty* was recaptured on 20 June by *Dart*, a privateer from Guernsey. For the circumstances surrounding her loss, see Midshipman Joel Abbot to Rodgers, 22 Oct. 1813, in DNA, RG45, BC, 1813,
Vol. 4, No. 50 (M148, Roll No. 12). Abbot was a member of *Kitty*'s prize crew.

SECRETARY OF THE NAVY JONES TO COMMODORE JOHN RODGERS

Commodore John Rodgers   Navy Department
Commanding the U S. Frigate *President*   October 4th 1813.
Providence R.I.

Sir

    I have received your Letters of the 27. 28, 29 & 29th. and congratulate you
and our Country upon your safe arrival after an active vigilant and useful
Cruize, in which if you have not added to "the Lustre of our Arms" it is because
the opportunity which alone is wanting to justify the entire confidence of your
Country, did not occur.

    The effects of your Cruize however is not the less felt by the enemy either in his
Commercial or Military Marine, for while you have harrassed and enhanced the
dangers of the one, you provoked the pursuit & abstracted the attention of the
other to an extent perhaps equal to the disproportion of our relative forces, and
which will not cease until his astonishment shall be excited by the Account of your
arrival.— I have now only to express my very earnest desire that such partial repairs
as the *President* may require may be speedily effected in order that you may make a
short cruize taking the Circuit of the West India Islands keeping well to windward of
Barbadoes running down the Coast of Surinam & through the Islands down the
South Side of Porto Rico through the Mona passage, down the North side of St.
Domingo and Jamaica in the track of the Jamaica fleets through the Florida passage
and along the Coast of Georgia South & North Carolina to New York if practicable.[1]

    I regret to find that according to your report by the time this Cruize is per-
formed, the *President* will want <u>a thorough repair</u>, which I presume must apply
not to her state of decay, but to the frames of her Decks having worked loose by
the pressure of her Canvas and metal,—

    The Schooner *High Flyer* your prize, will no doubt make an excellent light
Cruizer, with a suitable armament, and I am disposed to purchase her for the
service of the Navy, upon such terms as may be just and equitable, which may be

ascertained by your stating to me your opinion of her actual worth accompanied with a report of her capacity, state and condition of her materials, armament, hull &c. and an Inventory thereof—or by a public Sale at which I can authorize a person to attend on behalf of the Department;—

The first mode if we can agree will be the shortest, and will enable me immediately to put her into the service to attend you on your Cruize.

A sett of our new Signals general & private, together with those recently taken from the Enemy will be forwarded to you.— I am very respectfully Your Obedt. Servt.

W Jones.

LB Copy, DNA, RG45, CLS, 1813, pp. 73–74.

1. During the next two months, Rodgers refitted *President* for another voyage. Preparations were complete by the middle of November, but, owing to poor weather and the British blockade, the commodore could not put to sea until the first week of December. On the fourth of that month, he set out on his fourth and final cruise in *President.*

Converting a Privateer into a Naval Warship: The U.S. Schooner *Vixen*

The quickest way for the Navy Department to augment the number of ships in service was through purchase. One of the finest vessels purchased into the navy in 1813 was the prize schooner General Horsford. *The command of this schooner, renamed* Vixen, *was given to Lieutenant George C. Read. Unfortunately, the second* Vixen *was no luckier than her namesake,[1] for on 25 December, while en route from Wilmington, North Carolina, to New Castle, Delaware, she was captured by H.M. frigate* Belvidera. *The documents below chronicle a portion of this promising vessel's short-lived naval service.*

1. *The first* Vixen *was captured by H.M. frigate* Southampton *on 22 November 1812. See Dudley,* Naval War of 1812, *Vol. 1, pp. 594–95.*

SECRETARY OF THE NAVY JONES TO LIEUTENANT GEORGE C. READ

Lieut. G. C. Read,   Navy Department
Present.   Septr. 28th 1813.

Sir,

The Department having purchased for the Navy of the U. States, the Prize Schooner, *General Horsford,* at Savannah, you will immediately proceed to that place, and report yourself to the Commanding Officer of the Station, Commodore Campbell, as the commander of that vessel, whose name you will be informed of in due time.

As it will neither be convenient to man, nor arm the Schooner at Savannah, Com. Campbell will be instructed to order on board as many men of the *Troup,* or other vessels in the service there, as will be sufficient to navigate her to Wilmington N.C. under convoy of the Schooner *Carolina,* for which purpose Capt.

Dent, the Commanding Officer at Charleston, under whose command the *Carolina* is, will be instructed.

The men, employed to navigate her round, will be returned to Savannah in the *Carolina*.

The vessel to which you are ordered was originally the Privateer Schooner *Snapper*, built and equipped at Philada. after the Declaration of War, and is not exceeded by any of her class, in all the qualities of an excellent cruizer. She is, I think, upwards of 200 tons, and it is my intention to arm her with 16. 18 pd. Carronades and one long 18 pounder on a pivot. This armament will be prepared and forwarded, through the Canal and Sound, to Beaufort or to Wilmington as soon as possible.

If men cannot be had at Wilmington we can recruit them further North, and send them on in the same manner. It is, therefore, of importance that every exertion should be made to reach Wilmington with the schooner as soon as possible. Mr. Robertson, the Navy Agent at Charleston, will furnish you with a particular Inventory of every thing purchased with the Schooner, and if there is not Kentledge enough, Com. Campbell will make up the deficiency out of the *Troup*— About 30 to 35 tons of Kentledge will be sufficient. I am, respectfully, Your Obedient Servant,

W. Jones.

LB Copy, DNA, RG45, SNL, Vol. 11, p. 99 (M149, Roll No. 11).

LIEUTENANT GEORGE C. READ TO SECRETARY OF THE NAVY JONES

Savannah   November the 3rd 1813

Sir,

I had the honor to inform you of the state in which I found the Schooner on my arrival at this place, but not having strength enough to overhaul all belonging to her did not give you a particular account of the difficiencies on board. I find on examination there is not an ounce of Iron ballast in her— The running rigging is dificient and that which remains so bad, I shall be obliged to replace it with new

From the little care which was taken to preserve her from the heat of the weather during the time she has been here, her seams have become so open that daylight may be seen through her in every direction.

I have therefore got some caulkers employed on her, and shall as soon as they finish proceed to sea—

The *Carolina* has been here several days. I shall have some difficulty in procuring men enough to carry me round as the Crew of the *Troup* have almost to a man had the fever which prevails at this place—

The following are the dimensions of the masts and spars of the schooner under my Commd..

fore Mast	71
do. top mast	27
do. top Gt. mt. sliding quarter	31.6
main mst. – – – –	73.
do. top mt.	29

do. top Gt. sliding Quarter	34
Bow sprit.	26.
standing Jib boom	32
flying Jib-boom	28
sprit sail yard	25.6
Square sail yard	23.
Square sail boom	31.6
Fore yard	56.
Fore top s. yard	32
fore top Gt. yard	25
main boom	58
main Gaff	25
main Gaff top sail boom	18

I have the honor to be sir, with great respect, your Obt. servant

Geo. C. Read

ALS, DNA, RG45, BC, 1813, Vol. 4, No. 78 (M148, Roll No. 12).

LIEUTENANT GEORGE C. READ TO SECRETARY OF THE NAVY JONES

U. States Schooner *General Horsford*
Smithfield   Novr. the 22nd. 1813

Sir,

I have the honor to inform you I got in here on the 20th. inst. and am waiting for a wind to proceed to Wilmington.

I left Tybee light house at 12 PM on the 18th. ult. in company with the United States Schooner *Carolina* but in consequence of a heavy blow from W.S.W. and thick weather during the night, lost sight of her. We fell in however, with each other again on the morning of the 20th. close in with Wilmington bar, and came in together.

I am happy to say Sir, the *Horsford* sails well and in every trial I had with the *Carolina* beat her but the *Horsford* is very light being in ballast, and not even having a sufficiency of that; to which the disparity in sailing with the wind free may in some measure be attributed

From what I have seen of this Vessel I have reason to think she will always sail well, and I have found by experience she is a good sea boat. The *Carolina* is a superior Vessel of her class and is capable of carrying 24 lb. carronades with as much ease as she does her present Mettle.

I hope Sir, on the receipt of this I may be permitted to go about making such improvements as I may think necessary for the comfort of her officers and crew. she will want a considerable outfit, being without boats—Cables bad, and only sixty fathoms in length. A kedge and Cable of small hawsers—running rigging—a suit of sails—Iron ballast to complete the quantity you intended she should carry, having got but between 7 and 8 tons from the *Troup*

There is another thing to which I beg leave to call your attention— her copper is only up to light water mark— Were I permitted to carry it within a foot of the bends, the copper might be sent round with the armament. There will be a small quantity of copper required for the magazine. I have the honor to be sir, with great respect your obt. servant

Geo: C. Read

ALS, DNA, RG45, BC, 1813, Vol. 4, No. 112 (M148, Roll No. 12). Notation on back reads: "Has arrived with the *Vixen*— States Outfit that will be wanting &c." This is the first mention of *General Horsford*'s being renamed *Vixen*.

SECRETARY OF THE NAVY JONES TO LIEUTENANT GEORGE C. READ

Lieut. George C. Read, Navy Department
Comg. U.S. Schooner *Vixen*, Novr. 29th 1813.
Wilmington N.C.

Sir,

I am gratified to hear of your safe arrival at Wilmington, but as the Enemy still continues to interpose serious obstacles to the transportation of the armament of the U.S. Schooner *Vixen* under your command, and as Seamen are not to be had to the Southward of the Delaware, no alternative is left, but to order the *Vixen* round to New Castle, Delaware, immediately, where the necessary repairs and equipments can be effected, while the recruiting is going on.

I have, therefore, directed Mr. Potts, the Navy Agent, to put on board the *Vixen*, 100 Barrels Turpentine, 50 Tierces of Rice, if to be had, and as many Barrels of Tar, all in prime order, as will put her in complete sailing trim.

You will select one of the best qualified Sailing Masters on the Station, and put him in command of the *Vixen*; order Midshipmen Evans [1] and McChesney to join the vessel, and direct the Commander to proceed, immediately, for New Castle Delaware; but if prevented entering the Delaware, to proceed to New York, making every exertion, however, to enter the Delaware in preference.

The Crew will consist of as many Officers and Men as may be sufficient to navigate her to advantage, and no more; as men may be readily had at Philadelphia, and, I do not wish to take a man from the Southern station unnecessarily. The Sailing Master Commanding should be a good Coasting Pilot.

Having made all the necessary arrangements for the despatch of the *Vixen*, you will proceed to this place, as soon as possible, in order to receive instructions and join the *Vixen*. Her armament, in the interim, will be completely prepared.

As the Service is much in want of the Stores which she will carry round, it will be amply remunerated should she arrive safely; and not a moment should be lost in despatching her from Wilmington. I am, respectfully, Your Obedt. Servant.

W. Jones.

LB Copy, DNA, RG45, SNL, Vol. 11, p. 156 (M149, Roll, No. 11).

1. Jones incorrectly identified Sailing Master George Evans as a midshipman here.

A Captain's Prerogative

The commander of a naval vessel was permitted some discretion in the selection of the officers who were to serve under him. This rule, however, was not absolute, and no captain could veto the department's final decision on personnel assigned to his ship.

MASTER COMMANDANT LEWIS WARRINGTON TO
SECRETARY OF THE NAVY JONES

New-York   October 2d 1813

Sir

I am sorry to find that the arrangement of a first Officer, mentioned in your letter of the 28th. ult:, lays me under the necessity of offering an objection to it; which nothing but the importance and responsibility attached to that station, would induce me to do [1]

You ~~are~~ Sir are aware of the necessity there is for the Captain's reposing the most unlimited confidence in the 1st. Lieut:; and where there is any doubt as to his capability, this cannot be done— My knowledge of him, leads me to believe, that his experience and acquirements in his profession are not such as to entitle him to that situation— I certainly do not think him sailor enough to take charge of the ship in case of my death or indisposition at sea— With regard to the Carronades, there can be objection to the 42d. on the score of the vessel's capacity— I should prefer the 32d., but rather than wait a long time, will readily take those you recommend   I am respectfully Your Obdt. Servt.

L. Warrington

Will you have the goodness to send me a list of the crew— We have shipped 86 men; all but one or two Seamen

ALS, DNA, RG45, MC, 1813, No. 134 (M147, Roll No. 5).

1. On 28 September, Jones wrote Warrington that he had ordered Lieutenant Alexander J. Dallas, Jr., to report for duty as *Peacock*'s first lieutenant. See Jones to Warrington, 28 Sept. 1813, DNA, RG45, SNL, Vol. 11, pp. 109–10 (M149, Roll No. 11). Warrington's own choice for *Peacock*'s first was Lieutenant John B. Nicolson.

SECRETARY OF THE NAVY JONES TO
MASTER COMMANDANT LEWIS WARRINGTON

Lewis Warrington Esqr.
Master Commandant,
U.S. Navy.   New York.

Navy Department
Octr. 7th. 1813.

Sir,

Whilst I am sensible that the first Officer of a Ship of War should possess the requisite qualifications to challenge implicit confidence from his Commander, I am also aware of the delicacy of defining, precisely, what is the just ground for that confidence; because it is a case which enlists, involuntarily, a variety of feelings, which affect the judgement, and that many cases have occurred, in which different Commanders entertained opposite opinions of the qualifications of the same Officer. The principle, therefore, must have its limits, and those limits must be determined by this Department; otherwise the power and duty of appointing to particular Stations, Officers whose merits and services appear to entitle them to the confidence of the Executive, would be transferred from its lawful source, and subjected to the opinions and feelings of the several Commanders. The judgment and opinion of Commanders will always have, with me, their due weight; but this Department, in selecting Officers, has no other criterion than their general reputation, founded on the duration and nature of the service, which each individual has seen.

According to this rule, Mr. Dallas is conceived to be qualified for the station to which he was ordered. He has seen a great deal of active service in our best Ships, and from the length of time, and nature of the service in which he has been engaged, ought to be, not only a Sailor, but an accomplished Officer. He is, moreover, Senior to Mr. Nicholson, whom you wished as first Officer, and who would have been ordered to the *Peacock*, but as you had just left the Frigate *United States*, it was not thought expedient to order another Lieutenant from that Ship, under existing circumstances.

Wishing, however, to spare Mr. Dallas the discharge of an unpleasant duty, and to afford you a reasonable opportunity of obtaining a first officer, who may command your confidence, I shall order him to another Ship.

The suggestion I made to substitute forty two, for thirty two pounders, is superseded by the necessary number of the latter being completed, and will be transported, as soon as possible; no doubt, by the time the carriages are ready. I am, Sir, Very respectfully, Your Obedient Servt.

W. Jones.

LB Copy, DNA, RG45, SNL, Vol. 11, pp. 109–10 (M149, Roll No. 11).

The British Blockade Extended

Because the majority of Great Britain's land forces were committed to defeating Napoleon's armies in Europe, the most effective weapon the British government had at its disposal to end the American war in 1813 was economic coercion. To accomplish this, the Royal Navy instituted a blockade of the American coast. At first only the Chesapeake and Delaware Bays were blockaded. But as the strength of the North American Station increased, the number of U.S. ports placed under blockade grew. On 16 November, Admiral Warren took one more step in tightening the "noose around the American coastline." [1]

1. Horsman, War of 1812, p. 69. See also pp. 142–44 for the author's comments on the impact of the British blockade on the U.S. economy. See also Mahan, Sea Power, Vol. 2, pp. 177–87, 193–208.

ADMIRAL SIR JOHN B. WARREN, R.N., TO
FIRST SECRETARY OF THE ADMIRALTY JOHN W. CROKER

No. 224   Halifax   16th Octr. 1813.

Sir

It is with extreme regret I am under the necessity of communicating to you for their Lordships information that Commodore Rodgers has effected his arrival in the United States Frigate *President* at Newport, I had made the best disposition in my power to intercept his return into Port and I am sure that every Captain was anxiously vigilant to fall in with him— the following was the arrangement of the Squadrons employed on this particular service.

La Hogue and *Tenedos*—On the tail of the Banks of Newfoundland—
Poictiers and *Maidstone*—From Sambro lighthouse to Sable Island, thence in a S:E direction twenty Leagues and back by Cape Sable—
Ramillies and *Loire*—From Cape Sable, South East, along the edge of St. Georges Bank as far as Latde: 42°:'00 Sir Thos. Hardy having the Command off Boston
Nymphe, Majestic, Junon and *Wasp*—Inshore Squadron under the Orders. of Sir Thomas Hardy, off Boston— The *Nymphe* is refitting being relieved by the *Junon*
Orpheus and *Loup-Cervier*. From the Tuckanuck passage to Block Island—
Valiant and *Acasta* and *Atalante* Sloop also *Borer* Gun Brig. From Block Island to Entrance of Long Island Sound and off New London
Plantagenett—Off Sandy Hook
Belvidera Statira Morgiana Off the Entrance of the Delaware.
Dragon, Lacedemonian, Armide, Dotterall & *Mohawk* At the Entrance of the Chesapeak.

I am entertained the most confident hope that Commodore Rodgers would not have been able to escape through all these Ships, but in steering for the Tuckanuck passage he fell in with the *High[flyer]* Schooner Tender, which, on my way from the Chesapeak to this Port I had stationed upon Nantucket Shoals for the express purpose of watching that Channel, and in the event of seeing the *President*, to carry the information to the Squadron off Boston, & which from her very Superior Sailing and light draft of Water, she might have done in time to apprize his Majestys Ships.

The *Orpheus* having sprung her Mainmast was obliged to come into Halifax for a new one and I had no Ship to replace her so soon as she again, got ready and proceeded to her Station—

The *Albion* is now under Orders to reinforce the *Orpheus* and *Loup-Cervier* and the *Narcissus* just returned from Quebec proceedes to join the *Belvidera* off the Delaware.

The *Statira* is here, but so very bad in her top sides, knees &c that I purpose sending her to guard Long Island Sound and assist in blocking up the United States Frigates *United States, Macedonian* & *Hornet* Sloop in New London for a short time and so soon as I can replace her on that Station to order her to the West Indies to take home Convoy from thence   The *Victorious* is refitting at Halifax very short of compliment and her Crew slowly recovering from Sickness, many having been Invalided— I have the honour to be Sir Your most obedient humble Servant.

John Borlase Warren

LS, UkLPR, Adm. 1/504, pp. 417–20.

ADMIRAL SIR JOHN B. WARREN, R.N., TO
FIRST SECRETARY OF THE ADMIRALTY JOHN W. CROKER

No. 274   Halifax   20th: Novr: 1813.

Sir

Having consulted with his Excellency the Lieutenant Governor of this Province and considered the best means of enforcing the Blockade of the different Ports of the United States, I found it necessary to give full effect to the Orders of the Lords Commissioners of the Admiralty and to further their Lordships intentions therein, to direct an additional Blockade to be proclaimed which comprehends the line of Coast from the entrance by the Sound into New York to the Southern Ports & River Mississippi— I enclose a Copy of the Same and hope it will meet with their Lordships approbation— I have the honour to be Sir Your most obedient humble Servant

John Borlase Warren

LS, UkLPR, Adm. 1/504, pp. 551–53.

[Enclosure]

BY the Right-Honourable SIR JOHN BORLASE WARREN, BART. K.B. *Admiral of the Blue, and Commander in Chief of His Majesty's Ships and Vessels employed, and to be employed, on the American and West Indian Station, &c. &c. &c.*

A PROCLAMATION.

WHEREAS, His Royal Highness the Prince Regent hath caused his Pleasure to be signified to the Right Honorable the Lords Commissioners of the Admiralty, to direct that I should institute a strict and rigorous Blockade of the *Chesapeake,* the *Delaware,* and the Ports and Harbours of *New-York, Charlestown, Port Royal, Savannah,* and the *River Mississippi,* in the UNITED STATES OF AMERICA, and to maintain and enforce the same, according to the Usages of War in similar Cases, and the Ministers of Neutral Powers have been duly notified, agreeably to the Orders of His Royal Highness, that all the Measures authorized by the Law of Nations would be adopted and exercised with Respect to all Vessels which may attempt to violate the said Blockade.

AND WHEREAS, in obedience to His Royal Highness's Commands, I did without Delay, station a Naval Force off each of the before-mentioned Bays, Rivers, Ports and Harbours, sufficient to carry His Royal Highness's Order for the Blockade thereof, into strict and rigorous Effect; but finding that the Enemy by withdrawing his Naval force from the Port of New-York, and establishing at the Port of New-London a Naval Station, to cover the Trade to and from the Port of New-York, thereby endeavouring to prevent, as far as in his Power, the Execution of His Royal Highness's said Orders; and also finding, that the Enemy has through the Medium of Inland Carriage, established a Commercial Intercourse between the said Blockaded Ports, and the Rivers, Harbours, Creeks, Bays and Outlets contiguous thereto, whereby the full Effect of the said Blockade has been to a certain Degree prevented, in order to put a Stop to the same,—I do, by Virtue of the Power and Authority to me given, and in Obedience to the Orders I have received from the Right Honourable the Lords Commissioners of the Admiralty, Declare, that, not only the Ports and Harbours of the *Chesapeake, Delaware, New-York, Charleston, Port Royal, Savannah,* and the *River Mississippi* herein before-mentioned, are still continued in a state of strict and rigorous Blockade; but that I have also Ordered all that Part of *Long Island Sound,* so called, being the Sea Coast lying within Montuck Point, or the Eastern Point of Long Island, and the Point of Land opposite thereto, commonly called Black Point, situate on the Sea Coast of the Main Land or Continent, together with all the Ports, Harbours, Creeks and Entrances of the East and North Rivers of *New-York,* as well as all other the Ports, Creeks and Bays along the Sea Coast of *Long Island,* and the State of *New-York,* and all the Ports, Harbours, Rivers and Creeks, lying and being on the Sea Coasts of the States of *East and West Jersey, Pennsylvania,* the lower Countries on the *Delaware, Maryland, Virginia, North and South Carolina, Georgia,* and all the Entrances from the Sea, into the said River of *Mississippi,* to be strictly and rigorously Blockaded:— And I do therefore by Virtue of the Power and Authority in me vested, Declare the whole of the said Harbours, Bays, Rivers, Creeks and Sea Coasts of the said several States to be in a state of strict and rigorous Blockade. And I do further Declare, that I have stationed on the Sea Coasts, Bays, Rivers and Harbours of the said several States, a Naval Force, adequate and sufficient, to enforce, and maintain the Blockade thereof, in the most strict and rigorous Manner. And I do hereby require the respective Flag Officers, Captains, Commanders, and Commanding Officers of His Majesty's Ships and Vessels, employed and to be employed on the American and West Indian Station, and all others whom it may concern, to pay the strictest Regard and Attention to the Execution of the said Orders of His Royal Highness the Prince Regent, and also to the Execution of this Order. And I do caution and forbid, the Ships or Vessels of all, and every Nation in Peace and Amity with the Crown of Great-Britain, from entering, or attempting to enter, or from coming out, or attempting to come out of any of the Ports, Harbours, Bays, Rivers or Creeks before-mentioned, under any Pretence whatsoever; and that no Person hereafter may plead Ignorance of the Measures, which His Majesty has been reluctantly compelled to adopt, in Order to force his Enemy to put an End to a War, on their Part unjustly declared against his Majesty and all his Subjects, I have caused this Proclamation to be published.

GIVEN under my Hand, at HALIFAX, the 16th Day of NOVEMBER, 1813.

JOHN BORLASE WARREN,
Admiral of the Blue, and Commander in Chief, &c. &c. &c.

TO The Respective Flag Officers, Captains, Commanders, and Commanding Officers of His Majesty's Ships and Vessels, employed, and to be employed on the American and West-Indian Station, and all whom it may concern.

BY COMMAND OF THE ADMIRAL,
GEORGE REDMOND HULBERT, *Secretary.*

D, UkLPR, Adm. 1/504, pp. 551–53, enclosure.

The Use of American Prisoners to Man British Merchantmen

The war between the United States and Great Britain generated tremendous demand on both sides of the Atlantic for able-bodied seamen. Unfortunately for both belligerents, the pool of available seamen was too small to man all the merchantmen, privateers, and naval vessels each nation had afloat. As a result, many ships, public and private, were forced to lie idle until sufficient crews could be recruited to enable them to put to sea. In 1813, the scarcity of sailors at Halifax became so great that the owners of merchant vessels were forced to resort to extraordinary measures to man their ships. The Admiralty's disapproval of these measures prompted the following reply from Rear Admiral Edward Griffith.[1]

1. For the testimony of an American prisoner of war regarding this practice, see the deposition of Abraham Walter, pp. 600–602.

REAR ADMIRAL EDWARD GRIFFITH, R.N., TO FIRST SECRETARY OF THE ADMIRALTY JOHN W. CROKER

No. 15   *Centurion*   Halifax
                                                  18th: October 1813
Sir

I have received your letter of the 26th: August, with its enclosures from Captain McLeod of the *"Princess,"*[1] relating to the cases of ten Prisoners of War who have been allowed to go out of Prison at Halifax, for the purpose therein stated: and directing me to explain this circumstance for their Lordships information: In reply to which I have to acquaint you that the difficulty, if not impossibility, at times of procuring Seamen to navigate the trade from this Place to the United Kingdom, has induced the Senior Officer of His Majesty's Ships, when applied to by a Merchant Owner, to sanction a few Seamen being shipped from the Prison at Melville Island for the above purpose; The Agent for Prisoners of War taking proper security for their being delivered into Custody in the Vessel arriving at a Port of the United Kingdom. It is a Practice, I am informed, which has been common here, since the American War; and I have reason to think that, without such occasional assistance being afforded to the trade of this Port, many vessels would lose their Voyage, for want of Hands to navigate them. The men so granted have always been selected from amongst European foreigners or Americans, who have been Captured in Merchant Vessels; but as it is to be inferred from the tenor of your letter that their Lordships do not approve of this practice, I shall give directions for the discontinuance of it. I am, Sir, Your most obedient humble Servant

                                        Edw Griffith   Rear Admiral

LS, UkLPR, Adm. 1/504, pp. 439–40.

1. *Princess* was a stationary receiving ship.

Redesigning the 74s

The 74-gun ships building at Charlestown and Portsmouth had already undergone one major design change in the spring when it was decided to increase their dimensions both in length and in width.[1] In the fall Commodore William Bainbridge proposed a second alteration in these ships' design: that they be built with a frigate's bow rather than the traditional beakhead bulkhead[2] bow of a 74. Before deciding on the merits of this proposal, Secretary Jones solicited the opinions of both Bainbridge and Captain Isaac Hull.

1. See pp. 91–95.
2. The beakhead bulkhead closed in the forecastle on a 74-gun ship of the line. Its construction did not permit a ship of the line's deck to run so far forward as that of a frigate.

SECRETARY OF THE NAVY JONES TO COMMODORE WILLIAM BAINBRIDGE

Commodore Wm. Bainbridge.   Navy Depart.
Charlestown. Massts.   Octr. 22d. 1813.

The enclosed extract from a letter received this instant from Captain Hull will indicate the object of this letter. If in the progress of the Ship building under your direction any improvement shall suggest itself to you as preferable to the plan and mode of finishing Ships of her class I shall be glad to receive it for consideration, but I presume no important deviation from the original design will be determined upon without the previous approbation of this Department. The alteration hinted at is a very important one involving some weighty considerations. If you have had it in contemplation and will offer your reasons in support of your plan they will receive respectful attention. I am very respectfully your obedt. Servt.

                                                     W Jones.

LB Copy, DNA, RG45, CNA, Vol. 1, p. 525 (M441, Roll No. 1).

SECRETARY OF THE NAVY JONES TO CAPTAIN ISAAC HULL

Isaac Hull Esqr.   Navy Department
Commanding Naval Officer   Octr. 23rd. 1813.
Portsmouth. N.H.

I have received your letter of the 17th. current on the subject of changes intended by Commodore Bainbridge in the 74 building at Charlestown.

Commodore Bainbridge may have had the alteration mentioned in contemplation, but has not suggested it to the Department, of course he will do so before he determines to carry it into effect.

I have written him on the subject and requested the result of his reasoning on the subject, as the alteration is an important deviation from the practice of all the Naval powers in Europe, nevertheless, that alone would not induce a rigid adherence to their plans if good reasons existed for the deviation.

I have myself reflected upon the proposed alteration which certainly would combine many advantages, if it is not liable to objections of a nature to overbalance the advantages.

I cannot conceive that raising the Hawseholes seven feet would cause the Ship to ride much heavier, as the angle would be so acute with a long Scope of cable as to be almost imperceptible. Raising the Bowsprit in the bed would rather be advantageous than otherwise and would require less Steeve, but the more it is elevated the more it may be supposed to strain the nightheads and wooden ends, but the form of the upper Bow would by terminating at the Stem head at the height of the upper Deck instead of the Beak and Bulk head give additional strength; a great advantage would certainly be gained by working the cables on the upper gun Deck.—

I have thought that the retaining of the Beak head in Ships of the line might be the effect of old habits more than utility, for the Beak head was retained in frigates until within a few years.

I hall [*shall*] be glad of your opinion on the subject, as I have asked that of Commodore Bainbridge, on that as well as on the inboard works, copy of my letter to him is enclosed, which you will consider as addressed to you also.

The Agent under your advise as to the kinds of timber, will contract for as much as you can deck or cover to advantage. I am respectfully yr. obedt. Servt.

W Jones

LB Copy, DNA, RG45, CNA, Vol. 1, pp. 526–27 (M441, Roll No. 1).

COMMODORE WILLIAM BAINBRIDGE TO SECRETARY OF THE NAVY JONES

Navy Yard, Charlestn. Mss.
Octor. 27. 1813.

Sir,

I have the honor to acknowledge the receipt of your letter of the 22d. instant, Enclosing an extract of a letter from Captain Hull respecting the Beak head, Bulk heads of the seventy four gun ships building under our directions. The draught drawn by Mr. Hart, which I had the honor to forward to you some time since, did not lay down the Beak head, Bulk head timber, but showed a frigate's bows. Presuming the alteration intended, as per draught, had been noticed by you, and not receiving any objections from you on the subject of said alteration, I concluded it met your approbation and acted accordingly.— Indeed, I cannot conceive any good objection to this improvement of building the bows of two decked ships. The objection mentioned by Captain Hull, of making the ship ride heavier, is one I am confident, Sir, will not be considered so by you; as the original draught by Mr. Humphreys places the hawse holes just <u>under</u> the upper gun deck, and the alteration intended places them just <u>above</u>, thereby making a difference only of about 3 feet height for the angle of the cable. As great a difference often exists in ships of the same class as to the height of their hawse holes— In fact, frigates' hawse holes are much higher in proportion than the hawse hole laid above the upper gun deck in two decked Ships.— One of the most able and Scientific Ship builders, Gabriel Snodgrass, in a report made to one of the principal Secretaries of State in Great Britain, in 1796, makes the following observation:—"No line of Battle Ship should work their cables on the lower deck."— The character of that able builder is too well known to you, Sir, for me to doubt of respect being given to his opinion.— As to Captain Hull's other objection, of its bringing the bows of the Ship higher up, I cannot conceive it to be an objection but rather an advantage, for when the Bowsprit lies so very low, it is obliged to be steeved very much to keep it out of the water; and the head, railings &ca instead of running nearly horizontally, are consequently placed at a very acute angle of elevation. But Mr. Humphrey's original draught places the bowsprit on the upper gun deck (which is where the present draught places it), thereby laying it higher and giving it less steeve than the European mode of placing it on the lower gun deck, and is in my opinion much better— To follow the original plan, by Mr. Humphreys, of stepping the bowsprit on the upper gun deck, and giving a Beak head Bulk head, would leave the Bowsprit very insecure; and I presume that no Ship was ever so built. All the line of battle ships I have ever seen with a Beak head, Bulk head, have uniformly carried the bowsprit through the upper gun deck and stepped on the lower gun deck, thereby giving additional security to the bowsprit.

I Know no other reason why so many of the European nations continue the Beak head, Bulk head, than that old habits and practices are difficult to get clear of in those countries as well as in our own. Some of the finest ships of the line I ever saw, were built at Constantinople by the celebrated french Naval Architect, Le Brun, and they were built with frigate bows, and not with Beak head, Bulk heads. I believe the Russia, Swedish and Danish men of war are at present so built— But I feel confident, sir, that so long as you are at the head of our Navy, we shall not be tied down to European prejudices or customs, except the latter should carry conviction with them— Our country has certainly passed its novitiate in the art of ship building.—

The following are my additional objections to the Beak head, Bulkhead in our 74s. First, the ship is not so strong about her bows— her upper gun deck is not so well protected against a raking fire across the bows; for the Beak head Bulk head, cannot be made so resistible to the shot as the bows can. Second. It being a square across the bows, it holds much more wind in riding at anchor, than the circular form of the bows of Ships would do. Third. It carries the accommodation of the head much lower and more exposed. Fourth. It is a receptacle for water when the Ship pitches deep into the sea, and thereby gives a great additional draught in her bows which may Endanger the Beakhead Bulk head, besides Keeping the upper gun deck wet. It also takes away a great deal of forecastle-room which is of great importance in working the ship.

I am decidedly of Mr. Snodgrass' opinion respecting the cables working on the upper gun deck. The ship, in my opinion, will ride full as easy, and certainly be much drier on her decks: And the manger being low (as is the case if worked on the upper gun deck) makes it much more convenient for veering and heaving, than being high as must be the case if worked on the lower gun deck. The lower gun deck, being the birth deck for the crew, is also Kept much drier and clearer than it would be if the cables worked on it, which is a subject deserving consideration on account of the health of the crew.

Having given to you, sir, my reasons against the Beakhead Bulkhead, I beg leave most respectfully to solicit, that should they not correspond with your own ideas so as to decide in your mind to build our 74s. without the Beak head Bulk head, that you will (if only by way of experiment) indulge me in building the ship here, intended for my own command, as I have contemplated, with a

frigate bows. I am willing to take the responsibility of the risque of being condemned hereafter, on trial, for recommending the alteration. In doing so, I feel
confident I hazard nothing; but on the contrary, feel assured that the experiment will meet your approbation. I have the honor to be, sir, with the highest
respect, your obt. servt.

Wm Bainbridge

LS, DNA, RG45, CL, 1813, Vol. 7, No. 53 (M125, Roll No. 32). Two pages are missing
from the microfilm copy of this letter. They can be found bound with the original.

CAPTAIN ISAAC HULL TO SECRETARY OF THE NAVY JONES

Navy Yard   Portsmouth
2d November 1813

Sir,

In answer to that part of your letter of the 23rd asking my opinion as to the
proposed alteration in the bows of the 74, I have the honour to inform you that
I have reflected on the subject and find advantages and disadvantages, but having had but little experience in Ships of the Line, I do not feel competent to decide which ought to predominate.

One great argument against running the Deck forward like a Frigate is that
of its never having been done by any nation before us, and I cannot believe that
they would let old Customs carry them so far as to lay aside great improvements
were they to discover them, and this alteration is a very important one, the disadvantages that I have thought of are as follows:

lst. By carrying the Cables on the upper Gun Deck the Ship would ride heavier on her Cables and no doubt would strain much more in her timbers—

2d. By working the Cables on the upper Gun Deck the bits must be there
also, of course they will be between the Ports on the upper deck and come directly opposite & in the way of a gun on the lower Deck. This I think important.

3d. by working the Cables on the upper Gun Deck, the Capstans must be there
and fixed, as they could not well be lowered from the Upper Deck down into the
Orlope as is usual in ships of this rate. Besides, your upper Capstan aft, would be on
the quarter deck; much in the way of working what ropes you work on the deck.

4th. By working the Cables on the Upper Gun Deck, they with the Capstan
bars, Messenger, Nippers &c. will be much in the way of working the Ship,
which is generally done on that deck in Ships of the line. The Cables would also
have to be rowsed a greater distance, which would make it heavier to work
them, beside the wear and tear which would be greater.

These, and as I have said before, that of the practice of all Naval powers,
would be great objections.

On the other hand there would be <u>advantages</u>, such as that of having the lower
deck entirely clear, and (by the cables going on the upper deck) would be much
drier, and not so liable to get too large a quantity of water on her lower deck in
riding heavy, and there cannot be a doubt but the Ship would look better or more
snug, by running her upper deck forward like one of the large Frigates, than she
would with a Beak head, and her upper deck in my opinion would be stronger by
finishing with a hook than cut short as it must be for the Beak head

I differ very much from Commo. Bainbridge as to the Sheer of the Ship. It is clearly my opinion that they are to straight and that they will be hogged in six months after they are launched, if they are not in launching itself, for no ship of the length of these can be built so strong as to prevent their hogging or straightening from five to eight inches and very often, more. I therefore fear our ships have not sheer enough.

You did not ask my opinion on this subject, consequently it is an intrusion, but I hope you will pardon it when I assure you that I have been led to it from no other views than that of being devoted to the service, as, if you should think with me, it may not be too late to alter the sheer of those that are not quite so forward as the Ship here and at Charlestown. The old draft in my opinion was much too crooked, but the new one is, I think too straight   If therefore a Ship was built between the two, I think she would be a better vessel— With very great respect I have the honour to be Sir, Your Obedt. Servant

Isaac Hull

LS, DNA, RG45, CL, 1813, Vol. 7, No. 75 (M125, Roll No. 32).

SECRETARY OF THE NAVY JONES TO COMMODORE WILLIAM BAINBRIDGE

Commodore Wm. Bainbridge   Navy Depart.
Charlestown. Massts.   Novr. 3. 1813.

Your letter of the 27th. ulto. has been received. I recollect, perfectly well, Snodgrass' reasoning on the subject which always appeared to me to be conclusive in favor of the new method of finishing the upper bows, bedding the Bowsprit and working the Cables on the Second gun Deck. I have also heard the observations of many judicious Commanders, at home and abroad, in support of the improvement, and I must confess that I have never heard objections that I did not think strongly mixed with prejudice and the influence of old habits.— Yet the adherence of the British Navy to the old system appeared to demand a strong investigation and serious contemplation of the subject. I am decidedly in favor of the proposed improvement, which you will please to communicate to Capt. Hull, and also, give him the exact height and Steeve of the Bowsprit, height of hawseholes and finish of the upper bow and head, and send a copy of the same to this Department, in order that corresponding directions may be given to the builders in Philadelphia. I am, Sir, respectfully yr. obdt. Servt.

W Jones.

LB Copy, DNA, RG45, CNA, Vol. 1, p. 531 (M441, Roll No. 1).

Purchasing Ships into the Royal Navy

To increase the force under Admiral Warren's command, the Admiralty transferred dozens of ships from home and overseas stations to North America. It also granted Warren the authority to purchase ships into naval service. Captured American privateers were usually favored for such purchases because of their speed and superior sailing qualities.

ADMIRAL SIR JOHN B. WARREN, R.N., TO
FIRST SECRETARY OF THE ADMIRALTY JOHN W. CROKER

No. 234   Halifax, 25th October 1813.

Sir,

I beg you will please to acquaint the Lords Commissioners of the Admiralty, that in consequence of the authority conveyed in your letter dated the 18th Novr. 1812, for the Purchase of Six small Vessels and a Flotilla Force, I directed the Captured American Letters of Marque named on the back hereof to be Surveyed, which being found fit for His Majesty's Service, and of a description that were much wanted, I ordered them to be Purchased; they are all particularly fine Vessels of their Class and extremely fast Sailers. I have the honor to be Sir, Your most Obedient humble Servant.—

John Borlase Warren

LS, UkLPR, Adm. 1/504, p. 523.

[Enclosure]

The Privateer Brig *Rapid* of 310 Tons— Commissioned & called *Nova Scotia* Commanded by Lieutt. Bartlo. Kent.

The Letter of Marque Brig *Herald* of 315 Tons. Commissioned & called the *Barbadoes* Commanded by Captn. John Fleming.

The Do. Schr. *Lottery* of 225 Tons. Commissioned & called the *Canso* Commanded by Lieutt. Wentwth. P. Croke.

The Do. Do. *Syron* of 215 Tons. Commissioned & called the *Pictou* Commanded by Lieutt. Edward Stephens.—

The Do. Do. *Lynx* of 225 Tons. Commissioned & called the *Musquedobit* Commanded by Lieutt. John Murray

The Do. Do. *Racer* of 225 Tons. Commissioned & called the *Shelburne* Commanded by Lieutt. David Hope

The Do. Do. *Atlas* of 240 Tons. Commissioned & called the *St. Lawrence* Commanded by Lieutt. David Boyd

The Privateer Schr. *High Flyer* of 132 Tons. now called the *High Flyer*

The Do. Do. *Spencer* of 90 Tons. now called the *Cockchafer*

These Vessels were Purchased as Tenders, and to act as a Flotilla Force in Rivers and Harbours, in which Service they were found of the greatest ability; nor would it have been possible for me to have distressed the enemy in so great a degree as they have experienced, or to have carried the War into the interior of the Country, without some such class of Vessels.—

D, UkLPR, Adm 1/504, p. 525, enclosure.

Civilian Aid to the Enemy: Two Perspectives

The willingness of coastal New England towns to supply food, water, and wood to enemy vessels proved enormously advantageous to the Royal Navy. No doubt, such collaboration was an expression of the political and economic frustration New Englanders felt toward "Mr. Madison's War."[1] More practically, it was a response to British naval dominance in New England waters, a dominance that state and federal officials were powerless to challenge during the war. When British naval officers came ashore to solicit supplies, New Englanders had only to reflect on Cockburn's raids in the Chesapeake to know how they should respond: cooperation was preferable to devastation. The following documents offer two perspectives—one British, one American—on civilian aid to the enemy at Provincetown, Massachusetts.

1. Of New England Federalists, one British naval officer remarked, "They hate the war on their own account, hate the war because it prevents their making money, and like the English as a spendthrift loves an old rich wife." See Napier, Journal, p. 23.

Captain John Hayes, R.N., to Admiral Sir John B. Warren, R.N.

His Majestys Ship *Majestic* anchored in an outside berth in Cape Cod Bay on the 16th October 1813 where she procured seventy tons of water, Twenty Chords of Wood, and dry Fish with Fruit & Vegetables in abundance, and it appears to me particularly adapted to afford shelter to the Ships cruizing in Boston Bay, but it will be necessary in bad weather to gain the Anchorage in time, as the winds that blow onshore are directly out of the Bay; but should the Ships sustain any injury in a Gale of Wind they may safely repair here after it is over and be in smooth water to set all to rights again; It is of course presumed if the force at Boston is superior; that the Ships will not remain long enough at Anchor to afford the Enemy an opportunity to take advantage of their situation; The Inhabitants of Province Town are disposed to be on Friendly terms, and have promised to allow the Ships to take water from their Wells, and on reasonable terms will supply them with fish, Fruit, & Vegetables, and also good firewood; this article they cheaply procure from the Coast to the northward of Cape Ann, and to enable them to keep a supply of it I have given a note to several Owners of Schooners going for a Cargo stating the assistance afforded the *Majestic* and recommending their being permitted to pass—

Majestic's Anchorage was with the Light House and Windmill which stands near it in One, bearing about E b N and the outside low sandy point W b N in 13 fathoms Water. Off the sandy spit which partly forms the harbour 2 1/2 Miles and from the Town 5 Miles. from this berth you may safely run in for the Sandy Shore between the Town and Lighthouse and Anchor where you please, not going nearer than one Mile; In this Anchorage you will have the Harbour quite open, into which you may go if you think proper in Mid Channel and Anchor in a perfect Basin, with 9 or 10 fathoms Water: The American coasting pilot[1] gives so good a description of this place, that all which may be necessary for me to add is, that if you give the shore generally a berth of a mile you can get into no danger as nothing runs off above that distance, unless you go up to

Welsfleet where a reef of 6 Miles runs off the point in a W by S. or W.S.W. direction, and not generally noticed on the Charts, or in the Books of directions, every other part of the Bay is Clear, where 500 Sail may Anchor and a Fleet may work in and out together during the short time the *Majestic* remained at the Anchorage it blew a gale from Northward and Westward, and also from the Southward and Eastward in neither was it necessary to strike Topgallt. Masts, there not being any Sea to affect the Ship altho' the men of War outside were reduced to reefed Courses, The Ground was a mixture of mud and blue Clay very tenacious, farther in the ground is a close fine Sand equally good, but farther out the mud is too soft and loose to hold.—

A Spanish Flag hoisted at the Mizen Top Gallt. Masthead will be understood by the Inhabitants (in fine weather) that the ship stands in need of refreshments, and in bad weather as Wanting a Pilot

("Signed")   Jno. Hayes

Copy, UkLPR, Adm. 1/504, pp. 737–39. This undated report was enclosed with Captain Hayes's letter of 25 October to Admiral Warren. See Hayes to Warren, 25 Oct. 1813, UkLPR, Adm. 1/504, pp. 733–36.

1. Captain Lawrence Furlong's *The American Coast Pilot,* was first published in 1796 by Blunt and March of Newburyport, Massachusetts.

COMMODORE WILLIAM BAINBRIDGE TO SECRETARY OF THE NAVY JONES

Navy Yard   Charlestown M
31st Decemr. 1813

Sir.

I am informed that the British Vessels of war Cruizing on this Coast. rendevouse—at Province Town, Cape Cod Harbor—Where they have familiar Intercourse with the Shore, and receive all necessary supplies It is much to be regretted that they should have so Important shelter from the Gales, which will enable them to keep this Station throughout the Winter. In addition to which, it opens a wide door for illicet Trade with the Enemy, and gives a favorable opportunity for the Introduction of his Manufactures. Some Troops stationed in Province Town would prevent the Enemy from receiving a supply from the Shore at that place— And by having a few 18 or 24 pound Cannon might I presume annoy their Vessels lying in the Harbor— I have the honor Sir, to be with the highest respect yr. obt. St.

Wm Bainbridge

LS, DNA, RG45, CL, 1813, Vol. 8, No. 115 (M125, Roll No. 33).

The Royal Navy Punishes Deserters to the Enemy

The Royal Navy had always experienced a problem with desertion. The severity of the problem fluctuated, however, generally improving in time of peace and worsening in time of war. During the Napoleonic Wars losses experienced due to desertion were particularly acute.[1] *A significant number of those who fled service in the Royal Navy at this time found employment in the American merchant marine or in the U.S. Navy. Once hostilities between the United States and Great Britain commenced, it was the Admiralty's policy to deal harshly with British deserters discovered on American warships. Those so discovered were subject to the death penalty. It was believed that such sanctions would discourage further incidents of desertion to the enemy.*[2]

1. For a brief treatment of this topic, see Lavery, Nelson's Navy, pp. 143–44.

2. John D. Armstrong, surgeon's mate on board Constitution *and a British alien, was fearful enough of the treatment he would receive should "Old Ironsides" be captured that he asked Secretary Jones to transfer him to a shore station, a request to which Jones acceded. See Armstrong to Jones, 3 Dec. 1813, DNA, RG45, BC, 1813, Vol. 4, No. 130 (M148, Roll No. 12). See also the comments of British deserter Samuel Leech, whose ship, the U.S. brig* Siren, *was captured by H.M.S.* Medway, *in his autobiography* Thirty Years from Home, *pp. 197, 218, 224–25.*

ADMIRAL SIR JOHN B. WARREN, R.N., TO FIRST SECRETARY OF THE ADMIRALTY JOHN W. CROKER

No. 240   Halifax, 27th October 1813.—

Sir,

I have the honor to acknowledge the receipt of your letter of the 30th July, directing me to order the Captains and Commanders under my orders to make known to their respective Crews, that John Wiltshire[1] alias Jonathan Bowers, alias John Riley suffered the Sentence of Death passed on him at the last Admiralty Sessions for adhering to His Majesty's Enemy's on board the *True Blooded Yankee* American Privateer; and to impress on their minds the heniousness of taking up Arms against their Sovereign and Country &c; and I shall pay the strictest attention to their Lordship's directions thereby communicated.— I have the honor to be Sir, Your most Obedient humble Servant

John Borlase Warren

LS, UkLPR, Adm. 1/504, pp. 509–10.

1. Wiltshire was an Englishman imprisoned in a French jail at the time *True Blooded Yankee* was fitting out at Brest. In return for his release from prison, he agreed to serve on the American privateer. He was captured when *Margaret,* on which he was part of the prize crew, was taken by H.M. cutter *Nimrod.* See Maclay, *American Privateers,* pp. 275–76.

Charges of Neglect in the Care of *Argus*'s Wounded

Three days after their capture, Argus's wounded were landed at Mill Prison, Plymouth. When the prison surgeon, George Magrath, examined them, he was shocked at what he found: men with shattered limbs left untreated since the day of the battle and nearly all "in a state of Gangrene."[1] *Magrath's superiors at the Transport Board*[2] *forwarded his report to Reuben G. Beasley, the American agent for prisoners at London.*

Beasley was greatly disturbed by the apparent neglect suffered by Argus's *wounded following her action with* Pelican *and he immediately made inquiries to determine whether the ship's surgeon, James Inderwick, had been derelict in the performance of his duties. On 30 October, Beasley informed Secretary Jones of the result of his investigation.*

1. *See Magrath to Transport Board, dated August 1813, enclosed in Reuben G. Beasley to Jones, 18 Sept. 1813, DNA, RG59, Despatches from U.S. Consuls in London, England, 3 Aug. 1812–28 Nov. 1816 (T168, Roll No. 10). Magrath's motives for making these charges are explored in Estes and Dye, "Death on the* Argus.*"*
2. *Along with its other responsibilities, the Transport Board was charged with the care and treatment of prisoners of war.*

REUBEN G. BEASLEY TO SECRETARY OF THE NAVY JONES

(Copy)   London, October 30th 1813.

Sir,

With reference to my Letter of the 18th Ultimo, enclosing the copy of a communication made to me by the Transport Board, implicating the conduct of Mr. Inderwick, Surgeon of the *Argus*, I have now the satisfaction to inform you, that according to the assurance of the Officers of that Vessel, there was not the least foundation for the charges contained in that communication; on the contrary, the most prompt & particular attention was paid by Mr. Inderwick to the wounded under the most difficult circumstances. I have the honor to be, with great respect, Sir, Your most obedt. Servant

R G Beasley

LS, DNA, RG45, MLR, 1813, Vol. 7, No. 45 (M124, Roll No. 59).

REUBEN G. BEASLEY TO SECRETARY OF THE NAVY JONES

London, 15th November 1813.

Sir,

With reference to my Letter of the 30th October last, respecting Mr. Inderwick, late Surgeon of the *Argus*, I now transmit the copy of a Letter which I have received from the Transport Office enclosing that of one from the Surgeon of Mill Prison Hospital at Plymouth, explanatory of his former communication to the Board, on which the imputation on Mr. Inderwick was founded.— I have the honor to be very respectfully, Sir, Your most obedt. Servant,

R G Beasley

LS, DNA, RG45, MLR, 1813, Vol. 7, No. 44 (M124, Roll No. 59).

[Enclosure]
(Copy)   Transport Office,
                                                    13th November 1813.

Sir,

With reference to my Letter of the 16th of September last, transmitting to you an extract of a report from the Surgeon of Mill Prison Hospital relative to the deplorable state of the American Prisoners who were received wounded from on board the United States late Sloop of War *Argus*, I am now directed by

the Commissioners for the Transport service &c. to transmit the enclosed copy
of a Letter from that Officer explanatory of his former report.— I am, Sir, Your
most obedient, humble Servant,

(Signed)   J. Dixon
pro Secy.

R G Beasley Esqr.

Copy, DNA, RG45, MLR, 1813, Vol. 7, No. 46 (M124, Roll No. 59).

[Enclosure]
(Copy)   Mill Prison Hospital
8th November 1813.

Gentlemen,

I have the honor to acquaint you that I have received a Letter from Mr. Inderwick, Surgeon of the late United States Sloop of War *Argus,* which informs me,
that my official report to you, on the state of the wounded Prisoners admitted
into Mill Prison Hospital, from that Vessel, has been made the ground of a representation to the American Government, highly prejudicial to his professional
reputation, as well as injurious to his future prospects in the Naval service of
that Country.—

In stating that "every case, with one exception, was in a state of gangrene, as
they had not been dressed from the time of infliction, until admitted into the
Hospital," was incontestibly correct in point of fact; but it was most remote from
my intentions, thereby to impute blame to the Surgeon, or to imply that the existing condition of the wounds exclusively depended upon neglect of dressing:
although perhaps, the construction of the paragraph, might warrant such a
conclusion. I am therefore happy in the opportunity thus afforded me, of removing any misconception, which the ambiguous wording of the sentence may
have led to; as I am convinced the unfavorable character which the wounds had
assumed, did not arise from any culpable or wilful neglect on the part of Mr. Inderwick; but was more to be ascribed, to the scene of intemperance, riot and
disorder, which I am informed from good authority, pervaded the Crew, from
the moment of their capture; and whilst some with shattered limbs refused to
submit to amputation, others as obstinately resisted the adoption of such medical treatment as was considered necessary to their respective conditions. From
this it will appear evident that I meant not to reflect on the—professional skill
or conduct of this Gentleman; but on the contrary, I feel it a justice due to him
to assure the Board, that from the many conversations I had with him, on various subjects connected with surgery, and the science of medicine, I formed a
very favorable opinion of his acquirements, and have every reason to think
highly of his judgement and—competency in his profession.— I have the honor
to be, Gentlemen, Your most obedient, humble Servant,

(Signed)   Geo. Magrath

Transport Board

Copy, DNA, RG45, MLR, 1813, Vol. 7, No. 47 (M124, Roll No. 59).

Captures by the Royal Navy

One measure of the British blockade's effectiveness may be found in the large number of American vessels captured by the Royal Navy in 1813. The list printed below itemizes over one hundred such captures made by Admiral Warren's squadron between April and September. This list only records captured vessels sent into Halifax for condemnation. It would be far longer if it included ships that were sent into other ports, or were destroyed following their capture.

ADMIRAL SIR JOHN B. WARREN, R.N., TO
FIRST SECRETARY OF THE ADMIRALTY JOHN W. CROKER

No. 266   Halifax, 11th. Novr. 1813.

Sir,

I beg leave to enclose a List of Ships and Vessels Captured & detained by the Squadron under my Command between the 20th April and this date— I have the honor to be Sir, Your most Obedient humble Servant—

John Borlase Warren

LS, UkLPR, Adm. 1/504, p. 699.

[Enclosure]

A List of Ships and Vessels Captured and detained and sent into Halifax by the Squadron under the Commd. of the Rt. Honble Admiral Sir J. B. Warren K B between the 20th April and the 20th September 1813

Date of Capture	Name of Capture	How Rigged	Tons	Cargo	From Whence	Where Bound	By what Ships Captured	Remarks
1813								
28th April	Henry	Ship	181	Salt &c.	Liverpool	Boston	La Hogue	Restored
24 "	Sally	Brig	143	Lumber	Portland	St. Margarets	Curlew	Do.
30 "	Hector	"	156	Sugar & Coffee	Havannah	New York	Spartan	Cargo Condemned vessel restored
5th May	Montgomerary	"		Privateer	Salem	Cruizing	Nymphe	Condemned
10 "	Diomede	"	293	Indigo Redwood &c.	Salem	Manilla	La Hogue & Nymphe	Condemned
11 "	Juliana Smith		37	Privateer	Boston	Cruizing	Nymphe	Do.
5 "	Ann	Schr.	42	Cotton Skins &c.	New Orleans	Bourdeaux	Do. Shannon Tenedos & Emulous	Do.
9 "	Young Phœnix	Ship			Jersey		Orpheus recapture	Restored
6 "	Emperor	Schr.		Indian Corn	Carolina	Boston	Do. Ramillies	Condemned
19 "	Paragon	Brig			Aberdeen	N Brunswick	Recapd. by Shannon & Nova Scotia—	Restored
18 "	Duck	Ship		Provisions	Waterford	Newfoundland	recapd. by Bold	Restored
21 "	Enterprize	Schr.	225		Salem	Cruizing	Tenedos Curlew	Condemned
19 "	Fidelia	Ship	243	Flour, Corn &c	New York	Cadiz	Orpheus & Ramillies	Do.
10 "	Juliet	Sloop	92	Molasses	Cuba	Newport	Paz	Condemned
26 "	Branch		78	Ballast	Boston	Dear Island	Bream	Do.

Date	Vessel	Rig	Tons	Cargo	From	Bound to	Captor	Fate
23rd April	Semeramus[1]	Sloop	85	Timber	P River	Boston	Bream	Do.
10th May	Columbia	Schr	98	Lumber & Potatoes	Martinique	Oporto	Rattler	Do.
19 "	Dolphin	Brig	119	Corn Beef & Pork	New York	Lisbon	La Hogue	Do.
16 "	Orion	"	269	Flour & In. meal	Do.	Lisbon	Do.	Restored
18 "	Pilgrim	"		Flour	New Orleans	Cadiz	Do.	Do.
24 "	Post Boy	Schr.	154	Brandy Wine	Salem	St. Dominigo	Shannon Tenedos Rattler	Condemned
1st June	Chesapeake	Ship			Boston	Cruizing	Shannon	Do.
1 "	Joanna	Schr.	48	Corn	Do.	Eastport	Privateer Dart	Restored
5th "	Washington	Schr.	65	Boards	Portland	Boston	Privateer Dart	Do.
6 "	Cuba	Ship	176	Flour			Do.	Restored
16 "	Christiana	Brig	132	Lumber	In the Possession of the American Privateer Teaser		Wasp Rover	Do.
	Lark	Schr.					Do.	
18 "	Eunice	"	193	Salt	St. Ubes	Boston	Wasp	Do.
"	Thomas	Brig			Cadiz	Do.	Do.	Do.
22 "	Gustava		123	Sundries	Boston	Madeira	Sylph	
24 "	North Star		117	Do.	St. Salvador	Boston	Tenedos	
8 "	Belle	Schr.	105	Ballast	Madeira	Egg Harbour	Spartan, Statira and Martin	Restored
2 "	Flor de Lisbon	Brig		Sugar & Rice	Porto Rico	Philadelphia	Do. Do. Do. Spartan, Statira & Martin	Restored
2 "	Charllotta	"		Some money Cloth	Porto Rico	Do.		
14 "	Del Carmen	Schr.		Flour Corn &c.	New York	Havannah	Do. Do. Do.	Do.
1 "	Kitty	Brig	157	Ballast	Madeira	Philadelphia	Do. Do. Do.	Do.
30 May "	Commerce	"	185	Cotton	Philadelphia	Gottenburg	Do. Do. Do.	Do.
20 "	Volador	"		Some money Silk &c.	Do.	Havannah	Do. Do. Do.	Do.
12 June	Hero		165	Provisions	Limerick	Lisbon	Do. Do. Do.	
26 "	St. Jago	Brig	267	Sundries	Salem	Malaga	Woolwich	
17 "	Porcupine	"	330	Brandy Wine & Silk	Byona [Bayonne]	Boston	Valiant, Acasta Wasp	Recapture

Date of Capture	Name of Capture	How Rigged	Tons	Cargo	From Whence	Where Bound	By what Ships Captured	Remarks
30	Minerva	"	184	Beef & Pork	Boston	Lisbon	La Hogue Spartan Statira, & Martin	Condemned
"	Morning Star	Sloop						
30	Thomas	Schr.		Privateer	Portsmouth	Cruizing	Nymphe	Restored
"	Liverpool Packet	Ship					Dover	
17	Harriet	Schr.	292	Oil & Seal Skins	Newfoundld.	London	Dover	Condemned
18 June	Protectress	Ship		Flour	Alexandria	Halifax		Restored
27 "	Little Bill	Schr.		Sugar & Molasses	St. Barts.	N Carolina	Loup Cerviere	Condemned
24 "	Herman	Ship	413	Flour	Baltimore	Lisbon	Chesapeake Squadron	Condemned
14 "	Star	"	409	Do.	Alexandria	Do.	Do.	Do.
	Sea Flour						Recapd. by Fantome	Recapture
8th July	Fanny	Brig	146	Flour	Newhaven	Halifax	La Hogue	Condemned
7 "	Swift	Schr.	63	Salt	Cape Cod	Ipswich	Curlew	Do.
7 "	Two Brothers	Do.	53	Sundries	Kennebeck	Ipswich	Do.	Do.
9 "	Precilla	"	61	Fish	St. Barts.	Boston	Do.	Do.
	Ellen	Brig		Molasses		Portland	La Hogue	Restored
27 "	Rebecca	Schr.	86	Flour	N York	Cadiz or Halifax	Boxer	Cargo Condemned, vessel to stand to see if English owners will claim
28 "	Nancy	"	14	a variety	Taken in Harbour at Little River by Boxer			Condemned
7 "	Prudentia	"		Flour, Staves & Tar		Cadiz	Rattler	Restored
7 Augt.	Eunice	Sloop					Curlew	Condemned
13 "	Anna	Brig	125	Flour, Beef Gin &c.	New Haven	Laguira	Poictiers Maidstone & Nimrod	further proof ordered

Date	Vessel	Rig	Tons	Cargo	From	To	By whom captured	Remarks
11	Republican	Ship		Provisions &c.	New York	Port au Prince	Nimrod	Do.
"	York Town			Privateer			Do. Poictiers / Maidstone	Condemned
18	Manchester	Brig				Boston	Do. Do. Do.	Recapture
19	Isabella	Schr.	126	Wine Silks, Oil &c.	St. Thomas's	Halifax	Pictou	Restored
20	Lively	Ship	374	Ballast	N York	Beaufort	Eperviere	Recapture
14th June	Gustoff	Schr.				Philadelphia	Statira Martin	Restored
22nd July	Providence	Brig			Morrice River	Bordeaux	Nymphe	Recapture
1st June	Fanny	Brig	248	Cotton	Savannah	St. Barts.	Statira	Condemned
30th June	Ulysses	Scr.	223	Lumber	Portland	Portland	Majestic	
11th July	John Adams	Schr.			Tortola	Kennebeck	Rattler & / Retreive Pr.	
14	Betsey	"	117	Rum	St. Thomas's	Halifax	Bream	
14	Trilon	Brig	122	Rum and Molasses	Boston		Bream	
12	Jefferson	"	99	Ballast	Liverpool		Bream	
28	Stamper	Brig					Ringdove	Recapture
	Mary	Sloop	164	Fruit, Wine, Whalebone	Lisbon	Boston	Nimrod	Do.
	Flor de Fajo			Sugar, Coffee Nutmeg	Batavia	Providence	Manly	
2nd Augt.	Hope	Brig					Manly	
4	Four Brothers	Schr.					Emulous	Recapture
"	Roxanna	Ship					La Hogue	Restored by consent
31st July	Wm. & Ann	Sloop	77	Coals and Glass	Scotland	Ireland	Nimrod	recapture
11	Minter [2]	"	56	Lumber	Province Tn.	New Bedford	La Hogue	
8th Augt.	Wasp	Sloop		Privateer	Salem	Cruizing	Bream	
6th July	Two Brothers	Schr.	89	Flour and Corn	Tanfield	Eastport	Boxer	
6	Friendship	Sloop	100	Flour	Blackrock	Do.	Do.	
13th Augt.	Polly	Schr.					Statira	Recapture
18	King George	"	204	Salt	Liverpool		Recruit	Do.
12	Gennett [3]		35	Fish	Hingham	Fishing	Nymphe Curlew	
13	Paragon	Schr.	157	Cotton and Rice	Charleston	Boston	Do. Do.	

Date of Capture	Name of Capture	How Rigged	Tons	Cargo	From Whence	Where Bound	By what Ships Captured	Remarks
17 "	Endeavour	Sloop	104	Corn and Wood	Castine	Boston	Do. Do.	
3 "	Rebecca	Schr.	117	Wood and Barque	Townsend	Do.	Boxer	
25 July	Fairplay	Sloop					Boxer	
31 "	Porpoise	Schr.	32	Fishing Stores			Rattler	
	Anaconda	Brig					Sceptre	Condemned
27th Augt.	Euphemia	Schr.	90	Copper and logwood	Havannah	Boston	Majestic	
26 "	Elizabeth	Brig					Shelburne	recapture
24 "	Espozy Mina	Schr.		Hides and Indigo	La Guira	N York	Statira	
16	Flor de Mar	Ship	311	Wine and redwood	Fyal	Boston	La Hogue	
	Alicia	Brig					Loire and Martin	
	Jane	Ship					Do. Do.	
1st Septr.	Divina Pastora	"	380	Sugar Coffee Molasses	Havannah	New York	Statira	
3 "	Jerusalem	"	750	Sugar Coffee Copper &c.	Do.	Boston	Majestic	
	Dolphin	Sloop						Condemned
29th Augt.	Mariner	Brig					Poictiers	recapture
31 "	Fortune	Schr.					Boxer	
3rd Septr.	Watson	Brig					Poictiers	recapture
11 "	Torpedo	Schr.					Plantagenet	
16 "	Catalonia	Ship					Shannon	
16 "	Alliance	"					Do.	
17 "	Queen Charlotte	Schr.					Do.	recapture
11 "	Massachusetts	Ship					Canso	
14 "	Santa Cicilia	"		Salt and Dry Goods	Lisbon	New Bedford	Wasp	

20	"	Active				Epervierre
13	Schr.	Mary	61	Sugar and Coffee	Boston	Sylph
		Flor de Jago				Condemned

John Borlase Warren

DS, UkLPR, Adm. 1/504, pp. 703–11. Notation in upper right corner of first page: "not before gazetted"; and in lower left corner: "Dec 24 Gazette." One column, "What Colours," located between "How Rigged" and "Tons," is not printed here. That column had entries for only five prizes: *Hector* (Spanish), *Young Phœnix* (English), *Chesapeake* (American), *Prudentia* (Spanish), and *Anaconda* (American).

1. *Semerimes* and *Pleasant River*, according to Essex Institute, *American Vessels*, p. 155.
2. *Mentor*, ibid., p. 139.
3. *Gannett*, ibid., p. 121.

Hurricane Damage at Halifax

The Admiralty's efforts to build up its forces in North American waters were dealt a serious setback by a hurricane that struck Halifax on 12 November. Although no vessels were lost, the material damage was great, especially to the 74s at anchor in the harbor.

ADMIRAL SIR JOHN B. WARREN, R.N., TO
FIRST SECRETARY OF THE ADMIRALTY JOHN W. CROKER

No. 267.   Halifax.   13th. Novr. 1813.

Sir

I request you will please to state to the Lords Commissioners of the Admiralty, that last Evening about Six oClock, this Harbour was visited by one of the most violent Hurricanes ever known here, it lasted only an hour and a half, but in even that short period the direful effects of it are beyond belief, and the damages sustained by the Men of War and Shipping are extremely great, between fifty and Sixty Sail of Ships were driven onshore, many of them bilged, and others carried so far above high Water mark, as to prevent their being again got off. The Gale raged at low Water, but in a few minutes a torrent came in at a furious rate, and rose the Stream Several feet above the rise of the Tide—

The *San Domingo, La Hogue, Maidstone, Epervier, Fantome, Manly, Nemesis, Morgiana, Canso,* were parted from their Anchors and put onshore, the whole are afloat except the *Epervier* and *Manly,* & have not received material injury except the *Maidstone* and *Fantome* which must be hove down before they can leave the Port.

The *Nymph, Tenedos* were ready for Sea, the former lost her Bowsprit Foremast and Topmasts, had the Starboard Quarter entirely stove in— The *Tenedos* lost her Mizen Mast the *Victorious* received considerable injury by breaking adrift from Six Cables and getting onboard others, the *Shelburne* Schooner was totally dismasted, the *Nemesis* lost her Mizen Mast the *Success* her Bowsprit, and of the Convoy which awaited only a fair Wind to proceed with the *Poictiers* to England, only one Vessel is now likely to be able to be ready—

His Majestys Ships are materially crippled by this event, I shall however use every possible endeavour to have them repaired, with every dispatch which the Strength of this Yard and their own means admit of. I have the honour to be Sir Your most obedient humble Servant

John Borlase Warren

The Gale commenced at S.S.E. and finished at N.W.

LS, UkLPR, Adm. 1/504, pp. 713–15.

The Use of Flags of Truce

Under certain circumstances, communication between the enemy and U.S. citizens was legally permissible. Such communication, however, could take place only under a flag of truce by permission of military or naval authorities. The presence of both a naval and

military establishment in cities such as Charleston, South Carolina, raised questions as to whose authority was superior with regard to flags of truce—the navy's or the army's? As Acting Lieutenant Edward H. Haddaway discovered, it was a question fraught with professional hazard.

CAPTAIN JOHN H. DENT TO
OFFICERS COMMANDING BARGES ON GUARD IN CHARLESTON HARBOR

Charleston   23rd Nov 1813

Guard Orders,

The following orders are to be Strictly carried into execution by the officir having the guard in rebellion roads.

1st. Strict attention must be paid to the Guard orders issued from the department relative to intercourse with the Enemys vessels off the coast or harbours of the U.S.

2nd No vessel or craft is to leave the port without a regular clearance from the Custom House, and you are satisfied does not intend to proceed to a Situation occupied by the enemy,

3. No Craft or Boat to be permitted to go beyond the bar, without my permission

4th fishing smacks or boats are not to go beyond the bar to fish, if attempted they are to be seized and reported.

5th. No flags of truce or other communications are to be permitted with the enemy under any pretence whatever, without my written orders. if attempted the craft or boats with the persons on board are to be seized and reported in order that they may be proceeded against according to law.

6th No officer or other person to leave the Barges on guard without my permission

7th. Barges when on guard, and the weather permitting are to cruize near the bar, so as to observe the motions of the enemy,

8th All flags of truce from the Enemy approaching the harbour are to be received by the Senior officer of the guard near the bar, and the boat not permitted to come within the harbour & as soon as the communication is received dismissed

J H Dent

LB Copy, ScU, John H. Dent Letter Book.

CAPTAIN JOHN H. DENT TO SECRETARY OF THE NAVY JONES

The Honorable William Jones.   Charleston.   23rd Novr. 1813.

Sir

During my absence Genl. Pinckney granted a flag to a Mercantile agent of this city to go on board the Enemy's vessels off the Bar to close the sales of the purchase of *Inca*'s cargo. I am sorry to inform you Lieut Haddaway (Senior officer in Port) permitted the flag to proceed contrary to my orders and also permitted Mr. Jervey [1] to go on board, & not the person named by the General. I

Captain John H. Dent

must Sir protest against the late proceedings of Mr. Jervey (who has been lately appointed to an office in the Custom House) before the receipt of your late orders I directed the commanding officer of the guard to take the names of the persons going out and coming in with the flag, this gentleman considered the interference of the Navy an insult to him, and refused to have his and his companion's Names inserted on the list, observing to the officer that he knew what he was about, and that his authority was as great in the harbour as the commanding Naval officer, I saw him after the receipt of your orders, and informed him how incorrect his proceedings had been &c. And further Stated that if he again attempted to have any intercourse with the enemy I Should proceed against him according to law, and further I considered it important that your orders Should be made public in order that no person in future detected proceeding as heretofore Should plead ignorance [they were] [2] published in the papers of this City, five days after Mr. Jervey went on board the *Dotterel* with the permission of Lt Haddaway and as I am informed to shew that he still could do so. in defiance of my orders, I have arrested Lt Haddaway for disobedience of orders in permitting a flag to proceed to the Enemy in an irregular manner & contrary to orders, and permitting a civil officer to go on board the enemy not Specified in the permit given by the General. I Have the Honor to be With great respect Yr obt Svt

J H Dent

LS, DNA, RG45, CL, 1813, Vol. 7, No. 124 (M125, Roll No. 32).

1. Thomas H. Jervey had served briefly as a sailing master on the Charleston Station in 1809. On 1 December 1812 he was reappointed to that rank by Secretary Hamilton. He resigned his warrant the following August in order to assume the post of surveyor and inspector of the revenue for the port of Charleston.
2. Words in brackets are supplied from Dent's letter book copy of this letter.

CAPTAIN JOHN H. DENT TO SECRETARY OF THE NAVY JONES

The Honorable William Jones   Charleston.   26th Novr. 1813

Sir

In my letter of the 23rd. inst, I had the honor to report the arrest of Lieut Haddaway, commanding officer of the U.S. Schooner *Nonsuch*. I herewith forward the charge & Specifications.
Charge. Disobedience of Orders.
Specification 1st. In permitting a flag to proceed on the 20th inst to the Enemy, in an irregular manner, and contrary to orders.
Specification 2d. In permitting a civil officer to go on board the enemy not Specified in the flag granted by Major General Pinckney
On a full investigation of the circumstances attending this communication, with the enemy, I am satisfied, Lieut Haddaway was led into this error from the want of Judgement in similar cases, and the manner in which the General gave the permit a copy of which I enclose for your information, Lt. H. is a good officer, and heretofore active and attentive to orders; as a court Martial will be attended with much inconvenience to the Service, on this Station I would beg leave to observe, that a lecture from the department, and a restoration to duty would have the desired effect. I have taken the liberty Sir of suggesting this

method of punishment, and if it does not meet your approbation I beg you will consider it as such. I Have the Honor to be With great respect Your Most Obt Svt

J H Dent

LS, DNA, RG45, CL, 1813, Vol. 7, No. 132 (M125, Roll No. 32).

[Enclosure]
(Copy)
Head Quarters   Charleston.   4th. November 1813.
Sixth District

By. order of Major General Thomas Pinckney Commanding the Sixth Military District. U.S. Mr. Philip Cohen has permission to pass the Military Posts in this harbour, for the purpose of going with a flag of Truce, in the Sloop Pilot boat *Eagle* Clark Master on board the blockading Squadron of his Brittannic Majesty, on private business,
By the General's Command.

(Signed)   James Ferguson
Aid de Camp

Copy, DNA, RG45, CL, 1813, Vol. 7, No. 132, enclosure (M125, Roll No. 32).

[Enclosure]
16th November 1813

The above mentioned Mr. Philip Cohen having Stated that the ransom of the goods for which he had Contracted, has been partly effected, but cannot be finally completed, on account of the smallness of the vessel employed unless he be permitted to go once more on board the enemy's vessels off the bar, he has permission to proceed once more for this purpose but the President's pleasure concerning the mode of Sending Flags having been lately made public, he must conform thereto, by making application to the Commanding officer of the Naval Department that all the requisites in the order from the Secretary of the Navy may be complied with, By the General's Command.

(Signed)   James Ferguson
Aid de Camp

Copy, DNA, RG45, CL, 1813, Vol. 7, No. 132, enclosure (M125, Roll No. 32).

SECRETARY OF THE NAVY JONES TO ACTING LIEUTENANT EDWARD H. HADDAWAY

Lieut. Edward Hadaway,   Navy Department
U.S. Navy,   Decr. 6th 1813.
Charleston S.C.

Sir,
   Captain Dent has reported to this Department your arrest, with the charges and Specifications; but, at the same time, with great liberality represented the

general good conduct and correctness, which have hitherto distinguished you as an Officer, and attributes your error, on that occasion, to a defect of judgement.

The charge of disobedience of Orders, a charge of a most serious nature indeed, appears to be established on the face of the transaction, and were it not for the extenuating circumstances, and the liberality of the Commanding Officer, must have been brought to a serious issue. It is, therefore, expected that you will see the matter in its proper light, and carefully avoid committing yourself in future.

With these considerations, the Arrest is removed, and you are, again, ordered on duty. I am, respectfully, Yours, &c.

W. Jones.

LB Copy, DNA, RG45, SNL, Vol. 11, p. 160 (M149, Roll No. 11).

Court-Martial of Sailing Master William Harper [1]

No greater stigma could attach to a naval officer's reputation than to stand accused of cowardice in battle.[2] Six days following the capture of H.M. brig Boxer, Enterprise's *sailing master, William Harper, was arrested on just such a charge. For nearly three months, Harper waited for the Navy Department to act on his case, all the while enduring the gibes of his Portland neighbors and fellow shipmates. In early December, unable to bear his uncertain status any longer, the sailing master penned an appeal to William Jones, entreating the naval secretary for an opportunity to clear his name at a court-martial. Harper's letter reveals the mental anguish of a naval officer whose courage has been called into question. Secretary Jones's response illustrates the gravity with which the department viewed charges of cowardice.*

1. *William Harper was warranted a sailing master on 23 January 1809. In August 1813, he was transferred from the gunboat service at Portland to* Enterprise.

2. *During the War of 1812, four officers were court-martialed for cowardice: Lieutenant William S. Cox and Midshipman James Forrest of* Chesapeake, *Acting Lieutenant John T. Drury of Sackets Harbor and Sailing Master William Harper of* Enterprise. *A fifth officer, Master Commandant Samuel Angus, was acquitted of cowardice by a court of inquiry investigating the loss of Gunboat No. 121. For an insightful essay that addresses the issue of cowardice in combat, see Valle, "Navy's Battle Doctrine."*

SAILING MASTER WILLIAM HARPER TO SECRETARY OF THE NAVY JONES

Hon Secretary of the Navy—   Portland   Decr. 5th 1813

Having been arrested on the 11th day of September last past on a (1) complaint exhibited against me by Lieut Ed. R. McCall a transcript of which is subjoined, by Commodore Isaac Hull. With anxious solicitude I have desired & expected that a court Martial might be convened for my Trial, that I might ~~have~~ be indulged with an opportunety of vindicating my conduct, & defending & preserving my character. My feelings and my principles have impelled me to urge proceedings in my case, by frequent applications to Com. Hull. His (2) Letter a copy of which is annexed enclosed, refers to expected instructions concerning the Business from the Navy Department. Permit me Sir, to State to the chief of that Department whose respectabetely & interests are Identifyed with mine—I have Friends & connections whose sympathy & pride are allied to my Fame & Fortunes— I have feelings that cannot basely yeild to indignities, & I have rights that I cannot relinquish, but with, Life— By my Arrest I am reduced to a most mortifying & humiliating condition— I am set up as a Land mark for the direction of the glances of distrust & observations & remarks of levity & Malice. An officers honour, Sir, is his conscience. I need not say how much I am compelled to feell injured by groundless accusations, how earnestly I desire an investigation of my official conduct—& how confidently I believe that the direction of the Navy Department would prevent delay of Justice, even if I were singular & absolutely & entirely alone in my concerns respecting this subject—

But the claims of my Family for my personal exertions for provision for their maintenance when I am civilly paralized by this arrest, the demands of my Friends for exculpation from Blame & reproach, when I cannot obtain the means of Publick justification, the anxiety of myself, that I may stand erect in society, when I am virtually bound down with fetters constrain me most urgently to solicit immediate Trial. Other considerations of equal concern to the Govt., the accused & the accusor are additional motives to a speedy trial of this case, Witnesses, those persons who observed every transaction & occurance on board the U.S. Brig *Enterprise* in the action with his Brh. Majs. Brig *Boxer* may be dispersed & I may be deprived of the means of procuring & producing the evidence on which I rely for my Justification, & the U.S. may also by the disposition of the Officers and crew of the *Enterprise* be subjected to great expence in the production of the witnesses in support of the complaint made in its behalf against me, It is with the utmost reliance on the just & equitable & prudent disposition of the Honourable secy. of the Navy that I make this application, & beg leave to solicit immediate orders for the constitution of a Court to try me on the complaint prefered against— Sir, Most respectfully Your Obt. Servant

William Harper
Sailing Master U.S. Navy.

ALS, DNA, RG45, CL, 1813, Vol. 8, No. 16 1/2, enclosure (M125, Roll No. 33).

[Enclosure]

(No. 1)   The charge Exhibited against you is cowardice and the Specifications a follows—
Specification 1st
   In as much as he left his Station in the early part of the Engagement between the U.S. Brig *Enterprize* & the British Brig *Boxer* & endeavoured to screen himself from the Shott of the Enemy by getting behind the Foremast & under the heel of the Bowsprit while the Enemy lay under on our quarter by doing which he set an example to the crew of the *Enterprise* that might have led to her surrender and disgrace to the american character—

Specification 2d.

For having advised me to hawl down the colours at a time when the firing from the Enemy was much diminished and ours could be kept up with unabted effect—

Signed   E. R. McCall
Lieut   U.S. Brig *Enterprize*

Copy, DNA, RG45, CL, 1813, Vol. 8, No. 16 1/2, enclosure (M125, Roll No. 33).

[Enclosure]
(2)   Navy Yard Portsmouth
                                                5th Nov. 1813—

Sir,

I some days since received your letter and should have answered it immediately, had I not been in hourly expectation of hearing from the Department relative to your situation. About three weeks since I received a letter [1] from the Department saying that your case would be attended to immediately, but have not heard from there Since— I am Sir, Your Obet. Servant

Isaac Hull

Mr. William Harper
Portland

LS, DNA, RG45, CL, 1813, Vol. 7, No. 80 (M125, Roll No. 32). This enclosure became separated from Harper's cover letter and was inadvertently bound with a different volume of the Captains' Letters.

1. See Jones to Hull, 9 Oct. 1813, DNA, RG45, CNA, Vol. 1, p. 521 (M441, Roll No. 1).

SECRETARY OF THE NAVY JONES TO CAPTAIN ISAAC HULL

Captain Isaac Hull   Navy Department
U.S. Navy.   Portsmouth. N.H.   Decr. 13th 1813.

Sir,

Enclosed is the order of this Department, directing you to convene a Court Martial, for the trial of Sailing Master Harper, which you will convene with the least possible delay.[1]

It is presumed that the testimony of Lt. McCall can be dispensed with, as the crime, if committed, must have been witnessed by the Officers and Crew generally, the greater part of whom are still on board the *Enterprize*, and Lieut. Tillinghast can readily attend, being at Newburyport, attached to the U.S. Ship *Wasp*.

The presence of Lieut. McCall would be attended with serious inconvenience to the service, and to him, as he would have to travel, nearly one thousand miles by land at this inclement season, in order to return to his station, where his services are indispensable.

I should have followed the course suggested and dismissed Mr. Harper, upon the presumption that there is, at least, evidence sufficient to justify suspicion, which of itself is sufficient, when the charge involves the vital principle, which is paramount to every other requisite in the character of an Officer; but Mr.

Harper has written in a strain of wounded sensibility, demanding a speedy trial, to save him from ruin and disgrace, and his connexions from the deepest humiliation. It is a crime of all others which ought not to pass with impunity.

If he is guilty, let him meet the ignominious punishment which awaits him—if innocent, it is just that that innocence should be proclaimed.[2] I am, very respectfully, Your Obedient Servt.

W. Jones.

LB Copy, DNA, RG45, SNL, Vol. 11, pp. 168–69 (M149, Roll No. 11).

1. Harper's court-martial convened at Portsmouth on board *Enterprise* on 28 December. Because of a number of procedural delays, a verdict was not reached until 22 January 1814, when the court found Harper not guilty. The newly acquitted sailing master returned to duty in the gunboat service at Portland where he remained another five months before resigning. For the record of Harper's court-martial, see DNA, RG125, CM, Vol. 4, No. 156 (M273, Roll No. 4). A printed version of this court-martial appears in Picking, Enterprise *and* Boxer, pp. 133–76.
2. The penalty for any officer found guilty of cowardice was death or such punishment as a court-martial should decide to impose.

A Plan to Render *Constitution*'s Gunfire More Deadly

On 9 September, Secretary Jones ordered Captain Charles Stewart on a cruise in Constitution.[1] *Although Stewart had completed preparations for his voyage by month's end, unfavorable weather and the British blockade prevented him from putting to sea until the last day of the year. Shortly before his departure, Captain Stewart submitted a plan to the department that he believed would improve* Constitution *'s chances of successfully surviving encounters with enemy vessels of superior force.*

1. See Jones to Stewart, 19 Sept. 1813, DNA, RG45, CLS, 1813, pp. 66–69.

Captain Charles Stewart to Secretary of the Navy Jones

Boston   Decbr. 5th. 1813

Sir

I have constructed a portable Sheet iron furnace for heating <u>red-hot shot</u> of the following dimentions which would answer, as well for land service as sea service—Lenth 3 feet depth 3 feet width 18 inches, it heats red 21 shot 24 lbs. in 20 minuets, with a pine wood fire, the construction of the pipes is such as gives it a great drauft. from its dimentions you can readily conceive it occupies but little room, and is calculated to set to the back part of our Galley where it interfers with nothing— My purpose is only to use it against the enemies ships of such force as would render our safety precarious, (if we cannot otherwise escape,) by bringing them under our stern battery, and firing a few red-hot ball in their hull, They are not verry expensive, and I should recomend all our frigates haveing them, the use of which might facilitate their escape from a superior force, by the confusion they would be thrown into, if not the destruction of ~~the~~ an enemy that is not disposed to contend with us on fair and eaqual terms, I have the honor to be verry Respetfy. Sir your Obedt. Servt.

Chs. Stewart

ALS, DNA, RG45, CL, 1813, Vol. 8, No. 17 (M125, Roll No. 33).

SECRETARY OF THE NAVY JONES TO CAPTAIN CHARLES STEWART

Charles Stewart Esqr.   Navy Department
Comg. U.S. Frigate *Constitution,*   Decr. 14th 1813.
Boston.

Sir,
    I have Received your letter of the 5th. Instant, relative to the construction of a Furnace for heating Shot.
    I shall be pleased to have a drawing and description of the Furnace. I am, respectfully, Your Obedient Servt.

                                            W. Jones.

LB Copy, DNA, RG45, SNL, Vol. 11, p. 171 (M149, Roll No. 11).

CAPTAIN CHARLES STEWART TO SECRETARY OF THE NAVY JONES

                               Boston   Decbr. 25th. 1813
Sir
    Herewith you will receive a model of of the Furnace for heating red-hot shot The parts of Tin are to be made of thick sheat-iron rivited together as the dots represent, the grates of strong bar-iron which is represented by wood, the pan of tin goes under to receive the ashes and coals that fall, the construction of the drauft pipe is the most important,
    This model is made on a scale of one and a half inches to the foot and represents exactly the one mad for the Ship The shot is placed on the upper grate and the fire wood on the lower, they are verry portable and would answer for stationary or floating batteries, also for Gun boats, The season has been so uncomonly mild that I have not yet been able to make my escape from the force that is watching us, but I hope a few day will bring us a nort easterly wind and enable us to do so without much risque of meeting them, On Sunday last the Raza [1] and *Junon* Frigate was off Cape Ann, and under Cape Cod a 74 gun ship and two Frigates were at anchor, with two or three Brigs of war cruiseing betwene the capes. I have the honor to be verry Respectfuly Sir Your Most Obdt. Svt.

                                       Chas. Stewart

ALS, DNA, RG45, CL, 1813, Vol. 8, No. 106 (M125, Roll No. 33).

    1. A razee, a ship of the line that has been converted to a lower rate by having one of its decks removed. The *Majestic,* which had been razeed from a 74-gun to a 58-gun ship, was stationed off Boston Harbor in late 1813.

Cruising Orders for *Siren, Enterprise,* and *Rattlesnake*

In December, William Jones issued cruising orders for the brigs Siren, Enterprise, *and* Rattlesnake. *The emphatic wording of these instructions illustrates the secretary's firm conviction that the navy must wage war against Great Britain's commerce, not her battle fleet.*

SECRETARY OF THE NAVY JONES TO
MASTER COMMANDANT GEORGE PARKER

George Parker Esqr.   Navy Department
Master Comt. U S Navy   December 8th. 1813.
Commanding Brig *Siren*
Boston Harbour

Sir

As the *Siren* has long since been in perfect readiness for Sea, except her armament, which must ere this, have arrived, and trusting that the delay has afforded you a favorable Opportunity to practice & reduce your Crew to perfect order and discipline; You will take the earliest opportunity which a favorable Wind and the absence, or leward position of the enemy may afford, to run off the Coast and cross the Gulph Stream to the South East: thence in a direct course for the vicinity of Madeira, thence to the Southward, passing through the Canaries to Cape Blanco and along the Coast of Africa, running down the South Coast to the Gulph of Guinea and Isle of St. Thomas, looking into the principal Harbours; thence to the Southward, passing the Cape of Good Hope and running so far to the Eastward as to gain the Island of Rodrigues, where it will be proper to cruise for a convenient length of time, for the purpose of intercepting the trade between the Ports of India and the Isle of France and Bourbon, the Cape of Good Hope and the homeward bound trade.—

Whether this shall be the remotest point of your Cruise, must depend upon your success and resources at the time you are about to depart from that station; but, it is presumed, you will have had an opportunity, in the course of the preceding part of your route, to replenish your Water, and, in all probability provisions, from the prizes you may have made, as vast quantities of rice are brought from Bengal to the Isle of france, and Salt Provisions from Europe to the Cape of Good Hope Isles of France, Java, and other eastern possessions.— Your own observations must have proved to you how precarious & uncertain is the prospect of getting prizes into a friendly port, and that the manning of a few prizes will soon terminate your Cruise and diminish your force so as to jeopardise the safety of the *Siren* and your own reputation by a chance conflict with an Enemy nominally your equal, but fully manned. With every patriotic Officer, private motives will yield to considerations of public good, and as the great object and end of our public force is to harass and distress the enemy, and as the most effectual annoyance is the destruction of his trade and Commerce, it ought to be the ruling principle of Action with every Commander.

A Single Cruiser, if ever so successful, can man but a few prizes, and every prize is a serious diminution of her force; but a Single Cruiser, destroying every captured Vessel, has the capacity of continuing in full vigour her destructive power, so long as her provisions and stores can be replenished, either from friendly ports, or from the Vessels Captured.— Thus has a Single Cruiser, upon the destructive plan, the power perhaps, of twenty acting upon pecuniary views alone; and thus may the employment of our small force, in some degree compensate for the great inequality compared with that of the Enemy. Considered even in a pecuniary view, the chances of safe arrival of the Prize are so few, and of recapture by the enemy so many, that motives of interest alone are sufficient; but when we consider that it is in all probability, consigning the prize Crew to a loathsome prison in the hands of a perfidious and cruel Enemy, every just motive will combine to urge the destruction, rather than the manning of every prize.—

The American People and Government have given abundant proof that they are deficient neither in gratitude nor generosity.— I therefore strenuously urge and order the destruction of every captured Vessel and Cargo, unless so near to a friendly port as to leave little doubt of safe arrival, or that the merchandize shall be so valuable and compact as to admit of transhipment without injury to the Vessel under your Command, or to the public Service.—

When Circumstances shall indicate the expediency of leaving the station off Isle Rodrigues, either from a failure of success, or want of supplies your subsequent route must depend upon the state of your provisions and stores, and the prospect of replenishing them on the route you may take.— If your provisions are sufficient to enable you to reach the Coast of Chili, the run is not very long, and Captain Porter has found means to procure provisions at Valparazo.— In pursuing this route you will run from the Isle Rodrigues for the Isles of St. Paul and Amsterdam, thence gradually into a higher Southern Latitude, until you fall into the track of Captain Cook to the Southward of New Holland in a direction for Cape Horn, and in this course, with the strong and constant South West Gales, you will soon run down your easting, & edge away for the Coast of Chili, where the information you may receive of the Enemy's force will determine you whether to run to the northward, along the Coast of Peru, Guiaquil and Calafornia, to the mouth of Columbia River, or to return home round Cape Horn, keeping clear of the east Coast of Brazil (which is well watched) down the north Coast of Brazil and Guiana, and through the West India Islands to St Mary's in Georgia, where you will first touch for information.— If a view of your resources off Isle Rodrigues shall forbid the eastern route, you will then follow the track of the British trade from India & the Isle of France home, keeping about fourty Leagues South of Madagascar, when on its Meridian; then for the South East Coast of Africa, round the Bank of Augullas and Cape of Good Hope, in the track for St Helena and Ascension, thence down the north Coast of South America through the Islands and home, as before described.— On your outward Cruise your means of annoyance to the trade of the Enemy on the Coast of Africa will be very great.— He is there in fancied security, pursuing a lucrative trade, without protection.— The return Cargoes from that Coast are extremely valuable; Consisting of Elephants teeth, Gums, rich Woods and Gold Dust. Most of the harbours where this trade is carried on, will admit the *Siren*, and here you will replenish your water and obtain refreshments of fruits and roots, particularly yams, which are an inestimable article: the Vessels you may capture will also furnish you with European supplies.— In your route for the Southern Ocean, if you touch at the Isle Tristian de Cunha, you will procure water, vegitables and live Stock, and under all circumstances, policy will lead you to pass for a British Cruiser.— The cruel policy of the Enemy towards our Captured Countrymen, renders it very important to increase the number of prisoners in our hands, in order to counteract his measures; and whenever it can be done with safety, you will avoid liberating them on parole, or granting them Cartels, which he utterly disregards. In all cases it will be proper so to dispose of those you can not land in the United States, as to deprive him of their services as long as possible, by landing them in remote situations, without the means of speedily joining his Arms; but always with due regard to the dictates of humanity and the means of sustenance. Prisoners landed in France, or in any Country in hostility with Great Britain, will be subject to regular exchange for an equal number of our Countrymen.— You will on no account ransom any prize you may take.— The practice is strictly prohibited by a Statute of Great Britain, and therefore all ransoms of British Vessels are void.—

You are also strictly prohibited from giving or receiving a Challenge, to, or from, an Enemy's Vessel.— The Character of the American Navy does not require those feats of Chivalry. and your own reputation is too well established, to need factitious support Whenever you meet an equal Enemy, under fair Circumstances, I am sure, you will beat him; but it is not even good policy to meet an equal, unless, under special circumstances, where a great object is to be gained, without a great sacrifice.— His Commerce is our true Game, for there he is indeed vulnerable.— I am respectfully Your Obedt. Servt.

W Jones.

LB Copy, DNA, RG45, CLS, 1813, pp. 81–84.

SECRETARY OF THE NAVY JONES TO
MASTER COMMANDANT JOHN O. CREIGHTON [1]

John Orde Creighton Esqr.   Navy Department
Master Commandt. U S Navy   Decmr. 22d. 1813.—
Commanding US Brig *Rattlesnake,*

Sir

When the United States Brigs *Rattlesnake* & *Enterprize* under your command, are in an efficient state of preparation for a Cruise, you will proceed to Sea, and, passing to the eastward of Bermuda in such track as will be most likely to avoid the Enemy's heavy Cruisers, Shape a Course for the Island of Anagada; thence by St. Thomas', down the north sides of Porto Rico, St. Domingo & Jamaica, round the west end of Cuba through the Florida passage to Wilmington NC. There report the events of your Cruize and the State and condition of your Vessels to this Department, and await its further orders.—

In this route you will pass in the track of the trade of the British Virgin Islands and of the Jamaica fleets, homeward bound; and it will be well to cruise two or three weeks about the double headed Shot and Cat Key, on the edge of the Bahama Banks, on which you can retire with your own Vessels and prizes from the heavy Cruisers of the Enemy, should they appear.

The design of attaching the *Enterprize* to your Command, is to render you superior to any one of the Enemy's heavy Brigs of War, which are more numerous than any other of his Cruisers in those Seas. You will therefore, be careful not to seperate, and as either of the Brigs under your Command will be superior to any British Letter of Marque, should you fall in with a West India fleet you may together destroy a great number, and send in some of the most valuable, provided you are not distant from the Ports of Georgia, South and North Carolina.—

The Port of Charleston may, probably, be watched by a superior force, during the winter, and such prizes as you may determine to send in, had better run for the Ports of Georgia and North Carolina, particularly the latter if their draught of water will admit.— The great object however, is the destruction of the Commerce of the Enemy and bringing into Port the Prisoners, in order to exchange against our unfortunate Countrymen who may fall into his hands. You will therefore man no prize, unless the value, place of capture and other favorable circumstances, shall render her safe arrival morally certain. As the ransoming of british Vessels is prohibited by a statute and the Ransom bonds declared void, you will not agree to the ransoming of any prize.— The enemy has also, in violation of his own agreement and of good faith, refused to recognize Cartels granted at Sea: you will therefore, grant no Cartel nor liberate any prisoners, unless under circumstances of extreme and unavoidable necessity.— The Character of the American Navy stands upon a basis not to be shaken, and needs no sacrifices by unequal conflict to sustain its reputation. You will therefore avoid all unnecessary contact with the Cruisers of the Enemy. even with an equal, unless under circumstances that may ensure your triumph, without defeating the main object of your Cruise, or jeopardising the safety of the Vessels under your Command.—

Be assured Sir, that the confidence of our Country cannot be enhanced by any new achievements of our gallant Navy;— it is now entire and the services of an Officer will now be estimated by the extent of the injury he may inflict upon the vital interest of the enemy in the destruction of his Commerce.— You will please acknowledge the receipt of this Letter, of which you will furnish a Copy to Lieutenant Commt. Renshaw, and appoint a place of Rendezvous in case of unavoidable seperation.— wishing you a prosperous and honourable Cruise—I am very respectfully—Your Ob Servant

W. Jones—

LB Copy, DNA, RG45, CLS, 1813, pp. 85–86.

1. Creighton was promoted to master commandant on 24 July 1813.

Shipboard Hygiene

Within the wooden world of an American man-of-war, a strict regard for cleanliness was one of the first priorities of a commanding officer.[1] Aside from the obvious health benefits it conferred, proper sanitation promoted morale and discipline among a ship's company. To this end, captains of naval vessels established regulations requiring their crews to maintain a clean shipboard environment and to give regular attention to their own personal hygiene.[2] How the captain of the U.S. brig Rattlesnake dealt with a particularly egregious breach of these rules by one of his own officers is illustrated in the documents below.

1. *In his semiautobiographical novel* White Jacket, *detailing life aboard an American warship in the 1840s, Herman Melville writes, "Of all men-of-war, the American ships are the most excessively neat, and have the greatest reputation for it." Although penned more than thirty years after the War of 1812, Melville's comments seem apropos the navy of the early republic, for both of the captains he served under, James Armstrong and Cornelius K. Stribling, were veterans of the War of 1812. See Melville, White Jacket, p. 107.*

2. *For an example of such regulations, see pp. 616–21. For departmental regulations outlining the duties of captains in this regard, see Barbary Powers, Vol. 2, p. 33, no. 52.*

CAPTAIN ISAAC HULL TO SECRETARY OF THE NAVY JONES

U.S. Navy Yard
Portsmo. N.H.   10th Decr. 1813

Sir,

I have this day been informed by Captain Creighton of the *Rattlesnake* that the Surgeon of that Vessel has neglected his dress and person to such a degree that his body is filled with Vermin and on searching his bedding, it was found that that was in the same state, consequently no Officer can think of messing or associating with him, nor is it very honourable to the service that a man so lost to all sense of feeling should be permitted to remain in it.

A written report from Captain Creighton will be forwarded. I have the honour to be With great Respect Sir Your Obedt. Servant.

Isaac Hull

LS, DNA, RG45, CL, 1813, Vol. 8, No. 34 (M125, Roll No. 33).

[Enclosure]

U.S Brig *Rattle Snake*
Decr: 10th: 1813

sir

I am under the necessity of reporting to You one of the most Extraordinary cases of uncleanliness that I ever heard of in an officer during fourteen Years that I have served in the navy—

It has been reported to me, and has become public, that the acting surgeon (D: Yeates)[1] of the *Rattle Snake* is covered with Vermin, and by sending his clothes on shore to wash, has nearly fill'd a whole Neighbourhood with the same— I am Mortified beyond expression and have to request that the said D: Yeates may be removed from under my Command, as I cannot consent to his Messing with the other officers of the Brig or of myself serving with a man of his discreption. Very respectly. Your Obedt: St.

Jno. Orde Creighton
Commander

Isaac Hull Esqr:
Comg. Naval Officer
Portsmouth

ALS, DNA, RG45, CL, 1813, Vol. 8, No. 35 (M125, Roll No. 33).

1. Donaldson Yeates received his M.D. from the University of Pennsylvania in 1810. On 14 May 1812 he was commissioned a surgeon's mate and was ordered to join *Constitution*. He served on the frigate until October 1813 when he was transferred to the brig *Rattlesnake*. Yeates's uncleanliness no doubt was owing to his reduced state of health at this time. On 10 November he had solicited a furlough from Jones, citing his "absolute inability from Sickness & disease" to carry out his duties. See Yeates to Jones, 10 Nov. 1813, DNA, RG45, BC, 1813, Vol. 4, No. 92 (M148, Roll No. 12). Secretary Jones never responded to this letter.

[Enclosure]

U Brig *Rattlesnake*   Decembr. the 12 1813

Dear Sir

Heaven Can bear me witness how deep and heartfelt is my mortification and Chagrin, how agonizing my sensations, whilst I am now writing you. Excuse me

Sir, in imposing on your attention and time and permit me briefly to represent to you my Situation. You will I have no doubt dispassionately consider my claims. Capt. Creighton upon my requesting permission to visit the Town this day "replied" yes sir you may go ashore and Stay aShore—but as I retired, no Said he, Stay where you are and await 'till you hear from the Secretary" by which I presume he has exhibited to you Charges against me & petitiond. for my removal from office. I also presume you are acquaint with their nature— Should I not be too prolix, tedious and uninteresting to you, I think I could give some Cogent reasons, why Such an accident or misfortune has befallen me, and might happen to any one in, my Situation under Similar Circumstances. But waving all extenuation, nor presuming to exculpate myself I have only to say that a brother and Sister only are left to me of a family which never Knew disgrace, how inadequately then can I represent to you my situation and feelings, if Compelled to return to them, Covered with dishonor Casting a Stigma on their names and Sullying the bright inheritance of my forefathers. By their influence in part, I was placed here, and it has ever been my exultation and pride to retain my Situation and discharge its duties. I am not independent of the Navy, of the pecuniary emolument resulting from my pay. If dismissed, irrevocably lost, to my Country and my friends, I can never exercise my profession profession with advantage or Composure. Friendless and alone I must descend to more menial employments and associates. I conjure you therefore by an appeal to the best feelings of your nature, by the generosity of your heart & the finer and more Compassionate movements of your breast; not to discard me, but retain and allow me the privelege of retrieving and reestablishing my Credit and fame. It will imprint my heart with indelible gratitude and the Keen recollection of what I now Suffer, will forever prevent the recurrence of a Similar misfortune   With great consideration and respect Your Hbl. Servt.

Donaldson Yeates
<u>Surgeon</u>

I will Solicit the friendly interposition of Comdre. Wm. Bainbridge and of Come. Hull as I have Saild. with them both Since the War

D Yeates

ALS, DNA, RG45, CL, 1813, Vol. 8, No. 34, enclosure (M125, Roll No. 33). This letter was addressed to "The Honble. William Jones, Secretary of the Navy, Washington City."

SECRETARY OF THE NAVY JONES TO CAPTAIN ISAAC HULL

[Extract]
Captain Isaac Hull   Navy Department
Comg. Naval Officer,   Decr. 22nd. 1813.
Portsmouth N.H.

Sir,
. . . . I have received a letter from Doctor Yeates, couched in terms of such good sense and extreme sensibility, that, although my disgust and consequent determination had been previously formed, I am disposed to forgive the foul neglect,

and ask your indulgence and kind Offices for him, if you think it possible to reconcile the Officers of the *Rattlesnake* to him; but if not, you will order the best Surgeon's Mate from the *Congress* to join the *Rattlesnake*. If the Officers cannot forgive and forget the offence of Doctor Yeates, he had better resign, for the disgrace will follow him through the Service; but, if their magnanimity can overlook the fault, he may be restored, and, I am willing to believe, he would merit their generosity.[1] I am, very respectfully, Your Obedient Servant,

W. Jones

LB Copy, DNA, RG45, SNL, Vol. 11, p. 179 (M149, Roll No. 11).

1. Hull wrote Secretary Jones that the officers of *Rattlesnake* were "willing to receive . . . [Yeates] again into their mess," but the surgeon's continued poor health precluded it. See Hull to Jones, 1 Jan. 1814, DNA, RG45, CL, 1814, Vol. 1, No. 5, (M125, Roll No. 35). Yeates was later ordered to Sackets Harbor where health problems continued to bedevil him. His condition became so critical that his commanding officer granted him a furlough to return home to Maryland where he died on 28 October 1815.

Return of the U.S. Frigate *Congress*

In mid-December, the frigate Congress *put into Portsmouth Harbor, completing the second-longest cruise made by an American vessel during the war. Remarkably, during the nearly eight months that she was at sea,* Congress *captured only four prizes, making her cruise, in terms of time and resources spent, the least profitable of the entire war. Although Secretary Jones declared his desire to see* Congress *readied for another cruise as soon as possible,[1] the extensive damage the frigate had sustained during her long voyage precluded such action. In fact,* Congress *was found to be in such a state of decay after her return that it was deemed too costly to restore her to seaworthiness; consequently, her guns were removed and she was laid up for the rest of the war.*

1. See Secretary Jones's letter to Congress's *commander, Captain John Smith, 5 Jan. 1814, DNA, RG45, SNL., Vol. 11, pp. 184–85 (M149, Roll No. 11).*

CAPTAIN JOHN SMITH TO SECRETARY OF THE NAVY JONES

Hon. William Jones　　　　　　　　　　　　　　　　U.S. Frigate *Congress.*
　　　　　　　　　　Portsmouth Harbour　　December 14th 1813
　Sir
　I have the honor to communicate to you the arrival at this anchorage, of the U.S. Frigate *Congress* under my command, whose daily situation during the Cruize, I take the liberty of laying before you, in the abstract from the Ships Log, which accompanies this; In which there is accounted for, all vessels which were seen by us, from the period of our seperation from the *President*, untill our arrival at this place, with the exception of one Brig, which twice escaped, under the favor of dark nights; and whose great distance only enabled me to conjecture her to be an American Privateer—

The expiration of the term of Service, of the greater part of the crew, of the *Congress,* I am concern'd to advise you of; They have nevertheless for some months, been serving under those circumstances, with the Same zeal, and activity, I have always found them eminent for; Your sanction for their discharge, and order, to replace their number, I shall be thankful for.

The early departure of the mail, will deny me the opportunity of communicating to you the exact state and condition of the Ship, which shall be rendered the instant its extent can be enquired into; I am however apprehensive from the length of time her hold has been stow'd, that a great part of her ceiling may prove decay'd, that her Bowsprit must be taken to pieces, and the Coaging [1] repaired, the Ship to be thoroughly caulk'd, and the greater part of the lower Rigging renew'd— I have the honor to be with all respect Your Obt. Hbl Servt.

John Smith

LS, DNA, RG45, CL, 1813, Vol. 8, No. 49 (M125, Roll No. 33).

1. Probably coaking, a method of joining spars together.

CAPTAIN JOHN SMITH TO SECRETARY OF THE NAVY JONES

Hon. William Jones   U.S. Ship *Congress*
                                       Portsmouth N.H.   December 31st 1813

Sir

I have the honor to inform you that the *Congress,* did not get to her moorings at the Navy Yard at this place, until the 28th. inst. in consequence of contrary winds— The contiguity of the outer harbour to the Sea, forbid my dismantling the Ship preparatory to her refit. as it was both desirable & proper that She Should remain prepard. to interfere with the curiosity of any equal or inferior force of the enemy, which might have appeared in the neighborhood—

The great Severity of the weather must retard much our equipment, which we are anxiously, and industriously, engaged in—

The few men which the discharge of those whose times have expired will leave on board, cannot prepare the Ship for Sea, with the despatch desired; but I am sanguine that the Embargo may facilitate the entering of Seamen, which the different recruiting officers, have found very difficult—

I shall be enabled to acquaint you on monday whether it is necessary to renew or reprepare the Bowsprit— I have the pleasure to be With all respect Your Obt. & Hbl. Sevt.

John Smith

P.S. I have the honor to advise you of the Safe arrival at Boston of the British Brig *Atlantic* captured by the *Congress* on the 5th of December last— She is the Second valuable prize, which the perseverance, & skill, of Midshipman Robert M Rose, have preserved for us this war—

J. Smith

LS, DNA, RG45, CL, 1813, Vol. 8, No. 122 (M125, Roll No. 33).

Personnel Problems at St. Marys Station

Perhaps no station commander experienced greater difficulties in controlling his junior officers than Commodore Hugh G. Campbell. In 1813, four officers under Campbell's command were dismissed for gross misconduct.[1] The problem of ill discipline at St. Marys reflected the onerous nature of gunboat station service itself, a service in which commanders like Campbell found many impediments to the maintenance of strict discipline: inactivity, an enervating climate, and a dearth of good officers.[2]

1. *Lieutenant Charles Grandison, Midshipmen Andrew Pentland and James Vasse, and Sailing Master Robert Cutchin.*

2. *Campbell's efforts to maintain discipline may have been hampered by his own poor health. See Campbell's letter of 28 November to Secretary Jones in which the fifty-three-year-old captain declined command of a cruising vessel because of a debilitating old injury. Campbell to Jones, 28 Nov. 1813, DNA, RG45, CL, 1813, Vol. 7, No. 137 (M125, Roll No. 32).*

COMMODORE HUGH G. CAMPBELL TO SECRETARY OF THE NAVY JONES

St Mary's   18th Decr. 1813

Sir

Herewith I have the honor to enclose charges against Mr. Winslow Foster,[1] Sailing Master— I have the honor to be With Great Respect Sir Your obedient servant

Hugh G Campbell

LS, DNA, RG45, CL, 1813, Vol. 8, No. 71 (M125, Roll No. 33).

1. Winslow Foster was warranted a sailing master on 10 March 1811.

[Enclosure]

St Marys   Novr. 12th 1813

Sir

The improper conduct of Mr. Winslow Foster, as far as came within my observation, subsequently to the 5th of August last, has been as follows

While laying at the Cockspur in the savannah as a part of the convoy to the Transports bound to Beaufort, on the 24th August he took one of his boats and went up to Savanah for the purpose as he said to me of getting a further supply of bread (being nearly out) and was absent from the Vessel two Nights in Succession, during his absence a gale of wind came on which drove two of the Transports on shore   no detention was however occasioned by his absence as we remained there two days after his return getting ~~getting~~ off the Transports— The next improper conduct that I saw of his, was at this place, he came into Mr. Rothwells Lodgings at a late hour of the night on or about the 26th Sept. he appeared to be under the influence of Liquor and in a conversation directed principally to Messer. Paine & Rothwell he made use of Language highly derogatary to the character of an officer, on this occasion he subjected himself In my opinion to the Charges of Drunkeness improper language and unofficer like conduct— on the Night of the Illumination at this place 5th october in celebrating the Naval victory on lake Erie—he got very drunk and was quarreling and fighting with several persons, and finally he brought some of his men on shore to stand by him   I did not however see any of them armed, and when Mr. Trevett and myself ordered them off they complyed with the order— he appeared to be particularly anxious to get hold of a Man by the name of Amos who he said had struck him on the head with a stick and would have succeeded, had he not been prevented by some of the persons present, on hearing afterwards that this Amos had been taken to prison by the Civil authority. he run out in the street and endeavored to prevail on the Mob (if I may so express it, there being a great many people of various description ~~condition~~ collected) to accompany him to the Goal for the purpose of breaking it open to come at this Man but finding he was not followed by but few, he returned

After having said this much of Mr. Foster I hope I may be permited to declare in Justice to him that I never saw him act improperly on board his vessel but on the Contrary he always appeared active in the discharge of his duty and kept his vessel in good order and his men in a high state of discipline— he certainly is a good Seaman and Navigator, and was it not for the emproper use he occasionly makes of Liquor he would in my opinion be a valuable Officer I have the Honor to be very Respectfully Sir Your Obt. Servant

John R Grayson

Commodore Hugh G. Campbell

ALS, DNA, RG45, CL, 1813, Vol. 8, No. 71, enclosure (M125, Roll No. 33).

[Enclosure]

St Marys   Novemb 11th 1813

Sir

In reply to your order of to day I have to state, that painfull is the task to say any thing derogatory to the Carracter of an Officer, particularly to speak of an occurrence at My House, his conduct towards me, & When I did not feel it my duty to report personal abuse, alltho it was blended with general. impropriety, I shall therefore give a plain detail of Mr. Winslow Fosters conduct, in my House, toward mid Belt & my self, & other Officers—

On the evening of the 5th of Octbr last, after the Illumination in Honor of the Gallant Perrys victory on the Lakes, I with Mr. John R Grayson, repaired to my House & I immediately retird to Bed, several Officers & Gentm. soon after Came in among the Number Mr. Foster & Mids. Belt who had the Day or two before arrivd from New Providence. Conviviality was apparent in every Countinance, but that of Mr. Fosters, who made a wanton attack upon Mids. Belt for what cause I do not Know neither was there any alleg'd— he Call'd him a Contaminated Officer, & threatened to take his side arms from him & used the vilest language, unwarranted by any Conduct of Mr. Belts, that came under my Knowledge, previous or after— such conduct induce'd me to get out of Bed, & solicit Mr. Foster to use better language & not quarrel or <u>leave</u> my House, the request produs'd a torrent of abuse, indeckerous Language & an assail of my Carracter, his epithits were frequent & too redickalous to insert—

He afterwards left the Room & was absent some time, during his absence Mr. Grayson (then lodging in my House) return to Bed, he returnd & came violently into my Bed Room Accompany'd by a number of his Sailors as far as the Door, using those words, Stand by me Boys, or words to that import— I remaind in Bed at the Solicitation of Mr G and Mr. Trevett who I requested to clear the yard of the men which they did, by ordering them out; that was warmly oppos'd by Mr. Foster, he alledging that the Govm't paid my House Rent & he would bring as many men in It as he pleasd— he then attackd Mr Trevett with all the venom & opprobrious language that the foulest tongue could utter, such as <u>Damnd</u> <u>Liar</u> &c &c &c which not is merrited chastisement— he then Came to my Bed & renewd his infamous assertions— I have been informd that Mr. Foster went to the wharf & orderd his men on shore arm'd, as I did not leave my Birth did not See any Arms but Clubs, none others were visiable—

Within the limitation of your order I am compeld to notice Mr. Fosters conduct in my House in the presence of Respectable personages— his first attack was upon Mr. Cuchins S.M. accus'd him of repeated Drunkenness &c &c &c. he then attack Act Lt. Gibbs asserted he knew nothing of duty, Damd him & the Comdr. & swore he would not obey Lt Gibbs, or Comd. Campbell if he orderd him to serve under Gibbs, a dam'd Mids., with a swab on his shoulders, at the time Mr. Foster was making those remarks he was under the influence of the <u>Ardent</u>   I have the Honor to be verry Respectfully Sir Your Obt. Svt.

N W Rothwell

Comd. H G Campbell
St Marys Geo

ALS, DNA, RG45, CL, Vol. 8, No. 71, enclosure (M125, Roll No. 33).

DEPOSITION OF MARTHA ROGERS

State of Georgia   ⎫   Before Ed W Weyman
Camden—County ⎬   a Magistrate for this County

Personally appeared Martha Rogers who being duly Sworn doth depose and say that Winslow Foster hath been in the habit of frequenting her House for upwards of Eighteen Months last past, and that he hath frequently to this Deponents own Knowledge set up the whole Night playing at cards for Money, and generally became Intoxicated and abusive or Quarelsome in Company— This Deponent further Saith that on one Saturday Night within the Time above Described She requested the aforesaid Winslow Foster at Twelve OClock to cease playing at cards that he was encroaching on the Sabbath, whereupon the said Foster gave her very abusive Language and threats of a Violent Nature, such as saying that her being a Woman only prevented him from taking her Life—and Drew his Dirk at the same time— This Deponent saith further that she hath usually during her Residence in St. Marys Kept a Boarding House and public House

Martha Rogers

Sworn to this
18th. Novr. 1813 at St. Marys
E W Weyman J.P.

DS, DNA, RG45, MLR, 1813, Vol. 7, No. 75, enclosure (M124, Roll No. 59). A copy of this deposition was enclosed in Campbell's letter of 18 December to Secretary Jones.

DEPOSITION OF JOHN BABCOCK

Georgia   }   Before me Ed W Weyman
Camden County,   }   a Magistrate for this County

Personally appeared John Babcock Inn Keeper in the Town of St. Marys who being duly sworn, doth depose and say, That he is acquainted with Winslow Foster of the U S Navy—That he the said Foster hath frequently been in his House & very abusive and Troublesome to this Deponents Boarders— This Deponent further saith that he hath often seen the said Foster intoxicated with Liquor, and Quarelsome when so— He hath seen him in Scuffles, and particularly in one with Captn. Charles Stubbs

                                                             John Babcock

Sworn to at St Marys
this 18th. Novr. 1813
E W Weyman J.P.

DS, DNA, RG45, MLR, 1813, Vol. 7, No. 75, enclosure (M124, Roll No. 59). A copy of this deposition was enclosed in Campbell's letter of 18 December to Secretary Jones.

COMMODORE HUGH G. CAMPBELL TO SECRETARY OF THE NAVY JONES

                                        St Marys.   Decr. 20th. 1813
Sir
     I enclosed by the last Mail several charges against Mr. Winslow Foster (Sailing Master) all of which I beleive to be correct— I regret this circumstance Extremely as he is certainly the most Capable officer I have under my command, nor is this regret mitigated by his being the Son of an old Acquaintence Seth Foster[1] of Norfolk— His Foibles I must acknowledge has never Extended To his command afloat. They have been confind To the shore when accidently falling into company and has proceeded I am inclined to beleive from a gay disposition and Perhaps an irretable disposition— he has Never been Known to have acted out of the Line of his duty on board and has since the date of those Charges Conducted himself with great propriety— He is very Penetant and acknowledges the Emproprieties he has Been commited and ungenous [ungenerous] remarks towards His Brother officers—[2] The Charges of Robert Cutchins[3] wer made after he found himself disgraced and Considered foster the author of his Misfortunes
     Robert Cutchins received his dismisal Agreable to your orders. he is gone on to New York Holding his warrant, which he refused to deliver up to me. I [If] you deem further preof [proof] against him Necessary it can be procured immediately and sent on, as he has gone to the north as he says. to be reinstated— I have the Honor to be With great Respect Sir Your Obedient Servant

                                                        Hugh G Campbell
LS, DNA, RG45, CL, 1813, Vol. 8, No. 76 (M125, Roll No. 33).

     1. For a letter from the elder Foster to Secretary Jones regarding his son, see Seth Foster to Jones, 25 Oct. 1813, DNA, RG45, MLR, Vol. 6, No. 154 (M124, Roll No. 58).

2. Secretary Jones ordered Winslow Foster's dismissal after receiving Campbell's letter of 18 December. Upon receiving Campbell's letter of 20 December, the secretary reversed himself and ordered Foster reinstated. Foster did not long remain penitent, for in April 1814 the fractious sailing master was again under arrest. "It is much to be regretted," Campbell wrote of Foster, "that he has not been heretofore confined to the narrow Limits of a Ship of War Constantly under the Eye of a Commander where I am disposed to believe he would prove an ornament to the Service, but unfortunately for many of our officers commanding Gun Boats they too frequently make a false Estimate of their Command." Campbell to Jones, 23 Apr. 1814, DNA, RG45, CL, 1814, Vol. 2, No. 165 (M125, Roll No. 35).

3. See Robert Cutchin's letter of 8 November to Secretary Jones in which he charges Foster with unofficerlike conduct. Cutchin to Jones, 8 Nov. 1813, DNA, RG45, MLR, 1813, Vol. 7, No. 74 (M124, Roll No. 59). For additional charges against Foster, see Cutchin to Jones, 1 Dec. 1813, DNA, RG45, MLR, 1813, Vol. 7, No. 75 and enclosures (M124, Roll No. 59).

The Hospital Ship at Charleston

In late June, at the request of Surgeon George Logan, the Navy Department authorized the establishment of a hospital ship at Charleston.[1] Although by year's end it had been operational less than five months, Logan declared the new hospital ship an unqualified success.

1. See p. 122. Logan reported that the hospital ship was ready to receive patients on 3 August. See Logan to Jones, 3 Aug. 1813, DNA, RG45, BC, 1813, Vol. 3, No. 68 (M148, Roll No. 12).

SURGEON GEORGE LOGAN TO SECRETARY OF THE NAVY JONES

Charleston. S.C.

Sir!

I had the honour of addressing a Letter to you in July last, acquainting you with the transfer of the Hospital Depart. on this Station to the late Guard Vessel which had been filled up for the purpose, by order of the Commandg. Officer on it now affords me peculiar satisfaction to report the complete success whc has attended this Establishment and its superior advantages to a Hospital on Shore

In consideration of the exposed Situation of the Crews of the Barges, stationed at the inlets, the number of Invalids have exceeded what would have been expected from the Force stationed at Charleston, Georgetown & Beaufort— we have had constantly during the last Six Months from ten to five & twenty <u>Patients in</u> Hospital, Bilious Fevers, Pleurisey & violent Deseases have successively occurred; they have appeared satisfied with their <u>situation</u>, its healthiness has rendered the convalescent Stage short, none have been lost by desertion, & but four by death (two of these were incurable)— The Hospital Ship therefore in this climate unites the important advantages of Oeconomy—Safety & an exemption from the Epidemics prevailing in a City or its suburbs which our Convalescents from other deseases would be liable to—

The Condition of the Hospital has been regularly reported to the commandg. officer, who has occasionally (in compliance with your instructions) been consulted, & affords every necessary assistance altho' he assures me that he has no authority to do so (as he has not received your instructions), but considers the regulation of the Hospital Dept. as resting with myself— The Commanding Officer has however ordered a boats Crew, & authorised the hire of a Cook & nurse & assistant nurse, which the number and comfort of the Sick rendered indispensably necessary

I feel a reluctance, Sir, in occupiing your attention at a period when I presume you are much engrossed by important concerns but conceive it a duty encumbent upon me to sollecit your Opinion & further instructing respecting the regulation of the Hospital department   very respectfully Sir Your Obt humble &c

Geo Logan

29th. Decmbr. 1813.

ALS, DNA, RG45, BC, 1813, Vol. 4, No. 177 (M148, Roll No. 12).

The North American Station at Year's End

At the close of 1813, Admiral Warren still felt he lacked adequate resources to conduct naval operations against the United States—this despite the increased number of ships at his disposal and the growing effectiveness of the British blockade. Citing continuing difficulties on the North American Station, Warren renewed a familiar plea to the Admiralty.

ADMIRAL SIR JOHN B. WARREN, R.N., TO FIRST SECRETARY OF THE ADMIRALTY JOHN W. CROKER

No. 290   Bermuda   30: Decr: 1813.

Sir

I request you will be pleased to acquaint my Lords Commissioners of the Admiralty that having sent the *Barossa* to Jamaica to carry home specie, and every other Ship that could be spared without raising the Blockaded ports of the America, I lament to find that both the Leeward Islands and Jamaica are still very deficient of a Force adequate to their protection, or to perform the various extensive Convoy Service required to be done in those places—

The Hurricanes in the West Indies & at Halifax, have unfortunately encreased the difficulty of carrying forward the Service, and very considerably crippled and diminished the disposeable part of the Squadron, I have already Stated these circumstances to you in my letters from Halifax, but am compelled to repeat the same, in order to entreat their Lordships atten[tion] to the state of my Ships, and extreme necessity of encreasing the Force in every part of the West Indies.

The Americans are building a very large Class of Corvette Ships of Six hundred tons, with twenty four Ports on one Deck, Some are launched, many [?] are nearly ready— The *Adams* has been cut down to the size of a Twenty Gun Ship, She is Manned and in readiness with the *Constellation* to seize the first moment of putting to Sea— Every exertion is making at New York, Philadelphia and Baltimore to prepare Vessels of War, the rapidity with which the Americans, build and fit out their Ships, is scarcely credible, and I am very apprehensive of the mischief their Cruizers will do to our Trade—

Several large Clipper Schooners of from two to three hundred Tons, strongly manned and armed have run thro' the Blockade in the Chesapeak, in spite of every endeavour and of the most vigilant attention of our Ships to prevent their getting out, nor can any thing stop these Vessels escaping to Sea in dark Nights and Strong Winds, their Lordships will be pleased to observe by Captn. Barrie's letter which is herewith enclosed, an instance of Several of these Schooners passing out in a Squadron and outsailing every Ship in Chace.

Two Ships of the Line each to be called 76 Guns are to be finished and launched in March, one at Portsmouth the other at Charlestown near Boston.

The Southern Coast about Charlestown is a retreat for the Enemys Privateers and Letters of Marque, I am anxious to Send Small Cruizers thither to destroy and intercept them, the large Class of our fast sailing Brigs are the best adapted and I should be very happy if their Lordships w[ould] cause some to be Selected and ordered to join me.

I take the liberty likewise to represent that as all the American Men of War, Privateers and even Traders, are particularly good Sailing Vessels such of his Majesty's Ships as are appropriated to my Command, should be of the same description— I have the honour to be Sir Your most obedient humble Servant

John Borlase Warren

LS, UkLPR, Adm. 1/505, pp. 87–90.

Chapter Two

The Chesapeake Bay Theater:
January–December 1813

Given American offensive operations in Canada, the timing of the inevitable attempt of the British to prosecute the war in Chesapeake Bay was a matter of resources. During 1812 British land forces were thinly stretched in the defense of Canada, and the Royal Navy needed reinforcements to mount a meaningful blockade of the Atlantic coast of the United States. When a small squadron of British frigates made rendezvous at Lynnhaven Bay near the mouth of the Chesapeake in early February 1813, however, officials in Washington should not have been surprised. These ships were a portent of the trouble to come.

Henry, the third Earl Bathurst, British Secretary of State for War and the Colonies, had planned a military diversion on behalf of British forces in Canada by launching a series of amphibious raids in Chesapeake Bay intended to frighten American politicians into withdrawing troops from the Canadian border to defend the rich and vulnerable plantations of the Chesapeake, to say nothing of the safety of the capital and principal government officers. Bathurst provided Admiral Sir John B. Warren with an expeditionary force that totalled about 2,400 men, including two battalions of Royal Marines, some 300 infantry from Bermuda and another 300 French "chasseurs" who were in fact prisoners of war who had been persuaded that the risk of death in battle was preferable to languishing in British prisons. The Royal Marines were under the command of Colonel Sir Thomas Sidney Beckwith, a distinguished veteran of campaigns in India and the Iberian Peninsula.

To reinforce Admiral Warren's naval forces, the Admiralty sent Rear Admiral George Cockburn in H.M.S. Marlborough, *74, to the Chesapeake to take command of a squadron, including the 74s* Poictiers, Victorious, *and* Dragon, *the frigates* Maidstone, Junon, Belvidera, *and* Statira, *and several other vessels. Warren ordered Cockburn to blockade the Chesapeake and Delaware Bays, capture and destroy shipping in the James, York, Rappahannock, and Potomac Rivers and off Baltimore, gather intelligence of the American military and naval forces, obtain pilots and a safe anchorage for the squadron, discover the best way of capturing the U.S. frigate* Constellation, *cut off trade in Long Island Sound, maintain constant communication with other British squadrons, and send prizes in convoy to Bermuda. Cockburn arrived off Lynnhaven Bay on 3 March 1813 and was joined by Warren nineteen days later.*

In early April, Cockburn and Warren got underway with their squadron for a prolonged expedition up the bay, returning to Lynnhaven Bay nearly a month later. Warren sailed for Bermuda with forty prizes on 17 May. During the entire operation, the British had faced no serious opposition although there were some sharp battles and attacks on privateers and revenue cutters. In June, after Warren's return, the British attacked the American position on Craney Island in the Elizabeth River only to receive a harsh setback.

A combined force of Virginia militia, naval gun crews from Constellation, *and gunboats from the Gosport Navy Yard repulsed an amphibious attack of British Royal Marines, the 102nd Regiment, the two Independent Companies of Foreigners, and sailors from the fleet. Shortly afterward, the British attacked the town of Hampton near Newport News with shocking results. The French troops got out of hand, looting and killing defenseless civilians, much to their officers' consternation. They were sent back to the fleet in disgrace and did not fight again for the British.*

To counter the forces at Admiral Warren's disposal, the Americans had virtually no regular land forces and only a few small naval vessels in the Chesapeake. For defense, the inhabitants of the Chesapeake Bay coast had to depend on the Virginia and Maryland militias; three poorly manned naval gunboat squadrons at Norfolk, Washington, and Baltimore; the blockaded frigate Constellation; *the frigate* Adams *in the Potomac under the command of Captain Charles Morris; and a division of four privateer schooners operating out of Baltimore under Captain Charles Gordon, U.S.N.*

During the summer of 1813, Secretary of the Navy William Jones adopted a new idea for the defense of the bay proposed by Joshua Barney: a flotilla of well-armed barges. The Chesapeake Bay flotilla did not come into being until 1814, for it took an entire year for this concept to take shape. The Virginia militia's finest hour was its defense of Craney Island; otherwise, it showed itself to be active in reconnaissance and spirited in resistance, as British units using the elements of surprise and mobility by sea staged a series of hit and run raids along the shores of the Chesapeake Bay and her tributaries.

The Maryland militia was so divided in its command between Eastern and Western Shores, and so weakly armed and inexperienced, that little activity can be credited to its account. Admiral Cockburn bypassed Baltimore but attacked Havre de Grace, Frenchtown, and Georgetown on his first northerly expedition. In a second cruise, his vessels reconnoitered the Severn River off Annapolis and the Patapsco below Baltimore, but attacked neither city. Nevertheless, the inhabitants of these towns were fearful and prepared for the worst. The British landed on and occupied Kent Island in August and probed the Eastern Shore rivers for points of resistance. The Maryland militia made a creditable stand at St. Michaels on the Miles River in an artillery action in which the British naval patrol retreated. After this skirmish, the British under Cockburn withdrew from Kent Island to the southern reaches of the bay and left for Bermuda in September 1813. Captain Robert Barrie was left to maintain the blockade in H.M.S. Dragon, *74, in charge of some frigates, brigs, and schooners. Despite his best efforts, some American privateer "clippers" slipped through the blockade on northerly gales.*

For thousands of Americans in the middle Atlantic states, and particularly for those living in tidewater Maryland and Virginia, the events of 1813 brought fear, threats, loss and destruction of property, imprisonment on board British vessels, and death for some if, in the path of the enemy, they chose to stand and fight or were unable to escape. British vessels tested the defenses of the bay and probed the Potomac as high as Cedar and Maryland Points. By mid-July, the alarm had spread to Washington, as the British had intended, "to embarrass the enemy in the measures for the further invasion of Canada." The British withdrew but had learned much that would be useful in the next campaign season: the weakness of the American defenses, the wealth of the area to be plundered, a knowledge of navigation in the rivers of the Chesapeake, and how easy it would be to stage a raid in depth toward the national capital. The Madison administration might also have taken a lesson from these same factors: the strength of their opponent, his seaborne mobility, the vulnerability of the Chesapeake region to such attacks, and the likelihood that, if the war lasted another year, the British would return in force with a more strategic objective.

Constellation and the Defense of Norfolk

Captain Charles Stewart intended to take the refitted Constellation *on a cruise in February 1813, but the newly arrived British blockading squadron prevented his escape from the Virginia Capes. Retiring to the refuge of Norfolk Harbor, Stewart, senior officer on the station, in coordination with John Cassin, commandant of the Gosport Navy Yard, prepared plans to defend the Norfolk–Craney Island area. Their first task was to reorganize the gunboats into a fighting unit.*

CAPTAIN CHARLES STEWART TO SECRETARY OF THE NAVY JONES

United States frigate *Constellation*
February 5, 1813

Sir

I received your letter of the 25th ult. by Lieut. Biggs directing a further proof to be made of the quality of the *Constellation*'s powder. I endeavoured to accomplish the object of your instructions at Annapolis, and sent to the Navy Agent at Baltimore for a cask of Dupont's powder that had been ascertained to be of good proof, intending by comparison, (with the small means in my power) to ascertain their relative strength; but after waiting four days I was disappointed as the powder was not sent. It is probable it was at Annapolis but the severe weather that set in prevented my having any communication with the shore afterwards, and the ice making so fast obliged me to get under way on the morning of the 1st. inst. and proceed down to Hampton Roads. The ship has sustained some slight injury from the ice, a few sheets of copper being cut off the bows.

Yesterday morning we discovered two sail of the Line, three Frigates, a Brig and Schooner of the Enemy working up between the Middle ground and Horse Shoe for the Roads. It being calm we hove up and kedged the Ship up to the flats where the tide having fallen the Ship took the ground and lay untill the

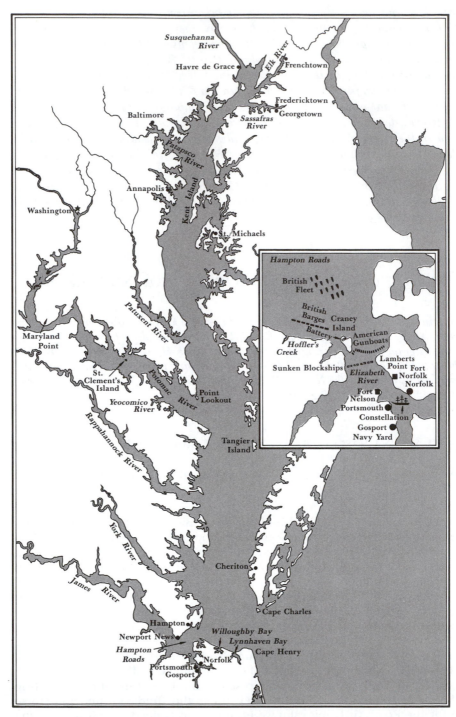

Map 2. Chesapeake Bay Theater

evening flood made, during which time we were engaged lightening the Ship, by taking out the provision Stores and starting the water. At seven P.M. she floated, and by placing our boats with lights along the narrows, the pilot, Mr. James Thomas brought her up in Safety to fort Norfolk. The object of the Enemy appeared to be this Ship, as they got under way (from information) on the evening's flood with a leading breeze and run up to the roads. Finding us gone they went down again and anchored in Lynnhaven Bay. As they are in force it is very probable some attempt may be made against Norfolk.

From the first I was desirous of avoiding this place, satisfied that our chance of getting to sea, would be rendered difficult, as the Enemy possesses, no doubt, the earliest information from their Agents here. We had not been twenty four hours in the Roads before they were apprised of it.

There are no means Captain Cassin informs me of proving powder at this place as he has no Provets.[1]

I shall now get the Ship in a state of readiness to proceed whenever the Enemy gives us an opportunity. Owing to the length of time we have been in the river and bay; and the exposure of our crew to the changeable weather, we have had a good many sick with colds and inflammatory fevers, but fortunately no deaths. I have the honor to be, Respectfully, Sir, Your obedient Servant.

Ch^S. Stewart

ALS, DNA, RG45, CL, 1813, Vol. 1, No. 53 (M125, Roll No. 26).

1. Provett is the aphetic form of eprouvette, an instrument for proving the strength of gunpowder.

SECRETARY OF THE NAVY JONES TO CAPTAIN JOHN CASSIN

Capt. John Cassin   Navy Depart.
Commandant at the   Feb: 16. 1813.
Navy Yard   Gosport.

The present menacing attitude of the enemy's Squadron in the waters of the Chesapeak immediately in the vicinity of your Command calls for the utmost exertion of your talents & vigilance and zeal to guard against an attack either by land or water.

You will therefore place the Gun Boats in the best condition for efficient Service and with the Crews already attached to them and such as may be collected from the local force, which in such a Crisis cannot fail to be sufficient for the purpose I trust when combined with the other means of defence will give perfect Security. The Flotilla is placed under your immediate Command, but in all general operations Capt. Stewart of the *Constellation* your Senior will command the whole naval force on the Station as long as he shall remain there.

The enemy having penetrated the Bay as far as New point with their tenders and Boats, and are now greatly annoying the trade all the force at this place and its vicinity will be employed for the protection of the Bay and in repelling the Marauders. For the same purpose you will despatch the *Scorpion* Cutter for Annapolis,[1] as soon as the safety of your Command will admit, there to report to this Department. If you can procure either by reasonable hire or purchase a well constructed Schooner of 80 to 90 tons of <u>easy draught of water</u> and have

Captain John Cassin

the means of manning her, you will equip her with one heavy long gun amidship and such other armament, as will render her the most efficient, and despatch her also for Annapolis.

As it is very important to give timely notice of the Blockade to vessels destined for the Chesapeak and Delaware and particularly to our public vessels, you will immediately employ a fast sailing pilot Boat to cruize on such Stations as will be most likely to avoid the enemy and meet such vessels, as may be coming in from S.E. to E.N.E.

You will return to this Department a list of the vessels and their force and the officers and Crews attached to your Command. In the pilot Boat you will take care to employ a trusty Crew and send with them a midshipman to communicate the intelligence.

If you deem a further supply of ammunition or other Stores necessary report the same to this Department.

According to your Suggestion I revoke the arrest of Lieutenant Kennedy as his acknowledgement to you is deemed sufficient by yourself.[2]

W Jones.

LB Copy, DNA, RG45, CNA, Vol. 1, pp. 359–61 (M441, Roll No. 1).

1. *Scorpion* was sent to the Potomac flotilla instead; see p. 333.
2. Cassin and Lieutenant Edmund P. Kennedy, commander of the cutter *Scorpion*, became embroiled over a question of command. See Cassin to Jones, Feb. 1813, DNA, RG45, CL, 1813, Vol. 1, No. 54 (M125, Roll No. 26). Cassin did not date this letter, but it was probably written about 10 February.

CAPTAIN CHARLES STEWART TO SECRETARY OF THE NAVY JONES

United States frigate *Constellation*
Norfolk Harbour   March 17. 1813.

Sir

On the 9th instant I got under way with the *Constellation* and went down to Crany Island lite. The Enemy on the 10th. moved up from Lynnhaven Bay with three Ships of the Line and two Frigates and came into Hampton Roads on the 11th. where they have since been joined by two other Ships of the Line. Their frigates, tenders, and armed boats are constantly in motion.

I found the Gun boats so weakly manned and so utterly incompetent to protect themselves, should the Enemy make the attempt to board them in the night, to prevent their falling into their hands I was under the necessity of withdrawing them within the fortifications of Norfolk and to return up from that position with the Ship. Ten of the boats have been sent up to the Navy Yard and their men put on board of those remaining which renders them about half manned. When the means and force of the Enemy are considered, and the state of this place for a defence, it presents but a gloomy prospect of Security, and although you may expect all will be done that can be done by resistance with the means of opposition which we possess, yet such is the state and limit of these means (the place has been so utterly neglected) that I do not think we ought to flatter ourselves that it will be effectually successful. Our dependance on the local forces for manning the gun boats, which is the only active force we have on these waters, has proved abortive, indeed some of the Militia have already deserted from an apprehension of being ordered into them. Many of the inhabitants have moved from Norfolk with their effects and many more are preparing to go. Four block ships have been sunk in the channel off Lamberts point, but that I fear will present very little opposition. One of their frigates passed up James river to day. I have the honor to be Respectfully Sir Your obedient Servant

Ch^S Stewart

P.S. I am getting out of the Ship all the Stores, Sails, Spars, &c. and sending them up the Elizabeth river, as it is now reduced to a certainty that this ship will not have an opportunity of getting to sea.

ALS, DNA, RG45, CL, 1813, Vol. 2, No. 53 (M125, Roll No. 27).

CAPTAIN CHARLES STEWART TO SECRETARY OF THE NAVY JONES

United States frigate *Constellation*
Norfolk Harbour   March 22. 1813

Sir

I had the honor to address you on the 17th inst informing you that I was under the necessity of withdrawing the Flotilla from Crany Island owing to the weak state and condition of the Gun Boats, since which time I have been busily engaged selecting and preparing as many of them, best sailing, as we could man and arm, holding them ready for any movement which may be required of them. The following number are all that we could put in such state and condition under the order issued the 18th instant

No. 67	Lieutenant Gardener
60	Henley
152	Neale
155	Wilkinson
149	Shubrick
61	Saunders
154	Sailing master Young.

Owing to a deficiency of all most every article required, (it taking from the other boats and Navy Yard all the small arms and stores to complete this number agreeable to the order) the two tenders *Franklin* and *Despatch* are manned and armed from this Ship with forty men each.

Yesterday Lieut. Ridgely went down to Admiral Cockburn in the *Franklin* tender as a Flag of Truce, to convey on board the Secretary to the Russians Embassador. He was treated with great civility, and learned that the night before they had despatched their launches and cutters with six hundred men above Crany Island for the purpose of suppressing this division of Gun Boats. The Guard boat from this Ship lay near them for two hours unperceived and heard most of their conversation; they retired however before day light finding the division of Gun Boats withdrawn.

There are still in Hampton Roads three sail of the Line and two Frigates. Their ships do not separate much. Their Frigates and tenders when we make a movement with the Flotilla retire under the protection of the ships of the Line. Their excursions have been confined to the shores of James's river, occasionally landing in strong parties to procure stocks &c. They have destroyed a number of the Oyster boats, and taken possession of the licensed vessels that had retired up that river.

It is much to be regretted that a strong work has not been erected on Crany Island, I mean a small work for eight or ten guns made sufficiently high to prevent an escalade or surprize; the Narrows piered and secured with strong booms and chains; should that have been done, the Gun Boats well manned and stationed above the booms, it appears to me we might bid defiance to their operations by water. I have the honor to be, Very Respectfully, Sir, Your obedient Servant.

Chs. Stewart

ALS, DNA, RG45, CL, 1813, Vol. 2, No. 78 (M125, Roll No. 27).

SECRETARY OF THE NAVY JONES TO CAPTAIN CHARLES STEWART

Capt. Chas. Stewart   Nav: Deptmt.
Comg. U S. naval force   nfolk   27. March 1813

Your letters of the 17th, 22d & 24th were received by the regular course of the mail— Capt. Cassin has instructions to recruit the deficiency of the crews of the gunboats, & for this purpose to give a reasonable bounty. If he succeeds, you will be enabled to act offensivly when occasion may offer: but sattisfied as I am, that the special object of the movements of the enemy is to draw your force out from the waters of norfolk with the hope of cutting off its return—it will be necessary to be extremely guarded in your movements, in order to avoid the possibility of an event so hazardous in its consequences: this your penetration has anticipated, & prudence will avert—considering the present force of the enemy, the defence of your present position is the object of chief solicitude, & the movement you made with the flotilla, is a proof that the enemy is not altogether insensible of your offensive power. I highly approve of the measure you have adopted—a few of the best gunboats, with the heaviest metal well manned, will prove more efficient than a greater number indifferently manned— Your two tenders, will also be found extremely usefull. It is some consolation, that while a strong squadron of the enemies Ships are employed in watching your little squadron & carrying on a Petty larceny kind of warfare, against the river craft & plantations, our gallant commanders are scouring the ocean, in search of a superior foe, & gathering laurels in such abundance, & in such rapid succession, as to afford the enemy scarcely time to soothe the chagrin of one defeat before he is subjected to the mortification of another. This days mail brought the account of the arrival at New York of the *Hornet* Capt. Lawrence, having, on the coast of Surinam captured the enemies Brig *Peacock*—rated 18. but mounting 21. The action was very short, & most decissive; The *Peacock* sunk before all the prisoners could be removed, 9 of them went down with her—of the enemy, 9. were drowned 9. killed, 33. wounded— The *Hornet*, one killed & two wounded

W. Jones

LB Copy, DNA, RG45, SNL, Vol. 10, pp. 324–25 (M149, Roll No. 10).

British Activity and Strategy

The Admiralty, desiring to take the offense in its Atlantic campaign, ordered Rear Admiral George Cockburn,[1] in November 1812, to join Admiral Sir John B. Warren in Bermuda. Arriving in mid-January 1813, Cockburn formed a squadron under his flag Marlborough, 74, and left for the Chesapeake about a month later. The Lords Commissioners chose the Chesapeake as their target for offensive operations because Baltimore privateers were devastating British commerce and they felt that marauding Royal Navy squadrons could attack the unprotected coastal towns there with impunity.

Frustrated by his inability to pursue Constellation *into the shallow Elizabeth River, and wary of Norfolk's defenses, Cockburn sent a force of small boats to forage for food along the James River. Similar raiding missions along the Chesapeake's inland waterways would follow throughout the year. Meanwhile, the British government, hoping to divert American troops from Canada, ordered Colonel Sir Thomas Sidney Beckwith[2] to America to coordinate military expeditions with the naval force in the Chesapeake.*

1. *For a recent biography of Cockburn, see Pack,* Man Who Burned the White House.
2. *Colonel Sir Thomas S. Beckwith had a long, distinguished career in the British Army, being considered one of the finest leaders of light troops. In 1812 he was appointed assistant quartermaster general in Canada.*

CAPTAIN GEORGE BURDETT, R.N.,[1] TO ADMIRAL SIR JOHN B. WARREN, R.N.

Copy

His Majesty's Ship
Maidstone   Lyn Haven Bay
Chesapeake, 9th Feby. 1813.

Sir,

I have the pleasure to inform you of a very gallant achievement that was performed by the boats of the Squadron you did me the honor to place under my command for the Blockade of this Port and its Rivers; Yesterday morning at 9 OClock AM a Schooner was observed in the NW standing down the Chesapeake Bay, at the same time I made the *Belvidera* & *Statira*'s Signal No. 239 with the North West Compass Signal; as the Stranger approached the Squadron I perceived her to be a Vessel of considerable Force, Captain Byron at the same time made the Signal for her being superior to the Boat in chace, but not to those of the Squadron United. I immediately made the Signal for all Barges, Cutters &c &c to proceed in the same direction upon which the Schooner made all Sail in the direction from whence she came, and I had the satisfaction to perceive she was quite becalmed, at One oClock P.M. the Stranger opened a well directed Fire upon the headmost of our Boats from her Stern chace Guns and I was happy to find the boats in advance rested on the Oars until they all formed up when a rigorous and Gallant attack was made by all the boats (nine in No.) under the Orders of Lieutt. Nazer Second Lieutt. of His Majesty's Ship under my Command who happened to be Senior Officer, through a very heavy Fire from all the Enemy's Guns, when he was Boarded & carried Sword in hand, after a most obstinate resistance which was maintained upon the Deck of the Enemy for a few Minutes. She proves to be the American Armed Schooner *Lottery* of Two Hundred and Ten Tons, mounting Six twelve pound Carronades (but pierced for Sixteen) with a Complement of Twenty eight

Rear Admiral George Cockburn, R.N.

men, from Baltimore bound to Bourdeaux with a Cargo of Coffee, Sugar and Log-wood, She is Coppered and Copper fastened.

I cannot sufficiently applaud the stile of Gallantry that this Service was performed with, for every Officer and man went away with the conviction the chace was a large Privateer, and I beg leave Sir particularly to recommend Lieutt. Nazer to your notice, and the conduct of every Officer and man in the boats of the Squadron employed upon this Service was most conspicuous.

I also have the honor to enclose a List of the killed & Wounded in the different Boats of the Squadron which I am happy to add is trifling, when compared to the obstinate resistance made by the Enemy whose loss was very great, the Captain & eight men dangerously Wounded.[2] I have the honor to remain Sir, Your most Obedient Servant

Signed: George Burdett   Captain

Copy, UkLPR, Adm. 1/503, pp. 137–38.

1. Captain George Burdett commanded a squadron of four frigates which entered Chesapeake Bay on 4 February. He relinquished that command to George Cockburn upon the latter's arrival in the bay a month later.

2. No enclosure of killed and wounded was found in the Admiralty records. The *Naval Chronicle* printed the following return: "*Maidstone*—2 wounded (1 severely). *Belvidera*—None. *Junon*—2 wounded (1 severely). *Statira*—2 wounded (both dangerously), 1 since dead." See Vol. 29 (Jan.–June 1813), p. 250.

REAR ADMIRAL GEORGE COCKBURN, R.N., TO ADMIRAL SIR JOHN B. WARREN, R.N.

No. 2   *Marlborough*   Hampton Roads
                                                    the 13th March 1813

Sir

1st   I have the honor to inform you that owing to strong WSW Winds which we met with in the Gulf Stream, it was not in my Power to reach Lynhaven Bay with the Squadron under my Orders before the Evening of the 3rd instant, and it was the 4th before the whole of the Ships—got in.

2nd   On my arrival I was most concerned at being informed by Captain Burdett, that although every possible exertion had been made by the Squadron of Frigates of which he had had Command, yet that it had not been within their Power to collect the slightest Intelligence either as to the force in Norfolk, as to the strength or Position of the Forts in this Neighbourhood, nor as to the actual situation of the *Constellation* Frigate, nor had any Survey been made of the position of the Middle Ground Sand, and other Shoals in the Mouth of the Chesapeake, in short that nothing further was Known than at the moment of your Sailing for Bermuda; It became therefore necessary for me to take immediate Measures for advancing at once on all these very essential Points.

3rd   I of course was most anxious previous to separating the Squadron (in obedience to the 6th Paragraph of your Orders to me) to ascertain how far our united Force would have any prospect of success in an Attack upon Norfolk and whilst taking Measures for obtaining this Information, I employed the Masters of this Ship and the *Poictiers* to Survey and Buoy off the Middle Ground Sand &c.

4th   On the 6th I gave the Order to Captain Burdett of which the enclosed No. 1 is a Copy, and on the 8th having tolerably well ascertained from Different corroborating Sources that the Military Force in Norfolk actually consisted of at least Three Thousand Men, 1500 of which were supposed to be well trained and composed principally of their best Rifle Corps the whole on the alert and expecting Attack, I was forced to give up the Idea of making any serious Debarkation from the Ships, and Judging how anxious you would be to have the Delaware secured as well as this Bay I determined on immediately detaching Sir Jno Beresford, to whom I therefore gave the Order of which No. 2 is a Copy.

But as on our Arrival off the Capes the Squadron captured two Pilot Boats at a considerable distance from the Shore, one of which was manned by the *United States* American frigate, and had on board an Officer belonging to that Ship, I thought it probable they were actually looking for the French Squadron which you intimated to me was to be expected, although the officer of course denied it, and stated that he was merely cruizing to warn off Merchant Vessels. I therefore Judged it wise not to send away the *Dragon* immediately to Cruize off New York, nor to make for the moment any further Detachments from this Squadron and as at the same time that I received the Intelligence as to the Land Force at Norfolk, I likewise learnt that the *Constellation* was laying some way below that Town surrounded by Gun Boats. I determined to move with the Line of Battle Ships towards Hampton Road to ascertain positively the actual strength and Position of the Enemy's Batteries on the different Points approaching Elizabeth River, and to see if it were practicable to get at and Capture or Destroy the Frigate; I therefore weighed on the 10th from Lynhaven Bay with the *Marlborough Victorious, Dragon* and *Acasta,* and I am happy to say we got safe up on the 11th although the weather was extremely unfavorable to us, and we were obliged to buoy off the whole of the Channel as we advanced not having any Person in the Squadron who was in the slightest degree acquainted with it, and as we found it much more intricate and very different to our Charts and Directions.

5th   There is not any Battery on Point Comfort, nor is there yet any upon Sewell or Willoughby Points.

The Frigate is I think about half way up Elizabeth River apparently protected by two Batteries and Seventeen Gun Boats each carrying (as I am informed) a 42 Pounder and the Channel into Elizabeth River is so intricate as to leave us but little chance of getting at her except by Boats, and for them I fear herself and Gunboats will prove somewhat too strong, we are however sounding and endeavouring to gain a Knowledge of the Entrance of the River and you may depend on it that no Opportunity will be lost of doing any thing I may find practicable and our means equal to, without unnecessarily risking His Majesty's Ships. And I have the greatest pleasure in assuring you that nothing can exceed the Zeal, Exertion Gallantry, and good Conduct invariably displayed by every Officer and Man in the Squadron.

6th   I think it also right to state to you, that if you can obtain from General Horsford or by any other means, One Regiment to add to the Marines of the Squadron I have no doubt that we should be able to get possession of Norfolk and from such a blow to them now the greatest Benefits might certainly result.

The Chief American Officers in this neighbourhood are acting with a severity that cannot be long tolerated, it is suspected in Norfolk that we have been assisted in getting up here by Pilots, and that we have received Information and other Aids from Agents in the Town. These Ideas have occasioned the arbitrary Imprisonment of many People (certainly innocent of the Charge) which must naturally add to their Confusion and Difficulties whenever they are seriously threatened, and should the Information which I have read in an American Paper prove Correct, that a large reinforcement of Ships with Major Williams's Division of the Marine Battalion are on their way here I have no hesitation in pronouncing that the whole of the Shores and Towns within this Vast Bay, not excepting the Capital itself will be wholly at your mercy, and subject if not to be permanently occupied, certainly to be successively insulted or destroyed at your Pleasure; I should however here remark to you that I conceive Bomb Ships or other Strong Vessels of light draught of Water would also be extremely useful in carrying into effect any extensive operations of this Nature.

7th   Our Masters are now tolerably well acquainted with the Middle Ground, Horse Shoe and Willoughby Shoals and I have placed Buoys on most of the Dangerous Projections of each of them for the guidance of any Ships which you may hereafter send here to me.

8th   On the 9th the *Sydney* a fine American Letter of Marque Schooner from Baltimore bound to Havannah carrying one long Gun Amidships on a Swivel and two Carronades endeavour'd to get from the Chesapeake round Point Comfort towards Norfolk, She being when discovered above eight Miles from any Ship of the Squadron, the Wind westerly and an Ebb Tide, the Signal was immediately made for the boats to chase her, and after a most fatiguing pull of Three Hours they succeeded in getting up to her and the headmost of them under the Command of Lieutenant Westphall (1st of the *Marlborough*) dashing at once alongside carried her, and I am happy to add without loss though she had kept up a constant fire on the Boats from their arriving within reach of her Shot 'till they got alongside.

9th   I have directed this Vessel and the several other Prizes that are manned and fit to proceed to endeavour to find their way to Bermuda without Convoy, as the *Statira* had unfortunately sailed for that place previous to my arrival, and I see no prospect of being able to spare another Ship, besides the one charged with this Dispatch, from the various Duties of this Bay, and I conceive your speedily getting this Letter to be so essential to the public Service that I cannot think of allowing the Frigate charged with it, to be subjected to the Detention which her taking such a Convoy would probably Occasion.

10th   It is not in my Power to send you by this opportunity a correct List of Captured Vessels, as I had not collected one previous to my quitting the lower anchorage.

11th   I have directed that the Frigate to be charged with this Dispatch, should carry to Bermuda all the Prisoners in the Squadron, I enclose you a letter on this Subject which I sent by a Flag of Truce to the Commanding Officer at Norfolk,[1] as also his answer thereto and I trust that this obstinate determination to refuse all overtures for a partial exchange here will induce you to send to England these Prisoners (as I have threatened them that you will do) and such others as we may take beyond the Number of

Englishmen actually restored to you for I am credibly informed that this is a measure which would be attended with much Inconvenience to the American Government, which begins already to find a difficulty in procuring the necessary Number of men for its Naval Operations—confined and trifling as they must of Course yet be.

12th   If the *Ramillies* has not sailed for this place previous to your receiving this Letter, I beg to submit to you the propriety of her being ordered here with as much Provision and Water as she can stow, as we shall by that Time be all getting short, and the *Victorious* still having in her sick List upwards of Seventy. I doubt whether I shall be able to Keep her with me even 'till so relieved.

13th   You will perceive by the above statements that I have not been yet able to make up a Squadron to Cruize off Block Island, indeed the *Narcissus* which I had stationed off the Light House having again parted Company from me, the only Vessel of War of any description whatever now in Lynhaven Bay is the *Junon*. I hope however by the Time the *Acasta* gets down there herewith, that the *Narcissus* will have found her way back, or that some other Frigate may have arrived equal to carrying this Letter and the Prisoners, without obliging me to lose for this Purpose the services of a Frigate of the largest Class.

14th   Should circumstances and my further observations induce me to think all our efforts to get at the *Constellation* likely to prove vain I shall probably drop down again myself to Lynhaven Bay to enable me the better to spare a greater Proportion of my Force on detached Services for whilst occupying this Anchorage, close to all the Enemy's Gun Boats and all his Resources, I am forced to Keep a sufficient Force with me to enable me to act offensively with my Boats by Night, and to overpower him therewith, should he attempt any Attack during Calms, or any Annoyance by Fire Vessels, or other Means, but in Lynhaven Bay the Distance the Enemy would be from Shelter is so great and the Expanse of Water so wide that it is impossible for him to cause the slightest Disturbance or Inconvenience to our Ships whilst there, in Return however our laying there is of course neither so annoying nor so disgraceful to him, as our being here threatening and holding in Consternation and Dismay one of his principal Towns with a Frigate and Flotilla before it equally or more seriously menaced with Destruction. I am therefore anxious to know from you whether you conceive it to be more advantageous to carry on here Operations of this Nature requiring our united Efforts, or by sacrificing Views of this Description to divide the Ships and by detaching them along the Coast to annoy more particularly any Trade Afloat which the Americans may still endeavour to carry on.

15th   I am not without Hopes that the Squadron here may be furnished from time to time (from the upper part of the Chesapeake) with supplies of Cattle and Vegetables, a Person having engaged to send me such, but whether he will be enabled for any continuance to elude the present great Vigilance of the American Government is I think extremely doubtful.

16th   Whenever I can spare another Vessel, I shall transmit you further Particulars and accounts of our Proceedings, but almost despair of having it within my power 'till you send me some Schooners or other dispatch Vessels from Bermuda, those taken and manned by the Squadron being wholly wanted and constantly occupied in Keeping up our requisite Communications. I have the Honor to be Sir Your very faithful and most obedient Humble Servant

"sd." G. Cockburn Rr. Admiral

LB Copy, DLC, Papers of George Cockburn, Container 9, Letters Sent, 3 Feb. 1812–6 Feb. 1814, pp. 117–29. This was addressed to Warren in Bermuda.

1. Robert B. Taylor was a brigadier general in the Virginia militia, commanding the defense of Norfolk.

REAR ADMIRAL GEORGE COCKBURN, R.N., TO LIEUTENANT COLONEL KENDALL ADDISON [1]

His Britannic Majesty's
Ship *Marlborough* Hampton
Road the 19th March 1813

Sir,

I have the Honor to acknowledge the receipt of your Letter under date the 18th Current requesting to Know,

1st Whether some Inhabitants of the County of Northampton who happen to be at this moment in Norfolk may be permitted to return to their families unmolested by the British Squadron.

2nd Whether the Packet accustomed to ply between Northampton and Norfolk may still continue so to do.

3rd Whether the Vessels accustomed to fish on the Eastern side of the Chesapeake and to carry their Fish to Norfolk may still continue so to do?

In answer to which Questions I have the Honor to inform you that any small unloaded Vessel coming from Norfolk with the Gentlemen alluded to in the 1st Question shall be permitted to proceed without molestation provided they pass immediately through the British Squadron, and do not shew any Disposition to avoid it.

I will also allow the Packet alluded to by you in the 2nd Question to pass under similar restrictions, and it being perfectly understood that she is not to have any Cargo on board but merely to convey Passengers and Letters.

With respect to the 3rd Question although I will certainly permit your fishing Vessels to follow unmolested their usual occupations, yet I am sorry I cannot meet your further wishes in permitting them to carry their Cargoes to Norfolk.[2] I have the Honor to be &c &c &c

("Sd") G. Cockburn Rr. Adml.

To Lt. Coll. Addison
of the United States
27th. Regt. Northampton.

LB Copy, DLC, Papers of George Cockburn, Container 9, Letters Sent, 3 Feb. 1812–6 Feb. 1814, pp. 130–31.

1. Addison commanded the 27th Regiment of the Northampton County, Virginia, militia.
2. For the Admiralty's reaction to permitting such communication, see p. 356.

THE RIGHT HONORABLE HENRY, EARL BATHURST TO
COLONEL SIR THOMAS SIDNEY BECKWITH, BRITISH ARMY

<u>Most Secret</u>.   Downing Street   20th March 1813

Sir,

It having been judged expedient to effect a diversion on the Coasts of the United States of America, in favour of Upper and Lower Canada, which the American Government have declared it to be their intention to wrest from His Majesty in the course of the ensuing Campaign, Sir J. B. Warren will receive Instructions to direct a Squadron to proceed with the Troops named in the Margin, towards those places on the Coast, where it may appear to him most adviseable that a descent should be made— And His Royal Highness the Prince Regent confiding in your Valour, Enterprize and Discretion, has been generously pleased to commit to you the Command of these Troops, in such Operations as you may judge it expedient when on shore to undertake.

The number and description of the Force placed under your Command, as well as the object of the Expedition itself, will point out to you that you are not to look to the permanent possession of any place, but to the reembarking the Force as soon as the immediate object of each particular attack shall have been accomplished.

While afloat, you will consider yourself as under the Command of the Naval Officer Commanding this Expedition. The Disembarkation of the Troops, and their Re:embarkation, will be directed by him; but he will be instructed to concert with you as to the best mode of effecting the same respectively. You will decide as to the time of re:embarking the Troops, as that must in a great measure be regulated by the success of your undertaking, and by the approach of the Enemy's Force; but you will previously ascertain, whether, in the opinion of the Commander of the Naval Force, there is any time peculiarly unfavourable for Re:embarkation.

As the object of the Expedition is to harrass the Enemy by different attacks, you will avoid the risk of a general action, unless it should become necessary to secure your retreat.

When the object of the Descent is to take possession of any Naval or Military Stores, you will not delay the destroying them, if there is reasonable ground of apprehension that the Enemy is advancing with a superior force to effect their recovery.

If you shall be enabled to take such a position as to threaten the Inhabitants with the destruction of their property, you are hereby authorized to levy upon them Contributions in plate and Money in return for your forbearance. But you will not by this understand that the Magazines belonging to the Government, or their Harbours, or their Shipping are to be included in such arrangement.

You will on no account give encouragement to any disposition which may be manifested by the Negroes to rise against their Masters. The Humanity which ever influences His Royal Highness must make Him anxious to protest against a system of Warfare which must be attended by the atrocities inseparable from commotions of such a description. If any Individual Negroes shall in the course of your operations have given you assistance, which may expose them to the vengeance of their Masters after your retreat, you are at liberty on their earnest desire to take them away with you. You are authorized to enlist them in any of the Black Corps if they are willing to enlist; but you must distinctly understand that you are in no case to take slaves away as Slaves, but as free persons whom the public become bound to maintain. This circumstance as well as the difficulty of transport, will make you necessarily cautious how you contract engagements of this nature, which it may be difficult for you to fulfill. I am Sir Your most obedient Humble Servant

Bathurst

LS, MiU–C, Thomas Brisbane Papers, 1813–15. The following was written in the left margin, first page: 1st. Battn. of Marines—842; 2nd Battn. of Marines—842; 103rd Regt., Detachment—300; 2 Independent Companies—300; A Detachment of Marine Artillery—50. Bathurst meant the 102d.

REAR ADMIRAL GEORGE COCKBURN, R.N., TO
ADMIRAL SIR JOHN B. WARREN, R.N.

No. 3   *Marlborough* Hampton
                                             Road   the 23rd March 1813

Sir

1st   Herewith I have the honor to enclose the duplicate of my Letter and its enclosures under date of the 13th Current which was transmitted to you by the *Laurestinus* and I have now the honor to state for your further information, that subsequent to sending away the abovementioned Dispatch the utmost possible endeavours and perseverance were exerted Night after Night by all the Boats of the Squadron to find and Buoy off (in the same manner as we had done to this Anchorage) the channel into Elizabeth River, but so intricate and difficult is it that all our efforts proved vain and the Boats were never able to get into the deep water abreast of Craney Island without passing occasionally in as little as <u>four feet</u>, and the smallest of them at times taking the ground, at last however one of the Pilots we had taken (and who 'till then had resisted all my offers and Solicitations) came forward and agreed for a Stipulated reward to shew us the Passage into the River, declaring however that it was so extremely narrow and difficult that neither himself nor any Pilot in the Place could possibly Keep in the deepest water during the night, or be able in the dark to carry thro' the Flats more than twelve feet, and that by day he conceived Three and a half and Three and a quarter fathoms would be the utmost depth he could insure to us, It became therefore necessary to take advantage of his assistance to prove what depth could actually be found in this difficult part of the Navigation, and to learn the marks for Keeping in the deepest water previous to attempting the Passage with any of the Ships—I consequently sent the Master of the *Marlborough* with him in the Barge well armed and guarded by other Boats, to run through the channel with the marks on to sound it and make the necessary Remarks relative thereto, and I am sorry to say on the return of the Master he informed me that through these Flats, which extend from this side of Sewells Point to abreast Craney Island, about four miles in distance, he had more casts of 3 1/4 than 3 1/2 Fathoms, very few deeper than the latter and none shoaler than the former, and that to ascertain whether the Pilot had kept him in the deepest water possible, he on returning occasionally hauled to either side of the marks pointed out, when he always almost instantaneously, shoaled the water; This report of course obliged me to give up at once all further Idea of carrying our Ships into Elizabeth River, and I therefore gave the necessary directions for converting some of our Prizes into Fire vessels to endeavour by means of these and our Boats with Congreve's Rockets,[1] to destroy the Enemy's Frigate, but the Americans having I suppose, observed our Boat stand in through the right channel. The Frigate was run up to Norfolk the next flood tide accompanied by the Gun Boats, which amount to nineteen (instead of Seventeen as is mentioned in my last letter) and immediately after she passed the Forts, three Merchant Ships, which were prepared for the purpose, were sunk across the Channel abreast the Lower Fort, which is called Fort Norfolk apparently a regular Stone Work having about Nineteen or twenty Guns mounted on Barbette and being somewhat below and on the opposite side to Fort Nelson, which is supposed to have from twenty to twenty four Guns; the appearance of these Forts and of the present position of the Frigate &c you may form some Idea of by the enclosed sketch made by one of my officers.

2nd   These movements of the Enemy having put it quite out of my power to attempt any thing further in Elizabeth River with adequate prospect of success until we should have a sufficient military Force to land at the same time on both its Banks, I determined on making a movement up James's River to distract the Enemy and to capture such of his vessels as might have taken shelter there, and I therefore moved one of the Frigates close to the mouth of it and sent the Tenders and Boats of the Squadron under the Command of Lieutenant Westphale of this Ship to penetrate as far up as might prove practicable for the aforesaid purposes and I am happy to add that they succeeded in getting up as high as Hog Island, and in capturing a number of Vessels which from their inland position had considered themselves in perfect safety, and I have the satisfaction to remark, from the Prisoners taken on this occasion and from some Americans who have since been on board here with Flags of Truce, that it appears the Capture of these Ships so high up one of their Rivers, the probability of their other Rivers being subject to similar visitations, the state of alarm in which our arrival has put the whole country, their late ineffectual application to Government for means of defence, added to the rigorous blockade of the Bay, and the Delaware, and the check lately given to the Licence trade by the recent orders on that head, have caused the continuation of Hostilities with us to be now as unpopular in this as it has been in other parts of the United States and the Virginians who a few Months back so loudly called for war are beginning to be as clamorous and axious for Peace.

3rd   It may be also useful for me Sir here to state to you that in a conversation I had an opportunity of entering into the other day, with an intelligent Merchant of Richmond he fairly explained to me that the Commencement of this War could not but have been popular in this part of the world from the increased Advantages which they appeared at the moment to derive from it for he assured me he never had seen since his entering into Business such Commercial activity in America, offering such Prospects of general Profit to all concerned in it as for the four or five Months immediately following the Declaration of Hostilities he said the demands for Supplies from Europe and the West Indies had been naturally very much increased by it, and the Superabundance of British Licences occasioning Plenty of them to be always in the market at as reasonable Rate, the Ship owners were able <u>without risk</u> to get Freight the moment their ships were ready to receive it, the Merchants had more orders for Shipments to Europe &c than they could well execute, and the Farmers and Cultivation of the land consequently got higher prices for the produce of their Labor, than had been known for many years; but the late measures of our Government having (he said) not only put a Stop to these advantageous prospects but having also thrown back into the Country an immense quantity of last years produce and caused an entire and complete stagnation of all Commerce to succeed so immediately to the late Scenes of activity and profit, had had a proportionate effect on the minds of the People, and there was now only to be heard from one end of the Country to the other Lamentations of Individuals who were now beginning to suffering from the effects of the war. He also added with much apparent pleasure that Mr. Maddison had lost all the latter measures he had proposed to Congress (previous to its breaking up) for prosecuting the War with rancour, and he assured me from the present state of the Country the President would neither be enabled nor permitted to continue it—within 48 hours after this conversation a Flag of Truce from Norfolk with Mr. De Siverskoff on board of her brought me the Letters of which the enclosures marked a and b, are copies, and the dispatch from Mr. Dashkoff which I had the honor of personally delivering to you this morning, which occasioned me to send the replies and order as marked C. D. E. & F.

4th Since my arrival at this anchorage I have also received by Flag of Truce from Lieutenant Coll. Addison Commanding the United States Forces at Northampton on the Eastern shore of Virginia a Midshipman and Eight men belonging to the *Victorious,* together with the Letters of which the enclosures G and H are copies, to which I returned the answers marked I and K.

5th On the 19th. Currt. the Guard Boats for the night whilst reconnoitring in Elizabeth River had the good Fortune to meet with the Carpenter and Seven men belonging to the *Tartarus,* who had just made their escape from the jail of Norfolk where they had been confined as Prisoners of War, and it is right I should mention to you that they complain much of the mode in which they have been disposed of, and fed during the time they have been in the power of the Americans.

6th I have now Sir only to assure you of the continuation of the same Zeal and good conduct of the officers and men of this Squadron which I had the satisfaction of noticing in my last dispatch.

7th I have the honor also to transmit herewith in a separate accompanying Packet copies of all the Memoranda and other orders which I have seen occasion to issue to the Squadron since parting from you as likewise a Return of Vessels Captured. I have the honor to be Sir &c. &c.

(Signed) G. Cockburn Rr. Adl.

LB Copy, DLC, Papers of George Cockburn, Container 9, Letters Sent, 3 Feb. 1812–6 Feb. 1814, pp. 136–46. Enclosure letters mentioned in the margin of the 3rd part: A—letter from Brig. Gen. Taylor; B—letter from Capt. Stewart; C—letter to Brig. Genl.

Taylor; D—letter to Captn. Stewart; E—letter to Exy. Mon. De Dashkoff; F—pass for a
Vessel to carry Dispatches to Russia. Enclosures G and H and responses I and K, all mentioned in part four, were neither identified nor included in the letter book.

1. Developed by William Congreve at the Royal Laboratory, Woolwich, England, Congreve's rockets were first used by the British at the seige of Boulogne in 1806. The 32-pound version, the most
successful model, consisted of a cylinder of sheet iron wrapped with wire, constituting a projectile
42 inches long and 4 inches in diameter. A composition akin to gunpowder served as propellant,
while a wooden stick 15 feet long extending from the rear provided stability in flight. The rockets'
range varied from 1500 to 3000 yards. Their great advantage was mobility, but their major defect
was unpredictability in flight. For further reading on these rockets, see Hobbs, *Congreve War Rockets*,
and Hogg, *Artillery*, pp. 248–50.

Baltimore Defense Plans

*News that the British blockading squadron was off Hampton Roads spread quickly
throughout the Chesapeake. By mid-February, a group of Baltimore insurance company
underwriters queried Secretary Jones about fitting out their own schooners to protect the
city's merchant trade from the British. Captain Charles Gordon, commander of the Baltimore Station since November 1811,[1] also solicited more vessels from Jones.*

1. *Gordon's rank as captain dated from 2 March 1813.*

Committee of Underwriters of Baltimore to
Secretary of the Navy Jones

Baltimore   February 1813

Sir,
    Under the Circumstances of the present Blockade of the Chesapeake, and
the extraordinary Hazards to which our Commerce is exposed, the public & private Underwriters of this City have been consulting on the best mode of affording some protection to our Homeward and Outward bound Trade.
    We find by experience, that the intrepid Navigators of our fast sailing and
War-built vessels, willingly encounter the Risk of passing the large British Ships,
which form the Blockade and have been unexpectedly successful in their attempts. But in executing their bold designs, they calculate only on the danger
to be apprehended from these Ships.— They are not aware that armed Boats
and small craft are prepared to decoy and intercept them in their passage, and
these are sometimes met at considerable distance from the Fleet, and are the
more dangerous, because least, if at all, expected.
    It was the opinion of a General Committee formed of Deputies from each In-
surance Company, that two, or more, not exceeding Four, fast sailing and well
equipped, and well armed Schooners, might be employed to great advantage in
destroying or checking these armed Boats and the other small Craft engaged in
the same service, and afford an effective protection to the Ships or vessels that
may evade, or dare to take the fire of, and to pass, the blockading Squadron.
They have accordingly appointed a Committee to engage Suitable vessels for

this purpose, and to cause them immediately to be fitted & equipped and despatched under vigilant Commanders & competent Crews, to render all the Service that may be found practicable.

The Committee are aware that the protection of Commerce is the proper provence of the General Government, with which they do not desire to interfere. But the occasion is urgent, and they are confident that their Exertion will be received as intended, as an auxiliary measure, that will procure temporary relief, until a more efficient plan can be devised & executed. They will provide for the present expence of the proposed armament, with a due regard to œconomy, and trust for reimbursement to the Justice of Government, sincerely hoping the present proceeding will be duly appreciated & approved.

We have been ordered to make this Communication to you, and shall be happy to hear from you in Reply, with as little delay as possible. With great Respect We have the honor to be in behalf of the Underwriters of Baltimore Sir Your humble Servts.—

Jn⁰ Hollins   presidt. of the Maryd. Insce. Co.
D Winchester   Prest. of the Baltimore Ins: Compy.
S. Sterett, Ps. Isn. Ins. Co.

LS, DNA, RG45, MLR, 1813, Vol. 1, No. 106 (M124, Roll No. 53).

SECRETARY OF THE NAVY JONES TO
COMMITTEE OF UNDERWRITERS OF BALTIMORE

Messrs John Hollins	Presidents of	Navy Depart.
Winchester	Baltimore Insurance	16 Feb: 1813
& S Sterett	Company	

Your letter of [?] [1] inst. has this moment reached me and I shall tomorrow lay it before the President. It is true that the Government of the United States is Constitutionally charged with the protection of Commerce, but its means are limited and inadequate to protect at all points our extensive Coast and coasters against a powerful Naval foe whose Superiority enables to attack a vulnerable point with a celerity and force that cannot be repelled but by the Cooperation of the voluntary local force, whose interests & feelings are directly assailed.

The Naval force of the Government in the waters of the Chesapeake is the Frigate *Constellation*— 17 Gun boats and a Cutter now at Norfolk and will be retained there for the defence of that place now directly menaced with an attack.

The force here is three Gun boats to which I expect to add a Schooner with a heavy gun amidship— these will be ready in two days and under the Command of Captain Sinclair of the Navy will immediately proceed to the Mouth of the River and cooperate with any other force that may offer and I trust will soon clear the Bay of the marauders, who now infest it.

The *Scorpion* Cutter is also ordered from Norfolk to join Capt Sinclair. This little flotilla will be well officered and manned with the crew of the *Adams* Frigate now fitting here.

The movements and object of the contemplated force both public and private had better be conducted with as much circumspection as may be, and if it were practicable to get below their tenders and launches in the night so as to intercept them and chastize their temerity, it would probably confine them to their ships in future. I am &c

W Jones.

P.S. I have ordered a fast Pilot Boat from New York to cruize off the Coast and warn our vessels public & private of the Blockade of the Chesapeake and Delaware.

LB Copy, DNA, RG45, MLS, Vol. 11, pp. 198–99 (M209, Roll No. 4).

1. The Baltimore underwriters' letter was undated.

Master Commandant Charles Gordon to Secretary of the Navy Jones

Baltimore   16th Feby. 1813

Sir/

In reply to yrs. of yesterdays date I have the honor to inform you that there is but one Gun Boat (*No. 138*) at this place— She has a Commander, one mate, a stewart & two ordinary seamen— She will be provisioned, watered & ready for service by tomorrow night if men can be procured— She has been detained here two months entirely for the want of men that could not be procured in consequence of the high wages & bounty offer'd to seamen for the Letter of Mark service—

There are nine other Gun Boats belonging to this station, which I contemplated keeping at Annapolis during this winter to be always ready for immediate service; But on my sending them round to Washington on duty, the greater part (I understand) were ordered from thence to Norfolk, & the remainder were caught in the Ice in the Eastern Branch— very respty. Sir yr. Obt. servt.

Cha^S. Gordon

ALS, DNA, RG45, MC, 1813, No. 17 (M147, Roll No. 5).

Captain Charles Gordon to Secretary of the Navy Jones

Baltimore   13th March 1813

Sir/

I have the honor to inform you that Governor Winder having placed the defence of this City under the direction of Genl. Saml. Smith, he has this day solicited of me my cooperation with the Land forces in the defence & protection of Baltimore Town & harbour against any attack which the Enemy may meditate—

I informed the Genl. that it would give me infinite pleasure to render any assistance in my power untill I could receive your further instructions; But that my force was now reduced to a single Gun Boat, and even that Boat was destined to join Captn. Sinclair in the Potomac—

In consequence of the reports (now in circulation) of part of the British squadron having advancd up the Bay, I had determined on suggesting to you the propriety of fitting out one or two small Tenders at this place for the purpose of cruising in the Bay between Annapolis & the Potomac in order to protect the Bay trade against those Tenders & boats of the Enemy, and also to give to Annapolis & Baltimore the most erly information of their advance & situation from time to time— Having stated this my intention to the Genl. he immediately urged the necessity, and requested I would solicite of you permission to procure & equip two or three such vessels for that service—

It being well ascertained that no heavy ship can enter the Patapsco without lightening more than is usual in such cases, we have nothing to apprehend from any force except the approach of Gun or Bomb Vessels, which if attempted could be repell'd with our Tenders well fitted & man'd— I confess I do not myself apprehend an attack on this place, still I believe the Enemy may without much difficulty distress Annapolis—

There are now laying at Fort McHenry ready for sea, two or three very fine Privateer Schooners which I am of opinion are well adapted to our Bay cruising & capable of contending with any of the Tenders & boats of the Enemy— I know not if the owners of those vessels would agree to their serving the United States on the present occasion— But with your permission I would suggest to them the idea of their loaning those vessels & armaments & Crews to the United States for 1 or 2 months or during the Blockade; the United States agreeing to return them in the same condition we receive them, and to put their Crews in the pay and establishment of the Navy for the time being—

I beg leave also to inform you that I am much in want of a Lieutt. to take charge of the recruiting service on this station, as I have no person with whom I can trust the necessary monies for the advances &c.— And should you determine on fitting out anything from this place I could find employment for 2 or 3 smart Lieutts. & Midshipmen— I have the honor to be most respectfy. Sir, yr Obt. servt.

Cha^S. Gordon

ALS, DNA, RG45, CL, 1813, Vol. 2, No. 36 (M125, Roll No. 27).

The Potomac Flotilla under Sinclair and Kennedy

William Jones considered Washington more vulnerable to attack than Baltimore or Annapolis and therefore established a Potomac flotilla in February 1813, under Master Commandant Arthur Sinclair, late of Argus. *Sinclair took his newly purchased schooner and three gunboats down the bay as far as Piankatank River to annoy the enemy and destroy small tenders from the blockading squadron. His orders required him to return his crew to Washington by 15 March for duty on board* Adams.[1]

At the end of March, Jones ordered Lieutenant Edmund P. Kennedy to relieve Sinclair. In an effort to insure greater protection of the Potomac River, Jones's new orders to Kennedy curtailed the flotilla's cruising range to just beyond the mouth of that river.

1. See Jones to Sinclair, 26 Feb. 1813, DNA, RG45, SNL, Vol. 10, pp. 278–79 (M149, Roll No. 10).

SECRETARY OF THE NAVY JONES TO MASTER COMMANDANT ARTHUR SINCLAIR

Capt. Arthur Sinclair [1]   Nav: Deptmt.
Present.   17. Feb: 1813.

The waters of the Chesapeak, being now under a vigourous blockade by a squadron of the Enemies Ships at the entrance of the Bay—& their Tenders & launches having penetratd as high as new point, to the very great hazard of the trade inward & outward bound, it has become necessary to direct the small force now here, to repel those predatory incursions, & confine the depredation of the enemy to the sphere of his ship.

For this purpose, I have directed the commandant of the Navy Yard, to procure a schooner calculated for the purpose & capable of bearing a heavy gun a mid-ships, & such other armament as may be deemed proper, & also to equip the three gunboats now at the Navy Yard, as soon as possible. You will therefore immediately take the command of this expedition, & with the utmost dispatch, proceed to the mouth of the Potomac, & thence, as your judgment & discretion may direct, to execute the object of this enterprize. You will immediately ascertain, the names of officers & men, now attached to the gunboats, & report to me, the additional number & rank of officers, & number of men required to render your force efficient, which will be furnished from the *Adams*, for this temporary purpose, to be returned to that ship, when the expedition is terminated. A voluntary force of at least two stout privateers is now equipping at Baltimore, for the same purpose, & a perfect co-operation is my desirable; they will probably meet you at the mouth of the Potomac. I have ordered the *Scorpion* cutter from Norfolk to Annapolis & if you meet her, you will take her under your command [2]

W. Jones.

LB Copy, DNA, RG45, SNL, Vol. 10, p. 262 (M149, Roll No. 10).

1. Master Commandant Sinclair was not promoted to captain until 24 July 1813.
2. *Scorpion*, the cutter at Norfolk originally intended for use at Annapolis, was sent to the Potomac instead.

MASTER COMMANDANT ARTHUR SINCLAIR TO SECRETARY OF THE NAVY JONES

U States Armed Schooner *Adeline*[1] in
the Mouth of the Peankitank River
March the 11th. 1813

Sir
Agreeable to your instructions I take the earliest opportunity to inform you of my proceeding with the Flotilla under my command— Oweing to contrary winds and the extreme dull sailing of the gunboats I was until the 10th Inst reaching the mouth of the Patowmack where I recd. direct information that the Enemy were in Lynhaven Bay with four 74's—five Frigates & some small vessels; and that two other Frigates with two armed, Baltimore built, Schooners and a Sloop, were off New Point light, committing depridations in every Inlet and on every Bay craft they could come across— I immediately proceeded down the Bay, and at mid-night made a harbour under Gwins Island, the wind being a head and a prospect of bad weather— After having anchored in a line across the Channel with two

gunboats in company (the other not being able to fetch in had gone into the Rappahannock) I was hailed from an armed Schooner,[2] within us, to know who we were— I informed him, and upon requiring to know who he was, he went to quarters immediately and ordered my Boat onbd. him— I had anchored with Springs upon our cables and our men at quarters— I ordered him to let me know who he was, and upon his insisting on my Boats being sent to him, I fired a musket a head of him, which he instantly returned with a Broadside of Round and grape with a constant fire of small arms— Being well assured, from this conduct that it was one of the Enemies Schooners, I opened a fire on her from this vessel and in 15 or 20 minutes silenced her— I now ceased firing and desired the nearest gunboat to hail him and know if he had struck to us, and who he was— He made no reply but immediately renewed the Action— I then ordered a genl. fire from all the vessels, and in about the same length of time silenced him a second time— He acted, upon our ceasing our fire, precisely as he had before done, and it was now half an hour before he was a third time silenced— Altho his conduct did not deserve a third indulgence, yet humanity induced me to stop the effusion of Blood which our well directed fire must evidently have caused onboard his vessel— I was now in the act of sending an officer on board him to take possession, when I discovered he had made Sail and was endeavouring to escape under cover of the darkness of the night— I immediately cut my cable and made sail after him; but after a running fight of half an Hour, his great superiority of sailing and the extreme darkness of the night effected his escape— The last we saw of him he appeared to be on wind down the Bay— This procedure, added to his other conduct, and his having, as I am informed by the inhabitants of this place, anchored here just at night without shewing any colours, confirms me in the opinion of his being one of their light cruizers— He has, no doubt, suffered severely in killed and wounded, as we were at all times in good grape and canister distance, and from the quantity of his Bull Works which were floated onshore near where he lay, his hull must have been as much shattered as we could see his rigging appeared to be, by the light from his guns,

Our damage has been very trifling, only one man severely wounded, and our Rigging a little cut— I cannot say too much in praize of all the officers and crew of this vessel— I find from the excessive unwealdiness of the gunboats that I can calculate on but little support from them on this Expedition. They cannot hold their own upon a wind in the Bay, and never will stay, but in perfectly smooth water— A few light, fast sailing schooners, of easy draft, would be of infinitely more utility on such a service as this—

I find from this days information that we are here almost in the midst of their upper Squadron— Two Frigates, a Brig & Sloop of war with a number of smaller vessels are in and about Mockjack [*Mobjack*] Bay, which is the next harbour below us— They are blocking in a number of valuable vessels from Baltimore now at Anchor in the Severn, making from that Bay— If the sailing of the Flotilla would by any means justify the attempt, I would endeavour to get over to that River, in order to protect them from being cut out by their Boats; but such is the situation of the heavy ships in that Bay, as I have just been informed, that such a movement could not be attended with success: however I shall govern my self as circumstances may accrue. I have the honor to remain with great respect, Sir, your obt. Servt.

A Sinclair

ALS, DNA, RG45, MC, 1813, No. 34 (M147, Roll No. 5).

1. *Adeline* was purchased by the navy in February 1813 and renamed *Asp*.

2. Two days later Sinclair identified the ship as H.M. schooner *Lottery* and noted that she had sunk before she could reach the fleet at New Point Comfort; see Sinclair to Jones, 13 Mar. 1813, DNA, RG45, MC, 1813, No. 34 (M147, Roll No. 5). Both this letter and Sinclair's of 11 March were given the document number 34. *Lottery* was the Baltimore privateer that the British had captured on 8 February and renamed *Canso*; see pp. 318, 320. This vessel remained in British naval service until 1816. Perhaps Sinclair mistakenly attacked an American privateer. There is an allusion to this in the following letter.

SECRETARY OF THE NAVY JONES TO LIEUTENANT EDMUND P. KENNEDY

Lt. Edmd. P. Kennedy   Nav: Deptmt.
Comg. the U S. flotilla Potomac River   29. March 1813

The Flotilla, consisting of the *Scorpion* cutter, Schooner *Asp*—& gunboats *Nos. 70. 71. & 137.* is placed under your command. The object of this force is to watch the mouth of the Potowmac & occasionally to observe the situation & movements of the enemies force below, availing yourself of any fair oppertunity of attacking with success, but taking especial care that your return to the mouth of the Potowmac, is not intercepted by the enemy. The main object of your command is the protection of this River.

Should the enemy attempt to enter it, with a force superior to yours, you will retire as he advances, until you reach Fort Warburton, where you will take a favorable position, on the spit of sand opposite, & in co-operation with the Fort defend the passage. If you observe the enemy, moving up the Bay, in force, you will if possible, employ a small Boat, to give information at Annapolis. It will be proper, to embrace every possible oppertunity of communicating with this Department, whatever may be interesting, & for that purpose, you will not be absent from the mouth of the Potowmac more than five days at any one time. The gunboats sail & work very heavily, & it will be necessary to observe some caution lest in the event of pursuit by a superior force, they should be cut off or seperated. It will require some circumspection lest you should come in contact with some of our private armed vessels in the Bay, which by the imprudence of the commander of one of them, was the case during the late cruise of the Flotilla. It is known that some of the gunboats under your command, are Latteen rigged, which is a conspicuous & sufficient distinction of itself.

W. Jones

LB Copy, DNA, RG45, SNL, Vol. 10, pp. 325–26 (M149, Roll No. 10).

LIEUTENANT EDMUND P. KENNEDY TO SECRETARY OF THE NAVY JONES

U. States Cutter *Scorpion*
Abreast Fort Washington
9th April 1813

Sir,

I have the Honr. of inclosing you the Guard report of the *Asp*, belonging to the <u>Flotilla</u> under my command— The Flotilla is anchor'd in the place directed in order to cooperate with the <u>Fort</u> but I really do not calculate on receiving any aid from that Quarter, the Platform being very badly constructed & in miserable Order—one Gun Boat well mann'd might attack it in the present Situation with certain Success.

I wish very much to proceed farther down the river Sir, but I have no Surgeon, & the Men are very Sickly; the Boats are badly Mann'd as well in Number as in quality of the Crew Shoul'd it meet your approbation Sir I woul'd be glad to have a few Men exchanged & permission to proceed to St. Marys— Respectfly. I have the Honr. to be Your Mst. Ob. Svt.

Edm^d. P. Kennedy

ALS, DNA, RG45, BC, 1813, Vol. 1, No. 178 (M148, Roll No. 11).

[Enclosure]

A Report of Vessels boarded by the U States Schooner *Asp* Jas. B. Sigourney Commander from Friday 9th At 8 am Until Saturday 10th At 8 AM Inclusive

Day date & Hour	description of Vessles	Vessles Names	Masters Names	Where from	Where bound	Cargo	Remarks
Friday Apr. 9							
1 PM	Sloop	*Little Liddy*	Bnj H Merick	Alexandria	French Town	Flour	Reported that the British Squadron was off Rappahannock
5 PM	Schooner	*Hariot*	Wm. Jackson	Wecomico	Alexandria	Wood	Reported that the British Squadron At Mouth of the River
1/2 5 PM	Schooner	*Polly*	Jos. Smith	Pottomack Creek	Alexandria	Plank	
9 PM	Schooner	*Adolphus*	Capt. Linavall	from the mouth Potomack	Alexandria	Flour	Put Back in consequence of the British Vessels being of the mouth of the River
1/2 9 PM	Schooner	*American*	Capt. Smith	from ditto	Alexandria	Flour	Put Back in consequence of the British cruisers being of the mouth of the River

Boarded a number of small Craft and Permitted to Pass
Also Boarded a Small fishing Schooner from Little Wecomico
Reported a heavy fireing was heard off patuxon on Tuesday

Saturday 10th April 1813
J B Sigourney

DS, DNA, RG45, BC, 1813, Vol. 1, No. 178, enclosure (M148, Roll No. 11).

American Privateer Schooner Dolphin and Others Captured in the Rappahannock River by British Boats, 3 April 1813

British Raiding Parties

Admiral Sir John B. Warren in his flagship San Domingo, 74, arrived in Lynn-haven Bay on 22 March accompanied by Ramillies, 74, Statira, 38, Mohawk, 12, and Highflyer, tender. Frustrated in their attempts to attack Constellation in the Elizabeth River, the British decided in early April to proceed up the bay to harass American merchantmen and coastal towns. Warren and his squadron sailed as far as Annapolis, leaving the amphibious operations in the upper bay to Rear Admiral Cockburn. Besides attacking several towns and a cannon foundry, Cockburn made charts of the waters through which he cruised, which would prove useful when the British returned with an even greater vengeance in 1814.

LIEUTENANT JAMES POLKINGHORNE, R.N.,[1] TO
ADMIRAL SIR JOHN B. WARREN, R.N.

Copy   His Majesty's Ship *San Domingo*
                                            in the Chesapeake   3d April 1813

Sir,

In pursuance of the Orders to proceed with the Boats of the Squadron you did me the honor to place under my Command, and attack the Enemys vessels at the Mouth of the River Rappahannock—

I have to inform you, that after rowing fifteen Miles I found they were four Armed Schooners drawn up in a line ahead, apparently determined to give us a warm reception, notwithstanding their formidable appearance and the advantage they would necessarily derive from mutual support, I determined to attack them, the Issue of which is such as might have been expected, from the brave Men you did me the honor to Command and is as follows (Vizt.)—

Arab--------	7 Guns 45 Men Run on Shore & boarded by two Boats of the *Marlborough* Under Lieut. Urmston & Scott
Lynx-------	6 Guns 40 Men Hauld her Colours down on my going along side in the *San Domingos* Pinnace—
Racer-------	6 Guns 36 Men boarded and carried after a sharp resistance by the *San Domingos* Pinnace–
Dolphin ----	12 Guns 98 Men the Guns of the *Racer* were turned upon her, and then gallantly Boarded by Lieut. Bishop in the *Statiras* large Cutter and Lieut. Liddon in *Maidstones* Launch—

From the scattered situation of the Squadron and strong Tide, only the fast rowing Boats were able to get up, and much credit is due to the Officers and Men in the heavy Boats for their great exertions and perseverance, and had they been up in time to join the attack, I am Confidant I should have received every support that could be expected—

Lieutenant Urmston & Scott of the *Marlborough* Lieut. Bishop of the *Statira* and Lieut. Liddon of the *Maidstone* speak in the highest terms of the gallantry of their respective Crews, and it would be an injustice to those Officers and Men were I not to bear testimony to their gallant and intrepid Conduct—

I must also beg leave to represent that the conduct of Lieut. Flint, and the Royal Marines in the Pinnace deserve great praise for the steady and well directed fire kept up by them when advanceing under the Enemies Grape and Musquettry, and that the assistance I received from Lieut. Brand Messrs. Pearce & Ridgeway Midshipmen (who have served their time and passed) as well as the Crew of the pinnace was such as to merit the highest encomium and to whom I shall ever feel much indebted

I herewith enclose a List of the Killed and Wounded[2] And have the honor to be Sir, Your most obedient Servant

(Signed)   J Puckinghorn

P.S. The Enemys loss as far as I have been able to ascertain, is Five Killed, and one died since of his Wounds, and Ten Wounded.

Copy, UkLPR, Adm. 1/503, pp. 482–85.

1. Variously spelled Puckinghorn, Puckinghorne, and Polkinghorne. Marshall's *Royal Naval Biography* refers to him as Polkinghorne.
2. The British suffered two killed and eleven wounded during the 3 April engagement on the Rappahannock River. See UkLPR, Adm. 1/503, p. 487.

Rear Admiral George Cockburn, R.N., to Admiral Sir John B. Warren, R.N.

No. 8   *Marlborough,* Swan Point East
                                                  2 miles   April 19th 1813.

Sir,

The *Mohawke* having come to me last night owing to a mistake of Signals and that Vessel drawing less Water by Three feet than the Tenders, which is of essential consequence in the difficult Navigation around this spot, I have ventured to keep her and send you the *Lynx* in her stead to inform you that I brought the Squadron to this Anchorage on Friday Evening without other accident than the *Racer* (Tender) taking the Ground on Swan Point spit from which however she was soon got off again without damage.

On opening the Patapsco River I was mortified to observe that there was no Vessel below the Fort, excepting one large Gun Boat advanced about a Gun shot from it, and some Schooners and Small Vessels under Sail near the mouth of the River apparently endeavouring to regain a safe anchorage in consequence of our approach, as soon as we anchored. I dispatched the *Hornet* and Boats in pursuit of these (the shallowness of the numerous Knowls around here not allowing me to make use of the larger Tenders.) Two of the *Statira*'s Boats pulling towards the Gun Boat she immediately weighed and instead of waiting to give Protection to the other Vessels she ran up beyond the Fort firing at these two Boats as she run away from them, and a constant fire was kept up on all the Boats from the Shore from small Guns or Field Pieces without however any effect, and every Vessel (except the Gun Boat which made such a timely retreat) was Captured and brought out. Enclosed I have the honor to transmit a List of these Vessels and how I have disposed of them, they not being of a description for sending into an English Port.

On Saturday morning learning from the Prisoners that all the Vessels in the Patapsco had been hauled as close up as possible, unloaded and disarmed, excepting only one Privateer and therefore there being little prospect of my being able to effect any advantageous operations in that River, I determined to avail myself of our advanced position to endeavour to procure a Supply of Fresh Water, that alongside and between us and Poole Island being however (contrary to the Information you had received) too Brackish to drink, I directed the *Maidstone* to move as much higher toward Turkey Point as from the depth of Water Captn. Burdett should find practicable and then to advance the Tenders again from him for the protection of the Watering Vessels into which I had converted the Prizes taken the day before, in spite however of the assistance of all our Masters and Pilots the *Maidstone* was not able to get above Five miles to the Northward of me and the Tenders not above a mile further, but the watering Vessels nevertheless succeeded in getting off Turkey Point under the Protection of Armed Boats & I am happy to say have just returned with a Load of Excellent Water and the *Mohawke* which on taking under my orders, I immediately dispatched to get as near Turkey Point as possible for the protection and furtherance of this Service, having succeeded in getting Six or Seven Miles higher than the Tenders, I have no doubt of being able to complete the whole Squadron in Water by tomorrow night or the next day at furthest without difficulty or risk, and all the Ships are completed in Fact from the Prizes.

I am endeavouring to have the position of the different Shoals and Knowls around us ascertained and buoyed off, and if I find it possible to get any thing into the entrance of Patapsco I shall do so, and should it appear practicable to annoy their Fort or Vessels above it with Rockets &c. I shall not hesitate in attempting it.

I transmit also an intercepted Letter which will give you Some Idea of the Effect our appearance here has had at Baltimore and of the Precautions taken in consequence thereof. I have the honor to be Sir Your very faithful and most obedient Humble Servant

G. Cockburn   Rr. Adml.

LB Copy, DLC, Papers of George Cockburn, Container 9, Letters Sent, 3 Feb. 1812–6 Feb. 1814, pp. 150–54.

REAR ADMIRAL GEORGE COCKBURN, R.N., TO ADMIRAL SIR JOHN B. WARREN, R.N.

No. 11

His Majesty's Ship *Maidstone*,
Tuesday Night 3rd May 1813
at Anchor off Turkey Point

Sir

I have the Honor to inform you that whilst anchoring the Brigs and Tenders off Spesucie Island agreeable to my Intentions notified to you in my official Report of the 29th Ulto. No. 10 I observed Guns fired and American Colours hoisted at a Battery lately erected at Havre-de-Grace at the entrance of the Susquehanna River, this of course immediately gave to the Place an Importance which I had not before attached to it, and I therefore determined on attacking it after the completion of our Operations at the Island, consequently having sounded in the direction towards it and found that the Shallowness of the Water would only admit of its being approached by Boats, I directed their assembling under Lieutenant Westphal, (1st of the *Marlborough*) last night at 12 O'Clock alongside the *Fantome*, when our Detachment of Marines consisting of about 150 Men (as before) under Captains Wybourn and Carter with the Small Party of Artillery men under Lt. Robertson of the Artillery, embarked in them and the whole being under the immediate direction of Captain Lawrence of the *Fantome*, (who with much Zeal and readiness took upon himself at my request the conducting of this Service) proceeded towards Havre to take up under cover of the Night the necessary Positions for Commencing the Attack at dawn of day— The *Dolphin* and *Highflyer* Tenders Commanded by Lieutenants Hutchinson and Lewis followed for the support of the Boats but the Shoalness of the Water prevented their getting within Six Miles of the Place. Captain Lawrence however having got up with the Boats and having very ably and judiciously placed them during the dark, a warm fire was opened on the Place at Daylight from our Launches and Rocket Boat, which was smartly returned from the Battery for a short time, but the Launches constantly closing with it and their Fire rather encreasing than decreasing, that from the Battery soon began to Slacken, and Captain Lawrence observing this, very judiciously directed the landing of the Marines on the Left, which movement added to the hot fire they were under, induced the Americans to commence withdrawing from the Battery to take Shelter in the Town— Lieut. G. A. Westphal who had taken his station in the Rocket Boat close to the Battery therefore now judging the moment to be favorable pulled directly up under the work and landing with his Boat's Crew got immediate possession of it, turned their own Guns on them, and thereby soon obliged them to retreat with their whole Force to the furthest Extremity of the Town, whither (the Marines having by this Time landed) they were closely pursued and no longer feeling themselves equal to a manly and open Resistance, they commenced a teazing and irritating fire from behind their Houses, Walls, Trees &c. from which I am sorry to say my gallant first Lieutenant received a Shot through his Hand whilst leading the pursuing Party, he however continued to Head the Advance with which he soon succeeded in dislodging the whole of the Enemy from their lurking Places and driving them for Shelter to the Neighbouring Woods &c whilst performing which Service he had the satisfaction to overtake and with his remaining Hand to make Prisoner and bring in a Captain of their Militia— We also took an Ensign and some armed Individuals but the rest of the Force which had been opposed to us having penetrated into the woods I did not judge it prudent to allow of their being further followed with our small Numbers, therefore after setting Fire to some of the Houses to cause the Proprietors (who had deserted them and formed Part of the Militia who had fled to the Woods) to understand and feel what they were liable to bring upon themselves by building Batteries and acting towards us with so much useless Rancor, I embarked in the Boats the Guns from the Battery, and having also taken and destroyed about 130 Stand of small arms, I detached a small division of Boats up the Susquehanna to take and destroy whatever they might meet with in it, and proceeded myself with the remaining Boats under Captain Lawrence in Search of a Cannon Foundery which I had gained Intelligence of whilst on shore in Havre as being situated about 3 or 4 Miles to the Northward where we found it accordingly and getting Possession of it without difficulty, commenced instantly its destruction and that of the Guns and other Materials we found there, to complete which occupied us during the Remainder of the Day as there were several Buildings and much complicated heavy Machinery attached to it,— It was known by the names of the Cecil or Principio Foundery, and was one of the most valuable Works of the Kind in America, the Destruction of it therefore at this moment will I trust prove of much national Importance—per Margin[1] I have stated the Ordnance taken and disabled by our small Division this day, during the whole of which we have been on Shore in the Centre of the Enemy's Country and on his high Road between Baltimore and Philadelphia. The Boats which I sent up the Susquehanna returned after destroying five Vessels in it and a large Store of Flour, when every thing being compleated to my utmost wishes, the whole division re-embarked and returned to the Ships where we arrived at 10 O'Clock after being Twenty two Hours in constant exertion without Nourishment of any kind, and I have much pleasure in being able to add that excepting Lt. Westphal's wound we have not suffered any Casualty whatever.

The Judicious Dispositions made by Captain Lawrence of the *Fantome* during the preceeding Night, and the able manner in which he conducted the attack of Havre in the Morning, added to the Gallantry, Zeal, and attention shewn by him during this whole day, most justly entitle him to my highest Encomiums and Acknowledgements and will I trust ensure to him your Approbation and I have the Pleasure to add that he speaks in the most favorable manner of the good conduct of all the Officers and Men employed in the Boats under his immediate Orders, particularly of Lieutenants Alexander and Reed of the *Dragon,* and, *Fantome* who each commanded a Division— Of Lieutenant G. A. Westphal whose exemplary and gallant Conduct it has been so necessary for me already to notice in detailing to you the operations of the day, I shall only now add that from a thorough Knowledge of his merits (he having served many years with me as 1st. Lieut.) I always on similar Occasions expect much from him, but this day he even outstripped these expectations, and though in considerable Pain from his wound he insisted on continuing to assist me to the last moment with his able Exertions, I therefore Sir cannot but entertain a confident hope that his Services of today, and the wound he has received added to what he so successfully executed at French Town (as detailed in my letter to you of the 29th Ultmo.) will obtain for him your favorable consideration and Notice and that of My Lords Commissioners of the Admiralty—[2] I should be wanting in justice did I not also mention to you particularly the able Assistance again afforded me this day by Lt. Robertson of the Artillery who is ever a Volunteer where Service is to be performed and always foremost in performing such Service, being equally conspicuous for his Gallantry and Ability and he also obliged me by superintending the destruction of the Ordnance taken at the Foundery. To Captains Wybourn and Carter who commanded the Marines and shewed much Skill in their Management of them, every Praise is likewise due, as are my acknowledgements to Lt. Lewis of the *Highflyer,* who not being able to bring his Vessel near enough to render us assistance, came himself with his usual active Zeal to offer his Personal Services— And it is my pleasing Duty to report to you in addition that all the other Officers and Men seemed to vie with each other in the Cheerful and Zealous Discharge of their Duty, and I have therefore the Satisfaction of recommending their general good Conduct on this Occasion to your Notice accordingly— I have the honor to be Sir, Your very faithful and most humble Servant

(Sd.)　　G. Cockburn　　Rr. Adml.

LB Copy, DLC, Papers of George Cockburn, Container 9, Letters Sent, 3 Feb. 1812–6 Feb. 1814, pp. 162–70. Another copy is in UkLPR, Adm. 1/503, pp. 669–77.

1. "Taken from the Battery at Havre, Six Guns—12 & 6 Prs. Disabled in the Battery for Protection of Foundery five 24 Prs. Disabled Ready for sending away from Foundery Twenty eight—32 Prs. Disabled in Boring House and Foundery, Eight Guns & four Carronades of different Calibres—Total 51 Guns and 130 Stand of Small Arms—"
2. In July 1813, the Admiralty rewarded George Augustus Westphal's exploits with the rank of commander. He led the division of boats that captured the privateer *Anaconda* at Ocracoke, North Carolina; see pp. 184–87.

REAR ADMIRAL GEORGE COCKBURN, R.N., TO ADMIRAL SIR JOHN B. WARREN, R.N.

No. 12   H.M.S. *Maidstone* off the
                                        Sasafras River   the 6th May 1813

Sir

I have the honor to acquaint you that understanding George Town and Fredericstown, situated up the Sasafras River were Places of some Trade and Importance, and the Sasafras being the only River or Place of Shelter for Vessels at this upper Extremity of the Chesapeake which I had not examined and cleared, I directed last Night the assembling of the Boats alongside the *Mohawke,* from whence, with the Marines as before under Captains Wyburn and Carter with my Friend Lt. Robertson of the Artillery and his small Party they proceeded up this River, being placed by me for this Operation under the immediate directions of Captn. Byng of the *Mohawke.*

I intended that they should arrive before the abovementioned Towns by Dawn of Day, but in this I was frustrated by the Intricacy of the River, our total want of local Knowledge in it, the darkness of the Night, and the great Distance the Towns lay up it; It therefore became unavoidably late in the morning before we approached them, when having intercepted a small Boat with two of the Inhabitants, I directed Captain Byng to halt our Boats about two Miles below the Town, and I sent forward the two Americans in their Boat to warn their Countrymen against acting in the same rash manner the People of Havre-de-Grace had done, assuring them if they did that their Towns would inevitably meet with a similar Fate, but on the contrary, if they did not attempt Resistance no Injury should be done to them or their Towns, that Vessels and Public Property only, would be seized, that the strictest Discipline would be maintained, and that whatever Provisions or other Property of Individuals I might require for the use of the Squadron should be instantly paid for in its fullest Value. After having allowed sufficient Time for this Message to be digested and their Resolution taken thereon I directed the boats to advance and I am sorry to say I soon found the more unwise alternative was adopted, for on our reaching within about a mile of the Town between two projected elevated Points of the River, a most heavy Fire of Musquetry was opened on us from about 400 Men divided and entrenched on the two opposite Banks, aided by one long Gun. The Launches and Rocket Boat smartly returned this Fire with good Effect, and with the other Boats and the Marines I pushed ashore immediately above the Enemy's Position, thereby ensuring the capture of his Towns or the bringing him to a decided action, he determined however not to risk the latter, for the moment he discovered we had gained the shore, and that the Marines had fixed their Bayonets, he fled with his whole Force to the Woods, and was neither seen or heard of afterwards, though several parties were sent out to ascertain whether he had taken up any new Position or what had become of him, I gave him however the Mortification of seeing from wherever he had hid himself that I was Keeping my word with Respect to his Towns, which (excepting the Houses of those who had continued peaceably in them and had taken no Part in the attack made on us) were forthwith destroyed as were four Vessels laying in the River, and some Stores of Sugar, of Lumber, of Leather, and other Merchandize; I then directed the re-embarkation of our small Force and we proceeded down the River again to a Town I had observed situated in a Branch of it about half way up, and here I had the satisfaction to find that what had passed at Havre, George Town, and Fredericstown had its Effects, and led these People to understand that they have more to hope for from our Generosity than from erecting Batteries and opposing us by the Means within their Power. The Inhabitants of this Place having met me at landing to say that they had not permitted either Guns or Militia to be stationed there, and that whilst there I should not meet with any opposition whatever, I therefore Landed with the Officers and a small Guard only, and having ascertained that there was not any Public Property of any Kind or warlike Stores, and having allowed of such Articles as we stood in need of being embarked in the Boats on Payment to the Owners of their full value, I again re-embarked leaving the People of this Place well pleased with the wisdom of their Determination on their mode of receiving us, I also had a Deputation from Charleston in the North East River, to assure me that that Place is considered by them as at your Mercy, and that neither Guns nor Militia Men shall be suffered there and as I am assured that all the Places in the upper Part of the Chesapeake have adopted similar Resolutions, and as there is now neither public Property, Vessels, nor Warlike Stores remaining in this Neighbourhood, I propose returning to you with the light Squadron Tomorrow Morning.

I am sorry to say the hot Fire we were under this Morning cost us five Men wounded one only however severely and I have much Satisfaction in being able again to bear Testimony to you, of the Zeal, Gallantry, and good Conduct of the different Officers and Men serving in this Division— To Captain Byng of the *Mohawke* who conducted the various arrangements on this Occasion with equal Skill and Bravery every possible Praise is most justly due, Captains Wybourne and Carter, likewise conducted the Marines much to my satisfaction, and Lt. Robertson of the Artillery as usual rendered me the greatest Service by his Advice Activity and Gallantry; Lt. Lewis of the *Highflyer* (who left his Tender after bringing her as near as the depth of Water would allow her to approach) having throughout the day acted as my Aid-de-Camp and rendered me much useful assistance, is entitled to my best acknowledgements and Recommendations to your Notice; Lt. Alexander of the *Dragon* the Senior Officer under Captn. Byng in Command of the Boats deserves also that I should particularly notice him to you for his Steadiness, Correctness, and the great ability with which he always executes whatever Service is entrusted to him, and I must beg permission to seize this opportunity of stating to you how much I have been indebted since on this Service, to Captain Burdett of this Ship who was good enough to receive me on board the *Maidstone* when I found it impracticable to advance higher in the *Marlborough* and has invariably accompanied me on every occasion, whilst directing these various operations and rendered me always the most able prompt and efficacious Assistance. I have the honor to be, Sir, Your very faithful and Most Humble Servant.

(Sd.)   G. Cockburn.   Rr. Admiral

LB Copy, DLC, Papers of George Cockburn, Container 9, Letters Sent, 3 Feb. 1812–6 Feb. 1814, pp. 171–79. Another copy is in UkLPR, Adm. 1/503, pp. 679–85.

Craney Island Defense Preparations

Captain Charles Stewart continued to fortify the Gosport Station during April and May, but was faced with the perennial manpower shortage. Jones concurred with Stewart's defense plans, but cautioned him to leave the erection of an artillery battery on Craney Island to the War Department.

Captain Charles Stewart to Secretary of the Navy Jones

United States frigate *Constellation*
Norfolk harbour   April 4. 1813

Sir

The Enemy's Squadron put to Sea on the evening of the 2d. inst. leaving the *Victorious* of 74 guns off Willoughby's point, one frigate on the tail of the horse shoe, and one in Lynnhaven bay. I presume the rest have gone to Bermuda to replenish their water and provisions. It appears to me that no time ought to be lost now to erect a battery on Crany Island, and to put the flotilla in a respectable condition, for I am persuaded they intend something more than a blockade in this quarter.

Something might be effected against the enemy with fire vessels and powder chests floated down in the night, but unless I am particularly instructed on this head I should not feel myself authorised to attempt it. I have the honor to be, Very Respectfully, Sir, Your obedient Servant

Ch^S. Stewart

ALS, DNA, RG45, CL, 1813, Vol. 2, No. 129 (M125, Roll No. 27).

Secretary of the Navy Jones to Captain Charles Stewart

Charles Stewart Esqr.   Navy Deptmt.
Commanding Naval Officer, Norfolk Harbour.   April 8. 1813.

Sir,

Yours of the 4th is received, and I am inclined to believe that part of the Squadron that left the Chesapeak on the 2nd of May[1] be those which it is said have appeared off Sandy Hook.[2]

Agreeably to the instructions I have already given I trust the recruiting of the Crews of the Flotilla will progress until the requisite number are obtained. But the demand for men and the great number of places not less exposed than Norfolk, and with <u>much less protection</u>, does not admit of a further diminution of the defence of those places in order to strengthen Norfolk: nor will it do to strip our Ships of their crews, because that would render the war on our part merely defensive, and completely release the enemy from the pressure of our active hostility. If you have any other mode of putting the "Flotilla in a respectable condition" than that of strengthening your force at the expense of other exposed situations, I shall be glad to hear it. I have already mentioned that our efforts to recruit for the Gun Boats have failed at Baltimore, and progress very slowly at Philadelphia, even for the small force ordered for the defence of the Delaware, now as effectually blockaded and annoyed as the Chesapeak.

Every possible <u>effort</u> and <u>resource</u> of Department will be employed for the defence of Norfolk, and every other exposed situation; but the defence of a <u>part</u> must be regulated by a view of the <u>whole</u>; for no reasonable man can suppose that our means are competent to the defence of <u>all</u> against a superior force, which can be concentrated against any one point. You will, therefore, make the best use of the means you possess, and encrease them by all the resources within your vicinity.—

The presence of a powerful hostile squadron is naturally calculated to excite alarm, thus we have urgent calls from Maine to Georgia, each conceiving itself the particular object of attack.

Whatever may be the ultimate design of the Enemy against Norfolk, nothing should relax our exertions for its defence; but I do not believe it his intention to attack that place, or the force in its waters. His prospect of success diminishes by delay, and if it is necessary for that end to increase his force, the object to be attained and the sacrifice to be made does not appear to warrant the undertaking. I yesterday authorised you to construct floating Battery you suggested, and if you think any thing of importance can be effected by means of Fire vessels and powder chests you are authorised to try the experiment. I am, very respectfully, Yours &ca.

W. Jones.—

P.S. The Battery you suggest on Crany Island comes within the scope of the Department of War, and not of this Department. It has long since been suggested to the Secretary of War.—

LB Copy, DNA, RG45, SNL, Vol. 10, pp. 339–40 (M149, Roll No. 10).

1. The clerk meant to write "2nd of April may be those. . . ."
2. *Acasta*, 40, arrived at Sandy Hook on 7 April.

CAPTAIN CHARLES STEWART TO SECRETARY OF THE NAVY JONES

United States frigate *Constellation*
off Norfolk   May 13. 1813

Sir

Yesterday afternoon the Enemy's squadron returned down the bay and came into Lynnhaven; they are now extended in line from Willoughby's point to cape Henry light and in all probability will move up into Hampton roads to day as the wind is fair; there are fifteen sail of ships of war. There is a party at work throwing up a battery on Crany island, but I fear they have been too tardy in their operations; there are about five hundred troops on the island, and I have stationed seven gun boats there to assist in covering the operations; in all probability Hampton or that place will be attacked soon.

I shall defer my departure in compliance with your orders of the 7th. inst, a few days, untill the enemy's intentions are developed.[1] I think it highly probable, if they design any thing against Norfolk, that active operations will commence immediately on these waters.

I have had the bomb-ketch *Spitfire* given some slight repairs, which will be completed this week, and she will answer very well on the bay or rivers. Captain Cassin is collecting logs for the floating battery which when done I feel persuaded will prove most formidable to a ship of the line She is designed to carry thirty four ~~long~~ heavy guns. I have the honor to be, Respectfully Sir Your Obedient Servant

Ch^S. Stewart

ALS, DNA, RG45, CL, 1813, Vol. 3, No. 126 (M125, Roll No. 28).

1. On 7 May Jones ordered Stewart to leave immediately for Washington and then proceed to command *Constitution,* refitting at Boston. Stewart was apparently more concerned about a possible British attack than Jones, because the captain asked to delay his departure. On reflection, the secretary agreed. See Jones to Stewart, 7 and 17 May 1813, SNL, Vol. 10, pp. 401 and 421–24 (M149, Roll No. 10).

Leasing Schooners for Baltimore's Defense

Reports of a British squadron in Chesapeake Bay prompted Secretary Jones to accept the proffer of leased vessels from Baltimore shipowners. Captain Charles Gordon spent April and May choosing four ships and recruiting the officers and crews to man them. On completing his flotilla's complement, he set out on a month-long cruise hoping that his naval presence in the bay would encourage American vessels to venture out. He saw no action because the larger British ships did not permit their smaller vessels to stray far from their protection. Gordon did succeed, however, in removing some of the British buoys, placing them elsewhere to confuse the enemy.[1]

1. *For further reading on Baltimore's leased schooners, see Calderhead, "Naval Innovation."*

SECRETARY OF THE NAVY JONES TO CAPTAIN CHARLES GORDON

Captain Charles Gordon,   Navy Department
U.S. Navy, Baltimore   April 15. 1813.—

Sir,

The President of the United States desirous of affording to the trade of the City of Baltimore and its intercourse with the waters of the Chesapeake, the aid of such a naval force as may be practicable with immediate effect, and having no regular Naval force near Baltimore, except the Gun Boat under your orders,

I hereby authorize you to enter into an engagement in behalf of the Navy Department with any of the Citizens of Baltimore, who may have Schooners of a
class and description suitable for the occasion, completely equipped for service,
and who may be disposed to loan the said vessels to the Government for the
purpose aforesaid, to accept of the loan of <u>four</u> such vessels, conditioned to restore the said vessels when demanded by the owners thereof, or directed by the
Secretary of the Navy, in the same condition in all respects in which they may be
delivered to you.—[1]

In order to ascertain the fair equitable value of such vessels at the time of receiving them into the service of the United States, you will, in conjunction with
the Navy Agent, cause an exact account of the State and condition, an inventory
of the appurtenances, and an impartial valuation of each vessel to be taken and
acknowledged by the Navy Agent in behalf of the Navy Department, and by the
owners of each of the said vessels on the other Part—

You are then to proceed to man and provision them for service with the utmost dispatch by recruiting such number of seamen, ordinary seamen and boys,
as the nature of the service may require, to serve during the time the said vessels
shall be employed, and you will also engage & appoint such acting officers, subordinate to the commanders, as may be necessary. The private commanders of
the vessels you may thus engage, if of approved character, conduct and qualifications may continue to command them in the public service, and in order to give
them the necessary authority and render them responsible to the Government,
the commanders will receive the appointment of Sailing Masters in the Navy of
the United States, to continue during the period of such service.—

The whole of the officers and of the crews will be entitled to the same pay, rations and prize money, and subject to the discipline and regulations as the
other officers and crews of the Navy of the United States. The purser of the Station will act as purser for the whole force under your command and forward to
the Department correct muster rolls of the whole.—

As those vessels will be, to all intents and purposes, vessels of the Navy of the
United States, whilst so employed, and the engagement to restore them in their
original condition provides for the wear and tear, and is equivalent to the hire
of said vessels, and, moreover, as the officers and crews if wounded or disabled
in the public service will be entitled to the benefit of the Navy pension fund, it
is to be clearly understood that that fund will be entitled to the one half of
whatever prizes may be made, and the officers and crews to the other half, except when the captured force may be equal, in which case the officers and crews
will be entitled to the whole.—

Your command will be independent of any authority but that of this Department; but in the possible event of the approach of the enemy towards the City of
Baltimore, you will on all proper occasions afford to the Commanding General[2]
the most effective co-operation in your power. Your force, comprising the four
schooners contemplated by this arrangement, and the United States Gun Boat
No. 138, will be very respectable, and admirably adapted for vigorous offensive
service; and I trust you will be enabled if not to cut off, at least to confine, the
light cruisers of the Enemy within the range of the Guns of his Squadron; but it
would be a more acceptable and important service to recapture those fine
Schooners which have recently and unfortunately fallen into his hands.

Should the enemy retire below the Potomac, the flotilla in that river consisting of the *Scorpion* cutter, Schooner *Asp* and three Gunboats, under the com-

mand of Lieutenant Kennedy, will be directed to join your command. I am, respectfully, your ob: servant

W. Jones.

LB Copy, DNA, RG45, SNL, Vol. 10, pp. 352–54 (M149, Roll No. 10).

1. For the Baltimore merchants' offer to lease ten armed schooners, see Joseph H. Nicholson to Jones, 13 Apr. 1813, DNA, RG45, MLR, 1813, Vol. 3, No. 15 (M124, Roll No. 55). For Gordon's description of the leased schooners, *Comet, Patapsco, Revenge,* and *Wasp,* see p. 352.

2. Major General Samuel Smith, Republican senator from Maryland, was in command of the Third Division of the Maryland militia and charged with the defense of Baltimore.

CAPTAIN CHARLES GORDON TO SECRETARY OF THE NAVY JONES

Baltimore   18th April 1813

Sir,

I have the honor to inform you that our last accounts from North point (this evening) reports a Ship of the Line & one Frigate off swan point, another Frigate a little above (apparently watering at swan point by floating their Casks) and a Brig with other small vessels a few miles higher up the Bay (no doubt) sounding— Another square rigg'd vessel was in sight coming up the Bay (supposed to be a Brig—

In compliance with yr. instructions, I engag'd the Schooners *Comet* & *Patapsco* on Friday evening; The *Comet* is haul'd off & only waiting for her crew 80 of which have enter'd today— The *Patapsco* requiring some alterations in her equipment besides ballasting, provisioning &c., will delay us a few days tho. I think she will be ready before her crew can be procured; For notwithstanding the great outcry of vessels & men in abundance I find (except in the case of the *Comet*) trouble & difficulty— A great number of the sailors now in port are still attach'd to the Letters of Marque laying here with there Cargo's, in which deprives us the use of those fine Schooners well fitted, and the services of those men; Still I hope, in a few days, we shall procure a sufficiency—

I have also engag'd the *Revenge,* she will haul off tomorrow, & be in readiness for her crew, 20 of which have already entered—

The fourth I have found it difficult to procure without taking a new unfinish'd vessel— I have applied for 4 or 5, but their owners have all made some objections, respecting their cargoes &c.—

The *Fox* privateer that is now heaving out to repare her false keel can be got ready as soon as any other vessel now idle— I have applied for her & shall receive a decisive answer from her owner to morrow—

As all the officers & crews of those vessels are unacquainted with our service & accustom'd to privateers, I think it necessary (to preserve order as well as to preserve the stores & to look out at night) to have a Corporals guard of U.S Marine (say 3 or 4) in each vessel for a week or untill their crews are organized & disciplin'd— We have 5 or 6 now fit for duty, those with an addition of 15 would answer our purpose, all of which will be requir'd on this station during the building of the ships— very respty. Sir, yr. Obt. Servt.

Cha^S. Gordon

ALS, DNA, RG45, CL, 1813, Vol. 3, No. 9 (M125, Roll No. 28).

CAPTAIN CHARLES GORDON TO SECRETARY OF THE NAVY JONES

Baltimore   27th April 1813

Sir

Nothing material has occur'd since the last, I had the honor to address you except, an increase of the Enemy's squadron— From our last reports there were 2 ships of the line & 2 Frigates off Swan point, one Frigate above, & two Brigs with 4 Schooners nearly about Elk river The Schooners cruise from one extreme of the Squadron to the other, & all the small craft appear occupied in watering— The alarm in Town appears to increase daily as it is reported that the Frigates are lightening to cross the shoal There are now five hulks in the Channel opposite the Fort ready for sinking, which if done must effectually keep them out of the harbour, & the Fort with such a body of Militia ought to be competent to repel vessels of light draft & any attempt to land; Still the alarm increases to such a degree that the Citizens are packing up their valuables, & it is rumour'd the specie will be removed from the Banks—

A surprise by Boats in the night appears to be their greatest fear, & in order that we may sound the alarm, I have 6 Guard Boats from my little force every night rowing Guard from 3 to 4 miles below the Fort with signals—

The *Comet* (being the only vessel I have yet been able to mann) we are exercising & preparing for the first opportunity to act— The *Revenge* & *Patapsco* have about half their Crews each— There is a little Privateer Schooner of 50 Tons loan'd to me which I contemplate using as a Tender, if men can be procur'd, which I doubt very much as a great number have already gone off to Philada. & N. York—

I have the promise of 8 long eighteens, which I contemplate putting in Scows, if on trial, they will stand the concussion, and if men can be had to man them— Those with the schooners all well mann'd would enable me to form a line across the Channel opposite the Fort, sufficient to oppose a formidable force of Boats &c.— And five Hulks when sunk, with the heavy pieces on Fort M'Henry most certainly ought to keep any heavy force at a respectful distance— But Sir, it is with the utmost concern I perceive through our whole forces, a want of confidence in ourselves from the Major Genl. Throughout the City & [Govt.?] on down to the Citizen Soldier on post upon the ramparts— I shall exert myself to take (as soon as possible) my contemplated position across the Channel, because the least movement on our part appears to inspire them all; And I believe was I enabled to make an advance for a few days it would give time to rouse the people & inspire them with confidence—

So soon as all the vessels are mann'd I should forward the names of the Commanders agreeable to yr. orders— I have the honor to be very respectfly. Sir, yr. Obt. servt.—

Cha^S. Gordon

ALS, DNA, RG45, CL, 1813, Vol. 3, No. 58 (M125, Roll No. 28).

CAPTAIN CHARLES GORDON TO SECRETARY OF THE NAVY JONES

Revenge off Baltimore   19th May 1813

Sir,

The difficulties attending the transfer of the Command of the *Patapsco* from Captn. Mortimer to Mr. Mull has detain'd me two days; But I am happy to say we have now all hands on board, and only wanting for the signal to weigh— As I contemplate cruising a few days about Kent Island & Annapolis to exercise and organize our crews, I shall be enabled to receive any communications or instructions you may wish to make by the way of Annapolis or Baltimore— Mr. J. S. Skinner, the Agent for Prisoners at Annapolis, has a lookout Boat, which he has promised to keep constantly running up & down the Bay to communicate with me & to forward any communications without delay.

My whole force consists of the *Revenge* mounting 14–12 lb. Carronades 2 long 12's & one long eighteen on a pivot in a midships, The *Comet* mounting 12–12 lb. Carronades & 2 long nines, The *Patapsco* mounting 12–12 lb. Carronades & 2 long twelves, The *Wasp* mounting 2 9 lb. Carronades shifting, & one long nine on a Pivot in a midships And the U.S. Gun Boat *No. 138* mounting one long four & twenty & two 12 lb. Carronades—

The compliment of officers & men as pr. muster roll forwarded by the Purser— The *Wasp* being small & in the character of a tender & Cruiser jointly, I have given her Commander an appointment as <u>acting</u> Sailing Master (for the time being—

The City Committee having refus'd Mr. Mix[1] the vessel he ask'd for, he left here last evening in a fast rowing boat with 6 men to join me in the bay—

In case the officers & men (alluded to by you in a former letter) should arrive here I leave orders seal'd (with the Agent for him). I have the honor to be very respectfly. Sir, yr Obt. servt.

Cha^S Gordon

ALS, DNA, RG45, CL, 1813, Vol. 3, No. 153 (M125, Roll No. 28).

1. See pp. 354–56 for more on Elijah Mix.

Captain Charles Gordon to Secretary of the Navy Jones

Baltimore   21st June 1813

Sir,

I have the honor to inform you of my arrival at this place today, with the 4 Schooners & the Gun Boat under my Command, after a Cruise of 30 days between this & the Middle ground at the entrance of the Chesapeake—

Since the date of my last communication, I have been laying off & on below the Potomac taking every opportunity to reconnoitre & observe the movements of the Enemy, whose force the day before yesterday consisted of 2 Ships of the Line (one bearing a Rear Admirals flag) 4 Frigates & 1 Brig—

After laying 2 days becalm'd off New point Comfort, with the fleet in sight from our decks part of the time, I received a breese at noon the day before yesterday & stood down to the head of the middle, from whence I could discover two Frigates under way near Old point Comfort & the rest of the fleet at Anchor in the Channel from the Roads to the Capes forming a line of communication from Cape Henry up into the Roads— The Admiral with the other Ship of the line off the Horse shoe 2 Frigates below, 2 off old point & the Brig (one of the objects of our persuit) at Anchor close under the Admirals stern—

Schooner Patapsco of Baltimore

Such a position, together with the constant protection given their small cruisers (particularly in the night) rendered any <u>offensive</u> operations on our part impracticable— The squadron being generally in want of water and all the small articles of provisions expended, together with the main mast of the *Revenge* being sprung, I conceived it a favorable time (while the Enemy were so low down) to return for a supply & to refit for another Cruise, I therefore bore up at 5 P.M. on Saturday & arrived here this afternoon—

They will be ready to proceede down again in a short time, when I will do myself the honor to report to you in order to receive any instructions you may contemplate giving—

The force under my Command being so totally different from vessels own'd by the United States, And the services of the vessels & Crews limited to the Bay, induces me to solicit of you some instructions to govern me in my movements as well as in the expences of repares, refittings &c.

There are many little occurrances that might drive us to sea, such as the Enemy's getting above us in the night or heavy squalls from the westd. in the night, such as we experienc'd the other night while laying off New point [Comfort.]

I feel extremely desirous of [knowing] yr. wishes in those situations, it would therefore be gratifying to me to be permitted to come on for a day or two, to communicate to you more fully on the subject of my situation— with great respect Sir yr. obt. servt.

Cha[S]. Gordon

ALS, DNA, RG45, CL, 1813, Vol. 4, No. 98 (M125, Roll No. 29). Two words in the document were obliterated by the seal. Conjectures are supplied in brackets.

Fulton's Torpedo

The tightening of the British blockade around the Chesapeake renewed interest in Robert Fulton's torpedo experiments. An article published in the Maryland Gazette *on 4 March extolled the use of his weapons against the enemy's ships. It is possible that Elijah Mix,[1] a Chesapeake mariner, read this piece and was inspired to destroy some vessels himself, because in April he requested President Madison's financial assistance in this endeavor.[2] The navy responded with supplies and Mix spent the month of May working closely with Captain Charles Gordon to perfect his weapon. Mix had intended to use torpedoes against the British when they were in the upper bay, but their departure in early May for the Virginia Capes necessitated his following them. His plan encompassed rowing a boat close to an anchored enemy vessel and dropping a torpedo into the water. The weapon would drift to the ship and explode on impact. The second letter in this grouping documents the sighting of one of these "Powder Machines," which might have been one of Mix's weapons.[3]*

1. *Elijah Mix was appointed sailing master in June 1813.*
2. *Elijah Mix to James Madison, 8 Apr. 1813, DLC, James Madison Papers, Ser. I, Vol. 51, No. 87.*
3. *For further reading on Mix's experiments, see Calderhead, "Naval Innovation," pp. 216–18.*

SECRETARY OF THE NAVY JONES TO CAPTAIN CHARLES GORDON

Charles Gordon Esq: Navy Department,
Commanding Naval officer   May 7th 1813.—
Baltimore.   (Confidential)

Sir,

  A Mr. Elijah Mix will call upon you by my order to furnish him with such aid in carrying into effect his plans for the destruction of the enemy's Ships now off the Patapsco as I have encouraged him to expect; viz:

  You will furnish him with 500 lbs. of powder, a Boat, or Boats, and Six men; provided he can prevail upon that number of men, fit for the enterprise, to volunteer their services. His plan is that of Fulton's Torpedo. He is an intrepid Zealous man and means to perform the service in person. The Mayor of Baltimore, I understand, has patronized his undertaking, but; if it is to be carried into execution, the greatest privacy ought to be observed. I am, very respectfully &c—

                                                              W. Jones.—

LB Copy, DNA, RG45, CLS, 1813, pp. 23–24.

REAR ADMIRAL GEORGE COCKBURN, R.N., TO ADMIRAL SIR JOHN B. WARREN, R.N.

No. 17   *Marlborough* off Willoughby
                                                    Point, 16 June 1813.
Sir,

  I have the honor to acquaint you that the boats of the *Victorious* picked up on the morning of the 5th Currt. drifting out with the Ebb Tide, one of the Powder Machines, commonly known by the name of Fulton's, made to explode under Water and thereby cause immediate destruction to whatever it may come in contact with. This was no doubt destined for the *Victorious* or some other of our Ships here. The American Government intending thus to dispose of us by wholesale Six Hundred at a time, without further trouble or risk, but as it is not likely their laudable Efforts in this way have been confined to <u>one</u> Machine only, and this having actually drifted outside of all the Ships prior to its being discovered by us, I think it extremely probable others of a similar Description have passed out to Sea unobserved, and as they will be as likely to come in contact with Neutrals, or indeed some of their own Countrymen as with English, it may be right that in such case it be generally known by whom such infernal Machines have been promiscuously turned adrift into the Ocean, for otherwise it will scarcely perhaps be attributed to a Government, the head of which has, in a public message to Congress so recently boasted of its "unvaried examples of Humanity," and whose public prints and authorized documents are so constantly harping on the same Theme, that it requires examples like these and such Communications as we have recently received from its officers to prove the real spirit predominating in its Councils.

  I have now closed with His Majesty's Ships towards Hampton Roads, which will enable the Enemy to try further humane Experiments with us with much more facility to himself and much less Risk to the Public at large, but the zealous activity of the Officers of this Squadron fully authorize me to assure you Sir that be the Enemy's attempts what they may, they will prove equally futile and unavailing with respect to their Effects upon us.[1] I have the honor to be &ca &ca

(Sd.)   G. Cockburn   Rr. Admiral

LB Copy, DLC, Papers of George Cockburn, Container 9, Letters Sent, 3 Feb. 1812–6 Feb. 1814, pp. 202–4. Another copy is found in UkLPR, Adm. 1/504, pp. 29–30.

1. During the summer of 1813, Mix made several attempts to destroy H.M.S. *Plantagenet,* which was guarding the Chesapeake Bay near Cape Henry. He nearly succeeded on 24 July, but his torpedo exploded too soon and the resulting damage was limited to a cascade of water on the decks.

Admiralty Criticizes Warren

The Admiralty's assessment of Admiral Sir John B. Warren's handling of the Chesapeake campaign was negative on several points. The Lords Commissioners criticized Warren for taking too active a role in peace negotiations, for being too permissive with the local American citizenry, for not allocating his resources equitably, and for not making regular returns on his ships' dispositions.

First Secretary of the Admiralty John W. Croker to Admiral Sir John B. Warren, R.N.

Secret   Admiralty Office   17 May 1813
Duplicate

Sir,

I have received and laid before my Lords Commissioners of the Admiralty your Letter No. 104 of the 28th of March last with its inclosures, relative to the offer made by M. de Dasckoff, of the mediation of His Imperial Majesty, the Emperor of all the Russias for reestablishing Peace between his Majesty and the United States of America, and I have their Lordships Commands to repeat to you their approbation that neither you or Rear Admiral Cockburn should have thought yourselves authorized to enter into any Negotiation, or to defer or relax your measures of hostility on the proposition from the Russian Minister, or from the American Government.

I have it further in Command to acquaint you that their Lordships see no reason why Rear Admiral Cockburn should have consented to permit the communication of the Americans with the Chesapeak to be continued, when he could have prevented it, and they cannot but express their opinion that the regular communication by Letter which he has granted may on several obvious occasions be of the greatest injury and danger to our Military operations.[1]

Their Lordships hope that as soon as it was ascertained that the *Constellation* was beyond the reach of Naval attack, you kept no more Ships in the Chesapeak than were necessary for the complete and secure Blockade of that River, and that in the distribution of your force, you have particularly attended to their Lordships former directions to keep as much as possible, a line of Battle Ship with each Squadron of Frigates, and above all that you will have attached at least one line of Battle Ship to the Squadron off Boston.

I have their Lordships Commands to refer you to my various Letters relative to sending to me your disposition of the Squadron under your Command, and to express their great surprize that you should not have sent home by the *Childers,* the account of the disposition of your ships, and as far as you could collect it, of the state and condition thereof. The want of these Accounts is a serious inconvenience to their Lordships, and one which you do not in any degree endeavour to obviate, by stating in your dispatches which have been received, any particulars relative to the situation of the Squadron under your Command. I am Sir Your Most Obedient humble Servant

J W Croker

LS, DLC, Alexander F. I. Cochrane Papers, MS 2340, fols. 75–76. Another copy is in UkLPR, Adm. 2/1377, pp. 14–16.

1. Cockburn permitted the American packet carrying mail and passengers between Northampton and Norfolk to continue to ply between those two places. See Cockburn to Addison, 19 Mar. 1813, p. 324.

Gunboat Flotilla Attacks British Frigate

Admirals Sir John B. Warren and George Cockburn returned to the mouth of the Chesapeake in mid-May after completing the initial phase of their raiding expeditions. Cockburn remained behind while Warren sailed for Bermuda with captured vessels under convoy. Warren rejoined Cockburn in mid-June with the reinforcements that the Admiralty had ordered in March for the Chesapeake. Now the British were prepared for extensive operations instead of forays. Before the British could attempt their planned attack on the Craney Island defenses, however, the American gunboat flotilla took the offensive for the first time and engaged H.M. frigate Junon on 20 June.

CAPTAIN JAMES SANDERS, R.N., TO
REAR ADMIRAL GEORGE COCKBURN, R.N.

His Majestys Ship *Junon* at the Mouth of
Norfolk River   Chesapeake   20th June 1813

Sir,

In obedience to your orders I anchored off Newport Neuse in this Ship last evening, the *Narcissus* and *Barossa,* as near to us as the wind and tide would allow them to get, at this time perceived the enemy's eight Gunboats stated to you in my report of yesterday had been strengthened by seven more; at 1/2 past 2 AM observed them in motion standing towards us with light and variable wind the ebb tide beginning to make, soon after they opened their fire upon us, I then got this Ship quietly under Sail, *Narcissus* and *Barossa* quickly following and opening their fire as they approached; the *Junon* was wore occasionly the more effectually to bring her Guns to bear, and as we found her getting into shoal water, at 1/2 past 6 AM ceased firing and again took up our anchorage Newport News bearing W by N and Sewels point E 3/4 S the *Narcissus* and *Barossa* anchoring E by S from us: I regret our ignorance of Norfolk River[1] would not allow the Squadron to follow higher up, indeed from the great attention of Mr. Griffiths the Master, this Ship was enabled to go considerably further than she had before; had the exertions of our little Squadron been called properly into Action I have no doubt but the result would have been highly creditable to His Majesty's Arms. I am very sorry to tell you our loss is one Marine killed and three Seamen wounded, and one Seaman killed by the exploding of a Gun after the Enemy withdrew, Several shot in our hull and some of the standing and running rigging cut, Captain Lumley and Sherriff report none killed or wounded. I have the honor to be Sir your most obedient humble Servant.

("Signed")   Jas. Sanders. Captain

Copy, UkLPR, Adm. 1/504, pp. 313–14.

1. Sanders meant James River. A similar error is in the dateline.

Captain John Cassin to Secretary of the Navy Jones

Navy Yard   Gosport
June 21st 1813

Sir,

On Saturday at 11 p.m. Captain Tarbell[1] moved with the Flotilla under his Command Consisting of Fifteen Gun Boats, in two Divisions, Lieutenant John M. Gardner 1st Division & Lieutenant Robert Henley the 2nd man'd from the Frigate & fifty Musketeers Genl. Taylor ordered from Craney Island, and proceeded down the river but adverse winds & squalls prevented his approaching the Enemy untill Sunday morning at 4 P.M.,[2] when the Flotilla commenced a heavy gawling fire on a Frigate at about three quarters of a mile distance laying well up the Roads, at half past four a breeze sprung up from E.N.E which enabled the two frigates to get under way, one a razee or very heavy Ship & the other a frigate to come nearer into Action the boats in consequence of their approach haul'd off tho Keeping up a well directed fire on the razee, & other Ship which gave us several broadsides; The Frigate first engaged supposed to be the *Junon* was certainly very severely handled for I heard the Shot distinctly strike her, had the calm continued one half hour, that frigate must have fallen into our hands or been destroyed, she must have slipt her mooring so as to drop nearer the razee, who had all sail set coming up to her with the other Frigate, the Action continued one hour & half with the three Ships, shortly after the Action the Razee got along side of the Ship and has her upon a deep careen in a little time with a number of boats & stages round her, I am satisfied considerable damage was done to her, for she was silenced some time untill the razee open'd her fire when she commenced again. Our loss is very trifling Mr. Allinson Masters Mate on board *No. 139* was kill'd early in the action by an Eighteen pound ball which past through him & lodged in the Mast. *No. 154* had a shot between wind & water. *No. 67* had her franklin shot away & several of them had some of their

Sweeps, as well their Stantions shot away but two men slightly injured by splinters from the Sweeps; on the flood tide several ships of the line and Frigates came into the roads & we did expect an attack last night, there is now in the roads, thirteen Ships of the Line & Frigates, one Brig & several Tenders—

I cannot say too much for the Officers & Crew on this occasion, for every man appeared to go into Action with so much chearfullness and appearently to do their duty, resolved to Conquer, having a better oppertunity of discovering their actions than any one else being in my boat the whole of the Action. I have the honor to be Sir, Your obt. hble. St.

John Cassin

LS, DNA, RG45, CL, 1813, Vol. 4, No. 97 (M125, Roll No. 29).

1. Jones ordered Captain Charles Stewart to leave Master Commandant Joseph Tarbell temporarily in command of *Constellation* when Stewart departed for his new command. Tarbell had been stationed at Norfolk since March. Seeing *Junon* becalmed, Captain John Cassin directed Tarbell to attack her with the gunboat flotilla.
2. Cassin meant a.m.

Attack on Craney Island

When Admiral Sir John B. Warren returned to the Chesapeake with reinforcements, he selected Norfolk as his first target. Craney Island, on the western side of the mouth of the Elizabeth River, was the first obstacle the British had to confront in approaching the harbor.

The official battle report from Captain John Cassin, commanding officer at Norfolk, neglected to mention the contributions made by the Virginia militia under Lieutenant Colonel Henry Beatty, whose men controlled all but one of the cannon on the northern edge of the island. Warren's account of the engagement minimized the British defeat.[1]

1. For more background on the attack, the events leading up to it, and the controversy regarding the nature of the joint American naval-militia operation, see Hallahan, Craney Island.

CAPTAIN JOHN CASSIN TO SECRETARY OF THE NAVY JONES

Navy Yard   Gosport
June 23rd 1813

Sir,

I have the honor to inform you on the 20th the Enemy got under way, in all thirteen Sail, and drop'd up to the mouth of James River, one Ship bearing a flag at the Mizen at 5 P.M were discovered making great preparation with troops for landing, having a number of boats for the purpose, finding Craney Island rather weak man'd, Captain Tarbell directed Lieutenants Neale, Shubrick, & Sanders[1] with One Hundred Seamen on shore at 11 P.M. to a small battery on the N.W. Point of the Island— Tuesday 22nd at the dawn the Enemy were discovered landing round the point of Nansemond river, Said to be Four thousand troops, and at 8 A.M. the barges attempted to land in front of the Island out of reach of the Shot from the Gun Boats, When Lieutenants Neale, Shubrick & Saunders and the Sailors with Lt. Brackinbridge [*Breckenridge*] & marines of the

Constellation One Hundred & fifty in number, opened their fire, which was so well directed that the Enemy were glad to get off, after sinking three of their largest boats, one of which called the *Santapee*,[2] Admiral Warrens boat, fifty feet in length, carrying seventy five men, the greater part of the Crew were lost by sinking; twenty Soldiers & Sailors were saved & the boat haul'd up; from the boats that were sunk I presume there was forty prisoners, the troops that were landed fell back in the rear of the Island & Commenced throwing rockets from Mr. Wise's house, when Gun Boat *67* throw'd a few shot over that way, they dispersed & went back; we have had all day deserters from the Army coming in, I have myself taken in twenty five and Eighteen prisoners belonging to the *Santapee;* the Officers of the *Constellation* fired their 18 pounder more like rifflemen than Artillerists, I never saw such shooting and seriously believe they saved the Island yesterday. In the evening their boats came round the point of Nansemond, and at sun set were seen returning to their Ships full of men, at dusk they strew the shore along with fires in order to run away be the light— I have the honor to be Sir, Your obt. Hble. Servt.

John Cassin

P.S. This moment Captain Tarbell has just come up, and informs me the enemy have withdrawn their Troops from Craney Island, and have landed at Newportnews—and were firing Congreve Rockets.

J. C.

LS, DNA, RG45, CL, 1813, Vol. 4, No. 107 (M125, Roll No. 29).

1. James Sanders was an acting lieutenant until his appointment was confirmed by the Senate in July 1813.
    2. *Centipede.*

ADMIRAL SIR JOHN B. WARREN, R.N., TO FIRST SECRETARY OF THE ADMIRALTY JOHN W. CROKER

San Domingo   Hampton Roads   Chesapeake,
June 24th 1813.

Sir,

I request you will inform their Lordship's that from the Information received of the Enemy's Fortifying Crany Island, and it being necessary to obtain possession of that place to enable the Light Ships and Vessels to proceed up the Narrow Channel towards Norfolk; to transport the Troops over on that side for them to attack the New Fort and Lines; in the Rear of which the *Constellation* Frigate was Anchored: I directed the Troops under Sir Sidney Beckwith to be landed upon the Continent wither the nearest Point to that Place, and a Re-inforcement of Seamen and Marines from the Ships; but upon approaching the Island, from the extreme Shoalness of the Water on the Sea Side, and the difficulty of getting across from the Land: as well as the Island itself being Fortified with a Number of Guns & Men from the Frigate, and Militia; and Flanked by Fifteen Gun Boats: I considered, in consequence of the representation of the Officer Commanding the Troops, of the difficulty of their passing over from the Land: that the persevering in the attempt would cost more Men than the numbers with us would permit: as the other Forts must have been Stormed before the Frigate and Dock Yard could be destroyed; I therefore ordered the Troops to be Re-embarked.

I am happy to say the Loss in the above affair (a Return of which is enclosed) has not been considerable, and only two Boats Sunk.

I have to regret that Captain Hanchett of His Majesty's Ship *Diadem* who Volunteered his Services and led the Division of Boats with great Gallantry was severely Wounded by a Ball in the Thigh.

The Officers and Men behaved with much Bravery, and if it had been possible to have got at the Enemy, I am persuaded we would soon have gained the place.

I shall endeavour to carry their Lordships further Orders into Execution upon every favourable occasion. I have the honor to be Sir, Your most obedient humble Servant

John Borlase Warren

LS, UkLPR, Adm. 1/503, pp. 743–46.

[Enclosure]

Return of Officers, Seamen, and Marines belonging to His Majesty's Ships, Killed, Wounded, and Missing, in the attack on Craney Island 22nd June 1813.

Killed— None
Wounded— One Officer & 7 Seamen
Missing— Ten Seamen
Name of the officer Wounded.
Captain Hanchett of His Majestys Ship *Diadem*,
Severely, but not Dangerously.

John Borlase Warren

DS, UkLPR, Adm. 1/503, p. 747.

Assault on Hampton

The British attack on Hampton followed quickly on the heels of their abortive attempt on Craney Island. Captain Samuel J. Pechell, commander of Warren's flagship, San Domingo, *had led the unsuccessful raid on Craney Island, but Rear Admiral George Cockburn directed the amphibious assault on Hampton. Sir Thomas Sidney Beckwith's initial report of the 25 June action did not indicate the slightest hint of misconduct among his regiments. A later version, however, substantiated American accounts of atrocities committed by the two Independent Companies of Foreigners.*

CAPTAIN JOHN CASSIN TO SECRETARY OF THE NAVY JONES

Navy Yard   Gosport
June 26th 1813

Sir,

I am sorry to inform you the Enemy succeeded in taking Hampton yesterday morning, after a very obstinate resistance, and no doubt great loss on both sides; the Enemy landed several hundred Troops near Newportnews at 4 A.M.

marched round, commencing the Action with their Rockets, while the barges forty in number entered the Creek, so few troops tho I believe brave as Ceazer did not exceed five hundred, were overpower'd by numbers, and the Rockets thrown in such way as to confuse them; from the best information we can receive the Inhabitants had flown and little or nothing left in town but the shells of houses, I have not heard of any more than two houses burnt as yet, after finishing watering I fear they will destroy the place being apprehensive of an attack from the land side—

I have only forty casks of powder and only one hundred 32 pound Shot left in the yard, no Grape or Cannister, of any description, I believe it might be procur'd at Richmond. The *Dispatch* laying at Cabbin point, I had sent her to Richmond with Captain Brooks & officers destined for Canada & on her return found the Enemy at the mouth of the river which compel'd her to return to that place, she could be ordered to Richmond for that purpose, should it meet your approbation—

I presume they have not forgotten us, and will pay us another visit ere long, very few days will make Craney Island very secure; they have had two extraordinary oppertunitys to attack the Gunboats, was their inclination that way by strong & favourable winds; I do most sincerely think they do not like our mettle in the boats since Sunday last— I have the honor to be Sir, your obt. hble servt.

John Cassin

LS, DNA, RG45, CL, 1813, Vol. 4, No. 119 (M125, Roll No. 29).

COLONEL SIR THOMAS SIDNEY BECKWITH, BRITISH ARMY, TO ADMIRAL SIR JOHN B. WARREN, R.N.

His Majestys Ship San Domingo
Hampton Roads   28th June 1813.

Sir,

I have the honor to report to you that in compliance with your orders to attack the enemy in town and Camp at Hampton, the troops under my command were put into light sailing vessels, and boats, during the night of the 25th Inst., and by the excellent arrangements of Rear Admiral Cockburn who was pleased in person to superintend; the advance under Lieut. Colonel Napier consisting of the 102nd Regt. two companies of Canadian Chasseurs,[1] three companies of Marines from the Squadron, with two 6 Prs. from the Royal Marine Arty. were landed half an hour before day light the next morning, about two miles to the westward of the town—and the Royal Marine Battalions under Lieut. Colonel Williams were brought on Shore so expeditiously that the column was speedily enabled to move forward.

With a view to turn the enemy's position our march was directed towards the great road leading from the country into the rear of the Town. Whilst the troops moved off in this direction Rear Admiral Cockburn, to engage the enemy's attention ordered the armed launches and rocket boats to commence a fire upon their batteries this succeeded so completely that the head of our advanced guard, had cleared a wood and were already on the enemy's flank before our approach was perceived. They then moved from their camp to their position in rear of the town and here they were vigorously attacked by Lieut. Colonel Napier, and the advance unable to Stand, which they continued their march to the rear of the town, where a detachment under Lieut. Colonel Williams conducted by Captn. Powell Asst. Qr. Mr. Genl. push'd thro' the town and forced their way across a bridge of planks into the enemy's Encampment, of which, and the batteries, immediate possession was gained— In the mean time some Artillery men stormed and took the enemy's remaining field force.

Enclosed I have the honor to transmit a return of ordnance taken— Lieut. Colonel Williams will have the honor of delivering to you a stand of colours of the 68th Regt. James City Light Infantry, and one of the 1st Battn. 85th Regt. The exact numbers of the enemy it is difficult to ascertain— From the woods country, and the strength of their position our troops have sustained some loss;[2] that of the enemy was very considerable. Every exertion was made to collect the wounded Americans, who were attended by a Surgeon of their own, and by the British Surgeons who performed amputations on such as required it, and afforded every assistance in their power; the dead bodies of such as could be collected were also carefully buried.

I beg leave on this occasion to express the obligations I owe to Lieut. Colonel Napier and Lieut. Colonel Williams for their kind and able assistance— The gallantry of Captn. Smith the officers and men of the two Companies Canadian Chasseurs who led the attack was highly conspicuous and praiseworthy; as well as the steadiness and good conduct of the officers, and men of the 102nd Regt. and the Royal Marines disembarked from His Majestys Ships *San Domingo, Malbro* and *Plantagenet*— My best thanks are also due to Captn. Parke the officers and men of the Royal Marine Artillery—to the officers & men of the 1st Royal Marine Battalion, as well as to Major Malcolm & the officers & men of the 2nd Royal Marine Battalion.

I beg leave to point out to you the exertions of Capt. Powell Asst. Qr. Mr. General; of acting A.D.C. Lieut. Frederick Robertson Royl. Artillery & of Capt. Romilly Royl. Engineers whose Zeal, and spirited conduct entitle them to my best acknowledgements. I am also much obliged to Captn. Gore Loyl. Cheshire Regt. whose services you were pleased to accept during these operations, and attach to me as an acting A.D.C. I have the honor to be Sir Your most obedient most humble Servant

Sidney Beckwith
Qr. Mr. Genl.

LS, UkLPR, Adm. 1/503, pp. 779–82.

1. These were not Canadian companies but two Independent Companies of Foreigners composed of French prisoners of war who chose fighting over prison. For more background on the Hampton attack and the confusion surrounding the nationality of these soldiers, see Hitsman and Sorby, "Independent Foreigners."

2. Beckwith enclosed a casualty chart reporting the following return of killed, wounded, and missing at Hampton, 26 June 1813: Royal Marine Artillery—1 rank and file killed, 4 rank and file wounded; (Ships) Three Companies of Royal Marines—1 rank and file wounded, 1 rank and file missing; 1st and 2d Canadian Chasseurs—3 rank and file killed, 13 rank and file wounded, 6 rank and file missing; 1st Batt. Royal Marines—1 rank and file killed, 1 lieutenant, 6 rank and file wounded; 2d Batt. Royal Marines—1 lieutenant, 1 sergeant, 6 rank and file wounded, 3 rank and file missing. Total—5 killed, 33 wounded, 10 missing; see UkLPR, Adm. 1/503, p. 785.

[Enclosure]

Return of Ordnance Stores &c taken in Hampton on the 25th[1] June 1813.—
Four 12 Pr. Iron Guns on travelling Carriages—
Three 6 Pr.   Do.—on Travelling Carriages with Timbers and a proportion of
Ammunition for each of the above Calibres—
Three Covered Waggons and their Horses.

T. A. Parke
Capt. & Senr. Offr.   R.M. Arty.

DS, UkLPR, Adm. 1/503, p. 783.

1. Parke meant 26th.

COLONEL SIR THOMAS SIDNEY BECKWITH, BRITISH ARMY, TO ADMIRAL SIR JOHN B. WARREN, R.N.

H.M.S. San Domingo
July 5th 1813.

Sir

It is with great Regret I am obliged to entreat your Attention to the Situation
& Conduct of the Two Independent Companies of Foreigners embarked on this
Service.

It may be necessary on this Occasion, that I should remind You of the Idea, I
entertained, of the Character & Description of the 2d. Company which saild
with me from England, which I had the Honor of stating to You at Bermuda:
and also my doubts of their Fidelity, whenever an Opportunity of deserting
should present itself.— That this apprehension was not a groundless one, will
appear when I state to You, that of this Company, an Officer and 30 Men have
already deserted to the Enemy.

With the Character of the 1st. Company, You were acquainted before we left
the Island of Bermuda: where their Conduct was so perfectly insubordinate,
that it was necessary to hold repeated Courts Martial upon them, and one Man
was actually shot there for Mutiny.

I learned also from Brigadier General Horsford, and from Lieutenant
Colonel Napier of the 102d Regiment, that the Company mutinied on Parade
in presence of the Garrison under Arms assembled for Punishment—

Of these also many have deserted; amongst others, the Quarter Master Serjeant, having previously robbed ~~the~~ his Captain & Officers of their Money—

Their Behaviour on the recent Landing at Hampton, has already been reported to You, together with the circumstances of their dispersing to plunder in
every direction; their brutal Treatment of several Peaceable Inhabitants, whose
Age or Infirmities rendered them unable to get out of their Way; the necessity of
sending them in from the Outposts; and upon the Representation of their Officers, who found it impossible to check them, and whose Lives they threatened,
the subsequent Necessity of re-embarking & sending them off to their Ship—

Since their Return on Board, their Conduct has been uniformly the same. Individuals have broken into open Mutiny, encourag'd & supported by the
rest—they have set their Officers at Defiance; and on being remonstrated with,

have not hesitated to say, that when next landed, they would chuse a Service for themselves— Capt. Smith, their Commanding Officer, whose Intelligence and Activity, deserve that he should be employed with better men, has been oblig'd, great as the disappointment must be to him, to report the Two Companies, a desperate Banditti, whom it is impossible to controul; & who, he does not doubt, will desert in a Body, the first Opportunity.

Impress'd with the Conviction that these Companies can no longer be safely employ'd on the present Service, & that retaining them may be productive of some serious Disaster: I take the Liberty of submitting to You, the necessity of their being sent away as soon as possible.

I need not recapitulate the pains that have been taken to conciliate these men, both by holding them up in a respectable Light—and by every Attention being paid to their Comforts—And, I trust, it will appear to You, the Trial of them, has been carried as far as Reason or Prudence can possibly justify—

For any further Information, I beg leave to refer You to Capt. Barclay, Commanding HMS *Success*, in which these companies are embarked. His report I am persuaded, will fully establish the Statement now laid before You. I have the Honor to be Sir Your most obedt. most humble servt.

Sidney Beckwith
Qr. Mr. Genl.

ALS, CaOOA, British Military and Naval Records, RG8, I, "C" Ser., Vol. 679, pp. 189–91.

Cockburn's Reflections on the Blockade

Rear Admiral George Cockburn's raid on Ocracoke[1] alerted him to the necessity of extending the blockade to North Carolina in order to stop the American diversion of the Chesapeake's trade southward through inland waterways.

1. See Cockburn to Warren, 12 July 1813, pp. 184–86.

REAR ADMIRAL GEORGE COCKBURN, R.N., TO
ADMIRAL SIR JOHN B. WARREN, R.N.

No. 21　　　　　　　　　　　　　　　　　　　　　　*Sceptre*[1]
the 19th July 1813

Sir,

From Observations which I had opportunities of making whilst executing your Orders at Ocracoke

I feel it right to state to you that the Blockade of the Chesapeake is very materially, if not entirely frustrated by the Port of Beaufort and the Ocracoke Inlet not having been hitherto declared to be also in a state of Blockade, for there being an easy inland navigation from Norfolk and Elizabeth Town to the before mentioned Places the Flour and other Produce of the neighbourhood of the Chesapeake, which can no longer be sent by the Capes of Virginia, is now sent in numerous small Craft to the Neutrals and other large vessels safely laying at Ocracoke and Beaufort to receive it, and nothing I believe can possibly interrupt or prevent this active Trafick by inland Navigation, but declaring that these Places are in future to be considered strictly Blockaded as well as the Chesapeake of which in fact they now form a part, owing to their immediate water Communication with it, and forming as they do not only an Outlet for its Produce but a Depôt likewise for whatever is to be important to it, as in a recent instance of the *Atlas* letter of Marque whose Cargo amounting to 600,000 Dollars was sent from Ocracoke to Norfolk by means of the inland Navigation here alluded to, the Vessels employed in which are I understand kept in constant activity from the immense Quantity of Goods in this manner sent from and received at the various Towns situated on the Shores of the Chesapeake

The putting an immediate Stop to the Enemy reaping these advantages, appearing to me an object of the highest Importance, and as it will be nearly if not wholly attained by declaring these Places to be Blockaded I have deemed it my Duty Sir to submit these Remarks for your consideration. I have the honor to be &c &c

(Sd.)   G. Cockburn   Rr. Admiral

LB Copy, DLC, Papers of George Cockburn, Container 9, Letters Sent, 3 Feb. 1812–6 Feb. 1814, pp. 222–24.

1. Before leaving the Chesapeake for an assault on Ocracoke Inlet, Cockburn shifted his flag from *Marlborough*, 74, to *Sceptre*, 74.

British Activity in the Potomac

Captain Charles Morris ordered Lieutenant George C. Read,[1] *on 5 July, to take* Scorpion *and* Asp *to the mouth of the Potomac for reconnoitering service. A day earlier, Warren's squadron arrived at that river, intending to sound the waters and proceed up as far as possible. Cutters from H.M. sloop* Contest *and brig* Mohawk *engaged* Asp *in fierce action.*

1. *George C. Read relieved Lieutenant Edmund P. Kennedy of the flotilla command on 4 May 1813. Kennedy was sent to the Charleston Station.*

COMMANDER JAMES RATTRAY, R.N., TO ADMIRAL SIR JOHN B. WARREN, R.N.

Copy   His Majesty's Sloop *Contest*
                                              Yeacomoco Creek   July 14th. 1813
Sir,

I have the honor to acquaint you that agreeable to your directions this morning, I chaced the strange sail in Company with His Majesty's Brig *Mohawk*, who took refuge in Yeacomoco Creek, but in consequence of the water being very shoal, I was oblidged to Anchor two or three Leagues distant from here and send the Cutter of his Majesty's Brig under my Command, under the directions of Lieut. Curry, accompanied by Lieut. Hutchinson with the Cutter of His Majesty's Brig *Mohawk* with Orders to bring her out (if possible) or to destroy her—

The Vessel proves to be the United States Schooner, *Asp*, mounting one long 18 pr. and two 18 pr. Carronades, Swivels, &c. Commanded by a Lieutenant and a Complement of twenty five Men, and fully prepared with boarding netting for a strong opposition

The Enemy had hauld the Schooner within her own width of the Beach, under the protection of a large Body of Militia and placed her in a position with a spring on her Cable to bring all the guns to bear on the two Boats. On their approach, a heavy & tremendous fire opened from the Schooner and the Shore, notwithstanding which, the cool and determined bravery of Lieut. Curry and his Crew, seconded by Lieut. Hutchinson and Crew of the *Mohawk*, she was carried by Boarding in a few minutes.—

On discovering the Schooner to be an Armed Vessel, I followed the Boats in my Gig, accompanied by Captain Litchfield of the *Mohawk*, and arrived alongside her at the moment of her Capture, which afforded us an opportunity of observing the gallant manner in which she was carried.—

In consequence of the *Asp* being three or four miles up the Creek, and the Channel extremely difficult and narrow, with a wind right and a vast number of Troops advancing towards the Beech, I deem'd it prudent to set her on fire, which I trust will meet your approbation—

I am sorry to state that two men have been Killed and Six Wounded, among whom is Lieut. Curry, slightly in the Arm whose distinguished conduct, with that of Lieut. Hutchinson, Messrs. Morey and Bradford, Midshipmen of the *Mohawk*, Mr. Tozar Midshipman of the *Contest* and the rest of the Crews cannot do otherwise than merit my warmest praise on this spirited occasion

I have taken ten of the Enemy Prisoners, the Lieutenant[1] was found Killed [on board the] Schooners Decks, and some others were drowned making their escape on Shore.—

I beg leave to subjoin a list of the Killed and Wounded in the Margin.— I have the honor to be Sir Your most obedient humble Servant

(Signed)   James Rattray   Captain

Contest

Wounded
R. C. Curry   Lieut. slightly
Killed
George Taylor   Marine

Mohawk

Killed
Geo. Marsh   Ordy
Wounded
T. Bennett   A.B. dangerously
R. Roberts   L.M.   Do.
A. Gordon   Qr. Mr. Slightly
B. Flynn   Marine   Do.
Jno. Sawyer   Supy.   Do.

Copy, UkLPR, Adm. 1/504, pp. 69–71.

1. Midshipman James B. Sigourney, commander of schooner *Asp*. He had been attached to the Potomac flotilla since February 1813.

MIDSHIPMAN HENRY M. MCLINTOCK [1] TO SECRETARY OF THE NAVY JONES

                                          Kinsale   July 19th, 1813
Sir
    I have to inform you of the unfortunate event which occured here on the 14th,
the action between the British barges and U.S. Schooner *Asp*, commanded by Mr
Sigouney, at 9 oclock A.M. the *Scorpion* & *Asp* got under way from Yeocomico
River and stood out, at 10 discovered a number of sail which proved to be the
enemy; the *Scorpion* then made signal to act at discretion and stood up the River,
the Schooner being a bad sailer and the wind ahead we where not able to get out;
finding the enemy approaching us we thought best to return, immediately two of
the Brigs stood towards us and anchered a short dist from the bar, when they
manned their boats. Mr Sigouney thought it would be for our advantage to run
further up the Creek which we did, but finding the enemy had left their vessels
we had not time to weigh anchor therefore we were obliged to cut our cable, we
were attacked by 3 boats well manned and armed we continued a well directed
fire on them and after a short time they were compelled retreat and obtain a reinforcement about an hour after we retired we were attacked by 5 boats we continued doing the same as before but having so few men we were unable to repel the
enemy, when they boarded us they refused giving any quarters, there was upwards
of fifty men on our decks which compelled us to leave the vessel, as the enemy
had [possest] it they put her on fire and retreated, a short time after they left her
we went on board and with much difficulty extinguished the flames, but it is with
deep regret that I inform you the death of Mr Sigouney, who fought most gallantly in defence of the vessel, and the utmost exertion was used by every man on
board, our crew only consisted of twenty one and there is ten killed wounded and
missing, we have our amunition and two of our carronades on shore, our men are
very much in want of cloathing as they were all taken from them. I shall remain
here until further orders. Your obd. Serv.

                                          H M MClintock
                                          Midn in U.S. Navy
ALS, DNA, RG45, BC, 1813, Vol. 3, No. 33 (M148, Roll No. 12).

    1. On 22 March 1813, the Navy Department ordered Midshipman Henry M. MClintock attached
to one of the gunboats in the Potomac flotilla.

ADMIRAL SIR JOHN B. WARREN, R.N., TO
FIRST SECRETARY OF THE ADMIRALTY JOHN W. CROKER

                                          San Domingo Off Point
                                          Lookout   Chesapeake,
                                          29th July 1813—
Sir,
    I beg you will inform their Lordship's that on the 14th July the Squadron and
Troops arrived at the entrance of the Potowmac, when two sail of small Vessels
being discovered I sent the *Contest* & *Mohawk* in pursuit of the smallest, which
was destroyed, as stated in my letter No. 170 of the 22nd July, the other a Sloop
of 12 Guns, also manned from the *Adams* Frigate from being far ahead escaped
and passed up the River.

The Ships of the Line proceeded up as far as Sandy Point where the Squadron was Anchored: I afterwards directed Clements Island to be taken possession of by a Company of Marines, for the purpose of obtaining Water, Cattle and Refreshments during our stay in the River, and the Boats burnt some small Vessels on the Virginia shore. I likewise detached Captain Shirreff with the Ships named in the margin,[1] after receiving on board a Corps of about 600 men from the 1st. Batallion of Marines and 102d. Regt. which Sir Sydney Beckwith accompanied, to proceed as far up the River as possible, in order to make an impression if practicable upon the Enemy's Frigate & small Vessels below Alexandria, as well as to create an Alarm at Washington and to embarrass the Enemy in the measures for the further Invasion of Canada during the setting of Congress in that City: I am sorry to say that in consequence of the Shoals between Cedar & Maryland Points, that the Frigates could not get higher up, without being lightened, than the former place: Several dis-embarkations however were made upon the Shores of the River by the Troops under Sir Sydney Beckwith's directions, as well as small detachments from the ships, and some Vessels destroyed which had the effect of obliging the Enemy to march down large Corps of Regulars and Militia on each side the River and in one instance the American Cavalry & Infantry on the Maryland Shore were accompanied by the Ministers of State and War: Colonels Monroe and Armstrong, and several persons from the Capitol where much confusion seems to have existed; and it appearing that it would be impossible for the Ships of War to go further up & that a larger Corps must be sent, which might probably engage our attention in measures that would take a longer period of Time and prove incompatable with our future operations: I directed the Light Squadron to join me, and returned down the River opposite Point Lookout where the 102nd Regts. and two Batallions of Marines and Artillery were landed under the direction of Rear Adml. Cockburn, and the Troops Commanded by Sir Sydney Beckwith marched across the Peninsula and took up a Position to protect the Party Employed in procuring Cattle and Forage for the use of the Squadron, where I am happy to say 120 head of Cattle and 100 Sheep were obtained, and the Troops Re-embarked after having undergone a very fatiguing March, with the utmost good Order and celerity, and the Squadron is again pursuing its course to the upper part of the Bay.— I have the honor to be Sir, Your most Obedient humble Servant.

John Borlase Warren

LS, UkLPR, Adm. 1/504, pp. 79–83.

1. "*Barossa, Laurestinus, Conflict, Mohawk,* and *High Flyer.*"

Defense Plans for Washington

Reports of British activity in the Potomac spurred Captain Charles Morris to propose defense plans for Washington. William Jones concurred with his general outline but cautioned Morris against retreating to an extreme defensive position because of the effect it would have on public opinion.

CAPTAIN CHARLES MORRIS TO SECRETARY OF THE NAVY JONES

U S Frigate *Adams*   July 18th. 1813.

Sir,

I have the honor to propose the following plan of defence for the city of Washington—and enclose a rough plan of the Ship channel from about 4 miles below Greenleaf's point to the Navy Yard, for convenience of reference—[1]

I would propose a battery on Greenleaf's point of as many heavy cannon as can be conveniently mounted, which would I should presume be at least twenty—

I would remove this ship, over the Bar and place her across the Channel opposite Windmill point with the gunboats on the flat toward the point marked A and the Galleys and barges between them and the point— on the point A mount a heavy Carronade or two if they can be made ready, to rake the full of the line of boats with Grape &c in case of attack

Construct a Battery for Ship guns on Windmill point, in which I would mount one half my gundeck Guns (13, 18 pounders) and as far as might be possible man them from the Ship— at all events have the battery under the command of our own officers— Let the Scows Guns be placed on the line of gunboats—

As a further defence let a hulk be sunk across the Channel one mile below Greenleafs point which will be near the line B, C on this plan. One of our old Ships at the yard might be soon prepared, would be quite sufficient and can never be better employed—

Defences may be easily and speedily erected on and opposite Mason's Island for the protection of the Foundery, as the Water is too shoal to admit the enemy using other than light force on that service. Such troops as can or may be collected to be stationed in such parts of the city as may be best adapted to repel an attempt to land—

I would leave the defence of the pass of Fort Warburton to the Fort itself and the water battery which we have constructed for them which mounts, 5–18 pr. & 2 32 prs, and to the other force which may be deemed requisite to protect its rear—

I will now proceed to state as concisely as possible my reasons for this arrangement—

I take for granted that should the enemy really intend proceeding as high as this place that their first object, is the destruction of the navy yard and its dependencies— the second object in point of Military importance is the destruction of the Foundery above Georgetown and the third, which in a moral point of view is equal to the others would be the removal of the seat of Government which though of no real injury in itself would depress the public mind in this country, and naturally affect our reputation in Europe—

To attempt either of these objects they would at least send six Frigates and I believe one or more ships of the line— Against such a force your own observation will have shown you that our force here could make no effective resistance— If we awaited their attack in that Ship, however gallant our defence might be, it must in all probability terminate in the destruction of our force—and they would then immediately proceed and find the passage to the navy yard without material obstruction. The breadth and depth of the channel here prevents the possibility of artificial obstruction— These are the defects of our present position—

My reason for sinking the hulk at B. C. is, that the Channel is of sufficient depth to admit any ship within 150 yards of Greenleafs point, and should they improve that advantage, I fear we have no troops sufficently disciplined to stand discharges of grape— I place it one mile below that it may be fairly under the protection of our batteries— It prevents the possibility of an attack on the Ship or yard except in Boats—

I place the Battery on Greenleafs' point, from its advantageous situation commanding the main channel by a <u>raking</u> fire and covering the diverging channels on each side of it with a powerful cross fire—

I erect a Battery for Ship guns on Windmill point because it raked the navy yard channel and because it enables us to use immediately our own guns, which are mounted and provided with all kinds of ammunition—

I place the Ship opposite Windmill point that we may act in concert with our own battery because she will so completely fill the channel as to prevent any other ship from passing us, which enables us to spare one half our guns—because it is the best position for repelling an attack from boats and because it is the best position to act in concert with our other floating force—

I place the gun boats, Scows and gallies in a line between Windmill point and point A because it is the narrowest place and easiest supported— And I place the carronades at A as a cover & support for that end of the line—

As the General defence of the other part of the city belongs more exclusively, to other officers more conversant and competant than myself with that subject I forbear making any observations upon it—

I proposed this plan this morning to the Secretary of War, who seemed to approve it, and has ordered Genl. Vanness, with the militia to proceed immediately to Washington for the purpose of fortifying Greenleafs point— He will I presume give you his opinion himself of the plan generally— He desires me to request you will endeavor to have the battery constructed on <u>Windmill point</u> for the reception of this ship's guns— Should you order it—please to let the platform be 13 feet wide, as long as the ground will allow—to face a point one mile below Greenleafs point in the Channel—with a breast work of Timber <u>two feet</u> above the platform so that our guns will play over it—

Your opinion on this subject, and further orders will be very desirable, in the mean time I shall continue to use every exertion for strengthening our present position

Should we be ordered up I propose bringing the gunboats, and leaving the scow—taking all our own men with us—

I enclose a letter from Lt. Read received last Evening since which I have received no further information   Very respectfully yr. Ob. Sert.

C Morris

ALS, DNA, RG45, CL, 1813, Vol. 5, No. 14 (M125, Roll No. 30).

1. Morris's rough sketch is bound after his letter.

SECRETARY OF THE NAVY JONES TO CAPTAIN CHARLES MORRIS

Captain Charles Morris   Navy Department
U.S. Frigate *Adams*   July 18th 1813

Sir,

Mr Morris [1] has delivered to me, your letters of this day, with the several enclosures therein referred to, which will receive deliberate attention. Mr Morris will hand to you the Night Signals, for the purpose of the alterations you suggest, which you will please transmit, as soon as your pressing duties will admit of the necessary attention. From the last article, in the enclosed hand bill, I fear the *Asp* has been captured, and poor Sigourney killed. I confide much in the vigilance of Lieutenant Read, and trust he will avoid approaching too near the enemy, lest, by a calm, or other casualty, their Barges should get hold of him. Your plan of defence, with very little exception, meets my full approbation, but only as a dernier resort.

To retire from your present position with the Naval force, before the enemy had approached its vicinity, with a decidedly superior force, would have the worst possible effect, in destroying the confidence, and depressing the spirits of the people. Those of Alexandria would consider their defence as abandoned, and though the enemy may not now seriously meditate the attempt, (and I firmly believe he does not,) yet, invited by the absence of the squadron, and the consequent panic, he would, in all probability, make the attempt, were it only to destroy Alexandria, and reconnoitre and menace this place.

If the maintenance of your position is at all doubtful, with the Fort and Squadron combined, its fall will be the necessary consequence of withdrawing the squadron.

My opinion is, therefore, that it will be better to remain until the enemy shall approach, in such force as to leave no doubt of the propriety of retiring, and in the interim, to prepare all the means of defence, you have pointed out as the ultimate stand. This I shall take immediate measures to do, as far as attaches to my Department.

The platform, for the Battery, shall be immediately commenced, if hands can be had, and the people of the yard, now out with the Militia, had better be detached by the Secretary, for the service of the Navy Yard; for without them, you must be sensible of the difficulty of making the contemplated preparations. Be pleased to suggest it to the Secretary of War. The Hulk of the old *Boston* will answer for the channel, and the line you have chosen, opposite Windmill point, is strong and judicious. I have some doubts of the propriety of the two Carronades, at the point A, unless the hill, in the rear, is covered by troops. These points, however, can easily be settled; the main design is agreed upon.

The great object will be, to retire in time, to reach the ultimate position, with the Frigate, and of that you will be the exclusive judge. Your knowledge of the Channel, and depth of water, will indicate to you the proper time— Your Ship draws much less water than any of theirs, and you could reduce your draught of water materially, by starting the water in the after hold. The Scows are clumsy, and must retire in time; these and the Gunboats, would cover the passage of the Frigate over the Bar. I have written in haste, and will again write to you tomorrow. I am, respectfully your Obt. Servant,

W. Jones.

Would it not be better to moor the *New York* at Windmill point, and put one half your Guns on her; she would, I think, answer the purpose better than a Land Battery.

LB Copy, DNA, RG45, CLS, 1813, pp. 54–56.

1. Lemuel Morris, an uncle of Captain Charles Morris, served as chaplain in *Adams* from 16 March to 8 August 1813.

Joshua Barney and the Defense of the Chesapeake

The Baltimore flotilla commanded by Captain Charles Gordon and composed of a gun-boat and four leased schooners was considered by Jones to be "a cheap prompt and efficient temporary force."[1] The navy knew that the owners of these vessels would want their ships back once privateering activity started again, but the return of these ships would leave the Chesapeake vulnerable. When Joshua Barney[2] in July 1813 proposed a defense force of twenty barges or row-galleys, a "flying Squadron," Secretary Jones jumped at the chance to fill the vacuum caused by the loss of the leased schooners and appointed Barney to the special command of the Chesapeake flotilla. Barney spent the summer and fall of 1813 super-intending the construction of eight barges and manning and outfitting vessels from the former Potomac flotilla that he also inherited.

1. Jones to James Madison, 17 Apr. 1813, DLC, James Madison Papers, Ser. I, Vol. 51, No. 97.
2. For background on Barney's earlier career and his successful cruise on the privateer Rossie, see Dudley, Naval War of 1812, Vol. 1, pp. 248–60.

JOSHUA BARNEY'S DEFENSE PROPOSAL

Defence of the Chesapeake Bay &c

The Enemy have on this Station, 11 ships of the line, 33 frigates, 38 Sloops of war, and a number of Schooners &c.

Each ship of the line, <u>now</u> has 110 Marines,   Total 1210
each frigate 50 1650
each Sloop of War 30 1140
Marines coming from England 2000
Two Batallions of Royal Artillery, ditto, ... 1000
Two Batallions of Seamen (men they can trust) . . . <u>1200</u>
                                                       8200

The <u>Avowed</u> object of the Enemy, is, the distruction of the <u>City & Navy yard</u>, at Washington, the <u>City and Navy yard</u> at Norfolk, and the City of <u>Baltimore</u>, we see by the above statement that upwards of <u>8000</u> men, can be landed from the Enemies ships.

Frigates, Sloops of War, Schooners with Barges and small craft will be employed against those places; Now, what force have we to oppose such an Armament, should they make the attempt in a short time, which in my opinion will be done the moment <u>Admiral Warren</u> returns from <u>Bermuda</u>, (where I conceive he is now gone to meet the <u>Marines and Royal Artillery from England</u>) there to organize, and provide every thing necessary for the Campaign; he has already tried our waters, knows our Channels, <u>received information</u>, and will no doubt speedily return prepared for Mischief—

The question is, how to meet this force with a probability of success. <u>Our</u> ships (two frigates) cannot act, our <u>old</u> gunboats will not answer, they are too heavy to Row, and too clumsy to sail, and are only fit to lay <u>moor'd</u>, to protect a pass, or Assist a Fort. I am therefore of opinion the only defence we have in our power, is a Kind of Barge or Row-galley, so constructed, as to draw a small draft of water, to carry Oars, light sails, and One heavy long gun, these vessels may be built in a short time, (say 3 weeks) Men may be had, the City of Baltimore could furnish Officers & men for twenty Barges, we have now in Baltimore 150 Masters and Mates of vessels, all of whom have seen, and some of them been, onboard such kind of vessels, in Sweden and Denmark, and among the Spaniards, these men can be relied on, and when no further services should be required, would again return into the Merchants service, by which means the officers of the U S Navy, need not be called into this service. Let as many of such Barges be built as can be mann'd, form them into a flying Squadron, have them continually watching & annoying the enemy in our waters, where we have the advantage of shoals & flats throughout the Chesepeake Bay, the Enemy could be followed by such boats in every direction, without danger, their force would be respectable, and the enemy dare not dispatch Small ships, Brigs, or Schooners upon any expedition whilst such a force lay near them, these boats may be constructed to Row, beyond all possibility of the enemy having it in their power to Injure them, each boat ought to carry 50 officers and Men, and 25 Soldiers; A Squadron of twenty Barges would require 1000 officers & men, and 500 Officers & Soldiers, which in a few hours could be transported to any given point, and if necessary 500 or 1000 additional troops might be added; let each boat have, one 24 pounder, and small arms compleat, with such a force there would be no necessity for Camps being formed at any given point, as this force would always be hovering round the Enemy, and prevent any partial attacks on our bay-shore, or within our Rivers; such vessels as are here discribed, might oblige the Enemy to quit our waters, for during the summer months, they could so harrass them at Night: by getting near the ships of War, and keeping up a constant fire upon them, when no object would appear as a mark for the enemy, so that little damage could be received, especially as the Barges would be fitted to prevent boarding from the enemy, even if they were disposed to make the attempt, but a force like this would be sufficient to deter such an undertaking.

Add to this squadron three or four, light fast-sailing vessels, prepared as fireships, which could with ease, (under cover of the Barges) be run onboard any of the enemies ships, if they should attempt to anchor, or remain in our Narrow rivers, or harbours. In the Winter the Enemy could not act, but then our Barges might be kept at Hampton or in York river and other places at the mouth of the Bay. Should the enemy land all their forces with a design on any of our large Cities, they must be met in the field, but unless their heavy ships can cover the landing, and receive them onboard again, the Barge squadron could cut off their retreat by acting in concert with our troops onshore.

I would recommend as absolutely necessary, that the channel in the Potomac, below Washington be Imediately stopped up by sinking of vessels, or other substance for that purpose, let the frigate *Adams*, and all the Gun-boats (Old ones) be stationed at that place above the Obstruction, and also a floating Battery, to prevent the enemy from coming up, this obstruction can be easily removed when necessary, by ourselves, I would also sink vessels &c and stop the channel at Hawkins's point, a few miles below the fort at Baltimore; and defend the pass by armed schooners now in service, and two floating Batteries, prepared with furnaces for hot shot, and so fitted as to prevent being boarded by the Enemy. The defence at Norfolk I am told is nearly compleat— The expense of these Barges

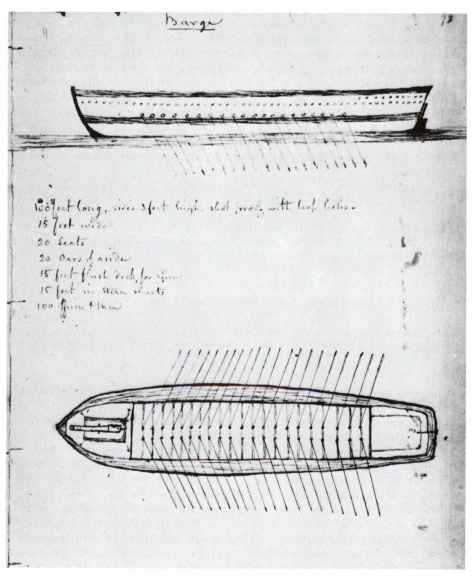

Barge for Use in the Defense of Chesapeake Bay

would not be great, they would cost about 3000$ each, and after the service was performed might be sold for <u>Coasters</u>, having only <u>a deck</u> to put on them.

This plan was before the <u>Assembly of Maryland</u>, a few days ago, and <u>a Bill passed the Senate</u> for building and manning <u>twenty</u> Barges, but was <u>rejected by the house of Delegates</u>, by which means our Bay harbours and Cities lay exposed to the fury of the Enemy. This is the <u>outlines</u> of a plan of Defence & offence, the details can be better explained verbally than in writing, when all the advantages could be pointed out, in fact we have no other mode of defence left us, but if we had, I conceive this by far the best, most effectual, and cheapest; <u>50 Barges</u> will not cost more than <u>One half</u> the price of <u>One frigate</u>, the officers and men will be on pay but a short time, and will have no further claim on the government. This <u>Marine</u> force would be <u>separate from</u>, and unconnected with the <u>Navy</u>, and could be so organized, as to have <u>One Regiment of troops</u>, annexed to it, the whole under the command of an able, active Naval officer, and <u>one Colonel</u>, with powers to correspond, not only with the General Government, but with the <u>Governors of Virginia & Maryland</u>, and to act in concert whenever circumstances required.

Joshua Barney
July 4t. 1813

ADS, DLC, James Madison Papers, Ser. 1, Vol. 52, No. 73. A draft copy is found in DNA, RG45, AF11 (M625, Roll No. 405). Barney's barge sketch is found with the copy at the National Archives.

SECRETARY OF THE NAVY JONES TO JOSHUA BARNEY

Joshua Barney Esqr. Navy Department
Baltimore August 20th 1813.

Sir,
The nature of the force, necessary for the defence of the extensive Bays and rivers of the United States, and the means of manning and employing that force, requiring an organization, in some degree, different from that in the general Naval Establishment, The President of the U. States, in order more effectually to accomplish the objects of the Legislature, as contemplated in the late law, providing for the building or procuring, and employing, such number of Barges, as he may deem necessary, has determined to select, for the special command of the Flotilla, on the upper part of the Chesapeake, a Citizen, in whose fidelity, skill, local knowledge, and commanding influence with the Mariners of the district, reliance may be placed, in cases of great emergency.

I have, therefore, the pleasure to offer to you that Special Command, subject only to the orders of this Department; and for the economy, and efficient employment of the force committed to your charge, you will be held responsible, and subject to the Rules and regulations for the government of the Navy of the United States.

It is not intended, because it would be incompatible with the rights of others, to appoint you, by Commission, to any regular and permanent rank in the Navy of the U. States; but, for the purpose and direction of your command, you will be considered as an Acting Master Commandant, in the Navy of the U. States, respected, and obeyed as such, within your special command, and be entitled to the pay, rations, and emoluments of a Master Commandant, exclusive of such reasonable allowances, for the extra expenses you may necessarily incur, in consequence of the peculiar nature of the service, and your superintendence of the objects, connected with your command on Shore. Your command will consist of the Barges, now building by contract at Baltimore for this Department, such of the City Barges, as may be purchased, or taken into the service of the U. States, and such other Barges, Gun Boats, or vessels, as may, from time to time, be attached thereto, by order of this Department.

The Officers immediately subordinate to you, as commanders, will be Sailing Masters in the Navy of the U. States, and such other subordinate and petty officers as this Department shall direct.

The Petty Officers and crews, will be regularly shipped, as in the Navy of the U. States, subject to the rules and regulations for the government thereof, and entitled to all the rights, privileges, and advantages of the Navy Pension fund, and Hospital, distribution of prize Money, pay, rations, &c. as in any other branch of the service.

They will moreover be shipped for twelve months, for the special service of the Flotilla, and not liable to be draughted for any other service.

You will, herewith, receive a special letter of appointment, with a copy of the rules and regulations of the Navy, and a blank oath of Office. Your acceptance will be signified by letter, and by taking and subscribing the oath, which you will transmit to this Department; from which time your pay, &c. will commence. I am, very respectfully, Your Obedt Servant,

W. Jones.

LB Copy, DNA, RG45, SNL, Vol. 11, pp. 56–58 (M149, Roll No. 11).

SECRETARY OF THE NAVY JONES TO
ACTING MASTER COMMANDANT JOSHUA BARNEY

Joshua Barney Esqr.   Navy Department
Comg. the U.S. Flotilla, Baltimore.   Augt. 27th 1813.

Sir,

James Beatty Esqr. Navy Agent Baltimore, having by order of this Department, contracted for the building of eight Barges, or Galleys, for the defence of the Chesapeake and its waters, four of which are to be 75 feet long, and 4 of 50 feet long, to be armed and equipped, as this Department shall direct; and considerable progress having been made in the construction thereof you will immediately superintend, and direct the equipment, with as much expedition as possible.

Mr. Beatty will state to you what the builders have engaged to perform, which you will cause to be faithfully executed; and for the residue of the equipment and finishing, Mr. Beatty will, upon your requisition, provide.

He is directed to have a number of 24 Pounders, belonging to the Navy Department, immediately transported to Baltimore; four of which you will appropriate to the four largest Galleys, in addition to which, they will each have a 42 pd. Carronade, if we have an opportunity of sending them round from this place; and if not, you will substitute four of the 32 pd. Carronades in Baltimore. The smaller

Galleys will be armed with long 18 pounders, to be sent from this place, and with 32, or 24 pd. Carronades. The opportunity you had of inspecting the new "*Black Snake*" Galley, at the Navy Yard here, will have conveyed to you a more perfect idea of the manner in which I wish them to be armed and equipped, than any written description; and if the movements of the enemy will admit, the "*Black Snake*" shall be sent round to you, completely fitted, to the most minute article, ready for action, from which all the rest can be fitted in exact conformity. In the interim you shall have the dimensions, description, and drawing of the Masts, Spars, Sails, &c. and, if the "*Black Snake*", cannot be sent round, either the Naval Constructor, Mr. Doughty, or our Master Boat builder will attend at Baltimore to give directions.

The Galleys, building at Baltimore, are upon the same plan and construction as those here, except that the former are a little fuller at each each end, the better to enable them to bear the heavy metal without hogging. The *Black Snake*, now with everything on board, ready for service, draws 21 inches water. Much pains have been taken to perfect those built here, in order to serve as an exact guide for those built elsewhere; and I am so perfectly satisfied with them, in all respects, that every possible effort will be made, to get one of them round to Baltimore in due time. I not only rely upon your exertions, to equip them in the shortest possible time; but upon your judgment, care, and economy, in doing it to the best advantage. The three Galleys, building here, will be added to your squadron, together with the *Scorpion* Cutter, Schooner *Asp*, and two or three Gunboats. Also such of the Barges, belonging to the City of Baltimore, as come within the description of the Act of Congress, provided the Agent, and Committee can agree upon terms. It will be necessary to look ahead, and take measures to prepare your ammunition, small stores, &c. If the Grape shot and stools are to be cast, it should be done immediately.

The small armament will be, for the largest Galley,

36 Muskets,
36 Boarding Pikes.
Ammunition for the long Gun,

	80 Round Shot,
	30 Stand of Grape.
For the Carronade—	60 Round Shot,
	30 Stand of Grape,
	30 Cannister.
For the Smaller Galley	26 Muskets,
	26 Boarding Pikes.

Ammunition same as for the large Galleys. Powder equivalent to the above, exclusive of 10 rounds of powder and round shot, for exercise at the target.

The Schooners[1] will soon be delivered up to their owners, and the crews, if practicable, transferred to the Barges. I am, respectfully, your Obedient Servt.

W. Jones.

LB Copy, DNA, RG45, SNL, Vol. 11, pp. 62–64 (M149, Roll No. 11).

1. For more information on the schooners *Patapsco, Comet, Revenge*, and *Wasp*, see pp. 348–54.

ACTING MASTER COMMANDANT JOSHUA BARNEY
TO SECRETARY OF THE NAVY JONES

Baltimore   Augt. 31st 1813

Sir

I had the honour, yesterday, to receive your letter of Instructions of the 27 Inst. I imediately waited upon Mr. Beatty the Navy Agent, and with him went to see the Barges building here, I am sorry to inform you that they are very backward, only <u>one</u> nearly ready to launch, several with the Ribbs up and neither floored or planked, and others merely floored, I do not see that they will be compleated in less time than four weeks, The Contractors appear to me, either not to understand what they are about, or will not understand, which will make it absolutely necessary to have either <u>Mr. Doughty</u> or the Master boat-builder here to give directions, and the sooner the better, could the "*Black-Snake*" be brought round, many difficulties, and much time & trouble would be avoided, and the work done in a more masterly Stile. Not knowing what Guns I shall be obliged to take for the Barges, I cannot prepare the ammunition for them, I have ordered the "Grape shot" and Stools to be cast imediately of <u>every</u> size.

The <u>small armament</u> mentiond in your letter, consists only of <u>Muskets and pikes</u>, we shall want <u>pistols</u> and <u>Sabres</u> in proportion; I would suggest having the Grape and Cannister made up at Washington, or, if you could spare a Gunner from the yard, to send here, he might be employed in fitting every Article of gunnery whilst we are fitting the Barges; Mr. Beatty informed me yesterday that he had agreed with the Baltimore Committee for three of their Barges, which I presume you intend should be imediately employed, and as the Schooners and the Barges are now about to be paid off, we must make a new agreement, on which subject I beg your Instructions, and whether in case the Commanders of the Barges does not wish to remain in them I may be permitted to appoint others. I have daily application from old Masters of vessels for employment but shall as you mentioned take the Masters of the <u>Schooners</u> if they are "disposed" to continue, some I am informed will, others will not, should you be of opinion that I should ship men imediately, I shall prepare a place for them untill called into service. If the Commanders of Barges were appointed, I could direct each of them to superintend the building and procure his men at the same time, which would prevent delay but for gods-sake send me the "*Black-Snake*", or I must come again to Washington, to see her, and make these thick-skuls here do their duty. If we could get the Guns &c round from Washington I should feel perfectly at ease. I am informed the Enemy has gone down from below Annapolis— A short correspondance has taken place between <u>Genrl Smith</u> and myself, I inclose a Copy of my letter—

AL, DNA, RG45, MLR, 1813, Vol. 5, No. 154 (M124, Roll No. 57). The last page of Barney's letter was not bound in with Vol. 5 but was in Vol. 6, No. 3 1/2 (M124, Roll No. 58). Barney did not sign this letter, but he did sign an enclosed copy of a letter to Samuel Smith relating to captured British signals. The enclosure is not printed here.

SECRETARY OF THE NAVY JONES TO
ACTING MASTER COMMANDANT JOSHUA BARNEY

Joshua Barney Esqr.   Navy Department
Comg. U.S. Flotilla, Baltimore.   Septr. 2nd 1813

Sir,

Your letter of the 31st Ulto. has been received. Mr. Doughty will be in Baltimore probably to-morrow. Four 18 pounders, such as the *Black Snake* carries, will be sent for the four large Barges; four 18 pounders, something shorter and lighter for the 50 feet Barges, and four 24 pd. carronades for the same. The 32 pd. carronades, for the large Barges, the Agent will deliver from Mr. Dorsey's works. Those are now shipping on board the *Scorpion* and *Asp*, which, together with the *Black Snake*, will proceed immediately to Baltimore, and deliver them to you. The *Scorpion* and *Asp*, having part of the crew of the *Adams* on board, will return to watch the mouth of the Potomac, until that Ship is ready.

With Muskets and pikes, I do not see much necessity for pistols and cutlasses; indeed pistols are not to be had. We shall endeavour to send you the Grape and Canister from this yard, or a part certainly.

You will open a Rendezvous, and recruit as many men as will man the whole of the new and old Barges. The Complement of Officers and men, and the rate of pay, &c. to be agreeable to the subjoined list.*

As soon as it is determined what number of the Sailing Masters of the Schooners and old Barges agree to continue, you will inform this Department. I am, Sir, respectfully, Your Obedient Servant,

W. Jones.

*Complement of Officers and Men for the new Barges, building at Baltimore for the U. States. viz.

75 feet Barges,   1 Sailing Master Commanding.
                    1 Master's Mate,
                    1 Gunner,
                    1 Boatswain,
                    1 Steward,
                    1 Cook,
                   10 Seamen and
                   <u>34</u> Ordinary Do.
Officers & Men   50.

50 feet Barges,   1 Sailing Master Commanding.
                    1 Masters Mate,
                    1 Gunner,
                    1 Boatswain,
                    1 Steward,
                    1 Cook,
                    8 Seamen and
                   <u>26</u> Ordinary Do.
Officers & Men   40.

Master's Mates $20, Gunners $20, Boatswains $20, Stewards $18, Cooks $18, Seamen $12, Ordinary Seamen $6 to $10 per Month, being the same pay, and will be entitled to the same rations, and privileges, as in the Navy of the U. States.

To be regularly shipped, under articles for 12 Months, subject to the Rules and Regulations for the Government of the Navy; but not liable to be drafted into any other service, than that of the Chesapeake Flotilla.

LB Copy, DNA, RG45, SNL, Vol. 11, pp. 72–74 (M149, Roll No. 11).

British Incursions in the Upper Bay

When Admiral Warren's frigates could not sail beyond Upper Cedar Point on the Potomac because of the shoals, he ordered his squadron to venture up the bay again. The British spent August attacking St. Michaels and Queenstown as well as establishing a base on Kent Island. The appearance of their ships off Baltimore and Annapolis caused great consternation. Fear for the safety of Maryland's capital prompted Navy Secretary Jones to permit Captain Charles Morris and the crew of Adams *to serve as artillerists at the Annapolis forts.*

LIEUTENANT JAMES POLKINGHORNE, R.N., TO COMMANDER HENRY LORAINE BAKER, R.N.[1]

Copy   His Majesty's Sloop *Conflict*
                                                                     10th August 1813

Sir,

In compliance with your orders I proceeded with the Division of Boats under my direction up the St. Michaels River; we advanced alongshore close to the Town of St. Michaels, and were discovered by the Enemy's Patrole who fired on us; a few minutes after a Battery mounting six twelve, and six pounders, gave us a round of Grape and Canister, when we immediately landed, got possession of the Battery, and drove the Enemy into the Town, After spiking the Guns spliting the Carriages, and destroying all the ammunition and stores, I re-embarked with the loss of only two wounded; by this time the Enemy had collected in considerable numbers, and commenced firing from two Field peices in the Town the destruction of the Battery being complete, and not a vessel to be seen,[2] I deemed the object of the enterprize fulfilled, and returned onboard with the Boats. The Conduct both of Officers and Men was exemplary and highly praise worthy for their steadiness in forming quickly in landing and driving the Enemy into the Town. Lieutenant Cairns and Roberts headed the small arm men and Royal Marines and Lieutenant Blood who had the care of the Launch with carronades, most effectually kept the Enemy on the defensive and rendered every assistance in covering our embarkation   I have the honor to be Sir, your most obedient humble Servant

                                                        Signed   J. Puckinghorn

Copy, UkLPR, Adm. 1/504, pp. 249–50.

1. Commander Henry Loraine Baker commanded H.M. sloop *Conflict.*
2. One reason the British had attacked St. Michaels was to destroy several privateers being built there.

ADMIRAL SIR JOHN B. WARREN, R.N., TO
FIRST SECRETARY OF THE ADMIRALTY JOHN W. CROKER

San Domingo Off the
South end of Kent Island
Chesapeake, 23rd August 1813.

Sir,

I request you will communicate to their Lordships' that on the 28th Ulto. I detached Captain Shirreff with the *Barossa, Laurestinus, Conflict,* and *Mohawk* Sloops, and *High Flyer* Tender up the Bay in hopes of cutting Off some of the Baltimore Flotilla amounting to Six or Seven sail of Schooners and some Row Galleys, likewise to secure the passes and Ferry round Kent Island, And I also directed Rear Admiral Cockburn to lead the Squadron up the Bay, it falling little Wind however on the 4th Instant several of the Ships on account of the Tide were obliged to Anchor, but the *Sceptre* from having a light breeze was enabled to get up as high as Kent Island; when the Rear Admiral, having three Companies of the 102nd Regiment on board very Judiciously and Zealously directed them to be dis-embarked with the Marines of that Ship and took possession of the above Island, secured the Ferry just as a considerable Number of Oxen and Sheep were at the Point ready to pass over to the Continent. On the 6th Instant the remainder of the Squadron arrived Off the Southern part of the Island and on the following day the Troops under the Command of Sir Sydney Beckwith were disembarked and Marched for the Northern part of the Island where they were placed in Camps and Sir Sydney established here several Posts and gave the necessary Orders on the occasion.

I was glad to obtain possession of this valuable & beauty Island which is half as large as the Isle of Wight not only on account of its' situation as a central Point between Annapolis, Baltimore, Washington and the Eastern Ports of the State of Maryland which joins the Delaware, but with the further view of refreshing the Troops and Crews of the Ships who had been so long Embarked and living upon Salt Provisions, and at the same time of receiving Cattle, Stock & Vegetables, which this Fertile and well Cultivated Spot furnished in the greatest abundance.

On the 12th. Instant Sir Sydney Beckwith marched with a part of the Troops upon a Reconnoissance against several Corps of the Enemy that had made their appearance near the Island: and the First Batallion of Marines were Embarked and proceeded under the direction of Captains Patterson and Maude toward Queen Town; & for a fuller description of the Operations on that occasion I beg leave to refer their Lordships' to the enclosed letter from the Quarter Master General: Upon the return of the Troops to the Island on the 13th the Army & Squadron remained near this place untill the 22nd, when after having large supplies of Fresh Provisions and Stock, and the Artillery & Officers having been furnished with Horses for their Service; And it having been ascertained that upwards of Eleven Thousand Troops were assembled at Baltimore exclusive of the Flotilla & Works established near that City, and that a Corps of Five Thousand men were around Annapolis and others expected from Washington, and the defenses of that Town much encreased: And Sir Sydney Beckwith having agreed with me that an Attack from the Force with us would prove very doubtful; I gave Orders for the whole of the several Corps to be Embarked, and proceeded down the Bay, in execution of their Lordships Orders.[1] I have the honor to be Sir, Your most Obedient humble Servant.

John Borlase Warren

LS, UkLPR, Adm. 1/504, pp. 137–41.

1. Warren had reported problems with desertions in the army and poor discipline among the marines. He wished to return to Halifax to avoid the hurricane season, to refit his ships, and to refresh the troops; see Warren to Croker, 14 Aug. 1813, UkLPR, Adm. 1/504, pp. 91–92.

SECRETARY OF THE NAVY JONES TO CAPTAIN CHARLES MORRIS

Captain Charles Morris,   Navy Department
U.S. Frigate *Adams*, Navy Yard.   August 12th 1813.

Sir,

The attitude of the enemy off Annapolis, indicating an immediate attack upon that place, and being informed that in the military force assembled for its defence, there is a great deficiency of Artillerists you will immediately repair, with the Officers and crew of the *Adams*, to Annapolis, and offer your cooperation to the commanding military officer, in conformity with the terms of the joint regulation of the War and Navy Departments, copy of which you will present to him.

As your force will not be prepared for field service, he will doubtless assign to you the command of one or both forts, in which you can act with most effect, as your men have been well trained to the use of great guns, of which the example of their brethren, on similar occasions, has furnished the fullest assurance you will take with you, a sufficiency of Pikes and Cutlasses, as the most convenient weapons for the occasion, and three days provision <u>cooked</u>. Mr. Buller Cocke, of the Navy Yard, will procure carriages for the speedy transportation of your force, and will take care to keep you provided, with all that may be necessary for the sustenance and comfort of your command; and you will make such requisitions on the Navy Agent, Mr. Randall, for other objects as your wants and the nature of the service may render expedient.

You will please keep me informed of such occurrences as may be interesting, and as soon as your services can be safely dispensed with, you will return to this place. I am, respectfully, your Obedt. Servt.

W. Jones.

LB Copy, DNA, RG45, SNL, Vol. 11, pp. 47–48 (M149, Roll No. 11).

SECRETARY OF THE NAVY JONES TO CAPTAIN CHARLES MORRIS

Capt. Charles Morris,   Navy Department
Comg. U.S. Naval Forces, Annapolis.   Augt. 29th 1813.

Sir,

I have received your letter of the 27th and though the position of the enemy may be still as favourable for an attack upon Annapolis, as at any period hitherto, yet I do not think the probability, or indication of an attack, by any means as great as it has been.

Indeed there are many who apprehend an attempt to debark at Herring Bay, and by a forced march for this place, in the absence of those who are called off from its defence, accomplish its destruction, then cross the country to Port Tobacco, and reach their ships without serious opposition. You will have found General Bloomfield of this opinion. I do not however believe, that the enemy is at all prepared, or disposed, for so bold and vigorous an enterprize. Although you are independent of the command of either the Governor, or General Bloomfield, yet it would have been more regular to have conferred with the latter than the former. The Governor is acting in his State capacity, and has no command of the forces of the U. States—the General is the U.S. Military commander of the District.

It is not at all certain that the enemy may not again enter the Potomac, were it only to keep up the alarm, and harrass the Country. The Naval force, though ready upon an emergency, to defend a fort as well as a Ship, cannot be expected to do Garrison duty; therefore, as you have put the Forts at Annapolis in order, and given time to collect the proper force for its defence, you will, without delay, return to this place, with the whole of the force under your command, and as symptoms of fever have appeared among your Seamen at Fort Madison, you cannot remove too soon.

I am, moreover, anxious to have the necessary alterations made in the *Adams* as soon as possible. I am, respectfully, Your Obdt. Servt.

W. Jones.

LB Copy, DNA, RG45, SNL, Vol. 11, p. 67 (M149, Roll No. 11).

Blockade Duty

By the beginning of September 1813, Admiral Warren had sailed for Halifax and Rear Admiral Cockburn had departed for Bermuda. They left behind Captain Robert Barrie with a skeleton force to blockade the Virginia Capes and conduct occasional raids on coastal towns. The latter helped to dispel the monotony of this unrewarding service.

CAPTAIN ROBERT BARRIE, R.N., TO MRS. GEORGE CLAYTON

Dragon   Sept 4th 1813
Chesapeak Bay

My Dear Mother

The *Bramble* Schooner arrived here yesterday in six weeks from Plymouth and I was sadly disappointed in not receiving a line from any of ye—your last letter was the 1 May— I wrote from Halifax to say that I was to rejoin the Squadron in the Chesapeak— I found it at anchor off Annapolis & in possession of Kent Island—this has been evacuated and we are now in Lynn haven bay—where I am to be left in charge of the blockade of the Chesapeak   I shall have a few frigates & small craft under my orders & if the Americans venture to run any of their French traders during the winter I hope to catch a few of them—but this Blockading affair is a sad disappointment to me who expected a Cruize off New

York for the winter— I have also a most serious charge on my hands and have a duty to perform with one ship of the line two frigates ~~and~~ two Brigs and three schooners that has hither to employed never less than four sail of the Line six frigates & Brigs & Schooners without end— I expect to remain on this service for at least five months, unless a Peace takes place before that time— The Enemy has one frigate & about twenty other armed Vessels at Norfolk—one frigate at Alexandria and a considerable collection of government armed Vessels at Baltimore and as Nathan has not had any trade whatever during the summer I hope he will dash a little now the bad weather is coming on— our news is very old from Europe— in Canada we are going on pretty well but I can not boast much of the exploits of our Chesapeak squadron—thank god the *Dragon* had no share in the attack of Craney Island, Hampton or any of the towns in the Chesapeak— Tubs has left me he got too old for old Thompson & was [sawing?] therefore I have sent him about his business he is now with the Commander in Chiefs Secretary—but I do not think he will remain in his service long Thompson is very well for an old one [?]

Cririe has gained great credit for his very gallant conduct in the *Narcissus* boats & should be promoted if merit had its due reward— Mr. Hamer is going on very well but he is not a particularly bright sailor   The Admiral has promised to send my letters from Halifax when the Packets arrive therefore I expect to hear from some of you evry month— The Squadron is very sickly but *dragon's* crew at present are in good health but they are a most troublesome set of blackguards— making best remembrance to all & ever believe me my dear Mother your truly affectionate & dutiful son

Robt. Barrie

We are sadly afraid of a dirty Peace with Nathan—

ALS, MiU–C, Barrie Papers. The brackets represent indecipherable words.

CAPTAIN SAMUEL JACKSON, R.N., TO CAPTAIN ROBERT BARRIE, R.N.

Copy   His Majesty's Ship *Lacedemonian*
                                    in the Chesapeake   23d Septr. 1813

Sir,

From the representation that was made by the Masters of the *Dragon* and *Lacedemonian* respecting the Enemy's Schooners in Chereton and Kings Creeks and the Evening of the day I left you proving favourable for an attack on them, for the purpose, not only of ascertaining what they were, but also of either bringing them out or destroying them.

I therefore at 12 O'Clock that night sent five Boats with two Carronades, Sixty Seamen and Twenty five Marines under the Orders of Lieutt. Maw first Lieutenant of this Ship (accompanied by Captain Litchfield who very handsomely volunteered his services upon the occasion— The *Mohawk* was also ordered as close inshore as possible for the purpose of giving any assistance to the Boats that might be requisite— From the intricacy of the navigation in bringing the Vessels down the Creeks, I judged dawn of day to be the best time for making the attack. The Brig and Boats were however discovered by the Enemy some time before they reached the Shore, and they soon collected a considerable body of Militia to oppose the Boats at the entrance of the Creek which was not above Musket shot across— Their Force at this time was about a Hundred Riflemen which covered themselves behind Trees, Sand Hills, and every where they could shelter themselves. Independent of this Force they have two Field Pieces, one of which was abandoned and it is thought dismounted— The Launch was stationed to keep clear and secure the entrance of the Creek, whilst the other Boats were employed in bringing down the Vessels, and after towing them down for nearly two miles exposed to a heavy fire of Musketry from both sides the Creek. I am sorry to say that there was not sufficient Water to get them over the Bar—the *Mohawk* at this time also took the ground, and upon which it was found necessary to set fire to the vessels in our possession—Their Cargoes consisted of Corn and Potatoes— By this time the Enemy had collected from two to three Hundred Men who were driven from one position to another whenever they came within the reach of our fire— Thus terminated this little but brilliant piece of Service, which I can bear testimony from the way it was performed deserved every success and certainly the whole of the Enemy's vessels would have been brought out had their been sufficient Water to have got them over the Bar which indeed when we left them was nearly dry, and scarcely Water left to float the Boats over.

Captain Litchfield and Lieutenant Maw speak in the highest terms of Lieut. Taylor, Mr. Franklin Master and of every Officer and Man employed upon this occasion.

I am extremely sorry to add that in heaving a <u>new Schooner</u> off <u>that was on shore</u>, I had one man killed and one wounded, I fear dangerously, of the *Lacedemonian,* and one wounded from the *Mohawk*— The Enemy's loss was considerable they were driven in every direction, and all the Officers agree in their having at least from Twenty to Thirty Killed and Wounded.

One Boat from the *Mohawk* accompanied the *Lacedemonian.* I have the honor to be Sir your most Obedient and very humble Servant

(Signed)   Saml. Jackson   Captain

Copy, UkLPR, Adm. 1/505, pp. 139–41. Enclosed in Warren to Croker, 29 Dec. 1813, pp. 129–30.

Changes in the Potomac Flotilla

Continuity of command did not mark the first seven months of the Potomac flotilla's existence. Lieutenant Alexander S. Wadsworth, late of Adams, replaced Lieutenant George C. Read as that group's commander on 28 September. Wadsworth was the flotilla's fourth leader since February. His duties remained essentially the same as those of his predecessors—to reconnoiter the river for British activity and to engage the enemy's small vessels if feasible.

SECRETARY OF THE NAVY JONES TO LIEUTENANT ALEXANDER S. WADSWORTH

Lt. Alexander Wadsworth   Nav. Deptmt.
US. Frigate *Adams.*   Nav. Yard   28 Sept. 1813.

Having receved information that a 74 a Frigate a Brig & a Tender part of the enemy's squadron, anchored in the Bay off the mouth of the Potomac on saturday last; You will immediately take the command of the Flotilla now at the Navy Yard—consisting of the *Scorpion* Cutter. Schr. *Asp.* Gun Boat no. *70. 71.* & *137.* the Galley *Shark.* & the small Barge mounting two 12 pd. caronades; & proceed toward the mouth of the river recoinnoitering the enemy's force with care, & if you shall be satisfied that his Boats & tenders cannot attack you with a superior force, you will endeavor, should a favorable opportunity occur, to annoy & drive him from his station: until you ascertain the enemy's force it will be prudent to direct the heaviest sailing gun Boats, to remain at Port Tobacco to be ordered, as circumstances may dictate: you will take especial care to prevent all intercourse with the enemy & suffer no vessel to pass whose destination either avowed, or such as you have good reason to suspect will lead her within the power of the enemy whatever intelligence you may wish to communicate, will reach the Department through the Post office at Port Tobacco.

W. Jones

LB Copy, DNA, RG45, A & R, Vol. 11, p. 58.

Condition of *Constellation*

Captain Charles Stewart departed Constellation *for* Constitution *in May 1813, leaving Master Commandant Joseph Tarbell in temporary command of that ship. Jones wanted Captain Charles Gordon to take charge of* Constellation *once the Baltimore flotilla could spare him. But British activity in the upper bay and the necessity of returning the leased schooners to their owners during the summer of 1813 precluded an early departure. Jones ordered Gordon in late August to restore all the leased schooners to their owners and assign his gunboats to Joshua Barney, who would succeed Gordon in command of the Chesapeake flotilla.*

On 15 September Gordon was still in Baltimore and Jones, unhappy with Captain Tarbell's[1] *command of* Constellation, *directed Gordon to proceed immediately to Norfolk via Washington. Once in Norfolk, Gordon discovered the neglected state of his ship and crew. Secretary Jones attempted to determine who was to blame for the frigate's poor condition.*

1. *Joseph Tarbell was promoted to captain on 24 July 1813.*

SECRETARY OF THE NAVY JONES TO CAPTAIN CHARLES GORDON

Capt. Charles Gordon,   Navy Department
Comg. U.S. Frigate *Constellation*, Norfolk.   Octr. 6th 1813.

Sir,

As the season is at hand when you will doubtless have an opportunity of eluding the vigilance of the enemy, and getting to Sea, but as it is first necessary to heave out and clean the bottom of the *Constellation,* you will use every exertion to accomplish that object, and re-equip without delay. Captain Cassin has my instructions to afford you every facility and assistance in his power, and to comply with your necessary requisitions. When the *Constellation* is ready to receive her crew, Captain Tarbell, the Commandant of the Flotilla, will deliver over to you all the men belonging to the

Constellation, who have been employed in the temporary service of the Flotilla. I am informed, that, during the time Capt. Tarbell had the temporary command of the *Constellation,* her powder was damaged, excessively, by inattention to the Pumps, and Captain Cassin informed me, that an enquiry was about to be made into the circumstances of the neglect;[1] but as I have heard nothing further on the subject, I have to request that you will make strict enquiry, and report to me what shall appear to you to be the facts of that case, and the nature and extent of the damage.

Should you require a new Cable or Cables, we have two or three here of a very superior quality, and you will not order them made, until we ascertain the practicability of transporting them from this place in due time. I am, very respectfully, Your Obedt. Servt.

W. Jones.

In everything relating to your command, you will receive orders direct from this Department.

W. J.

LB Copy, DNA, RG45, SNL, Vol. 11, pp. 107–8 (M149, Roll No. 11).

1. See John Cassin to Jones, 7 Sept. 1813, DNA, RG45, CL, 1813, Vol. 6, No. 7 (M125, Roll No. 31).

CAPTAIN CHARLES GORDON TO SECRETARY OF THE NAVY JONES

U S.F. *Constellation*
Gosport   12th Octr. 1813

Sir,

Ever since my arrival I have been collecting my Crew from the different Vessels of the Flotilla to enable me to prepare the Ship for sea— Not untill the day before yesterday was it in my power to have a general muster— Enclosed herewith is a copy of the Pursers report after Muster—

The ship is entirely stripp'd & every thing landed with a swept hold— The preparations of Pendants, Blocks &c. which had to be <u>made</u> (the yard being deficient in those articles) may delay us a little But I am happy to say Captn. Cassin uses every exertion to forward us and, I hope will not detain the Ship as I shall try to commence getting the outriggers out & pendants up to day— The Hull, Masts & standing rigging appear to require nothing of importance. But there are great deficiencies in every thing else— She will require a quantity of running rigging, One set of Top sails & Courses to replace those that have been bent & have become mildew'd & rotten, Two Bower Cables, One Mizen Top mast to replace a white pine one she has now And, to compleat her original indent for stores in the different Departments which I find are (in most cases) entirely gone— There being no inventory taken & no receipt from Captn. Tarbel to Captn. Stewart when the change took place, I find it difficult to assertain <u>precisely</u> what is deficient or where the deficiencies are gone particularly the Cabin furniture— But having every thing now on shore, with officers attending to them I shall be enabled to compleat the indents by the time the Ship will be ready for them, except such as are not to be had here And for which I shall immediately forward my requisition on the Navy Yard Washington enclosed to you for approval— I found the Ship without order or arrangement in any degree owing to her Crew being so long absent & indeed had become almost strangers to the Ship, to their stations & to every thing like system & regularity. For in the Gun Boat service they cannot be kept in that state of discipline necessary for a man of war— In fact the Ship will require re-fitting from her Keelson up and her Crew reorganis'd & train'd as tho. she were just from the Ordinary— my Commission'd officers are very inexperienc'd. And we are entirely deficient in warrant officers as you may perceive by the enclosed return— Mr Laughton an old midsn. on the Charleston station has applied to join us & I think would be an acquisition—

The report of the officers who were orderd by Captn. Cassin to enquire into the causes of the damag'd powder, I shall have the honor to forward by tomorrows mail—my men (25 in number) that left Baltimore with me arrived this day & are included in the enclosed report— The Powder is still on its way under charge of an officer, It has been detain'd unexpectedly at Urbanna, in the Rappahannock, for want of Waggons, And the Tender (*Franklin*) has now gone up James River with a smart officer to meet it & to assist in getting it across—

The Enemy being now in Lynhaven bay I am of opinion a Vessel may get into York river & send across to Hampton such articles as will admit of land transportation— If you contemplate sending us men from Washington they, with the sails & indeed everything the Ship will require, except the Cables, may be very readily sent a cross from Little York, and if the Cables could be landed we could send from here for them or even waggon them if necessary— I have the honor to be Sir, yr. obt Servt.

Chas Gordon

ALS, DNA, RG45, CL, 1813, Vol. 7, No. 96 (M125, Roll No. 32). This letter and the following enclosure are bound in with the November 1813 Captains' Letters.

[Enclosure]
(Copy)

An abstract of the Crew of the U. States Frigate *Constellation*, Charles Gordon Esqr. Commander—

One Captain	Four, Boatswain's Mates
Five Lieutenants	One, Carpenters— Do.
One, Surgeon	One, Boatswain Yeoman
One, Purser	One, Carpenters— Do.
One, Master	One, Gunners— Do.
Two, Surgeon's Mates	Five, Quarter Masters
Eleven, Midshipman	Eight, Quarter Gunners
One, Sailmaker	One Hundd. & fifty Seaman
One, Cook	Eighty, Ordiy, Seamen
One, Steward	Six, Boys
One, Cooper	One, Coxswain
One, Master At Arms	288 Total
One, Armourer	_44 Marines
Two, Master's Mates	332 Grand Total

(Sign'd)   Isaac Garretson
Purser
October 11th 1813

Copy, DNA, RG45, CL, 1813, Vol. 7, No. 96, enclosure (M125, Roll No. 32).

CAPTAIN CHARLES STEWART TO SECRETARY OF THE NAVY JONES

Boston   October 18. 1813

Sir

I have received your letter of the 12th. instant covering a copy of one from Captain Gordon of the *Constellation* to the Commandant of the Navy Yard at Washington detailing certain deficiencies on board that ship.

It is truly mortifying to me that there should have arisen any necessity for calling on me at this period to shew the state and condition of that ship at the time I surrendered her to the charge of Captain Tarbell; particularly as her books of indent and expenditure were left on board, made up to the day of my leaving her; by reference to them it will be seen what had been received on board, as stores, and what was expended. I also regret that you may have considered it a neglect on my part in not having taken an inventory, which I certainly should have done under any other circumstances. But, Sir, I deem it necessary to explain to you what appeared to render it unnecessary. An order from the Department directing that ship to be held in readiness for sea, which was fully complied with, agreeable to my report to you, dated May 12th, which stated her to be in every respect ready for a Cruise, except a small deficiency in her complement of men, and having, agreeable to that order, kept her so untill my leaving her, I did not consider there was any necessity for breaking up her store rooms &c to inventory her materials, to command the receipt of a temporary Commander who would in all probability be superceded in a few days. With respect to the Cabin furniture, I had taken the precaution to see all the articles (but chairs and tables) placed carefully into the Captains Store room, and locked up, except such as was necessary to take in the *Franklin* tender with me to Richmond, for our convenience—while on board; the return of which to the ship Lieut. Wilkinson and Mr. McCauley were charged with, who I presume complied accordingly. A list of them is enclosed.

Considering that Captain Tarbell's abode was with his family at the Navy Yard, and his command of the Ship but temporary, I did not presume any thing relative to the Cabin-furniture would be changed from the place in which I had left it, untill his sucessor had joind the ship; but in this I may have been mistaken. Enclosed you will receive a copy of the articles got at Washington, Annappolis, and Norfolk for the Cabin; also a list of what was broke and lost during the time I was on board.

Of the general stores and furniture of that ship belonging to the Boatswain's, Gunner's, Sailmakers, Carpenter's and Master's departments, the bills or receipts bearing my Signature at the several places, will show what was received on board; the expenditure book will show what was used; the difference will be what was on board at the time I left her, except six hundred stand of grape shot loaned to Forts Norfolk and Nelson, the receipts for which was left with the first lieutenant Neale, and was to have been returned on demand if not used.

My indents for furniture and stores, when fitting out that ship, were made with the strictest regard to Economy so far as I had control, (which only consisted in quantity), and therefore she was more bare in that respect than any outfit that preceded her; if they were costly the fault was the market price, and the extravagance of the agents in quality; if she has been expensive in her general stores the fault has been, the bad quality of her original Supplies, as heretofore reported to the Department, and no fault of mine.

It now remains for me to assure you, on the honour of an Officer, that the only articles taken with me from that ship and belonging to the Government, were, her Chronometer, Letter Book, Order Book, and one set of signal books, one towell left among my cloaths in the bag by mistake of my steward, and an edition of Bowditch's Practical Navigator among my books, which articles are now applied to the Public use in the *Constitution*, and that no other article was taken from her by me, or by my orders, but what belonged to myself. If positive proof of the above is necessary it is in my power to give it. Captain Ridgeley who is near you, and who is perfectly aware of the state and condition of the ship being such as I reported her to be at that time, can satisfy you that nothing was wanting to render her complete for her intended cruise, and Mr. McCauley can inform you whether the articles on board the *Franklin* were returned. If then, such proves to be the case, and any deficiencies have arisen afterwards, the fault was not mine, and must be attributed to the neglect of some other person. Had I thought it necessary at the time to have taken an inventory and receipt, it should have been done, but I deem it equally the duty of an Officer, to guard the property of the Navy, as much without having receipted for it, as though he had. If any articles have been distributed among the gun-boats, as appears by Captain Gordon's letter, it has occurred since I left there; for while on that station, I permitted nothing to go on board them but arms and ammunition, which were always returned to the ship immediately on the object being accomplished for which they were put there; this was at all times strictly complied with by the officers.

With respect to Bunting, there was none, if I recollect right, received on board, although indented for; and I believe there was great difficulty in getting sufficient, at that time, to make her Signal flags.

With respect to her sails, one entire suit was bent at the time; and all the spare sails, which had been received on board a few days before from Captain Cassin agreable to the receipt when deposited with him, were in the Sail Room.

Although desirous at all times of the good opinion of the Government, for correctness as an Officer, and a Gentleman, yet I wish them, at no time, to give me credit on that account in advance; and assure you, that at no time, will your doing so, oblige, or serve me; fairness of intention is all I claim, and that I am as liable to err in judgement as most men, there can be no doubt. Therefore on all such occasions as the present, I shall be infinitely more thankful to you to communicate them to me as you have now done; and I assure you that I shall always, very gladly, afford every elucidation in the case, of which I am capable and have the means of doing. Very thankfully, I have the honour to be Your obedient Servant

Ch^S. Stewart

ALS, DNA, RG45, CL, 1813, Vol. 7, No. 18 (M125, Roll No. 32).

[Enclosure]

Cabin furniture received onboard the U.S.F. *Constellation* at Washington &c &c

1 Dineing table with ends.	2 tin cannisters
12 Chairs.	3 dozn. glass tumblers
3 dozn. Table cloaths/large & small	3 dozn. wine glasses
1 green Table cover.	6 quart decanturs
24 China dishes/assorted.	6 pint ditto
2 dozn. Soup plates.	2 warter decanturs
3 dozn. Shallow plates	2 pr. Candlesticks & Muffers
12 vedgitable plates	1 table bell
6 sauce tureens	4 hair brushes
4 Salt Cellars.	1 tin dirt pan
18 desert plates	1 frying pan
1 Block-tin Tureene	4 stew pans
12 tin dish covers	4 tin bake pans
2 Cork screws.	1 Cullender
1 tin bread basket	1 Cleaver and tormentors [1]/Cook
24 Silver table spoons	4 brass cocks, assorted
12 ditto Tea Do.	2 wash hand basons
1 Silver Soup ladle	1 set cot curtains
1 set of plated Castors	1 set Knives & forks.
4 Waiters Japaned.	1 set Tea China.
2 tea kettles.	

Articles lost and broken onboard the U.S. Frigate *Constitution* [2]

2 Dishes/Broken	1 milk jug Broken
2 vedgitable dishes/Broken	2 silver table spoons/lost
1 sauce turine/broken	14 towels/lost.
4 plates/broken	

Sundries taken onboard the *Franklin* tender to Richmond and returned onboard the *Constellation* at Norfolk

1 Quart decantur	1 dozn. plates
2 pint ditto	4 dishes
6 Tumblers	6 cups & saucers
6 wine glasses	1 frying pan
6 Table spoons } silver	2 stew pans
6 Tea spoons }	1 Tea Kettle
3 table cloaths/small	8 Knives & forks
6 towels	1 set Castors

D, DNA, RG45, CL, 1813, Vol. 7, No. 18, enclosure (M125, Roll No. 32).

1. A tormentor is a long iron meat fork used by sea cooks.
2. Stewart meant *Constellation*.

Secretary of the Navy Jones to Captain Charles Stewart

Charles Stewart Esqr.   Navy Department
Comg. U.S. Frigate *Constitution*, Boston   Octr. 28th 1813

Sir,

I have received your letter of the 18th current, relative to the Stores of the *Constellation*, which is perfectly satisfactory, and such as I had no doubt of receiving from you on the subject.

The disorganization, waste, and negligence, on board the *Constellation*, subsequent to your command, are, I believe, without a parallel in the service; sails rotting on the yards, seven feet water in her hold, 2000 lbs. of powder utterly destroyed, and great part of the furniture, &c. dilapidated or lost; and the responsibility attempted to be shifted from the Commander to a Warrant Officer, who is said to have been left with the entire command, under the pretext of the Commander and Lieutenants, being engaged in Flotilla expeditions, and on Craney Island.

This may account to you for the necessity of my enquiry, in order to investigate and trace the negligence to its proper source.

Wishing you a prosperous and honourable Cruize, I am, very respectfully, Your Obedt. Servant,

W. Jones.

LB Copy, DNA, RG45, SNL, Vol. 11, pp. 131–32 (M149, Roll No. 11).

Sailing Master Benjamin Bryan [1] to Secretary of the Navy Jones

The Honbl. William Jones   Norfolk   13th Nov 1813
Secretary of the Navy

Sir

It has recently come to my knowledge that an attempt has been made to fix on me the blame of damaging a quantity of powder, on board the Frigate *Constellation*, of which I was lately master; to enable you to judge to whom it justly belongs. I beg leave to submit the following extracts from the Log Book of the Ship.

Thursday 4 Feby 1813, the ship warping from Hampton Roads up towards Norfolk for Safety from three British frigates then in Chase, she grounded on the flats near the diamond rock: at 2 P.M. the master (myself) was ordered to start the water in the hold, which was immediately done, & the provisions discharged on board of four Schooners hired by Capt Stewart for the purpose of Lightnening the ship. at 6 P.M. the ship floated, made sail, and at 11 P.M. anchored between Forts Norfolk & Nelson.—

To the following question propounded by Commodore Cassin viz

What was the situation of the Frigate *Constellation* between the 20th of June & 12th July 1813 (when the operations vs the enemy at Craney Island required the officers & crew of the ship)

I, answer

Capt Tarbell Commanding the Flotilla, manned it from the *Constellation*, on the 20th of June and proceeded to attack an English Frigate in Hampton Roads, on the 21st at 4 P.M all hands returned on board from the Gun Boats; at 6 P.M all hands repaired on board the Gun boats again and sailed for Craney Island, where they remained till the 23rd; at 9 am on the 23rd returned from Craney Island on board the ship, at 3 P.M on the 24th all hands embarked on board boats and proceeded to Craney Island again and remained till the 27th when they returned on board; the ship during their absence having been in charge of the master & 12 men— On the 28th at 6 a.m. all hands embarked again for Craney Island, and remained there till the 30th and on that day at 5 a.m. returned on board, and on the 2nd July the boats and crew left the ship again for Craney Island— On the third of July at 6 P.M. all hands and the boats returned on board the ship; On the 5th at 4 P.M. the men were again embarked for Craney Island; at 6 a.m. the 6th all hands returned on board from the Island.

On the 7th at 4 P.M. all hands embarked again for Craney Island—

On the 8th at 6 a.m. all hands returned from the Island—

On the 9th at 6 P.M. all hands returned to the Island for the night.

On the 10th @ 6 a.m. all hands returned from the Island to the Ship and remained on board till the 12th (except those stationed on board Gun Boats) & boats were on the 12th sent to Craney Island to remove the ships arms & ammunition, from the Gun Boats, on board her.

The foregoing extracts embracing, nearly all the proceedings from the time of the ships grounding, to the return of her Crew after the expedition of the Enemy against Craney Island; I flatter myself with an opinion, that an examination of them (with ~~a~~ an ~~remark~~ assurance that the ship did not make more than from 12 to 15 inches water in 24 hours) will be sufficient to satisfy you, that I do not merit the stigma attempted to be Cast on me, and that the powder in all probability, was damaged by the water being started in the hold, and it was not my duty to interfere in the pumping it out—

And it will appear from the foregoing statement, that I was not at any one time longer ~~enough~~ in charge of the ship, ~~more~~ than 48 hours[2]   I am Sir most respectfully Yr. Humble Servt.

Benjamin Bryan

ALS, DNA, RG45, BC, 1813, Vol. 4, No. 100 (M148, Roll No. 12).

1. Sailing Master Benjamin Bryan was ordered to *Constellation* on 7 August 1812.
2. For Joseph Tarbell's account, which substantiates Bryan's, see Tarbell to Jones, 7 Dec. 1813, DNA, RG45, CL, 1813, Vol. 8, No. 27 (M125, Roll No. 33).

British Blockade: Successes and Failures

Captain Robert Barrie continued to enforce the British blockade of the Chesapeake and harass coastal towns with forays against American merchant vessels during the last two months of 1813. The British were kept busy seeking new sites for replenishing their water reserves. The Americans found the British presence in the bay strong enough to prevent shipment of construction supplies for the sloops building at Baltimore.

LIEUTENANT GEORGE PEDLAR, R.N., TO CAPTAIN ROBERT BARRIE, R.N.

Copy   H.M. Ship *Dragon*   Potowmac
                                                     River   Novr. 5th 1813

Sir,

In compliance with your directions I beg leave to state the proceedings of the Boats you did me the honor to place under my orders on the night of the 5th Instant

On leaving the Ship with three boats of the *Dragon* and two of the *Sophie* I proceeded onshore to the entrance of St. Mary's and with the greatest silence rowed up the River a distance of four or five Miles without meeting the least resistance until within an hundred Yards of some Vessels moored to the Shore in a small Creek, when a Party of the Enemy from a Wood on the bank of the River gave three cheers and commenced a fire of Musquetry. The superior fire of Guns and small Arms from the Boats soon dislodged them. we then took possession of the Vessels named in the margin[1] and towed them out the Enemy having taken the whole of their Sails onshore.

I have great pleasure in acquainting you that this Service has been performed without any loss on our part and have only to regret that in this trifling affair no opportunity occurred where the Officers and men could particularly distinguish themselves as I am certain they would have fully answered your expectations. To Lieuts. Douglas and Fitzmaurice of this Ship the latter a Volunteer on this occasion one Pearson of the *Sophie*, the Petty Officers, Seamen & Marines employed in Boats I feel much indebted for their assistance and steady good conduct   I have the honor to be Sir, Your most Obedient and humble Servant

"Signed"   George Pedlar

Copy, UkLPR, Adm. 1/505, pp. 137–38.

1. "*Quintessence.* Sloop Packet of Alexandria—Sundries—Coppered & sails very fast   *John.* Schooner. Corn and Glass   *Alexandria* Schooner Wood."

CAPTAIN ROBERT BARRIE, R.N., TO ADMIRAL SIR JOHN B. WARREN, R.N.

Copy   H M Ship *Dragon*   Lynhaven
                                                     Bay, 14th Novr. 1813

Sir,

As the severe Weather and sudden changes of Wind rendered the Watering at Cape Henry extremely precarious, I thought it best to secure a supply of that Article in time. I therefore left the *Lacedaemonian, Armide,* and *Actaeon* here, and proceeded with the *Dragon* and *Sophie* up the Potowmac, where I took possession of St. Georges Island and having completed the Wood & Water of both Vessels returned to this Anchorage yesterday.

During my absence there was a Weeks continuance of fine Weather which enabled Captn. Jackson to complete the Water of the Frigates and *Actaeon.*

In spite of our utmost endeavours the Enemy's Clippers continue to pass us every Northerly Wind. The *Armide* chaced one 120 miles going ten and eleven knots without being able to come up with her.

The *Lacedaemonian, Armide* and *Sophie* are now outside the Cape, the *Lacedaemonian* slipped after a Schooner and as she and the *Sophie* are very fast Vessels I hope they will be fortunate. The *Actaeon* has chaced several of their Clippers but she has no chance with them; I chaced a Settee rigged Privateer yesterday in *Dragon* but I had the mortification to observe that we have lost our Sailing and the Privateer easily escaped us by the Tangier Shoals through the Cape Charles Passage.

The Enemy's Frigates have not attempted to make any movement; a Sloop of War was lately launched at Baltimore, but she is not yet Masted.

The Slaves continue to come off by every opportunity and I have now upwards of 120 men, women and Children on board, I shall send about 50 of them to Bermuda in the *Conflict.*

Amongst the Slaves are several very intelligent fellows who are willing to act as local guides should their Services be required in that way, and if their assertions be true, there is no doubt but the Blacks of Virginia & Maryland would cheerfully take up Arms & join us against the Americans.

Several Flags of Truce have been off to make application for their Slaves &ca., but not a single black would return to his former owner. I have the honor to be Sir, Your most obedient humble servant

"Signed"   Robt. Barrie   Captn.

Copy, UkLPR, Adm. 1/505, pp. 131–33.

JOHN S. SKINNER [1] TO SECRETARY OF THE NAVY JONES

Baltimore   December 6th 1813. Sir—

As I have understood that you propose soon to send round the sails and rigging for the Sloops of war at this place, I feel it my duty to apprize you, that in my opinion, formed upon observations recently made while on a visit to the enemy at the Capes, this property coming here from the Potowmac is exposed to imminent risque of being captured by the Brigs *Acteon* and *Sophie.* While the *Dragon* and the *Armide* remain stationary at the Capes watching the *Constellation* these two Brigs are employed either in intercepting the coasting trade or in looking into the mouths of the waters on the Chesapeake— A Traitor whose name is Lewis, lately captured in a Schooner the *"Lucy and Sally"* from ~~Richmond~~ Fredericksburgh volunteered to conduct them into Piankatank to cut out some Baltimore Schooners— We left them on Wednesday night last at the mouth of, and I think from appearances about to enter that River— The boarding Officer said they designed to put Lewis on shore at Rappahannock the next day— American Prisoners who were on board these Brigs represent the *Sophie* to carry 18 guns and from 120 to 150 Men she has a broad yellow Streak along her Ports— The *Acteon* has 14 or 16 guns and 100 men— The *Sophie* is a remarkably fast Sailor— I should suppose it would be well for a vessel coming round with public property to fell her way 10 or 15 miles ahead and having ascertained that those Brigs were not in sight of the mouth of Potomac she ought then to beat up with the wind from N.W. to the mouth of Patuxent or farther if practicable. There is reason to believe that an expedition will be fitted out from this place to attempt the capture of these Brigs—

I heard Sir T. Trowbridge, tell Com Barry that his men had gone aft that morning to ask him, as the *Lacedamonian* was going to Bermuda for provisions, if he would send up a challenge to the *Constellation* and the Prisoners who were on board the *Lacedamonian* say that when it was be[lieve]d the *Dragon* would have gone to Bermuda it was the intention of Capt Jackson who commands that Frigate and would have been the Senior officer, to send out the *Armide* and invite Capt Gordon to meet him. There is besides the vessels mentioned, a small schooner (tender) the *Cockchaffer* carrying 2 guns and twenty men   I do not think that any inducements could draw the 74 and Frigate above Hampton Roads, while the *Constellation* remains at Norfolk— very respectfully your Obt. Sevt.

John S Skinner

ALS, DNA, RG45, MLR, 1813, Vol. 7, No. 82 (M124, Roll No. 59).

1. John S. Skinner served at Annapolis during the war as agent for British packets, flags of truce, and dispatches and as agent for prisoners. His frequent contacts with the British fleet in the Chesapeake made Skinner an important source of military intelligence.

Offensive Actions in York River

When Captain Charles Gordon assumed command of Constellation *in the fall of 1813, he joined two other captains at Norfolk—John Cassin and Joseph Tarbell. Cassin, who oversaw the Gosport Navy Yard, had commanded the gunboat flotilla until relieved by Tarbell in May. Gordon resented Tarbell's undertaking a naval expedition in the York River on his own initiative without consulting him first and asked Jones to clarify the lines of authority at Norfolk. Secretary Jones did not answer this query until April 1814, when Gordon was made commanding officer of all naval forces at Norfolk.*

CAPTAIN CHARLES GORDON TO SECRETARY OF THE NAVY JONES

Constellation off Norfolk
December 13th 1813

Sir

For the last three or four days, I have been extremely anxious to hear from you, in answer to mine of the 3rd inst. as Linhaven Bay has been left for that time, with only one Frigate, the rest of the force on this Station having gone up the Bay in pursuit of Capt. Tarbell, who had taken seven Gun Boats & the two schooners well manned up to York river, in pursuit of two English Brigs—

Capt. Tarbell has this moment returned. I presume the rest of the Enemy's Squadron, will now resume their station off the Horse shoe—

The Expidition of Capt. Tarbell, caused much uneasiness & talk in Norfolk, fearful the Gun Boats might be blockaded in some of the rivers, and deprive Norfolk of that part of their defence— They were als apprehensive it might induce the enemy to send one or two Ships into the Roads, to shut the boats out and, keep them up the Bay—

There were repeated applications to me by the citizens, to know the Amount or object of this expidition. But as it was kept intire secret from me and my officers particularly, I could make no reply whatever, except that the Flotilla was under way & below Crany island before I had any knowledge of it. The strange and <u>distant</u> conduct of Capt. Tarbell to me on this occasion, and the great risk of having all his disposable force cut off from Norfolk by such an imprudent step, (when in my Opinion) the object which I now learn he had in view, could have been as well effected (<u>if at all</u>) with the two Schooners and launches without taking a Gun Boat, induced me to make some enquiry, into the state of those Boats, he left at Crany Island, and I found they only had a few men each to take care of them, and none capable of making any defence— Considering them exposed, and knowing the citizens were aware of this state, and felt uneasy; I had determined this day, (had not the Others returned) to order them all up in a situation to be ready to mann them from my ship, rather than leave them their, in the power of the Enemy— Those circumstances induces me to trouble you again, to know if any <u>responsibility</u> of this Flotilla, or its operations are attached to me, or if <u>any interfearence is expected</u> from me in any act or undertaking of Capt. Tarbell, as the commander of Said Flotilla. I have the Honor to be Sir your Obt. Servt.

Cha^S Gordon

ALS, DNA, RG45, CL, 1813, Vol. 8, No. 43 (M125, Roll No. 33).

Recruiting for Barney's Flotilla

In December 1813, Secretary Jones was concerned that Acting Master Commandant Joshua Barney's Chesapeake flotilla might not be strong enough in the spring to meet with "vigor" the return of the enemy whose "exertions will doubtless be great, and the theatre of his malignant hostility, will be our Barges, Waters, and Seaport towns."[1] He ordered Joshua Barney to contract for the construction of ten more barges and to continue his efforts to recruit seamen.

1. *Jones to Barney, 8 Dec. 1813, DNA, RG45, SNL, Vol. 11, p. 164 (M149, Roll No. 11).*

ACTING MASTER COMMANDANT JOSHUA BARNEY TO SECRETARY OF THE NAVY JONES

Annapolis   Decr. 15th 1813

Sir—

I had the honor to write you on the 9th Instant   since then I have received your letter of the 8th directing me to confer with Mr. Beatty, respecting the building of 6 or 8 barges of the 2d Class, At "St. Mary's", on the Eastern shore, from a former letter of yours I rather suppose you meant <u>St. Michaels</u>, and have this day wrote to <u>Mr. Perry Spencer</u>, the only Builder of Note on the Eastern shore on that subject, my letter went by Mr. Spencer's Son, who is a Delegate in the Assembly of Maryland, and <u>he</u> thinks his father will undertake the Contract—

I am fully of your opinion, "that every possible exertion must be made during the Winter to meet the Enemy with Vigor in the Spring," under that Idea I have turned my views to the best means of procuring men, and beg leave to ask your permission to employ Captain Soloman Frazier a Senator, now here, from the Eastern shore, he is well known as a Character, perhaps the most popular among the seafaring men on the Eastern shore, of any man in Maryland; he was in the service of this State the latter end of the War, and commanded at that time a Galley, in which service he behaved on several occasions with great Gallantry and honour to himself—he is Rich and at his ease, but declares if you will give him an appointment, he will quit the Senate and serve under me, I have promised to write you on the subject, and with your consent have also agreed to give him the Command of One division of my flotilla, of course he will expect to be put on the same footing with Capt Rutter,[1] I am fully of opinion he will be able to procure men sufficient to mann his division, between this and the spring, and should Mr. Spencer agree to build the Barges, Capt. Frazier will have it in his power (being on the shot) to superintend the building, at the same time to recruit his men. I shall leave here the moment I receive your answer to mine of the 9th Inst. Since then two more men have shipped from the 38th Regt. whose discharge from the War Department I will thank you to order sent me to Baltimore from whence I will send for the men, whose names are Henry Davidson & Francis Davenport. I am Sir with Respect your Ob Servt.

Joshua Barney

My delay here distresses me much, as my presence is wanting in Baltimore

ALS, DNA, RG45, MLR, 1813, Vol. 7, No. 96 (M124, Roll No. 59).

1. On 15 September 1813, Jones appointed Solomon Rutter an acting lieutenant in the Chesapeake flotilla. He was commissioned a lieutenant in the flotilla service on 25 April 1814. Solomon Frazier received his appointment as lieutenant in the flotilla on 26 April 1814.

SECRETARY OF THE NAVY JONES TO
ACTING MASTER COMMANDANT JOSHUA BARNEY

Joshua Barney Esqr.   Navy Department
Comg. U.S. Flotilla, Baltimore   Decr. 17th 1813.

Sir,
    Your letter of the 15th is before me. St. Michaels was the place intended to be designated in my letter of the 8th instant. Your representation of the character and qualifications of Capt. Solomon Frazier is very satisfactory; and as nothing will prevent our organizing such a Flotilla, as will enable us to repel all the force the enemy can employ, in the same way, if not to drive his Ships from the Bays, but the difficulty of getting men, it is of the utmost importance to employ able and enterprising Officers, who are popular among the Seamen and Watermen of their local Districts.
    The services of Captain Frazier will, therefore, be accepted with pleasure; and I accede to your proposal of giving him the command of one division of your

Flotilla, with the same appointment, pay, &c. as Captain Rutter now holds by the authority of this Department.

Mr. Beatty will, therefore, with your advice and assistance, take measures for contracting for ten Barges of the second Class at St. Michaels, to be built as fast as possible, under the superintendance of Mr. Frazier, whom you will particularly instruct on that subject. If you have not already accurate drawings, and detailed instructions for the building, (which I believe were forwarded to Baltimore by the Constructor,) they can be forwarded from this place; but if you have one of the barges of that class, completely fitted, it will be well to send her as a model.

The order, from the War Department to discharge the men belonging to the 36th Regt. was sent to the Commanding Officer at Annapolis; and a general order, to discharge all the men who are willing to enlist with you, was this day forwarded to him, which will include the two men mentioned in your last.

Push the Recruiting service as fast as possible. I am, respectfully, Your Obedient Servt.

W. Jones.

LB Copy, DNA, RG45, SNL, Vol. 11, pp. 174–75 (M149, Roll No. 11).

Constellation and *Adams* Waiting to Get to Sea

By year's end Constellation *and* Adams, *under Captains Charles Gordon and Charles Morris, were both ready to put to sea. Gordon had several opportunities to escape the blockade in December, but Secretary Jones did not forward him his cruising orders until January 1814. Morris, despite grave misgivings about the fitness of the redesigned* Adams, *was able to elude Captain Robert Barrie's blockading squadron in January 1814.* Constellation *was not so lucky.*

Captain Charles Gordon to Secretary of the Navy Jones

Constellation   Norfolk
28th Decr. 1813

Sir,

I have the honor to inform you that the Ship is waiting yr. orders only— The favvorable opportunities which have offered of late for our escape; And particularly the present moment induces me to trouble you again on the subject of some instructions— I have a good Hampton Pilot, and think on a certainty I could have gone out last evening—

Under the daily expectation of hearing from you (in answer to mine of the 13th Inst. &) I have delay'd going to Craney Island, as I knew the Enemy would then be more vigilant; And, if I could receive yr. instructions before dropping down, I might proceede on to the roads if there was a prospect of getting out the same night— But as I have not heard from you, I have determined on going to my moorings at the Island so soon as the weather clears up—

Owing to the threatening weather of late & a want of confidence in my old Cables, I have been induced to get one new Bower; And will (with your permission) compleat them—

I am collecting all the old Charts I can find among the Ship Masters in Norfolk which (with my Book of Charts) will enable me to proceede on a Cruise at any moment—

The Bay is at times entirely clear for a Day &, but seldom more than one Ship at Anchor; The other one or two is either looking out off the Capes or up the Bay; And with such thick blustering & variable weather as we have had of late their situation must be very uncertain—

The Ship of the Line is generally at Anchor & rides out all Gales; The Frigates are kept under way (I presume) for the want of Cables—

This Ship having been now so long Idle &, under sailing orders twelve months ago, I have concluded it is not your intention that I should let a very favorable opportunity elude me; I however, shall not fail to communicate to you my movements on all occasions, keeping constantly in view the good of the service, And the honor of the Flag— with great respect Sir, yr. obt. servt.—

Cha^S Gordon

ALS, DNA, RG45, CL, 1813, Vol. 8, No. 111 (M125, Roll No. 33).

Captain Charles Morris to Secretary of the Navy Jones

Private, or public.   U S.S. *Adams*   Decr. 31st 1813
                                                       Chesapeake Bay off Point Lookout

Sir,

I had the honor to receive yours of the 27th to day— I take the liberty of enclosing you a copy of Capt Stewart's letter in reply to mine of the 7th inst. I regret that his desire for one of the new frigates is not stronger than his anxiety and impatience for a cruise.[1]

I took my present position two days since that I might be ready to improve the first Northeast snowstorm or thick weather which may happen, as I find the Northwest winds though sometimes violent during the day are invariably moderate or calm in the night

The increase of the moon renders thick weather absolutely necessary for our purpose and may perhaps compel us to wait its wane— Should no favorable opportunity occur soon I shall proceed near to Annapolis for the purpose of keeping our provisions and water full until the nights become darker and more favorable—

I regret that the Ship gives but little satisfaction either to myself or officers— They are so little satisfied with her that they would willingly change to any other vessel that can get to sea, but will not apply for a removal while I remain in her— They do not consider her a safe cruising vessel, owing to the motion of her rudder which I formerly mentioned— I believe myself that this continual motion, which increases in violence in propertion to the Ships way in the water, must materially affect the durability of the Ship, and would probably soon wear out the rudder pintles— But I do not think there effects would produce immediate danger—though it is impossible to calculate how long first as none of us have ever met a similar case—I can only account for this motion by supposing her main breadth so far aft that the water thrown off by it does not unite till it passes the rudder which is left to the action of an eddy violent in proportion to the Ship's velocity—This opinion is strengthened by the circumstance of the motion ceasing when she goes less than four knots and becoming exceedingly violent when going ten which is the most we can get out of her—

For myself although I should prefer almost every other vessel yet I trust my sense of duty will always secure my exertions to make the best use of such means as may be placed in my power— I should feel disposed to expose the Ship and crew to greater hazard if I believed they would be able to perform greater service when at sea— As it is I certainly shall neglect no opportunity which offers a reasonable hope of eluding the vigilance of the Enemy

I have ever felt a confidence that you would favor my wishes when the interest of the service would allow you to do it with propriety, and in this confidence shall wait such oppertunity, and am Sir with Esteem and respect your Obd. Servant

C: Morris.

ALS, DNA, RG45, CL, 1813, Vol. 8, No. 120 (M125, Roll No. 33).

1. Morris, unhappy with *Adams*'s seaworthiness, had asked Charles Stewart to relinquish the command of *Constitution* to him, leaving one of the new frigates being built for Stewart. The latter refused the proposition. Stewart's letter to Morris of 17 December 1813 was enclosed with Morris's letter to Jones.

Chapter Three

The Northern Lakes Theater:
January–December 1813

The first campaign season of the War of 1812 demonstrated that successful military operations contiguous to the eastern Great Lakes and Lake Champlain required naval control of those lakes. Land transportation was laborious, slow, and expensive. Neither the United States nor Great Britain had made adequate preparations to use sea power effectively on the northern lakes. As military operations progressed, leaders on both sides realized that they must either exert themselves to establish competent naval forces on the lakes or risk military failure.

On the Canadian side of Lake Erie, the British Army Quartermaster General's Department controlled the Provincial Marine vessels Queen Charlotte, *16 guns, and* General Hunter, *6 guns. The American army had purchased and armed the brig* Adams *on Lake Erie. General William Hull had used* Adams *to carry his personal possessions and papers in attacking Detroit but lost all with the vessel when he surrendered in August 1812.* Adams, *captured without a contest, was taken into the Provincial Marine and renamed* Detroit. *On Lake Ontario, the Provincial Marine corvette* Royal George, *22, the sloop of war* Earl of Moira, *14, and the schooner* Duke of Gloucester *faced the lone American naval vessel, the brig* Oneida, *16, stationed at Sackets Harbor. With these sparse naval resources, the contestants had begun the war on and around the lakes.*

During September 1812, Commodore Isaac Chauncey, newly appointed commander on Lakes Ontario and Erie, took charge of building a naval squadron on Lake Ontario, combining purchased schooners and the corvette Madison, *built by shipwright Henry Eckford and a team of skilled ship carpenters from New York City. At the same time, Daniel Dobbins, a lake mariner from Presque Isle (Erie), Pennsylvania, visited Washington to report on British naval activity in that area. Secretary of the Navy Paul Hamilton sent him back to Erie as a sailing master with gunboat plans and orders to construct the vessels at that place under Commodore Chauncey's command.*

Later that month, Navy Secretary Paul Hamilton gave Lieutenant Thomas Macdonough an independent command on Lake Champlain, a strategically vital link in the United States' line of defense. American control of this lake would give access to the St. Lawrence River via the Richelieu River that flows northward from the lake. If the British were to gain control of Champlain, they would have a way of striking at the heart of New York State and of severing the disaffected New England states from the rest of the country. At Macdonough's disposal were two decaying navy gunboats aground near Burlington, Vermont, to which would be

403

added four that had been purchased by the army. Macdonough arrived at Platts-
burg by mid-October to confer with his counterpart, Major General Henry Dear-
born. Afterwards, he crossed Lake Champlain to Burlington to commence work
on his squadron. By December he had equipped and armed three sloops, President, Growler, *and* Eagle *and two gunboats. He reported the enemy in posses-*
sion of three armed sloops and a schooner being fitted out at Isle aux Noix. His
pleas for additional ordnance and ship carpenters were heeded. In early May
1813, Macdonough's vessels were ready, yet he still lacked a sufficient number of
ordinary seamen to commence operations. In the coming months, Macdonough's
force encountered several setbacks. In June Lieutenant Sidney Smith was captured
along with the two armed sloops under his command, Eagle *and* Growler. *The*
British soon embarked with a joint force from Isle aux Noix and staged attacks at
Plattsburg and Burlington, destroying warehouses, naval stores, and gunboats.
Owing to this enemy activity, Macdonough was confined to the defensive and to
preparing for a joint action with Major General Wade Hampton's army, which
was intended for a thrust against Montreal.

By late November 1812, Chauncey had achieved dominance over the Provin-
cial Marine's Lake Ontario force and had fortified his ice-locked vessels at Sackets
Harbor for the winter. At Erie, Dobbins had still not received Chauncey's autho-
rization to begin work, though he had obtained men and materials. Finally, in
late December 1812, Chauncey made a tour of inspection to Buffalo, Black Rock,
and Erie that demonstrated the urgency of commencing construction. From New-
port, Rhode Island, Master Commandant Oliver Hazard Perry applied for duty
on the lakes, fearing that he might be retained for coastal gunboat service instead
of seeing action at sea. In January the newly appointed secretary of the navy,
William Jones, approved and placed Perry under Chauncey's command. Mean-
while, the British government, recognizing that the weak and ineffective Provin-
cial Marine would be no match for newly built American naval squadrons, de-
cided to dispatch Royal Navy officers, men, and materiel to Upper Canada.

In Canada and the United States, preparations went ahead for the 1813 cam-
paign that would commence as soon as the ice broke up on the lakes. Chauncey au-
thorized Dobbins to construct two brigs and to arm several schooners at Erie. At
Sackets Harbor, Eckford and his men labored to build a large sloop of war, a light
dispatch schooner, and strengthen the armed schooners purchased the previous year.
While this work went on, the Madison administration made plans for a spring
military offensive aimed at Kingston, intending to sever Upper Canada from its
administrative and logistical bases at Quebec and Montreal. During February it
appeared that British reinforcements had begun to trickle into Upper Canada. Ex-
aggerated intelligence reports suggested that a considerable force had passed up
river to Kingston. Hearing this, Dearborn and Chauncey agreed that it would be
best to shift their campaign objective further west to York and Fort George with
Kingston as a final target. These operations commenced in late April with a joint
attack against York under Chauncey, Dearborn, and Brigadier General Zebulon
M. Pike. York was without a naval defense, and the small force posted there under
Major General Sir Roger H. Sheaffe beat a hasty retreat. Although Pike lost his life

in the action, it was a successful raid, resulting in the destruction of British ord-
nance stores and naval supplies intended for the Lake Erie squadron at Amherst-
burg. From York the joint American force returned to Sackets Harbor, then sailed to
Fort Niagara; after some weeks delay, Dearborn and Chauncey landed troops before
Fort George and succeeded in pushing British troops out of the immediate area, in-
cluding Fort Erie on the upper Niagara River. The victory was short lived because
of the mishandling of American troops advancing westward toward Burlington.
After the British captured two American generals and a number of their men, the
Americans withdrew to the banks of the Niagara.

The British Admiralty in March sent naval reinforcements to the lakes in the
troopship Woolwich. *These reinforcements, under the command of Commodore*
Sir James L. Yeo, were officers and seamen destined for operations on Lakes On-
tario, Erie, and Champlain. Yeo's Royal Navy contingent reached Kingston in
May and replaced the Provincial Marine and took control of naval operations,
with orders to remain on the defensive and to cooperate closely with Governor-
General Sir George Prevost. Within weeks Yeo and Prevost had placed Chauncey
on the defensive with an amphibious attack on his Sackets Harbor base.
Chauncey, who had just completed the attack on Fort George, raced for Sackets
Harbor and remained there until the General Pike *was ready for sea. For several*
weeks in late summer, with the opposing armies stalemated at Niagara, the two
squadrons maneuvered for position at the western end of Lake Ontario.
Chauncey, who had an initial numerical advantage, lost four schooners in this
skirmishing. Hamilton *and* Scourge *capsized and sank during a severe squall;*
Julia *and* Growler *were captured after Yeo's squadron cut them off from the rest*
of Chauncey's line of battle. After these events, the American commodore grew ex-
ceedingly cautious about venturing out of Sackets Harbor without knowing in
advance the location of Yeo's squadron.

American plans for the rest of the military campaign had depended on the cap-
ture of Kingston after obtaining command of the lake and defeating the British
forces on land at Niagara. Although the two preliminary steps were not accom-
plished, Secretary of War John Armstrong insisted on carrying out the plan. He
replaced the ailing and aged Dearborn with the equally aged but mercurial Major
General James Wilkinson and ordered him to prepare an attack on Kingston or
Montreal. There was a great difference involved in considering the two objectives.
At Kingston, Chauncey's naval squadron could give needed assistance, but if an
attack were launched against Montreal, the navy could do little but blockade the
head of the St. Lawrence.

On Lake Erie, the military outcome depended on the naval contest between
Oliver H. Perry and Robert H. Barclay. Each was to cooperate with an army gen-
eral needing naval superiority on the lake to move his army and supplies. Major
General Henry Procter, who was running short of supplies for his troops, con-
stantly urged Barclay to bring Perry to action. Major General William H. Harri-
son, commanding the American Northwest Army, likewise awaited a victory from
Perry's squadron so that he could restore American control of Detroit and the upper
Great Lakes. The battle was finally joined on 10 September 1813, when the

*squadrons met near the Bass Islands in light, variable winds. Perry's bravery fi-
nally decided an uncertain battle, and he captured Barclay's entire squadron.
American naval superiority on Lake Erie enabled General Harrison to transport
his army by water in pursuit of Procter's retreating troops and Indians. Procter's
defeat at Moraviantown on the Thames River completely altered the British defensive posture in Upper Canada. The remnants of Procter's forces retreated eastward
to join Major General John Vincent's Army of the Centre at Burlington Heights.*

*During the summer, Secretary of War Armstrong traveled to Sackets Harbor to
join Wilkinson and to participate directly in planning the forthcoming attack. The
expedition required, as had the others, at least temporary American superiority on
Lake Ontario. This much Commodore Chauncey accomplished. On 28 September,
he discovered and engaged Yeo's squadron off York. The British withdrew to the
west, fighting a stubborn rearguard action. Commodore Chauncey pursued Yeo's
damaged squadron to Burlington Bay. Not willing to risk his squadron under the
enemy's land batteries on a stormy lee shore, Chauncey withdrew and returned to
Sackets Harbor. To his dismay he discovered that Armstrong and Wilkinson had decided that the British were too strong at Kingston to afford the Americans a reasonable chance of success. The American descent of the St. Lawrence in late October
and early November is an example of a campaign hastily planned and poorly timed
and executed. Chauncey positioned his squadron at the head of the St. Lawrence to
protect the army transports as they went down river. Wilkinson's expeditionary
troops were defeated at the Battle of Chrysler's Farm on 11 November. General
Hampton's army, approaching Montreal from the south, ran into stiff resistance at
the Battle of Chateauguay on 25 October. Hampton retreated and prepared to go
into winter quarters rather than join Wilkinson's force for a renewal of the offensive.*

Building the Fleet on Lake Erie

*Commodore Isaac Chauncey found the naval establishment on Lake Erie in poor condi-
tion when he visited Black Rock and Erie during his tour of inspection in December 1812
and January 1813. He was displeased with the four gunboats then under construction at
Presque Isle, and he knew that the four vessels grounded at Black Rock could not be freed
until the Americans gained possession of Fort Erie across the Niagara River. Commodore
Chauncey, however, pushed forward the construction of a new brig and the alteration of
two of the four gunboats then building at Erie; he would continue to superintend the construction of the Lake Erie fleet from his headquarters at Sackets Harbor.*

COMMODORE ISAAC CHAUNCEY TO SECRETARY OF THE NAVY HAMILTON

Erie Pennsylvania, 1st Jan'y 1813

Sir/

I arrived here yesterday and found that Mr. Dobbins had commenced the
building of four gun Boats two of the frames was already raised and the other

two nearly ready these boats are too small to cruise upon this lake and the two that are the most forward are in a state ~~not~~ I cannot alter them but the other two I have aded ten feet to their lenth which will make them safe vessels

Mr. Dobbins has already expended three thousand dollars— he sent me a copy of his instructions in October last I then wrote to him not to commence building untill he heard further from me upon the subject he however states that he never received that letter which was the reason that he commenced the boats without instructions

These boats will not be ready to Launch before the middle of april there is but few carpenters to be got here and most of these are house carpenters— I have however ordered three good Ship Carpenters from Sacketts Harbour to this place which will enable Mr. Dobbins to progress with the work pretty fast untill the spring when I will furnish more workmen—

The Harbour of Presque Isle is large and capasous and would be a very fine rendezvous for our Vessels on this lake if there was ~~water~~ more water on the bar which unfortunately only admits vessels drawing from 4 to 5 feet yet in my opinion it is the best and indeed the only place that we can build at. The situation is healthy and good accommodations may be procured for the workmen and the place can be easily defended—

Before I leave here I shall inform myself of the resources of this part of the country in furnishing materials for building and equiping vessels for war my present impression is that it abounds with fine timber and Iron and cordage may be procured with facility from Pittsburgh— I have the honor to be Very Respectfully Sir your Obt. H. Servt

Isaac Chauncey

ALS, DNA, RG45, CL, 1813, Vol. 1, No. 1 (M125, Roll No. 26).

COMMODORE ISAAC CHAUNCEY TO SECRETARY OF THE NAVY HAMILTON

Black Rock 8th. Jany. 1812 [*1813*]

Sir

I arrived here from Erie yesterday and found things much as I left them, the vessels at this place purchased for acct. of the Navy Department (four in number, besides the *Caledonia*[1]) are in that state that they cannot be removed until we have possession of the opposite side of the ~~shore~~ river I have therefore determined to procure materials at Erie this winter to build a Brig of about 300 tons to mount the Guns of the *Oneida* upon her The cost of the materials will not be great and can be sold with little loss if not wanted, I shall be in a situation in the spring (if we get the vessels out of this river) to build the Brig in the course of a few weeks which will enable me to seek the enemy upon this Lake, unfortunately Lieut. Elliott (from the best motives however) had the Decks of the vessels at this place taken up for the purpose of entering into a more extensive alteration than I wished or contemplated, soon after the Carpenters got at work, the enemy commenced a fire upon this place which induced them to break off, and return to New York the consequence has been, that the vessels still remain in the state in which the Carpenters left them in Octr. last, that is with their Decks and sides all tore up. I have not deemed it adviseable under all circumstances to do any thing to them this winter, as the weather is unfavorable and

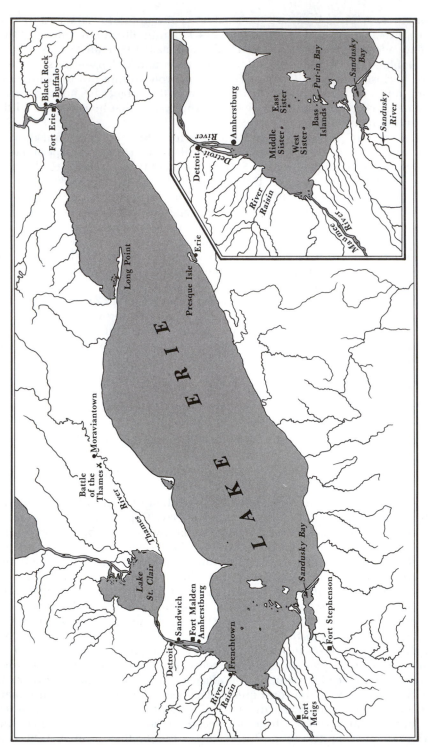

Map 3. Lake Erie

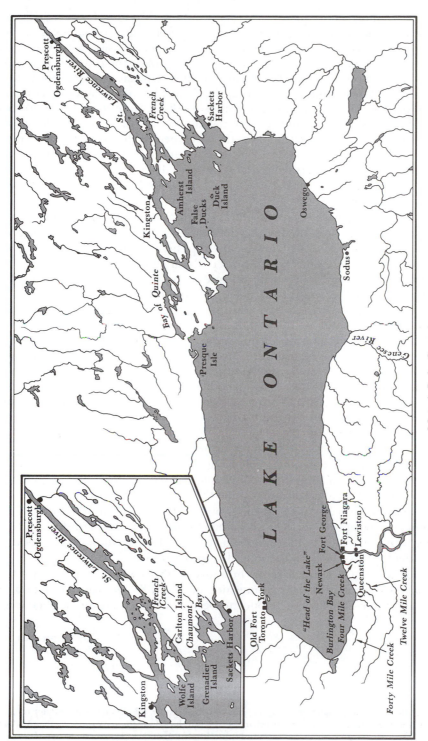

Map 4. Lake Ontario

the days are short, consequently the men would work under disadvantages, that will be removed in the Spring, moreover I do not wish to incur expense that may prove useless for unless we get possession of the other side these vessels can be of no use to us consequently, any repairs put upon them would be thrown away. I have however, contracted for all the stuff requisite to repair them to be delivered here this winter, and in the spring I shall be in a situation to complete their repairs and mount their Guns in a few weeks, if there should be a prospect of gaining the opposite shore if there was no other obstruction the Ice in this River would prevent our getting into the Lake before the first of June and as I shall be able to get out of Sackets Harbour about the first of april I contemplate bringing all the Carpenters from that station, to this by water which will give us an abundance of time to fit these vessels or build the Brig at Erie or both as circumstances may require—

The vessels here have been hauled into a small creek in rear of Squaw Island where they are safe from the Ice and the shot of the Enemy, and I am erecting a Block House to mount four Guns on the top, besides musquetry, near the vessels which will enable our men to protect them completely even if the enemy should attempt to cross over with an intent to burn them, both officers and men have suffered very much this fall and winter for the want of quarters. They have been living about in the woods in small huts, made of the leaves of trees, ever since they arrived on this station, and Lieuts. Elliott and Angus have not been able to procure quarters for them the consequence has been that we have lost many by sickness, and a number by desertion. I am only astonished that so many have remained true to their Country, under all the privations which they have suffered. I am in hopes to get both men and officers into comfortable quarters by the 15th. Inst. as the building for their accommodation is now under cover and will be ready I think by that time, to receive them when they all will be more happy and more healthy. The wounded officers and men are doing very well. Midshipman Graham has suffered an amputation of his leg—

I am making arrangements for collecting all our stores into one building which are now distributed in almost every direction for twenty miles round, owing to the great confusion which has prevailed upon this frontier ever since the war—

I have been induced (as I informed you by a former communication) in consequence of losing the services of so many officers, by death and wounds, together with the conduct of Lt. Angus to appoint Midsns. Dudley and Holdup to act as Lieutenants which I hope you will approve of—

I hope to be able to arrange my business on this station, so as to leave here for Sackets Harbor next week from which place I will write you the state of my command there— I Have the Honor to be very Respectfully Sir yr. obed. servt.

Isaac Chauncey

LS, DNA, RG45, CL, 1813, Vol. 1, No. 13 (M125, Roll No. 26). This letter was misdated 1812.

1. The sloop *Contractor* (later renamed *Trippe*), schooner *Amelia,* schooner *Catherine* (later renamed *Somers*), and the schooner *Ohio* were merchant vessels purchased for the navy in December 1812 and January 1813. The brig *Caledonia* was captured from the British off Fort Erie on 8 October 1812.

COMMODORE ISAAC CHAUNCEY TO LIEUTENANT JOHN PETTIGREW [1]

Lieut. John Pettigrew,   Black Rock
U.S. Navy   9 Jany 1813
present.

The situation in which you are now placed you must be sensible is a very responsible one, but from your zeal for the service I have no doubt but that you will exert yourself to the utmost to discharge the various and important duties attached to your station with credit to yourself and benefit to your country. I wish however to call your early attention to the situation of the officers and men. There must be no time lost in getting them into their quarters as made as comfortable as the nature of the Service will admit of. Your next care will be to prevent desertions and whenever they do take place every exertion must be used to retake them. The men must not be suffered to ramble about the Village or even leave their quarters without a <u>written</u> pass. They must be frequently mustered and punished for selling their clothes, or frequent intoxication, or in fact for any other crime committed against "the rules for the Government of the Navy."—

The Block House must be completed with all possible expedition and 4 guns mounted on the top of it and every precaution used to guard against a surprize by the enemy. You will cause all the Stores of every description belonging to the navy department which are now scattered about this village and Buffaloe and vicinity to be collected and such as are liable to embezzlement you will have put into some good store under lock and key. You will also have an Inventory taken of the whole, and a copy transmitted to me as soon as an officer can be spared. You will send one to Genesee or further if necessary to ascertain where and what property belonging to the navy department has been left on the road and to get an account of the whole and to transmit it to me.

I request that you will have collected immediately and put into the upper story of the new Barracks all the rigging, sails, & other stores belonging to the *Contractor, Amelia, Catherine, Ohio,* and *Caledonia.* Have their spars, cables, anchors, &c. collected in one place. I also request that you will have the rigging and sails of these vessels overhawled, and put in good order ready to be used in the spring.

You will keep me informed of every occurrence of importance that takes place in my absence, and I trust that when I again visit the station I shall only find cause of praise not of censure. I have the honor &c.

Isaac Chauncey—

LB Copy, MiU–C, Isaac Chauncey Letter Book.

1. Lieutenant John Pettigrew was placed in charge at Black Rock, New York, following the arrest of Lieutenant Samuel Angus in December 1812.

ACTING LIEUTENANT THOMAS HOLDUP TO RALPH IZARD, JR.

Buffaloe   Niagara County
State of New York   Jany. 11th. 1813

My Dr. Father/ [1]
I was highly gratified yesterday by receiving your truly welcome Letter dated Philadelphia Decr. 14th. but the pleasure I enjoyed from the perusal of it was

partly destroyed when I observed the sorrowful manner in which you conclude your Epistle. The firmness which I know you are possessed of will bear you through the ills of this life better than any consolations which myself or your numerous Friends might be enduced to give on the occasion I shall therefore dismiss this painful subject for the present & shall proceed according to your request to give "a detailed account" of the occurrences that have taken place since our leaving Albany— Lt. Pettigrew our then Commanding Officer received orders from Commodore Chauncey to proceed to Utica where other orders would be given him. We accordingly set off & after dashing through mud, hail, & rain we arrived at the above place— Upon opening his orders (instead of repairing to Sacketts Harbor which we all calculated upon) Lt. P. was directed to make the best of his way to this place, where worn out with fatigue & disappointment we arrived on the 16th. of October— Still anxious to render a service to our Country we immediately proceeded in to get the Guns from the *Detroit* (one of the Vessels cut out from under Fort Erie by the Gallant Lt Elliot & which owing to the ignorance or fear of the Pilot was run on shore & compelled Lt E. to burn her to prevent the Enemy from again obtaining possession of her.) After much trouble we succeeded in getting all the Guns from her hold amounting to 4 & stripping her of every particle of rigging &ca. We also procured about 600–12 lb. Shot & about 80 stand of Grape for the 4 Twele pounders— From that period 'till the 28th. of Novr. nothing particular occurred except our pursuing the *Queen Charlotte* in two open Boats; as what few vessels we have on this Lake amounting to Six Schooners & the Brig *Caledonia* taken by Lt. Elliot were all (except the Brig) hauled to pieces & our Ship Carpenters haven taken fright upon the English opening their Batteries on us they fled & have never since returned We however were not able to get sight of her Royal Highness & I think it fortunate we did not for I have no doubt but she would have given us a Queenly reception— I almost forgot to mention that a few days after we arrived here Lt. Angus (your old Shipmate) took command of this station—

Accordingly on the morning of the 27th. Novr in pursuance of Genl. Smyth's request Lt. Angus ordered ten Boats to be prepared & 80 Seaman directed to prepare themselves for an Expedition on the Canada Shore for the purpose of Spiking their Cannon &c &c— About 1 oClock on the morning of the 28th every thing was in order when we were joined by about 100 Soldiers under the command of Capt King

We immediately shoved off & rowed up shore a considerable Distance, when we hove too & Lt Angus directed the Officers to follow him as closely as possible— We then struck over & when within about a quarter of a mile of the Canada shore were discovered by the Enemy who opened a heavy & destructive fire of Grape Shot & from 2 Six pounders & musketry from about 250 Soldiers— We Out of the 10 Boats but 5 succeeded in landing—owing to which cause, I know not— Among the Boats that got ashore I mine was lucky enough to be one— We immediately charged upon the English & after a spirited skirmish engagement forced him to retire. They then retreated to a large Red House & opened a most dreadful fire from the Windows but our brave Sailors immediately burst open the Door & in a few minutes the House was in flames— After that the En[emy] [2] retreated as fast as possible— Capt. King [& a] few Soldiers & Sailors took peaceable pos[session] of the Batteries & spiked the Cannon. The [?] Pieces were also spiked— By some means [or] other the word <u>Retreat</u> was sounded & [?] men & the greater part of the Office[rs] returned to our Shore— Lt. Wragg, Dud[ley and] myself were left on the Canada Shore [with] about 20 men—when returning dow[n] towards the beach I met the brave Sai[ling Master] Watts lying wounded on the ground & [wan]ting to assist him I received a Ball in my right Hand; ~~but~~ which passing through from under the Thumb came out at the Ring finger I am now almost well but am still obliged to write with my left Hand—you will therefore make allowances— Wragg & Brailsford were also wounded but are doing well— We had 9 out of 12 naval officers Killed & wounded & 22 Sailors Killed & wounded   The Doctor assures me I shall have the perfect use of my right hand— Lt Angus has despatched an Official Report to the Secty of the Navy which you will see in a few days[3]— Comdr. Chauncey has been with for about 2 Weeks & has been pleased to appoint your humble servant a Lieutenant & also our Countryman Dudley who from the Gallantry he displayed on the night of the 28 richly merited it— As respects myself I have no business to say any thing but I will say this that a clear conscience is the greatest blessing a man can feel— Farewell—my respects to your amiable Lady— Lt. Angus desires his respects—so does Dudley & Brailsford   Write me soon as I am always rejoiced at hearing from my Dr Father. Yr affectionate

Tho[S]. Holdup

ALS, DLC, Naval Historical Foundation Collection, Stevens Family Papers, Folder 1.

1. Thomas Holdup, orphaned in his youth, was befriended by former navy lieutenant Ralph Izard, Jr. Holdup used the term "father" as a sign of respect and affection for the older man. Holdup was adopted by Colonel Daniel Stevens and legally took the name Thomas Holdup Stevens in 1815.
2. The manuscript is torn at this point and a section along the right edge is missing; the bracketed words that follow have been supplied by conjecture.
3. For a copy of this report, see Dudley, *Naval War of 1812*, Vol. 1, pp. 355–59.

The Provincial Marine on Lake Ontario

A tour of inspection conducted by officers of the British army's quartermaster general staff revealed the inadequacies of British naval preparations as late as six months after the declaration of war. The British fleets on the northern lakes were under the command of the Provincial Marine, essentially a transport service for the British army, before naval affairs were taken over by officers and seamen from the Royal Navy in May 1813. The principal vessels were still in need of extensive repairs, while their crews from the Provincial Marine lacked adequate discipline and training. Defenses at Kingston, the primary port, and York (known as Toronto after 1834), an important secondary shipping center, needed to be strengthened through the construction of block houses to protect the fleets moored in those ports.

CAPTAIN ALEXANDER GRAY, BRITISH ARMY,[1] TO
LIEUTENANT COLONEL JOHN VINCENT, BRITISH ARMY[2]

Point Frederick   16 Jany 1813—

Sir

I beg leave to acquaint you that I have this day inspected the Two Ships of War laying in this Harbour, and have the honor of Reporting for your information, the State of those vessels—

I commenced my inspection with the *Royal George*, by first ordering the Crew to be turned up and mustered,—which consisted as follows

	No.
Ships Company, including Officers	80
Detatcht. of the Newfoundld. actg. as Marines	22
Total	102

off the above number there were 23 of the seamen [sick] reducing the total effective strength to 79.— The General appearance of the men bespeak the greatest want of attention to cleanliness, and good order— After the inspection of the ships company I directed them to be ordered to their quarters, and the shot drawn, and the Cartridges fired off, to scale the Guns, This operation occupied 50 minutes, such was the state of the Guns— The greater part of them missed fire repeatedly in consequence of the vents being choaked up, and would not go off till they were cleared out with the Pricking Needles and fresh primed.—

I next examined the State of the vessel, as to cleanliness and interior œconomy, and found her every where in the most filthy condition.—

I next proceeded to inspect the *Moira*, and found

	No.
her Ships Company, including officers	35
Detatcht. of the Newfoundld. actg. as Marines	16
Total	51

off the above number there were 6 sick, reducing the Total effective Strength to 45.—

The Men, Guns, and State of the vessel very much resembled the *Royal George*— Not quite so bad; or rather, the state of the *Moira* was <u>bad</u>, and that of the *Royal George* <u>Worse</u>—

As I have reason to believe that a <u>Radical reform</u> in the Provincial Marine will Soon take place, I do not conceive it necessary to recommend any partial changes as I have reason to believe no Material benefit would result to the Service from such a measure— This Statement will however shew the absolute necessity there is of making Suitable provision for the protection of these vessels, untill they are in a condition to defend themselves   I have the honor to be Sir, Your Most Obedient Humble Servant

A Gray
actg. Dy. Q M Gl.

LS, CaOOA, British Military and Naval Records, RG8, I, "C" Ser., Vol. 729, pp. 28–30.

1. Captain Alexander Gray, 24th Infantry, Acting Deputy Quartermaster General.
2. Lieutenant Colonel John Vincent, 49th Regiment of Foot, was commander of the British army forces in Kingston; he was promoted to the rank of brigadier general in February 1813 and transferred to the command of the British forces on the Niagara frontier.

LIEUTENANT COLONEL RALPH HENRY BRUYÈRES, BRITISH ARMY,[1] TO GOVERNOR-GENERAL SIR GEORGE PREVOST

Kingston　　19th January 1813

Dear Sir

I left Prescott on Friday last after having given the necessary directions to Lieut. de Gaugreben to proceed with the Survey of that Post, and to erect without delay a Block House on a small commanding spot in the rear of the present Battery which it will completely protect; it is also intended to improve, and close this Battery as soon as it is possible to break ground.— I slept that night at Brockville, twelve Miles from Prescott which is the most improved Village on the communication; it has some very handsome Houses with a Church, and Court House, and is situated on an elevated, & commanding spot of ground. there is a small Troop of Cavalry, with a Volunteer Rifle Company and some Militia stationed here; they are however very inefficient, a large proportion of them being absent, and returned to their own homes.— The only position that is occupied from hence to Kingston is at the River Canonoqui about 36 Miles from Brockville. this is a good Post with a Company of Militia stationed under the command of Col: Stone; they are Building a Block House on a strong point of ground near the River; the lower story is nearly raised, and the whole will be completed in about six Weeks.

I arrived late on Saturday Evening at Kingston about 24 Miles from the River Canonoqui.— I have been fully occupied since that time in minutely examining this important place, and communicating with Colonel Vincent on the measures necessary to be adopted for the security of the Post; and the Marine establishment so as to retain our ascendancy on the Lake.— The latter is a very serious, and difficult task which must require the greatest exertion, and assistance from the Lower Province, in order to Arm the new Ship that is now Building; for unless this Vessel is completely armed, and well Manned it will not be possible to effect a junction with the Ships at York.— The following statement will explain to your Excellency the Shipping, and resources in this Port which I trust will be equal to meet that of the Enemy, and to effect their passage to York Harbor, which if once accomplished you will then have the decided superiority on the Lake which may be easily maintain'd.

Royal George	{ 20	32 Pdrs. Carronades
	{ 2	9 Pdrs. long Guns
Moira	{ 10	18 Pdrs. Carronades
	{ 4	9 Pdrs. long Guns
New Ship [2]	{ 20	12 Pdrs. long Guns temporary armament.
Total	56	

there are besides four Merchant Vessels in the Port that may be Manned, and Armed equal to oppose the smaller Vessels of the Enemy.—

To oppose this Force the Enemy have

One Ship of. . . . . . 18 Guns
One ditto . . . . 24 ditto.

with seven or eight well armed Schooners.—

Taking advantage of a fair Wind there is every reasonable expectation to hope you may force your passage to York.

In order to put the Naval force at present here in a state to venture on the Lake it is indispensably necessary to send up without loss of time twenty 12 Pdrs. Guns with Ship Carriage complete to arm the new Vessel in a temporary manner untill the armament required from England shall arrive here. these long Guns may then be most usefully employed, and are required to Arm the different positions on the communication from hence down the St. Lawrence.

It will be further necessary to lower and alter the *Moira* (as proposed) as that Ship is now totally inefficient. The Merchants I have no doubt will very willingly permit their Vessels to be made use of for one Voyage. They must all be well armed, and altered to contain the Guns. It will be also be requisite to send Officers, and Sailors for the whole of this Flotilla; that each Vessel may be well Manned and have good Officers for those at present employed, are totally incapable for any hasardous undertaking. Captain Gray has most positively assured me that the new Ship will be ready in time; the progress hitherto made is not equal to realize that expectation, and many have their doubts on the subject. The Keel is at present only laid, but many of the Timbers are prepared for raising, and the Work once in fair train the progress will be more expeditious.

It is much to be regretted under present circumstances that the whole of the Naval establishment had not been concentrated at this Post. it would have saved much time, and expence in Transport,—united all the Workmen under one Head,—and insured the armament of your Ships.— It would then have been only necessary to secure this Post against attack untill your Fleet was fully prepared, and equipped to proceed on the Lake.

The evil is now without remedy, and the best must be done to concentrate, and unite as soon as possible, but by no means to venture from hence till your Vessels are rendered fully efficient with Men, and Arms.—

I have consulted with Colonel Vincent on the practicability of an expedition to destroy the American Ships in Sackett's Harbor. It is now so long since any information has been obtained from that Post (being previous to the closing of the Navigation) that it is indispensably necessary first to procure a correct knowledge of the force at present there, and whether they have Fortified and strengthened their position with the Ship Guns, for it is ascertained they have nearly 100 pieces of Artillery in that Harbor for Naval purposes,—much will therefore depend to what use they have applied these Guns during the Winter.— Col: Vincent intends to take advantage of a circumstance that has lately occurred at Prescott in consequence of an attempt to form a predatory attack on the Post to serve as a plea to send an intelligent Officer as a Flag of Truce to the Commanding Officer at Sacket Harbor, besides which he will endeavor to procure a confidential Man that will undertake to examine the Post, so that I am in hopes that on my return from Fort George we shall be enabled to give your Excellency correct information on this subject for could this expedition be undertaken with any hope of success all our difficulties would be immediately obviated.—

It is expected that the first effort of Commodore Chauncey will be to endeavor to destroy York previous to the Ice being dispersed in the narrow part of the Lake towards this place, and then to proceed here; but I hope we shall be well prepared to resist him. I have directed the Block House on Point Henry to be raised and improved; also to erect another Block House on Point Frederick which will effectually protect the Dock Yard. The Batteries can only be repaired, and enclosed as soon as the first thaw takes place. It is indispensable to erect a new Powder Magazine at this Post; the present one is an old Wind Mill converted to this purpose very insecure, and improperly situated surrounded with Wooden Buildings in the Barrack Yard. The present Building may be very usefully applied as a place of defense by placing a Gun on the top of the Arch when the Powder is removed. I very earnestly beg leave to impress upon your Excellency the necessity of keeping this Post as strong as possible in point of Garrison untill our Naval force shall be prepared to quit the Harbor for it is reasonable to expect that every possible effort will be made to destroy it. This is a very defendable position but owing to the extent of the Posts (which cannot possibly be contracted) it will require at least 800 effective Men not including the Militia of the Country with more of the Royl. Artillery to defend the position with more certainty of success.— Col: Vincent is fully of this opinion, and has approved of all the measures herein suggested.

I shall depart from hence for York tomorrow morning, and shall arrive there on Saturday next.— I have the honor to remain with the greatest Respect Your Excellency's Most obedient, and most faithful Servant

R H Bruyeres.—

ALS, CaOOA, British Military and Naval Records, RG8, I, "C" Ser., Vol. 387, pp. 10–14.

1. Lieutenant Colonel Ralph Henry Bruyeres was the commanding British military engineer in the Canadas. He had conducted a survey of defenses in Upper Canada in 1802 and was familiar with the frontier defenses of that province. Bruyeres was made acting colonel 1 March 1813, and died the following year.
2. *Sir George Prevost*, built at Kingston and launched 28 April 1813, was renamed *Wolfe* after launching.

American Strategy on the Lakes

American control of the Northwest depended on a successful naval campaign in 1813. The surrender of the American outposts at Mackinac and Detroit in July and August 1812 and the humiliating defeat of Major General Stephen Van Rensselaer's army at Queenston in October 1812 had opened up the entire northwest frontier to enemy attack.

In order for the American forces to regain their position in the Northwest, control of Lakes Ontario and Erie had to be assured. This could be accomplished only through the combined effort of the American army and navy working in close cooperation. While both military and naval leaders realized that Kingston was the key to controlling the Saint Lawrence River, the Great Lakes, and Montreal, the apparent strength of that city's fortifications proved daunting.

COMMODORE ISAAC CHAUNCEY TO THE SECRETARY OF THE NAVY

Sackets Harbour
January 20. 1813.

Sir

I arrived here yesterday and found every thing much as I left it— There has no reinforcement of troops arrived, nor are the Block houses completed; they are however progressing and I presume will be finished by the first of next month, after which I presume we should be able to give the Enemy a warm reception if he should pay us a visit this Winter.

Four deserters that left the *Royal George* on Sunday night last arrived here to day, they are two Sailors and two Soldiers; they corroborate the information previously received from various sources, and which may be relied on, to wit, that the Enemy's regular force at Kingston is about one thousand men; that they are building a ship at Kingston which they think is to rate 36 guns. She is

120 feet keel and 36 feet beam, and is to be launched early in April: they are also building two other vessels at York; their size they do not know, but think one of them is to be a frigate— the cables, anchors, and rigging which were taken up in the *Royal George* last summer to York they think are about the size of the Cables and rigging of that ship—

One hundred and thirty ship carpenters and fifty sailors arrived at Kingston about the middle of December; seventy of the carpenters were sent off for York: I obtained the same information at Utica from a man whose sleigh had been pressed to convey them— Every deserter that comes over, (and there are many) gives the same account, and say that it is the opinion of the officers and inhabitants generally that if they do not make a desperate effort to regain the command of the Lake that Canada must fall: it is therefore their determination to build a sufficient force this Winter to insure them the command of the Lakes next Summer—

With this information I have deemed it my duty to provide materials to build another ship here—the roads are now good, the materials can be got with facility and brought in for little expense, and, if not wanted, sold for little loss—

If the President should determine to authorise another ship to be built here it will be proper for me to receive your instructions as early as possible in order that I may prepare her armament &c to be ready to meet the Enemy upon equal terms next Spring. I have the honor to be, Very respectfully, Sir, your obdt. servt.

Isaac Chauncey

LS, DNA, RG45, CL, 1813, Vol. 1, No. 25 (M125, Roll No. 26).

COMMODORE ISAAC CHAUNCEY TO THE SECRETARY OF THE NAVY

Confidential   Sackett's Harbor   21st Jan'y 1813

Sir/

The information detailed in my letter of yesterday respecting the exertions of the Enemy to create a force this winter superior to ours, is unquestionably correct. It will therefore require correspondent exertions on our part to defeat their plans and destroy their hopes— I have therefore determined (provided it meets with your approbation) to attempt the destruction of their fleet the next spring before they have an opportunity of forming a Junction.

My plan is this, to prepare all my force this winter and in the spring as soon as the Ice breaks up to take onboard 1,000 picked troops and proceed to Kingston land them about three miles to the westward of the town in a bay which I have marked on the chart herewith enclosed leave two Vessels to cover their retreat (if such a measure should be found necessary) proceed with the remainder of the squadron to the Harbor of Kingston and attack the Forts and Ships at the same time the troops would attack in the rear with this force I have no doubt but that we should succeed in taking or destroying their ships and Forts and of course preserve our ascendancy upon this Lake

With a view of making some arrangements with Major General Dearborn for the Troops that will be required for this enterprize as well as to forme some plan of co-opperation with the Army generally next Summer it will be necessary for me to visit that officer this winter

It is my intention to leave here about the first of next month for Albany and return immediately after making my arrangements with the general but if you should determine to build another ship here it would be proper for me to visit New York for a few days to make the necessary arrangements— I therefore take the liberty to ask you to send a duplicate of the order to Albany which would save me a long journey

I beg you to be assured that every exertion in my power shall be used to preserve the ascendency that we have obtained upon this lake   I have the honor to be Very respectfully Sir your obt. H. St.

Isaac Chauncey

ALS, DNA, RG45, CL, 1813, Vol. 1, No. 29 (M125, Roll No. 26). A sketch of Kingston Harbor, with "Proposed place of landing troops" marked to the west of the city, is on file with this letter.

SECRETARY OF THE NAVY JONES TO COMMODORE ISAAC CHAUNCEY

Comre. Chauncey   Navy Dep'mt
Sacketts harbor NY.   27. Jany. 1813

Having just entered upon the duties of the Department, I have not yet had a convenient opportunity of perusing with due attention, the whole of your correspondence during the period of your important command. It is impossible to attach too much importance to our naval operations on the Lakes—the success of the ensuing campaign will depend absolutely upon our superiority on all the lakes—& every effort, & resource, must be directed to that object. It is to me, exceedingly gratifying, that a trust, so honorable & momentous, is committed to the direction of an officer, who has given such commanding evidence of capacity, energy & judgement. Persevere then Sir, in accomplishing what you have so judiciously arranged—the preparations you have made for completing the vessels at black rock are well adapted to the emergency; but lest obstacles should continue to oppose their passage into Lake Erie, it will be proper to construct a force at Erie, sufficient to ensure our ascendancy, on the whole of the upper Lakes, independent of the force at black rock; for this purpose, you are authorized to prepare, the materials for building & equiping a Brig, of such size as you may deem expedient, in addition to the gunboats & the Brig, which you have already made arrangements to build & equip. Iron, cordage, & shot, can be procured at Pittsburg & I will immediately contract here, for as many caronades 32 pdrs. as will arm the two Brigs at Erie—all the Armament & stores, necessary to be procured here, & at Pittsburg, can be transported from thence, up the Allegheny and French creek, in due time, to reach Erie, before the Lake is navigable: This force would facilitate beyond calculation the operations of Genl. Harrisons Army,[1] & in the event of the fall of Malden & Detroit, would enable you to detach a part of your force to Lake Huron, to take post at the mouth of French River on the N.E. side of Lake Huron, were you will intercept the supplies for the western Indians, which are sent up Grand river to this post, as soon as the waters of those Rivers are navigable, & from them distributed through the waters of Huron & Michigan to the tribes, even beyond the Mississippi. It is this commanding position, which gives to the Enemy the absolute controul of the Indians. This force would also enable you to take Michelmacinack & command the waters of Lake Michigan. Whatever force the Enemy may create, we must surpass; & with this view, it will require all your vigilance, to penetrate their designs. The command of Lake Ontario is no less important, & to secure this object, you are authorized to build at Sackets harbor, another corvette of such dimensions, as you may deem proper; Indeed you are to consider the absolute superiority on all the Lakes, as the only limit to your authority. Immediately on receipt of this letter, you will report to me, your plans, & forward your requisitions of stores of every kind, with your opinion of the places most convenient to procure the supplies, & from whence they may be transported with the greatest facility economy & despatch—also the number & description of mechanics, & of officers & men, & the time at which they should reach their destination; Forty or fifty good carpenters can be sent from Philada. as early as you please; If you wish any particular officers, name them, & they shall join you. I understand, from persons resident on the shore of the Lake, that the navigation at Buffaloe & black rock is not open until the 15th. May, although it is open at & above Erie about the 15. April; not a moments time, is therefore to be lost, in the accomplishment of our object. You will communicate freely & generally, all such information as may enable me to furnish you in due season, with the best means of carrying into execution the object of the Government & ensuring to yourself, the imperishable fame which achievements so important & brilliant, cannot fail to produce. For your information, I enclose an extract from genl. Harrisons letter, dated 1812, which will enable you to form some idea of the contemplated military operations & of your means of co-operation—

W Jones.

LB Copy, DNA, RG45, SNL, Vol. 10, pp. 231–32 (M149, Roll No. 10).

1. William Henry Harrison, governor of the Indiana Territory from 1800 to 1813, was appointed a brigadier general on 22 August 1812 and made commander of the Northwest army; he was promoted to major general on 2 March 1813.

Chauncey Requests Perry's Service on the Lakes

Commodore Isaac Chauncey intervened to hasten the appointment of Master Commandant Oliver Hazard Perry to the lakes. Perry had served in the navy for 14 of his 28 years, but lacked experience in battle. He had superintended the gunboat flotilla at Newport, Rhode Island, for two years and was anxious for a more active assignment.[1]

Perry had a reputation as an ambitious, intelligent officer willing to take chances. He had also offered to bring with him one hundred experienced seamen from Rhode Island—an offer that no doubt appealed to Commodore Chauncey who was faced with the difficult task of recruiting sailors in a wilderness.

1. On Perry's earlier career and his requests for a transfer to another station, see Dudley, Naval War of 1812, Vol. 1, pp. 126–27, 354, 563–65.

Captain Oliver H. Perry

COMMODORE ISAAC CHAUNCEY TO MASTER COMMANDANT OLIVER H. PERRY

Capt. O. H. Perry,   Sackets' Harbor
commg. naval officer   20 Jany. 1813.
Newport, R I

I arrived here yesterday from Buffaloe and found your favor of the 1st. inst. Independent of the pleasure of hearing from an old acquaintance, nothing could be more agreeable to me than your offer of service. I accept of them with great pleasure provided the Secretary agrees to it. You are the very person I want for a particular service where you may gain honor for yourself & reputation for your Country.—

I shall write to the Secretary this day requesting that you may be ordered to join me with your men. If you should receive such an order I wish that you would lose no time in coming on. There will be a fine field here ~~next~~ this Summer. The enemy are building 2 frigates. With great regard I am dear Sir Your friend &c.

                                                     Isaac Chauncey

LB Copy, MiU–C, Isaac Chauncey Letter Book.

COMMODORE ISAAC CHAUNCEY TO THE SECRETARY OF THE NAVY

                                                     Sacket's Harbour
                                                     January 21st. 1813.
Sir

    Captain O. H. Perry having offered his services, I request, (if not interfering with your other arrangements) that you will be pleased to order that officer to this station.

    He can be employed to great advantage, particularly upon Lake Erie where I shall not be able to go myself so early as I expected owing to the encreasing force of the Enemy upon this Lake. We are also in want of men and he tells me that he has upwards of a hundred at Newport who are anxious to join me: if these men could be ordered also it would save much time in recruiting. I have the honor to be Very respectfully Sir, your obdt. servt.

                                                     Isaac Chauncey

ALS, DNA, RG45, CL, 1813, Vol. 1, No. 28 (M125, Roll No. 26).

COMMODORE ISAAC CHAUNCEY TO MASTER COMMANDANT OLIVER H. PERRY

Captain O. H. Perry—   Sackets' harbor
U.S. Navy   15th. March 1813—
present.—

    You will proceed immediately to Presqu'Isle upon lake Erie and assume the command at that place. I have contracted with a Mr. Noah Brown to build for account of the Navy Department 2 Brigs to mount 20 guns each, and compleat 4 gun boats that are partly finished. These vessels are to be completed as far as respects the carpenters, Joiners, Blockmakers, and Smith's work by Mr. Brown in the best manner and in the shortest time possible. I have engaged a Mr. Sacket [1] a Sailmaker at New York to [make the Sails] [2] take a gang of men with him to Erie to make the sails. You will therefore be pleased to cause a suitable loft to be prepared for him to work in. I have also engaged a rigger to fit the rigging &c.— you will take with you from this place such officers and men as you may want in fitting these vessels. There are a number of guns and stores at Black Rock; you will select such as may be wanted to fit and equip the vessels at Erie and order them sent up to that place. You are at liberty also to order any of the officers and men now at Black-Rock to accompany you at Erie. I have ordered all the light canvas for the sails to be sent from Philadelphia, presuming that we could procure the heavy duck at Pittsburgh. You will however ascertain that fact as soon as you get there and if it is not to be got you will write to george Harrison esqr. navy Agent at Phila. to send it to you immediately. The rigging you can get made at Pittsburgh, & I should advise you to contract for it immediately. ascertain whether you can get the Anchors made at Pittsburgh and let me know. You will find the guns already at Erie when you arrive there, but whether the slides &c belonging to them have been sent with them I do not know. The shot I presume you will be obliged to procure at Pittsburgh. Let me know whether cabooses can be got there.—

Being so far separated from you I must necessarily leave much to your own judgement and discretion both of which I have the fullest confidence in. I will barely remind you that it is an object of the very first importance to have these vessels built & fit for service as soon as possible. You will therefore take care that every thing is prepared and ready to go on board as soon as the vessels are in the water. After taking into view the stores at Erie and those to be got at Buffaloe and this place you will supply the deficiencies in the best way you can either from Pittsburgh or Phila. I shall write the agent at the latter place to furnish upon your requisitions. You will keep me informed of your progress and your wants and whenever you deem it advisable you will send a copy of your communication to me to the Dept.— I hope to be able to join you with the greater part of my officers and men by the first of June, therefore hope to find you completely ready by that time. Provisions for 500 men for 6 months have been ordered to be got ready and one half of it deposited at Erie subject to the order of the commanding officer there. You will cause it to be well taken care of.—

I have again to request that you will not suffer any obstacles to prevent your getting the vessels at Erie ready for service by the 1st. of June at which time I hope to join you with such a force as will ensure us success against the enemy which will at the same time ensure us the applause and gratitude of our Countrymen. I have the honor to be with great respect and esteem Sir yr. obt. H St.

Isaac Chauncey

P.S. For your information I enclose you copy of a letter from The Secretary of the Navy to me dated 27th. ulto., and an extract of a letter from Genl. Harrison to the Secy. of the Navy dated 20th. ulto.—

LB Copy, MiU–C, Isaac Chauncey Letter Book.

1. James L. Sackett, a sailmaker from New York, was sent to Erie by Isaac Chauncey on 24 February 1813.
2. The square brackets appeared in the letter book copy, possibly denoting the incorrect copying of this line.

Preparing the Fleets on the Northern Lakes

The winter of 1812–13 saw the construction of three separate fleets on Lakes Erie, Ontario, and Champlain. This building program presented tremendous obstacles in procuring men, materials, and supplies. The American bases at Erie, Pennsylvania, and at Sackets Harbor and Plattsburg, New York, had few local industries to tap for shipbuilding supplies and were remote from other industrial centers.

Although timber was plentiful along the shores of the lakes, all other materials had to be transported hundreds of miles along shallow rivers and unimproved roads. New York City supplied the ship carpenters, workmen, sailors, guns, and naval stores for Lakes Ontario and Champlain; Philadelphia and Pittsburgh provided men and supplies for the Lake Erie fleet.

LIEUTENANT THOMAS MACDONOUGH TO SECRETARY OF THE NAVY JONES

Shelburn   January 22d. 1813

Sir,

I have the honor to submit a few observations in relation to the U. States Naval force on Lake Champlain and hope you will concur in the arrangement proposed— The sloops which were fitted as well as time and circumstances would permit could be made with a little expence much more effective by taking off their long and high Quarter decks on which no guns can with safety be mounted, and were it removed, four, in addition to what now is, could be mounted on each sloop; say twenty four or Eighteen pound cannonades— These quarter decks extend one third forward so that the guns are only on the Main deck—and three of a side on board each vessel, where as they could with ease and safety carry five on a side making on board each sloop ten guns besides the one on a circle forward—and without any additional force to work them— It is generally understood that the British intend to have the superior Naval force on this Lake next summer, which will be the case unless, the alteration takes place in our sloops which I have mentioned— I suppose the comg. genl. is aware of this circumstance, as he is not here I have not his opinion on the Subject— I saw a Man a few days since whose information may be relied on, that he says the British were making preparations for considerable Naval operations, and it is well known that they have three sloops, fitted in the manner that I wish ours, besides, other small vessels like gallies, and that they are to be well manned— To insure our superiority on the water, these sloops should, sir, be fitted to the best advantage and manned with at least Thirty 0. Seamen, I consider the twenty men, that I now have, as seamen enough for all the Vessells, there are no men to be got here and Soldiers are Miserable creatures on shipboard, and I very much fear ~~unless~~ that unless I get the above 0. Seamen, and not Soldiers, there will be a dark spot in our Navy— The carpenters could be sent on from New York, twelve or fifteen of them and have all repairs, finished by the last of March, by which time the Ice will clear away— Men also might be sent from New York with the twelve guns to be Mounted of twenty four or Eighteen (calibre) cannonades— I have all equipments but swords which we are intirely deficient of, which might also be forwarded to me from N. York—

The carpenters could also repair one of the Gun Boats which went on shore in a blow, and received some injury in her bottom. I have her now in a situation to be haul'd up, for the carpenters— I have the honor to be Sir your most obt. servt.

T. Macdonough

ALS, DNA, RG45, BC, 1813, Vol. 1, No. 16 (M148, Roll No. 11). Notation on reverse of letter reads, "I agree to the alterations he proposes in the Sloops— Instruct the N. Agent at New York to send on 15 carpenters instantly— to mount 12. 18 pd Carronades and forward them with the swords as soon as possible. The [?] will also send the Seamen he requires in due time—."

COMMODORE ISAAC CHAUNCEY TO SECRETARY OF THE NAVY JONES

Sackets' harbor
5 feb 1813—

Sir,
I shall leave here this day for Albany for the purpose of consulting with Major Genl. Dearborn respecting our operations in the spring. Brigd. Genl. Dodge resigned his command at this post on the 30th. ulto.: the command of the troops here has devolved upon Col. Van Alston of the Militia, a very plain man. I shall urge General Dearborn to find an officer of the regular Army to command at this post, as I deem it of great importance that we should have an officer of experience to command the troops here.—

I have 22 guns mounted upon the *Madison* and have got her well manned. We keep the ice cut from around her and have every thing in a state of preparation to repel an attack at a moments' notice either night or day. All the other vessels are so arranged that they are calculated to protect each other, and as no Officer or man is permitted to leave his vessel after 8 o'clock, I think that we can protect each other our fleet against any force that will be brought against us by the Enemy, provided the Army will keep the Forts and prevent the assailants from turning our own guns upon the vessels.—

Two Block-houses are nearly completed and I have 8 guns prepared, with all their ammunition, ready to mount upon them the moment they are ready. These houses will add much to the means of protecting the Fleet and Forts against any sudden attack.

The Marines which I required in my letter of the 1st. of December last I hope will be ordered to join me as early as possible.—

I hope Sir that you will not order any more Sailing Masters to my command. I have now a number of that Grade of officer which I have not employment for. I have the honor to be very respectfully Sir yr. obt. Servt.

Isaac Chauncey

LS, DNA, RG45, CL, 1813, Vol. 1, No. 50 1/2 (M125, Roll No. 26).

COMMODORE ISAAC CHAUNCEY TO SECRETARY OF THE NAVY JONES

New York   16th. Feby. 1813

Sir/
I arrived here on Saturday last from Albany Sunday having intervened prevented my doing much before yesterday. I have now made my arrangements

with the carpenters and a part of them will leave here this week for Sacketts Harbor and Erie but I shall depend chiefly upon Philadelphia to furnish mechanicks and stores for the station at Erie for which purpose I have the honor of inclosing a list of Carpenters and stores which I wish to be sent forward immediately— I have enclosed a copy of the list to George Harrison Esqr. in order that he might be prepared to comply immediately ~~upon the~~ with your order upon the subject— before I left Erie I contracted for the frame of a Brig of 360 tons   I have wrote from this place to Mr. Dobbins to procure timber for another vessel of the same dimentions—the Master builder with a few picked men will leave here on friday and will arrive at Erie about the last of this month the Carpenters which are to be sent from Philadelphia I should recommend to be placed in charge of a trusty man of their own class who will answer for a foreman in the yard at Erie. Captain Perry will be required at Erie as soon as he can get there I therefore think that it would promote the publick service to order him to proceed direct from this place. The 37–32 pd. carronades which you have ordered from Washington will arme the two Brigs we however shall require four long 32 pounders for the gun Boats as there may be a difficulty in geting those guns up from Buffaloe all the Iron and Cordage can be procured at Pittsburgh. It will be necessary to inshure a suply of provissions for our men upon Erie will you make that arrangement or shall I? I will complete the Indents for the force at Erie as soon as possible and will forward them to you. With respect to Ontario before I left Sacketts Harbor I made arrangements for procuring the Materiels for building a Ship of the size of the *Madison* therefor there will be no detention upon that Lake except from the armament, and I presume that can be sent forward in time— I should wish if not attended with too much expense that 42 pdr. carronades might be sent for the New Ship at Sacketts Harbor but least that may be attended with some difficulty I shall make arrangements for long 12 pds. being sent from this place as there is no carronades to be got here

There is some excellent men onboard of the *John Adams* and *Alert* who would Volunteer for the Lake service May they be permitted? I have the honor to be Very Respectfully Sir your Obt H Servt

Isaac Chauncey

ALS, DNA, RG45, CL, 1813, Vol. 1, No. 78 (M125, Roll No. 26).

Commodore Isaac Chauncey to Noah Brown [1]

Mr. Noah Brown   New york
New york   18 feb. 1813.

I wish you to proceed with all possible despatch for Erie upon Lake Erie in the State of Pennsylvania, and there build in the shortest time possible 2 Brigs capable of mounting 18–32 pounders carronades & 2 long 9s. These vessels must be so constructed that they can be made to draw not exceeding 6 1/2 or 7 feet water, and at the same time possess the qualities of sailing fast and bearing their guns with ease. Their frame &c. will be left entirely to yourself. You will procure the materials and workmen on the best terms possible. I have ordered about 40 Ship Carpenters from Philadelphia which I presume will join you early in March. You must bear in mind that I do not limit you as to the number and kind of workmen to be employed by you upon this business. My object is to have the vessels built in the shortest time possible. You will find at Erie 4 Gun Boats in a considerable state of forwardness. I shall expect that you will take charge of them also and have them finished as soon as possible. When you require funds you will make out your bills against the navy department and send them to me at Sackets' Harbor for my examination and approval.—

Be pleased to keep me informed from time to time of your progress, and at what time you will be able to launch these vessels. I have the honor &c.—

Isaac Chauncey.—

LB Copy, MiU–C, Isaac Chauncey Letter Book.

1. Noah Brown, a New York shipbuilder, was selected by Chauncey to complete the vessels under construction at Presque Isle. He later built vessels on Lake Champlain and on Lake Ontario.

COMMODORE ISAAC CHAUNCEY TO SECRETARY OF THE NAVY JONES

New York   22d. Feb'y 1813

Sir/

On friday last Mr. Noah Brown (a very respectable ship carpenter) with 15 prime men left here for Erie where I hope they will be joined by the men from Philadelphia as soon as possible— Mr. Eckford has already despatched about 30 men for Sacketts Harbor and will leave here himself with about the same number on Wednesday next   I shall complete my arrangements with a rigger and sail makers to proceed this day to proceed to Erie about the 15th of March, and I shall send an officer to Pittsburgh to contract for the cordage and canvass so that there will be no detention when those people arrive at Erie— I shall select a gang of sailors from the men at Black Rock to go to Erie for the purpose of assisting in fitting the riggin &c. the remainder I shall take onboard of the fleet upon Lake Ontario and am in hopes to finish our business upon that Lake before Erie is Navigable so that we shall be able to transfer the men from one lake to the other as we may want them—at any rate the men intended for Lake Erie had better be sent in the first place to Sacketts Harbor from which place we can transport them by water to Niagara and from thence in boats along shore to Erie—

Having completed my arrangements as far as practicable at this place I shall leave here tomorrow for Sacketts Harbor from which place I will write you the state and condition of the fleet— I have the honor to be Very Respectfully Sir your obt. H. St.

I Chauncey

ALS, DNA, RG45, CL, 1813, Vol. 1, No. 106 (M125, Roll No. 26).

Sailors for the Lakes

A critical shortage of experienced and disciplined seamen would trouble the navy throughout the War of 1812. Recruiting for the northern lakes proved especially difficult because the countryside was sparsely settled and few local men had experience as sailors. A few ambi-

tious young officers, like Midshipman William W. Edwards, recognized the opportunities that would be available for personal glory and prize money once the season opened on the lakes in 1813 and requested to be transferred. Most seasoned officers and seamen, however, preferred service on a seagoing frigate to that on a smaller vessel confined to inland waters.

In order to find sufficient men for the vessels building on Lakes Ontario and Erie, the navy took to drafting crews from vessels which were either undergoing extensive repairs or were blockaded in the ports on the East Coast. Much to the consternation of their commanding officers, seamen from Argus, John Adams, Alert, *and* Constitution *were transferred to serve on the northern lakes.*

MIDSHIPMAN WILLIAM W. EDWARDS [1] TO SENATOR JAMES TURNER [2]

U.S.F. *U.S.*   February 1. 1813.
Harbour of New-York

Sir

When I entered the service of my country, it was with a view to excel in my profession, and to gain "a name in arms." It was my choice to sail with Commodore Decatur, because I entertain'd the highest opinion of his skill and valor: in this I have been confirmed by experience.— But however desirable my situation on board this ship may appear I am desirous to change it: because I can see no chance of speedy promotion there being a large proportion of Midshipmen on board who are older in service than myself, and whose expectations must of course be fulfilled before I can reasonably hope for promotion.

Under these circumstances I am desirous of being sent to the Lakes, as I think the ensuing spring will open a wide field for young men of enterprize in that quarter.

If you Sir, would be so good as to request the Secretary of the Navy to order me to that station it would be conferring a particular obligation on me, and it might probably be of the utmost benefit to my future prosperity. I have the honor to be With the highest respect Your most obd. servt.

W: W: Edwards

Honble. James Turner
Washington City

ALS, DNA, RG45, MLR, 1813, Vol. 1, No. 161 (M124, Roll No. 53).

1. There is no record of any official response to Midshipman Edwards's request for a transfer to the lakes. He was assigned to the brig *Argus* on 24 March 1813 and received a promotion to lieutenant four months later. Edwards was killed 14 August 1813 when *Argus* encountered the brig *Pelican* off the Irish coast.
2. James Turner, a Republican, served as U.S. Senator from North Carolina from 1811 to 1816.

COMMODORE STEPHEN DECATUR TO SECRETARY OF THE NAVY JONES

U.S.F. *United States*
New york   Feby 18th 1813

Sir,

The men order'd from the *Argus*, for the Lakes, have been selected, and are now at the disposal of Lt. Chauncey—[1] As it is probable that there will be time to hear again from the department, before the men will leave this, I have taken the liberty to address you upon this subject, begging that my zeal for the good of the service may plead my excuse for so doing— The *Argus* is now nearly ready for sea— She may in the course of two weeks meet the enemy, and with her old crew, which were well disciplin'd, I shou'd not fear the result of a contest with an equal force— She will not be near as efficient with a new crew until time shall be afforded to discipline them— Fifty volunteers might have been obtain'd from the *Jno. Adams* the *Alert* and the Gun boats— Those men are not liable to be drafted for service other than the defence of the harbour of New York, having been enter'd expressly for that purpose— These men are equally good with those of the *Argus*, and will not require more reorganization than those of the *Argus* wou'd when turn'd over to other vessels— If Sir this view of the subject shou'd induce you to alter your former determination, there may be yet time to countermand your first order   very respectfully I have the honor to be your obt. svt.

                                                                    Stephen Decatur

LS, DNA, RG45, CL, 1813, Vol. 1, No. 89 (M125, Roll No. 26).

   1. Lieutenant Wolcott Chauncey, younger brother of Commodore Isaac Chauncey, was ordered to the lakes in February 1813.

COMMODORE ISAAC CHAUNCEY TO SECRETARY OF THE NAVY JONES

                                                            Sackets' Harbor
                                                        18th. March 1813.—

Sir,
   I had the honor of informing you from Newyork that the crews of the *John Adams* and *Alert* were anxious to join me upon the Lakes. Not having heard from you upon the subject I am apprehensive that letter may have miscarried. As we shall require 500 more men by the first of June I shall esteem it a favor if you will permit the whole or any part of the crews of those ships to join me, which will save much time and expence in recruiting.—
   To guard however against a disappointment in the supply of men I have requested Capt. Hull to cause a rendezvous to be opened at Boston and to recruit as many men for the Lakes as he can until I hear further from the Department upon the subject. I should have ordered another rendezvous opened at Newyork but as they are recruiting there for 2 large Frigates already I thought a third rendezvous might interfere.—
   These arrangements I hope will meet your approbation. I have the honor to be very respectfully Sir Yr. Ob. St.
                                                                    Isaac Chauncey

LS, DNA, RG45, CL, 1813, Vol. 2, No. 59 (M125, Roll No. 27).

COMMODORE WILLIAM BAINBRIDGE TO SECRETARY OF THE NAVY JONES

                                                    Navy Yard   Charlestown, Mass.
                                                        27th. April 1813

Sir
   I have the honor to inform you, that I have this day transferred fifty more of the Frigate *Constitution*'s Crew and forwarded them to Sacket Harbor to serve

under the command of Capn. Isaac Chauncey—which number makes one hundred & fifty (150) of the Crew of the *Constitution* sent to the Lakes— the urgent manner in which Captain Chauncey pressed the necessity of having an additional number of Seamen for our successful operations on those waters, induced me, from motives of the public good, to make the said transfers, and trust they will meet with your approbation— I respectfully recommend the giving immediate orders to the Captain of the *Constitution* (presuming that one is already appointed) to open Rendezvouses for recruiting his Crew as the repairs of said Ship are rapidly progressing and would have been much more forward then they are, if I had not been detained for the Beams—

In pursuance to your Instructions relative to hastening the necessary repairs of the Frigate *Chesapeake*—I have the pleasure to inform you, that they are already in great forwardness and that they will not be expensive. I have the honor Sir, to be with the greatest respect yr. ob. st.

W^m. Bainbridge

LS, DNA, RG45, CL, 1813, Vol. 3, No. 60 (M125, Roll No. 27).

A Change in Strategy on Lake Ontario

There was much apprehension among the American military commanders at Sackets Harbor in the early months of 1813. A British force from Prescott had crossed the St. Lawrence River on 23 February and gained control of that vital waterway by capturing the American post at Ogdensburg, New York. Commodore Isaac Chauncey and Major General Henry Dearborn, commanding at Sackets Harbor, fearing that their post would be the next target, readied the town for a British attack from across the frozen lake.

Although the attack never materialized, a sense of unease prevailed at Sackets Harbor. Sir George Prevost had recently arrived at Kingston with additional army troops. In the mistaken belief that Kingston was strongly fortified, Chauncey and Dearborn concluded by mid-March that an attack on the British headquarters in the spring would be unwise. Chauncey, in his letter to the secretary of the navy of 18 March, recommended that York be the first object, followed by an assault on the forts on the Niagara frontier. Dearborn, writing to the secretary of war, proposed much the same plan for the campaign of 1813.[1]

1. Hitsman, "Alarum on Lake Ontario"; Skeen, John Armstrong, pp. 145–49.

COMMODORE ISAAC CHAUNCEY TO SECRETARY OF THE NAVY JONES

Sackets' Harbor
18 March 1813.—

Sir,

In my letter to you of the 21st. Jany. last I had the honor of submitting for your consideration my ideas of a plan to attack the Enemy this Spring which you were pleased to approve. Since that period, the complection of things has changed considerably and the objections to that plan as a <u>first</u> object are these.— The Enemy possessing the means of obtaining the most accurate information from this side will be informed of the force collected and collecting at this place together with the preparations making evidently for an attack upon Kingston; he will unquestionably prepare himself for such an event and will oppose all the force in his power to the accomplishment of our object. I have no kind of doubt as to the final result, but as the opposing force would be considerable, it would protract the general operations of the campaign to a later period than I think would be advisable, particularly when we take into view the probability that large re-inforcements will arrive at Quebec in the course of 2 months. My idea is, that we should continue to keep up the appearance that an attack upon Kingston was intended to be made as soon as the Lake was navigable, and the preparations now making will give currency to such an opinion. This will oblidge the Enemy to concentrate his force at Kingston and have the effect of preventing re-inforcements from being sent to the upper part of the province, and eventually facilitate our main object.—

I would propose in lieu of my first plan that we should make every preparation for an attack upon Kingston and when, completely prepared (which we ought to be, as soon as the Lake is navigable) I would take on board 1,000 or 1,500 <u>picked</u> Troops under the command of a judicious officer and 4 or 6 pieces of light Field-Artillery and proceed directly to York (where the Enemy has but a small force) land the Troops under cover of the Fleet, & then proceed with the small vessels into the Harbor and take possession of the Town and vessels. This I think can be accomplished without loss on our part and will have the effect of giving us the complete command of this Lake. The Enemy's naval force at York consists of the *prince Regent* of 18 guns, the *Duke of Gloucester* of 16 guns, and 2 brigs building calculated to carry 18 guns each. By possessing ourselves of these vessels and taking or destroying all the public stores and munitions of war at York, will give us a decided advantage in the commencement of the campaign.— I would propose in the next place to keep possession of York long enough to induce the Enemy to detach a force from Fort George to dislodge us. of his movements we could be informed by means of our small vessels. When the Enemy has approached sufficiently near York as to prevent his immediate return to Fort George I would re-imbark the Troops and proceed immediately to the neighbourhood of that Fort, land the Troops and Sailors a few miles north of it at 4 mile creek, and then in conjunction with the Troops at Lewistown and Black-Rock (with which previous arrangements must necessarily be made in order that our operations may be simultaneous) I would make a general attack upon Fort George and the Niagara Frontier which I am persuaded we could carry, and the advantages resulting from a successful attack of this kind, to the service, (even if we were not able to hold it but for a few days) would be immense, for it would immediately release five vessels which are now lying useless in the Niagara river and must continue so long as the Enemy has possession of that frontier. With that addition to the force preparing at Erie it would give us, a decided superiority upon the upper Lakes. If this Enterprize should prove successful (which I see no reason to doubt) I would leave a force sufficient upon this Lake to watch and blockade the Enemys' force at Kingston, and proceed myself with all the officers and men that could be spared direct to Erie—and as soon as possible get the whole Force into operation upon that Lake, destroy their naval power there as soon as possible, attack and take

Malden and Detroit, & proceed into Lake Huron and attack & carry Machili-mackinac <u>at all hazards</u>. This would give us such a decided advantage in the upper province and such an influence over the Indians that I think the Enemy would abandon the upper country altogether and concentrate his forces about Kingston and Montreal. In that event it would leave us at liberty to bring nearly the whole of our force (naval as well as military) to act upon any one point.—

You, Sir, may conceive that I am sanguine as to the results of this Enterprize. I have thought much upon the subject and after making every Deduction for every possible contingency, I am persuaded in my own mind that we should succeed.—

I have communicated my ideas to but two persons and to these in confidence—to wit—Genl. Dearborn and Col Macomb. They both approved of my plan and thought that it would succeed.— I will observe, however, if it is to be adopted that the most scrupulous silence ought to be observed with respect to the real object of our operations, and no one made acquainted with our destination except the commanding General and the officer who is to accompany me, for we have daily evidence that our officers cannot keep a <u>Secret</u>. The officer commanding at Niagara and Black Rock should be instructed to co-operate with me whenever I should make him acquainted with my object.—

There will be many details attending the operations (the outlines of which I have the honor of herewith submitting for your consideration) which I have not noticed, as in a service of this nature much must always be left to the discretion of the Officer Commanding. I however beg to assure you that I shall so time the operations as to give us all the advantages of a proper selection.—

There is one subject, Sir, which I feel a reluctance to agitate, but the conviction upon my mind of the importance of a Decision has induced me to submit it for your consideration.—

It is this.— From the very nature of my command it will frequently become necessary for me to act on shore with the Army or parts thereof and that with a large Body of men under my immediate orders. Now Sir, although I have an order from the Department to consider my rank as that of a Brigadier General, yet some of the officers of the Army may be disposed to dispute the legality of such an order and refuse to recognize me as holding any military rank whatever, and as the field of Battle is not the proper place to settle that point, I should wish, Sir, that some order may be taken upon the subject. My idea is that the President may give some Brevet rank that the officers of the Army would recognize while I was acting on shore. I beg, however, to be clearly understood as disclaiming all idea or wish of obtaining permanent military rank; my only object is, to place my relative rank with officers of the Army (when acting together) upon that footing, that neither they or myself shall be led into error by entertaining erroneous opinions whereby the publick service may suffer—

I am authorized to state that Col Macomb coincides with me in opinion as respects the relative rank of officers in the two services and that he has no objection to serve under me whenever the public service may require me to act on shore.—

I have to apologize to you Sir for the length of this communication, but the motives which have prompted it, will, I trust be a sufficient excuse for occupying so much of your time.— I have the honor to be with great respect Sir your most ob. and very Hble. sevt.

Isaac Chauncey

LS, DNA, RG45, CL, 1813, Vol. 2, No. 58 (M125, Roll No. 27).

SECRETARY OF THE NAVY JONES TO COMMODORE ISAAC CHAUNCEY

(No. 13)

Commodore Isaac Chauncey,   Navy Dep'tm't
Commanding U.S. Naval Forces,   April 8th. 1813.—
Sacket's Harbour, NY.

Sir,

On the 6th. instant, I received your letter of the 18th. ulto. comprising your plan of operations for the ensuing season on the Lakes.

The subject has received all the attention and deliberation which ought to precede the adoption of measures upon which, not only the fate of the campaign in that quarter, but the character and duration of the war, and the final object of that war, an honorable and secure peace may depend.

The President has been pleased to express his approbation of the general outline, and his particular satisfaction with the judicious and zealous execution of the preparatory arrangements under your direction. But, as the campaign combines extensive military and Naval operations, it is of primary importance to reconcile and harmonize the designs and movements of the combined forces, so that the most perfect understanding and efficient concert may result from their mutual co-operation.

The plan of operations for the army of the United States, in that quarter, contemplates a movement, with all the troops and train that can be transported in the fleet under your command, and in the Boats constructed by order of the War department, to attack and carry the Town of York; and after the capture and destruction of the shipping and stores there, proceed directly to Fort George, and carry it by assault; while the army at Niagara makes a simultaneous movement upon Forts Erie and Chipaway; with a view to subdue and retain the whole of those posts. This would, at once, release the Naval force at Black Rock, and enable you, without loss of time, to commence your operations on Lake Erie.— The importance of the effects which must flow from the successful issue of your enterprize on this Lake, is even greater than that of the lower Lake; because, it at once erects a Naval barrier between our civilised and savage Enemies from Niagara to Michigan. In the whole of your operations there is nothing so precious as time. A rapid movement from Niagara to Malden, taking such part of the force at Erie as may be even in a partial state of preparation, with as many chosen troops as can be transported, would, at once, annihilate the Naval force and the hopes of the Enemy; and leave you a free passage to Michilimackinac and the mouth of French River; where all the Indian supplies are deposited, and furs collected in return.

With a prospect so auspicious, and a result so glorious and decisive, to animate our gallant forces, I cannot deny myself the pleasure of anticipating the fame which, I am sure, you will deserve, and trust you will achieve.— The delay you contemplate at York, after its subjugation, it is conceived, would be a loss of time upon a very uncertain contingency.

I am aware that under unfavorable circumstances of winds and weather, the Boats of the Army may embarrass, or retard your movements: indeed, your squadron may reach its destination whilst the boats cannot move at all. It must, therefore, depend upon the degree of force to be encountered, whether it will be prudent to proceed with the force you contemplate, on board the Squadron, or await a more favorable state of things, and move with the whole force contemplated by the War Department, which I understand to be 2500 men; 1000 of whom, I presume, can be conveniently transported in the vessels of the Squadron, and the residue in 15 Boats, which you can take in tow. This can only be determined by the mutual concert of the military and naval commanders with the knowledge of existing circumstances, and reference to the instructions under which they act.—

There is no difficulty in settling the subject of relative Rank between Naval and military commanders; but that of <u>command</u> is a subject of great delicacy and can be approached but with great caution. The British Government which has more experience on this subject than any other, and cannot be accused of indisposition to cherish the pretensions and feelings of its Naval officers, has been obliged to confine itself to a prohibitory regulation, which absolutely excludes her Naval officers from commanding on shore, under any pretence, and her military commanders from commanding, under any pretence, the Ships and vessels of the Navy.— The Secretaries of War and of the Navy of the United States, have adopted a regulation which, it is hoped, will meet any case that can possibly arise of that nature, between officers whose intelligence and patriotism will cherish harmony, rather than punctilio. I enclose the Regulation for your information and Government.

I have no doubt, from the character of Captain Perry, and the urgent instructions you have given him, that our affairs will progress rapidly at Erie.—

I have felt some solicitude about the four 32 pdr. cannons you required for the Gun boats at Erie; it has been, and will be, impossible to transport them in waggons, until the Roads are perfectly good. Indeed, they are so heavy that I doubt whether they can be carried by waggons at any time.—

I have heard of a 24 pounder, on a Ship carriage, at Pittsburg, belonging to the War Department, which I shall order to Erie; and, there is, at that place, a long 18 pounder which can be had.—

The success of the campaign absolutely depends upon the judicious movements and vigorous direction of the Naval force under your command; and, as nautical skill and experience can alone determine the time, circumstances and manner of employing that force, in cooperation with the military, of these you will be the exclusive judge. Relying upon your cordial and Zealous exertions to give full effect to the joint operations of the land and naval forces, and with much confidence in the result of those exertions, I am, very respectfully, your ob. servant

W: Jones

LB Copy, DNA, RG45, CLS, 1813, pp. 5–9.

AGREEMENT GOVERNING JOINT OPERATIONS

Regulations of the War & Navy Departments for the government of their respective commanders when acting in concert:—

1st. No Officer of the Army of the United States shall on any pretence command any of the Ships or Vessels of the Navy of the United States—nor shall any Officer of the said Navy command, under any pretence, any Troops of the Army of the United States.—

2nd. When the services of the Naval forces or any part thereof may be necessary on Land, in cooperation with the Military, the said naval forces shall have a distinct & independant service assigned to them under their own commander, by agreement between the Military & Naval commanders.—

War Department
April 8th 1813.—

LB Copy, DNA, RG107, Letters Sent by the Secretary of War Relating to Military Affairs, 1813, p. 355 (M6, Roll No. 6).

Sir James Lucas Yeo's Instructions

Sir James Lucas Yeo, appointed Commodore and Commander of His Majesty's Forces on the Lakes of Canada, earned his rank and reputation with daring and initiative. Yeo had joined the Royal Navy as a boy at the age of eleven, attaining the rank of post-captain by the time he was twenty-five. He was awarded a knighthood by the Portuguese for a daring assault on a garrison in French Guiana in 1809 that resulted in the expulsion of the French from South America.

Yeo's natural daring was to be tempered by his instructions from the Admiralty. He was to place himself under both Governor-General Sir George Prevost, Commander in Chief of the Canadas, and Admiral Sir John Borlase Warren, Commander of the North American and West Indian Stations. Moreover, he was directed to take a defensive position on the lakes, and was expected to cooperate and coordinate his movements with the British army forces in Canada.[1]

1. *See also Drake, "Yeo and Prevost."*

LORDS COMMISSIONERS OF THE ADMIRALTY TO COMMODORE SIR JAMES LUCAS YEO, R.N.

Copy

By the Commissioners &c

Whereas the Earl Bathurst, one of His Majesty's Principal Secretaries of State, hath signified to us the Pleasure of His Royal Highness The Prince Regent that We should take under our direction and control His Majesty's Ships and Vessels employed on the Lakes of Canada; We having the greatest confidence in your gallantry, Judgement and zeal for His Majesty's Service, have thought fit to select you for the command of the said Naval Force; and We do hereby require and direct you to proceed to the said Lakes of Canada, and there take the command of the several Ships and Vessels belonging to His Majesty on those Lakes, appointing and distributing amongst them the Officers and Men under your orders, according to the Instructions which we have directed our Secretary to transmit herewith for your guidance.

The first and paramount object for which this Naval Force is maintained being the defence of His Majesty's Provinces of North America; We do hereby require and direct you in the Employment thereof to cooperate most cordially with His

Excellency the Captain General and Governor in Chief of the said Provinces, not undertaking any operations without the full concurrence and approbation of him or of the Commanders of the Forces employed under him; and on all occasions conforming yourself and employing the Force under your command according to the Requisitions which you may from time to time receive to this Effect, from the said Governor or Commander of the Forces.

During the continuance of your command you are hereby authorized to hoist a distinguishing Pendant as Commodore on Board such one of His Majesty's Ships as you may select—

You are further required and directed to pay particular attention and obedience to the Instructions herewith transmitted, & to all other Instructions or directions which you may hereafter receive from us or from Our Secretary by Our Command.—

Given under Our hands 19th March, 1813—

Signed   Melville
W Domett
J S Yorke
J Osborn

By Command of their Lordships
Signed J. W. Croker

Copy, CaOOA, British Military and Naval Records, RG8, I, "C" Ser., Vol. 729, pp. 132–34. This duplicate copy and enclosure were sent to Sir George Prevost under a cover letter of 20 March 1813.

[Enclosure]

Admiralty office
19th. March 1813—

Sir/

Referring you in the first instance to the order of my Lords Comm'ers of the Admiralty of this day's date which you will receive herewith, I have their Lordship's commands to acquaint you that arrangements have been made for conveying you and the officers & men under your command to Quebec in His Majesty's Troop Frigate the *Woolwich*—

On board this Ship the commissioned warrant and petty officers and Seamen stated in the enclosed list have received directions to embark, and to follow your orders for their further proceedings

On your arrival in the river St. Lawrence you are to take the earliest opportunity of communicating your Instructions to Lieut. General Sir Geo. Prevost, Captain General and Governor in Chief of His Majesty's Provinces in North America of explaining the amount of the Force under your Orders, of learning from him all the details of the Ships and Vessels employed on the Lakes, and of consulting and arranging with him with regard to all the various particulars of the important Services to which your joint efforts are to be directed.

You will on your arrival at the Lakes (the means of conveyance to which for the officers men and stores from Quebec you are to request the Governor to supply) distribute the officers men and stores amongst the ships and vessels in such manner as you shall think best for His Majesty's Service, giving the Commanders Lieutenants and other Officers according to their respective ranks, acting orders or warrants for the different vessels to which you may appoint them—

The ships and vessels now on the Lakes have been hitherto entirely, <u>manned provisioned and stored</u> under the direction of the Governor in Chief; with regard to the manning it is obvious that the number of seamen under your orders will not more than enable you to distribute a due proportion of able seamen among the different vessels, and that you will not be able to dispense with the services of the Persons now employed in those vessels, most, if not all of whom, must still continue in them and you will arrange with His Ex'cy. Sir George Prevost, a scheme for manning the ships as nearly as may be according to the system established in the Navy, of able seamen, ordinary landsmen and marines; the latter to be supplied as their Lordships understand from the Newfoundland Fencibles or some other Military Corps which may be at the Governor's disposal: on this subject however of proportioning the classes of Men, you are at liberty to make such deviation from the ordinary practice as local circumstances may seem to require. . . .[1]

It can scarcely be necessary to recommend to your particular attention all subjects connected with the health comfort and good discipline of the officers and men under your orders in the latter point especially their Lordships feel that the trust committed to you is in the peculiar circumstance of the Service in which you are employed, one of great delicacy, they however are satisfied that as on the one hand by any too great relaxation which might impair the good order that must ever be maintained in His Majesty's Ships of all Classes and descriptions, as on the other, you will endeavour by a judicious attention and by all reasonable indulgence to the Men under your orders, to obviate the risks and temptations t/w a new and very peculiar service might expose them—

I am not to conceal from you that their Lordships feel some anxiety on this subject, occasioned as well by the proximity of the scene of your operations to the Enemy's Territory, as by the efforts which the Americans have made on as many occasions to seduce His Majesty's Subjects from their duty and allegiance—

You will not fail by every opportunity to transmit to me for their Lordships information, a detailed report of all your proceedings, and you will collect and send as soon as possible a detailed and accurate account of the number, force and state of Equipment of the ships and vessels of War on the Lakes, as well those belonging to the Enemy as to His Majesty, and you will consider and report what you may under all circumstances conceive the best mode of putting and maintaining His Majesty's squadron in the most effective state, and of furnishing its future supplies of stores, should it be found necessary or advisable to alter the present system.

I am further to acquaint you by the act of the 29th. of Geo: 2d. Chap. 27 the Provisions of act of the 22d. Geo: 2d. Chapter 33 for amending explaining and reducing into one Act of Parliament the laws relating to the Government of His Majesty's ships vessels and forces by Sea are extended to the Lakes of Canada: as however you are not likely even to have officers sufficient to compose a Court Martial, you are to send any offenders for trial to Halifax by such opportunity as may offer—I am &c

(signed)   J. W. Croker—

Copy, CaOOA, British Military and Naval Records, RG8, I, "C" Ser., Vol. 729, pp. 135–45.

1. Beginning at this point, seven paragraphs that relate to pay, the keeping of muster books, and expenditures for provisions have been omitted from this transcription.

The Chauncey-Angus Feud Resolved

A protracted feud between Commodore Isaac Chauncey and Lieutenant Samuel Angus followed the junior officer's arrest on 26 December 1812 under charges of disobedience of orders and unofficerlike conduct.[1] The two men's quarrel was fueled by a broader disagreement over military discipline and personal honor: Chauncey demanded subordination from his junior officers, but Angus refused to show deference to Chauncey as a matter of personal honor. Only upon receiving an apology from Angus would the Commodore withdraw the charges and allow Angus to be transferred to another station.[2] Angus reluctantly offered his apology in his letter of 8 April, over three months after his arrest.

1. *See Dudley*, Naval War of 1812, *Vol. 1, pp. 371–74.*
2. *For the entire exchange of correspondence between Chauncey and Angus, see Chauncey to Jones, 2 April 1813 and its enclosures, in DNA, RG45, CL, 1813, Vol. 2, Nos. 121–22 (M125, Roll No. 27).*

COMMODORE ISAAC CHAUNCEY TO LIEUTENANT SAMUEL ANGUS

Lieut Saml Angus,   Sackets' Harbor
U.S. Navy   Mar 27th 1813.—
Buffaloe
St. Newyork,

I have received your letter of the 18th. by Mr Holdup together with a copy of one from the honorable the Secretary of the navy of the 3d. to you, upon the subject of your arrest.—[1]

I must confess that I had anticipated a different letter from you particularly when I take into view the length of time which has elapsed since the affair alluded to, took place. You must certainly be sensible that you forced upon me the alternative which I adopted. Contrary to my wishes and most earnest endeavours to save you from disgrace, you not only put me and my authority at defiance, but boasted that no Court Martial could <u>break</u> you. And now, Sir, what is the reparation you tender for the Indignity offered to me as your commanding officer and the injury done to the service by your insubordination? Why it is merely this, that as the honorable the Secretary of the navy has declined interfering in your case without my consent, "<u>you are sensible from the purport of his letter that you have acted incorrectly in refusing to do your duty</u>"; but there does not appear to be any conviction upon your own mind that you have acted "incorrectly" towards me, or even that you have acted incorrectly at all. You only appear to be sensible that as the Secretary does not approve of your conduct that from that circumstance alone you think that you may have done wrong.

Now sir if you are really & sincerely convinced in your own mind that you have committed an error, there would be no disgrace in acknowledging it fully & offering such reparation as the nature of the case would require; but on the contrary if there is no such conviction upon your mind, you ought not to make any apology whatever, but abide the decision of a Court martial.

After having given the subject all the consideration that its' importance requires your own judgment and experience in Service will point out to you the proper course to be pursued. I most sincerely hope that it may be such as to induce me to intercede with the Honorable the Secretary of the Navy to withdraw your arrest and suffer you to return to your duty. I have the honor to be respectfully Sir yr. obt. Svt.

Isaac Chauncey

LB Copy, MiU–C, Isaac Chauncey Letter Book.

1. Angus to Chauncey, 18 March 1813, DNA, RG45, CL, 1813, Vol. 2, No. 122, enclosure (M125, Roll No. 27); Jones to Angus, 3 March 1813, DNA, RG45, SNL, Vol. 10, p. 289 (M149, Roll No. 10).

LIEUTENANT SAMUEL ANGUS TO COMMODORE ISAAC CHAUNCEY

(Copy) Buffaloe   April 8th. 1813—

Sir,

"I was in hopes that my last Letter to you by Lt. Holdup would have done away all impression on your mind relative to the circumstances that occasioned the arrest and that the meaning I would have wished to convey was to that amount— I have been lead away since the commencement of the affair with an idea that under particular circumstances an Officer had a right to refuse duty when he conceived himself insulted by his commanding Officer— I am now fully convinced that under no circumstances whatever an Officer has a right to refuse the orders of his commanding Officer.— I therefore sincerely acknowledge that I have treated you with indignity in refusing your order but be assured at the same time that it was under mistaken impressions, for never intentionally would I have offerred You an indignity for I have always thought it more honorable to acknowledge than persist in an error— under this view of the circumstances that led to my arrest—and my full <u>conviction</u>—of having acted incorrectly—and your personal knowledge of me for many years—I hope will induce you to intercede with the Honble. Secretary of the Navy in having my arrest withdrawn so that I may return to duty— In full confidence that you can have no personal animosity to me and assuring you it is my warmest wishes that the affair may be adjusted to Your perfect Satisfaction from a view of my Statement. I have the honor to Subscribe myself with high respect." Yr. Obt. Servt.

(Signed)   Sam[l] Angus

Copy, DNA, RG45, BC, 1813, Vol. 1, No. 177 (M148, Roll No. 11). This copy was sent to the secretary of the navy.

Supplies for the Lake Erie Fleet

The spring of 1813 saw considerable progress in the construction of the fleet on Lake Erie. Sailing Master Daniel Dobbins pushed forward the construction of four gunboats and two brigs according to Commodore Isaac Chauncey's instructions. Noah Brown, the New York shipbuilder selected by Chauncey to be the master shipbuilder on the lake, arrived at Erie with some of his workmen about 2 March and lost no time in beginning work. Master Commandant Oliver H. Perry arrived at Erie on 27 March, when the ship-

building was already well advanced. While construction progressed rapidly, all essential supplies—canvas, rigging, iron fittings, guns, and shot—had to be manufactured and sent from Pittsburgh or Philadelphia.[1]

1. Rosenberg, Building Perry's Fleet, *pp. 21–28.*

SAILING MASTER DANIEL DOBBINS TO COMMODORE ISAAC CHAUNCEY

Sir

I Recevd a line a few days since from you handed by Mr. Noah Brown who apears to be the man that we want at this Place in order to drive the business and I shall make it a point to do all that is in my Power to facillitate the business— Mr Brown has been here but a few days and has but a small gang (as not one of the Phila. Carpenters have arived yet and no word of them) he has gone on very fast the keels of the two brigs are laid or Ready to lay ~~the~~ and a number of the frames Made and a house built to live in (but not finished) the gun boats two of them are geting the Clamps in for the beams in the bottoms Ready for Caulking.

but notwithstanding all these Prospects a Cloud hangs over all having no Guard the boats might be burnt without any discovery I have been Proposing to get volunteers to keep watch till I hear from you which I may perhaps effect My fears arise from some of the People amongst us more than those at a distance I am very Respectfully yours,

Daniel Dobbins

Since writing the within I find that I cannot Rais volunteers to stand guard but can hire the workmen to stand which Method I mean to addopt untill I hear from you   Mr Brown joins with me in opinion both with respect to the danger and and the Mode to pursue

Daniel Dobbins

Evn the 14th March 1813

Copy, NBuHi, Daniel Dobbins Papers. Endorsed: "Copy of a letter to Commodore Chauncey Sacketts Harbor."

MASTER COMMANDANT OLIVER H. PERRY TO COMMODORE ISAAC CHAUNCEY

Copy   Erie   10th. April 1813

Sir

I have the honor to inform you, I have just now returned from Pittsburg— most of the articles, we shall want can be procured there, such as anchors, rigging &c and cambooses by sending to Phila. for a pattern to cast by, Mr. Ormsby[1] appears to be very zealous, but to insure greater dispatch I shall send Mr. Taylor[2] (actg. Sailing Master) to Pittsburg to drive every thing on with all possible celerity— The canvass must come from Phila. I have written Mr. Harrison on that subject and for such other things as cannot be had at Pittsburg—

Most of the carpenters have at length arrived <u>without</u> their tools, which will probably be here in ten days. The <u>two</u> blacksmiths from Philadelphia have arrived. Mr. Brown does not expect much from them, as one of them is almost a boy, and the other is merely a <u>striker</u> to him—the number of Carpenters, short of what was ordered from Phila. is 8, and blacksmiths 3— Many are the difficulties we have to enccounter but we <u>will</u> surmount them all—

Not a single article has yet arrived from any direction for the Vessels, and will be ten days before any of the 32 pdrs. Carronades get here. Mr. Dobbins I expect in 4 or 5 days with One 12 pr. muskets &c. &c from Buffaloe—

I wrote you on my arrival here on the subject of the defenceless situation of this Place— I of course know not whether the Enemy will make an attempt to destroy the vessels we are building, but from the importance (to them) of so doing it may confidently be expected they will, I should feel seriously alarmed if I was not sensible the government must know how we are situated here, as well as I do myself, and that troops must now be on their march for the defence—although I cannot here of any— I have commenced clearing the hill in the rear of the Brigs where we shall erect a temporary Block house, two gun boats will be launched in about a week which will be anchored with the 12 pr. on one of them off the Brigs— with the 20 officers and men, now here, and the forty I expect, and about 70 artificers, who will assist us, they will not be given up lightly, every Officer and man feels the importance of the duty in which they are now engaged, and whether it is in the exertions of preparing those vessels for immediate service, or for their defence, their country will have no cause to blush for them— With sentiments of Respect I have the honor to be Your Obd. Servt.

Signed　O. H. Perry

The Ice is broken up and in a week the navigation will be open, between this and West end of the Lake—

Copy, DNA, RG45, MC, 1813, No. 46, enclosure (M147, Roll No. 5). This copy was sent to Secretary of the Navy Jones with a cover letter dated 11 April 1813 in which Perry added, "The frames of the two Brigs have been up several days."

　1. Oliver Ormsby, a Pittsburgh merchant, was appointed navy agent for that city in February 1813.
　2. William V. Taylor, acting sailing master, served in the gunboat flotilla in Rhode Island and transferred with Oliver H. Perry to the lakes in 1813.

Arrest of Master Commandant James T. Leonard

The arrest of Master Commandant James T. Leonard offers a rare glimpse into the private life and morals of a naval officer in the years of the early republic. Leonard was an experienced and capable officer but also something of a maverick. He had been in naval service for fourteen years and had served under Commodore Thomas Truxtun in the Quasi-War with France, participating in Constellation's *night action against* La Vengeance *in 1800. Leonard subsequently served on the New Orleans Station and commanded the gunboat flotilla in New York.*

When Leonard was ordered to Sackets Harbor in December 1812, he was accompanied by a woman from New York who was his mistress. He introduced her as his wife, and she mingled freely in the polite society of officers' wives in the village of Sackets Harbor. When it was discovered they were not married, the woman was ostracized. Commodore Isaac Chauncey ordered Leonard to send the woman away, but Leonard brazenly disregarded Chauncey's demand. Chauncey had Leonard arrested on charges of disobedience of orders, neglect of duty, and dissolute and immoral practices.

Leonard repeatedly asked the secretary of the navy to intervene on his behalf, claiming that Chauncey was trying to persecute him, delaying a trial as a way to draw out his punishment.[1] While awaiting court-martial, Leonard was not allowed to serve on active duty, leave the vicinity of Sackets Harbor, or transfer to another station. Although the secretary urged Chauncey to convene a court, the commodore postponed the trial; it would be almost eight months before Leonard's case was heard. Chauncey firmly held that the reputation of the navy was tarnished by Leonard's private conduct.

1. *There are numerous letters from Leonard to the secretary of the navy about his case; for the most important, see Leonard to Jones, 23 April, 3 June, 7 July, 26 July, and 5 August 1813, all in DNA, RG45, MC, 1813, Nos. 51, 69, 82, 89, and 94 (M147, Roll No. 5); and his court-martial of 1 December 1813 in DNA, RG125, CM, Vol. 4, No. 152 (M273, Roll No. 4).*

COMMODORE ISAAC CHAUNCEY TO MASTER COMMANDANT JAMES T. LEONARD

James T. Leonard Esq.   Sacketts Harbor   13 April 1813
acg. Master Commn.
in the Navy of U. States

Sir
    You will hereby consider yourself arrested upon the following charges and specifications, to wit
Charge first—Disobedience of orders—Specification—contrary to my general orders of the 4th. of December 1812 and my Letter of instructions to you of the 1st. of February 1813—you have Slept on shore frequently between the 30th. March and this date, particularly on the Night of the 12th. April inst.—
Charge Second—Neglect of duty—Specification— first for not using your best exertions, in preparing the U.S. Ship *Madison* under your command for service— Second for leaving the Same Ship in the ice, and in an unprepared State outside the Harbor on the Night of the 12th. of April in a gale of Wind, when there was every prospect of the Ice breaking up, and which did actually break up some time during the same night and the ship drifted out in the Bay, and was only saved from total loss by extraordinary exertions of Officers and Men   Third—for not visiting your Ship untill after 10 oClock on the Morning of the 13th. April, when she had been for many hours in a very exposed & dangerous situation   Fourth— for not having the Sheet Cable bent and the Ship otherwise prepared to meet any contingency of Wind or Weather— fifth—for leaving the Ship in the afternoon of the 13th. of April, inst. after the Court martial adjourned, of which you was a Member, before She was either Secured or in a place of Safety.
Charge third—Dissolute and immoral practices—Specification—For introducing some time in December last, your Mistress, to the family of Major Samuel Brown[1] and Suffering her afterwards to pass as your Wife and in violation of

your promise to me, you are now living with the same Woman in the most public manner, whereby you neglect your duty to your Country and to your Ship, and Set a bad example to the officers generally, and the young Midshipmen in particular one of which lives in the House with you and your Mistress.

Upon the receipt of this arrest, you will deliver to Captain Smith your Sword and confine yourself to a district of four Miles Square in or about this Village untill the decision of a Court Martial can be had upon your conduct— I have the honor to be Respectfully Sir Yr Mo Ob S

Isaac Chauncey

LB Copy, MiU–C, Isaac Chauncey Letter Book.

1. Major Samuel Brown, U.S.A., deputy quartermaster general of Military District No. 9.

COMMODORE ISAAC CHAUNCEY TO SECRETARY OF THE NAVY JONES

(No. 3)   Sackett's Harbor   16th. April 1813.

Sir—

I have been under the painful necessity of arresting Captain James T. Leonard upon various charges a copy of which are enclosed— I have been led to this painful alternative at this time from a conviction upon my own mind that such a step was absolutely necessary.— It will perhaps be proper for me at this time to state to you generally the circumstances which has led to the arrest of Captain Leonard.— This gentleman arrived here some time in December last, while I was absent on my tour to the Westward— he brought with him from New York a woman of the Town which passed for his Wife— on my return to this place in January, as I passed through Utica several gentlemen of respectability waited upon me, and stated that Captain Leonard's conduct in this particular was doing the officers and service an injury— upon my arrival here I stated to Captain Leonard the impropriety of his conduct— he promised to send his Mistress back to New York which he did a few days after, but in the latter part of March she returned to this place and he now lives with her as publickly as if she was his wife— however criminal this conduct may be in itself by putting publick opinion so much at defiance—I should not have noticed it at this time if it had not led to a criminal neglect of his duty, not only by disobeying my possitive order but by leaving the Ship outside the bar in the Ice in so unprepared a state that nothing saved her from total loss but my anxiety in consequence of the severity of the gale induced me to go on board at day light and by extraordinary exertions I got the Ship in a place of safety— this is not the only neglect of Captain Leonards— I found upon a closer examination that he had neglected to station the Men or prepare the Ship in many other respects for the approaching Campaign.— An officer at this time who could be so regardless of his own reputation and that of his Country, as to neglect his duty in so important a particular as might lead to the defeat of the whole campaign is not worthy of so important a command— altho' my duties will be very much increased by Captain Leonard's conduct, yet my reputation will be preserved, for I shall now see myself that every thing is prepared and not trust to any one that might deceive me.—

I hope Sir, that you will consider that I have acted correctly in this business— and that you will replace Capn. Leonard by an officer of the same grade as soon as it can be done with convenience to the department   I have the honor to be very respectfully Sir Yr. Mo. Ob. St.

Isaac Chauncey

LS, DNA, RG45, CL, 1813, Vol. 3, No. 2 (M125, Roll No. 28).

A British Midshipman on Lake Ontario

John Johnston, a young midshipman in the Royal Navy, sailed with Sir James Yeo when the British commodore left England to take command of the naval forces on the Great Lakes. Johnston's extant letters to his mother document the point of view of a junior naval officer in Canada.[1]

Johnston was from a well-placed British family; his grandfather was the Earl De La Warr, and his uncle Lord Frederick Campbell. With promises of promotion from Lord Melville, First Lord of the Admiralty, he had signed on for service in North America. He would soon learn not only that family connections meant little in the provinces of Canada, but also that life on the Lake Ontario station could be rigorous.

1. *Ritchie and Ritchie, "Laker's Log."*

MIDSHIPMAN JOHN JOHNSTON, R.N., TO JANE JOHNSTON

H M S. *Woolwich*   April 28th. 1813—
At Sea

My dear Mother

As we are now within a few days sail of Quebeck, I shall begin and give you an account of our voyage since our departure from Plymouth, which I am sorry to say has been one of the most uncomfortable I ever heard of or can imagine. To begin with Sir Jas. who talked so smoothly in London quite altered his tone in Blue Water, particularly with the Mids, who he looks upon as a poor set of wretches sent out to be butchered for their Commissions and not worthy the name of Officers; We are not only obliged to attend particularly to our own men, but to keep our Watch as if we belong'd to her, the Ship is so lumbered we cannot by any chance get to our Chests under 3 Hours so that when we get wet on our Watch we cannot Shift ourselves by which means half of us are in the Doctors list; and I have gone into it today; for this Week we have been Sailing through immense Islands of Ice, so you may guess how intolerably cold the weather is. Sir Jas. was very angry when he heard I mess'd in the wardroom and hinted which I suspect will be the case that I should be the last Promoted, he has already made one so I am sure of not being the first as he promised Lady S. Smith, if it was not that we are going purposely to fight therefore would appear Cowardly I certainly wou'd leave him at Quebeck & return home never to go to Sea more. I am afraid my Letter will not be very consolatory, but it makes me easy to unburthen my Griefs. The scene around me is not very apt to infuse fresh Spirits in me; Ice as far as the Eye can see every thing looking Cold Bleak and Dreary. At Quebeck we shall disembark and I believe proceed to the Lakes immediately; so that for the first Month we shall almost be Froze by the cold as I believe we have 500 miles to go from Quebeck to the Lakes. I hope if you can you wou'd try & get a commission sent out to me, as perhaps now I am on a Foreign Station Lord Melville might do it. I do not write with pleasure as I know how seldom Letters go safe from a Foreign Station, but I hope you will learn the best way to direct to me, they will most likely be able to tell you at the Admiralty, though I almost fear we shall get few letters there. I forgot to tell you that I was obliged to take my things out of the Wardroom and to sleep in such a horrid place so crowded & Jam'd up in such manner that I frequently feel suffocated; the passage home from India was completely Paradise compared to it——

Quebec May 5th. We are just arrived here this morning. Everything is in the utmost confusion, the Americans have burnt some of our Ships in the Lakes; Sir Jas. is very vex'd and I believe we all march away today without Baggage or any thing but our Arms. The beginning of my Letter was written in a dull moment, but it is a true account of our Passage The Idea of so soon being alongside the <u>Yankees</u> has dispel'd those gloomy Ideas; and I am now on the *qui vive* I now more than ever feel the Want of my Sword. As we are all packing & busy I must make a finish. I now take my leave, and may Heaven bless you all my dearest Mother my very kindest & most Affectionate Love to Grandmama & Fredk. and all my good Relations so adieu And Believe me Ever Your Dutiful & Affectionate Son

<u>John Johnston</u>

ALS, Hertfordshire County Archives, #16292. Addressed to Mrs. Johnston, Hampton Court Palace, Kingston on Thames, Middlesex.

Midshipman John Johnston, R.N., to Jane Johnston

Kingston June 23d. 1813—

My dear Mother

I have now set down with the intention of writing you an account of our Adventures since our departure from Quebec; which from our continual bustle & being at Sea I have not had time before to do. I wrote you about half a dozen Lines the other day just to let you Know I was in the Land of the Living, and one from Quebec which I hope & suppose you have recd. before now. We all left Quebec the same day we arrived there & made the best of our way to Montreal (200 Miles) which was very pleasant the weather being very fine & both sides of the River Cultivated & Villages every 4 or 5 Miles. From Montreal we had a very Fatiguing Journey to Kingston (200 Miles) sometimes going by Land & sometimes by Boats frequently having to track them over Tremendous Rapids; at last we arrived at Kingston where we were encamped, and began fitting out the Ships we found lying here; our Force consists of Two 20 Gun Ships a Brig & 2 Schooners, we keep at Sea or rather on the Lake in General and anoy the American Coast as much as possible, the American Naval Force is stronger than ours, and they are only waiting for one of the Ships which is not quite ready, to Engage us, as they Know as well as ourselves that Fate of upper Cannada depends on our being the Conquerors or the Conquered, Both Fleets are anxiously waiting the event. The American Fleet lay in Sackets Harbour about 45 Miles from Kingston, which place we attacked 3 Weeks ago, the reason was this, their Fleet went away with Soldiers to take Fort George at the Head of Lake, we immediately Embarked 900 Soldiers and attacked Sackets intending to burn the Ship which was on the Stocks and all the Publick Stores, but they were to Strong for us. We landed at day Break under a most destructive fire of Cannon & Musquetry, the Country being very woody their Riflemen picked us off without being Hurt or perceived, the Action lasted 4 Hours and I suppose a Hotter never was for the time it lasted, We burnt their Stores but not the Ship, I commanded a Gun Boat, but my boat being soon filled with Killed & Wounded and I myself wounded in the leg the Boat being no longer able to act I landed with & fought with the Soldiers and luckily escaped any further damage. My wound is now almost well and I can walk quite well. If you get a Map of Cannada you will then be better able to understand my Letters and to judge of the Situation of the different places. There is no promotion going on as Sir John Warren sent officers, who arrived here before us, to fill up the vacancies. I am heartily tired of this Lake cruizing and am very much afraid I shall not be able to get Home before next summer as in the Winter all the places are Froze up, and then it will be very difficult as the next Campaign will begin. Promotion is quite out of the case.[1] Adieu and believe me ever Your Dutiful & Affectionate Son

John Johnston

I shall come home if Possible immediately after the Action   I hope you are all well   Give my Duty & Love to Grandmama and to Fredk. when you write. I am on board one of the 20 Gun Ships Commanded by Capt. Mulcaster, who I like very much & I believe he does me. We Labor under every disadvantage things excessively dear and a great loss upon Bills. I have spent a great deal coming up from Quebec, so that I shall have to draw soon & be a looser by my Bills—

ALS, Hertfordshire County Archives, #16294. Addressed to "Mrs. Johnston, Hampton Court Palace, Kingston upon Thames, Middx."

1. Johnston was in fact promoted to the rank of acting lieutenant on 12 July 1813 in recognition of his "conspicuous valor" in the attack on Sackets Harbor. See Yeo to Johnston, 12 July 1813, Hertfordshire County Archives, #16373. He was later mortally wounded in the British expedition against Algiers under Admiral Lord Viscount Exmouth on 27 August 1816 and died on 3 October 1816.

First Attack on York, Upper Canada, 27 April 1813

The ice that confined the American ships to their winter stations on Lake Ontario finally broke up on the night of 18 April, giving the American commanders the opportunity to make their first move against the British fleet. Their target was York, the provincial capital of Upper Canada. Several British vessels were undergoing repairs there, and the town was less well guarded than was Kingston.

Commodore Isaac Chauncey's fleet, consisting of fourteen sail, first attempted the assault on 23 April, but a gale forced them back to port. A few days later, this naval contingent, with a force of 1,700 army troops under the command of Major General Henry

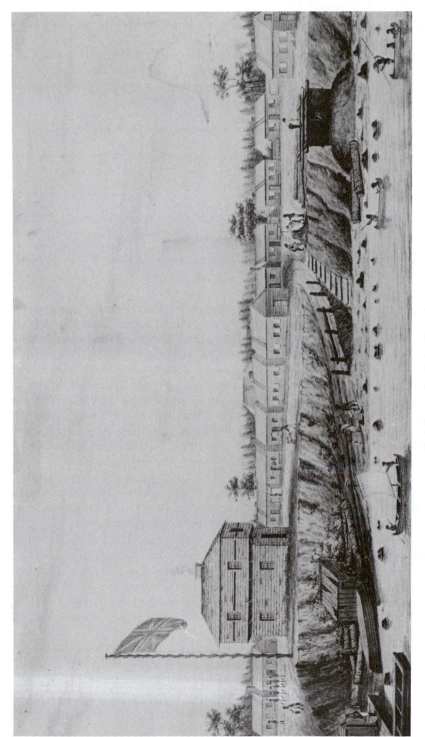

York Barracks, Lake Ontario

Dearborn and led by Brigadier General Zebulon Montgomery Pike,[1] succeeded in captur-
ing the town.

The Americans seized or destroyed valuable stores and supplies, part of which were in-
tended for the British fleet then building on Lake Erie. The town was looted and several
government buildings burned by the Americans, acts that would be recalled in August
1814 when the British burned Washington, D.C., in retaliation.[2]

1. *Zebulon Montgomery Pike, 15th Regiment U.S. Infantry, was commissioned brigadier general on 12*
March 1813.

2. *On the Battle of York, see Dudley, "Chauncey and Joint Operations," pp. 142–43; Humphries, "Capture of*
York"; and Hickey, War of 1812, pp. 129–30.

COMMODORE ISAAC CHAUNCEY TO SECRETARY OF THE NAVY JONES

No. 11—   U.S. Ship *Madison*, Sacketts Harbor   24 April 1813

Sir

At the urgent request of Major Genl. Dearborn, (but contrary to my own judgement) I got under way yesterday with the whole Squadron, with the intention of
proceeding upon our contemplated enterprize— The Wind was from the S.S.E and
the appearance of a Storm— we stretched out towards the Lake as far as Stony
point— at about 2 P.M—it blew heavy in Squalls with heavy rain and thick
weather— not more than one half of the Troops could get below at one time—
those in the Small vessels particularly were very uncomfortable and the Vessels
themselves (being very deep) were not in a Situation to encounter a gale of Wind
upon the open Lake which there was every appearance of— these circumstances together with having Sprung my Main Top Sail Yard and the *Hamilton* having lost her
fore gaft induced me to bear up for this Harbor where we arrived about Sun down
and it was fortunate we did so, for it blew very heavy last night attended with rain. I
am convinced that if we had kept the lake we should have lost some of our small
vessels, with perhaps their Crews, at any rate the fleet would have been seperated
which might have been attended with disastrous consequences.—

I am now completely ready and will proceed as soon as I think the wind and
weather is such as I ought to risk this Fleet upon the Lake situated as it is.—

I am particularly anxious to get the Troops to the place of their destination as
soon as possible for crowded as they are now on board of the different vessels,
they as well as my own Men, will very Soon become Sickly— We have on board of
the *Madison* about 600 Souls and many of the small vessels even more crowded
than ourselves.—

I shall use every exertion to carry your instructions into complete execution
and shall co-operate with the Army with zeal— It will be my pride so to conduct
the <u>Naval</u> part of the expedition as to merit your approbation. I have the honor
to be very respectfully Sir yr. mo. ob. st.

                                                        Isaac Chauncey

LS, DNA, RG45, CL, 1813, Vol. 3, No. 51 (M125, Roll No. 28).

COMMODORE ISAAC CHAUNCEY TO SECRETARY OF THE NAVY JONES

(Dupt.)   U.S. Ship *Madison* at Anchor
No. 12   off York.   8 o'clock P.M.   27 April 1813

Sir

I have the satisfaction to inform you that the American Flag is flying upon the Fort at York.

The Town capitulated this afternoon at 4 O'Clock.

Br. Gen. Pike was killed.—

I have the honor to be very respectfully Sir Yr. Mo. Ob. St.

Isaac Chauncey

LS, DNA, RG45, CL., 1813, Vol. 3, No. 56 (M125, Roll No. 28).

COMMODORE ISAAC CHAUNCEY TO SECRETARY OF THE NAVY JONES

(No. 13)   U.S. Ship *Madison*
               at Anchor off York   28 April 1813

Sir/

Agreeably to your instructions and ~~previous~~ arrangements made with Major General Dearborn—I took on board of the Squadron under my command the General and Suite and about 1700 Troops and left Sacketts Harbor on the 25th. inst. for this place— we arrived here yesterday Morning and took a position about one Mile to the South and Westward of the Enemy's principal Fort and as near the Shore as we could with Safety to the Vessels— the place fixed upon by the Major General and myself for landing the Troops was the scite of the old French Fort Taranto—

The debarkation commenced about 8 o'clock A.M. and was completed about 10— the Wind blowing heavy from the Eastward the boats fell to leeward of the position fixed upon and were in consequence exposed to a galling fire from the Enemy, who had taken a position in a thick wood near where the first Troops landed—however the cool intrepidity of the Officers and Men overcame every obstacle— their attack upon the Enemy was so vigorous that he fled in every direction leaving a great many of his killed and wounded upon the field— as soon as the Troops were landed I directed the Schooners to take a position near the Forts in order that the attack upon them by the Army and Navy might be simultaneous— the Schooners were obliged to beat up to their position which they did in very handsome order under a very heavy fire from the Enemy's Batteries and took a position within about Six hundred yards of their principal fort and opened a heavy cannonade upon the Enemy which did great execution and very much contributed to their final destruction. The Troops as soon as landed was formed under the immediate orders of Br. Genl. Pike who led in a most gallant manner the attack upon the Forts and after having carried two redoubts in their approach to the principal work (the enemy having previously laid a train) blew up his Magazine which in its effects upon our Troops was dreadful having killed and wounded a great many and amongst the former the ever to be lamented Brigadier General Pike who fell at the head of his column by a contusion received by a heavy Stone from the Magazine— his death at this time is much to be regretted, as he had the perfect confidence of the Major General—and his known activity zeal and experience makes his loss a national one.—

In consequence of the fall of General Pike, the command of the Troops devolved for a time upon Col. Pierce [1] who soon after took possession of the Town— at about 2 P.M. the American Flag was Substituted for the British and at about 4 our Troops were in quiet possession of the Town— as soon as General Dearborn learn'd of the situation of General Pike he landed and assumed the command. I have the honor of inclosing a copy of the capitulation which was entered into, and approved by General Dearborn and myself by the next opportunity

The Enemy set fire to some of his principal Stores, containing large quantities of Naval and Military Stores, as well as a large Ship upon the Stocks,[2] nearly finished— the only vessel found here is the *Duke of Glouster* undergoing repairs— the *Prince Regent* left here on the 24th. for Kingston.— We have not yet had a return made of the Naval and Military Stores, consequently can form no correct idea of the quantity, but have made arrangements to have all taken on board that we can receive the rest will be destroyed.—

I have to regret the death of Midshipmen Thompson and Hatfield [3] and several Seamen killed— the exact number I do not know as the returns from the different vessels have not yet been received.

From the judicious arrangements made by General Dearborn I presume that the Public Stores will be disposed of, so that the Troops will be ready to re-embark tomorrow and proceed to execute other objects of the expedition the first fair Wind. I cannot speak in too much praise of the cool intrepidity of the officers and Men generally under my command, and I feel myself particularly indebted to the Officers Commanding Vessels for their zeal in seconding all my views. I have the honor to be very respectfully Sir yr. ob. st.

Isaac Chauncey

LS, DNA, RG45, CL, 1813, Vol. 3, No. 63 (M125, Roll No. 28).

1. Colonel Cromwell Pearce, 16th U.S. Infantry.
2. *Sir Issac Brock* was built at York for the Provincial Marine and destroyed 27 April 1813.
3. Benjamin Thompson, warranted midshipman 1 December 1804; John Hatfield, warranted midshipman 18 June 1812.

MAJOR GENERAL HENRY DEARBORN, U.S.A., TO SECRETARY OF WAR JOHN ARMSTRONG

Honorable John Armstrong   Head quarters—York—Upper
Secretary of War   Canada—April 28th. 1813.

Sir,

After a detention of some days by adverse winds we arrived here yesterday morning and at 8 o'clock commenced landing our troops about three miles westward of the Town and one and an half from the Enemy's works; the wind was high and in an unfavorable direction for our boats, which prevented the Troops landing at a clear field (the ancient site of the french fort Terento) The unfavorable wind prevented as many of the armed vessels from taking such positions as would as effectually cover our landing as they otherwise would have done: but every thing that could be done was effected. Our Riflemen under Major Forsyth first landed under a heavy fire from Indians & other troops.— General Sheaffe[1] commanded in person; he had collected his whole force in the woods near where the wind obliged our troops to Land, consisting of about 700 regulars & militia and one hundred Indians. Majr. Forsyth was supported as promptly as possible with other troops; but the contest was sharp and severe for near half an hour:— the Enemy were repulsed by a far less number than their own, and as soon as General Pike landed with seven or eight hundred men, and the remainder of the troops were pushing for the shore the Enemy retreated to their works, and as soon as the whole of the Troops had landed and formed on the clear ground intended for the first landing, they advanced thro' a thick wood to the open ground near the Enemy's works, and after carrying one battery by assault, were moving on in collumns towards the main works, when the head of the collumns was within about sixty rods of the Enemy a tremenduous explosion occurred from a large magazine prepared for the purpose, which discharged such immense quantities of stone as to produce a most unfortunate effect on our troops;— I have not yet been able to collect the returns of our killed and wounded, but our loss by the explosion must I fear exceed one hundred— and among them I have to lament the loss of the brave and excellent Officer Brigr. Genl. Pike, who received such a contusion from a large stone, as terminated his valuable life within a few hours:—his loss will be severely felt. Previous to the explosion the Enemy had retired into the Town, excepting a party of regular troops which did not retire, early enough to avoid the shock; it is said that upwards of forty of them were destroyed. General Sheaffe moved off with the regular troops and left directions with the commanding officer of the Militia to make the best terms he could; in the mean time all further resistance on the part of the Enemy ceased, and the outlines of a capitulation were agreed on. As soon as I was informed of Genl. Pike being wounded, I went on shore. I had been induced to confide the immediate command of the Troops in action to Genl. Pike, from a conviction that he fully expected it, and would be much mortified at being deprived of the honour, which he highly appreciated.— Every movement was under my view—our Troops behaved with great firmness, and deserve much applause, especially those who were first engaged, under circumstances that would have tried the firmness of veterans.— Our loss in the action in the morning and in carrying the first battery, was not great, probably about fifty Killed and wounded, among them were a full proportion of officers and altho' the Enemy had a decided advantage in point of numbers and position, at the commencement, their loss was greater than ours, particularly in officers.—

It was with the greatest exertion that the small vessels of the fleet could work into the harbour against a gale of wind directly ahead;—but as soon as they got in contact with the batteries a tremenduous cannonade commenced from 24 & 32 pounders and was kept up without intermission under a heavy fire from two batteries until the Enemy's batteries were carried, or blown up by the explosion, which undoubtedly had a powerfull effect on the Enemy.— I am under the greatest obligations to Commodore Chauncey for his able and indefatigable exertions in every possible manner that could give facility and effect to the expedition— he is equally estimable for deliberate sound judgement, bravery and industry.— The Government could not have made a more fortunate selection for the important trust he holds.— unfortunately the Enemy's armed ship the "*Prince Regent*" left this place for Kingston four days before we arrived.— A large ship on the stocks and nearly planked up, with a large store of naval stores, were set on fire by the Enemy soon after the explosion of the magazine.— there are no vessels fit for use in the harbour, a considerable quantity of Military stores and provisions remained.— We shall not possess the means of transporting the prisoners from this place and must of course leave them on parole.— I hope we shall so far complete the necessary measures at this place in the course of this day as to be able to sail to morrow for Niagara—by which route I send this by a small vessel with notice to Genl. Lewis[2] of our approach. I am Sir your Obedt. Servt.

H. Dearborn

ALS, DNA, RG107, Letters Received by the Secretary of War, Registered Series, D–125(7) (M221, Roll No. 52).

1. Major General Sir Roger Hale Sheaffe, British Army, commander in chief and administrator of Upper Canada.
2. Morgan Lewis, commander of U.S. troops on the Niagara frontier; he was appointed major general 2 March 1813.

COMMODORE ISAAC CHAUNCEY TO SECRETARY OF THE NAVY JONES

No. 15.

U.S. Ship Madison
at Anchor off York.   7th May, 1813

Sir,

When I had the honor of addressing you on the 28th. Ulto, I expected to have dated my next letter in an other part of the Enemy's Territory—but the Winds and Weather have been against us— We made arrangements for reimbarking the Troops as soon as the public stores found here could be got off or destroyed and on Saturday the 1st. inst. the whole of the Troops were reimbarked in good order with an intention of sailing the next morning, for the purpose of executing the remaining part of your instructions.— The wind which had been moderate, from the Eastward, increased to a gale, accompanied with rain and has continued to blow so very heavy that we have been riding ever since with two anchors ahead and lower Yards and Top Gallant Masts down and there is every appearance of its continuing— this is particularly unfortunate as it gives the Enemy an opportunity to be better prepared to meet us—and our own Troops are becoming Sickley, crowded as they are on board of the small vessels, where not more than one half can get below at one time— they are not only exposed to the rain, but the Sea makes a fair breack over them.

Immediately after the action of the 27th. Ulto. I put as many wounded on board of the *Asp*,[1] and *Gold Hunter*[2] as they could carry and ordered them to Sacketts Harbor, but the Easterly Winds prevailing and blowing so heavy that they could not keep the Lake— they returned to this anchorage on the 2d. inst.— I have since succeeded in landing the wounded from those two vessels, as well as those from the *Lady of the Lake*[3] at Niagara— We still have a number of sick and wounded on board of the Fleet which I shall land as soon as the Weather moderates— I shall leave here the first moment, that the weather moderates so as to make it proper for the small vessels to be upon the Lake—

The stores found at this place are considerable but it will be impossible for me to get a return untill they are landed— each vessel had orders to take on board as much as they could carry, and we succeeded in getting the *Glouster* off and caulking her, so as to load her with stores also— We found at this place 28 Cannon of different calibre, from 32 to 6 pounders a number of Muskets large quantities of fixed ammunition—shot—shells and munitions of War of various kinds a great deal of which was put up in boxes and marked for Niagara and Malden— the ship building at this place was intended to mount 30 Guns and was to be launched in about 4 weeks— The *Glouster* was undergoing a thorough repair and intended to mount 16 Guns— We found a small schooner here, which was claimed by an individual— General Dearborn thought it best to pay for, and burn her— We also destroyed or brought off many boats which had been prepared for the transportation of Troops, Stores, &c. the store which the Enemy burned was filled with Cables, Cordage, Canvass, Tools and Stores of every kind for the use of this Lake and Lake Erie, supposed to be worth $500,000— the loss of stores at this place will be an irreparable one to the Enemy, for independent of the difficulty of transportation, the articles cannot be replaced in this Country— the provisions and Cloathing also taken and destroyed will be a serious loss to him—in fact I believe that he has received a blow, that he cannot recover and if we succeed in our next enterprize (which I see no reason to doubt) we may consider the upper Province as conquered—however to put nothing at hazard I directed Mr. Eckford to take 30 Carpenters from Sacketts Harbor and proceed in the *Lady of the Lake* to Niagara where he has been landed and gone to Black Rock to put the vessels laying at that place in a perfect state of repair, ready to leave the River for <u>Presque Isle</u> the moment that we are in possession of the opposite Shore— I have no doubt but that he will have the vessels ready by the end of this month. I have the honor to be Very respectfully Sir Yr. Mo. Ob. St.

Isaac Chauncey

LS, DNA, RG45, CL, 1813, Vol. 3, No. 101 (M125, Roll No. 28).

1. The schooner *Asp* was formerly the Canadian merchantman *Elizabeth*, captured by *Growler* in November 1812 and purchased by the United States as a prize vessel in February 1813.

2. The schooner *Gold Hunter* has not been identified; she was convoyed to Sackets Harbor following the Battle of York, but was not owned by the Navy Department.

3. The U.S. schooner *Lady of the Lake* was launched at Sackets Harbor on 5 April 1813.

The British Forces in the Aftermath of the York Attack

The British lost two vessels in the American attack on York on 27 April 1813. Sir Isaac Brock *(under construction) was burned to keep her from falling into American hands;* Duke of Gloucester, *built in 1807 for the Provincial Marine, was captured but was too rotten ever to see active service as an American warship. Fortunately for the British,* Prince Regent, *a twelve-gun schooner, had been moved to Kingston a few days before the attack.*

The need for a reorganization of the British marine establishment on Lake Ontario be-
came even more clear after the attack on York. Lieutenant Robert Heriot Barclay [1] *along*
with several officers from Admiral Sir John B. Warren's squadron had arrived at
Kingston on 5 May to take command until Sir James Lucas Yeo arrived from England.

Sir Roger Hale Sheaffe, who had led the hasty retreat from York, offered a weak expla-
nation for his defense of the town, but the Canadians had lost confidence in their com-
mander. He was recalled as commander in chief a few months later.

1. *Barclay was later sent to Amherstburg, Upper Canada, to command the fleet on Lake Erie.*

CAPTAIN ALEXANDER GRAY, BRITISH ARMY, TO
MAJOR GENERAL SIR ROGER HALE SHEAFFE, BRITISH ARMY

Kingston Dock Yard
4th May 1813

Sir/

I have the honor to report the present state of our Marine force at this Post.

					Total
1 *Royal George* ---------	20–32 pr.	Carronades	2 long 9 prs.------	22.---
2 *Moira* ---------------	10–10	------Do.------	4 do.--do. --------	14 ---
3 *Prince Regent* ---------	10–12	------Do.------	2 do.--6 prs.------	12.---

The above are completely equipped and ready for Sea.

4 *Sir George Prevost* pierced for 24 Guns now lying along side the Wharf taking in her Masts will be ready for her Guns and Crew in about three weeks.

5 The Brig now on the Stocks[1] is intended to carry 16 Guns (24 or 32 pr. Carronades) This vessel is seventy feet Keel, and twenty four feet Beam, and will be ready for sea in about five weeks or probably sooner if our stores arrive from below.

In reporting upon the state of the Marine of Lake Ontario, I beg leave to suggest the Propriety of laying down a vessel of a large class, upon the Slip, from whence the *Sir George Prevost* was launched, to replace the *Sir Isaac Brock* recently destroyed. This measure may easily be carried into effect, as I have engaged (provisionally) as much Timber as will effect this object, and the Shipwrights on their way from York will furnish an abundant supply of workmen.

There is every reason to suppose that a vessel of this Description may be built in four or five weeks. In short something must be done to recover the loss we have sustained at York, and this appears to me to be the only mode of recovering our Naval ascendancy.

I am far from thinking the cause lost, as we have, still entire, the principal part of our Naval force, and with the addition of the *Sir George Prevost,* and the Brig on the Stocks, I have every reason to believe we shall be enabled to cope with the Enemy. It is however advisable to put this matter past a doubt by persevering in our exertions in the Dock Yard.

If this measure meets your approbation, the Keel of the new ship may be laid the instant the Shipwrights from York, arrive. I have the honor to be, Sir, your most obedient humble servant

(signed) A Gray
Actg. Dy. Q Mr. Genl.
True Copy
Robert R. Lossing ADC

Copy, CaOOA, British Military and Naval Records, RG8, I, "C" Ser., Vol. 678, pp. 232–33.

1. H.M. brig *Lord Melville* was laid down as a schooner and altered to a brig during construction; she was launched in July 1813.

MAJOR GENERAL SIR ROGER HALE SHEAFFE, BRITISH ARMY, TO GOVERNOR-GENERAL SIR GEORGE PREVOST

Kingston 5th. May 1813.

Sir,

I did myself the honour of writing to Your Excellency on my route from York to communicate the mortifying intelligence that the Enemy had obtained possession of that place on the 27th of April, and I shall now enter into a fuller detail, than I was enabled to do at the date of that letter.

In the evening of the 26th of April I received information that many Vessels had been seen from the Highlands to the eastward of York, soon after daylight the next morning the Enemy's Vessels were discovered lying to not far from the shore of the peninsula in front of the town; they soon afterwards, made sail with a fresh breeze from the eastward, led by the Ship lately built at Sackett's harbour, and anchored off the point where the french fort formerly stood; many boats full of troops were soon discerned assembling near the Commodore's Ship, apparently with an intention of effecting a landing on the ground off which he was anchored; our troops were ordered into the Ravine in the rear of the Government Garden and fields; Major Givins and the Indians with him were sent forward through the wood to oppose the landing of the Enemy—the Company of Glengary Light Infantry was directed to support them, and the Militia not having arrived at the Ravine, The Grenadiers of the King's Regiment and the small portion of the Royal Newfoundland Fencibles belonging to the Garrison of York were moved on, led by Lt. Colonel Heathcote of that corps commanding the [?] this movement was directed to be made within the [?] parallel to the Lake side, and only so far from it, as not to be discovered by the Enemy's Vessels, several of which were not at a great distance from the shore: Captain Eustace's company of the King's Regiment, and some Militia that were quartered at the east end of the town, and had been left there during the night, lest the Enemy might make some attempt on that flank, were ordered, with the exception of a small party of the Militia, to join these troops—which was soon effected: while these operations were going on Major General Shaw Adjutant General of Militia led a portion of the Militia on a road at the back of the wood to watch our rear, and to act according to circumstances; by some mistake he led the Glengary Company ~~was drawn~~ away from the direction assigned to it, to accompany this detachment, so that it came late into action, instead of being near the Indians at its commencement; the movement of the other troops was retarded by the difficulty of the wood, while the Enemy being aided by the wind, rapidly gained the shore under cover of a fire from the Commodore's ship and other vessels, and landed in spite of a spirited opposition from Major Givens and his small band of Indians; the Enemy was shortly afterwards encountered by our handful of troops, Captain McNeal of the King's Regiment was early killed while gallantly leading his Company which suffered severely: the troops fell back, I succeeded in rallying them several times, and a detachment of the King's with some Militia, whom I had placed near the edge of the wood to protect our left flank repulsed a column of the Enemy which was advancing along the bank at the Lake side: but our troops could not maintain the contest against the greatly superior and increasing numbers of the Enemy— they retired under cover of our batteries, which were engaged with some of their Vessels, that had begun to beat up towards the harbour, when their troops landed, occasionally firing, and had anchored a short distance to the Westward of the line from the Barracks to Gibraltar Point; from that situation they kept up a heavy fire on our batteries, on the Block house and Barracks, and on the communications between them, some of their Guns being thirty two pounders; to return their fire, we had two complete twelve pounders, and two old condemned guns without trunnions (—eighteen— pounders) which, after being proved, had been stocked and mounted under the direction of Lieut. Ingouville of the Royal Newfoundland Regiment whom I had appointed Assistant Engineer; a twelve pounder of the same description was added during the engagement; with these defective means the Enemy was kept at bay for some time, when, by some unfortunate accident, the travelling Magazine at the Western battery blew up, and killed and wounded a considerable number of Men; many of them belonging to the Grenadier company of the King's Regiment, the battery was crippled, the platform being torn up, and one of the eighteen pounders overturned: the magazine was replaced and the battery restored to some order, but it was evident that our numbers and means of defence were inadequate to the task of maintaining possession of York against the vast superiority of force brought against it, though providentially little mischief had hitherto been done by the long continued cannonade of the Enemy, except to some of the buildings: the troops were withdrawn towards the town, and the grand Magazine was at the same time blown up, the Enemy was so near to it, that he sustained great loss, and was, for a time, driven back by the explosion; some of our own troops were not beyond the reach of fragments of the stone, though they escaped with very little injury; Captain Loring my Aide de Camp received a severe contusion, and the horse he rode was killed.

The troops were halted at a ravine not far to the westward of the Shipyard, I there consulted with the superior Officers, and it being too apparent that a further opposition would but render the result more disastrous, some of the Enemy's Vessels indicating an intention to move up the harbour in order to cooperate with their land forces, I ordered the troops of the line to retreat on the road to Kingston, which was effected without any annoyance from the Enemy; when we had proceeded some miles we met the Light company of the King's Regiment on its march for Fort George, I had sent an express the preceding evening to hasten its movement, but it was at too great a distance to be able to join us at York.

The Ship on the Stocks and the Naval stores were destroyed to prevent the Enemy from getting possession of them, an attempt to set fire to the *Gloucester*, that was fitting out for purposes of transport, proved abortive; she was aground a mere hulk, her repairs not being half finished: I have been informed that the Enemy succeeded in getting her off, and putting her into a state to be towed away, a number of Shipwrights having arrived from Sackett's harbour with the expectation of employing them in a similar task on our New Ship.

The accounts of the number of the Enemy landed vary from eighteen hundred and ninety to three thousand; our force consisted of a Bombardier and twelve Gunners of the Royal Artillery to assist whom Men were drawn from other Corps, two Companies of the 8th or King's Regiment, one of them, the Grenadier, being on its route for Fort George, about a Company in number, of the Royal Newfoundland regiment, and one of the Glengary Light Infantry, and about three hundred Militia and Dock Yard Men; the quality of some of these troops was of so superior a description, and their general disposition so good, that, under less unfavourable circumstances, we might have repulsed the Enemy in spite of his numbers, or have made him pay very dearly for success; as it was, according to the reports that have reached me, his loss was much greater than ours, a return of which I have the honour of transmitting, except of that of the Militia, of which a return has not yet been received; but I believe it to have been inconsiderable: Donald McLean Esqr. Clerk of the House of Assembly gallantly volunteered his Services with a musket, and was killed.

Captain Jarvis of the Incorporated Militia, a meritorious Officer, who had a share in the successes at Detroit and Queenston, had been sent with a party of Militia in three batteaux for the Militia clothing, which had been left on the road from Kingston, he came to me during the action to report his arrival, and soon afterwards he was severely wounded; a few of the Indians (Missasagus & Chipeways) were killed and wounded, among the latter were two Chiefs.

Thinking it highly probable that the Enemy would pay, an early visit to York, I had remained there long beyond the period I had originally assigned for my departure to Fort George, in order to expedite the preparations which the means in my power enabled me to make for the defence of the place; Your Excellency knows that I had intended to place Colonel Myers, Acting Quarter Master General, in the command there, at least for a time; I afterwards learnt that Colonel Young was in movement towards me with the 8th or Kings Regt., I then decided to give him the command, to avoid the inconvenience of seperating the head of a department from me, and being informed that he was to move up by himself as speedily as possible, I was for some time in daily expectation of seeing him; at length, having reason to believe that he was to accompany one of the divisions of his Regiment, I wrote to him both by the land and by the water route to come to me without delay; about the 25th of April I received certain intelligence, of what had been before rumoured, that he was detained at Kingston by a severe illness, and on the 26th I learnt that Colonel Myers was to leave Fort George that day for York; I therefore determined to wait for his arrival, and to leave him in the command until Colonel Young might be in a state to relieve him; it was in the evening of the same day that I heard of the approach of the Enemy: I have thought it proper to enter into this explanation, as Your Excellency may have expected that I had returned to Fort George before the period at which the attack was made on York. I propose remaining here until I shall have received Your Excellency's commands. I have the honour to be, With great respect, Your Excellency's Most obedient humble servant,

R H Sheaffe
M Genl. &c. &c.

LS, CaOOA, British Military and Naval Records, RG8, I, "C" Ser., Vol. 695A, pp. 195–206.

LIEUTENANT ROBERT H. BARCLAY, R.N., TO
NOAH FREER, BRITISH MILITARY SECRETARY

(Duplicate)   H.M.S. *Wolf* Kingston   Lake Ontario
                                                      May 9th. 1813—

Sir/

I had the honor of receiving His Excellency's letter dated the 26th. of April, and am happy to say that all the Naval force, with the Exception of the *Glouces-ter*, is now in Kingston, and that the Ship formerly named the "*Sir George Prevost*" now by his Excellency's desire named the "*Wolf*" was launched without any accident on the 27th. of April, and is now in a considerable state of forwardness.

You will be pleased to assure His Excellency that no exertion on my part, or on that of the other Naval Officers shall be wanting, to put in force his wishes of having His Majesty's Squadron on the Lake equal to going out, and utterly destroying that of the Enemy—

I enclose lists of Stores &c which are required to supply the immediate wants of the Squadron, and have to beg His Excellency will be pleased to cause them to be sent up with all convenient despatch, as they will much accelerate the equipment of it, particularly the Cables, Cabouses, Pitch and tar; of these four articles we are totally destitute, and although all the requisition is highly requisite, if there in an opertunity of procuring these before the rest, it would be adviseable to do so—

In the Royal Navy, the sea men are allowed Butter, and cheese, or in cases where these are not to be obtained Cocoa, and Sugar; I perceive that neither is allowed in the Provincial Marine— I beg leave to suggest to His Excy. the propriety of sending up from Quebec a sufficient supply of these provisions to be ready to issue to the crews when they arrive, as part of their accustomed Rations—

As at the Capture of York the Enemy deprived us of the finest vessel on the establishment—I propose to His Excy. to lay down a ship here of the same force— The Shipwrights from York furnish us with men, and Capt: Gray has with the greatest promptitude provided a sufficient quantity of wood, (provisionally) to carry the project into execution, should it be approved of—

I have taken on myself, with the concurrence of Sir Roger H. Sheaffe to order Six Gun boats to be laid down, capable of carrying a long 24, or 18 pounder, as the guns can be procured. I hope they will be ready in time to be useful, and that His Excy. will approve of the measure—

The state in which I found the executive part of the Dock Yard reflects the highest credit on Capt: Gray—but it will require a great change in the System to prevent the great abuse of public Stores; which shall be adopted as soon as possible; He retains his situation as Commissioner and I have no doubt, that every thing will be amply provided for by him

The Ships are I think as fine vessels of their kind as I have ever seen. The *Moira* is small, it is true, but she is by no means so despicable as was represented— The *Regent* is a fine vessel for a despatch boat, but I do not think her capable of much severe active service—

The Provincial Officers appear to feel the loss of their commands more sensibly than was expected, and with the exception of two or three, will, I think apply for retirement or any other situation they may be judged fit for— Capt: Earl [1] would accept the post of Master Attendant of this arsenal, and in the event of

Lieut. Platt[2] preffering active service, I should think him a very fit person for it— I can easily feel for Capt: Earl, but as to the rest who have been placed in their situations from so low a sphere, I think it requires his Excellency's consideration what remuneration they deserve, if any, on their retirement from active service at this time when their local knowledge is so much wanted—

I enclose also a list of the distribution of officers for His Excellency's information those of the Provincial Marine therein mentioned told me that they would serve with pleasure, if their <u>local</u> rank and pay was continued, <u>subordinate</u> to the officers of the Royal Navy; but since that they have, I suspect, been tampered with, and I understand wish to rank with us according to the dates of their Commissions which is totally inadmissable—

Tobacco is another great essential to the comforts of a seaman, the want of it would be seriously felt, and there is none here— I think it might be sent up with the cocoa and sugar; I know that a seaman would forego almost any comfort rather than his tobacco. They are accustomed to have it provided with the slop cloathing and may of course expect it here.

As I understand that the Ships on the Lakes are intended to be put on the list of the Navy; would it not be better to alter the name of the "*Royal George*" as there already appears one bearing the same on the Navy List—not that I think it of any great consequence, I merely mention that it is so—

As I am not aware of what slop clothing may come from Halifax I shall only state in a general manner what will be necessary to begin with—

Captain Sampson[3] was put in arrest by Captain Gray, and Mr. Smith[4] from the *Royal George* was put in Command of the *Moira* instead of him— When Captain Finnis[5] joined Mr. Smith returned to his ship again, and Lt. Sampson is out of Employment I shall enquire into his case and make a report to you for his Excellency's information   I have the Honor to be Sir Your most obdt. & Humble Servant

R. H. Barclay   Comr. & Senior Officer

LS, CaOOA, British Military and Naval Records, RG8, I, "C" Ser., Vol. 729, pp. 183–88. Duplicate copy sent. Attached was a two-page list of ships' stores and shipbuilding supplies, "Required to Complete the Fitting of His Majesty's Ships at Kingston," signed by Barclay and dated 9 May 1813.

1. First Lieutenant Hugh Earle, Provincial Marine.
2. A Lieutenant Platt was not found in the records of the Provincial Marine.
3. First Lieutenant Theophilus Sampson, Provincial Marine.
4. Second Lieutenant George Smith, Provincial Marine.
5. Lieutenant Robert A. Finnis, R.N.

The American Fleet on Lake Champlain

Progress in shipbuilding on Lake Champlain had proceeded slowly during the winter of 1812–13. In February fifteen ship carpenters arrived from New York, and in March naval ordnance was shipped to Whitehall. Lieutenant Thomas Macdonough's three largest vessels, the sloops President, Eagle *(formerly* Bulldog*), and* Growler *(formerly* Hunter*), were overhauled to carry more guns. By May Macdonough had moved the fleet* *from its station at Burlington, Vermont, to Plattsburg, New York, which would be the center of military operations during the active season of the year. Macdonough still waited for a reinforcement of sailors to man his fleet adequately.*[1]

1. *Everest,* War of 1812, *pp. 92–93, 108.*

LIEUTENANT THOMAS MACDONOUGH TO SECRETARY OF THE NAVY JONES

U.S. Cutter *President*
Plattsburgh   May 1st. 1813—

Sir

I have the honor to inform you of the arrival at this place of the vessels under my command on Lake Champlain, and of their being ready for service with the exception of the remainder of the men from New York and the mounting of the carronades which we are now employed about   I have received the Powder shot &c which you directed to be sent me, I have at present about fifty men and officers whom I intend to put on board the three sloops, and lay the two gun Boats up untill I receive more men or there should be a necessity for their being equipped, as the present force of the enemy consists of three vessels carrying two guns each, with about forty men each, calculated for boarding, which force I consider myself superior to, without the Gun Boats; the timely increase of our force has in all probability prevented the augmentation of that of the enemy which it was well understood they intended last winter— I shall as soon as the carronades are mounted proceed down in the vicinity of the lines prepared to accomplish such service as will be in my power to effect— Since the removal of Mr. Beale[1] (Purser) the duties of that office have devolved on me, which under the present manner of procuring supplies (as directed by the Honble. Mr. Hamilton and I believe the best one that could be adopted) is attended with much difficulty—and perplexity of account'g independent of those immediately of the men & officers   I have in consequence to inform you that the purser whom you intended sending to me in the place of Mr. Beale has not come on and I consider the presence of that officer at a place like this where, there is no agent of whom supplies might be procured essential— I have the honor to be Sir your most Obt. Servt.

T. Macdonough

ALS, DNA, RG45, BC, 1813, Vol. 2, No. 5 (M148, Roll No. 11).

1. George Beale was appointed a purser and ordered to Lake Champlain 14 October 1812. Because the Senate failed to confirm his nomination, Beale's appointment was revoked on 6 March by Secretary Jones. The Senate finally confirmed his nomination on 24 July, and on 4 August Beale was ordered once again to Lake Champlain.

Joint Operations on the Niagara Frontier: Attack on Fort George

The American strategy on Lake Ontario called for an attack on Forts George and Erie, located on the Canadian side of the Niagara River, following the attack on York. Com-

Capture of Fort George

modore Isaac Chauncey cooperated with Major General Henry Dearborn in the planned assault on 27 May 1813. The navy's vessels bombarded Fort George with a heavy fire, allowing American army troops to land west of the fort. The amphibious assault was jointly directed by Colonel Winfield Scott and Master Commandant Oliver H. Perry in an action remarkable for its cooperation between the services.

Following the loss of Fort George, British general John Vincent ordered the evacuation of the other forts on the Canadian side of the river. The American ships that had been trapped at Black Rock opposite Fort Erie were thus able to join the fleet building at Erie. Control of the Niagara frontier would be contested for the remainder of the year as American and British troops attempted to hold and regain these strategic points.[1]

1. Hickey, War of 1812, pp. 139–43; Dudley, "Chauncey and Joint Operations," pp. 144–45; Skaggs, "Joint Operations," p. 125.

COMMODORE ISAAC CHAUNCEY TO SECRETARY OF THE NAVY JONES

No. 21   U.S. Ship *Madison*
                                                Sacketts Harbor   15 May 1813

Sir

Wishing to obtain the true situation of the Enemy's vessels at Kingston, before I left here for Niagara I thought it a good opportunity to send a flag over with Lieut. M. L. Green, of the Royal Navy (taken at York) upon his parole— I accordingly dispatched the *Lady of the Lake,* with that Officer and two Seamen on the 14th.— She returned this day, and the Officer reports to me, that the *Royal George, Earl Moira, Prince Regent* and *Simcoe,*[1] were ready for Sea, and that the New Ship had her lower Mast in and rigging and tops overhead and apparently nearly ready in other respects—that a Post Captain of the Royal Navy was on board of the "*Lady of the Lake*" and made many enquiries respecting the Ship building at this place &c.— I have also a Montreal Paper of the 1st. Inst. which mentions that eight Officers of the Royal Navy (amongst whom was a Rear Admiral) passed through that City for Kingston, a few days before—under all these circumstances I have determined not to leave this place entirely without Naval protection— I have therefore ordered Lieutenant Chauncey in the *Fair American* & Actg. Lieutenant Adams in the *Pert,* to take on board their proportion of Troops and proceed to Niagara—land them, and return to this place as soon as possible, where I shall keep them Cruizing, until my return—the remainder of the Squadron except the Ship will take on board Troops and proceed to Niagara tomorrow— I shall remain with 300 of Col. Macombs Artillery, untill a reinforcement arrives which I understand is on the road. I do this from a conviction of its necessity,—for if I should leave here now, I should leave this important post to be protected by about 300 or 350 effective Men and those Volunteers, and I think Sir, that you will consider the Ship building at this place of too much importance to be left with such protection— The moment that the reinforcements arrive I shall not loose any time, in joining the Squadron at Niagara, and carrying into execution your instructions.— I have the honor to be Very respectfully Sir Yr. Mo. Ob. St.

                                                          Isaac Chauncey

LS, DNA, RG45, CL, 1813, Vol. 3, No. 141 (M125, Roll No. 28).

1. The brig *Governor Simcoe* was later renamed *Sir Sidney Smith.*

COMMODORE ISAAC CHAUNCEY TO SECRETARY OF THE NAVY JONES

No. 28   U.S. Ship *Madison*
                                              Niagara River.   27th. May 1813

Sir

I am happy to have it in my power to say, that the American Flag is flying upon Fort George— We were in quiet possession of all the Forts at 12 O Clock. I have the honor to be very respectfully Sir, Yr. Mo. Ob. St.

                                                              Isaac Chauncey

LS, DNA, RG45, CL, 1813, Vol. 3, No. 187 (M125, Roll No. 28).

COMMODORE ISAAC CHAUNCEY TO SECRETARY OF THE NAVY JONES

No. 29   U.S. Ship *Madison*
                                              Niagara River.   28th. May 1813

Sir

Agreeably to arrangements which I have already had the honor of detailing to you—I left Sacketts Harbor with this Ship on the 22d. inst. with about 350 of Col. Macombs Regiment on board— the Winds being light from the Westward I did not arrive in the vicinity of Niagara before the 25th. the other parts of the Squadron had arrived Several days before, and landed their Troops— The *Fair American* and *Pert* I had ordered to Sacketts Harbor, for the purpose of watching the Enemy's movements at Kingston— I immediately had an interview with General Dearborn for the purpose of making arrangements to attack the Enemy as soon as possible and it was agreed between him and myself to make the attack the moment that the Weather was such as to allow the Vessels, and Boats to approach the shore with safety.— On the 26th. I reconnoitred the position for landing the Troops and at Night sounded the shore and placed Buoys to [point?] out the Stations for the small vessels— It was agreed between the General and myself to make the attack the next Morning (as the Weather had moderated, and had every appearance of being favorable)— I took on board of the *Madison, Oneida* and *Lady of the Lake* all the heavy artillery and as many Troops as could be stowed—the remainder were to embark in Boats and follow the Fleet— at 3 yesterday Morning the signal was made for the Fleet to weigh and the Troops were all embarked on board of the boats before 4 and soon after Generals Dearborn and Lewis came on board of this Ship, with their Suites—it being however nearly calm the Schooners were obliged to sweep into their positions— Mr. Trant in the *Julia* and Mr Mix in the *Growler*, I directed to take a position in the Mouth of the River and silence a battery near the Light House which from its position commanded the Shore where our Troops were to land— Mr Stevens in the *Ontario*, was directed to take a position to the North of the Light House so near in shore as to infilade the battery and cross the Fire of the *Julia* and *Growler*— Lieut. Brown in the *Governor Tompkins* I directed to take a position near to two Mile Creek where the Enemy had a Battery, with one heavy Gun— Lieut. Petti-grew in the *Conquest* was directed to anchor to the S.E. of the same Battery so near in as to open it in the rear, and cross the Fire of the *Governor Tompkins*— Lieut. MacPherson in the *Hamilton*, Lieut. Smith in the *Asp*, and Mr. Osgood in the *Scourge* was directed to anchor close to the Shore and cover the landing of the Troops, and to scour the Woods and plain whenever the Enemy made his appearance— all these Orders were most promptly and gallantly executed— all the Vessels anchored within Musket shot of the Shore, and in ten minutes after they opened upon the batteries, they were completely silenced and abandoned. Our Troops then advanced in three Brigades—the advance led by Col. Scott and landed near the Fort, which had been silenced by Lieut. Brown—the Enemy who had been concealed in a ravine now advanced in great force to the edge of the Bank to charge our Troops— the Schooners opened so well directed and tremenduous a fire of grape and canister that the Enemy soon retreated from the Bank— our Troops formed as soon as they landed, and immediately assended the Bank and charged and routed the Enemy in every direction—the Schooners keeping up a constant and well directed fire upon him,—in his retreat towards the Town— Owing to the Winds having Sprung up very fresh from the Eastward which caused a heavy Sea directly on Shore, I was not able to get the Boats off to land the Troops from the *Madison* and *Oneida*, before the first and Second Brigades had advanced.— Capt. Smith with the Marines, landed with Col. Macombs' Regiment and I had prepared 400 Seamen which I intended to land with myself, if the Enemy had made a stand, but our Troops pursued him so rapidly into the Town and Fort George, that I found that there was no necessity for more force— moreover the Wind had increased so much and hove such a sea on Shore that the situation of the Fleet had become dangerous and critical— I therefore made the signal for the Fleet to weigh and ordered them into the River, where they anchored immediately after the Enemy had abandoned Fort George— The Town and Forts were in quiet possession of our troops at 12 O Clock and the Enemy retreated in a direction towards Queenstown.—

Where all behave so well, it is difficult to select any one for commendation, yet in doing justice to Lieutenant Macpherson, I do not detract from the merits of others— he was fortunate in placing himself in a Situation where he rendered very important service in covering the Troops so completely, that their loss was triffling.

Captain Perry joined me from Erie on the Evening of the 25th. and very gallantly volunteered his services and I have much pleasure in acknowledging the great assistance which I received from him in arranging and Superintending the debarkation of the Troops— he was present at every point where he could be useful, under a shower of Musketry, but fortunately escaped unhurt— We lost but one killed and two wounded, and no injury done to the Vessels   I have the honor to be very respectfully Sir, Yr. Mo. Ob. St.

Isaac Chauncey

LS, DNA, RG45, CL, 1813, Vol. 3, No. 190 (M125, Roll No. 28).

BRIGADIER GENERAL JOHN VINCENT, BRITISH ARMY, TO
GOVERNOR-GENERAL SIR GEORGE PREVOST

40 Mile Creek
May 28th. 1813—

Sir/

I have the honor to inform your Excellency that yesterday morning about daybreak the Enemy again opened his Batteries upon Fort George; the Fire not being immediately returned, it ceased for some time.— About 4 o'clock A.M. a combination of circumstances led to a belief that an invasion was meditated; the morning being exceedingly hazy, neither his means or his intention could be ascertained, until the mist clearing away at intervals, the Enemy's Fleet consisting of fourteen or fifteen vessels was discovered under weigh standing towards the Light House in an extended line of more than two miles covering from ninety to one hundred large boats, and scows, each containing an average of fifty or sixty men.— Though at this time no doubt could be entertained of the Enemy's intention his points of attack could only be conjectured;—having again commenced a heavy fire from his Fort, line of Batteries and Shipping, it became necessary to withdraw all the ~~shipping~~ Guards and Piquets stationed along the Coast between the Fort and Light House, and a landing was effected at the two mile creek, about half a mile below the latter place. The party of Troops and Indians stationed at this point, after opposing the enemy and annoying him as long as possible, were obliged to fall back, and the fire from the Shipping so completely enfiladed and scoured the plains that it became impossible to approach the beach.— As the day dawned the Enemy's plan was clearly developed, and every effort to oppose his landing having failed, I lost not a moment in concentrating my Force, and taking up a position between the Town of Fort George and the Enemy, there waiting his approach. This movement was admirably covered by the Glengarry Light Infantry joined by detachments from the Royal Newfoundland Regiment and Militia, which commenced skirmishing with the Enemy's Riflemen, who were advancing through the Brush-wood. The Enemy having perfect command of the Beach, he quickly landed from three to four thousand men with several pieces of artillery, and this Force was instantly seen advancing in three solid columns, along the Lake Bank, his right covered by a large body of Riflemen, and his left and front by the fire of the Shipping and Batteries in their Fort. As our Light Troops fell back upon the main body which was moved forwards to their support, they were gallantly sustained by the 8th. King's Regiment commanded by Major Ogilvie, the whole being under the immediate direction of Colonel Myers Acting Quarter Master General, who had charge of the Right Wing. In the execution of this important duty, gallantry, zeal, and decision were eminently conspicuous, and I lament to report that I was deprived of the services of Colonel Myers, who having received three wounds was obliged to quit the Field— Lieut. Colonel Harvey the Deputy Adjutant General whose activity and gallantry had been displayed the whole morning, succeeded Colonel Myers, and brought up the right division consisting of the 49th. Regt. and some Militia.— The Light artillery under Major Holcroft, were already in position waiting the Enemy's advance on the plains.— At this moment the very inferior force under my command had experienced a severe loss in officers and men, yet nothing could exceed the ardour and gallantry of the Troops who shewed the most marked devotion in the service of their King and Country and appeared regardless of the consequence of the unequal contest.

Being on the spot, and seeing that the Force under my command was opposed with tenfold numbers who were rapidly advancing under cover of their shipping and Batteries from which our positions were immediately seen and exposed to a tremendous fire of shot and shells, I decided on retiring my little force to a position which I hoped might be less assailable by the heavy ordnance of the enemy, and from which a retreat would be left open in the event of that measure becoming necessary.— There after waiting the approach of the Enemy for about half an hour, I received authentic information, that his force consisting of from four to five thousand men had reformed his columns and was making an effort to turn my right flank.— At this critical juncture not a moment was to be lost, and sensible that every effort had been made by the officers and Men under my command to maintain the Post of Fort George, I could not consider myself justified in continuing so unequal a contest, the issue of which promised no advantage to the interests of His Majestys Service.

Having given orders for the Fort, to be evacuated, the guns to be spiked, and the ammunition destroyed, the Troops under my command were put in motion and marched across the Country in a line parallel to the Niagara River, towards the position near the Beaver Dam beyond Queenston Mountain, at which place I had the honour of reporting to Your Excellency a depôt of provisions and ammunition had been formed some time since. The rear guard of the army reached that position during the night, and we were soon afterwards joined by Lieut. Col. Bishopp with all the detachments from Chippewa to Fort Erie.— The Light and one Battalion Company of the 8th. King's joined us about the same time as did Captain Barclay with a detachment of the Royal Navy.—

Having assembled my whole force the next morning, which did not exceed sixteen hundred men, I continued my march towards the head of the Lake, where it is my intention to take up a position and shall endeavour to maintain it until I may be honoured with Your Excellency's Instructions which I shall feel most anxious to receive. I beg leave to suggest the great importance there exists for a communication being opened with me through the medium of the Fleet; the anchorage under Mr. Brandts house is perfectly good and very safe.— I believe Your Excellency need not be informed that in the event of its becoming necessary that I should fall back upon York the assistance of shipping would be requisite for the transport of my artillery— I cannot conclude this long communication without Expressing a well merited tribute of approbation to the gallantry & assiduity of every officer of the Staff and indeed of every individual composing my little army; every one most gallantly discharged the duties of his respective station— The struggle on the 27th. continued from three to four hours and I lament to add it was attended with very severe loss.

I have the honour to enclose a list of killed and wounded and missing with as much accuracy as the nature of existing circumstances will admit; many of the missing will I hope be found to be only stragglers, and will soon rejoin their corps. I shall reach the Head of the Lake tomorrow evening.— Hitherto the enemy has not attempted to interrupt my movements: information reached me this morning through an authentic channel that he has pushed on three thousand infantry and a considerable body of Cavalry towards Queenston.— His whole force is stated to amount to nearly ten thousand men and I cannot conceal from Your Excellency my conviction that unless some disaster attends their progress, that force will daily increase. My sentiments respecting the Militia are already known, and it will not be supposed that their attachment to our cause can be very steady under the peculiar complexion of the present times.—I have the &c &c.

John Vincent
Brig Genl.

P.S. I send this despatch by Mr. Matheson who acted as a volunteer on the 27th. and I am happy to inform Your Excellency—that his conduct was very honourable to his character, and merits my marked approbation.— Ammunition will be wanted by the first vessel.— Captain Milnes has been kind enough to remain with me 'till my next Despatch.—

ALS, CaOOA, British Military and Naval Records, RG8, I, "C" Ser., Vol. 678, pp. 318–26. The list of killed, missing, and wounded referred to in this letter can be found in CaOOA, British Military and Naval Records, RG8, I, "C" Ser., Vol. 678, pp. 336–37. It lists a total of 358 casualties or missing: 52 killed, 44 wounded, and 262 wounded and missing.

The Battle of Sackets Harbor, 29 May 1813

While Chauncey's fleet was at Niagara, Commodore Sir James Lucas Yeo, who had been at Kingston only a fortnight, and Governor-General Sir George Prevost launched an attack on the American naval base at Sackets Harbor. Their goal was to destroy General Pike, *the new ship under construction, and to disrupt shipbuilding at the American station.*

Although the Americans repelled the attack, the day went poorly on all fronts. Sir James Yeo was under the direction of Governor Prevost, who hesitated about making an attack after nightfall. The attack was delayed overnight, allowing the Americans sufficient time to rally the army and militia and prepare for the defense of the town.. During the assault, the inexperienced militia broke and ran when faced with British regulars, leaving Brigadier General Jacob Brown of the New York militia to try to rally them. An anxious junior naval officer, fearing that the town had fallen to the British, ordered the ships and storehouses burned, thus partially accomplishing for the British what they could not do themselves by force.[1]

1. Drake, "Yeo and Prevost," pp. 160–61.

COMMODORE ISAAC CHAUNCEY TO LIEUTENANT WOLCOTT CHAUNCEY

Lieut. W. Chauncey
commg. U.S. Schooner
Fair American—

U.S. Ship *Madison*
S.H.   20 May 1813.

Upon your arrival here you will cruize with the *Fair American* & *Pert* between this place and the Island of Fonti in order to watch the movements of the Enemy. You will be careful however in your approaches towards Kingston, and not get so near in as to endanger the loss of your vessels by a calm or sudden shift of wind. You are not to cruize to the Westward of the real ducks nor at any time go far out as to endanger your being cut off from this harbor. If the enemy should come out and make any movements towards this place, you will immediately return to port, moor your vessels inside the bar, and defend the new Ship to the last extremity. If you are drove from your vessels, retreat to the Blockhouses where I recommend you to mount 2–6 or 4 pdrs. At all events if this place should be attacked, let the defence of the new Ship be such, as to do yourself credit and silence clamour. I leave the officers and men on the point under your direction. They ought to be frequently exercised at the guns mounted there, and see that they are well supplied with powder and Balls. If the enemy should make a movement before I return you will dispatch some fast sailing Boat to give me the information as soon as possible. Trusting much to your discretion and judgement I shall forbear dwelling longer upon the importance of your command and am with great respect Dear Sir your most ob. H. St.

Isaac Chauncey

LB Copy, MiU–C, Isaac Chauncey Letter Book.

"South-east view of Sackett's harbour"

COMMODORE SIR JAMES LUCAS YEO, R.N., TO
FIRST SECRETARY OF THE ADMIRALTY JOHN W. CROKER

No. 3   His Majesty's Ship *Wolfe*
                                              at Kingston, in Upper Canada,
                                                    the 26th. of May 1813

Sir/

I have the Honor to acquaint you for the information of the Lords Commissioners of the Admiralty, that I arrived here on the 15th. Instant, with 150 of the Officers and Seamen under my Command, the remainder have also arrived here at different periods between that and the 24th.—

The Ships and Vessels here were in a very weak state the *Royal George*, had 18–32 Pounder Carronades, and two long nine pdr. Guns, the *Moira*, 10–18 Pounder Carronades, the *Beresford*[1] 10–12 pdr. Carronades, and two long six Pounder Guns, the *Wolfe* was launched but not Decked, or Rigged, nor any Guns on board, she has since been furnished, at different times, with twenty Guns and Carronades of various Calibers, collected from the Forts and which have arrived from Quebec, the Enemy have burnt on their taking possession of York a Ship that was Building there intended to carry 30 Guns, as was stated in my Letter No. 1 at Quebec on the 5th. instant.

From the arrival of the Establishment, to the present date, all hands have been very actively employed in fitting and preparing the Squadron, in the best possible manner the short time would allow, in a state to put to Sea, or defend themselves in case of surprize.

The Enemy's Squadron are very superior, both, in number and the complete way they are equiped, their force consist of one Ship of 20–32 Pounder Carronades and 6 long 18 Pounder Guns, a Brig with 18–24 Pounder Carronades, and 16 smaller Vessels, each carrying a long 32 Pounder Gun some 4 and others 6 Carronades besides, they have also a Ship of thirty and a Brig of Eighteen Guns nearly ready for launching at Sacketts harbour.[2]

They having the above stated advantage on the Lake at present, and the certainty of their shortly being reinforced by those Building it will appear evident to their Lordships that the Enemy (now possess a force which are equal if not superior,) if not checked will soon get too formidable for an attack to be made on them that might prove advantageous, I am therefore about to proceed to Sea to meet them, as the possession of upper Canada must depend on whoever can maintain the Naval Superiority on Lake Ontario.

I beg leave to draw their Lordships attention that even in the event of being successful, the Superiority cannot long be maintained without an immediate reinforcement of Seamen, as the Enemy from their proximity to New York, can obtain any supply of Men, or, Stores at a few hours notice.

I have further to state to their Lordships that I found on my arrival, Messrs. Barclay, Pring,[3] and Finnis, Commanders, and four Lieutenants, which had been sent from Halifax, by Sir John B. Warren, Bt.

Also transmit a list of Acting appointments and removals, up to this period, of Commissioned, and Warrant, Officers, and a Report of Survey on Thomas England Esqr. Commander Invalided, and have the Honor to be Sir your most obedient humble Servant

James Lucas Yeo.   Commodore

LS, UkLPR, Adm. 1/2736, pp. 80–83.

1. The schooner *General Beresford*, formerly called *Prince Regent*, was built at York for the Provincial Marine in June 1812; she was renamed about May 1813.
2. *General Pike*, launched 12 June 1813, was under construction at Sackets Harbor; the prize schooner *Duke of Gloucester*, captured by the Americans at York on 27 April, may have been undergoing repairs at the harbor, but would never see active service as an American ship of war.
3. Lieutenant Daniel Pring, R.N., was transferred from Halifax to the lakes in May 1813; he was given command of the squadron on Lake Champlain on 19 July 1813.

MEMOIR OF LIEUTENANT DAVID WINGFIELD, R.N.[1]

[Extract]

The ships were ready for sea by the latter part of May, and a strong body of troops were assembled at Kingston to make an attack upon the enemy's works at Sacketts harbour, which, if once in our possession, would have put an end to the naval war on Lake Ontario, and saved some millions of pounds, and thousand of lives, as the Americans had no other harbour along the coast fit for a naval depôt, an excellent opportunity likewise offered for putting the plan into execution, their fleet having sailed about 100 miles up the Lake to attack one of our Forts on the bank of the river Niagara, and not believing that our ships could be prepared for sea so early, they had left the place nearly defenceless: in the afternoon we weighed and stood out of the harbour, anchoring about six miles off Kingston to await the troops who were embarked in batteus and gun boats; the latter had 24 pounders mounted on circular platforms; the troops did not join the fleet till late in the evening, when it being quite calm the boats were made fast to the ships

At daybreak a light breeze sprung up and we got under weigh, the boats occasionally laying on their oars to keep company; having but light breezes, and frequent calms we made but little ~~way~~ progress, about noon, on rounding a point we came in full view of the enemy about 10 miles distant, who, immediately they perceived us, commenced firing alarm guns to call in the surrounding militia, at 2 PM we were totally becalmed within six miles of the town of Sacketts; Sir James Yeo had gone in shore in his gig some time before to reconnoitre, and perceiving several shots fired at the boat, a gun vessel was ordered to cover her retreat, if necessary; on her return we received orders to prepare for disembarking the troops, the ships cleared for action, and nothing was wanting but a good breeze to take them close enough in shore to cover the landing; about 6 PM a fresh breeze sprung up dead on the land, the ships bore up and took in their small sails, the guns were prepared in the gunboats, and soldiers, who were not employed at the oars, in place of the seamen who had to fight the gun, had their muskets in their hands, and lay down at the bottom of the boats to prevent confusion; every heart now beat high with eagerness and expectation, but when nearly within gun shot of the shore, the ships suddenly hauled their wind and stood out to sea, making a signal for the boats to follow; as soon as they got a good offing, they hove too, and the boats assembled round the Commodore's ship, where we learned that the attack was suspended till the following morning; this order emanated from the Governor general of the two Provinces, who was on board the flag ship, and of course, commanded in chief, and the officers ~~and~~ being in the provincial service, and pay, Sir James was obliged to obey, though much against his will, this caused some altercation between the two Commanders, on board, Sir James urging the expediency of an immediate attack, and the Governor alleging the decline of the day to defer it; the delay, however put a great damp upon out spirits, as we plainly saw by our glasses, several boats well manned, enter the harbour to reinforce the garrison, and well knew they would be receiving reinforcements all the night, as they kept up an incessant firing of minute guns; whereas if we had made a bold dash at once, it is most probable that few, if any, guns would have been fired upon us and the troops would have been landed immediately under their batteries, and in the town, under cover of the shipping who would have run right into Sacketts harbour; we soon after learned that the Americans were not above 300 strong when we first hove in sight, and had made every preparation for destroying the public buildings and stores, particularly a large ship upon the stocks, we knowing it would be the utmost folly to attempt standing against such a force as they must perceive we had, independent of the shipping: this days work ended with ordering the troops on board the ships, and the boats to be made fast to their sterns, except some to row guard along shore during the night, where they captured about 150 of the enemy coming down the Lake for Sackets

When the troops were on board the ships, they made sail further off shore, as the breeze freshened and continued blowing dead on the land; at midnight it fell calm and left us about five miles off the town: at dawn of day the hands were turned up, the soldiers embarked in the boats, and the ships stood in for land, but having light baffleing winds, they made but little progress and none came within gun shot except a schooner of 10 guns, and she did not arrive untill the men had made good their landing

After some consultation, the boats were ordered to proceed under cover of the gun boats only, but our favourable opportunity was gone, and the troops knew it as well as ourselves, for, though there was no murmuring, or attempt to disobey orders, their countenances, so different to what they were the evening before, plainly shewed they did not obey the orders with that cheerfulness which confidence inspires; the enemy had nearly 24 hours notice, and had made the best use of their time by minute guns, and expresses, to receive strong reinforcements, and it being daylight before the boats shoved off from the ships, our motions were distinctly perceived by the Americans, who, not being awed by the shipping had drawn great numbers of men from the town, concealing them among the bushes, behind trees, logs, and rising grounds, just above the beach, which enabled them to take deliberate aim as we approached the shore; they had likewise brought out four field pieces to annoy us

About 3 am we formed the line, the gun boats leading the van, and commenced pulling in shore about a mile above the town in order to keep out of the range of the shot from the forts and block houses; the boats were heavily laden, and proceeded but slowly, while the enemy kept up an ill directed fire from their field pieces: when within musquet shot of the beach, the gun boats pulled ahead and fired a few rounds of grape and canister shot to scour the

beach, but the Yankies had anticipated us, and were so well sheltered, that I believe none were killed or wounded; the batteus and ships boats advanced, and I
observed to an officer of the 104th Regt, who commanded the troops in the
boat under my charge, that the Americans intended to let us land unmolested,
but it soon appeared I was mistaken, for when about pistol shot from the beach,
and we had encouraged each other with the usual salutation of three cheers,
they opened a well directed fire from their field pieces, and rifles, that almost
every shot did execution, which for the moment staggered us, but soon recovering from the surprise, every boat made the best of her way to land; the gun
boats kept up a continued fire, but having no other mark than the smoke from
the enemy's guns, but little execution was done and in a very short time there
was fifteen killed and wounded in my boat, principally picked off from, and
about the gun; in passing one of the boats, which appeared in great distress, I
hailed the officer, who was wounded, and had but three men who had escaped
the effects of the shot of the enemy; as the military officer, and myself were
obliged to stand up and cheer on the men, we were too prominent a mark to
remain long and I took a mental leave of the few friends I had left; the men
being so deliberately picked off from the gun, the crew got in some confusion,
for as the seamen were disabled, others took their place, and were relieved at
the oars by the soldiers; while occupied in this double transfer, the army officer,
with his glass, had discovered a body of men drawn up a short distance from the
beach, who being dressed in green, the uniform of all the American foot soldiers, could scarcely be perceived among the trees and underwood, he called
me and pointed them out, while so occupied the coxswain of the boat was
struck with two balls and fell, the soldier took the tiller, while I went forward to
the gun which being loaded with grape and canister shot, I had it pointed to
the spot and made a great havock among the bushes, if not the men; by this
time some of the boats had made good their landing, and the troops formed,
upon which the enemy made a precipitate retreat into the town

When the soldiers were all landed, and the wounded men placed on the
beach, those gun boats which were not disabled, rowed towards the batteries,
and commenced firing, to draw off some of the attention of the enemy from
the advancing party; here we were kept till half past seven, when we were recalled to the landing place to take on board the troops who were retreating in
great haste; they were once in the town, but being dreadfully cut up from some
block houses, and a great dust seen rising from the opposite entrance ~~to the
town~~, supposed to proceed from a reinforcement to the garrison, a retreat was
sounded, but who gave the orders no one knew, the Governor and his staff positively denying having done so, however it was not the less obeyed; in a few minutes a smoke was seen rising from their dock yard, which caused an attempt to
be made to rally the troops, but did not succeed: before the soldiers were all
embarked it was known to a certainty that, what was supposed to be a reinforcement, was nothing else but the main body of the Americans retreating, leaving
some block houses manned, until their new ship, and public store houses were
on fire, and then to follow

I was informed by several officers of the American Army and Navy, when I was
taken prisoner,[2] that had the attack commenced immediately after we hove in
sight the day before, so far from defending themselves, the number of men in
the garrison would have scarcely been sufficient to destroy the public works

We lost nearly 400 men killed and wounded in this disgraceful affair, when, in every probability the place would have been taken without the loss of a single man had things been conducted as they ought: this failure caused a coolness between the Governor, and Commodore, and at length broke out into an open rupture, in consequence of the loss of our flotilla on Lake Champlain[3] which, in Sir James Yeo's public dispatches he attributed to the misconduct of the Governor, who was soon after suspended, and a court martial called, but he died soon after his arrival in England

The soldiers were greatly disheartened, and it was well for us that the troops at Fort George, the place the Americans had gone to attack, were better commanded, otherwise their ships would have been down upon us, and from our crowded state, most probably would have taken us all; we arrived in Navy bay the same evening and disembarked the troops and wounded men: thus ended an expedition begun under the most favourable auspices

I before remarked that, could we get possession of Sackets harbour, it would have saved an immensity of blood and treasure

D, CaOOA, David Wingfield, "Four Years on the Lakes of Canada, in 1813, 1814, 1815, and 1816; by a Naval Officer under the command of the late Sir James Lucas Yeo. . . ," MG24, F18, extract from pp. 6–10. The memoir is not dated, but internal evidence suggests it was written after 1834.

1. David Wingfield, born in 1792, was a Royal Navy midshipman in 1813; he was promoted to the rank of lieutenant on 20 March 1815, the highest rank he attained during his career. For the attack on Sackets Harbor, see Ellison, "David Wingfield."
2. Wingfield was commander of *Confiance* when that vessel was captured by the American fleet on 5 October 1813.
3. The Battle of Lake Champlain took place 11 September 1814.

BRIGADIER GENERAL JACOB BROWN[1] TO SECRETARY OF WAR ARMSTRONG

Head Quarters
Sackets Harbour   June 1, 1813

Sir

You will have recd. mine of the 29th. Ulto. from the field of Battle.— All that I then stated is so—

I have now to add that on the 25th. Ulto. I recd. a communication from Genl. Dearborn desiring me to take the command at this Post— I hesitated— Col. Backus was here, an officer of experience in whom I placed the most implicit confidence and I could not do an act which I feared might wound his feelings— In the night of the 27th. Col. Backus wrote me by Majr. Swan desiring that I would come & take the command— I could no longer hesitate— Early in the morning of the 28th. I was here—

As the day opened Lieut. Chauncey ~~the Brother of our worthy Commodore~~ came in from the Lake firing alarm guns, the signal guns that had been agreed upon some days previous to rally the Militia were fired in answer and I sent out expresses in evry direction to alarm the country— As soon as Lieut. Chauncey came into Port he advised me that the Fleet approaching was an enemy & with the Glass we could distinctly see that they had a verry liberal supply of Boats. I then no longer doubted but that they were resolved to land with a chosen body of Troops and storm our works—

The ~~few~~ Artillerists ~~we had to man the Guns of Fort Tompkins~~ & Volunteers ~~prepared themselves for the event~~ and Lt. Chauncey did every thing possible to support & strengthen Navy Point the guns on which were altogether under his command and mand. with his Officers and Men— As Col. Backus had recently arrived on this station I invited him and others to accompany me in a thorough examination of the Grounds arround our position and as soon as this had been done we settled a regular place of defense ~~with Lieut. Chauncey~~. I had ever been of opinion that no military man would ~~ever~~ risque the Landing of Men in the mouth of Sackets Harbour for reasons which would be superfluous here to explain—

I knew that there was a place where determined men might land with considerable safety under cover of the fire from their small flat bottomed Gun-Boats which I also knew had recently arrived from Montreal and were in all probability, with the fleet— At the waters edge near Horse Island where I believed the enemy would land I was resolved to meet them and with this view the plan of defence was settled between myself Col. Backus Col. Mills Lieut. Chauncey Majr. Swan & Majr. Brown—

I was myself destined to meet the Enemy at the waters edge ~~where I believed that they would land~~ with all the Militia that came in and the Albany Volunteers under command of Col. Mills— At the alarm an order given by me Col. Backus was to order a body of Regulars to advance so as to meet the enemy after they had broken or disposed of the force with me— This force ~~with me~~ being broken I was to rally them and fall upon the enemys right Flank, so as to retard their approach toward Fort Tompkins as long as possible always hoping that the country would send forth all its means to our assistance and believing that to gain time was to ensure Victory—if however the enemy should overcome the assembled Regulars & Militia and drive us the whole length of way from Horse Island to Fort Tompkins and carry that Fort Lieut. Chauncey would then and in that case see the stores on Navy Point destroyed the New Ship Burnt and retire with his schooners & the men he had left to the south shore of the Bay east of Fort Volunteer— the Force remaining with me were to retire to Fort Volunteer (being the highest Ground) as our last and dearnier [*dernier*] resort—and if the enemy should prove too hard for Lieut. Chauncey, he was to land his men blow up his vessels and join me in fort Volunteer where we would be governed by circumstances. This being our plan & the enemy having first struck us as contemplated it remains to see how well our Plan was executed— The Wind being verry light during the whole of the 28th. and the enemy having arrangements to make for landing they moved slowly up the Bay but no doubt would have attacked us in the course of the Afternoon had it not been for the approach of Boats from Oswego with reinforcements— This circumstance diverted them for a time—they attacked the Boats—took [?] [2] of them and a number of our men with what loss to them or to us In other respects I am yet uninformed— In the course of the 28th. & night of the 28th. & 29th. a considerable number of militia collected—they were as they arrived ordered to a small improvement on the main just within Horse Island and such provisions as could be furnished were carted to the Ground where they all eat in common paying no attention to the ordinary mode of drawing rations— Col Mills with the Albany Volunteers was on Horse Island— In the evening of the 28th. I joined the Force assembled near Horse Island and explained to the leading officers my views as I feared a night attack—it being of the first importance to the enemy to be rapid in their movements to prevent the fatal effects to them of the Force that I would have would be assembled by morning and of those brave men as I supposed that would generously fly to their country's standard, ambitious to have a name in the victory which I most firmly believed was certain As the morning of the 29th approached I found myself with a part of three Regiments of militia and a part of the Albany Volunteers amounting altogether say to five Hundred men—all anxious for the fight were you to believe their professions— The moment it was so light as to see an object on the Bay the Enemys ships were discovered in nearly a direct line between the head of Horse Island and Stoney point and within Ten minutes Thirty three Boats filled with men approached us from the larger Indian or Gardener Island when the action in fact began as the enemy immediately opened upon us with his Gun Boats— I immediately directed Col. Backus to advance and ordered Col. Mills to join me on the main—

The moment Col. Mills had joined me I ordered [?][3] of the Albany Volunteers who had the command of a traveling Brass Six pounder to open upon the enemy— the Albany Volunteers under Col. Mills were then laid down on the right behind a small natural Breast work on the Beach, and all the Militia under Col. Sprague behind the same breast work on the left and those under Col. Tuttle to take a position that I pointed out about 30 Rods upon my left flank by the edge of the woods near the Bay to prevent a surprise from savages that I expected would come in from that quarter the enemy by this time had landed a body of men at the head of Horse Island who were advancing in open column upon a line with the enemys front Boats—evry exertion was then made to inspire my little force with confidence & if they would but lay firm and restrain their fire I was confident that evry man must [merely?] kill his man. I then took my position in the centre by the left of the men at the Six pounder directly in front of the column approaching from the Island and all was silent with me excepting this 6— The enemy rapidly approaching and keeping up as heavy a fire as possible from their gun Boats—not a shot was fired from their column the Front approached charging Bayonets— It appears impossible to restrain raw troops so as to make them in any high degree useful—those with me did fire and would fire before I intended— the enemy were however pretty near and as I was attentively watching their movements and the happy effects of our fire to my utter astonishment my men arose from their cover broke & before I could realize the disgraceful scene, there was scarcely a man within several rods of where I stood— Col. Mills fell gallantly strugling to stop his men— I was more fortunate— I made all the noise I could for my men—put my pocket handkerchief on the point of my sword and made evry sort of flourish signal possible that they might notice me but in vain—at a little distance however I had the good fortune to come up with Capt. McNitt who had succeeded in rallying a few men and they were doing all they could from behind some large logs by the edge of the Field. I complimented them and curst complained of those who had left me— Ordered Capt. McNitt to stand fast and I would go and call up Col. Tuttle from the point where I had ordered him— I went—but no Col. Tuttle could I find or any other man— By the time I returned Capt. Mayo and a few others had joined Capt. McNitt   I then ordered an advance upon the rear of the enemy's right flank and I trust some execution was done but as my party did not exceed one Hundred & as I deemed it verry important for me to know how things stood in front of the enemy where the regulars were most nobly contending I orderd. a rapid movement forward to pass the enemy and as we were advancing a fire came at some distance upon <u>our</u> right flank we halted, faced about, and McNitt was in the act of Firing when I ordered a little delay saying they might be our Friends—in a moment we saw the red Coats approaching from the right of the path along which we had passd. McNitt gave them his best fire & we made a rapid retreat upon the extreme left of the few Brave men who had sustain'd the contest in front

As I last turn'd from the enemy & come out of the woods upon the left of my friends I saw an ~~awful and damned~~ alarming flame arising from Navy point the position which contained the spoils of York and some few of Commodore Chaunceys effects— With all possible expedition I made my way into fort Tompkins and found the Officer Lieut. Ketchum I had left there in the act of firing the long thirty two at the enemy's shipping I desired him to keep up as heavy a fire as possible and assured him that victory was ours— He replied "Genl. I can not discharge this piece again, the flame from the Marine Barracks is so hot that my men cannot exist here"— I felt the force of his answer and replied "do the best you can" & left him, being alarmed for the ship, the object of the contest I hurried towards her and found Major Brown who assured me the ship was safe and that what had happened was owing to the infamous conduct of those in whom Lieut. Chauncey had placed confidence—that it was without his knowledge—that they had gone from Navy point and informed Chauncey that all was lost upon the right of our line of Battle— I ordered Major Brown to send forthwith and assure him that all was safe on the right and that Victory was ours

In passing up to the Brownville, Middle & Adams Road where I perceived some hundreds of Idle men were assembled at a verry respectfull distance from danger Major Swan rode up to me & informed me that the fixed ammunition was expended— I replied "it may be so, I do not believe it— ~~but~~ if it is so tell no Man" I then rode among those people and they tried to impose upon me as they had upon the Major, but I knew them better and could admit of no such excuse many of them had drawn their boxes full the day before and never fired a gun at the enemy   With much ado I got them to move towards the right flank of the enemy in hopes of throwing them into the woods behind Sir George should he presume further to advance— I then orderd. Major Lucket who I knew would not hesitate to advance with his mounted light dragoons into the open space west of Judge Sackets old House and nearly in a line between the enemy & the ship— <u>It was done</u>— Hurrying then to where the American & Brittish Regulars fought I verry soon felt that victory was really ours—and if Sir George had not been off with almost the rapidity of thought—he would not have returned that day—

The closing scene of this Glorious Day for the officers and soldiers of the regular Army who had the honor to be on the spot, you have in my despatch of the 29th. Ulto.— I have only to add in relation to the officers generally that they are men who do honour to their Country and that they would do honour to any age or nation

To Capt. McNitt of the Militia I presented the sword which I wore on the 29th Ulto. as testimony of my esteem & regard for his gallant conduct And I would be gratified if you would cause him to be commissioned in the regular army—

To Col. Backus, who, praised be God still lives, I have presented the sword taken from ~~the~~ Adjt. Genl. Gray who was killed not distant from where Backus fell and by the side of Sir George Prevost

I have directed Majr. Swan who had the goodness to volunteer his services as my acting adjt. Genl. and to whom I feel myself under the greatest obligations for his attentions during the arduous scene through which we have passd, to make out and transmit with this despatch a return of the killed wounded & prisoners on Both sides and also of the parts of Regiments of the regular army engaged, that you may have a correct idea of the amt. of Force on our side and that those parts of Regts. may have the honour which they have so fairly earned— The Enemy that landed were at least one thousand picked men and their fleet consisted of the new ship *Wolfe*—the *Royal George*—the *Prince Regent*—the *Earl Moira* & two schooners besides their Gun & other Boats— As I am closing this communication Commodore Chauncey has arrived with his Squadron & as I can be no longer useful here I shall return home in the morning—

I must yet add in justice to a brave honourable man that Lieut Chauncey stands higher in my estimation than ~~he did~~ before he was associated with me for the protection of this place— no blame I know by any possibility can attach to him for what happened on navy point—

He was deceived by the materials on whom he relied and nothing short of Divinity can guard against such occurrences—

Lieut. Col. Tuttle of the Regular Army who was on the march to this place made evry exertion that an officer or a soldier could make to get into the action but camc too late for the fight & I am confident that Col Tuttle and evry officer under his command feels it as a misfortune individually that it was not in their power to get up in time— Respectfully

Jac: Brown
<u>Brig: Genrl. Militia</u>

LS, DNA, RG107, Letters Received by the Secretary of War, Registered Series, B–204(7) (M221, Roll No. 50).

1. Jacob Brown was brigadier general of the New York state militia; he was appointed brigadier general in the U.S. Army on 19 July 1813 in recognition of his successful defense of Sackets Harbor.
2. Blank.
3. Blank.

COMMODORE ISAAC CHAUNCEY TO SECRETARY OF THE NAVY JONES

(No. 30)   U.S. Ship *Madison*
                                    Sacketts Harbor   2d. June 1813

Sir

On the Evening of the 30th. Ulto. I received an Express from Lieut. Chauncey, stating that the Enemy was off Sacketts Harbor, with his whole Fleet— I immediately prepared to leave Niagara with the Squadron, but as I had sent the *Hamilton* with the detachment of Seamen ordered with Captain Perry as far as Lewiston and had ordered Lieut. Macpherson to proceed to Black Rock to bring down powder and grape shot for the Squadron— I was obliged to wait his return, which detained me untill the morning of the 31st.— I immediately weighed and ran over to York to see whether the Enemy had run for that port— not finding him there I run down along the Canada Shore under an expectation of meeting him going up with reinforcements— I passed within sight of Kingston yesterday about

1 P.M. and arrived here about 4, without having seen any thing of the Enemy.— I found however that he had paid this place a visit on the 29th. Ulto. and landed about 1200 Men, supported by his whole Naval force aided by a number of Gun Boats, mounting 68 pounder Carronades.[1] The Troops were commanded by Sir George Prevost in person and the Naval Forces by Sir James L. Yeo—who lately arrived at Kingston with about 500 Seamen.— The Enemy penetrated to Fort Tompkins, but as every inch of ground was disputed with him, his loss by this time was so great that he retreated with some precipitation, leaving many of his killed and wounded upon the Field of Battle— he also took off many of his wounded as the Sailors were observed to be constantly employed upon that Service as the Enemy advanced.— He also gained time to get off many by sending in several flags of truce upon frivolous pretenses— the Enemy's loss must have been severe, otherwise he would not have retreated without accomplishing the object of his Visit, and one of primary importance to him—to wit, the destruction of the Ship building at this place.—

The Regular Forces stationed here behaved uncommonly well, they disputed every inch of ground with the Enemy, although double our numbers— the two Schooners were of infinite service in keeping the Enemy's small Vessels and Gun Boats in check in his approach to the Harbor, and the Officers and Men did their duty.

In this repulse of the Enemy so honorable to the American Arms—I am sorry that I am oblidged to state an occurence which has tended much to lessen our exultation which would otherwise have been complete.—

The Officer having charge of Navy Point and the Guns mounted there was directed by Lieut. Chauncey to defend it to the last extremity, but if the Enemy got complete possession of the Town and Batteries—then to fire the Barracks and retreat in Boats to the Schooners— this Officer from some cause not yet accounted for set Fire to all the Buildings upon Navy Point without necessity and retreated to the Woods— The Buildings were of no value they however contained a part of the Stores, for the New Ship and nearly all the property brought from York—the loss of the Canvass is a serious inconvenience as the Sail Makers must remain idle, until I can replace it from New York— I shall loose no time in replacing all the Stores lost by this accident— I shall also institute an enquiry into the Conduct of all the Officers concerned and report to you the result as soon as known. I have the honor to be very Respectfully Sir Yr. Mo. Ob. St.—

Isaac Chauncey

LS, DNA, RG45, CL, 1813, Vol. 4, No. 8 (M125, Roll No. 29).

1. In the letter book copy of this document, the armament is correctly stated as 18 pounder carronades (MiU–C, Isaac Chauncey Letter Book).

CAPTAIN RICHARD SMITH, U.S.M.C., TO
LIEUTENANT COLONEL COMMANDANT FRANKLIN WHARTON, U.S.M.C.

Sir,

Before this you must be aware of the attack made on this place on the 29th. ulto. by the enemy & of the result & circumstances attending that day— Commodore Chauncey with all the Squadron except two of the Schooners was absent at the time, but owing unfortunately to some misunderstanding on the part of the commanding Naval officer then present the Marine & Navy Barracks with all the Naval Stores of every description on this Station, all the prize goods taken at York & every article of public property belonging to the Marine Corps I am sorry to inform you was set on fire & entirely destroy'd— My officers & men suffer'd much they have nearly lost all their clothing camp utensils &c— My loss is a serious one, most of my public accounts, vouchers, baggage &c, were also destroy'd, which with the public property could have been saved if the commanding Naval officer had given any previous notice of his intention to do that, which could not have been possibly effected by the enemy— Many of my men is entirely without shoes & several almost naked in consequence of the fire, to relieve them is out of my power; the clothing spoken of by you I hope may reach me soon, untill then, I shall not be able to relieve their distress'd situation— I now require clothing of every description as most of the men have it due them— Lt. Sterne has been restored to duty by order of the Secretary of the Navy— The Sick report of this morning states Twenty Six unfit for duty— Robert Forster of the detachment died on the 23d ulto. John Smith, Fifer, gave him self up to me while at Fort George, upper Canada on the 30th. ulto. as a deserter from the Command of Capt Hall Newyork— In consequence of the loss of some of my returns, it will be out of my power for the present, to forward the usual returns of pay clothing &c to the different Staff— We sail in a few days for Kingston, the enemies fleet it is said is ready for sea & willing to meet us on the Lake—the force of the two is about equal— Our new ship will be launched tomorrow but will not be ready for sea for some weeks in consequence of the late fire, her sails rigging &c were all destroy'd— Respectfully yr. obdt. servt.

R^d. Smith   Capt.

Marine encampment
Sacketts Harbour   June 11th. 1813.—

ALS, DNA, RG127, CMC, 1813, Letters Received.

Freeing the Ships at Black Rock

The evacuation of Fort Erie by the British gave the Americans the opportunity to free the five vessels left in an unfinished state of repair at Black Rock, New York. Henry Eckford and twenty-five ship carpenters from Sackets Harbor repaired the ships, and two hundred soldiers from Major General Henry Dearborn's army helped to move the vessels down river. It proved to be a daunting task. Strong currents in the Niagara River and contrary winds precluded sailing the craft out, so that they had to be towed using a few oxen and human force alone. After a week of effort, the vessels—Caledonia, Somers, Trippe, Ohio, and *Amelia—were free and sailed to join the squadron at Erie.[1]*

1. *Rosenberg,* Building Perry's Fleet, *pp. 55–56.*

COMMODORE ISAAC CHAUNCEY TO SECRETARY OF THE NAVY JONES

No. 30   U.S. Ship *Madison*
                                                    Niagara River, 29th. May 1813

Sir

Deeming the command of Lake Erie of primary importance I dispatched Captain Perry yesterday with 55 Seamen to Black Rock, to take the Five Vessels there to Erie as soon as possible and to prepare the whole Squadron for Service by the 15th. of June.— General Dearborn has promised me 200 Soldiers to put on board of the vessels at Black Rock, to assist in protecting them to Erie— Mr. Eckford has with uncommon exertions prepared these Vessels for service, since the capture of York, and I think that Captain Perry will be ready to proceed for Presque Isle, about the 3d. or 4th. of June, provided I can get the Gun carriages up, which I brought from Sacketts Harbor for the Vessels at the Rock— we are however still much in want of Men, and if none arrive before my return to Sacketts Harbor I shall be obliged to dismantle the Fleet upon this Lake, to man that upon Erie— The two Brigs building at Erie have been launched.

The *Queen Charlotte* and three others of the Enemy's vessels came down to Fort Erie, on the 26th. Inst. but as soon as they heard of the capture of Fort George, and its dependencies they proceeded up the Lake, I presume for Malden— I have the honor to be very respectfully Sir Yr. Mo. Ob. St.

                                                              Isaac Chauncey

LS, DNA, RG45, CL, 1813, Vol. 3, No. 196 (M125, Roll No. 28).

MASTER COMMANDANT OLIVER H. PERRY TO COMMODORE ISAAC CHAUNCEY

copy   U.S. Brig *Caledonia*   June 12 1813.—
                                                         off Buffaloe Creek.

I have the honor to inform you that I have at length succeeded in getting the vessels from Black Rock above the rapids after almost incredible fatigue both to officers and men the wind having blown from the Westward nearly a fortnight. Without the assistance of the Soldiers sent me by Genl. Dearborn we could not have ascended the Rapids, having tracked every Vessel by main Strength.

I have received a letter from Lt. Turner who tells me the Anchors for the Brigs will not be finished before the 20th. of July, although when I was at Pittsburgh they were promised by the 1st. of May. I make no comments on this abominable deception. If you Sir have two spare anchors and would send them to Niagara with the men, I think with some contrivance, I should not be delayed for the misconduct of the Anchor Maker at Pittsburgh—

Copy, DNA, RG45, CL, 1813, Vol. 4, No. 103, enclosure (M125, Roll No. 29). This copy was enclosed in a letter from Commodore Isaac Chauncey to Secretary of the Navy Jones of 24 June 1813.

Preparations on Lake Erie

Master Commandant Oliver H. Perry and Lieutenant Robert H. Barclay worked tirelessly during the summer of 1813 to build, equip, and man their respective fleets on Lake Erie. They each faced similar shortages of supplies, provisions, and men. The only material available locally was timber; virtually all other material, including iron, guns, shot, canvas, and rope, had to be made and shipped from great distances over bad roads or along the lake.

The greatest problem facing both commanders was a shortage of men. Perry and Barclay would complain that their respective commanding officers—Commodore Isaac Chauncey and Commodore Sir James Lucas Yeo—were deliberately holding back men and were keeping the most skilled seamen for their own fleets on Lake Ontario.

MASTER COMMANDANT OLIVER H. PERRY TO SECRETARY OF THE NAVY JONES

Erie Penna.   June 19th. 1813

Sir

I had the honor of receiving your letter of the 25th. Ult.[1] last eveg. The very flattering manner in which you are pleased to speak of me, is highly gratifying to a young officer whose ardent desire it is to possess the good opinion of his Government and countrymen, and who has at the same time a due sense of the responsibility of his situation, and doubts of his capacity to meet fully the expectations of Government. I can only promise Sir, not to be wanting in activity and exertions for the honor and good of the service.

I left Buffalo on the eveg. of the 14 Inst. with the vessels named in the margin[2] and arrived last evening without seeing the enemy although they were watching for us and from information derived from judge Sackett, it appears we were both in sight at the same time from Chatocque. I have the honor to enclose a list of the Naval Force at this place and a roll of officers & men, the vessels can be ready to go over the bar in a day after the arrival of the crews, provided the anchors and shot arrive in time from Pittsburgh, which I have no doubt will be the case from letters I have recd. from Mr. Ormsby. The sails of both Brigs are nearly finished, and the rigging of one fitted, and guns mounted the other will be rigged very shortly and the guns mounted— The Gun Boats are fitted wanting only an additional quantity of shot. The vessels from Buffalo although not well fitted are considered as ready for service at a moments notice.— The fifty men Comr. Chauncey has spared me from the other Lake will allow me to progress rapidly in the equipment of those vessels, In fact Sir the moment the crews arrive the whole force shall be on the Lake unless some unforeseen accident prevents.

From the best information I can get it appears the enemy have the vessels named in the enclosed list. Their new Ship[3] (the officers of the *Queen Charlotte* reported when at Fort Erie) was to be launched on the 1st. of June. I could not learn whether they had got her guns up or not— She is said to be larger than the *Charlotte*. It appears Capt. Barclay with his men have arrived and are now onboard their fleet.

I beg leave to observe to you Sir, my great deficiency in officers of experience, those that are here, although very valuable young officers are without much naval knowledge and as I have neither a regular Boatn. or Gunner, the detail of their duties occupies a great part of my time.

I enclose an estimate of the number of officers Seamen & marines required to complete the crews of the vessels here   Very Respectfully I have the honor to be Sir Your Obdt. Servt.

O. H. Perry

LS, DNA, RG45, AF7 (M625, Roll No. 76).

1. In his letter of 25 May, Secretary of the Navy Jones directed Perry to correspond directly with him regarding preparations on Lake Erie and the movements of the enemy rather than writing through Commodore Isaac Chauncey. Jones also informed him that cannon were sent to Erie, and that he was sending additional seamen and marines. See DNA, RG45, SNL, Vol. 10, pp. 439–40 (M149, Roll No. 10).

2. Text at bottom of last page of document:

Vessels From Buffalo
Caledonia	Brig		
Ohio	Schooner		
Amelia	"		
Sommers	"	formerly	*Catherine*
Trippe	Sloop	"	*Contractor*

Allow me to ask the favor of knowing the names you intend for the two Brigs.

O. H. Perry

3. H.M. ship *Detroit* was launched at Amherstburg in late July 1813.

[Enclosure]

Estimate of the number of Officers, seamen, & Marines required for the Vessels of War on Lake Erie—viz

```
2 Brigs—            130 ea . . . . . . . . . . 260
4 Schooners . . . . .  28 . . . . . . . . . . . . 112
1 small Brig, Caledonia . . . . . . . . . . . .  50
3 schooners ⎫
            ⎬ from Buffalo. . . 35 . . . 140
1 sloop     ⎭
                                             562
deduct, number now here . . . . . . . . . 159
                        Wanted     403
```

Erie, June 20. 1813
S. Hambleton
Purser.

I shall consider myself equal to the enemy with a smaller number than the above.

O. H. Perry

DS, DNA, RG45, AF7 (M625, Roll No. 76). Postscript is in the hand of Oliver H. Perry. Two other enclosures provided a list of British vessels on Lake Erie, and a list by rank of the 159 officers and men then serving on Lake Erie.

LIEUTENANT ROBERT H. BARCLAY, R.N., TO
MAJOR GENERAL HENRY PROCTER, BRITISH ARMY

HMS: *Queen Charlotte* June 29th. 1813

Sir/

In reply to your letter, requesting a statement of what is wanted to make His Majesty's Squadron effective on Lake Erie, that you sought transmitted to His Excellency the Governor in chief—

I have to state that there is a general want of stores of every description at this post but more especially <u>Iron</u> for chain plates, and other uses all of which have been demanded long ago, also an abstract of former requisitions has been sent by me to hasten the supply of those things which I judged indispensably necessary—

The *Detroit* may be launched in ten days, but there is no chance of her being ready for any active service until a large proportion of stores, and guns are sent here— And even admitting that she could be equipped—there is not a seaman to put on board her— The absolute necessity of Seamen being immediately sent up is so obvious that I need hardly point it out to you— The Ships are manned with a crew, part of whom cannot even speak English—none of them seamen and very few even in numbers.— The Enemy have two corvettes in a forward state at Presqu' isle, and from their resources being so contiguous I have no doubt but that they will be ready to sail very soon in a much superior force than any exertion of mine can get ready to oppose them.—

I have repeatedly pointed out to Commodore Sir James Yeo the manner in which the squadron under my command is manned, and I have no doubt of his sending as many seamen as he can spare—but I have little hopes of his sending a sufficient number, until some method is adopted to get another supply of good Seamen from England or Quebec—

A party of 12 good shipwrights is also much wanted here, the builder represents that his present party are most ignorant of their profession, and the difficulties he labours under from that circumstance must be very great. If His Excellency would cause a party to be sent here, in the event of damages by action taking place they could soon be repaired and the squadron rendered effective again— At Present when any repair or alteration is required, (of which many are indispensably requisite) from the small number of men employed, every thing must stand still until that is finished—such is the case at present but under every disadvantageous circumstance the *Detroit* will be fully ready to receive her guns and men, as soon as they are sent up— I am Sir Your most obd. & Hble. Servant

R H Barclay   Comd.
H M Ships & vessels on Lake Erie

LS, CaOOA, British Military and Naval Records, RG8, I, "C" Ser., Vol. 730, pp. 27–30.

[Enclosure]

A Statement of the Forces of the American Squadron as last reconnoitred in the Harbour of Presque Isle June 20

> Two new Brigs or Corvettes in a forward state
> Seven Schooners ⎫ Number of Guns unknown
> Two Brigs   ⎭ but all Armed & Manned

The Corvettes appear to be both as large as the *Queen Charlotte* but they are still in the inner harbour, not rigged or armed but from their resources being so near at hand I cannot reasonably expect they will be long in that situation

> R H Barclay   Sen Offr
> on Lake Erie

DS, CaOOA, British Military and Naval Records, RG8, I, "C" Ser., Vol. 730, p. 31.

[Enclosure]

A Statement of the Force of His Majesty's Squadron employed on Lake Erie

Names	Guns	Calibres	Canadians	Newfoundland	41st Regiment
Queen Charlotte	18	24 Prs. Caronades	40	25	45
Lady Prevost	12	10, 12 prs. Cds. & 2 long 9s.	30	10	36
Hunter	6	4 long 6s & 2, 18 prs. Cds.	20	4	15
Erie	2	1 Traversing long 12 prs. & 1, 12 prs. Caronade	6	4	5
Little Belt	2	1 Do. long 9 prs. & 1, 24 pr. Cds.	6	4	5
*Chippewa	2	2, 8 Inch Howitzers	6	7	

Detroit— pierced for 20 but not yet launched

*Left with Brigadier Genl. Procter

R H: Barclay   Senr. Offr.
on Lake Erie

DS, CaOOA, British Military and Naval Records, RG8, I, "C" Ser., Vol. 730, p. 32.

View of Amherstburg

SECRETARY OF THE NAVY JONES TO MASTER COMMANDANT OLIVER H. PERRY

O. H. Perry Esqr.   Navy Department
Comg. Naval Officer   July 3d. 1813.
Erie.

Sir,

I have received your letters of the 19th. and 24th. with the papers therein referred to, and trust the moment is near at hand, when we shall have the command of both Lakes.

I have reason to believe, that Commodore Chauncey will, ere this, have despatched a reinforcement to you, as there are now, on the way to Sackett's Harbour, 500 Officers, Seamen and Marines, who will reach that place from the 7th to the 15th. Instant.

Commodore Chauncey will be ready to meet the enemy with his whole force, about the 15th. and I trust, under such advantages as will insure a complete victory, unless the enemy shall previously have taken shelter at Kingston.— But in any event, when the force above mentioned shall have arrived, he will detach a sufficient number of Officers and men to complete the crews of the whole force under your command. Presuming that you will have such information of the force and designs of the enemy as will enable you to appreciate the consequences of hazarding a contest before you receive reinforcements, and have the other sloop of war ready for action, the determination is submitted to your judgement and discretion.

The following is a quotation from my letter of this date, to Commodore Chauncey, which you will consider as an instruction to yourself.

> "I have informed Capt Perry, that as the entire command was given to you, with the most perfect confidence, a very great degree of reluctance is felt by the Department, in interposing its authority; and nothing but the apprehension of suffering the enemy to escape, under circumstances so favourable for offensive operations on our part—the probability of his being reinforced—of the Ship at Malden being brought into action sooner than expected, and of delay, or adverse circumstances on the Lakes below, could induce me to anticipate your commands. I have therefore advised him, to weigh, with great caution, the probable issue of an attempt to meet the enemy as he proposes, and if, upon mature deliberation, he is clearly of opinion, that, (with the one Sloop and 9 smaller vessels, manned with 159 officers, Seamen and Marines, and 200 regular soldiers, and such volunteers as he can pick up,) he can succeed, in cutting off the enemy's squadron, he has my authority to make the attempt;—but, immediately on receipt of my order, to communicate with you, and if he shall receive your instructions to suspend the execution of the design, or to pursue any other course, that he will substitute your orders for those of the Department."

The testimony of the deserters from the *Charlotte* is highly probable, and there is a remarkable coincidence in their narratives; yet it must be received with caution, and compared with information from other sources. According to their account, the British Naval force in men cannot be above 220 or 30, which would give you, even without any further reinforcement, a decided superiority.

The consequences of cutting off, at once, his Naval force on Erie, would be incalculably great, and probably would be immediately followed by his abandonment of Malden, and the upper country; which would immediately induce the desertion of the Savages, and release a great part of General Harrison's army, which might immediately be transported, by our fleet, to Niagara, and produce a decisive blow in that quarter also. This is the bright side of the picture, and we must not forget to look at the reverse. Under all circumstances and with these precautionary admonitions, the President relies upon your prudence, skill, and enterprize, to determine upon, and execute that plan, which shall appear to you best adapted to advance the public cause, and, with it, your own reputation and honour.

The Secretary of War has allowed the 200 regulars to remain under your command, until you shall receive the reinforcement of Officers and Seamen, destined for your command.

One of the sloops of war, (the first ready) is to be called the "*Lawrence*," after our brave countryman, Captain James Lawrence, late of the United States Navy;—the other the *Niagara*.[1] I am, very respectfully, Your obedient Servant,

W. Jones

LB Copy, DNA, RG45, CLS, 1813, pp. 48–51.

1. The brigs *Lawrence* and *Niagara* were built at Presque Isle and launched in early June 1813.

The Capture of *Growler* and *Eagle* on Lake Champlain

The first naval action of the year on Lake Champlain ended badly for the Americans. With his flagship grounded and needing repairs, Lieutenant Thomas Macdonough sent his two other large vessels, the sloops Growler *and* Eagle, *to patrol the line and try to control British gunboat activity. Lieutenant Sidney Smith, eager for action and ignoring the hazards of navigating in the narrow Richelieu River, proceeded farther north towards the British base at Isle aux Noix. The sloops encountered heavy fire from British row galleys and shore batteries, and in attempting to turn in the narrow river, ran aground and were captured. The loss was a serious one for the Americans: about one hundred men were made prisoners,[1] and Macdonough's fleet was reduced to only the crippled* President *and two small unmanned gunboats. The balance of power on the lake had shifted in favor of the British, who lost no time in planning to use it to their advantage.[2]*

1. *For the statement of Abraham Walter, pilot of* Growler, *on the treatment of the prisoners of war, see pp. 600–602.*
2. *Everest, War of 1812, pp. 108–10.*

MAJOR GEORGE TAYLOR, BRITISH ARMY, TO
MAJOR GENERAL RICHARD STOVIN, BRITISH ARMY

Isle aux Noix   3 June 1813.

Sir,—

In the absence of Lieut. Col. Hamilton I have the honor to acquaint you that one of the Enemys Armed Vessels was discerned from the Garrison at half past five o'Clock this morning when I judged it expedient to order the three Gun Boats under way, and before they reached the point above the Garrison another Vessel appeared in sight—when the Gun Boats commenced firing; observing the Vessels to be near enough the shore for Musquetry, I ordered the Crews of two Batteaux & row boat, which I took with me from the Garrison to act according to circumstances, to land on each side the River and to take a position to rake the Vessels. The firing was briskly kept up on both sides, (the enemy with small arms & grape shot occasionally)—near the close of the action an express came off to me in a Canoe with intelligence that more armed vessels were approaching and about three thousand men from the Enemy's Lines by Land, on this information I returned to put the Garrison in the best order for their reception, leaving directions with the Gun Boats & parties not to suffer their retreat to be cut off from it, and before I reached the Garrison the Enemys Vessels struck their Colours after a well contested action of three hours & a half— They proved to be the United States Armed Vessels *Growler* & *Eagle*, burthens from 90 to 100 Tons & Carrying Eleven Guns each— between them 12 eighteen & 10 six Pounder Carronades, Completely equipped under the Orders of the Senior Officer of the *Growler* Captain Sydney Smith with a complement of Fifty Men each; they had one man killed & eight severely wounded— We had only three men wounded, one of them severely from the enemys Grape Shot on the Parties on Shore— The alacrity of the Garrison on this occasion calls forth my warmest approbation, Ensigns Dawson, Gibbon & Humphreys & acting Qr. Masters Pilkington and Crews of the 100th (Prince Regents) Regiment and Lieutt. Low[1] of the Marine Department with three Gunners Royal Artillery to each Boat behaved with the greatest gallantry—and am particularly indebted to Capt. Gordon of the Royal Artillery and Lieut. Williams with the parties of the 100th. Regiment on Shore who materially contributed to the Surrender of the Enemy. The *Growler* is arrived at the Garrison in good order & apparently a fine Vessel, and the Boats are employed in getting off the *Eagle* which was run aground to prevent her sinking, I have hopes she will be saved, but in the mean time have had her dismantled, her Guns & Stores brought to the Garrison.—

Ensign Dawson of the 100th. Regt. a most intelligent officer will have the honor of delivering you this— I have the honor to be, Sir, Your Most Obedt. & Humble Servant

Geo. Taylor
Major 100th (Prince Regents)
Regt. & Lt. Col.

Names of Officers taken on board the United States armed vessels *Growler* and *Eagle* in action with His Majestys Gun Boats &c off Hospital Island above Isle aux Noix 3d. June 1813—

Captains { Sydney Smith Comdg.
{ Jarius Loomis

Masters Mates { John Trambler
{ John Freeburn

Midshipmen { Walter Neil Monteith
{ Horace Sawyer

and

Captain Oliver Herricksen[2] } of the United
Ensign Washington Dennison } States Army.

Number of Men Killed, wounded and Prisoners onboard the United States armed vessells, *Growler* & *Eagle* 3d. June 1813.—

       1 Killed—
       8 Wounded severely
       <u>91</u> Prisoners—
      100 Total—

Geo: Taylor
Major & Lt. Col.

LS, CaOOA, British Military and Naval Records, RG8, I, "C" Ser., Vol. 679, pp. 10–11.

1. Lieutenant William Lowe, Provincial Marine.
2. Captain Oliver Herrick, U.S. Army.

LIEUTENANT THOMAS MACDONOUGH TO SECRETARY OF THE NAVY JONES

U.S. Sloop *President* at anchor
Plattsburgh   4th. June 1813

Sir.

I am sorry to acquaint you with the loss of the U.S. sloops, *Growler* and *Eagle*, under the command of Lieut. Sidney Smith— those vessels were stationed in the vicinity of the lines to prevent smuggling and the enemys Gun Boats (or galleys) making excurtions in our waters— I cannot give you the particulars of this unfortunate and unlooked for capture untill Lt. Smith states them to me, I shall then forward to you his statement—[1] I have the honor to be Sir your most obt. servt.

T. Macdonough

I should require for me to get, again, the command of this Lake two sloops in the place of those captured and they can be purchased here. I hear the comdr. of this section of the army is about purchasing them, of which I shall inform you as soon as I see, or hear from him—and three experienced Lieutenants, six midshipmen, three gunners, thirty seamen and seventy ordinary seamen— my guns are gone sir, and there is not a spare one on the Lake   18 pr Cannonades I think the best kind for these vessels, as they are light and carry a greater quantity of grape shot than long guns of about the same weight and it is likely they will be used principally against small vessels with many men exposed in them, or against sloops. I should require also one thousand cylanders[2] for the twenty guns which I calculate to mount on the two sloops ten on each one— I also request your permission to receive from the Navy Yard at New York such supplies of rigging as I may require.

I avail myself sir, of this opportunity to recommend Midshipman Joseph Smith of Massachusetts as a suitable person to command one of these sloops, he is old in the Navy has been much in the merchants service to India &c and in the capacity of Lieutenant I am confident you would not regret the appointment—

I shall not want either grape or round shot as I have those in abundance, and the cylinders I wish to be sent filled— I have the honor to be Sir your most obt. servt.

T. Macdonough

ALS, DNA, RG45, BC, 1813, Vol. 2, No. 110 (M148, Roll No. 11).

1. For this report, see Macdonough to Jones, 22 July 1813, pp. 515–16.
2. Cylinder (or canister) shot consisted of a cylindrical tin filled with ball shot which scattered on being fired.

MAJOR GENERAL FRANCIS DE ROTTENBURG, BRITISH ARMY, TO MAJOR GENERAL GEORGE GLASGOW, BRITISH ARMY

Copy
Secret & Confidential

Hd. Qr. Montreal
5 June 1813

Sir

In consequence of our having succeeded in taking two of the Enemy's largest vessels on Lake Champlain, an opportunity now offers for destroying the whole of their naval force Boats &c on that Lake, and I wish you immediately to consult with the Senior Officer of the Navy now at Quebec, on the possibility of his allowing about 60 or even more of the best sailors with a proportion of officers for three vessels for that purpose—as it will be a business of but a few days, the Men may return in the Steam boat— I beg you will state to the Senior Captain that it is a thing of the greatest importance to this Country, and if effected would enable us to send troops in boats to any part of the Lake, and I am convinced he cannot object to sending them.— It must be done with the greatest secrecy, and the men informed & might be even given out, that they are to reinforce the Navy at Kingston;—but you will prior to taking any other ships, let me know the naval officers' opinion, as I would wish to make my arrangements here that they might leave this place in the night they arrive, and the distance being so short, they can be put on board, and set off immediately. I think if there are no objections a naval officer should be sent up immediateley (but in colored clothes) and not saying who he is, that he might not create suspicion to see what arrangements may be necessary. I have &c

(signed)   F. de R.
M. Genl. Comg.

Copy, CaOOA, British Military and Naval Records, RG8, I, "C" Ser., Vol. 679, pp. 64–65.

MAJOR GENERAL GEORGE GLASGOW, BRITISH ARMY, TO MAJOR GENERAL FRANCIS DE ROTTENBURG, BRITISH ARMY

Quebec   Monday Evening   7th June
9 1/2 oCk

Sir,

I had the honor to receive your secret and confidential Letter of the 5th. Inst. by the Mail which arrived this evening at Eight oClock, and have given immediate attention to your wishes expressed in it. I have communicated with Capt.

Russell of H.M.S. *Cygnet* the Senior Officer of the Navy in port, upon the matter proposed by you, and I have received from him a ready acquiescence therein— I have also had Capt. Kempt the agent of Transports with me, who has offered a cooperation from his Department; Capt. Russell intends to furnish from the *Cygnet* for the particular service you require, One Lieut., two Midshipmen, two petty officers, and 30 Seamen, and Captain Kempt will supply from the Transports under his directions, One Lieut. of the Navy and seventy men, including mates who will act as petty officers— The whole of the above will take their departure from hence in their own boats, tomorrow evening for Montreal; Capt. Russell & Capt. Kempt have both handsomely made an offer of their services upon the occasion which I have accepted, and it is proposed that they will leave Quebec tomorrow morning at 10 oClock, after having made the necessary arrangements for the departure of their men, and will proceed express in colored Clothes to Montreal, to communicate with you & to prepare for the arrival of their boats, which may probably reach Montreal, in a day or two after them.

Capt. Russell of the *Cygnet* has consented to spare his men for this Service from the assurance I have given him of an Embargo being laid upon all Vessels in the port from the 10th. Inst. & until further Orders, and for which purpose I must request you will give the necessary directions— I am the more urgent in requesting your compliance with this measure, there being but few vessels about to sail with the present Convoy on the 10th. and confident that the trade will not suffer in the least from the circumstances.— As the departure of the *Cygnet* & Convoy has been positively fixed for the 10th, from which no deviation should have been admitted by Capt. Russell but under the peculiar urgency of the case, & my promise to him of an embargo being laid on, I must beg to repeat my request that your instructions to this effect, may be sent off express, so as to reach Quebec if possible on the morning of the 10th. I have the honor to be Sir your most obedient humble servant

George Glasgow
Maj Genl.

LS, CaOOA, British Military and Naval Records, RG8, I, "C" Ser., Vol. 679, pp. 66–69.

British Ascendancy on Lake Ontario

After Commodore Isaac Chauncey returned to Sackets Harbor from the Niagara campaign, he was reluctant to go out again until General Pike, which was partially burned during the British attack, was completed and he judged his force was superior to the enemy's. Chauncey adopted a slower and more cautious approach —"to put nothing at hazard"—rather than to risk losing his squadron in an engagement in which he did not have the upper hand. Chauncey remained at Sackets Harbor from 1 June until 21 July. In the interim, Yeo's squadron sailed Lake Ontario almost unchecked.

The British attacked Major General Henry Dearborn's encampment at Forty Mile Creek, captured valuable army stores at the Genesee River and at Sodus, threatened the American naval base at Oswego, and attempted a secret land attack on Sackets Harbor. Chauncey sent out some of his smaller schooners with some success: On 16 June, Lady of the Lake *captured* Lady Murray. *Chauncey, however, refused to bring his fleet out, depriving Yeo of the opportunity to bring his opponent to action.*

COMMODORE ISAAC CHAUNCEY TO SECRETARY OF THE NAVY JONES

No. 38.   U.S. Ship *Madison*
                              Sackets Harbour   11th. June 1813.

Sir,

Ever since my return to this place I have kept one of the small vessels cruising between the Ducks and Kingston for the purpose of watching the movements of the enemy; and they have occasionally looked into Kingston when the wind was such as to do it with safety. The officer has always brought me word that he saw the enemy's fleet at anchor in the harbour, but within a few days we have picked up several canoes upon the Lake with people who said that they was deserters from the other side. These people reported that the enemy's fleet had gone up the lake with troops and a determination to risque the fate of the upper province upon the issue of a battle with me, but so many deserters coming over at this time created in my mind a suspicion that a part if not the whole of them had been employed by the enemy as spys and incendiarys, for the purpose of inducing me to leave the protection of the new ship and go in quest of the enemy, in order to renew their attack upon this place or burn the ship by means of incendiarys. I therefore kept all the deserters that came over, confined, and increased the guards around the ship to near 100 men every night.— a boat however arrived last evening from Niagara, the master of which reports that he saw the enemys fleet off Niagara on Monday the 7th Inst. beating in, and that the officers at the forts thought them to be the american squadron. He also reports that generals Chandler and Winder had been surprised and made prisoners of;[1] that a reinforcement had gone to the head of the Lake which had left Forts George and Niagara with not more than 200 men in each. If this mans statement should be correct and our officers should suffer themselves to be luled into security from a belief that the fleet then beating in was American, I am apprehensive for the consequences. Immediately upon receiving this information, I prepared to proceed in quest of the enemy, but upon more mature reflection I have determined to remain at this place and preserve the new ship at all hazards. My feelings upon this occasion can better be immagined than described: on the one hand I had the prospect (if I succeeded against the enemy) of immortalizing myself; on the other hand if I was beaten, the loss and disappointment to my country would be great and irreparable.— the only question then was, whether I was to fight for my own agrandisement or that of my country? if the latter, there could be no question as to the course that I ought to pursue, which was to put nothing at hazard: for by remaining here four weeks I could prepare the new ship for service, and with her I should consider myself as having the complete and uncontrouled command of this Lake; without her, the enemy has near a fourth more guns than I have, as many men and as good, and his officers are experienced and brave. With such a disparity of force I trust that you will approve of my determination of puting nothing at hazard untill the new ship is fited. I have the satisfaction of knowing that every commissioned officer on this station coincides with me in opinion as to the propriety of remaining in port untill we can fit the New Ship.

I shall use every exertion to have her got ready for service as soon as possible and I think that I shall be able to proceed with her upon the Lake on or before the 15th of July, provided her stores and men arrive in time. The burning of the public stores here on the 29th ulto. has been a serious misfortune independent of the loss; for the detention of the new ship in consequence will be at least three weeks longer than it otherwise would have been. We however must remedy the evil by industry. I have infamation that the canvass to replace the sails and canvass that was burnt, left Albany on the 8th., we may therefore look for it in about three or four days. A part of the guns has arrived at Oswego and other stores are coming on. I have a number of boats waiting at Oswego to receive the stores as they arrive, and officers stationed there to superintend their shipment. I have the honor to be Very Respectfully Sir your most obt. servt.

Isaac Chauncey

LS, DNA, RG45, CL, 1813, Vol. 4, No. 47 (M125, Roll No. 29).

1. Brigadier Generals John Chandler and William Winder were captured in the Battle of Stoney Creek, 5 June 1813.

SECRETARY OF THE NAVY JONES TO COMMODORE ISAAC CHAUNCEY

(No. 22.)

Commodore Isaac Chauncey   Navy Department
Comg. the U.S. Naval forces   June 17th. 1813.
on the Lakes.

Sir,

In my last I mentioned the crew of the U.S. late Brig *Vixen*, as having been ordered on to join you, but some obstacle having intervened, in respect to their exchange, I am obliged to detain them in New York, until the difficulty is removed, in the meantime the residue of the crew of the *Alert*, and all that can be recruited, will be sent on to you, by Lieutenant Renshaw; and moreover, I have directed Commodore Bainbridge, to send on to you, with the utmost expedition, 120 of the crew of the U.S. Brig *Siren*, just arrived at Boston.

The moment is critical, and the issue of our contest, for the ascendency on Lake Ontario, must ere this be decided; every thing that can inspire confidence, and rational hope, is on our side; the casualty and fortune of war, alone, can turn the scale against us. You have doubtless weighed well the chances, before you risqued the encounter, as the addition of the New Ship *General Pike*, for which the greater part of a complete crew will have arrived before she was ready to take the Lake, would have ensured to you the decided superiority.

To have remained in port, and suffered the enemy to range the Lake unmolested, would have been mortifying; and perhaps would have frustrated our military operations, which appear to depend, essentially, for success upon our Naval support, and cooperation.

Of this I am persuaded, that whatever may be the issue, your determination has been governed by mature deliberation, and zealous devotion to the cause, and honour of our country.

With this conviction, and the most perfect confidence in your skill, vigilance, and intrepidity, I await the issue, which is to decide the fate of Upper Canada, and the future character of the War in which we are engaged. I am, very respectfully, your Obedient Servant,

W^m. Jones.

LB Copy, DNA, RG45, CLS, 1813, pp. 32–33.

COMMODORE ISAAC CHAUNCEY TO SECRETARY OF THE NAVY JONES

No. 45.—   U.S. Ship *Madison*
                                        Sackets' Harbor   18 June 1813.—

Sir,

On the 14th. Instant the Enemy sent a Flag over with six wounded prisoners. It struck me forcibly that his object was to ascertain whether our fleet was in or not and that he intended to send Troops and Stores up the Lake. I therefore determined to intercept them and for that purpose I directed Lt. Chauncey to proceed with the "*Lady of the Lake*" that night off Presqu' Isle and cruize close in with the Enemy's shore the better to enable him to cut any thing off from the Land that might be passing up or down. I also thought it possible that he might fall in with Generals Chandler & Winder on their way down to Kingston. On the 16th. Lieut. Chauncey fell in with and captured the Schooner *Lady Murray* from Kingston bound to York with an Ensign and 15 non commissioned officers and privates belonging to the 41st. and 104th. regiments, loaded with provisions, powder, Shot, and fixed ammunition. Lt. Chauncey arrived this Morning with his prize. I shall dispatch the "*Lady of the Lake*" immediately with the hope of intercepting some of their troops passing up.—

The prisoners report that the new Brig[1] at Kingston is launched, and will soon be upon the Lake. She is to carry 20 Guns. They also state that several Gun Boats are in a state of forwardness.—

I enclose herewith a List of the Prisoners.— I have the honor to be very respectfully Sir yr. ob. servant,

Isaac Chauncey

P.S. I enclose a copy of Lt. Chauncey's Letter to me.

LS, DNA, RG45, CL, 1813, Vol. 4, No. 77 (M125, Roll No. 29). A copy of a letter from Lieutenant Wolcott Chauncey to Isaac Chauncey, dated 18 June 1813, was enclosed. Enclosure in DNA, RG45, AF7 (M625, Roll No. 76).

1. H.M. brig *Lord Melville.*

LIEUTENANT MELANCTHON T. WOOLSEY TO COMMODORE ISAAC CHAUNCEY

Copy   Oswego   June 19, 1813   3 p.m.

Sir,

I have the honor to inform you that the British Squadron appeared off here this morning at 11 Oclock. They were in sight to the Westward at Daylight. We had been working all night and had nearly completed a battery on the Town side in which are mounted 2–18 pdrs. & 2–12s Brass guns. The Enemy stood in about noon but meeting with a pretty warm reception from the guns on shore and the *Growler* moored across the river, hauled off. They are now lying too with their heads off shore just out of gunshot, and are embarking troops in 2 small schooners, and 4 Boats which have just joined them apparently from the Ducks. Whether they will attempt a landing this day or not, is uncertain. From the number apparently on board these vessels I am not uneasy about the event.

The Fleet consists of the *Wolfe, Royal George, Earl Moira, Prince regent, Simcoe*, one Gun Boat and a prize schooner lately taken by them at Gennessee River with Mr. Hooker's goods on board. I have no doubt but that the boats which have just joined the fleet have been to the Ducks to land a part of the Booty with which their ships were deeply laden before they left Gennessee River. The Stores for the Ship are by this time at the Falls. I shall, if nothing prevents, forward them to Big Stoney or Big Sandy Creeks there to wait your orders. If I can procure a Guard I will give directions to have an Express dispatched to you from either of the above mentioned places immediately on their arrival. We muster about 300 Regulars and 200 Militia: the latter so so—not enough for a powerful invading foe. Mr. Montgomery carries this Express.

Copy, DNA, RG45, CL, 1813, Vol. 4, No. 93, enclosure (M125, Roll No. 29). This copy was enclosed in a letter from Commodore Isaac Chauncey to Secretary of the Navy Jones dated 21 June 1813.

COMMODORE ISAAC CHAUNCEY TO LIEUTENANT MELANCTHON T. WOOLSEY

M. T. Woolsey esqr.   U.S. Ship *Madison*
commg. naval officer,   S.H.   12 O Clock   20 June 1813
Oswego,

Yours by Mr. Montgomery I have this moment received and am extremely apprehensive that the enemy will be able to effect a landing & drive your little force from the batteries. If they should the consequences to us will be serious. I am persuaded that you are aware of the importance of preserving the *Growler* and the guns and rigging for the *Genl. Pike* and that they will not be given up without a struggle. At all events the *Growler* ought to be destroyed in preference to her falling into the Enemy's hands, and the stores for this place ought to be sent into the woods for safety until the enemy has left the coast, and then they may be sent along shore in boats taking advantage of Westerly winds.

Col Macomb has ordered major Duvall with 100 men to Oswego: others will be sent if the enemy has not already done the Mischief. I shall wait with impatience to hear again from you, remember that you have much at stake and that the fate of the campaign depends in a very great degree on your exertions to preserve the guns and stores for the *Genl. Pike*. With great respect I have &c.

                                                    Isaac Chauncey.—

LB Copy, MiU–C, Isaac Chauncey Letter Book.

LIEUTENANT MELANCTHON T. WOOLSEY TO COMMODORE ISAAC CHAUNCEY

Copy   Oswego June 21, 1813.   8 o'clock p.m.—

Major Carr is about sending a dispatch to Sackets' Harbor and I avail myself of the opportunity to inform you that I have information from Mr. Vaughan at the Falls that there are 2 cables and 10 guns and their tackle at the upper landing. A boat load of cordage has just come down and is now loading on board the *Gold Hunter*, as soon as she is loaded I shall send her with a strong guard to Sandy Creek. Under existing circumstances I dare not take upon myself to send her further than Sandy Creek. This express will supercede the necessity of sending an Express from that place after the arrival of the boat and I shall give Capt. Dominick orders to wait at Sandy Creek for your further orders.

The British Squadron landed yesterday morning a body of men at Great Sodus and burned it. I think this savage warfare calls for vengeance. A Dr. Baldwin and a Capt. Tappen have just got in here from Sodus which place they left about 11 O'Clock this morning, at that time the Fleet appeared to be about Pultney Ville. Mr Vaughan informs me that 3 more guns are on the way: how far back he does not know. I am busily employed building a Battery to mount 7 guns. This place is in a wretched state of defense. The Militia are all returning home, and between 2 and 300 regulars are by no means competent to defend it.—

Copy, DNA, RG45, CL, 1813, Vol. 4, No. 93, enclosure (M125, Roll No. 29). This copy was enclosed in a letter from Commodore Isaac Chauncey to Secretary of the Navy Jones dated 21 June 1813.

COMMODORE ISAAC CHAUNCEY TO SECRETARY OF THE NAVY JONES

No. 52

U.S. Ship *Madison*
Sackets Harbor
24th June 1813

Sir,

I have been this day honored with your letter of the 14th inst. and am extremely flattered with your approbation.

Under existing Circumstances I have thought it advisable to be prepared to build another vessel. I have therefore directed Mr. Eckford to prepare the Materials to build a fast sailing schooner of about 250 Tons to mount 3 long 32 pounders. I prefer this kind of Vessel for the following reasons: First, we have nearly all the ~~Timber~~ Materials in the yard left from the new Ship: she can be sooner built; will cost less money; be more efficient, and lastly we have her Armament on the spot. This vessel will not be required if the enemy keeps the Lake until I get the *Genl. Pike* ready, for whenever the two Fleets meet upon the Lake the mastery will be decided and the Conqueror left without a Rival. I am only apprehensive that he may go into Kingston and wait there until all his force is ready in which case he would have the Superiority, for in addition to his present force he has a Brig nearly ready for service which will mount 18 to 20 guns and from 6 to 10 gunboats. I shall be able to ascertain in a few days whether it will be advisable to build another vessel or not. I shall however go on in preparing the materials so that she can be built in about 4 weeks if required. I am anxious not to create expense unnecessarily but at the same time endeavour to be prepared to meet any event.

In order not to alarm the Enemy I have circulated a Report (which is generally believed even amongst the Officers) that the *Genl. Pike* cannot be got ready before the first of August, and to give currency to that report I have directed her cables and anchors to be kept above the Falls at Oswego and when I do go out I shall take two of the *Madison's* which will answer for the Cruise. all these reports are faithfully transmitted to the Enemy which I think will put him less on his guard. I shall not rig the *Genl. Pike* until I am perfectly ready to sail which I think I shall be on or before the 15th of next Month: at any rate I shall use every exertion to get ready as soon as possible. If the Seamen should not arrive in time I shall try and obtain a sufficient number of Soldiers to replace the Men taken from this ship and the other vessels to man the *General Pike.*— I have the honor to be very respectfully Sir yr. most ob. servt.

Isaac Chauncey

LS, DNA, RG45, CL, 1813, Vol. 4, No. 104 (M125, Roll No. 29).

COMMODORE SIR JAMES LUCAS YEO, R.N., TO FIRST SECRETARY OF THE ADMIRALTY JOHN W. CROKER

No. 5   His Majesty's Ship *Wolfe*, at
                        Kingston, Upper Canada, the 29th. June 1813

Sir/

   I have the Honor to inform you, for the information of the Lords Commissioners of the Admiralty, that on the 3rd. Instant, I sailed with His Majesty's Squadron under my Command, from this Port, to co-operate with our Army at the Head of the Lake, and annoy the Enemy, by intercepting all supplies going to his Army, and thereby oblige his Squadron, to come out for its protection.

   At day light on the 8th. the Enemys Camp was discovered close to us, at 40 Mile Creek, it being calm the large Vessels could not get in, but the *Beresford*, Captain Spilsbury, the *Sir Sidney Smith* Lieutenant Majoribanks, and the Gun Boats, under the orders of Lieutenant Anthony (first of this ship) succeeded in getting close under the Enemy's Batteries, and by a sharp and well directed fire, soon obliged him to make a precipitate Retreat, leaving all his Camp Equipage, Provisions, Stores &c. behind, which fell into our hands, the *Beresford*, also captured all his Bateaux, laden with Stores, &c., our Troops immediately occupied the Post, I then proceeded along shore to the Westward of the Enemys Camp, leaving our Army in his front, on the 13th. we captured two Schooners, and some Boats, going to the Enemy with Supplies, by them I received information, that there was a Depôt of Provisions, at Genesee River, I accordingly proceeded off that River, landed some Seamen, and Marines of the Squadron, and brought off all the Provisions found in the Government Stores, as also a sloop laden with Grain, for the Army, on the 19th. I anchored off the great Sodus, landed a party of the 1st. Regiment of Royal Scotts, and took off six hundred Barrels of Flour, and Pork, which had arrived there for their Army. Yesterday I returned to this anchorage to Victual and Refit the Squadron. I have the Honor to be Sir/ your most obedient humble Servant

James Lucas Yeo   Commodore

LS, UkLPR, Adm. 1/2736, pp. 110–12. Duplicate copy sent.

COMMODORE ISAAC CHAUNCEY TO SECRETARY OF THE NAVY JONES

No. 54.

U.S. Ship *Madison*
Sackets' Harbor
3d. July 1813.

Sir,

At 6 o'clock on the evening of the 1st. inst. I received information by a deserter that Sir James Yeo, with 800 to 1000 picked men, was secreted in the woods in Chaumont Bay about 7 miles from this harbor: that he left Kingston the evening before with about 20 large Boats and landed in Chaumont Bay about daylight in the morning of the 1st. hawled all his Boats on shore and covered them with the Branches of Trees and kept their men close in the Woods. It was Sir James's intention to remain concealed all day and make a desperate attack upon the fleet the following night. The *Madison* was to be boarded by 400 picked men headed by Sir James himself, and the other vessels boarded at the same instant and carried at all hazards. The plan was well arranged, and if it had been attempted there would have been a dreadful slaughter on both sides. As soon as I was informed of the plan and situation of Sir James and his party, I made my arrangements so as to have ensured defeat to the Enemy, and I think, a total annihilation of his force. We remained at our quarters all night under the anxious expectation of an attack but day light appeared without hearing any thing from the Enemy. I immediately got under way with the whole Squadron and run outside of Point Peninsula in order to cut him off from Kingston if he should be still in his hiding place. I went on board of the *Lady of the Lake* and examined the whole shore from Grenadier Island round the West Shore of Chaumont Bay without being able to discover any Enemy or the signs of any Boats. I returned to the harbor about Sundown and anchored the Squadron as before and made the same preparations for defense. At about 8 o'clock two Seamen were brought in by the Guard Boats: they deserted from the Enemy the Evening before. They stated the force and arrangements to be the same as mentioned by the first Deserter: they also stated that they left their party about 8 o'clock the preceding evening at which time they were reimbarking on board of their Boats for the purpose of returning to Kingston. The reason assigned by Sir James Yeo for relinquishing the Enterprize was that some person had just given him information from the Harbor that we knew of his being there, & that we were making preparations to cut him off, & what confirmed him in this belief was that two of our guard vessels were then cruising outside of him. He assured his party that the Enterprize was only relinquished for a few days, that he meant to return the first dark and stormy Night and had no doubt of complete success. These two men lay concealed in the woods until Sir James with his party put off, which was about 10 o'clock. This day 3 other Deserters have been brought in by the guard-boats: they corroborate the account given by the others in every particular.

We are prepared to receive Sir James whenever he may think proper to make so desperate an attack. I have 16 guns mounted upon the *General Pike* and the others have all arrived and will be mounted in a few days. Nearly the whole of the rigging has arrived and fitted: her sails nearly finished, and the other parts of her Armament will be here I presume in time. I have made arrangements with the Military commanding officer at this post to furnish me with a sufficient number of men from the Army (many of whom are sailors) to compleat the crew of the *Genl. Pike*, we therefore shall not be detained an hour for men, and you may depend

upon my exertions to get upon the Lake as soon as possible for it is mortifying beyond expression to be obliged to remain here while the Enemy is cruising. I have
the honor to be very respectfully Sir yr. ob. servt.

Isaac Chauncey

LS, DNA, RG45, CL, 1813, Vol. 4, No. 147 (M125, Roll No. 29).

COMMODORE ISAAC CHAUNCEY TO MAJOR GENERAL HENRY DEARBORN, U.S.A.

Major Genl.   U.S. Ship *Genl. Pike*
H. Dearborn   12 July 1813.—
commdr &c &c
Fort George

I was yesterday honored with your letter of the 1st. inst., and regret extremely
to learn that you have met with any losses, particularly as the Enemy's force in
that quarter is constantly augmenting.

The *Genl. Pike* is nearly ready, her guns are all mounted, her sails finished,
and she has a full complement of men, and if the Enemy should be upon the
Lake, I hope to leave here in 5 days; but if he should be in Kingston I shall remain here a few days longer in hopes to induce him to go out. It will however
be out of my power consistent with my present arrangements to visit the upper
part of the Lake with the fleet as long as the Enemy remains in this neighbourhood with so powerful a force, and as to taking any troops on board as long as
the Enemy's force is superior in point of guns, I shd. deem it unsafe and im-
politic, and might hazard the safety of the fleet, but as soon as Sir James and
Myself have had a Meeting and the result should be what I expect it will be, I
will transport troops to any point that you may wish.—

I am much pleased to hear that your health is re-established, and that you are
again able to attend to the various and important duties of your command. I
hope soon to have the pleasure of seeing you and that I shall have it in my power
to say that we have no Enemy to contend with upon the Lake.— I have the honor
to be with great regard and esteem Dr. Sir Yr. most ob. S.

Isaac Chauncey

LB Copy, MiU–C, Isaac Chauncey Letter Book.

SECRETARY OF THE NAVY JONES TO COMMODORE ISAAC CHAUNCEY

(No. 27.)

Commodore Chauncey   Navy Department
Commanding the U.S.   July 14th 1813.
Naval forces on the Lakes.

Sir,
I have this day received your letters, Nos. 53, 54, 55, 56, & 57. No. 54 was
under a cover, superscribed in the handwriting of Mr. Anderson, with the Albany Post-Mark of the 9th, and <u>without seal</u>, on either the letter or cover. The
hazardous plans of the British commander, evince the desperation of his case,

and are characterized more by despair than marked by judgment. I suspect the most prominent feature in his character, is impetuosity, in English phraseology, "dashing". A knowledge of the personal character of our adversary is of material importance, and may often be turned to great advantage. It is highly probable their casual success, by boarding the *Chesapeake*, may have inflated their vanity, and prompted the adoption of that mode of attack.

I wish it may—an equal foe has nothing to apprehend on that score, and copious phlebotomy is the best cure for Knight Errantry. His plan, at Chaumont Bay, was "well arranged"; but marked with desperation. What prudent commander would have abandoned his fleet, and ventured upon a hostile shore, with 800 or a 1000 men, within 7 miles of a vigorous enemy, 4000 strong. What would have been his fate, had not his fears corrected his judgment, the only evidence of which, is, his retiring.

The moment is critical, and the suspence irksome; but a certainty of superiority, is vastly more important, than the lapse of a few days.

His object may be Sackett's Harbour, and it certainly would be more judicious to make a vigorous effort, to destroy you there, than to meet you with a superior force on the Lake, or by an expedition against Fort George, expose Kingston to the attack of your whole force, Naval and Military, in the absence of his fleet and 4000 of his troops, which, I have no doubt, you would avail yourself of.

Captain Crane would be with you, with 250 or 60 men, by the 10th. and by this time, I trust, you are ready to meet the enemy.[1]

It is of vast importance to make an early movement on the Upper Lake, as a few men only, are wanting there, to give us immediate possession of the enemy's force on Erie, which delay may render more difficult. I find, by my letters from Mr. Harrison, that Captain Perry will be disappointed in his heavy anchor as the Agent at Pittsburg, in a late letter to Mr. H. says he is of opinion, "the anchors may yet be sent from Philadelphia, or New York, sooner than they can be had from Pittsburg." I hope Capt. Perry will not be detained on that account, but adopt some expedient, or substitute, to increase the weight, or number of his small anchors. I have, however immediately, ordered the anchors from Philadelphia, to be at Pittsburg, positively, in 15 days; and if you have any to spare, you had better send them up the Lake, to avoid uncertainty. My accounts from Capt. Perry are to the 2nd of July; the 2nd sloop of war would be ready in 3 weeks, from the 24th of June, I have directed the first, to be called, the *Lawrence*, the 2nd the *Niagara*.

You were perfectly correct in arresting Mr. Saml. Stacy, as a spy; and you will hold him, until the President shall direct the course to be pursued with him, which I will ascertain tomorrow. It is indeed time that traitors were brought to punishment.[2]

Tell Lieutenant Elliot, that I early represented his claims to remuneration, for the capture and destruction of the *Detroit*, and that Congress have voted to him, and his companions in that affair, $12,000

When promotions are under consideration, the brave Officers of the Lakes will not be forgotten. I am, very respectfully, Your Obedt. Servant

W. Jones

LB Copy, DNA, RG45, CLS, 1813, pp. 51–53.

1. Master Commandant William M. Crane and the officers and crew of *John Adams* were ordered to the lakes on 26 June 1813. See Crane to Jones, 30 June 1813, DNA, RG45, MC, 1813, No. 78 (M147, Roll No. 5).

2. For the arrest of Samuel Stacy as a spy, see pp. 520–21.

COMMODORE SIR JAMES LUCAS YEO, R.N., TO
FIRST SECRETARY OF THE ADMIRALTY JOHN W. CROKER

No. 6   His Majesty's Ship *Wolfe*, at
                                         Kingston, Upper Canada,
                                         the 16th July 1813

Sir/

I have the Honor to transmit to you, for the information of the Lords Commissioners of the Admiralty, a detailed account of the Enemy's Naval Force on Lakes Ontario, Eire, and Champlain, as also that of His Majestys, by which their Lordships will perceive how inadequate the Force under my Command, is to meet them with any thing like an equal Force at every point, as the Officers, and Men, which come from England are scarcely sufficient to Man the Squadron on this Lake, I have therefore appointed Captain Barclay, and Finnis with three Lieutenants, (sent here by Admiral Sir John B. Warren) to the Vessels, on Lake Eire, and Captain Pring, to command the Naval Force on Lake Champlain, I have also judged it expedient to promote two Midshipmen, to the Rank of Lieutenant, to serve under that Officer.

I have ever since my arrival, been so much occupied in the equipment of the Squadron, and co-operating with the Army at the head of the Lake, that I have not had time or opportunity to communicate so fully to you, for their Lordships information, as I otherwise should have done.

I have used every device in my power, to induce the Enemy's Squadron to come out, before his new Ship was ready, but to no effect. I am sorry to say she is now manned and will be ready for Sea in a few days.

Our new Brig the *Melville*, will be Launched this Week, when the two Squadrons will be in as great force, as they can be for this Year, and immediately we are both ready a general Action must take place, as every Military operation or success, depends intirely on whoever can maintain the Naval superiority on this Lake.

I am happy to state that only one Seaman, has deserted to the Enemy, and their conduct in general has been orderly, and good, every reasonable, and proper, indulgence has been given them, to keep them in this temper, but the encouragement that is held out by the Agents, of the Enemy, of which there are many in this Province, may I fear seduce them in time.

With respect to the Payment of the Seamen, I am sorry to say that at present, it is absolutely out of my power to meet their Lordships wishes, the Provincial, or old, Marine have always been regularly paid every two Months, at the rate of 10 Dollars for Able seamen and 8 Dollars for Ordinary, and Landmen, per Month, most of the Men of the former Marine, are retained in the Squadron, I represented the business to His Excellency Sir George Prevost Bt. the Governor of the Canadas and also shewed him their Lordships Instructions, on that head, at the same time expressed my anxiety to adhere as close as possible to them. His Excellency was of Opinion it would be attended with the greatest danger, if not totally impracticable to make any alteration in the Payment of the Seamen, at this momentous crisis, and to make a distinction, between the new, and the old Marine, could not be done. I have therefore been obliged to yield to necessity, and what I feel I cannot take upon myself to alter.

I consequently trust their Lordships, seeing the peculiar state of the case, will approve of the steps I have taken, or furnish me with their further directions on that subject, indeed it has been a task of infinite Labour, and perseverance, since my arrival, to throw the former arrangements, in some measure, into a system agreeably to the Rules of the Navy.

There is one more point I wish to draw the attention of their Lordships, which is the absolute necessity of sending out more grown up young Men, as Midshipmen, and Seamen, for even a Victory over the Enemy, would not enable us to maintain the superiority without a reinforcement, being sent immediately, as the Enemy from their Rivers, have every facility, and means, of obtaining whatever they stand in need of in a few days.

I beg leave further to state that, the Seamen will receive but one Months Wages out of every two that may become due, until they are six Months in Arrear, and enclose herewith a List of the Acting appointments, and Removals, of Commissioned Officers, between the 26th. of May and 16th of July 1813, and of Warrant Officers from 27th. May to this period—also an abstract of the Weekly Accounts of the Squadron, and have the Honor to be Sir/ your most obedient humble Servant

James Lucas Yeo   Commodore

LS, UkLPR, Adm. 1/2736, pp. 116–118A.

Commodore Sir James Lucas Yeo, R.N.

[Enclosure]

A List of the American Naval Force on the Lakes in Canada the 15th July 1813

Place Where	Names	How Rigged	Guns		Carronades		Men	Remarks
			No.	Caliber	No.	Caliber		
Lake Ontario	*General Pike*	Ship	long 30	prs 24	"	"	300	new ship nearly ready for sea
	Madison	Ship	"	"	26	32		Fit for sea
	Onieda	Brig	"	"	18	24		Fit for sea
	Fourteen	Schooners each mounting one or two long 32 pds long guns & 4 or 6 Carronades						
Lake Erie	Two	Corvettes launched but not ready for Sea			18	32 prs		
Lake Champlain	*President*	Schooners	18	"	"	"	"	To mount each
	Two other	Schooners and several Gun Boats						Dont know of what caliber they are.

They have also some larger vessels Building on this Lake but of what Force or Rig I have not been able to learn

James Lucas Yeo   Commodore

DS, UkLPR, Adm. 1/2736, p. 123.

[Enclosure]

A List of His Majesty's Ships, and Vessels on the Lakes in Canada, 15th July 1813

Place Where	Ships or Vessels Names	How Rigged	Guns No.	Guns Caliber	Carronades No.	Carronades Caliber	Men	Remarks
Lake Ontario	Wolfe	Ship	8	18	10 & 4	32 & 68		22
	Royal George	Ship	2	18	16 & 2	32 & 68		20
	Melville	Brig	2	18	12	32		14
	Moira	Schooner	2	9	12	24		14
	Beresford	Schooner	"	"	12	18		12
	Sir Sidney Smith[1]		"	"	12	24		12
Lake Erie	Detroit[2]	Ship	18	"	when launched			
	Queen Charlotte	Schooner	"	"	16	24		
	Lady Prevost	Schooner	2	6	10	12		
	General Hunter[3]	Schooner	2	6	4	12		
	Chipewa[4]		2	6	2	12		
Lake Champlain	Growler	Sloop	"	"	12	18		
	Eagle	Do	11	6	"	"		
	Four Gun Boats				1	24 each		
	Government	Schooner	4	6	"	"		

James Lucas Yeo   Commodore

DS, UkLPR, Adm. 1/2736, p. 124.

1. Sir Sidney Smith, a schooner, was probably the former merchant schooner Simcoe, launched at Kingston in November 1806.
2. Detroit, a ship of 12 guns, was built at Malden in 1813; she was later captured by the Americans in the Battle of Lake Erie, 10 September 1813. An earlier Detroit (formerly U.S.S. Adams) was built at Detroit in July 1812, captured by the British in August of that year, recaptured by the Americans at Black Rock in October 1812, and burned to prevent recapture.
3. General Hunter, a 6-gun brig, was built at Malden in 1806 for the Provincial Marine; she was captured in the Battle of Lake Erie, 10 September 1813.
4. Chipewa, a 4-gun schooner, was formerly a merchant vessel.

Manning the Northern Lakes Fleets

As shipbuilding on Lakes Ontario and Erie progressed during the spring and summer of 1813, Commodore Isaac Chauncey requested more and more sailors to be transferred to the lakes to man the new vessels. Secretary of the Navy Jones, growing weary of these requests from Chauncey and pressed by the need for crews for other naval vessels as well as demands for protection of cities on the eastern seaboard, responded with a letter of reproach to Chauncey.

Commodore Isaac Chauncey to Secretary of the Navy Jones

No. 31   U S Ship *Madison*   Sacketts Harbour
                                                                June 4th. 1813—

Sir,

I beg to call your attention to the situation of the Naval forces upon the Lakes— I have under my command upon this Lake 14 vessels of every description mounting 82 Guns, well man'd & well appointed. The Enemy have seven vessels & 6 Gun Boats mounting 106 Guns, well Officer'd & man'd if he leaves Kingston I shall meet him   The result may be doubtful but worth the trial— I should have prefer'd having the new Ship with me but the accident of the Fire has deprived me of her stores & sails; more over when she is ready we have not an officer or man to put on board of her, and she can be of no manner of use unless we have men— I had the Honour of addressing you on this subject last winter   You informed me that the men could not be spared from the *John Adams* & *Alert* at New York but authorised me to open Rendezvous to recruit men for the Lakes   I accordingly wrote to Commodres. Bainbridge & Hull requesting that they would open rendezvous at New Port, Boston, Salem & Portsmouth   I have since been informed by Comre. Bainbridge that I must not calculate upon men being enter'd for the Lakes that he had not got more than 3 or 4— he however sent me 150 of the *Constitutions* crew otherwise we could not have man'd our present fleet. If men are not transfer'd from other Ships the Ship building at this place & which will be launch'd in six days cannot be man'd nor can the fleet upon Lake Erie be of any manner of use as the whole number of men upon that Lake does not exceed 120 and there will be required for the vessels upon that Lake 680 men. I had calculated to have finished my operations upon this lake before this time & then to have transfer'd the Officers & Men with myself to Lake Erie but as I have been much longer detained by the operations of the Army than I had contemplated, and the Enemy having made extraordinary exertions to encrease his force & he is now in such force as to render it improper for me to leave this lake for the present I presume that you will perceive the necessity of ordering a reinforcement both of Officers & Men as soon as possible. I hope that it will not be deem'd impertinent for me to suggest the propriety of ordering Capn. Morris with all his crew to this place. He would have as good a ship as he now commands and could in my opinion render more important services to his country than he possibly can in the Potomack. It will also I think be obvious to you that an Officer of a higher grade than a Lieut. ought to succeed me in Command in case of my Death or other accident. I trust that you will do me the justice to believe that I will do every thing in my power to support the Honor and dignity of the American flag; yet I have not the temerity to believe that I can effect impossibilitys, I cannot fight a ship without men— from the information which I have received this day I have every reason to believe that the Enemy will renew their attack in 5 or 6 days with augmented force. I can only assure you that the result will either make him compleately master of this Lake or me—

I have deem'd this Communication of sufficient importance to dispatch acting Lieut. Dudley with it particularly as he is upon his parole and can be better spared than any other officer.[1] If his exchange can be effected I hope that he may be permitted to return. I refer you to him for a more detail'd account of our situation, force, preparations, & prospects—

You will find him an Officer of intelligence & great promise and I avail myself of this opportunity to recommend him to your notice & protection, he is deserving of both. I have the honour to be very Respectfully Sir your Most Obt. H. St.

Isaac Chauncey

LS, DNA, RG45, CL, 1813, Vol. 4, No. 14 (M125, Roll No. 29).

1. Acting Lieutenant James A. Dudley was captured on 13 April 1813 while shooting ducks on Strawberry Island, a place considered to be neutral ground by both British and American officers.

SECRETARY OF THE NAVY JONES TO COMMODORE ISAAC CHAUNCEY

(No. 23)
Commodore Isaac Chauncey,   Navy Department,
Commanding the U.S. Naval   June 26th. 1813.
Forces on the Lakes.

Sir,
    I have this instant received several of your letters and packets from the 10th. to the 18th. Inst. which shall be noticed in detail hereafter.
    I have also received a letter of the 19th. from Capt. Perry, at Erie, with a statement of our own, and of the enemy's force on that Lake. Captain P. has 159 Officers, Seamen, and Marines; and requires to man the whole force completely 450 more; but says he will be equal to the enemy with less. You will perceive, by the enclosed copy, of my letter to Capt. Crane, that I have ordered himself, and the whole of the officers, and crew of the *John Adams* to join you instantly. Commodore Bainbridge is ordered to send you 120 of the *Syren*'s crew. Captain Wainwright, with 100 Marines, are on their march to the eastward of this, to join you, Lieutenant Renshaw is recruiting rapidly in New York; and part of the *Vixen*'s crew, will be exchanged, and sent on to you, in a few days. Thus you may detach, immediately, a part of your force to Captain Perry; and assuredly, any temporary deficiency can be made up from the Military, as the enemy does, and the less inconvenience will be felt on that account, as undoubtedly you will have the finest body of Seamen in America. You may arrange the commands among the several Officers, in such way, as you shall think, will best promote the public interest and private harmony. It will be proper, I presume, to give Captain Crane the command of the *Madison,* and Lieutenant Elliot one of the Brigs at Erie. If you find Lieut. Deacon, a supernumerary, you may send him back to New York, or Philadelphia.

The Sailing Masters you have mentioned, shall receive their warrants immediately. Captain Leonard, having been a long time under arrest, you will bring him to trial immediately. I am, respectfully, Your obedient Servant

W^m. Jones

LB Copy, DNA, RG45, CLS, 1813, pp. 37–39.

SECRETARY OF THE NAVY JONES TO COMMODORE ISAAC CHAUNCEY

(No. 25)

Commodore Isaac Chauncey   Navy Department
Commanding Naval Officer   July 3d. 1813.
on the Lakes.

Sir,

I this day received your Nos. 50, 51, & 52,[1] and look with anxious solicitude for the completion of the *General Pike,* the issue of which, I trust, will accomplish the original design of the Campaign on Lake Ontario. The retarded operations of which, will materially affect our designs on the Upper Lakes.

As my letters will have assured you, of an ample force in men, before the *General Pike* would be ready for action, I trust you will have detached a sufficient number to complete the crews of at least one of the sloops of war, and all the other smaller vessels at Erie, with which Captain Perry would be decidedly superior to the whole of the enemy's force, and would be enabled to clear that lake, by the time you will be ready to decide the fate of Ontario.

In conformity to the original design of our Naval operations under your command, the power and the means afforded you, have been as unlimited, as the confidence of the President, in the prompt, vigorous, and skilful execution of the plans, submitted to your direction.

With this view, and to remove all doubt, or casualty, I have ordered the following Detachments of Officers, Seamen, and Marines, the whole of which are on their way, and will be with you, by the 7th. or 8th. Inst. except Capt. Wainwright with the Marines, who will reach the Harbour certainly by the 15th. viz.

From Boston	105 Officers and Seamen	
Residue of the *Alert*'s crew and recruits by Lieut Renshaw }	90	
Capt Crane and entire crew of the *John Adams* }	190	
Capt Wainwright and Marines }	<u>110</u>	495.

This force, united to that you now have on both Lakes, will, most assuredly, more than man the whole of the vessels on both Lakes, <u>better</u> than the same number and description of vessels, ever were in any service.

After your return from York, in taking a comparative view, of your own and the enemys force, you say that the whole of your squadron was perfectly well appointed and manned, but that you had not a man for the *General Pike,* subsequent to that period, Captain Sinclair and Lieutenants Trenchard & Bullus arrived with

80 men from the *Alert,* which would of course be applicable to the *General Pike.* But, Sir, whether you had men enough to man the *General Pike* or not, must depend upon a view of your aggregate number, distributed according to the best established rules of our service, among the several classes of our vessels comprising your squadron. According to this rule, you had sufficient to man the whole squadron, including the *General Pike,* and allowing 10 per Cent for the sick list.

Our vessels are better manned than those in any other service, both in numbers and quality. With the exception of the draught of men, brought up by Sir James Yeo, his crews were very indifferent, and you observe yourself, that his small vessels are "manned principally with soldiers," and although they are commanded by a <u>Knight</u>, and <u>three Post Captains</u>, I feel that the untitled republican Commodore, and his gallant and able officers, though not "Post Captains", have nothing to apprehend from the charm of a name, or the fortuitous circumstance of superior grade.

In corroboration of what I have said, in respect to your force <u>in men</u>, I would just observe, that your statement exhibits 274 officers and seamen, for the *Madison* of 24 Guns; when, upon a fair comparison with the *Wasp* & *Hornet,* 180 would be a <u>full</u> complement for the *Madison,* without taking into view the difference of distant service, manning of prizes, a long cruize, &c. Captain Crane, for instance, in the *John Adams,* (a heavier ship than the *Madison,*) manned for a two years cruize, in the fullest manner, 190 in number. I have no means of testing the accuracy of your information as to the enemy's force in men, but it is certainly very extraordinary, that the *Wolfe,* a corvette built ship, of 28 Guns, should have 300 men, the full complement of a British <u>rated</u> 38. The number is greatly superfluous, and would be a real injury to the service. It is, moreover, certainly known, that the number of Seamen, your informant has stated Sir James Yeo to have taken up with him, say 550, is greatly overrated. Wishing to possess correct and early information from Erie, and as the route through Sackett's Harbour is tedious and uncertain, I desired Captain Perry to communicate, direct to the Department, the state of the Public force on that lake, together with that of the enemy, and such other information as he may deem interesting to the Government. Under date of the 19th. Ulto. at Erie, he transmitted, to the Department, a statement of his force, and the number of Officers and men required to man the whole.

Viz.	2 Brigs 130 each	260
	4 Schooners 28 each	112
	1 small Brig, *Caledonia*	50
	3 Schooners } from Buffaloe 35 each	140
	1 Sloop	
		562
	Deduct number here	159
	Wanting Officers & men	403

With a note, at foot, "I shall think myself equal to the enemy, with a smaller number than the above."

On the 24th of June, he says, "I have great pleasure in stating to you, Sir, that one of the sloops of war will be ready for service in a few days, provided the Bower Anchor, (which I hear is on the way,) and the shot arrive; the stream anchors having already arrived, I can make out with them and one Bower. I shall bend sails

day after tomorrow. I shall be ready to execute your orders, the moment a sufficiency of officers and men arrive, with one sloop of war, and 9 smaller vessels—
the other sloop will be ready as soon as the anchors arrive from Pittsburg, which I
hope will be in three weeks. I omitted, in my last of the 19th. (written under severe indisposition,) to mention, that General Dearborn had placed 200 troops
under my command, to assist in navigating the vessels from Black Rock, and that
they are now here, still on board the vessels, subject to my order. The *Queen Charlotte* & *Lady Prevost* were at anchor off Carradaway yesterday.

"I shall expect your orders, Sir, with great anxiety, as I am in hopes to intercept those vessels before their return to Malden. The communication from
Sacketts Harbour, to this place, occupies nearly a month, which makes it very
difficult to obtain orders from Com. Chauncey, in time to execute them with
any advantage."

I enclose to you the examination of three deserters from the *Queen Charlotte*,
received from Capt Perry, which, after due allowance for the source from which
it is derived, is nearly corroborated by previous information; the substance you
will find as follows.

Ship *Queen Charlotte* 14. 24 lb carronades & 3 long 12's $\left\{ \begin{array}{l} \text{2 Lieuts} \\ \text{1 master} \end{array} \right\}$ 87 men

Sch. *Lady Prevost* - - - - 12. 18 lb.   Do -   30
Sch. *Hunter* - - - - - - - - 8   Guns - supposed   30
Chippeway - - - - - - - - - - 4   Do   (Capt. Perry's statement) - - - - - - Do   25
2 Gun Boats - - - - - - - - 2   Do each and 25 men each - - - - - - - - - Do   50
                    Guns 51 (as per original) [2]   Men 222

"New ship 5 feet longer and 3 feet wider than the *Charlotte*, Deck not laid—would
not be launched in less than a month—few carpenters—one, says Guns were
ready, 24 pd carronades—Another, Guns were not ready, saw 4 or 5 24 pound
Carronades at the Beach—Another does not think guns were provided."

In other respects there is a remarkable coincidence of testimony—5 feet
longer would allow but two Guns more than the *Charlotte*.

I have informed Capt. Perry, that as the entire command was given to you,
with the most perfect confidence, a very great degree of reluctance is felt, by
the Department, in interposing its authority; and nothing but the apprehension of suffering the enemy to escape, under circumstances so favourable for
offensive operations, on our part—the possibility of his being reinforced—of
the Ship at Malden being brought into action sooner than expected and of
delay, or adverse circumstances in the Lake below, could induce me to anticipate your commands. I have, therefore, advised him to weigh, with great caution, the probable issue of an attempt to meet the enemy as he proposes; and
if, upon mature deliberation, he is clearly of opinion, that, (with the one
sloop, and 9 smaller vessels, manned with 159 officers, Seamen and Marines,
and 200 regular soldiers, and such volunteers as he can pick up,) he can succeed in cutting off the enemy's squadron, he has my authority to make the attempt—but, immediately on receipt of my order, to communicate with you,
and if he shall receive your instructions, to suspend the execution of the
design, or pursue any other course, that he will substitute your orders for those
of the Department.

The President approves of the preparation you are making, for the encrease of our force, (and particularly of the nature of that force,) which he wishes to be carried into effect, with the least possible delay; as it is evident, that any Military advantage, must be succeeded by a retrograde and disastrous movement, unless supported by a decisive Naval superiority; and for this end, nothing shall be withheld, that the Government can command. I am, very respectfully, your Obedient Servt,

W. Jones

P.S. The Secretary at War, has directed, that the 200 regulars shall remain under the command of Capt. Perry, until the proper force shall join him.

LB Copy, DNA, RG45, CLS, 1813, pp. 41–47.

1. This letter was written in reply to Commodore Chauncey's letters No. 30 (29 May), No. 31 (4 June), and No. 32 (4 June). See pp. 480, 507–8 for the first two letters cited.
2. The number of guns stated here totals forty-five. The original statement provided with Perry's letter of 19 June 1813 was added incorrectly. See Perry's enclosure, "According to examination of Deserters 24 June 13 at Erie," in Perry to Jones, 19 June 1813, DNA, RG45, AF7. See also p. 485 for Robert H. Barclay's statement of the force of his squadron on Lake Erie on 29 June 1813.

American Setbacks on Lake Champlain

Following the capture of Growler *and* Eagle *on 3 June 1813, Lieutenant Thomas Macdonough was forced to rebuild his fleet for the second time within a year. Secretary of the Navy Jones urged him to do everything he could to prevent the British from gaining superiority on the lake. Macdonough purchased two additional sloops, which were renamed* Commodore Preble *and* Montgomery, *and continued to rebuild his gunboats. Major General Wade Hampton, newly arrived on Lake Champlain, was amassing troops and provisions at Burlington for an intended assault on Canada in conjunction with Major General James Wilkinson's army.*

While the American vessels were undergoing repairs and refitting, the British were making preparations for an amphibious assault on the shores of Lake Champlain in order to capture army provisions and to provide a diversion in favor of their troops in Upper Canada. Lieutenant Daniel Pring, senior naval officer at Isle aux Noix, Commander Thomas Everard, whose vessel was laid up in Quebec, and Lieutenant Colonel John Murray, military commandant at St. Johns, launched a joint assault that came to be known as Murray's Raid. From 29 July until 3 August, the British burned the military blockhouses, barracks, and storehouses at Plattsburg, Champlain, and Swanton; attempted to cannonade Macdonough's vessels at Burlington; and captured eight merchant ships, virtually all the private vessels on Lake Champlain. Macdonough could do little except utilize his ship guns and shore batteries to protect the American fleet, for his vessels were neither fully manned nor fitted out to meet the enemy.[1]

1. Everest, War of 1812, *pp. 115–19.*

Secretary of the Navy Jones to Lieutenant Thomas Macdonough

Lieut. Thos. McDonnough,
commanding the U.S. Naval forces
on Lake Champlain.

Navy Department
June 17th. 1813.

Sir,

I have received your letter, announcing the unfortunate disaster and loss of the two Sloops under the command of Lieutenant Smith, as it would appear by the imprudence of that officer, of which, however, you will enquire into, and report to me the result.

It now only remains, to regain by every possible exertion, the ascendancy which we have lost; for which purpose, you are authorized to purchase, arm, and equip, in an efficient manner, two of the best sloops, or other vessels to be procured on the Lake. I have written to Commodore Bainbridge, Commandant of the Navy Yard at Charlestown Massachusetts, to send on to you 20, 18 pounder carronades, if to be procured; and you are authorized to make such requisitions as the service may require, either on John Bullus Esqr. Navy Agent New York, and if not to be had there, upon Mr. Binney, the N. Agent at Boston, to whom, when you write, you will quote this authority. You are to understand, that upon no account are you to suffer the enemy to gain the ascendancy on Lake Champlain; and as you have now unlimited authority, to procure the necessary resources of men, materials, and munitions for that purpose, I rely upon your efficient and prudent use of the authority vested in you.

General Hampton,[1] an officer of talents and energy, is appointed to the military command on Lake Champlain, with whom you will heartily <u>cooperate</u>, in every measure calculated to promote the efficient objects of the War. But you are to observe, that the Naval command is exclusively vested in you, and for which you are held responsible.

General Hampton will afford you every assistance in the Quarter Master's Department, with Mechanics, Labourers, &c. and if you deem it necessary to construct 4 or 5 Barges, of 50 or 60 feet long, to carry a 12 or 18 pound carronade, you are at liberty so to do.

I shall order a Purser to your station immediately. I am very respectfully yours,

W^m. Jones

LB Copy, DNA, RG45, SNL, Vol. 10, pp. 469–70 (M149, Roll No. 10).

1. Major General Wade Hampton was appointed commander of the U.S. Army's Right Wing, Military District No. 9, which encompassed Lake Champlain; he arrived at Burlington, Vermont, on 3 July.

Governor-General Sir George Prevost to Major General George Glasgow, British Army

Copy

Headquarters   Kingston
4th July 1813

Sir

You will communicate to the Senior officer of H M Ships at Quebec my earnest desire that he should proceed promptly to St. Johns to take the Commd. of the

Vessels and Gun Boats on the Richelieu, bringing with him as many Officers and Seamen as he can possibly spare from his Ship, and obtain from the Transport and Merchant Service, for the purpose of Cruizing on Lake Champlain, with a just expectation of being enabled materially to annoy the Enemy on that Sheet of water, and if fortunate to destroy the remainder of their Shipping on it, and under all circumstances to create a powerfull diversion in favour of the Army in Upper Canada— I need not dwell with you on the importance of this Service to His Majesty's North American Provinces, if it is carried into effect with Zeal and Promptitude, nor do I entertain a doubt of either of these qualifications being displayed by the Officers of His Majesty's Navy, provided circumstances admit of the undertaking. You will not fail in taking such precautionary steps as shall preclude the possibility of delay or embarrassment in the execution of so highly important a Service as the one now entrusted to your arrangement and I trust you will find Major General Sir Roger Sheaffe fully prepared to perform that part in it which must devolve upon him— I have the honor to be, Sir, Your most obedient, humble Servant,

("Signed")   George Prevost

Copy, UkLPR, Adm. 1/504, pp. 321–22. This copy was enclosed in a letter from Lieutenant Thomas Everard, R.N., to Admiral Sir John B. Warren, R.N., dated 21 July 1813.

Lieutenant Thomas Macdonough to Secretary of the Navy Jones

Burlington   July 11th. 1813—

Sir,

In obedience to your order of the 3d. inst. I have the honor to acquaint you with my proceedings in conformity with your order of the 17th June immediately on receipt of which I purchased a sloop and have so far prepared her that the Guns & Men can be taken on board in four days from to day. I have planned her to mount ten 18 pr. carronades and one long 18 pr. on a circle forward two such long 18 prs. I have now here, procured from the Army, the other one of these Guns I calculate to Mount on the other sloop in the same manner (on a circle) and shall prepare her likewise to carry ten 18 Pr. carronades. I consider that no time has been lost in not purchasing the second sloop yet, as I have been enabled to get on so much faster with the present one and have been employed getting in timber & other Materials to begin with the sloop to be purchased immediately, which I shall do and calculate to have her in readiness for her guns & Men in two weeks from this day   I had another reason for defering the purchase of the second sloop as long as I could without causing any detention to the ultimate efficiency of the force to be equiped, which was the disappointment of getting the Guns from Boston which Commre. Bainbridge early advised me of, in consequence I was at a loss what guns to prepare for, in addition to which circumstance I was in hopes the owner of the vessell would fall to a reasonable price he asked me upwards of two thousand dollars more than the vessel is worth she is a sloop of about 90 Tons very flat consequently for that tonnage roomy on deck, I have offered him $4000—& unless he accepts this price I shall take her tomorrow & have her value appreciated. I suppose the Navy Agent in New York will immediately inform me of the Guns to be sent me no material difference will be necessary in the work of these sloops for mounting 18 pr. carronades or long twelves or nines. I shall consequently continue in the present manner of fitting them— Two of the Boats which I mentioned to you in reply to your order of the 17th June are completed—they carry each a long heavy 12 pr the other two are ready for their guns which are to come from the Army at this place as soon as I get a little more forward with the naval force to make it prudent to take them from the battery they are long 18 prs.—

I can equip the force contemplated on this lake sooner than I at first thought I could and were the officers & men now here I have little hesitation in saying we should have the ascendency before the expiration of July— The officers I now have are three midshipmen one only of whom is acquainted with a vessel a surgeons mate—and fifty Men (the crew of the *President*) no purser has yet Sir, made his appearance and I, now more particularly feel the want of the services of that officer, his orders were I presume of the date of the surgeons mates, & he has been on a month, the duties of the purser of this station have been in some measure unavoidably unattended to & at present my attention to those duties is still more withdrawn—

I avail myself here to acknowledge the receipt of the regulations of the War & Navy Departments and am happy to find that my opinion on this subject has been correspondent thereto and that I have been so governed during my co op-eration with the Army with the exception (after the loss of the sloops) of having placed two Capts of the army with a suitable number of their men in the two Gun Boats subject to my orders, this should not have been done had I had officers & men of my own to man them, they have been as guard vessels & have prevented & taken quantities of smugglers goods I shall however Sir have these Boats moored near the *President* untill I can officer & man them myself which I hope will soon be the case. I have the honor to be Sir your most obt. servt.

T. Macdonough

ALS, DNA, RG45, BC, 1813, Vol. 3, No. 21 (M148, Roll No. 12).

LIEUTENANT THOMAS MACDONOUGH TO SECRETARY OF THE NAVY JONES

Burlington   July 22d. 1813—

Sir,

No officers to command the vessels preparing for Guns on Lake Champlain having yet come on, I am induced to suspect that I have not been full enough in stating to you the necessity of them— These vessels are now ready for their crews & in a few days ~~could mount~~ their Guns might be mounted some detention has been caused by Wet blowing weather there being no shelter here from heavy winds, which the lake is very subject to, I shall in order to have these vessels under proper regulations & efficient require a Lieutenant to command each—there will then be three Lieutenants; there should be six or eight Midshipmen, in the whole, to allow two or three to each vessel— John Bullus Esqr. Navy Agent has advised me of his having shipped my guns, their carriages &c complete, I expect them here by the day after to morrow, I shall use every exertion to have these vessels ready for service by the first of August— Genl. Hampton is extremely desirous, & anxious for me to have the command on the lake as soon as possible; officers of Merit & talent he says have lately joined him but the command of the lake is necessary for a movement—

I have sir, received some particulars of the affair of the sloops on June 3d, by one of the pilots who was wounded, he states that on the 3d June at day break Lt. Smith made the signal to get under weigh to the *Eagle* (commanded by Sailing-Master Loomis who was attached to this station by the late Capt Ludlow) and follow his motions, that the pilots remonstrated against going over the lines with the wind from the southward, assuring Lt. Smith that if he went down with the wind as it then was he could not return he however stood down the lake to within two miles of the Isle aux Noix bringing the batteries plain in sight, then hauled his wind to beat back the Gun Boats then came up from the Isle aux Noix and attacked him (three in number) the enemy seeing that the vessels could not beat back against the tide, sent about three hundred men on the shores opposite to the vessels, the channel being about one hundred yards wide & the water about two hundred yards, the vessels were obliged to stand close in under the Musquetry on either shore in order to gather head way enough to tack. In this situation their running rigging was cut away which rendered them unmanageable & many men would have fallen on board the vessels had not the quarters been so thick that a musquet ball could not pass through, one 24 pr. shot struck the *Eagle* at the waters edge, she could not keep the hole long on the weather side having to make such short tacks, she filled & sank her deck under, Lt. Smith shortly after gave his vessel up Many of the enemy were killed & wounded but the number we shall never know— I have not heard a word from Lt Smith since his capture, I shall forward to you the statement he may make with his reasons for so doing

The purser has not yet made his appearance Sir, although he must be aware of the necessity of his services— I have the honor to be Sir, your most obt. sert.

T. Macdonough

ALS, DNA, RG45, BC, 1813, Vol. 3, No. 42 (M148, Roll No. 12).

Major General Sir Roger Hale Sheaffe, British Army, to Governor-General Sir George Prevost

Montreal   25th. July 1813.

Sir,

I have the honour of informing Your Excellency that Captain Everard and some Officers and Seamen of the *Wasp* sloop of war, with other seamen from various sources, in all about eighty, arrived last evening—and proceeded early this morning for Isle aux Noix,—to which post the flank companies of the 13th. Regiment and of the 103rd. Regiment, and the Light Company of the Canadian Regiment, completed to eighty rank & File each, will follow tomorrow— the companies of the 13th Regiment having been removed to La Prairie before the arrival of the Seamen:—those Companies with a detachment of a hundred men from the 100th Regiment, and with the troops already attached to the Vessels and gun boats will form a Corps of nearly six hundred Men— it is proposed to add two three pounders to this force, and to employ it, with the cooperation of the flotilla, in destroying buildings and stores for warlike purposes, or vessels and boats on the west shore of Lake Champlain; on which, our latest informa-tion states, there is no force capable of opposing such attempts: the Enemy's troops having been withdrawn from that side and concentrated at Burlington, where they are in too great strength, and in too populous a country for any at-tempt to be made against them, with the means we possess.—

I shall proceed tomorrow to Isle aux Noix.—

One of the three frigates armed in flute which were dispatched to the Mediterra-nean for the Regiment De Meuron has been reported in the River by telegraph.—

I believe that Wind Mill point is too low and sandy to afford a good posi-tion— I expect, however, more precise information respecting it, and shall for-ward it when obtained. I have the honour to be, With great respect, Your Excel-lency's, Most obedient, humble servant,

R H Sheaffe
M Genl. &c

LS, CaOOA, British Military and Naval Records, RG8, I, "C" Ser., Vol. 730, pp. 67–70.

Instructions for Lieutenant Colonel John Murray, British Army

Instructions for Lieut. Colonel Murray Commanding a Corps to act on the Banks of Lake Champlain.

Isle aux Noix   27th of July 1813

As the force under your Command is not sufficient to justify an attempt on Burlington, where the Enemy has concentrated his troops, Armed vessels, Craft and Boats, and has his Depôt of Stores, the chief object of the movement to the Lake will be to create a diversion in favor of the Army in Upper Canada, by alarming the Enemy with his expectation of Attack and thereby checking the movement of reinforcements to their troops in that Province.

At the points on the Western side of the Lake from which the Enemy has lately withdrawn his Troops there are probably public buildings, if not stores for Military purposes— These may be destroyed, and likewise all Vessels Boats &c found along the shore which can aid the Enemy, but All private property, and the persons of the unarmed and inoffensive are to be respected, every care and precaution must be taken to preserve them inviolate, for which purpose in case of disembarkation the vigilance of the officers will be particularly required to prevent straggling

It is expected that the Naval Armament and the Troops will act in concert, so that they shall at all times be ready to aid and support each other

The operations are to be confined to the banks of the Lake, and are not to be extended higher than Platsburg, unless it be ascertained that an important ob-ject can be effected at no great distance above it and without incurring a risk of consequences which would render it imprudent; if any of the Enemy troops be taken they are to be brought away to be sent to Quebec

The preservation of silence, good order and subordination especially in dis-embarkation, acting on shore, or in reembarking, the security of the Boats, Arms, Ammunition and provisions are objects which will require peculiar atten-tion, in aid of which much will be effected by insisting on a strict adherence to the order assigned to the Batteaux, and to the distribution of the Men, and of the several Articles in the Boats originally allotted to them.

In proceeding up the Lake, and in returning, reconnoisances are to be made to discover if the Enemy has collected a force to oppose, or has established a Battery at any point from which he may be able to annoy you

You will of course consult with Captain Everard on the operations, and concert with Him the plan of execution

In the conduct of the Service intrusted to you, I have chiefly to recommend caution, it is an important Military quality in such situations as those in which you are likely to be placed; you will avail yourself of all opportunities of obtaining information, and have Notes taken of whatever may deserve it, to be communicated to me as early as practicable, with reports of your movements, and of all interesting occurrences

The Expedition will of course return at the expiration of the period assigned for our enjoying the benefit of the aid and cooperation of Captn. Everard, his officers and Seamen, and even earlier if its remaining on the Lake will no longer promise any advantage to His Majestys Service

D, CaOOA, British Military and Naval Records, RG8, I, "C" Ser., Vol. 679, pp. 291–93. Enclosed in a letter from Major General Sir Roger Hale Sheaffe, British Army, to Governor-General Sir George Prevost.

MASTER COMMANDANT THOMAS MACDONOUGH [1] TO SECRETARY OF THE NAVY JONES

Burlington   August 3d 1813

Sir

I regret having to inform you that the enemy after having been a short time within our waters made their appearance off this place yesterday Morning with two sloops and a galley and soon after commenced firing on the shipping and Batteries which they continued for a short time, the Vessels being moored with springs on, acting on the defensive, opened upon them in concert with the batteries, when they hauled off and stood to the southward— they have taken two small craft one of which they burnt last night the other I suppose they will mount a gun on, My unfinished state in point of officers to command the two vessels lately fitted (with few exceptions) prevented my not meeting the enemy, I have Sir but one officer & he a Midn. with whom I could trust the Command of one of these vessels on an occasion of less importance than the one of yesterday— The enemy have very lately received a reinforcement of seamen from Quebec. I have in consequence requested Capt Evans to send me on fifty more men with the two Lieutenants to command the two new vessels ~~and those~~ and this additional number of men the enemy cannot keep within our waters, I should consider this force sufficient to command the lake which Genl. Hampton is very desirous should be obtained— I have the honor to be Sir your most obt. Sert.

T. Macdonough

ALS, DNA, RG45, BC, 1813, Vol. 3, No. 66 (M148, Roll No. 12).

1. Thomas Macdonough was promoted to master commandant on 24 July 1813.

COMMANDER THOMAS EVERARD, R.N., TO
GOVERNOR-GENERAL SIR GEORGE PREVOST

H M. Sloop *Broke*[1]   Augst. 3rd
Lake Champlain

Sir,

Major General Glasgow has apprized your Excellency of my repairing with a party of Officers and Seamen to man the Sloops and Gun boats at the Isle aux Noix, in consequence of your Letter of the 4th ult. addressed to the senior Officer of H M ships at Quebec, stating it to be of great importance to the public service that an attempt should be made to alarm the Enemy on the Montreal frontier &c— And agreeable to your wish that I should communicate any thing interesting that might occur, I have the honour to acquaint you that the object for which the corps under the command of Lt. Cl. Murray had been detached having been fully accomplished by the destruction of the Enemy's Blockhouse, Arsenal, Barracks and public Store-houses at Plattsburgh, and the Troops having embarked on the 1st Inst. to return, there being neither public buildings nor store-houses remaining on the West side of the Lake beyond Plattsburgh, I stood over to Burlington with the *Shannon* and one Gun-Boat to observe the state of the Enemy's force there, and to afford him an opportunity of deciding the naval superiority on the Lake. We were close in on the fore-noon of the 2nd and found two Sloops of about 100 Tons burthen, one armed with eleven Guns, the other with thirteen, ready for Sea, a third Sloop (somewhat larger) fitting out, with guns on board and 2 Gun Schooners laying under the protection of ten Guns mounted on a bank of 100 feet high without a breast work. Two scows mounting one Gun each as floating Batteries, and several field pieces on the shore— Having captured and destroyed four Vessels, without any attempt on the part of the Enemy's armed Vessels to prevent it, and seeing no prospect of inducing him to quit his position, where it was impossible for us to attack him, I am now returning to execute my original orders—

There were several Barracks and store-houses (one not yet finished) erected on the high Bank in the Rear of the Guns, a small wood immediately behind these buildings, and in the rear of it (the wood) an Encampment of some Extent, the whole would probably contain 5000 Men. I could not ascertain the amount of their military force, but it appeared about the strength that we had been led to expect. No satisfactory account could be collected from the Prisoners. The statement of the sea-defence is I believe accurate, as the Sloops and Gun Boat were swept within shot in order to attract their fire. I beg leave to add that the best place for effecting a Landing appears to me to be on the North side of the Town nearly two Miles from the Camp and Battery. The alarm occasioned by the appearance of a military force on the shores of the Lake appears to have been very general, our Boats were 20 Miles above Burlington in the night & heard Musketry and Drums on both Sides of the Lake   I have the honor to be Your Excellency's most obedient & very Humble Servant

Thos: Everard
Commander, HMS *Wasp*

LS, CaOOA, British Military and Naval Records, RG8, I, "C" Ser., Vol. 679, pp. 340–42.

1. The U.S. sloop *Eagle*, captured by the British at Isle aux Noix on 3 June 1813, was taken into British service under the name of *Broke*; she was later renamed *Finch*. The former U.S. sloop *Growler* was given the name *Shannon*; she was later renamed *Chub*. Both vessels were used in Murray's raid on Lake Champlain.

MASTER COMMANDANT THOMAS MACDONOUGH TO
SECRETARY OF THE NAVY JONES

Burlington   August 14th. 1813

Sir,

I have the honor to inform you that I have received my commission as Master-commandant in the Navy of the United States, to assure you that this preferment is highly gratifying to me and that it shall be my duty and ambition to merit the confidence you have placed in me—

Lieut. George Pearce has this day joined me and taken command of one of the sloops, Mr. Horace F. Marcelin acting Master has also joined me— George Beale purser has not yet come on—

Those sloops are now compleated, and with the additional number of men, (one hundred) whom I have required of Capt. Evans at New York, for them and the other smaller craft, I shall have the ascendency on the lake— The enemy have fitted out two small sloops in addition to those they before had, making in all four sloops, three galleys & two Gun Boats in consequence of this late augmentation of their force I have purchased another sloop of about fifty tons to carry four twelves and one eighteen pr. I have also anticipated your permission and have taken the masts out of our two Gun-Boats, which Boats from their rig and construction would only carry a light twelve pr. and have fitted them with thirty oars each & to carry a long twenty-four, but not having such guns here they are completed with an eighteen pr. on each— From the last accounts of the enemy they are preparing all their force, which, when compleated I shall endeavour to keep within their own waters thereby prevent all annoyance to of the movements of the army—and aid its movements when the comng. Genl. may wish— I have the honor to be Sir your most obt. Sert.

T. Macdonough

ALS, DNA, RG45, MC, 1813, No. 106 (M147, Roll No. 5).

Espionage on the Lakes

Loyalties of those who resided along the Canadian-American border were divided during the War of 1812. Most families had relatives or business acquaintances along both sides of the line. The Saint Lawrence River and the Great Lakes served not as a barrier but as a route for communication and exchange between similar peoples. An illicit trade in provisions and military intelligence developed on both sides of the border.

The cases of two men, Samuel Stacy and Peter Hogeboom, shed some light on such clandestine activities. Stacy, a citizen of New York, was arrested in July by Commodore Isaac Chauncey. He was suspected of providing intelligence of American troop and fleet movements that allowed the British to attack the lightly guarded base at Sackets Harbor on 29 May during the absence of the American fleet. Hogeboom, a Dutchman who resided in the Canadian provinces and had relatives on the American side, presented a detailed proposal to the British commanders on how he could provide information on American military activities. Hogeboom apparently had second thoughts about the matter, for he recanted his offer shortly after.

Accurate information regarding enemy strength and movements could be invaluable in a closely matched contest. Both British and American officers denounced spies as traitors to their country; at the same time, however, they continued to make good use of the information such persons provided.

COMMODORE ISAAC CHAUNCEY TO SECRETARY OF THE NAVY JONES

No. 55.—
                                                        U.S. Ship *Madison*
                                                        Sackets' Harbor
                                                        4th. July 1813.—

Sir,

On the 1st. inst. I caused a Mr. Saml. Stacy to be apprehended as a spy. Mr. Stacy lives upon the St. Lawrence a few miles below Ogdensburgh, and I have the most positive information that he has been in the habit of conveying information to the Enemy for many Months. He visited this place a few days before the British made the attack on the 29th. of May, and I have no doubt but that he is the person that gave them information that most of the Troops had been sent to Niagara. I had information from the person that I employ on the other side that this man would visit the Harbor about the last of June: He was accordingly watched. When he left Ogdensburgh he said that he was going to Utica upon important business. He told others that he was going into the Western Country to collect Money, instead of which he came to the Harbor without any ostensible business and made a great many inquiries respecting the Fleet—when they would sail—and the force of the new Ship &c. &c. &c.; I therefore thought it my duty to detain this Man for trial. I can prove his frequent intercourse with the Enemy, at any rate I shall deprive the Enemy of the information which he would have conveyed to him which is all important at this time.—

It would be very desireable to hang this Traitor to his country—as he is considered respectable in the country in which he lives and I think that it is full time to make an example of some of our Countrymen who are so base, and degenerate as to betray their country by becoming the Spies & Informers of our Enemy. I hope the Steps which I have taken with respect to Mr. Stacy will meet with your approbation.—[1] I have the honor to be very respectfully Sir yr. ob. sert.

                                                        Isaac Chauncey

DNA, RG45, CL, 1813, Vol. 4, No. 152 (M125, Roll No. 29).

1. Secretary of War John Armstrong gave orders on 26 July 1813 that Mr. Stacy be released, "on the ground that a citizen cannot be considered as a spy." See John Armstrong to Joseph Anderson, *ASP: Military Affairs*, Vol. 1, p. 384. Stacy was released and later applied to the British for aid; it is not known if he ever received any assistance from the Canadian government following his release. See Hitsman, "Spying."

LIEUTENANT COLONEL JOHN HARVEY, BRITISH ARMY, TO COLONEL EDWARD BAYNES, BRITISH ARMY

<u>Secret</u>
                                                        Head Qr.   St. Davids
                                                        23d July 1813—

My dear Col.

I am desired to enclose to you a Letter containing a Proposal the object of which without explanation you may be puzzled exactly to make out— Mr. Hogeboom is (as his name implies) a Dutchman, who has been long resident in this Country engaged in trade with Colonel Clarke of Chippeway who has the highest opinion of his integrity and attachment to the British Govt— The Mercantile connexion betwixt them is dissolved (by the circumstance of the times) and Mr. Hogeboom is <u>disposable</u> in any way that may best promote his <u>personal advantage</u> of which it is not the practice of his Nation to lose sight— Mr H's <u>family</u> is now and has long been resident <u>in the States</u> and he has taken it into his Head that by passing there himself he might be useful to us as a secret agent— of his zeal & fidelity I feel no doubt but of his talents the specimen which his Epistle affords is not quite so satisfactory—

His demand appears most exorbitant *prima facie* though if the important service he is inclined to undertake was really well executed no Price would be too great to pay for it—

In the event of his Proposal being declined his Plan is I understand to fix himself in trade in Lower Canada—

Clarke advances him money   I am my Dr Col. yours

J Harvey

LS, CaOOA, British Military and Naval Records, RG8, I, "C" Ser., Vol. 679, pp. 275–77.

PETER HOGEBOOM TO MAJOR GENERAL FRANCIS DE ROTTENBURG, BRITISH ARMY

Niagara Falls   23rd. July 1813—

Sir

agreeable to your request, I have make a statement, on the subject of asstablishing a line of inteligence Between lake Erie & Lake Ontario, and else where as circumstances will admit, & Also, as I have some particular friend in the neighborhood of Sackets Harbor. at the same time after black a person in the vicinit of that place to communicate, inteligence ~~of~~ over to Kingston or some place in that Quarter,—Particular Persons & places to be asstablished on the lines on this side, this of corse will be the Duty of the Commanders to whom the communication is to be made, at either of the places   The mode to be persued on the Enemy's side to convey the inteligence, of course must be to the person engaged, one a week if practable and on particular occation oftener if circumstances will admit, the expense of hiring person to bring over the Dispatches, will be a separate Charge, the person Imployed of corse will do his endevour to get their person upon the best possible terms— From the nature of this Business matter may Transpire, ~~that the Commander~~ that communication could not at times be made once a week, in such cases, the person engaged will be the best Judge, of corse he will do his best endevour to send them as soon as may be, at the same time all such News Papers as can be got from various parts of the U.S. will be sent over, the Politicks of the U.S. will be communicated as far as the person employed will be Capable, of Doing— And if it should so happen that the Commander in Chief should have occation to send Dispatces over land to the Sea Board or to N. York, such matters also will be attended too, but of corse will be a separate Charge— the sum that will be Required for 12 Months will be five Thousand Dollars $2000 to be advanced, in order to Commence the Opperation,—

If any thing should farther occur to your mind you will be pleased to Communicate the same   I am Sir Yrs. with Due Respect

Peter Hogeboom

ALS, CaOOA, British Military and Naval Records, RG8, I, "C" Ser., Vol. 679, pp. 279–80.

PETER HOGEBOOM TO MAJOR GENERAL FRANCIS DE ROTTENBURG, BRITISH ARMY

Sir

Upon reflection I have concluded to Decline the matter on which we have had some conversation, as I told you I had not the Idea of the Extent &c. I you will pardon me for the trouble his Exclency has been put to, as well as your Self— I am yrs. with Due Respect

Peter Hogeboom

ALS, CaOOA, British Military and Naval Records, RG8, I, "C" Ser., Vol. 679, p. 278.

An American Privateer Action on the Saint Lawrence

In the early morning hours of 19 July, Neptune *and* Fox, *privateers from Sackets Harbor, captured the British gunboat* Spitfire *on the Saint Lawrence River along with her convoy of fifteen batteaux loaded with provisions for the British army. It was a daring feat. Since the capture of Ogdensburg in February, the Saint Lawrence had been in British control, heavily guarded from Prescott on the north and Kingston on the south. The privateer captains managed to repel an attack by four additional British gunboats and then slipped out of the river past the eighteen-gun brig* Earl of Moira.*

An anonymous letter, published in the Buffalo Gazette, *provides an amusing account of the action, but also expresses the outrage felt by many citizens of the area against recent depredations committed by the British against American villages on the lake shore.*

COMMODORE ISAAC CHAUNCEY TO SECRETARY OF THE NAVY JONES

No. 66.   U.S. Ship *Genl. Pike*
                                                                    Sackets' Harbor
                                                                    21st July 1813.

Sir,

Yesterday I received information that two Boats from this place fitted as privateers had succeeded in surprizing and capturing 1 gun boat and 15 batteaux with stores on their way up the St. Laurence.

I immediately dispatched the *Governor Tompkins, Conquest* and *Fair American* to cruise between Grenadier Island and the mouth of the River, in order to afford the privateers and their prizes protection to this harbor. This morning I directed Captain Crane in the *Madison,* to weigh and proceed with the remaining parts of the Squadron off Grenadier Island and cruise between that Island and the Ducks until I joined him, keeping up a communication by Signal with the *Genl. Pike.*—

I shall leave here this evening or tomorrow morning. I have been detained thus long for the purpose of fitting my guns completely.—

We still continue to be very sickly. Capt. Sinclair and every Lieutenant of this Ship but one, are sick, and we have 60 of the crew upon the Sick List. I hope, however, that when we get upon the open Lake, the Sick List will be very much diminished. I have the honor to be very respectfully Sir yr. ob. servt.

Isaac Chauncey

LS, DNA, RG45, CL, 1813, Vol. 5, No. 24 (M125, Roll No. 30).

AN ACCOUNT OF THE AMERICAN PRIVATEERS *NEPTUNE* AND *FOX*

From the *Utica Patriot.*

The following detailed account, (on the correctness of which we fully rely,) of the capture of the British boats, mentioned in our last, we extract from a letter received last evening from a gentleman at Sacket's Harbor, to his friend in this village, dated

July 28, 1813.

Dear Sir— On the 27th inst. arrived the privateer *Neptune,* carrying a 6-pr. and the *Fox,* an 18-pr. commanded by Major Dimock, and Captain Dixon, from a cruise to the St. Lawrence. On the 19th inst. at 4 o'clock A.M. they surprised and captured the British Gun Boat *Spit Fire,* mounting one 12-lb. carronade, and 15 Canadian batteaux, loaded with provisions, on their way up the St. Lawrence. The surprise was so complete and well arranged, that not a single shot was fired, or life lost on either side. The batteaux were laden with 27,000 wt. of sea bread, and 270 barrels of Irish pork, intended for the British army at Kingston. Our privateersmen retired into Cranberry Creek, where, having erected a breast work of the captured barrels of pork and hard bread, on the 21st, at sunrise, were attacked by four gunboats, mounting two 32-prs. one 9-pr. and a 6-pounder, and carrying from 250 to 300 men. The attack continued about two hours, when the enemy retired with considerable loss, and were pursued some distance. Our loss was but 3 killed, and 1 wounded. However, just before this, with a view, if possible, to succeed by menaces, or if not, to cover their retreat, they sent in a flag demanding a surrender of the PORK-and-BREAD FORT; and threatened, in case of a refusal, to bring up a reinforcement, let loose their Indians upon them, & that no quarter should be given! Maj. Dimock replied, that they should not surrender but at the point of the bayonet, and indignantly ordered off the officer requiring the surrender. The enemy's loss must have been considerable, as our men were well entrenched behind the *substantials of life,* and had a fair opportunity of dealing out a full measure of *death* to their antagonists. This is evidenced also by the precipitate retreat of the enemy. The number of men engaged on our part did not exceed 60. Upon coming out of the St. Lawrence, on their return to this place, they had a new and more formidable enemy to contend with. The British brig *Earl of Moira,* of 18 guns was purposely stationed to intercept their return. They nevertheless, by making a vigorous and daring effort, passed her without much injury. The *Fox,* Captain Dixon, who brought up the rear, passed within half musket shot of the brig: 3 9 pound shot struck the *Fox,* one of which passed through her magazine, but without any essential injury.

This expedition reflect much honor, upon the officers commanded and the men engaged in it. It was fitted out by, and composed chiefly of volunteers who have been injured by the depredations of the British. It was to be hoped that the war, upon this part of the frontier at least, would have been conducted according to the rules of civilized warfare: and that accordingly private property would be respected. But flushed with a temporary success, the British have committed repeated acts of wanton destruction and capture of the property of individuals. This experiment will convince them that it is no longer to be continued with impunity; & that a spirit of retaliation is arising, which, if it does no more, will at least check their career, and make full amends for the past as well as indemnity for the future.

A cannonade was heard in the direction of Presque Isle, (situate about midway on the north shore of the lake,) 2 days since, supposed to be an attempt of our fleet to destroy a large ship building there.

Buffalo Gazette, 10 August 1813.

Second Assault on York, 30 July 1813

Commodore Isaac Chauncey sailed from Sackets Harbor on 21 July with his new flagship General Pike, *26, and twelve other vessels in expectation of meeting the British squadron on the lake. When he did not find his opponent, Chauncey, in conjuction with Brigadier General John P. Boyd, planned an amphibious attack on a cache of provisions near Burlington Bay. Six hundred American soldiers, sailors, and marines advanced on shore on 30 July but quickly withdrew when they learned that a large reinforcement from York had arrived and the depot was well defended.*

Chauncey's fleet then sailed for York. The Americans landed and captured or destroyed provisions and supplies and set fire to the barracks and storehouses. The loss of flour and provisions would later cause a critical shortage of food for General Henry Procter's army on Lake Erie and would be a factor in Lieutenant Robert H. Barclay's sailing to meet Perry's fleet. After leaving York, Chauncey returned to Niagara, where he sent on eleven officers and one hundred men to join Perry's squadron at Erie.

COMMODORE ISAAC CHAUNCEY TO
BRIGADIER GENERAL JOHN P. BOYD, U.S.A.[1]

Brigadier General   U.S. Ship *Genl. Pike*
John P. Boyd   Lake Ontario   24 July 1813
commg. the forces of the U States
at Fort George & its vicinity

Sir

I was this day honored with your Letter of the 21 inst. by S. Master Mix and as I required the *Lady of the Lake* for special service I sent the prisoners to Sacketts Harbor in the *Raven*.—[2]

I am now on my way to show myself off Fort George, but as I find by your Letter that the Enemy has a deposit of Stores at the head of the Lake I think that it may be an object to make a push for them without alarming him and giving time to collect a force to defend them— I have therefore determined to run for the head of the Lake without stopping at Fort George, I in consequence take the liberty of requesting you to send by the *Lady of the Lake* the best guides that you can procure to direct us to the deposit of stores &c &c   I think that this movement of mine will have the effect of alarming the Enemy so that he will break up at Ten Mile Creek and retreat towards the Forty Mile Creek where if I had a force to meet him he would be in a perilous situation.

I hope to be with you on or before the 1st. I have the honor to be, very resp. Sir Yr. ob st.

I. C.—

LB Copy, MiU–C, Isaac Chauncey Letter Book.

1. Brigadier General John P. Boyd succeeded Morgan Lewis as commander of Fort George.

2. *Raven*, a one-gun schooner purchased by the Navy Department on 6 February 1813, was used as a transport and supply vessel.

JOHN STRACHAN [1] AND GRANT POWELL [2] TO
COLONEL EDWARD BAYNES, BRITISH ARMY

York   2 August 1813.

Sir

We beg leave to state for the information of his Excellency The Governor General, that about eleven oclock on Saturday morning, the enemy's fleet consisting of twelve Sail were seen standing for this harbour. Almost all the Gentlemen of the town having retired, we proceeded to the garrison about two oclock, and waited till half past three when the *Pyke*, the *Madison* & *Oneida*, came to anchor in the Offing, and the Schooners continued to press up the harbour with their sweeps, as the wind had become light—three coming too abreast of the town, the remainder near the Garrison. About four p.m. several boats full of troops landed at the garrison, and we having a white flag desired the first officer we met to conduct us to Commodore Chauncey—

We mentioned to the Commodore, that the Inhabitants of York consisting chiefly of women and children were alarmed at the approach of his fleet, and that we had come to know his intentions respecting the town—that if it were to be pillaged or destroyed we might take such measures as were still in our power, for their removal, and protection. We added, that the town was totally defenceless, the Militia being still on parole, and that the Gentlemen had left it having heard that the principal inhabitants of Niagara had been carried away captive, a severity unusual in war. Commodore Chauncey replied, that it was far from his intention to molest the inhabitants of York in person or property, ~~and~~ that he was sorry any of the Gentlemen had thought it necessary to retire, and that he did not know of any person taken from Niagara of the description mentioned. Col: Scott the Commander of the troops said, that a few persons had certainly been taken away, but it was for corresponding with the British army. The Commodore told us, that his coming to York at present was a sort of retaliation for the visits our fleet had made on the other side of the Lake, and to possess himself of the public stores, and destroy the fortifications, but that he would burn no houses. He mentioned something of Sodus and the necessity of retaliation should such measures be taken in future. He likewise expressed much regret at the destruction of our public library on the 27th of April—informed us, that he had made a strict search through his fleet for the books, many of them had been found, which he would send back by the first flag of truce. He then asked what public stores were here, a question which we could not answer. On parting both the Commodore & Col Scott pledged their honor, that our persons and property should be respected, and that even the town should not be entered by the troops much less any Gentlemens House

As we were quieting the minds of the Inhabitants, the troops took possession of the town, opened the jail, liberated the Prisoners, taking three Soldiers confined for felony with them. They visited the Hospitals & paroled the few men, that could not be removed they next entered the Stores of Major Allan[3] & Mr. St. George,[4] and seised the contents, consisting chiefly of flour. Observing this we went to Col Scott & informed him, that he was taking private property. He replied, that a great deal of Officers baggage had been found in Major Allans store, and that altho' private property was to be respected, provisions of all sorts were lawful prise, because they were subsistence of armies. That if we prevailed in the contest the British Govt. would make up the loss and if they were successful their Govt. would most willingly reimburse the Sufferers. He concluded by declaring, that he would scise upon all provisions he could find. The three Schooners, which had anchored abreast of the town towed out between eleven and twelve oclock on Saturday night, and we supposed, that the fleet would have sailed immediately; but having been informed by some Traitors, that valuable stores had been sent up the Don, two Schooners came up the harbour yesterday morning— the troops were again landed, and three armed boats went up the Don in search of the Stores. I have since learned that through the meritorious exertions of a few young men two of the name of Platter,[5] every thing was conveyed away, and the boats sunk before the enemy reached the place. Two or three boats containing trifling articles, which had been hid on the march were discovered & taken but in the main object the enemy was disappointed— As soon as the armed boats returned the troops went on board, and by Sun Set both Sailors and Soldiers had evacuated the town. The Barracks the wood yard, and the Store Houses on Gibraltar Point were then set on fire, and this morning at day light the enemys fleet sailed.

The troops which were landed act as marines and appear to be all they had on board, not certainly more than 240 men— the fleet consists of 14 armed vessels One is left at Sackets harbour. It is but justice to Commodore Chauncey & Col Scott to state, that their men while on shore behaved well and no private house was entered or disturbed   We have the Honor to be With Respect Your Most Obt. Humble. Servants

John Strachan
Grant Powell

ALS, CaOOA, British Military and Naval Records, RG8, I, "C" Ser., Vol. 679, pp. 324–26. Written in the hand of John Strachan.

1. John Strachan was Anglican minister at York and chaplain at Fort York. He later became the first Anglican bishop of Toronto and was active in Canadian politics as a member of the "Family Compact."

2. Grant Powell was acting surgeon in the Canadian Provincial Marine. He was the son of William Dummer Powell, an influential judge and politician in York.

3. William Allan was a York merchant and major of the Third Regiment York Militia. He was, with the other men of the local militia, captured 27 April 1813 and was released on parole awaiting formal exchange, and so was duty bound not to fight.

4. Laurent Quetton St. George was a wealthy York merchant and son-in-law of William Dummer Powell.

5. Ely and George Playter are credited with moving and concealing two boatloads of arms, baggage, and ammunition up the Don River.

COMMODORE ISAAC CHAUNCEY TO SECRETARY OF THE NAVY JONES

> U. States Ship *Genl. Pike* at anchor
> off Niagara   4th Augt. 1813

Sir

After leaving Sacketts Harbor I stretched over for the enemys shore, and from thence stood up the Lake; the winds being light I did not arive off this post untill the evening of the 27th Ulto. on the 24th I fell in with the *Lady of the Lake* on her return to Sacketts Harbor with prisoners from Fort George, I transfered the prisoners to the *Raven*, and ordered her to Sacketts Harbor. The *Lady of the Lake* I dispatched to Fort George for guides for the head of the Lake. Genl. Boyd having informed me that the enemy had a considerable deposit of provisions and stores at Burling Bay, I was determined to attempt their destruction— On the 25th I was joined by the *Pert,* and on the 27th by the *Lady of the Lake,* with guides and Capt. Cranes Company of Artillery, and Col. Scott who had very handsomely volunteered for the service— After converseing with Colo. Scott upon the subject it was thought adviseable to take on board 250 Infantry, which by the extraordinary exertions of that excellent officer were embarked before 6 oclock the next morning, and the Fleet immediately proceeded for the head of the Lake, but owing to light winds and calms we did not arive to our anchorage before the evening of the 29th; sent two partys on shore and surprised and took some of the inhabitants from whom we learned that the enemy had received considerable reinforcements within a day or two, and that his force in regulars was from 600 to 800 men, we however landed the Troops and Marines, and some sailors the next morning and reconoitred the enemys position; found him posted upon a peninsula of very high ground and strongly intrenched, and his Camp defended by about eight pieces of cannon, in this situation it was thought not adviseable to attack him with a force scarcely half his numbers and without artiliary, we ~~was~~ were also deficient in Boats, not having a sufficient number to cross the Bay with all the Troops at the same time, the men were all reembarked in the course of the afternoon and in the evening of the 30 Ultimo we weighed and stood for York, arived and anchored in that Harbor at about 3 P.M. on the 31st run the schooners into the uper Harbor landed the Marines and soldiers under command of Colo. Scott, without opposition, found several hundred Barrels of Flour and provisions in the public store houses, five pieces of cannon, Eleven boats, and a quantity of shot, shells, and other stores, all which ~~was~~ were either destroyed or brought away. On the 1st Inst. after having received on board all that the vessels could take, I directed the Barracks and the public store houses to be burnt we then reembarked the men and proceeded for this place, where I arrived yesterday— Between 4 and 500 men left York for the head of the Lake two days before we arived there some few prisoners ~~was~~ were taken some of which ~~was~~ were parroled the others have been landed at Fort George— I dispatched Lts. Eliott, Smith, and Conckling,[1] with eight midshipmen and about one hundred petty officers and seamen for Erie this morning where (from the arrangements that have been made) I think they will arive about the 7th or 8th. This force with what has allready been sent forward, will enable Captain Perry to proceed upon the Lake— I have directed him to open an intercourse, and coopperate with Genl. Harrison without delay—

In consequence of taking so many men from this ship it has so deranged her batterys that I have been loth to go on shore before I had the men requartered and stationed and seen them exercised at their Guns, consequently I have not seen the Genl. commanding at this Post, nor do I know any thing of his views, if after an interview I find that my presence is not imperiously required here, I shall return to the visinity of Sacketts Harbor and if I should not meet with the enemys Fleet on my way down, I shall Blockade him in Kingston. I have the honor to be Very Respectfully Sir Your obt. Servt.

Isaac Chauncey

ALS, DNA, RG45, CL, 1813, Vol. 5, No. 69 (M125, Roll No. 30).

1. Lieutenant Augustus H. M. Conkling; he would command *Tigress* in the Battle of Lake Erie.

A Dispute over Reinforcements for Lake Erie

The need for sailors on Lake Erie grew critical in July. Master Commandant Oliver H. Perry's ships were completed, but he still lacked sufficient men to sail them. Perry was frustrated when he received a desperate appeal from Brigadier General William Henry Harrison in late July to help repel an attack on Fort Meigs but could offer no aid to the army.

After a reinforcement of sixty men from Sackets Harbor arrived at Erie in July, Perry sent a curt letter to Commodore Isaac Chauncey complaining about the quality of the men who had been sent. His letter implied that Chauncey had kept all the best sailors for his own squadron, and had sent only the "dregs," which included landsmen and Black sailors, to Lake Erie. Chauncey upbraided Perry for his comments, maintaining that he had distributed officers and men fairly between the two squadrons. Chauncey was still smarting that Perry had in effect obtained a separate command by corresponding directly with the secretary of the navy, thereby overstepping the chain of command. This exchange provoked Perry's request for removal from Lake Erie.

MASTER COMMANDANT OLIVER H. PERRY TO COMMODORE ISAAC CHAUNCEY

"Copy"   Erie   27th. July 1813—

Sir

I have this moment received by Express the enclosed letter from Genl. Harrison,—[1] If I had officers & men (and I have no doubt you will send them)—I can fight the Enemy and proceed up the Lake—but having no one to command the *Niagara* and only one Commissioned Lieut and two actg. Lieuts., whatever my wishes may be, going out is out of the question— The men that came by Mr. Champlin[2] are a motley set, blacks, Soldiers and boys, I cannot think you saw them after they were selected— I am however pleased to see any thing in the shape of a man— Very respectfully I have the honor to be Sir Your Obd. Servt.

Signed, O. H. Perry

Copy, DNA, RG45, MC, 1813, No. 91 1/2, enclosure (M147, Roll No. 5).

1. General William Henry Harrison's army at Fort Meigs was under seige by the British and their Indian allies from 23–27 July 1813. The attack failed and the British army withdrew to attack Fort Stephenson near Sandusky. Harrison's letter to Perry requesting aid has not been found. In his reply to Harrison, Perry stated that he felt "inexpressible mortification in stating to you that I am ~~unable~~ not yet able to go out, owing to a sufficient number of officers & men not having yet arrived," (extract from Perry to Jones, 2 Sept. 1813, DNA, RG45, MC, 1813, No. 116 [M147, Roll No. 5]). See also Clanin, "Correspondence of Harrison and Perry," p. 164.

2. Sailing Master Steven Champlin and sixty men were sent from Sackets Harbor to Erie on 16 July 1813. Champlin was Perry's nephew and had served in the gunboat flotilla at Newport, Rhode Island.

Commodore Isaac Chauncey to Master Commandant Oliver H. Perry

"Copy"   U States Ship *Genl. Pike*
at anchor off Burlington Bay—
30th. July 1813—

Sir

I have been duly honored with your letters of the 23d. and 26th ult. and notice your anxiety, for men and officers. I am equally anxious to furnish you, and no time shall be lost in sending officers and men to you, as soon as the public service will allow me to send them from this Lake—

I regret that you are not pleased with the men sent you by Messrs. Champlin and Forrest,[1] for to my knowledge a part of them are not surpassed by any seamen we have in the fleet, and I have yet to learn that the Colour of the skin, or cut and trimmings of the coat, can affect a mans qualifications or usefullness— I have nearly 50 Blacks on board of this Ship and many of them are amongst my best men, and those people you call Soldiers have been to Sea from 2 to 17 years, and I presume you will find them as good and usefull as any men on board your vessel, at least if I can judge by comparison, for those that we have on board of this Ship, are attentive and obedient, and as far as I can judge many of them excellent seamen, at any rate the men sent to Lake Erie, have been selected with a view of sending a fair proportion of petty officers and Seamen, and I presume upon examination that it will be found that they are equal to those on this Lake—

I have received several letters from the Secretary of the Navy urging the necessity of the Naval Force upon Lake Erie acting immediately, you will therefore as soon as you receive a sufficient number of men commence your opperations against the Enemy, and as soon as possible Co-operate with the Army under Genl. Harrison—

As you assured the Secretary that you should conceive yourself equal or superior to the enemy with a force in men so much less than I had deemed necessary, there will be a great deal expected from you by your Country, and I trust that they will not be disappointed in the high expectations formed of your gallantry and judgement. I will barely make an observation which was impressed upon my mind by an old Soldier, that is "never despise your Enemy"

I was mortifyed to see by your letters to the Secretary (extracts & Copy's of which has been forwarded to me) that you complain that the "distance was so great between Sacketts Harbor and Erie, that you could not get instructions from me in time to execute with any advantages to the service," thereby intimating the necessity of a <u>separate command</u>— would it not have been as well to have made the complaint to me instead of the Secretary—

My confidence in your Zeal and abillities is undiminished and I sincerely hope that your success may equal your utmost wishes—

I shall dispatch to you some officers and Seamen and further instructions, upon my return to Niagara where I hope to be the day after tomorrow— I have the honor to be Very respectfully Sir, Your obt. Servt.

Signed   Isaac Chauncey

Copy, DNA, RG45, MC, 1813, No. 91 1/2, enclosure (M147, Roll No. 5).

1. Midshipman Dulany Forrest and sixty men were sent from Sackets Harbor to Erie on 16 July 1813.

MAJOR GENERAL WILLIAM HENRY HARRISON, U.S.A., TO
MASTER COMMANDANT OLIVER H. PERRY

Head Quarters
Seneca Town 9 miles from
L. Sandusky   4th Augt. 1813

Sir

Your favor of the 27th. Ultimo was received a few days ago— I have now the satisfaction to inform you that the seige of Fort Meigs was abandoned by the enemy on the 27th ulo.— on the evening of the 1st Inst. they appeared before the Post of Lower Sandusky and about 5 oclock P.M. of the 2nd attempted to carry it by Storm— In this rash attempt they were repulsed with great loss, two officers (a Lt. Col. by Brevet and a Lt.) with about 50 men penetrated to the ditch where they were all killed or wounded, but two or three, who were sheltered by the dead bodies by which they were covered— We have 26 prisoners— Genl. Proctor retreated down the Sandusky River with the utmost precipitation— I have examined some of the most inteligent Prisoners— They all agree that the new Ship was launched on Saturday the 17th ultimo—that neither her guns or seamen had arrived (a very few of the former being on the warf) but that both were expected from Long Point— One of the Prisoners says that they were about to take some of the Guns from the ramparts of Malden to put in her and that they expected to make up the Compliment by taking Fort Meigs— From this statement you will at once perceive that Sailing from Presquille a single day sooner or later may be of the greatest importance to your success against the enemys Fleet— I had much rather that such Stores as are intended for the army and not yet arrived at Erie should be left and brought up hereafter than they should be the cause of your delay—

Make what use you may think proper of Colo. Hill's Regt.[1] I should suppose that some marksmen might be selected from it who could render you great Service in an action with the enemy— With great Respect and consideration I am yr. Humble Servt.

Willm. Henry Harrison

on our side but one man killed and a few slightly wounded

LS, MiU–C, Oliver Hazard Perry Papers.

1. Colonel Rees Hill, a Pennsylvania militia officer from Greene County, Pennsylvania. Hill was directed in late July to put his regiment at Perry's disposal and to sail on board Perry's fleet if they could be of use. See Andrew H. Holmes to Oliver H. Perry, 23 July 1813, in Clanin, "Correspondence of Harrison and Perry," p. 163.

Master Commandant Oliver H. Perry to Secretary of the Navy Jones

U.S.S. *Lawrence* off Erie   Augt. 10th 1813

Sir,

I am under the disagreeable necessity of requesting a removal from this station, the enclosed copy of a letter from Comr. Chauncey[1] will I am satisfied convince you that I cannot serve longer under an officer who has been so totally regardless of my feelings— The men spoken of by Comr. Chauncey, were those mentioned in the roll I did myself the honor to send you—they may Sir, be as good as are on the other Lake, but if so, that squadron must be poorly manned indeed—

In the requisition for men, sent by your order, I made a note saying, "I should consider myself equal or superior with a smaller number of men to the enemy," that requisition Sir, was made nearly two months since—what then might have been considered certain, may from lapse of time be deemed problematical. The Comr. insinuates that I have taken measures to obtain a separate command. I beg leave to ask you Sir, if any thing in any of my letters to you could be construed into such a meaning— on my return to this place in June last, I wrote you, the *Queen Charlotte* and *Lady Prevost* were off this harbor, and if they remained a few days might possibly be able to intercept their return to Malden— I had no orders to act—and the only way of obtaining them in time was to write to you Sir—as the communication between Comr. Chauncey and myself occupied considerably upwards of a month— in my request, I meant this as a reason for applying to you on the emergency instead of the Comr.— I have been on this station upwards of five months and during that time have submitted cheerfully and with pleasure, to fatigue and anxiety, hitherto to me unknown in the service— I have had a very resposible situation, without an officer, (except one sailg. master) of the least experience,—however seriously I have felt my situation, not a murmur has escaped me. The critical state of Genl. Harrison was such that I took upon myself the very great responsibility of going out, with the few young officers you had been pleased to send me, with the few seamen I had, and as many volunteers as I could muster from the militia—I did not shrink from this responsibility—but Sir, at that very moment I did not surely anticipate the rect. of a letter in every line of which there is insult— Under all these circumstances, I beg most <u>respectfully</u> and <u>most earnestly</u> that I may be immediately removed from this station   I am willing to forego that reward which I have considered for two months past almost within my grasp— If Sir I have rendered my country any service in the equipment of this Squadron I beg it may be considered as an inducement to grant my request— I shall proceed with the squadron and whatever is in my power shall be done to promote the honor and interest of the service— When I volunteered to join Comr. Chauncey I left a respectable command at Newport if Sir I could be ordered to that place until more active service could be found for me—it would add very much to the obligation— If this is impossible I beg I may be indulged with a short furlough the situation of my family requiring my presence. Very respectfully I have the honor to be Sir Your obt. Servt.

O. H. Perry

I enclose to you Sir a copy of the letter which Comr. Chauncey takes exception at—[2]

O. H. P.

ALS, DNA, RG45, MC, 1813, No. 103 (M147, Roll No. 5).

1. Perry here refers to Commodore Isaac Chauncey's letter of 30 July; see pp. 530–31.
2. See Perry to Chauncey, 27 July 1813, pp. 529–30.

SECRETARY OF THE NAVY JONES TO MASTER COMMANDANT OLIVER H. PERRY

O. H. Perry Esqr.   Navy Department
Comg. U.S. Naval Forces,   August 18th. 1813.
on Lake Erie.

Sir,

I have received your letters of the 10th. and 11th. with much anxiety, as they indicate a state of things unfriendly to harmony, and reciprocal confidence, between the Commander in Chief and yourself, which was the less to have been expected, as he selected you for the command of the Erie Squadron, and has never ceased to speak of you, in terms of the highest approbation and confidence.

Sensible as I am of your love of Country, high sense of honour, and zealous devotion to the service, I cannot but believe, that reflection will allay the feelings of discontent which you have expressed. The indulgence of such feelings, must terminate in the most serious injury to the service, and probably ruin to yourself. Avoid recrimination—persevere in the zealous and honourable path of duty which you have hitherto pursued, with so much credit to yourself, and utility to your Country; and the result, I have no doubt, will enhance the fame of both. A change of Commander, under existing circumstances, is equally inadmissible, as it respects the interest of the service, and your own reputation. It is right that you should reap the harvest which you have sown. The season is short, and when active operations have ceased, if you continue to desire a transfer to some other station, you shall be indulged.

It is the duty of an Officer, (and in none does his character shine more conspicuous,) to sacrifice all personal motives & feelings when in collision with the public good. This sacrifice you are called upon to make, and I calculate, with confidence, upon your efforts to restore and preserve harmony, and to concentrate the vigorous exertions of all, in carrying into effect, the great objects of your enterprize. I am, Sir, respectfully, your obedient servant,

W. Jones

LB Copy, DNA, RG45, CLS, 1813, pp. 60–61.

Engagement on Lake Ontario:
Loss of *Hamilton, Scourge, Julia,* and *Growler*

The British squadron, newly fitted and armed, sailed from Kingston on 31 July in order to seek a decisive action with Commodore Isaac Chauncey's fleet. The Americans had more ships and were superior in armament, but the vessels of the British fleet were better manned and could fight more effectively as a squadron. Chauncey often found it necessary to tow his smaller, dull sailing schooners in order to keep his ships together.

Calm weather and light breezes kept the two fleets apart until 7 August, when they both appeared off the head of Lake Ontario near Niagara. The crews of both squadrons remained at quarters all evening, waiting for a change of wind to engage their opponents. In the early morning hours of 8 August, a sudden squall carried two American schooners, Hamilton and Scourge, to the bottom, with the loss of all but sixteen of their crews. These schooners had been built as merchant vessels of shallow draft; they were not designed to carry the weight of heavy cannon on deck and were unstable in stormy weather. Hamilton had been refitted to carry nine guns and Scourge ten, far more than the other schooners of comparable size in the American squadron.

The opposing fleets continued to maneuver in the light breezes for two more days until the evening of 10 August, when Yeo bore down for the American line and succeeded in cutting off and capturing two vessels, the schooners Julia and Growler.[1] The Americans had lost nearly 160 men and twenty-three guns in two days. The loss of four of his eleven schooners was a serious blow to Chauncey and no doubt shook the confidence of the usually cautious American commodore.

1. *A vivid, first-person account of the loss of* Scourge *and the capture of* Julia *is found in Cooper,* Ned Myers, *pp. 77–100. For an account of the recent discovery and documentation of* Hamilton *and* Scourge, *see Cain,* Ghost Ships; *and Nelson, "Ghost Ships."*

MAJOR WILLOUGHBY MORGAN, U.S.A.,[1] TO
LIEUTENANT COLONEL DAVID CAMPBELL, U.S.A.[2]

Fort George 9th August 1813

Dear Colonel.

The fleets have done nothing yet. Commodore Chauncey has endeavoured to bring the enemy to action; but having the advantage of the wind he has been able to avoid a rencontre. The reason he avoids an action at present is pretty evident. He wishes to make sure work; there is no necessity now for his risking any thing, and in the course of six weeks he will be uncontrouled master of the lake—having a large ship building at Kingston which will be finished by that time.

The Commodore is out now endeavouring to bring the enemy to a fight, but I am much afraid he will not be able to effect his purpose.

A most distressing occurrence has happened to our fleet. The night after the enemys fleet came in view whilst the fleet was out Cruising a squal came up so suddenly that two of the sloops were capsized and entirely lost. Only twelve of the crew were saved. No vestage of the vessels is to be seen. Independant of the deep sorrow this unfortunate event excites we have sustained a loss of nine Guns.[3] Nevertheless the Commodore is trying to bring Sir James to battle; but

Sir James still avoids it with all his dexterity. To my apprehension Sir James in prudence has every reason to avoid a recontre; the Commodore every reason to desire it— Why did Sir James leave Kingston? It is not Known; but the Officers of the Navy Conjecture that he hoped to have surprised our fleet—

I believe ere this we should have tried our hands again in conjunction with the fleet if the British vessels had not appeared— But of this say nothing— I believe the mail does not go out till tomorrow. I will keep my letter open till that time.

9 O'clock at night The wind blows fresh but is diametrically against us. This has been the case ever since the enemys ~~flight~~ fleet appeared insight. Fortune declares for Sir James or something superior to [fortune?]. The Commodore is still out trying to prevent Sir James' escape, but unless the wind changes I am fearfull that it is all to no purpose.

10th. in the morning the British fleet is in view, ours is not but no doubt it is near at hand. Sir James finds it difficult to get out of the head of the lake. He has attempted it once or twice. The wind is still against Chauncy, If he can once get to the windward action [will be sure?]. Adieu

Willoughby Morgan   Major

ALS, NcD, Campbell Family Papers. Addressed to Lieutenant Colonel David Campbell, 20th Infantry, Winchester, Virginia.

1. Willoughby Morgan, 12th U.S. Infantry, was promoted to major on 26 June 1813.
2. Lieutenant Colonel David Campbell, 20th U.S. Infantry, was appointed 12 March 1812.
3. Nineteen guns were actually lost in the accident.

COMMODORE SIR JAMES LUCAS YEO, R.N., TO
GOVERNOR-GENERAL SIR GEORGE PREVOST

Wolfe off York   11th. August 1813
1/2 past 1 P.M.

My Dear Sir,

Yesterday evening the Enemy's Squadron stood for us with a fine breeze from the Eastd. Our's was becalmed off the Post at 12 Miles Creek.— At sun set a breeze came off the land which gave us the wind of the Enemy, And I stood for them. On which he immediately stood from us under as much sail as his schooners could keep up with him.

He was in a long line, the *Pike, Maddison, Oneida,* six schooners and two to-windward to rake our Masts as we came up.— At 11 we came within Gun shot of the schooners when they opened a brisk fire and from going so fast it was more than an hour before we could pass them. At this time all our squadron was two & three miles astern of the *Wolfe.* On coming up with the *Maddison & Pike* they put before the Wind made sail firing their stern chase Guns—and I found it impossible to get the Squadron up with them, as the *Wolfe* was the only Ship that could keep up. I therefore made sail between Him and the two schooners to windward which I captured the *Julia & Growler* each mounting one long 32 & one long 12 Pr. with a compliment of forty Men.

I am also happy to acquaint You that two of his largest schooners the *Hamilton* of nine guns & the *Scourge* of ten guns up-set the night before last in carrying sail to keep from us, and all on-board perished, in numbers about one hundred. This has reduced his Squadron to ten and increased ours to eight but they will take men from the Ships.

I feel confident that by watching every proper opportunity we shall get the better of him, but as long as he is determined to sacrifice every thing to his own safety, I shall never in this narrow water be able to bring the two ships to action as I have no vessel that sails sufficiently well to second me.

This conduct He cannot persevere in long for His own Honor as the loss of all his schooners (which I ever must have in my power) will be an indelible disgrace to him, and I am at a loss to know how he will account to His Government for it. The *Pike* mounts 28 long 24 Ps. & four hundred and twenty men. The *Maddison* 22–32 Pr. carronades and three hundred & forty men (<u>Good Head Money</u>[1])   Their squadron took on board the day before Yesterday nine boats full of Troops I suppose to repel boarders.

I am happy to add that the *Wolfe* has not received any material damage and no one hurt on-board. I am now landing the Prisoners and repairing the damages of the *Growler* who has lost her Bowsprit & otherwise much cut up.

It concerns me to find I have such a wary opponent as it harasses me beyond my strength. I am very unwell and I believe nothing but the nature of the service keeps me up.

I must close this which is more than I have my eyes for these forty eight hours—and hope my next will be more acceptable. I have the Honor to remain Dear Sir Your Excellency's obedient humble Servant

James Lucas Yeo.

ALS, CaOOA, British Military and Naval Records, RG8, I, "C" Ser., Vol. 730, pp. 81–84.

1. A bounty (or head money) for each person on board a captured ship was added to the valuation of the prize, and the sum was divided among the officers and crew.

An Unknown Midshipman to J. Jones

Sackets Harbour on board the *Madison*   Augt. 13th. 1813—

Most Respected Uncle

Dear Sir

In my last I informed you in haste of our sailing which was at the moment rather unexpected. I now hasten to inform you of my safe return to the Harbour. Would to God I could say of the safe return of us all. From the 21st. Ult nothing worth mentioning occured untill the 29th. when we arrived at 4 mile creek and anchored. We took on board the fleet 150 Soldiers—Weighed and directed our course for Burlington where we arrived the following day (the 30th.) B. is a deposit for public stores supposed to contain of flour only, 10,000 barrels. We landed Soldiers, Marines and Sailors about 600 before advancing for we were informed of the enemy's strength which was so great that had we advanced to the enemy's stores situated about 4 miles up the bay we should have been surrounded and massacred by the Savages and English. We then returned to the place of our landing, and reembarked. I was informed by an inhabitant that our men who fell or were taken at the battle of 40 Mile Creek were most shockingly butchered.

Their heads skinned, their hearts taken out and put in their mouths, their privates cut off and put in the places of their hearts— We owing to <u>someones</u> imprudence, narrowly escaped a similar fate. 31st. we weighed, and stood down the lake— August 1st. we came to anchor in 14 fathoms water. York light house bearing 3 1/2 north distant 2 miles. We landed and took some stores. August 2nd. at 2 1/2 P.M. we got under way and stood for Fort George where we arrived Augst. 3rd.— Augst. 7th. while at anchor off Fort George at 4 A.M. discovered 6 sail supposed to be the enemy's fleet bearing W.N.W. 10 miles distant. at 5 Com. made signal and we got under way. at 7 signal was made for battle, the American Ensign was hoisted. Sir George displayed the English Union, being within long shot the Com. fired 5 or 6 guns which they did not return but continued bearing down upon us. The Com. thunder struck (and no doubt frightened) at their coolness and determined bravery, tacked ship and left them! under pretence of endeavouring to get the weathergage. Never again will we have the opportunity we have this day had, of settling the contest with so small a sacrifice. This night also sunday and S'night continued endeavouring to get the weathergage, sunday at midnight we were struck by a heavy squall and were near experiencing the fate of two of our finest schooners, which were lost the Crews excepting 16 perished. This is only part of the evil arising from not attacking the enemy on the third, for which the Com. is answerable and perhaps highly censurable, (you know he is a peace man) Monday, Tuesday, and Wednesday still in chace and manoevering, on Wednesday night at 1/2 past 9 (in the afternoon we had the weathergage but wind shifted) notwithstanding having lost the weathergage by change of wind our schooners opened a heavy fire on the enemy's ships which no doubt did them much injury, we were all ready for the fight the enemy's balls flew briskly round us. We kept closing, two of our Schooners were in the midst of the enemys fleet when the Com. wore ship and left the enemy! the two schooners were taken— They fought like heroes and it is feared every man was killed, we being out of provisions returned to S. Harbour, where we this moment arrived. Our boats are bringing off provisions and we will no doubt sail immediately.

Excuse my haste and remember me to Mrs. and to all your family whom I am anxious to see and hear from, and believe me my dear uncle most affectionately yours—

Copy, DNA, RG45, CL, 1814, Vol. 2, No. 70 (M125, Roll No. 35). A copy of this letter was enclosed in a letter from J. Jones of 114 Water Street, New York, to Secretary of the Navy Jones dated 25 March 1814.

COMMODORE ISAAC CHAUNCEY TO SECRETARY OF THE NAVY JONES

No. 71— U.S. Ship *Genl. Pike*
Sacketts Harbor. 13 Aug. 1813
Sir

I arrived here this day with this Ship, *Madison, Oneida, Governor Tompkins, Conquest, Ontario, Pert* and *Lady of the Lake,*—the *Fair American* and *Asp* I left at Niagara.— Since I had the honor of addressing you last, I have been much distressed and mortified,— distressed at the loss of a part of the force intrusted to my command and mortified at not being able to bring the Enemy to action.— The following movements and transactions of the Squadron since the 6th. inst. will give you the best idea of the difficulties and mortifications that I have had to encounter.—

On the 6th. inst. I had a conference with Generals Boyd and Williams and it was determined to attack the Enemy immediately and to insure the capture or destruction of his whole army. I was to take on board of the Fleet, the next day Fifteen Hundred Men, under the command of Genl. Williams and land them at Burlington Bay, and after carrying the Enemy's position at that place, Genl. Williams was to march upon the road for Fort George in order to attack the Enemy in rear, while Genl. Boyd made a simultaneous movement and attacked him in front— by these arrangements (the fleet acting in concert) the enemy's ~~fleet~~ would have been completely cut off, and his whole army must have surrendered in the course of a few days— On the 7th at day light the Enemy's fleet, consisting of two Ships, two Brigs, and two large Schooners were discovered bearing W.N.W.—distant about five or Six Miles—Wind at West.— at 5 weighed with the Fleet, and manouv'red to gain the Wind— at 9 having passed to Leeward of the Enemy's line and abreast of his van (the *Wolf*) hoisted our colours and fired a few guns to ascertain whether we could reach him, with our Shot, finding they fell short, I wore and hauled upon a wind on the Starboard Tack— the rear of our Schooners then about 6 miles astern the enemy wore in Succession and hauled upon a Wind, on the same tack, but soon finding that we should be able to weather him upon the next Tack, he tacked and made all Sail to the Northward— as soon as our rear Vessels could fetch his wake, tacked and made all sail in chase— in the afternoon the Wind became very light and towards night quite calm, the Schooners used their Sweeps all the afternoon in order to close with the Enemy, but without Success— late in the afternoon I made the signal of recall and formed in close order— Wind during the Night from the Westward and after midnight Squally— kept all hands at Quarters, and beat to Windward in hopes to gain the Wind of the enemy— at 2 A.M. missed Two of our Schooners at daylight discovered the missing Schooners to be the *Hamilton* & *Scourge*, Soon after Spoke the *Govr. Tompkins* who informed me that the *Hamilton* and *Scourge* both over-set and sunk in a heavy Squall about 2 O'Clock, and distressing to relate every Soul perished except 16— this fatal accident, deprived me at once of the Services of two valuable Officers (Lieut Winter and Sailing Master Osgood) and two of my best Schooners, mounting together 19 Guns— this accident giving to the Enemy decidedly the Superiority. I thought he would take advantage of it particularly as by a change of Wind he was again brought dead to Windward of me—formed the line upon the larboard Tack, and hove too— Soon after 6 A.M. the enemy bore up and set studding-sails apparently with an intention to bring us to action— when he had approached us within about four miles he brought too on Starboard Tack— I wore and brought too on same tack, finding that the Enemy had no intention of bringing us to action I edged away to gain the land in order to have the advantage of the land breeze in the afternoon— it soon after fell calm— I directed the Schooners to sweep up, and engage the Enemy, about noon we got a light breeze from the Eastward,— I took the *Oneida* in tow (as she sails badly) and Stood for the Enemy when the Van of our Schooners was within about 1 1/2 to 2 Miles of his rear— the Wind Shifted to the Westward, which again brought him to Windward— as soon as the breeze struck him, he bore up for the Schooners in order to cut them off, before they could rejoin me, but with their Sweeps and the breeze soon reaching them also they were soon in their Station— the Enemy finding himself foiled in his attempt upon the Schooners hauled his Wind, and hove

A SCENE ON LAKE ONTARIO.

United States Ship of War Gen.Pike/Commodore Chauncey and the British Sloop of War Wolf, sir James Yeo. Preparing for action Sep.t 28.1813.

Published and Sold by Shelton & Kensett Cheshire Con. Novem.r 1.st 1813.

too.— It soon after became very Squally and the appearance of its continuing so during the Night and as we had been at quarters for nearly forty hours and being apprehensive of separating from some of the heavy sailing Schooners in the Squalls induced me to run in towards Niagara and anchor outside the bar— Genl. Boyd very handsomely offered any assistance in Men that I might require— I received 150 Soldiers and distributed them in the different Vessels to assist in boarding or repelling boarders as circumstances might require, blew very heavy in Squalls during the Night— Soon after day light discovered the Enemy's Fleet, bearing North weighed and stood after him— the Wind soon became light and variable and before 12 O'Clock quite calm at 5 fresh breezes from North the Enemys fleet bearing North distant about 4 or 5 leagues, wore the fleet in succession and hauled upon a wind on the larboard Tack— at Sun down the enemy bore N.W. by N. on the Starboard tack— the Wind hauling to the Westward, I stood to the Northward all night in order to gain the North Shore— at day light tacked to the Westward the Wind having changed to N.N.W. soon after discovered the Enemy's fleet, bearing S.W.— I took the *Asp* and the *Madison,* the *Fair American* in tow and made all sail in chase— It was at this time that we thought of realizing what we had been so long toiling for—but before 12 OClock—the Wind changed to W.S.W. which brought the enemy to Windward tacked to the Northward at 3 the Wind inclining to the Northward wore to the Southward and Westward and made the Signal for the Fleet to make all Sail— at 4—the Enemy bore S.S.W., bore up and steered for him— at 5 observed the Enemy becalmed under the Land, nearing him very fast with a fine breeze from N.N.W.— at 6—formed the order of battle within about 4 Miles of the Enemy—the Wind at this time very light— at 7, the Wind changed to S.W. and a fresh breeze which again placed the enemy to Windward of me tacked and hauled upon a wind on the larboard tack under easy Sail— the Enemy standing after us at 9 when within about two gun Shot of our rear, he wore to the Southward— I stood on to the Northward under easy Sail— the fleet formed in two lines—a part of the Schooners forming the weather line, with orders to commence the fire upon the Enemy—as soon as their Shot would take effect and as the enemy neared them to edge down upon the Line to Leeward and pass through the intervals and form to Leeward— at about half past 10 the enemy tacked and stood after us,— at 11 the rear of our line opened his fire upon the Enemy— in about 15 minutes the fire became general from the weather line which was returned from the enemy at half past 11 the weather line bore up and passed to the Leeward except the *Growler* and *Julia* which soon after tacked to the Southward, which brought the Enemy, between them and me— filled the maintopsail and edged away two points to lead the enemy down, not only to engage him to more advantage but to lead him from the *Growler* and *Julia*— he however kept his Wind, untill he completely separated those two vessels from the rest of the Squadron— exchanged a few Shot with this Ship as he passed, without injury to us, and made Sail after our Two Schooners tacked and stood after him at 12 (midnight) finding that I must either separate from the rest of the Squadron or relinquish the hope of saveing the two which had seperated, I reluctantly gave up the pursuit rejoined the Squadron then to Leeward and formed the line on the starboard tack— the firing was continued between our Two Schooners and the Enemy's Fleet, untill about 1 A.M. when I presume they were obliged to surrender to a force so much their Superior— saw nothing more of the enemy that night, soon after day light discovered them close in, with the North Shore, with one of our Schooners in tow the other not to be seen, presume she may have been Sunk— the enemy showing no disposition to come down upon us, altho to windward and blowing heavy from West— The Schooners laboring very much, I ordered two of the dullest to run into Niagara, and anchor the gale increasing very much and as I could not go into Niagara with this Ship—I determined to run for Genesee Bay as a shelter for the small vessels—and with the expectation of being able to obtain provisions for the Squadron as we were all nearly out the *Madison* and *Oneida* not a single days on board when we arrived opposite Genessee Bay— I found there was every prospect of the gales continuing, and if it did I could run to this place and provision the whole squadron with more certainty and nearly the same time that I could at Genessee admitting that I could obtain provisions at that place after bringing the breeze as far as Oswego, the Wind became light inclining to a calm which has prolonged our passage to this day.— I shall provision the Squadron for Five weeks and proceed up the Lake this Evening, and when I return again I hope to be able to communicate more agreeable news than this communication contains.

The loss of the *Growler* and *Julia* in the manner in which they have been lost is mortifying in the extreme and altho' their Commanders disobeyed my positive orders, I am willing to believe that it arose from an error of Judgement and an excess of zeal to do more than was required of them thinking probably that the enemy intended to bring us to a general action, they thought by gaining the Wind of him they would have it more in their power to annoy and injure him than they could by forming to Leeward of our Line.— From what I have been able to discover of the movements of the Enemy he has no intention of engaging us except he can get decidedly the advantage of Wind and Weather and as his Vessels in Squadron sail better than our Squadron he can always avoid an action unless I can gain the Wind and have Sufficient daylight to bring him to action before dark, his object is evidently to harrass us by Night attacks by which means he thinks to cut off our Small dull Sailing Schooners in detail fortune has evidently favored him thus far, I hope that it will be my turn next and altho inferior in point of force—I feel very confident of success. I have the honor to be Very Respectfully Sir Yr. Mo. Ob. St.

Isaac Chauncey

P.S. I enclose herewith a plan of the order of battle on the Night of the 9th. inst.—[1]

I. C.

LS, DNA, RG45, CL, 1813, Vol. 5, No. 99 (M125, Roll No. 30).

1. This plan can be found in DNA, RG45, CL, 1813, Vol. 5, bound between Nos. 100 and 101 (M125, Roll No. 30).

Life of a Naval Surgeon on Lake Ontario

In response to a proposed cut in his pay, Dr. Walter W. Buchanan wrote a letter of protest to the secretary of the navy in which he provided many details about his role as a surgeon in the U.S. Navy. Dr. Buchanan first entered naval service in October 1800 during the Quasi-War with France when he was appointed surgeon and ordered to join Ganges. *That ship had just returned from a cruise to the West Indies, where virtually the entire crew had contracted a debilitating fever. The vessel was refitting when Buchanan joined her. Her next cruise proved to be a short one: while en route to Havana in January 1801, Ganges was damaged in a storm and found unfit for sea. Buchanan was discharged in August 1801 with the reduction in the navy under the Peace Establishment Act.*

Buchanan returned to New York where, in 1808, he became professor of midwifery at Columbia's College of Physicians and Surgeons and practiced at the New York Almshouse (predecessor to Bellevue Hospital).[1] He was later recruited by Isaac Chauncey for service on the lakes and was appointed naval surgeon on 31 August 1812.[2] Buchanan participated in all naval engagements on the lake and was in charge of the makeshift naval hospital at Sackets Harbor.

1. Cushman, "Columbia Alumni."

2. Buchanan's appointment as surgeon was confirmed on 21 December 1812; he formally accepted his commission on 15 March 1813.

Surgeon Walter W. Buchanan to Secretary of the Navy Jones

The Honourable   Sackets' Harbour   August 27th 1813.
Wm. Jones
Secretary of the Navy U.S.

Sir

Mr. Fitzgerald, Purser on this station has just submitted to my perusal, a communication from Mr. Turner, relative to my extra pay as Hospital Surgeon, referring to an indorsement made by you on that subject, stating "that as living cannot be as high at Sackets Harbour as at Newyork—he must make a deduction of 25 per cent upon the usual allowance"— I cannot presume Sir, to suppose that you are acquainted with the grounds upon which I was induced to relinquish a respectable private practice of 11 or 12 years standing & adopt the perilous & arduous duties of a navy Surgeon— Permit me therefore to submit to your candid consideration the reasons which influenced my decision

In 1800 I was appointed a surgeon in the navy— I then became acquainted with Commodore Chauncey & my attattchment to him has encreased with my knowledge of the man— Upon the reduction of the Navy I retired to the paths of private life & my ambition never lead me to expect, or even wish again to wear the uniform of our Country— Upon the contemplation of the expedition to the Lakes, Dr. Bullus & Comr. Chauncey both solicited me to embark in the enterprize—in a manner flattering to my professional feelings—& eventually succeeded in gaining my acquiesence, by your predecessor placing me on the same footing as other Hospital Surgeons.

Considering that this would be a permanent establishment—I relinquished my private practice, gave up a situation in the Newyork alms house of 300$ per ann:—vacated a Professional chair in Columbia College in that city—left the bosom of a young & rising family—& aged parents who are indebted to me for support & whose reduced circumstances are known to have resulted from the Part my father took in our revolutionary war—& excluded myself from society by following Comr. Chauncey at a few days notice, to this inhospitable clime— There in common with my brother officers we have suffered every hardship & every privation that men can suffer even the necessaries of life, instead of "not being as high as at New York" is infinitely beyond what I have ever paid during 12 years I have been master of a family in that city— The article of potatoes alone were lately 12/ per Bushel— During my residence here I have submitted to every deprivation— I have been engaged in every expedition from the attack upon Kingston last November—to the two late interviews with Sir James Yeo's squadron— In consequence of excessive fatigue & professional exertions at York, I was seized with a complaint which confined me to Bed for 4 Weeks & 2 days— During the last winter, in consequence of the illness of Messrs. Cook & Caton[1]—I attended the Hospital & squadron in the most inclement season—almost unassisted & during 10 months disagreeable service, I am not conscious of having been guilty of any act, that could impair the confidence that Com: Chauncey & the Government were pleased to place in me— I entered the service under (I presumed) an implied obligation on the part of Government to make good that salary—(whether I could expend it here or not)—which Com: Chauncey was authorized by the then Secretary of the Navy to offer me— I have conscientiously fulfilled according to the Best of my abilities—the duties delegated to me by my Country— But there is also, Sir another duty which must be as imperiously fulfilled—it is the duty I owe myself my family to my Profession— I therefore Sir Respectfully submit my case to your reconsideration— I do not appeal to your generosity or that of my Government—But to a more exalted & a more noble principle— I Remain, Sir Very Respectfully your Obdt. Humble Servt.[2]

W. W. Buchanan

ALS, DNA, RG45, BC, 1813, Vol. 3, No. 130 (M148, Roll No. 12).

1. Surgeon's Mate Andrew B. Cook and Surgeon William Caton.
2. Secretary of the Navy Jones agreed to continue Dr. Buchanan's extra pay as hospital surgeon; see Jones to Buchanan, 5 Oct. 1813, DNA, RG45, SNL, Vol. 11, p. 106 (M149, Roll No. 11).

Perry Gains the Lake

Lieutenant Robert H. Barclay was frustrated in his attempts to build and adequately man and equip his squadron on Lake Erie. The guns and stores intended for his fleet were captured by the Americans in their two attacks on York in April and July, and a sufficient reinforcement of sailors was not forthcoming from Commodore Sir James L. Yeo. If Barclay could not build a superior naval force on the lake, he hoped he could at least destroy the enemy's ships before they could get out of Presque Isle Bay. Major General Henry Procter and Barclay planned to launch an attack on the American base; they only awaited reinforcements to carry out the assault. Their plan was halted when Brigadier General Francis de Rottenburg was made administrator and commander of the forces in Upper Canada on 19 June and refused to provide the additional troops needed for the assault.

Despite his own disappointed hopes for an adequate number of trained sailors, Master Commandant Oliver H. Perry was ready to sail by late July. His final obstacle was getting his ships across the bar that sheltered Presque Isle harbor. This was accomplished by the use of "camels," watertight boxes that were submerged alongside a ship, then pumped out to help float it through shallow water. The American vessels were lightened by removing their guns and ballast, but they were in danger of attack until rearmed.[1]

Although Barclay kept a close watch on the American base, he withdrew his ships about 30 July—allowing Perry time to move his vessels onto the lake. Barclay probably went to Long Point, the British depot for stores and the main point of communication between Lakes Erie and Ontario, to ready the sails and armament for his new ship Detroit, which had been launched and was then fitting out for service. He also anticipated the imminent arrival of reinforcements of sailors and soldiers; without additional men, Barclay could not meet the Americans either inside or outside of Presque Isle harbor. The British vessels were also running short of provisions after a fortnight on the lake and had to return to Long Point to resupply.

1. *On the use of camels to move Perry's vessels, see Rosenberg,* Building Perry's Fleet, *pp. 50–52.*

LIEUTENANT ROBERT H. BARCLAY, R.N., TO GOVERNOR-GENERAL SIR GEORGE PREVOST

H.M.S. *Queen Charlotte*
Long point—July 16th 1813

Sir/

The present state of His Majesty's Naval force on Lake Erie induces me to call your Excellency's serious attention to it—more particularly as the means that I possess, have been so entirely misrepresented—

On my taking the command here, I instantly reconnoitred the Enemy's naval stations, and on finding so great a force getting ready at Presqu'isle, I judged that an immediate attack by Land and the Lake would decidedly be the best mode of anihilating their naval equipments at once— Under that impression I wrote to Genl. Vincent for a sufficient body of regulars, to join what Genl. Procter could bring with him from Amherstburg, and a body of Indians (which he could at all times command) to enable me to attack Presqu'isle at once— Genl. Vincent having promised the remainder of the 41st. Regt. I sail'd from this bay, to apprize Genl. Procter of it— He perfectly coincided in the propriety of the measure, and prepared to come down with his troops and Indians—but, just when all was ready Genl. de Rottenburg gave him to understand that no assistance could be given from that quarter, he was obliged in consequence to desist from an enterprise ~~that~~ for which he had not sufficient numbers to make the success even probable—

I left Amherstburg with all the vessels that I could employ as men of war— and manned with the former Canadian crew, strengthened by 50 of the 41st. Regt.—but our actual force being so much inferior, to that of the Enemy when they get equipment for them renders the situation of this squadron in a most hazardous situation—

I have further received from Lt. Colonel Evans 70 of the 41st Regt. and intend proceeding early to morrow for Presqu'isle— and take advantage of their not being yet on the Lake, and endeavour to prevent it by a blockade until the *Detroit* is ready for sea— But that circumstance will never take place, if seamen, and ordnance, together with stores of every description are not immediately sent up— It is the more to be insisted on, as if the Enemy do gain the ascendancy on this Lake, all supplies must necessarily be cut off.

I enclose a statement of the force of the rival squadrons, and if prompt assistance is not sent up, although my officers and crews will do every thing that zeal and intrepidity can do; the great superiority of the enemy may prove fatal—

I write this to Your Excellency in the hope that you will take the squadron on Lake Erie into consideration—and that you will see the immense advantage that will accrue to the Enemy by being enabled to transport troops either to annoy the right of the army under Genl. de Rottenburg, or to cut off Genl. Procters communication with the lower province except by Land—

Indeed the whole line under Genl. Procter must lay open to the Enemy, in the event of their being able to make His Majesty's Squadron retire—

The *Detroit* will be ready to launch on the 20th. instant—but there is neither a sufficient quantity of ordnance, Amunition or any other stores—and not a man to put in her— If that vessel was on the Lake I would feel confident as to the result of any action they might chuse to risk—but at present although for the good of H.M. Provinces I must attack them— I cannot help saying—that it is possible that they may have an advantage—'though I trust not a decided one—

I have communicated with Sir James Yeo on the same subject—and if he, from the exigencies of the service on the Lake Ontario will not admit of his sending many seamen, even fifty would be of the greatest service for the present—but it will require at least from 250, to 300 seamen, to render His Majesty's Squadron perfectly effective— I have the Honor to be Your Excellency's Most obdt. and Humble Servant

R. H. Barclay   Senr. Offr.
on Lake Erie

ALS, CaOOA, British Military and Naval Records, RG8, I, "C" Ser., Vol. 730, pp. 33–38. An extract of this letter (found in CaOOA, British Military and Naval Records, RG8, I, "C" Ser., Vol. 679, pp. 256b–c, 257a–b) includes Barclay's signed "Statement of the Force of His Majesty's Squadron employed on Lake Erie," which is not found with this copy.

GOVERNOR-GENERAL SIR GEORGE PREVOST TO
LIEUTENANT ROBERT H. BARCLAY, R.N.

Kingston   21st July 1813

Sir,

I have received your Letter of the 16th Inst. upon the subject of your wants for the manning and equipment of the Naval Force under your command— I am fully aware of all the difficulties you have to contend with & shall endeavour as far as lays in my power to enable you to surmount them but you must be sensible of the impossibility in the present state of the Country part of which is in the occupation of the Enemy of supplying you with all the articles of which you stand in need—

I repeat to you what I have already said to General Proctor that you must endeavour to obtain your Ordnance and Naval Stores from the Enemy— I am satisfied that this cannot be effected without an addition to your present strength and have therefore strongly pressed upon Sir James Yeo the necessity of sending forward to you immediately a supply of Petty Officers & Seamen and he has assured me that he will do so without delay

I have also given possitive directions for the remainder of the 41st to be sent to Br. Genl. Proctor, I am in hopes that the arrival of these reinforcements aided by your own resources will in time afford the means of attempting something against the Enemy's Flotilla before they shall be in a state to venture out up the Lake— You will please to communicate this Letter to Br. Genl. Proctor— I am Sir &c. &c.

(signed)   George Prevost
Commander of the Forces

LB Copy, CaOOA, British Military and Naval Records, RG8, I, "C" Ser., Vol. 1221, pp. 3–4.

Master Commandant Oliver H. Perry to Secretary of the Navy Jones

U.S.S. *Lawrence* at anchor
out side of Erie Bar   Augt. 4th 1813
9 P.M.

Sir,
    I have great pleasure in informing you that I have succeeded after almost incredible labour and fatigue to the men, in getting all the vessels I have been able to man, over the bar, Viz. *Lawrence, Niagara, Caledonia, Ariel, Scorpion, Somers, Tigress* and *Porcupine.*— They are neither well officered or manned but as the exigency of Genl. Harrison, and the whole of the western country is such, I have determined to proceed on Service— My Government should I be unsuccessfull I trust will justly appreciate the motives which have governed me, in this determination.— I have sent an express to Comr. Chauncey requesting in the most urgent manner, officers and men,— he has however sent me no answer, and, as it is doubtfull whether I am to receive any more reinforcements, I have distributed the few I have in the best manner I am capable among the different vessels.— Lt. Turner has charge of the *Niagara,* and Mr. Magrath[1] (a gentleman of experience) has the *Caledonia.* The enemy have been in sight all day and are now about four leagues from us— We shall sail in pursuit of them, at three tomorrow morning. Very Respectfully I am Sir Your Obd. Servt.

O. H. Perry

ALS, DNA, RG45, MC, 1813, No. 93 (M147, Roll No. 5).

    1. Humphrey Magrath was appointed a midshipman in 1800, made sailing master in 1803, lieutenant in 1809, and purser in 1812. As staff officers, pursers were not generally given sea commands. Magrath resigned his commission on 4 June 1814 and committed suicide on 11 July 1814.

Lieutenant Robert H. Barclay, R.N., to Commodore Sir James Lucas Yeo, R.N.

No. 15

H.M. Ship *Queen Charlotte*
Augt. 5th. 1813   off Presque Isle

Sir
    The time is now come which I have so long feared; that of being obliged to withdraw from this without supplies.

On reconnoitreing the Enemy's Squadron this Morning I found them all over the Bar: Viz. two large Brigs—1 Smaller and 7 Schooners.

I before did myself the honor to state to you our Comparative force and I hope that taking into consideration the great disparity, and also the certainty of Speedy reinforcement by having the *Detroit*—You will approve of what I have done: for what in my opinion is best for the preservation of His Majesty's Squadron, and also for ultimately having the Superiority on this Lake

But the greatest misfortune attending their being on the Lake, is that no farther Supplies can be sent from Long Point & that the Seamen will now have to be sent by Land; there are no boats at Long Point that could convey many, even if you choose to risk their coming by Water; when it is probable the Enemy will be doing all he can to prevent any thing coming up that way, there are only one large Boat and a common <u>Battoe</u>.

And as to the Guns I should recommend their being kept at Burlington and I will run the *Detroit* with such Guns as I can procure at Amherstburg, then come down and have them immediately sent over.

They have not as yet made any shew of following us: but if they were not ready for Service they would hardly venture over the bar, although under the protection of their Batteries, and I think it more probable, from the great addition to their Military Strength at Presque Isle that their first attempt will be to reinforce Harrison and cut off Genl. Procter's retreat but it is to be hoped from the length of time that he has been there that he may have effected his purpose.

I have sent Lieut. O'Keefe of the 41st. Regt. to ensure your receiving this letter and I have directed him to join me again without delay at Amherstburg, in the event of meeting any body of Seamen that he may assist them in every way to cause their speedy arrival at Amherstburg as certain as is in my power. I have the honor to be Sir Your Obedt. Servant

(Signed)   R. H. B.

From my information from below I have great hopes that you will soon meet your Enemy in which I am joined by Captn. Finnis and also most sincerely that you will have a noble addition to your Squadron.

(Signed)   R. H. B.

Copy, UkLPR, Adm. 1/5445, pp. 139–40. This copy was introduced as evidence in the court-martial of Lieutenant Robert H. Barclay.

LIEUTENANT ROBERT H. BARCLAY, R.N., TO MAJOR GENERAL HENRY PROCTER, BRITISH ARMY

No. 14

H.M.S. *Queen Charlotte*
Off the Islands   August 9th 1813

Sir

On the 3rd Inst. I wrote, advising you that from the forward state in which the Enemy's Squadron were at Presque Isle I doubted the propriety of remaining off that port with so inferior a force longer than the 6th and that I should then return to Amherstburg and employ all my means in fitting out the *Detroit*. But the Winds being light and Westerly—I came up with the *Miami* [1] by which vessel I sent it.

On last reconnoitreing Presque Isle I found the Enemy's Squadron <u>over</u> the <u>Bar</u> and Anchored under the protection of their Batteries.

Knowing their force and supposing that they would not venture out unless well prepared, I thought it more prudent to sail at once for Amherstburg, leaving the *Erie* with orders to bring any dispatch that might have arrived during my last absence from Long Point Anchorage.

I was the more induced to do so, from the total silence held relative to Seamen, or Stores coming up; for surely there was time enough during the Month I have been out for that purpose—

From the great increase of Military at Presque Isle I rather think their object must be an expedition to some point—Whether against you, to co-operate with Harrison—or in your absence, against Amherstburg, I cannot determine.

Having 150 of the 41st. Regiment on board, should they attempt the latter place; such an addition to the force will be very seasonable

On my leaving Presque Isle Lt. OKeefe of the 41st volunteered his services to carry a letter to Burlington to advise any Officer, or Men, of my removal from that place, also to render them any assistance in his power to forward them by Land. I accepted his offer, and he left me on the 6th.

I send this by Lt. Purvis to whom I have given directions to follow your wishes relative to the Transports and *Chippewa*—for it would be a serious loss, these Vessels to us, and a very great accession to the force of the Enemy

I enclose a Copy [2] of a Letter I recd. from His Excellency Sir George Prevost: which is in answer to one I wrote him relative to our wants and of the imperious necessity of their being supplied.

You will receive any particular information relative to the Enemy from Lt. Purvis. I have the Honor to be Sir Your Most Obedt. Hble. Servant

(Signed)   R. H. B.

Be pleased to send to me what instructions you have relative to the Detachment of the 41st. They are healthy and in good spirits. I shall need their assistance more than ever.

(Signed)   R. H. B.

P.S. I had forgot to say that 60 of the R.N.F.L. [3] Regt. had gone to Amherstburg by Land for the Squadron.

Copy, UkLPR, Adm. 1/5445, pp. 137–39. This copy was introduced as evidence in the court-martial of Lieutenant Robert H. Barclay.

1. *Miami* was a British gunboat on Lake Erie.
2. The enclosure was not found with this letter. Barclay is probably referring to Prevost's letter of 21 July 1813; see pp. 545–46.
3. Royal Newfoundland.

MASTER COMMANDANT OLIVER H. PERRY TO
CHRISTOPHER RAYMOND PERRY

U.S.S. *Lawrence* at Anchor off Erie
Aug 9th. 1813

Dear Father

I have this morng. recd. your letter of the 26th. July and beg you to accept my thanks for the circumstantial detail of events passing in your quarter.— I have at length got my little squadron out, but am only half man'd and officer'd— I hear of about 90 men being on their way to join me this will not be half enough— I have made one short cruise, after the enemy he however retreated up the Lake in a great hurry—we shall be after him the moment those men arrive— I am pleased with co-operating with Genl. Harrison, he is the only <u>officer</u> we have of enterprize—

I intend writing you a long letter as soon as I get underweigh at present I am entirely overrun with business— Alexr. is well and is as smart a midn. onboard the vessels as any I have—will make a fine officer.[1] My love to all. I shall write in a day or two Your aff. son

O. H. P.

our force here is

Brigs	The *Lawrence*	20 Guns
	Niagara	20
	Caledonia	3 heavy
Schor	*Ariel*	3 light
	Scorpion	2 heavy
	Somers	4 light & heavy
	Porcupine	1
	Tigress	1
Sloop	*Trippe*	2 } heavy
Schoors	*Ohio*	1
	Amelia	1

ALS, MiU–C, Oliver H. Perry Papers. Addressed to "Chris. R. Perry Esqr., Chelsea Landing, Norwich, Cont." A handwritten copy of this letter, evidently transcribed by one of Perry's siblings, had the following notation written at the bottom: "note by copyist *I cannot make out the name of the last vessel, The letter was evidently written in great haste—and I remember that when it was received our parents were very much depressed at his saying there were not half men enough, for, as they said, it required much to make him complain—."

1. Perry's younger brother, James Alexander Perry, served as a midshipman on board *Lawrence*.

The British Fleet on Lake Erie

By mid-summer, the situation of the British army and navy on Lake Erie had grown more desperate. Their fleet still lacked sufficient cannon, ammunition, and stores; the guns were removed from Fort Malden in order to fit out the new ship Detroit. *The British army's attempt to capture needed supplies from Fort Meigs in July had failed, and by August provisions were desperately low.*

In addition to his own army, Major General Henry Procter was feeding his Indian warriors and their wives and children. Procter, who never really controlled his Indian allies, feared the consequences if he could no longer placate them with food and presents.

Lieutenant Robert H. Barclay's vessels were ill-prepared to cruise the lake for want of naval stores. However, he faced an even greater problem—an acute shortage of experienced sailors. His crews were completed with drafts of soldiers who knew nothing of sailing; many were French Canadians who could not even speak English.

While Perry was on the lake exercising his men and meeting with Major General William Henry Harrison to plan strategy, Barclay was still waiting for reinforcements. On 9 September, with provisions at Amherstburg nearly exhausted, Barclay's squadron left port for its inevitable encounter with the American fleet.[1]

1. On British naval preparations on Lake Erie, see Drake, "Loss of Mastery."

MAJOR GENERAL HENRY PROCTER, BRITISH ARMY, TO
GOVERNOR-GENERAL SIR GEORGE PREVOST

Sandwich
August 26th 1813

Sir

I have had the Honor to receive your Excellency's Letter of the 22d Inst. Captain Barclay was immediately acquainted that an officer and fifty or sixty Seamen were on the Way here. I beg to say that a more essential Piece of Service could not be rendered to us here by an active zealous Officer than to push them on by the quickest possible means for I assure your Excellency we are peculiarly in need of them, both Officers and Seamen. If I had not even received your Commands to communicate with your Excellency with the Frankness of a zealous Soldier, I should have felt it my Duty to expose to you whatever the Good of the Service made it requisite you should know. Your Excellency speaks of Seamen valorous and well disciplined. Except, I believe, the 25 whom Captain Barclay brought with him, there are none of that Description on this Lake, at least on Board His Majesty's vessels. These are scarcely enough, and of a miserable Description to work the Vessels, some of which cannot be used for want of Hands, such even as we have. I have the highest Opinion of Captain Barclay and have afforded him every Aid I possibly could. We have set too strong an Example of Cordiality, not to have it prevail thro' both Services. We have but the one Object in View, the Good of His Majesty's Service or Preservation of this District. Captain Barclay has, besides the Royal Newf'd Land, one hundred and fifty of the 41 Reg., better Soldiers these cannot be, but they are only Landsmen. I beg to observe that Sir James Yeo was over manned with prime Seamen, British. I have Reason to believe that the Indians will heartily oppose the Enemy and that we stand rather high in their Opinion, tho' they observe the Enemy's Fleet on the Lake, possessing the Command of it. Your Excellency is aware that the Indian Body is seldom disposable, never so, contrary to their opinion, or Inclination. Mr. Harrison has informed them of his Intention to advance, and they expect him; therefore no Influence will or can prevail on them, or any Part of them, to leave their Families; especially whilst the Enemy can choose his Points of Attack, that is whilst he has the Command of the Lake. I will venture to offer my Opinion to your Excellency that as long as Captain Barclay, without Seamen, can avoid the Enemy he should do so. All my Ordnance is on Board except the Fields and in the Event of any Disaster to the Fleet, the Arrival of any Body of Seamen would be of no use whatever. Seamen should be pushed on even by Dozens. I shall send to have Conveyances ready for them, a few Hours gained is or may be of the greatest Consequence not only to us but to the upper Province. The Fleet once manned, one Flank secured I have no Doubt that a Body of Indians may be induced to move to the centre Division on a Prospect of being actively employed with the Troops. The Enemy's Fleet reconnoitered ours laying off Hartley's Point, three Miles below Amherstburg. They anchored off the Settlement twenty Miles below Amherstburg. Boats are collecting in numbers at the Islands. I have the honor to be with the highest respect, Your Excellency's Obedient Servant

Henry Procter
Major General
commt.

ALS, CaOOA, British Military and Naval Records, RG8, I, "C" Ser., Vol. 679, pp. 494–99.

LIEUTENANT ROBERT H. BARCLAY, R.N., TO COMMODORE SIR JAMES LUCAS YEO, R.N.

Private,   September 1st. 1813—
A Copy

My dear Sir/

We are now in most anxious expectation of being able to meet the Enemy who are still about the Islands, but have never shewn since their first appearance, what they are about I cannot imagine, every day to them is a loss not to be regained. I have not sent any thing to reconnoitre them lately except a Canoe (which is now out) fearing that from the frequent Calms, and their vessels being so well qualified to sweep they might take her, and increase their force at our expense.—

By dint of exercising the Soldiers on board I hope they will make a good hand of it, when they are backed by a few Seamen, I hope you will add to this gang from the *Dover*,[1] as they will be a small reinforcement of themselves however valuable even a small number is.—

As to our coming to Long point, it much depends on the motion of the Enemy's Squadron whether they chuse to fight us or not, for if they have made themselves works in the harbour among the Islands and take shelter under them we must remain and watch their motions; lest, that in our absence, they might take advantage of it and come here.— But I shall send a Transport the moment I can with safety, both for what Stores, and Guns there may be coming to me; and for provisions which are beginning to be very much wanted here.—

The quantity of Beef and flour consumed here is tremendous, there are such hordes of Indians with their wives, and children.—

The *Detroit* is a very fine Ship, but I fear with her Shores (for she has one under every beam) she will sail heavily: but at all events fast enough to ensure a general action if they run, and wish to save their small craft.—

The Officers and Seamen whom you send would much better be forwarded to Amherstburg by land, that is a certain mode, by the Lake in boats it is most uncertain,— I am sure, Sir James if you saw my Canadians, you would condemn every one (with perhaps two or three exception) as a poor devil not worth his Salt.— Captn. Finnis begs to be kindly remembered to you and Mulcaster, and he is sincerely joined by My dear Sir Yours most faithfully

R H Barclay

Copy, CaOOA, British Military and Naval Records, RG8, I, "C" Ser., Vol. 730, pp. 126–28.

1. *Dover* was a Royal Navy troopship; forty-one officers and men were sent from *Dover* at Quebec to reinforce the squadron on Lake Erie, arriving 5 September.

Major General Henry Procter, British Army, to Noah Freer, British Military Secretary

Sandwich
September 6th 1813

Sir.

The probable Consequences of any further Delay in sending an adequate Supply of Indian Stores to this District are of so serious a Nature, that I cannot refrain from urging the necessity of their being pushed forward by every possible Means: and that if unfortunately they should not have arrived in the Country, they may be procured, if possible, immediately from the North West Company for the present at least. His Excellency the Commander of the Forces is well aware that the scanty Supplies, and Purchases were barely adequate to the necessities of the moment. The long expected Supplies cannot any longer be delayed without the most frightfull consequences. The Indian's and his Family's suffering from Cold will no longer be amused with Promises, His Wants he will naturally attribute to our neglect at least; and Defection is the least of Evils we may expect from him. There have not been among the Indians, with whom we are concerned, any Traders; consequently their necessities can be supplied by us only or the Enemy, who are not inattentive to any Circumstances respecting the Indians, that may be turned to their Advantage. I do not hesitate to say, that if we do not receive a timely and adequate Supply of Indian Goods, and Ammunition, we shall be inevitably subjected to Ills of the greatest magnitude. Mr. Robert Dickson,[1] to whose Zeal and Ability, which from Circumstances have not had full Scope, I must offer full Testimony, will have the Honor more fully to speak to the Purport of this Letter as well as another Subject on which we are fully agreed, the Indian Department. I have the honor to be Sir Your most obedient humble Servant

Henry Procter
Major General comg.

ALS, CaOOA, British Military and Naval Records, RG8, I, "C" Ser., Vol. 680, pp. 26–29.

1. Robert Dickson, a fur trader, was appointed assistant superintendent of the Indians of the western nations in 1813. During the summer of 1813, he rallied and led the Indian troops in the vicinity of Amherstburg.

The Battle of Lake Erie, 10 September 1813

After a hard-fought action lasting upwards of three hours, Master Commandant Oliver Hazard Perry claimed a decisive victory over the British fleet on Lake Erie. His actions on that day, and the words he wrote announcing his victory, would be among the most celebrated in American naval history.

Perry's victory secured American control of Lake Erie for the remainder of the war. More importantly, it allowed Major General William Henry Harrison's army to advance in the northwest territory and reclaim the American military posts on the Ohio and Michigan frontier that had been lost the previous year. Because the British could not keep open their lines of communication and supply to the westward without a naval force on the lake, the American victory in the Battle of Lake Erie changed the balance of both military and naval power in the northwest.

MASTER COMMANDANT OLIVER H. PERRY TO
SECRETARY OF THE NAVY JONES

U.S. Brig *Lawrence,*
off Sandusky Bay, Sept. 2. 1813.

Sir,

I have the honour to inform you that I anchored this afternoon with the squadron at this place for the purpose of communicating with Genl. Harrison.

Since I last did myself the honour of writing you I have been twice off Malden—first on the 24th & 25th of last month and again yesterday.

Owing to a severe Indisposition which confined me to my Birth I was under the necessity of anchoring the squadron off Bass Island, a situation which commanded the principal passage. The moment I was able to be on Deck I again sailed for Malden and was yesterday all day off that place—close in.— Their new ship is rigged, has Top Gallant yards athwart and is anchored at the mouth of the Harbour under the Guns of a Battery, together with their other vessels—viz. the *Queen Charlotte, Hunter, Lady Prevost,* a Sloop and Schooner. Three other vessels are lying at the Navy Wharf.

The crews of the different vessels have suffered much from a complaint occasioned, it is supposed, by the water. Many are still sick.

It is said by some Deserters who have arrived at Camp Meigs from Malden that the small vessel chased by the squadron run ashore in her attempt to escape and was lost. I have the honor to be Sir Very Respectfully Your Obdt. Servt.

O. H. Perry

ALS, DNA, RG45, MC, 1813, No. 115 (M147, Roll No. 5).

CAPTAIN OLIVER H. PERRY[1] TO
MAJOR GENERAL WILLIAM HENRY HARRISON, U.S.A.

We have met the enemy and they are ours: Two Ships, two Brigs one Schooner & one Sloop.[2] Yours, with great respect and esteem

O H Perry.

Facsimile, DNA, RG45, AF7 (M625, Roll No. 76). Reproduced in Lossing, *Pictorial Field-Book*. The location of the original document is not known.

1. Oliver H. Perry was promoted to the rank of captain retroactive to the date of the Battle of Lake Erie.

2. The British fleet actually consisted of two ships (*Queen Charlotte* and *Detroit*), one brig (*General Hunter*), two schooners (*Lady Prevost* and *Chippewa*), and one sloop (*Little Belt*). *Lady Prevost*, a large schooner, was mistaken for a brig; both vessels are two-masted, but a brig carries square sails and a schooner fore-and-aft sails. The error was first recorded in the logbook of *Lawrence* when the British fleet was sighted at a distance on the day of the battle: "At 7 discovered the whole of the Enemys Squadron Viz, two Ships—two Brigs—One Schooner & one Sloop with their larboard tacks aboard to the W'd about 10 miles dist." (RNHi, William V. Taylor Papers, Logbook of U.S.S. *Lawrence*, entry for 10 Sept. 1813). At that distance, *Lady Prevost*, of about 230 tons, was mistaken for a second brig since she was larger and carried more guns than the brig *General Hunter*, of 180 tons. The error was repeated in subsequent reports, which were based on information in the logbook.

CAPTAIN OLIVER H. PERRY TO SECRETARY OF THE NAVY JONES

U.S. Brig *Niagara* off the Western
Sister   Head of Lake Erie, Sepr. 10th. 1813
4 p.m.

Sir

It has pleased the Almighty to give to the arms of the United States a signal victory over their enemies on this Lake— The British squadron consisting of two Ships, two Brigs one Schooner & one Sloop have this moment surrendered to the force under my command, after a Sharp conflict. I have the honor to be Sir Very Respectfully Your Obdt. Servt.

O. H. Perry

ALS, DNA, RG45, CL, 1813, Vol. 6, No. 33 (M125, Roll No. 31).

LIEUTENANT GEORGE INGLIS, R.N., TO LIEUTENANT ROBERT H. BARCLAY, R.N.

Copy—   His Majesty's late Ship *Detroit*,
September 10th. 1813—

Sir,

I have the honor to transmit to you an account of the termination of the late unfortunate Action with the Enemy's Squadron—

On coming on the Quarter Deck, after your being wounded the Enemy's Second Brig, at that time on our weather beam, shortly afterwards took a position on our weather bow, to rake us, to prevent which in attempting to wear to get our Starboard broadside to bear upon her, as a number of the Guns on the Larboard broadside being at this time disabled, fell on board the *Queen Charlotte*, at this time running up to Leeward of us in this Situation the two Ships remained for some time, as soon as we got clear of her I ordered the *Queen Charlotte* to shoot a head of us if possible and attempted to back our Fore Topsail to get astern, but that Ship laying completely unmanageable, every brace cut away, the Mizen Topmast and Gaff down, all the other Masts badly wounded, not a Stay left forward, Hull shattered very much, a number of the Guns disabled, and the Enemy's Squadron raking both Ships ahead and astern, none of our own in a Situation to support us, I was under the painful necessity of answering the Enemy to say we had struck, the *Queen Charlotte* having previously done so— I have the honor to remain Sir, your obedient, humble Servant—

(Signed)   George Inglis   Lieutt.

Copy, UkLPR, Adm. 1/504, pp. 387–89.

LIEUTENANT ROBERT H. BARCLAY, R.N., TO COMMODORE SIR JAMES LUCAS YEO, R.N.

Copy

His Majesty's late ship *Detroit*
Putin Bay, Lake Erie, 12th. Sept. 1813.

Sir,

The last letter I had the honor of writing to you dated the 6th Instant, I informed you that unless certain intimation was received of more Seamen being on their way to Amhersburg, I should be obliged to sail with the Squadron, deplorably manned as it was, to fight the Enemy (who Blockaded the Port) to enable us to get supplies of Provisions and Stores of every description, so perfectly destitute of Provisions was the Post that there was not a days Flour in store, and the Crews of the Squadron under my Command were on half allowance of many things, and when that was done there was no more; Such were the motives which induced Major Genl. Proctor (whom by your Instructions I was directed to consult, and whose wishes I was enjoined to execute as far as related to the good of the Country) to concur in the necessity of a Battle being risqued under the many disadvantages which I laboured, and it now remains for me, the most melancholy task, to relate to you the unfortunate issue of that Battle, as well as the many untoward circumstances that led to that event.

No Intelligence of Seamen having arrived I sailed on the 9th Inst. fully expecting to meet the Enemy next morning as they had been seen among the Islands, nor was I mistaken, soon after daylight they were seen in motion in Putin Bay, the Wind then at S W, and light, giving us the Weather gage, I bore up for them, in hopes of bringing them to Action amongst the Islands, but that intention was soon frustrated by the Wind suddenly shifting to the South East, which brought the Enemy directly to Windward.

The Line was formed according to a given plan, so that each Ship might be supported against the superior Force of the two Brigs opposed to them. About ten the Enemy had cleared the Islands and immediately bore up under easy sail in a line abreast, each Brig being also supported by the small Vessels; At a quarter before twelve I commenced the Action by firing a few long Guns, about a quarter past the American Commodore, also supported by two Schooners, one carrying four long twelve Prs., the other a long thirty two and twenty four pr. came to close action with the *Detroit*, the other Brig of the Enemy apparently destined to engage the *Queen Charlotte*, supported in like manner by two Schooners, kept so far to Windward as to render the *Queen Charlotte*'s 24 pr. Carronades useless, while she was with the *Lady Prevost*, exposed to the heavy and destructive Fire of the *Caledonia* and four other Schooners armed with heavy Guns like those I have already described.

Too soon, alas, was I deprived of the Services of the noble & intrepid Captn. Finnis, who, soon after the commencement of the action fell, and with him fell my greatest support. Soon after Lieut. Stokoe of the *Queen Charlotte* was struck senseless by a Splinter which deprived the Country of his Services at this very critical period, as I perceived the *Detroit* had enough to contend with, without the prospect of a fresh Brig; Provincial Lieut. Irvine who then had charge of the *Queen Charlotte* behaved with great courage, but his experience was much too limited to supply the place of such an officer as Capt. Finnis, hence she proved of far less assistance than I expected.

The Action continued with great fury until half past two, when I perceived my opponent drop astern and a Boat passing from him to the *Niagara* (which Vessel was at this time perfectly fresh) the American Commodore seeing that as yet the day was against him (his Vessel having struck soon after he left her) and also the very defenseless state of the *Detroit*, which Ship was now a perfect Wreck, principally from the Raking Fire of the Gun Boats, and also that the *Queen Charlotte* was in such a situation that I could receive very little assistance from her, and the *Lady Prevost* being at this time too far to Leeward from her Rudder being injured, made a noble, and alas, too successful an effort to regain it, for he bore up and supported by his small Vessels passed within Pistol Shot and took a raking position on our Bow, nor could I prevent it, as the unfortunate situation of the *Queen Charlotte* prevented us from wearing, in attempting it we fell onboard her. My Gallant first Lieut. Garland was now mortally wounded and myself so severely that I was obliged to quit the deck.

Manned as the Squadron was with not more than Fifty British Seamen, the rest a mixed Crew of Canadians and Soldiers, and who were totally unacquainted with such Service, rendered the loss of Officers more sensibly felt— And never in any Action was the loss more severe, every Officer Commanding Vessels and their Seconds was either killed, or Wounded so severely as to be unable to keep the deck.

Lieutenant Buchan, in the *Lady Prevost*, behaved most nobly and did every thing that a brave and experienced Officer could do in a Vessel armed with 12 pr. Carronades against Vessels carrying long Guns, I regret to state that he was very severely Wounded.

Lieut. Bignell of the *Dover*, Commanding the *Hunter*, displayed the greatest intrepidity, but his Guns being small, 2, 4, & 6 prs., he could be of much less service than he wished.

Every officer in the *Detroit* behaved in the most exemplary manner. Lieut. Inglis shewed such calm intrepidity, that I was fully convinced that on leaving the deck, I left the Ship in excellent hands, and for an account of the Battle after that, I refer you to his letter, which he wrote me, for your information.

Mr. Hoffmeister Purser of the *Detroit* nobly volunteered his services on deck and behaved in a manner that reflects the highest honor on him, I regret to add that he is very severely Wounded in the knee.

Provincial Lieut. Purvis, and the Military officers Lieuts. Garden of the Royal Newfoundland Rangers, and O'Keefe of the 41st. Regt. behaved in a manner which excited my warmest admiration. The few British Seamen I had behaved with their usual intrepidity, and as long as I was on deck the Troops behaved with a calmness and courage, worthy of a more fortunate issue to their exertions.

The Weather Gage gave the Enemy a prodigous advantage, as it enabled them, not only to choose their position, but their distance also, which they did in such a manner as to prevent the Carronades of the *Queen Charlotte* and *Lady Prevost* from having much effect, while their long Guns did great execution, particularly against the *Queen Charlotte*, But the great cause of losing His Majesty's Squadron on Lake Erie was the want of a competent number of Seamen: until the thirty six arrived from the *Dover*, I had not more than ten or fifteen, and those you know Sir, were of the very worst quality, the rest consisted of Canadians, who could [not?] even speak English, and Soldiers, who except crossing the Atlantic, had never seen a ship.

Such was the means I had to defend the Squadron entrusted to my charge against a Force superior in itself and fully equipped and manned, and in a situation where an Action was inevitable, or probably we must have at last surrendered for want of Provisions.

Captain Perry has behaved in a most humane and attentive manner, not only to myself and Officers but to all the Wounded.

I trust that although unsuccessful, you will approve of the motives that induced me to sail under so many disadvantages, and that it may be hereafter proved that under such circumstances the Honour of His Majesty's Flag has not been tarnished.

I enclose the List of killed and Wounded And have the honor to be Sir, Your most obedient humble Servant

"Signed"   R. H. Barclay
Commander and late Senr. Officer

Copy, UkLPR, Adm. 1/505, pp. 379–86. The enclosed list of killed and wounded is in Adm. 1/505, following p. 289.

CAPTAIN OLIVER H. PERRY TO SECRETARY OF THE NAVY JONES

<table>
<tr><td>(Copy.)</td><td align="right">U.S. Schooner Ariel,
Put in Bay   13th. Septr. 1813.</td></tr>
</table>

Sir,

In my last I informed you that we had captured the Enemy's Fleet on this Lake. I have now the honour to give you the most important particulars of the Action.

On the morning of the 10th. Inst., at sunrise, they were discovered from Put in Bay, where I lay at anchor with the Squadron under my command. We got under way, the wind light at S.W., and stood for them. At 10 A.M. the wind hauled to S.E. and brought us to windward; formed the Line, and bore up. At 15 minutes before twelve, the Enemy commenced firing; at 5 minutes before twelve, the action commenced on our part. Finding their fire very destructive, owing to their long guns, and its being mostly directed at the *Lawrence*, I made sail, and directed the other vessels to follow, for the purpose of closing with the Enemy. Every brace and bowline being soon shot away, she became unmanageable, notwithstanding the great exertions of the Sailing Master. In this situation, she sustained the action upwards of two hours, within canister distance, until every gun was rendered useless, and the greater part of her crew either killed or wounded. Finding she could no longer annoy the Enemy, I left her in charge of Lieut. Yarnall, who, I was convinced, from the bravery already displayed by him, would do what would comport with the honour of the Flag. At half past two, the wind springing up, Capt. Elliott was enabled to bring his vessel, the *Niagara*, gallantly into close action. I immediately went on board of her, when he anticipated my wishes, by volunteering to bring the Schooners, which had been kept astern by the lightness of the wind, into closer action. It was with unspeakable pain that I saw, soon after I got on board the *Niagara,* the Flag of the *Lawrence* come down; although I was perfectly sensible that she had been defended to the last, and that to have continued to make a shew of resistance would have been a wanton sacrifice of the remains of her brave crew. But the Enemy was not able to take possession of her, and circumstances soon permitted her Flag again to be hoisted. At 45 minutes past two the signal was made for "closer action." The *Niagara* being very little injured, I determined to pass through the Enemy's line; bore up, and passed ahead of their two Ships and a Brig, giving a raking fire to them from the Starboard Guns, and to a large Schooner and Sloop from the Larboard side, at half Pistol shot distance. The smaller vessels, at this time, having got within Grape and Canister distance, under the direction of Captain Elliott, and keeping up a well directed fire, the two Ships, a Brig, and Schooner, surrendered, a Schooner and Sloop making a vain attempt to escape.

Those Officers and Men, who were immediately under my observation, evinced the greatest gallantry; and I have no doubt that all the others conducted themselves as became American Officers and Seamen.

Lieut. Yarnall, first of the *Lawrence,* although several times wounded, refused to quit the Deck.

Midshipman Forrest, (doing duty as Lieut.) and Sailing Master Taylor, were of great assistance to me.

I have great pain in stating to you the death of Lieut. Brooks of the Marines, and Midn. Laub, both of the *Lawrence,* and Midn. John Clark, of the *Scorpion*; they were valuable and promising officers.

Mr. Hambleton, Purser, who volunteered his services on Deck, was severely wounded, late in the Action. Midn. Claxton, and Swartwout, of the *Lawrence,* were severely wounded.

On board the *Niagara,* Lieuts. Smith and Edwards, and Midn. Webster, (doing duty as Sailing Master,) behaved in a very handsome manner.

Captain Brevoort, of the Army, who acted as a volunteer, in the capacity of a Marine Officer, on board that vessel, is an excellent and brave officer, and with his musketry did great execution.

Lieut. Turner, commanding the *Caledonia,* brought that vessel into action in the most able manner, and is an officer that, in all situations, may be relied on.

The *Ariel,* Lieut. Packet, and *Scorpion,* Sailing master Champlin, were enabled to get early into action, and were of great service.

Capt. Elliott speaks in the highest terms of Mr. Magrath, Purser, who had been despatched, in a boat, on service, previous to my getting on board the *Niagara*; and being a Seaman, since the action, has rendered essential service, in taking charge of one of the prizes.

Of Capt. Elliott, already so well known to the Government, it would almost be superfluous to speak. In this action he evinced his characteristic bravery and judgment; and, since the close of the action, has given me the most able and essential assistance.

I have the honour to enclose you a return of the killed and wounded, together with a statement of the relative force of the Squadrons. The Captain and first Lieut. of the *Queen Charlotte,* and first Lieut. of the *Detroit,* were killed;— Capt. Barclay, Senior Officer, and the Commander of the *Lady Prevost,* severely wounded. The Commanders of the *Hunter* and *Chippeway,* slightly wounded.

Their loss in killed and wounded I have not yet been able to ascertain; it must, however, have been very great.

Very respectfully, I have the honour to be, Sir, Your Obedt. Servant,

(signed.)   O. H. Perry.

Copy, DNA, RG46, Records of the U.S. Senate, Committee on Naval Affairs, Petitions and Memorials, SEN 13A–F6. The original manuscript copy of Perry's letter to the secretary of the navy has not been located.

Sailing Master William V. Taylor to Abby Taylor

U.S. Sloop of War *Lawrence*
Put in Bay— 15th. Sepr.—

Heaven has allow'd us, My dear Wife, to gain a most decisive victory & preserved your husband unhurt. I say unhurt because my wound was trifling, I scarcely felt it—a flesh wound in my thigh— The Action commenced on the 10 Sepr. on the British side at 1/4 before 12 on our Side at 12— the *Lawrence* alone rec'd the fire of the whole British squadron 2 1/2 hours within Pistol shot—we were not supported as we ought to have been— Capt. Perry led the *Lawrence* into [ac]tion & sustain'd the most destructive fire with the most [gall]ant spirit perhaps that ever was witnessed under similar circumstances— they observing us to be the flag ship directed their whole fire at us viz. Ship *Detroit* of 19 long 24's 18's & 12's *Queen Charlotte* of 19 guns carronades Brig *Lady Prevost* 13 guns Brig *Hunter* of 10 guns *Chippewa* of 3 guns & *Little Belt* of 1 gun

Judge the scene at 1/2 2 P M when 22 Men & officers lay dead on decks & 66 wounded, every gun dismounted carriages knock'd to pieces—every strand of rigging cut off—masts & spars shot & tottering over head & in fact an unmanageable wreck. I say at this time when not another gun could be worked or fir'd or man'd Capt. Perry determined to leave her— got a Boat along side haul'd down his own private flag which we fought under with the last words of Lawrence on it—Dont give up the Ship—& bore it in triumph on board of the *Niagara*—leaving Lts. Yarnell, Forrest & myself to act as we thought proper we at this time all wounded— about 10 minutes after he got on board the *Niagara*—we concluded as no further resistance could possibly be made from this Brig & likewise to save the further effusion of human blood as at this time they kept up a galling fire on us, agreed to haul down our colours— many poor fellows men as well as officers that lay wounded on our decks, shed tears of grief saying Oh dont haul down our colours— No ship my dear girl this war has been fought so obstinately & suffer'd so much as the *Lawrence*— their long guns carried shot through & through us—two shots pass'd through our Magazine—it was a narrow escape for us—— When Capt. Perry assumed the command of the *Niagara* he found she had not lost a man kill'd or wounded—he immediately made sail & led her most gallantly into close action—sending Capt Elliot in the Boat to bring up the small vessels— this was a proud moment for our beloved Commander— he engaged the two ships & brig on one Side & a brig on the other & obliged them to haul down their colours in five minutes— soon after the other two small vessels haul'd down theirs & we all came to anchor & secured the prisoners— when Capt. Perry returned to the *Lawrence*, every poor fellow rais'd himself from the decks to greet him with three hearty cheers—I do not ~~say~~ hesitate to say there was not a dry eye in the Ship

Lt. Brooks of Marines was kill'd early in the action—by my side— Midn. Laub kill'd— Midn. Claxton—severely wounded. Midn. Swartwout severely wounded— Lt. Yarnell wounded Lt. Forrest do—I will not mention myself— Mr. Hamilton [*Hambleton*] was severely wounded—this was all the officers on board except Capt. Perry & his brother—neither of whom was touched   I forgot to mention Mr. Breese who likewise escaped with myself—total loss in our Squadron was 29 kill'd & 25 Wounded the British acknowledged a loss of about 45 kill'd & upwards of 100 wounded— Capt. Barkley their commander was severely wounded his 1st. Lt. kill'd— the Capt. of the *Queen Charlotte* Kill'd 1st. Lt. severely wounded & many other commissioned officers who I cannot mention kill'd & wounded— Lt. Turner—Mr. Almy—Mr. Brownell—Mr. Dunham are all well— I expect to go to <u>Erie</u> to day with the <u>*Lawrence*</u> & all the sick & wounded—where I will write you again— My love to our dear Parents Brothers & Sisters—friends & acquaintances—kiss my little children— I felt perfectly cool in action—my prayers were for you & my little children— God be praised that I was spared, to take care of you all— may I never lose that confidence which I placed in him on that day it animated me to exertion.—— Heaven bless you

Wm. V. Taylor

The British were 10 guns & 200 men superior to us.

ALS, RNHi, William V. Taylor Papers.

SECRETARY OF THE NAVY JONES TO CAPTAIN OLIVER H. PERRY

<table>
<tr><td>O. H. Perry Esqr.
Comg. U.S. Naval Forces
on Lake Erie.</td><td align="right">Naval Department
Septr. 21st. 1813.</td></tr>
</table>

Sir,

Rumour had preceded and prepared the Public mind for the enthusiastic reception of the glorious tidings, confirmed by your letter of the 10th. received and published in handbills this day.

Every demonstration of joy and admiration, that a victory so transcendently brilliant, decisive, and important in its consequences, could excite, was exhibited as far and as fast as the roar of cannon and the splendour of illumination could travel.

In the absence of the President I have no hesitation in anticipating his warmest admiration and thanks, in behalf of our Country, for this splendid achievement, which must ever continue among the brightest honours of the Nation. You will please accept, for yourself, an ample share, and communicate to the gallant officers, seamen, and others, under your command, the full measure of those sentiments and feelings, which it is my duty to express, and my delight to cherish.

Tomorrow, I trust, will bring the interesting details, for which so many hearts are palpitating between the Laurel and the Cypress. I am, very respectfully, your obedient Servant

W. Jones

LB Copy, DNA, RG45, SNL, Vol. 11, p. 93 (M149, Roll No. 11).

A Surgeon's Account of the Battle of Lake Erie

Dr. Usher Parsons, a twenty-five-year-old surgeon's mate on the Lake Erie squadron, found himself the only physician available for duty on the day of the decisive battle; the two senior surgeons were too ill with fever to attend. Dr. Parsons was an enthusiastic and competent physician despite his youth and lack of experience in treating battle injuries. Like many surgeon's mates, Parsons received his medical training through an apprenticeship rather than through college education. He completed his medical training under Dr. John Warren, an eminent Revolutionary War physician from Boston, in 1812. Realizing that prospects for physicians in the military would be good during the war, Parsons entered naval service. He was assigned to John Adams *and was transferred with her crew to the lakes in 1812.*

Dr. Parsons had to treat about one hundred sick and wounded on the day of the battle. He reported a remarkable rate of success in the treatment of the wounded. This was no doubt due in part to the doctor's insistence on boiling all drinking water, keeping hospital quarters clean and ventilated, and providing an adequate diet of fresh food for the injured. Moreover, there were so many wounded that Parsons had to delay a day or two before performing amputations, which allowed the patients time to recover somewhat from the trauma of their injuries.

Parson's letters to his parents, his diary, and his daybook of practice provide a remarkable glimpse into his naval career and the treatment of the sick and injured during the War of 1812.[1]

1. On Parson's career, see Goldowsky, Yankee Surgeon.

SURGEON'S MATE USHER PARSONS TO WILLIAM PARSONS

Off Lower Sandusky, near Put In
Bay and near the head of Lake Erie
on board Brig *Lawrence* Sept. 22nd. 1813

Dear Parents

Before the arrival of this an account of our victorious engagement with the British squadron on this Lake will reach you. I can only add a few particulars.— Most of the action was supported by this vessel as you will be led to suppose when informed that out of 150 men (our ships crew) 31 of whom were sick previous to the action we had rising 80 killed and wounded, among whom ~~where~~ were nearly all our officers save the intrepid commander— On board all the others were about 30 killed and wounded. This vessel supported a destructive fire from the enemy's two ships on one side and a brig astern raking us ~~fore and aft~~ for two hours all within musket shot, during which we so disabled the ships that when the Commodore left this vessel to bring another into her assistance he succeeded in 15 minutes in making all three strike. It may seem misterious to one how some of the other vessels could see us slaughtered in such a manner but it is equally so to us— Nor can the commanders of some of them offer satisfactory reasons for remaining behind. Unfortunately for the wounded the two Surgeons had been confined for some days with fever and could render them but little assistance. It however has operated in my favour as I have had all the amputating to perform and it affords me the greatest pleasure to reflect that in no case have

I failed of the best success. This has impressed the Commodore with so favourable an opinion toward me that I have not the least doubt of his rendering me assistance to a better situation.— He is the first warm friend I have met with in the service ~~who was~~ capable of assisting me. I am now on my way in the *Lawrence* for Erie, having all the sick and wounded on board and shall continue with them in the hospital 'til the most of them recover, and then intend to shape my course for Cape Home. Gen. Harrison was on board the *Lawrence* this morning and his army was on an Island within half a mile of the vessel consisting of about 7000. Tomorrow they cross to Malden a distance of about 18 miles.— Since the loss of the British fleet the Indians have deserted Detroit after leaving the place and (as is reported) massacreing the inhabitants— I had some narrow escapes for my life during the action five cannon balls passed through the room in which I was attending to the wounded. Two that I had dressed and laid aside were afterwards killed during the action.— The enemy's squadron mounted more guns than ours and carried at least one fourth more men.— In the course of a year I hope to obtain a little prize money.—

I have enjoyed very bad health during this cruize and am reduced to a skeleton and will never cross this or any other Lake again.—

I have lately received a letter from Dr. A Hall jr and one from Charlotte Parsons,[1] dated August 28th.—

Remember me to enquiring friends   Yr. affectionate son

Usher Parsons

Saml.[2] is steady & well.

ALS, RHi, Usher Parsons, "A Diary Kept During the Expedition to Lake Erie, Under Captain O. H. Perry, 1812–14." This letter was bound into the diary.

1. Dr. Abiel Hall, Jr., of Alfred, Maine, was a friend of Usher Parsons's, and the son of Dr. Abiel Hall, Sr., with whom Usher had studied medicine; Charlotte Parsons was Usher's sister-in-law.
2. Usher's older brother Samuel Parsons also served on the lakes.

SURGEON USHER PARSONS'S ACCOUNT OF THE BATTLE OF LAKE ERIE [1]

Surgical account of the Naval engagement on Lake Erie on the 10th Sept. 1813—
        By Usher Parsons M.D.
                Surgeon U.S. Navy—

<u>Mess: Editors</u>. To such of your readers as are unacquainted with the duties of a surgeon in a sea engagement and with the description of wounds that fall under his care, the following sketch may be acceptable—

The U. States' force employed in this action, consisted of 9 vessels with about 600 officers and men, and had been out of port four weeks, either cruising, or lying at anchor in Put-in bay, a safe harbor, among a cluster of islands, near the head of the Lake. The crews left port in good health, but shortly after were visited with an epidemic, which spread through the fleet attacking about 20 or 30 in a day, It answered the descriptions of a bilious remittent fever; was of short duration; except in a few instances, in which it degenerated into a Typhus; and in only one instance proved fatal. So rapid were the recoveries, that, of above two hundred cases, only seventy eight were reported unfit for duty, on the day previous to the action. Thirty one of these were on board the *Lawrence,* and about the same number on board the *Niagara,* their whole crews being about one hundred and forty men each.—

About 12 Oclock on a clear pleasant day we met the enemy. The action soon became general and was severely felt, especially on board the *Lawrence,* the flag ship, two of the enemy's largest vessels engaging her at short distance for nearly two hours, part of which time the men fell on board her faster than they could be taken below The vessels being shallow built, afforded no Cockelpit or place of shelter the wounded were therefore received on the wardroom floor, which was about on a level with the surface of the water. Being only nine or ten feet square this floor was soon covered which made it necessary to pass the wounded out into another apartment as fast as the bleeding could be stanched either by ligature or tourniquettes. Indeed this was all that was attempted for their benefit during the engagement, except that in some instances division was made of a small portion of flesh by which a dangling limb that annoyed the patient was hanging to the body. Some after this treatment were again wounded; among whom were Midn. Laub who was moving from me with a tourniquette on the arm when he received a cannon ball in the chest—and Charles Pohig a seaman brought down with both arms fractured was afterwards struck by a cannon ball in both lower extremeties which he survived about one hour.

An hour's engagement had so far swept the decks that new appeals for surgical aid were ~~more~~ less frequent a remission at this time very desirable both to the wounded and myself for the repeated request of the Commodore to spare him another man had taken from me the last one I had to assist in moving the wounded; indeed many of the wounded themselves took the deck again at this critical moment. Our prospects nevertheless darkened; every new visiter from the deck bringing tidings still more dismal than the last 'till finally it was announced that we had struck— The effect of this on the wounded was distressing in the extreme—medical aid was rejected and little else could be heard from them than "sink the ship" "Let us all sink together"— But this state of despair was short. The commodore was still unhurt, had gone on board the *Niagara* and with the small vessels bearing down upon the enemy soon brought down the flags of their two heaviest ships and thus changed the horrors of defeat into shouts of victory. But all the wounded were not permitted to mingle in the joy. The gallant Brooks and some others were no more. They were too much exhausted by their wounds to survive the confusion that immediately preceeded this happy transition.

The action terminated shortly after 3 o'clock; and of about one hundred men, reported fit for duty in the morning, twenty were found dead, and sixty one wounded. The wounded [arteries] occupied my first attention, all which, except where amputation was required, were rendered secure before dark. Having no assistant, I deemed it safer to defer amputating till morning in the meantime suffered the tourniquettes to remain on the [limbs]. Nothing more was done through the night than to administer opiates, and preserve shattered limbs in a uniform position. At day light a subject was on the table for amputation of the thigh, and at 11 o'clock all amputations were finished. The impatience of this class of the wounded to meet the operation, rendered it necessary to take them in the same succession in which they fell. The compound and simple fractures were next attended to; then luxations, lacerations, and contusions; all which occupied my time till 12 o'clock at night.—

The day following I visited the wounded of the *Niagara*, who had lain till that time, with their wounds undressed. I found the surgeon sick in bed, with hands too feeble to execute the dictates of a feeling heart. Twenty one were mustered, most of whom were taken on board the *Lawrence* and dressed; and afterwards such as were lying in like manner, on board the small vessels. In the course of the evening, the sick were prescribed for, which was the first attention I had been able to render them since the action.

The whole number of wounded was ninety six. Of these, twenty five were cases of compound fracture; viz. of the arm, six; of the thigh, four; of the leg, eight; of the shoulder, three; and of the skull and ribs, three.— Of simple fracture there were four cases, viz. of the thigh, leg, arm, and ribs.— Grape shot wounds were three; and canister, four. The splinter and lacerated wounds, large and small, were thirty seven. There were two cases of concussion of the brain; of the chest, three; and of the pelvis, two. The contusions, large and small, were ten; and the sprains six.

Of the whole number there died three; viz. midshipman Claxton, with compound fracture of the shoulder, in which a part of the clavicle, scapula, and humerus, was carried away: also a seaman with a mortification of the lower extremity, in which there had been a compound fracture; and another with a fracture of the scull, where a part of the cerebral substance was carried away.—

The compound fractures of the extremities, were much retarded in their cure, by the frequent displacement of the bones, by the motion of the ship in rough weather, or by some other unlucky disturbance of the limb. In this way the bones in one case did not unite, until after forty days had elapsed, and in two or three other cases, not till after twenty five days.

The delay of amputations, already mentioned, had no effect on the success of the operations. Every case did well.

There were not more than two very singular wounds, or such as would be unlikely to occur in any sea engagement. In one of these cases, grape shot, four times as large as a musket ball, passed under the pyramidal muscle, without injuring the peritoneum. In the other, a canister shot, twice the size of a musket ball, entered the eye, and on the fifth or sixth day, was detected at the inside of the angle of the lower jaw, and cut out. In its passage, it must have fractured the orbitar plate of the superior maxillary bone, the orbito-temporal process of the splenoid bone, and, passing under the temporal arch, inside the coronal process of the lower jaw, must have done great injury to the temporal muscle and other soft parts, lying in its way. ~~This subject was a Kentucky rifleman, and the loss of his right eye is rather calculated to spoil his sport.~~

The recovery of so great a proportion of the wounded may in some measure be attributed to the following causes.— First, the purity of the air. The patients were ranged along on the upper deck, with no other shelter from the weather, than a high awning to shade them. They continued lying in this situation for a fortnight, and, when taken on shore, were placed in very spacious apartments well ventilated.— Secondly, to the supply of food best adapted to their cases, as fowls, fresh meat, milk, eggs, and an abundance of vegetables. The second day after the action, the farmers on the Ohio shore brought along side every article of the above description, that could be desired. Thirdly to the happy state of mind, which victory occasioned. The observations, which I have been enabled to make on the wounded of three engagements, have convinced me, that this state of mind has greater effect, than has generally been supposed; and that the surgeon on the conquering side will, *caeteris paribus*,[2] always be more successful, than the one, who has charge of the vanquished crew: and that it is of the first importance ~~to keep the mind as tranquil and cheerful~~ in such cases to soothe and cheer the patient as much as circumstances will permit.

Lastly to the assistance rendered me by a Mr. Davidson[3] and Commodore Perry. The former was a volunteer among the Kentucky troops ~~under Col John-son~~ and volunteered to serve on board the fleet during the engagement— The day after the action he ~~assisted me~~ rendered ~~me~~ the wounded every aid in his power and remained with them three months— And the Commodore's solicitude for the welfare of the wounded ~~was quite~~ seemed to equal what he could have felt for the success of the action.

Draft, RPB, Usher Parsons Papers. With slight changes, this paper was published in *The New England Journal of Medicine and Surgery,* Vol. 7, No. 4 (Oct. 1818), pp. 313–16.

1. Usher Parsons was promoted to surgeon on 15 April 1814. He wrote this account about 1818 based on his notes and diaries.
2. *Caeteris paribus,* other things being equal.
3. Private Joseph Davidson served in Captain John Payne's Company of Colonel Richard M. Johnson's Regiment of Kentucky Volunteers.

Operations on the Detroit Frontier

American control of Lake Erie enabled Major General William Henry Harrison and Captain Oliver H. Perry to launch a major offensive against the retreating British army in Canada. Perry served as a volunteer aide de camp to Harrison and offered support to the army by assisting with the transportation of men and supplies in naval vessels and by providing cannon fire to cover army troop movements.[1]

The British outposts of Amherstburg and Detroit fell without resistance on 27 September; the Americans then defeated the British in the Battle of the Thames on 5 October. The close cooperation between Harrison and Perry in these joint operations assured an American victory on the Detroit frontier and led to the breakdown of the British alliance with the Northwest Indian tribes.

1. *Skaggs, "Joint Operations"; Skaggs, "And They Are Ours."*

Major General William Henry Harrison, U.S.A., to Secretary of War Armstrong

H.Q.   Mouth of Portage River
on Lake Erie   15th. Septr. 1813

Sir

You will have been informed from the letter of Com. Perry to the Sec. of the Navy of the Brilliant Naval victory obtained by him & the capture of the whole of the enemy's flotilla on this Lake. I arrived here the day before yesterday with a part of the troops from Seneca Town & this morning Genl. Cass has brot. on the remainder. Gov. Shelby has also arrived with his militia. We are busily engaged in embarking the Stores & Artillery & by the day after tomorrow the whole will be afloat— Genl. McArthur will join me the day after at the Bass Islands with the troops from Fort Meigs & on the following night if the weather permits we shall sail for the Canada Shore. As soon as I have driven the Enemy from Malden & Detroit I shall despatch a detachment for the reduction of Macinac & St. Josephs & will expect your orders for my further movements. The upper part of the province of U.C. being cleared of the enemy, unless it should appear expedient to pursue the Indians the army under my command might move down the Lake to Long point or below it & cooperate with that under General Wilkinson. From my present impressions with regard to our affairs in that quarter I should if I considered myself authorized to do so immediately proceed to the Lower end of the Lake.

Com. Perry had out with him in the late action about 130 of my men, he speaks in the highest terms of their Conduct. Major Wood had arrived at this place with two Companies when the Com. returned to Putinbay, he immediately sent him a reinforcement of fifty men which were of great service in securing the prisoners. I have the honor to be &c. &c.

W. H. Harrison

ALS, DNA, RG107, Department of the Army, Letters Received by the Secretary of War, Registered Series, H–231 (M221, Roll No. 53).

MAJOR GENERAL FRANCIS DE ROTTENBURG, BRITISH ARMY, TO GOVERNOR-GENERAL SIR GEORGE PREVOST

Head Quarters of the Centre Division
4 Mile Creek   17th September 1813

Sir

With feelings of Sorrow and affliction I transmit to your Excellency a Dispatch from Genl. Proctor which I received last night and a copy of the answer I send him in consequence— This terrible disaster if not counterbalanced by a complete Victory on this Lake must eventually change all my dispositions and force me back to the Position of Burlington Heights— I shall now stop the sailors at Burlington until I hear from Sir James. Every exertion shall be used to provide General Proctor with provisions by land   I have the Honor to be most respectfully Your Excellency's Most obedient and most humble Servant

Francis De Rottenburg
M. General

By mistake Your Excellency's letter which was forwarded from this yesterday was dated the 17th instead of the 16th

LS, CaOOA, British Military and Naval Records, RG8, I, "C" Ser., Vol. 680, p. 78.

[Enclosure]

Sandwich
September 12th. 1813

Sir

With the Deepest Regret I acquaint you that the Squadron of His Majesty's Vessels* under the Command of Captain Barclay sailed at 3 O Clock P M on the 9th Instant to seek that of the Enemy**, and that on the 10th Inst. the two

Fleets were seen engaged between the Islands, about 25 Miles from the Settlement below Amherstburg. The Action lasted from twelve to nearly half past three, and I understand from Lt. Colonel Warburton who saw the Action from an elevated situation fifteen Miles below Amherstburg, that the Firing was incessant, and the Vessels appeared to be very near each other. The Spectators were fully impressed with the Idea that our Fleet were the Victors, but circumstances have since placed it beyond a Doubt, that the whole of our Fleet have been taken or destroyed. The Wind was fair for Amherstburg, the whole of the 10th. & the 11th Inst. no Accounts from or of Capt. Barclay, and on the latter Day, the vessels*** evidently under one Flag worked down the Lake. The Commissariat might have preserved this District, or a due Attention to the naval Establishment on this Lake. I have no neglects to upbraid myself with, that could have the slightest Effect on the Safety of this Country, tho' one is implied in your Letter, "not employing the *Queen Charlotte* and my Craft diligently in conveying Provisions from Long Point, at the opening of the Navigation." I beg Leave to observe in Answer that those from whom you received that Information, might have mentioned that the unfortunate Ship *Queen Charlotte* could not be used at the Period alluded to, for want of Hands, who were in the Craft employed on the Expedition to the Miami which has received the approval of His Excellency the Commander of the Forces. I take the Liberty of suggesting, the Expediency of occupying immediately an eligible Piece of Ground at Turkey Point, by Blockhouses connected by Picketting, that may be defended by from three to five hundred men. I do not see the least Chance of occupying to advantage my present extensive Position, which can be so easily turned by means of the entire command of the Waters here which the Enemy now has. A Circumstance that would render my Indian Force very inefficient. It is my Opinion that I should retire on the Thames, without Delay, preparatory to any other movement that may be found requisite, or determined on. I have written to Colonel Talbot to send to the Thames whatever Articles of Food there may be in his Reach, also to have the Road, as far as possible, repaired, thro' the Wilderness. I feel myself much at a Loss with Respect to the Indians. The Loss of the Fleet is a most calamitous Circumstance. Michilimackinac will require immediate attention. It is to be apprehended that the Enemy may make an immediate Attempt to pass up some of their Vessels to possess themselves of that Place, and some Vessels we must send to the upper Lake. Requesting to hear from you by Return of the Express   I have the Honor to be Sir Your Obedient humble Servant

Henry Procter
Major General
commr.

Major General de Rottenburg

* *Detroit, Queen Charlotte, Lady Prevost, Hunter, Chippewa, Ariel,* two ships, schooner, brig, small schooner, Sloop, six Sail

** Nine sail, two Brigs carrying 20 32 Pound carronades each and two long 12 Pounders

*** Eleven

ALS, CaOOA, British Military and Naval Records, RG8, I, "C" Ser., Vol. 680, pp. 71–74.

[Enclosure]

Head Quarters   Centre
Division   17th. Septemb. 1813

Sir/

Major G. De Rottenburg received your letter of the 12th. Inst. yesterday evening. He directs me to ask in the first place whether the sailing of Captain Barclays Squadron to meet the Enemy at a time when it was so incompetently manned, was the consequence of a positive order to that purport from Commodore Sir Jas. Yeo, or the commander of the Forces, or whether that measure was adopted by you, and in that case that you will be pleased to state the circumstances or motives by which you was led to the adoption of so hazardous a measure, with the knowledge which you possessed of the intention to urge forward seamen, with all possible expedition and the assurance which you had received, that they were actually on their way—

Secondly I have Major General De Rottenburgs direction to say, that he does not clearly see the necessity or expediency, of your immediately retiring from your present position— There certainly may be reasons which you have not stated, or with which the Major General is consequently unacquainted, which may point more urgently to the necessity of such a movement, than he is at present aware of— But the View M. Genl. De Rottenburg is inclined to take of your situation as connected with the loss of the Squadron, is that, that event cannot affect you as immediately as to make any precipitate retrograde movement necessary— After an action of three hours and a half the Enemys Vessels must have received so much damage as not to be in a situation to undertake any thing further for some time— This interval you will employ in looking well at your situation, in communication with Tecumseh, and the Indians, in ascertaining the impression which this disaster has produced on them, and in concerting with them the measures best calculated, to lessen the consequences of that disaster— concentrating on making such a disposition of your remaining Force, as may prove to them the sincerity of the British Government, in its intention not to abandon them, so long as they are true to their own interests— An officer of Engineers proceeds immediately to Long Point to construct the Block Houses you recommend, and such other defensive works as may appear to him to be required— Colonel Murray who has lately joined this Division of the Army, will also proceed to assume the command at Long Point— He will be instructed to call out the Militia—

With reference to the concluding Paragraph of your letter, I am directed to inquire what means we possess in vessels &c, by which to send assistance to Michilmackinac. Does the Enemy possess any vessels at present on Lake Huron, and would it be practicable to prevent their possessing the Narrows of the Sinclair, and thus to preserve the ascendancy on that Lake (Huron) the Enemy possessing that of Lake Erie? Would the Seamen now hourly expected be of any service, or may their progress be stopped? Do you wish the 10 24 prd. carronades intended for the *Detroit* to be sent on and to what Place? Your answers to these Queries and a full communication of every thing relating to your situation, intentions and wants, it is requested may be transmitted by the most expeditious means at your disposal—

(signed)   J. Harvey
D.A.G.

(copy)

Major Genl. Proctor
&c   &c   &c

Copy, CaOOA, British Military and Naval Records, RG8, I, "C" Ser., Vol. 680, pp. 75–77.

CAPTAIN OLIVER H. PERRY TO SECRETARY OF THE NAVY JONES

U.S. Schoor. *Ariel*   Put in Bay
Sepr. 24th. 1813

Sir

I have the honor to acquaint you that about twelve hundred troops were yesterday transported to a small Island distant about 4 leagues from Malden, notwithstanding it blew hard, with frequent squalls this day although the weather is not settled, the squadron will again take over as many more.— We only waite for favorable weather to make a final move.— I need not assure you Sir, that every possible exertion will be made by the officers & men under my command to assist the advance of the army, and it affords me great pleasure, to have it in my power to say, that the utmost harmony prevails between the army & Navy. I have the honor to be Sir Very Respectfully Your Obdt. Servt.

O. H. Perry

ALS, DNA, RG45, CL, 1813, Vol. 6, No. 81 (M125, Roll No. 31).

CAPTAIN OLIVER H. PERRY TO SECRETARY OF THE NAVY JONES

U.S. Schooner *Ariel*
Septemr. 1813—

Sir

I have the honor to acquaint you, that on the 26th Inst, the commander in chief of the N.W. Army, and myself, in the *Ariel*, reconnoitered the enemys shore, and determined on the place to land the Army.

At 3 a.m. of the 27th. commenced the embarkation from the middle Sister (Island) at 9. the troops being on board, and in boats, the squadron weighed, and stood for the place of landing. At 2 P.M. the vessels anchored in a line (1/4 of a mile distant from the shore) about 1 1/2 miles to the Eastward of Bar Point, for the purpose of covering the landing of the Troops. At 45 minutes past two, those in the boats, landed without opposition, in excellent order.

Finding on enquiry, that the Enemy had evacuated Malden, the Squadron got underweigh, and anchored off the Town of Amherstburg, where the remaining troops were landed.

No opportunity offered to the officers under my command, to shew their Gallantry, but Sir, they evinced throughout, the greatest disposition to be serviceable in transporting the Army and rendering it, every assistance in their power.

The arrangement for the debarkation of the Troops, I had intrusted to Capt. Elliott, from the cordial assistance he received from every officer of the Army, and his own exertion and judgement, that service was most admirably performed. Very Respectfully I have the honor to be Sir Your Obd. Servt.

O. H. Perry

LS, DNA, RG45, CL, 1813, Vol. 6, No. 1 (M125, Roll No. 31).

Captain Oliver H. Perry to Secretary of the Navy Jones

U.S. Schooner *Ariel*

Sir

I arrived off Sandwich with a part of the force under my command on the 29th. Ult, and immediately proceeded with Genl. Harrison at the head of a Division of his Army to repossess Detroit. A considerable body of Indians were in, and about the Town, at the time of our crossing, but they fled without making any resistance.

The wind being favourable on the 30th Septr. I detached the *Niagara, Lady Prevost, Scorpion, & Tigress* under the Orders of Capt. Elliott, up Lake St. Clair in pursuit of the Enemys vessels said to be loaded with the baggage and Artillery of the Enemy.

I shall proceed immediately with the *Ariel,* and *Caledonia* to the river Thames to cooperate with the Army. The other Vessels of this Squadron are employed in the transportation of troops, provisions &c for the Army. Very Respecty. I am Sir your obd. Servt.

O. H. Perry

LS, DNA, RG45, CL, 1813, Vol. 7, No. 21 (M125, Roll No. 32).

Captain Oliver H. Perry to Secretary of the Navy Jones

U.S. Schooner *Ariel*
Detroit   7th. October 1813—

Sir

I have the honor to inform you, that I have returned to this Place, after having had the pleasure of witnessing the capture of the Brittish Army, and the defeat of their Indians, by the Army under Majr. Genl. Harrison.

On the 2nd Inst. I proceeded to the mouth of the Thames and joined the Vessels that I had previously detached. On the morning of the 3d, on our Army's advancing, immediately stood into the River with the Gun boats, *Scorpion & Tigress,* & was soon after joined by the *Porcupine,* the only vessels that could cross the bar. They proceeded up as far as McCrea's under the direction of Capt. Elliott, in company with the Army. There, they were obliged to stop as the banks of the River were too high for their guns to be of any service. Since the capture of the Enemy, have been employed in bringing down the large quantity of ammunition and stores taken from them.

The Vessels not employed in this service have been transporting provisions, Baggage &c for the Army— Very Respectfully I have the honor to be Sir your obd. sert.

O. H. Perry

LS, DNA, RG45, CL, 1813, Vol. 6, No. 131 (M125, Roll No. 31).

Major General William Henry Harrison, U.S.A., to Secretary of War Armstrong

Head Quarters
Detroit   9th October 1813

Sir

In my letter from Sandwich of the 30th ultimo, I did myself the honour to inform you, that I was preparing to pursue the enemy, the following day. From various causes however, I was unable to put the troops in motion until the morning of the 2nd. Instant and then to take with me only about one hundred and forty of the Regular Troops, Johnson's mounted Regiment and such of Gov. Shelby's volunteers as were fit for a rapid march, the whole amounting to about three thousand five hundred men. To Genl. McArthur (with about seven hundred effectives) the protecting of this place and the sick was committed. Genl. Cass's Brigade and the Corps of Lt. Col. Ball were left at Sandwich, with orders to follow me as soon as the men received their knapsacks and blankets, which had been left on an Island in Lake Erie.

The unavoidable delay at Sandwich was attended with no disadvantage to us. Genl. Proctor had posted himself at Dolson's on the right bank of the Thames (or French) fifty six miles from this place, where I was informed, he intended to fortify and wait to receive me. He must have believed, however, that I had no disposition to follow him, or that he had secured my continuance here, by the reports that were circulated that the Indians would attack and destroy this place upon the advance of the Army; as he neglected to commence the breaking up the bridges until the night of the second instant. On that night our army reached the river which is twenty five miles from Sandwich and is one of four streams crossing our route, over all of which are bridges; and being deep and muddy, are unfordable for a considerable distance into the Country— the bridge here was found entire and in the morning I proceeded with Johnson's Regiment to save if possible the others— At the second bridge over a branch of the river Thames, we were fortunate enough to capture a Lieut. of Dragoons and eleven privates, who had been sent by Genl. Proctor, to destroy them. From the prisoners I learned that the third bridge was broken up and that the enemy had no certain information of our advance. The bridge having been imperfectly destroyed, was soon repaired and the army encamped at Drake's farm, four miles below Dolson's.

The river Thames, along the banks of which our route lay, is a fine deep stream, navigable for vessels of considerable burthen, after the passage of the bar at its mouth, over which, there is six and a half feet water.

The baggage of the army was brought from Detroit in boats protected by three Gun boats, which Commodore Perry had furnished for the purpose, as well as to cover the passage of the army over the Thames itself, or the mouths of its tributary streams; the banks being low and the Country generally open (Prairies) as high as Dolson's, these vessels, were well calculated for that purpose—above Dolson's however, the character of the river and adjacent Country is considerably changed. The former, though still deep, is very narrow and its banks high and woody. The Commodore and myself therefore agreed upon the propriety of leaving the boats under a guard of one hundred and fifty Infantry, and I determined to trust to fortune and the bravery of my troops to effect the passage of the river. Below a place called Chatham and for miles above Dolson's is the third unfordable branch of the Thames; the bridge over its mouth had been taken up by the Indians, as well as that at McGregor's Mills, one mile above,—several hundred of the Indians remained to dispute our passage and upon the arrival of the advanced Guard, commenced a heavy fire from the opposite bank of the Creek as well as that of the river. Believing that the whole force of the enemy was there I halted the army, formed in order of battle, and brought up our two six pounders to cover the party, that were ordered to repair the bridge. A few shot from those peices, soon drove off the Indians and en-

abled us, in two hours to repair the bridge and cross the troops— Col. Johnson's mounted regiment being upon the right of the army, had seized the remains of the bridge at the Mills under a heavy fire from the Indians. Our loss
upon this occasion, was two killed and three or four wounded—that of the
enemy was ascertained to be considerably greater. A house near the bridge, containing a very considerable number of muskets had been set on fire—but it was
extinguished by our troops and the arms saved. At the first farm above the
bridge, we found one of the enemy's vessels on fire, loaded with arms and ordnance Stores and learned that they were a few miles ahead of us, still on the
right bank of the river with the great body of the Indians— At Bowles's farm,
four miles from the bridge, we halted for the night, found two other vessels and
a large distillery filled with ordnance and other valuable stores to an immense
amount, in flames—it was impossible to put out the fire— two twenty four
pounders with their carriages were taken and a large quantity of ball and shells
of various sizes— The army was put in motion early on the morning of the 5th.
I pushed on in advance with the mounted Regiment and requested Gov. Shelby
to follow as expeditiously as possible with the Infantry; the Govs. zeal and that
of his ~~troops~~ men, enabled them to keep up with the Cavalry, and by 9 Oclock,
we were at Arnold's Mills, having taken in the course of the morning, two Gun
boats and several batteaux, loaded with provisions and ammunition.

A rapid in the river at Arnolds Mills affords the only fording to be met with,
for a very considerable distance, but upon examination, it was found too deep
for the Infantry— Having however fortunately taken two or three boats and
some Indian Canoes on the spot and obliging the horsemen to take a foot man
behind each, the whole were safely crossed by 12 Oclock.— 8 miles from the
Crossing we passed a farm, where a part of the British Troops had encamped
the night before under the command of Col. Warburton.— The detachment
with Genl. Proctor had arrived the day before at the Moravian Town, four miles
higher up. Being now certainly near the enemy, I directed the advance of Johnson's Regiment to accellerate their march, for the purpose of procuring intelligence— The officer commanding it, in a short time, sent to inform me, that his
progress was stopped by the enemy, who were formed across our line of march.
One of the enemy's Waggoners being also taken prisoner, from the information
received from him, and my own observation, assisted by some of my officers, I
soon ascertained enough of their position and order of battle, to determine
that, which it was proper for me to adopt.

I have the honour herewith to enclose you, my general order, of the 27 ultimo
prescribing the order of March and of battle when the whole army should act together— But as the number and description of the troops had been essentially
changed since the issuing of the order, it became necessary to make a corresponding alteration in their disposition— From the place where our army was last
halted, to the Moravian Town, a distance of about three & a half miles—the road
passes through a beech forest without any clearing and for the first two miles near
to the bank of the River.— At from two to three hundred yards from the river, a
swamp extends parallel to it, throughout the whole distance— The intermediate
ground is dry and although the trees are tolerably thick, it is in many places clear
of underbrush— across this strip of land, its left appayed[1] upon the river, supported by artillery placed in the wood, their right in the swamp covered by the
whole of their Indian force, the British Troops were drawn up.—

Major General William Henry Harrison, U.S.A.

The troops at my disposal consisted of about one hundred and twenty regulars of the 27th Regiment, five brigades of Kentucky volunteer Militia Infantry under his Excellency Gov. Shelby, averaging less than five hundred men and Col. Johnson's Regiment of Mounted Infantry, making in the whole an aggregate something above three thousand. No disposition of an army opposed to an Indian force can be safe unless it is secured on the flanks and in the rear— I had therefore no difficulty in arranging the Infantry conformably to my General order of battle— Genl. Trotters brigade of five hundred men formed the front line, his right upon the road and his left upon the swamp— Genl. Kings brigade as a second line one hundred and fifty yards in the rear of Trotters and Chiles's brigade as a *corps de reserve* in the rear of it— these three brigades formed the command of Major Genl. Henry the whole of Genl. Desha's Division consisting of two brigades were formed *en potence*[2] upon the left of Trotter

Whilst I was engaged in forming the Infantry, I had directed Col. Johnsons Regiment, which was still in front, to be formed in two lines opposite to the enemy and upon the advance of the Infantry to take ground to the left and forming upon that flank the endeavour to turn the right of the Indians. A moments reflection however convinced me that from the thickness of the Woods and swampiness of the ground, they would be unable to do any thing on horseback, and there was no time to dismount them and place their horses in security; I therefore determined to refuse my left to the Indians and to break the British lines at once by a charge of the Mounted Infantry— the measure was not sanctioned by any thing that I had seen or heard of—but I was fully convinced that it would succeed. The American backwoodsmen ride better in the woods than any other people.— A musket or rifle is no impediment to them, being accustomed to carry them on horseback from their earliest youth. I was persuaded too that the enemy would be quite unprepared for the shock and that they could not resist it— Conformably to this idea, I directed the regiment to be drawn up in close column, with its right at the distance of fifty yards from the road, (that it might be in some measure protected by the trees from the artillery) its left upon the swamp and to charge at full speed as soon as the enemy delivered their fire.— The few regular troops of the 27th Regiment under their Colo. (Paul) occupied in column of sections of four, the small space between the road & the river for the purpose of seizing the enemy's artillery and some ten or twelve friendly Indians were directed to move under the bank— The Crotchet[3] formed by the front line and Genl. Desha's division was an important point— at that place, the Venerable Governor of Kentucky was posted, who at the age of sixty six preserves all the vigor of youth, the ardent zeal which distinguished him in the Revolutionary War and the undaunted bravery which he manifested at King's Mountain. With my Aids de Camp, the acting assistant adjutant General Capt. Butler, my Gallant friend Commodore Perry who did me the honour to serve as my Volunteer aid de Camp and Brigadier General Cass, who having no command tendered me his assistance— I placed myself at the head of the front line of Infantry, to direct the movements of the Cavalry and give them the necessary support.— The army had moved on in this order but a short distance, when the mounted Men received the fire of the British line and were ordered to charge— the horses in the front of the column recoiled from the fire, another was given by the enemy and our Column at length getting in motion broke through the enemy with irresistible force, in one minute, the contest in front was over; the British officers seeing no hopes of reducing their disordered ranks to order, and our mounted men wheeling upon them and pouring in a destructive fire immediately surrendered— it is certain that three only of our troops were wounded in this charge (upon the left however, the contest was more severe with the Indians—Col. Johnson, who commanded on that flank of his regiment received a most galling fire from them, which was returned with great effect.) The Indians still further to the right advanced and fell in with our front line of Infantry, near its junction with Desha's division and for a moment made an impression upon it.— His Excellency Gov. Shelby however brought up a regiment to its support and the enemy receiving a severe fire in front, and a part of Johnson's Regiment having gained their rear, retreated with precipitation— their loss was very considerable in the action and many were killed in their retreat.

I can give no satisfactory information of the number of Indians that were in the action but they must have been considerably upwards of one thousand— From the documents in my possession (Genl. Proctor's official letters all of which were taken) and from the information of respectable inhabitants of this Territory, the Indians kept in pay by the British were much more numerous than has been generally supposed   In a letter to Genl. De Rottenburg of the 27th. Inst. Genl. Proctor speaks of having prevailed upon most of the Indians to accompany him— Of these it is certain that fifty or sixty Wyandot Warriors abandoned him.*

The number of our troops was certainly greater than that of the enemy—but when it is recollected that they had chosen a position that effectually secured their flank which it was impossible for us to turn and that we could not present to them a line more extended than their own, it will not be considered arrogant to claim for my troops, the palm of superior bravery.

In communicating to the President through you, Sir my opinion of the conduct of the officers who served under my command I am at a loss how to mention that of Gov. Shelby being convinced that no eulogium of mine can reach his merits—

The Governor of an independent state, greatly my superior in years, in experience and in military character, he placed himself under my command and is not more remarkable for his zeal and activity than for the promptitude and cheerfulness with which he obeyed my orders. The Major Generals Henry and Desha and the brigadiers Allen, Caldwell, King, Chiles and Trotter all of the Kentucky Volunteers manifested great zeal and activity— Of Gov. Shelby's staff His adjutant General Col. McDowell and his Quarter Master Genl. Col. Walker rendered great service, as did his Aids de Camp Genl. Adair and Majors Barry and Crittenden—the military skill of the former was of great service to us and the activity of the two latter Gentlemen could not be surpassed. Illness deprived me of the talents of my Adjutant General Col. Gaines who was left at Sandwich. His duties were however ably performed by the acting assistant Adjutant General Capt. Butler— My aids de camp Lt. O'Fallon and Capt. Todd of the Line and my volunteer aids John Speed Smith and John Chambers Esq. have rendered me the most important services from the opening of the Campaign. I have already stated that Genl. Cass and Commodore Perry assisted me in forming the troops for action— the former is an officer of the highest merit and the appearance of the brave Commodore cheered and animated every breast.

It would be useless Sir after stating the circumstances of the action, to pass encomium upon Col. Johnson and his regiment. Veterans could not have manifested more firmness— the Colonel's numerous wounds prove that he was in the post of danger. Lt. Col. James Johnson and the Majors Payne and Thompson were equally active though more fortunate— Major Wood of the Engineers, already distinguished by his conduct at Fort Meigs attended the army with two six pounders— Having no use for them in the action, he joined in the pursuit of the enemy and with Major Payne of the Mounted regiment, two of my aids de Camp, Todd and Chambers and three privates, continued it for several miles after the rest of the troops had halted and made many prisoners.

I left the army before an official return of the prisoners or that of the killed and wounded was made out— it was however ascertained that the former amounts to six hundred and one regulars including twenty five officers. Our loss is seven killed and twenty two wounded—five of which have since died. Of the British Troops twelve were killed and twenty two wounded the Indians suffered most—thirty three of them having been found upon the Ground, besides those killed on the retreat.

On the day of the action, six pieces of brass artillery were taken, and two iron twenty four pounders the day before. Several others were discovered in the River and can be easily procured— of the Brass pieces, three are the Trophies of our Revolutionary War, that were taken at Saratoga and York and surrendered by General Hull—

The number of small arms taken by us and destroyed by the enemy must amount to upwards of five thousand— most of them, had been ours and taken by the enemy at the surrender of Detroit, at the river raisin and Colo. Dudley's defeat. I believe that the enemy retain no other military trophy of their Victories than the standard of the 4th Regiment— They were not magnanimous enough to bring that of the 41st Regiment into the field or it would have been taken—

You have been informed, Sir, of the conduct of the Troops under my command in action—it gives me great pleasure to inform you that they merit also the approbation of their country for their conduct, in submitting to the greatest privations with the utmost cheerfulness

The Infantry were entirely without tents and for several days, the whole army subsisted upon fresh beef without bread or salt. I have the honor to be with great respect, Sir, your Humble Servt.

Willm. Henry Harrison

* A British officer of high rank, assured one of my Aids de Camp, that on the day of our landing Genl. Proctor had at his disposal, upwards of three thousand Indian Warriors but asserted that the greatest part had left him previous to the action—

P.S. Genl. Proctor escaped by the fleetness of his horses, escorted by forty dragoons and a number of Mounted Indians—

LS, DNA, RG107, Letters Received by the Secretary of War, Unregistered Series, H–1813 (M222, Roll No. 7).

1. From the French term *appuyer*, a military maneuver in which the flank of a line of troops is supported by placing them alongside an obstruction such as a river, woods, or fortification.

2. A military formation in which a part of a line is thrown forward or backward at an angle to the main line.

3. The intersection of two lines of troops arranged at an angle to each other.

Perry Resigns His Command on Lake Erie

The bitter dispute between Captain Oliver H. Perry and Commodore Isaac Chauncey over manning the fleets hampered cordial relations between the two officers. Perry again asked for removal from the Lake Erie station; his request was granted by the secretary of the navy in the same letter that informed Perry of his promotion to the coveted rank of captain.

Chauncey protested this "indulgence" in a letter to the secretary of the navy dated 13 October. The letter reveals much about Chauncey's ideas of duty and personal sacrifice to the naval service and offers insight into his thoughts and opinions.

Secretary of the Navy Jones to Captain Oliver H. Perry

Capt. O. H. Perry,   Navy Department
Comg. the U.S. Squadron,   Septr. 29th. 1813.
on Lake Erie.

Sir,

The President has confirmed the sentiments, which I anticipated, in my letter to you of the 21st. Inst. in a manner the most ample and expressive.

I have, by his direction, executed a Commission promoting you to the rank of Captain in the Navy of the United States, which I will forward to whatever place you shall please to direct.

I am, this morning, favoured with yours of the 20th.[1] and, although there is much of importance yet to be done upon the Upper Lakes, which I should like you to bring to maturity, yet, if you think the service will not suffer by your absence, you are at liberty, as soon as the public interest shall admit of your departure, to proceed to Rhode Island and resume your command there, until a Ship, suitable to your rank, shall be at the disposal of the Department.

In the event of your resigning the command of the Erie Squadron, it will, of course, devolve on Captain Elliot, who will communicate with, and receive the instructions of Commodore Chauncey, the Commander in chief, who will be furnished with a copy of this Letter.

Capt. Elliot will communicate direct to this Department, (in order to save time,) whatever may be of importance to be speedily known.

The commissary General of Prisoners has given the necessary directions, in relation to those captured by you, and you will not parole <u>any person</u>, except Captain Barclay, without his special authority. I am, very respectfully, your obedient Servant,

W. Jones.

LB Copy, DNA, RG45, SNL, Vol. 11, pp. 102–3 (M125, Roll No. 11).

1. In his letter of 20 September 1813, Oliver H. Perry reiterated his request to leave the Lake Erie station and asked for permission to parole Lieutenant Robert Heriot Barclay on account of the severity of his wounds.

COMMODORE ISAAC CHAUNCEY TO SECRETARY OF THE NAVY JONES

No. 95   U.S. Ship *General Pike*
                                            Sacketts Harbor   13th Octo. 1813

Sir,

I have this moment been honored with your Letter of the 29th Ulto. and notice with regret that you have consented to suffer Captain Perry to resign his command upon Lake Erie and retire from the Lake service— altho Captain Perry is as much entitled to indulgence as any other Officer, yet the principal which it establishes will be found to be a troublesome one—for the moment that it is discovered that the Department is disposed to indulge all who are dissatisfied with the Lake Service it will be inundated with applications and I shall be left without an Officer of experience to support and assist me in the various duties of my command—

I have not been disposed to complain from a wish not to be troublesome knowing at the same time that it was not always convenient for the Department to order Officers from one Station to another— I have therefore been satisfied with such Officers as I have had, but which with very few exceptions were much too young and inexperienced for the important situations that they held, but if the few who have experience should be withdrawn my reputation as a Naval Commander will rest upon a very uncertain tenor.

The Idea which I have of Service and which I have cherished ever since I have had the honor to bear a Commission, is that an Officer has no right to question the propriety of an order which he receives from his Superior—it is his business and his duty to obey it—he has no right to select for himself a particular service or be dissatisfied with that assigned to him for it is to be presumed that the head of that Department under which he serves or the Commanding Officer who selects him has done it with a view of his peculiar fitness to perform the service assigned to him— with these impressions I have never asked a change in any order that I have ever received and I should have accepted of the command of a half dozen bark canoes on Lake Superior with as much alacrity as I did the command on these Lakes—

It is a fact that I believe is generally known amongst my Naval Brotherun, that few, if any Officers made greater Sacrifices than myself, both in a pecuniary point of view and in domestic comforts yet I have no disposition to complain— the Government of my Country has thought that I could serve them better upon the Lakes than upon the Atlantic— I am satisfied and altho I have not been fortunate in gathering Laurels, I have the consolation to believe that I have done my duty and I have certainly provided the means for others to reap the harvest— It will be recollected that when I received my appointment 13 months since, that the only vessel owned by the government of the United States upon Lakes Ontario, Erie, Huron, and Michigan, was the little Brig *Oneida*. Since that period there has been two fleets created, one of which has covered itself with glory—the other tho' less fortunate has been quite as industrious— I however acknowledge with gratitude that all this could not have been done but from the unlimited confidence and plenary powers conferred on me by the Navy Department for which I am grateful and my unremitting exertions shall be used to merit a continuance of such confidence.

If the Lake Service is a hard one I have not been exempt from its hardships and its privations, but have shared in common with the other Officers the fatigues and anxieties incident to such a service, yet I should be ashamed to ask a removal before I had accomplished the object for which I was sent.

The removal of Captain Perry from Lake Erie will subject the Department to inconvenience if not loss. I mean in the final settlement of the accounts upon that Lake, for as Captain Perry had discretionary power most of the expenditures were by his orders and if he does not examine and certify to the correctness of the accounts before he leaves the station the Department will not only be subject to imposition, but I shall have much trouble in a final settlement of the accounts upon that Lake.

I have the highest opinion of the zeal and talents of Captain Elliott and as this opinion coincides with yours I shall leave him in command upon Lake Erie after Captain Perry retires— I have instructed him accordingly— Copies of my Letters to him and Captain Perry are herewith inclosed. I have the honor to be very respectfully Sir Yr. Mo. ob. St.

Isaac Chauncey

LS, DNA, RG45, CL, 1813, Vol. 6, No. 168 (M125, Roll No. 31).

Engagement Near the False Ducks

Following the loss of his four schooners in August, Commodore Isaac Chauncey briefly returned to Sackets Harbor to take on provisions. His new schooner Sylph, *carrying sixteen guns, joined the American squadron when they set forth again. She had been launched on 18 August, only twenty-one days after her keel was laid.*

The American fleet encountered the enemy on 11 September amid the False Duck Islands near Kingston. The British at first had the advantage, but when the wind changed Yeo ran for safety into Amherst Bay. Chauncey, with his dull sailing schooners in tow, chased the British squadron but could not bring them to action. The Americans had the advantage of the weather gauge, but Chauncey would not cast off his heavy schooners, nor would he risk taking his vessels into the unknown waters of Amherst Bay.

The encounter off the False Ducks was indecisive but is noteworthy for the degree of caution shown by both commanders. As the stakes in men and ships increased, neither Chauncey nor Yeo seemed willing to risk a battle in which they did not clearly have the upper hand—an attitude that would make a decisive naval battle on Lake Ontario unlikely.

COMMODORE SIR JAMES LUCAS YEO, R.N., TO
ADMIRAL SIR JOHN B. WARREN, R.N.

Copy

His Majestys Ship *Wolfe* off the
false Duck Islands, on Lake
Ontario the 12th. of September 1813.

Sir,

I have the Honor to acquaint you that His Majesty's Squadron under my command, being becalmed off Genesee River, on the 11th. Instant, the Enemys fleet of eleven sail having a partial Wind, succeeded in getting within range of their long twenty four, and thirty two Pounders, and from their having the Wind of us, and the dull sailing of some of our Squadron, I found it impossible to bring them to close Action, we remained in this Mortifying situation five hours, having only six Guns in all the Squadron, that would reach the Enemy, (not a Carronade being fired) at sun set a breeze sprang up from the Westward, when I steered for the false Duck Islands, under which the Enemy could not keep the Weather gage, but be obliged to meet us on equal terms, this however he carefully avoided.

Altho I have to regret the loss of Mr. William Ellery, Midshipman and three Seamen Killed, and Seven Wounded, I cannot but conceive it fortunate that none of the Squadron have received any material damage which must have been considerable, had the Enemy acted with the least spirit, and taken advantage of the Superiority of position they possessed.

I found the Enemy this Cruize reinforced by a new Schooner of 18 Guns 4 of which are long 32 or 42 Pounders, this Vessel is 85 feet Keel, was intended for a large Brig, and was Actually laid down, Built and ready for Sea in Six Weeks.[1] Inclosed is a List of Killed and Wounded— I have the Honor to be Sir Your most obedient humble Servant

(Signed)   James L. Yeo   Commodore

Copy, UkLPR, Adm. 1/2736, pp. 137–38.

1. *Sylph*, a schooner built by Henry Eckford at Sackets Harbor, was laid down 26 July and launched 18 August 1813. She carried 4 long 32-pounders and 12 6-pounders. During the winter of 1813–14, she was rerigged as a brig, and her armament was changed to 2 9-pounders and 16 24-pounder carronades.

Commodore Isaac Chauncey to Secretary of the Navy Jones

U. States Ship Genl Pike
off the Ducks Islands   13th Sepr. 1813

Sir

On the 7th at daylight the Enemies fleet was discovered close in with Niagara River, and from the southward made the signal and weighed with the fleet (prepared for action) and stood out of the River after him; he immediately made all sail to the Northward, we made sail in chase with our heavy schooners in tow and have continued the chase round the Lake night and day untill yesterday morning, when he succeeded in geting into Amherst Bay which is so little known to our pilots and said to be full of shoals that they are not willing to take me in there.— I shall however (unless drove from this station by a Gale of wind) indeavour to watch him so close, as to prevent his geting out upon the Lake.—

During our long chase we frequently got within from one to two miles of the enemy, but our heavy sailing schooners prevented our closing with him untill the 11th off Genesee River we carried a breaze with us while he lay becalmed to within about 3/4 of a mile of him when he took the breaze and we had a runing fight of three & a 1/2 hours, but by his superior sailing he esscaped me and run into Amherst Bay yesterday morning— In the course of our chase on the 11th I got several broadsides from this ship upon the enemy, which must have done him considerable injury as many of the shot was seen to strike him and people was observed over the side pluging shot holes; a few shot struck our Hull and a little riging was cut but nothing of importance not a man was hurt.—

I was much disappointed that Sir James refused to fight me as he was so much superior in point of force, both in Guns and men having upwards of twenty Guns more than we have and heaves a greater weight of shot— I think his object is to gain time to add to his force and play a sure game, or as the boisterous season is approching he may wish to defer an action untill he meets me upon the Lake when it is blowing heavy and to Leeward of him, when my small vessels would be off no service and he might succeed in cuting some of them off—

This ship, the *Madison,* and the *Sylph* has each a Schooner constantly in tow yet the others can not sail as fast as the Enemies squadron which gives him decidedly the advantage and puts it in his power to engage me when and how he chusses— I shall however indeavour to manage this little fleet so as to make it answer the main object for which it was created, even if I am not able to take or destroy the enemies Naval force on this Lake. I have the honor to be Very Res. Sir Your most obt. Humble Servt.

Isaac Chauncey

LS, DNA, RG45, CL, 1813, Vol. 6, No. 43 (M125, Roll No. 31).

SECRETARY OF THE NAVY JONES TO COMMODORE ISAAC CHAUNCEY

Commodore Isaac Chauncey   Navy Department
Commanding the United States Naval forces   Septemr 19th. 1813.
on the Lakes,
Sacketts Harbour

Sir

Your Letters No. 73 to 82 inclusive have been received and your Official Account of the transactions during your efforts to bring the enemy to action, has been published as you will have seen.—

To the elements we must submit for it is not for valor skill and enterprize, to counteract their influence, or command success.

I would not depreciate the talents or the prowess of your antagonist, but an impartial world must impeach his candour and veracity, and unhappily there are those, who appear more disposed to give Credit to the enemy than to those, whose talents and lives are devoted to the protection of the national rights & honor.

The last private advices from Fort George are of the 7th. which place you in pursuit of the enemy with a fine wind, and every prospect of bringing him to close action.

Your Country and its entire Government have seen nothing in your conduct but proofs of zeal skill and intrepidity, and look with confidence to the issue of a combat which it is hoped and believed the fickle elements cannot much longer avert.

Your numerical force in Guns is inferior to that of the enemy, but in everything which constitutes real efficiency you are his equal and I trust will be found his superior.

The Schooner *Sylph* I am persuaded has concentrated more efficient strength than you lost by tempest and capture. Indeed the issue of your present cruize will determine the nature and extent of the force which it will be proper subsequently to employ.— Should you be victorious, your present force will be ample for the future but should the conflict prove indicisive, it will be proper to abandon the least serviceable of the small Vessels and increase our force in Vessels of a more formidable Class. For this purpose, I have recently and privately sounded Messrs. Browns the builders on the subject of building at Sacketts Harbour in the least possible time three sloops of war from the draughts and moulds of the "*Peacock*" now nearly completed by them.[1] Their answer is prompt and decisive, they will undertake it immediately & transport 400 Carpenters to that place the instant we engage. They propose to find all the materials for the Hulls complete. If it shall be determined upon, perhaps Mr. Eckford might be united with them, or undertake one of the Sloops. I await only the issue of your present cruize and your sentiments on the subject.—

The "*Peacock*" is a noble and elegant Vessel 118 feet Gun Deck & 32 feet Beam, capable of carrying 20, 42 pd. Carronades & 2 long 24s.— Her form combines all the properties of fleetness stability and accomodation.— I have sent from this place by the way of Delaware and Jersey, 45 42 pr. Carronades with a special view to this object, they will be in New York in a few days, also a few 24 pd. Carronades which I have desired to be retained there for the Lake service.—

Your Letter to Capt. Perry is certainly calculated to correct the impressions he had cherished, and I trust will have a good effect. By the express mail of yesterday from Pittsburg, a Letter from the Deputy Comissary of Ordnance has a postscript in his hand writing on the cover dated the 15th. instant saying "Com Perry has captured Six British Vessels."— I sincerely hope this may prove to be true.

The Secretary of War will communicate to you his plans of operation, and I have only to request a continuance of that prompt & zealous co-operation which has hitherto distinguished your command.—

I trust you will seize the first possible moment to convene a Court Martial for the trial of Capt. Leonard, and as soon as may be convenient, transmit to this Department correct Muster Rolls of the Officers and Crews, of the several Vessels under your Command, & an approximate estimate of the supplies for the Lake Service during the year 1814.— I am very respectfully Your Obedt. Servt.

W Jones

LB Copy, DNA, RG45, CLS, 1813, pp. 69–71.

1. *Peacock* was built by Adam and Noah Brown at the New York Navy Yard; she was laid down 9 July and launched 19 September 1813, although she did not make her first cruise until March 1814. See pp. 225–29 for more on *Peacock* and the sloops of war built in 1813.

Contest for the Command of Lake Ontario

The movements of the two opposing fleets were watched with great interest from the shores of Lake Ontario. British and American military commanders realized that control of the water route was necessary before a successful land campaign could be waged, and they urged their naval counterparts to action. Both fleets manuevered in an attempt to gain command of the lake.

Commodore Isaac Chauncey conferred with Secretary of War John Armstrong at Sackets Harbor before his fleet sailed on 18 September. Armstrong wanted to move troops from Nia-

gara to Sackets Harbor for the planned assault on Kingston and Montreal, and he re-
quested naval protection for the convoy.

On 28 September, Commodore Chauncey engaged his opponent in a three-hour battle
that came to be known as the "Burlington Races." In the encounter, several vessels on each
side were dismasted, but there were few casualties. The British ran for the protection of the
batteries on Burlington Heights; the American fleet pursued them for several hours, but
broke off the chase when the winds increased to gale force.

While the British repaired their damaged vessels, the American army used the opportu-
nity to convoy troops from Niagara to Sackets Harbor. The British fleet slipped past
Chauncey's blockade and sailed for the eastern end of the lake in order to cooperate with
the British army in protecting Kingston and the Saint Lawrence River. On 4 October, the
Americans captured four schooners and sloops transporting British troops near the False
Ducks off Kingston.

SECRETARY OF WAR ARMSTRONG TO PRESIDENT JAMES MADISON

Sackets harbor   21 Sept. 1813.

Dear Sir,

Commodore Chauncey left this place on the 18th for Fort George. It is obvious that Yeo will continue to refuse a battle. His object will be better answered,
by waiting the campaign & hazarding nothing. I have therefore endeavord to impress the Commodore with the necessity of counteracting this policy—not by
pursuing an enemy who escapes him on system, but by convoying the troops immediately to this post & thus enabling us, to go to our particular object. Several
small measures have been taken to carry the mass of the British land force to the
westward. Even our errors at Fort George, have fortunately favored this plan &
Prevost has so far given into it, as at this moment to have at Kingston and
Prescot, somewhat less than three thousand troops, eleven hundred of which
only, are troops of the line. Prevost himself is again at Kingston. The corps at this
place is now healthy—well supplied and under a course of regular instruction. It
improves daily and will render efficient service. Gen. Hampton has crossed the
lake and will be ready to move by the 25th. I had directed him to carry the Isle
aux Noix, St. John's &c before him, on his way to La Chine. He states this to be
impossible, as Lt. McDonough has not the command of the narrow waters on
which these posts stand. We must therefore, by a well chose position on the
plains, pass up the enemy in their fortresses untill our main object is carried. Of
Gen. Harrison I have heard only, that he would be ready to embark, on the 13th
inst. I have thought it important in various aspects to hold Fort George. The
works, (with a small garrison) as now constructed, will be sufficient against an assault; & a seige, under the present circumstances of the enemy and at the present advanced season of the year is not to be expected. Gen. W. has authority to
organize the friendly Indians and a Corps of volunteers, which, with a body of
militia, will cover our own frontier. Gen. Dearborn's aid de camp is now here &
will perhaps explain the General's wishes. To ask a Court of enquiry, where no
imputation has been made by any agent of the Govt. or officer of the army, is un-
reasonable. Were the removal of an officer from one Mil. command to another,
sufficient cause for courts of enquiry—we should have much (& very useless) occupation, besides that of combating the enemy. We must be cautious therefore

of making a precedent, which will draw after it such consequences. I offer this as an opinion—& am most respectfully, Dear Sir, Your faithful & obedt. servant

J. Armstrong.

Mr. Ellicot was recommended by Mr. Jones—Mr. Roberdeau (who has been his pupil) & several others, highly respectable men from Pena. We have the use of his mathl. astronomical & Philose. apparatus. I never saw, nor had any other kind of intercourse with Mr. Ellicot—& was prompted only by his high character as a Mathematician. The Engineer Corps, or rather its head, Col. Swift, is much pleased with the appointment. If however there are substantial reasons against it—he may be set aside.[1]

ALS, DLC, James Madison Papers, Ser. I, Vol. 53, No. 47.

1. The army was recruiting a force of eight topographical engineers in 1813. Isaac Roberdeau was appointed and assigned to Fort Mifflin; Andrew Ellicott, professor of mathematics at West Point, was a candidate but was not appointed.

COMMODORE ISAAC CHAUNCEY TO SECRETARY OF THE NAVY JONES

U S Ship *Genl. Pike*
Niagara River   25th September 1813

Sir

After I had the honor of addressing you on the 13th, I continued to Blockade the Enemy untill the 17th, when the wind blowing heavy from the westward, the Enemy having run into Kingston, and knowing that he could not move from that place before a change of wind, I took the opportunity of runing into Sackett's Harbor for the purpose of having a personal conference with Genl. Armstrong, the result of which determined me to proceede to this place for the purpose of protecting the Troops down the Lake and also to induce the Enemy to leave his station at Kingston to follow me which would enable me to get between him and that place and either force him to risque an action or suffer us to accomplish our object without it—

I remained but a few hours at the Harbor and left it at daylight on the morning of the 18th, but did not arive here untill yesterday, owing to continual head winds, not having laid our course during the passage. On the 19th I saw the Enemies fleet near the false ducks, but took no notice of him. I wished him to follow me up the Lake.

Genl. Wilkinson informs me that the last of the Troops will be ready to embark on the 28th when himself and suite will come on board of this ship and I shall proceed down the Lake with all the expedition that the nature of the service will admit of— The Troops at the Harbor will be ready to move by the time that we arive there and I calculate that the result of the contemplated opperations will be such as not to disappoint the just expectations of our country

There is a report here, and generally believed, that Capt. Perry has captured the whole of the enemies fleet, on Lake Erie. If this should prove true in all its details (and God grant that it may) he has immortalised himself and not disappointed the high expectations formed of his talents and bravery

I have learnt from a source which can be depended upon that we did the enemy much more injury in our rencounter on the 11th than I had expected— I find that we killed Captain Mulcaster of the *Royal George* and a number of his men and did considerable injury to the ship as well as several of the other vessels.[1] It was truly unfortunate that we could not have brought the enemy to a general action on that day as I am confident that the Victory would have been as complete as that upon Lake Erie— I however have the consolation to know that every exertion was used to bring him to close action if we did not succeede it was not our fault. I yet hope to have the proud satisfaction of communicating to you that Sir Jas. L. Yoe is my prisoner. I have the honor to be Very Respectfully Sir Your obt. Humble Servt.

Isaac Chauncey

LS, DNA, RG45, CL, 1813, Vol. 6, No. 92 (M125, Roll No. 31).

1. Commodore Chauncey was mistaken about the death of William Howe Mulcaster; five seamen were killed and thirteen wounded in that action, but Mulcaster was not among them.

COMMODORE SIR JAMES LUCAS YEO, R.N., TO ADMIRAL SIR JOHN B. WARREN, R.N.

(Copy)

His Majestys Ship *Wolfe* at
the Head of Lake Ontario the
29th September 1813

Sir/

I have the Honor to acquaint you that the Squadron under my Command, having landed supplies for our Army, at the Head of the Lake, proceeded in quest of the Enemys Squadron, which was discovered, (eleven in number that of His Majesty's five,) to Windward of York yesterday morning, the Wind blowing strong from the Eastward. They immediately bore down in a long extended line, our Squadron keeping their Wind under a press of sail, at 12 OClock the *Pike* Commodore Chaunceys Ship being nearly within Gun Shot, our Squadron tacked in succession to close with the Centre and Rear of their line, the Enemy wore at the same time, and the action became general, at one the Main and Mizen Topmasts of this Ship were shot away, by which she became unmanageable on a Wind, and the *Pike* immediately hauled off and took her distance for her long Guns, I therefore put the Squadron before the Wind, for a small Bay at the Head of the Lake where he would have been under the necessity of engaging on more equal terms, this however he declined contenting himself with keeping at the utmost range of his long Guns, and on approaching the Bay he hauled off, leaving us in this state perfectly unmolested to refit the Squadron.

I have deeply to lament the loss of our Masts as otherwise we should in a quarter of an hour have brought them to close Action, but I can assure you Sir, that the great advantage the Enemy have over us from their long 24 Pounders almost precludes the possibility of success, unless we can force them to close action, which they have ever avoided with the most studied circumspection.

The *Pike* had her Main Top Gallant Mast shot away, and appeared cut up in her sails, and Rigging.

The very zealous and active support, I have received from the Captains, Officers, Seamen, and Soldiers, on this as on every occasion justly excites my warmest praise.

On the *Wolfe* losing her Top Masts, the Enemy directed their attention chiefly to disable the *Royal George,* but the steady and well directed fire from that Ship frustrated their design, she was altogether conducted by Captain Mulcaster, with his accustomed energy and zeal.

Captain Spilsbury of the *Melville,* Lieut. Charles Anthony, acting in Command of the *Moira,* during the illness of Captain Dobbs also merit my mark'd approbation, which is likewise due to Lieutenants Cunliffe Owen, in Command of the *Sir Sydney Smith,* and Charles Radcliffe, commanding the *Beresford.*

I return a List of the Killed, and Wounded, and also a statement of the relative strength of the two Squadrons. I have the honor to be with respect Sir, your most obedient humble servant.

(Signed) James Lucas Yeo. Commodore

Copy, UkLPR, Adm. 1/2736, pp. 154–57.

COMMODORE ISAAC CHAUNCEY TO SECRETARY OF THE NAVY JONES

(No. 85) U.S. Ship *General Pike*
Off Niagara 1st. Octor. 1813.

Sir

On the 26th. Ulto. it was reported to me that the Enemy's Fleet was in York— I immediately dispatched the *Lady of the Lake,* to look into York, and ascertain the fact she returned in the Evening with the information that the Enemy was in York Bay— I immediately prepared to weigh but owing to a strong wind from N.N.E. was not able to get out of the River before the Evening of the 27th—and owing to the extreme darkness of the Night, a part of the Squadron got seperated and did not join before next Morning at 8 A.M.— On the 28th. the *General Pike, Madison* and *Sylph,* each took a Schooner in tow and made all sail for York, soon after discovered the Enemy's Fleet under way in York Bay, shaped our course for him and prepared for action— he perceiving our intention of engaging him in his position, tacked and stood out of the Bay—wind at East— I formed the Line and run down for his Centre,—when we had approached within about 3 Miles he made all Sail to the Southward— I wore in succession and stood on the same Tack with him edging down gradually in order to close— at 10 minutes past meridian the Enemy finding that we were closing fast with him and that he must either risk an action or suffer his two rear vessels to be cut off he tacked in succession, beginning at the van, hoisted his Colors and commenced a well directed fire at this Ship, for the purpose of covering his rear, and attacking our rear as he passed to Leeward— perceiving his intention, I was determined to disappoint him— therefore as soon as the *Wolf* (the Leading Ship) passed the centre of his line and abeam of us I bore up in succession (preserving our Line) for the Enemy's Centre— this manoeuvre not only covered our rear but hove him in confusion—he immediately bore away— we had however closed so near as to bring our Guns to bear with effect, and in 20 minutes the Main and Mizen Top Mast and Main Yard of the *Wolf* was shot away— he immediately put before the Wind and set all sail upon his foremast— I made the signal for the Fleet to make all Sail—the Enemy however Keeping dead before the Wind was enabled to out-sail most of our Squadron, as it brought all the Sail upon one Mast, he did not feel the loss of his Main and Mizzen Top Mast— I continued the chase untill near 3 O'Clock during which time I was enabled in this Ship (with the *Asp* in tow) to keep within point blank shot of the Enemy and sustained the whole of his fire during the chase, Capt. Crane in the *Madison* and Lieut. Brown in the *Oneida* used every exertion to close with the Enemy, but the *Madison* having a heavy Schooner in tow and the *Oneida* sailing very dull before the Wind, prevented those Officers from closeing near enough to do any execution with their Carronades. The *Governor Tompkins* kept in her Station, untill her Foremast was so badly wounded as to oblige her to shorten sail— Lieut. Finch of the *Madison* who commanded her for this Cruise (owing to the indisposition of Lieut. Pettigrew) behaved with great gallantry and is an Officer of much promise   Captain Woolsey in the *Sylph* was kept astern, by the *Ontario* which he had in tow, but did considerable exertion with his heavy guns.—

At 15 minutes before 3 P.M. I very reluctantly relinquished the pursuit of a beaten Enemy— the reasons that led to this determination, were such as I flatter myself that you will approve— they were these, at the time I gave up the chase this Ship was making so much water, that it required all our Pumps to keep her free (owing to our receiving several Shot so much below the Water edge, that we could not plug the holes from the outside) the *Governor Tompkins* with her foremast gone and the Squadron within about Six miles of the head of the Lake, blowing a gale of Wind from East and increasing with a heavy Sea on, and every appearance of the Equinox, I considered that if I chased the Enemy to his anchorage at the head of the Lake I should be obliged to anchor also, and altho' we might succeed in driving him on Shore, the probability was that we should go on shore also—he amongst his friends, we amongst our Enemies and after the gale abated, if he could succeed in getting off one or two vessels out of the two Fleets, it would give him as completely the command of the Lake as if he had Twenty Vessels,— moreover he was covered at his anchorage by a part of his army and several small Batteries thrown up, for the purpose, therefore if we could have rode out the gale we should have been cut up by their ~~hot~~ Shot from the Shore— under all these circumstances and taking into view the consequences resulting from the loss of our Superiority on the Lakes at this time, I without hesitation relinquished the opportunity then presenting itself of acquiring individual reputation at the expense of my Country—

The loss sustained by this Ship was considerable owing to her being so long exposed to the fire of the whole of the Enemys Fleet, but our most serious loss was occasioned by the bursting of one of our Guns, which killed and wounded 22 Men and tore up the Top Gallant forecastle which rendered the Gun upon that deck useless.— we had four other Guns cracked in the Muzzle which rendered their use extremely doubtful— our Main Top gallant Mast was shot away in the early part of the action, and the Bow Spirit, Fore and Main Mast wounded, rigging and Sails much cut up and a number of Shot in our hull, several of which were between wind and water and 27 Men killed and wounded including those by the bursting of the Gun— The *Madison* received a few Shot, but no person hurt on board   The *Governor Tompkins* lost her Foremast and the *Oneida* her Main Top Mast badly wounded— we have however repaired nearly all our damage and are ready to meet the Enemy— during our chase one if not two of the Enemys small vessels was completely in our power, if I could have been satisfied with so partial a victory, but I was so sure of the whole that I passed them unnoticed, by which means they finally escaped—

The Gale continued untill last Night, but the Wind still blows from the Eastward— I thought it important to communicate with General Wilkinson to ascertain when he meant to move with the Army— I therefore run off this place for that purpose and he thinks that the public service will be promoted by my watching Sir James at the head of the Lake and if possible prevent his return to Kingston, while he proceeds with the Army for Sacketts Harbor, I shall therefore proceed immediately in quest of the Enemy.—

I have great pleasure in acknowledging the assistance I received from Captain Sinclair[1] during our Chase in using his best exertions to bring this Ship into close action, the other officers and Men behaved to my perfect satisfaction, and were extremely anxious to close with the Enemy even singly, and if he ever gives us an opportunity for close action, they will show that they are not inferior to any of their Countrymen. I have the hononor to be very respectfully Sir Yr. Mo. Ob. St.

Isaac Chauncey

LS, DNA, RG45, CL, 1813, Vol. 6, No. 115 (M125, Roll No. 31). The enclosed list of killed and wounded on board *General Pike* has not been reproduced here.

1. Arthur Sinclair was promoted to captain on 24 July 1813.

COMMODORE SIR JAMES LUCAS YEO, R.N., TO
GOVERNOR-GENERAL SIR GEORGE PREVOST

Sir Sidney Kingston
7th. Octr. 1813.

Sir,

The Courier being on the point of going off I have only time to announce to Your Excellency the arrival of the Squadron off Collinses Bay in the Bay of Cante, where I have left them for the purpose of protecting Kingston to the Westward, and ready to go down either Channel to the Eastd. as circumstances may make necessary.

It is with much regret I find the Convoy Captured by the Enemy's Squadron—particularly as it proceeded from the obstinacy or stupidity of Lieutt. Macklean who instead of keeping in with our shore as he was ordered & was recommended the evening he was captured—stood over to the Real Duck Islands and the wind coming [from] the NNE he could not regain his own shore.

The *Enterprize* which was the worst sailing Vessel, came in safe— she was in tow of the *Hamilton* at the time they saw the Enemy & recommended ~~going~~ Lieutt. Macklean to go inside the False Ducks—or be cast off—which they did & had they all followed his example, would have escaped also.

General de Rottenburg will have informed Your Excellency of his motive for himself & the squadron coming down the Lake— I left him at the Head of the Lake on the 5th. in the Evening.

Colonel Drummond with his party will be here this Evening.

I am doing every thing in my power to get as many Gun-Boats ready as possible & shall man them from the squadron until the Seamen arrive.

Your letter to me left this for York, four hours before my arrival. I have the Honor to remain with respect Sir Your Excellency's Most obedient humble Servant.

James Lucas Yeo

ALS, CaOOA, British Military and Naval Records, RG8, I, "C" Ser., Vol. 731, pp. 5–7.

COMMODORE ISAAC CHAUNCEY TO SECRETARY OF THE NAVY JONES

No. 91   U.S. Ship *General Pike*—
                                              Sacketts Harbor   8 Octo. 1813

Sir

As soon as the last of the Flotilla with the Troops cleared the Niagara I proceeded in quest of the Enemy—on 2d inst. at 10 a.m. discovered him steering a course for Niagara with Studding sails and all sails set—Wind from the South & Westward, we made all sail in chace but as soon as we shot out from the Land so that he could fairly make us out he took in Studdingsails and hauled upon a wind to the Westward and made all sail from us the Wind being light all day we made but little progress against the Current and at Sun down the Enemy was off the 20 Mile Creek and had evidently gained considerably from us, during the night the Wind continued so light that we altered our position but very little and at day light on the 3d. saw the Enemy at anchor close in with the Land between the 12 and 20 Mile Creek as soon as he saw us he weighed and made all sail to the Westward. Wind from South to South West and squally I made Sail in chase and continued the chase the whole day it blowing very heavy in Squalls— at Sundown we could barely make him out from the Mast head when he appeared nearly up to the Head of the Lake it continued squally, with rain and the Night very dark— at day-light on the 4th hazy could see nothing of the Enemy—continued working up for the head of the Lake, towards Meridian it became calm I ordered the *Lady of the Lake* to sweep up to Burlington Bay and ascertain whether the Fleet was there— at half past 9 P.M. She returned with information that the fleet was not there. Saw but two Gun Boats— It struck me at once that he had availed himself of the darkness of the preceding night and had either run for Kingston or down the Lake, for the purpose of intercepting the Flotilla with the Army, I therefore made all sail and shaped my course for the Ducks, with a view of intercepting him or his prizes if he should have made any. The Wind increased to a strong gale from the Northward and Westward and continued during the whole day on the 5th we therefore made a great run for at 1 P.M. we passed Long Point— at 3 discovered 7 Sail near the False Ducks presuming them to be the Fleet made Sail in chase at 4 made them out to be Sloops and Schooners I made the Signal for the *Sylph* and the *Lady of the Lake* to cast off their Tow and chace N.E. soon after perceiving the Enemy seperateing on different Tacks, I cast off the *Governor Tompkins* from this Ship, gave the squadron in charge of Capt. Crane and made all sail in chase, at 5 the Enemy finding us to gain fast upon him and one of his Gun vessels sailing much worse than the rest he took the people out and set her on fire at Sundown, when opposite the real ducks, the *Hamilton* (late *Growler*) *Confiance* (late *Julia*) and *Mary Ann* struck to us— the *Sylph* soon after brought down the *Drummond* cutter rigged— the *Lady Gore* run into the Ducks, but the *Sylph* (which was left to watch her) took possession of her early the next morning— the *Enterprize* a small Schooner is the only one that escaped and she owed her safety to the darkness of the Night.

Finding much difficulty in shifting the prisoners, owing to the smallness of our boats and a heavy Sea I determined to take the prizes in tow and run for this place and land the prisoners and Troops that I had on board we arrived here at day light— on the 6th the *Lady of the Lake* having towed one of the prizes in I dispatched her immediately to cruise between the real and False Ducks She returned the same afternoon, having discovered the Enemy's Squadron going into Kingston.—

I have repaired the principal damage sustained by this Ship in the action on the 28th. Ulto. and have put a new Fore mast into the *Governor Tompkins*— we are now ready and waiting the movement of the Army which is contemplated will leave here on the 10th.

The vessels captured on the 5th. are Gun vessels mounting from 1 to 3 Guns each with Troops from the head of the Lake (but last from York) bound to Kingston— We learn't from the Prisoners that the Enemy was very much cut up in their Hulls and Spars and a great many men killed and wounded particularly on board of the *Wolf* and *Royal George*. I inclose herewith a List of the prisoners taken on the 5th. I have the honor to be very respectfully Sir yr. Mo. Obt. St.

                                                    Isaac Chauncey

LS, DNA, RG45, CL, 1813, Vol. 6, No. 147 (M125, Roll No. 31).

COMMODORE ISAAC CHAUNCEY TO SECRETARY OF THE NAVY JONES

No. 92   U.S. Ship *General Pike*
                                          Sacketts Harbor.   8th Octo. 1813
Sir
    Your Letter of the 19th Ulto.[1] conveying to me the undiminished confidence of yourself and government was truly gratefull to my feelings, particularly at this time, and will stimulate to still greater exertions, (if greater was possible) for the accomplishment of the object and wishes of the Executive, altho' an Officer may be conscius himself of having done all that it was possible for him to do in the execution of his duty, yet he may fall far short of the expectations and wishes of his Employers, consequently suffer (tho' innocently) in his reputation.—

    Fifteen years of the best part of my life has been devoted to the Service of my Country, the remaining years and the small portion of talents that I possess, with life itself, is still at her service and if I am so fortunate as to execute the various duties intrusted to me by the Government of my Country to its satisfaction, it is immaterial what the opinions of the opposition may be with respect to me and my conduct—

    I am still in hopes to be able to bring the Enemy to close action, if I do, I am confident of success— a few days must determine— I have no idea, that Sir

James will come out and fight me upon the open Lake, but in a few days I shall take a possition for the purpose of covering the Troops in landing near Kingston which I think will induce the British Commodore to risk an action in which the Supremacy of this Lake must be determined— if I am as successfull as I hope to be we have force enough— but if the Enemy should be triumphant he not only destroys this Fleet, but preserves Kingston, which will enable him to encrease his present force so, as to preserve his ascendancy upon the Lake— but if any circumstance should prevent a meeting of the Two Fleets this Fall, and the Enemy should retain possession of Kingston it would be necessary for us to build a sufficient number of Vessels to meet him in the Spring upon equal terms,—to do this we must build vessels of an equal class— From the best information that I can get, there is materials prepared at Kingston for three vessels— Two of them are in some state of forwardness,—one of these Vessels is to be a Frigate— the length of her keel obtained from various sources is 150 feet—a part of her frame is already raised— the other two are to be 20 Gun Ships or Brigs.

Altho' I have the highest opinion of Messrs. A. & N. Brown—yet as Mr. Eckford has built 4 vessels at this place, and has become acquainted with the resources and people of this part of the Country, I think that he could have built sooner, and perhaps cheaper than any other Man, and as to his talents as a Ship Carpenter I am bold to say, that there is not his equal in the U. States, or perhaps in the World— his exertions here was unexampled— the *Madison* was built in 45 working days in a new Country, where every thing was transported from New York except the Timber— The *General Pike* would have been launched in 40 days, except from the circumstance of my being obliged to send Mr. Eckford with 35 of his best workmen to Black Rock where he rebuilt and fitted out five vessels in less than 30 days,—returned to this place and launched the *Pike* in 62 days from the time her keel was laid— The *Sylph* a Schooner of 340 Tons was built in 21 days—

Such exertions on the part of Mr. Eckford, I should humbly hope would entitle him to a share of public patronage and from your known liberality I trust that you will at least make him an Offer, as it must be extremely mortifying to him to see others preferred after his best exertions had been used to obtain the confidence of his government—

With respect to Captain Leonard I do assure you Sir, that I am as anxious as he possibly can be, to bring him to trial, and not one moment shall be lost in doing so, whenever it will not interfere with the public service, a few weeks cannot make so great a difference to him—the cruizing Season is almost over— when the trial can take place without injury to the public service.— In fact it may be convenient to convene a Court when the Squadron next returns to Port—if so it shall be done.

Muster Rolls shall be forwarded to the Department, as soon as they can be made out—as also estimates for the ensuing year— I have the honor to be very Respectfully Sir Yr. Ob. Hbe. St.

Isaac Chauncey

LS, DNA, RG45, CL, 1813, Vol. 6, No. 146 (M125, Roll No. 31).

1. See pp. 581–82.

Joint Operations on the Saint Lawrence River

The army's campaign against Kingston and Montreal seemed doomed from the start. Delays postponed the embarkation of the troops until mid-October, a time when early winter storms made navigation uncertain. Secretary of War John Armstrong tried to direct the attack from Sackets Harbor, but he could not extract cooperation between his two commanders, Major General Wade Hampton on Lake Champlain and Major General James Wilkinson on Lake Ontario. Even the objective of the campaign was still undecided when the army embarked troops on the Saint Lawrence River in mid-October.

Commodore Isaac Chauncey was angered when he learned that the army had finally determined to attack Montreal instead of Kingston (which had been the original objective of the 1813 campaign). A reduction of the British naval base at Kingston would benefit the navy the following season, but an attack on Montreal offered no such advantage. Chauncey objected to the navy's being used as a mere transport service for the army with little role in strategic planning.

The American armies did not fare well in the late fall season. General Hampton's division, on its movement from Plattsburg, was defeated in the Battle of Chauteauguay on 25–26 October. General Wilkinson's army was attacked by British vessels at French Creek on 1 November and was defeated in the Battle of Chrysler's Farm ten days later. These setbacks ended the campaign on the Saint Lawrence River for the year.

SECRETARY OF WAR ARMSTRONG TO PRESIDENT JAMES MADISON

Sackets harbor
17th Oct. 1813.

Dear Sir,

Our troops left Fort George for this place under the command of Gen. Boyd on the 30th ult. On the 3d. instant the enemy had notice of this movement. On the 9th. after burning his surplus stores & baggage, he began his march for Burlington bay, which he reached on the night of the 11th & whence, it is said, he has arrived at Kingston, by the bay of Quanta, with 1200 sick and convalescent and 1500 effective rank & file. The whole of Boyd's division is not yet here! With nine days start of the enemy, what might not have been done? At Kingston, we shall no longer find him naked & napping. He is sufficiently awake to our designs and sufficiently strong to make an obstinate resistance. Before De Rottenberg's arrival, his whole regular force did not exceed 1200 men. What we do now at this point, must be done by hard blows, perhaps by tedious operations. Frost, hail and snow admonish us against the latter. To reinstate our superiority of force, Hampton's Division may be brought up to join us—but this also would produce delay & compel us to abandon the other and better object below. Under these circumstances it remains to choose whether we shall attempt Kingston by assault or proceed directly to Montreal. This will be decided at Grenadier Island, whither the first division of the army sailed yesterday. The second would have followed to-day but for the intervention of a most violent storm. Wilkinson is indisposed, but better than he has been.

I have received two letters from Gen. Williams wishing employment in the Creek war. This arrangement would I think be very useful. The British fleet having gone to Halifax, there is no probability that he will be wanted on the Sea-board. I should accordingly have ordered him on the south western service, had I been sure that it would have entirely conserted with your arrangements. If under these he cannot be first, he may perhaps be second. Should this suggestion be approved, it would save time were he informed directly of it. I am Sir, with the highest respect, Your most obedient & faithful servant

John Armstrong

ALS, DLC, James Madison Papers, Ser. I, Vol. 53, No. 66.

COMMODORE SIR JAMES LUCAS YEO, R.N., TO GOVERNOR-GENERAL SIR GEORGE PREVOST

His Majesty's Ship *Wolfe*
at Kingston   17th. October 1813

Sir/

I have had the Honor to receive your Excellencys Letter of the 14th. Inst. as also seen your communication to Major General De Rottenburgh, by which I perceive your anxiety that every effort should be made by the Squadron to stop and defeat the Enemys Flotilla going down the St. Lawrence.

I have therefore (as the only alternative left to accomplish that object) ordered such part of the Squadron, as can act in the River, down to the East End of long or Wolfe Island, until all the Gun Boats, can be collected from Prescott, as that narrow Channel properly Blockaded, will in my opinion leave the Navigation as safe as if the Gun Boats were with the Convoys, that is for a few days until we can be assured of the Enemys real intention, for if they go down the River, it would be necessary to have all the Gun Boats, collected and ready to follow them up. I have consulted every Pilot as to the practicability of the two Ships being of any use in the narrow Waters, and they all agree that they can go down the River to Prescott, with a fair Wind, but that, there is not room to manoeuvre or Work them in the narrow Channel, I therefore do not like to risk them unless the Enemys Squadron go down, in which case they are all ready to follow, or to do their utmost in repeling the Enemy on an Attack on this place.

It is with the greatest reluctance I divide the Squadron, and nothing but your Excellencys pointed Instructions on that head could have induced me to do it, as I have a strong presentiment that Kingston is the place they will Attack, particularly if they hear that we have divided our force—or they may take advantage of it and go up to York, these being my sentiments, I request your Excellency will explicitly make known to me your opinion as to the disposition I have made that any other arrangement may be made without delay.

I am both surprised and disappointed at Captain Barclays not having written or dictated a line on the Subject of his Action.

Your Excellency having in your note of the 19th. of September requested me to make known to you my unreserved sentiments upon subjects of Public concerns, was my reason for informing you of the Shipwrights leaving the Yard, as I am convinced that unless some effort is made to retain those we have, and obtain a number of others to join,—the present force of the Yard is very inadequate to the service they have to perform, as the Total Number of Shipwrights now Employed in the Yard only amounts to fifty four. I have the Honor to be with respect Sir, your Excellency's most obedient humble servant

James Lucas Yeo   Commodore

P.S. 10 P.M. a Man has this moment returned from Sackets Harbour by whom we have received such information, as to make it more necessary than ever keeping the Squadron together a chain of signals post are Established between this and the East End of long Island, [and] also one on the Island opposite Kingston, I therefore have no doubt but that I shall receive any information of the Enemys movements in sufficient time to repair to any Point

J. L. Y.

LS, CaOOA, British Military and Naval Records, RG8, I, "C" Ser., Vol. 731, pp. 47–51.

COMMODORE ISAAC CHAUNCEY TO SECRETARY OF THE NAVY JONES

No. 101   U States Ship *Genl Pike*
                                    off Stony Island   30th October 1813

Sir

By request of Majr. General Wilkinson, I visited him yesterday at his Quarters on Grenidear Island for the purpose of making final arrangements as to the co-operation of the Fleet, with the Army, in its opperations against the enemy—

I was much disapointed and mortifyed to find that the General had taken his determination to decend the St. Lawrence and attack Montreall in preference to Kingston, disapointed because in all our consultations upon this subject for the last four weeks Kingston was fixed upon as the point to be first attacked, and when I parted with the Secretary at War on the 16th I understood that it was his decided oppinion that Kingston should be first reduced, mortifyed to find that the Navy had been used as a mear attendant upon the Army for the purpose of Transport and protection and when it could be no longer used for those purposes and the season too far advanced to cruise on the Lake with safety it is left to protect itself in the best manner it can without the possibility of participating in any enterprize against the enemy this season

To my mind there are various and important objections to attacking Montre-all at this advanced season of the year and leaving Kingston in full possession of the enemy in the rear, I will state those that strike me as the most prominent

1st   The enemy for the last month has been under the impression that Mon-treall was the point to be attacked consequently he is better prepared there than Kingston and we have certain information that he has fortifyed the differ-ent passes in the river particularly about the rapids so as to annoy and cut up our troops in their passage down the River; this will oblige the Genl. to land at each of those fortifyed passes and take possession of them to insure a safe pas-sage to his Army these necessary detentions will probably prevent his arrival in the visinity of Montreall, untill late in November, this will enable the enemy to draw the whole of his disposeable force from Quebeck to the protection of that Island, and possibly be able to keep our Army in check for ten or fifteen days longer and when he is eventually obliged to abandon the city and Island, to our troops, we shall be reduced by sickness and death, to probably, eight or nine thousand men this force will be constantly diminishing during the winter and in the spring, the enemy may and probably will transport an army of double that force to Montreall which he can readily do as sloops of war and transports can assend the river quite to that Island.

If therefore the force that may be collected at Kingston, this winter should act, in concert with those from Quebeck in the spring it would place our Army in a perilous situation and possibly eventuate in their defeat and surrender

The second objection to the Generals determination to attack Montreall in preference to Kingston, is, that the latter place may be occupied by our troops in ten days and I think with less loss than we shall sustain at Montreall,— The possession of Kingston would place in our hands an immense quantity of stores both of provisions clothing and munitions of war and also the whole of the enemies fleet on this Lake which would enable the army to persue its conquests uninteruptedly, it would also enable the Government to withdraw a large number of officers and seamen for other objects besides avoiding the expense of making any addition to our Naval force on this Lake which can be no longer usefull, than while the enemy has possession of the province above Kingston

Another view of this subject is that the occupation of Kingston presents as many advantages to the final conquest of the uper province as that of Montreall and many more to our own troops; for if the army landed below Kingston (as proposed) the enemy would be obliged to retreat upon York where he could not procure supplys for such a body of men, moreover it would place him between General Harrison's Army and the one at Kingston, which would oblige him to surender at discretion, and place in our power between four and five thousand men; besides this advantage over the enemy, our own troops would occupy a position perfectly secure from any attack, either this winter or spring and at the same time be in the visinity of a deposit at Sacketts Harbor; (made safe by their situation,) from which they could draw supplys or reinforcements— I will venture to say that in one month after our troops occupy Kingston there would not be a hostile soldier to the Westward of Montreall, which would render that city less an object of protection to the enemy.

The third and not the least objection to the determination of the General, of leaving Kingston in the full and quiet possession of the enemy and withdrawing the whole of the force from Sacketts Harbor, is that it exposes the fleet and stores to certain and total distruction the ensueing winter; for if the enemy collects the whole of his force from the different points of the upper province at Kingston he will have, from the best information between from four and five thousand regular soldiers; with this force he can (after the first of January) cross on the Ice to Sacketts Harbor in one day, burn the fleet and Town and return to Kingston, without difficulty; in fact I should not be astonished if Sir James should take advantage of a westerly wind while I am down the St. Lawrence and run over to the Harbor and burn it which he certainly can do if he knows its defenseless situation; for to the best of my knowledge there is no troops left there except sick and invalids nor is there more than three Guns mounted.

I however concieve it to be my duty to afford to the Army every facility of Transport and protection in my power, I shall therefore accompany and protect it untill it passes a point beyond which it will be perfectly secure from annoyance by the enemies fleet. I shall then make the best of my way out of the St.

Lawrence as it is deemed unsafe to be in that River after the first of November, on account of the Ice—

I have deemed it to be my duty, thus briefly to state to you, Sir, my objections to the contemplated movement of the Army, and my fears for the consequences of such movement; I beg at the same time to assure you, that my exertions shall not be relaxed for the preservation of this fleet and the protection of the Army; nor my prayers, withheld for the complete success of our arms, against the enemy, both by land and water   I have the honor to be with great respect Sir Yr. most obt. humble Servt.

Isaac Chauncey

LS, DNA, RG45, CL, 1813, Vol. 7, No. 63 (M125, Roll No. 32).

Acting Captain William Howe Mulcaster, R.N., to Commodore Sir James Lucas Yeo, R.N.

(Copy)
His Majesty's Sloop Melville,
East End of long Island
2nd. November 1813

Sir/

I have the Honor to acquaint you that His Majestys Sloops *Melville*, and *Moira*, accompanied by 4 Gun Boats, formed a junction with the *Sir Sidney Smith*, and *Beresford* Schooners, yesterday morning, and I instantly made an arrangement with the Commanders of those Vessels for an immediate attack on the Enemy's Position at French Creek, as soon as we could see through the Snow. The Squadron Weighed, and made Sail, the Enemy had posted a strong detachment of Infantry on the Bluff, at the entrance of the Creek, to pour Musquetry on the Vessels Decks, the Bluff, was passed by His Majesty's Squadron within hail, receiving the fire of the Enemy, and returning discharges of Grape and Canister,—they were compelled to abandon their Post with precipitation, nor was it again reoccupied during our stay.

On rounding the Bluff the Enemy appeared in great force, drawn up in three Columns, with a Battery of two brass 18 Pounders in Front, and a numerous train of Artillery on their Flanks, I anchored the *Melville, Moira,* and *Sir Sidney Smith,* in Order of Battle, (there not being room for the *Beresford,* owing to the narrow Entrance of the Creek) a sharp Cannonading now commenced from the Ships, which was well returned from the shore, for near an hour.

On a preconcerted Signal being made the Gun Boats, under Capt. Spilsbury, put off and pulling along the Eastern bank, kept up an animated fire; as the day was closing fast, and the Enemys Troops could no longer be discerned from the thickness of the Trees, so as to fire at them with precision, and the Squadron having received several shot in their Hulls, and a few between Wind and Water, I thought it right to haul off for the night.

The Wind was too strong for the Gun Boats, to pull in, and annoy the Enemy in the middle of the night, as had been intended; however at Daylight the Wind abated, and the Squadron again passed, and Exchanged fire with the Batteries;— The Enemy had mounted several Guns in the night, and some red-hot Shot, came on board the Squadron.

The Scows, and Bateaux, of the Enemy were hauled upon the Shore, to have brought off or destroyed them, would have cost an immense number of Men (considering the fine Position of the Enemy) which I could not afford, having to guard against the Enemys Squadron in the morning.

One Merchant Schooner without a Soul on board, was afloat, but a Boat came off and cut her Cables, as we rounded the Bluff, and she drifted on the Rocks; I am happy to say our loss has been trifling, one Seamen Killed, Mr. Walter Leslie, Master's Mate, and 4 Seamen Wounded.

From the manner in which the Enemys Troops were at times exposed, I am warranted in saying they must have lost Men.

I have much satisfaction in Reporting to you the great exertions of Captains, Spilsbury and Dobbs, of Lieuts., Radcliffe, of the *Beresford*, and Owen, of the *Sir Sidney Smith*, and all the Officers, and Men, both in the Squadron, and Gun Boats, whom you did me the Honor to place under my command. I have the Honor to be Sir your most obedient humble Servant

(Signed)　　W. H. Mulcaster　Actg. Captain

Copy, UkLPR, Adm. 1/2736, pp. 186–89. Copy enclosed in letter from Commodore Sir James Lucas Yeo to Admiral Sir John B. Warren of 3 November 1813.

COMMODORE ISAAC CHAUNCEY TO SECRETARY OF THE NAVY JONES

No. 106　　　　　　　　　　　　　　　　　U.S. Ship *General Pike*
　　　　　　　　　　　　Sacketts Harbor　11th. Novemr. 1813

Sir

I had the honor on the 4th inst. of informing you that the Squadron was then at anchor off the East end of Long Island and that the Army was collected at French Creek a little below me.—

I have now the honor to inform you that the whole of the Army left its position at French Creek on the 5th and proceeded down the River with a fair Wind and fine Weather.— The same day the Enemy's fleet dropped down below Kingston on the North side of Long Island and anchored off Sir Johns Island within about five Miles of me— the North and South Channels, in which the two Fleets lay are separated by a chain of Small Islands, connected by reefs of Rocks, and there is but one passage (which is situated near the foot of Long Island) that Vessels can pass from one channel to the other, and in this passage vessels drawing more than twelve feet Water, cannot pass— I however determined to attack the Enemy, if he remained in his position, and I could get this Ship through the reef which separated us—for this purpose I meant to lighten the *General Pike* and *Sylph* and warp them through— early on the Morning of the 6th I sent boats to sound out the best Water in the channel and buoy it out— the moment that the Enemy perceived us, he weighed and run up under the Guns at Kingston, which made it unnecessary for us to get our Fleet into the North Channel.

I was apprehensive that when the Enemy found that our Army had descended the St. Lawrence and that he had nothing to apprehend for the safety of Kingston, that he would take on board a thousand Men and take possession of Carlton Island which would have given us much trouble, and perhaps led to the final destruction of the Fleet.—

Upon Carlton Island there is a regular work and very strong both by nature and Art and a thousand Men with a few pieces of Cannon would command the Channel most completely and would prevent a fleet much stronger than ours from passing up or down— knowing the commanding situation of this Island I felt anxious (after the Enemy returned to Kingston) to take a position near it, so as to command the passage from the Westward and prevent him from taking possession. I accordingly shifted my station from the foot of Long Island to Carlton Island where I remained untill the Evening of the 9th. when I changed my anchorage to Gravelly Point— there I lay untill yesterday, when from the threatening appearance of the Weather I was induced to leave the River and proceed for this place, where the Squadron arrived safe this Morning— It is now blowing a heavy Gale from the Westward with Snow, and every appearance of the Winter having set in.

From the 2d. to the 10th. the Weather has been uncommonly fine—the Winds prevailed from the Southward and Westward and clear dry Weather, and as mild as the Autumns are in the Middle States— the Army could not have asked for a more favorable time, which I have no doubt, but that the General has taken advantage of and I presume by this time is in Montreal. I have the honor to be very respectfully Sir Yr. Mo. Obt. St.

Isaac Chauncey

LS, DNA, RG45, CL, 1813, Vol. 7, No. 93 (M125, Roll No. 32).

Commodore Isaac Chauncey to Major General James Wilkinson, U.S.A.

Major General James Wilkinson   U.S. Ship *General Pike*
Commr. in Chief of the Amn. forces   Sacketts Harbor   12th. Novem 1813
at or near Montreal— &c &c &c

Dear General

I arrived here yesterday and left the River the day before in consequence of the threatening appearance of the Weather which has really set in now to be Winter— from the time that you left French Creek untill the 10th. I never in my life saw finer Weather which rejoiced me on your account and I have no doubt but that you profited by it and reached Montreal before this bad Weather commenced and are now in Snug Quarters taking a Comfortable Glass of Wine, which I will do this day to your health

Your rear was not out of Sight on the 5th. when the whole of the Enemys fleet with several Gun Boats dropped down within about five Miles of me where they lay untill the next day when observing me making some preparations to get into the North Channel where he lay he moved up under the Guns at Kingston.—

I shall endeavour to run up to Fort George to bring a part of General Harrison's Army down for the protection of this place, after which I shall lay up for the Winter.—

Will you, my Dear General have the goodness to send me an order to take possession of Fort Tompkins and the Block House near it   I don't know whether you are knowing to the circumstance, but the fact is nevertheless true, that the ground upon which Fort Tompkins and the Block House stand, is under lease to the Navy Department for which I pay a heavy Ground Rent— The Fort was built by the labor and materials of the Navy and was lent to the Army at a time, when we had no use for it— the Block House, tho' built at the expense of the War Department was delivered over to the Navy by order of General Dearborn and has been occupied by us untill within a few Days, when Col. Dennis ordered all our people out of it— my reason for wishing the Block House and Fort Tompkins is to occupy them with Marines and Seamen for the Protection of the fleet during the Winter. Wishing you Health Honor, and Happiness, I have the honor to be Dear Sir Yr. Mo. Ob. St.

I. C.—

LB Copy, NHi, Isaac Chauncey Letter Book.

COMMODORE ISAAC CHAUNCEY TO SECRETARY OF THE NAVY JONES

No. 111.   U.S. Ship *General Pike*
Sacketts Harbor   21 Novemr. 1813

Sir

I had the honor of addressing you on the 15th inst. from off Niagara— On the 16th I received on board of the fleet General Harrison and Suite and about 1100 Troops and got the whole of the fleet out of the River— the Wind however continued from the Eastward, and on the 17th increased to a gale and continued to blow with increasing violence attended with Snow and heavy rains untill the Night of the 19th when it changed to the Westward which enabled me to arrive here last Evening with this Ship.

The Fleet was separated the first Night of the gale, and as the Weather continued thick I was not able to collect them afterwards— I was drove by the violence of the Gale to nearly the head of the Lake and as I knew that this Ship was a much better Sailor than the rest of the fleet I was extremely anxious for their safety— I was however somewhat relieved on the 19th when in Stretching in towards Niagara, I found that the *Madison* was at anchor in that River— at 12 OClock that Night the Wind changed to the Westward and blew with some violence— I shaped my course for this place as I had ordered the vessels in case of seperation to run for Sacketts Harbor and as it was in my power to amuse the Enemy (in case he was out) and give the Small vessels an opportunity to get in— I arrived last Evening, and the *Sylph* in about one hour after me, the *Oneida, Lady of the Lake, Conquest, Pert,* and *Ontario* arrived this Morning—the four former from Niagara where they put in during the Gale without any material injury— they left at that place the *Madison, Fair American* and *Governor Tompkins,* the *Madison* with but little injury—the *Governor Tompkins* with the loss of her rudder, and the *Fair American* on shore, but expected to be got off this day— I am sorry however to inform you that the *Julia* is missing— She has not been seen by any of the Squadron, since the first night of our Separation, and I am apprehensive that She has either foundered or gone on shore.[1]

The Troops and Seamen suffered extremely, as they were wet from the commencement of the Gale, untill their arrival here—the Water was so deep on the birth deck, that we were obliged to scuttle it to let the Water off,—yet the Men arrived in better health, than could have been expected.—

I am in great hopes, that the *Madison* and *Governor Tompkins,* will be in this Evening as the Wind is fair if they Should not I shall proceed tomorrow off the Ducks, to Watch the movements of the Enemy, untill the arrival of all our Vessels, or untill I am satisfactorily informed of their situation. I have the honor to be very respectfully Sir Yr. Mo. ob. st.

Isaac Chauncey

LS, DNA, RG45, CL, 1813, Vol. 7, No. 114 (M125, Roll No. 32).

1. All the American vessels returned safely to Sackets Harbor; see Chauncey to Jones, 24 Nov. 1813, DNA, RG45, CL, 1813, Vol. 7, No. 126 (M125, Roll No. 32).

Prisoners of War in Canada

What constituted just treatment of prisoners during the War of 1812 was never satisfactorily resolved by the United States and Great Britain. Charges of harsh treatment on both sides were frequent. Americans told of being forced to navigate British vessels or even to fight against their own countrymen. Both American and British seamen complained of crowded and dirty housing, spoiled food, and mistreatment.

British authorities sent naturalized American citizens whom they claimed as British subjects to England to be tried on charges of treason—a crime punishable by death. The United States, in May 1813, determined to retaliate for the imprisonment of twenty-three Irish-Americans captured at the Battle of Queenston in 1812. When these prisoners were sent to England as royal subjects to await trial, American officials ordered twenty-three British prisoners held in close confinement, to suffer the same fate if their counterparts in England were put to death. Great Britain responded by holding an additional forty-six men as hostages, with the United States following suit. The situation escalated until virtually all American and British officers were held in close confinement by 1814. Officers had previously been released on parole and allowed to return home or to enjoy the freedom of a town until they were formally exchanged. The system of retaliations practiced by the United States and Great Britain in 1813 and 1814 resulted in worsening conditions for prisoners of both nations.[1]

1. On the topic of prisoners of war, see Dietz, "Cartel Vessels"; Dye, "Maritime Prisoners"; and Robinson, "Prisoners." For a description of the treatment of seamen captured in Canada and sent to Melville Island, Halifax, see Cooper, Ned Myers, pp. 99–136.

DEPOSITION OF ABRAHAM WALTER

State of New York
<u>Clinton County</u>

Abraham Walter formerly Pilot to the Sloop of War *Growler* on Lake Champlain, being duly sworn deposeth and Saith, that he was employed on board that Sloop when it was taken by the British in June last that after the Sloops *Growler* and *Eagle* were surrendered, the prisioners both Officers and Sailors were taken to Quebec where they were immediately confined on board a Prision Ship. there they were examined by a Public officer or Examiner and about Eight or ten of the prisioners were declared to be British Subjects; these were immediately separated from the rest put on board a Man of War and Sent to England to be tried for treason. One of these was Known to be a native of New hampshire by Capt. Herrick of the Newhampshire Volunteers who was also a Prisioner, & who had known him from his infancy—and several of the rest were declared by others of their acquantance to be native citizens of the United States. these representations were unavailing to with british Officers who commanded & they were torn thus from their Compainions to defend themselves against the Charge of treason in England.— The residue were still confined to their Prision Ships in a situation more disagreeable than can will be imagined—

Some time after a number of British Vessels were wishing to proceed to Hallifax the Crews of which had mostly been pressed out of them to fight the american forces on the upper lakes; & seaman were wanted to supply their place— Gov. Provost sent an order to Gen. Glascow who then commanded there, directing him to proceed on board the Prision Ship and to induse the Prisioners to volunteer to man their Fleet for Hallifax, & in case they refused to comply, to force them on board for that purpose. the application was made, but the American Prisioners considering the measure unjustifiable towards their own government refused to volunteer; and were accordingly forced on board the Vessels by a brittish press gang; where this Deponent understood they had Quarters assigned them & were compelled to assist in navigating Brittish Vessels to hallifax, & afterwards to England as this deponent has since been informed— and further that not one of the Seamen who was Prisioner there was exempted from this proceeding—

And this Deponent further Saith that in the beginning of the Present Month of November an order was received in conformity to the Prince Regents Order & Proclamation to seize forty Six american Officers and noncommissioned Officers who were then Prisioners of War & to imprision them to be keept in close confinement agreeable to the tenor of that Proclamation— Prisioners to that number most of whom were Officers there on their Parole many of them in a delicate State of health, were immediately put under arrest and marched guarded to the Public Prision and immured for what fate God only Knows is to him unknown, among those destined for close imprision are Lieut. Smith then in a declining state of Health and Doct. James Wood a citizen of Champlain who was taken from his home while he was in the Employment of the Revenue but as this Deponent believes no way connected with the Army— they were imprisiond on the fifth of Nov. instant

This deponent further saith that the Enemy has uniformly at that place treated American Prisioners, Both Officers & Privates with extreme rigour. that sometime since an american Midshipman and two masters mates, merely for having proceeded on a Party of Pleasure about a half a mile beyond the Limits assigned them though they immediate returned within them, were seized & put into prision and kept in Irons, till the general imprisionment of Officers & noncommissioned Officers as above related took place. and this Deponent further saith that all that was allowed for the American Prisioners on board the prision Ship was Daily—one pound of Old wormy bread, which the Inhabitants declared had been twise to the commissioners & condemned for spoiled bread & one half pound of exceedingly bad Meat which in almost any other situation would be absolutely not Eatable; no Liquors, no soap to prevent themselves from becoming Lousy, no candles no & none of the other comforts of Life; and that it was the opinion of all the prisoners that many of them had actually starved to death not being able to eat the Provisions and further that immediately on the Prince Regents Proclamation being received Col Gardner[1] the american agent there who had been Occupied in paying off the sick & Privates of the Land Service, was immediately notified by Gov. Provost to Consider himself confined to the same Limits which were assigned for the Officers at Beaufort. and when this Deponent Left that Place he was compelled to remain with Genl. Winchester & others & was not permitted to visit the prisioners who were in distress on board the Prision Ships or to visit the the town to negociate his bills for the relief of the Officers & had already been obliged to share what little private money he had with him Among them for their temporary relief. This Deponent further saith that he started from the neighborhood of quebec and came by the way of Derby in Vermont and arrived at this Place two Days since and farther this deponent saith not

Abraham Walter

Sworn before me
This 23d day of November 1813
Henry Delord one of the Judges of the Court of Common Pleas in and for the County of Clinton

DS, DNA, RG45, AF7 (M625, Roll No. 76).

   1. Robert Gardner, U.S. Army Pay Department; American agent for prisoners of war in Canada, appointed 3 Aug. 1813.

PAROLE OF LIEUTENANT DAVID DEACON [1]

Copy   Head Quarters
                                              Montreal   25 novr. 1813

   These are to certify that the bearer hereof David Deacon Lieutenant in the navy of the united States as described on the back hereof has permission to return to the united States, he having given his Parole of honour, that he will not enter into any naval Military or other service whatever against the united Kingdom of Great Britain or any of the dominions thereunto belonging or against any power at peace with Great Britain, untill a regular exchange shall have been made and tatified [ratified] by an agent of the British Government duly authorised so to do.— By command of his Excellency

Edward Baynes
Adj. General
U C

Name – David Deacon
Rank – Lieutenant in the navy
Age – Thirty two
Stature – five feet ten & a half inches

Person – thin
Visage – Round
Complexion – Sallow
Hair – Dark
Eyes – Gray
marks or
wounds &c. } none

Copy, DNR, Operational Archives, ZB File.

1. Deacon was commanding officer of *Growler* when that ship was captured on Lake Ontario on 10 August 1813.

LIEUTENANT DAVID DEACON TO SECRETARY OF THE NAVY JONES

Honble. William Jones   Phila.   Decr. 11th. 1813.

Sir

I have just arrived at this place from Quebec. In company with Lieut. Colonel Borstler,[1] we were permitted to return to the U States in consequence of the same Indulgence haveing been granted to Lieut Col Myers and Capt. Gordon of the British armcy. Proposals arc likewise made by Sir George Provost to exchange me for Capt. Gordon. Should this arrangement take place I have most urgently to request your permition to visit you at the Navy Dept.— I have much to say Both for your Information as wel as for my own Justification— I have been unfortunate Sir, But am confident I have Done my Duty— I shall retire to my place of residence Burlington N. Jersey, at which place I shall wait your orders. I have the Honour to Be Sir your Obt. St.

D. Deacon

ALS, DNA, RG45, BC, Vol. 4, No. 142 (M148, Roll No. 12).

1. Lieutenant Colonel Charles G. Boerstler, 14th U.S. Infantry, was the commander at Black Rock, New York; he was captured in the Battle of Beaver Dams, 24 June 1813.

Rebuilding on Lake Champlain

Master Commandant Thomas Macdonough's force was seriously weakened by the loss of Growler *and* Eagle *in June, and by the destruction of stores and boats during Murray's raid in July. At the close of 1813, the American fleet on Lake Champlain consisted of the sloops* President, Commodore Preble, *and* Montgomery, *and four gunboats. Macdonough's two hired vessels,* Frances *and* Wasp, *sailed so poorly that they would later be returned to their owners. With this makeshift fleet, the Americans were able to chase the British back into the Richelieu River whenever they attempted to enter American waters. Macdonough maintained a precarious balance of power on the lake, but it was clear the British were strengthening their force at Isle aux Noix for the coming year.*

Macdonough's task during the winter of 1813–14 was to rebuild his weakened squadron in order to gain control of Lake Champlain early in the spring. Secretary of the Navy Jones gave Macdonough his full support for the effort, but supplies and men were still slow in coming. With his vessels in winter quarters on Otter Creek, Macdonough drew on local forges, rolling mills, and lumber mills at Vergennes, Vermont, to provide timber, cannonballs, and iron fittings for the vessels built there during the winter.

MASTER COMMANDANT THOMAS MACDONOUGH TO SECRETARY OF THE NAVY JONES

Plattsburg Bay   23 Nov. 1813

Sir

I have the honor to inform you that the enemy still continues within his own waters and that I keep prepared to meet him should he come out.

The North and South ends of the lake will be frozen in the course of a few days which will make it necessary for the enemy as well as us to go into Winter quarters but I calculate for the protection of the public stores on the shores of this lake to keep out longer than the enemy the most northern deposit of those stores being at Plattsburg. I find, Sir, the enemy can and have brought over from the river St. Lawrence gallies, by land, on large trucks which they have constructed for that purpose— they have now at the Isle Aux Noix from nine to twelve of those boats some of which carry a long 24 pounder in the bow which fire only on a line with the keel and a 32 pr. cannonade in the stern which fires abeam or in any other direction as it traverses and carrying upwards of fifty men.— they have a number of those boats (though probably small and carrying only gun) in the river St. Lawrence and is it not probable, as the seat of war may be in the vicinity of this lake next summer that they will transport some of those boats into this water and thereby make an increase of our naval force necessary.

If not in anticipation of this measure of the enemy, I should propose building twenty or five and twenty boats this winter some to carry an 18 or 24 pr. with a cannonade in the stern, then should they not bring their boats from the St. Lawrence we should be prepared as the Army advanced into Canida to go down the Sorrell river, pass the Chamblee rapids (of six miles) and enter the St. Lawrence, there to co-operate with the army as it progresses against Montreal or Quebec—these boats should carry about 30 men each. The transportation of cannon &c. will be easy this winter on the Snow to Vergennes at which place materials are at hand for building also shot contracted for by Government and as soon as the ice would permit they could be all ready for service. The force would probably prevent the enemy endeavouring to raise a force to cope with us on the lake which has been their system. Having been twelve months absent from my family I beg you will favour me with permission to pass a part of this winter with them in Middletown, Connecticut, as soon as I shall have laid the vessels up, leaving them in charge of a very capable officer, Lieut. Cassin—from thence to go on to New York and select the cannon &c. necessary for those boats should the building of them meet your approbation.

Accompanying this is the voluntary statement of Abraham Walters who was pilot of one of the Sloops taken last summer—he made his escape from Quebec and after a severe journey of ten days reported himself to me yesterday.— I have the honor to be Sir Yr. mo. obd. Servt.

T. Macdonough

ALS, DNA, RG45, MC, 1813, No. 169 (M147, Roll No. 5). See pp. 600–602 for the deposition of Abraham Walter.

SECRETARY OF THE NAVY JONES TO
MASTER COMMANDANT THOMAS MACDONOUGH

Thomas MacDonough Esqr.
Comg. U.S. Naval Forces,
on Lake Champlain,
Plattsburg.

Navy Department
Decr. 7th 1813.

Sir,

I have received your letter of the 23d Novr. I wish early preparations to be made, for building fifteen Galleys, for which plans and Draughts will be immediately forwarded to you, similar to those now constructing here, and at Baltimore, for the Flotilla of the Chesapeake.[1]

The first Class, 75 feet long and 15 wide, to carry a long 24 and a 42 pound Carronade, row 40 oars, and drawing but 22 inches water, with all on board.

Second class, 50 feet long and 12 feet wide, to carry a long 18 and 32 pd. carronade, and row 26 oars; they have been tried, and are the most perfect of their kind.

Large supplies of Naval and Ordnance Stores are ordered to Albany, before the close of the Hudson, for the Lake service.

Your visit to your family had better be made soon, and as short as possible; as great exertions will be required to meet the Enemy on the first opening of the Navigation.

I wish a correct return of your present force, with Muster rolls of the officers and men attached to each vessel, to be forwarded to the Department as soon as possible. I am, respectfully, Your obedient Servant,

W. Jones

LB Copy, DNA, RG45, SNL, 1813, Vol. 11, p. 163 (M149, Roll No. 11).

1. See pp. 373–81 for the construction of gunboats for the Chesapeake Bay flotilla.

MASTER COMMANDANT THOMAS MACDONOUGH TO
SECRETARY OF THE NAVY JONES

Plattsburgh   18 Decr. 1813

Sir

I have the honor to inform you that I shall proceed tomorrow with the United States Flotilla under my command to winter quarters in the mouth of Otter Creek. I hope Sir it will be considered that I have fulfiled the duties required of me on this lake and that I have merited the trust and confidence reposed in me by my government.— Since the completion of a force adequate to the meeting of our enemy he has never appeared except in predatory excursions at the most favourable times for him. I can assure you Sir that we have always been prepared to repel or defeat him—we have frequently sought him and he has as frequently avoided us. It has never been my good fortune to fall in with the enemy and I have to lament the apparent tacit disapprobation of the President of the United States in his late communication to Congress by finding no mention made of this part of our force employed against our enemy in Canada. You will please to observe that the most northern deposit of the provisions and military stores belonging to the Army are at Plattsburgh— this deposit as well as all others on the margin of the lake I considered immediately under my particular charge and keeping what I supposed one great object of the war in view (the conquest of Canada) I hazarded not their loss by unnecessarily exposing my vessels in the northern end of the lake where it is very narrow, full of reefs and decidedly advantageous for an action for the enemy with the heavy gallies which they lately brought up the Sorrell river from Quebec. The Flotilla under my command has I am very conscious always manifested a perfect willingness to see the enemy on fair terms. In October past arrangements were made for it to precede a part of the Army against the Isle Aux Noix but this was I presume deemed inexpedient by the commanding General in consequence of intelligence received by him of the strength of that place. Should you deem this letter improper I beg you will consider it as emanating from feelings not at ease because it may be considered that I have not done that which it was in my power to do.— I have the honor to be with the highest respect Sir Yr. mo. obd. Servt.

T. Macdonough

ALS, DNA, RG45, MC, 1813, No. 190 (M147, Roll No. 5).

MASTER COMMANDANT THOMAS MACDONOUGH TO SECRETARY OF THE NAVY JONES

Vergennes   Decr. 28th. 1813—

Sir

Herewith I have the honor to send you a statement of our Naval force on this lake, the purser will in a day or two forward to the Depmt. muster rolls of the officers & men attached to each vessel this sir, should have been done before, but during the time that this station was without a purser irregularities inevitably occurred which has caused the delay—

Sloop	*President*	6–18 pr. Columbiads— 4. Twelves
Sloop	*Commre. Preble*	7–12 prs. and 2 18 pr. Columbiads
Do	*Montgomery*	7–9 prs. and 2 18 pr. Columbiads
Do	*Wasp*	3–12 prs.

Four Gallies each carrying a long 18 pr.

The sloop *Wasp* is a small vessel & sails badly, I took her last summer from a Merchant of this place and promised to pay him what she should be appraised at, this however being little I suspect her owner will take her again & will be satisfied for the time I have had her by the repairs done to her I shall endeavour to make this arrangement as the sloop is not fit for the service. I calculate to mount on the bow of the sloop *President* a long 24 pr. on a pivot— I have the honor to be most respectfully Sir, your Obt. Sert.

T. Macdonough

ALS, DNA, RG45, MC, 1813, No. 197 (M147, Roll No. 5).

The American Fleet on Lake Erie

While the United States controlled Lake Erie at the close of 1813, fear of a British counteroffensive left the Americans uneasy as winter approached. Virtually all the ships on the lake had been damaged in the Battle of Lake Erie or in the operations on Lake St. Clair and the Thames River; most needed extensive repairs. Moreover, the vessels were widely dispersed—the largest ships were at Erie, and others were at Put-in-Bay or ashore at Buffalo. This rendered them vulnerable to British attack during the winter. The transport of Major General William Henry Harrison's army to Sackets Harbor and the St. Lawrence River left the Lake Erie fleet largely unprotected.

Master Commandant Jesse D. Elliott had assumed command of the Lake Erie station on 25 October 1813 after Captain Oliver H. Perry returned to Rhode Island. Elliott was anxious to leave the station—he had requested leave of absence numerous times since his first request on 11 September 1813, the day following the Battle of Lake Erie. As the senior officer on the lake, Elliott was denied leave each time. He was forced to remain in charge of an officer corps that was bitterly divided by a growing controversy over Elliott's role in the battle.[1]

1. Elliott, commanding Niagara, had failed to bring his vessel into close action during the heat of the Battle of Lake Erie. He later claimed a large role in the American victory, although other officers of the fleet thought he deliberately held back his ship. For the next thirty years, Elliott would try to exonerate his reputation. See Roske and Donley, "Perry-Elliott Controversy"; Belovarac, "Brief Overview"; and Friedman and Skaggs, "Jesse Duncan Elliott."

SECRETARY OF THE NAVY JONES TO MASTER COMMANDANT JESSE D. ELLIOTT

Jesse D Elliott Esqr.   Navy Department
Commanding Naval Officer   Novemr. 30th. 1813—
Lake Erie.

Sir

The Army under the command of Genl. Wilkinson having gone into Winter Quarters short of the contemplated object of the Campaign and so low down upon the St. Laurence as to forbid its return to the Lakes should circumstances require its presence; and as that under the command of Genl. Harrison has also descended to the foot of Lake Ontario, leaving the force at Niagara & Detroit very feeble, it is not improbable that the Enemy, should his red Allies remain with him in any considerable force, may make an effort to regain some of his lost ground by a vigorous push for Detroit, with the hope of cutting off Genl. Cass, destroying any naval force we may have in that River or at Malden, and of restoring the confidence and regaining the services of the Savages.— It is therefore deemed important to take the earliest moment to apprize you of the existing state of things below, in order that you may adopt the most effectual means in your power, to guard against the consequences and defeat the object of the enemy.—

I trust that as much of our Naval force under your Command, has been collected at Erie as was practicable.— And in order that early measures may be taken to repair and equip such force as may be deemed expedient on Lake Erie for the ensuing Campaign, you will <u>immediately forward to me</u>, the duplicate of a report which you will make to Commodore Chauncey, relative to the whole

Naval force on Lake Erie including the captured fleet, describing the state and condition of the several Vessels, the repairs & equipments which each will require, and the local situation of each.— Also a general view of the stores and supplies on hand and contracted for and the probable wants of the most necessary articles not attainable on the shores of the Lake or at Pittsburgh.—

A correct Muster Roll of the Officers and Men under your command is also required.— You will communicate to Genl. Cass such parts of this Letter as may be proper for his information.—I am very respectfully Your Obedt. Servt.

W. Jones—

LB Copy, DNA, RG45, CLS, 1813, p. 77.

COMMODORE ISAAC CHAUNCEY TO MASTER COMMANDANT JESSE D. ELLIOTT

Captain Jesse D Elliott   U.S. Ship *General Pike*
Commandg. Naval Officer   Sacketts Harbor   1st. Decemr. 1813
at Erie Pennsylva.

Sir

Your Communication of the 8th Ulto. by Mr. Webster has been duly received and the manner in which you have laid the vessels up approved of—but I think that the force left with the two Ships at Put In Bay is much too small unless you can add to it from the Army I therefore recommend you to make immediate application to the Commanding Officer at Detroit for fifty more Men

The Block House for the protection of the Vessels at Erie ought to be built immediately but the Hospital and Store House I think may be dispensed with, you may substitute some of the small vessels for those purposes

I have to request that you loose no time in having the *Laurence* and *Niagara* repaired in their Masts Spars ~~and~~ rigging and Sails and put in the best order for Service— You will also have all the necessary repairs put to the other vessels of the Squadron—except the two Prize Ships which you will leave in their present state untill further Orders— I presume that the Mechanics of the Fleet will be found sufficient to do all the repair required during the Winter—if they should not you will employ others so as to have all the Vessels in a complete state of preparation for actual service the moment that the Lake becomes navigable in the Spring.

With respect to the vessels that have unfortunately got on Shore at Buffaloe [1] if you have not been able to get them off you will cause them to be stripped and all their Guns and Stores taken out and deposited with their Rigging and sails in some good Store House near Buffaloe. I should recommend you to Store them 2 or 3 Miles from Buffaloe upon the Main Post road— You might leave one Midshipman and two Seamen to watch them during the Winter and order all the rest to join me at Erie as they can be better taken care of there and at less expense than at Buffaloe. You will recruit all the Marines that offer during the Winter.

With respect to the many promotions made by Captain Perry upon Lake Erie I presume that he has the Secretary's authority for so doing as he has never consulted me upon the Subject I shall not therefore interfere with them

Your request to visit your family (which at first view might be considered a reasonable one) I request [*regret*] that I cannot grant— to an Officer of your

Master Commandant Jesse D. Elliott

merits and experience a single glance at the situation of the Fleet upon Erie will convince you that the request ought not to have been made and I am well persuaded that upon reflection that you will acquiesce in my decision with great cheerfulness— Your situation is a responsible one and you must be aware that it is all important to the Government that the Vessels upon Erie should not only be preserved but prepared in every respect for any Service that they may be required for in the Spring—and who is so proper to attend to the various duties appertaining to the Station as yourself.

Your presence is absolutely necessary to curtail as much as possible the expenses of the Station—to examine and approve all Bills and to regulate expenditures generally and also to provide for the Wants of the Station by making timely requisitions for stores Provisions Clothing &c &c— I do assure you that it would have afforded me infinite pleasure to have gratified you with a visit to your friends if I could have done it without injury to the public service as it is you must submit as I am obliged to   I have the honor to be very Respectfully Sir Yr. Mo. Ob. St.

                                                                                    I. C.

LB Copy, NHi, Isaac Chauncey Letter Book.

1. Four vessels, *Ariel*, *Trippe*, *Chippewa*, and *Little Belt*, were driven on shore in a gale during the last week in October. These ships were later destroyed by the British when they attacked the town on 30 December 1813.

Master Commandant Jesse D. Elliott to Commodore Isaac Chauncey

Copy of a letter to Comr. Isaac Chauncey   U.S. Sloop *Niagara*
dated   Erie   19th December 1813.

Sir
    Your letter of the 1th Inst. I have had the pleasure to receive, and agreeable to instructions from the Honorable the Secretary of the Navy (a copy of which I enclose you) I inform you of the exact situation of the Naval Force on Lake Erie. In my last I stated to you my intention of visiting Buffalo, for the purpose of endeavouring to get the Vessels off that had been driven on shore in the storm of October. I remained at that place two weeks without being able to accomplish that end, caused by continual winds from the westward, the <u>ways</u> are prepared, and early in the Spring, they can be got into the water. The *Lawrence, Niagara, Caledonia, Scorpion, Ohio, Porcupine,* and *Amelia,* are at this place, the *Somers* & *Tigress,* are up the Lake. (I expect them down in a few days) the *Ariel* and *Trippe,* are on shore at Buffalo, their masts out, Rigging, Sails and Stores placed in a Store House at that place, the three first will want considerable repairs. Of the Prize Vessels, the *Detroit* and *Queen Charlotte,* are at Put in Bay, in charge of a Sailing Master, M. Mate, a Midshipman and twenty seamen, an officer of the Army and forty men, they are dismasted, and will want considerable repairs, the *Lady Prevost* and *Hunter,* are at this place the former, in want of many repairs, the latter few, the *Little Belt* and *Chipawa* on shore at Buffalo, little injured. I regret excessively you should have delayed so long in letting me hear from you on the subject of the defense of the vessels, It is my opinion (as Fort George has been evacuated) that the Enemy may make an attempt to destroy the shipping at this Place however with what force I have, they shall be a dear privelege   I am fearful we shall not be able

to recruit marines, I would suggest the Idea to you, of naming to the Honorable the Secretary of the Navy, the necessity of having a few of the Army as a substitute, they may be ordered from the Pittsburg Rendevous. Every thing requisite for Sailing the fleet, can be obtained on the Lake Shore or at Pittsburg.

I most cheerfully recall my application, for permission to return to my family, and Sir, will be most happy, that, in the Spring, I may be superceded in this command, and join you as your Captain in the *Genl. Pike.*

When the fleet is in a situation of defence, I shall visit Pittsburg for the purpose of obtaining supply's for the ensuing summer. The wounded of the Enemy as well as our own are recovering fast. I have sent sixty of the former to Pittsburg for safe keeping, the remainder will follow in a day or two— Very Respectfully I have the honor to be Sir your obd. Servt.

Signed   Jesse D. Elliott

Copy, DNA, RG45, MC, 1813, No. 195 (M147, Roll No. 5). This copy was enclosed in a letter from Jesse D. Elliott to Secretary of the Navy Jones dated 22 December 1813 (reproduced below).

Master Commandant Jesse D. Elliott to Secretary of the Navy Jones

U.S. Sloop, *Niagara*
Erie   22nd December 1813—

Sir

Your letter of the 30th Ult. I have the honor to acknowledge the receipt of, and herewith enclose you the duplicate of a report made to the Commander in chief, of the situation of the Naval Force under my command on Lake Erie, together with the muster Roll of the Station. Agreeable to your instructions, strengthened by the recent occurrences on the Niagara River, I dispatched an express for Detroit, with information to Brigr. Genl. Cass of the situation of our Troops in Lower Canada, together with their evacuation of Fort George, and the Force the Enemy have at Burlington Heights. You will in one moment observe the situation of Detroit when I inform you that Genl. Cass has stated to me, in a letter dated the 9th Novemr. that he has only an effective force of 400 men, and surrounded by disaffected persons I am apprehensive our force at Put in Bay will not be sufficiently strong to resist the Enemy if in numbers, therefore would suggest to you the propriety of having an additional number of Soldiers, And Sir, I presume you are acquainted with the situation of this Lake, when the winter will have set in. When the Ice forms it is sufficiently strong to bear any weight from Point Ebans to Cateragus a distance of about 25 miles, thence up our side of the Lake to this place, entirely unseen when approaching. Therefore to make my force as strong and as effectual as possible, I have moored the Vessels close [in?] and in an Eight Square, presenting a fire all round the Compass, and covered by a Block House, that I expect will be finished by the time the Ice will make on the Lake, I would also suggest to you the necessity of having a few Soldiers at this place, as substitutes for Marines.

In a former communication to Comr. Chauncey, I mentioned to him that the terms of service, of almost all the men will have expired, before the vessels can be in service in the Spring and I am fearfull that from the many privations seamen have on Lake Service, that few will reenter.

Some time since I wrote you on the subject of a young Gentlemen who has in two actions served with me, as an acting midshipman and has on each occasion been severely wounded, will you Sir, do me the favour to warrant him as a midshipman, dating it when he received his first wound, 8th October 1812—[1]

I beg leave to enclose to you the memorial of Doctr. John Kennedy, Late Surgeon of his Brit. Majys. Ship *Queen Charlotte* who has rendered essential service, since the Action of the 10th Septr. to the wounded of the Enemy, as well as our own.

On this Station we are at great inconvenience in consequence of the great delay of the mail between this place and Pittsburg. Letters are delayed 12 days, probably the thing may be remedied at the General Post Office— Very Respectfully I have the honor to be Sir your obt. servt.

Jesse D. Elliott

LS, DNA, RG45, MC, 1813, No. 195 (M147, Roll No. 5). The enclosed copy of a letter to Isaac Chauncey is reproduced above; the enclosed statement of Dr. John Kennedy has not been located.

1. Acting Midshipman John L. Cummings was involved in the capture of the brigs *Detroit* and *Caledonia* in 1812; for Elliott's report, see Dudley, *Naval War of 1812*, Vol. 1, pp. 327–31.

Shipbuilding on Lake Ontario

As winter approached, Commodores Isaac Chauncey and Sir James Lucas Yeo turned their attentions to readying their respective squadrons for the 1814 campaign. Intelligence of their enemy's rapid progress in shipbuilding spurred each commander to greater exertions in building new vessels for the coming season. The winter months would set the stage for the great shipbuilding contest on Lake Ontario the following year.

The British had two new frigates and four gunboats under construction at Kingston during the winter of 1813–14. Their new ships, Prince Regent *of 58 guns and* Princess Charlotte *of 42, were launched in April 1814. Plans were underway to construct an immense ship of the line at Kingston the following spring. The Americans built two large brigs,* Jefferson *and* Jones, *at Sackets Harbor during the winter. They also were making plans to build two large 44-gun frigates the next year.*

Commodore Isaac Chauncey left Sackets Harbor late in December to travel to Washington in order to confer with Secretary of the Navy Jones and President James Madison on the campaign for the coming year. During his two-month absence, shipbuilding would progress under the direction of his second in command, Master Commandant William M. Crane.

COMMODORE SIR JAMES LUCAS YEO, R.N., TO ADMIRAL SIR JOHN B. WARREN, R.N.

Copy.

His Majestys Ship *Wolfe*
at Kingston, Upper Canada
the 6th December 1813.

Sir.

Being apprehensive that written Communications may meet with delay, or miscarry at this Season of the Year, and conceiving it of the first importance that you should be informed of our exact Situation, and what we stand in need of to insure Success on the opening of the navigation, I have judged it expedient to send Mr. Scott, my first Lieutenant overland to Halifax who having a thorough Knowledge of every thing that is going on here—will be enabled to lay before you Sir, the nature, and wants of this Service more clearly than if I was to write Volumes on the Subject.

The two new Ships are in a very forward State, and I am almost certain of having a force in the Spring sufficiently strong to meet the enemy with effect and decision. I need not point out to you Sir the great advantages that are to be hoped for by this Squadron being on the Lake three weeks or a month before that of the Enemy. This I think is certain if I receive a Reinforcement of Seamen by the beginning of April, but not otherwise, and I know of no other possible means of obtaining them but by their marching across to Quebec. This Service Lieutenant Scott is well qualified to conduct having travelled that Road before.

I trust whatever Men are sent from Halifax may be selected for this particular Service, as I have not the Power of keeping up that strict discipline and Subordination which I could do on the Atlantic I therefore must depend much on the good disposition of the Seamen. The Marlbros[1] have been guilty of every extravagance, and given more trouble than all the establishment put together; there were also several Black and American Citizens among them, the latter of which I of course immediately discharged.

From the unavoidable exposure of the Seamen in the Gun boats at this Season of the Year, we have a great number Sick (nearly eighty) I therefore am certain (to insure Success) we shall require 200 or 250 additional Seamen.

I beg leave to refer you to Lieutenant Scott for any further Particulars as that Officer is in full Possession of my Sentiments.

I am informed that the Enemy have added Sixty Eight Shipwrights to their Naval Yard at Sackets Harbour to assist in building two Frigates. I have the honor to be with the highest respect, Sir Your most obedient humble Servant

Signed   James Lucas Yeo.
Commodore

Copy, UkLPR, Adm. 1/505, pp. 225–27.

1. Four officers and 110 men, drafted from H.M.S. *Marlborough,* a 74-gun ship, were sent from Quebec to Lake Ontario by Admiral Edward Griffith in October. These sailors replaced the men previously sent from H.M. troopship *Dover* when they were ordered to return to Quebec.

COMMODORE ISAAC CHAUNCEY TO SECRETARY OF THE NAVY JONES

No. 130.
U.S. Ship General Pike
Sacketts Harbor   17th Decemr. 1813

Sir

I was last evening honored with your Letter of the 1st inst. with the enclosures therein referred to.

I trust that in a day or two after the date of your Letter that you was relieved from your anxiety for the safety of the Fleet by the receipt of my Letters from this place.

I have had the honor in former communications of stating to you that the Enemy had two vessels in a considerable state of forwardness and that the keel of a third was laid and recent advices state that, materials are preparing for a fourth of this however there may be some doubts, but none whatever that he is building three vessels and that the length of keels as stated is pretty nearly correct, but of the breadth of beam or the number of Guns that they are to mount I can obtain no information that can be relied on— I have however employed a Man who has promised to obtain that information for me from a friend in Kingston   The Enemy has received between the first of October and last of November a reinforcement of about five hundred Seamen with a proportionable number of Officers— this additional force I presume is intended for the vessels building, but by the last accounts no stores either to arm or equip these New Vessels had arrived at Kingston but from the situation of our Army no obstruction can be offerred to the Enemy's sending from Quebec or Montreal any quantities that he may require and no doubt but that he will profit by the opportunity.

The Enemys physical force at this time is certainly equal if not superior to ours, add to that force the three vessels which he is building it will make him vastly superior— therefore to place ourselves upon an equality with him we necessarily must build three vessels of a force corresponding with his—but I should recommend to add a fourth vessel of the size of the *Sylph* in lieu of all the heavy Sailing Schooners, for really they are of no manner of Service except to carry Troops, or use as Gun Boats.

If it is determined to prosecute the War offensively and secure our Conquests in Upper Canada—Kingston ought unquestionably to be the first object of attack, and that so early in the Spring as to prevent the Enemy from useing the whole of the Naval force that he is prepareing— with this view of the subject we should require to be built this Winter two vessels that would insure our ascendancy even if the Enemy should have ready at the breaking up of the ice in the Spring the two vessels that are the most forward.

But on the other hand if it should be determined to act on the defensive untill our Troops are collected and disciplined the additional Naval force required upon this Lake may be better built in the spring than now and I presume 20 per cent cheaper—moreover the transportation of stores from New York at this Season of the Year would not only be attended with difficulty, but a vast expence.

The Enemy is collecting a considerable force at Kingston and no doubt will push forward a part of it to the neighborhood of Fort George and when an opportunity offers he will attempt and probably succeed in recovering that Fortress in which case he will reoccupy Fort Erie and the whole of the North Side of the Niagara frontier which will expose the ~~whole~~ four vessels that are on shore at Buffaloe to be burnt by him unless a small force should be stationed there— I have however directed Captain Elliott, that in case he could not get the vessels off to dismantle them and deposit the stores a few Miles from Buffaloe.

Whether the Enemy will extend himself as far as Malden will I presume depend much upon the disposition of the Indians to second his views by re-uniting their force with his— If he should reoccupy Malden the two prize ships at "Put in Bay" I consider in a dangerous situation and the force left with them quite inadequate to their defence. If the Enemy should be in sufficient force to defend these ships it would be his policy not to destroy but preserve them and by building attempt to regain his ascendancy on the Lake— I have directed Captain Elliott to apply to the Commanding Officer at Detroit for an additional guard for those Vessels—would it not be adviseable to order them destroyed in preference to their falling into the Enemys hands?

Captain Perry has never made a return to me of the prisoners taken upon Lake Erie, or Said one word to me on the subject and I am still ignorant of the number or grade or in what manner they were disposed of—and I am almost as ignorant of the Prizes, as no particular return of them has ever reached me.

I shall loose no time in having the Prizes valued agreeably to your instructions and transmit the valuation to the Department.

I directed Captain Perry in October last to transmit to me correct Muster Lists of the Officers and Men upon Lake Erie—these Lists I received a few days since from Captain Elliott which I will transmit to the Department as soon as copied together with Muster Rolls of the Officers and Men on this Station.

I shall continue to make all the necessary preparations here for building and collect all the timber that will be first required but shall recommend to Doctor Bullus to detain the Ship Carpenters in New York untill he receives further instructions from you upon the subject   I adopt this course lest we might incur expense, that by a little delay might be avoided. I have the honor to be very Respectfully Sir Yr. Mo. Obt. St.

Isaac Chauncey

LS, DNA, RG45, CL, 1813, Vol. 8, No. 67 (M125, Roll No. 33).

COMMODORE ISAAC CHAUNCEY TO SECRETARY OF THE NAVY JONES

No. 138   U.S. Ship *G. Pike*
                                    Sacketts Harbor   24th Decr. 1813

Sir,

I shall leave here on the 26th for Washington and shall make no stop on the way except one day with my family at New York.

The fleet is moored in two lines at right angles with each other, so that each line is calculated to support the other and also to afford protection to the Block Houses, situated on the two sides of the Harbor.

I consider the fleet as safe from any attack of the Enemy, unless he comes in such force as to take possession of the Harbor, and by geting possession of the Batteries, drive us from the vessels with hot shot; at any rate there is no probability that the St. Lawrence will be sufficiently frozen to bear Troops before some time in Feby. The season is uncommonly open and mild although the Harbor and Bay has been several times frozen over, it is now perfectly open and free from Ice.

I leave Capt. Crane in command during my absence, who is an officer of more than common merit, and who will, from his known industry and talents, be always prepared to meet any contingency or repel any attack that may be made by the enemy.

With the view to promote the public Interest add, to the safety of the fleet and insure a more rigid and a better discipline amongst the officers and men, I have thought it best to put out of commission the schooners mentioned below, and have distributed the officers and men, on board of the larger vessels of the fleet; which measure I hope you will approve. I have the honor to be Very Respectfully Sir yr. most obt. Humbe. Servt.

Isaac Chauncey

Conquest
Fair American
Pert
Julia
_____

Asp, exchanged for *Julia* in October,
Raven Growler and other prize vessels has been used as transports to the Army.

LS, DNA, RG45, CL, 1813, Vol. 8, No. 101 (M125, Roll No. 33).

Winter on the Lake Ontario Station

The Americans stationed on the northern lakes fared much better during the second winter of the war than they had during the first, yet conditions remained harsh. Housing had improved with the construction of barracks, but sickness still prevailed. "Lake fever" (probably malaria) was common throughout the late summer into the winter months, and secondary cases recurred at any time. Dysentery and other disorders also weakened the American forces. When the lakes froze over and crews of the vessels became idle, discipline problems increased. The prices of goods in the local markets were exorbitantly high, and pay was irregular. Morale ran low as winter set in and hopes for an end to the war diminished.

Master Commandant William M. Crane, formerly commander of John Adams, *assumed temporary charge of the Lake Ontario station when Commodore Isaac Chauncey left for Washington. Crane's orders for governing shipboard life, prepared in December 1813 and July 1814, provide insights into the discipline problems on the station and into the habits and practices of common sailors.*[1]

1. These regulations were adapted from Crane's earlier "Rules and Regulations for the Internal Government of the U.S. Sloop Argus," *Oct. 1811, in DNA, RG45, William M. Crane, "Journal Kept on Board* Argus *and* Nautilus, *October 1811–July 1812."*

MASTER COMMANDANT WILLIAM M. CRANE'S
RULES FOR THE REGULATION OF SHIPBOARD LIFE

On board U S S *Madison* in
Sacketts Harbor   Decr. 19th. 1813

Sir

You will cause the following regulations for the internal government of the United States Ship *Madison* under my command to be carried into effect   Respectfully Yr. Obd. Sevt.

W. M. Crane

To the Senior Lieut.
On board U S Ship *Madison*
Prest.

Art 1st.   The Laws for the Government of the Navy and the President of the United States printed Instructions must be strictly adhered to.

Art 2d   The Deck is always to be in charge of a Lieut. or Sailing Master, who will on assuming the command acquaint himself with the precise situation of the vessel and <u>battery</u> which is at all times to be kept in readiness for service.

Art 3d   All the Lieuts. of Divisions will keep correct Lists of their Mens Cloath-
            ing, Mattrasses and Blankets, and the Master those of the brace men
            and others stationed in the Magazines, passages, pumps, and Shot
            Lockers, there will be a general Inspection every Sunday— Watch and
            Quarter Bills are also to be kept by every Officer.—

Art 4th.   The Officers will individually charge the men against the shameful
            practice of selling their Cloaths, or the Tobacco and small stores
            which they may draw from the Purser as <u>I am</u> determined to punish
            with the utmost severity all those found guilty.—

Art 5th.   The Purser is forbidden to furnish any supplies of cloathing, or
            Stores to the crew without my written order, which will be given pro-
            vided the Division Officer deems them necessary for their comfort.
            All requisitions by the Crew for Cloathing, or small stores, are to be
            made out in writing, and if approved signed by the Division Officer
            and presented to me

Art 6th.   No Officer or other Person belonging to the Ship is to sleep out of
            her, without special permission from me.—

Art. 7th.   The Lights and Fires are to be extinguished under the Forecastle, on
            the Birth Deck and in the Steerage at 9 P M and no lights to be per-
            mitted there again <u>but in Lanthorns, leave first having been ob-
            tained from the Officer Commanding the Watch</u>.—

Art. 8th.   The First or Senior Lieut. will execute all the Watching Quartering
            messing & birthing & stationing of the Crew, he will also superintend
            all the general duties of the Ship, in which he is to be aided by every
            Officer in the vessel he will grant permission to Officers (and Sea-
            men who have conducted with propriety) when they can be spared
            from duty, keeping in view however, the unequivocal order in the
            6th. Article, he will also appoint a Midshipman or Masters Mate to
            take charge of the Birth Deck which he will carefully inspect every
            day, no Ships stores are to be converted to any other purpose, or
            given out by those having charge of them but by a written order
            from the first Lieutenant

Art. 9th.   Cleanliness promotes health, perhaps as much as any other circum-
            stance, I therefore request that the Officers will be particularly care-
            ful to keep their Apartments and Servants clean— they must also im-
            press it on the men of their Divisions— no particular day can be
            assigned for washing bags and cloaths, the weather will govern in
            this respect— but the Beds and Blankets must be frequently aired
            and the Dust beaten out—

Art. 10th. The Officer of the Deck will muster all the boys at 9 A.M. and in-
            spect their appearance punishing those who have dirty Cloaths, face
            feet or hands, and it would be well in the Division Officers to care-
            fully examine their men in this respect at muster.

Art. 11th. The Officer in charge of the Birth Deck will daily inspect the Mess
            Chests and Bread Bags keeping them clean and free from Grease &c
            the Birth Deck is not to be washed in Winter without an order from the
            first Lieut. who will consult the Surgeon before he directs it   it should
            be white washed once a fortnight and fumigated morning and evening.

Art. 12th   The Crew are to be mustered and inspected at Quarters every morn-
            ing at 1/4 past 9 again in the afternoon, and an exercise provided

the weather will permit, at all events there must be a muster at sun set when the <u>battery</u> must be cleared of Lumber, Pikes &c distributed and all arrangements made to meet an attack

Art 13th.   All filth and rubbish must be removed from about the Ship, by cutting holes in the Ice and depositing it in the water as often as may be necessary

Art. 14th.   The Sailing Master will be careful in noting all the transactions in the Log Book, Wind, weather, Public Stores recd. or landed and the particular manner in which the Ships company are employed— he will also frequently examine the situation of the Cables and Rigging, acquainting me with their situation and condition—

Art. 15th.   The sick are under the immediate and sole care of the Surgeon, whose skill and humanity creates the highest confidence, they are to be visited at least twice every day, no comforts the service admits of must be withheld from them, extra attendants may be had on application to the first Lieut. or Officer of the Watch   The Surgeon or his assistant will daily inspect the boilers and cooking utensils, in order that they may be kept perfectly clean, their situation he will report to the first Lieut. The Surgeon and Mate are not to be absent from the Ship at the same time with out permission from me— The Sick mens cloaths will be washed by their mess mates, their Bedding frequently aired and their persons kept clean

Art. 16th   The Gunner will have always filled Thirty round of Cartridges, one Powder Horn and Sixty Tubes with priming cartridges for each gun forty eight primed matches. Gun Locks Division Bags Guns & Gun Carriages and Tackles in complete readiness for actual service, also the small arms are to be kept in perfect repair, fifty rounds for each Musket and thirty for each Pistol Pikes and Cutlasses at hand— he is never to open the Magasines without an order from the Commanding Officer— all deficiencies are to be reported to me

Art. 17th.   The Boatswain will turn his attention to the fitment and preservation of the Rigging which he will carefully inspect and frequently examine.—

Art. 18th.   The Sail Maker will carefully examine the Sails and repair such as require it.—

Art. 19th.   The Carpenter will keep the Pumps in perfect order, inspect Boats and Spars and keep them in Repair, he will also superintend all the work performed by his crew, the Hull of the Ship must be frequently examined as well as the Masts and Spars—

Art. 20th.   The Crew are to be divided into four watches with a proportionate number of petty officers loggerheads always kept in the Galley during the night, and the Snow thrown off the Guns and Deck; all persons approaching the Ship after dark are to be hailed and if suspicious examined & detained for this purpose a good look out must be kept on all sides.

Art. 21st.   The good conduct of the Petty Officers and Seamen will receive every encouragement and all indulgences the service admits of will be granted to those who are distinguished by their correctness, they are expressly guarded against <u>fighting</u> with each other, <u>drunkenness, selling cloaths, small stores tobacco or grog</u>, nor are they permitted to <u>exchange</u> their <u>apparel</u>, every Saturday, after the ordinary work is over, they will be allowed to mend their cloaths— all promotions will be made, from those who are cleanly, obedient, and seamen like in their deportment—

Art. 22d. If any man has cause for complaint, he is to apply in a respectful manner to the Officer of the Deck, who will redress his grievance unless it is of a nature to require my interference—

Art. 23d. The Mates and Midshipmen are to be divided into three watches, they are never to leave the Deck untill regularly relieved, either at the expiration of their watch or to their Meals, whenever they are sent with a wooding or watering party, or in a Boat they will recollect the men are confided to their care, and no circumstance can warrant a breach of this important duty— they will receive every proper attention and the Commander in Chief will be made acquainted with their merits.

Art. 24th. In case of an alarm of Fire the Ships Company will immediately assemble at Quarters when the Sail Trimmers will procure wet swabs and the firemen fill their Buckets with water—

Art. 25th. The first Lt. only is allowed to flog the men for misconduct, and he is never to give them more than one dozen for an offence with a piece of nine thread ratline—

W. M. Crane.

U S Ship *Genl. Pike*
Sacketts Harbour   July 28th. 1814

The regulations for the internal government of the *Madison* dated Decr. 19th. 1813 will be the rule of action on board the U S Ship *Genl Pike*

W. M. Crane

Art. 26th   The Marine Officer will take charge of all Soldiers that may come on board as well as Marines, unless a Senior Officer should embark with them, he is to inspect the Arms, Ammunition Cloathing and Messing of the Marines he will exercise them daily and whenever the Crew are called to Quarters; they are also to be trained to the great guns— Offences committed by the Marines not requiring my interference may be punished by the Marine Officer, not exceeding One Dozen with a piece of nine thread ratline, a morning report will be made to me acquainting me with the strength & situation of the detachment, no reductions, or promotions must be made amongst the Marines without my concurrence

Art 27th.   Cursing and Swearing at the men it is hoped will cease, all Officers are expressly enjoined to discountenance it

Art 28th.   If any of the Crew, neglect either to turn out in their watch, or duty such persons may be confined, or the first Lieut. sent for, but no person save the first Lieut. is permitted to flog them—

July 28th. 1814   W. M. Crane.

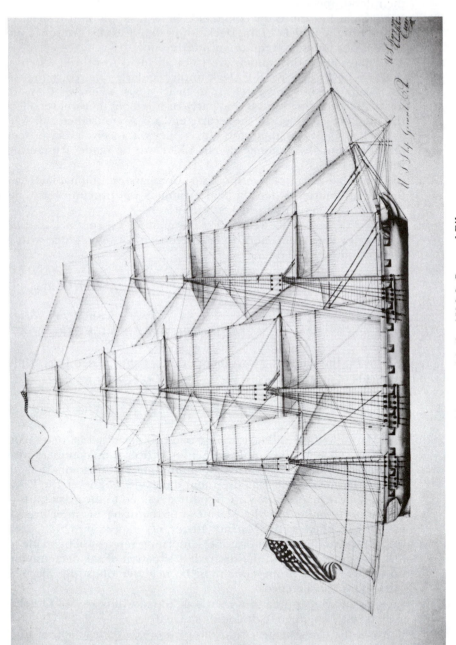

Plan of Spars and Sails of U.S.S. General Pike

Articl. 29. The Spirit room is never to be opened but in the presence of a Commissioned, or warrant officer, the Master at Arms will also attend to guard against accident from the lights, which are never to be out of a good lanthorn

W. M. Crane

Art 30th. All the Lieutenants, Master, Masters Mates, and Midshipmen will be particularly careful to keep a correct cloaths list, watch, quarter and Station Bills

W. M. Crane

DS, NCooHi, General Orders (NM 45.57).

COMMODORE ISAAC CHAUNCEY TO SECRETARY OF THE NAVY JONES

No. 131   U.S. Ship *General Pike*
Sacketts Harbor   19th Decemr. 1813

Sir

Since our return from Niagara the crews of the different vessels have become extremely sickly particularly the *Madison*—the deaths from that Ship for the last twenty days have averaged nearly one a day— the Marines are also very sickly averageing from 35 to 40 every day on the Sick report.— The Men have every thing that this place can afford to make them comfortable, yet the very best constitutions sink under the effects of the Climate for notwithstanding the best medical attendance they frequently die after two or three days sickness— It is really disheartening to see so many fine fellows sinking under disease with scarcely a possibility of saving them.—

Beleiving that it would benefit the Service and meet your approbation—I have directed all the Wounded, Ruptured and those rendered unfit for duty by long and fixed diseases to be discharged from the service of the United States as their continuance here would endanger their own lives and add to the expence of the Station without rendering service— I have the honor to be very respectfully Sir, Yr. Mo. Ob. St.

Isaac Chauncey

LS, DNA, RG45, CL, 1813, Vol. 8, No. 72 (M125, Roll No. 33).

AN UNKNOWN MIDSHIPMAN TO J. JONES

Sackets Harbour   December 21st. 1813

Most Esteemed Uncle,

I this moment recd. yours of the 10th. Inst. and am surprised to learn you have not received my letters. I wrote you on the 10th. Ulto. and also on the first Inst. Informing you of my having been attacked with the fever. You may be assured nothing gives me more pleasure than to write to or hear from you my dear uncle, who have been more than a parent to me.

Opperations of an offensive nature are suspended here for this season. 'tis' exceedingly cold, and every article we have to pay the most extravigant prices for. 'tis' reported we are going to build two ships and a brig. I hope it may be true, for if I may be allowed an opinion I conceive it of more importance that our forces on the Lakes should be strengthened than on the Ocean. 'Tis' also reported that our prize agent, J. N. Heard is coming on to pay us our prize money. I know not whether 'tis' correct, would to God it may be so. You may judge how much we have need—

The Como. has given the men one dollar apiece to celebrate Christmas and there are not five Officers who have money sufficient to take their letters from the Post Office. It is much to be regretted that our land forces have been so unfortunate; but <u>Montreal</u> must and will be ours. We have nothing to do here of any consequence. I ardently wish I could visit you this winter and my health requires it.

In case my prize money should be as much as it is supposed, with your consent, I will resign visit Washington and obtain a Lieutenancy in Macomb's Regiment. This situation will be more lucrative and promotion more rapid. I may then safely calculate on a Captaincy in 18 months, war or peace. I cannot think of any thing like a Lieutenancy in the Navy these four years—

My health is recovering tho' I am far from being well, my love to yourself and family and respects to any who may enquire after me. While I have the honor to be &c.

Copy, DNA, RG45, CL, 1814, Vol. 2, No. 70 (M125, Roll No. 35). A copy of this letter was enclosed in a letter from J. Jones of 114 Water Street, New York, to Secretary of the Navy Jones dated 25 March 1814.

Destruction along the Niagara Frontier

The campaign on the Niagara in 1813 ended with the wanton destruction of homes and villages on both the Canadian and American sides of the border. Fort George, held by the Americans since April 1813, was only weakly garrisoned as winter set in. The militia stationed there trickled away as their times of service expired, and many were discharged before they were even paid. When a British force advanced on Fort George on 10 December, the commander, Brigadier General George McClure of the New York State militia, gave orders to abandon and destroy the post. Residents of nearby Newark, Ontario, were given short notice to evacuate their homes, and the village was burned, ostensibly to keep the British army from finding shelter there during the winter. In their retreat, the Americans did not have time to destroy the fort or its supplies and ammunition, and Fort George fell to the British.

The Americans retreated across the river to Fort Niagara. On 18 December, the British surprised and captured the American troops, who were unprepared for an attack despite earlier warnings that one was likely to occur. The nearby village of Lewiston was plundered and burned by the British army and its Indian allies.

On 30 December, the British army advanced to Black Rock, which was only weakly defended by local militia units. They plundered and burned the villages of Black Rock and Buffalo and destroyed the two American vessels and two prizes that lay aground there. Master Commandant Jesse D. Elliott feared that the British intended to advance on the naval base at Erie next.

The year ended with the British in control of the entire Niagara frontier; the Americans had lost all the territory on the Niagara that they had gained that year. Hundreds of families, both Canadian and American, could only watch as their homes and possessions were destroyed as winter set in on the Niagara.

BRIGADIER GENERAL GEORGE McCLURE TO SECRETARY OF WAR ARMSTRONG

Fort Niagara   10 Dec: 1813.—

Sir

This day found Fort George left to be defended by only sixty effective Regular Troops under Capts. Rodgers and Hampton of the 24th. Regt. U.S. Infy. and probably forty volunteers—

Within the last three days, the term of service of the militia has been expiring and they have recrossed the river almost to a man— Foreseeing the defenseless situation in which the Fort would be left, I had authorized some of my most active subalterns to raise volunteer companies for two months, and offered a bounty in addition to the monthly pay— It is with regret I have to say that this expedient failed of producing the desired effect—a very inconsiderable number indeed was willing to engage for a further term of service on any conditions— From the most indubitable information, I learn that the Enemy are advancing in force— this day a scouting party of Col: Wilcocks'[1] volunteers came in contact with their advance at twelve mile creek—lost four prisoners and one killed—one of the former they gave up to their savages— This movement determined me in calling a Council of the principal Regular and Militia officers left at Fort George this morning— They all accorded in opinion that the Fort was not tenable with the remnant of a force left in it— I, in consequence, gave orders for evacuating the Fort since dark and with but three boats have brought over already all the light artillery and most of the arms, equippage ammunition &c and shall doubtless have time to dispose of the heavy cannon before the Enemy makes his appearance— The village of Newark is now in flames—the few remaining inhabitants in it, having been noticed of our intention, were enabled to remove their property—The houses were generally vacant, long before— This step has not been taken without council, and is in conformity with the views of your Excellency disclosed to me in a former communication*

The Enemy are now completely shut out from any hopes or means of wintering in the vicinity of Fort George— It is truly mortifying to me that a part of the Militia at least could not have been prevailed on to continue in service for a longer term, but the circumstance of their having to live in tents at this inclement Season, added to that of the Paymaster's coming on only prepared to furnish them with one out of three months pay, has had all the bad effects that can be imagined— The best and most subordinate militia, that has yet been on this frontier, finding that their wages were not ready for them, became with some meritorious exceptions, a disaffected and ungovernable multitude—**

I am much surprized at not having received long before this time some instructions from your Department for my government—***

Having received none—the Militia all returning to their homes and no troops to supply their places—I am driven to the only alternative left me—

I shall remain at this garrison myself untill I can hear either from you or from his Excellency the Governor of this State— I have the Honor to be yr. most obt. servt.

Geo. McClure   Br. Genl.
Commdg.

* not true, my letter authorized it only in case it should be necessary to the <u>defense</u> of Fort Geo. In that case the measure would be justifiable.

** Major Lee was expressly ordered to pay these Troops & the Indians.

*** Letters were sent by the Presidents direction enabling him to give bounties—& I made a requisition early in Nov. on Gov. Tompkins for 1000 men & gave gen. instructions for keeping the fort & furnishing a competent garrison.

LS, DNA, RG107, Department of the Army, Letters Sent to the Secretary of War, Registered Series, M–257(7) (M221, Roll No. 55). Footnotes denoted by asterisks were written in another hand and were probably added by the secretary of war.

1. Joseph Willcocks, an Irish immigrant, held minor government appointments in Upper Canada from 1800 to 1807. He came to sympathize with the cause of revolutionary Ireland and the whig tradition; as an elected member of the legislature of Upper Canada from 1808 to 1812, he was the leader of the parliamentary opposition group. In July 1813 he raised and commanded a unit of expatriate Upper Canadians fighting on the American side.

LIEUTENANT GENERAL GORDON DRUMMOND,[1] BRITISH ARMY, TO GOVERNOR-GENERAL SIR GEORGE PREVOST

Fort Niagara,   Decr. 20th. 1813.—

Sir,

Conceiving the possession of Fort Niagara to be of the highest importance, in every point of view, to the tranquillity and security of this Frontier, immediately on my arrival at St. David's, I determined upon it's reduction, if practicable without too great a sacrifice.— There being, however, but two Batteaux at this side the water, I did not think proper to make the attempt, until a sufficient number should be brought from Burlington; at this season of the year a most difficult undertaking. But, by the indefatigable exertions of Captain Elliott, Deputy Assistant Quarter Master General, every difficulty, particularly in the carriage of the Batteaux by land for several miles, notwithstanding the inclemency of the weather, (the ground being covered with snow, & the frost severe,) was overcome; they were again launched; and the troops, consisting of a small Detachment of Royal Artillery, the Grenadier Company of the Royal Scots, the Flank Companies of 41st. and the 100th. Regts. amounting in the whole to about 550, which I had placed under the immediate orders of Colonel Murray, Inspecting Field Officer, were embarked.— The enclosed report of that most zealous, and judicious Officer, will point out to you the detail of their further proceedings.— At 5 O'Clock, A:M: the Fort was attacked by Assault, at the point of the Bayonet; two Picquets, posted at the distance of a mile, and of a mile and half, from the Works, having previously been destroyed, to a man, by the same weapon: and at half an hour afterwards this important place was completely in our possession.

By this gallant atchievement, 27 Pieces of Ordnance, (mounted on the several Defences,) 3000 Stands of Arms, a number of Rifles, a quantity of Ammunition, Blankets, Clothing, several thousand pairs of Shoes, &c, have fallen into our hands; besides 14 Officers, and 330 others, Prisoners. And 8 respectable inhabitants of this part of the Country, who had been dragged from the peacable enjoyment of their property to a most unwarrantable confinement, were released; together with some Indian Warriors of the Cocknawaga, and Six Nation, Tribes.— The Enemy's loss amounted to 65 in killed; and to but 12 in wounded; which clearly proves how irresistable a weapon the Bayonet is in the hands of British Soldiers. Our loss was only 5 killed; and 3 wounded.— I have to regret the death of a very promising young Officer, Lieutenant Nolan, of the 100th. Regt.

I beg leave to bear the highest testimony of the anxious, active, and meritorious exertions of Colonel Murray; who, I regret to say, received a severe, though not dangerous wound in the wrist; (which I hope will not, at this critical period, deprive me, for any great length of time, of his valuable services;) and to Lieutenant Colonel Hamilton, of the 100th. Regt. and the Officers, Non Commissioned Officers, and Soldiers, who so gallantly achieved this most daring and brilliant enterprize.—

The Militia came forward with alacrity; and assisted much in launching, and transporting the Batteaux across the River, in a very rapid current, for which service they are deserving of the highest praise.— Captain Norton, the Indian Chief, volunteered his services; and accompanied the Troops.— And I beg to recommend in the strongest terms to the favor and protection of His Royal Highness, The Prince Regent, Captain Elliott, of the 103rd. Regt., Deputy Assistant Quarter Master General; whose conduct on this, as on every other occasion, has been so distinguished; as also Lieutenant Dawson, of the 100th. Regt. who commanded the Forlorn Hope; Captain Fawcett, of the same Regiment, who immediately supported him with the Grenadiers; and Captain Martin, who, with three Companies, gallantly stormed the Eastern DemiBastion.—

My best acknowledgements are due to Major Generals Riall, and Vincent, for the cordial and zealous assistance I received from them in making the arrangements; to Lieutenant Colonel Harvey, Deputy Adjutant General; and to the Officers of my personal staff.—

I have the honor to forward to Your Excellency the American Colours, taken on this occasion, by Captain Porter, my Aide de Camp; who being in my fullest confidence will give Your Excellency such further information as you may require. I have the honor to be, Sir, Your Excellency's most obedient, humble servant,

Gordon Drummond
Lt. General

LS, CaOOA, British Military and Naval Records, RG8, I, "C" Ser., Vol. 681, pp. 253–57. The return of the killed and wounded enclosed with this letter is not reproduced here.

1. Lieutenant General Gordon Drummond succeeded Major General Francis de Rottenburg as commander in chief and administrator of Upper Canada; Drummond arrived in Canada in December 1813.

MASTER COMMANDANT JESSE D. ELLIOTT TO SECRETARY OF THE NAVY JONES

U.S.S. *Niagara*,
Decr. 31. (11 PM.) 1813

Sir,

I have the honour herewith to enclose you a copy of a Dispatch this moment received from Majr. Isaac Barnes commanding a force on the retreat from Buffalo and Black Rock. The Ice will soon make sufficiently strong to bear a force which no doubt is advancing for the destruction of Erie and the fleet under my command— The latter will be defended as long as ammunition, Provisions & men will last—a disposition to defend the helpless village of Erie has induced me to require of the commg. militia officer present together with the officer commanding the Division that the former would order his Regiment under arms immediately and that the Divisional Officer would with all possible despatch repair to this place with such number of men as he may think advisable—

A few days since I had the honour to enclose you the copy of a Report made Commodore Isaac Chauncey as to the situation of our naval force on this Lake— In my letter accompanying that Report I suggested the propriety of having one hundred & fifty men detached from the army to do duty as marines— I have now Sir addressed a Letter to the commanding military officer at Pittsburgh, a copy of which is enclosed together with one to the officer on the retreat, the commanding militia officer present and Majr. Genl. Meade, commg. Division— The bearer of the despatch has informed me verbally that the Troops retreated on without ammunition, and as this will be the most proper place for meeting the Enemy I have advised him to move on—when on his arrival such arrangements as our means will admit of will be made— Impressed with the idea that the Enemy will make any sacrifice to regain the command of this Lake I have collected what Provisions I could obtain and placed them on board the shipping— I shall detatch an officer with a sufficient number of men to attend four pieces of state artillery and shall command in person— Respectfully I have the Hon. to be yr.

Jesse D. Elliott

LS, DNA, RG45, MC, 1813, No. 198 (M147, Roll No. 5).

[Enclosure]
"Copy"

To the Commandant of Erie or to whom it concerns—

The British this morning landed about three thousand Regulars, militia, and Indians at Black Rock and after a severe engagement with our militia under command of Majr. Genl. Hall forced them to retreat to the Village of Buffalo and about sun rise to surrender themselves prisoners of war. The houses in the Village were immediately committed to flames and about three oclock this afternoon almost entirely consumed—at the same time two large Vessels lying above Black Rock were set on fire, and consumed. It is the avowed object of the British (as received by good authority) to proceed in a short time to Erie, for the purpose of burning the vessels in that Port, and as an inducement to the Indians to aid and assist them in this nefarious plan, full liberty is given them to plunder for their own benefit, wherever they may go, as the communication from this place to the Eastward is entirely interrupted by the said Indians &c. and as it is important for you to have the earliest information of the above, we recommend to you every exertion, for to be in readiness in case of an attempt to burn as aforesaid and request of you some assistance of men, arms and ammunition as we have but few arms and no amunition— The time is alarming! Distruction is the order of the day—

On the retreat from Buffalo, 30th. December 1813,

Isaac Barnes, Majr.
Comdg. Militia near Buffalo

N.B. Information is just received that the Enemy have advanced up Lake Erie 8 or 10 miles and destroy every thing as they pass——

Copy, DNA, RG45, MC, 1813, No. 198, enclosure (M147, Roll No. 5).

[Enclosure]

Erie, Decr. 31, 1813.
11 o'clock P.M.

Sir,

I have this moment received a Despatch by Express, of which the enclosed is a copy, & request you to order out the militia as soon as possible for the defense of this place—

Should the Ice make so as to bear Troops I shall not be able to afford any protection to the Town. I have the honour to be, yr. obt. servt.

(signed)   Jesse D Elliott
commg. force on Lake Erie

Major Genl. Meade
Meadville

Copy, DNA, RG45, MC, 1813, No. 198, enclosure (M147, Roll No. 5).

[Enclosure]
"Copy"

U.S.S. *Niagara*
Erie   31st. December 1813—

Sir

A few days since, I addressed the Honl. the Secy. of the Navy, on the subject of the defense of the vessels at this place. I then suggested to him the propriety of requiring from the war depart. a force of One hundred and fifty men, and that they could be received more readily from Pittsburg than any other place. I herewith enclose you a Copy of a Dispatch this moment received from the Commanding and surviving officer of a force that has been in action with the Enemys* fleet have arrived at Niagara with a large number of men, and from present appearances, are destined for this Place, for the distruction of the Fleet as well as the Town of Erie, I would therefore suggest to you Sir the necessity of using all possible dispatch in repairing to this place with what Regular force, you may have, under your command, a Copy of this communication, I have forwarded to the Genl. Government. With Great Respect I have the honor to be Sir your &c—

signed   Jesse D. Elliott
Comdg. Naval officer
Lake Erie

Commanding Military Officer
Pittsburg

*This must be a mistake the enemy's fleet cannot have arrived at Niagara—The sentence is ambiguous.

Copy, DNA, RG45, MC, 1813, No. 198, enclosure (M147, Roll No 5). The footnote denoted by an asterisk was added by William Jones.

[Enclosure]
"<u>Copy</u>"   Erie   31st December 1813

Sir,
    Enclosed you have the copy of a Dispatch this moment received from Majr. Isaac Barnes on his retreat before the Enemy from Buffalo, and I have the honor to suggest to you the propriety of calling out the Regiment of Militia under your command— Very respectfully your obd. sert,

Signed   Jesse D. Elliott

Col. Wallace
Erie

Copy, DNA, RG45, MC, 1813, No. 198, enclosure (M147, Roll No. 5).

Chapter Four

The Gulf Coast Theater:
January–December 1813

Captain John Shaw, commander of the New Orleans Station, was an old hand on the Gulf Coast. He had been appointed to the post soon after the Louisiana Purchase, was stationed there from 1803 to 1805, and returned in 1811. Although he was familiar with the geography and environment of the Mississippi Delta, he disliked serving under the military officers usually given overall command of U.S. troops in the Louisiana Territory. He especially disliked Major General James Wilkinson, who had held that post since 1803. Wilkinson had earned a strange reputation among regular army officers. He was given to intrigue and had been involved in the Aaron Burr conspiracy before betraying Burr. Investigated by courts-martial, Wilkinson managed to gain acquittal each time. He returned to New Orleans at the beginning of the War of 1812 having cleared his name once again. As soon as he was back in Wilkinson's grasp, Shaw began to communicate his distaste for the unsatisfactory command relationship. All the same, Wilkinson was the senior officer and the navy secretary ordered Shaw to cooperate.

The naval force available at New Orleans was unusually weak for an area so dominated by water approaches. A glance at a chart indicates at least five possible routes an enemy force could use to assault the city. All, save the Mississippi River, are shallow-water estuaries and bays, suggesting that the ideal defensive vessel would be a gunboat of the type admired by Thomas Jefferson. Yet, there were only ten operable gunboats out of fourteen assigned in late 1812. Of heavier vessels the station commenced the war with the brigs Siren, 16 guns, commanded by Lieutenant Michael B. Carroll; Viper, 12 guns, commanded by Lieutenant Daniel S. Dexter; and Enterprise, 12 guns, commanded by Lieutenant Johnston Blakeley. Lieutenant Joseph Bainbridge, Commodore William Bainbridge's younger brother, succeeded Carroll as commander of Siren in November 1812. Two other vessels remain to be mentioned: Shaw had purchased and renamed a ship Louisiana, formerly the merchantman Remittance, on the account of the navy, and had begun to convert her into an armed cruiser. Criticized for her rotten condition, Louisiana would one day give a good account of herself at the Battle of New Orleans. Shaw, an energetic officer, pressed hard to use the meager resources at his disposal to prepare for the enemy. He was, however, bedeviled by higher costs than those at other naval stations, a lack of willing recruits, and a disease-ridden, enervating climate.

Although unknown to Shaw for many months, he lost the brig Viper, now commanded by Lieutenant John Henley, to the frigate H.M.S. Narcissus, 32

629

guns, in mid-January 1813. Johnston Blakeley's Enterprise *sailed from New Orleans in company with* Viper, *separated, and put in at St. Marys, Georgia, without encountering the enemy. The department ordered Shaw to release Bainbridge to sail in* Siren *for the Delaware or Boston in March 1813.*

Meanwhile, Shaw had to contend with the extensive smuggling and piracy along the coast. With the rebellion of Spain's Central and South American colonies in 1810, new republics emerged in Colombia and Venezuela. The flags of these would-be nations provided a convenient cover for "privateers" intent on piracy. Enterprising seamen, aware that money was to be made capturing Spanish shipping, established their bases along the Gulf Coast. Lake Barataria, west of the delta, was one of the best known of these pirate bases. These activities had been a problem in peacetime, but now that war was at hand it was a question how these pirates would behave in the face of the British. Shaw's gunboats, however, were no match for the swift sailing schooners preferred by the Baratarians. The pirates were allowed to exist undisturbed until the autumn of 1814.

One of Shaw's more creative ideas was the establishment of a shipyard on the banks of the heavily wooded Tchefuncte River that drained from the north into Lake Pontchartrain. It was a remote, protected site, easily approached from Mississippi Sound by vessels needing repairs. They would enter the narrow pass called the Rigolets from the south and sail northwest across the lake to the yard. Shaw commenced the building of a large blockship to protect the passes north and east of New Orleans. Without the yard and blockship, it is difficult to see how the naval station could function effectively in wartime. Yet, Shaw had to defend the Tchefuncte yard and the blockship from the cost-cutting knife of the new navy secretary, William Jones, who seems to have decided they were expensive, useless appendages. Shaw also had a critic within the naval station, Purser Thomas Shields, as well as civilians who wrote to the navy secretary, casting aspersions on Shaw's activities.

In the one joint military and naval operation conducted during Shaw's tenure at New Orleans, he collaborated successfully with General Wilkinson, providing gunboats for transportation and protection of the military force that captured Fort Charlotte from the Spanish at Mobile during May 1813. Following this event, the War Department ordered Wilkinson to relieve General Henry Dearborn of command of the army at Sackets Harbor.

Shaw was delighted to find that General Thomas Flournoy, Wilkinson's successor, was a man he could like and respect. Several months later, when a full-scale uprising of Creek Indians erupted north of Mobile, Shaw feared that nearby Choctaws might join, endangering the settlements at Bay St. Louis and even Tchefuncte. Andrew Jackson's Tennessee militia suppressed the Creek insurrection during 1813–14, but not before Shaw became concerned that the military forces needed at New Orleans were being sent to fight Indians at the very moment when the British might attack his base.

In October 1813 the Navy Department finally granted Shaw's request for a transfer from the New Orleans Station. He was replaced by his capable second-in-command, Master Commandant Daniel T. Patterson. Departing his long-held command, Shaw wrote Patterson a prescient letter warning him of possible inva-

sion routes and advising him of the measures needed to protect New Orleans from an expected British attack. Shaw then reported to Washington to settle his accounts before proceeding to a seagoing command.

Capture of U.S. Brig *Viper*

On 2 January the U.S. brig Viper, Lieutenant John D. Henley commanding, departed the Balize on a cruise in the Gulf. The cruise was a short one, for only ten days out, the ship sprung a leak, forcing Henley to return to New Orleans for repairs. During the homeward voyage a strange sail was spied and Henley altered course to intercept the unknown vessel. The American commander discovered too late that he was closing with an enemy warship of superior size. Henley bore his ship away in an attempt to escape, but all efforts to outsail his foe proved futile. After a chase of five hours, Viper was overhauled by H.M. frigate Narcissus.

CAPTAIN JOHN R. LUMLEY, R.N., TO
ADMIRAL SIR JOHN B. WARREN, R.N.

Copy.

His Majesty's Ship *Narcissus*
at Sea, 17th Jany. 1813.—

Sir,

I beg leave to acquaint you, that His Majesty's Ship under my command Captured this day the United States Brig of War *Viper* mounting twelve Guns & having on board a Complement of 93 men— She had been Cruizing Seven Weeks off the Havanna, and had made no Captures— I have the honor to be Sir, Your most Obedient Humble Servant

Signed   Jno. Richd. Lumley   Captn.

Copy, UkLPR, Adm. 1/503, p. 283.

LIEUTENANT JOHN D. HENLEY TO SECRETARY OF THE NAVY HAMILTON

New Providence   Feby. 1st 1813

Sir,

It is my misfortune to address you as a prisoner, On the 2nd. of Jany. I saild. in company with the U.S. Brig *Enterprize,* on the 7 we parted off the Tortugas where I continued to cruise untill the 12. when it was discovered that the *Viper* has sprung a leak   as the leak continued to increase I determined to run in to have a fair opportunity to examine it. on the 17th. about 50 miles to the Eastward of the Balise a large sail was discovered to windward it was soon discovered that she was a cruiser   I bore up immediately for cat & Ship Island but the Superiority of the Sailing of the Frigate enabled the Enemy to get along side after five hours chase when I was compelled to surrender to H.M. Frigate *Narcissus* Capt. Lumley of 40 guns, during the chase I cut away my stern Boat & hove four of my guns over board but without effect. Myself purser [1] Docter [2] Midshipman [3]

& crew was landed at this place on the 29th. the Brig with the Lieuts.[4] has gone to Bermuda; every exertion will be made to get my Officers & crew to the U. States as early as possible and hope on examination that it will be found that the hr. of the Flag has not suffered by being struck to such superior force.[5] I have the hr. to be Respectfully yr. Obt. Sevt.

John D Henley

ALS, DNA, RG45, BC, 1813, Vol. 1, No. 30 (M148, Roll No. 11).

1. Humphrey Magrath.
2. Acting Surgeon's Mate Gerard Dayers was appointed a surgeon on 7 May 1813. His commission was confirmed by the Senate on 24 July 1813.
3. Henry Laub, Joseph Boussier, David C. Nicholls, Erasmus Watkins, and John B. Rousseau.
4. Acting Lieutenants Frederick W. Smith and Laurence Rousseau. They arrived in *Narcissus* at Bermuda on 10 February. Both officers were promoted to lieutenant on 24 July 1813.
5. A court of inquiry convened at the Washington Navy Yard on 18 May 1813 absolved Henley of any blame in the loss of *Viper.* For the record of this court, see DNA, RG125, CM, Vol. 4, No. 136 (M273, Roll No. 4).

The Campaign against Smugglers and Pirates

As commanding officer of the New Orleans Station, Captain John Shaw's most important responsibility was defending the American Gulf Coast against British attack. But the Royal Navy was not the only enemy with whom Shaw had to contend. He also had to suppress the numerous smugglers and banditti that infested the waterways of the Mississippi Delta. With limited resources at his disposal and denied adequate support from the department, Shaw was clearly overmatched by both opponents. It is not surprising, then, that the commandant responded with pique when criticized for not combatting piracy more vigorously.

Captain John Shaw to Secretary of the Navy Hamilton

The Honb. Paul Hamilton,   New Orleans, January 18th. 1813

Sir,

I was honored by yesterday's Mail, with yours of the 14th. Ult. enclosing a copy of a letter, from the Naval officer of the Customs,[1] at this port, to the Honorable the Secretary of the Treasury;[2] and must beg leave to make reference to the several letters to you, in which I have pointed out, from time to time, the many outrages committed on this coast, by <u>privateers</u>, <u>pirates</u>, and <u>smugglers</u>; and in which I have endeavored to demonstrate, that the force heretofore under my command, had been rendered by decay, altogether inadequate to the protection of the coast, and the support of the revenue laws, even in a time of peace:— On the latter subject, the incompitency of the force,—lest it may have been intercepted, for the receipt neither of it, nor of scarcely any other, has for a long time, been acknowledged; I beg leave to insert here, the second paragraph of my letter of the 10th. July last,[3] to the Honorable Secretary:

"From my former communications to the Honorable Secretary of the Navy, it will have been observed, that the force under my command, is by no means adequate to the defence of the extensive coast which it has to guard, even against pirates & privateers, in a state of peace; and how much less so, must it be in a time of War!— In addition to the Gun boats, which have been ordered to this station, from New York, but which, by the bye, have not yet arrived,—I would suggest, that a few copper-bottomed Schooners, mounting from 10 to 12 Guns each, are almost indispensably necessary. Such vessels would enable us, if sent out amongst the West-India-Islands, greatly to annoy the Commerce of the enemy, on its passage from Jamaica to England."

As the whole circumstance, taken together, of the round which Mr. Croudson's letter has taken, through two Departments of the Government, and thence back again to this place, cannot possibly be viewed in any other light than, as conveying, however delicately, an oblique glance at censure; it necessarily compels me again to advert, to a subject, to which my feelings had almost ceased to vibrate, and on which, I had intended, never again to trouble you:—

I have never, at any time, or on any occasion, declined or neglected to employ every mean within my power, towards the inforcement, not only of the revenue laws, but of every other law of our Country, so far as the duties of my office may have rendered the employment of these means proper; but as, from the subordinate situation under a Military General,[4] and, as circumstances may by chance require, in the case of his absence, under the command of a Military officer of almost any grade, in which you have judged it expedient to place me;—the disposal of the Naval force is entirely wrested out of my hands; I cannot conceive how any responsibility or censure, on account of such disposition, good or bad, of the force nominally under my Command, can possibly attach itself to me; I have in truth no manner of control over them; they are ordered by the Military Chief, from place to place, as he thinks proper, while I have become the mere trumpeter of his will and pleasure. Should any censure therefore be conceived to be due, on account of the neglect, apparently insinuated, by Mr. Croudson, in his letter; I trust that it will be directed to its proper object. In short, having no claim on any praise which may be judged due, to any judicious dispositions which may happen to be made, of the forces here, I hope to stand exonerated from the consequences of those of a contrary character.

I shall conclude with a sincere repetition of the assurances which I have heretofore offered so frequently; that every effort shall be used on my part, towards strengthening, by number and condition, the Naval forces on this station; and with informing you that nothing now detains the Ship *Louisiana*, but want of men,—and that a staunch brig of 229 Tons burthen,[5] lately purchased into the service, for the purpose of being turned into a bomb vessel, will, as I hope, be shortly ready for service. Sir, I have the honor to be with great respect your Most Obt Servt.

John Shaw

I have the honor to enclose herewith a copy of an order[6] from General Wilkinson, to exemplify the subject of this letter

LS, DNA, RG45, CL, 1813, Vol. 1, No. 23 (M125, Roll No. 26).

1. Samuel Croudson.
2. Albert Gallatin.

3. See Dudley, *Naval War of 1812*, Vol. 1, pp. 383–84.

4. Shaw is referring here to Major General James Wilkinson, U.S.A. For background on the Shaw-Wilkinson feud, see *ibid*, pp. 388–98.

5. *Etna.*

6. Enclosure not printed.

CAPTAIN JOHN SHAW TO THOMAS H. WILLIAMS [1]

New Orleans   February 24th. 1813.

Sir,

I have been honored with the receipt of your note of yesterday, covering an "extract of a letter from the Secretary of the Treasurer, to the Collector at New Orleans, dated December 10. 1813";—and I am, myself, perfectly aware, how desirable it is, that efficient measures should be adopted by the authority which Controls the Naval & Military forces on this station, for breaking up the hordes of Marine banditti, by whom the revenue, & other laws of the United States, have been so long outraged within your district.— I have always, so far as I have been enabled by the means placed at my disposal, answered with alacrity, the several Calls which have from time to time, been made on me, for aid towards the accomplishment of that object; and I have made frequent representations to the Navy Department of the entire insufficiency of these means:—

It remains for me to inform you, however,—and the emotions with which I now do it, are remotely different from those of exultation,—that the situation in which I have been placed, by a letter from the Honorable Secretary of the Navy, dated 12th. October,—is such as to make it utterly impossible for me, without subjecting myself to trial & sentence, by a Military Court Martial, to render you any assistance whatever, without an order from General Wilkinson   Sir, I have the honor to be yours respectfully

(Signed)   John Shaw

LB Copy, DLC, Naval Historical Foundation Collection, John Shaw Papers, 1813 Letter Book.

1. Thomas H. Williams was collector of customs for the port of New Orleans.

Problems of Ill Discipline

The nature of naval service on the New Orleans Station made the maintenance of strict discipline among subordinate officers and enlisted men a difficult task for Captain John Shaw. Unlike the commander of a man-of-war, Shaw did not have the advantage of having his men confined within wooden walls, where a vigilant eye could be kept on one and all from the quarterdeck. Instead, Shaw's men were deployed in gunboats along waterways stretching from New Orleans to Mobile Bay. Such physical separation impeded his ability to exert authority consistently and effectively and increased the likelihood that disciplinary lapses might occur.

The most important instrument Captain Shaw had at his disposal to insure adherence to naval law was the court-martial. Courts-martial could, and often did, mete out harsh corporal punishments to those guilty of breaching regulations. Naval officers believed that it was this type of punishment, and the fear it inspired, that helped maintain order among their men. Yet Shaw often lacked the necessary number of officers to convene courts-martial, a situation he feared would erode discipline on the station.[1] It is noteworthy that among all naval stations in 1813, the second highest number of courts-martial were convened at New Orleans.[2]

1. *For example, see p. 666.*
2. *Thirty-two courts-martial and courts of enquiry were convened in 1813. Eight were held at New Orleans—seven of the former and one of the latter. For additional reading on discipline in the early sailing navy, see Valle,* Rocks & Shoals; *Langley,* Social Reform; *and C. McKee,* U.S. Naval Officer Corps.

COURT-MARTIAL OF ORDINARY SEAMAN JOHN PERRY

New Orleans   2d. Feby. 1813.

Proceedings of a Naval Court Martial convened by order of Commodore John Shaw—

Present

Lieut. Commt. Joseph Bainbridge	⎫	President
" " Danl. T. Patterson	⎪	
" " Danl. S. Dexter	⎬	Members
" " Louis Alexis	⎪	
" " Tho: Ap Catesby Jones	⎭	
Wm. Wilson		Judge Advocate

The case of John Perry, ordinary Seaman, was taken up on the following charges—

To wit: A repeated breach of the 17th article of an act for the better government of the Navy of the U.S. passed in 1800—

Specifi 1st.   Deserting from the Goal in Bayou St. Johns while on duty on or about the 12th of Decr. 1812.

"   2d.   Deserting from Mr. Dealy Masters mate of Gun Vessel *No. 162* on the 13th of the same when under confinement.

"   3d.   Deserting from the Marine Guard at the ~~Hospital~~ Arsenal on the 15th of the same month under similar circumstances.

The prisoner challenged two of the members of the court, and it appearing that he had already been punished in a summary way for the same offences that were now charged against him, the prosecution dropped—

The prisoner was then arraigned on a charge of, "Threatening and mutinous language while in confinement onboard of Gun Vessel *No. 24* at Tchifonté and a repetition of the same on board Gun Vessel *No. 156* on her passage from Tchifonté to Fort St. Johns on or about the 20th Inst."

Specification—   "Saying publickly that he would have satisfaction and threatening to take the life of Lieut. Louis Alexis whenever he should have an opportunity"

Plea "<u>Not Guilty</u>"

1st. Witness George Parker   I heard the prisoner say about 4 weeks ago that if Lieut. Alexis punished him, he would take his life—that he had no right to punish him and that he would have Satisfaction— I heard the prisr. afterwards say the same thing on the passage to Fort St. Johns aboard *156*— He was sober when he use thos expressions—

Q by Court   What was the reason of the prisoners using those expressions?

Ansr.   Because, as he said, he had been frequently and severely punished without cause.

Q. by Court   Did you ever hear him assign any reason why Lieut. Alexis had no right to punish him?

Ansr.   The reason was that he had asked Lieut. Alexis for his discharge & that he had denied it to him— That the prisr. came to the Bayou bridge in a boat, came to town and shipped on board the *Louisiana* leaving the boat without permission.

Q by Court   Did you ever hear the prisr. mention the occasions on which he had been punished?

Ansr.   He mentioned his having been ordered to repair a drum—that he had been called upon by Lieut. Alexis to do so and that he had refused to comply— the prisr. told me that he knew how to do it but that he would not—

2d. Wit   Jas. Rowley   The prisr. said on board of *24* that if Lieut. Alexis punished him at his own discretion, he would have his life— afterwards on board of *156* on his passage to Fort St. Johns he said that Lieut. Alexis was the greatest villain that ever he heard of and repeated that he would take his life if he were punished— He said that he would bring Alexis up for the transactions in Tchifonte— The prisr. was sober at the time.

Q by Court   To what transactions did he allude?

Ansr.   In the first place to bringing up the Marine Minus belonging to *66* and flogging him and keeping him standing in the cold without a shirt during 3 hours and pickling his back every half hour— And he said he would see whether it was lawful for a man to put a halter round anothers neck and drum him about town—and that if there was no satisfaction to be got he would write on to Head-quarters— The witness further Stated that he had recd. about 16 doz: aboard of Capt. Alexis—

Lieut. Jones Witness   Stated that the expressions used on board of Gun Vessel *24* occurred between the 25th Decr. & the 7th Jany.—

The Court found the prisr. guilty and pronounced the following sentence—

"That he receive three hundred lashes on his bare back with a cat of nine tails, in the most public manner at the time and place that the commander in chief shall direct"

Joseph Bainbridge   Prest.
Dan[l] T. Patterson
Dan[l] S. Dexter
Louis Alexis
Thos" Ap Catesby Jones

Sentence approved—and to receive it—<u>one</u> half alongside the U.S. Brig *Siren*— the one half alongside the Ship *Louisiana* at 10 oclock on Saturday the 27th. Inst.

John Shaw

DS, DNA, RG125, CM, Vol. 4, No. 122 (M273, Roll No. 4).

COURT-MARTIAL OF PRIVATE PATRICK GARREY, U.S.M.C.

New Orleans   Wednesday 3d. Feby. 1813

Proceedings of a General Naval Court Martial convened by order of Commodore John Shaw—

Present

Lieut. Commt.	Joseph Bainbridge			President
"	"	Danl. T. Patterson		
"	"	Danl. S. Dexter		Members
"	"	Louis Alexis		
"	"	Tho: Ap Catesby Jones		
		Wm. Wilson		Judge Advocate

The Court occupied itself with the case of Patrick Garrey private of marines on the following charges.

1st. Charge   Drunkenness—

Specif—   Being drunk on post at the large gate of the lower Navy Yard on the afternoon of the 26th Jany.

2d. Charge   Assaulting a man belonging to the ship *Louisiana*—

Specif—   Stabbing or wounding with his bayonet James Curry & striking him with his musket unprovoked and while doing his duty cooking on the afternoon of the 26th Jany.

Plea "Not Guilty"

Thos. Watts Witness   "The prisr. appeared to be groggy on post, I believe on the 26th Jany. I did not see the pris. wound the man but I saw the wound afterwards—which seemed to be done—not by a thrust, but by a slanting stroke while doing his duty— Curry bled freely"

Jas. Berthe Witness   The pris. seemed to be drunk about the time stated in the charge— I saw the pris. give a side stroke to Jas. Curry but it was not a thrust

Jas. Curry Witness   The prisr. appeared to be tipsey— He shoved the bayonet into my thigh— He left his post to attack me—

Lieut. Patterson Witness   On the afternoon of the 26th Jany. I saw the prisr., off his post strike Curry with his Muskett— My attention was attracted by the noise Curry made when attacked by the prisr.— I went up and Curry shewed me his wound— Curry was at his station The prisr. I beleive struck him over the Caboose, behind which Curry was taking refuge— The prisr. appeared to me intoxicated—

Here closed the testimony for the prosecution.

Farragut Witness for prisoner   Thinks that the prisr: was intoxicated

Thomas   Witness—   thinks that the prisr. was only tipsy—

The prisr. have threw himself on the mercy of the Court.

The Court found him "Guilty" of both charges and pronounced the following sentence:

"That Patrick Garrey receive seventy lashes with the cat of nine tails on his bare back at such time and place as the commander in chief shall direct."

Joseph Bainbridge   Prest.
Danl T. Patterson
Danl S. Dexter
Louis Alexis
Thos" Ap Catesby Jones

Sentence Approved—and to receive it on Board the U.S. Brig *Siren* on Friday 26th. Inst.— (weather not favourable) the next good day

John Shaw

DS, DNA, RG125, CM, Vol. 4, No. 125 (M273, Roll No. 4).

Orders to Economize

Throughout the war, most of the materiel required to build, repair, and refit naval warships—cannon shot, gunpowder, cordage, canvas, kentledge—was unobtainable at New Orleans. It had to be shipped to the Gulf Coast from manufacturing centers in the Northeast. The heavy expense incurred in transporting these stores greatly inflated their price and was the primary reason the naval station at New Orleans proved so costly to maintain.[1] In 1813 expenditures at New Orleans escalated even higher as additional monies were needed to repair hurricane damage sustained the previous summer and to establish a new shipyard on the Tchefuncte River.

The large sums of money expended on the naval establishment at New Orleans so troubled the new secretary of the navy, William Jones, that on 5 February, he warned Navy Agent John K. Smith to curb spending. Further economies were ordered the following March, when Shaw was directed to reduce the number of gunboats and men under his command. The department's call for fiscal restraint at New Orleans would remain a familiar refrain the remainder of the war.

1. For Shaw's complaints to Secretary Jones concerning the high price of naval stores at New Orleans, see p. 666.

SECRETARY OF THE NAVY JONES TO NAVY AGENT JOHN K. SMITH

John K. Smith   Navy Depart.
New Orleans,.   5. febry 1813

Your letter dated 31st. Decr 1812 advising of your having drawn on this Department for the sum of 20 m. $ has just been handed to me.

The Accountant of the Navy has informed, that you have not forwarded your accounts—and I confess to you that with this information before me, and, perceiving as I have with great concern that the expenses on the New Orleans are extravagant beyond all reasonable bounds— I hesitated whether I should pay the bill in question or not. The solvency of your circumstances & that of your

Sureties has however induced me to accept this Bill— It is proper however that I should distinctly state to you, that after having allowed you sufficient time to transmit your accounts for settlement, I shall not, unless they shall be received, accept any more of your drafts— My determination is to check the great & astonishing extravagance of the New Orleans station: tho' I do not allow myself to attribute to you such extravagance.

W Jones.

LB Copy, DNA, RG45, MLS, Vol. 11, pp. 183–84 (M209, Roll No. 11).

SECRETARY OF THE NAVY JONES TO CAPTAIN JOHN SHAW

Capt. John Shaw   Nav: Dep'mt.
New Orleans.   1. March 1813

It has been determined to retain in commission at New Orleans only ten gunboats—& the two block Ships—& the Bomb Brig, all the other gun boats, must be immediately laid up in ordinary in the care of the officer of the Yard— Each of the boats in commission must have:

a commander
2 Masters Mates or Midshipmen
1. Acting Gunner
1. Steward
1. Cook
8 able Seamen, & 6 ordinary seamen & boys. The block Ships & bomb Brig, must have no more men attached to them, than may be indispensibly necessary

The *Siren* you will immediately order to the Delaware giving to her commander, special instructions to keep a good look out for the enemy squadron now blockading the Chesapeak. & supposed to be lying, between the Delaware & the Chesapeak

Every officer & man, now on the orleans Station, not required to complete the above arrangement must be immediately paid off, & discharged from the Service.

I have to issue to you, my most positive injunctions, not again to purchase any vessel, of any description, or Even to do any important repairs—or to make requisitions on the agent, for any extensive supplies. without the previous approbation of this Department—otherwise you must be charged with the amount in, your individual capacity.

W. Jones

LB Copy, DNA, RG45, SNL, Vol. 10, pp. 286–87 (M149, Roll No. 10).

Public Criticism of Captain John Shaw

Critics of Captain John Shaw were to be found not only among officers of the army and navy at New Orleans, but also among the city's civilian population. Some complained of a want of energy and judgment in Shaw's direction of the station's affairs. Others leveled a more serious charge: that the captain was guilty of grossly mismanaging department funds. Such allegations no doubt fueled Secretary Jones's suspicion that the New Orleans Station was run with too much laxity.

[EDMOND?] JOHNSTON TO SECRETARY OF THE NAVY HAMILTON [1]

New Orleans   March 8th 1813—

As I am a man who never meddles himself with the private affairs of other People, but when it becomes public I think that everyman who feels a particular welfare for his Country & Nation ought to concern himself especially when he hears and sees dicernably a part of the Naval Institution of this Port now dwelling upon the verge of an ~~eternal~~ eternal extermination. I will now acquaint you of the actions of Comodore Shaw, he ~~has~~ is a man slow in execution, decision and Judgement; He has [lately?] [purcha]sed a Merchantman & fitted her out for the defence [of?] [this?] port. Now you would be surprized and astonished [it?] [would?] alarm you, she is good for Nothing, she mounts from [?] [to?] [?] guns and the other day when they were firing salutes on [the?] birthday of Washington she was very much shattered and I have likewise heard an Old experienced Naval Officer express himself verry warmly on the subject, he says that as soon as she is ordered on a cruise and ever came into a contact with the Enemy she would directly sink; the Captain [2] who commands her, says that as soon as he is ordered on a cruise he will ~~ab~~ abdicate his ~~com~~ office before he would place his life in such a perilous situation not that he is pusillanimous but he dreads at the thought of coming in Contact with the Enemy and would inevetilably crown his efforts with opprobrium and sorrow. her Name is the *Louisana* cost $98.000. He spends one week with another $5.000 and the Citizens of the City exclaims loudly at his extravagance and it is the perpetual conversation that the Government ought to be informed of his actions and that he ought to be displaced. [3]

I have now volunteered my services in performing the desires of the people and I think Sir that you would be doing a very patriotic thing to your Country to displace him immediately and place a Man of Reputation who would act with descision, Judgement, Judiciousness, and execute with the greatest velocity You have now an apparent elucidation of the subject. I have the honor to be with the highest consideration and respect Sir your most obedient humble servant

[Edmond?] Johnston
New Orleans   March 8th 1813

ALS, DNA, RG45, MLR, 1813, Vol. 2, No. 55 (M124, Roll No. 54).

1. Johnston was not aware that William Jones had replaced Paul Hamilton as navy secretary.
2. Lieutenant Daniel S. Dexter.
3. For similar complaints concerning Shaw, see Benjamin Morgan's letters of 11 January and 15 March 1813 to Chandler Price, PHi, U. C. Smith Collection, Papers of William Jones.

U.S. Brig *Siren* Departs New Orleans

With the departure of Enterprise and the capture of Viper, the only cruising vessel left on the Gulf Station was the brig Siren. But in March, she too was ordered to the northward[1] *thus reducing Captain John Shaw's active force to the ship Louisiana and seven gunboats. Siren, commanded by Master Commandant Joseph Bainbridge,*[2] *departed Balize on 3 April, cruised for a month in the Gulf, then sailed for Boston where she arrived on 10 June.*[3]

1. For Siren's original sailing instructions, see p. 639. These instructions were countermanded in Jones to Shaw, 23 March 1813, DNA, RG45, SNL, Vol. 10, p. 318 (M149, Roll No. 11).
2. Bainbridge was promoted to master commandant on 3 March 1813.
3. For Joseph Bainbridge's report of Siren's arrival at Boston, see Bainbridge to Jones, 15 June 1813, DNA, RG45, MC, 1813, No. 73 (M147, Roll No. 5). See also William Bainbridge to Jones, 11 June 1813, CL, 1813, Vol. 4, No. 49 (M125, Roll No. 29).

MASTER COMMANDANT JOSEPH BAINBRIDGE TO SECRETARY OF THE NAVY JONES

U.S. Brig *Siren*
Balize   30th March 1813

Sir,

Having fitted out my vessel in the best manner our means will allow on this station, for there are many things which are necessary to a vessel which can't at all be procured here; and being about to put to sea again, I do myself the honor of writing to you to inform my readiness for a cruise and of my being about to go out; thereby performing a pleasing as well as necessary duty— After going into dock and being given up to the officers of the Navy Yard; the Vessel in heaving out accidentally fell beyond her bearings, filled and sunk: but by the skill and unremitted exertions of Lt. Patterson the commander of the Navy Yard, she was raised in two or three days without any injury whatever and got the partial repairs that her accident of striking on the shoal on the coast of Florida rendered necessary— In crossing the bar at the Balize we had the Mishap added to our other accident of grounding, from the extreme shoalness of the water, notwithstanding we had started all our water, and brought her to an even keel, to put her in condition to pass the bar; this circumstance added to the rapidity of the current slewed her across the bar which twisted her rudder off at the neck, and left it barely sufficient (as it hung by a small piece) to guide the Brig as far as Orleans; we were obliged to take out the Guns, and after being in that situation between two, and three days we got her off and out of danger— This is an additional proof of the difficulties which a vessel of this draught of water must always find on this station, which difficulties render her situation extremely hazardous, the want of harbours and the shoalness and unevenness of the coast would make her very liable to capture if chased by an enemy of superior force—

After my arrival I demanded in justice to myself and respect to those to whom I feel myself amenable, a court of enquiry on my conduct in getting my vessel on shore, and having been honorably acquitted of all blame in the affair, I hope the proceedings of the court which I presume Comod. Shaw has enclosed to

you, and their opinion as published, will be perfectly satisfactory to yourself—[1]
I beg leave to mention to you the appointment of young Mr. Thos. Brown of
Philadelphia, as a Midshipman on board this vessel, with the approbation of the
Commodore, and which I hope will also meet yours—

Duty and respect to the Merits of Lt. Norris who is actg. as first Lieutt. on
board this vessel who is really a deserving young man and has been a long time
acting as Lieutt. require that I should endeavour to entreat you in his behalf,
and thereby gain if possible his commission for him; his long experience, and
his great merit as an Officer and a man justly entitle him to claim it—

Mr. S Henley who is also actg. as second Lieutt. is an extremely deserving
young man, and having acted in that capacity for a long time I hope you will be
pleased to confirm the appointment—

I must now Sir, speak to you on a subject very near my heart, and deeply interesting to me in my official capacity; my rise in the navy is all that I or any
other Officer can promise himself, this from want of occupation, for our navy
has at all times been slow, but when after having devoted the best part of his life
to the service of his country there should be promotions made above an Officer, it excites emotions of wounded pride which are extremely poignant— I
have felt it in its fullest extent in the promotion of Lieutt. Morris,[2] and I find by
the papers and common report that Lieutts. Allen and Biddle are spoken of—
This is a boon I have long laboured to deserve, and to acquire which I have entirely devoted myself since I first entered the service of my country— I have the
honor to be Sir, with the greatest respect Your Obdt. Servt.

<u>Joseph Bainbridge</u>

ALS, DNA, RG45, MC, 1813, No. 44 (M147, Roll No. 5).

1. For the record of this court of inquiry, see RG125, CM, Vol. 4, No. 129 (M273, Roll No. 4).
2. The negative response of other officers to Charles Morris's promotion to captain is docu-
mented in Dudley, *Naval War of 1812*, Vol. 1, pp. 516–23.

The Mobile Campaign

*In early February, the U.S. Congress, voting in secret session, authorized the occupation
of Spanish West Florida.[1] Within days of Congress's action, Secretary of War Armstrong
issued orders to Major General James Wilkinson instructing him to seize Mobile and the
surrounding territory as far east as the Perdido River.[2] Wilkinson received these orders on
14 March, and, acting with great dispatch, assembled an expeditionary force by the end
of the month. In making his preparations, the general called on Captain John Shaw to
provide naval escort for the army's troop transports.*

*The transports, convoyed by six gunboats, arrived at the entrance of Mobile Bay on the
evening of 10 April. While Wilkinson's troops debarked and made preparations to invest
Mobile and nearby Fort Charlotte, Shaw and his flotilla blockaded the entrance to the bay.
The seige that followed was a brief and bloodless affair with the Spanish garrison's com-
mander, Captain Don Cayetano Perez, agreeing to articles of capitulation on 13 April.
Two days later Fort Charlotte changed hands.*

Although the capture of Mobile had been a modest enterprise, undertaken against forces of a neutral power, it was one of the few military successes the United States could point to in 1813. It was also "the only permanent gain of territory made during the war."[3]

---

1. For background on American designs on West Florida, see Adams, History of the United States, *Vol. 1, pp. 206–15; and Pratt,* Expansionists of 1812, *especially Chapter 2.*

2. *A copy of these orders, dated 16 February 1813, may be found in Wilkinson,* Memoirs, *Vol. 3, p. 339.*

3. Adams, History of the United States, *Vol. 1, p. 215.*

Major General James Wilkinson, U.S.A., to Secretary of War Armstrong

Pass of Christian
April 3d. 1813   Evening

Sir

After many unexpected delays & cross accidents, one of which had nearly brought me to an antiprofessional end, (by drowning instead of Shooting) I reached this place, last evening in rear of the Detachment destined to take possession of fort charlotte, excepting a party of thirty or forty men whom I hourly expect; and the day Capt. Shaw overtakes me with two Gun Boats which I left at the Bayou St. John I Shall proceed: orders had anticipated my arrival here, for three of those vessels Supposed to be in this vicinity at the Bay of St. Louis to take possession of Mobile bay & guard the pass to the town, but those vessels left this Station on the 24th. ultmo. contrary to my arrangements, & have not since been heard of. I have Shifted my baggage twice, by necessity Since I left New Orleans, and finally was obliged to leave it, in a grounded Gun Boat, last evening; This morning I dispatched a Small vessel with a three pounder & about twenty men to get into Mobile bay, by the inland pass and prevent all communication between Pensacola & the Town if possible, at the Same time the Troops at Fort Stoddart are ordered to descend Mobile River & fortify opposite that town to cut off all Intercourse over land. A crazy Gun Boat which I have observed in the Bay of St. Louis will also be ordered to intercept all communication between the Spanish Ports the moment a Gale which now prevents all Intercourse with her shall abate; and if Capt Shaw does not detain me, I will if I live & am not opposed by Superior force, be before Fort Charlotte in eight days. For your Satisfaction & that of the President I Send this by express, to meet the mail at Fort Stoddert, and am in much in haste most respectfully Sir, Your obedt. Servt.

Ja: Wilkinson

N.B. I have with me Seven companies of the 2d. & 3d. Regts. Infantry & one of Artillery— I inclose the copy of a letter from Capt Shaw received the last Instant.

LS, DNA, RG107, Letters Sent to the Secretary of War, Registered Series, July 1812–May 1814, W–148(7) (M221, Roll No. 58).

[Enclosure]

New Orleans   April 1st. 1813

Dear Sir:

It has been with much regret I have just learnt that the Barge which you had been on board of have been upset, and that from the act of provadence alone both yourself and those Gentlemen whom accompanied you were arrested from being drowned. Presuming that all your baggage must have been with you in the boat, and the letter to Lt. Merrel [*Merrill*] must have been lost I have thought it adviseable to forward a duplicate of that dispached by Mr. Roany [*Roney*] to him. I shall sail positivily tomorrow— I will have to remain in the Chefuncta a few hours from thence I shall proceed to the Eastward Sir, I have the honor to be yr. ob St.

(Signed)   John Shaw

Copy, DNA, RG107, Letters Received by the Secretary of War, Registered Series, July 1812–May 1814, W–148(7), enclosure.

CAPTAIN JOHN SHAW TO SECRETARY OF THE NAVY JONES

Honorable William Jones.   Mobile   April the 19th. 1813.

Sir,

I have the Honor to Inform you that Fort Charlotte is now in our possession.

The Expedition sailed from the Pass Christian on the night of the 8th. Instant, the wind being ahead prevented our progress as fast as we could have Wish'd, On the 11th. Inst., Four hundred men were landed about three Miles below this place, and on the Evening of the 14th Inst. I anchor'd the following Gun vessels *Nos. 5. 22. 65. 156 & 163* in a close line ahead <u>on Springs</u> within 200 yards of Fort Charlotte, Articles of Surrender of the Fort was Enter'd into between the Spanish Commandant, and General Wilkinson & on the Evening of the 15th. Inst. our Flag was display'd within their Works, The Spanish Troops about Eighty in Number immediately took shipping and proceeded to Pensacola. Fifty Peices of Cannon has been got within the Work, Forty of which are mounted, but the Carriages much decay'd.

We have now Sir, an Extensive Coast, full of Shallows, which require light Vessels for Easy draughts of Water to navigate them, from the mouth of the Lafourche to this place is at least in Extent 300 Miles, the Naval force under my command has decreas'd to almost nothing, I have now with me nearly our whole Strength, *Nos. 5. 22. 65. 156 162 & 163*, Gun vessel *No. 22* with difficulty got here, I shall moor her for a guard Boat for the defence of this Harbour. & for the protection of the Bay, It will require for its defence 15 Sail of Gun Vessels, for the defence of the Regolets and the Island nearly Eastwardly 10 Sail, for the Mississippi and the Balize 10 Sail, for the La Fourche and Barrataria 6 Sail, with this Force I am satisfied that no Enemy's Vessels could anchor within our Waters with Safety, There is now but one Gun Vessel at New Orleans, which is under orders to sail for this place as soon as ready, Should an attack be made by the Enemy wherein the Naval force is required to act, It is too Evident that the small force under my command could make but a feeble resistance, Under these Circumstances, my

Honor as an Officer of the Navy may be liable to much censure & abuse, I trust that the Honorable Secretary of the Navy In the event of an attack being made on me by an Enemy, and my Incompetency to oppose the same, will be placed in a proper point of view, In all my communications to the Honorable Secretary for some months previous to the War, I have given him a true & faithfull statement of the real state and condition of the Force under my Command.

The General and myself will leave here in a few days In order to take a Survey of Mobile Point, to fix on the most Suitable place to Establish a Battery for its defence.[1]

Enclosed is a List of the whole Naval force now on this station Sir I have the Honor to be Your mo Obt. Servt.

John Shaw

LS, DNA, RG45, CL, 1813, Vol. 3, No. 16 (M125, Roll No. 28).

1. Relations between Shaw and Wilkinson during the Mobile campaign were free of the acrimony that had characterized their earlier dealings with one another. Indeed, the general was generous in his praise of Shaw's contributions to the expedition, and over the next several weeks the two commanders cooperated effectively to strengthen Mobile's defenses. A new fort was constructed at Mobile Point and four gunboats were stationed at the bay's entrance to protect the town from sea assault.

[Enclosure]

A List Exhibiting the whole Naval Force under my Command on this Station.—

What No.	No Guns	Callibre.	Number of Men	Where at
Ship *Louisiana*	22	1 24 pounder / 4 6 do }	136	Balize
G Vessel *No. 5*	5	1 24 do / 2 6 do }	44	Mobile
" " *65*	3	1 24 do / 2 6 do }	40	do
" *156*	5	1 18 pr. / 2 18 / 2 12 }	44	do
" *162*	5	1 18 pr. / 4 12 do Carronades }	46	do
" *163*	3	1 24 pr. / 2 6 }	40	do.
" *22*	3	1 12 pr. / 2 6 " }	26	do
" *23*	5	1 32 pr. / 4 6 pr. }	45 will be required, but at present—not man'd	
	51 Guns Total		421 Men Total	

Gun Vessel *No. 27.*, Condemned & is now laying at the Bay St. Louis.

Mobile   April 19. 1813.

John Shaw

DS, DNA, RG45, AF8 (M625, Roll No. 200).

Louisiana

By April 1813, Lieutenant Daniel S. Dexter had completed fitting out the ship Louisiana *for service.[1] Over the next five months,* Louisiana *alternated duty between stations at Plaquemine and the Balize. Dexter's most pressing concern during this time was the health of his crew, which, due to the effects of heat and disease, steadily deteriorated over the course of the summer. By August the numbers of men felled by death and sickness had become so great that there were scarcely enough healthy crewmen to work the ship. Dexter himself finally succumbed to illness, forcing his return to New Orleans in September.*

Another problem demanding Lieutenant Dexter's attention was the decayed condition of Louisiana*'s gun deck. In May it was discovered that all of the beams and some of the knees supporting the vessel's gun deck were rotten. As a temporary measure, Dexter had the gun deck reinforced with stanchions, but he warned Captain John Shaw that* Louisiana *could not engage the enemy and safely bear her current weight of metal. It was not until the end of the year that* Louisiana*'s heavy armament was removed in favor of lighter guns.*

1. *For additional documentation on the purchase, manning, and fitting out of* Louisiana, *see Dudley,* Naval War of 1812, *Vol. 1, pp. 382–83, 417–19, 434–35.*

LIEUTENANT DANIEL S. DEXTER TO CAPTAIN JOHN SHAW

U.S. Ship *Louisiana*, Plaquemine, 6th Aprl. 1813.

Sir,

I had the honor this morning to receive your two communications of the 25th March and 5th inst. and shall pay particular attention to the injunctions contained in them.

I arrived here on the 27th ult. and have remained here since for the purpose of getting the Ship in complete readiness for any event that may occur, and to exercise my men at quarters, the necessity of which your own reflection will convince you, as few of them were ever on board a man of war before.

I am sorry to inform you it is absolutely necessary that this Ship should be furnished with 40 or 50 more men; With her present complement I am unable fully to man the guns, even by stationing every man on board at them (including the Marines.) One gun is worked entirely by officers. In the event of going to sea, I should not be able to fight more than six guns, after manning the braces, tops, &c. and have none at small arms.

By a boat from the Balize last night, I learn that the Brig *Siren* sailed on Saturday last; that Gun Vessels *No. 5, No. 156,* and *No. 163,* arrived there a few days since; and that an English Sloop of war [1] appeared off the bar on Friday— I am unacquainted with the nature of Lieut. Merrill's orders, but from what you mention respecting Mobile, I conceive you expect to find these gun Vessels at the Bay St. Louis; and have accordingly dispatched a letter to Lieut. Merrill, apprizing him of your intentions.

I have caused the power of attorney to be copied, and again inclose it to you, with the signatures of all on board this Vessel who formerly to G B *No. 162* and *66.*

I must likewise apprize you of the great need I am in of more boats for the use of this Vessel. A launch, and another cutter are requisite. I have the honor to be, Sir, With great Respect, Your's &c. &c.

(Signed)   Dan[1] S. Dexter

LB Copy, DNA, RG45, Daniel Dexter Letter Book, pp. 53–54. In Dexter's hand.

1. *Herald*, 6th rate, 20 guns.

ACTING SURGEON GEORGE MARSHALL[1] TO ABRAHAM MARSHALL

U.S. Ship of War *Louisiana*
Balize   May 3rd 1813

Dear Father

I must again express my astonishment at not hearing more frequently from my family— You certainly might without much inconvenience indulge me occasionally in that respect— A few lines from you will be more interesting to me, than all I could write would be to you— I shall expect after you receive this, to have the pleasure of hearing from some of you every week— I shall not be much at N. Orleans, but you will continue to direct letters to that place— I have continual intercourse with Gentlemen who will forward them to me immediately—

In my last Letter I requested thee to offer a few observations on the Political state of affairs— There appears to be some prospect of a cessation of hostilities thro the intervention of the <u>Emperor of Russia</u>   I hope for a speedy & honorable peace— We have given our enemy positive evidence of the American Eagle being an <u>Amphibious</u> Animal, & capable of supporting her rights upon either Element— We have <u>won</u> all where nothing was expected—& <u>lost</u> all where everything was to have been gained— This reverse of fortune has reflected great light upon the Minds of our <u>learned Wiseacres</u>— They have, after a tedeous <u>Embargo</u> & [<u>Tarifs</u>?] system, <u>wisely</u> discovered tha [*that*] a Naval establishment is not "<u>an unnecessary & dangerous expence</u>" but an indespensable appendage to our government, & the only means by which we will be able to establish, & preserve peace— I conceive a <u>moderate Naval force</u> to be as essential to a commercial people, as positive Laws are to the peace and tranquility of Society—

We are just on our way to New Orleans with a prize—[2] she is a fine Brig—& it is presumed has considerable specie on board— I have plenty of business to attend to— You must not be allarmed for my safety when I inform you, that my <u>report</u> of this morning to the Captain, contained thirteen cases of <u>Yellow fever</u> five of dysentery—three of Hepatitis (Inflimation of the Liver) & seven of Intermittent fever, exclusive of Convalescents & slight cases— My candour will almost be questioned when when I inform you that out of the numerous patients which I have had since I commenced the practice of Medicine—the most part of whom were violent cases—I have not had the painful task of recording the fatal termination of but one case—& he was not properly my patient—as I was called in consultation— This almost unprecedented success in this Country did not arise from any peculiar mode of practice but to my singularly good fortune— I have one <u>Mate</u> to assist me, but neither of us get much rest day or night— New Orleans & the adjacent Country continues healthy—but the Troops at the Balize have the Fever among them

Present my love to my affectionate mother & family—& all my relations & friends—but particulary to [Uncl] J. Marshall & receive to thyself assurances of my sincere affection

GEO. Marshall

ALS, DNA, RG45, AF8 (M625, Roll No. 200). The address on this letter reads, "Mr. Abraham Marshall Senr., Marshalton Post Office, Pennsylvania."

1. George Marshall was appointed acting surgeon by Captain Shaw on 29 June 1812.
2. Probably the brig *Sao Pablo*. See Dexter's letter containing his interrogatories to *Sao Pablo*'s captain in Dexter to Shaw, 29 April 1813, DNA, RG45, Daniel Dexter Letter Book, pp. 59–61.

LIEUTENANT DANIEL S. DEXTER TO CAPTAIN JOHN SHAW

U.S. Ship *Louisiana*
Balize, 24th May 1813

Sir,

It is with regret that I yield to the necessity of informing you of the decayed state of the Gun Deck beams of this Vessel. My Carpenters have for some days past been Employed in Caulking the Gun Deck, which had become very leaky, and in several places were obliged to repair the plank which were decayed; in removing them, we discovered that the beams under them were quite rotten. I then caused <u>all</u> the beams to be bored, and found them more or less decayed; some of them so much so, that after boring into them about an inch or more was able to thrust the augur, without turning, almost entirely through the beam

Some of the Gun Deck Knees are also a little rotten, which with the decayed situation in which I found the beams, render me apprehensive that the vessel will not be able to support her present weight of metal for any length of time; particularly should it be necessary to fire her guns very often in succession.

Were it possible to procure them, I am of opinion that it would be most advisable to put 12 pounders on her Gun Deck which she would be able to bear much longer and in that time do more execution with them, than with a few broadsides of the 24 pounders.

During your absence from town, I inclosed in a letter to Capt. Patterson, which you have probably seen, the inadequacy of my crew to work the Guns. I now, more than ever, feel the deficiency in that point as 27 out of the before too small Complement are on the sick Report. In fact, I have seldom less than twenty and often as many as thirty unfit for duty.

Thus, Sir, having made you acquainted with the circumstances in which this Vessel is at present, I leave it with yourself to determine as to the expediency of making an alteration in her armament, and encreasing the number of her crew. I have the honor to be Sir, Most Respectfully Yours &c. &c.

(Signed)   Danl S. Dexter

LB Copy, DNA, RG45, Daniel Dexter Letter Book, pp. 62–63. In Dexter's hand.

Captain John Shaw to Brigadier General Thomas Flournoy,[1] U.S.A.

New Orleans   June 8th. 1813

Sir,

It has hitherto been found impracticable to procure a sufficient number of seamen to complete the crew of the ship *Louisiana,* now stationed for the defence of the Balize; nor has she at this moment, men enough on board, fit for duty, to man more than one half of her guns, while the Enemy have a force stationed actually in sight:— The Marine fencibles, a Corps formerly under the Command of Captain Allan, one of the pilots, stationed also at the Balize, are made up, chiefly, of sea-faring men, who are anxious to be transferred to their proper element; in which, could they be accommodated, our embarrassments, with regard to the *Louisiana,* would be at once removed; an object, which, under existing circumstances, is all-important to the interests of the public service. These considerations, therefore, induce me to solicit your authority, for the transfer of of so many of them, to the *Louisiana* as shall be found sufficient to work her guns, or, in other words, to complete her crew.

This transfer, at the desire, or with the consent, of the men themselves, will be no more a departure from principles, as you must readily perceive, than the inlisting of men from Volunteer Corps, into the regular service of the United States; the authority for the two measures, differing only in this, that the <u>latter</u> is <u>directly</u> authorized by an order from the Government, while the <u>former</u> is only <u>indirectly</u> authorized, by orders from the same source, for a strict co-operation between the land and Naval forces on this station.— The only possible objection which can ever be raised to arrangements of the kind now requested, is that of its being an interference with the command of the officers, who may thus loose their men. I believe it will be granted, however, that where the views of individuals happen to come in contact with the publick interest or safety, as in the present case, and they cannot be made to harmonize, the former should always be made to yield. Sir, I have the honor to be, very respectfully your obt. servt.

(signed)   John Shaw

LB Copy, DLC, Naval Historical Foundation Collection, John Shaw Papers, 1813 Letter Book.

1. Flournoy succeeded Major General James Wilkinson as commander of the Seventh Military District after the latter's departure from New Orleans in June 1813. The Seventh Military District comprised Louisiana, the Mississippi Territory, and Tennessee.

Lieutenant Daniel S. Dexter to Captain John Shaw

U.S. Ship *Louisiana,*
Plaquemine, 1st August 1813.

Sir,

I had the honor, last evening, to receive your two letters of the 26th ult. by a boat from G V *No. 5,* off Britain Island. She brought a Masters Mate, 4 Seamen, a serjeant and 12 soldiers, all of whom I have sent on board *No. 23,* and ordered Mr. Pollock to proceed in her immediately to Britain Island, where he will join *No. 5.*

Inclosed is a list of the sick belonging to this vessel;[1] though there are many not included in it, whose state of convalesence is not so well established as to prevent fears of relapses and who will not, probably, be able to do duty during the warm months evening; and also a list of the deaths.

Immediately after Dr. Marshall's departure, I dispatched a boat to New Orleans, for a Surgeon, medicines, and Hospital stores, and Doctor William Barnwell, junr. has, by Lt. Comdt. Patterson's orders, served on board, with a supply of the necessary articles. Every assistance and nourishment that Could possibly be procured, has been administered to the sick, and no pains or expence spared to render their situation comfortable. I am sometimes induced to hope a gradual and general recovery is about taking place, but am as frequently drawn back to despondency by relapses, deaths, & new cases.

Could I for a moment have conceived myself justifiable in the measure, I should long since have proceeded in this Vessel to one of the places mentioned in your letter, for the preservation of my crew; I could, by that means perhaps have saved the lives of 14 or 15 of them; But, of course, unauthorised, I dare not leave my station. Since I know your wishes on the subject, I shall, as soon as it is in my power, attempt it, though I fear tis too late, for I have now scarcely well men enough to weigh the anchor. I dispatched Mr. McKeever to New Orleans on the 28th ult. to open a rendezvous for this ship. Should he be have good success I may yet soon be able to extricate myself from this second Terre aux Buoeff's scene.[2]

I have given Mr. Edward Herries[3] permission to proceed to the Bay St. Louis for the benefit of his health. He is anxious to visit his friends at Baton Rouge, for which permission I have directed him to apply to you of his arrival at the Bay. I have the honor to be Sir, With Respect Your Obt. Servt.

(Signed) Dan[l] S. Dexter.

Commodore John Shaw
Bay St. Louis

LB Copy, DNA, RG45, Daniel Dexter Letter Book, pp. 83–84. In Dexter's hand.

1. Not found.
2. Dexter is referring here to the terrible suffering endured by the army while it was encamped at Bayou Terre aux Boeufs in 1809. Within a year losses due to disease and desertion had reduced the size of Wilkinson's 2,000 man force by over fifty percent; see Jacobs, *U.S. Army*, pp. 345-52.
3. Acting Midshipman Edward Herries died on 10 August 1813.

English Pilots at the Balize

On 31 May Lieutenant Daniel S. Dexter wrote Captain John Shaw that he suspected the river pilots at the Balize, most of whom were English, of providing intelligence to the enemy.[1] Because their work gave them an intimate knowledge of all ship movements in and out of the Mississippi River, these pilots were in a unique position to assist the Royal Navy in striking a blow not only against American commerce, but against Shaw's command as well. Readily perceiving the threat such men posed to the safety of the New Orleans Station, Captain Shaw promptly requested Governor William C. C. Claiborne to dismiss all pilots at the Balize who were British subjects.

1. See *Dexter to Shaw, 31 May 1813, DNA, RG45, Daniel Dexter Letter Book, pp. 65–66.*

Captain John Shaw to Governor William C. C. Claiborne

New Orleans   June 7th. 1813.

Sir,

By a letter just received from the commanding officer of the *Louisiana,* stationed at the Balize, I am informed that an English man of war, had appeared off the mouth of the river on the 27th. ultimo; that she had continued generally in sight, close in with the land, off the S.W. pass, until the 30th.; that the pilots, on board a pilot-boat, which had been out, and which was boarded, as they say, by a boat from the British ship,—learned that she was the *Herald* sloop of war, carrying 24 guns—16 long twelves, on the main deck, & eight on her upper deck; that she is stationed off the Balize, & is expected to be joined in a few days, by a brig of 22 guns; and that the Lieutenant from whom this information was obtained, inquired where the *Siren* was.

Lieut. Dexter expresses his strong suspicion, of the pilots having been on board the enemy's vessel, which, however, they deny; and that, as almost all the pilots* at the Balize, are, as he assures me English subjects, he has no doubt but they will give the enemy all the information which they may acquire, while they will conceal the real truth from us; or, in other words, that they will act agreeably to such instructions, as they may receive from the enemy:—

Your Excellency will readily perceive the obvious danger, to the safety of the country, to be apprehended, from permitting such a description of spies, to continue to act in the character of pilots; and I must therefore pray you to cause such of them as may be found to be British subjects, to be removed from their present situation. Sir, I have the honor to be your Excellency's Most obt. servt.

(signed)   John Shaw.

*The assistant pilots are here wished to be distinctly understood; and not those regularly appointed by the Executive of the state.

LB Copy, DLC, Naval Historical Foundation Collection, John Shaw Papers, 1813 Letter Book.

Governor William C. C. Claiborne's Circular to Pilots

New Orleans   June 10th 1813

Sir,

If any of the deputy Pilots in your employ at the Balize should be British subjects, you are hereby instructed to dismiss them & to report their names to the marshal of the ——— You will also dismiss from your service every other person against whom there exists the smallest suspicion of holding intercourse with the enemy, & you will report to me by every mail, whether any & what vessels of the enemy are to your knowledge or belief hovering on our Coast. I am, Sir, &c

Signed/   W. C. C. Claiborne.

Claiborne, *Letter Books,* Vol. 6, pp. 219–20.

GOVERNOR WILLIAM C. C. CLAIBORNE TO CAPTAIN JOHN SHAW

New. Orleans   June 10th 1813

Sir,

I have received the letter in which you inform me, that several persons employed by the Branch Pilot at the Balize, were British subjects, & strongly suspected of holding Intercourse with the enemy.— I have in consequence directed that all persons of the above description, be dismissed from service, & that their names be reported, in order that the necessary measures may be taken to remove them from the sea board. I am sir &c.

Signed)   W. C. C. Claiborne.

Claiborne, *Letter Books*, Vol. 6, pp. 221–22.

A Purser's Authority: Shaw *vs.* Shields, Part II

In December 1812, Captain John Shaw and Purser Thomas Shields became embroiled in a dispute over Shaw's appointment of a purser to Louisiana.[1] *Protesting this infringement of his prerogatives as station purser, Shields appealed to the Navy Department for relief. The newly appointed secretary, William Jones, decided in favor of Shields, ordering Captain Shaw to dismiss* Louisiana*'s purser.[2] The bickering between the two men had scarcely subsided when a new altercation arose. This time the quarrel centered on Shields's authority to refuse advance monies to men on the New Orleans Station, even when ordered to pay out such monies by Captain Shaw. Once again, both officers called on the navy secretary to arbitrate their dispute.*

1. *See Dudley,* Naval War of 1812, *Vol. 1, pp. 435–40.*
2. *See Jones to Shaw, 31 Jan. 1813, DNA, RG45, SNL, Vol. 10, p. 238 (M149, Roll No. 10).*

PURSER THOMAS SHIELDS TO SECRETARY OF THE NAVY JONES

The Honble. Wm. Jones,   New Orleans   12 June 1813

Sir,

I have the honor to herewith to Enclose for your perusal and decision copies of a correspondence between Comde. Jno. Shaw & myself, on the Subject of an order given me by Tho Turner Esqr. the Accountant of the Navy— I beg leave sir, most respectfully to suggest to you the delicacy of my situation & to ask yr instructions how to proceed. I have the honor to be Most Respectfully Sir, Yr. Ob. St.

Tho. Shields
Purser

ALS, DNA, RG45, CL, 1813, Vol. 6, No. 163 (M125, Roll No. 31). The four enclosures that follow were individually numbered. They are bound in reverse order following Shields's cover letter.

Captain John Shaw

Purser Thomas Shields

[Enclosure]

1   New Orleans   June 5th. 1813

Sir,

It has become my duty to inquire of you, upon what authority, Mr Boswell, who, I understand, acts for you in your absence from Town, refused to comply with a request made by me, on or about the first of April last, during your absence from New Orleans,—to pay up Mr. Ballard, what might then be due to him; and in addition, to advance to him, on my responsibility, one or two month's pay; as he was then on the eve of his departure, on an expedition, in company with myself, against Mobile?

You will also be pleased to inform me whether or not Mr. Boswell (rated in your last return as a purser's steward) is considered by you as amenable to the laws & regulations of our service?— Hurry of duty alone, has so long prevented me from addressing you on this subject. Sir, I have the honor to be yours respectfully

John Shaw

Thomas Shields esq.
Purser of the N.O. station
New Orleans

LS, DNA, RG45, CL, 1813, Vol. 6, No. 163, enclosure (M125, Roll No. 31).

[Enclosure]

2

Commodore John Shaw.   New Orleans   7th June 1813.

Sir

Your Letter of the 5th. Inst. was not handed me until the night of its date, it otherwise would have been immediately replied to.

My instructions from the Navy Dept. are positive in regard to pecuniary transactions, and are couch'd in the following terms— "You will in no instance make advances to the Officers & Seamen, on your Station except the usual advance on joining a Vessel, unless the same is bona fida due, even if the same should be order'd by the Commanding Naval Officer."

Mr. Boswell holds the same situation now, that he did when I arrived on this Station, sanctioned, I presume by the Department as Mr. Hambleton has settled his transactions here, at the Accountants Office.—

My inclinations have ever led me to further, as far as in my power lay, the Interest of the Public service   My orders to Mr. Boswell have ever been preremptory to advance no money unless due, to any one— I am forbidden to keep a contingent Acct. if the Service requires additional aid in a pecuniary way, I beg leave to suggest the propriety of calling on the Agent. From the Tenor of your Letter, I fear Mr. Ballard has said, that he could not get what money was actually due him, on the date of yr. order,— the enclosed will shew that he received more.^x

I do not conceive that Mr. Boswell is subject to, or amenable to Naval Law, he is not on the Articles— But even were he, the Censure in this instance, if any, must attach to me.—

I am heavily bonded Sir, to account for the monies drawn by me, & tho I most certainly should not hesitate to obey your orders directed to me personally, supposing my instructions were Known to you it would compell me at the time I obey'd them to solemly protest against the proceedure,—this proceedure, I should in justice owe to myself— at the same time I know & acknowledge the necessity of obedience to orders, but I have to settle & am held responsible hereafter for the correctness of my accts.— I beg you Sir, most respectfully, to reflect on this subject seriously & before censuring me, to ascertain whether I am really in an error.— I have the honor, to be, Yr. Most Obt. Servt.

Signd.   Thos. Shields
Purser

XMr. Ballards acct transmitted to Comdr. Shaw.—

LS, DNA, RG45, CL, 1813, Vol. 6, No. 163, enclosure (M125, Roll No. 31). This copy was signed by Shields.

[Enclosure]

<u>3</u>   New Orleans, June 9th. 1813.

Sir,

I have received your letter of the day before yesterday, in reply to mine of the 5th. instant, and should consider it a perfect waste of time for you & I, at this late period, to enter into a contest on the subject of rank; that being a point long since established by the laws of our country & the usages of the service; I shall at once, therefore, and without further comment, dismiss that part of the subject of the present letter.—

You state in your letter, now before me, that your 'instructions from the Navy-Department, are positive in regard to pecuniary transactions, and' that they 'are couched in the terms,' which you there recite, namely, that you should not perform certain acts, apertaining to your office as purser—"even if the same should be ordered by the Commanding Naval officer."— As an order of this nature, forbiding a subordinate, to be obedient to his superior officer, must be considered perfectly anomalous, a precedent for which might in vain be sought for in the annals of Naval transactions throughout the civilized world; and as, to my recollection, I have never yet been favored with the sight of your orders from Government to join this station,—which I presume, includes your general instructions,—I must request of you to allow me the perusal, or to furnish me with a fair transcript, of your original orders referred to.

It is perfectly true, indeed, that I formerly in 180[8?] or 1809, saw a <u>circular letter</u>, from Mr. Thomas Turner, purporting to have the same effect, which you ascribe to your instructions; and I had the perusal, also, of a letter from Commodore Decatur, to Mr. Paul Hamilton, the then Secretary of the Navy, produced by that very extraordinary occurrence; and in reply to which he was informed that the <u>circular</u> in question, could by no means interfere with his authority, but on the contrary, that every officer & other person on board his ship, must of course yield obedience to his orders.— As a Post Captain in the Navy, I was ordered here by my Government, in command of this station; & I should be extremely sorry to perceive a disposition in any officer under my command, to court the issue of a contest with me, or the consequences of a disobedience of orders, on the subject of duties incident to my command. I have never on any occasion, attempted an unwarrantable interference with the duties, either of the Navy-agent, or the purser, on this station; and as I shall continue, as heretofore, to guard against the issuing of any other than legal orders, holding myself in the meanwhile responsible for all, as well for those, which may to any person happen to appear doubtful, as for others, I shall take care in future to enforce prompt obedience to them: To permit the contrary, would be a departure from duty; inasmuch, as it could not fail to have a direct tendency to degrade the command entrusted to me by Government, and thus completely deprive it of its naval character & respectability.

It would seem to appear, however, from the view which you take of the subject, that the commanding officer of this station, is to be considered as a mere automaton, without any authority whatever, not possessing so much as the right to expect obedience, during your absence at any time from this city—even from one of your deputed assistants—a person who is rated on your general return as a purser's steward:— On this subject, sir, you will permit me to observe, that such a mode of doing duty is disapproved; that every person in your office must be subject to legal orders, and amenable to the consequences of disobedience; and that I shall take the most prompt steps to punish the officer who may represent you in your absence, & who shall make a reply to an order from me, similar to the one made to Mr. Ballards, by Mr. Boswell. It seems proper further to remark, that I know Mr. Turner only as a Gentleman, and as a clerk in the Navy-Department; that it yet remains for me to learn that he possesses the power of interfering with my command, or that I am subject to his orders (if he possess such transcendent authority let it be produced;) and that, until such authority be shown I shall not consider communications from him as possessing the force of law, or of orders.

I shall conclude by setting you right on the score of your conjecture respecting the representations which Mr. Ballard might have made to me; his statement corresponded with your own, and was no more I presume, than a simple report of the fact as it had actually occurred. Sir, I have the honor to be yours respectfully

                                                                    John Shaw

Thomas Shields, esq.
Purser of the N.O. station
New Orleans

LS, DNA, RG45, CL, 1813, Vol. 6, No. 163, enclosure (M125, Roll No. 31).

[Enclosure]
4
Commdr. John Shaw   New Orleans   10 June 1813.

Sir,

I had the honor to receive your letter of yesterday   It certainly never was my wish or intention to court the issue of a contest or even a contest itself with my commanding Officer, enclosed is a copy of my orders which I presented you on the morning of my arrival in this city— I beg leave most respectfully to assure you Sir, that I feel too high a regard for the honor & prosperity of the Navy, ever Knowingly to degrade it by disrespectful conduct on my part

This is the first moment Sir, that I ever heard an order issued from the accountants office, to the Purser's, & wherein the authority of the Commanding Officers cannot be concern'd, should be questioned as illegal, and the more especially so, as it must unquestionably have been by the order of the Hon'ble Secretary of the Navy himself.— I take the liberty of enclosing Mr. Turner's Letter on the subject.—

I beg leave to call a circumstance that has occurr'd to the Knowledge of Comdr. Shaw— Lieut. Trippe while commanding the Schooner *Enterprize* on a distant or foreign station, drew on his own responsibilty several large sums of money— after his decease, Mr. Timberlake her Purser, now on board the *U. States* Frigate with Commdr. Decatur, was order'd to settle his Accounts; on their adjustment, Lt. Trippe was found indebted to the Governmt. from actual receipts upwards of $3,000.— Which sum was actually charged to the private account of Mr. Timberlake & deducted from, the earnings of his industry, without an act of Congress has been passd. since I left the Atlantic States in his favor.— This circumstance Sir, I believe was the cause of the order given by the direction of the Secretary of the Navy.— It occurred early in the winter of 1809.—

To put this subject at rest for ever, as well as to convince you of my sincerity in declaring, that nothing is more distant from my wishes or intentions than to disobey orders—I have this day written to the Hon'ble William Jones, for a final answer to the question. I again beg leave to inform you, that I am not allow'd to keep a contingent account, nor have I ever drawn a dollar for that purpose since I have had the honor to be under your command— I respectfully suggested in my note of the 7th inst. the propriety of directing yr. orders to the Agent, when the interest of the Public required other appropriations than what I am authorized to make; I was in hopes Sir, this observation would not have been deemed indecorous, it certainly was not intended so— as it regards Mr. Boswell's being amenable to Naval Law, in my opinion was given because askd.— it is only matter of opinion— my duties on this station, are arduous & perplexing, not like as tho it was on board a single ship; Mr. Boswell is rated on, or was rated on the Muster Roll a Steward   I did not conceive from the circumstance of his never having signd. the shipping articles that he was subject to Naval Law— I have erased his name from the Books, my instructions to him during my absence from Orleans were "to comply with all orders emanating from the Commdg. Naval Officer, be him whom it might, the advances of money where not due excepted—unless the usual advances on joining a Vessel when any new appointments of Officers should be made—" I am not inform'd that he has, acted contrary to his instructions— A steward Sir, by Naval Law you know is subject to Corporeal punishment— Mr. Boswell never will consent to the exercise of this power nor do I believe, I can find a man of sensibility who will— I am not allow'd by Law a Clerk, consequently am obliged to pay him out of my own pocket— this decision makes a difference of 500$ a year against me— I will be much obliged to Commodore Shaw, to inform me, whether I can visit the Bay St. Louis, or have leave of absence for a month. My office will be shut, but all supplies will be as readily furnished as tho I was here.—Respectfully, I am Sir, Yr Most Ob Servt.

Signd.   Thos. Shields
Purser

After perusal be pleased to return the enclosed orders

Signd.   T. S.—

LS, DNA, RG45, CL, 1813, Vol. 6, No. 163, enclosure (M125, Roll No. 31). This copy was signed by Shields.

CAPTAIN JOHN SHAW TO SECRETARY OF THE NAVY JONES

The Honl. William Jones   New Orleans   June 14th 1813

Sir,

It has become an object of the most interesting inquiry with me,—to know with precision, in what light the Government considers me at this place,—whether as a land, or as a Naval officer,—and in either case, what rank I am allowed to hold among my brother officers. The doubts and difficulties which have pressed themselves on my mind, in relation to this subject, have been produced by the several mutations which the command, originally assigned to me, has underwent, since my arrival at New Orleans, nearly three years ago:—

On joining this station, in the latter part of 1810, I was placed under the immediate command, of the Governor of the Orleans Territory: Again, on the arrival of General Wilkinson, another transfer was made (a copy of the order for which I have the honor to enclose) placing me in the line, and, together with all my disposable force, under the command of that officer; to which I have continued amenable, until he, on the 10th. instant, took his departure from this place, for the City of Washington.

There have, I assure you, Sir, been great confusion & much vexatious bickering, produced by these (as they have appeared to me) unusual & irregular transfers; and as I believe it to be well known, that the older officers in the Navy, are men of experience in their profession—who have approved themselves worthy (by a faithful & patriotic discharge of duty) of the trust usually reposed in officers of their rank in service,—a very unpleasant question, which still remains without a solution, frequently & unavoidably obtrudes itself on the mind;—why have our Government thought necessary or proper, to place a Post Captain in the Navy, under the immediate orders of a Brigadier General, or, the Military Commanding officer near New Orleans? An order, by which, without any forced construction, of the disjunctive member of the sentence, with which it ends,—and without any very extraordinary change of the military arrangement of the district,—I have all along been liable to come under the unqualified command of a Major or Captain of Militia,—Officers who, it must indeed be confessed, generally Know pretty nearly as much about Naval, as military, duty.

Having heretofore, so strongly & so frequently, remonstrated on the fluctuating circumstances of my Command, to the late Honorable Secretary of the Navy without effect, I had almost determined to trouble the Navy Department no more on the subject. As however, you cannot but be perfectly sensible of the heart-burnings, which these Circumstances must necessarily produce; I still entertain hopes of being restored to such a state of respectable responsibility, & independence on on the military as may restore the spirit of emulation & enterprise, which late regulations on the station have almost driven out of the service. To maintain a perfectly good understanding with the Military, & to Co-operate with them, in the strictest & most spirited manner, would exactly accord with the feelings of us all; but I pray you let it be a cooperation: Such an arrangement as this,—making the naval commanding officer responsible to the government alone, for his official acts,—is all that is wished,—& this, I still hope, will be granted by the Government.

I must also beg particular attention to the enclosed Copies of a Correspondence, which has recently taken place, between Mr. Shields, the purser of the station & myself. It was produced, as will appear by the Correspondence itself,—by an order of mine to his office, to advance one or two months pay, to Mr. John P Ballard, my Clerk (on my own personal responsibility) who was then making preparations, to accompany me on the expedition, of which you have been informed, to <u>Mobile</u>. Mr. Shields himself was absent from Town, & the order was rejected by the person who acted for him in his absence, & who is rated on the pursers books as a steward. It appears that he had received peremptory orders from Mr. Shields, to disobey any orders from me, which might require advances of money to any person during his absence; notwithstanding this was a solitary instance, within my recollection, since I have been on this station of my having given such an order. The propriety of the order under the circumstances of the case, will not, I presume be questioned, but will I hope, on the contrary, be approved; while the attitude taken by Mr. Shields, & the language used in the discussion especially in his letter of the 7th., was improper & unwarrantable, & will, I doubt not, be so considered, as long as the necessity of regularity, subordination & obedience to orders, shall continue to be admitted, in public service.[1] Sir, I have the honor to be with great respect &c.

John Shaw

LS, DNA, RG45, MLR, 1813, Vol. 4, No. 51 (M125, Roll No. 29).

1. After reviewing the above correspondence, Secretary Jones decided in favor of Purser Shields. See Jones's handwritten memo of 12 July 1813, probably to accountant of the navy, Thomas Turner, in which he writes, "I wish to correct the errors of Captain Shaw who appears to fancy himself supreme and to forget that there is any other authority," in DNA, RG45, MLR, 1813, Vol. 4, No. 154 (M124, Roll No. 56).

Protesting Reductions at New Orleans

By mid-year, Captain John Shaw's command at New Orleans had reached its nadir. With just six gunboats and one ship to guard over three hundred miles of coastline, U.S. strength in the Gulf was at its lowest ebb since the commencement of the war. It was a particularly frustrating time for Shaw because, just as the threat to the station was increasing, the forces he had at his disposal to oppose it were dwindling. In a letter to the secretary of the navy dated 12 June, Shaw protested the reductions Jones had ordered the previous March; and, as he had numerous times before, the captain warned of his inability to counter British sea power effectively. Secretary Jones's continued silence in the face of Shaw's repeated pleas for more resources starkly illustrates the low priority given by the department to the needs of the New Orleans Station.

CAPTAIN JOHN SHAW TO SECRETARY OF THE NAVY JONES

The Honl. William Jones   New Orleans   June 12th. 1813

Sir,

The circumstance of my having been, for some time past, absent from New Orleans, on the public duty, must be offered as an apology for not having, until now, acknowledged the receipts of your several letters of the 1st. 23rd. & 30th. of March last; which came duly to hand, & was acted upon by Lieut. Patterson, agreeably to instructions which I had left with him,—as the officer next in Command at this place,—on my departure for Mobile in the beginning of April:—

Agreeably to your instructions of the 1st. March, I have issued orders for the reduction of the crews of the several Gun Vessels; but I should be sensible of, and very justly chargeable with a remissness in my duty, were I to omit to express to you my decided opinion,—produced by a personal knowledge of the exposed & vulnerable situation of the extensive coast which they are designed to protect,—that this reduction of their crews, is directly opposed to every idea of even a tolerable defence of this station, which is now strictly blockaded by the enemy.

The whole force at present attached to this Station, and intended for the protection of three hundred miles of Coast,—from the Perdido, eastwardly to Vermillon Bay on the West, every point of which is open to the inroads of the enemy's boats,—consists of the Ship *Louisiana*, stationed for the defence of the Balize; and Six sail of Gun Vessels—four of which have been stationed at Mobile since the time of taking possession of that place—one at the out-let of the Rigoletts—and the other (newly fitted out) attempting to make up a crew at New Orleans; in which, however, notwithstanding the transfers made to her from other vessels, on the reduction of their crews, she has, as yet, owing to the extreme scarcity of Seamen, but half succeeded. This force, even were the crews aug-mented to the full number of men who could be usefully employed on board, would, there can be no doubt, be absolutely inadequate to the purposes of an efficient defence against a vigorous attack of the enemy. I shall consider it my duty, occasionally, as I have heretofore done, in my letters to the Navy-Department, of Feby. 17th. April 11th. June 2nd. July 10th. August 17th. & 27th. October 1812;[1] and of the 19th. April last (the three first before the declaration of War) to all of which I beg leave to refer you,—to state to the Honorable Secretary of the Navy, my own ideas of force necessary for the defence of this station, or at least, of the insufficiency of what is at present allotted to it; sincerely hoping that I may not be considered as chargeable with what might be the consequences of an attack from a superior & overwhelming force from the enemy. All that I can possibly do, in addition to the making of correct representations of the incompetency of the means which may be placed at my disposal, is to take care that the reasonable expectations which may be entertained by our country, respecting the efficient employment of these means, shall not be disappointed; and for this I pledge myself.

The Bomb Brig is now nearly complete in her carpenters work. She is constructed for mounting 12 Guns—6 or 9 pounders,—and a 13 inch sea-Mortar: There are however, no seamen at New Orleans; owing to which, the difficulty of manning her, must be selfevident.

The building of the block Ship on the Tchifoncta, is progressing with all the activity which I have found it possible to give to it. Her frame will, I expect, be entirely moulded in the course of three or four weeks; after which it will not take us long to have her plank sheers on. Her frame consists altogether of live-oak & pitch-pine timber; & with the latter kind she will be planked The spot which I have selected for building this vessel on, is incomparably the best one on that river. It is in part a rising ground, forming an inclined plane, in short, just such as was desirable for that purpose,— A very trifling expense has been incurred in preparing the foundation on which to place her blocks. The site together with nearly 20 acres of well timbered pine land annexed, forming a spacious front on the river, has been obtained from a Mr. Lorens,[2] a french gentleman, residing near the spot, on a lease, renewable every ten years at the option of the Government, forever, at the moderate rent of $20 per annum. When the lease shall be completed & put on record, I shall do myself the honor of forwarding to you a Notarial Copy. The advantages of the situation selected on the Tchifoncta for a Ship-yard over any other place within the limits of this station; and the advantageous terms on which live-oak timber for Ships of any size could be procured on the margin of the lakes in the vicinity of Tchifoncta,—shall be made the subjects of a subsequent communication.

The Brig *Siren*, Captain Joseph Bainbridge, sailed from Ship Island on the 8th. or 9th. of last month, for Boston or Portsmouth, in New-Hampshire, agreeably to your order of the 23rd. of March last. Sir, I have the honor to be with great respect your Most Obt Servt.

John Shaw

LS, DNA, RG45, CL, 1813, Vol. 4, No. 58 (M125, Roll No. 29).

1. The letters of 10 July, 17 August, and 27 October 1812 referred to by Shaw are printed in Dudley, *Naval War of 1812*, Vol. 1, pp. 383–85, 392–95, 417–19.
2. Jacques Lorreins.

Progress on the Blockship at Tchefuncte

Between June and September, Captain John Shaw spent most of his energy superintending the building of the blockship at the Tchefuncte shipyard. Progress on the blockship through the summer months was steady if not spectacular. Work was hampered chiefly by a shortage of skilled shipwrights, though construction did halt for a brief time when the yard appeared in danger from an Indian attack.

Shaw's major concern while at Tchefuncte was in keeping the cost of the blockship under control. He found this very difficult to do because the iron and canvas needed to finish the ship were very scarce, and therefore very costly. The one item that Shaw was able to obtain plentifully and cheaply was timber. White oak and live oak—prime woods for shipbuilding—were readily available for cutting and hauling in the forests surrounding the yard. Their use enabled Captain Shaw to boast that the blockship was constructed of the finest materials.

CAPTAIN JOHN SHAW TO SECRETARY OF THE NAVY JONES

The Honl. William Jones   New Orleans, June 28th. 1813

Sir,

I have just returned from the Tchifoncta, where the building of the block ship is fast progressing. This Vessel, I hope to have launched in November or December next. I have experienced some difficulty, however, in procuring a sufficient number of good Ship-Carpenters, for the wages ($50 per month & a ration) which I have attempted to establish; nor am I certain but that I shall yet be compelled to raise them to $60 per <u>month</u>, of 26 <u>working</u> days, made good to each.

The whole extent of the river Tchifoncta, & within a small distance of its banks, is thickly timbered with yellow & pitch-pine, well calculated for Ship-building; while the margin of Lake Ponchartrain, into which the Tchifoncta discharges itself, abounds in live-oak—is easy of access—and from which, I presume, that timber can be procured, & landed at the Ship-yard, at about a third of a dollar per cubic foot. Plenty of large white oak timber, also grows, & can be procured within the short distance of from 1 to 2 1/2 miles, in the country, back of the Ship-yard; of which 130 knees have already been collected, & with a part of which the Navy-yard at New Orleans, has been supplied. We pay as I have formerly taken occasion to state to you, a dollar per tree, standing, for pine timber; for live-oak, however, where it is obtained from land belonging to individuals, we pay double that sum. The hauling is far from being expensive: The timber for the masts & spars complete, for the block ship, will cost the Government less than $75; whereas, had it been necessary to purchase them at New Orleans, they could not have been procured for less than six hundred dollars.

There could not, in my opinion, be a more eligible situation found in the United States, at which to collect, & prepare any quantity of live-oak, of the very best quality, for our Naval service. The trees being large, the timbers for vessels of all sizes—from a first rate Ship of war, down to those of Gun boats, can be procured with great facility. From the pass of Manchac,—which connects the lakes, Maurepas & Ponchartrain,—all along the sea-coast to the eastward, as far as Mobile bay, this timber can be procured in great abundance. The eastern extremity of the coast just mentioned (near to Mobile bay) would, however, on account of the more easy approach of vessels be the preferable part at which to cut live oak, intended to be transported to a distant Navy-yard. I feel pursuaded;—from every calculation I have been able to make on the subject,—that the complete frame of a line-of-battle ship, or a Frigate, could be cut & prepared on this coast, agreeably to the mould which might be designated, with advantages over that of any other part of the United States, in a ratio of, at least, 5 to 3; and that, were even 100 frames of such vessels required, they could be procured on this coast, within the limits I have mentioned, with great facility. Should the Honl. Secretary of the Navy, conceive these suggestions to be of any importance to the service, in the event of any number of frames being required by Government; I should willingly volunteer my services—between this, & the time when I may have to leave the Station—in making all the arrangements, for the accomplishment of such object.

The expense of the Naval establishment at this place, has, unavoidably, been very considerable; but I can truly say, that since I have had the honor of being in the command of this station, none of these expenses, have, with my knowledge or approbation, been wantonly incurred. The Hurricane of last year, as must be well known, was productive of a very large portion of expense; but the consequences of that gale, were unavoidable; as neither precaution nor exertion, could in any degree, counteract its devastation: This is manifest from the destruction of private property,—of which, the proportion was at least as great as that sustained by the public— Some individuals were entirely ruined by it:— Our store in the Navy-yard, was blown down; & our vessels afloat, were all, either driven ashore, or almost torn to pieces. These vessels were ordered by Government, to be immediately repaired & equipped for active service and with that order I strictly complied.

After the hurricane, the Honl. Secretary of the Navy, placed me under the command of Brig. Gen. Wilkinson; & having thus become a subordinate officer, I knew my duty too well to be guilty of disobedience of orders; or to court the issue of a trial by a General Court Martial, by opposing the measure, although in my private opinion, I could not rid myself of the idea of its being, if not actually wrong, at least without a precedent. Hence, if any improper expence shall have been incurred, in my department of the service, in the purchase of Ships &c for the defence of this City—having in every instance, acted under orders—I trust that no just grounds for censure; can attach itself to me, for having in these cases merely obeyed orders.

The British Sloop of War *Herald*, anchored off the bar of Mobile, on the 3rd. instant. Gun Vessels *No. 156, 163* & *65*, went out, attacked, &, in ten minutes, drove her from her anchorage; since which, she has not re-appeared.

The last account received from Pensacola, states that 10 or 12 Gun boats, are fitting out at the Havanah, for that place—were to be convoyed by the British—&, as I presume, to be employed by them. A report is also current, and seems to gain ground, that E. Florida, has been either sold or ceded to Great Britain.— An official account reached this place last evening, from Mobile, that a small party of spanish Troops, had crossed the Perdido, & burned down a new block-house & other buildings which had been recently erected there, under the superintendence of Lt. Col. Boyer of the 2nd Infantry. Col. Boyer with the Troops under his command, had been previously ordered to Mobile Point, to relieve a detachment of the 3rd. regt. who were under marching orders from Government, for the borders of Upper Canada.

The 24 pounder Guns, now on board the Ship *Louisiana,* are found to be quite too heavy for her; & as they will answer, and be required, for the block-ship, building at Tchifoncta, I must beg the attention of the Honl. Secretary to the subject of ordering a tier of 16 medium 9 or 12 pounders, to be forwarded as early as possible from Pittsburgh. Unless this arrangement be attended to, and the present armament be continued on board the *Louisiana,* 16 twenty-fours will be required, in the fall, for the blockship.

I am happy to inform you, for the honor of the contractors, that the Gun powder, which has been sometime since received from Tennessee, has on trial, greatly exceeded in strength the conditions of the contract. The average range of a twenty-four pound shot, with an ounce of powder from the provette, was found to be (instead of 75, the terms of the contract) 115 yards.

I have no officers here, unemployed. I have been compelled to move about, myself, in every situation of my command. The circumstances of the service, will this summer, require the greater part of my time to be spent, in the superintendence of the building of the block-ship on the Tchifoncta. Sir, I have the honor to be with great respect your most Obt. servt.

John Shaw

LS, DNA, RG45, CL, 1813, Vol. 4, No. 128 (M125, Roll No. 29). A duplicate of this letter was bound along with the original.

CAPTAIN JOHN SHAW TO SECRETARY OF THE NAVY JONES

Honl. William Jones.   New Orleans, July 12th. 1813

Sir,

I have the honor to enclose you herewith a duplicate of my last communication;—& shall, in a few days, proceed eastwardly, in order to join General Flournoy at the pass of Christiana; from whence we shall visit Mobile & the river Perdido. On this excursion, I may perhaps be absent from this City, about thirty days.

We experience much difficulty, in obtaining a sufficiency of Iron for the Block-ship; that article being extremely scarce, and now selling at, from 15 to 19 cents per pound: We have no Canvass in store, nor can there, at this time, be even a very moderate quantity of it purchased in this City; what little there is sells—English at forty, & Russia at even sixty, dollars per bolt. And in short, every other article, wanted for service, seems to have taken a proportionate rise: Hence the expenses, necessarily to be incurred on this station, owing to the enormous prices, which must be thus, unavoidably paid, for articles of first necessity, for the use of our armed vessels, must, of course, be very considerable. Having nothing to do, however, with the purchase of supplies no share of the responsibility can possibly attach to me. I do most earnestly recommend, & I have all along recommended, the purchasing by whole-sale instead of retail, to be deposited in store, such supplies, as, it, must be Known, will ultimately be wanted: An obvious consequence, resulting, under existing circumstances, from this retail mode of purchasing small articles as they happen to be wanted, is, that the retail prices, even if they were not subject to any kind of change, must always be much higher than those of whole-sale; while, on the on the other hand, our supplies having been almost wholly cut off for sometime past, the prices daily & rapidly encrease with the scarcity of the articles required. They ought to have been laid in twelve months ago at least, when they might have been purchased here, on comparatively moderate terms; whereas, they will now have to be obtained, at advanced prices, elsewhere.— I have therefore to request of the Honl. Secretary, to cause to be forwarded to this place, as early as may be, by the way of Pittsburgh, a sufficient quantity of Russia duck & of canvass (from No. 1 to No. 7) to make the sails complete for the Block-ship; also a supply of bar-iron assorted—and, as I have formerly suggested, sixteen or twenty—nine or twelve pounder cannons, to be mounted here, for the Ship *Louisiana*; the 24 pounders which She now carries on her Gun deck, having been found to be quite too heavy for her.

It appears necessary to repeat to the Honl. Secretary, what I have formerly represented to the Navy Department, that the scarcity of commissioned Lieutenants on this station, is such, as to render the convening of Naval Courts-Martial, extremely inconvenient & embarrassing to the Service; a consequence of which is, that offenders cannot, without manifest injury to our arrangements, be dealt with, agreeably to the nature of their crimes, and have thus to be allowed to pass with impunity.

The 3rd. Regt. of Infantry, 850 strong, under the command of Col. Constant, left this city, yesterday in barges, for Cincinati, Ohio. Sir, I have the honor to be with great respect your Most Obt Servt.

John Shaw

P.S. The present hostile disposition of the creek indians has temporarily, though perfectly shut up the Southern Mail route via Fort Stoddert.

J. Shaw

LS, DNA, RG45, CL, 1813, Vol. 4, No. 185 (M125, Roll No. 29). A duplicate of this letter was bound along with the original.

CAPTAIN JOHN SHAW TO SECRETARY OF THE NAVY JONES

Honorable William Jones   Tchifoncta   September the 11th: 1813.

Sir

Nothing particular has transpired in the Division, under my Command Since I last had the Honor to address you. General Flournoy and myself have been together to the Eastward for these Six Weeks, The Gun Vessels have some time Since transported from the Pass of Christian to Fort Charlotte, Mobile, 400 of the 7t. Regiment, 500 men of the 2d Regiment is now Stationd at the Point of Mobile in Cooperation with four Sail of Gun Vessels viz, *nos. 65: 156. 162 & 163,* The Bomb Brig *AETNA,* I have also orderd to Mobile Bay where she will proceed as soon as her Crew is Completed.

Since the arrival of General Flournoy on this Station the greatest Harmony has Existed between us, duty goes on very pleasantly, the Officers of the Navy feel Emulated in a Strict Cooperation with the Army, As it must be naturally Expected that the Enemy will not let us rest Idle much longer in peace or quietness on the Frontiers, Should it meet the Views of the Honorable Secretary of the Navy, I should wish to continue in my present command, in preference of being recall'd to the North. General Flournoy has Sollicited me to remain with him, if it meets with your approbation.

The Crew of the Ship *Louisiana,* stationd in the Early part of the Season, for the defence of the Balize, has unhappily been cut up by Sickness, from 90 to 100, of her crew have been Violently attack'd by a malignant Fever & are now in the Hospital under the particular care of Doctor Heermann, only one Officer onboard of this vessel has Escap'd this Fever, I have order'd her to New Orleans where she arriv'd on the 9t Instant,

The Block Ship is progressing as fast as the nature of our Force will admit, She is built of the Very first materials, will be able to mount 26. 32 pound heavy Cannon on her Deck, her draft of Water all on board, will not Exceed 6 feet, 6 In: The perpendicular of her Gun Deck in length 148' feet, beam molded 42 feet, This Ship will when ready for service in my Opinion be better calculated to defend our Waters than all the Forts & Batterys Erected for the defence of the country, I shall do myself the honor of writing more fully in my next

Fort Mims on the Tensaw was attack'd by a large party of Indians on the 30th. Ulto., the americans consisting of 300 men were all distroyd by the Savages, and the Fort fell into their possession.

I beg leave again to remind the Honorable Secretary of the Navy, of the great necessity of the Canvass & Cannon being forwarded Early as possible, both of these articles are at present of the first necessity. I have the honor to be Your obt. St.

John Shaw

LS, DNA, RG45, MLR, 1813, Vol. 6, No. 37 (M124, Roll No. 58).

CAPTAIN JOHN SHAW TO SECRETARY OF THE NAVY JONES

Tchifonta   September the 15th. 1813.

Sir

I have the Honor to Enclose you a Copy of my last communication.

Governor Claiborne & myself have been in company for these three days past, and have call'd together the militia Officers of this Parish, apprising them of their danger., the Governor has recommended that strong Stockade Forts should be built in Each Parish, and I have no doubt, but that the Inhabitants will Immediately avail themselves of this Salutary advice,. I am of an opinion that little or no danger can happen to the Inhabitants here from the Creek Indians, the distance is too far, and I apprehend could not be attended with any success to them.; Should however the Chactaws join them against us, all this frontier would no doubt be immediately abandoned and would be left subject to their ravages.—

I have Organized all the Mechanicks and workmen here, Employ'd at the Block Ship, into a Corps., in addition I shall have a subalterans guard of marines, a stockade Fort will be built by the different residents for their protection. I shall mount a few peices of heavy cannon, as soon as the work is completed I shall then not feel the same anxiety of being attacked by the Indians should they attempt it. I feel very confident of defeating them. This morning I received a dispatch from General Flournoy, requesting my joining him at Mobile. I shall depart from this place tomorrow Evening and join him agreeable to his wishes.

I shall, Sir, be very much mistaken if an attack will not be attempted by the British ere long, on some part of our Sea Boards, the progress of the Indian War, sufficiently, in my opinion bespeaks their design., whilst it is necessary to require the attention of all the Physical force of the country to places far distant from any part of our sea board, will afford the British an opportunity to land their forces on any part of the Coast, between the Pass Heroine and Pearl River, In the Event of their succeeding in this object, the standard of Revolt would be hoisted, and the Chactaw Indians invited by them to take up the Tomahawk & scalping Knife against us., These few remarks may be consider'd as a Visionary Calculation Emanating solely from Timidity, but sir since I have had the honor to command on this Station my personal exertion has been Employ'd from time to time, in gaining a most perfect Knowledge of our Sea board, and as it is well Known that very many Enemys to our Country have an Equal share of the Knowledge of the nature and Extent of the Sea Coast, with myself, convinces me the more, that at any time the Enemy may require Pilots to Effect their landing, they will succeed in obtaining them. in this Situation they would meet with a very feeble opposition by the small force under my command which as I have heretofore stated is now at Mobile Bay. I must again repeat to the Honorable Secretary of the Navy the great necessity there is of augmenting this force at this Critical moment. I have now at this yard as much live Oak Timber, calculated to build four gun Boats, the Live Oak in the Lake, is allready cut calculated to build 6 or 8 more, The Small Timber has been taken from the large live Oak Trees cut down for the Block Ship. I have received no communication from the Honorable Secretary of the, Navy Since last June. I have the honor to be Your Obt Servant

John Shaw

LS, DNA, RG45, CL, 1813, Vol. 6, No. 54 (M125, Roll No. 31).

A New Commandant at New Orleans

On 18 October Secretary Jones ordered Master Commandant Daniel T. Patterson[1] to relieve Captain John Shaw as commander of the New Orleans Station.[2] Patterson was a seasoned, professional officer with more than thirteen years of naval service. He had been stationed at New Orleans since 1807, and his knowledge of the Gulf coupled with his experience made him the logical choice to succeed Shaw. Patterson embarked on his new duties with energy and resolve, and his performance at New Orleans in the months that followed would demonstrate the wisdom of Jones's selection.

1. *Patterson was promoted to master commandant on 24 July 1813.*
2. *Like many of his subordinates, Shaw had made repeated requests to the Navy Department for a transfer from the New Orleans Station. After leaving New Orleans, the captain returned to Washington to settle his accounts. On 19 October 1814 he was given command of the frigate* United States. *For letters expressing the dissatisfaction of naval officers with service on the Gulf Station, see Dudley,* Naval War of 1812, *Vol. 1, pp. 421–28 and C. McKee,* U.S. Naval Officer Corps, *pp. 306–7.*

SECRETARY OF THE NAVY JONES TO
MASTER COMMANDANT DANIEL T. PATTERSON

Daniel T. Patterson Esqr.   Navy Department
Master Commandant, U.S. Navy,   Octr 18th 1813.
New Orleans.

Sir,

I enclose to you a duplicate of my letter of this date to Commodore Shaw, lest he should be absent from New Orleans, in order that you may immediately communicate it to him, and carry into execution the object of its contents; in conformity with which, you are invested with the command of the Naval Forces of the U. States on the New Orleans Station, which you will immediately assume, on communicating with Com. Shaw on the subject of this Order.

I entertain the most perfect assurance, that this mark of the confidence of the President, will be returned by the most diligent, faithful, and zealous discharge of the very important duties of your command; and, that whilst you maintain the force under your command in the most efficient order, and employ it to the best advantage for the defence of the Coast and Country, and annoyance of the Enemy, you will also exercise your best discretion and care, to check the enormous expenditure and waste, which has hitherto marked the Naval Service on that Station, and confine your requisitions to what may be absolutely necessary for the substantial benefit of the service; avoiding all superfluities, and particularly restraining the extravagant propensity of the Officers, to indulge in costly and luxurious equipments and furniture, which, whatever may have been the practice hitherto, will no longer be tolerated; as the Navy Agent will be positively prohibited from paying all bills, not absolutely necessary for the plain, substantial, and indispensable equipments, repairs, and Supplies, according to law and the Regulations of the Naval Service.

The first step required of you, will be a comprehensive and accurate report, of the number, force, state, and condition of all the vessels under your command; and a correct Muster roll of all the Officers and men, as well those attached to the vessels, (which you will distinguish,) as all those who may be connected with the Establishment, directly or indirectly.

You are to understand, explicitly, that no vessels are to be purchased, or built; nor no alterations in the Hull, Rigging, or Armament; nor any extensive repairs to be made, without the previous approbation of this Department; unless such repairs as may arise from casualty, and not admitting of delay, without manifest injury to the Service.

You will also report to me, such supplies as you deem necessary for the station, for the ensuing year, of a nature not to be obtained on favourable terms on the spot; taking into view, those on board the Squadron at the time, and in the hands of the Agent. You will also take care that the Purser makes his regular, periodical returns to this Department, according to instructions.

I am not informed of the actual progress and condition of the Block Ship, which, I perceive, will be a most costly object; and I am yet unapprised of the probable extent of her cost. Had I known the actual state of her progress, when I came into the Department, her further progress would have been instantly arrested; and I have no doubt, to the saving of an enormous, useless expense. I wish, therefore, to have particular information on this subject.

Should any of the Gun Boats be in a state of great decay, it will be proper to forego any repair; as I contemplate substituting large Barges, or Galleys, to go in very shoal water, row and sail fast, and carry heavy. We have now, on the Chesapeake, several of this description, 75 feet long, 15 feet wide, 4 feet deep, with two lug sails, and 40 oars; mounting a 24 Pounder, in one end, & a 42 pound Carronade in the other. They have a wide Gangway, but open amidships, to row double banked, under cover of a cedar awning, with Curtains at the sides, which afford complete Shelter for the men. They row either end foremost, indifferently, and draw, with all on board, but 22 inches water. Draughts and plans will be sent to you.

On all important occasions, where the military operations may require the co-operation of the Naval forces, you will use every effort in your power, to render it effectual; but this will be by mutual concert, between the Commanding General and Yourself, not by his command. For the Naval and Military commands are separate, and independent, and governed by the enclosed joint regulations of the War and Navy Departments; of which the Commanding General has, doubtless, the Counterpart. Nevertheless it is all important, and I am sure you will cherish the Sentiment, that the utmost harmony should prevail; and indeed it is equally honourable to both branches of the service, that wherever they have been combined, the harmony and emulation, that have prevailed, are without example. The Detachment of Marines you will also consider as attached to your command, and subject to your order.

As it is important that the command of the Flotilla would be kept distinct and entire, should a superior Officer appear on the Station, he is not to interfere with your special command, for which you are held directly responsible to this Department. I am, Sir, respectfully, Your Obedient Servant,

W. Jones.

LB Copy, DNA, RG45, SNL, Vol. 11, pp. 122–24 (M149, Roll No. 11).

MASTER COMMANDANT DANIEL T. PATTERSON TO
SECRETARY OF THE NAVY JONES

New Orleans   Novr. 22d 1813

Sir,

I do myself the honour to acknowledge the receipt by yesterday's mail of the Triplicates of your instructions to me of the 18th. and 19th. ult. investing me with the Command of the United States naval forces on this Station, and permit me to repeat that I Sensibly feel this flattering mark of Confidence which the President of the United States and yourself have honoured me with, and that my utmost exertion Shall be used to fulfill every expectation you may have Kindly formed from it, and I feel highly gratified to find my Command responsible only to the navy Department.

Commodore Shaw not having yet returned to this City the transfer of Command has Consequently not taken place but having forwarded to him by two Several Conveyances Copies of your letter to him, as transmitted me, I expect him almost hourly, as soon as in Command you may rely upon receiving from me every information, you have required, and Such other as I may find necessary.

I beg leave at present to remark only on that part of your letter, relative to Substituting large Galleys in place of Such Gun Boats, as may require material repairs, the Species of Galley or Barge as Stated by you, would be the most efficient kind of force for our Shoal Waters, would be formidable and of infinite Service, with Such Boats, the piratical depredations on the Commerce of this place might be destroyed, their Hounts [*Haunts*] on our Western Coast discovered and the Band Broken up, As we could then with a Strong force follow them into their harbours of Shoals. They have now arrived at such a pitch of insolence and Confidence from numbers as to Set the revenue laws and force at defience, and Should they not be Soon destroyed, it will be extremely hazardous for an unarmed vessel even American to approach this Coast. they have even dared to rescue property which had been Seized by the Officers of the Customs in the river Mississippi; the property Smuggled by them into this place is immense, the honest merchant Cannot obtain a livelihood, by his Sales while those robbers roll in riches piratically captured on the high Seas and brought and Sold in face of day in this place in violation and defience of all our revenue laws this evil which is I feel of great magnitude, I am extremely desirous of Correcting and the force you Speak of is peculiarly well adapted for Such Service and for defence, these could here be built and put in the water Complete except Sails, and armament, for $2400. in a Short time, and the Timber of this Country is remarkably good. By the monthly return of the navy Agent, you will perceive that we have no Carronades on this Station of any description; but on the Subject of Supply, I Shall as Soon as possible make you a particular Statement. I have the honour to be with much respect Sir, Your most Obedt. Servt.

Dan[l] T. Patterson

LS, DNA, RG45, MC, 1813, No. 166 (M147, Roll No. 5).

A Petition for Promotion

If a naval officer had a grievance concerning rank, his only course of redress was to write a letter to the Navy Department laying the merits of his case before the secretary. Sometimes these letters carried the endorsement of the aggrieved officer's superior. More often than not, such attempts to solicit promotion failed. What is singular about Lieutenant Daniel S. Dexter's petition for promotion is that it was addressed to the U.S. Senate. Dexter must have chosen this route for his memorial because he had something most officers did not—politically influential friends. It is not known whether Dexter's memorial was ever laid before the Senate. Perhaps it was suppressed on the advice of his supporters, Senator James Brown and Congressman Thomas B. Robertson, both representatives of Louisiana. Nevertheless, Lieutenant Dexter's wish for promotion was finally gratified thirteen months later when he was commissioned a master commandant on 20 December 1814.

Lieutenant Daniel S. Dexter to Senator James Brown

New Orleans, 14th November, 1813.

Sir,

I should, long since, have done myself the honor of writing to you, had not a severe and lingering illness prevented me; and I now beg you will consider the <u>cause</u> of my past <u>silence</u> an excuse for it.

Capt. Patterson has politely favoured me with a sight of that part of your letter to him which mentions the interest and exertions you were so good as to use in behalf of my promotion;[1] and I have the pleasure of informing you that I hope soon to enjoy the gratification of making you my acknowledgements <u>personally</u> for your friendly attention; as I have just received the Secretary's permission[2] to return to the Atlantic States with all Convenient speed.;—I shall accordingly Leave this for head quarters, and soon as my state of health which is yet delicate, will permit.

I have it in contemplation to forward by next mail a Memorial to the Senate relative to my advancement; but, as you have already with such obliging promptitude espoused my cause, and are best acquainted with the dispositions and intentions of Government, I shall take the liberty of inclosing it in a letter to yourself, and request you will decide on the propriety of presenting it. In the meantime, dear Sir, permit me to hope, should any further promotions be brought on the Carpet this winter, that the services you have so kindly proffered will be continued in my favour.

We have no news here.— Considerable activity prevails in <u>preparation</u>, but no actual service is going on, either Naval or Military. With sentiments of the highest respect and esteem I have the honor to be, Dr. Sir, Your Obt. Servt.

(Signed)   <u>Danl S Dexter</u>

LB Copy, DNA, RG45, Daniel Dexter Letter Book, pp. 92–93. In Dexter's hand.

1. See p. 208.
2. Dexter was ordered to report to the department on 18 October. See Jones to Dexter, 18 Oct. 1813, DNA, RG45, Letters Sent Conveying Appointments and Orders and Accepting Resignations, No. 11, p. 69.

LIEUTENANT DANIEL S. DEXTER TO SENATOR JAMES BROWN

New Orleans, 29th Novr. 1813.

Dear Sir,

Inclosed is the Memorial I mentioned to you in my last letter.— I am not aware that it contains any thing which might militate against my chance of speedy promotion, nor am I certain that it will operate in favour of it; I have therfore to request you will be so good as to peruse and determine on its merits and the effects it will probably produce; which your being present and perfectly acquainted with the disposition of the Senate, will enable you to do with a degree of correctness and precision which my absence and want of Knowledge prevents me from doing; and aceeding to your own opinion on the subject, either present or repress the Memorial.

I anticipate the pleasure of seeing you in Washington in about a month, as I have taken passage in a schooner that sails for Baltimore next Sunday. I have been induced to adopt this mode of proceeding to the North by the advice of my friends, and the assurance of Dr. Heerman that my low state of health would not allow me to undertake the journey by land in less than two or three months, without danger of a relapse. As I shall so soon be with you, I could wish, should no existing circumstances make it necessary to present the Memorial immediately, that you would retain it till my arrival; of this, however, you will be the best judge.

Capt. Patterson has also forwarded a Memorial on the same subject; I believe, under cover to the Secretary of the Navy.— We have nothing new here worth mentioning. With much Respect, I have the honor to be, Sir, Your Obt. Servt.

(Signed)   Dan[l] S. Dexter

Honorable James Brown,
Senator, City of Washington.

LB Copy, DNA, RG45, Daniel Dexter Letter Book, pp. 94–95. In Dexter's hand.

LIEUTENANT DANIEL S. DEXTER TO U.S. SENATE

To the Honorable the Senate of the U. States of America in Congress Assembled

Danl. S. Dexter, of Providence R.I. a Lieutenant in the Navy, most respectfully presents this memorial to the Senate of the U. States, conceiving himself entitled to a Rank superior to the one he now holds in the naval service, & that he feels himself injured & agrieved in having with held from him rights which he considers his due, in as much as other Officers his juniors in service have been promoted over him posessing no greater claims than himself to such reward

He appeals therefore to yr. honorable body as forming an integrel part of this Source from whence promotion flows & begs leave to narrate the Services in which he has been engaged that you may the better judge of the justice of his claims, and apply to them the relief your wisdom & liberality may think they deserve & which your high attributes under the Constitution enable you to give—

Yr. Memorialist respectfully represents that he entered the ~~Naval~~ Service as a Midsn. in Apl. 1800, & in June joined the Frigate *Geo Washington*, Lt. Jacobs Comde. at N. Port. R.I. and proceeded to Philaa. where Capn. Wm. Bainbridge assumed the comd. & from whence she saild for the Mediteranean early in Augt. that he continued in this capacity to serve onboard of different Vessels & under different Commanders Generally on the Mediterranean Station until Septr. 1804 when he was promoted to an acting Lieutenantcy by the late Comde. Prebble, with whom he was during all the attacks made on Tripoli & continued with him until Comde. Saml. Barron took command of the Squadron— ~~when~~ & Cap. Decatur that of the *Constitution* With Capn. Decatur yr Memorialist continued to act as a Lt. and was transferred with him when he assumed the command of the *Congress* Frigate, and continued on board that ship in the same capacity until her return to the U States in Novr. 1805—

In Jany 1806 your Memorialist was orderd by Comde. Prebble to Portland, to superintend the building of the Bomb Ketch *Etna*, whence he was shortly after orderd by the Hon. Secy. of the Navy to Newberry Port to direct the building of Gun boat *No. 12*—& where he remaind until she was equipt for sea, when he was orderd by the navy Department to take command of her & proceed for New Orleans under the Command of Lt. Jones & when he arrivd in Novr. 1806—

Your Memorialist has remaind on this unhealthy station ever since, generally in comd. of a Division of G.B. in the Mississippi, on the coast of Florida & on the waters of Mobile—

Your Memorialist was not commissioned as a lieut. until Feby. 1807 altho he distinctly understood that Comde. Prebble was authorized to confer that rank & from the year 1804 he was always addressd by that title from the N Dept.—

In Octr. 1811 yr Memorialist took command of the late US Brig *Viper* & was employd in her Cruizing off the Coast about six months when Lt. J. D. Henley, as a senior officer, applied for her & she was given up to his comd.— He then re-assumed the command of the Gun Vessels in which service he remained until after the declaration of war when in Novr. 1812 he was orderd to take charge of the ship of war *Louisiana* & in which command he still continues—

Thus has yr Memorialist ~~served~~ for thirteen years served in the navy of his country with activity and without intermission & with the proud conciousness of ever enjoying the confidence of his different commanders and of being as serviceable to the Republic as the limited situation in which he acted would allow, yet have his services been overlookd, or forgotten & his claims to promotion denied or neglected while others his juniors have been promoted & rewarded whose pretensions are certainly not fairer than his own—

This exclusion from his rank, this forgetfulness of his rights, Yr Memorialist has felt to be a amortifying and grevious wrong—equally derogatory to his character as destructive to his honor as an Officer, for it cannot but strike yr honorable body as a tacit avowal of ~~my~~ his inability to fill the office He now claims—

Since the declaration of War yr Memorialist has repeatedly but in vain solicited a recall from this most unpleasant station & requestd more active duty— Upwards of seven years the prime of his life has been consigned in this pestilential clime & what might be termd meritorious in him has been made the ~~reason for~~ plea to justify injustice— He cannot descend to particulars which might seem invidous & unmanly, for while he acknowledges the pretensions of some of his brother Officers, juniors to himself, to the thanks & highest rewards of his country Yet there are others who have not surpassed him in devotedness to his duty & with whom he would not blush to be compared were their brightest actions to be contrasted with his own—

Under these circumstances & considerations yr Memorialist most respectfully presents a view of his Grievances to yr Honbe. body, He would also suggest that regular promotions, unless obviated by brilliant actions terminating in the honor & Glory of our Common Country & which yr Memorialist could never for one moment think of objecting to He humbly conceives to be the Officers right, as it is his hope, tis the spring that gives activity to his valor & inspiration to his ability, it sooths him when environd by difficulties & danger & consoles him when separated from his Kindred & his Country Rob him of this expectd boon & you rob him of hope;— the sources of emulation are dried up and the proud Chaplet with which fancy had encircled his brow, when Merit & Services brought reward fades in uncertain perspective beneath the Chilling influence of favoritism and neglect

Your memorialist hesitated long, before he resolved on addressing yr H— body, but the goading remembrance of unrequited service, the humiliating & almost daily examples of junior officers being placed over him, added to protracted hopes & the ill Success attending reitterated applications for recall from a disagreeable & distant station, at last compelld him to claim yr interposition in his behalf an interposition that he cannot doubt will be accorded in such amanner as to advance him, to that rank he feels so justly his due— And etc.—

AD, DNA, RG45, AF8 (M625, Roll No. 200). Memorial is dated 29 November 1813 in a hand other than Dexter's.

LIEUTENANT DANIEL S. DEXTER TO CONGRESSMAN THOMAS B. ROBERTSON

New Orleans, 29th November 1813.

Dear Sir,

Long and severe illness has deprived me of the pleasure of writing to you for some months past, and even now, I cannot boast of good health; but my recovery has been and will continue to be greatly accellerated by the pleasing idea of shortly enjoying a personal interview with my friend in the City of Washington, as I have just received an order of recall from this station, and engaged in a Schooner that sails for Baltimore in four days. Dr. Heerman's advice and assurance that it would be a long time ere my health would warrant attempting the journey by land, has induced me to adopt this mode of returning.

I have written to Mr. Brown, of the Senate, inclosing a Memorial relative the unjust delay in my promotion, and requested him to determine on the expediency of presenting or repressing it. As a friend in whose judgment and good wishes towards me, I have all confidence, I could wish that you would advise with Mr. Brown on the subject, should it be agreeable to both.

We have no <u>news</u> here. In about a month I hope to be with you. Till then adieu. With much Respect & esteem, Your friend & Servt.

(Signed)   <u>Dan[l] S Dexter</u>

Hon Thos. B. Robinson [1]
City of Washington.

LB Copy, DNA, RG45, Daniel Dexter Letter Book, pp. 93–94. In Dexter's hand.

1. Dexter meant Robertson.

New Orleans at Year's End

At year's end, the situation on the New Orleans Station had not measurably improved from that of the preceding summer. While a new ship, the bomb brig Etna, had been added to the station's force, two others, Gunboat No. 65 and Louisiana, were temporarily out of service. What was particularly mortifying to Master Commandant Daniel T. Patterson, the new commander at New Orleans, was that he had no ships strong enough to challenge any of the British vessels hovering off the Gulf Coast. As had his predecessor, Captain John Shaw, Patterson pleaded with Secretary Jones to provide the New Orleans Station with enough officers, men, and craft to contest the enemy effectively.

Master Commandant Daniel T. Patterson to
Secretary of the Navy Jones

New Orleans   7th. December 1813.

Sir,

I have forborne touching on the various points of your letter of instructions of the 18th Octr. till the transfer of the command should have taken place; but the unexpected and protracted absence of Comr. Shaw, from this place renders it a duty I owe to the station to, remark on one or two points, 1st. as it respects the number, force & State of the Vessels on this station, I have the honor to inform you that, there are at this moment in commission only 11 vessels of every description, viz: One Ship (*Louisiana*) one Brig (Bomb *Etna*), Six Gun Boats & their dispatch Vessels or Tenders.—

The *Louisiana* has heretofore mounted 14 long 24 pdr. on her Gun Deck, six 12 pd. Carronades on her Qr. deck, & two long 12s. on her Forecastle, but her main deck battery is now changing by an order of Comdr. Shaw's dated in Octr. last, to 10–9s & 6 12s long guns; which will make her a much more Formidable Vessel, & enable her to cross the Bar, as she is fully capable of bearing that armament with safety; the other Guns it would have been impossible to fight to advantage, nor would her Frame have been able to support many discharges. she will be ready to proceed on Service in a few days except her crew, which is very much reduced from the sickness last season, the Bomb Brig *Etna* mounts 6–6s. 2–8s. two breech Brass Howitzers, is ready for service, except a crew, but will drop down the River as low as Fort St. Philips in a day or two, she has on board 50 Souls.— Gun Boats *nos 156* & *162.* mount each a long 18 pr. and four carronades 12s & 18's. *nos 163* one long 24, & four sixes *no 5* one long 24 & 4–6's *no 23* one long 32. & 4 sixes and are on duty with full crews, *No. 65* mounts one long 24 & 4–6's [ordered?] a few days ago by the comdr. for repairs, but upon enquiry I find she will require so material a repair, that I shall lay her up: the crew's time having expired will be paid off— the dispatch vessels are two of them armed with 4 prs. and all with muskets.

This force you will perceive Sir, is inadequate to the defence of such a great extent of coast as requires defending, independently of annoying the enemy, which is extremely desirable, [?] permit me to suggest the great advantage two fast schooners [that?] could mount 12. to 16. 18 pd. carronades with long Gun on a Pivot amidships would be to this station, both for defence & offence, they could hang on the rear of the Jamaica convoys & cut out of their Fleet, & when occasion required act in squadron with the Ship & Brig; this coast would then require so large a force to maintain a Blockade that the enemy would scarcely be able to spare it for that purpose.— 2nd. Lieut. Dexter having been taken from this station, deprives me of one if not my best officer & leaves not Lieutenants enough to form a court Martial, nor enough to place in such commands as in my opinion req[uires] a Lieutenant.— There are only three Warranted Masters now in service, & 5 Warranted midshipmen, all others are A[cting] appts.. granted by Commdr. Shaw.— With two more Lieuts. & three who are acting on this Station Command.—, three or four Sailing M[asters] 8 or 10 midshipmen, & 150 to 200 Seamen, this Station would be [?] formidable; & I should hope that even then the expences would not exceed 20,000$ per mo: This number of Officers & men who in the winter cannot be employed on the lakes & now not required much I presume on Lake Erie, could embark at Pittsburgh & be here in a short time; seamen have at all times been extremely difficult to obtain here, & now more so than ever, indeed there are none in this [place?] to be had for any wages— As Mr. Smith Navy Agent is at Washington, he can fully inform you how very requisite 'tis that this station should be reinforced—with active, enterprising, trusty Officers, & a number of Seamen;—& many Changes which it will be highly necessary to make, could more readily be effected, with new Officers; than with only those, who, are now here, by the next mail I hope to be able, to reply satisfactorily to every part of your letter which requires it.—

The enemy have on this coast at this moment three men of War viz: Sloop *Herald* mounting 26 Guns 18–32 pound carronades. 6–18's & two long Guns, with about 150 men, Brig *Forester* Mounting 22–32 lb. carronades & 200 men & Brig *Contest* 14 Guns,[1] & I feel truly mortified, that I have no vessel with which to give either of them a meeting, with the ship & Brig I shall watch them closely, & seize the first favorable opportunity that may Offer of bringing them to action, but theirs all sail well ours very indifferently, consequently they can if they wish it, avoid at most times a contest.— but should you coincide with me in opinion, & give me the additional force of Vessels, Officers, & men, I should hope to add another Flag to those already so gloriously won from the foe: & indeed the two latter are indispensably necessary, to support our present force, as they cannot be obtained here.— I have the honour to be Sir with Great Respect Your Obedt. Servant

Danl T. Patterson

ALS, DNA, RG45, MC, 1813, No. 185 (M147, Roll No. 5).

1. According to the Admiralty's list of ships in sea pay, both *Forester* and *Contest* were rated sloops, the former mounting 18 guns and the latter 14 guns. See pp. 170, 172.

MASTER COMMANDANT DANIEL T. PATTERSON TO
SECRETARY OF THE NAVY JONES

New Orleans   Decr. 13th. 1813

Sir,

I have the honour to inform you that Commodore Shaw arrived here on the 7th instant, and on the 10th resigned all Command of the naval forces on this

Station, tho' a regular transfer of Official papers relative thereto, has not yet taken place but will in a day or two.

By the next mail I shall hope to give you full information on every remaining unanswered point of your letter of instructions of the 18th. Octr. On the 6th inst. I had the honour to State to you the number, Force, and Condition of all the vessels under my Command, duplicate of which accompanies this [1]

In consequence of the force of the enemy on this coast (as stated in my last) the Strict Blockade maintained by them; believing that no vessel can depart from this port, without falling into the hands of the enemy, and that none would depart, unless to aid the enemy, by furnishing them Supplies or giving information it has been deemed by the Commanding Genl. and myself necessary to inforce most rigidly the naval General Order of 29th July last that of the war Department of the 5th Augt. and which are Consequently Strictly inforced by the Commanders of the vessels under my Command, with Such vessels, as may be laden with provisions or munitions of war. that it is the intention of the Spaniards to Supply our enemy with provisions & from [this?] place, we have certain intelligence by letter from Pensacola, a [copy?] of which letter Genl. Flournoy forwards by this mail to the war Department, that Spanish vessels for that purpose, with a Pass from the Commander of the Blockading Squadron are to Come to this place and load with Such articles as they may Stand in need of, is I think unquestionable, Should the Spanish Colonies Suffer from the exportation of flour &c. being Stopped from this port, they have only their great ally to blame for it; but while [ ] [2] continues the Same certainties of Such Supplies falling into the hands of our enemy as at present exist. I Should feel myself wanting in duty to my Country, were I permit it to pass, and that you Sir, will Support me in the execution of my duty. However, it may militate against the interest of individuals, I am fully Confident, I have the honour to be Sir, with great respect, Your Obedt. Servt.

Dan[l] T. Patterson

LS, DNA, RG45, MC, 1813, No. 189 (M147, Roll No. 5).

1. Patterson means his letter of 7 December printed above. The duplicate he is referring to has not been found.
2. There is a blank space in the text of Patterson's letter here.

CAPTAIN JOHN SHAW TO MASTER COMMANDANT DANIEL T. PATTERSON

New Orleans　　December 21st. 1813

Sir

In consequence of arrangements sometime since made, but which was afterwards suspended, the Honorable Secretary of the Navy, has at length been pleased to indulge me in a desire I had previously expressed, of being withdrawn from this Station; and as you have been ordered to the command, it becomes my duty to make to you as my successor, a few observations relating to the strength of the force, now about to be transferred to you, and my opinion of the proper mode of disposing of it, in case of an attack made by a formidable force from the Enemy:—

For information, respecting the public vessels on the station, together with a statement of their force, respectively, I must beg leave to refer you to an accompanying paper, marked A; which contains every thing necessary on that subject. Although it is impossible for me to furnish you with a correct statement of the various articles, at present on board each of them, yet I believe I can assure you of their having at least one hundred rounds of ammunition on board for each gun; of their being well supplied with the necessary Naval stores & equipments; and, upon the whole of their being in excellent order to perform any kind of service.

In taking a view of the nature and extent of the sea-board—its bays, bayaus, &c. I have all along been of opinion, that, if ever, or whenever, an attempt should be made by the Enemy to capture this City, the approach would not be either by way of the Balize or the S.W. Pass; as the rapidity of the current, and other difficulties, arising from its numerous meanderings, must be insuperable objections to those routes. The approach by the way of Lake Barritaria, would, I apprehend, be found equally objectionable; for the narrowness of the Bayaus, and, indeed, their shallowness, as must be apparent, would render almost impossible, the transportation, to this place, of a force adequate to such an object. The Bayau, or river, La Fourche, is however known to be a stream of considerable magnitude & importance,—being navigable for vessels of considerable size. I must give it as my opinion therefore, & strongly recommend it to you, that a vigilant look-out should be constantly kept up on that route; and that a regular express to pass between this City and a Military post which will probably be established on that river, ought to be urgently recommended to the Commanding General, as essentially necessary, during the Winter & Spring months, to the safety of this part of the Country.

The eastern section of this state & the Bay and waters of Mobile, appear to me much more vulnerable to the attack of an invading enemy, than any of the points to the westward of the Balize; for what obstacle is there to oppose the landing of British troops, should an expedition be undertaken for that purpose, at any spot, between Pearl river & the Pasgagola? Were such an attempt to be made on that part of our Coast, the enemy would immediately find himself on terra-firma—would have an open pine-woods-country to march through—would be able to procure beef cattle in abundance, for his support—and, what is more, Sir, he would, in my opinion, obtain pilots with great facility, to conduct him either to Natchez or to Baton Rouge; from either of which places it must be obvious, he would meet with nothing to arrest, either his progress or his ravages, in his descent towards this City— The mouth of the Rigoletts—from thence eastwardly, across Lake Bourne, to the Malheureux Islands—& the pass of chef menteur, will also claim your attention:— Through these passes if not properly guarded, owing to their proximity to this place, an expedition from the enemy, might with great facility, approach New Orleans. I would therefore, recommend, that you, in co-operation with the commanding General, should use the utmost vigilence towards the defence of those positions, during the winter & spring months. During the sickly season of summer & autumn, I imagine that nothing need be apprehended from the enemy; as the unhealthiness of the climate will be their best protection.

The coasting trade between this and Mobile, will, I apprehend, require the particular attention of the Naval Commanding officer. The keeping of our waters, along the Islands, as far as pass Heron, free of the enemy, will probably afford a pretty steady, and a very important exercise, for his utmost vigilence & efforts; while the fort on Mobile point, if made tenable by the Military, and supported by a small Division of Gun Vessels, may prevent the enemy from obtaining possession of that Bay. The free navigation of that part of our coast, being thus kept open, will afford almost the only practicable means of conveying supplies of provisions, munitions of war &c. to such Military force as may be stationed by our government within the Creek Nation & elsewhere, along our eastern frontier. These Sir, are my views on this particular subject; & which I hope may accord with your own, when turned to them, as I imagine they must soon be.

The only unfinished duty, now in progress, under orders from the Secretary of the Navy, which has to be transferred for your completion, is the building of the Block-ship now on the stocks on the Tchifoncta river, that the advancement of that duty has been as rapid, as the means in my power admitted; and that no exertions on my part, or on the part of any other officer concerned in it, have been spared for bringing it to a speedy & successful termination, must be too well known to yourself to admit of any doubt on the subject. On this subject, therefore, it only remains for me to recommend to you, the continuance of the necessary exertions, in getting her afloat and put in Commission. If well officered and manned, she will form a battery for any point where she may be required, on which reliance may be confidently placed in time of danger.

I transfer to you, herewith, marked B, a list of the names & respective grades of the officers attached to this station:— Your personal knowledge of them all renders it unnecessary for me to make any other particular mention of them to you by name; yet I cannot on this occasion, refrain from expressing the high sense I entertain of their unremitted attention, in general, to duty, & their strict observance of orders, since I have had of the honor to command of this station. I am also much indebted to the medical Gentlemen, for their humane & skilful attention to the sick under their charge; more especially, during the rage of the most malignant diseases among our men. On these occasions, no complaint has been made, nor any desire expressed by them, to withdraw from the posts assigned them, notwithstanding the perilous situations in which they were placed. The consideration of these circumstances, induces me to express for those gentlemen, sentiments of the highest respect & esteem.

The general state of the magazine—the cannon powder on hand—the number of cannon—sea-mortars—cannon-shot, shells &c. are so well known to yourself, that I should consider it useless and unnecessary, to make any return of, or particular observations respecting them, to you: The same may be observed, with regard to the state of the Navy-store, and the various Naval supplies which it contains.

Accompanying this I hand over to you the following official letters, from the Navy-Department, which you will find numbered from 1, to 8, inclusively: Viz. No. 1, dated February 14th. 1811, authorizing the appointment of sailing Masters &c.: No. 2, dated August 28th. 1811, directing the appointment of Midshipmen: No. 3, dated 20th. June, 1812, which mentions an arrangement between the War & Navy-Departments, respecting a mutual interchange of munitions of war &c. &c. and directing a conformity therewith: No. 4, dated 26th. August, 1812, communicating the appointment of John Mitchell esquire, and the fixing of his residence a Halifax, as agent for Prisoners; & containing orders relating thereto: No. 5, dated September, 1812, authorizing the procuring of two Block-ships, in case of indispensible necessity; & enjoining economy: No. 6, dated 28th October 1812, which authorizes the convening of Courts Martial: No. 7th. dated the lst. March 1813, communicating the determination of that Department, of the amount of force allowed to this station, and containing orders arising out of that subject: and No. 8 dated March 30th. 1813, accompanying twenty blank certificates to be furnished to disabled & wounded persons in service, and containing directions for filling them up.

I also transfer to you a letter from the Navy-Department, which I have marked (C) together with the copy of the signals, transmitted with it, to be observed between our public & private armed vessels; which latter you will perceive to be strictly confidential.

I have requested the Honorable secretary of the Navy to permit the Block-ship building on the Tchifoncta, to be coppered, if it were but up to her first ribbands; and I beg leave to recommend it to you to make a similar application. I have urged its necessity on the ground of the probable difficulty and indeed the almost impossibility (owing to her extremely flat form) there will be of heaving her out for the purpose of paying her bottom, after she shall have been once launched, in order to secure her against the destruction of the insects so prevalent in these waters.

I have often represented to the honorable secretary of the Navy, the extensive practice of smugling Kept up on this coast, and especially to the Westward of the Balize; and the insufficiency of the Naval force on this station to effectually arrest its progress. The same subject will no doubt, necessarily employ no small portion of your attention—as will also the subject of a rigid economy, so justly and strongly urged by our government.

Before closing this communication I must beg to be permitted, sir, to tender to you individually, my most sincere thanks, for the very able & important support which you have afforded me in the execution of the various duties, appertaining to the command of the station, since I have been honored with it; and to assure you, that while I cordially congratulate you on your appointment, as my successor to the command, I am truly mortified, at its not being in my power to turn over to you such a naval force (I speak of the vessels) as if called into action would be productive of honor to our country and tars which you will have the honor to command Sir, I have the honor to be very respectfully your most obt servt.

John Shaw

LS, DNA, RG45, CL, 1813, Vol. 8, No. 94 (M125, Roll No. 33).

MASTER COMMANDANT DANIEL T. PATTERSON TO
SECRETARY OF THE NAVY JONES

New Orleans   27th December 1813

Sir,

In my last dated the 13th inst, I had the honor to inform you of Commodore Shaw's having transferred the Command of this Station to me; since then Viz: on the 21st inst he transferred all the public letters from the Navy Department relative to the Station.

In a few days I shall visit the Block Ship Building on the Tchifuncte, when I will make A particular report to you of her State, progress, the probable length of time yet required to finish her; and the extent of her cost &c., After which I shall proceed to Mobile Bay, visit every Vessel under my Command, with the Purser of the Station; muster their crews, and make to the Department a correct return thereof, in the manner prescribed by your instructions of the 18th. of Octr.—

Enclosed I have the honor to transmit a list[1] of such articles, with the quantities of each, as are required for the ensuing year; and which cannot be obtained here, except at the most extravagant prices, and many not at all; I have inserted yarns, instead of ready made Cordage as it can be made here, on as good terms, and of better quality, and Sizes; than in the Western States, the last parcel Sent from Tennessee is indifferent in quality and nearly useless in size, except it may be applied to the Block Ship.—

The carronades may become extremely servicible, on this Station, from the enemy's Vessels using that Species of Gun; and as we can then be on a more equal footing with them; when fortunate enough to be able to encounter them.—

The Ship muskets, on this Station are of a very bad quality, and require continual repairs; nor are there more than Sufficient for the few Vessels at present in Commission; that can be rendered fit for Service. the Pistols are too much worn to be put in Such order as to be depended on, nor are there sufficient for the Station; all that the Military could possibly spare they [have?] furnished us with. Cutlasses, and Battle Axes, you will perceive by the monthly return of the Navy agent; we are entirely destitute of, of course in want of those articles, these things cannot be obtained here on any terms

Excuse me Sir for repeating my urgent Solicitations, for an increase of Officers, Seamen, and Vessels; I have not now Sufficient to protect efficiently the coasting trade between this and Mobile; and which 'tis highly important to maintain; particularly during the War with the Creek Indians in order to furnish the necessary provisions &c for the army, in that Country as the Capture of any of the Convoys by the enemy, would be a most serious loss to that Army, might compel them to abandon their Conquest and would at the Same time greatly relieve the latter; the approaches to this City too; by Water are so numerous, that they require many Vessels and Vigilant Officers; to guard them effectually:— The Ship _Louisiana_ will be in readiness to drop down the River in a few days, except the want of <u>Seamen</u>, & where or how to obtain them, I Know not; for there are none in this City; had I <u>Seamen</u> for <u>her</u> the _Herald_ Should be mine.

By letters from Jamaica it appears the enemy are there fitting out a number of Gun Brigs &c of light draft of water, supposed for an expedition against this Country; Should they come, what can be effected with the force under my command Shall be   I can only express my regret that 'tis not greater, or Such as to afford a reasonable prospect of Success.— I have the Honor to be Sir with great respect yr Obt. Sevt.

Dan[l] T. Patterson

ALS, DNA, RG45, MC, 1814, Vol. 2, No. 105 (M147, Roll No. 5).

1. Enclosure not found.

Chapter Five

The Pacific Theater: January–December 1813

Writing from Constitution *on 13 October 1812, Commodore William Bainbridge informed Captain David Porter that* Constitution *would set sail within two weeks on a commerce-raiding cruise that would pass the Cape Verde Islands and then shape a course for the island of Fernando de Noronha in the south central Atlantic. From there, he intended to head south, searching for British prizes along the coast of Brazil as far as the island of "St. Catherine's" (Santa Catarina), with a final destination of St. Helena where he would try to intercept merchant ships returning from India. Bainbridge hoped* Essex *would be able to join him at the Cape Verde Islands or at one of the other locations no later than 1 April 1813. Should this be impossible, he allowed Porter complete discretion to act "for the good of the service." When* Essex *finally sailed from the Delaware River in late October, Porter steered for the south Atlantic, expecting to meet Bainbridge at Fernando de Noronha. He arrived one day before Bainbridge's planned arrival date, but there was no sign of the commodore.* Constitution *and* Hornet *had already passed by, leaving a letter for Porter with orders for a new rendezvous off Cape Frio, about 60 miles north of Rio de Janeiro. Porter again arrived at the designated place on the appointed day, but Bainbridge had been detained at Bahia (Salvador) where he and Master Commandant James Lawrence, in* Hornet, *were blockading H.M. sloop of war* Bonne Citoyenne. Porter *remained in the vicinity of Cape Frio until 13 January 1813. He sailed for Santa Catarina off southern Brazil and waited again for Bainbridge, but the commodore by this time had defeated H.M.S.* Java *and was en route to the United States. Having missed rendezvous a third time, Porter implemented the discretionary part of his orders. On 26 January, he set sail for the Pacific and an extraordinary naval adventure.*

Several years earlier, Porter had dreamed of a voyage of discovery in the Pacific. He wrote a lengthy letter to Secretary Hamilton proposing an elaborate navigational plan for the acquisition of new territory for the United States and the exploration of uncharted coasts. Hamilton did not endorse the idea. In setting sail for Cape Horn, Porter combined his yearning for Pacific exploration with his cruising orders and carried the war against Britain into a new theater. There was much that could be done, against little serious opposition, until word reached London that an American frigate was at large in a British sphere of influence along the western coast of South America.

The Spanish colonies of South America were in rebellion against the Napoleonic regime in Spain which had been invaded and occupied by French armies in 1807.

Using the occupation of the Spanish throne by Joseph Bonaparte as a pretext, local juntas sprang up in a burst of patriotic rhetoric and self-determination. In the viceroyalty of the Rio de la Plata, the royalists rallied to the throne in Lima, while local patriots in Santiago and Buenos Aires urged their overthrow, claiming the viceroy was a minion of the Bonapartists in Spain. The British government favored the break with Bonaparte, encouraged merchants to trade directly with the Spanish colonies, and maintained good relations with the viceroys. In Lima, Viceroy Don Fernando de Abascal y Sousa played a waiting game, disclaimed loyalty to the Bonapartists and pledged fealty to the dethroned King Ferdinand VII. At the same time, the example of the United States's Revolutionary War provided a lingering inspiration for Latin American patriots who fought to overthrow Spanish rule. José Miguel Carrera and his brothers had revolted against the Chilean loyalists in 1811 and were still in charge at Santiago in 1813, although Viceroy Abascal was raising a counter-revolutionary army to oust them. The arrival of Captain Porter's Essex *at Valparaiso on 15 March 1813 caused a flurry of excitement among the Chilean revolutionaries who solicited his aid against royalist naval vessels and privateers. Porter saw this as an opportunity to court local favor while awaiting an opportunity to attack British shipping and whaling fleets.*

Recapture of H.M. Packet Brig *Nocton*

Of the fourteen ships captured during Essex*'s cruise, her richest prize was H.M. packet brig* Nocton, *taken off Brazil on 12 December 1812 with $55,000 in specie in her hold.*[1] *Impressed with her sailing qualities, and believing her to be a suitable replacement for the recently captured* Nautilus, *Captain David Porter dispatched* Nocton *to the United States as a prize with the hope that she would be purchased into naval service. Porter placed Acting Lieutenant William B. Finch*[2] *in command of* Nocton *with a crew of fourteen men to work the ship and guard the prisoners on board. On her journey to the northward,* Nocton *was retaken by a British warship—a fate that was to be shared by four more of* Essex*'s prizes.*

1. *For details of* Nocton*'s capture, see Dudley,* Naval War of 1812, *Vol. 1, pp. 625–27.*
2. *Finch was promoted to lieutenant on 4 January 1813.*

LIEUTENANT WILLIAM B. FINCH TO SECRETARY OF THE NAVY JONES

New York
February 13th. 1813

Sir,

I have the Honor to inform you that I arrived here this day in the Cartel *Bostock* from Bermuda—having left the U.S. frigate *Essex* on the 12th day of Decr. in charge of H.M's packet brig *Nocton* carrying ten Guns from Rio de Janeiro for Falmouth captured the day previous in Lat. 00°.39'S and Longe. 29°.30'W without cargo— having on board fifteen thousand pounds sterling in Specie which was removed to the *Essex* for safekeeping—with a prize crew consisting of Midn. Connover and 13 seamen (one an invalid) also seventeen prisoners part of her former Crew—

In consideration of her bearing the character of a King's Vessel and well calculated to supply the loss of the *Nautilus* Capt. Porter I believe was induced at that distance to dispatch her for the United States—

Having reached the Lat. 31°. 30' N and Longe. 66°. W while lying too (at day light on the Morning of Jany. 5th) with the Wind from the Westward a large Sail was descried on our Weather beam— I immediately bore up made N carried sail through heavy squalls from her but to my mortification perceived my chance of escape hopeless— and after a chace of three hours and twenty minutes the frigate *Belvidera* going at the rate of Eleven Knots and an half ranged alongside and took possession of me having in the chace sprung her mizen cap & Topmast badly and necessitated in consequence to furl her mizen top sail—

I shall report myself to Como. Decatur and await your further orders and if consistent request permission to proceed to Washn.

I regret that I am necessitated to conclude my letter by informing you of the detention of one of the prize crew as a French-man—who has been sent to french prison at Halifax— I could receive no other satisfaction by remonstrance than the assurance that all recognized as frenchmen would be detained. With Respect I am Sir Your obdt. servt.

Wm. Finch

List of Officers and Men detached from the U.S. frigate *Essex*—(Capt. Porter) composing the Crew of the British packet *Nocton* prize to the *Essex* recaptured by the *Belvidera* Jany. 5th 1813 and carried to Bermuda—

Wm. Finch	—	Lt.
Thos. A. Conover	—	Midn.
John Williams	—	Sea:
Jno. C. Porter	—	"
Wm. Bussell	—	"
Betlin F. Rose	—	Mar. (detained)

ALS, DNA, RG45, BC, 1813, Vol. 1, No. 61 (M148, Roll No. 11).

Essex at Valparaiso, Chile

On 15 March 1813 Essex *arrived at Valparaiso, Chile. After eight weeks at sea the American frigate was in dire need of reprovisioning. But because of Spain's traditional hostility toward foreign contacts with her American colonies, and because of American filibustering in the Floridas, Captain David Porter was not confident of his chances of obtaining succor there. To his relief, the people of Valparaiso greeted* Essex *and her crew with enthusiasm and hospitality. Chile was fighting for her independence, and, as Porter learned, the Chileans "looked up to the United States for example and protection."[1]*

Over the next eight days Porter directed the replenishing of his ship's food, water, and wood. Completing this task with speed was essential, for British whalers to the northward

"U.S.S. Essex, 1799"

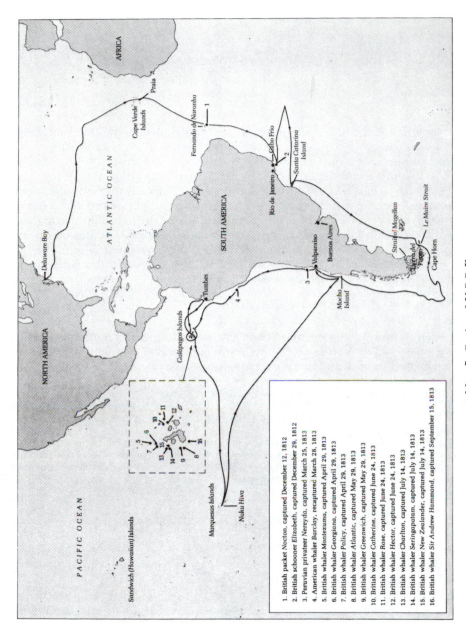

Map 5. Cruise of U.S.S. Essex

were ignorant of Essex's arrival in the Pacific. If Porter tarried too long in preparing Essex for sea, his quarry would be alerted to her presence, thus sacrificing one of the American captain's greatest advantages—the element of surprise.

1. Porter, Journal of a Cruise, Vol. 1, p. 102.

Journal of Midshipman William W. Feltus [1]

[Extract]

March 22d 1813

Commences Pleasant   at 2 having dressed the ship sent the boats on shore for the company   at 4 discd. a sail standing for this Port. sent word to Capt Porter on shore   at 1/4 past 4 PM the boats came on board with Capt Porter the consul [2] and some spanish officers   at 5 (perceiving that the strange sail was very large) cut down the awning and flags the Ship was dressed in, cut one cable and sliped the other   made sail cleared ship for action and stood out of Valpriso in chase   at 6 P.M. shortened sail and spoke the chase the Porteguese ship *fame* from Rio Janerio 87 days passage   made sail stood off and on during the night   at 7 AM ran into the port of Valpriso the porteguese ship in the offing   at 10 came too by the cable we sliped   at 1/2 past 10 the *Fame* ran in came too fired a salute ~~which we returnd~~ Ends Pleasant

W W Feltus

N.B when we were going out the Spaniards flocked on the Neighbouring Hills crying—*Bravo*—*Vive le Americanòs*   the above ship was very much like a frigate she having a Gun deck and her ports being out— she mounted 22 Guns

ADS, PHi, Journal of Midshipman William W. Feltus.

1. William W. Feltus was the son of Henry J. Feltus, rector of St. Ann's Episcopal Church, Brooklyn, New York.
2. Joel R. Poinsett, American consul general for Buenos Aires, Chile, and Peru. Poinsett served as an intermediary between Porter and the Chilean junta, helping the American naval officer to obtain supplies for his ship while at Valparaiso. For a discussion of Poinsett's role in South American politics, see Rippy, *Joel R. Poinsett*, especially Chapter 5.

Captain David Porter to Commodore William Bainbridge

(Copy)

U S Frigate *Essex*
Port of Valparaiso, March 23d 13

Sir,

Agreeable to your orders of the 13th Octr. 1812, I sailed from the River Delaware on the 26th Octr. shaping my course for Port Praya in the Island of St. Iago, where I arrived agreeable to appointment on the 27th Novr., I there took in some water and refreshments and sailed on the 2d Decr. making the best of my way for Fernando de Noronha, on the 11th Decr. I captured H B M Packet the *Nocton*, and sent her to the United States after taking some money out of her to the Amount of about £11,000 Sterling— On the 15th Decr. agreeable to appointment I arrived at Fernando de Noronha where I sent my boat on shore and received your letter of the 3d Decr. directing me to cruize off Cape Frio until the 1st Jany. to this last place I proceeded and (as I frequently heard of your being off Bahia) cruized there until the 12th Jany. capturing only the Schooner *Elizabeth*,[1] when my water and provisions getting short and feeling apprehensive of the scurvy I determined to put into port, and as I had certain intelligence that the British Admiral[2] had sailed from Rio on the 5th Jany. in pursuit of us I considered it adviseable to go to a place where there would be the least likelihood of his getting intelligence of me in a short time, and therefore proceeded to St. Catherines where I procured wood & water and some refreshments, but found it impossible to procure any sea stock except some Rum and a few Bags of flour— I here obtained intelligence of your action with a British Frigate, and of the capture of the *Hornet*, of a considerable augmentation of the British force on the Coast of Brazils, and saw no hopes of being able to join you except at the last appointed rendezvous and there my stock of provisions would not admit of my going to cruize until the time specified, to go else where than to the places appointed would be a departure from your instructions and as it now became necessary for me to act discretionary I determined to proceed to the nearest port that would render my supplies certain and at the same time put it out of the power of the enemy to blockade me and thus be enabled to extend my cruize, with this view I proceeded to this place where I arrived on the 15th. March after a tempestuous passage in which however we suffered but little except from short allowance of provisions— I here in six days after my arrival had on board as much provisions wood & water as my ship could conveniently stow, and shall sail on my cruize to day— My reception here has been of the most friendly nature, the political state of the country is most favourable to our cause, and every advantage that a port of the United States could afford to us has already been offered to me by the President & Junto—[3] their cause is Liberty and Independence, and the arrival of this Ship has given them fresh vigor—

Our Commerce has been much harrassed in those seas and at the mouth of this harbour by several corsairs or pirates from Lima, and as I have as complete power in the Pacific as the whole British Navy can have in the Atlantic I shall be enabled to afford it that protection it now stands in need of both from the aforesaid corsairs and the armed British Ships in this part of the world that have already made some captures of our Whalers which are numerous here—

Be assured Sir, that I shall use the most active exertions to annoy the enemy, my prospects I think will justify the most sanguine expectations, and I shall endeavour as often as possible to communicate to you the result— I have endeavoured from time to time to get intelligence to you of my movements through our minister[4] at Rio Janeiro, I shall continue to pursue the same plan— You know my intentions I shall say nothing respecting them—

With the utmost regret that circumstances should have prevented our meeting, and the most fervent wishes for your health, happiness & prosperity, I have the honor to remain Your Very huml. Servt.

Signed, D— Porter—

Commre. Wm. Bainbridge
Comdg. US Frigate *Constitution*—

Copy, DNA, RG45, CL, 1813, Vol. 4, No. 139, enclosure (M125, Roll No. 29).

1. *Elizabeth* was captured on 28 December 1812 and sent on to Rio de Janeiro as prize under the command of Midshipman William Clarke. Denied sanctuary in Brazil, she was burned, being deemed too unseaworthy to make the voyage to the United States. See Porter, *Journal of a Cruise*, Vol. 1, pp. 47–48; and Long, *Nothing Too Daring*, p. 78.

2. Rear Admiral Manley Dixon, R.N.

3. President José Miguel Carrera and junta members Don Santiago Portales and Don Pedro José de Prado.

4. Thomas Sumpter.

UNIDENTIFIED AGENT TO MESSRS. WATSON AND BROWN

The United States Frigate the *Essex* Capt: Porter arrived in this Port on the 15th. March & took in Water & Provisions with the greatest dispatch; She remained here only 6 days & was received with the loudest acclamations of Joy by the Governmt: & people, it is supposed she will return to this Port again, & has only gone out to take & destroy the English Whalers on the Coast; She mounts 40 Guns, viz. 28—24Lbs. Carronades & 12 long nines with a complement of 340 Men, She landed some of the *Nocton* Packets Sailors here;

The Capt: of the *Essex* is said to have demanded the restoration of all the American Property, which has been confiscated by order of the Court at Lima with a positive declaration that if they do not accede to it He will sink every thing He meets with under Spanish Colours, & it is said, He has disarmed six of the largest of the Lima Cruizers—

Copy, Adm. 1/21, pp. 253–54. The above document was extracted from a letter written by Brown's and Watson's agent at Valparaiso dated 8 April 1813, and was enclosed in Dixon to Croker, 9 June 1813, Adm. 1/21, pp. 249–54.

Capture of the Peruvian Privateer *Neryeda*

While at Valparaiso, Captain David Porter learned that the Viceroy of Peru had ordered all American vessels trading with Chile seized. Upon putting to sea, it was Porter's aim to halt this harassment of American commerce. Such a course of action was diplomatically hazardous, for Spain's relations with the United States were already strained, and attacks on her colonial shipping might drive her from neutrality into armed belligerency. Porter therefore had to temper force with restraint in dealing with the Peruvian corsairs. In disarming the Peruvian privateer Neryeda, *and ordering her home to Lima, Porter sought to achieve the proper balance between force and restraint.*

JOURNAL OF MIDSHIPMAN WILLIAM W. FELTUS

[Extract]

At Sea   March. 25th 1813

Commences thick.   at 5 AM light airs   discd. a sail on the weather bow   at 7 came up with and spoke the chase an American Ship the *charles* a Whaler from Nantacket about 13 Months ago. she informed us that she was chased by a spanish privateer off Coquimbo   her 2d mate came on board in order to pilot us up to Coquimbo. (the land in sight)   at 8 made sail the *Charles* being in company with us   at 1/2 past 8 discd. a sail ahead which we believe to be the Spanish privateer   Ends Pleasant   Chase dead to windward   the wind having shifted cleard. away for action

Lat Ob. 30°21' South
Long 71°49' West
Wm. W Feltus

Mar. 26th   at Sea

Comences Pleasant   chase to windward   at 1 fired a gun to Leward & Hoisted english Colors   the American Ship *Charles* Hoisted English over the American Colors   at 1/2 past 1 PM the chase fired a gun to Leward & Hoisted Spanish Colors   at 2 she fired a shot across our bows which we returnd. with 6 at which she hove too and got her boat out & sent it on board   when it came along side Capt Porter ordered her back for the Capt the boat having an armed officer in. fired another shot at her when she stood down to us. her boat came on board again with the ~~first~~ 2d Lieut & ~~an American~~ who brought Her papers he said that they had taken several American Whalers that she was a Spanish privater out of Lima that she had also taken some English vessells, Examined her papers & found that she had a commission to cruiz 5 months as a privateer after Counterbanders & she had been cruizing 8 months. sent the boat again after the Capt & some of the american prisoners she had on board. the boat returned with the 1st Lieut & Capt of an American Ship she had captured   put the 2 Lieutenants under the charge of a centry. then we understood by the american Capt that she was a Pirate that she took evry thing she came across hoisted American Colors & fired 2 shot into the ~~American~~ Privateer at which she struck her colors   sent Mr. Downs on board with some men (secured the Guns)   at 4 PM Mr. Downs came on board with the Spaniards Mr. Macknight & Cowan[1] went on board with orders to follow the *essex*   made sail for Coquimbo at 8 hoisted a light at Mizen Peak   stood off and on during the night   in the Morning Made sail for Coquimbo   sent Mr. Downs on board the Privateer to heave evring thing like arms or ammunition over board and cut away her Royal & top yards & masts to heave all her light sails spare spar sails &c. overboard   at 9 AM Mr. Downs returned with the men he had taken with him & the American Prisoners   put the spanish officers & men on board with orders to proceed to Lima   Capt Porter sent a letter by the privateer to the Viceroy of Peru stating the Buziness. Ends Pleasant the Privateer standing to the nd. wd. & the American ship following us

Lat Ob. 30°30' South
Long Ob. 71°20' West
Wm. W Feltus

ADS, PHi, Journal of Midshipman William W. Feltus.

1. John S. Cowan was warranted a midshipman on 17 December 1810. He was killed in a duel with one of *Essex*'s officers in August 1813.

CAPTAIN DAVID PORTER TO
THE VICEROY OF PERU, DON FERNANDO DE ABASCAL Y SOUSA

U S Frigate *Essex*
At Sea   26th March 1813

Your Excellency,

I have this day met with the Ship *Nereyda* mounting fifteen Guns, bearing your Excellencies Patent and sailing under the Spanish flag—

On examination of said Ship I found on board of her as prisoners the Officers and crews of two vessels belonging to the United States of America employed solely in the Whale fishery of those seas captured by her and sent for Lima, after being plundered of boats, cordage, provisions, clothes and various other articles, and was informed by her officers that they were cruizing as the allies of Great Britain to capture and send in for adjudication all American Vessels they should meet with, alleging at the same time that they had not your Excellencies authority for such proceedings—

I have therefore to preserve the good understanding which should ever exist between the Government of the United States and the provinces of Spanish America determined to prevent in future such vexatious and piratical conduct, and with this view have deprived the *Neryeda* of the means of doing the American commerce any further injury for the present, And have sent her to Lima in order that her commander may meet with such punishment from your excellency as his offence may deserve— I have the honor to be With the highest respect and consideration Your Excellencies Obt. Huml. Servt.

Signed, D Porter—

His Excellency
The Vice Roy of Peru, Lima—[1]

Copy, DNA, RG45, CL, 1813, Vol. 4, No. 139, enclosure (M125, Roll No. 29). The text of this letter was excerpted from the enclosure printed on pp. 697–99.

1. In retaliation for the seizure of the privateer *Neryeda*, the Viceroy had sixteen American seamen from the *Colt*, an American privateer purchased into Chilean service, "put in irons, and condemned to labour on the public works" at Callao. See Johnston, *Three Years in Chili*, p. 122.

Operations in the Galapagos Islands

Essex arrived at the Galapagos archipelago in mid-April and remained there, with the exception of a brief voyage to the coast of Peru, until the first week of October. During this time she and her consorts captured twelve British whaling ships. Captain David Porter's success in the Galapagos was due largely to his ability to maintain his vessel at sea for an extended period of time. Captured whalers provided ships' stores to replace Essex's own, and the islands' exotic fauna—turtles, iguanas, sea birds—provided an ample supply of fresh food for Essex's crew. The factors that hampered Porter's operations most were the scarcity of water and the limited number of officers and men available to man prizes.

Captain David Porter

Porter calculated that his cruise in the Galapagos Islands cost Great Britain over five million dollars. While this figure grossly exaggerates the amount of damage he inflicted on the enemy, there can be no denying that Captain Porter had dealt British commerce a heavy blow.

JOURNAL OF MIDSHIPMAN WILLIAM W. FELTUS

[Extract]

31 March

Commences Pleasant. at sun down finished painting ship (painted her in the following manner Viz 1 broad yellow streak round her Hull as far as the fore chan- nels   rigged false waist cloths as high as the quarter deck nettings and painted ports on them, got tarpaulins up and rigged a poop and painted windows thereon painted the quarter Galleries different colours, At 3 AM taken aback took in the steering sails and Royals Braced on the Larbd tacks wind died away   at 8 a breeze sprung up aft made sail   employ'd mending sails. Ends bon tems. . . .

April 24th 1813   Banks Bay

Commences hot with light Breezes from the Wd. at 6 PM the Capt returned with a number of Green Turtle also some Aiguanas which were of a red and yel- low colour a great number of fish Seal skins et cetaera   they had turned 30 tur- tle and left them on the beach. Capt Porter ordered Mr. Cowell Master to go on shore with 2 Boats and bring them off and when the Moon rose to turn as many as possible and to come off at day light. Accordinly he took jolly boat and sent Mr. Isaccs & myself in the Green Cutter. we landed about 7 o clock to the Nd. of the place where ships usualy anchor. we made a large fire on the Beach & got 6 turtle in the Boat pulled out of the Bay & ran farthur North where we landed not without diffulty for there was a great many Rocks near the shore & also a surf setting on the shore   ~~also~~ it was very dark we got on the Rocks several times. when we landed we found that Jolly Boats even were here and were build- ing a fire   there were only 11 turtle here out of 30 thirty that had been turn'd on their backs   the tide had risen so much that it had carried the rest off. I turned in on the sand having my great coat under my head   at 1 AM or at moon rise we went in search of turtle but found but one   at 8 AM went on board made sail out of the Bay in search of the *Bartly*[1] that we had not seen since we came into the Bay   soon after she hove in sight   at 10 we were taken aback with all sail set Ends hot. . . .

April 29th 1813

Commences Hot   at [?] clear   at day light Fortune smiled on us for we discd. a sail   soon after we disd 2 more close together   gave chase   at 7 came up with and took the British ship *Montezuma* laden with Sperm. oil   soon after it fell calm those other two ships were Hull down Manned all the Boats and rowed after them in the following manner

Gig	Whale Boat	3d cutter	the Boats were
Pinnace		Jolly Boat	armed
1st. cutter		2d Cutter	

Lat 1°4' North
Long 91°20' W. . . .

April 30th 1813

Commences Warm rowing after the ships (I was in the 2d cutter) at 1/2 past 1 the ships fired 2 Guns a piece to windward and Hoisted the British flag we pulled up under one of their sterns she had 2 Guns pointed at us we immediately Hoisted the American Ensign. the ship Gave us 3 cherrs which we did not returned and boarded her she immediately struck to us. we manned her and went to the next she Had 1 Gun run out abaft and 1 in each Gangway and ready to fire we ran along side and boarded Hauled down her <u>Colors</u> this last ship the *policy* threw overboard near 100 tarapin. the first ship was named the <u>*Georgeannah*</u>. made sail for the *essex* sent the Prisoners on board and sent officers and men on board, in the morning employ'd sending for the peoples things Ends Hot

Long 91° 18' W
Lat 1° 5' Nor. . . .

Friday June 25th 1813

Commences Pleasant the strange sail proved to be the U S Sloop *Georgeannah*.[2] Mr. Downs command. went on board the *Essex* the Frigate gave him 6 Cheers the Prizes gave 3 a peice soon after 2 more ships hove in sight I went on board the Frigate. Mr. Downes told me that he Had captured 3 English Whalers Viz the *Rose* the *Hector* & the *Catharine* at the *Hector* He fired 5 Broadsides before she struck <u>killed</u> 2 & wounded 4 men. the *Rose* he sent in as a cartell with the Prisoners at 6 PM the *Georgeannah* & Her 2 prizes came too in company with us At 7 AM I recieved orders to go on board and take command of the Prize ship <u>*Montezuma*</u> at 10 AM went on board Ends bon temps

AD, PHi, Journal of Midshipman William W. Feltus. Entry for 25 June made at Tumbes, Peru.

1. *Barclay*, Captain Gideon Randall, a whaler captured by the British privateer *Nimrod*, was retaken by *Essex* on 28 March.

2. Captain Porter had armed the prize *Georgiana* and sent her on an independent cruise on 12 May under the command of *Essex*'s first lieutenant John Downes. For Porter's instructions of 12 May to Downes, see Porter, *Journal of a Cruise*, Vol. 1, pp. 167–69.

CAPTAIN DAVID PORTER TO SECRETARY OF THE NAVY HAMILTON [1]

U S Frigate *Essex* at Sea
July 2d 1813, Lat: 2°26'S   Long 82°W.

Sir,

I have the honor to inform you that on the morning of the 29th April in Lat: 0°40' North, Longde. 91°15' West, about 20 miles to the northward of the Island of Albemarle one of the Gallapagos in the Pacific Ocean I captured the British Ship *Montezuma*, two others being in sight close together distant from us about 7 miles which we were informed were the British Letter of Marque Ships *Policy* and *Georgiana*, the first mounting 10 Guns 6 & 9 pounders, the other six eighteen pounders 4 Swivels and 6 large blunderbusses mounted on swivels; the winds being light and variable and confiding greatly in the bravery and enterprize of my officers and men, and apprehensive of their escape from the prevalance of fogs in that climate, I directed the boats of this ship to be armed & manned and divided into two divisions, placing the first under the command of Lt. Downes, 1st Lt. in a Whale boat accompanied by Midsn. David G Farragutt, the officers in command of Boats under Lt. Downes were Lt. S D McKnight in the 3d Cutter accompanied by Midsn. Odenheimer, Sg. Master Jno: G Cowell in the Jolly Boat accompanied by Midsn. Henry W Ogden and Midsn. George Isaacs in the 2d Cutter— The Second division under the command of Lt. Wilmer 2d Lt. in the Pinnace accompanied by Midsn. Henry Gray & Masters Mate James Terry, Lt. Wilson & Mr. Shaw, Purser in the 1st Cutter, and Lt. Gamble of the Marines in the Gig— suitable signals were established, and each boat had her particular station pointed out for the attack, and every other previous arrangement was made to prevent confusion— the boats 7 in number rowed off in admirable order— Guns were fired from the enemy to terrify them— they rowed up under the muzzles of the Guns and took their stations for attacking the first ship, and no sooner was the American flag displayed by Lt. Downes as a signal for boarding and the intention was discovered by the enemy than the colours were struck without a shot being fired, so much was they daunted by the intrepidity of our brave officers and men, they then left a crew on board the prize and took their stations for attacking the other vessel when her flag was also struck on the first call to surrender, thus were two fine British Ships each pierced for 20 Guns worth near half a million of Dollars mounting between them 16 Guns and manned with 55 men well supplied with ammunition and small arms surrendered without the slightest resistance to seven small open boats with fifty men armed only with muskets, pistols, boarding axes & Cutlasses!

Be assured Sir, that Britons have either learnt to respect the courage of Americans or they are not so couragous themselves as they would wish us to believe— I have the honor to be With great respect Your Obt. Servt.—

D Porter

LS, DNA, RG45, CL, 1813, Vol. 4, No. 139, enclosure (M125, Roll No. 29).

1. Because he had been at sea for nine months, Porter did not know of Hamilton's replacement by William Jones.

CAPTAIN DAVID PORTER TO SECRETARY OF THE NAVY HAMILTON

[Extract]

U S Frigate *Essex* at Sea,
July 2d 1813, Lat 2°26'S, Long 82°W

Sir,

On the 23d of March last I sailed from Valparaiso shaping my course to the Northward and on the 26th of the same month fell in with the Peruvian Corsair Ship *Nereyda* mounting 15 Guns   she had a few days before captured two American Whale Ships, the crews of which (amounting in number to 24 men) were then detained prisoners on board her, and they could assign no other motive for the capture than that they were the allies of Great Britain and as such should capture all American Vessels they could fall in with; therefore to prevent in future such vexatious proceedings I threw all her armament into the sea, liberated the americans and addressed to the Vice Roy of Peru the following letter[1]. . . .

I then proceeded with all possible dispatch for Lima to intercept one of the detained Vessels which had parted with the *Nereyda* only three days before and I was so fortunate as to arrive there and recapture her on the 5th April at the moment she was entering the port, this vessel (the ship *Barclay,* Capt. Gideon Randall of New Bedford) I took under my protection and have had her with me ever since

From Lima I proceeded for the Gallapagos Islands where I captured the following British Ships

Montezuma	270 tons,	21 men,	2 Guns	⎫
Policy —	275 "	26 "	10 "	⎬ Letters of Marque
Georgiana	280 "	25 "	6 "	⎬
Atlantic	351 "	24 "	8 "	⎬
Greenwich —	338 "	25 "	10 "	⎭

The *Georgiana* being reputed a very fast sailor and apparently well calculated for a cruizer I mounted Sixteen Guns on her and gave the command of her to that excellent Officer Lt. John Downes with a complement of 42 men, appointing Midsn. W. H. Haddaway Acting Lieutenant on board her and sent her on a cruize—

Lt. Downes joined me at Tumbez near Guiaquill on the coast of Peru, on the 24th. June after capturing three prizes—to wit—

Letter of Marque Ships {	*Hector*	270 tons	25 men,	11 Guns
	Catherine	270 "	29 "	8 "
	Rose	220 "	21 "	8 "

The first had two men killed and six badly wounded in her recontre with the *Georgiana*— And the *Rose* was discharged (after being deprived of her Armamment) with all the prisoners captured by the *Georgiana* as they amounted to nearly double her crew; she was furnished with a passport to proceed to St. Helena— My own prisoners I liberated at Tumbez on parole—

I found that the *Georgiana* did not deserve the character given her for sailing, I therefore shifted her Officers and crew to the *Atlantic* and mounted on her twenty Guns with a complement of 60 men and appointed Midsn. Dashiell Acting

Sailing Master on board her—to this Vessel I gave the name of the *Essex Junior*— I also fitted up the Ship *Greenwich* as a Store Ship and mounted on her twenty Guns placing her under the command of Lieut. John Gamble of the Marines, on board of her I have put all the provisions and other stores of my other prizes except a supply of [three and a half][2] months for each, and have by this means secured myself a full supply of every necessary article for seven months— I had hoped to dispose of my other prizes at Guiaquil; the Governors in Peru however, are excessively alarmed at my appearance on the coast as my fleet amounts now to nine sail of vessels all formidable in their appe[arance] and they would if they dare, treat us with a ho[stility] little short of declared enemies—

I have given to Mr. John G Cowell Sailing Master an appointment to Act third Lieutenant Midsn. Cowan to Act fourth Lieutenant, and Midsn. W H Odenheimer as Sailing Master, I beg Sir, that the appointment of those officers as well as that of Lt. S D McKnight who is acting second Lieutenant, and those serving on board the *Essex Junior*, may be confirmed by the Department—

I have given to Mr. M W Bostwick my Clerk the appointment of Acting Midshipman not that he is desirous of coming forward in the Navy in that line but I hoped by this means to introduce him to the notice of the Department as I shall take the liberty to recommend him strongly as a suitable person to hold the appointment of Purser— Doctors Richd. K Hoffman and Alexander M Montgomery two gentlemen of great merit who volunteered their services with me at the commencement of hostilities have received Acting appointments from me, the first as Surgeon to fill the vacancy occasioned by the death of Doctr. Miller, the other as Surgeons Mate, to the great care and attention of those gentlemen may in a considerable degree be attributed the extraordinary health of the crew, and as they are both desirous of joining the Navay I hope their appointments may be confirmed— I have suffered greatly for the want of officers and you must be well persuaded of my deficiency when you are informed that I am under the necessity of appointing my Marine Officer[3] & Chaplain[4] to the command of prizes— they all however enter with cheerfulness into their new duties, and if the expedition should prove unsuccessful it will not be (I am [persua]ded) owing to our want of activity or vigilance and of this you must be satisfied as for the last eight months we have been constantly at sea, with the exception of twenty three days, and yet Sir we have enjoyed extraordinary health and spirits, no symptom of the scurvy having yet appeared in the ship nor have we at this moment more than two on the sick list and their diseases are owing more to the infirmities of old age than any other cause, Indeed Sir, when I compare my present situation with what it was when I doubled Cape Horn I cannot but esteem myself fortunate in an [extra]ordinary degree— then my ship was shattered by tempestuous weather and destitute of every thing my officers and crew half starved naked and worn out with fatigue— Now Sir, my ship is in prime order abundantly supplied with every thing necessary for her, I have a noble Ship for a consort of twenty Guns and well manned, a Store Ship of Twenty Guns well supplied with every thing we may want and prizes which would be worth in England two Millions of Dollars, and what renders the comparison more pleasing, the enemy has furnished all—

Excuse me Sir, for not making known my present intentions as this letter may not reach you, it may however be satisfactory to you to know how I intend to dispose of my prizes, let it suffice to say that I shall endeavour to .qd66. 94dk. c7. .g4c66c. [*sell them in Chilli.*][5]

British Letters of Marque are numerous in those seas and were it not for my arrival our Whale fishers would have been much harrassed, but they now find it necessary to keep together for mutual protection— I expect to be .a58q5d2. [*pursued*] but shall be .a8daf8d2. [*prepared*]

The State Department will no doubt inform you of the effect our presence has produced in A .ax6c9cgf6. [*political*] view on that head I shall be silent—

Subjoined is a list of deaths since I left the United States, and I beg you will relieve the anxiety of my family and all our friends by communicating as much of this letter as you may think proper—

The times of my best men have expired but their attachment to the Ship and their zeal for the service we are engaged on prevent all complaints on that account, it is not probable you will hear of me for several months to come unless some disaster happens, but I beg leave to assure you Sir, that I shall not be idle and I hope before I return to make the services of the *Essex* as important as those of any other single Ship— We may not be individually beni[fitted] but we shall do the enemy much injury which will be a sufficient compensation to us in for all the hardships and privations we must naturally experience while cut off from all communication with the rest of the world and are dependant on the precarious supplies the enemy may afford—

A British Ship shall .7w9 .7focbf9d. .94d .afgc3cg .c7. .qf3d98. [*not navigate the Pacific in safety*]

To decipher part of this letter I must refer you to the Cypher sent me at New Orleans dated [?] June 1809— I have the honor to be With great respect Your Obt. Servt.

D Porter.

List of deaths since my departure from the United States

1812 Decr.	3d	Levi Holmes,	Sea—	Palsy—
1813 Jany.	24th	Edwd. Sweeny—	OS—	Old Age
"	"	Saml. Groce—	S—	Concussion of the brain by a fall from the Main Yard—
"	March 1st	Lewis Price,	Marine,	Consumption—
"	April 4th	James Spafford	Gr. Mate,	Accidental Gun shot wound of the lungs—
"	May 25th	Doct. R Miller,	Surg:	Disease of the liver—
"	May 26th	Benj Geers—	Qt. Gr.	Inflammation of the stomach,
"	June 19th	John Rodger	Qt. Gr.	fall from the Main Yard—

LS, DNA, RG45, CL, 1813, Vol. 4, No. 139, enclosure (M125, Roll No. 29). Two pages are missing from the microfilm copy of this letter. They can be found bound with the original.

1. For the text of the letter omitted here, see Porter to Viceroy of Peru, 26 March 1813, p. 692.
2. Text of bracketed words supplied from Brannan, *Official Letters*, pp. 176–79.
3. 1st Lieutenant John M. Gamble, U.S.M.C.
4. David P. Adams.
5. Bracketed words that follow the code have been supplied by a typescript of the final five paragraphs of letter No. 139, which deciphers the coded words. This typescript immediately precedes letter No. 139. There is an error in the last decoded word, the two g's erroneously being read as q's. As a result, the word "Pacific" is improperly decoded as "passes".

Captain John Downes

CAPTAIN DAVID PORTER TO SECRETARY OF THE NAVY HAMILTON

(Duplicate)   U S Frigate *Essex*, at Sea
                              July 2d 1813, Lat 2°26'S. Long 81°W.

Sir,
     Permit me to recommend to your notice that brave intelligent and enterpriz-
ing Officer Lieut. John Downes whose conduct from his earliest introduction
into the Navy to the present time has always been uniform— If any officer deserves in an extraordinary degree the attention of the Department Lt. Downes
certainly does who has shewn innumerable instances of his courage, and if he
has not yet had an opportunity of distinguishing himself in a desperate engagement, it is because the enemy has always been precipitate in striking his flag—
     If however he should meet with that manly resistance which Britons would
have led us to expect, I pledge myself that he will do honor both to himself and
country— I have the honor to be With great Respect Your Obt. Servt.—

                                                            D Porter

LS, DNA, RG45, CL, 1813, Vol. 4, No. 140 (M125, Roll No. 29).

CAPTAIN DAVID PORTER TO SECRETARY OF THE NAVY HAMILTON

                                              U S Frigate *Essex*, At Sea
                                                        July 22d 1813—

Sir,
     On the 2d July I had the honor to inform you that I had captured in those seas
and on my passage from the United States the following British Vessels To wit,

H.B.M. Packet Brig *Nocton*	175 tons,	31 men	10 Guns.
Schooner *Elizabeth*	120 "	10 "	6 "
Ship *Montezuma*	270 "	21 "	2 "
" *Policy*	275 "	26 "	10 "
" *Georgiana*	280 "	25 "	6 "
" *Atlantic*	351 "	24 "	8 "
" *Greenwich*	338 "	25 "	10 "
" *Hector*	270 "	25 "	11 "
" *Catharine*	270 "	29 "	8 "
" *Rose*	220 "	21 "	8 "

Since which I have captured—

Ship *Seringapatam*	357 tons,	31 men,	14 Guns,
" *New Zealand*	259 "	23 "	8 "
" *Charlton*	274 "	21 "	10 "—

The *Seringapatam* is an elegant India Tick [*teak*] built Corvette Ship, pierced for 22 Guns, sails fast, and is well calculated for the service, she is remarkably strong and was formerly one of Tippo Saibs [1] men of war—

The *Charlton* being an old ship I have given her up to her Captain on condition that he lands my prisoners at Rio de Janeiro, the *Rose* was also given up on similar terms. I have the honor to be With great respect Your Obt. Servt.—

D Porter

LS, MiU–C, David Porter Papers.

1. Tippoo Sahib was sultan of Mysore from December 1782 until his death in May 1799. The capital of Mysore was Seringapatam.

CAPTAIN DAVID PORTER TO EDWARD CARY

U S Frigate *Essex*, at Sea
in the Pacific Ocean   July 23d 1813—

Sir,

Your ship *Edward* was taken by the British Whale Ship *Seringapatam* commanded by William Stavers, sent into Lima and from thence to England— The *Seringapatam* had no commission, and this fact must have been known to Capt. Folger, he had it in his power while at Lima to recover his vessel on a simple representation of the case to the vice Roy, this he did not make, but entered into an agreement with Stavers, in consideration of his Slops &c., to assist in taking the Vessel to England where he was to be paid the amount of his proportion of the Oil, his officers also entered into the same agreement, and thus, to secure themselves, have sacrificed the interest of their owners and become traitors to their country— Stavers was afterwards captured by me, and I have sent him to America in the vessel which carries this to be tried for Piracy—[1] The Secretary of the Navy is in possession of papers relative to the facts stated, and on application to him I have no doubt he will give you every information in his power— Stavers is said to be a man of property, his owners are very wealthy, and your own interest will probably dictate to you the course to be pursued— Very Respectfully Your Obt. Servant

D Porter

Mr. Edward Cary
Merchant   Nantucket—

LS, MiU–C, David Porter Papers.

1. Stavers was sent back to the United States under arrest in the prize ship *Georgiana*, commanded by Lieutenant James Wilson. Before reaching America, *Georgiana* was captured by H.M. frigate *Barrosa*.

Essex in the Marquesas Islands

By the end of September, Captain David Porter was compelled by the deteriorating condition of Essex *to terminate his cruise in the Galapagos Islands. Eleven months at sea had taken a severe toll on the frigate's hull, sails, and rigging, rendering her less and less seawor-*

thy. *The ship was also in danger from the hundreds of rats infesting her holds. So great had their numbers become that they literally threatened to eat "their way through every part of the ship."* [1] *Porter knew that* Essex *stood little chance of returning home safely, or of engaging enemy warships successfully, if these conditions were not remedied by an overhaul.*

On 3 October Essex *and her four remaining prizes* [2] *set sail for the Marquesas Islands. For Porter, these islands were the logical site for overhauling* Essex. *Their isolation guaranteed that repairs could proceed without the threat of enemy interference; moreover, they offered diversion to a ship's company that had toiled long at sea without "a run on shore." After a voyage of three weeks, the American frigate and her consorts arrived at their destination. An anchorage was established off the island of Nuku Hiva and repairs on* Essex *were immediately begun.*

1. Porter, Journal of a Cruise, Vol. 1, p. 251.
2. Essex Junior, New Zealander, Seringapatam, *and* Sir Andrew Hammond. *The preceding August, Porter had ordered Lieutenant John Downes to escort the prize ships* Catherine, Hector, Montezuma, *and* Policy *into Valparaiso for condemnation and sale. Unable to sell any of the vessels, Downes had them laid up.*

JOURNAL OF MIDSHIPMAN WILLIAM W. FELTUS

[Extract]

Sunday Oct. 24th

At 5 PM saw the Land on the Lee Bow   at day light Hood isle in sight on the Lee quarter & Rooahoga ahead   Bent the Cables   At Merd. near the Latter

Monday 25th 1813

At 1 Hove too off the Isle   Capt Porter went on shore & ~~some~~ one of the Cutters   the Native sold them Bananas & Plantons for old iron hoops. they are all naked and of a copper colour. the isle is rocky and High & ~~but~~ the Valleys are coverd with wood & Herbage   filled away and stood for Nooahevah   at 10 AM the Frigate came too in the Bay of Port Anna Maria   the other ships lay off and on   discd. a sail which proved to be the *Essex Junior* Ends Warm

Tuesday Oct. 26th 1813

At 5 PM attempted to run in but the wind being ahead were obliged to stand out after evening   every man going on shore   At 9 AM attempted to get in but was obliged to come too in the mouth of the Harbour   the other ships took a light Breeze & got in   the Frigate warped up into the Bay

Wednesday Oct. 27th 1813

Went on board of the Frigate with an intention of going ashore but perceived the Mountain indians [1] (who are at war with those near the shore) [2] were coming down from the mountains to make an attack. the Frigate Hoisted the cornet & fired several guns for the Boats. at which they immediately turned back. at 4 PM went on shore. the Men are naked excepting a britch clout the Girls have a piece of the cuntry cloth (which is made of bark) hung over their shoulders reaching to their knees   they value Iron & Whales teeth greatly with which they ornament themselves. they tatoo themselves all over their body Legs & arms. their arms are a Sling Spear & stone which they send an astonishing distance when they take an enemy they eat him or her either raw or roasted guts & all. the party near the shore say they are our friends. At 9 AM Mr downs took sails & 2 Guns on shore for to mak a tent for the Frigates crew   they fired the 2 Guns several times at which the natives were much pleased   all the ships got down their M & top S Yards & masts.

Thursday Oct. 28th 1813

Frigates people employed Clearing out the Hold   Went on shore   At sun down the 1/4 of the Frigates crew came on shore for to sleep. Came off, an attack is expicted daily to be made by the Mountain savages upon those in the Valley   At Meridian Warm

Friday Oct. 29th 1813

The mountain savages shewed themselves & threw stones at the tent on shore (as I undersand by one of the officers) Capt Porter had several muskets fired at them. they dispersed and sent word down that they would destroy the sails we had Landed from the Frigate & that they would fight us. At 6 AM Lieut Downes with about 50 men & Lieut Gamble with the Marines went up the Hill. the savages shewed themselves about 11 O clock on the top of the Hill   Meridian warm none of our men in sight but we can hear at times the report of their musketry

Saturday Oct. 30th 1813

At 4 PM the Men returned having routed the natives (or rather mountain savages) & killed 5: the friendly party plundered the plantations of the others & brought the dead down and buried them   At meridian warm.

Sunday Oct. 31st 1813

At 5 PM one of the mountain chiefs came down and made peace[3]   the Frigates men employed caulking ship & clearing out the Hold. At Merd. Pleasant   1/4 of the men in the fleet on shore as usual to sleep in the tent

Monday Novr. 1st 1813

Pleasant   at 9 AM got the powder out of the frigate & got the main top mast down it being rotten   Ends warm   thermt. at 84°

Tuesday Novr. 2d 1813

Got casks ready for watering the ship (I forgot to mention that Yesterday the mountain Savages came down with fruit &c.) the inhabtants of this island are divided into several tribes they live to a great age & are of a very stout build   the Productions of the isle are cocoanuts Bannanas Plantons Bread fruit & the Ava & Cavva Roots   the sandle wood is to be found here. At Meridian the Frigate smoked ship & we got off 2 Rafts of water. . . .

Draw by Capt Porter   Engraved by W. Strickland

Mouina.

Chief Warrior of the Taychs.

Friday Novr. 12th

Went on shore   visited the Houses of the Natives also some Houses where they kept their dead. When one of their relations die they lay the body in a trough & either keep it in their Houses or lock it (or rather fasten it up) in a small House until the flesh is entirely decayed   they then scrape the Bones & Hang them up in their Houses   Ends Warm. . . .

Sunday Novr. 14th 1813

At 1 PM a sail hove in sight from behind the Point of the Isle   the Gun on shore was fired & the different ships hailed & ordered to prepare to weigh   the *Essex Junior* took some of the frigates Hands & got under way & made all sail in chase   At sun down both Vessels out of sight   at day light saw one sail   at 10 lost sight of her again   At Meridian Warm—

Monday Novr. 15th 1813

At 2 PM the *Essex Junior* came too having spoke the strange vessel, an american ship[4] from the Sanwich Isles Last Bound to this place for Sandle wood. At sun down the American Vessel in sight off the Harbour   At 9 AM the American Ship in the mouth of the Bay   Meridian Ship Beating in—

Tuesday Novr 16th 1813

At 1 PM the American Ship came too in shore of the Prizes (Capt Porter had Several Casks filled with sand on a small Hill. also mounted 4 Guns between them As a fort   Went on shore but returned at sundown as usual. Meridian Warm!

NB the Prizoners had formed a plan last night to cut out the *Essex Junior* but were detected[5]. . . .

Thursday Novr. 18th

Warm   employed on board the frigate painting caulking & stowing the Hold At 8 AM Capt. Porter sent for the Prizoners & punished 2 of them one for theft & the other for improper Language   the 2 mates & the rest of the Prizoners were put in chains & sent on shore to work   Ends Warm

Friday Novr. 19th

Warm   went on shore but returned at sun down   at 10 AM parted our Hawzer   Meridian Warm therm—at 82°— Yesterday afternoon Capt. Porter took posession of the Island in the in the name of the U.S. & fired a Salute of 17 Guns from the little fort on the Hill. the *Essex Junior* returned the same number. the isle Capt. Porter named Maddisons isle the fort Maddisons fort & the Encampment Maddisons Village also the Bay Massachusetts Bay. . . .

Sunday Novr. 28th

At 4 PM the *Essex Junior* went up to Controolers bay   at 4 AM a boat from each Ship followed   ends warm—

Monday Novr. 29th 1813

The Boats returned and gave us the following information Viz that they Landed 30 men but were unsuccesful Lieut Downs had his Leg Broke by a stone & 3 men ~~were~~ were wounded   at 8 AM the *Essex Junior* returned & came too   Ends Warm

Tuesday Novr. 30th 1813

At 6 PM Capt. Porter and some of the officers with about 155 men went over the Hills in order to attack the tipees [*Taipis*]   Ends Cloudy with Rain. . . .

Thursday Dec 2d

At 8 AM our officers and men returned   3 of them being wounded Slightly; they had burnt all their Houses & destroyed some fruit trees   Ends squally

Saturday Dec 4th

Warm   At 8 AM Corporal Mahand died   Ends ditto

Sunday Dec 5th

At 11 AM buried the dead on shore with the Honors of War— the tipee tribe made Peace & brought in their Hogs [6]. . . .

Monday Dec 13th

At 5 PM the Frigate & *Essex Junior* went to Sea & left Mr. Gamble in charge of the Prizes.[7] Ends warm

AD, PHi, Journal of Midshipman William W. Feltus.

1. The Happahs.
2. The Taii (spelled "Taeehs" by Porter). These were the natives among whom Porter and his men settled while repairing *Essex*. The Taii requested Porter's assistance in fighting their enemies the Happahs.
3. For background on Porter's war against the Happahs, see Porter, *Journal of a Cruise*, Vol. 2, Chapter 13.
4. *Albatross*, William Smith, master.
5. For Porter's account of this prisoners' plot, see Porter, *Journal of a Cruise*, Vol. 2, pp. 77–79.
6. The clash between *Essex*'s crew and the Taipis tribe is detailed in Porter, *Journal of a Cruise*, Vol. 2, Chapter 15.
7. Marine Lieutenant John M. Gamble had orders to proceed to Valparaiso the following May with the prize ships *Seringapatam* and *Sir Andrew Hammond*. *New Zealander* was placed under the command of Master's Mate John J. King with orders to proceed to the United States as soon as she was laden with whale oil. *New Zealander* was captured on her voyage to the States by H.M. frigate *Belvidera*.

Declaration of Captain David Porter

It is hereby made known to the World that I David Porter a Captain in the Navy of the U States of America and now in command of the United States Frigate the *Essex*, have on the part of the said United States taken possession of the Island called by the natives Nooahevah, generally known by the name of Sir Henry Martins Island, but now called Madison's Island, that by the assistance

"Madisonville in Massachusetts bay—Essex & her Prizes"

and request of the freindly tribes residing in the valley of Tieuhoy, as well as of the Tribes residing in the mountains whom we have conquered and rendered Tributary to our Flag, I have caused the village of Madison, to be built consisting of six convenient Houses, a Rope Walk, Bakery and other appurtenances, and for the protection of the same, as well as for that of the freindly Natives, I have constructed a Fort calculated for mounting 16 Guns, whereon I have mounted four and called the same Fort Madison—

Our right to this Island being founded on priority of discovery conquest and possession, cannot be disputed, but the natives to secure to themselves, that freindly protection which their defenceless situation so much require have requested to be admitted into the great American Family, whose pure Republican Policy approaches so near to their own and in order to encourage those veiws to their own Interest and hapiness, as well as to render secure our claim to an Island valuable on many considerations, I have taken upon myself to promise them that our cheif shall be their Cheif and they have given assurances that such of their bretheren as may hereafter visit them from the United States shall enjoy a welcome and hospitable reception among them, and be furnished with whatever refreshments and supplies the Island may afford, that they will protect them against all their enemies, and that so far as lays in their Power they will prevent the subjects of Great Brittain (knowing them to be such) from coming among them untill peace shall take place between the two nations— Presents consisting of the Produce of the Island to a great amount have been bro't in by every tribe in the Island not excepting the most remote, & have been enumerated as follows—

Six Tribes in the valley of Tieuhoy called as a body Ta-eeh. "Seperately," 1st Hoattas 2nd Maouh. 3d "Houecah," 4th Paheuh, 5 Hekuah & Havouhs— Six Tribes of the Happahs vizt. 1st Nieekees, 2nd Tat-to-evouhs, 3d Pachas 4 Keekahs, 5 Teekauhs 6th Matawhoahs.— Three tribes of the Matamatuahs vizt. Maama Biciahs, 2d Givah 3d Ca-ha-ahs, 1st tribe of the Atta-to-hahs—2nd Ja-kee-ah 3d Paahewtah, Ni-kah one tribe   12 Tribes of the Ty-pees Vizt. 1st Po.he.guh.ah, 2d He.guh.ah 3d Otto.ye.ya 4th Cah.hu.nokah 5th To.mah.va.henah 7th Mo.vaeekah, & Atteshow, 9th Attelapneyhanah, 10th Attehacos. 11th Atta.to.meahhoy 12 Atta.ka.ka.ha.neu.ah, Most of the above have requested to be taken under the protection of the American Flag and all have been willing to purchase on any terms a freindship which promises to them so many advantages— Influenced by considerations of humanity which promise a speedy civilization to a race of men who enjoy every mental as well as bodily endowment which nature can bestow, and which requires art only to perfect, as well as by veiws of Policy, which secures to my country a fruitfull and Populas Island possessing every advantage of security and supplies for Vessels, and which of all others is the most happily situated as respects climate & local position, I do declare that I have in the most solemn maner under the American Flag display'd in Fort Madison & in the presence of numerous Witnes's taken possession of the said Island, called Madisons Island for the use of the United States whereof I am a citizen, & that the act of takeing possession was announced by a discharge of 17 Guns from Fort Madison & returned by the Shipping in the Harbour, which is hereafter to be called Massachusetts Bay— and that our claim to this Island may not hereafter be disputed, I have buried in a bottle at the foot of the Flag Staff in Fort Madison a copy of this Instrument together with several pieces of money of the coin of the united States [1]

In witness wherof I have hereunto affix'd my signature this 19 day Novembr—
1813

                                          Signed   David Porter

Witnesis Present

Jno. Downes   Lieut   U.S. Navy
James P Wilmer   L.   USN
Lt. D McKnight   Do
D P Adams   Chaplain   Do
Jno. M Gamble   Lt. Marines   Do
Jno. R Shaw   Purser   Do
Richard Hoffman   acting Surgeon   Do
William Smith   master of the American Ship *Albatross*
Wilson P Hunt [2]   agent of the American North Pacific Fur Compy.
Jno. M Maury. [3]   Midn.   US Navy
P DeMestre
Benja. Clapp [4]   Citizens of the U S America
W W Bostrick   act. mid   do
Jno. G. Cowell   actg. Lieut   do
H. H Odenhammer   SM.   USN—

Copy, MdAN, Harbeck Collection.

    1. The United States government never acknowledged Porter's annexation of Nuku Hiva.
    2. Wilson P. Hunt was the principal agent for John J. Astor's Pacific Fur Company. He oversaw
trading operations at company settlements along the Columbia River. In a letter to Secretary of
State James Monroe, Astor described Hunt as "a Real American and a man of talents and honnour."
See Astor to Monroe, Feb. 1813, in Bridgwater, "John Jacob Astor," p. 51.
    3. John M. Maury, an older brother of famed naval oceanographer Matthew F. Maury, was pro-
moted to lieutenant on 28 June 1811. Maury had been furloughed by the department to make a
voyage in the merchant service. He met with ill fortune and was stranded on Nuku Hiva when *Essex*
arrived with her prizes. Porter permitted him to become part of *Essex*'s company.
    4. Benjamin Clapp was probably a passenger on *Albatross* or perhaps had been a member of her crew.
He was appointed an acting midshipman by Porter on 8 December 1813 and remained on Nuku Hiva
under Lieutenant Gamble's command. Clapp was warranted a midshipman by the department on 21
November 1815, but upon Porter's request, his warrant was antedated to 8 December 1813.

The Royal Navy in the Pacific

In March 1813 the British Admiralty dispatched the frigate Phoebe, *under the command of Captain James Hillyar, on a secret mission to the Pacific Northwest. Hillyar's
sealed orders directed him "to destroy, and if possible totally annihilate any settlements
which the Americans may have formed either on the Columbia River or on the neighbouring Coasts."* [1] *The Admiralty's action had been prompted by pleas from the Canadian
Northwest Company for assistance in eliminating the trading posts of their American com-
petitor, John Jacob Astor.*

Phoebe *arrived at Rio de Janeiro on 10 June 1813 in convoy with the Northwest Company store ship* Isaac Todd. *Upon learning of* Phoebe*'s destination and mission, Rear Admiral Manley Dixon, commander of the South American Station, placed the sloops* Cherub *and* Racoon *under Hillyar's command to insure that he had enough force to engage* Essex *successfully should he encounter that vessel en route to the Pacific Northwest.*

Captain Hillyar's squadron left Rio on 6 July. While rounding Cape Horn, the three warships became separated from Isaac Todd. *Failing to reunite with the store ship, Hillyar proceeded on course to the Columbia River. In October, just north of the equator, Hillyar received intelligence that led him to conclude incorrectly that* Isaac Todd *had been captured by* Essex. *He then made a decision to depart from his orders.* Racoon *he sent on to the Columbia River to complete* Phoebe*'s original mission.* Phoebe *and* Cherub *he turned to the southward to cruise in search of the American frigate.*

1. *Admiralty to Hillyar, 12 Mar. 1813, Adm. 2/1380, pp. 370–75, quoted in Gough,* Royal Navy, *pp. 14–15. For additional background on the British expedition to the Columbia River, see Hussey,* Voyage of the Racoon.

REAR ADMIRAL MANLEY DIXON, R.N., TO
FIRST SECRETARY OF THE ADMIRALTY JOHN W. CROKER

Duplicate His Majesty's Ship *Montagu,*
No. 84. rio de Janeiro   21st. June 1813

Sir,

I request you will acquaint the Lords Commissioners of the Admiralty, that since the arrival of His Majesty's ship *Phoebe* and the *Isaac Todd,* at this Port on the 10th. instant, every means have been taken to expedite them for Sea; the latter Ship, Captain Hillyar, has found the greatest difficulty in keeping Company with, owing to her uncommon heavy sailing, occasioned probably in part to her being badly stowed, heavy Masts and rigging, and too many Guns on her Deck, however, no alteration I understand will make her sail even tolerably The Crew have been extremely discontented,—two mates have left her, and seven Seamen, in a dark Night, took away her Boat, neither of which have been since heard of.

Captain Hillyar found it necessary to punish some of the Crew previous to her arrival here:—and as soon as I heard of her state, I desired Captain Hillyar to interrogate the Master, Mates and Crew for the purpose of finding out their cause of discontent, the two latter said, the Ship was not safe at Sea, that they had been deceived and so forth; but, since these people have left the *Isaac Todd,* it appears they go on better, and the Ship will be soon ready to prosecute her Voyage.

The two Gentlemen, Messrs. McTavish and McDonald,[1] whether from an apprehension that the bad state of the *Isaac Todd,* or the discontent of her Crew might prove prejudicial to the Voyage, or, for other reasons have made generally known the destination of the Ship, and which came to my knowledge, before I saw those Gentlemen; and having had an interview with them relative to the state of the Ship, they immediately made me acquainted with the nature of the Voyage, as likewise the purport of a conversation they had with some of the Lords of the Admiralty, respecting the *Phoebe*'s accompanying the *Isaac Todd* to the N.W. Coast, as far as the River Columbia

This Information respecting the *Isaac Todd* and the probable destination of the *Phoebe* for her protection to the Southern Pacific, with the Intelligence relative to the Enemy, have operated powerfully on my mind to give the fullest effect I am able towards the Success of the Expedition to the N.W. Coast, and have therefore given the necessary Orders for the *Cherub* and *Racoon* to accompany the *Phoebe*, particularly as they were destined for the Southern Pacific; Captain Hillyar will therefore have the Command of this small Squadron, and it has been judged as the best mode to adopt, in case the *Isaac Todd* should part Company, that each of the three ships should take on board 4 or 5 Tons of such Articles of Provisions and stores as may be requisite to take to Columbia and that Mr. McDonald should take his passage in the *Phoebe*, leaving Mr. McTavish to proceed in the *Isaac Todd*.

I am likewise to acquaint you, that in consequence of my having received certain Information of the Arrival of the United states frigate *Essex* at Lima and Valparaiso.—

I had determined, previous to the arrival of the *Phoebe*, to dispatch the first frigate, I had, at my disposal with the *Racoon* to that Coast, in search of the Enemy and protection of the Whale fishery, but now, that another important object of Commerce is in view, I trust their Lordships' will approve of my sending an additional Ship, as in the event of the *Phoebe*'s falling in with the *Essex*, altho' an Action would most probably be favorable in its result, yet the crippled state of the former would be likely to disqualify Captain Hillyar, from executing not only his most Secret Orders, but such others, as in case of his separation from the *Isaac Todd*, I think it my duty to give that Officer under the circumstances related, for the double purpose of looking for the *Essex* and protecting the Whalers.

The object of the Expedition to the NW. Coast will (I am given to understand) be conveyed to the Spanish Ports in the South Pacific by a Merchant Brig which left England in the same Convoy with the *Isaac Todd* and parted Company on the separation of the Convoy, to proceed thither.

The Minister from the United States of America has clandestinely conveyed intelligence on matters of great National importance to Buenos Ayres and from thence it soon finds its way to Chili;— He will most likely do the same respecting this Expedition, which I lament to say appears to be too well known, but, I am in hopes Captain Hillyar with his little Squadron will effect every purpose of the Expedition and other service entrusted to his Judgement to execute.

You will be pleased to further acquaint their Lordships, that it will be only in the event of the *Isaac Todd*'s parting Company that I presume to give any additional Orders to Captain Hillyar, as I leave him entirely to the due execution of his most secret Orders, which their Lordships' have directed me to give them when ready for Sea, and which are not to be opened until the *Phoebe* has arrived 30 leagues to the Southward of this Port.

Captain Hillyar acquaints me, that he will be ready to leave this Port in six or seven days. I have the honor to be, Sir, your most obedient and humble Servant.

<u>Manley Dixon</u>

LS, UkLPR, Adm. 1/21, pp. 289–91.

1. Northwest Company partners Donald McTavish and John McDonald.

REAR ADMIRAL MANLEY DIXON, R.N., TO
CAPTAIN JAMES HILLYAR, R.N.

<u>Copy</u>. His Majesty's Ship *Montagu*,
<u>Secret</u>. Rio de Janeiro, 1st. July 1813.

Sir,

In delivering to you the Most Secret Orders of the Lords Commissioners of the Admiralty, the purport of which I have made myself acquainted with, in consequence of having received very important Intelligence relating to the Enemy, and other points of Service; and the manifest destination of the *Phoebe* and the *Isaac Todd,* having been made known to me in your presence, by Messrs. McTavish and McDonald;

I consider it a duty incumbent upon me (on taking the object of the Expedition into my most serious consideration, and in order to give every possible facility and effect in my power to a successful termination of the same) to place under your immediate Orders the *Cherub* and *Racoon,* which ships were about to sail to the Southern Pacific, for the protection of the Whale fishery from the 17° of South Latitude to the Equator, or Gallipegas Islands, cruizing from ten to one hundred leagues from the Land.

The first object that I have in view, is not only to afford to you the better prospect of keeping Company with the *Isaac Todd,* but to materially strengthen your force in the event of your meeting an Enemy of superior force; the United States frigate *Essex* has been in the Southern Pacific and late accounts from Spanish Ports, speak positively to her arrival at Lima and Valparaiso in March last, and sailed again from the latter Port, for the avowed purpose of destroying the Whalers.

The additional force of the two Ships will likewise afford you the double prospect of succeeding on the Service pointed out in your Most Secret Orders, for should the *Isaac Todd,* not reach the places of rendezvous or destination, the division of several of the Articles of Provisions and Stores taken out of that ship, and put on board the Ships of War at the particular recommendation of Messrs. McTavish and McDonald, with one of the Partners on board the *Phoebe,* will enable you to persevere in the first object of the Expedition with a much greater prospect of Success, than, if the *Phoebe* was to be alone, the more particularly as I think it very probable, you may have to encounter with an Enemy of force at the extent of your destination.

This Expedition with its object, I am sorry to say, appears to be, too generally known and I have no doubt it will reach the Western coast of America long before you arrive there and which will give the Enemy's Ships time to collect with a view of opposing the frigate under your Command; but, I am in hopes, the additional strength of the two smaller Ships will put it in your power to effect every purpose of the Expedition and other Service without difficulty.

I beg to recommend to your particular attention the original destination of the *Cherub* and *Racoon,* and as every thing relating thereto must depend upon the Information you may gain relating to the Enemy, and the state of the Fishery, it must solely depend upon you to exercise your Judgement and discretion, how far it may be necessary either to take both Ships on to the extent of your destination, or leave one or both; supposing the *Isaac Todd* to be in Company; for the purpose of Cruising in the aforementioned Latitude, for the protection of the Whale-fishery.

When you have completed the Service, of the expedition, it must depend upon the state of your Provisions before you return to the Spanish Ports for a further supply and in your route round Cape Horn, when you reach the length of the Plata, you will dispatch the *Cherub* and *Racoon* to Rio de Janeiro, unless you previously gain intelligence, in the Ports of the Western Coast of sufficient importance to render it necessary, that those Ships should cruize for a longer period for the protection of the Whalers.

When on their return, you will direct them to put into Lima for Water and refreshments. On your arrival at the Spanish Ports, you are to use every endeavour to cultivate the most friendly understanding between the two Nations, and if you should find, any reprisals to have been made of British Vessels or their Cargoes by Spanish Privateers or Guarda Costas, or by the authorities of their Ports (relative to which the accompanying intelligence speaks positively) You are to inquire the cause thereof and to do your utmost by conciliation, to leave them restored, according to the Laws subsisting between the two Nations, and if there should be any refusal to what you may consider a just demand made by you relative to British Commerce, you are to have the case drawn up, in the best manner you are able for the Information of the Lords Commissioners of the Admiralty, taking every possible care yourself and recommending the same to the Captains and Officers of the respective Ships, to take up no cause of Politics between Spain and her Colonies, but to act with the most perfect neutrality towards them both.

Finally you are to consider these additional Orders as auxiliary to the due execution of their Lordships' Most Secret Orders, having no intention whatever to interfere further than using every means in my power, to enable you to execute with honor and success, the Service, they expect you to perform on the N.W. Coast of America. I am Sir, your most obedient and humble Servant

Manley Dixon

LS, UkLPR, Adm. 1/21, pp. 330–31.

COMMANDER WILLIAM BLACK, R.N., TO
FIRST SECRETARY OF THE ADMIRALTY JOHN W. CROKER

Copy No. 1   *Racoon.*   Columbia River
                                                        15th December 1813
Sir

Agreable to order from Captn. Hillyar, I succeeded entering Columbia River, in Majestys Sloop *Racoon.* Novr. 30th 1813   found party of North west Company here, who had made arrangements with the American party before my arrival.

Country and Fort I have taken possession of in name and for British Majesty   latter I have named Fort George and left in possession and charge North west Company.

Enemies party quite broke up, they have no settlement whatever on this River or Coast.

Enemies Vessels said on Coast and about Islands, while Provisions last, shall endeavour to destroy them; Weather here set in very bad.

Left *Phoebe*, and *Cherub* Longitude 82°"20'W. Latitude 4°"33'S well   Consort parted from Squadron before reaching Cape Horn, not yet arrived. Natives appear well disposed towards English. Sir Your Obedt. Servt.

(signed)   W Black

Copy, Adm. 1/21, p. 464.

Index

Certain aspects of the treatment of persons and vessels in this index supplement annotation in the volume.

PERSONS: The rank of military personnel is the highest rank attained by the individual during 1813 when it could be ascertained. When all references to an individual lie outside that span, the rank is the highest applicable to the person at the times to which the text refers. Civilian masters of vessels are identified simply as "Capt." Vessels that civilians and naval personnel commanded during 1813 are noted in parentheses at the end of the man's entry.

VESSELS: In most cases, vessels are identified according to their use and rig—such as *Columbia*, US frigate; *Columbia*, American merchant schooner; *Columbia*, HM sloop of war—according to the best information available. Since the use and rig of a vessel could vary, nomenclature used to identify vessels refers to the year 1813. When all references to a vessel lie outside that year, the nomenclature is that applicable to the vessel at the time to which the text refers. The names of commanders of warships for 1813, including privateers but not most gunboats, are noted in parentheses at the end of the vessel's entry. The names of masters of commercial vessels are so listed when they could be ascertained.

Portugal: U.S. naval cruise proposed off, 47, 52, 105; availability of ports of, to U.S. cruisers, 50; merchant vessels of, 100, 120; British trade with, 141; outward-bound vessels, 220; awards Yeo knighthood, 435; mentioned, 165

Post Boy, American letter of marque schooner, 279 (William Cook)

Postmasters-General, British, 157

Post Office Service, British, 158*n*, 159*n*

Potomac Creek, Va., 337

Potomac flotilla: *Scorpion* sent to, 315*n*; command of, 330, 332, 335, 366*n*, 373, 386; gunboat to be sent to, 331; establishment of, 332; operational orders, 332, 335, 349, 386–87; sails to Gwynn I., 333; engages armed schooner, 333–35; manning of, 333, 336; stationed near Fort Warburton, 335; vessels comprising, 335, 387; sickness in, 336; officers, 367*n*, 368*n*

Potomac River: Potomac flotilla's operations in, 146, 330, 333, 335, 336, 387; British operations in, 309, 311, 366, 368–69, 381, 395, 396; defense of, 332, 374; outward-bound vessels, 337; British squadron off, 337, 349, 352, 368–69, 386–87; Baltimore flotilla near, 352; *Asp* and *Scorpion* reconnoiter, 366, 380; fortifications of, 370–71; British expedition in, expected, 384; mentioned, 507

Potomac River, Eastern Branch, 331

Potts, Joshua (Navy Agent, Wilmington, N.C.), 62 and *n*, 153, 258

Powell, —— (Capt., British Army), 363

Powell, Grant, 528*n*; **to:** Baynes, Edward, 526–27

Powell, William D., 528*n*

Prado, Pedro José de, 689, 690*n*

Praia, São Tiago, Cape Verde Islands, 688

Preble, Edward (Capt., USN), 47, 55, 674

Precilla, American merchant schooner, 280 (J. Small)

Prescott, Upper Canada, 414–15, 416, 430, 523, 583, 593

President, US frigate: **captures:** *Alert*, 253; *Bedford*, 5; *Daphne*, 253; *Duke of Montrose*, 157, 158, 159, 253; *Eliza Swan*, 253; *Falcon*, 253; *Fly*, 254; *Jean and Ann*, 253; *Kitty*, 158, 253; *Lion*, 254; *Maria*, 158, 253; *Shannon*, 254; **recaptures:** *Highflyer*, 27*n*, 252, 254, 261; as squadron flagship, 2; arrives at Boston, 4, 5; cruise of, in 1812, 4, 5; departs from Boston, 5, 48*n*, 104, 105–6, 251; fitting out, 5, 31, 51, 255*n*; requires repair, 5, 254; provides officers and crew for *Commodore Hull*, 31–32; Burbank confined on, 33; cruising plans, 47, 50–51, 104–5, 254; sailing qualities of, 50; plan to break blockade of Chesapeake with, 50–51; in Massachusetts Bay, 105; chases warships, 106, 251; at sea, 165; hunted by Royal Navy, 250; cruises, 250–55, 255*n*; makes captures, 250–54 passim; arrives at Newport, 250, 261; in North Sea, 251; sails in company with *Congress*, 251; waters and provisions at Shetland I., 251; waters at Bergen, Norway, 251; and British warships, 251, 252;

prisoners in, 252; sails in company with *Scourge*, 252; shortage of provisions in, 252, 253; health of crew in, 253; *Shannon* and *Tenedos* challenge, 253; *Highflyer* to serve as tender to, 255; to receive new set of signals, 255; cruise delayed by blockade, 255*n*; parts company with *Congress*, 300 (John Rodgers)

President, US sloop, 404, 459, 488, 505, 515, 603, 606 (Thomas Macdonough)

Presque Isle, Lake Erie, Pa.: U.S. naval vessels at, 147, 453, 480, 484, 543, 544, 547; description of bay, 407; Oliver H. Perry ordered to, 422; shipbuilding at, 488*n*; U.S. naval vessels moved over bar at, 543, 546, 548; as British target, 544; American military forces at, 547, 548; mentioned, 531. *See also* Erie, Pa.

Presque Isle, Lake Ontario, Upper Canada, 495, 525

Prevost, Sir George (Governor-General of British North America and Gov. of Lower Canada, 1811–16): **to:** Barclay, Robert H., 545–46; Glasgow, George, 513–14; **from:** Barclay, Robert H., 544–45; Bruyeres, Ralph H., 414–17; de Rottenburg, Francis, 566; Drummond, Gordon, 624–25; Everard, Thomas, 519; Procter, Henry, 550–51; Sheaffe, Roger H., 455–57, 516–17; Vincent, John, 464–66; Yeo, James L., 535–36, 588–89, 593–94; relations with Yeo, 405, 435–36, 437, 473; in attack on Sackets Harbor, 405, 467, 471, 472, 473, 476, 478; commands army troops at Kingston, 430, 583; receives copy of Yeo's orders from Admiralty, 436; and British naval forces on Great Lakes, 437, 483, 502; receives report on capture of York, 455–57; orders joint operations on Lake Champlain, 514; informed of second attack on York, 526; and reinforcements for Lake Erie, 545–46; correspondence with Robert H. Barclay, 548; and American prisoners at Quebec, 601, 602, 603

Price, Chandler, 86, 87, 640*n*

Price, Lewis (Pvt., USMC), 699

Prince, James (U.S. Marshal, District of Mass.), 194, 249

Prince de Neufchatel, American privateer brig, 225*n*

Prince Regent, HM frigate, 612, 613

Prince Regent, HM schooner: American intelligence of, 431; moved to Kingston, 451, 453; armament of, 454; readiness of, 458, 462; renamed *General Beresford*, 470*n*; in attack on Sackets Harbor, 477; in attack on Oswego, 496. See also *General Beresford*

Princess, HM 6th rate, 264 and *n* (Daniel McLeod)

Princess Charlotte, HM frigate, 612, 613

Principio Foundry, Md., 342–43

Pring, Daniel (Comdr., RN), 469, 470*n*, 502, 512

Prisoners: liberated at York, 527; French, 685

—American: taken to Jamaica, 41, 42; taken in *Vixen*, 41, 42, 183*n*, 494; released, 41, 57, 97; treatment of, 42, 245–49, 295, 600–601;

A ... of ... ... Running Fight of 15 Aug ... U.S. ... Between The U.S. Fleet Und ... and the British Fleet of ... Superior Force commanded B ... Sir James